Chapter	Developmentally Appropriate Practice (DAP) Guidelines	NAEYC Professional Prep Standards	NAEYC Preschool/Program Accreditation Standards	DEC Recommended Practices
	3A1. Teachers consider what children should know, understand, and be able to do across the domains of physical, social, emotional, and cognitive development and across the disciplines, including language, literacy, mathematics, social studies, science, art, music, physical education, and health, pp. 36–39			
Chapter 3: Building Positive Relationships through Nonverbal Communication	**2B1.** Teachers establish positive, personal relationships with each child and with each child's family to better understand that child's individual needs, interests, and abilities and that family's goals, values, expectations, and childrearing practices, pp. 74–78 **2B2.** Teachers continually gather information about children in a variety of ways and monitor each child's learning and development to make plans to help children progress, pp. 60–74 **2F.** Teachers possess an extensive repertoire of skills and strategies they are able to draw on, and they know how and when to choose among them, to effectively promote each child's learning and development at that moment, pp. 78–81	**1b.** Use developmental knowledge to create healthy, environments for young children, pp. 60–74 **2c.** Involve families and communities in young children's development and learning, pp. 74–77 **4a.** Understanding positive relationships and supportive interactions as the foundation of their work with young children, pp. 77–78, **5c.** Using own knowledge, appropriate early learning standards, and other resources to design, implement, and evaluate developmentally meaningful and challenging curriculum for each child, pp. 78–81	**1.B.11.** Teaching staff engage infants in frequent face-to-face social interactions each day. These include nonverbal behaviors (e.g., smiling, touching, holding), pp. 60–74, 78–81 **2.D.03.** Children have varied opportunities to develop competence in verbal and nonverbal-communication, pp. 61–74, 78–81 **3.B.03.** Teaching staff develop individual relationships with children by providing care that is: responsive, attentive, consistent, comforting, supportive, and culturally sensitive, pp. 74–78 **3.B.09.** Teaching staff create a climate of respect for infants by looking for as well as listening and responding to nonverbal cues, pp. 60–74, 78–81 **3.E.07.** Teaching staff actively seek to understand infants' needs and desires by recognizing and responding to their nonverbal cues, pp. 60–74, 78–81	**INT3.** Practitioners promote the child's communication development by observing, interpreting, responding contingently, and providing natural consequences for the child's verbal and non-verbal communication and by using language to label and expand on the child's requests, needs, preferences, or interests, pp. 60–74, 78–81
Chapter 4: Promoting Children's Positive Sense of Self through Verbal Communication	**2B2.** Teachers continually gather information about children in a variety of ways and monitor each child's learning and development to make plans to help children progress, pp. 102–116 **2F.** Teachers possess an extensive repertoire of skills and strategies they are able to draw on, and they know how and when to choose among them, to effectively promote each child's learning and development at that moment, pp. 92–102	**1b.** Use developmental knowledge to create healthy, environments for young children, pp. 92–101 **3d.** Knowing about assessment partnerships with families and with professional colleagues to build effective learning environments, pp. 102–116 **4c.** Using a broad repertoire of developmentally appropriate teaching/learning approaches, pp. 92–101 **5c.** Using own knowledge, appropriate early learning standards, and other resources to design, implement, and evaluate developmentally meaningful and challenging curriculum for each child, pp. 92–102	**1.D.01.** Teaching staff counter potential bias and discrimination by treating all children with equal respect and consideration; initiating activities and discussions that build positive self-identity and teach the valuing of differences; intervening when children tease or reject others; providing models and visual images of adult roles, differing abilities, and ethnic or cultural backgrounds that counter stereotypical limitations, upon ethnicity, gender, ability, geography, or age; and avoiding stereotypes in language references, pp. 92–101 **2.D.03.** Children have varied opportunities to develop competence in verbal and non-verbal communication by responding to questions; communicating needs, thoughts, and experiences; and describing things and events, pp. 101–116 **2.L.01.** Children are provided varied learning opportunities that foster positive identity and an emerging sense of self and others, pp. 92–101 **3.D.02.** Teaching staff use routine care to facilitate children's self-awareness, language, and social interaction, pp. 92–101 **3.F.05.** Teaching staff support the development and maintenance of children's home language whenever possible, pp. 114–116	**INS11.** Practitioners provide instructional support for young children with disabilities who are dual language learners to assist them in learning English and in continuing to develop skills through the use of their home language, pp. 114–116 **INT3.** Practitioners promote the child's communication development by observing, interpreting, responding contingently, and providing natural consequences for the child's verbal and non-verbal communication and by using language to label and expand on the child's requests, needs, preferences, or interests, pp. 101–116 **INT5.** Practitioners promote the child's problem-solving behavior by observing, interpreting, and scaffolding in response to the child's growing level of autonomy and self-regulation, pp. 92–101

Chapter	Developmentally Appropriate Practice (DAP) Guidelines	NAEYC Professional Prep Standards	NAEYC Preschool/Program Accreditation Standards	DEC Recommended Practices
Chapter 5: Supporting Children's Emotional Development and Learning	**1C4.** Teachers listen to and acknowledge children's feelings and frustrations, respond with respect in ways that children can understand, guide children to resolve conflicts, and model skills that help children to solve their own problems, pp. 141–144 **2B1.** Teachers establish positive, personal relationships with each child and with each child's family to better understand that child's individual needs, interests, and abilities and that family's goals, values, expectations, and childrearing practices, pp. 139–141 **3A.** Desired goals that are important in young children's learning and development have been identified and clearly articulated, pp. 127–139	**1a.** Know and understand children's characteristics and needs (0–8), pp. 127–139 **1b.** Use developmental knowledge to create healthy environments for young children, pp. 141–144 **4a.** Understanding positive relationships and supportive interactions as the foundation of their work with young children, pp. 139–141 **4c.** Using a broad repertoire of developmentally appropriate teaching/learning approaches, pp. 144–147	**1.B.01.** Teaching staff foster children's emotional well-being by demonstrating respect for children and creating a positive emotional climate as reflected in behaviors such as frequent social conversations, joint laughter, and affection, pp. 129–147 **1.B.05.** Teaching staff function as secure bases for children. They respond promptly in developmentally appropriate ways to children's positive initiations, negative emotions, and feelings of hurt and fear by providing comfort, support, and assistance, pp. 129–147 **1.B.06.** Teaching staff encourage children's appropriate expression of emotions, both positive (e.g., joy, pleasure, excitement) and negative (e.g., anger, frustration, sadness), pp. 144–147 **1.D.04.** Teachers help children talk about their own and others' emotions. They provide opportunities for children to explore a wide range of feelings and the different ways that those feelings can be expressed, pp. 144–147 **2.B.02.** Children have varied opportunities to recognize and name their own and others' feelings, pp. 130–139 **2.B.03.** Children have varied opportunities to learn the skills needed to regulate their emotions, behavior and attention, pp. 139–144	**INT1.** Practitioners promote the child's social–emotional development by observing, interpreting, and responding contingently to the range of the child's emotional expressions, pp. 129–147
Chapter 6: Building Resilience in Children	**2B3.** Teachers are alert to signs of undue stress and traumatic events in each child's life and employ strategies to reduce stress and support the development of resilience, pp. 161–181	**1a.** Know and understand children's characteristics and needs (0–8), pp. 159–161 **2a.** Use diverse family and community characteristics, pp. 161–181 **2c.** Involve families and communities in young children's development and learning, pp. 181–182 **3d.** Knowing about assessment partnerships with families and with professional colleagues to build effective learning environments, pp. 161–181 **4c.** Using a broad repertoire of developmentally appropriate teaching/learning approaches, pp. 161–181 **5c.** Using own knowledge, appropriate early learning standards, and other resources to design, implement, and evaluate developmentally meaningful and challenging curriculum for each child, pp. 161–181 **6d.** Integrating knowledgeable, reflective, and critical perspectives on early education, pp. 181–182	**10.D.01.** The program has written policies to promote wellness and safeguard the health and safety of children and adults, pp. 161–181	**INS1.** Practitioners, with the family, identify each child's strengths, preferences, and interests to engage the child in active learning, pp. 181–182 **INS2.** Practitioners, with the family, identify skills to target for instruction that help a child become adaptive, competent, socially connected, and engaged and that promote learning in natural and inclusive environments, pp. 173–181
Chapter 7: Play as a Context for Social Development and Learning	**1E2.** Teachers foster in children an enjoyment of and engagement in learning, pp. 191–196 **2E4.** Teachers provide experiences, materials, and interactions to enable children to engage in play that allows them to stretch their boundaries to the fullest in their imagination, language, interaction, and self-regulation as well as to practice their newly acquired skills, pp. 196–216	**1b.** Use developmental knowledge to create healthy environments for young children, pp. 191–196 **4c.** Using a broad repertoire of developmentally appropriate teaching/learning approaches, pp. 191–196	**1.C.02.** Teaching staff support children's development of friendships and provide opportunities for children to play with and learn from each other, pp. 191–216 **1.C.03.** Teaching staff support children as they practice social skills and build friendships by helping them: enter into [play], sustain [play], and enhance play, pp. 191–216	**INS7.** Practitioners use explicit feedback and consequences to increase child engagement, play, and skills, pp. 191–216 **INT4.** Practitioners promote the child's cognitive development by observing, interpreting, and responding intentionally to the child's exploration, play, and social activity by joining in and expanding on the child's focus, actions, and intent, pp. 191–216

(continued on back endsheet)

8e

Guiding
Children's
Social
Development
and Learning

THEORY AND SKILLS

8e

Guiding Children's Social Development and Learning

THEORY AND SKILLS

Marjorie J. Kostelnik, Ph.D.
University of Nebraska–Lincoln

Anne K. Soderman, Ph.D.
Michigan State University

Alice Phipps Whiren, Ph.D.
Michigan State University

Michelle L. Rupiper, Ph.D
University of Nebraska–Lincoln

Kara Murphy Gregory, Ph.D.
Michigan State University

CENGAGE
Learning®

Australia • Brazil • Japan • Korea • Mexico • Singapore • Spain • United Kingdom • United States

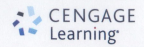

Guiding Children's Social Development and Learning: Theory and Skills, Eighth Edition

Marjorie J. Kostelnik, Ph.D., Anne K. Soderman, Ph.D., Alice Phipps Whiren, Ph.D., Michelle L. Rupiper, Ph.D., and Kara Murphy Gregory, Ph.D.

Product Manager: Mark D. Kerr

Content Developer: Julie Martinez

Content Coordinator: Paige Leeds

Product Assistant: Nicole Bator

Media Developer: Renee C. Schaaf

Marketing Manager: Kara Kindstrom

Production Management, and Composition: Charu Khanna, MPS Limited

Manufacturing Planner: Doug Bertke

Rights Acquisitions Specialist: Dean Dauphinais

Photo Researcher: PreMedia Global

Text Researcher: PreMedia Global

Art and Cover Direction: Carolyn Deacy, MPS Limited

Cover Image: Blue Jean Images / SuperStock JGI/Blend Images/Getty Images
©Cengage Learning

Library of Congress Control Number: 2013944270

ISBN-13: 9781285743707

ISBN-10: 1285743709

Cengage Learning
200 First Stamford Place, 4th Floor
Stamford, CT 06902
USA

Cengage Learning is a leading provider of customized learning solutions with office locations around the globe, including Singapore, the United Kingdom, Australia, Mexico, Brazil, and Japan. Locate your local office at **www.cengage.com/global**.

Cengage Learning products are represented in Canada by Nelson Education, Ltd.

To learn more about Cengage Learning Solutions, visit **www.cengage.com**.

Purchase any of our products at your local college store or at our preferred online store **www.cengagebrain.com**.

Printed in the U.S.A.
3 4 5 6 7 17 16

Contents

Preface   xv

1   **Making a Difference in Children's Lives**   1
    Objectives   1
    NAEYC Standards   1

naeyc **Social Competence Defined**   2
  Individual Variations in Social Competence   3
    Highlight 1-1 Observable Behaviors of Socially Competent Children   5
  The Benefits of Being Socially Competent   5
    Highlight 1-2 Learning Is a Social Process   6

naeyc **What Early Childhood Professionals Need to Know about Children's Development and Social Competence**   6
  All Development Is Interrelated   7
  Social Development Occurs in an Orderly Sequence   7
  Rates of Development Vary Among Children   8
  There Are Optimal Periods of Social Development   8
  Social Development Has Cumulative and Delayed Effects   8

naeyc **Learning and Social Competence**   9
  Children Are Active Social Learners   9
  Children Have Multiple Ways of Learning about the Social World   9
  Social Competence Involves Continuous Challenge and Mastery   10
    Digital Download Social Competence Anecdotal Record   10
  Social Learning Takes Time   11

naeyc **The Social Environment**   11
  Family Influences   11
    Challenging Behavior Meet Patrick   12

  Peer Group Influences   12
  Caregiver and Teacher Influences   12
    TeachSource Video 1-1 *Learning through Play*   13
  Cultural Contexts   13
    Highlight 1-3 Cultural Variations   13
  Seeing the Big Picture!   14

naeyc **Your Role in Fostering Children's Social Competence**   15
  Working with Children as a Professional   16
    Digital Download Specialized Knowledge   17

naeyc **Developmentally Appropriate Practices and Social Competence**   18
  Age-Appropriate Practices   19
  Individually Appropriate Practices   20
  Socially and Culturally Appropriate Practices   20
    TeachSource Video 1-2 *5–11 Years: Lev Vygotsky, the Zone of Proximal Development, and Scaffolding*   21

naeyc **A Framework for Guiding Children's Social Development and Learning**   21
  Establishing Positive Relationships with Children   22
  Creating Supportive Environments   22
  Teaching and Coaching   23
  Intensive Individualized Interventions   23

naeyc **Chapter Structure**   23
  Specialized Knowledge   23
  Demonstrated Competence   24
  Standards of Practice   24
  Continuing Education   24
  Code of Ethics   24

Summary   24

Key Terms   25

Discussion Questions   25

2 **Good Beginnings: Establishing Relationships with Infants and Toddlers** 27

Objectives 27

NAEYC Standards 27

naeyc Essentials of All Positive Adult–Child Relationships 28

Warmth 28

Acceptance 28

Genuineness 29

Empathy 29

Respect 29

naeyc Attachment as a Foundation of Relationships 29

Highlight 2-1 How Strong Is Your Relationship with the Infants and Toddlers in Your Care? 31

naeyc Reading Infant/Toddler Cues 31

TeachSource Video 2-1 *0–2 Years: Attachment in Infants and Toddlers* 31

Influence of Temperament on Social Relationships 31

Behavioral States 33

Highlight 2-2 Soothing with the Five S's 35

Movement and Social Interaction 36

naeyc Supporting Individuation and Socialization 36

Infants 36

Toddlers 37

Individual Differences in Outcomes 37

Adult–Child Separation 38

naeyc Fostering Children's Competence in Communicating 39

Beginning Communication 39

Challenging Behavior Meet Mary 40

More Advanced Communication 41

Tuning in to Children's Communications 42

naeyc Friendliness 43

Friends 44

naeyc Fostering Self-Regulation 45

Highlight 2-3 Beginner's Guide for Supporting Toilet Learning 46

Digital Download Check Your Understanding 47

naeyc Relating to Infants and Toddlers with Special Needs 47

naeyc Skills for Developing Positive Social Relationships with Infants and Toddlers 48

Digital Download Hints about Infant/Toddler Toy Play 51

TeachSource Video 2-2 *Infants and Toddlers: Guidance* 52

naeyc Pitfalls to Avoid 55

Summary 56

Key Terms 57

Discussion Questions 57

3 **Building Positive Relationships through Nonverbal Communication** 59

Objectives 59

NAEYC Standards 59

naeyc Functions of Nonverbal Communication 60

naeyc Channels of Nonverbal Communication 61

Position in Space 62

Body Motion 64

Body Orientation 65

Gestures 65

Touch 66

Facial Expression 68

TeachSource Video 3-1 *Infants and Toddlers: Family Interactions, School, and Community* 71

Paralinguistics 71

naeyc Nurturing Relationships Nonverbally 74

Warmth 75

Acceptance 75

Genuineness 76

Empathy 76

Respect 76

How the Concept of Time Influences Relationships 76

naeyc Communicating Authority and Security through Nonverbal Behavior 77

Potential Challenges in Sending and Interpreting Nonverbal Messages 78

Challenging Behavior Meet Jay 79

 Children's Acquisition of Nonverbal Communication Skills 79

Where Nonverbal Communication Fits in the Curriculum 80

Methods of Acquiring Nonverbal Skills 80

 Skills for Developing Positive Relationships with Children Nonverbally 82

Digital Download How to Show Warmth and Respect 83

Digital Download Providing Security through Authority Noverbal Signals 84

 Pitfalls to Avoid 86

Summary 87

Key Terms 88

Discussion Questions 88

4 Promoting Children's Positive Sense of Self through Verbal Communication 90

Objectives 90

NAEYC Standards 90

 Children's Emerging Sense of Self 92

Self-Awareness 92

Self-Concept 92

Digital Download ME Books 93

TeachSource Video 4-1 *5–11 Years: Self-Concept in Middle Childhood* 94

Self-Esteem 94

The Evolution of Self-Esteem 96

Highlight 4-1 Teresa and the Trio of Self-Esteem 96

Variations in Children's Self-Esteem 98

How Adult Practices Influence Children's Self-Esteem 100

 The Verbal Environment 101

The Negative Verbal Environment 102

Positive Verbal Environments 102

 Establishing a Positive Verbal Environment 102

Behavior Reflections 105

Effective Praise 107

Conversations 108

Questions 109

Paraphrase Reflections 110

Shared Narratives 113

Supporting Linguistically Diverse Children: Verbal Strategies 114

 Skills for Promoting Children's Self-Awareness and Self-Esteem through Verbal Communication 116

Digital Download Effective Praise Classroom Record 118

TeachSource Video 4-2 *Language Development: Oral and Literacy-Related Activities – Bonus Video 3* 120

Challenging Behavior Meet Celia 121

 Pitfalls to Avoid in Using Skills to Promote Children's Self-Understanding 121

Summary 123

Key Terms 124

Discussion Questions 124

5 Supporting Children's Emotional Development and Learning 126

Objectives 126

NAEYC Standards 126

 What Emotions Are and Where They Come From 127

 Why Emotions Are Important 127

Where Emotions Fit in the Curriculum 129

 What Early Childhood Professionals Need to Know about Children's Emotional Development 129

How Children's Emotions Emerge and Mature 130

Highlight 5-1 The Appearance of Joy Is Celebrated in Traditional Navajo Families 131

How Children Develop Emotional Self-Awareness 131

How Children Learn to Identify Other People's Emotions 133

How Children Learn to Regulate Their Emotions 134

Highlight 5-2 The Emotional Lessons of Early Childhood 136

Highlight 5-3 The Costs of Emotional Illiteracy Are High   136

The Emotional Tasks of Childhood   136

Highlight 5-4 A Lesson in "Initiative"   138

naeyc Individual Variations in How Children Express Emotions   139

Differences in Children's Expressive Styles   139

Gender Differences in Children's Emotional Expression   139

Family and Cultural Variations in Children's Emotional Expression   140

naeyc Challenges Children Encounter When Dealing with Emotions   141

Emotional Difficulties Experienced by Children from Infancy through Age 7   141

Emotional Difficulties Experienced by Children Ages 7 to 12   141

Challenging Behavior Meet Sam   142

Counterproductive Ways of Responding to Children's Emotions   143

naeyc Constructive Ways of Responding to Children's Emotions   144

Talking to Children about Their Emotions   144

Affective Reflections   144

Highlight 5-5 Benefits of Reflecting Children's Emotions   145

Helping Children Use Words to Express Their Emotions to Others   146

naeyc Skills for Supporting Children's Emotional Development and Learning   147

Digital Download Common Feeling Words   148

TeachSource Video 5-1 *2–5 Years: Language Development for Early Childhood*   149

Digital Download Story Prompts   150

naeyc Pitfalls to Avoid in Dealing with Children's Emotions   155

Summary   155

Key Terms   156

Discussion Questions   156

Digital Download Reflect on Your Practice CourseMate   157

 **Building Resilience in Children**   158

Objectives   158

NAEYC Standards   158

naeyc Defining Resilience   159

What Do Resilient Children Look Like?   159

naeyc How Does Resilience Develop?   160

naeyc The Influence of Stress, Risk Factors, and Adversity on Resilience   161

The Concept of Stress   161

When Stress-Coping Mechanisms Fail   162

Multiple Risk Factors   163

TeachSource Video 6-1 *Divorce and Children*   165

naeyc Assets and Protective Factors   172

Highlight 6-1 Examples of Assets and Protective Factors   172

Developing Stress Hardiness and Resilience in Children   173

Monitoring Children's Health   174

Coaching Children in Decision Making, Planning, Implementing, and Evaluating   175

Sharing the Value of Optimism   176

Fostering Self-Efficacy and Self-Determination   178

Modifying Difficult Temperaments   178

TeachSource Video 6-2 *0–2: Temperament in Infants and Toddlers*   179

Strengthening Skills of Friendship Building and Social Connections   179

Challenging Behavior Meet Julie   180

Scaffolding Children's Intellectual and Scholastic Competence   180

naeyc Working with Families as Partners in Developing Resilience   181

naeyc Skills for Developing Stress Hardy and Resilient Children   182

naeyc Pitfalls to Avoid When Building Resilience   185

Summary   187

Key Terms   188

Discussion Questions   188

Digital Download Reflect on Your Practice CourseMate   189

7 **Play as a Context for Social Development and Learning** 190

  Objectives 190

  NAEYC Standards 190

naeyc The Nature of Play and Social Competence 191

Genetic Foundations 191

  Highlight 7-1 Characteristics of Play 191

Where Play Fits in the Curriculum 192

Social Development and Play 192

  TeachSource Video 7-1 *2–5 Years: Play in Early Childhood* 195

naeyc Types of Play 196

Exploratory Behavior 196

Play with Objects 197

Dramatic Play 199

  Digital Download Observation of Dramatic Play Skills for Younger or Less Experienced Children 202

  Digital Download Observation of Dramatic Play Skills for Older or More Experienced Children 202

Construction Play 208

  Digital Download Check Your Understanding 209

Play with Movement 209

Games 213

Humor 215

naeyc Skills for Supporting, Enhancing, and Expanding Children's Play 216

  Challenging Behavior Meet Jonathan 218

  TeachSource Video 7-2 *Young Children's Stages of Play: An Illustrated Guide* 221

naeyc Pitfalls to Avoid 224

Summary 226

Key Terms 226

Discussion Questions 226

8 **Supporting Children's Peer Relationships and Friendships** 229

  Objectives 229

  NAEYC Standards 229

naeyc The Importance of Children's Relations with Peers and Friends 230

Adult–Child Relationships 230

Peer Relationships 230

Friendships 231

What Happens When Children Cannot Find a Friend 233

naeyc Children's Ideas About Friends and Friendship 233

Friendship Framework 233

  TeachSource Video 8-1 *5–11 Years: Peer Acceptance in Middle Childhood* 235

naeyc How Children Choose Their Friends 237

Physical Appearance 237

Ethnicity 239

Gender 239

  TeachSource Video 8-2 *2–5 Years: Gender in Early Childhood* 239

Age 239

Behavior Characteristics 239

Attitudes/Preferences 240

Social Competence 240

Unsuccessful Peer Interactions 241

naeyc The Friendship Skills Every Child Needs to Know 242

Making Contact 242

Maintaining Positive Relationships 243

  TeachSource Video 8-3 *Including Students with Physical Disabilities: Best Practice* 243

Negotiating Conflict 244

naeyc Where Friendship Development Fits in the Curriculum 245

Typical Challenges Children Face in Meeting Friendship-Related Learning Standards 245

naeyc The Adult Role in Supporting Children's Friendships 246

Creating Friendship-Supportive Classroom Environments 246

Demonstrating Friendship Skills with Puppets and Props 247

  Digital Download Sample Friendship Skits 248

Teaching Friendship Skills Through Role-Playing 250

Buddy Skills Training 250

One-on-One Intensive Coaching 251

  Challenging Behavior Meet Jacob—a Child with No Friends 251

  HIGHLIGHT 8-1 Coaching to Enhance Peer Communication 251

naeyc **Skills for Supporting Children's Peer Relationships and Friendships** 252

naeyc **Pitfalls to Avoid in Promoting Peer Relations and Friendships** 258

Summary 259

Key Terms 260

Discussion Questions 260

> **Digital Download** Reflect on Your Practice CourseMate 261

9 **Influencing Children's Social Development by Structuring the Physical Environment** 262

> Objectives 262
> NAEYC Standards 262

naeyc **Structuring Space and Materials** 263

Building and Grounds 264

Adjusting Exterior Spaces to Promote Social Development 266

Arranging Furnishings and Equipment 268

Controllable Dimensions 270

Choosing Appropriate Materials 272

> **Highlight 9-1** Evaluating the Effectiveness of the Space 273

Adding or Removing Materials, and Childproofing the Environment 275

> **Challenging Behavior** Children "Running Wild" 278

naeyc **Structuring Time** 279

The Daily Schedule 279

> **Digital Download** Warning Signs that the Physical Environment Is Problematic 281

Rate and Intensity of Programs 282

naeyc **Skills for Structuring the Physical Environment to Foster Social Development and Prevent or Diminish Undesirable Behavior** 283

naeyc **Pitfalls to Avoid** 289

Summary 290

Key Terms 290

Discussion Questions 291

10 **Fostering Self-Regulation in Children: Communicating Expectations and Rules** 293

> Objectives 293
> NAEYC Standards 293

naeyc **What is Self-Regulation?** 294

How Self-Regulation Evolves 294

Amoral Orientation (No Regulation) 294

Adherence (External Regulation) 295

Identification (Shared Regulation) 296

Internalization (Internal Regulation) 296

naeyc **How Development Influences Self-Regulation** 298

Emotional Development 298

Cognitive Development 299

> **Highlight 10-1** The Link between Moral Thinking and Moral Behavior 299

Language and Memory Development 301

naeyc **How Experience Influences Self-Regulation** 302

Direct Instruction 303

Modeling 303

Reinforcement and Negative Consequences 304

Integrating Development and Experience 304

> **TeachSource Video 10-1** *5–11 Years: Moral Development in Middle Childhood* 304

naeyc **Adult Approaches to Child Guidance** 305

The Authoritarian Style 306

The Permissive Style 306

The Uninvolved Style 306

The Authoritative Style 307

The Dynamic Interaction between Children's Temperament and Adult Approaches to Guidance 307

> **Highlight 10-2** Becoming an Authoritative Adult 309

Becoming Authoritative 309

naeyc **Stating Your Expectations** 309

Knowing When Behavior Change is Necessary 310

Part One of the Personal Message 311

> **Highlight 10-3** Setting Limits with Rosie: A Child with Special Needs 312

Highlight 10-4 Why Reflections Come First in the Personal Message 313

Part Two of the Personal Message 313

Highlight 10-5 Reasons Strengthen Cognitive Connections! 314

Part Three of the Personal Message 316

Articulating the Entire Personal Message—The Four R's 317

Highlight 10-6 Creating a Complete Personal Message 318

Positive Personal Messages 318

The Connection between the Authoritative Style and Developmentally Appropriate Practice 319

naeyc Skills for Expressing Expectations and Rules to Children 320

Digital Download Analyzing Potential Rules and Expectations 322

Digital Download Do's & Don'ts Analysis 323

TeachSource Video 10-2 *Guidance for Young Children: Teacher Techniques for Encouraging Positive Social Behaviors* 324

Digital Download Dear Families of Children in the 6-Year-Old Class 324

naeyc Pitfalls to Avoid 325

naeyc Combining Personal Messages with Other Skills You Have Learned 327

Challenging Behavior Meet Ethan 327

Summary 328

Key Terms 328

Discussion Questions 329

11 Fostering Self-Regulation in Children: The Role of Consequences 331

Objectives 331

NAEYC Standards 331

naeyc Problem Behaviors and Their Potential Solutions 332

naeyc Consequences 334

Consequences that Increase Desirable Behaviors 334

Consequences that Reduce Mistaken Behaviors 334

Highlight 11-1 Potential Reinforcers 335

Types of Corrective Consequences 336

Deciding which Corrective Consequences to Use 338

Implementing Corrective Consequences 340

Following Through with Consequences 341

When to Implement Consequences 342

naeyc Combining the Warning and Follow-Through with the Personal Message 342

Rationale for This Verbal Sequence 342

Successive Use of the Skill Sequence 344

What to Do about Young Children's Temper Tantrums 344

Where Consequences Fit in Your Daily Repertoire of Guidance Strategies 346

naeyc The Need for Intensive Individualized Intervention 346

Intensive Individualized Interventions 346

Challenging Behavior Meet Katie 348

naeyc Adapting Rules and Consequences for Children with Special Needs 351

Highlight 11-2 Strategies for Adapting Rules and Consequences for Children with Special Needs 352

naeyc Skills for Implementing Consequences 353

Digital Download Anticipating Consequences that Fit the Rules You Make 353

Digital Download A-B-C Analysis Template 356

Digital Download Positive Behavior Support Plan Template 357

naeyc Pitfalls to Avoid 358

TeachSource Video 11-1 *Lauren and Beth: Serving Students with Special Needs in Inclusive Environments* 358

Summary 361

Key Terms 361

Discussion Questions 362

12 Handling Children's Aggressive Behavior 364

Objectives 364

NAEYC Standards 364

naeyc Defining Aggression 365

Types of Aggression 365

Assertiveness 366

naeyc Why Children Are Aggressive 366

Biology 367

The Frustration-Aggression Hypothesis 367

The Distorted-Perception Hypothesis 367

Reinforcement and Direct Experience 367

Modeling and Observational Experience 368

Lack of Knowledge and Skills 368

naeyc The Emergence of Aggression 368

Changes in Aggression over Time 368

   Highlight 12-1 A Toddler's View of "WHAT'S MINE!" 369

Gender Differences in Aggression 370

naeyc Ineffective Strategies Adults Use to Handle Children's Aggressive Behavior 371

Ignoring Aggression 371

Displacement 371

Inconsistency 371

Physical Punishment 371

Lesson 1: Aggression Looks Like This 372

Lesson 2: Might Makes Right 372

Lesson 3: Aggression Is the Only Option 372

Lesson 4: This Adult Can't Be Trusted 372

Lesson 5: Watch Out for Number #1 372

Lesson 6: Don't Get Caught! 372

naeyc How to Effectively Address Childhood Aggression 374

All-Purpose Strategies to Counter Aggression 375

The Special Case of Instrumental Aggression 377

   Challenging Behavior Meet Brian: A Child Struggling to Communicate 378

naeyc A Model for Conflict Mediation 379

Step 1: Initiate the Mediation Process 379

Step 2: Clarify Each Child's Perspective 379

Step 3: Sum Up 379

Step 4: Generate Alternatives 380

Step 5: Agree on a Solution 380

Step 6: Reinforce the Problem-Solving Process 381

Step 7: Follow Through 381

Conflict Mediation in Action 381

   Highlight 12-2 Summary of Conflict Mediation Model 381

How Children Think about Conflict Resolution 382

Does Conflict Mediation Work? 383

naeyc When Aggression Turns into Bullying 384

Victims of Bullying 384

Bullies 385

Witnesses to Bullying 386

The Role of Adults in Bully Prevention 386

naeyc Skills for Handling Aggressive Behavior 388

   TeachSource Video 12-1 *School Age: Emotional Development (Bullying)* 388

   Digital Download BULLY BUSTER Checklist 392

naeyc Pitfalls to Avoid 394

Summary 396

Key Terms 397

Discussion Questions 397

13 **Promoting Prosocial Behavior** 399

   Objectives 399

   NAEYC Standards 399

naeyc Defining Prosocial Behavior 400

Benefits of Prosocial Behavior 400

   Highlight 13-1 Benefits of Engaging in Prosocial Behavior 401

Children's Motivation to Act in a Prosocial Way 401

Steps to Becoming Prosocial 401

   TeachSource Video 13-1 *Maddie: Positive Collaboration between School Professionals and Parents to Serve a Student with Physical Disabilities* 404

naeyc Influences on Children's Prosocial Behavior 404

Biology and Prosocial Behavior 405

Social Cognition and Prosocial Behavior 405

Language and Prosocial Behavior 405

Sharing   405

Social Experiences and Prosocial Behavior   407

TeachSource Video 13-2 *Benefits of Preschool*   408

Cultural Expectations and Experiences and Prosocial Behavior   408

Adult Behavior and Prosocial Behavior   408

Challenging Behavior Meet Courtney   411

naeyc **Skills for Promoting Prosocial Behavior in Children   411**

Digital Download Activities that Encourage Cooperation and Sharing   412

Highlight 13-2 Strategies to Teach Children to Share   414

Highlight 13-3 Sample Activity to Promote Prosocial Behavior   417

naeyc **Pitfalls to Avoid   418**

Summary   420

Key Terms   420

Discussion Questions   420

 14 **Fostering Healthy Attitudes about Sexuality and Diversity**   423

Objectives   423

NAEYC Standards   423

naeyc **Children's Psychosexual Development   424**

Gender-Role Development   424

Adult Responses to Young Children's Psychosexual Behavior and Development   425

Highlight 14-1 Responding to Unexpected Behaviors   427

naeyc **Ethnic Identity, Preferences, and Attitudes in Children   428**

Highlight 14-2 Identifying Your Social Identity   430

naeyc **Inclusion of Children with Exceptional Needs   433**

Council for Exceptional Children (CEC) Standards of Professional and Ethical Practice for Teachers of Children with Disabilities   434

Developing Individualized Family Service Programs (IFSPs) and Individualized Education Programs (IEPs)   435

The Individualized Education Program (IEP)   436

Categories of Disabling Conditions   436

Challenging Behavior Social Goal for Gavin, a Kindergarten Child with Down Syndrome: Eating Snack at the Table   436

Digital Download Categories of Disabilities   437

Inclusion   441

Children's Perceptions of Disabling Conditions   442

Children's Attitudes toward Peers Who Have Special Needs   442

Guidelines for Integrating Children with Disabling Conditions into Formal Group Settings   443

naeyc **The Impact of Precocious Behavior, Shyness, and Difficult Temperament on Children's Social Development   444**

Advanced and Precocious Children   445

Excessively Shy Children   445

Temperament and Individuality   446

Challenging Behavior Meet Adam   447

naeyc **Skills for Fostering Healthy Attitudes about Sexuality and Diversity   448**

naeyc **Pitfalls to Avoid   453**

Highlight 14-3 Letter to Parent from International School Principal   453

Summary   455

Key Terms   455

Discussion Questions   456

Digital Download Reflect on Your Practice CourseMate   458

15 **Making Ethical Judgments and Decisions**   459

Objectives   459

NAEYC Standards   459

naeyc **Ethical Judgments and the Variables that Influence Making Such Judgments   460**

How Program Goals, Strategies, and Standards Relate to Ethical Judgments   460

Variables that Affect Ethical Judgments   463

Highlight 15-1 The Public Rates Teachers Highly on Ethics and Trustworthiness   464

naeyc **Principles Involved in Making Ethical Judgments   467**

Priority Principles   468

naeyc **Ethical Judgments Related to Children's Extreme Behavior   470**

What Constitutes Extreme Behavior?   470

   Challenging Behavior Meet Adrian   471

Frequently Reported Sources of Extreme Behavior   472

naeyc **Ethical Codes of Conduct Focused on Child Abuse and Neglect   474**

Defining Abuse and Neglect   474

Scope of the Problem   475

The Abusers   475

The Victims   477

   Highlight 15-2   Signs of Physical Abuse and Neglect   478

   Highlight 15-3   Signs of Sexual Abuse   479

Reporting Child Abuse   480

Child Abuse Prevention in the Formal Group Setting   482

naeyc **Ethical Dimensions of Working with Families   482**

naeyc **Skills for Making Ethical Judgments   483**

naeyc **Pitfalls to Avoid   489**

Summary   490

Key Terms   490

Discussion Questions   491

   Digital Download Reflect on Your Practice CourseMate   492

Appendix A Code of Ethical Conduct and Statement of Commitment   493

Appendix B Case Studies   501

Appendix C Professional Skills Inventory Rating Form   511

Glossary   514

References   522

Index   546

Preface

NTMU
HIG
MIHAP

We live in a fast-paced social environment in which people can reach hundreds of "friends" with the click of a mouse and keep up with the lives of people all over the world through texting and other social media. Clearly, technology has revolutionized the way we connect with others. Yet, at the heart of it all, people continue to need close human relationships to feel fulfilled. In addition, certain elements of social competence must still be mastered for individuals to achieve ultimate life success. As someone who aspires to work with young children professionally, this is where you can make a difference.

Every day, children in community programs and schools interact with peers and adults, learning valuable social and emotional lessons about themselves and the people around them. What you say and do with children has a tremendous impact on them, and shapes them for good or ill in ways you will never fully know. Even as you teach them, children will teach you new things about child development, family life, social learning, and yourself. *Guiding Children's Social Development and Learning: Theory and Skills*, eighth edition, will help you make the most of all these learning opportunities.

Teachers and professional caregivers have a primary role in providing emotional support and guidance to the children with whom they work. This includes helping children develop positive feelings about themselves, increasing their ability to interact effectively with others, and teaching them socially acceptable means of behavior. Such learning is facilitated when children view the adult as a source of comfort and encouragement as well as behavioral guidance. How well adults perform these roles is affected by how deeply they understand child development, their ability to establish positive relationships with children, and their grasp of principles related to behavior management. This comprehensive blend of developmental and behavioral knowledge and practice makes a qualitative difference in how aspiring professionals think about children's social development and how they respond to it.

Too often, we have encountered students and practitioners whose interactions with children are wholly intuitive. They rely on "gut level" responses or approach child guidance as a series of tricks to meet short-range objectives, such as getting a child to stop interrupting. They have no purposeful or integrated set of strategies that address long-range goals, such as teaching a child to delay gratification. Other adults have more knowledge about broad principles regarding relationship building and behavior management but have difficulty integrating those principles into a systematic, consistent plan of action. Most distressing to us are adults whose lack of training leads them to conclude that the normal behaviors children exhibit as part of the socialization process somehow are abnormal or malicious. These people also often fail to recognize the impact of their own behavior on children. As a result, when children do not comply with their expectations, they think condemnation, rather than teaching, is appropriate for the situation. *Guiding Children's Social Development and Learning* has been written to address these shortcomings. We hope to eliminate much of the guesswork and frustration experienced by professionals in the field as well as to improve the conditions under which children are socialized in formal group settings. To accomplish this, we provide a solid foundation of current research on child and adult behavior. We translate that research for real-life use, connect it to skills that are proven to work, and assist students in applying knowledge and practicing skills to effectively support children's social development and learning.

New to This Edition

The eighth edition of *Guiding Children's Social Development and Learning* has been extensively updated. Here are the major changes you will see in *every* chapter within this volume:

- More than one-third of the previous references have been replaced with new research-based material dating from 2006 through 2014.
- Examples of state standards are presented to illustrate the concepts being discussed. A variety of states are featured, highlighting early childhood benchmarks nationwide.
- NAEYC standards are emphasized throughout the text. Each chapter designates the standards it covers.
- A detailed correlation chart highlighting the NAEYC coverage is presented on the front and back inside covers of the book.

- Each chapter incorporates several **Highlight Boxes**. These are short features designed to provide brief summaries of material or examples to further illustrate the material in the text.

- **Digital Downloads** provide information and complete versions of the forms in the textbook for students to download, customize, and use to review key concepts and in the classroom! Look for the Digital Downloads label that identifies these items.

- **TeachSource Videos** feature footage from the classroom to help students relate key chapter content to real-life scenarios. Critical-thinking questions, artifacts, and bonus video help the student reflect on the content in the video.

- Four case studies of children who pose special challenges to adults are available in Appendix B. Case study analyses at the end of each chapter help readers apply what they have learned to a case-related scenario.

- Each chapter ends with a **Reflect on Your Practice feature**. These involve sample checklists students can use to monitor and reflect on their use of particular chapter-related skills in their interactions with children.

- The **Professional Skills Inventory** provided in Appendix C is a comprehensive field-tested classroom observation tool for instructors to use in evaluating student performance in student's practicum sites.

Distinctive Features of this Text

Guiding Children's Social Development and Learning:

- Introduces the Social Support Pyramid in Chapter 1 to describe four phases in guiding children's social behavior. This pyramid appears in each chapter, highlighting how the skills presented in that chapter fit into an overall program of social support and intervention.

- Draws upon research and practice from a variety of fields, linking theory and practice to illuminate research and show readers how it can be translated into practical classroom applications.

- Identifies clear objectives for student learning.

- Offers up-to-date, research-based rationales for skills and methods presented.

- Includes many real-life examples to illustrate key points.

- Offers step-by-step instructions for how to implement skills associated with the content presented in each chapter.

- Describes typical pitfalls associated with learning each skill and how to avoid them.

- Discusses the strong links between social competence and academic success.

- Presents information about children with special needs in all chapters, as well as examples and guidelines on how teachers can adapt the material to their work with children with special needs.

- Presents featured examples about how to work effectively with children whose behavior may present challenges to other children and adults.

- Provides examples of children's art as a way to represent authentic "young voices" in the text.

Presentation

Together, the chapters in this book comprise a thorough picture of children's social development and the classroom practices professionals use to enhance children's social development and learning. We have included traditional areas of study such as self-esteem, aggression, decision-making, rules, and consequences. We also have addressed more current topics such as infant and toddler communication, self-regulation, resilience, friendship, prosocial behavior, bullying prevention, and positive behavior support. Considered individually, each chapter offers an in-depth literature review backed by research findings from many fields (psychology, physiology, education, medicine, sociology, family consumer sciences, interior design). The sequence of chapters also has been thoughtfully planned so that each serves as a foundation for the next—simple concepts and/or skills precede more complex ones; chapters that focus on relationship enhancement come before those that discuss behavior management. We have made liberal use of real-life examples to illustrate concepts and related skills. This is to assist students in making the connection between what they read and "flesh-and-blood" children.

Our scope of study encompasses the social development of children from birth to 12 years of age, with particular emphasis on children birth to age 8. We have targeted this period of childhood because it is during the formative years that the foundation for all socialization takes place. Furthermore, the skills taught have been specially designed to take into account the cognitive structures and social abilities particular to children of this age. Because children live and develop within the context of a family, a community, a nation, and a world, they are constantly influenced by, and in turn affect, the people and events around them. Thus, our perspective is an ecological one in which children are viewed as dynamic, ever-changing beings in an equally dynamic, ever-changing milieu. Additionally, it has been our experience that students learn professional behavior best when they are given clear, succinct directions for how to carry out a procedure. Defining a procedure, offering examples, and giving a rationale for its use are necessary, but not sufficient. Thus, our approach to skill training is to point out to the student research-based strategies related to chapter content. We then break those strategies down into a series of discrete, observable skills that students can implement. We have been direct in articulating the specific steps involved. This forthrightness should not be taken to mean that there is no room for students to use the skills creatively. We anticipate that students will internalize and modify skills according to their own needs, personality, interaction style, and circumstance after they have learned them.

In addition, we recognize that an important component of using skills correctly is determining which alternatives from the entire available array are best suited to a given situation. Hence, knowing when to use a particular skill and when to refrain from using it is as important as knowing how to use it. For this reason, we discuss these issues throughout each chapter, both in the body of the text and in the pitfalls section at the end. We also have incorporated specific guidelines for how the skills can be adapted for use with children of varying ages and differing ability levels.

Supplementary Materials

In addition to the textbook, we have designed an *online resource* to help students master the skills presented in the textbook and an *instructor's manual* for the teacher.

Student CourseMate

Cengage Learning's Education CourseMate brings course concepts to life with interactive learning, study, and exam preparation tools that support the printed textbook. Visit the Education CourseMate for this textbook to access the eBook, Digital Downloads, TeachSource Videos, and quizzes. Go to CengageBrain.com to log in, register, or purchase access.

Instructor CourseMate

CourseMate includes the eBook, quizzes, Digital Downloads, TeachSource Videos, flashcards, and more—as well as EngagementTracker, a first-of-its-kind tool that monitors student engagement in the course. The accompanying instructor website, available through *login.cengage.com*, offers access to password-protected resources such as PowerPoint® lecture slides and the online Instructor's Manual with Test Bank. Course-

Mate can be bundled with the student text. Contact your Cengage sales representative for information on getting access to CourseMate.

Online Instructor's Manual with Test Bank

An online Instructor's Manual accompanies this book. It contains information to assist the instructor in designing the course, including sample syllabi, discussion questions, teaching and learning activities, field experiences, learning objectives, and additional online resources.

In addition, we have included a series of rehearsal exercises, which are role-play activities to be carried out in class. They acquaint students with how to use particular skills prior to implementing them with children and clarify basic concepts as they emerge during discussion or interaction. Finally, the Instructor's Manual contains a criterion-referenced observational tool, the PSI (Professional Skills Inventory). This is a unique feature of our instructional package. This instrument has been validated with hundreds of students and can be used by instructors and/or practitioners to evaluate the degree to which students demonstrate the skills taught. It includes the actual instrument that appears in Appendix C, as well as a coding manual to provide more specific examples of behaviors associated with each of the 10 observational categories identified on the Professional Skills Inventory Rating form. For assessment support, the accompanying updated Test Bank includes true/false, multiple-choice, matching, short-answer, and essay questions for each chapter.

PowerPoint Lecture Slides

These vibrant Microsoft® PowerPoint lecture slides for each chapter assist you with your lecture by providing concept coverage using images, figures, and tables directly from the textbook!

To the Student

This book will give you a foundation of knowledge and skills necessary for guiding children's social development and learning in professional practice. We hope it contributes to your enthusiasm about the field and to your confidence in working with children and their families. Although what you read here is not everything you will ever need to know, it will give you a secure base from which to develop your own professional style. You will have the advantage of learning, in one course, information and strategies that otherwise might take many years to discover.

Finally, you are reading a book authored by people with extensive practical experience in working with children, engaging in research, and teaching this content to learners much like yourselves. As a result, we are well aware of the issues related to children's social development that are important to students, and we have focused on those. We also have anticipated some of the questions you might ask and some of the difficulties you might encounter in working with this material. Consequently, we have made a conscious effort to discuss these in relevant places throughout the book.

Hints for Using the Materials

1. Read each chapter carefully. Plan to read them more than once. Use the first reading to gain a broad grasp of the subject matter; then, read a second time, paying particular attention to the sequence of development presented. Identify major concepts regarding adult behavior, and focus on the actual procedures related to each skill.

2. Make notes in the margin and highlight points you want to remember.

3. Go beyond simply memorizing terminology. Concentrate on how you might recognize the concepts you are studying in real children's behavior and how you might apply this knowledge in your interactions with children.

4. Ask questions. Share with classmates and the instructor your experiences in using the material. Participate fully in class discussions and role-play exercises.

5. Try out what you are learning with children. If you are in a field placement, are volunteering, or are employed in a program, take full advantage of that opportunity. Do not hesitate to practice your skills simply because they are new to you and you are not sure how well you will perform them. Persist in spite of your awkwardness or mistakes, and make note of what you might do to improve. Focus on your successes and your increasing skill, not just on things that don't go perfectly.

Acknowledgements and Thanks

We thank the following persons for their contributions to our work: Louise F. Guerney, professor emeritus The Pennsylvania State University, and Steven J. Danish, Commonwealth University of Virginia, were original sources of information regarding the philosophy and skills presented here. Laura C. Stein, coauthor and master teacher of children and students at Michigan State University, and Kara Murphy Gregory, early childhood instructor extraordinaire and consultant, worked hand in hand with us in developing the several editions of this textbook that preceded this one. We owe them much for their insights and for helping our ideas come alive on the page. Special thanks must also go to the Gregory children, whose artwork graces many of these pages. The following reviewers provided valuable feedback throughout the revision process for this edition:

Linda Aiken, Southwestern Community College, Sylva; Johnny Castro, Brookhaven College; Stephanie Daniel, J. Sargeant Reynolds Community College; Jennifer DeFrance, Three Rivers Community College; Elizabeth Elliott, Florida Gulf Coast University; Lisa Fuller, Cerro Coso Community College; Monica Garcia, University of Texas at San Antonio; Rea Gubler, Southern Utah University; Delora J. Hade, Des Moines Area Community College; Gale Hall, NHTI, Concord's Community College; Sharon Hirschy, Collin County Community College; Jennifer Johnson, Vance Granville Community College; Mary Larue, J. Sargeant Reynolds Community College; Elizabeth McCarroll, Texas Woman's University; Linda Rivers, University of Tennessee at Chattanooga; Jana Sanders, Texas A&M University–Corpus Christi; Grace Spalding, Michigan State University, Child Development Laboratory; Kathy Lynn Sullivan, Columbia College; Cathy Twyman, Daytona State College; and Christina Wake, Southwestern Michigan College.

Finally, over the years, we have worked with many students whose enthusiasm and excitement have invigorated us. Simultaneously, we have been privileged to know hundreds of children during their formative years. From them, we have gained insight and the motivation to pursue this project. We dedicate this book to them.

1 Making a Difference in Children's Lives

OBJECTIVES

On completion of this chapter, you should be able to:

Define social competence, and explain how it affects children's lives.

Describe how child development influences social competence.

Explain the role of learning in achieving social competence.

Identify the contexts in which children develop socially.

Talk about your professional role in supporting children's social competence.

Discuss how developmentally appropriate practices support the development of social competence.

NAEYC STANDARDS naeyc

1. Promoting Child Development and Learning
2. Building Family and Community Relationships
3. Using Developmentally Effective Approaches to Connect with Children and Families
4. Using Content Knowledge to Build Meaningful Curriculum
5. Becoming a Professional

Think about the aspects of everyday living that are most important to you—family life, time with friends, school, work, and play. They all involve human relationships. People are social beings. From the moment we are born, we spend a lifetime actively engaged with others. Through social interactions, we gain companionship, stimulation, and a sense of belonging. We obtain knowledge of who we are and how the world works. We develop personal and interpersonal skills and become familiar with the expectations and values of the society in which we live. Lessons learned during the early years about how to act and interact with others set the foundation for our success as adults. This is such a crucial facet of the human experience that much of children's attention during childhood centers on how to effectively navigate the social environment.

The social environment is complicated. Think about meeting someone for the first time. What do you do? How do you greet this person? You are probably thinking, "It depends," and you are correct. There is a lot to know and many things you must be able to do to function successfully in society. To interact effectively, you need to know a variety of scripts and what physical actions others will interpret as friendly. You have to make judgments about what is polite or impolite based on how well you know a person, his or her role, your role, the time, the place, and the culture in which you are operating. Based on all this, you will form an idea of how to best greet the person you have just met. Likewise, you will adopt a very different manner to greet someone at a football game than you might use at a funeral. Although such variations make common sense to adults, children are new to the world, and many of the social understandings and behaviors we take for granted are things children are just learning.

Imagine you are working with children in a child-care setting or elementary classroom. You observe the following behaviors among three 6-year-olds in your group: Dennis, Rosalie, and Sarah Jo.

Dennis is an active child. He has strong reactions to the people and things around him. He is imaginative, with many ideas for how to play. In an effort to translate his ideas into action, Dennis spends a lot of time telling the other children what to do and what to say. When peers suggest alternate play themes or strategies, Dennis tends to resist their ideas and yell to make things go his way. When other children ask if they can play with something he is using, Dennis often answers, "No." If they persist, it is not unusual for him to push or hit to keep things for himself.

Rosalie is a quiet child who seldom misbehaves. Typically, she wanders from one activity to the next without talking to the other children. Rosalie responds when spoken to but rarely initiates social interactions with peers or adults. She cannot name anyone in the group who is her friend, and no other children identify her as a favorite playmate. Although children do not actively reject her, they have come to ignore her and seldom include her in their activities. Most days, Rosalie is a solitary figure in the room.

Sarah Jo is keenly interested in the other children and often invites them to interact with her. Frequently, she is willing to try games or play in ways proposed by peers, yet she also expresses ideas of her own. Sarah Jo shares easily and can usually figure out how to keep the play going. Although she has her ups and downs, she is generally cheerful. Other children seek her out as a playmate and notice when Sarah Jo is absent from the group.

As you can see, each of these children is exhibiting a variety of social behaviors. Unfortunately, Dennis and Rosalie are displaying interaction patterns that are not serving them well. In fact, if they maintain these patterns over time, their prospects for life success will be weakened (Goleman, 2011). On the other hand, Sarah Jo has skills that predict a positive future.

As an early childhood professional, you could help Dennis and Rosalie develop better ways of getting along with others. You could also support Sarah Jo in expanding her skills. In doing these things, you would be contributing to each child's social competence. To promote social competence, you must first know what it is and what behaviors characterize socially competent children.

Social Competence Defined naeyc

Social competence includes the knowledge and skills children need to achieve their goals and to effectively interact with others (Davidson, Welsh, & Bierman, 2006; Rose-Krasnor & Denham, 2009). Consider the social, emotional, language, and cognitive skills the children are displaying in the following classroom interaction:

Claude and Alex are both building in the block area. When Alex takes a block from the shelf, Claude protests, "I need all the long blocks for my airport! Give it to me!" He yanks the block from Alex, who yells, "I need it for my bridge!" The boys each begin to tug on the block. After a few seconds, Claude suggests, "Hey, let's make your bridge go to the airport. All the people have to go on the bridge if they want to go to the airport!" Alex replies, "Yeah! That's a good idea! A big bridge for all the cars to drive on!" The boys begin to work together to create a road connecting the airport and bridge.

Think about the skills Alex and Claude demonstrated as they solved their problem in the block area. They used cognitive skills in recognizing a mutual problem, language skills in expressing their individual needs, and social skills when they developed a strategy for working together. By inhibiting an initial impulse to fight over the blocks, Alex and Claude exhibited emotional self-regulation and an awareness of how the other might feel. As you can see, a variety of knowledge and skills are evident in this simple interaction.

Many behaviors are associated with social competence. Typical categories include the following:

- Social values
- Personal identity
- Emotional intelligence
- Interpersonal skills
- Self-regulation
- Planning, organizing, and decision making
- Cultural competence

Early childhood professionals should observe the behavior of the children they are working with to evaluate the social skills they are exhibiting. What social behaviors are these children exhibiting?

As you can tell by examining Figure 1-1, social competence integrates a broad range of values, attitudes, knowledge, and skills involving both self and others.

In the United States and in many societies throughout the world, people tend to view children as more socially competent when they are responsible rather than irresponsible; friendly, not hostile; cooperative instead of oppositional; purposeful rather than aimless; and self-controlled, not impulsive (Hastings et al., 2006; Denham, Bassett, & Wyatt, 2008). Based on this perspective, Keisha, who notices that Gary is unhappy and attempts to comfort him, is more socially competent than Ralph, who walks by unaware of Gary's distress. Dinah, who often blurts out whatever comes to mind the instant it occurs to her, is less socially competent than if she were able to wait without interrupting. When Dante uses verbal reasoning to persuade his friends to give him a turn with a Wii game, he is demonstrating more social competence than a classmate who whines or relies on physical force to make his point. The profile of a socially competent child presented in Highlight 1-1 will give you a sense of how social competence translates into child attributes and behaviors (McClellan & Katz, 2001).

Note that the words *usually, frequently,* and *sometimes* best describe socially competent children's behavior. Children will not always be in a positive mood, nor will they always experience success in asserting their rights appropriately. "Any child may occasionally have some social difficulty ... for most children, these events are short-lived and constitute opportunities to learn and to practice new skills" (Hastings et al., 2006, p. 4). Children who take advantage of these opportunities (rather than becoming hostile or giving up) become increasingly successful in their social interactions and in achieving their personal goals effectively.

Individual Variations in Social Competence

Consider the following personal attributes:

- Kindness
- Honesty
- Shyness
- Generosity
- Friendliness
- Assertiveness

Which of these do you associate with social competence?

If you were to compare your answers with those of other readers, you would find many choices in common but probably not all because definitions of social competence are fairly similar worldwide and incorporate most

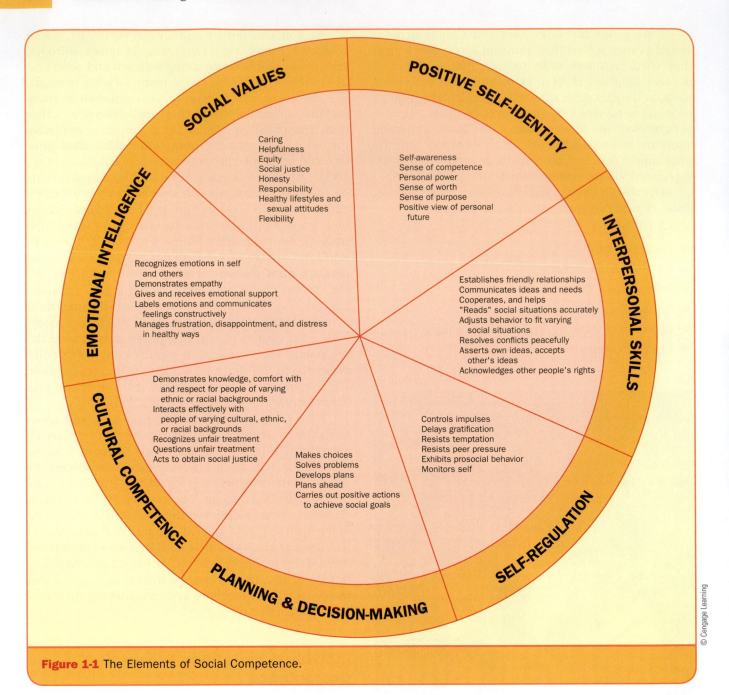

Figure 1-1 The Elements of Social Competence.

of the categories identified in Figure 1-1 (van Hamond & Haccou, 2006). However, some behaviors defined as socially competent in one culture are not defined that same way in others. For instance, people in Canada, China, Sweden, and the United States describe qualities such as friendly, kind, helpful, generous, and good problem solvers as socially competent (Ladd, 2005). However, although each country identified several qualities in common, there were also differences. For example, people in China identified "shy" as being socially competent while "not shy" was listed as competent by the other countries. To further complicate things, the same social value may be demonstrated through different behaviors in different groups. For instance, although many societies value respect, the combination of words and actions considered respectful in one family or culture may not match what is viewed as respectful in another (e.g., in some households, it is respectful to take your shoes off before entering the main living area; in other households, this is not expected).

Such variations contribute to distinct definitions of social competence across and within cultures. Yet, regardless of which behaviors equate with social competence in a given group, all children eventually develop behavior patterns that can be described as more or less socially competent within the society in

---

HIGHLIGHT 1-1

Observable Behaviors of Socially Competent Children

Individual Attributes

The child
1. is usually in a positive mood
2. is not excessively dependent on the teacher
3. usually comes to the program willingly
4. usually copes with rebuffs adequately
5. shows the capacity to empathize
6. has positive relationships with one or two peers; shows the capacity to really care about them and misses them if they are absent
7. displays a capacity for humor
8. does not seem to be acutely lonely

Social Skills

The child usually
1. approaches others positively
2. expresses wishes and preferences clearly; gives reasons for actions and positions
3. asserts own rights and needs appropriately
4. is not easily intimidated by bullies
5. expresses frustration and anger effectively and without escalating disagreements or harming others
6. gains access to ongoing groups at play and work
7. enters ongoing discussions; makes relevant contributions to ongoing activities
8. takes turns fairly easily
9. shows interest in others; exchanges information with and requests information from others appropriately
10. negotiates and compromises with others appropriately
11. does not draw inappropriate attention to self or disrupt the play or work of others
12. accepts and enjoys peers and adults of ethnic groups other than his or her own
13. interacts nonverbally with other children using smiles, waves, nods, and so on

Peer Relationships

The child is
1. usually accepted rather than neglected or rejected by other children
2. sometimes invited by other children to join them in play, friendship, and work
3. named by other children as someone they are friends with or like to play and work with

Source: Reprinted with permission from *Assessing Young Children's Social Competence,* by D. McClellan and L. Katz, 2001, ERIC Clearinghouse on Elementary and Early Childhood Education, Champaign, IL. (ERIC Document Reproduction Service No. ED450953).

---

which they live. These behavior patterns will have a powerful influence on their lives.

The Benefits of Being Socially Competent

. . . the single best childhood predictor of adult adaptation is not IQ nor school grades, but rather the adequacy with which a child gets along with others.

Children who are generally disliked, who are aggressive and disruptive, who are unable to sustain close relationships with others . . . are seriously "at risk."

—Willard Hartup (early childhood researcher)

Social competence is not a luxury. It makes a tremendous difference in how children feel about themselves and in how others perceive them. Research tells us that socially competent children are happier than their less competent peers. They are more successful in their interactions with others, more popular, and more satisfied with life. In addition, children's social relations have been linked to academic achievement, with positive social skills being associated with greater success in school (Epstein, 2009). See Highlight Box 1-2.

As a result of these favorable outcomes, socially competent children tend to see themselves as worthwhile human beings who can make a difference in the world. Other people perceive them as desirable companions and competent members of society. The same cannot be said for children whose social competence is poor. Youngsters unable to function successfully in the social world often experience distress and loneliness, even in the early years. They frequently are rejected by peers, suffer low self-esteem, and do more poorly in

Socially competent children are more successful in their interactions with others.

© Cengage Learning

HIGHLIGHT 1-2

Learning Is a Social Process

Academic success in the early school years is based on social and emotional skills. Young children can't learn to read, do their sums, or solve a science problem if they have difficulty getting along with others and controlling their emotions, if they are impulsive, and if they have no idea about how to consider options, carry out a plan, or get help.

Students who demonstrate strong social and emotional skills also tend to exhibit the following:

- Greater academic motivation
- More positive attitudes toward school
- Fewer absences
- More classroom participation
- Higher math achievement
- Higher language arts achievement
- Higher social studies achievement
- Higher grades
- Fewer suspensions
- Less tendency to drop out in high school

Source: Zins, J., Bloodworth, M., Weissberg, R., & Walberg, H. (2004). The scientific base linking social and emotional learning to school success. In J. Zins, R. Weissberg, M. Wang, & H. J. Walberg (Eds.), *Building academic success on social and emotional learning: What does the research say?* (pp. 1–22). New York: Teachers College Press, Columbia University; Ladd, G. W. (2008). Social competence and peer relations: Significance for young children and their service providers. *Early Childhood Services*, 2(3), 129–148.

school (Miles & Stipek, 2006). To make matters worse, socially incompetent children are at risk of continuing these problematic behavior patterns as they mature (Ladd, 2008).

Whether children eventually become more or less socially competent is influenced by many factors, including child development, childhood learning, and the contexts in which children function. You will need to know more about all of these things to support children in their journey toward social competence.

What Early Childhood Professionals Need to Know about Children's Development and Social Competence naeyc

Katie and Sandra, two 5-year-olds, are rocking their dolls in the housekeeping area.

Katie: We're friends, right?

Sandra: Yeah. You have a baby, and I have a baby boy.

Katie: These babies can't be friends. They don't talk or nothin'.

Sandra: Babies can't play games or save swings.

Katie: Not yet!

Sandra: Not like us!

Katie: Yeah!

Katie and Sandra are pleased to be friends and are proud of the social abilities they possess at 5 years of age that "their babies" have not yet developed. As children mature, developmental changes gradually occur that increase their social capacities. Such changes are governed by certain developmental principles that help us recognize commonalities among children and characteristics typical within age ranges (Copple & Bredekamp, 2009). These five principles remind us that children's social development is complex, requiring the support of knowledgeable adults who appreciate the unique qualities of the children they serve.

All Development Is Interrelated

All threads of development (social, emotional, cognitive, language, and physical) interweave and exist simultaneously. No aspect of development is more important than another, nor can any single thread exist independent of the rest. The truth of this principle is illustrated as children try to make friends. Their ability to establish relations with peers is dependent on a whole host of developmental skills and understandings.

- **Social:** Negotiating the rules of a game; waiting to take a turn; working out who will go first
- **Emotional:** Having confidence to approach another child; responding with enthusiasm when invited to play by a peer; expressing empathy toward another child
- **Cognitive:** Remembering another child's name; developing alternate strategies for how to solve conflicts that arise; knowing which scripts fit which social situations
- **Language:** Using words to greet another child or to describe how a game could be played; responding with appropriate comments to questions from a potential friend
- **Physical:** Making room for a new player; having the motor skills necessary to play a video game or a game of chase with a potential friend

Recognizing that all development is interrelated will enable you to better appreciate the many social behaviors children are striving to master. It will also help you identify opportunities to guide children's social development and learning throughout the day. Such chances come up as children play in the pretend grocery store, discuss rules for building with blocks, proceed through the steps in a science experiment, or work out a math problem in a group. These opportunities may occur indoors, outside, at the lunch table, in the gym, on the bus, during a field trip, or at a home visit. Social development is happening all the time and everywhere children are found.

Social Development Occurs in an Orderly Sequence

Try putting these developmental milestones related to self-awareness in the order in which they tend to appear during childhood:

- Children define themselves by comparing themselves to others. (I ride bikes better than Susan. I am shorter than Marc.)
- Children define themselves based on their personality traits. (I am honest. I am fun to be with.)
- Children define themselves based on what they look like. (I am a boy. I have brown eyes.)

What did you decide? In their proper order, social benchmarks such as these illustrate the principle of developmental sequence.

Social development proceeds in a stepwise fashion and is relatively predictable. Scientists worldwide have identified typical sequences of behavior or understanding related to various aspects of social development and social competence (Berk, 2013). For instance, children develop their concept of self over several years.

Preschoolers tend to focus primarily on physical traits. As they grow older, children gradually incorporate comparisons into their definition of self. By age 8 or 9, children become more conscious of the internal characteristics that comprise their personality. Although children spend differing amounts of time on each step and sometimes skip steps altogether, self-awareness seems to progress in roughly the same order for everyone.

There are developmental sequences for many aspects of social competence—self-regulation, empathy, prosocial behavior, moral understanding, ideas about friendship, and so forth. As you learn these sequences, you will gain insights into what comes first, second, and third in social maturation. Such knowledge will help you determine reasonable expectations for individual children and decide what new understandings or behaviors might logically expand children's current levels of functioning. For example, knowing that 3- and 4-year-olds focus on the physical traits that characterize who they are, you might plan classroom activities such as self-portraits or body tracings to enhance their self-awareness. On the other hand, you might ask early elementary-aged children, whose physical sense of self is more established, to tell or write stories focused on the personal qualities they value in themselves, such as honesty or being a good friend.

Rates of Development Vary Among Children

> Darlene is 4 years old; so is Emma. Darlene could use whole phrases to describe her feelings by age 2. She has numerous strategies for getting what she wants, including taking turns and making plans for the order in which children will get to use a favored toy. Emma only began using multiword sentences around age 3. Her approaches to getting something she wants include asking a child who has it if she can have it next or getting the teacher to help her find another one like it. Darlene and Emma are alike in many ways, but they are different from one another as well. Both children are developing in a typical manner.

As illustrated by Darlene and Emma, all children develop according to their own timetable. No two children are exactly alike. Although the principle of orderly sequences still applies, the pace at which individuals go through the various sequences differs.

This explains why Darlene could express her feelings in words by age 2, and Emma accomplished the same skill several months later. Both children are exhibiting typical development, but the timing is different.

Based on the principle of varying rates, you can presume children of the same age will exhibit a wide range of social abilities. Some will be in the early developmental phases of a particular skill, and others will be farther along in the sequence. These variations are not a question of bad or good, worse or better, but simply typical differences in children's social development. Understanding this will help you to be more patient with children and more realistic in what you expect of them.

There Are Optimal Periods of Social Development

There are certain moments in childhood when the door opens and lets the future in.

—Graham Greene (novelist)

Certain times in people's lives provide critical foundations for future development (Brophy-Herb, Schiffman, & Fitzgerald, 2007). During these periods, children are developmentally primed to acquire new understandings and skills. Conversely, if children are denied the kinds of experiences that will enhance development during this time, it may be harder for them to acquire certain skills or abilities later on. This is the principle of optimal periods of development.

Between the ages of birth and 12 years, children are eager, motivated social learners. They want to connect—to become socially engaged. Concurrently, negative behavior patterns are not so entrenched that they cannot be changed. This makes childhood an ideal time for enhancing many essential attitudes and behaviors related to social competence. Some of these include the following:

- Trust
- Self-awareness and self-esteem
- Interpersonal communication skills
- Prosocial attitudes and behaviors
- Friendship dispositions and skills
- Problem-solving strategies
- Coping skills
- Executive function (decision making, organizing, planning ahead)
- Self-regulation

If the preceding developmental tasks are ignored, it is harder for children to become socially adept as adolescents or adults. The principle of optimal periods compels us to focus on children's social development beginning when they are babies and well into the second decade of life.

Social Development Has Cumulative and Delayed Effects

An experience that has a minimal effect on a child's development if it occurs once in a while may have a positive or harmful influence if it happens repeatedly over a long period of time (Katz & Chard, 2000). This is the principle of cumulative effects. For instance, being the target of occasional criticism is not likely to cause permanent damage to children's self-esteem; however, youngsters who are subjected to steady fault finding are likely to develop lasting feelings of inferiority and pessimism (Seligman, 2007). On the other hand, reasoning with a child only once will not have a lasting impact on that child. However, adults who make a habit of reasoning with children will gradually see those children become better able to reason for themselves.

In addition to these accumulated impacts, developmental outcomes may be delayed. Some early experiences influence children's functioning in ways that only appear much later in life. For instance, children's development of self-regulation takes years to accomplish. Adults may even begin to wonder if their early efforts at reasoning with children will ever yield positive results. However, research shows that when adults consistently explain their point of view while also considering the child's perspective, children eventually become better able to monitor their behavior without constant supervision (Shaffer & Kipp, 2013). These strategies must be used for a long time before children can reason on their own.

Knowing the principle of cumulative and delayed effects will help you consider the long-range implications of your efforts to guide children's social development and behavior. As a result, there will be times when you reject a quick solution because it could undermine your long-term goals. For instance, even though it is faster to simply tell children "No," when they disobey, if you want children to develop self-regulation, you will take the time to talk to them about their actions. In doing so, both the cumulative and delayed effects of reasoning support children's eventual development of social competence.

As you can see, development plays a significant role in the extent to which children gain social competence. Understanding developmental principles will influence your interpretations of child behavior as well as your professional practices. Childhood learning is another factor to consider.

Learning and Social Competence naeyc

Cooperation, generosity, loyalty, and honesty are not inborn. They must be passed on to the child by older people, whether they are parents, other adults, or older youngsters.

—Urie Bronfenbrenner (human ecologist)

Some of the social learning we pass on to children includes saying, "Excuse me" when they bump into someone, crossing streets at the corner, and deriving pleasure from sharing with another child. We communicate such lessons through our words and our deeds. How well children learn these lessons is governed by several principles of learning that impact social competence.

Children Are Active Social Learners

Consider the following Chinese proverb:

> I hear, and I forget,
> I see, and I remember,
> I do, and I understand.

This saying captures a central truth about childhood learning: Children are doers. They do not wait passively for others to load them up with information. Children have active bodies and minds, which they use to make sense of social experiences in whatever they do. They accomplish this by observing, acting

on objects, and interacting with other people (Copple & Bredekamp, 2009). As a result of their experiences, children form ideas about how the social world works. (For instance, Cory might think, "If I say 'Please,' Mohammed will give me the scissors right now.") Sometimes children's ideas are confirmed (Mohammed says, "Okay"). Sometimes children encounter evidence that is contrary to what they believe (Mohammed says "No" because he still needs the scissors). By observing, experimenting, and reflecting on what happens, children gradually make adjustments in their thinking (Cory decides, "I will have to wait for the scissors, but I'll get them next"). Through hundreds of experiences like these, children construct ideas about codes of behavior to follow and strategies to use (Piaget, 1962; Vygotsky, 1978).

Because children are active learners, they need many opportunities to experience the social world firsthand. For instance, children become more skillful at sharing when they practice sharing with others in their daily encounters, rather than simply hearing or talking about sharing. Figuring out how to divide the crackers at snack time, how two people can use the computer together, or how to fit an extra person into a game are tangible problems children can solve on their own or with support from you. Such natural opportunities for social learning become teachable moments, in which children are motivated to learn new strategies. A typical teachable moment occurs when Celia wants to jump rope with a group of children already jumping. Her teacher uses this chance to help Celia figure out words she might use to approach the other children. On-the-spot mini-lessons like these are powerful. Children have immediate opportunities to practice relevant new skills as well as get feedback on the strategies they use. As you guide children's social development and behavior, you will need to look for these teachable moments and take advantage of the learning opportunities they offer.

Children Have Multiple Ways of Learning about the Social World

Although all children are active learners, they perceive, act on, and process social information in many ways. Consider the following examples:

> Gary has a real feel for music and uses that medium as a way to express his feelings. When a problem comes up, he likes to figure it out on his own.
>
> Samantha has a way with words. It's easy for her to communicate needs and feelings to others verbally. In problem situations, she prefers strategizing with a friend.

Children benefit from having many opportunities to interact with minimal adult intervention.

Gary and Samantha are demonstrating different combinations of knowing and learning.

Children learn best when they have access to learning opportunities that match the learning modes they favor. Because you cannot always be sure which manner of learning suits an individual child best, children benefit when you use a variety of modes in your social teaching. For instance, assume you want children to learn about helping. Some children may find it useful to:

- Carry out a classroom job on their own or read a book to themselves about helpful people.
- Interact with another child to carry out a classroom job.
- Rehearse a helpful act before trying it out for real.
- Talk about helpful actions they observed or carried out.
- Sing or make up a catchy song about helping.
- Reflect on a helpful act they have seen or heard about.

Most children combine such experiences, extracting important information from the ones that match their preferred ways of learning. As you guide children's social development, you will have to be sensitive to these different learning styles and make use of strategies that address each of them. See the downloadable observation tool you might use to learn more about an individual child's social competence. [insert link here]

Social Competence Involves Continuous Challenge and Mastery

Children enjoy the challenge of learning what they nearly understand, but do not quite grasp, and of trying things they can almost, but not quite, do on their own. This means they benefit from tackling concepts

Social Competence Anecdotal Record

Child's Name: _____ **Date:** _____

- Strengths in social competence:

- What I observed that demonstrates these strengths:

- Areas for improvement:

- What I observed that demonstrates an opportunity for improvement:

- Steps I will take to assist this child in developing further social competence:

Digital Download   **Download from CourseMate**

and skills just slightly beyond their current levels of proficiency and from working at them until they achieve greater competence (Bodrova & Leong, 2007). At the same time, research shows that children need to successfully negotiate learning tasks most of the time if they are to remain motivated to learn. Youngsters who are overwhelmed will fail. If failure becomes routine, most children will simply stop trying (Copple & Bredekamp, 2009). Thus, positive social learning is most likely to occur when children feel both stimulated and successful. Knowing this, your role is to monitor social situations, challenge children to stretch their understandings, support children as they attempt new social skills, and help children figure out more successful approaches. At times, peers may provide these supports instead. As children become more adept, you will gradually withdraw from the scene, allowing them to pursue mastery on their own.

Two-year-old Callie wants more snack but does not know how to ask for it—this example can be used to illustrate the process of challenge and mastery. Some on-the-spot coaching by you or a more knowledgeable peer could facilitate Callie's learning. Coaching might involve suggesting a simple script for Callie to use to get her peers to pass the cracker basket. If your words are too complex or too abstract, Callie will not absorb the lesson. If the script is just slightly more involved than Callie is used to, however, she may stretch her thinking to encompass the new words. Chances are, Callie will not learn the new script in a single episode, but this interaction may prompt her to try the new script in a variety of situations, practicing until she eventually gains mastery without prompting from someone else. In doing this, she will actually move to a higher order of social learning.

Social Learning Takes Time

There is more to life than simply increasing its speed.

—Mahatma Gandhi (political and spiritual leader)

Social learning is a gradual process. Although children are social beings at birth, they are not born socially competent. Nor do they attain mature levels of competence quickly (Shaffer & Kipp, 2013). Thus, when they come to preschool, kindergarten, or even fifth grade, youngsters are not yet socially mature. Throughout the preschool and elementary years, children spend much of their time exploring social ideas, experimenting with various strategies, and seeking clues about what works in the social world and what does not. This social learning cannot be unduly hurried. Numerous opportunities to engage in social interactions are needed to perfect social concepts and skills. This is true for typically developing children

as well as for children with special needs. While all young children need time and guidance to develop social skills, some children require extra help. Consider this as you think about Patrick, who is described on the following page.

As an early childhood professional, you have the responsibility to see that children, including youngsters like Patrick, get the time and opportunity to develop their social skills. In line with this task, you will need to exercise patience and provide support as children practice new techniques. That practice will take place in a variety of social contexts, including the early childhood setting. However, teachers do not socialize children all on their own. Many others are involved in the process too. This requires you to take into account all of the environments in which children acquire social competence.

The Social Environment naeyc

Some of the many settings where children form ideas and behaviors associated with social competence include at home, at Grandma's house, at the childcare center, at school, on the playground, in a peer group, at synagogue, and in the neighborhood. Things that happen in any one or all of these environments affect children in various ways, ultimately influencing the degree of social competence they achieve. To guide children's social development and behavior effectively, you must consider how such forces combine to affect children's lives (Arnett, 2008).

The most immediate social environment includes the people, materials, activities, and interpersonal relationships children experience directly in face-to-face settings such as home or school.

In these settings, children gain social experience through interactions with people and things. Now let's examine three influences especially important to children early in life: family, peer group, and early childhood settings.

Family Influences

Families throughout the world bear primary responsibility for meeting children's physical needs, nurturing children, and socializing them (Turnbull, Turnbull, Erwin, & Soodak, 2006). Family members have long-term attachments to children, providing links to their past as well as visions for their future (Gonzalez-Mena & Eyer, 2011). Parents and sometimes grandparents, aunts and uncles, or brothers and sisters are children's first teachers. They provide children with their earliest social relationships, models for behaviors and roles, a framework of values and beliefs, and intellectual stimulation. The initial attitudes toward other people, education, work,

Meet Patrick

Four-year-old Patrick is enrolled in Head Start. He likes to build with blocks, create things at the art table, ride trikes on the playground, and jump on the trampoline at home. He is a high-energy child with a charming smile. Patrick is also very curious. However, his attention moves from one thing to the next quickly, and he is easily distracted. It is hard for Patrick to listen to a story the whole way through, to pay attention when an adult is giving directions, to sit in his chair at snack, or to follow along when someone is explaining what will happen next. Although most young children fidget and squirm sometimes, Patrick is in perpetual motion most of the time. His impulsivity is very high, and his ability to deal with frustration is extremely low. These behaviors contribute to poor social relations with peers. Recently, Patrick's parents, caregiver, and pediatrician have been exploring the idea that Patrick may have ADHD.

Children with ADHD (attention-deficit hyperactive disorder) are hyperalert, responding to everything they see or hear. This leads to impulsiveness and the inability to attend to any one thing very long. These behaviors are present at levels much higher than expected for the child's developmental stage and actually interfere with the child's daily functioning. ADHD affects approximately 3–7% of the U.S. population and is diagnosed three times more often in boys than in girls (CDC, 2006). Because of their distracted, impulsive nature, children with ADHD need ongoing assistance from caring adults to develop greater social competence.

and society that children encounter are in the family. These functions take place through direct and indirect teaching, in constructive and sometimes destructive ways, more or less successfully. Through their actions and choices, families play the lead role in transmitting to children the manners, views, beliefs, and ideas held and accepted by the society in which they live. Eventually, however, children's social worlds expand beyond the home or extended family.

Peer Group Influences

As children interact with peers in childcare settings, at school, and in the neighborhood, a significant amount of social learning occurs. Within peer relationships, children learn concepts of reciprocity and fairness through the give and take that happens among equals. The social negotiation, discussion, and conflict found among peers help children learn to understand others' thoughts, emotions, motives, and intentions. This understanding enables children to think about the consequences of their behavior both for themselves and for others (Doll, Zucker, & Brehm, 2004). Then, as they receive feedback from their peers, children begin to evaluate the appropriateness of their actions and modify their behavior accordingly (Santrock, 2012). Consequently, peer relations provide critical contexts for social cognition (i.e., thinking about social phenomena) and social action. Such thinking and acting may result in either negative or positive social outcomes. This process is illustrated when 7-year-old Marvin has a "meltdown" each time he strikes out in T-ball. At first, his peers

say nothing, but after a few instances, they tell him to stop and complain that he is acting like a baby. Marvin eventually stops protesting so loudly if his turn at bat goes poorly. He wants the other children to accept him and comes to realize that they are more tolerant of his striking out than of his tantrums. Chances are you can think of many additional examples of how the peer group provides an important context for social learning.

Caregiver and Teacher Influences

Caregivers and teachers play key roles in promoting children's social competence (Wentzel & Looney, 2008; Ladd, 2008). They do this by engaging in a variety of social behaviors such as the following:

- Forming relationships with children
- Communicating values to children
- Instructing children
- Modeling social behaviors and attitudes
- Designing activities that highlight and give children practice in relevant knowledge and skills
- Planning the physical environment
- Formulating routines
- Communicating rules to children
- Enacting positive or corrective consequences to help children comply with societal expectations

Both social and emotional competence are essential for optimal success. The Head Start Child Outcomes Framework asserts that early social and emotional development is critical to later academic

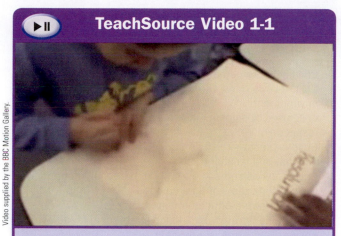

TeachSource Video 1-1

BBC Motion Gallery: *Learning through Play*

Go online and view *Learning through Play*. In this video, you will observe early childhood education in Wales.

1. How might education based on play assist children in developing social competence?

2. What opportunities did you see for children to interact with one another? How might this contribute to social competence?

3. How would teaching children in small groups contribute to social competence?

Watch on CourseMate

- Live in the same place
- See themselves as members of a particular generation
- Consider themselves to be of a particular economic/social class

Social values and beliefs vary from society to society and within societies among various subcultures. Some examples of typical variations among groups are depicted in Highlight 1-3.

These beliefs are transmitted from generation to generation. Children learn them explicitly through direct teaching and implicitly through the behavior of those around them (Copple & Bredekamp, 2009). As a result of how different groups approach these issues, children learn different things. For instance, in some societies, children learn that competition is good; in others, children learn to value cooperation more highly. In one group, time may be treated as a finite commodity not to be wasted; in another group, time may be seen as more fluid and less pressing. Such beliefs and values shape how people believe children should be treated, what they should be taught, and what behaviors and attitudes represent social competence (Berns, 2012).

achievement in school and to preventing future social and behavioral difficulty (Bierman et al., 2008). Social competence is also addressed in the formal learning standards designated for state-sponsored early childhood programs and elementary education programs throughout the United States. These standards describe what children should know and be able to do in the program. Although each state has its own standards, all of the states address social competence in some way. See Table 1-1 for examples.

Cultural Contexts

Family members, peers, caregivers, and teachers interact with children within a cultural context. Thus, children are influenced by their culture every day. Culture involves the values, beliefs, laws, and traditions held in common among groups of people. Individuals may share certain values, traditions, and beliefs because they do the following:

- Speak the same language
- Have certain historic experiences in common
- Trace their ancestors to the same country or region
- Share a common religion

HIGHLIGHT 1-3

Cultural Variations

People vary in their beliefs, values, and behaviors regarding the following:

- The way human beings relate to one another
- How people think about time and personal space
- What personality traits are highly prized
- Fundamental notions of whether human beings are naturally good or bad
- How to show respect
- How to interact with people you know as well as people you just met
- How to dress
- What and when to eat
- Ways positive and negative feelings are to be expressed
- When, how, and with whom affection, anger, resistance, and other feelings are appropriate or inappropriate
- What may be shared and how much
- In what ways individuals may touch each other
- What may and may not be communicated directly
- How to worship
- How to respond to life transitions and celebrations

Sources: Cole & Tan, 2008; Copple & Bredekamp, 2009; Rogoff et al., 2008; Rothbaum & Trommsdorff, 2008.

Table 1-1   Early Learning Standards Related to Social Competence

State	Level	Expectations	Benchmarks/Learning Outcomes
Georgia	Preschool ages 4–5	Children will increase their capacity for self-control. Children will develop confidence and positive self-awareness.	• Child helps to establish classroom rules and routines. • Child follows rules and routines within the learning environment. • Child uses classroom materials purposefully and respectfully. • Child expresses feelings through appropriate gestures, actions, and language. • Child demonstrates knowledge of personal information. • Child recognizes self as a unique individual and becomes aware of uniqueness of others. • Child demonstrates confidence in personal range of abilities and expresses pride in accomplishments. • Child develops personal preferences.
Arizona	Preschool ages 3–5	Children acknowledge the rights and property of self and others.	• Child asks permission before using items that belong to others. • Child defends own rights and the rights of others. • Child uses courteous words and actions. • Child participates in cleaning up the learning environment.
Illinois	Early elementary Later elementary	Children apply decision-making skills to deal responsibly with daily academic and social situations.	• Child identifies a range of decisions that children make in school. • Child makes positive choices when interacting with classmates. • Child identifies and applies steps of systematic decision making. • Child generates alternative solutions and evaluates the consequences for a range of academic and social situations.
New Jersey	Preschool	Children demonstrate self-direction.	• Child makes independent choices and plans from a broad range of diverse interest centers. • Child demonstrates self-help skills (e.g., clean up, pour juice, use soap when washing hands, put away belongings). • Child moves through classroom routines and activities with minimal teacher direction and transitions easily from one activity to the next.

Sources: *Georgia's Pre-K Program Content Standards*, Georgia Department of Early Care and Learning 2011, Atlanta, GA; *Arizona Early Learning Standards*, Arizona Department of Education 2005, Phoenix, AZ; *Illinois Learning Standards*, Illinois State Board of Education 2010, Springfield, IL; *Preschool Teaching and Learning Standards*, State of New Jersey Department of Education 2009, Trenton, NJ.

Seeing the Big Picture!

As you can see, many influences impact how children develop and learn. Because all of these factors interact and shape one another, it pays to keep the following ideas in mind as you work with children, their families, and your colleagues.

● **Programs for children complement but do not replace families in enhancing children's social competence.** Early childhood professionals

and families are partners in the socialization process. Such partnerships are enhanced when you establish respectful relationships with families and when you recognize that family members will have valuable insights from which you will learn and benefit.

● **Many factors affect children's social behavior.** For instance, when Gordon hits another child, he may be hungry, ill, or unsure of how to enter a game. He may have witnessed someone using physical force to achieve a goal and is imitating what he has seen. He may simply have run out of strategies to try. How effectively you react to Gordon will be influenced by your ability to consider all these things as well as sort out such factors.

- **Children's social competence is enhanced when there is communication among the settings central in children's lives (family members talk to teachers, teachers talk to childcare providers, etc.).** Such communication helps parents and early childhood professionals get a more complete understanding of the child and coordinate their efforts so that children experience similar expectations and approaches in each setting. Children benefit when this occurs. In contrast, when communication is lacking, adults may operate without full information or at cross-purposes. Neither circumstance enhances child development. This is why it is important for you to communicate with the important people in children's lives, providing them with relevant information and inviting them to offer their perspectives about children's social experiences.

- **Early childhood programs can moderate some of the negative circumstances children experience in other social contexts.** For example, in 2012, Hurricane Sandy affected dozens of U.S. states with particularly severe damage in New Jersey and New York. As a result, buildings were damaged, public transportation was closed, and many people were without power for several weeks. Daily activity was interrupted for months. Professionals in the area quickly rose to the challenge, reestablishing programs in which children could receive services while members of the community attempted to restore reasonable living conditions. Programs focused on helping children feel secure by providing them with safe environments and predictable routines, conditions that contrasted greatly with the upheaval children were experiencing in their community at the time.

In many ways, adults in childcare settings and schools can lessen the impact of negative conditions children experience elsewhere in the social system. Some examples are listed in Table 1-2.

As you can see, social contexts play a significant part in children's social development and learning. Now it is time to consider more specifically the role you will play in this network of influence.

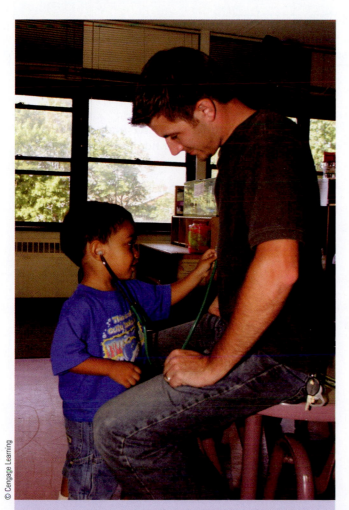

When children have positive relationships with their caregivers, they become more socially competent.

© Cengage Learning

Your Role in Fostering Children's Social Competence naeyc

If asked, "Why do you want to work with children?" think of what you would answer. Chances are, no matter what else you might say, your dreams for the future include making a positive difference in children's lives. There is no place where that difference will be more felt than in the social/emotional domain. Every day, you will be faced with situations in which you will have to make judgments about how to support and guide the children with whom you work. These are challenging tasks. On any given occasion, you may wonder about the following:

Should I pick up the crying baby, or should I let her cry it out?

What should I do about a child who bites others?

When is it reasonable to expect children to know how to share?

How can children learn better ways to resolve their differences?

Where can I turn if I suspect a child is being sexually abused?

Table 1-2   Program Conditions That Offset System Pressures

If Children/Families Experience . . .	You Can Provide . . .
Rejection	Acceptance
Feelings of isolation	Support and connections
Uncertainty due to divorce, death, changing family relationships	Consistent relationships, information for family members about these issues
Chaos in the environment	Predictable settings and routines
Fear, anger, shame	Safety, empathy, acceptance
Stress and pressure	Calm, patient interactions; time to explore and think; strategies for coping and handling stress more effectively
Poverty	Access to human resources and learning opportunities
Homelessness	A sense of safety, security, stability, and belonging within the classroom community
Violence at home, in the community, in the media	Nonviolent classrooms, peaceful strategies for dealing with conflict
Abuse or neglect	Protection, care, and compassion
Bias and discrimination	Equitable treatment, support in developing positive self-identity, awareness of others, and antibias behaviors

© Cengage Learning

How you answer such questions and what actions you take can be more or less helpful to children and their families. Some responses may even be harmful. For instance, your actions could enhance children's feelings of self-worth or detract from them. They could increase children's interpersonal abilities or leave children at a loss about how to interact effectively. Your response could either promote or inhibit children's development of self-control.

Although there is no one right answer for any situation, the things you say and do will make a real difference in children's lives. What resources will you tap to formulate effective responses?

As a caring person interested in supporting children's development and learning, you could draw on your past experiences with children, information you have read, advice provided by colleagues, and your intuition about what is best. Indeed, such sources might provide valuable insights. However, these sources are not sufficient to help you formulate a truly professional reaction to such situations. For that, you will need a greater array of knowledge and skills than those based solely on life experience. Although some people have certain personality traits and previous experiences that enhance their ability to guide children's social development and behavior, that background must be supplemented by additional

knowledge and competencies to make the journey from talented novice to bona fide professional.

Working with Children as a Professional

Think of the qualities adults need to relate well to young children. Perhaps you think adults need to be:

- Patient
- Caring
- Respectful
- Open-minded
- Humorous and fun

Someone can possess such qualities but still not be a professional. Whether your title is teacher, caregiver, counselor, group leader, social worker, or child life specialist, certain other characteristics will differentiate you as a professional. There are five characteristics of a professional: specialized knowledge, demonstrated competence, formalized standards of practice, lifelong education, and adoption of an ethical code of conduct. Use the downloadable list of ways to enhance knowledge and skills in each area. [insert link here]

Now, let's examine each of these characteristics and how they relate to your journey as a professional.

Specialized Knowledge

- Read three professional articles related to children's social competence.
- Participate in an online webinar related to social development.

Demonstrated Competence

- Examine the observation tool in Appendix C. Identify three specific skills you would like to improve. Outline concrete steps you will take to increase your abilities in these areas. Ask a peer or field placement supervisor to observe your actions and provide feedback.

Standards of Practice

- Visit professional websites related to early childhood education and read several position papers. Suggested sites include www.naeyc.org, www.dec-sped.org, and www.nea.org.

Continuing Education

- Join a local, state, or national professional organization.
- Identify workshops available in your area for early childhood professionals.
- Visit the library and review several early childhood professional journals.

Adopting a Code of Ethics

- Review the NAEYC Code of Ethics in Appendix A of this text.
- Review the Code of Ethics of the Division for Early Childhood (EDC) of the Council for Exceptional Children (www.dec-sped.org).
- Review the Code of Ethics of the National Education Association (www.nea.org/home/30442.htm).
- Conduct an online search to determine if your state has developed a specific code of ethics for educators.

Digital Download   Download from CourseMate

Specialized knowledge. Professionals have access to a body of knowledge that goes beyond what is known by the average layperson. This knowledge base is derived from a combination of theories and research that professionals gain through reading, reflection, observation, and experience. It includes terms, facts, principles, and concepts that help us understand why children behave as they do. It also provides guidance regarding which intervention strategies might be useful and which might not. Acquisition of relevant content happens as a result of prolonged education and specialized training (Ryan & Cooper, 2013; Horowitz, Darling-Hammond, & Bransford, 2005). The American Association of Colleges of Teacher Education (AACTE), the Association of Childhood Education International (ACEI), and the National Association for the Education of Young Children

(NAEYC) have all made recommendations for training professionals in a variety of fields involving children. They recommend a knowledge base that includes general studies (humanities, mathematics, technology, social sciences, biological and physical sciences, the arts, physical health, and fitness); child development; teaching and learning; curriculum development and implementation; family and community relationships; assessment, documentation, and evaluation; and field experiences with young children under appropriate supervision. Other professional groups such as the Child Life Specialist Association (CLSA) advocate similar content with the addition of specific information about health care settings.

Demonstrated competence. Professionals distinguish themselves from laypeople by demonstrating specific competencies related to their field. Many professions require licensing and certification, which are usually governed by state or national standards. Less formal monitoring occurs when aspiring professionals take tests, pass courses, and demonstrate effective practices either in a practicum setting or on the job. These experiences take place under the supervision of qualified members of the profession.

Regardless of how competence is assessed, being a professional goes beyond simply memorizing facts for a test; it requires you to translate the knowledge base into effective practices or skills. **Skills** consist of observable actions that, when used in combination, represent mastery of certain strategies. They can be observed, learned, and evaluated (Gazda, Balzer, Childers, & Nealy, 2005). For example, research tells us that an effective strategy for enhancing children's emotional development is to label children's emotions in a variety of situations (Denham, Bassett, & Wyatt, 2008). Although this sounds simple enough, it requires adults to use a broad feeling word vocabulary, to accurately interpret children's moods, to make nonjudgmental statements to children, and to determine when and where to best use the strategy. These actions fit the definition of a skill. First, they are all observable. You can see and hear the extent to which people use different feeling words and whether their statements are objective. Second, if individuals have limited vocabularies, they can learn additional feeling words; if they speak to children in judgmental ways, they can learn to be more objective. Third, a qualified observer could evaluate the person's use of the skill as well as provide feedback that would contribute to improved performance.

It is only when a person performs the entire combination of strategies correctly that it can be said that he or she has demonstrated the skill. Most aspiring professionals find that it takes time and practice to achieve this.

Some skills are simple to understand and easy to learn; others are more complex and difficult. In all cases, skill mastery will require you to know what to do, why to do it, and how to do it. Even when all of this is accomplished, true mastery is attained only when you can successfully carry out strategies in the setting for which they were intended. It is not enough to understand the importance of children's emotions or even to use feeling words in role-playing situations in class or at a workshop. You must also label children's emotions accurately in the center, on the playground, or in the classroom. This transfer of training from practice situations to real-life encounters is the ultimate demonstration of professional competence.

Standards of practice. Professionals perform their duties in keeping with standards of practice generally accepted for the field (Business Roundtable, 2004). Such standards come about through research and professional discourse. They are enforced through self-monitoring within the profession and sometimes through governmental regulation. In early childhood education, for instance, practices have been identified that support and assist children's social, emotional, cognitive, language, and physical development. Some of these include health and safety provisions that ensure children's well-being; staff-to-child ratios that enable frequent personal interactions between each child and staff member; requiring adults to have special training in child development and early education; stable staffing so children have chances to develop trusting relationships with adults; and programming that is appropriate for children's developmental levels and interests (NAEYC, 2009). Professionals who strive to maintain such standards are more likely to provide high-quality programs for the children in their charge. Deviation from these standards can be detrimental to children. Knowing the professional standards that govern the field provides a gauge by which practitioners assess their own performance as well as the overall quality of the services they offer children and families. NAEYC has developed standards for professional preparation. These standards are listed on the inside cover of your text along with the content in this book to help you achieve each standard.

Continuing education. To keep up with the standards in their field, professionals participate in continuing education throughout their careers (NAEYC, 2009). They constantly upgrade their knowledge and skills by attending workshops, consulting with colleagues, participating in professional organizations, reading professional journals, and pursuing additional schooling. Thus, professionals treat learning as a lifelong process that continues throughout the course of their careers.

Adopting a code of ethics. All professions have an ethical code that guides the behavior of their members on the job. These codes include statements of professional values as well as standards of conduct to help people distinguish good from evil, right from wrong, and proper from improper professional behavior (Ryan & Cooper, 2013). Such codes supplement the personal morals people bring with them to the profession.

Although having strong moral character is an important asset to your professional development, knowing right from wrong in a professional sense requires more than personal judgment (Feeney, 2010). It involves knowing the agreed-upon ethical standards within the field. Thus, professionalism requires you to adopt an ethical code of conduct that has been formally approved by the members of a profession. One such code prepared by NAEYC is presented in Appendix A.

A code of ethics provides a guide for decision making and a standard against which you can judge the appropriateness of your actions in different circumstances. It gives you a tool for talking about ethical dilemmas with others and gives you access to the collective wisdom of our colleagues even when no one else is available in person. Laypersons do not have access to these same ethical supports.

Take a moment to consider how the five elements of professionalism just outlined influence your response to the question, "What should I do about a child who bites others?" Examples of what professionals might think about, know, and do related to each element are presented in Table 1-3. As you can see, professionals have a rich background of knowledge, skills, and standards they call on to enhance children's social development. Evidence indicates that practitioners who have this kind of professional background are most likely to engage in the most effective practices that foster children's social competence (Gestwicki, 2011). Such practices are often described as being developmentally appropriate.

Developmentally Appropriate Practices and Social Competence

Developmentally appropriate practices (DAP) are associated both with professionalism among practitioners and high-quality programs for children (Horowitz et al., 2005). To engage in developmentally appropriate practices, you will make decisions based on the following information (Copple & Bredekamp, 2009):

- What you know about how all children develop and learn
- What you know about the strengths, needs, and interests of individual children

Table 1-3 Elements of Professionalism

| What Do I Do about a Child Who Bites Others? | |
Elements of Professionalism	Things to Think About, Know, and Do
Specialized knowledge	Awareness of age-related characteristics of young children.
	Theoretical explanations for why children bite.
	Research related to various strategies aimed at reducing biting among children.
Demonstrated competence	Intervene with children who bite using redirection, substitution, logical consequences, and/or stress reduction strategies.
	Address the needs of victims through restitution, self-talk, and/or assertiveness strategies.
	Use conflict-mediation strategies to reduce aggression.
	Use prevention and assertion strategies with onlookers.
	Demonstrate effective communication skills in working with the families of children who bite and their victims.
Standards of practice	State licensing requirements.
	Accreditation criteria and procedures of the NAEYC programs.
	Accreditation criteria for family group homes.
	Developmentally appropriate practices in early childhood programs.
	National Council of Teachers of English (NCTE) accreditation standards.
	State guidelines for teacher certification.
	Child development associate criteria.
	Schoolwide discipline policies.
Continuing education	Learn the latest information on emotional self-regulation.
	Become familiar with recent research on biting among toddlers.
Ethical code of conduct	Consider and act on ethical guidelines related to safety, confidentiality, and responsibility to children and families.

© Cengage Learning

- What you know about the social and cultural contexts in which children live

These three criteria help to ensure that your approaches to guiding children's social development and learning are age appropriate, individually appropriate, and socially and culturally appropriate.

Age-Appropriate Practices

Jack is 3. Amy is 10. Both want to play a game. Would you select the same game for each of them? Would you expect them to have similar social skills or the same understanding of how games are played?

As someone who is familiar with child development, you undoubtedly answered "No" to these questions because you are aware that age makes a difference in what children know and what they can do. Consequently, to choose games that would be fun and doable for Jack and Amy, you must take into account the age appropriateness of the different games available for them to play. For instance, a simple game of stacking blocks, then pushing them over might please Jack, but quickly bore Amy. Conversely, Amy might enthusiastically engage in an action game with other children outdoors that Jack would find too difficult to play. In both cases, your idea of a suitable game would be influenced by your knowledge of Jack's and Amy's motor skills, their cognitive understandings, their language abilities, and their social skills (such as their ability to wait, to follow rules, to take turns, to accommodate other people's needs, and to share). Although chronological age is not a foolproof indicator of children's thoughts and abilities, it does serve as a helpful gauge. This, in turn, allows you to make reasonable assumptions of what might be safe, interesting, achievable, and challenging for children at different times in their lives (Copple & Bredekamp, 2009). Therefore, you can better recognize that children's social competencies are influenced by age-related variables and that children at different ages will demonstrate different understandings and levels of skill.

Individually Appropriate Practices

The children are visiting a farm. Walter runs to the fence calling out, "Here horsy. Come here!" Margaret hangs back from the group, unsure of how close she wants to get to the big, hairy creatures. Carlos moves to the fence with Ms. Lopez. He is happy to watch as long as she is nearby.

Three different children have three different reactions. Each calls for an individualized response from you.

Every child who comes into this world is a unique being, the result of a combination of tens of thousands of genes inherited from his or her parents. Even the size, shape, and operation of a child's brain are slightly different from those of all other children. Children's temperaments are so distinct at birth that family members often make remarks such as, "Lucida has been that way ever since she was a baby." These biological differences are complemented by experiential factors that further differentiate one child from another. Each child in any group setting brings a set of experiences and understandings that influence social competence. A child who has few group experiences will have different needs and strengths than a child who has been in group care since birth. Likewise, youngsters who have played a certain game at home will be more capable of explaining the rules to others than children who have never played the game before. The kinds of experiences children have, and the amount, quality, and outcomes of those experiences all combine to yield a different result for each child.

Thinking about children as individuals enables you to adapt programs and strategies appropriately and to be responsive to the variations that exist among children in a group (Copple & Bredekamp, 2009). You can see the notion of individually appropriate practice at work during the children's visit to the farm.

One adult walks up to the fence with Walter, sharing his pleasure in the horses and helping him to control the impulse to immediately stick his hand through the fence to pet them. Another adult stands back with Margaret and Carlos, providing emotional support as they watch the animals from a comfortable distance. These individualized responses take into account the children's differing reactions and needs. Requiring all the children to stand far back would deny Walter the opportunity to examine the horses more closely, and

making everyone stand up close would force Carlos and Margaret into a situation they fear. Thus, treating all the children in exactly the same way would be inappropriate under the circumstances. The concept of individually appropriate practice reminds us that treating children fairly requires us to treat them as individuals and sometimes that means treating them differentially according to their needs.

Socially and Culturally Appropriate Practices

In addition to considering age and individuality, you will have to look at children within the context of their family, community, and culture to effectively support their development of social competence. Consider the following classroom scenes:

Scene 1

Ms. Hayes notices two children arguing over a doll in the pretend play area. She carefully separates the children and begins to talk with them about their disagreement. Juanita looks down at the floor. Ms. Hayes says, "Now Juanita, I want you to listen carefully. Look at me when I'm talking to you." Juanita keeps her eyes on the floor. Ms. Hayes gently raises Juanita's chin and insists that Juanita look her in the eye to show that she is listening to what is being said.

Scene 2

Ms. Freelander notices two children arguing over a steam shovel in the block area. She carefully separates the children and begins to talk with them about their disagreement. Carlos looks down at the floor. Ms. Freelander continues talking with the children. Eventually they agree to look for another vehicle so both children can have one to use.

In both cases, the adults were trying to help children resolve their differences within the context of a typical classroom disagreement. Both teachers relied on reasoning to support the children's efforts to solve the problem. These are accepted standards within the profession. Yet, Ms. Hayes insisted that Juanita look at her to show she was being attentive; Ms. Freelander did not make the same demand of Carlos. Ms. Freelander was engaging in socially and culturally appropriate practices; Ms. Hayes was not. What Ms. Freelander realized, and Ms. Hayes did not, was that in Carlos's and Juanita's families, children are taught to cast their eyes downward in the presence of adults, especially if they are being scolded. To do otherwise is to demonstrate lack of respect (Trawick-Smith, 2013).

Without realizing it, Ms. Hayes had ignored the social context in which Juanita lives. The adult inaccurately presumed that because her own upbringing taught her to look at someone directly as a sign of attentiveness, the children in her group had been taught the same.

When we ignore the cultural facets of children's lives, we lose access to the rich background children bring with them from home (Arnett, 2008). To avoid this problematic outcome, you will have to make a special effort to learn about the cultural backgrounds of the children in your charge. By interacting with children and families in ways that demonstrate appreciation and interest, you will learn more about what they interpret as meaningful and respectful. You will discover what expectations families have regarding their children's social development. You will find out more about what is happening in children's lives at home. These understandings will go a long way toward helping you interpret children's behaviors, emotions, and needs more accurately and respectfully.

TeachSource Video 1-2

Development Videos: *5–11 Years: Lev Vygotsky, the Zone of Proximal Development, and Scaffolding*

Go online and view *5–11 Years: Lev Vygotsky, the Zone of Proximal Development, and Scaffolding*. In this video, you will observe the concept of scaffolding.

1. How does the concept of scaffolding relate to developmentally appropriate practice?

2. What information would you need in order to scaffold children's developing social competence?

3. How might social context influence how you scaffold children's learning?

Watch on CourseMate

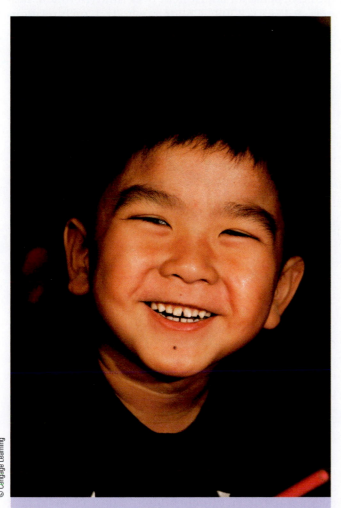

Chao is 3 years old. What are some things that might be true about Chao, based on what you know about children his age? How might Chao be different from other 3-year-olds in the program?

Keeping developmentally appropriate practice in mind, let us now consider a social intervention framework that helps professionals determine which practices to use, when to use them, and with whom.

A Framework for Guiding Children's Social Development and Learning

At the beginning of this chapter, we asked you to imagine working with three 6-year-old children in a child-care setting or elementary classroom:

Dennis	(described as active, imaginative, resistant to other children's ideas, relies on using hurtful behaviors to get what he wants)
Rosalie	(described as quiet, ignored by peers, alone in the classroom)
Sarah Jo	(described as cheerful, socially skilled, sought out by other children)

There are literally hundreds of ways you could help these children increase their social competence.

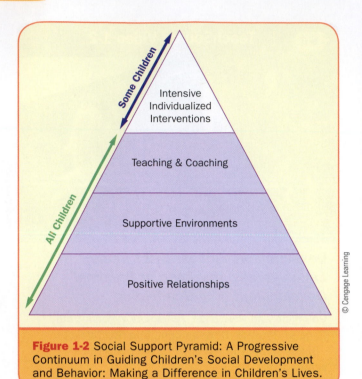

Figure 1-2 Social Support Pyramid: A Progressive Continuum in Guiding Children's Social Development and Behavior: Making a Difference in Children's Lives.

Sources: Adapted from Fox, Dunlap, Hemmeter, Joseph, & Strain (2003).

Which strategies might you choose? How would you know what to do when? Where would you begin?

Fortunately, you do not have to rely on intuition or guesswork to gauge your starting point or to consider how to progress from there. Effective teachers develop positive, nurturing relationships with each child, provide a stimulating and supportive learning environment, intentionally teach children social skills and coach them in how to use these skills, and create intensive individualized interventions when needed. These steps demonstrate a developmental progression in how to best guide children's social competence. This progression is depicted in Figure 1-2 and is described in greater detail next. From now on, we will call this the **Social Support Pyramid**. It is a variation on the Teaching Pyramid Model developed by special educators to support children's social development and learning (Fox et al., 2009). In fact, the Social Support Pyramid is an effective way to think about guiding the social development and learning of all children.

Establishing Positive Relationships with Children

Children flourish in a classroom where they sense that the teacher cares deeply about them—as people, about what they are learning, and about the skills they are developing.

—Claudia Eliason and Loa Jenkins (early childhood educators)

The first and most important step in promoting children's social competence is for adults to establish caring relationships with children (Hemmeter, Ostrosky, & Fox, 2006). Positive relations provide the base on which all other interventions build, and therefore, constitute the broadest phase of the Social Support Pyramid. This is because children need to feel psychologically safe and secure to learn best and to thrive (Goleman, 2011). Security comes from consistent trusting relationships with adults. Children who know their mistakes will be tolerated and their efforts to learn will be supported and encouraged are open to learning new things, such as how to express their emotions in words, how to wait, or how to treat others with kindness. Children who are frightened and suspicious are less likely to absorb such lessons. The same is true for children who feel rejected or inept. Consequently, children who experience warm accepting relationships with adults tend to increase their social abilities and positive behavior adjustment over time (Denham, Bassett, & Wyatt, 2008). Children who lack such relationships are more likely to display behavior problems, have a lower tolerance for frustration, and exhibit poorer social skills with peers.

Creating Supportive Environments

Phase two of the Social Support Pyramid involves creating supportive physical and verbal environments. The physical environment is a powerful force. It affects how we feel and what we do, determines how we interact with others, and makes a difference in how successful we are in reaching our goals (Weinstein, Romano, & Mignano, 2010). This is the case for everyone but especially for children. Children's social behavior is affected by environmental elements such as color, light, materials, room arrangement, sounds, and routines. Well-planned early learning settings enable children to interact comfortably, help children behave in socially acceptable ways, and give them opportunities to practice skills associated with self-regulation (Kostelnik & Grady, 2009).

How adults talk to children, how well they listen to what children have to say, the degree to which they align their nonverbal and verbal communication, and the extent to which they use language to expand children's social understandings greatly influences children's social behavior. In teaching and learning, demeanor and tone are just as important, if not more important, than the exact words you choose (Nabobo-Baba & Tiko, 2009). Similarly, words can harm, heal, support, or detract from children's sense of well-being and confidence. Nonverbal and verbal strategies connected to this phase of the Social Support Pyramid promote self-awareness as well as language and communication development.

Teaching and Coaching

Children aren't born with the capacity to navigate the social world very proficiently. The social and emotional skills needed to get along well with others and function successfully in society are developed gradually over time and must be learned. Your role is to teach children specific skills and coach them on how to use these skills effectively in order to facilitate their social understanding. Thus, the third phase of the Social Support Pyramid promotes children's skill learning and social development. Adult practices expand children's repertoire of social and emotional strategies and help children maintain desirable behaviors or change inappropriate ones to more acceptable alternatives. Reminding children to "Walk, don't run" or guiding children as they resolve a verbal conflict are examples of teaching and coaching (Epstein, 2007). In situations like these, adults help children achieve desirable standards of behavior, rather than simply restricting or punishing them for inappropriate conduct. Typical teaching and coaching strategies include discussing, modeling, instructing on the spot, redirecting, reminding, reinforcing, implementing consequences, and following through. Such strategies benefit every child at one time or another. However, what strategies to use, how to use them, when to use them, and what variations to employ will differ with the child and the circumstance.

Intensive Individualized Interventions

Most children develop greater social competence in response to the practices described within the first three phases of the Social Support Pyramid. In fact, if the strategies outlined previously are applied consistently and appropriately throughout early childhood, a significant percentage of children will enter kindergarten with the basic skills they need to interact positively (not perfectly) with both their peers and adults (see Figure 1-3). These early skills provide a strong foundation for further social skill development in elementary school.

However, some children (approximately 3% to 15%) exhibit persistent challenging behaviors that are not responsive to Phases 1, 2, and 3. These children require additional intensive interventions to resolve problem behaviors and develop new skills (Hemmeter, Ostrosky, & Fox, 2006; Kaiser & Rasminsky, 2012). Teams of professionals and family members most often develop this level of intervention together and then systematically implement it in multiple social environments. Such interventions appear at the top of the Social Support Pyramid because they are applied only after more preventa-

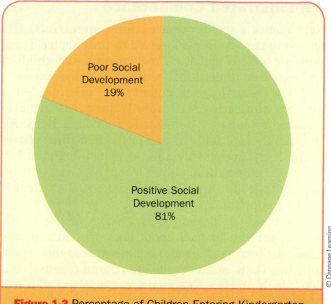

Figure 1-3 Percentage of Children Entering Kindergarten Who Exhibit Positive Social Behaviors When Interacting with Their Peers.

© Cengage Learning

tive measures have been tried and only with a small number of children.

No one marches lockstep through the phases depicted in Figure 1-2. Nor does anyone focus on just one phase at a time. Instead, early childhood professionals understand when and how to use each component of the Social Support Pyramid and are skilled in effectively implementing practices that correspond with each phase. All of this is what you will be learning in the remaining chapters of this text.

Chapter Structure

Guiding Children's Social Development and Learning is designed to help you acquire the necessary knowledge, skills, and attitudes to function as a professional working with children. Therefore, every chapter that follows is structured around the five elements of professionalism.

Specialized Knowledge

A statement of objectives opens each chapter to guide you in your reading and learning. The objectives are followed by the knowledge base for the chapter, which begins with a **discussion of the latest empirical findings and research** regarding a particular topic, such as children's emotional development or play, and includes definitions of **key terms**.

Demonstrated Competence

Next comes a section that outlines **specific skills** related to the research addressed in the chapter. These skills are directly applicable to your work with children and represent professional competencies that promote children's social development and learning. Skills for communicating with family members are also included to enhance home/program connections. All chapters include skills related to the first three phases of the Social Support Pyramid depicted in Figure 1-2. Specific information about intensive intervention skills is offered in the chapters where such content is most appropriate.

Each skill is presented as a series of observable actions for you to read about and then incorporate into your own professional behavior. Students report that the skills often "read like common sense" but take much practice to actually use effectively in real life. (To assist you in transitioning from "hypothetical" to "actual," we have provided the Online Companion, already mentioned in the Preface.) The skill sections are set off with color to make them easy to reference.

To enhance your skill development, we describe pitfalls you may experience as you begin to incorporate new behaviors into your interactions with children and families. The pitfalls are designed to help you recognize common errors beginners make and to gauge your progress in using specific skills.

Standards of Practice

The skills outlined in each chapter correspond to standards of practice commonly accepted for the field. They have their basis in developmentally appropriate practice and can be used to address all phases of the social intervention continuum depicted in Figure 1-2.

Continuing Education

All chapters conclude with a **summary** that provides a brief overview of the chapter's topic. **Discussion questions** follow to help you assess your understanding of the material. Four **case studies** are provided in Appendix B. Each chapter will refer to a particular case study allowing you to apply specific strategies related to that chapter which you might use when working with a child with specific needs. **Field assignments** give you an opportunity to apply what you have learned with real children in early childhood programs. These sections are designed to help you generalize what you are learning beyond the college classroom and to provide a base for future practice. As you become more involved in the field, you will update what you have learned in these pages by reading journals, attending conferences, and pursuing additional means of continuing education.

Code of Ethics

Each chapter takes into account ethics associated with the topic it addresses. Because ethics are so integral to professionalism, **ethics-related discussion questions** are included in each chapter as well. Although there is no single correct answer for any of the questions, talking them over with peers and supervisors will hone your ethical judgments.

Throughout the course of the book, every aspect of the NAEYC Code of Ethics will be covered. Our expectation is that you will be thoroughly familiar with the entire code by the time you complete this text.

Summary

Social competence refers to a person's ability to achieve personal goals in ways deemed appropriate by society. The acquisition of social competence begins in childhood and occurs as a result of both development and learning.

Children acquire social competence within an interdependent network of social settings. Considering how these settings combine to affect children's lives involves adopting a contextual perspective.

Maintaining this perspective enables you to see children holistically, to appreciate various influences on children's development, and to communicate more successfully with the central people in children's lives. The most basic influence is the family. As children mature, peers and settings outside the home (childcare or school) play ever-increasing roles in their lives. As children engage in such settings, they often come in contact with professionals in the field. Professionals demonstrate five characteristics that differentiate them from laypersons: specialized knowledge, demonstrated competence, standards of performance, continuing education, and a code of ethics.

Professionals who work with children refer to the Social Support Pyramid to guide their professional practice. The pyramid includes four intervention phases that range from establishing positive relationships with children, to creating supportive environments, to teaching and coaching, to developing intensive individualized interventions as necessary. As you learn to effectively carry out practices represented within the Social Support Pyramid, you will be well on your way to making a positive difference in children's lives.

Key Terms

code of ethics
developmentally appropriate
    practices

ethical dilemma
skills

social competencies
Social Support Pyramid

Discussion Questions

1. Refer to Figure 1-1. Define social competence. Randomly select one of the elements of social competence to discuss. Describe examples of behaviors that would illustrate the knowledge, skills, and values encompassed by that element.

2. A recent study involving Russian parents and early childhood professionals revealed that the following elements of social competence were particularly valued:

    - Kindness
    - Good manners
    - Respect for individual differences
    - Independent thinking and acting
    - Self-confidence
    - Self-direction
    - Spontaneity
    - Happiness

    Discuss how these behaviors/values compare with the elements of social competence described in relation to children in the United States identified in this chapter.

3. Evidence shows that approximately 75% of students with learning disabilities manifest social skills deficits during the early years. In addition, children with mental retardation are much more likely to experience problems in socialization and communication than their nondisabled peers (McCay & Keyes, 2002). Discuss what implications this has for families and early childhood professionals working with young children.

4. Some scientists say, "Remember that children are whole people in their own right, not deficient adults." Based on your knowledge of child development and learning as well as the content of this chapter, what significance does this have for children's development of social competence?

5. Imagine that you have been invited to speak to a group of families whose children are newly enrolled in your program. What are the three key things you would want to communicate to them about children's social competence and ways in which your program supports the development of social competence in children?

6. Consider the five characteristics of a professional—specialized knowledge, demonstrated competence, standards of practice, continuing education, and a code of ethics. List these on a piece of paper and then discuss various ways in which you are involved in acquiring these characteristics.

7. Refer to the NAEYC Code of Ethical Conduct outlined in Appendix A. Read Section I: Ethical Responsibilities to Children. Identify principles and concepts described in Chapter 1 that support the ideals and principles covered in this section of the code.

8. Not all children develop typically; some children experience challenges or delays in their development and learning. Discuss how you would adapt the notion of developmentally appropriate practice to take this into account.

9. Briefly describe the four phases of the Social Support Pyramid depicted in Figure 1-2. Discuss examples of adult behavior that would correspond to these four phases.

Case Study Analysis

After reading the case study for Seth in Appendix B, consider the following:

1. Refer to Figure 1-1. Describe Seth's abilities in three different elements of social competence presented in the figure.

2. Two social contexts (home, preschool) are referred to in the case study. What other social contexts might exist that influence Seth's development?

3. Discuss age-appropriate, individually appropriate, and socially/culturally appropriate practices you might use with Seth. Differentiate how these practices might be similar to or different from the practices you might use with his peers in his preschool class.

4. Describe the specialized knowledge and specific skills you would want to possess if you were Seth's primary teacher. Identify opportunities and strategies you could use to obtain the knowledge and skills identified.

5. Think about the Social Support Pyramid in relation to the case study. Identify what you would do to develop a positive relationship with Seth. Describe how the classroom environment might affect Seth's behavior. Point out potential opportunities that may exist to increase Seth's interaction with his peers. What skills would you want to teach Seth to take advantage of these opportunities? What skills would you want to teach Seth's peers so that they would be more successful in interacting with Seth?

Field Assignments

1. Make a diagram of the classroom or other childhood setting in which you will be practicing your skills this semester. Be sure to include details related to doors, windows, and furniture. Write a daily schedule for the formal group setting in which you will be participating, and identify your role at each time of the day. Name at least three adults with whom you will interact and briefly describe each person's role in the program. Name at least 10 of the children in your setting. What are two goals related to social competence you believe the supervisor has for the children in the setting, and what evidence did you use to determine this?

2. Select one principle of social development or learning described in this chapter. Name the principle, and give an example of children demonstrating that principle in your field placement or practicum site. Remember to write objectively, focusing on observable behaviors.

3. Refer to Table 1-2. Make a copy of this table, share it with a childhood professional, and ask

which elements of the table may represent his or her program. Ask for examples of how the program provides children with the conditions that offset system pressures.

4. Observe an early childhood setting. Write out examples of age-appropriate, individually appropriate, and socially/culturally appropriate practices you observe in the setting.

5. Consider the four phases of the Social Support Pyramid depicted in Figure 1-2. Observe in a childhood program, and provide examples of adult behaviors that demonstrate each of the first three phases. Find out if there is a plan for a child that corresponds to Phase 4, Intensive Individualized Interventions.

Reflect on Your Practice

Here is a sample checklist you can use to reflect on your use of the skills as a beginning professional. A more detailed classroom observation tool is available in Appendix C.

Teachers who support children's social and emotional development:

✓ Take the initiative in finding out their responsibilities for the day.

✓ Arrive promptly and stay for the entire session.

✓ Help to prepare and maintain the environment.

✓ Participate in all aspects of daily classroom activity.

✓ Cooperate as a team member.

✓ Support other adults in group activities, during transitions, and within activity areas or outside.

✓ Remain available for interaction with children.

CourseMate. Visit the Education CourseMate for this textbook to access the eBook, Digital Downloads, TeachSource Videos, and Did You Get It? quizzes. Go to CengageBrain.com to log in, register, or purchase access.

2 Good Beginnings: Establishing Relationships with Infants and Toddlers

OBJECTIVES

On completion of this chapter, you should be able to:

Recognize the essential elements of positive adult–child relationships.

Articulate how attachment is a foundation for relationships.

Describe cues children send that influence relationship building

Explain how infants and toddlers become their "own person" through individuation and separation.

Talk about how children's emerging communication skills influence their social competence.

Discuss the early development of children's peer relationships.

Tell how early self-regulation contributes to social learning.

Identify ways to support infants and toddlers with special needs.

Demonstrate strategies to enhance your relationships with infants and toddlers.

Outline pitfalls to avoid in interacting with infants, toddlers, and their families.

NAEYC STANDARDS naeyc

1. Promoting Child Development and Learning
2. Building Family and Community Relationships
3. Observing, Documenting, and Assessing to Support Young Children and Families
4. Using Developmentally Effective Approaches to Connect with Children and Families
5. Using Content Knowledge to Build Meaningful Curriculum

Ms. Peifer smiled brightly as she rose from the floor and walked toward 14-month-old Brandt, as he and his father entered the room. "We were hoping you were coming today," she spoke softly as she responded to Brandt's big grin and outstretched arms by reaching for him. Brandt's father nodded and gave her a brief report of Brandt's pediatric visit. Brandt gave her a hug.

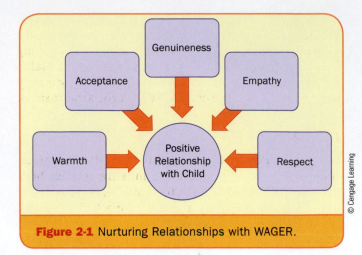

Figure 2-1 Nurturing Relationships with WAGER.

From this brief glimpse of Brandt's arrival, we observe that Ms. Peifer and Brandt are pleased to see one another and that they enjoy a comfortable, affectionate relationship. For infants and toddlers, a caring relationship with one or more adults is essential for optimum development (Raikes & Edwards, 2009). Of course, parents are usually the first adults with whom strong ties are forged. However, as children venture into the world, other family members, friends, and helping professionals may establish close relationships with young children too. Such relationships provide children with a safe context for early learning and development. They enable children to explore their environments freely, trusting the adults to nurture them, protect them, and guide them (Thompson & Goodman, 2009). Under these conditions, very young children flourish emotionally, socially, and cognitively (Labile & Thompson, 2008).

As you work with infants and toddlers, you will become one of the people from whom they seek security and affection. This is a significant responsibility as well as an enjoyable one. How you approach children, what you notice about them, and how you respond to them will either boost or detract from their confidence and social competence. To have the most positive effect, you need to understand the following:

- Adult qualities that contribute most to establishing relationships with children
- How children's emerging capabilities in the first three years influence their connections to you and to others
- Ways to translate your understandings into developmentally appropriate practice

Essentials of All Positive Adult–Child Relationships naeyc

The five key elements that contribute to establishing positive relationships with all children are warmth, acceptance, genuineness, empathy, and respect. These are depicted in Figure 2-1.

To help you remember all five elements, we suggest using the pneumonic device, WAGER:

W = warmth
A = Acceptance
G = Genuineness
E = Empathy
R = Respect

Let's take a moment to explore each dimension of WAGER more closely.

Warmth

Showing sincere interest in children, being friendly toward them, and being responsive are all aspects of **warmth.** Adults help children feel comfortable, supported, and valued by smiling, touching them gently, adopting a pleasant tone of voice, and using verbal behaviors that are attentive and understanding. Ms. Hamouz is demonstrating warmth when she greets 2-year-old Sarah by squatting down to her eye level, smiling, and nodding as Sarah tells her about last night.

Acceptance

To accept a child means to value that child unconditionally. This involves caring about children regardless of their personal attributes, family background, or behavior (Remland, 2009). Adults demonstrate **acceptance** by caring for and about babies and toddlers when they are dirty, smelly, or noisy as well as when they are pleasant, smiling, and joyful. They accept each child "no matter what" and believe that all children are worthy of their time, attention, and affection (Egan, 2010).

Acceptance should not be confused with condoning every child action, including destructive or hurtful behaviors. As you will discover throughout this text, there are ways to communicate acceptance to children while at the same time guiding them toward more appropriate behaviors. This dual agenda is illustrated when Ms. Chigubu moves quickly toward two toddlers who are throwing sand in the sandbox. One child is amused and laughing, while the other is angry. Ms. Chigubu communicates acceptance by acknowledging both of their emotions. At the same time, she makes it clear that throwing sand is not allowed for safety reasons and helps the children dig in the sand instead.

Genuineness

Positive adult–child relationships are also characterized by **genuineness.** Genuine adults are never dishonest with children. They remain truthful, yet reasonable and encouraging. They also take time to individualize their response to each child and each situation. Mr. Stauffer is demonstrating genuineness when he acknowledges Anna's desire to have her mom come "right now!" but also explains that mom won't be coming until after lunch. He consoles Anna for a moment and then leads her to the art table where he keeps her company as she begins using the markers.

Empathy

The single most important manifestation of caring is **empathy** (Carkhuff, 2012). Empathy involves recognizing and understanding another person's perspective even when that perspective is different from your own. An empathic person responds to another's affective or emotional state by experiencing some of the same emotion. Empathy, therefore, involves the cognitive processes of examining and knowing, as well as the affective process of feeling. This idea is captured in such sayings as "walking in someone else's shoes" or "seeing the world through another person's eyes." We can see and hear empathy in Mr. Jones's response when Tula slips on the steps and falls down. Mr. Jones winces in pain and responds sincerely, "Ow! You really fell hard. That must hurt. Let me help you up."

Respect

Respect involves believing that children are capable of learning and acting competently for their age. Adults show respect when they allow children to explore and function independently, think for themselves, make decisions, work toward their own solutions, and communicate ideas (Morrison, 2009). Lack of respect is evident when adults do things for children that they can do on their own, tell them how to think and feel, ignore their point of view, or deprive them of genuine opportunities to grow and learn. Disrespect is apparent when adults believe that children cannot learn because of their age, gender, culture, or socioeconomic background. Ms. Long shows respect for Carl as she waits patiently for him to put on his boots. She does not rush him or jump in to complete the task herself. When the

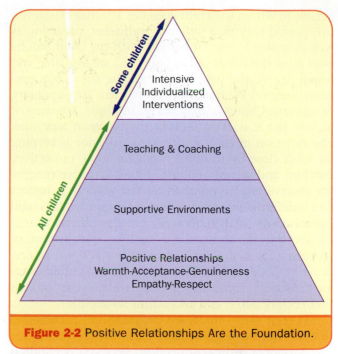

Figure 2-2 Positive Relationships Are the Foundation.

Source: National Scientific Council on the Developing Child, 2004.

boots are finally on, she smiles and nods in affirmation. Carl looks up, pleased with his accomplishment.

Adults who incorporate warmth, acceptance, genuineness, empathy, and respect in their interactions with young children show children that they like them, enjoy being with them, are having fun with them, and are pleased with their efforts and accomplishments. These aspects of adult behavior combine to establish a reassuring and comfortable tone in the classroom. They also create a strong base for the Social Support Pyramid you learned about in Chapter 1. Figure 2-2 is an illustration of how these five elements underscore the process of relationship building. As you can see, everything you are learning about guiding children's social development is predicated on this foundation. The whole progression begins as children form their first attachments with significant adults.

Attachment as a Foundation of Relationships

Mrs. Hsu cuddles baby Jacob against her body. She sings softly while patting him gently on the back. Jacob snuggles into her shoulder. It is a quiet, caring moment for each of them.

When there is a positive connection between an infant (or toddler) and a special adult, an **attachment** exists between them (Thompson, 2006). A mother who provides consistent, responsive care is frequently the first person to whom the child becomes attached. However, this person may be a father, grandparent, or sibling as well as others in regular contact with the child. Adults who meet the needs of the baby and are available and responsive to the baby's cues become the baby's preferred persons. We typically refer to them as the primary caregivers. Children may have multiple attachment figures, but it is essential that they have at least one. The function of early attachment behavior is keeping an adult close by to fulfill needs for food, protection, comfort, and security (Hinde, 2006). Sensitive caregivers observe and respond to all the ways that infants and toddlers communicate their interests, feelings, and desires. These adult actions elicit reciprocal attachment behaviors in the child such as smiling, reaching out, or seeking a favored adult to hold them (Copple & Bredekamp, 2009). Adults find these types of child behavior satisfying. Thus, attachment is a two-way process that both children and adults find rewarding.

Within early childhood programs, all infants and toddlers need a single reliable person with whom they can develop a strong connection. Very young children who have consistent caregivers and secure relationships gain the self-belief that they are deserving of attention and love, and they trust that someone is there to meet their needs (Riley et al., 2008). From their early relationships, infants and toddlers develop a concept of "relationship" and form expectations for future relationships with other adults and peers (Ziv, Oppenheim, & Sagi-Schwartz, 2004). In this way, the adult to whom the child is attached forms the secure base from which the child can then explore and reach out to others.

Attachment is maintained through sensitive care. In addition to using the nurturing behaviors described previously, you must determine as quickly as possible if the infant or toddler is comfortable, fed, rested, or bored, and then act appropriately to care for the child. Through many interactions that meet their needs and by responding in calm and predictable ways, adults help little ones develop their positive sense of self in the world.

When Janelle is dropped at the center early in the morning, her mom takes her daughter's coat off as the child glances around the room. Spotting Ms. Alice, she brightens with a smile. She looks up at her mom and says, "Bye-bye." She then looks to Ms. Alice who is approaching and waves, "I-O!" Ms. Alice waves back, "Hi-ho!" She then greets Janelle's mom pleasantly and asks about last evening's sleep and this morning's routine. As Ms. Alice bids mother goodbye, Janelle points to her diaper bag, saying "Milk." "I will get it right now," responds Ms. Alice.

Besides developing their own attachments with children, early childhood professionals also support the attachments between parents and their children by modeling and providing information. When caregivers share factual information regarding children's development, they help families better understand the natural progression of development as well as appropriate expectations for behavior. Informing families about children's daily experiences keeps them feeling part of their babies' world. If the child's caregiver and the family communicate about daily occurrences, then both the child and the adult family members feel more securely connected (Riley et al., 2008). This is illustrated when Mrs. Murphy comes to pick up her daughter, Jacqui, at the child-care center.

Ms. Allison greets Mrs. Murphy at the end of the day. She is smiling and holding pictures in her hand. "Jacqui had a marvelous day today. She especially enjoyed drawing. She made many pictures, and, interestingly, they were all of you and her together. Here is her stack. I recorded her words as she made the top one because I thought you would enjoy them. As she drew this, she said, 'Look, this is me. I have curly hair. And this is Mommy again. She has curly hair too. We are holding hands 'cause we love each other!' What a treasure for you two!" Mrs. Murphy's eyes sparkled as she gazed at her daughter's creation.

"Jacqui and Mommy"

© Cengage Learning

HIGHLIGHT 2-1

How Strong Is Your Relationship with the Infants and Toddlers in Your Care?

It is important to continuously reflect on your actions to be sure you are forming strong ties with *all* the children in your care. See the following checklist for questions to use in this self-evaluation.

• Do you both seek eye contact with each other?
• Do you brighten at the sight of each other?
• Do you adjust your responses to each other?
• Does the child relax when you hold him or her or if you are physically near?
• Is your presence calming to the child?
• Does the child play comfortably when you are near?
• Does the child glance your way to check in?

Source: Adapted from Riley et al. (2008).

▶❚❚ **TeachSource Video 2-1**

0–2 Years: *Attachment in Infants and Toddlers*

Go online and view *Attachment in Infants and Toddlers.*

In this video, you will see several children with their parents and with other professionals. Pay attention to the behavior of the adults as they interact with the children. Note how these very young children communicate with the adults.

1. **Describe how the adults demonstrated warmth, acceptance, genuineness, empathy, and respect.**
2. **How was attachment displayed in each of the children? Was it obviously present in all of them?**
3. **Listen carefully to Olivia just after her mother leaves the room. How would you describe the initial vocalization?**

Watch on CourseMate

Attachment does not happen by chance. Certain adult–child behaviors contribute to the process. Several of these are outlined in Highlight 2-1.

All of the attachment behaviors identified in Highlight 2–1 rely on your being observant and aware of children's reactions to their own internal states as well as to the world around them. Infants and toddlers provide cues about how they are feeling all the time. How well you read these cues will influence your ability to develop strong attachments with children and to support their social development over time. Let's take a look at some of the cues to which you must be sensitive.

Reading Infant/Toddler Cues **naeyc**

Seven-month-old Brandy Marie is quietly awake in her crib. Her caregiver approaches and says, "Hel-l-o-o-o-. Hel-l-o-o, Brandy, h-e-l-l-o, little girl." Brandy smiles openly and waves her arms. "So you want to play... want to play," says the caregiver in a lyrical tone of voice, repeating many phrases. Brandy chortles in delight.

When 6-month-old Jerome cried, his caregiver Joe immediately picked him up and held him close to his own face. This made Jerome pause, but then he cried louder. Joe turned the infant around and allowed him to see the world face outward. After he was turned around, Jerome stopped crying and enjoyed the view.

In both of these situations, the adults took careful note of each child's reaction and adjusted their behavior to match the children's needs. Luckily, infants and toddlers signal what those needs are. Temperament, behavioral states, crying, and body movements each provide important clues for the observant adult.

Influence of Temperament on Social Relationships

Infants are not all alike. Every child has a genetically based temperament that affects his or her development throughout life (Bates & Pettit, 2008; Rothbart & Bates, 2006). Temperament refers to the innate differences children display in the intensity of their reactions to stimuli, in how long they attend to stimuli, in their level of motor activity, in the extent to which their biological rhythms are regular or irregular, and in their degree of emotional self-regulation (Rothbart & Bates, 2006). As a consequence of temperament, an infant may be timid or intrepid, passive or actively curious, quick tempered or slow to anger, as regular as clockwork in her eating and sleeping habits or highly erratic, amenable to soothing or generally inconsolable. These inborn characteristics serve as the filters through which children form ideas and shape their view of the world and their place in it (Caspi & Shiner, 2006). They also influence how people react to children, inviting or inhibiting social interactions. For example, some temperamental traits are challenging to caregivers and influence the quality of social experiences between caregivers and children, as well as children's adjustment to group settings (Coplan, Bowker, & Cooper, 2003). However, even the most challenging temperaments children possess can have positive attributes. For example, Harry, who is extremely active and very intense, explores his environment with interest and gusto. He has many opportunities to learn and to interact with others. (See Table 2-1 for more on temperaments.) When adults recognize the strengths amid the challenges, they can assist children to balance their reactions and to become more regulated (Wittmer, 2008). Thus, recognizing and accepting infants' and

toddlers' individual temperaments leads to more positive interactions.

Three distinct types of temperament have been described by child development experts and are useful for understanding children's natural patterns of acting on the world: easy, slow to warm up, and complex (Thomas & Chess, 1986; Berk, 2013). The *easy* child (about 40%) is generally happy, friendly, predictable, and adaptable with an even-tempered affect. The *slow-to-warm-up* child (about 15% of children) is mildly responsive affectively, predictable in terms of his or her personal schedule, but hesitant in new situations. This child will eventually engage with new people or in new situations but only after repeated exposures. The *complex* child (about 10% of children) is likely to laugh loudly and long, or throw a tantrum. The affective intensity is strong. The pattern of sleeping and waking is irregular and unpredictable, and the child is frequently irritable and generally very active. Some children (about 35%) do not fit cleanly into one of these three temperament types; instead, their temperaments may be combinations of traits from all of the categories. Unless we pay very close attention to our reactions to temperament, we may unconsciously react differently to children solely due to our comfort with their temperaments.

Table 2-1 Temperament Strengths and Challenges

Temperament Traits	Strengths	Challenges
Positive affect: Cooperative, happy smiling, easily amused	Social exchanges with adults and peers are pleasant	Vulnerable to strangers May be too trusting for all situations
Irritable distress: Fussy, unhappy Easily frustrated Irritable, angry	Needs are noticed and met	Requires assistance and "translations" for social interactions and developing empathy for others
Fearful distress: Difficulty in adjusting to new situations	Remains within proximity of caregiver; experiences more language and assistance from caregivers	Requires reassurance and assistance with changes Often needs extra time and support for transitions
Extremely active	Encounters more stimuli (objects and people) in environment	Requires assistance focusing to complete activities Requires close supervision for safety and more defined boundaries
Focused attention/high persistence	Sticks to activity for long amounts of time	Requires encouragement to explore environment further and try new opportunities
Highly predictable patterns of behavior	Enjoys rhythms and routines and easily learns and loves to follow these	May require assistance with changes in routines or patterns that differ from child's expectations

© Cengage Learning

For example, two children who differ markedly in temperament may elicit different responses from adults.

Mike moves slowly, watches what is going on, seldom cries, and plays in his crib contentedly for long periods after awakening. Every movement or noise, on the other hand, distracts Todd. He moves quickly; cries vigorously, long, and frequently; and rarely is content to play in his crib after awakening. Both boys are 8 months old. Mr. McKinnon, who takes care of them, interacts less frequently with Mike and finds him satisfying and restful, though less exciting to play with. Todd gets much more attention, although Mr. McKinnon frequently feels irritated with him. The only time Todd seems to settle down is when he plays with an adult. Mr. McKinnon is aware of his tendency to ignore Mike and pursue Todd, so he carefully remembers to check on Mike regularly and involve him in play.

Gradually, patterns of interaction between adults and children emerge and become habitual. **Goodness of fit** between the temperament of the adult and that of the child is important because both parties of the relationship have characteristic styles of handling behaviors and emotions. The experience of an infant like Mike, who is somewhat inactive and not very sociable, with an adult who is impulsive, impatient, and expects quick social responses would be very different from his experience with an easygoing, patient adult who is willing to wait for him to respond in his own good time without forgoing the interaction.

The goodness of fit among the infant, the caregiver's temperament and expectations, and the infant's general living environment may be more important to the long-term outcome for the child than temperament alone. Even infants with complex temperaments can be happy and successful if caregivers are calm and accepting, working with the babies' strengths. If expectations for the child are clear and suitable for the child's age, and if caregivers use skills that enable them to be sensitive and responsive to children's cues, children thrive. To do so, adults must meet children's needs effectively, which means learning to read additional clues such as those conveyed by children's behavioral states.

Behavioral States

Infants do not behave the same way all the time. Sometimes they are wide awake and active. Sometimes they are quiet but alert. Sometimes they are drowsy, sleeping, or crying. These varied **behavioral states** influence how babies perceive the world and how they respond to social encounters. For example, an infant who is sleeping or crying vigorously is less able to engage in patty-cake than a child who is watching and ready to engage. On the other hand, a child who is quiet and alert may enjoy soft words and gentle touches but not a bouncing game more suited for a child who is completely awake. Newborns change states rapidly and irregularly. However, by the second or third month of life, changes in state become more regular, and infants establish their own rhythm or predictable pattern of behavior. Also, as infants mature, the duration of each state alters. For example, the quiet alert state is about 10% of waking time at birth, 50% at 3 months, and 80% by 6 months of age (Lock & Zukow-Goldring, 2012). Adults who quickly recognize each behavioral state and learn the infant's typical pattern are able to select and time their responses to best match the child's needs. The baby's cues either invite engagement or signal disengagement with others (Martin &

Understanding and warmth are key to supporting the social development of children with difficult temperaments.

Infants are ready to learn and to interact when they are in the quiet alert state.

Table 2-2   Infant Behavioral States and Appropriate Adult Responses

Behavioral State	Facial Expression	Action	Adult Response
Regular sleep	Eyes closed and still; face relaxed	Little movement; fingers slightly curled; thumbs extended	Do not disturb
Irregular sleep	Eyes closed; occasional rapid eye movement; smiles and grimaces	Gentle movement	Do not disturb
Periodic sleep	Alternates between regular and irregular sleep	Infants move slowly, may startle intermittently	Do not disturb
Drowsiness	Eyes open and close or remain halfway open; eyes dull/glazed	Less movement than in irregular sleep; hands open and relaxed; fingers extended	Pick up if follows sleeping; do not disturb if follows awake periods
Quiet alert	Bright eyes, fully open; face relaxed; eyes focused	Slight activity; hands open, fingers extended; arms bent at elbow; stares	Talk to infant; present with objects; perform any assessment
Waking activity	Face flushed; less able to focus than in quiet alert	Extremities and body move; vocalizes, makes noises	Engage: talk, sing, play; perform basic care
Crying	Red skin; facial grimaces; eyes partially or fully open	Vigorous activity; crying vocalizations; fists are clenched	Pick up immediately; soothe infant; identify source of discomfort

© Cengage Learning

Berke, 2007). When read well, harmonious relationships occur. Such synchronous caregiving is often called sensitive caregiving. See Table 2-2 for direction on the types of adult attention and action required in response to each **behavioral state.**

Crying. Crying is one of the infant's earliest means of communicating needs to the caregiver and has the expected effect of drawing an adult near. At 3 to 4 months of age, crying is usually physiological in nature due to sleepiness, hunger, digestive problems, or physical distress. Later, crying increasingly becomes psychological and is used to indicate fear, overstimulation, boredom, anger, or protest (Kovach & Da Ros-Voseles, 2008). Babies of about 4 months of age may cry because they have not been placed in the preferred sleeping position. In the second half of the first year, they may cry from rage at having tossed a toy out of reach. Frequently, crying between 9 and 15 months of age is accompanied by gestures. After the source of the distress is identified and attended to, the infant usually can be soothed and the crying stopped.

At all ages, infant cries range from general fussiness to intense fear, anger, frustration, or pain (Gustafson, Wood, & Green, 2000). Hunger, discomfort, and sleepiness tend to increase in intensity over time if the source of distress is not removed. Knowing the typical reasons for infant crying may assist you in locating the source of the outburst more readily. Usually, caregivers

use the context of the situation, as well as auditory cues and their knowledge of the individual infant, to determine the probable cause of the cry.

The cry caused by pain is a long, piercing wail followed by a long silence, and then gasping. This cry is a signal that something is wrong (Gustafson, Wood, & Green, 2000). It is quite different from speech sounds and is an extremely effective signal in getting the attention of the caregiver. You may not be able to reliably distinguish infant's cries initially, but over time your ability to decipher between the child's bid for attention and distress, anger, or pain will increase.

Philip, who was only 4 months old, was crying hard when his caregiver, Mrs. Smith, picked him up and carried him to the refrigerator to get his formula. He sniffled and stopped his loud cries gradually. However, when the phone rang, she put him down to answer it. His crying resumed loudly.

Seven-month-old Hannah woke up hungry and crying. Her caregiver, who was reliably prompt in feeding and changing her, started walking toward her, and she stopped her crying even before being picked up.

At about 12:15 P.M., Alberto toddled to the refrigerator and pointed. His mother was cleaning another room and did not see him. He began jabbering, pointing, and crying until she came to investigate. Alberto stopped crying as soon as he saw her walk into the kitchen.

When adults are responsive, babies learn to self-regulate crying. Infants discover that they will be comforted, fed, changed, or attended when prompt care is quickly forthcoming. Ignoring the cries of infants in the first six months is not effective in reducing the duration or frequency of crying. In general, the longer the infant has been crying, the longer and more difficult the soothing time. Each behavioral state elicits potential responses from caregivers. After the physical needs of infants are addressed, the most typical behavior elicited in caregivers to a crying infant is soothing.

Soothing. A very effective strategy for soothing a crying child is to pick the child up and hold him or her to your shoulder. Five other methods—known as the 5 S's—are also useful: swaddle, side/stomach, shush, swing/sway, and suck (Karp, 2012). (See Highlight 2-2.)

When it comes to soothing, the more senses that receive continuous stimulation, the calmer babies become (Karp, 2012). Picking up crying babies, swaddling them, walking or rocking them, and singing lullabies singly or simultaneously are all possible solutions. Older babies prefer the soothing strategy with which they are familiar. Communicate with families about children's individual preferences for calming. Infants whose caregivers are most responsive to cries in the first few months of life cry the least. These children also become more effective in other forms of communication later (Bell & Ainsworth, 1972).

Unfortunately, sometimes crying occurs for no apparent reason, and normally effective ways of soothing the infant are futile. Often labeled *colic*, this begins during the first three weeks of life and increases through the second month, decreasing

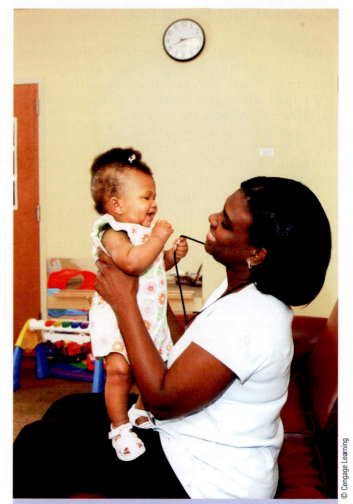

Infants whose caregivers are most responsive to their needs learn that the environment is predictable and the caregiver can be counted on.

© Cengage Learning

rapidly to more normal levels by the fourth month (Barr & Gunnar, 2000). Infants with colic have recurrent crying spells that last more than three hours per day for at least three days a week. They cry at predictable times of day and are otherwise well nourished and healthy.

Sometimes adults may become overstressed with their inability to sooth a crying infant, particularly one with colic. When that happens, the baby may tune in to their stress and become more upset. In such cases, it is useful to locate another available adult to take the child and provide the original caregiver with a break. Regardless of the cause for crying, when adults use soothing strategies, infants learn that the caregiver can be counted on to respond to their signals of distress predictably. This is an important element of trust. Another way that adults establish trust is by accurately interpreting children's communication through movement.

HIGHLIGHT 2-2

Soothing with the Five S's

- **Swaddle:** Wrap baby gently, but snugly in a blanket. Tuck arms down at the sides as you wrap.
- **Side or stomach position for holding (not sleeping):** Lay baby on side or stomach with your arm under baby's stomach.
- **Swing or Sway:** Move the baby in a motion that moves in the direction of head to feet, not sideways.
- **Shush:** Make a shushing noise over and over. (This imitates sounds in the uterus.)
- **Sucking:** Give the baby something to suck. This promotes future self-soothing.

Source: Karp, 2012.

Movement and Social Interaction

Infants move their bodies and reveal their needs for engagement (or not). Even after words are acquired, toddlers will continue to send cues through their movements. With the gradual increase in control of the head, arms, and shoulders, infants are able to manipulate their social interaction.

Initially, babies are only able to lift their heads to look briefly and then they flop back down. After a month, infants have control of their necks. By 3 months of age, they use their head position and gaze as a means of influencing communication with the caregiver. In the face-to-face position, infants are fully engaged, gazing at their caregivers. When infants turn their heads slightly, they maintain contact but signal that the play may be too fast or too slow. When the head is fully turned and the gaze lowered, contact is broken, and interaction is purposely stopped (Beebe & Stern, 1977; March of Dimes, 2003). When infants are completely overwhelmed by interactions that are too intense, they avert their gaze, go to sleep, cry, or become limp.

By the third month, infants are capable of tracking people as they move around the room. They stare at other people for long periods and, as they get older, will shift into a better position to watch what others are doing. For many sensitive caregivers, this is an invitation for conversation or play. Table 2-3 provides a summary of infant behaviors relating to head, gaze, and facial expression and corresponding typical meanings to the caregiver.

Once infants can sit up, between 6 and 10 months of age, they develop greater eye–hand coordination skills and a corresponding increase of interest in objects. They also may turn completely away from the caregiver to focus on an object. This is not a rejection of the caregiver but an exploration of the environment made possible by a comfortable relationship with a trustworthy adult. At about the same time, babies can creep successfully and physically follow their caregivers from room to room.

With increased mobility, infants' and toddlers' social horizons are greatly expanded. So, too, are the opportunities to encounter unsafe objects and environments, get into others' things, and explore their world. In doing so, they need consistent, sensitive guidance to keep them safe while encouraging them simultaneously to learn. Children's actions, along with adult interactions, scaffold children's understanding of the world.

Supporting Individuation and Socialization naeyc

Babies are immersed in two related, but separate lifelong processes: figuring out who they are as individuals and deciphering how they fit into the social world. These processes are called individuation and socialization. **Individuation** is the means by which personal identity is developed and one's individual place in the social order is acquired. When the emerging areas of self (e.g., senses, thoughts, emotions, and behaviors) are integrated, a unified personality or self-identity is formed. This takes place within the social context of human relationships and begins in infancy. **Socialization** is the process that includes one's capacity to cooperate in a group, to regulate one's behavior according to society, and to get along with others. Both individuation and socialization are absolutely essential to successful adaptation in life, and each evolves gradually.

Infants

Newborns show an innate interest in people, paying acute attention to them with all sensory modalities. When alert, they are likely to imitate simple adult actions such as opening the mouth. If the adult imitates the infant, the baby is likely to respond with another open mouth, thus inviting the interaction to continue. Self-awareness unfolds gradually as the infant matures. Early social participation such as molding to the adult's body when held, engaging in mutual cueing with the primary caregiver, being easily soothed by the preferred adult, and responding to signals contingently with the adult are early signs of a sense of self. **Contingent behavior** is like a conversation with turn-taking—but using only gesture, facial expressions, touching, or

Table 2-3 Infant Gaze and Social Meaning to Caregivers

Position and Expression	Typical Interpretation
Face to face, sober	Fully, engaged, intent
Face to face, smiling	Pleased, interested
Head turned slightly away	Maintaining interest; interaction too fast or too slow
Complete head rotation	Uninterested; stop for awhile
Head lowered	Stop!
Rapid head rotation	Dislikes something
Glances away, tilts head up; partial head aversion	Stop or change strategy
Head lowered, body limp	Has given up fighting off overstimulation

© Cengage Learning

playing—and often occurs with vocalizing. For example, baby Joey moves his arms. Mrs. Reynolds moves her arms. Joey opens his mouth. Mrs. Reynolds smiles and imitates him. By imitating the infant, the caregiver scaffolds the process of imitation for the baby setting the stage for reciprocal interactions where the infant learns about the self and others (Rochat, 2012).

Babies begin to engage in greater reciprocal (give-and-take) relationships with caregivers that require an understanding of self and others, remembering more from previous experiences and eventually learning positive social behavior by 6 months of age. Routine care and predictable adult–child face-to-face interactions lead to social expectations in the infant. The more promptly adults respond, the more likely infants will learn associations between their own and another person's behavior. They will show surprise if the adult behaves unexpectedly but may become sober, agitated, and then distressed.

In the last third of their first year, babies not only figure out that they can do things but that other people can too. For example, Randy could not get into a box, so she reached over to pull her caregiver to the box (with the expectation that help was at hand). Eventually children appear to detect "who is doing what to whom," identifying a process as well as perceiving the person and objects affected.

By the age of 1, babies are able to cooperate with a caregiver, such as by lifting their legs when a diaper is being changed. They begin to read subtle differences between people and begin to understand the dispositional world in which peoples' feelings and inclinations are revealed. They act with the clear intention of influencing the behavior of the adult. The foundation of social cognition emerges as a result of the intimate encounters repeated daily in which adults and infants respond synchronously to one another (Raikes & Edwards, 2009). Regular, frequent contact is essential to this process. Otherwise, social expectations are not rewarded. Infants can cope with a few caregivers such as the parents and the childcare worker, but they give up trying to build social connectedness if they encounter several adults a day or over a week. Infants in group care are capable of developing expectations of their regular caregivers who are consistently with them. When there is inconsistency in adults, the babies do not have the opportunities to learn what to expect. The lack of predictability elicits insecurity in babies and toddlers.

Toddlers

The toddler is practicing being a separate person and having a will, thus beginning to develop a sense of autonomy. Creeping and walking enable these older children to experiment with new ways to achieve desired goals. The exploits of this period require persistence and patience in adults. Barriers that previously protected children from falls are surmounted. Climbing makes forbidden objects high on shelves accessible. The emergence of self-will is accompanied by the gradual development of enough self-control to enable the child to act and accomplish! If toddlers can control their own bodies, then they can exert their will over their own actions and experience power. However, children who are not permitted to exert control over their movements doubt their ability to do so.

Sometime in the middle of the second year of life, children develop an objective self-awareness. Conscious, self-reflective behavior becomes possible. Assertions of "mine" and use of personal pronouns are cues of this. Verbalizations of "I want" signify that the child can think about thoughts and feelings that he or she has experienced. In addition, children begin to think about the thoughts of others in a very rudimentary fashion, believing that they are thinking alike (Thompson, 2006). For example, Kendyl is afraid of spiders, so everyone must stand on the chair to get away from the spiders because in her toddler mind, everyone must also be scared of arachnids!

Individual Differences in Outcomes

Developing a wholesome sense of trust is central to the process of individuation (Erikson, 1963). If feelings from the sensory world are typically pleasant, an infant will develop a sense of trust. However, if sensory stimulation is harsh, the child will develop a sense of mistrust or a sense that the world is a dangerous place. When adults meet (or do not meet) children's basic needs, this influences children's trust and mistrust. Trust and mistrust are the endpoints of a continuum, with each child needing some of both.

Complete trust is as maladaptive as complete mistrust. On one hand, a completely trusting child may be oblivious to the real dangers of the world, such as rapidly moving cars, because of the inappropriate expectation that she or he will always be taken care of. On the other hand, a completely mistrustful child may be unable to interact with things or people because nothing but pain and danger are expected.

The ideal is to have children on the trusting end of the continuum so that they can risk exploration and learn to tolerate frustration and delay gratification. Such children expect to be safe and comfortable most of the time. Their view of the world is hopeful. Trust is acquired through communication. The interaction between the infant's behavior and the caregiver's response is the basis of affective bonds, security, and the confidence felt by the infant and toddler, all of which help determine the degree to which children thrive.

Another outcome of the process of socialization and individuation is the child's self-concept. If adults are available, responsive, and loving, children perceive themselves as endearing, worthy, and lovable. However, if adults are inaccessible, unresponsive, or unloving, infants perceive themselves as disgusting, unworthy, or unlovable. The adult's general pattern of expressing affection and rejection will influence how well a baby's strong need for affection and comfort are met (Thompson, 2006).

Although the process of becoming a person and then becoming a member of a group begins in infancy, it is never really finished. Answering the questions of who am I and how do I fit into the world continue to challenge each person as he or she is socialized as a member of the culture. As such, one of the most difficult things that infants and toddlers learn to do is to separate from their parent or key attachment figure to be with others in a social situation.

Adult–Child Separation

The age when separation anxiety occurs varies, as does its intensity and duration. It is most often described as uncertainty in a new situation with unknown people. Generally, it occurs around 8 or 9 months of age and peaks between 13 to 15 months of age (Martin & Berke, 2007). When a child is first introduced to an unfamiliar caregiver, especially when stranger fears exist, it can be a very stressful experience for everyone. Children demonstrate separation anxiety by crying, grabbing at the parent, and showing other signs of distress. To the onlooker (and the parent holding the unhappy child), this appears quite terrible. However, when you consider the developmental milestones that it takes for a child to be at this point, it is really an awesome feat.

Just months ago, this little one did not know she was an individual. Slowly, she began recognizing that her actions would bring reactions. It was only around 6 months old that this screaming child began to think of herself as separate from the parent (or primary caregiver). It was at 8 or 9 months of age that she was able to know that objects exist even when she cannot see them. Therefore, when the child cries because her parent or primary person is leaving her, she is showing that she is not happy and would like to change the situation and remain with her safe and known person. It is the early childhood professional's role to help her adjust to the new situation so that she learns over time that she can have both: another safe place with kind, sensitive, caring people who meet her needs and her parent (or other significant person) who comes back predictably.

Early childhood professionals can model certain behaviors and recommend these behaviors to parents to assist in their child's transition from home to childcare (Deiner, 2009). Parents handle separations best by first allowing the child to become familiar with an alternative adult in the new setting while in the parent's presence. After the child seems more comfortable, the parent or caregiver should explain to the child that the parent is leaving soon. As the new adult engages with the child, the parent (having given the warning) departs. Some children begin to cry or chase after their parent. Helping professionals must, of course, provide comfort and reassurance and support the child in exploration of the environment and play with objects as soon as possible. Practices such as lying to or deceiving the child, encouraging parents to sneak out, or pulling a screaming infant from the parent's arms are to be avoided because the infant is quite capable of associating these terrifying and painful experiences with the caregiver as a person. These behaviors also betray the child's trust in the parent, the caregiver, and the new environment.

One important role for childcare providers is to aid families in the separation process. Some children may take a few days to become comfortable with a transition into the care of another. Others may take weeks or months, depending on their past experiences and their temperaments. Sometimes, children who were seemingly fine suddenly develop separation anxiety. This may occur because of changes within the child (such as cognition), changes within the family (such as a new sibling or a death), or changes within the environment (moving houses). When we use warmth, acceptance, genuineness, empathy, and respect with both the children and their parents, we strengthen our relationship with everyone involved. Ultimately, if adults deal with separation using understanding, warmth, and sensitivity, infants and toddlers will settle comfortably into their new situation. A goodbye routine developed ahead of time and implemented consistently can be very useful for everyone. See Table 2-4 for suggestions.

The more consistently the goodbye routine is followed, the more quickly the separation will occur. The success of the separation and the time it will take for a child to become confident and secure in his or her new environment will depend on the child and his or her individual temperament as well as on the consistency with which this routine is warmly followed. Although using such a routine may initially take more time for the parent and caregiver to create and implement, it will ultimately benefit everyone, especially the infant or toddler.

After a toddler adjusts to the new situation, you may see crying at the end of the day when the parent arrives. A toddler who had been happy and playing eagerly all day long, may collapse into tears at the sight of the parent. This, too, is an important sign that we should explain to disheartened parents. It means that the attachment with the parent is so strong that the child was able to hold it together all day but can

Table 2-4	Helping Families Separate: Establishing a Goodbye Routine

Before arriving at the center:

Parents tell the child of the day's activities by confidently stating that "Mommy (or Daddy) is going to work today, and you will be going to school." Help families understand the importance of sounding positive and sure about this and not waffling on its occurrence.

At the center:

Welcome the child and the parent into the environment. Treat them with warmth, acceptance, genuineness, empathy, and respect. (Sometimes, this event is not easy for either the child or the parent.) Invite parents to assist their baby or toddler in transitioning into your space. This may include taking off the child's jacket or hanging the child's bag on the child's hook. Encourage the parent to walk with the baby or toddler into the room.

In the room:

Point out to the child an interesting activity you believe the child will like. (For babies, take them gently into your arms and over to the objects; for toddlers, point them in the direction or take them by the hand to guide them.) Get the baby or toddler engaged in the activity right away. This is the transition from parent to caregiver. Some children will want to stay in their parents' arms a little longer and may not transition to you until engaged in the activity. Take your cues from the child.

Be sure the child has his or her transitional object (such as a favored toy or blanket) at this moment. Remind the child that the parent is leaving. Encourage the parent to tell the child how much he or she is loved and that Mommy or Daddy will return. Give the child a concrete specific for the return time such as after snack or at outside time. When the child is engaged, the departure should be brief. Long goodbyes do not help the child feel secure. Encourage parents to leave with smiles on their faces and with confidence. This will send their child the message that this is a safe place where his or her needs will be met.

Sensitively soothe sad children. Hold them or take them by the hand. Offer warm touch and kind compassionate words. Give reminders about the parent's love and return, as you continue to engage in an activity pleasing to the child.

Call parents within the hour to share their child's progress with the separation.

© Cengage Learning

demonstrate relief that it is time to go home with Mom or Dad. Parents appreciate these interpretations of their child's separation behaviors. By helping children adjust to new situations and assisting parents in understanding how to do to this well, you create trust among the child, parents, and you!

Now that you have read about separation anxiety, read about Mary and consider what you would recommend.

From this discussion, you can see that no two infants emerge from the early individuation process alike. Differences in temperament, daily relationships with the parents and other caregivers, and various pleasant or unpleasant experiences influence the degree of trust, the quality of attachment, and their sense of self. The patterns of communication in their world are of great significance in establishing who children are and who they will become.

Fostering Children's Competence in Communicating naeyc

"Ah-Boo! Ah-Boo! I'm looking at YOU!" chants Ms. Ella in a sing-song voice. Gregory watches her intently and grins ear to ear. Ms. Ella replies to his grin with a giggle of her own, gently taking him from his mother's arms

as she states with enthusiasm, "Let's see who else is here today." Gregory moves his body eagerly as if saying back, "Ok, let's go!" Ms. Ella responds with a laugh, "You are excited to find your friends!"

Ms. Ella and Gregory are engaged in a very rhythmic dialog. She invites, he responds. He reacts, she continues. Although this conversation seems "natural," it is actually the result of skill and effort by Ms. Ella. She recognizes her role as interpreting and scaffolding children's communication with their world.

Beginning Communication

Babies are innately prepared to learn language. They are capable of conveying signals that engage caregivers in social interactions. Neonates make pleasure sounds, and adults respond with satisfaction. An infant gazes into the adult's eyes for prolonged intervals, and the adult begins to talk as though the infant understands the message, even pausing when it would be the infant's turn to speak. Infants turn their heads toward the speaker, are calmed by the voice of the caregiver, and show preferences for their own parent's voice (Gleason & Ratner, 2012). In this early beginning, babies learn to signal nonverbally and begin to learn the rudiments of oral communication, with voice variations in pitch, volume, and turn-taking.

Meet Mary

Mary, age 18 months, and her mother, Rosene, were on their way to the childcare center near their home. Mary was strapped into her car seat firmly, which held her even though she wiggled and squirmed. Rosene said in a singsong tone, "Mary, you know mommy has to go work. You like Mrs. Bridges. You will have lots of fun at school."

"No go!" shouted Mary as her mother pulled into the parking lot. Retrieving Mary, she took her by the hand, even though Mary pulled against her mother's grasp, and moved into the childcare center.

Mrs. Bridges smiled a greeting to both Rosene and Mary, "Good morning, Rosene. Hi Mary. There is some play dough on the table ready for you to work."

Rosene, looking very uncomfortable, said in a fragile voice, "Mommy has to go to work now, Mary. You aren't going to cry, are you?" Rosene stood by the door looking at Mary anxiously as she approached the table with the dough. "Bye honey!"

Not yet involved with the dough, Mary turned and ran to her mom.

Mary hugged her mom tightly and began to cry.

Rosene walked her back to the table with the dough, turned and hurried from the room.

Mary hurried to the door and pounded on it, still crying very hard. Mrs. Bridges knelt down to hold her gently, and reassured him, "Your mom will come back to pick you up late this afternoon, just like she did yesterday. I know you really would like to have her right now. She has to go to work, though. I am here for you. Let's see if there is a rolling pin you can use."

Mary fingered a small stuffed toy frog that she carried in her pocket. It was her most favored thing that went everywhere with her. Sniffling, Mary went to the bucket and pulled out the rolling pin with one hand and held tightly to her frog in the other. Soon she set the frog down and was working on the dough with both hands. Mrs. Bridges helped her wipe her nose and stayed near her for several minutes while she began to play with interest. In a half hour, Mrs. Bridges quickly phoned Rosene, "Mary is fine. She is playing with the dough, and her frog is nearby. She stopped crying a few minutes after you left. I think we could work out a routine to help both of you feel better about the separation. Can you plan a little extra time at pick up today so that we can work out a goodbye routine?"

Using the information that you have already read, what are some of the strategies that Mrs. Bridges used to support the transition from family to childcare? What still needs to be done? How could a transition routine help Mary and her Mom? What do you think Mrs. Bridges will suggest for the separation plan?

Nearly all adult speech directed toward preverbal infants is used to convey social connectedness. The melody is important—rise-and-fall phrasing communicates warmth and loving approval. Short, staccato bursts signal "stop," "pay attention," or "don't touch." Soft murmurs are used to comfort and soothe. These patterns are true of all language speakers (Otto, 2009).

Between 1 and 3 months of age, babies make cooing sounds in response to speech. They smile, laugh, and make speech-like sounds when elicited. As the length of the quiet alert state increases, opportunities for communication with people increase. Between 3 and 7 months of age, babies respond distinctly to different intonations in people's speech.

By 8 months of age, babies repeat some simple babbling sounds such as "bababa" or "mamama" and may attempt to imitate sounds produced by adults. Though much of the babble practice occurs when infants are alone or resting before and after a nap, they will also babble when an older child or adult speaks to them. Babbling brings caregivers into conversations. Solitary babbling is different from the vocalizations heard when infants are "talking" in a "conversation" with their caregivers. Throughout the infancy period, babies need the back-and-forth patterning of face-to-face speech in the context of joint activity (Kovach & Da Ros-Voseles, 2008). The baby and the caregiver are constantly influencing one another during these conversation-like interactions well before the child uses words (Zero to Three, 2008).

The range of communication skills expands considerably in the middle of the first year. Young children show pleasure in simple games such as peek-a-boo and "tug the blanket"; they cry in rage when disappointed; and they express caution by looking away, knitting the brows, and having a sober facial expression. The flow of social interaction between the caregiver and the infant depends on the adult's ability to read the child's cues and to spend the time and energy to engage with the child. Adults bear most of the burden of social interaction, with infants gradually taking greater part during the course of the first three years.

Even quite young infants are able to read, decode, and interpret the facial expressions of their caregivers (Thompson & Lagattuta, 2008). They improve greatly in the understanding and use of gestures.

They exert some limited control in turn-taking and respond expressively to communications directed to them. Thus, they gradually learn the patterns of social engagement (Burgoon, Guerrero, & Floyd, 2010).

When a child is about 6 months of age, infant–adult interactions become focused on joint object involvement. Adults briefly point out and offer objects while commenting on them. Babies may turn their backs toward the adult when their interest is engaged in a toy to concentrate on the object. This behavior should not be interpreted as dislike; instead, it can be explained by the fact that the infant cannot focus on several things at the same time.

Between 9 and 15 months of age, infants gradually develop an increasing ability to deliberately initiate communication that influences the behavior of their caregivers (Carpenter, Nagell, & Tomasello, 1998). They first engage in **joint attention**. The most typical example is when the baby looks at the toy and then looks at the adult face to see that the caregiver is also looking at the toy. **Communicative gestures** such as pointing to an object desired with an urgent vocalization may be an imperative demand for the object, or the baby may point to an object with a vocalization indicating "isn't this interesting?" In both ways, the child is checking to see if the adult is responding to the overture. **Gaze following** occurs when the infant notices that the adult is focused elsewhere in the distance, and the child orients to the same place. By 12 months old, babies will look to where the caregiver is pointing. Babies continue to try to communicate when the caregiver does not respond appropriately and may modify or elaborate gestures. For example, Harry wanted the revolving ornament on the table. He opened and closed his hands and vocalized, "Eh, Eh!" with increasing volume. Unsuccessful, he pointed and increased the length of the vocalization to "Eehh …!" Finally his caregiver came over to him, picked him up, and then moved the item from view while telling him why he could not have it.

At a year or so, children develop some alternative ways of handling certain emotions. They might appraise a new situation before responding to it instead of responding immediately. One means of evaluating a situation is called **social referencing**. Babies use their developing communication abilities to read the caregiver's facial expression and tone of voice. If the adult responds to a new situation with comfortable posture and a neutral or smiling face, the infant will respond with exploratory behavior. On the other hand, if the caregiver appears fretful or upset, the infant is likely to behave warily (Labile & Thompson, 2008). Social referencing continues throughout childhood as children pick up emotional cues from other children and adults when determining how to act in an unfamiliar situation or with an unexpected occurrence.

Babies send messages, too. They clearly can "tell" the caregiver when they want to do something, using combinations of gesture, gaze, and vocalization. Most adults quickly recognize lifted arms as a request to be picked up. Older infants and toddlers have a variety of noncrying sounds that get and keep attention. These gradually develop into words. At about 13 months of age, symbolic communication emerges, and toddlers and their adult partners become increasingly ritualized as they expand upon their ways to interact.

Imitative learning begins to appear around this time too. Toddlers show awareness when either an adult or another toddler mimics what they are doing. They often gaze and smile at the person copying them before continuing their play. Earliest forms of pretend play (such as a baby washing his face) are examples of imitative behavior. The emotional displays one sees in other people are also eventually imitated. Thus, the older infant and toddler are likely to display pleasure, interest, anger, or fear in ways similar to the important adults in their environments.

More Advanced Communication

"Me do!"
"NO!"
"Big much."
"Thank you."
"!@#&!"
There comes a point when the language that children have heard becomes the words that they now use to express themselves and exert personal power into their world.

Words. Between 18 and 24 months of age, the understanding and use of language explodes. By the end of the second year, the child can function as a social partner and can communicate intentionally through words to influence the behavior of others. For this to happen, toddlers are simultaneously learning to use both facets of language: receptive language and expressive language. **Receptive language** is what one hears directed at oneself, "You are *so* smart!" **Expressive language** is what one says (to others), "No, MINE!"

From birth, children have been immersed in oral language. Now, they are actively incorporating what is said to them and what they are able to say into their notion of who they are (Martin & Berke, 2007). Children learn about the sounds that make up language, the meanings of words, the rules for putting words together, and the many ways that speech is used in social situations (Byrnes & Wasik, 2009; Genishi &

Dyson, 2009). Moving from babbling to individual words (usually nouns and names) to two-word phrases to full sentences is no easy task. It requires continuous support and feedback from the people in the child's environment. The sensitive periods for communication and social interactions occur in the first three years and require adults who interact with them to engage in conversations (National Scientific Council on the Developing Child, 2007).

Signs. When babies begin to be fed with a spoon, many families introduce sign language. Parents teach simple signs such as the one for "more" or "all done." This allows the baby to communicate more specifically, increases autonomy, and eliminates some mealtime stress. Babies may use between 50 and 100 signs before they begin to speak. Generally, professionals find this strategy very useful as well. If caregivers are fluent in sign, the children become bilingual as they would if there were two languages spoken by caregivers.

There may be dual-language learners in any classroom or center. Because they are learning vocabulary in both languages, their acquisition may take slightly longer than if only learning one language (Otto, 2009). Therefore, professionals should make sure that common objects are clearly named (chair, toilet) and verbs demonstrated (wash, put) as soon as possible in the program so that everyone can readily communicate.

In spoken languages, children initially understand much more than they speak (Byrnes & Wasik, 2009). The importance of connecting vocabulary to clear meanings cannot be overstated. It is usually easier to support the learning of a second language when the child is a competent communicator for his or her age in the home language. Some caregivers outside the home have successfully used key sign words (come, clean up, stop, toilet, rest, etc.) as the bridge between when children can initially understand spoken language and when they can speak the language.

The 2-year-old group had half of the children whose home language was English. The other children's families were speakers of Finnish, Korean, and Chinese. Miss Eppinger taught all of the children American Sign Language (ASL). Beginning on the first day of school, to ease their social interactions, she shared the signs for "stop," "help," and "look." To assist them in following routines and resolving conflicts, she used both English words and their corresponding ASL signs. All of the children used these signs months before many of the dual-language learners actually spoke English, enabling them to engage in social play successfully.

Tuning in To Children's Communications

Children learn the communication skills of the caregivers with whom they interact. They learn the sociocultural meanings of words and gestures in daily interactions (Genishi & Dyson, 2009). Sensitive and effective caregivers learn how each infant and toddler engages in social bouts and respects signals for disengagement. Observation of children's state, gaze, spatial positioning, posture, and distance from the adult will provide cues to the adult of whether to initiate social activity. Forcing social interaction on an infant who is tired or otherwise engaged leads to tears and irritability. The same is true for toddlers. Exhausted toddlers do not make for easy language participants. Pay attention to their cues.

For optimum development, children should be "bathed" in language that is connected meaningfully to what they are doing. Adults who talk to infants and toddlers within the routine settings of the day about ordinary things that are happening tend to increase the amount of vocalization of the children. Turn-taking conversations, lullabies and songs, and comments on the task at hand are all effective. Speech directed to other adults or general talking in the room is not effective. For toddlers, songs, silliness with words, and stories about themselves are all great ways to help surround them in meaningful language.

Words and gestures have meaning for babies long before they begin to use words. When adults begin to label young children's feelings according to how they are interpreting a particular event, they are providing appropriate useful vocabulary. Simultaneously, this vocabulary gives cues to the child as to the appropriate social response. "Oh, you don't know Mr. Rogers, do you? He is a new face that you're uncertain about. Come sit with me and we will talk to him together," will both calm a baby and describe what is happening when murmured in a soothing voice.

Early in their language development, toddlers tend to overgeneralize. "Dada" may be applied to all males indiscriminately. However, when adults use only the correct names for objects and actions, babies soon learn correct vocabulary (Gleason & Ratner, 2012). "Dada" will be applied to one important male and "Bompa" to the grandfather. Because some sounds are difficult to produce, babies typically substitute easier sounds until the necessary speech sounds are acquired. When adults use precise language for objects, actions, locations, and people, toddlers will also use precise words by the end of the second year.

Friendliness naeyc

Adults may not think of babies as being friendly with one another, but as more infants are experiencing group care, more of them have the opportunity for true peer interaction. In fact, they seem to show a preference for children close in age (Ross, Vickar, & Perlman, 2012). It seems that infants acquire social styles and an enduring orientation toward other people from their families. Typical early peer behavior is summarized in Table 2-5.

Babies show more interest than fear when babies unknown to them approach. Children with past interactions with peers do better than those with fewer social experiences. Babies initiate more and more complex interactions with familiar peers, but they cannot engage in complex play with more than one child at a time. Play episodes in which babies interact are typically short lived. Most consist of careful watching, sometimes with vocalizations, imitations, and toys being offered and retrieved.

Toddlers in a group setting attempt many different methods to engage with one another. They may try to connect from a distance, come very close and touch the peer, or do a combination of verbalizing with one of these. Often these are unsuccessful bids, but with adult assistance, they can work. Sometimes when toddlers are attracted to an object or a person, they gather rapidly together, tumbling over one another in an effort to get near the person or obtain the object. This group approach has been described as "swarming" and is most frequently an unsuccessful social interaction.

Toys attract children and bring babies together, but they also may draw attention away from another player. Toddlers usually can start a friendly approach but have difficulty keeping the interaction going. Those 15 to 20 months old are capable of engaging in an activity that involves taking turns, repetition, and imitation along with much smiling and laughing. As toddlers mature, their interactions with age-mates become longer, and their ability to share intentions and purpose increases the scope of their play. As they become more adept at this, their ability to work with others and engage in socially expected activities, such as sharing, increases. To share, children have to have some rudimentary understanding that they will give the toy to another person for an amount of time and

Table 2-5	Peer Relationships in Infancy and Toddlerhood
Age	**Infant and Toddler Behavior**
0–2 months	Contagious peer crying; intense visual regard between familiar infants
2–6 months	Mutual touching
6–9 months	Smiling; approaching and following; vocalizing; watching
9–12 months	Giving and accepting toys; simple games: "chase," "peek-a-boo"; waving; purposeful efforts to engage others
12–15 months	Vocal exchanges with turn-taking; social imitation; conflicts over toys, "swarming" may occur with groups of infants
15–24 months	Early words; mutual roles: hide and seek; "offer and receive"; imitates peers and imitative games with turns; aware of being imitated; beginning understanding of what is "mine" and what is "yours"; share toys

© Cengage Learning

© Cengage Learning

Toddlers enjoy one another's company.

that it will come back again. This is no small cognitive accomplishment, but it has been found to occur between very close toddlers (Wittmer, 2008).

Friends

Many parents and caregivers want to know, "Can infants and toddlers form friendships?" Children who see each other often have been found to have mutually caring affection for each other, which is the definition of friendship. These children look for each other and miss their friends when they are not available (Howes, 2000). They hug and smile when they are reunited (Wittmer, 2008). These friendships have been found to last over time and include elements of helping, intimacy, loyalty, sharing, and ritual activities (Whaley & Rubenstein, 1994). Activities such as run and chase (or follow), copying vocalizations or specific motor acts, usually with much laughter as well as themes such as dogs, cats, babies, and monsters, are played over and over again between toddler friends (Wittmer, 2012). Once established, these early friendships tend to continue, and some toddlers have two or more friends (Ross, Vickar, & Perlman 2012). These

intimate relationships are a wonderful starting place for the early practice of empathy and prosocial behavior. Toddler empathy is demonstrated when a 2-year-old comforts a peer who is crying by patting him on the arm or by giving up a toy to try to stop the friend's tears (Wittmer, 2008).

Adults can encourage toddlers' peer relationships and friendships through their language, presence, and the objects and opportunities that they provide. Describing infant and toddler behavior, intentions, and emotions aloud helps to translate children's interactions for all to better understand. For example, "Oh, Jared fell on you, Katie! He was trying to walk around to get a toy. Let's help him. Jared, what toy did you want?" By playing games and inviting children over by name, they are welcomed into simple situations in which adults can then guide their interactions. "Katie, Jared and I were just going to play with these trains. You could use this one...." Merely sitting on the floor with children attracts them to come over and play. Supporting children's interactions with other children is a wonderful starting point for practicing social skills.

Conflicts are usually brief struggles over toys and most frequent with friends with whom they have the

Even the youngest children form close relationships with others of their own age when they have many opportunities to interact.

most positive interactions as well. Babies 11–12 months old often show limited interest in the toy they fought over and turn to the next object that a peer is interested in. Between 18 and 30 months, children may protest or withdraw when they think a child is interested in their possessions with notions of "ownership" emerging at about 19 months of age (Ross, Vickar, & Perlman, 2012).

Adult nurturance and guidance makes young children's attempts with others more successful. Children's early displays of friendship and peer relationships become possible because of their beginning development of self-regulation.

Fostering Self-Regulation naeyc

Self-regulation is the ability to monitor and manage one's thinking, attention, feelings, and behaviors *internally* to cope with situations and events (Thompson, 2006, p. 33). This includes people's ability to adjust their emotions, ideas, and reactions to the demands at hand (Calkins & Williford, 2009). Although self-regulation takes a long time to develop, it has its beginnings in infancy.

When babies as young as 3 months vocalize instead of cry to get their needs met, they are starting to regulate themselves (Field, 2007). Another example occurs when infants are presented with a stress-inducing event. Some babies will start sucking on their hands or blankets and may turn their heads away. These are attempts to manage the event. Also, babies who go to sleep on their own demonstrate early self-regulation. When adults meet infants' needs consistently and follow predictable, peaceful routines, beginning levels of self-regulation become possible to achieve.

Mobile babies demonstrate self-regulation when they pay attention to events such as diapering (and even cooperate in the process) and when they solve their own problems such as getting a toy just out of reach. Adults assist them in attending by talking to them about what is happening step by step, and by allowing them to try to solve developmentally appropriate problems on their own before intervening (Elliot & Gonzalez-Mena, 2011.)

Another example of early self-regulation can be found in children's progression with the use of the toilet. With walking and the development of language, along with muscle control over the bladder and the

© Cengage Learning 2015

Toddlers are quite pleased with themselves when they are successful in learning to regulate body functions.

Beginner's Guide for Supporting Toilet Learning

1. Coordinate your efforts with parents and other caregivers. Aim for giving children consistent cues as to what to do and how to do it within the program. Keep your voice calm and matter-of-fact. Find out the words that family members use to refer to toileting. Use those words initially.

2. Have all supplies stored at hand ready to use, and stay with the toddler all the time.

3. Begin by incorporating some steps or practices while diapering.
   - Washing the baby's hands after diapering
   - Explaining what is occurring as you diaper
   - Asking babies to participate as much as possible (holding still or lifting legs, climbing up to the changing tabletop with help)

4. Take each toddler to the toilet about 10–15 minutes before the child typically eliminates in the diaper. This requires some observation and your keen attention. Most toddlers are regular in elimination. Put on plastic gloves and/or follow state sanitation standards.

5. Guide with physical assistance and language for each of these steps. It takes repetition and understanding to teach toddlers the following steps, which they usually learn one step at a time:
   - Child unfastens clothing and pulls down pull-ups or unfastens diaper.
   - Child backs up to the toilet seat and sits; later boys will stand. Adult directs them to aim the penis toward the toilet bowl, whether sitting or standing.
   - Child remains sitting for a few minutes. Adult holds a conversation with the child.
   - Child tears off tissue, folds it and eventually wipes front to back independently. Adult demonstrates and cleans the child as necessary. This is often the last step learned.
   - Child gets down from toilet and refastens clothing. Clean, dry clothing may be needed.
   - Child flushes the toilet.
   - Child washes and dries hands.

6. Adult assists the child as necessary to return to play.

7. Adult cleans all surfaces used. This will include walls and floors if you forgot to remind boys to aim into the toilet bowl. Rinse feces in the toilet out of cloth clothing, if necessary, and put soiled clothing in a plastic bag to return to parents. Remove your plastic gloves and roll up diaper or pull-up and place all of it in a sealed container.

8. Wash your own hands with soap and water.

9. When toddlers are experienced and are successful most of the time, confer with parents about switching from pull-ups to training pants or underwear.

10. Celebrate the child's successful move to wearing underwear with the child and family.

Digital Download Download from CourseMate

rectum, toddlers eventually become quite successful with independent elimination. They take great pride in learning the routine of the entire event. With calm straightforward instruction from adults in a low-key manner, power struggles are less likely to occur, and autonomy is achieved! See Highlight 2-3 for a simple guide.

Although eventual self-regulation is the goal for many areas of life, it is a complex process in which each child falls along a continuum from very little regulation to greater dependence on self. Infants and toddlers need support in handling prohibitions (Elliot & Gonzalez-Mena, 2011). Sometimes, the best avenue for fostering self-regulation is to begin with **shared-regulation.** This is a process in which the adult shares some of the responsibility for the management of an event or breaks a task into manageable pieces so that the child can experience success. Shared-regulation empowers children to feel successful while teaching them the steps to be independent in the future (Bath, 2008).

Using the toilet is again an example in which co-regulation is helpful. For instance, initially, the child can tell the adult when it is time "to go" and can assist in pulling pants off. Then the child may progress to independently removing pants, with the adult wiping. Finally, the child performs the entire series of steps alone. Breaking large tasks into more doable steps for toddlers eliminates much frustration and allows children to feel in control and thus successful.

"Temper tantrums" are physical demonstrations by toddlers that communicate their feelings of loss

Check Your Understanding

Identify the strategies that support co-regulation in infants and toddlers.

- Provide predictable peaceful routines.
- Help mobile babies focus their attention by talking to them and pointing out things.
- Encourage babies to solve their own problems (such as reaching for a toy) while talking about what is happening step by step.
- Use short, simple statements to give directions, comment on children's actions, or to encourage each child's attempts.
- Break difficult tasks (eating independently and toileting independently) into manageable chunks where toddlers can be increasingly successful.
- Remain calm and supportive when toddlers get frustrated and lose control (tantrums).
- Refrain from overreacting and overcontrolling. Use WAGER skills instead.
- Provide plenty of floor time for children to learn and practice social interactions.

Digital Download   Download from CourseMate

need for autonomy. After they have regained control, adults may suggest alternate strategies to help children achieve their goals.

With increasing cognitive development comes greater social skill because toddlers have more tools for social problem solving. They are able to imitate, plan, form expectations of future events, and remember others exist even if not present (Martin & Berke, 2007). They are curious, focus attention, solve problems, and persist even when frustrated (Petersen, 2012). They learn about causal relations and increase their ability to understand social experiences. When they are allowed practice and repetition, they are able to consolidate their learning into memory. These memories are then called upon and altered as new information occurs, thus creating strong neural pathways for social problem solving (Bauer, 2009). The more social experiences, the more opportunities for toddlers to grow in ability!

With the guidance and support of caring, responsive, and sensitive teachers, very young children develop the self-regulation, intellectual, and communication skills appropriate to their age and experiences (Petersen, 2012). These emerging abilities are relevant to their long-term success as learners as they are reflected in the educational standards of states. In Figure 2-3, you will see two sample standards from different states.

of control. While struggling with their desires for independence and dependency at the same time, toddlers sometimes share their frustration with the world by throwing their bodies on the ground, yelling, and thrashing their arms. When adults are calm and understanding, they can help toddlers regain composure. Adults who overreact and are overcontrolling toward toddlers interfere with their attempts at managing their world. Accepting children who have tantrums and then assisting, if needed, in helping them regain self-control contributes to their growing

Relating to Infants and Toddlers with Special Needs naeyc

Up to this point, the discussion and description of infants and toddlers has been based on typical development. However, some infants are identified at birth as having conditions that will alter the speed or the outcome in their growth and development, and others as having a high risk of not developing typically.

Michigan Board of Education

Program Standard: The program promotes the development of positive relationships between and among children:
- Children interact informally with one another.
- Children negotiate and resolve conflicts peacefully with caregiver intervention and guidance when necessary. (no. 9)

Pennsylvania Department of Education

Program Standard: Children will express feelings, thoughts, and needs appropriately to adults and peers:
- Children self-soothe by calming and being talked to, held, or rocked.
- Children manage frustration with adult support.
- Children show a strong sense of self as a powerful doer by demonstrating pride in accomplishments. (no. 25.2)

Figure 2-3 Examples of State Learning Standards Associated with Infants and Toddlers (Michigan Board of Education, 2006; Pennsylvania Department of Education and Department of Public Welfare, 2009).

Sometimes the challenges they face may not become apparent until later. For example, children experiencing delays in language development generally are not identified until well into the second year or even later. Professionals have a responsibility to refer children for special services or to cooperate with the intervention team in providing optimal conditions for their development. Physicians and childcare workers are most likely to be among the first to identify irregularities in the child's developmental progress because they see children regularly during their first three years. Early intervention has moderate and positive effects on the developmental progress of many children with disabilities who are less than 3 years of age.

In some states, infants and toddlers who are at high risk are also eligible for services. High risk is defined by the states but is likely to include infants born to chemically dependent mothers, abused and neglected youngsters, children who have had lead poisoning, and low birth-weight infants. Language problems are among the most frequent and have a substantial impact on children's social development as well as future educational outcomes.

Early childhood professionals play a significant role in the surveillance of all the children in their programs. They must observe skillfully, communicate with parents, and refer children for assessment when necessary. Information on development is available on the Internet from professional organizations for most areas that might concern you. For example, the American Speech–Language–Hearing Association (ASHA) posts a guide for typical language development by ages on its website. Consulting with the administrators of the program and sharing concerns with the family are necessary prerequisites for making a referral to the appropriate agency in the community so that no child "slips through the cracks." (Local public schools will be able to identify the specific agency in any community.) A referral means that someone with specialized skill will make a detailed assessment of a child. Some youngsters are on the edge of normal ranges and may not require specialized interventions, and others may be missed because caregivers and families continue to think that the problem will correct itself in time.

Many early childcare professionals do not recognize that the skills they have can and should be applied to working with infants and toddlers who have special needs. For example, children with Down syndrome learn more slowly than others. They will need more repetition and will achieve milestones of self-feeding and toileting later than their age-mates. Their social development will progress in the same direction but more slowly. These children can fit into a program for typically developing peers with minimal alteration of the environment, using the same strategies you use to nurture and guide all children.

By now, you have read a great deal about the importance of establishing positive relationships with infants and toddlers and how both you and the child contribute to this process. Now it is time to translate that knowledge into action. Although you may be attracted to infants and toddlers and feel affection for them, the skills to help them develop social competence are not entirely intuitive. They must be learned. The following strategies will help you accomplish this. Most importantly, they will give you the tools to demonstrate warmth, acceptance, genuineness, empathy, and respect routinely and in ways that children will interpret as trustworthy and supportive.

SKILLS FOR DEVELOPING POSITIVE SOCIAL RELATIONSHIPS WITH INFANTS AND TODDLERS naeyc

Providing Prompt Basic Care

1. **Respond promptly to infants' bids for aid.** When an infant 6 months of age or younger cries, pick up the infant quickly and attend to his or her needs. Older infants have an increased ability to wait and will respond to speech and other signs of attention while waiting for care, but their patience is limited. No child under a year of age should wait long for routine care such as feeding, diapering, or being put to bed for a nap.

2. **Establish a regular pattern in giving care when responding to infant signals.** Develop an individual pattern of picking up, talking, soothing, changing diapers, feeding, or holding each infant. What works with one child may not suit another. Adjust accordingly.

3. **Confer with parents about the child's routine.** Avoid undue stress by finding out the child's particular pattern of sleeping, playing, and eating at home. Cultural differences often affect how families provide routine care. Listen carefully, and when possible within the group setting, adapt your patterns of care to more closely conform to those of the child's parents.

4. **Handle infants gently, but firmly, moving them so they can see your face or other interesting sights.** Place them at your shoulder when walking so they can see the environment.

Support them in the crook of your arm for feeding so they can gaze into your face. Carry older infants at your side with their backs supported so that when they pull away from your body, they will not fall backward out of your arms. At the end of the first year, some infants may protest at being carried at all. In such a case, if for any reason you must carry the child, hold her closely and firmly to your body, wrapping the arms and legs with your arms so the child does not strike you in the process of protesting. When held, an infant should be safe and secure, and should not experience falling, being squeezed too tightly, or other discomfort.

5. **Ensure that the infant experiences tactile comfort.**
   a. Change wet diapers and clothing promptly. Babies who urinate several times in a disposable diaper before being changed get a painful rash.
   b. Pat gently when burping the baby; a thump is not required.
   c. Wash the baby's skin as needed.
   d. Caress the infant whenever opportunities arise. Loving touches are pleasurable to them. Back rubs or massage also may be effective in helping infants to relax.

6. **Adjust the environment to keep it safe and sanitary as infants begin to move on their own.** Protect babies from harm. As babies begin to roll, crawl, or walk, it is better to keep space orderly, safe, and clean than it is to restrict the baby or engage in rounds of limit-setting and upset. Remove breakables, keep floors free of clutter, securely fasten cupboards, and add gates to stairways.

Detecting Individual Needs

1. **Use multiple senses to gain information about the children.** Scan all the children under your supervision regularly. Look for signs of drowsiness, level of activity, degree of involvement with objects, potential opportunities for social engagement, and possible safety hazards. Listen to their vocalizations as well as their cries.

2. **Write down the time and date of significant behaviors.** Describe specifics of the circumstances and how adults and children acted rather than writing your conclusions about such experiences.

3. **Use your knowledge of development and the child's typical behavior to interpret events.** Draw on your knowledge of child development in general, and of individual children in particular, in responding to each child.

4. **Take into account the temperament and experience of all the children in your care.** Be sure to provide adequate stimulation for the very quiet child as well as the fussy baby. If you are more comfortable with peaceful babies, do not ignore the frequent crying of infants whose responses are less satisfying to you. Distribute attention among all infants and toddlers assigned to you.

5. **Keep pace with the changing needs of children as they mature.** During the first three years of life, infants' and toddlers' abilities and interests change rapidly, and a response appropriate to a child only a short time ago now may be outdated. Remain observant to children's cues and adjust accordingly.

6. **Encourage older infants and toddlers to participate in their own care.** Guide children in turning on the water at the "low sink." Let toddlers pour their own juice from small plastic pitchers with lids. Invite young children to select a cracker from the basket. Encourage children to choose a toy from the shelf.

7. **Report new skills and abilities to adult family members as soon as you observe them.** Help parents understand each day's achievement. Be careful not to report the *big* milestones right away. Instead, alert the family to be "on the lookout for" the firsts so that they may "discover" them and tell you, thus avoiding jealousy.

Establishing and Maintaining Effective Communication

1. **Respond to child signals in a way that is consistent with your interpretation of the meaning and appropriate for the developmental level of the child.** The behavioral state of the infant, the nonverbal cues of facial expression and vocalizations, the gestures and words, the context of the situation, and the child's typical behaviors are useful in determining appropriate responses to individual children.

2. **Talk to every child.** Words are never wasted on infants or toddlers. Maintain a face-to-face position and eye contact while speaking. Use short, simple sentences or phrases. Increase the complexity of your language according to individual children's abilities and ages. With babies, use a higher-pitched voice, emphasizing vowel sounds, and allow time for the infant to respond.

After you begin to converse with a baby, she or he will respond with coos, smiles, laughter, babbling, and attentiveness, depending on the baby's age. Pause for the child to respond in much the same way that you would carry on an adult conversation. Allow older infants enough time to respond to your speech with words or gestures.

3. **Talk while engaged in routine care. Describe what you are doing, what you see, what you hear.** Use specific vocabulary, simple grammar, and short sentences. Speak slowly and distinctly (Otto, 2009). The following script is based on an interaction between a 3-month-old child and his caregiver:

   Charlie begins to cry and Ms. Nu approaches. "Charlie, are you hungry? The bottle is warming." (She picks the infant up and walks toward the changing table.) "I'll bet you are wet … a diaper, yes …" (Charlie has stopped crying and appears to be watching her hands.) "Lay you down … now, unfasten this diaper … take it off, oooofff, ooooff." (She smiles and looks into Charlie's face as he wiggles his body and moves his arms.) Ms. Nu continues to tell Charlie what she is doing as she completes the diaper change, puts him in an infant seat near the sink, and washes her hands.

4. **Slow down or discontinue the interaction if the infant looks away for a few seconds, lowers the head, or cries.** He may be experiencing overstimulation. Going to sleep or shutting the eyes is another means for younger infants to terminate an interaction. Older babies may simply crawl or walk away.

5. **Use language to respond to older infants' gestures.** When a toddler points to a cookie, say, "Cookie?" Or, when an older infant bangs the cup after drinking juice, say, "Looks like you're finished." Name actions that the child is doing. For example, when Jeff was bobbing up and down while music was playing, his caregiver smiled and said, "Gee, Jeff, you're dancing!" Simple, short, direct statements are best.

6. **Tell infants and toddlers what you are going to do before you do it, and wait a second or two before acting.** Engage children in participating in their own care whenever possible. Announce, "I am going to pick you up now" before you do it. Allow the baby time to reach for you. Avoid quick, impersonal actions that treat the baby as an object rather than a social person.

7. **Repeat and expand toddler utterances.** At the end of the first year, infants may begin to say their first words. Simply use their word in a way that seems to make sense: "Mama!" exclaims Diedra. Her caregiver responds, "Mama's gone to

work." Sometimes people outside the family do not readily recognize a baby's word; family members must be consulted if the word is used regularly. "Manky" may mean a particular blanket; "Doe" may mean, "Look at that." In either case, respond with words such as "Do you want your blanket?" or "Blanket?"

8. **Use the context of the situation to interpret the meaning of one-word utterances.** Observe children to see if you have responded appropriately to their attempts at communication. Repeating the intended word (or your assumption of what it was) often helps as children recognize the meaning of a much larger vocabulary than the one they are able to produce. Introduce new words paired with old words to help children's language understanding and vocabulary growth.

9. **"Talk your ideas out loud."** Talk with children about what you are thinking and what others may be thinking. Give them reasons for your behavior and that of others, describing emotions, thoughts, ideas, and desires. *As Mrs. Peters was drawing, she said, "I'm making a big head because I have one. Now I'm making curly hair because I think I have a lot of big hair on the top and on the side of my head."*

Encouraging Exploration and Learning

1. **Provide play materials and interaction experiences that encourage infants and toddlers to explore the environment.** Allow young infants to explore your body by touching your hair or skin or by patting your clothing. Provide toys and materials that are within children's developmental range but that challenge their awakening interest in objects. Be sure you add in new toys to continue stimulation. As you rotate the new toys in and take some away, keep some of the favorites available. Never change all of the toys at once; this is very upsetting to infants and toddlers.

2. **Entice babies into play with toys by offering them and demonstrating play.** Play impromptu interactive games such as "peek-a-boo," "where's the toy," or "making faces." Allow children to set the pace. Do not intrude on their activities.

3. **Rejoice in the infants' and toddlers' accomplishments with them.** Finding a toy that has rolled behind a box is a significant achievement for an 8-month-old. Getting food from the plate onto the spoon and into the mouth is a feat for a

1-year-old. The first time to sit, to crawl, or to walk is the result of concentration, effort, and practice for the developing infant. Let children know you are proud of their successes. Laugh with them. Hug them. Talk to them. Let them know how glad you are that they can do something new.

4. **Encourage exploration by being physically available to children during play.** Infants and toddlers not asleep or engaged in other routine care should be on the floor for play. Stay in close proximity as they move out into the world of objects. Do not walk away as soon as they are engaged or leave them alone in a strange environment or with strange people without giving them a chance to acclimate themselves to the new situation. Timid infants and toddlers especially need patient support because, to them, the world may appear to be a frightening, dangerous place.

5. **Play with toddlers and organize the play so that more than one adult at a time is sitting on the floor and interacting with toddlers in groups.** Nothing is more appealing to a toddler than an adult who is doing something that they can play too. Some additional hints to support play are:

Hints about Infant/Toddler Toy Play

- At about 5-6 months, babies turn their backs on people to focus on toys.
- At about 12 months, the very best toy is the one someone else has.
- Putting toys away in a box or on a shelf is great fun when an adult plays too, dumping them all out again can prolong the game.
- Having two toys just alike is better than two similar toys when young toddlers want the same thing.
- Offering toys and retrieving them from others is early social play and may last only seconds.

Digital Download   **Download from CourseMate**

Helping Infants and Toddlers Comply with Adult Requests

1. **Use simple, common verbs to make requests of older infants and toddlers.** Say things like "Come here," "Look," and "Show me." A baby can understand and comply with these oral requests sometime between 8 and 10 months of age. Sign language, if used by the adults in an appropriate context, can be imitated by children sooner than they can speak the words. Use a warm tone of voice that is relaxed and in your usual pitch, and make requests or suggestions in a conversational volume, and children will be more likely to comply. Avoid harsh voices and physical force. They are ineffective and will generate only fear and withdrawal.

2. **Show infants and toddlers what you are requesting.** Demonstrate the action that you want the child to perform. At the same time, describe it in words. For example, if you want an infant to place a toy in a storage box, you might sit on the floor, pick up a toy, place it in the box, offer another toy to the infant, and, pointing to the box, ask her to put it in.

3. **Repeat suggestions or requests.** Babies and toddlers need to hear directions and see demonstrations frequently. Use a warm voice as you speak. Children under the age of 3 cannot stop an action in progress on their own, but a simple repetition of the request with a few moments of delay is likely to be effective. Sometimes toddlers respond with "No!" when asked to do something. Wait a moment or so and repeat the request. This assertion of self is not the same as defiance, and many toddlers will happily comply a minute or so later. Try not to be impatient or convey urgency or hurry. All toddlers take many repetitions, and youngsters with special needs take even more.

4. **Distract a child's attention by offering a substitute action or object.** Get the child's attention first. Offer an alternative object or point something out that might be of interest. Use simple substitution; infants often let go of what they are holding to get something else. To distract a very young child, engage his attention, make alternative suggestions about what to do, and show him how to do it. These will avoid power struggles and are likely to achieve compliant behavior. Verbal demands and pulling objects out of the children's hands are less effective and lead to angry confrontations that need not occur.

5. **Physically pick up and move the child who does not comply with your requests when safety is at stake.** Never delay action when safety is involved! Simple, firm, friendly physical removal with appropriate redirection of the child's interest is both appropriate and effective. Quietly voiced explanations, such as "It's not safe for you outside all by yourself," or "You can play in the tub of water when it's out, not the toilet," should accompany the removal and be followed by helping the child into another exploratory experience.

6. **Offer toddlers simple choices that will accomplish the task.** *"Would you like the red cup or the blue cup?" "Will you put your boots on first or your jacket?"*

TeachSource Video 2-2

Infants and Toddlers: Guidance

Go online and view *Infants and Toddlers: Guidance.* In this video, you will view a scene with four toddlers and a teacher in a group activity—an adult dressing an older infant.

1. List three ideas presented in the video and in the text in this section.

2. What did the teacher do to engage the infant in a social interaction during the dressing activity?

3. How did the teacher in the group activity encourage appropriate social behavior?

Watch on CourseMate

© Cengage Learning 2015

Supporting the Beginnings of Peer Relationships and Friendships

1. **Arrange social experiences between infants when they are comfortable and alert.** Arrange infants in such a manner that they can see each other close up for short periods of time. Provide opportunities for creeping infants to explore objects in the same area.

2. **Provide adequate space and materials for toddlers to use while playing together.** Toddlers are unable to stop quickly and often have poor balance as they acquire locomotor skills and are therefore likely to inadvertently lurch into other children. They should have enough uncluttered space to avoid getting into one another's way when engaging in active movement. Duplicate play materials are useful in minimizing conflict over toys and for increasing social play. Although sharing can occur spontaneously, in general, sharing toys is an unrealistic expectation for children before the age of 3. Toddlers are just beginning to act on their own goals and are less able to comprehend that others also have goals. Quick action that prevents interpersonal

stress between children supports the eventual development of more positive relationships.

3. **Demonstrate simple actions or words that can extend peer play.** One strategy is to "talk for the baby" or explain nonverbal play bids to the other child. *"When Cassandra points to the dough, she is letting you know that she wants to play with some of it here beside you."* In another instance, Spencer walked into the housekeeping area and picked up a doll, looking at Austin. Their teacher said, *"Austin, you are fixing food to eat. I think Spencer's baby might be hungry. Do you think that you could fix something good for the baby to eat?"* Austin brought the high chair to the table and began to prepare food as Spencer placed the doll in the high chair. The teacher observed carefully and expressed the toddler's wishes and intentions in words so the social exchange could get started and be maintained.

   A second strategy is to encourage one toddler to imitate another; this can transition into mutual turn-taking. *"See Rolly push the truck. Here is a truck that you can push, too."*

4. **Read books about social interactions.** Talk about the social events in the book as you look at the pictures and read the words. Relate these to personal experiences of the children. Compare the book character events with the children's real live events. *"Look, Jenny, the boy in the book is playing with his friend on the swing just like you and Suzy did just now outside."*

5. **Create books with classmates' photos in them or pictures of classroom events.** Photograph children in your care. Put these photos into books and use them to engage in discussions about social behaviors, to practice names of classmates, and to identify emotions. Relate the photos to the child with whom you are reading. *"Hmmm. This is you and Kamal. You are painting very colorful pictures. Do you remember that day? You were having soooo much fun. Look at your faces…."*

6. **Help children learn each other's names.** Refer to all children by name using correct pronunciations. Sing name games. Play simple games to practice names. When children know the names of others in their class, they have labels for their "friends." They will use these to refer to their peers and to form an identity of themselves as having friends… lots of them!

Being Available to Interact with Infants and Toddlers

Even though you know what to do and how to do it, there inevitably will be times when you are unavailable to respond promptly. You will experience time and energy constraints. Infants and toddlers whose caregivers usually respond sensitively receive the beneficial effects of developing expectations of adults, acquiring a sense of effectiveness, and associating their own actions with the outcome. Being available is not always the same as being physically present. You must be both mentally and physically present with children.

1. **Do housekeeping chores when infants and toddlers are asleep or when another caregiver is available to interact with the children**. Any task that diminishes your attentiveness to the children makes you unavailable.

2. **Limit the frequency and duration of adult-to-adult communication while children are present.** Focus your attention on the children. Limit phone conversations and texting when children are on site. Only parents need the phone number in the childcare room; personal cell phones should be off. Tell people who think you have plenty of time to talk, that you will contact them later. Keep adult conversations brief and limited to child issues.

3. **Send long-distance cues to cruising babies and exploring toddlers that you are available for a hug, a lap, or general sharing of delight.** Smile at them from across the room. Outdoors, hold your arms open to catch a running child joyfully. Clap your hands when you see a new accomplishment. Nod your head and smile when they look up at you when they finish a task. Offer your lap for a rest spot after a quick run. All of these specific actions let the child know that you are there for them. Demonstrate that you are present wholly for them.

Supporting Children Who Have Special Needs

1. **Read the individualized family service plan that has been prepared by the local agency providing specialized services.** Babies who have been identified as having specialized needs prior to entry into the program will have a written plan of intervention.

   In addition, some babies have particular medical or dietary needs with which you must be familiar. Find out as much information as you can from family members or other professionals working with the family.

2. **Ask for and participate in any specific training that will enable you to provide safe, healthy care of a specific child enrolled in the program.** Ask a knowledgeable person to demonstrate the use and care of any specific devices before the child is left in your care. Find out about the specialized needs of these young children, and understand clearly your responsibilities.

3. **Cooperate with the parents and other professionals by communicating regularly about the child who is receiving special services.** Often a journal that travels with the child is used to keep everyone informed about the child's progress. Parents, special intervention professionals, and childcare providers often need to share information. Babies cannot speak for themselves. Additionally, they frequently will not perform for an occasional visitor those behaviors that are more frequent in settings with adults they see daily. The traveling journal is useful for all children who move between settings.

4. **Maintain open communication with the family.** Share the child's accomplishments. Ask questions of family members to enhance your understanding of the child's needs and progress, as well as to receive updates on other important events in the family.

5. **Follow the process of your agency or program for obtaining written consent to share information with others or to refer families for special services.** Share information with others outside the program only with the consent of the parents. The behavior of all children should be treated as confidential information.

6. **Make detailed written observations on the child's behavior and development as you see it.** Be objective in describing what you see. Organize observations in a way that is meaningful to you so that you may contribute to the plan for intervention for the child. Note things that are typical for any child as well as those that seem to you to be unusual or atypical. Seek counsel of administrative leadership or experienced professionals in your program if the behavior seems atypical before conferring with parents. There is considerable variation in the rates of development.

7. **Participate in new and renewed individualized family service plans as appropriate.** Offer factual information about your interactions in relation to the goals and strategies being discussed. Listen carefully to

what others have to say to learn more about the children in your care. Ask questions about anything you may not understand.

8. **Adjust your interaction strategies to match the capability and specific needs of the infant and toddler.** Each child will be unique. However, very young children with special needs may require more frequent communication bouts, more consistent information talk, more help in focusing attention, more support in attaining self-regulation, and more guidance in social interactions with peers.

Supporting the Adult Family Members of Infants and Toddlers

1. **Listen to what family members tell you about their infant/toddler.** Adults who are caring for an infant full time since birth know a lot about that particular baby. They will tell you about what the child can do at this point, what other professionals have said regarding the child's development, how well the baby sleeps or eats, and if there is a change in behavior.

2. **Record pertinent information for other adults who provide care for the child in the program.** If a parent reports that a child has had a poor rest during the night or if stressful family events or other experiences have disrupted the tranquility of the home, make a note for other staff members who will be providing care when you leave for the day. Many infants and toddlers are in care for 9 or 10 hours. Be sure that private information is communicated only to those who need to know and is not shared indiscriminately.

3. **Allow parents opportunities to discuss how they feel about leaving their infant or toddler with a caregiver.** Nearly all parents feel some misgivings, and many are ambivalent about childcare.

Mrs. Walinsak brought her 7-month-old son into the center looking a little worried. "I think he is feeling cranky," she commented, as she started to give him to the caregiver. Ms. Biggs took Kelvin and smiled. He reached out for his mother and began to howl. Mrs. Walinsak began to tear up, looking as if she were about to cry. She said, "Goodbye Kelvin" and hurried out the door as Ms. Biggs assured her she would let her know how Kelvin was doing. Mrs. Walinsak went to her car, sat a moment, and came back to a window to peek in. Kelvin was still whimpering but no longer crying so gustily. She hesitated, then went to the car and drove off. Ms. Biggs waited for about 45 minutes before

phoning Mrs. Walinsak at work: "I just wanted you to know that Kelvin started playing just after you left. He's rolling balls right now and laughing." Mrs. Walinsak sighed, "I really need to work, but it is hard you know." "Yes, most parents find it hard. You want to stay and go at the same time," replied Ms. Biggs. "You can say that again!" responded Mrs. Walinsak.

4. **Ask questions periodically so that parents will have an opportunity to share concerns or inquire about typical behavior.** Simple questions can be asked, such as the following:

   - "What changes have you seen in Aida recently?"
   - "What are you finding most difficult about caring for Ian just now?"
   - "What are Kala's favorite play activities at home?"
   - "Do you have anything that you are wondering about in regard to Sandra's development?"

5. **Provide accurate developmental information based on observations of the child to family members.** Inform parents of typically developing behavior. Parents who are away from their infants and toddlers are interested in hearing about the developmental milestones and daily events of the child. As necessary, share the atypical behavior that you have observed so that parents may adjust their own care accordingly. This may be as simple as noting fussiness or fretfulness.

   Other observations may be more serious. If you have noted that a baby does not babble between 5 and 7 months of age and rarely responds to noises that appear to surprise other infants, share this information with the parents. The behavior may be caused by recurring ear infections or be a result of other problems. Regardless, the responsibility of the head teacher is to share these observations with the parents and recommend that someone qualified examine the child.

6. **Demonstrate respect for the families' cultures and languages by becoming informed.** If necessary, seek a translator if no adult member of the family speaks English. Learn the correct form of address for both the mother and father. Use the name of the child that the family uses; do not rename Ja-Young to June or any other more familiar name. Seek out additional written resources to help you understand the patterns of family behavior that will help you communicate with a family who has entrusted a child in your care. Keep in mind that individual differences *within* a cultural group are as varied as those *between* cultural groups.

7. **Check with family members about key child rearing beliefs and practices.** Cultural continuity between home and group settings is desirable to support both the family and the infants (Day & Parlakian, 2004). There are cultural differences in basic beliefs and expectations in ordinary things such as how much the baby should be held. For example, Korean mothers hold or carry their infants more during their first year than do mainstream American parents. What might appear as warm and caring to a mainstream parent may appear to be cold and neglectful to the Korean mother. There are cultural differences in when toddlers are expected to learn to use the toilet, when they feed themselves, when they contribute to picking up their toys, and when they should exhibit some emotional self-control. Explain what you are doing and why as you attempt to accommodate cultural differences. "I will carry An Sook in the sling as much as I can, without neglecting the needs of other children to be held."

8. **Know resources for information about child development and parenting as well as community resources.** Various local, state, and government agencies and professional groups provide free or low-cost written materials that are very useful to parents. Sometimes commercial organizations such as insurance companies provide safety information. The childcare sections of local bookstores have many titles, some more useful than others. Increasingly, materials related to health and to concerns of parents are available on the Internet.

Pitfalls to Avoid naeyc

Regardless of whether you are working with infants and toddlers individually or in groups, informally or in structured activities, there are certain pitfalls you should avoid.

1. **Ignoring infant cries.** Such notions as "Let him cry it out" or "You'll spoil the baby if you pick her up when she cries" are not true and do not work. The infant continues to cry because crying is the only signal for pain, hunger, or distress that is available. Infants cannot be spoiled in the first six months of life (Santrock, 2006). Providing quick, responsive, sensitive care to infants is likely to produce a compliant, cooperative, competent infant rather than one with unacceptable behavior.

2. **Attributing intentionality to infants' and toddlers' behavior before age 2.** Infants do not cry to make you run; they cry because of some discomfort. Infants do not get into things to annoy you; they are exploring the environment and are mentally incapable of planning to aggravate an adult. In the second half of the first year, intentional behavior begins when the child notes the effects of his or her behavior on adults. Children stumble on these behaviors through trial and error, so ignoring whining or screeching and suggesting another alternative to get your attention is fine. *"Show me,"* or *"I can't tell what you want when you make that noise! Point to it."*

3. **Attributing moral characteristics to infants and toddlers.** Certain infants are easy to care for, whereas others are very difficult or challenging. These children are neither "good" nor "bad." Sometimes, adults project their feelings onto a baby. A child is born with a temperament not of his or her choosing. Colic is a painful condition that makes life as difficult for the infant as for the caregiver. A sunny, happy temperament does not make an "angel," nor does an intestinal complaint make a baby a "perfect devil." The ability to make choices based on a value system is not acquired for several years. Avoid the trap of "good child–bad child" by focusing on actual behavior and emerging competencies.

4. **Focusing your attention only on the attractive, cuddly, or responsive children.** Distribute attention to all children, and be sure that infants who are slow to warm up or who are not cuddlers get reasonable and appropriate care. The more passive, less demanding infant should not be left alone in the crib for more than 15 minutes after awakening. Give this child the encouragement to explore and to socialize even if she or he appears content to do nothing at all.

5. **Assuming that nonspeakers cannot communicate.** Communication includes a wide range of verbal and nonverbal behaviors that allow us to send and receive messages. Speech is universally understood if everyone shares the same language. Infants and toddlers have an array of abilities to both send and receive information long before they develop speech. Sign language is useful to bridge the gap between primarily nonverbal and verbal communication.

6. **Ignoring cues that development is not progressing well and/or discounting parental concerns.** Nothing is less helpful than the phrase, "He will outgrow that." Infants and toddlers grow out of shoes and clothing with little intervention, but language, cognitive, motor, and social development usually require adjustments in adult behavior to facilitate improvement in

problem behavior. Sometimes simple adjustments are not enough, and children need more intensive intervention from specialists. No concern of a parent is trivial to the parent, so each concern should be treated respectfully. If concerns are treated as insignificant, parents will stop expressing them.

7. **Communicating important information or significant concerns about the child's behavior or development casually or in a hurry.** Sometimes caregivers do not want to see parents become upset, and other times they are so busy with children, they do not have time to interact. However, casual, fast communications that may be difficult or stressful for the parent to handle must be avoided. Think of how a parent would feel if the only thing you said was, "Mitchell had a bad day today. He bit four other children hard enough to leave tooth marks," and then went on to do something else. Instead, ask the parent to stay until you are free for about 15 minutes, try to set up an

appointment, or arrange to talk to the parent by phone later. Rapid communications that are positive, "K. C. and Carl played in the blocks for a half-hour today," or statements that affirm the parent, "The book you sent with Peter was really enjoyed by the other children," are always appropriate.

8. **Treating all families alike.** Families are no more all the same than are a group of children. An outstanding feature of the United States is its collection of diverse people. Families vary in composition, economic resources, religion, and education as well as in cultural affiliation or language of preference. Developing a relationship with families requires the same sensitivity to individual differences as developing a relationship with children. Avoid rushing to judgment about family caregiving practices; they may be just culturally different, not incorrect. Never assume that the parents are uninterested. Take the time to listen, learn, and share ideas.

Summary

Infants and toddlers begin life as social beings within their families. It is through interactions with their families as well as through meaningful positive relationships with other adults and peers that they truly learn about life. Adults support children's social competence when they establish positive relationships with them as defined by warmth, acceptance, genuineness, empathy, and respect (WAGER).

Using these aspects in our daily interactions with children sets them up to feel safe and secure so that they can explore and learn about the world. The attachment of infants and caregivers is an outgrowth of the sensitive care where adults read infant cues and respond promptly. Babies need consistency and predictability for attachment to occur; this is usually with the mother but may also be with a primary caregiver in a professional setting.

Babies are born with a temperament that generally includes how intense and how frequent certain behaviors occur, which influences how adults respond to them in turn. Behavioral states change rapidly over the first months of life with increasing time in the quiet alert state and less time sleeping as infants mature. Crying is an obvious cue that care is needed, and this too changes over time and can be diminished by soothing. In addition, babies use gestures and physical movement in space as means of communication.

The processes of individuation enable babies to perceive themselves as separate beings by the time they are 3 years old. Gradually, they increase their social awareness of themselves and correspondingly begin to understand that others have goals of their own. During the second and third years, children become increasingly socialized to act independently. Separation from the preferred adult is always difficult, and guidance in supporting parents and children is offered.

Infants are biologically equipped to communicate through gaze, vocalization, joint attention, and gestures, among other strategies, with adults during their first year. Adults provide both stimulation and practice by modifying their speech and responding to infant cues.

As more children are in group settings, babies have demonstrated great interest in their peers, particularly age-mates. Initial response is interest, and interaction skills develop slowly with adult support, though toddlers can maintain friendships with others with whom they have regular contact.

Infants begin to regulate their crying when they hear a caregiver approaching sometime near the sixth month. Adults support or co-regulate behavior in the earliest years with many strategies such as having predictable routines, helping babies focus their attention, giving short directions, and teaching children how to do difficult tasks such as using the toilet.

Some children encounter challenges from the beginning of life and may need the intervention of specialists as well as the cooperation of teachers to support their development. Early childhood professionals may be the first to recognize that development is irregular and have a responsibility to refer the family for assessment and intervention by specialists.

Skills that will enable you to become a sensitive, responsive adult who can support each child's individuation process were presented so that children in your care may establish a system of maintaining proximity to you, of exploring the environment, of establishing an identity, and of beginning social relationships with adults and other children. Basic skills for communicating with the adult family members support continuity and understanding between professionals and children's families.

Using these skills, you can recognize individual differences among children, quickly perceive their needs, accurately interpret their signals, and select appropriate alternatives for action. Integrating social interaction into the basic care of infants and toddlers and using an array of communication skills will help you nurture young children's development of social competence.

Pitfalls to avoid while you are learning to implement the skills are identified.

Key Terms

acceptance
attachment
behavioral state
communicative gestures
contingent behavior
empathy
expressive language
gaze following

genuineness
goodness of fit
imitative learning
individuation
joint attention
receptive language
respect
self-regulation

sensitive caregiving
shared-regulation
social referencing
socialization
temperament
warmth

Discussion Questions

1. Explain why positive adult–child relationships are critical to social development, and identify the key elements.

2. Explain what is meant by the statement, "Infants participate in their own development."

3. Describe the cues that infant and toddlers send and how they influence relationship building.

4. Describe the techniques that are most effective in soothing a crying infant.

5. Look at Table 2-1. Without repeating concepts suggested as strengths or challenges, generate one strength and one challenge for each temperament trait. Now select any two traits, and describe how that combination might prove advantageous or disadvantageous to the child's interaction with his or her caregiver.

6. How does the way in which basic care is given to an infant or toddler influence the course of the child's development?

7. Describe the process of individuation, clarifying how and when self-awareness is displayed.

8. Pretend you are working with 18-month-old toddlers. You notice some are really talking and making more sounds than others, and you wonder if everyone is fine. Where would you find information on language development to be sure? Download this information, and discuss five things children at this age can "typically" do.

9. Describe how the communication skills of infants/toddlers influence their social competence.

10. From the readings, what social behaviors would you expect to see in a 12-month-old?

11. Trevor is a timid, fearful child at a year and a half who is truly frightened when his mother leaves him at the center. Based on your reading, what do you think is his fear? What could you do to help the family with this situation? What other information could you share with the family about this situation to help them also make adjustments to their behavior?

12. Mick is a fast-acting, rapidly moving explorer. He usually perceives possibilities for play and exploration that you do not anticipate. He approaches other children eagerly and is sometimes successful and sometimes not. When he is angry, he is furious and may bite or hit. Rarely still or quiet, he is difficult to get to sleep and naps only a short time. He wriggles away when an adult tries to pick him up and protests

loudly. At 18 months of age, he seems to have the ability to exhaust all of the adults in the program, although his general disposition seems to be cheerful eagerness. Generate a plan to help Mick develop his social skills.

13. Patsy is 9 months old and does not babble and does not appear to respond much to environmental noise. You are concerned about her ability to hear. List in order what you should do to approach this problem.

14. Select one pitfall that is a problem for you, and describe how you plan to avoid it.

Case Study Analysis

Read the case study in Appendix B about Marco, a lively toddler, and consider the following:

1. What strategies did the head teacher use to coordinate with Marco's family members, and how well did they appear to work? If you cannot tell, list the information that you would need to know to answer.

2. List the words in the case study that might give you clues to Marco's temperament.

3. Make a plan to encourage Marco's friendships. Identify children and list some strategies that you think might work. Explain why you made these choices.

4. What evidence of self-regulation did Marco display?

5. What strategies did the teachers use to support Marco's appropriate behavior?

Field Assignments

1. Visit a childcare center or a family childcare home and observe how children respond to routine events of the day, such as being brought to the center and left by their parents, being fed, being diapered, and being put down for a nap. Record the caregiver's communication with the child and the infant's responses in these situations. Carefully monitor for evidence of WAGER. Where do you see this?

2. Note at least two instances of infant crying. How did the caregiver respond? What cues were there as to the meaning or message of the cry? Sometimes adults have difficulty in interpreting a cry and try several responses. If you observed this, note what the baby did in reaction to the adult behaviors on each occasion. What soothing techniques worked for each infant?

3. Observe two toddlers at separate times. Describe the social cues that each displayed. How were they the same, and how did they differ? What would you do to personalize your interactions with each according to their cues?

4. Watch an older infant play with a toy and then play with the baby yourself. Take cues from the infant, imitate the baby, and then elaborate on what the child has previously done. Note what you say and do and how the infant responds to your behavior.

5. Select one toddler to observe intently during the day. Watch how the child approaches other children. Under what conditions does he or she just observe a peer playing? Note how the toddler responds to the social approaches of other children and adults and the duration and quality of social engagements with adults and peers. After the session, write three descriptions of the child engaging in some social or communicative event.

6. Use the self-evaluation checklist in Figure 2-4 when you interact in a group of infants and toddlers. Record what the skilled adults do and what you do. Keep in mind that you may not have the opportunity to do all of the skills. Reflect on what you have done well.

Reflect on Your Practice

Here is a sample checklist you can use to reflect on your use of the skills as a beginning professional. A more detailed classroom observation tool is available in Appendix C.

Teachers who support social competence for infants and toddlers:

✓ Scan the environment with a quick check on each child.

✓ Sit on the floor where infants and toddlers can touch and be near one another.

✓ Hold conversations while diapering and assisting in toilet learning.

✓ Speak in simple sentences, and provide physical assistance in helping children comply with requests.

✓ Arrange opportunities for infants and toddlers to interact with age-mates.

CourseMate. Visit the Education CourseMate for this textbook to access the eBook, Digital Downloads, TeachSource Videos, and Did You Get It? quizzes. Go to CengageBrain.com to log in, register, or purchase access.

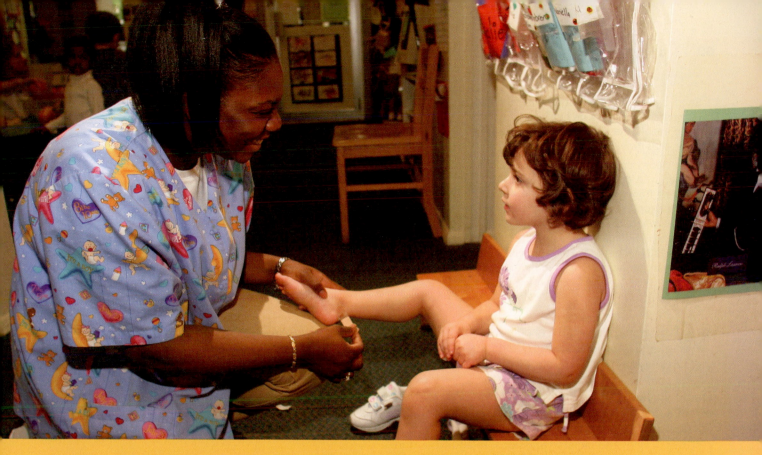

3 Building Positive Relationships through Nonverbal Communication

OBJECTIVES

On completion of this chapter, you should be able to:

Discuss the functions of nonverbal communication.

Describe channels of nonverbal communication and how they influence social interaction.

Tell how nonverbal behavior contributes to relationship building.

Demonstrate nonverbal behaviors that convey authority.

Identify potential challenges in sending and interpreting nonverbal messages.

Explain how children acquire effective nonverbal communication skills.

Identify nonverbal skills adults use to foster children's social competence.

Point out the pitfalls to avoid when interacting nonverbally with children and families.

NAEYC STANDARDS naeyc

1. Promoting Child Development and Learning
2. Building Family and Community Relationships
3. Using Developmentally Effective Approaches to Connect with Children and Families
4. Using Content Knowledge to Build Meaningful Curriculum

Shari, age 5, saw her mother enter the kitchen, silent, with an annoyed look on her face. Before her mother could speak, the child quickly protested: "Don't look at me in that tone of voice!"

Shari clearly understood the message conveyed by her mother, who stood stiffly with feet apart, hands on hips, scowling from the doorway as she viewed a clutter of baking supplies and flour spilled on the counters and shelves where Shari was "making cookies." Like most children, Shari could easily interpret the meaning of her mother's stance and facial expression. No words were necessary for her to grasp her mother's displeasure.

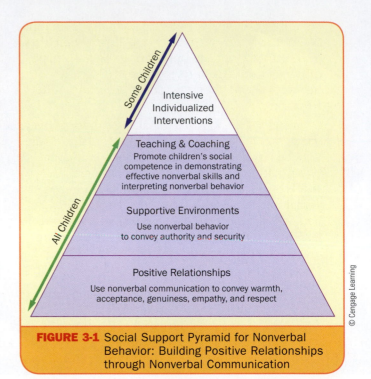

FIGURE 3-1 Social Support Pyramid for Nonverbal Behavior: Building Positive Relationships through Nonverbal Communication

With or without words, people within visual range of one another constantly send and receive messages through nonverbal cues. **Nonverbal communication** is composed of all messages sent or received except for words (Matsumoto, Frank, & Hwang, 2013). Nonverbal behavior includes body motion, the orientation of your body in relation to someone or something else, gestures, touch, and facial expressions. In addition, nonverbal communication includes paralinguistic, or vocal behaviors. These involve sounds that are not words, the rhythm of your speech, how loudly or softly you speak, pitch and voice tone, pauses, how quickly or how slowly you talk, and how much or how little you speak (Gazda et al., 2006; Matsumoto, Frank, & Hwang, 2013).

Unlike spoken language, in which words are explicitly defined, nonverbal codes are implicit, with the meaning derived from the context of the situation and the flow of the interaction. Thus, the same act in different contexts may have very different intents (e.g., a nod in one situation may mean hello, and a nod in another circumstance may mean you are dismissed). Sometimes, as illustrated by Shari and her mom, nonverbal communications are clear; at other times, they can be ambiguous or confusing. In either case, nonverbal signals are present in most social interactions, and people use them to convey and interpret a range of information and feelings (Doherty-Sneddon, 2004). This makes nonverbal communication a major medium of communication in everyday life (Remland, 2009).

Monitoring, regulating, and controlling nonverbal communication influences the flow and outcome of human interactions and contributes to interpersonal effectiveness (Riggio, 2006). Consequently, both adults and children need to pay attention to nonverbal signals in order to communicate accurately and effectively. Most importantly, from infancy onward, nonverbal communication links children to the adults in their world (Butterfield, Martin, & Prairie, 2004). In order to strengthen these interpersonal ties, in this chapter, we will pay particular attention to how adults demonstrate warmth, acceptance, genuineness, empathy, and respect (i.e., WAGER) nonverbally in their interactions with children. How nonverbal communication can be used to convey authority and security will also be described. Finally, we will discuss strategies for helping children accurately interpret others' nonverbal communications as well as learn positive nonverbal skills themselves. All three emphases correspond to levels one, two, and three of the Social Support Pyramid depicted in Figure 3-1.

To carry out nonverbal support strategies well, you must first understand the roles nonverbal communication plays in people's lives.

Functions of Nonverbal Communication naeyc

Nonverbal behavior plays many roles in human communication (Knapp, Hall, & Horgan, 2013):

- **To substitute for entire ideas:** Gestures such as handshaking, nodding the head, or waving the hand are used as **emblems**. Such gestures can be directly translated into words, but they are efficient, meaningful signals by themselves. Thus, an extended hand may be interpreted as an emblem of respect or friendliness; a smile may represent a greeting, permission to continue, or encouragement in a difficult situation.

- **To enhance verbal communication:** Young children most often use **illustrator gestures** to supplement the spoken word, especially when the child has a limited vocabulary (Doherty-Sneddon, 2004). For instance, Tommy, age 3, "drew pictures in the air" to indicate the relative size and shape of the box to explain its location. "It's really heavy!" he said, dropping down his arm as if he were carrying it.

- **To share emotions:** Words alone cannot convey the depth of meaning present in a verbal message enriched by nonverbal cues. Usually, emotional or evaluative content is conveyed nonverbally and is more accurate than communication by verbal means alone. Feelings of pleasure, surprise, happiness, anger, interest, disgust, sadness, and fear are all expressed more fully when words are accompanied by facial expressions, gestures, and other nonverbal actions.

- **To regulate social interaction:** For example, turn-taking in a conversation is indicated by changes in eye contact, which increases while listening and decreases while speaking, with corresponding changes in voice pitch and body position. The person speaking may involve the receiver in the communication by signaling a message such as "As you know," with the hands or acknowledging the listener's response with a nod to indicate, "I see you understood me" (Burgoon, Guerrero, & Floyd, 2010). Other gestures such as tapping the forehead are information-seeking gestures: "Now what is that person's name?" (Bavelas, Chovil, Coates, & Roe, 1995.)

- **To provide information as to how the message should be understood:** Nonverbal cues may serve a metacommunication function; that is, they may communicate about the message itself. For example, facial expressions can convey a notion about the way the total message is to be interpreted, such as, "I'm only kidding" or "Now, seriously speaking."

- **To clarify identity and status:** This has been referred to as the process of impression formation and management. A person's posture, tone of voice, facial expressions, gestures, and so forth provide information to others about their status, degree of confidence, temperament, disposition, and other characteristics of personality. For example, Ms. Kitchen hurried to intervene as two children were struggling over the last seat at the snack table. While she was speaking to the children, she noticed that her voice was shrill and her rate of speech was very rapid. She realized these nonverbal attributes interfered with the children's recognition of her status as the adult mediator and undermined her ability to gain control of the situation. She took a deep breath, lowered the pitch of her voice, and slowed down her speech. This prompted the children to focus more intently on what she was saying.

- **To hide or to mask:** Older children who have learned to use nonverbal cues as suggestions may adopt an amazed look of innocence when a misdeed has been discovered. The "Who, me?" expression is not usually considered to be a falsehood, as a verbal denial would be. The "Who, me?" expression requires that they be able to suppress their natural feelings of anxiety in that type of situation. Similarly, an older child might smile to be polite but not be genuinely pleased about what is occurring.

- **To pretend:** Nonverbal cues represent the most suitable vehicle for suggestion. Because nonverbal cues are not explicit and can potentially be misinterpreted, they also may be denied. Adults may use these deliberately as they try to "act a part" in a socially uncomfortable situation. Such "acting" requires that the adult perform as though he or she is at ease in the situation. Some evidence suggests that if children deliberately act in a way that they think would be socially appropriate for an unfamiliar situation, their feelings actually become modified (Saarni & Weber, 1999). Typical situations include giving a demonstration at a county fair, playing in a recital, or even answering questions in a classroom.

A clear relationship exists between the level of development of an individual's social skills and his or her successful use and interpretation of nonverbal behavior. Having a broad array of nonverbal skills is important to social success and psychological well-being (Riggio, 2006). Children who monitor and understand other's nonverbal behaviors are perceived as being sensitive and are highly desired as playmates by their peers (Doherty-Sneddon, 2004). Adults who use nonverbal behavior effectively tend to be seen by children as both credible and trustworthy. Ultimately, as you become increasingly alert to children's nonverbal signals, your skills in active observation become enhanced, thus improving the accuracy of your interpretations (Matsumoto, Frank, & Hwang, 2013).

Channels of Nonverbal Communication naeyc

A channel of communication is one of the modes or types of nonverbal communication. For example, the tone of voice itself is one mode, or channel; posture and position in space are others. Each channel of nonverbal communication may function independently and may be congruent with the verbal message sent.

Under ordinary circumstances, nonverbal messages are not likely to be under conscious control. For example, a person may "look daggers" at another, "deliberately ignore" someone, or perhaps give the appearance of mental abstraction or boredom. On a more subtle level, the relationships of people interacting in a group can be discerned by observation of nonverbal cues. Noting the body orientations, head tilt, and arm gestures of all the group members usually can identify the leader or speaker. For example, when observing a group of children on the other side of the playground, one could pick out the leader by watching the children interact. One child is gesturing; her head is tilted up, and she is looking at the others in sequence. The others in the group are looking and nodding in response to her gesturing. There is little doubt as to which child is the center of attention, even though the conversation cannot be heard.

In the following section, selected components of nonverbal behavior will be described as they relate to your ability to deliberately send and receive messages while working with children.

Position in Space

Children are exposed gradually to various distances for interpersonal interaction with friends and acquaintances until about the age of 7. At that time, they reflect the adult norms for their culture. Typically, younger children getting closer to adults and older children is tolerated. Generally, both males and females approach females more closely than males; both the very young and the very old are also approached more closely. People viewed as friendly, especially in an informal setting, can approach closer comfortably. People retreat when the approach seems unfriendly, the situation is unfamiliar, and the person approaching is male (Knapp, Hall, & Horgan, 2013). It is not surprising then if children entering a new situation appear to stand back a bit in the beginning.

Personal space, radiating from the center of the body, has specific boundaries that can be described by measurement or by function. Comfortable distances for interacting with others are from 0 to 1 1/2 feet for intimate distance, 1 1/2 to 4 feet for casual personal interaction, from 4 to 10 feet for social or consultative contact, and 10 feet or more for public interaction (Krannich & Krannich, 2001; Knapp, Hall, & Horgan, 2013, Matsumoto & Hwang, 2013a). These distances vary somewhat by the age, sex, culture, setting for the interaction, emotional climate, and other characteristics. Another description of personal space places the boundaries in relation to body parts or functions (Machotka & Spiegel, 1982). The personal space "rules" are important to pay attention to when working with young children because children treat violations of their personal

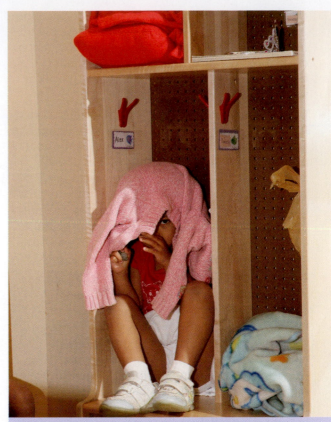

© Cengage Learning 2015

"Keep away!" is signaled nonverbally when children close themselves off from others. Insofar as possible, this child has blocked access to her personal space while still keeping a lookout for what is occurring nearby.

space as potentially threatening. Figure 3-2 illustrates internal, proximal, axial, and distal space.

Internal space is the area between the inner core of the body and the skin, and it is the most intimate and personal of all spaces. Openings to the body, such as the mouth, ears, nostrils, anus, and vagina, all represent access to internal space. Internal space also is entered when the skin is broken in injury or when a hypodermic needle is inserted. For example, Nick protested and pulled away when Ms. Payne took out the sharp, pointed tweezers even though the sliver in his hand was painful. She was invading his internal space and, in his opinion, causing him pain.

Proximal space is the area between the body and its covering of clothing, hair, or ornament. Uncovered body parts, such as the face, are not physically restricted but are psychologically restricted. For example, casual acquaintances do not touch one another's arms, legs, or face, even though they are uncovered. Some uncovered sections of proximal space, such as the hands, are freely accessible unless otherwise protected by countermoves such as crossing the arms or turning away. This means that, ordinarily, people do not touch portions

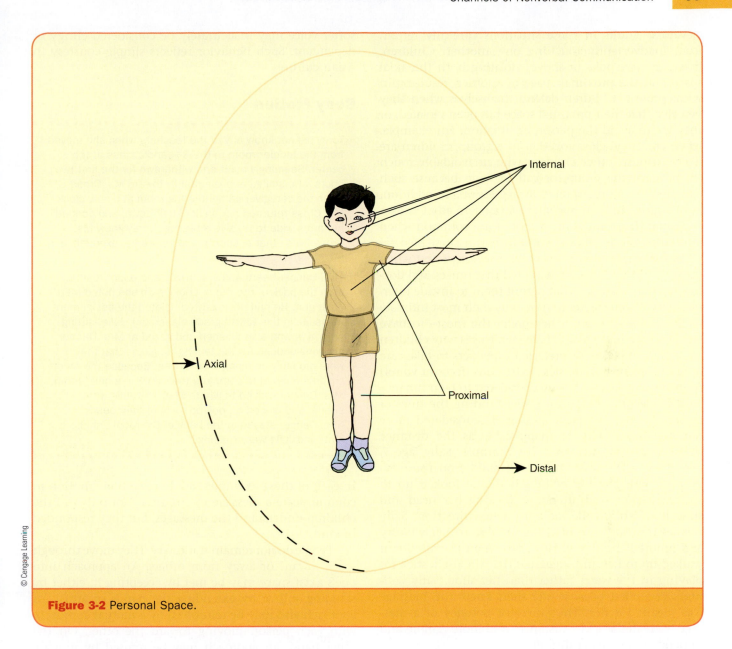

Figure 3-2 Personal Space.

of another's body that are clothed and limit touching the skin of others except when invited, as in shaking hands or giving a hug. A child sitting close to you on a sofa while you read a book is in your proximal space.

Axial space is bounded by the full extension of the arms and legs in all directions. Invitation to enter the axial space is indicated by open arms, in contrast to crossed arms or legs. Children are in your axial space when seated at a small table where you are also seated, for example.

Distal space is located between the axial boundary and the outer limits that the eye or ear can scan. The knowable world, or the impersonal world, exists in distal space. Usually young children run and chase each other on the playground in your distal space.

Children are also in your distal space when engaging in activities in a gym or lunchroom.

Professionals should understand the implicit rules of interpersonal space for three reasons:

1. Personal space generates negative feelings when violated.
2. Personal space determines the relevance of oral communications.
3. Personal space is influenced by culture and subculture.

First, violation of personal space generates negative feelings (Hall, 2002; Knapp, Hall, & Horgan, 2013). These negative feelings may be only mild irritation, such as that experienced in overcrowded hallways or elevators. Adults in these situations carefully refrain from inadvertently touching one another. Children, however, may poke or shove, violating both the axial space and the proximal space of another, resulting in vocal protest. Children defend themselves when they perceive that their proximal space has been violated, or they try to avoid the person or situation. For example, when crammed close together in a group, children are likely to push other children who unavoidably touch them, leave the group, or call for help because such experiences are interpreted as aggression. In addition, even young children may move away if an adult strokes their hair. Rage and violent protest are common when internal space is entered without permission. Medical personnel can expect to meet with severe protest when young children have not accepted that nurses and doctors have special roles that permit them to invade internal space. People prefer to have only their most intimate companions—the ones they prefer the most—to have any access to internal space. In fact, this is why children want their mothers or preferred caregivers to take care of them when they are sick. Extrusions (feces or vomit) from internal space also are considered to be intimate.

The second reason for understanding the rules of personal space is that a message is considered more remote, impersonal, or inapplicable as the distance between people increases. For example, Sally, age 7, was stirring the water in a mud puddle on the playground with the toe of her shoe. She looked up to see the playground attendant shaking her head and shouting "No!" while looking in her direction. Sally was aware that a lot of children were in her vicinity and ignored the signal. However, when the attendant walked up to her and suggested that she use a stick for playing in the water rather than her shoe, Sally willingly complied because she then knew the message was meant for her. The power or potency of a message is greater at lesser distances and more remote and impersonal at greater distances.

The third reason for understanding the concept of personal space is that concepts of "how close is close enough" vary by culture and subculture. Adults may misinterpret the meaning of a behavior because it does not meet their expectations. Although cultural differences exist for all channels of nonverbal communication, variations in the distance factor may be the most apparent. For example, a child who stands very close, speaks in a slightly louder voice than expected, orients the body in a face-to-face position, and maintains eye contact longer than expected may be considered by a teacher of European ancestry to be pushy, brassy, or aggressive, when the behavior actually is rather typical for an Arabic male child. Another child who also stands close to the adult while conversing but maintains less eye contact than expected and speaks in a

softer voice may inaccurately be considered clingy or dependent. Such behavior reflects simple courtesy in Asian cultures.

Body Motion

> Torey did not know any of the teachers when she moved from the toddler room to the 3-year-old class at the center. Seemingly quiet and withdrawn for the first two hours, she smiled and ran rapidly toward Ms. Cross when the caregiver came into the room at nine o'clock. Ms. Cross returned her smile, knelt down, and opened her arms wide to receive a big hug. Torey knew Ms. Cross from other encounters in her earlier experience in the program.
>
> Mrs. Danner heard some scuffling and paper rustling from the back of the room. Looking up she noted Matt's quiet grin. He had obviously completed the assignment, as usual, in this fourth grade classroom. Julie, sitting near him, was also finished and gazed at Mrs. Danner just long enough for the teacher to guess that they were probably amusing themselves. Because the other children needed to complete their work in a quiet room, Mrs. Danner walked to where Matt and Julie were sitting, and placed a book on each of their desks. Mrs. Danner stayed in the back of the room until both Matt and Julie were reading.

In each of these examples, adults used body motion to communicate a message to children. Not only did the children understand the messages, but they responded in kind.

People do not remain stationary. They move through space toward or away from others. An approach into one's axial space may be met by accepting it, either by standing still or by extending the hands or arms. An approach also may be reinforced by a mutual approach, with each person moving toward the other. On the other hand, an approach may be refused by moving away slightly, by simply avoiding the person approaching, or by closing the axial space by folding the arms. All of these signals are important cues as to how receptive a person is to an interaction. You will observe them in children, and children will observe them in you.

For instance, grasping another person is one way children initiate contact. A child might hug someone or grasp his or her hand to communicate, "I want to be with you." A hug back is a clear sign that the contact is welcome. When there is no reciprocity, and a peer remains immobile, that child is indicating that the contact is undesired. He or she could also avert the grasp by throwing it off, shaking it off, or pushing the person away. For example, when Marta tried holding hands with Kevin, he moved slightly away and shook his hand free of her grasp without saying a word.

When adults unfamiliar to one another make contact, initiating and accepting movements usually are ritualized, through a handshake, a salutation, or other formal introduction or greeting. Frequently, adults are much less polite to children, particularly when the children are in a group. Children may experience being shoved into a line by an unfamiliar adult or may be patted on the head, pinched on the cheek, or chucked under the chin. Often, children correctly interpret these as unwarranted invasions of proximal space and attempt to avoid the approach or avert the contact as best they can. It is better to approach children using a face-to-face orientation (which will be described next) and to use verbal means of gaining their attention.

The simplest sign that an interaction is over is when both people walk away simultaneously. On the other hand, if one child advances and the other retreats, they may need an adult to move near them to provide support if they are unable to work it out themselves. For instance, in one kindergarten class, Molly really preferred to be next to Kendra all the time. Kendra would play with Molly occasionally but frequently would move to another spot for story time to avoid her and sit by other children whom she preferred. Sometimes Molly would attempt to follow, and Kendra would move again. Usually Molly accepted the separation from Kendra when her teacher was nearby. On a few occasions, Kendra pushed Molly away from her. A child who does not want a separation may slow down his or her retreat, turn and stand, or show defiance against the other's intentions by facial expression or posture. Sometimes, forced separations are accepted by a rapid retreat. In this case, Molly might need the comfort of an explanation of the situation to both understand Kendra's cues and to find another child with whom to interact.

Body Orientation

Lannie and Rachel are seated at the science table examining live worms. Ms. Carter comes by and with hands on her hips, stands over them for a little while as they work.

Later, Ms. Jackson comes by, squats down near the table, facing the girls directly for a little while as they work.

Who is communicating more interest in what the girls are doing, Ms. Carter or Ms. Jackson?

According to all we know about body orientation, the children will interpret Ms. Jackson as more interested and more approachable because of how she is using her body to communicate her attention to their work with the worms.

How you position the front of your body in relation to the body of another person conveys meaningful information. The face-to-face position is the most direct body orientation. This is the position used in greeting, comforting, fighting, and conversing intimately. Avoiding this position usually indicates evasion or the desire to conceal. When people are facing the backs of others, they are proceeding in turn, following, or chasing. The side-by-side position implies companionship, togetherness, or a united front. The back-to-back position is associated with disengagement that is not simple separation, but hostility or protection in a hostile situation. Slight turns of the body usually are a transition from one position to another but may convey lack of interest, distrust, or impending separation if carried out continuously.

The relationship between body orientations of people who are interacting also has a vertical dimension. The term "one-upmanship" is descriptive both visually and in meaning. The position of being higher, or on the top, denotes status, authority, or power. The position of being lower denotes incapacity, humility, or servility. In the natural course of things, adults are big and powerful, and children are small and weak. Moving to diminish the vertical space between adults and children signals that an important message is about to be conveyed. This leveling can be done by squatting to the child's level or by lifting the child into a face-to-face position with the adult, as is commonly done with babies and very young toddlers. Between adults, leveling may be accomplished by sitting down, as height differentials among adults are usually in the legs. Squatting down may indicate friendliness or a willingness to interact on a cooperative basis.

Body orientation has other dimensions as well. Leaning toward another implies interest or regard, and leaning away suggests interpersonal distancing, offense, or lack of interest. An inclusion, in which another surrounds the axial space of a person, usually is either an emotionally positive experience, such as an embrace, or a negative one, such as a struggle. Professionals who work with children use inclusion (wrapping a youngster in your arms) in giving affection or comfort or when they use their bodies to keep children from harming themselves or others. This is exemplified when Ms. Torvimina holds 3-year-old Jacob securely to her body at a right angle so that he does not hurt himself or anyone else when he has a tantrum and is flailing his arms about vigorously.

Gestures

Movements of the head, hands, arms, legs, and body, or **gestures**, accompany speech and may be used to illustrate a word, such as moving the hands apart to show how large a fish was; to emphasize a statement, such as bringing the fist down on the table; and to replace speech, such as pointing to where the missing truck went or by how a person walks expresses sadness or happiness. Gestures may be used as insults, such as in raising the middle finger from a clenched fist, or as terms of endearment, such as a caress. They also convey emotions and attitudes of the speaker about the content of the message and about the listener (Feyereisen & deLannoy, 1991; Janssen, Schöllhorn et al., 2008). Unlike other aspects of nonverbal communications, gestures express deliberate thought or the process of thinking. They may increase accuracy of a task such as pointing while counting. Gestures also are used to enhance memory such as enumerating a remembered list by tapping fingers in sequence (Matsumoto & Hwang, 2013a).

Most gestures occur in the axial space of the sender and may be made without any speech. Although gestures commonly are learned with spoken language, young children frequently use illustrative gestures when they don't know the words to use. Intentional messages are sent by older babies through gestures such as pointing to a cup to indicate the need to drink. Hearing children who know sign language use these emblems in combination with oral language when communicating. Likewise, preschool children resort to pantomime. Gesturing increases in efficiency throughout childhood. Even older elementary-school-aged children are more effective in giving directions when the listener can see as well as hear them (Doherty-Sneedon, 2004). Gestures increase in frequency when the speaker is enthusiastic, when concerned that the listener understands, and when they are trying to dominate the conversation. Three-year-olds can interpret more gestures than they use, and by age 5, children are very skillful in doing this (Knapp, Hall, & Horgan, 2013).

Communication problems occur whenever a person's gestures suggest a meaning different from the verbal message (O'Hair & Ropo, 1994). Although occasionally deliberate, frequently these problems are a result of differing cultural patterns. People in lower social positions gesture more, and more vividly, than people of higher social status in all cultural groups. Distinct differences exist, however, between ethnic groups in the amount and expansiveness of the gestures commonly used. People from Asian countries use fewer and subtler gestures than persons of either European or African culture. People from northern Europe tend to be more restrictive as well, with southern Europeans using more expansive gestures and using them more frequently. North American children of English or Swedish descent are likely to make less expansive gestures than

children of Latino(a) descent. Youngsters of Chinese background move their hands and body even less while speaking. The longer children participate in the mixed American culture, the more they tend to move their bodies at a moderate level of activity (Ting-Toomey, 1999).

Some gestures are widely used and understood, such as the finger click or snap for attention. Others, such as the fingers in a claw position (contempt in Saudi Arabia), are used only in one part of the world. These emblems are cultural-specific gestures that have direct verbal referents (Ting-Toomey, 1999). Every cultural group has a wide variety of emblems understood by members of that particular group; however, this leaves much room for error because the same movement may mean a vastly different thing to other cultural groups. For example, moving the head from side to side means "no" to Bulgarians, but "yes" to several other cultures. The gesture meaning "OK," made by holding up the hand and forming a circle with the first finger and the thumb, means "money" in Japan, is a sexual insult in Brazil, is a vulgar gesture in Russia, and means "zero" in France. There is much potential for misunderstanding and confusion, especially for adults working in multicultural settings.

Touch

Situations in which touching occurs may be the most intimate, loving experiences, or the most hostile, angry, or hurtful ones. Situations in which touching is least likely to occur also are the most emotionally neutral. The probability of touch occurring is implied in the discussions of position in space (nearness to one another) and body orientation (face-to-face encounters).

The skin is both a communication sender and receiver. Touch conveys warmth like no other practice, and tactile calming is based on our biology (Gartrell, 2012). Feelings related to affection, fear, detachment, anger, and playfulness can be conveyed by touch. Gentle strokes, cuddling, caresses, and pats of affection are associated with nurturance and healthy development (Hansen, 2007). Games of walking fingers up a child's arm or "buzzing the bee to the tummy" illustrate playful touches. Slaps, kicks, pinches, and pokes that hurt are clearly understood as being hostile.

Touch is used to control or to influence others, such as grasping the hand of a child who is about to hit another. Touch is used less forcefully in getting a child's attention by gently tapping on the shoulder, or a child getting attention by tugging on the

With a glance, you can tell that the relationship between this adult and child is warm and close (intimate distance, touching, bodies of both relaxed, encircling arms) though at the moment the child is not happy (slight frown, gesture of raised left arm), and the adult has leaned back a little in response.

© Cengage Learning 2015

than themselves (Hall, 1996). Touching is more likely to occur in less formal situations, with higher-status individuals using more relaxed and affectionate strategies and lower-status persons using more formal strategies such as handshaking (Hall, 1996). Children use touch with each other to establish friendly relationships, reduce social distance, and indicate levels of intimacy (Hansen, 2007).

The accessibility of the body to touch is limited by age, relationship, and gender. Obviously, infants must be changed, fed, and otherwise handled extensively by caregivers of either sex. As children mature, direct touch of the skin between the chest and the knees is taboo. In adulthood, most direct touching of the skin is limited to the hands, arms, neck, and face for parents and same-sexed friends. Mothers and other close relatives are more likely to touch children than are other people. However, caregivers who have established a relationship with a child also have more freedom to touch or be touched by a child.

Touching the clothed body of a child in an appropriate public situation is acceptable for caregivers of either sex. For example, lifting a child so that a climber can be reached, putting an arm around a child who has suffered a mishap, or cleaning a cut are acceptable regardless of the age and sex of child or adult.

Men frequently initiate backslapping and handshaking, but the regions of the body that are acceptable to touch are more limited (Richmond, McCroskey, & Hickson, 2011). Women touch both children and other adults more frequently as well as receive more touching from them (Hall, 2006). The touching behavior of children less than 6 years old is prevalent but decreases steadily through later childhood, with marked sex differences emerging gradually until adult patterns are reached in adolescence.

The channel of touch may be the primary mode of establishing a sense of identity in the first three years. Physical contact also may be necessary for the development of satisfactory interpersonal relationships (Sansone, 2004; Hansen, 2007). It is also necessary for healthy physical development, which in turn is crucial for future social competence (Hansen, 2007). Therefore, appropriate physical contact with adult caregivers, especially for children under 6, should be available to them. Touch is an important means for establishing personal regard. Being "close" to someone implies being close enough to touch, as well as having strong affectionate bonds.

In addition to expressing ritualistic interactions (shaking hands), playfulness (tag), expressing affection (cuddling), and a task-related function (cleaning a scraped knee), touch may also be used as a control function (firmly grasping the hand of a young

teacher's clothing. Touch also indicates the level of involvement or interpersonal responsiveness in the communication. Both adults and children use touch this way (Knapp, Hall, & Horgan, 2013). Interestingly, touch is related to compliance. When someone is touched as they are being asked to do something, they are more likely to do it (Matsumoto & Hwang, 2013a).

Three factors influence the quality of tactile communication: the quantity (how much touching takes place or the duration of the touch), the region of the body where one is touched, and the strength of the touch (McCornack, 2012). People touch friends and family more than casual acquaintances. People tend to touch peers or younger persons more than those older

child who is crossing the street). The amount and frequency of touch as well as the rules about who may touch whom are also culturally specific, though much of the caregiving adult–child touching is more general. Both adults and children have personal preferences as to how much they touch others and the amount of touching that is comfortable for them to receive.

Facial Expression

> Mark marched around the tree in the playground. His face was pulled downward, and the muscles were very tight. Mr. Decker approached him saying, "You look upset, Mark." Mark glowered at him and answered, "Not upset, mad! I wanted to stay home!"

Facial expression is the most obvious component of body language and conveys the greatest amount of information nonverbally, particularly about emotions (Matsumoto & Hwang, 2013b). In dialogues, speakers use facial expression and gesture integrated into oral language to convey information as well as feelings (Bavelas & Chovil, 2006). Facial expressions can be consciously controlled and used to deceive. Ordinarily, facial expressions supplement and complement the verbal message, and both the sender and receiver benefit from it (Fridlund & Russell, 2006).

Many dimensions of meaning can be communicated by facial expression. The face communicates evaluative judgments, the degree of interest, and the intensity or degree of involvement through pleasant and unpleasant expressions. Although the face can clearly convey specific emotions—happiness, surprise, fear, anger, sadness, disgust, contempt, and interest—it is very mobile, and combinations of affect also may be displayed. Younger children are more open in showing feelings by their facial expressions than older children and adults, though the differences are a matter of degree, not of kind. Adults have more control and sometimes subdue their facial expressions using more subtle expressions.

Children display affect through facial expressions from early infancy onward. We must pay close attention

Children communicate clearly with body motion and facial expressions in these four pictures.

Displays of emotion are clear even in the very young—from the delight of discovery in the mirror or distress from a mishap in the snow.

to the cues these expressions are communicating. Pouting is a well-known expression of displeasure, and sticking out the tongue is a widely known expression of insult in Western cultures. Wrinkling of the nose when smelling an unpleasant odor and the disgust displayed when children taste new or different foods are readily understood. More subtle expressions, such as surprise quickly followed by interest or anger, sometimes are more difficult to detect.

Generally, even young children are fairly accurate in understanding facial expressions. Peers reject playmates whose facial expression is not appropriate for the situation (Doherty-Sneddon, 2004). Some children do not seem to know when to smile, look serious, or appear concerned. Such children can be coached so that they are more responsive in their expressions.

Smile. The smile is one of the earliest facial expressions acquired. The simple smile, the broad open smile, and the grin convey different meanings and use different muscles. When the smile is broad and lines form at the corners of the eyes, the person is amused or very pleased. A grin frequently is associated with mischief and may also indicate pleasure with oneself. A simple smile, sometimes called a social smile, is the gesture of slight pleasure,

greeting, and appeasement or obligation in that situation. It may be used to avert aggression or to indicate submissiveness—the display of the lower-status person is intended to placate the higher-status person (LaFrance & Hecht, 1999). Often, a relaxed smile in the presence of others is a way to convey friendliness and sociability rather than inner happiness (Kraut & Johnston, 2008). The simple smile with an otherwise neutral expression is called a **mask smile** (Key, 1975) because it is used to hide unpleasant or unacceptable feelings. The mask smile often has been described as being "painted on the face" or "plastered on" and has a rather immobile quality.

The combination of a mask smile or a habitual smile and either very serious or emotionally negative verbal content is particularly offensive to children. Insincere smiles lack warmth and feeling. Children interpret neutral or hypocritical facial expressions as disinterest, lack of caring, or phoniness. See Figure 3-3 for a cartoon drawn by a child who does not trust one of the adults in her school. This adult often wears a "frozen" smile but is frequently disrespectful to children. When adults use facial expressions inconsistent with their emotions and are unsuccessful, youngsters are often confused and wary (O'Hair & Friedrich, 2001). However, both children and adults tend to smile

FIGURE 3-3 Third Grader's Depiction of the "Mask" Smile of an Adult She Does Not Trust.

back at felt smiles and to respond positively to facial expressions that are friendly and interested (Knapp, Hall, & Horgan, 2013).

The cultural meaning of the smile varies. For example, children of Western European descent traditionally smile when greeting another person, and Japanese children offer greetings with a sober face. Cultural variations in the use of the smile are modified as children interact in the context of the larger society.

Finally, adults must be careful in interpreting children's facial expressions as well as in using their own expressiveness to highlight the message they intend to convey. For example, a young child may smile when a person slips on the ice and falls because the movements of the arms and legs are unusual, not because the child is amused that someone has been hurt.

Eye contact. Gaze is associated with dominance, power, or aggression, and also with attachment and nurturing (Matsumoto, 2006). Eye contact between two persons is a special kind of communication that can rapidly move an interaction to a personal or intimate level even though considerable physical space may separate the communicators. Latino(a) Americans tend to engage in longer eye contact during conversations than Europeans and African Americans (Ting-Toomey, 1999). The eye lock, or prolonged gaze, implies a more intimate holding or communication.

TeachSource Video 3-1

© Cengage Learning 2015

Infants and Toddlers: Family Interactions, School, and Community

Go online and view *Infants and Toddlers: Family Interactions, School, and Community*. In this video, you will see a teacher working with a parent and with children. First view the video with the sound on your computer turned off. Focus on all channels of nonverbal communication except the voice.

1. Note facial expressions of adults and of children. What did you see that told you how children felt at arrival, during the jumping activity, and during the matching activity?

2. How did the adults in this video use touch in their interactions?

3. Did you notice how adults exchanged eye contact, the gestures they used, their facial expressions, and their position in space? How would you describe the tone of this interaction?

4. How did the teachers move their bodies (position in space, orientation, leans and gestures) as they interacted with the adult or with the children?

Watch on CourseMate

The very long gaze between an infant and an adult is normal communication, but a similarly long eye lock between an older child and an adult is a glare and may be interpreted as hostility or aggression. The glance also holds meaning between persons who know each other well. A shared moment of eye contact may mean anything from "Have you ever seen anything so ridiculous?" to "Let's go!" Culturally appropriate eye contact denotes interest and the willingness to engage in social contact.

Eye aversion also is used to indicate turn-taking in normal conversation. In Western cultures, people tend to look more when listening than when speaking (Krannich & Krannich, 2001). Speakers glance away

briefly at the end of an utterance and then return the gaze to the other. They expect the listener to be looking at them at this point. This pattern is essentially reversed in African cultures and modified in mixed racial interaction (Fehr & Exline, 1987). In mixed racial interaction, Black listeners gaze less at the speaker than do White listeners. The pattern of looking down to show respect is common to Japanese, Puerto Ricans, Mexican Americans, and African Americans (Johnson, 1998).

Unfortunately, adults sometimes become very angry when a child violates the rules of establishing rapport through eye contact and may not recognize that the child is behaving correctly within a different set of culturally defined rules. There are normal variations among families as well as regional variations in the same cultural group.

Paralinguistics

Paralinguistics are the sounds people make that carry meaning but are not used as regular words in a sentence or the way in which a speaker says something. Paralinguistics provide additional meaning so that the listener will understand the intent of the speaker better. Usually these communicate affective content as well. Some types of paralinguistic behaviors are listed in Table 3-1.

One type of paralinguistic is **nonlexical sounds**, which are meaningful sounds that are not words. They are produced by everyone and can serve all the functions of nonverbal communication. Physiological acts such as coughing, clearing the throat, sneezing, spitting, belching, sucking the teeth, hiccupping, swallowing, choking, yawning, and sighing can be used solely as adaptive mechanisms or to demonstrate affect. For example, the cough, besides clearing the throat, may be used to communicate tension, anxiety, criticism, doubt, surprise, a prompting to pay attention, or recognition of one's own lies while talking. Several familiar sounds are used as emblems, or in place of words, such as "Uh, uh" (no), "Ah, ah" (warning), "Mmhmm" (yes), "Mmmmmmmm" (good!), "Psst" (look here), and "Ugh!" (how unpleasant!).

Much of the affective content of a message is conveyed by particular vocal qualities expressed simultaneously with speech. In addition, vocal variations facilitate interpersonal interactions. Intonation, for example, is used to denote the end of a sentence, an exclamation, or a question and serves as an indicator in conversational turn-taking.

The **rhythm** of speech is composed of differential stress on words, the **duration** sounds are held while

Table 3-1   Common Paralinguistic Behaviors and Examples

Type of Behavior	Examples	Meanings
Nonlexical sounds	Cough	Physiological need or tension, surprise, or doubt
Nonlexical sounds/emblems	Uh, um	No
Rhythm of speech	Stresses and pauses	Emphasis on stressed words
	Elongating a consonant	Dramatic effect, fear
Tempo of speech	Very fast speech	Excitement or urgency
	Slow speech	Emphasis or hesitancy
Rhythm provided by listener	Repetitious phrases such, as "Yes, ma'am," "Right on"	Confirms speaker's meanings, agreement
Hesitations	Um, ah	Fills up time between words allowing the speaker to get his or her thoughts together
	Repetition of a consonant when the speaker does not usually stutter	Excitement
Intensity	Force and volume of speech: Loud and forceful	High intensity usually means very strong feelings such as joy or terror or rage
	Softer, may be more or less forceful	Whispering usually means secrecy or private communication
Silence	No movement, no sound, direct eye contact	Provocation, resistance
	No sound	Being polite, avoiding embarrassment for self or others
	No sound	Used before or after to stress words
Pitch and Tone	High pitch, light or strong tone	Panic
	Medium tone, medium pitch	In control, firmness
	Fluctuating pitches and tones beyond typical use	Speaker is unpredictable in that circumstance
	Lower tones and pitches	May be soothing or commanding

© Cengage Learning

speaking, and pauses as well as accents on specific words. The stress given to each part of a sentence can determine its meaning. For example, when different words are stressed in the following sentence, the meaning of the pure lexical, or word, content is altered. "*Philip* is sharing the book with Harriet" implies that it is truly Philip, not someone else, who is interacting with Harriet. However, "Philip is *sharing* the book with Harriet" indicates that sharing is the focus of attention.

In the English language, the lengthening of consonants gives a terrifying or dramatic effect. "Runnnnnn!" is a serious, urgent, frightened demand for haste. Adults are likely to lengthen sounds for dramatic appeal when reading stories to children. Variations in the lengths of vowel sounds in ordinary speech, though, simply may reflect dialectal patterns.

Another aspect of rhythm is interpersonal, synchronous interaction. As one person speaks, the conversa-

tion partner may vocalize, "That's true," "Right on," or "Um-hum" in rhythm with the other's spoken words. This is not interruption but confirmation of the speaker's meaning. Nodding of the head and other gestures and body motions may all be used. African-American and Latin-American cultures that are highly sensitive to context are much more likely to use this rhythmic manner of total communication than are European Americans.

The **tempo** of a child's speech may be fast or slow, and the total rhythm smooth, jerky, or abrupt. The timing of speech bouts varies regionally and culturally, with some people allowing more silence between sentences than others (Remland, 2009). Adults who adapt the speed of their own speech to the age and experience of children are more likely to be understood. For example, toddlers and second language speakers have more difficulty in understanding high-speed adult speech. In addition, adults should allow plenty of time for children to complete their thoughts, should refrain from jumping in to finish the sentence for them, and should suppress the urge to take a talking turn prematurely. Such restraint shows respect for the child.

Hesitations, or pauses in speech, allow the speaker to retain the floor or a speaking turn while gathering the next thought. People may pause to think when they have been interrupted or react to an external disturbance such as a slamming door. Pauses may be filled with verbalizations such as "Er," "Um," or "Ah"; nonlexical sounds such as a cough; or unvoiced expressions such as swallowing. Major pauses in children's speech to adults usually occur because the child needs time to organize his or her thoughts.

Variations in **pitch and tone** convey a variety of emotional messages. High-pitched voices are associated with strong emotions such as great excitement or panic. Fluctuations in pitch are characteristic of the angry tone of voice. The pitch and tone of the voice are difficult to control; therefore, subtle interpersonal attitudes and emotions can "leak through" particularly among people who try not to show their emotions (Frank, Maroulis, & Griffin 2013). The quality of the voice itself conveys meaning to the listener, often adding emotional content to the message. Voice quality can be described as follows (Key, 1975, p. 61):

raspy	heavy	gruff	shrill	dull	full
gravelly	reedy	squeaky	soft	moaning	deep
thin	harsh	smooth	breaking	guttural	groaning
singing	resonant	rough			

People with warm, expressive voices are often viewed as more likable, trustworthy, influential, and competent than people with less pleasant voices (Semic, 2008). This applies to children as well as to adults. Toddlers who screech, people who whine, or youngsters who have quiet, inarticulate voices may be shunned by peers and be perceived less intelligent by their teachers (Semic, 2008). Therefore, adults should help children modulate their voices into more attractive displays when possible. For example, Ms. Winterspoon regularly told one child who whined a lot, "I don't understand you well when you talk like that, please tell me in your ordinary voice." Alternatively, with a child who tended to look at his feet and mumble, she asked, "Tell me in a bigger voice."

In an emergency situation, an adult who is distraught may speak rapidly in a shrill, fluctuating tone. Such speech is not likely to instill confidence in his or her ability to handle the problem. On the other hand, an adult's voice that is within the normal range of speech tone and volume enhances the message that the adult can cope with the circumstances (Mehrabian, 2007).

An increase in **intensity**, the force and volume with which something is said, usually is associated with strong feelings such as excitement, joy, eager anticipation, terror, rage, and coercion. However, how loud is "too loud" usually is situationally and culturally determined. For example, speaking intensely and loudly may be perfectly appropriate in a gym or on the street, but speech of the same volume would be inappropriate in a classroom or movie theater. High-volume speech in situations that call for moderate-to-low volume is considered by adults to be boorish, inappropriate, and annoying. People on cell phones tend not to monitor their volume and offend others nearby.

Whispering or simply mouthing words may be interpreted as attempts at secrecy or intimacy. When a voiced utterance dwindles to a whisper, it may be embarrassment that is being expressed. In any case, because a whisper lacks pitch and volume, a listener must attend to it more intently than to regular speech to receive the message.

Silence, the absence of sound when sound is expected, also is a powerful communicator. Deliberate silence in response to a question may be an insult or a provocation or may indicate resistance or lack of information. Silence may also be used selectively in an attempt to be polite, to avoid an imposition on another, or to allow someone else to avoid embarrassment (Sifianou, 1995; Jaworski, 2008). Silence also stresses the utterance following it, making the message stand out as being of extreme importance. A relaxed, attentive silence from an adult to a beginning speaker or a second language speaker is simple wait time for the child to speak.

All interactions between people occur in a specific time and place with a host of contextual features. Both senders and receivers need to understand some common principles to communicate effectively. Communications are inferential—that is, meanings are based on what is actually said in conjunction with the nonverbal signals that accompany the message. Communications are intentional—people generally send the messages that they intend to send. Communications are conventional—within a culture group, the same nonverbal signals have consistent meanings. Usually communication is negotiated between the listener and the speaker, is sequential with turn-taking, is systematic, and varies according to the participant's social relationships (Haslett & Samter, 1997). Therefore, it behooves adults to reflect on messages that they send to children so that they are communicating accurately and to deliberately attend to children so that they understand what the child is communicating. The burden is mostly on the more experienced of the communicators.

Read the following scenario, and then try to answer the questions posed at the end. Keep in mind that nonverbal communication is continuous, fast, and changes rapidly throughout an interaction. The nonverbal communications contain strong identity and relational messages that may be misinterpreted.

Jenny's mother admonished her to pay attention to the teacher and to not talk back to her before helping Jenny, in her clean, wrinkled dress, onto the Head Start bus. Trying to comply, Jenny, brushing her fine, flyaway blond hair from her face, stood close to her teacher. Careful to be still and quiet and gazing steadily at Ms. Sable, her African American teacher, she listened intently, with an immobile expression, to her teacher's greeting and directions.

Ms. Sable smiled at Jenny and tried to reassure her, but with the distinct impression that this child might be difficult to deal with this year. The notion that the child seemed resentful and maybe difficult flitted through her mind as she gazed at the rest of the mostly African American children in the class. She hoped the family would not create problems because she was an African American teacher.

1. What nonverbal cues about Jenny's identity did Ms. Sable probably process quickly?

2. What more subtle cues left the impression that Jenny might be resentful and difficult?

3. Why do you think this first impression might be made on a busy first day?

Warmth, acceptance, genuineness, empathy, and respect are communicated nonverbally though all channels. Notice the relaxed body of the teacher, the supporting and comforting touch, and the direction of the teacher's gaze.

© Cengage Learning 2015

Nonverbal messages clearly convey messages about interest and boredom, friendliness and hostility, as well as about dominance and submissiveness among others. Most of the time, these are taken for granted and do not come under conscious control. It is through the effective receiving of children's nonverbal messages that the sensitive adult comes to understand the child's meanings and feelings and is thereby able to be more effectively responsive.

Nurturing Relationships Nonverbally naeyc

People communicate specific messages nonverbally in the course of everyday interaction. In addition, through a combination of various nonverbal channels,

people convey impressions about their overall relationships with others. Messages that communicate warmth, acceptance, genuineness, empathy, and respect are conveyed to a great extent nonverbally.

When adults are mindful of their own nonverbal messages, children with whom they are communicating are more likely to feel understood, respected, and supported. When nonverbal communication is unfamiliar or unexpected, children feel vulnerable. When it is predictable and familiar, they feel secure. Adults who think about their own nonverbal behaviors, and those of the children with whom they work, can monitor and possibly modify their actions to provide a more secure and comfortable climate.

Warmth

How do children know that you like them? Only a small portion of the message of liking a child is conveyed by words; much more of the message is communicated by vocal characteristics and most by facial expression. Warmth is communicated primarily nonverbally (Gazda et al., 2006).

Adults who want to communicate caring and concern are more likely to approach the child and interact close to them. They will maintain frequent but not continuous eye contact and will face the child directly, keeping their head at about the same level as the child's. They may lean or reach toward the child while gesturing or speaking. Smiling, nodding, and a relaxed, friendly facial expression and body also indicate warmth and interest. Speech is at normal pitch, speed, and volume, and the tone is relaxed and melodious. Statements that express agreement, approval, or validation contribute as well. Warm adults appear willing to take time with the child (Andersen, Guerrero, & Jones, 2006). The overall impression is smooth, comfortable, and relaxed. These behaviors also tend to reduce the power differential between adults and children.

Fidgeting, turning away, a mask expression or sneer, a sharp tone of voice, or standing up and looking or moving far away communicates coolness, aloofness, or the absence of warmth. Crossing the arms or legs and either staring or failing to maintain normal conversational eye contact communicates maximum coldness. Self-grooming, frowns, looking at the ceiling, negative head shakes, or a fake yawn are all cold behaviors. The overall impression is either tense or carelessly offhand and disinterested. Unfortunately, adults such as students who are unsure of themselves or who are afraid of doing the wrong thing also use some of these mannerisms when feeling anxious. Children and other adults may misinterpret this behavior as uncaring and uninterested.

Acceptance

Acceptance requires that adults send positive messages nonverbally, consistently. Without acceptance from valued adults in their lives, constructive social development is impossible. To be accepted fully means to be valued unconditionally. Adults who demonstrate acceptance toward children care about them regardless of their personal attributes, family background, or behavior—and they show it (Remland, 2009). Teachers who use positive nonverbal immediacy in the classroom (smile, use eye contact, gesture, walk around, and have an open, relaxed body position) create a positive climate where students feel good about themselves and the learning context (Burgoon, Guerrero, & Floyd,

2010). The following behaviors demonstrate a positive evaluation:

- More forward lean
- More eye gaze
- Closer proximity
- More openness of arms and body
- More direct body orientation
- More touching
- More postural relaxation
- More positive facial and vocal expressions (Knapp, Hall, & Horgan, 2013)
- More vocal variety and expressiveness (Ray & Floyd, 2006)

Acceptance is widely misunderstood. Some adults assume that acceptance translates into condoning all

© Cengage Learning

What message is the adult conveying to this child through her body orientation and gestures?

child behaviors, even antisocial ones. Skilled adults communicate acceptance and liking of the child while guiding them toward more appropriate behavior. This dual agenda is illustrated when Ms. Niblock moves quickly over to two children who are hitting each other with sticks on the playground, squats down, and gazes at each one. They are obviously angry. She communicates acceptance by acknowledging their anger, by her posture, and by reaching out to each of them with her arms. At the same time, she makes it clear that hitting is not permitted in a quiet, firm voice, and helps the children put the sticks down.

Genuineness

As you know from Chapter 2, positive adult–child relationships are also characterized by genuineness. Genuineness is communicated when nonverbal behaviors and words match. When they are giving children positive feedback, their body motion, facial expressions, and voice tone support the message. When the message is in the opposite vein, their nonverbal communication is congruent as well. Being authentic and genuine is actually easier than trying to mask your true feelings. People are more relaxed and forthcoming, and their smiles do not include traces of disgust, fear, contempt, or sadness. Language is more fluent, and the pitch of the voice is more expressive when adults are being truthful. Children are quite adept at discerning genuine adults from infancy onward.

Authentic adults gain children's trust because children know that their words and nonverbal reactions are believable. Mrs. Tashima demonstrates genuineness when she takes time to look carefully at the children's artwork and points out something particularly interesting about each child's painting ("You used a lot of bright colors" or "You found a way to make the house look far away") rather than simply telling each child "Good job," without necessarily examining the art and meaning it.

Empathy

Empathy requires accurate decoding of children's nonverbal messages and alert listening to what they say as well as observation of what they are doing in a specific context. The adult must understand what the child is feeling and then communicate similarity of feelings back to the child, matching the child's nonverbal cues simultaneously or in a coordinated fashion. In contrast, adults who are inattentive, nonobservant, or focused on other matters are not empathic. Compare two teacher's reactions to Emily, a third grader, who spent an hour gluing and nail-

ing a creation made entirely from wood (Steiner & Whelan, 2004).

Emily, smiling shyly: "It's a wishing tree. You talk to it and things come true."

Mr. Daley, glancing briefly before quickly moving on "Don't get slivers from that thing. Did you finish your math assignment?"

Later in the afternoon, Mr. Bewick stops by the after-school program. Emily hesitantly shows him the wishing tree.

Mr. Bewick, kneeling down and grinning says: "Wow, a wishing tree. I've never seen a wishing tree before. Can I make a wish?" The adult waits for Emily's reply.

Mr. Bewick's response was empathic; Mr. Daley's was not. Mr. Daley focused on his agenda and was insensitive to the value of Emily's creation to her. He conveyed his lack of interest by looking at her work in a perfunctory manner and by moving along quickly. Mr. Bewick, on the other hand, recognized the importance of Emily's message and let her know that he felt some of her same excitement. He conveyed his interest with his nonverbal behavior as well as with his words.

Respect

You show respect for children when you are attentive to their ideas and when you give them opportunities to try things on their own, with no visible sign that you believe they will fail. Disrespect is apparent when adults communicate that children cannot learn or function effectively. See Table 3-2 for a comparison of respectful and disrespectful behavior.

How the Concept of Time Influences Relationships

Many social expectations are based on the shared meaning of time. You must be aware of your concept of time so that you can more easily understand your responses to children's behavior. In addition, you must learn how others, particularly people of different cultural backgrounds, interpret time. Otherwise, misunderstandings about time between adults and children will be inevitable. An adult may interpret that an 8-year-old is late for a Cub Scout meeting because the child arrived several minutes after the scheduled meeting time. However, the child may consider himself "on time" because he arrived before the major activities that were important to him had begun.

Table 3-2 Comparing Respectful and Disrespectful Behavior

Respectful Nonverbal Behavior	Disrespectful Nonverbal Behavior
Listens quietly and politely while a child speaks	Snorts, rolls eyes, sniffs, sighs, gasps, or makes other derisive sounds
Looks at the child	Looks over the child's head or out the window when the child is speaking
Focuses on the meaning that the child is trying to convey; provides enough time for the child to complete a thought	Interrupts the child; finishes the child's sentences
Tactfully, and privately assists the child in achieving cleanliness	Turns away or shows disgust when a child has a toilet accident or has body odor
Adjusts to cultural differences and preferences for interpersonal space, touch, and approach to time	Bases movement in space and touching of children solely on the adult's cultural preference

Children must learn a complex set of rules for the use of time in American culture. Children from Native American and Hispanic cultures may perceive clock time as less important than **subjective time**, which may cause additional misunderstanding (DeCapua & Wintergerst, 2007). Subjective time, in contrast to clock time, is ambiguous. It is based on an internal feeling of the people using it. Native American adults attending a powwow may know the dancing will be done on a particular weekend, but it may be at any hour during that period. It is the timing of the event that is important rather than the specific time of day.

The control of time is an indicator of status. This means that adults are likely to become angry with children who are slow, who dawdle, or who use what the adult perceives as too much time for a task. On the other hand, adults get angry with children who are impatient and do not wait for them for "just a minute." The duration of an event may be either too long or too short depending upon the perspective of the people involved.

Adults who take the time to listen to a child demonstrate that the child is important and the conversation is interesting. Adults who interrupt children, who are obviously ready to leave the interaction at the first opportunity, or who are excessively distracted by the events around them demonstrate a lack of interest. Attending to children promptly, keeping appointments or commitments, and taking the time to observe the child's work or play communicate to the child that she or he is important. On the other hand, you must keep in mind that although children understand these cues in others, they are just learning to adopt such actions in their own behavior. As a result, their own use of time to convey respect and interest is not fully developed.

Besides nurturance, nonverbal behaviors also play a part in conveying authority. This is true both in terms of adult behavior and in terms of children's interactions with peers.

Communicating Authority and Security through Nonverbal Behavior naeyc

Fortunately, adults have the legitimate power, or **authority**, to provide for the safety, security, and well-being of the children in their care. Obviously, adults control the resources needed for survival, learning, or play, and the ability to reward appropriate behavior. Adults have power in that they have skills and knowledge that children need. Most adults working with children have power based on warm, positive relationships with children and the children's desire to please. In addition, they have greater strength and size, which may be necessary to pick up and move a child who may be in a dangerous place or situation (Guerrero & Floyd, 2006). Perhaps less obvious is the fact that adults also provide for the order, safety, and feeling of security that children need.

Much of this sense of authority is conveyed to children nonverbally. Adults demonstrate their assertiveness when they interact in close physical proximity, maintain eye contact, and use a firm, even confident tone of voice. A simple touch to a child's arm is useful in getting compliance (Segrin, 2008). They may need to grasp a child firmly to prevent an injury to the child or someone else. Socially skilled dominant behavior that displays confidence and energy is more successful in influencing behavior in the long term than coercive (physical or verbal) strategies (Guerrero & Floyd, 2006). Children know that teachers have the authority to reward appropriate behavior, distribute resources fairly, and keep them safe from harm. Adults who use social skill to gain compliance have greater influence that lasts longer than those who use more coercive strategies (Burgoon, Guerrero, & Floyd, 2010). As your skill in reading the nonverbal messages of children increases, your judgment of when and how to act may improve as well (Langford, 2013).

Nonassertiveness implies lack of control of the situation or unwillingness to act responsibly. Both of these are communicated nonverbally, and even very young children can detect the fluctuating, intense, loud voice of anger, and the weak, wavering, hesitant voice of the timid adult. As a result, they are likely to respond to these aspects of that adult message rather than to the words that are used.

Adults are not the only ones to communicate authority in relation to others. Young children appear to display status and power through control of space or toys; through size and strength; by using vigorous, energetic movements; and through arguments with one another (Burgoon & Dunbar, 2006). Dominant children are more successful in getting other children to do what they want them to do, and submissive children tend to avoid arguments in favor of using more polite requests. The strategies that appear to work for the dominant child to gain power include boasting, leaning close to the other or invading the play area, standing up while the opponent is sitting, exerting superior strength while pulling or struggling, or offering empty compromises. Those who are dominant are more expressive, more bodily open, maintain smaller interpersonal distances, have less vocal variability, have louder voices, interrupt more, and have fewer hesitations (Knapp, Hall, & Horgan, 2013). Such interchanges do not necessarily lead to violence or personal injury and may be necessary for children to learn how to deal with a social system in which individuals have incompatible goals and varying degrees of power in the group.

Rudy entered the block area that he had left 15 minutes previously and asserted, "I didn't say you could move these blocks," as he moved in closely and loomed over the players. David, Devan, and Forrest initially tried to ignore him. Rudy moved forward, scowled, and said, "Put those back, over there.... Don't you hear me?" as he grasped one of the offending blocks and moved it. Devan protested and told Rudy that he had left and they were building. Rudy responded in a firm, loud voice, "I left and came right back." More softly and casually he continued, "You can do it when I am not here." Because Rudy is rarely absent, this compromise offer is essentially meaningless. The play continued with Rudy directing, asserting, and demanding, and the other three complying. This is essentially a collaborative arrangement between the ones who dominate and the ones who submit, as all the children know that adults would intervene if a vigorous altercation took place.

Rudy used the following strategies to exert dominance over his playmates: elevation, spatial violations, loud voice, conversational control, and control of materials. The other children attempted withdrawal to avoid conflict and then submitted. Rudy also offered a compromise or a solution to the problem, which, if sincere, would be an effective strategy to minimize injuring other's feelings.

Potential Challenges in Sending and Interpreting Nonverbal Messages naeyc

One or all channels of nonverbal communication transmit unspoken messages. In addition, it is possible to communicate one message in one channel of communication, such as facial expression, while communicating something quite different in another channel, such as the tone of voice. Neither of these may correspond to the meaning of the actual words spoken, resulting in a **mixed message**. For instance, an adult may smile and say, "Sure, have another helping," while displaying a rigid posture, a tense voice tone, and a clenched hand, which clearly demonstrate disapproval. Discrepant messages can be detected from what is said and can be linked to four nonverbal processes: control, arousal, negative affect, and cognitive complexity. The untruthful communicator tends to select words carefully and use grammar differently than when being truthful. In addition, the voice is more controlled while the body is tense. Often, unnecessary detail is added. Apparently, it is much easier to be an accurate, honest communicator (Remland, 2009).

By 9 months of age, infants can both identify when words and feelings of a speaker are discrepant and apply this confusing message to a social context (Blanck & Rosenthal, 1982). Babies rely entirely on nonverbal cues in their interactions with caregivers and become quite skillful communicators (Burgoon, Guerrero, & Floyd, 2010). Children of preschool age are sensitive to and wary of messages when the facial expression and tone of voice do not match. They assume the worst. Younger children also have difficulty in decoding mixed messages that are used to express dominance (Burgoon, Guerrero, & Floyd, 2010). As children get older, they show greater accuracy and speed in decoding facial expressions. They shift from depending mostly on what they hear to using facial expression as the primary key to understanding without losing their previously developed skills. As they become more skilled, children are able to extract more subtle emotional messages from visual nonverbal communications, and their dependence on the words that people use is decreased. They are less easily fooled, more accurate, and more competent in receiving the totality of the communication. Visual

Meet Jay

Jay is small for his 7 years. Always wearing long-sleeved shirts, even when it is warm outside, he is watchful of adults and bigger children. He appears to always check for exits when entering new spaces. His facial expression is generally blank except when he scans the room warily from time to time. If anyone approaches suddenly, he withdraws quickly or moves out of the way. Occasionally, he flinches when his teacher reaches out to touch him. Miss Planalp finds him hard to understand and unreachable. She has learned to approach him only when he can see her and to stay a couple of feet away from him until she asks if she can show him how to do a task.

Jay's nonverbal behavior may be overlooked in a busy classroom. He does not cause a problem for other children or for the teacher. However, his ability to learn social skills is limited by his defensiveness and his mistrust of others. He is one of the very quiet children that are challenging because he is so difficult to attune to.

If you were Jay's teacher, what nonverbal behaviors would you use; which ones would you avoid? Why?

cues are primarily used in decoding mixed messages by older children and adults.

However, children with learning disabilities are substantially less accurate in interpreting emotions in others. Boys, in particular, may not use facial cues to judge another's feelings, relying instead on motion cues (large gestures and movement through space). Although the trend of greater accuracy is maintained over time, many of these youngsters may still be confused as they enter adolescence (Nabuzoka & Smith, 1995). This can be especially serious; for example, a smiling child who is running fast toward another who is disabled in this way may be seen as an aggressor rather than a potential playmate. Nearly all social interactions will pose potential problems of misinterpretation for children who are playing with their more skilled age-mates. Likewise, children with autism require intensive intervention to be able to read nonverbal cues. They have difficulty with requesting, joint attention, social interaction, and turn-taking (Chiang, Soong, Lin, & Rogers, 2008).

Sarcasm combines negative lexical (word) content and a scathing tone of voice with a pleasant facial expression. Sarcasm is a strategy used to convey contempt, that the other person is incompetent, and is at the least a put down (Guerrero & Floyd, 2006). When verbal messages contradict nonverbal ones, adults tend to believe the nonverbal message, but children tend to believe the verbal one (Burgoon, Guerrero, & Floyd, 2010). Young children are disturbed by it because the words and tone of voice are both strongly negative, and these are the cues they rely on to interpret the affective meaning of a message. Preadolescents interpret such behavior as negative in tone or a bad joke. Adults may perceive this markedly mixed message as funny or a joke.

As you work to establish positive, warm relationships with children, you will likely encounter situations where you are confused about the meaning of some child's nonverbal cues. A child may misinterpret your good intentions. Cultural membership may be one factor, as may the child's life experience at home, in the community, or even in school. You cannot always know what to do. Reflecting on what you do know so far, consider the dilemma of how to interact with Jay, described above.

Children's Acquisition of Nonverbal Communication Skills naeyc

Your skillful and appropriate use of nonverbal communication sets the stage for children to learn from your example. Nonverbal behaviors, including the style and degree of expressiveness, are socialized from birth through adulthood. Children of families who use overtly expressive nonverbal behavior decode these cues accurately earlier than children whose families are less expressive. However, when families use subtler, less overtly expressive nonverbal cues, the children's decoding abilities are keener and more skilled as they mature because they have more practice in decoding nuances (Halberstadt, 1991). Unfortunately, some typically developing children experience difficulties in acquiring these skills. Children 8 to 10 years old who are socially anxious and afraid of not being accepted by their peers may be at risk because they withdraw and avoid the social situations that would enable them to learn and to become more skillful. They are substantially less accurate than their peers in decoding facial expressions and voice qualities for emotional content (McClure & Nowicki, 2001). For these reasons, professionals incorporate nonverbal skills into their program planning.

Where Nonverbal Communication Fits in the Curriculum

You have many opportunities to help children:

- Interpret nonverbal messages more accurately.
- Use nonverbal skills effective in interpersonal communication.
- Apply display rules for nonverbal behavior appropriately.

These understandings and skills represent core competencies associated with nonverbal communication. As such, they inform educational program content for children and are incorporated in the learning standards for most states. See Table 3-3 for typical examples.

Methods of Acquiring Nonverbal Skills

Children learn nonverbal communication patterns in three distinct ways: through imitation, through interaction with adults, and through teaching and coaching. Each of these are discussed in the following subsections.

Children learn through imitation. They mimic the specifics of the communication strategies of their immediate family, peers, and neighbors. From the earliest years, children pick up the nonverbal behaviors typical of their gender and cultural group. Viewing media

---

Table 3-3 Examples of State Learning Standards Associated with Nonverbal Communication

State	Grade/Age	Standard
Indiana	3–5 years	Use eye gaze, proximity, and gestures to communicate.
New Hampshire	Grades K–2	Understand that communication is verbal and nonverbal.
Connecticut	Grade 4	Use volume, pitch, phrasing, pace, modulation, and gestures to enhance meaning.

Sources: Indiana Department of Education (2012); Connecticut State Department of Education, Bureau of Teaching and Learning (2006); New Hampshire Department of Education (2006).

---

also helps children decode and imitate nonverbal behaviors (Feldman, Coats, & Philippot, 1999).

Not surprisingly, Americans' communication patterns vary systematically by racial groups, cultural heritage, gender, and even region of the country (Richmond, McCroskey, & Hickson, 2011). In fact, although adults may speak the same language, nonverbal patterns may still be closely linked to the country of origin of the family. For example, an individual may use the gestures more typical of Italians while speaking American English as a primary language.

The same variations are true for Spanish-speaking families. For example, although comfortable communicating distances are closer for all Spanish-speaking adults than for North Americans of northern European descent, there is a considerable difference between groups coming from different Spanish-speaking countries. Be aware that systematic differences in nonverbal communication exist, and observe carefully the adults close to the child to pick up the typical nonverbal behavioral cues that they use. In this way, you will more quickly understand the total message that the child is communicating.

Children learn through social interactions with adults. Children who interact with skillful, expressive adults also will eventually become skilled in nonverbal communication. Also, a child who has a cultural experience at home that differs from the larger culture at school or in other community settings will gradually modify his or her nonverbal communications, in essence becoming nonverbally bilingual.

Adults share in the responsibility for learning the meaning of the child's nonverbal environment, particularly for children under 6 years of age. Some rules of nonverbal behavior are pointed out by admonition. When adults see a child doing something that "everyone" finds inappropriate, such as spitting on the floor, they respond with a strong statement such as, "You spit on the floor. That spreads germs. Use a tissue." Cultural expectations are learned when a child makes an error and is corrected. Americans have firm rules about nudity and all interactions with internal space. Children simply cannot urinate in public! Rarely are these nonverbal rules formally explained as a part of classroom instruction.

Children learn through teaching and coaching. Adults may give children suggestions on how to "be friendly" or how to stand up for their rights. Family members may also provide scripts and coaching for younger children with cues as to nonverbal congruence: "Say, 'Thank you very much'" or "Tell him you are sorry if you mean it." Children receive formal instruction in English in schools. However, they seldom receive similar instruction for nonverbal behaviors except when they are engaged in theatrical experiences and must assume a role unfamiliar to them. Adults may give formal instruction as to nonverbal communications when children attend a performance ("Sit still. Don't whisper during the play."). However, much of the teaching is informal and generally on an individual level. Often classroom expectations for nonverbal behaviors are conveyed in this way (see Table 3-4).

The pattern of development of nonverbal language is very similar to that of speech. Children become increasingly skillful as they get older. Their messages become more complex and come increasingly under their control. Understanding of discrepant messages becomes easier with age and experience. By the age of 4, children can successfully tell a white lie in a politeness situation (Talwar & Lee, 2002). Comprehension precedes expression, and children shift from reliance on the verbal channel to the adult pattern of major reliance on facial expression between 7 and 10 years of age.

Display rules are a particularly important means of nonverbal behavior that children learn through instruction. **Display rules** are culturally specific guidelines that govern the demonstration of nonverbal behavior. Children learn to exaggerate, minimize, or mask expressions of their feelings depending on the

setting and the social situation. Preschool-age children learn from their parents, teachers, and friends about what is and is not polite or acceptable to express. For example, boys in the United States are schooled to mask negative emotions such as sadness or grief and not to display an overabundance of tenderness and affection, and girls are trained to maintain a pleasant front and to minimize aggressive displays such as anger (Burgoon, Guerrero, & Floyd, 2010).

> Mickey, who is only 3, made a face when tasting a new food at home, and said "Yuck!" as he pushed his plate away. Later in the week when Mickey ate at the childcare center and encountered a disliked food, he tasted it, refrained from comment, managing to keep his expression more subdued, almost neutral, and avoided eating it thereafter.

By the time children are 8 years of age, they can explain the use of display rules to others (Saarni & Weber, 1999).

> Falling on the ice, just after bragging to some other 8-year-old girls, embarrassed Martha. She got up, smiled, and tried the fall again deliberately to make the others laugh. To her best friend, she admitted later that she was hurt but did not want to look "stupid" in front of the other girls.

You will learn more about these behaviors in Chapter 5, Supporting Children's Emotional Development and Learning. For now, keep in mind that children who are better at decoding nonverbal behavior and who understand the display rules governing such communication are considered more socially competent both by their peers and by adults (Haslett & Samter, 1997).

Thoughtful adults who use nonverbal communication effectively are able to help children feel safe and secure as they guide their behavior. Usually, we do not think about our nonverbal messages. However, professionals who are mindful of their own and other's nonverbal messages think about these deliberately and consider the culture, the specific setting and situation, and the developmental level of children involved. Thoughtful observation and deliberate choices of nonverbal messages will enable you to be more sensitive to children and more effective when communicating emotions and expectations. The following guidelines will help you increase the effectiveness and accuracy of your nonverbal communication skills with children.

Table 3-4 Conveying Classroom Expectations for Nonverbal Behavior

Channel	Situation	Adult Statement
Voice	Children talking loudly	*Use your quiet voices inside.* (Teacher demonstrates appropriate volume.)
Touch	Children sitting closely in group time	*Put your hands in your lap.* or *Keep your hands to yourself.*
Position in space	Children attempting to get into a line	*Douglas, please stand behind William. Michael, stand behind Douglas please. You should be far enough behind the person ahead of you so that you can easily see your own shoes when you look down.*

SKILLS FOR DEVELOPING POSITIVE RELATIONSHIPS WITH CHILDREN NONVERBALLY naeyc

Tuning In To Children

1. **Tune in to the nonverbal behavior of the children in your care.** Observing your typical interactions with a child, those between the child and other children, and those between the child and other adults will help you understand various movements and gestures for that particular child. For example, Anne Janette's teacher checked for a fever when she had been playing quietly by herself at the puzzle table. Ordinarily, Anne Janette was noisy, boisterous, social, and physically active. Her temperature was over 100°F. The teacher was alert to the change in the child's typical behavior.

2. **Recognize and learn cultural and family variations in children's nonverbal behavior.** With so many variations among cultural groups, only direct observation within an appropriate context will provide enough information to understand the meanings of particular behaviors. Does the child usually look toward the speaker or away from the speaker when listening? Does the quiet wriggling of a 3-year-old when listening to a story mean that the child is uncomfortable, is bored, or has to go to the bathroom? Be alert for consistent sequences of behavior in individual children to learn what these cues mean. Respect children's nonverbal indications of violations of personal space.

3. **Respect children's proximal space.** Pat children on the back; shake their hands; give them congratulatory hugs. Avoid absentminded fondling or patting children on the head or buttocks. These gestures communicate patronization or disrespect.

4. **Walk up to children with whom you want to communicate, and orient yourself in a face-to-face position at their eye level.** Move your body into the axial space of the child to get the child's attention before trying to deliver a message. Stand, sit, or squat close to the child, not more than an arm's length away for conversation. Do not allow furniture or materials to act as a barrier between you and the child. Make sure your head is at the same level as the child's. Children should be able to see your face. Verbal messages can otherwise go literally "over their heads"! Facial expressions that reinforce your words help children to understand what you are saying. Maintain frequent but not continuous eye contact. When children are engaged in activities, move from child to child and speak to them individually. You will have to squat down to achieve face-to-face communication with small children.

5. **Lean slightly toward the child.** Leaning toward the child communicates interest and also helps you hear what the child is saying. Maintain a relaxed body posture. Slouching or rigidity does not convey interest or concern. Your body should not appear "ready to leave immediately." The arms and legs should be open, not tightly closed or crossed. Use movements that convey alertness. Nod your head or use other gestures to indicate your understanding. This should not be confused with fidgeting, which usually indicates lack of interest or boredom. Feet should be unobtrusive, not moving about. Mannerisms (hair flicking, lint picking, or table tapping) should be unobtrusive or absent. None of your movements should compete for attention with the child's words.

6. **Tune in to children's nonverbal messages, and make every effort to demonstrate that you are attempting to understand.** Avoid being dismissive and rushing to interpretation, particularly when the child is relatively unfamiliar or a member of a culture group other than your own. Pay close attention to what children say, how they say it, and what they do. Make judgments about displays of emotion, appropriate behavior, and the message intent using what you understand about the culture, gender, age, and skills of the child. When people believe that you are attempting to understand (whether you do or not), they feel your care and warmth.

7. **Respond as quickly as possible when spoken to, and take the time to listen.** Taking time to really listen to a child is sometimes very difficult to do. If you do not have time to listen to what a child has to say, let the child know that you are interested and will be able to attend more fully later. Then, be sure to do so. For example, Mr. Wardlich had begun reading a story aloud to the class when Carrie announced that she was going to Florida during spring break. Mr. Wardlich told her that she could tell him about it when the children were working on their penmanship, but that now it was time to read a story.

8. **Keep all channels of communication consistent when communicating about your feelings.** When expressing your feelings to a child,

your words should match your behavior. During the course of working with children, you are likely to experience a variety of feelings such as joy, amusement, annoyance, anger, surprise, puzzlement, and interest. Communications that are consistent across all channels are authentic, genuine, and honest. You can achieve clarity and understanding by using all channels to convey one message. Multiple feelings can be expressed in rapid sequence and still be genuine.

When adults try to suppress, mask, or simulate feelings, they are not being authentic, genuine, or honest. If you are angry, you should look and sound angry, without loss of self-control; if you are happy, your face, body, and voice should reflect your joy.

9. **Touch children with warmth and respect.** The younger the child, the more likely it is that he or she will find physical touching acceptable and even desirable. Ask older children's permission before touching them. Frequently, boys over 8 years of age resent being touched. The adult must, of course, respect the child's preference. However, when trust has been established, touching or patting a child in a friendly or congratulatory manner on the shoulders, hands, and upper back is acceptable regardless of age. When used appropriately, touch is soothing, comforting, and emotionally healing because it is a tangible link between you and the child. Something as simple as a nurse holding a child's hand while someone else is drawing a blood sample can reduce the child's anxiety.

10. **Use voice tones that are moderate in loudness and normal to low in pitch, and use a voice quality that is relaxed, serious, and concerned.** Keep your rate of speed moderate. Your voice should be clear, audible, and free of many "filled" pauses such as "Ah" or "Um." The speech should be regular and even in tempo, not impatient or excessively slow. Your speech should be fluent when answering simple questions or commenting on a topic rather than staccato or full of hesitations.

11. **Use nonverbal skills to communicate acceptance and respect even when a child is rejecting.** Sometimes young children withdraw or reject you when distressed ("Go away!"; "I don't want you!"; "I hate you!"). An accepting adult is able to provide reassurance, comfort, and guidance. Avoid using rejecting nonverbal behaviors.

12. **Catch yourself forgetting to use effective nonverbal behaviors, and make on-the-spot corrections.** Monitor your nonverbal behavior as you interact with children. If you find yourself towering over children, stoop down to their level and engage in face-to-face communication. If your voice becomes too loud, too soft, too fast, or too slow, then stop and resume your message using a more moderate volume and speed. If you find your eyes wandering away from the child, refocus, and listen more attentively to what the child is saying. Note which nonverbal behaviors you need to continue working on and make an intentional effort to improve your skills in these areas. General guides to showing warmth and respect are listed for you.

How to Show Warmth and Respect

Warmth

✓ Move physically close to the child.

✓ Bend, sit, or squat so you are at eye level.

✓ Smile, or display a pleasant friendly facial expression.

✓ Lean toward the child.

Respect

✓ Listen attentively.

✓ Look at the child in a conversation.

✓ Maintain a face-to-face orientation.

✓ Encourage the child to do as much as possible for himself or herself.

✓ Avoid being distracted, interrupting, or speaking at the same time as the child.

Digital Download **Download from CourseMate**

Conveying Authority and Security

1. **Dress appropriately.** Clothing, grooming, hairstyle, and general appearance convey messages, particularly of authority. A person responsible for the supervision and education of children, especially those younger than the children's parents, may be ignored. Unfamiliar young children will not approach you for assistance, and the 10- to 12-year-old is likely to treat you as a peer if your appearance suggests a peer relationship. Because appropriate dress varies from setting to setting, the

easiest guide is to observe the dress of the highest-status adults in the group.

2. **Maintain a tone of voice that is firm, warm, and confident.** The pitch should be even and the volume normal. Avoid shouting or using an overly loud voice. Tonal quality should be open (sound is full and melodious) and the speed steady. Dropping the jaw, relaxing the throat, and projecting through the mouth rather than the nose can achieve the desired tonal quality. Variations in pitch during a sentence or very rapid speech give the impression of uncertainty. A weak, distant, wavering, or very soft voice is nonassertive and may convey the message: "I am telling you to do this, but I don't think you will. And if you don't, I won't follow through." Adults whose normal voices are very soft or very high may need to add extra depth or intensity to their very important messages in order to be taken seriously.

3. **Look directly at the child when speaking, and maintain regular eye contact.** Eye contact may be maintained while speaking firmly to a child for longer periods than is typical of usual conversation, but staring or glaring at a child usually is not necessary. A steady, firm look at a child who is misbehaving sometimes is sufficient to remind the child to redirect the behavior in question. Aversion of eye contact or a pleading look is nonassertive. Because some adults are shorter than tall 11- and 12-year-olds, serious messages will be more effective if both child and adult are seated. Differences in height are usually differences in leg length. When a child towers over an adult, assertive messages are unusually difficult to deliver. Face-to-face interaction is more effective.

4. **Use your hands to gesture appropriately or, if necessary, to gently hold the child until the communication is complete.** Little children are quite capable of darting away when they do not want to hear what you have to say. They may also twist about, turn their backs toward you, or put their hands over their ears. The child can be held firmly and steadily without pinching or excessive force until the message is completed. Use gestures that enumerate points, that describe the meanings of the words used, or that indicate position in space are appropriate. Do not wag a finger in the child's face or point at the child to reinforce what you are saying.

5. **Relax, maintain close physical proximity, and maintain arms and legs in either an open or semi-open position.** You are in a naturally authoritative role. It is unnecessary to display aggressiveness, as demonstrated by hands on hips, feet apart, and a tense body, to achieve compliance. However, having a stooped or dejected-looking posture or leaning on something for support certainly is not assertive, and children may not comply with requests when they detect a nonassertive stance. Combine all of these strategies when individual children appear to lose control or are very distressed.

Providing Security through Authority Nonverbal Signals

✓ Get down to the child's level for face-to-face communication.

✓ Establish eye contact.

✓ Hold and touch the child gently to comfort or firmly for safety as needed.

✓ Express empathy through all nonverbal channels as appropriate.

✓ Keep your voice firm and moderate in tone and volume, or remain silent if the child is extremely loud or overwrought.

✓ Maintain a relaxed body posture.

✓ Keep all nonverbal channels consistent with your language. Give one clear message that you will keep the child safe.

Digital Download   **Download from CourseMate**

---

6. **Use nonverbal signals to gain the attention of a group of children who are engaged in an activity or who are dispersed in space.** Indoors, playing a chord on a piano, flicking the lights on and off, singing a specific tune, clapping your hands, sitting quietly and waiting for children to join you, or changing your tone of voice are effective signals to get the attention of the children. Then, you may signal for silence by putting a finger over your pursed lips or beckoning the children nearer with your hand. Outdoors, whistling, waving a hand or flag, holding an arm high with flattened palm toward the children, ringing a bell, or blowing a whistle are effective.

Children cannot be expected to receive and understand spoken messages if they do not know that you are trying to communicate with them. You can tell that they have received a signal if they turn toward you or begin to quiet down. Begin speaking after you have gained their attention. Very young children will need to be taught the meaning of nonverbal signals such as those mentioned in the preceding paragraph, as they are seldom used by families: "When I turn the lights on and off like this (demonstrate), stop what you are doing, stop talking, and look at me. Let's practice it once."

7. **Distribute your time and attention fairly.** One of the aspects of authority is the control of time and attention. Distribute these fairly. To be fair does not necessarily mean to be exactly the same. Some children will need more assistance than others. If it is based on obvious needs, then children perceive that this is fair and that you are a supportive adult in their world.

Enhancing Children's Nonverbal Behavior through Teaching and Coaching

1. **Model effective nonverbal behaviors, and point these out to children as necessary.** Make sure your voice, facial expression, and words match as you communicate with children. Get down to children's level. Make eye contact. All of these behaviors model interest. Periodically, draw younger children's attention to the nonverbal cues you are displaying. For instance, "Look at my face. I am not smiling. I am worried someone will get hurt." More subtly, you might do something like suggest that a child smile at another if they want to be friends, while smiling at them.

2. **Help children decipher other children's nonverbal cues.** Occasionally, a child will overlook or misunderstand another child's nonverbal behavior. Reinforce the meaning of the cue verbally and explain the other child's intent. "Look at Sam. He is frowning. He doesn't want you to take crackers from his plate." Or, "Tanya is laughing a little. That may not mean she is happy right now. Sometimes people laugh when they feel uncomfortable or embarrassed." Or, "Raj is pulling back. He doesn't want to hold the snake just yet." Or, "Watch Rob. See how he is looking at you. Rob is showing that he is interested in your idea."

3. **Teach children nonverbal skills they may not demonstrate on their own.** Some children need help remembering to make periodic eye contact, or to smile when someone smiles at them, or to use a moderately pitched voice instead of squealing or whining. Remind children

of these nonverbal actions and model as necessary. Teach children how to behave in new situations. Demonstrate what to do, if necessary. How to shake hands, how to vary one's voice when giving a speech or reading a story, or how to establish a comfortable distance when talking to someone else, are examples of situations in which some children might benefit from coaching.

Applying Nonverbal Communication Skills to Interactions with Family Members

1. **Approach family members with a relaxed body posture and a smile of welcome.** Family members come to the program for a variety of reasons. If child safety is not jeopardized by your doing so, walk up to the parents, greet them, and ask if you can be of assistance. Some beginning professionals may appear to be cold and indifferent when they are feeling a little shy or timid in initial interactions with parents, so remember that the professional role is to help parents feel at ease and comfortable.

2. **Orient your body for a face-to-face interaction in close proximity to the family member with whom you are interacting.** This is the normal pattern for personal interaction between adults and should be comfortable for both of you. However, if you are observing children at the same time, ask the parent to step further inside the room or position yourself so that you can continue to supervise children, and explain this to the parent.

3. **Maintain eye contact for brief interactions or alternate between child focus and adult focus.** For example, shift your focus from the parent to the child as appropriate to maintain the interaction while assisting children to enter and leave. In a classroom, you might seat yourself while the parent is seated or stand as necessary to maintain eye contact.

4. **Speak with normal to soft volume and normal to low pitch.** Try to achieve a voice quality that is relaxed, serious, and concerned. The nonverbal communication strategies for warmth, respect, and acceptance are the same for adults and children. Many friendly encounters help to establish rapport between adult family members and the staff.

5. **When family members communicate, pay attention to their nonverbal behavior, and maintain your nonverbal channels**

appropriately for their message to you and the message you want them to receive. For a worried family member, a look of confidence in the professional is reassuring. When someone is distressed or angered, a serious expression and a firm, quiet tone is appropriate; a nervous giggle or laugh would irritate them even more. A smiling face and general tone of friendliness are appropriate when a child tells a funny story but probably would not be appropriate if a parent of the opposite sex told an off-color joke at pickup time. The nonverbal messages that you send parents are much better communicators about your professionalism and your feelings about them than any other mode of communication.

6. **Maintain expressiveness in your written electronic communications with families, but keep them at a minimum!** The ☺ at the end of a short information message is perceived as you being more warm and approachable. Make wise choices in the photographs you select to present directly to families or through other adult venues. Parents know how to Google!

Pitfalls to Avoid naeyc

Regardless of whether you are using nonverbal communication techniques with children individually or in groups, informally or in structured activities, you should try to avoid certain pitfalls.

1. **Giving inconsistent nonverbal messages or nonverbal messages inconsistent with the verbal content.** Do not smile when you are angry, stating a rule, or trying to convey an admonition or your displeasure. Do not use a loving tone of voice while giving an admonition, or use a cold, distant tone while expressing approval or affection. Such double-bind messages result in confusion or distrust on the part of children.

2. **Acting before thinking.** Uninformed, unthinking adults sometimes behave nonverbally in ways that may be insensitive or insulting to others. Using a loud voice and speaking slowly will not help a non-English-speaking person understand. Quickly judging a 12-year-old with purple, spiked hair and responding angrily toward him is more likely to elicit rebellion than cooperation. Although genuine and honest responses are appropriate, thoughtful responses are also necessary to move toward positive relationships and understanding others. This is one of the differences between professionals and untrained persons. Professionals have and use information that will enable them to be more effective than do others who must rely solely on their own life experiences.

3. **Demonstrating warmth, acceptance, genuineness, empathy, and respect only to those children who comply or who meet with your approval.** Using nonverbal behavior to help develop positive relationships with children is necessary if you are to influence improved social development in every child. Without it, you will be ineffective. Additionally, other children are keen observers of your behavior and may perceive that you are untrustworthy, diminishing your overall effectiveness with all children.

4. **Hurting or threatening to hurt children.** Some nonverbal means of getting attention, such as rapping children on the head with a pencil, yanking them to get into line, or using excessive force to hold them in place so you can talk, are aggressive and inappropriate. Imminent violence is signaled by a raised hand or fist, looming over, forceful grasping, or glaring in extremely close proximity. Causing fear and pain to a child is definitely inconsistent with the NAEYC Code of Ethics, which affirms that professionals first do no harm.

5. **Using "baby talk."** Parents and intimates may use baby talk as a form of affection. Professionals who work with children must establish clear communication based on respect for the child (Denton, 2007). Avoid using a falsetto voice, using the diminutive form of common words (horsie, doggie), using sound substitutions (twain instead of train), or using the first person plural instead of "you" ("How are we today?"). Particularly offensive is adding diminutives on personal names when the family uses the regular form (Ralphie instead of Ralph).

6. **Interrupting children.** Allow children the chance to speak. Do not complete sentences for them even if you think you know what they mean. Do not try to fill the normal hesitations of a child's speech with your own words. Interrupting children and finishing sentences for them is intrusive, patronizing, and disrespectful. Let children choose the words to use, and do not hurry them along. This demonstrates good listening skills, providing a positive example for children to follow (Jalongo, 2008).

7. **Yelling or shouting at children.** More effective ways have been described for getting the attention of children. In addition, loud or shrill voices can be frightening. Such behavior in adults usually indicates that the adult has lost self-control.

8. **Calling to children from across the room.** In neutral or positive situations, adults usually remember to walk over to children and speak to them directly. However, in emergencies or when danger threatens, this procedure often is forgotten. In such a situation, you may attempt to regulate a child by calling out a warning. Unfortunately, this usually is ineffective because children do not always know the message is directed toward them. In addition, they may startle and thereby get hurt. Take a few seconds and move toward the child to deliver the message.

9. **Placing your hand over your mouth, on the chin, or otherwise covering your face and mouth.** If you are covering part of your face when speaking, your speech may be unclear or misunderstood, and your facial expressions may not be fully visible. Wearing hats such as baseball caps indoors may shadow your face so much that your expressions cannot be readily seen. Give children the chance to see your face clearly.

10. **Ignoring family members who are in reasonably close proximity.** When any adult approaches a caregiver, simple courtesy is always appropriate. Ignoring them gives the impression of indifference or of being rude. Adults may or may not be parents, so identifying them appropriately is also a safety issue for the children in your care.

Summary

People use nonverbal behaviors to efficiently and subtly communicate their feelings about a relationship as well as to convey the substance of the verbal message they are sending. Other functions for nonverbal communications are to substitute for the spoken word, regulate interactions, indicate identity and status, share emotions, hide real feelings, and pretend. They can be used to build a relationship and strengthen children's social competence. Nonverbal messages usually are implicit and often fleeting and therefore can be denied or misinterpreted.

Each of the channels, or modes, of nonverbal communication can work independently of the others and can complement or contradict the spoken message. Channels of position in space, body motion, body orientation, touch, and gesture all require physical movement in relation to the other person. Facial expression and paralinguistics are also very powerful communicators.

In the course of their every day interactions with others, people communicate impressions related to the relationship between them. Most often, these messages are conveyed nonverbally, rather than verbally, to express warmth, acceptance, genuineness, empathy, and respect.

Adults convey authority and security to children nonverbally by maintaining eye contact, using a firm confident voice, touching the child or being near the child. Children demonstrate dominance similarly, with smaller distances, with a relaxed open body orientation, fewer hesitations, louder voices, and vocal variability.

Messages that are consistent across all channels are more easily understood; in addition, the speaker sends the general message of honesty, genuineness, and integrity. Mixed messages—those that are not consistent across channels—are confusing to children, convey a general sense of deception or disinterest, cause children to distrust the adult, and are less likely to elicit the desired response.

Children learn to interpret nonverbal messages before they learn to deliberately send them. Most of their learning is based on imitation and in interaction with skilled communicators. Therefore, children exposed to effective communicators will themselves become more effective communicators. They also learn from direct instruction. Infants are able to detect mixed messages, and they rely substantially on the paralinguistic features of the message. As children get older, they become more skillful in understanding and sending nonverbal messages. They also tend to rely more on facial expressions in decoding messages, except when they detect deception.

Adults who understand the meanings of nonverbal messages can deliberately use them to enhance their effectiveness in communication. Skills have been presented that will increase your ability to nonverbally convey warmth, acceptance, genuineness, empathy, and respect, as well as authority. Using these skills will help you communicate clearly and develop positive relationships with children and their families.

Pitfalls have been identified that should be avoided. These will either prove ineffective or interfere with building positive relationships with children. Now that you understand some of the most basic components of communication with children, you are ready to explore ways in which these can be combined with verbal communication skills to facilitate the development of positive, growth-enhancing relationships with children and their adult family members.

Key Terms

acceptance
authority
axial space
channel of communication
display rules
distal space
duration
emblems
empathy
gestures

hesitations
illustrator gestures
intensity
internal space
mask smile
metacommunication
mixed message
nonlexical sounds
nonverbal communication

paralinguistics
personal space
pitch and tone
proximal space
respect
rhythm
silence
subjective time
tempo

Discussion Questions

1. Describe the functions of nonverbal communication, and how each is used in ordinary interactions.

2. How does nonverbal communication regulate social interaction?

3. Why is it necessary to describe how the different channels of nonverbal communication operate when discussing building relationships with young children?

4. Imagine watching two 10-year-olds in a face-to-face situation in which one is thrusting a stick at the other. What would be your interpretation of this event if the children were 12 feet apart; 3 feet apart; or quite close together? Why would you interpret these differently? What would you do?

5. Answer question 4 in relation to proximal, axial, and distal space. How would your interpretation and follow-up action be different if the children were 2 years old?

6. Why is it important to know something about the cultural heritage of children when interpreting the meaning of their nonverbal behaviors?

7. How do age, relationship, and gender affect nonverbal communication behaviors? Give examples.

8. Why should helping professionals use congruent verbal and nonverbal communications with children and strictly avoid incongruent messages?

9. Nonverbal communication, unlike language arts, is not formally taught in school. How do children learn about it?

10. How does your use of time in interactions with other people denote your social relationship to them?

11. Which nonverbal behaviors are most likely to convey warmth? Assertiveness?

12. Recall a time when you have been misinterpreted or when you misinterpreted someone else. Did you send or receive a mixed message (whether intentional or not)? Were cultural differences involved in the misunderstanding?

13. How do the nonverbal communications of adults contribute to building positive relationships with children?

14. Describe how nonverbal skills for adults compare with those for children.

Case Study Analysis

Read the case study on Marco in Appendix B and answer the following questions:

1. List the words or phrases that describe how (how much and when) Marco moves in one column, a word to describe the setting in the second, and how you would interpret his behavior in a third column.

2. List words or phrases that describe Marco's facial expressions, the situations when they occurred, and how you would interpret them.

3. Under what circumstances did the adults touch Marco? Who did Marco touch and under what circumstances?

4. In the episode dated 9/6, identify the nonverbal behaviors that Miss Snyder used that you consider effective. Were there moments that you think she

should have or could have been more effective? If so, what action should she have taken?

5. In what ways did the adults demonstrate warmth and inclusion to Marco by their actions?

6. What evidence did you see that the adults in this case study were sensitive to Marco's nonverbal signals?

Field Assignments

1. Observe two adults anywhere you can see them but not hear them. This may be in a mall, grocery store, or restaurant. Watch them and describe what you see. Record what you think the emotional tone or content of the interaction is. Include a description of the setting, position in space of each participant, body motions and orientation, gestures, and facial expressions.

2. Reread the guides for behavior to demonstrate warmth and caring as well as to demonstrate authority. Practice each one with one or two children in your field placement. Describe what you did and how the children responded. Evaluate how well you were able to use these skills.

3. In a group of children, practice smiling, keeping eye contact on a face-to-face level, and using strategies for conveying warmth. Observe the response of the children to your behavior. Describe their nonverbal behaviors as a response to your own.

4. Listen to a skilled adult giving directions to children. Note position in space, gestures, facial expression, tone of voice, and eye contact with the children. What did this person actually do? Compare to any other person interacting with children.

5. Compare the dress of any two adults in group situations with children. Listing all things that the people wore, determine whether or not the apparel was functional, and what you think it communicated to children and their parents.

6. Imagine that you are describing the behavior of a coworker. Use the following sentences in quotation marks and speak them aloud to another classmate to convey: (1) your respect and admiration for this person and then (2) your disdain and disrespect for the person. Use gestures, facial expression, paralinguistics, or other strategies to convey your meanings. Ask your listener if he or she could easily tell which message was which. "Ms. Reardson is a real professional. She knows a lot about the families. The children know that she means what she says. I could tell you a lot more if I had the time." What articles of the NAEYC Code of Ethics would you select to judge whether these communications are appropriate?

Reflect on Your Practice

Here is a sample checklist you can use to reflect on your use of the skills as a beginning professional. A more detailed classroom observation tool is available in Appendix C.

To promote children's effective communication through nonverbal communication:

✓ Move toward a child to whom you want to speak; respect personal space.

✓ Bend, sit, or squat to talk in a face-to-face conversation.

✓ Touch gently to comfort, show support, or to gain and keep a child's attention.

✓ Wait attentively for the child to finish speaking. Refrain from interrupting.

✓ Observe children, interpret their nonverbal signals, and respond to meet their needs or desires.

✓ Maintain the integrity of children's personal space.

✓ Use congruent verbal and nonverbal messages.

✓ Use medium volume, tempo, and pitch in talking to children.

✓ Employ a variety of nonverbal cues (facial expression, voice changes, gestures etc.) to support verbal communication.

4 Promoting Children's Positive Sense of Self through Verbal Communication

OBJECTIVES

On completion of this chapter, you should be able to:

Describe the developmental benchmarks associated with self-awareness, self-concept, and self-esteem.

Differentiate the characteristics of a positive verbal environment from a negative one.

Identify teacher practices that contribute to positive verbal environments.

Demonstrate verbal communication skills associated with promoting children's self-awareness and self-esteem

Recognize pitfalls to avoid in communicating verbally with children and their families.

NAEYC STANDARDS naeyc

1. Promoting Child Development and Learning
2. Building Family and Community Relationships
3. Observing, Documenting, and Assessing to Support Young Children and Families
4. Using Developmentally Effective Approaches to Connect with Children and Families
5. Using Content Knowledge to Build Meaningful Curriculum
6. Becoming a Professional

One day, Maddie was busy drawing this picture (Figure 4-1) at the table. She squinted her eyes, pursed her lips, and worked a long time. She carefully included the parts of her body and her family on her drawing. When she finished, she put down her marker with a satisfied, "There." followed by, "Want to see my picture? It's me and my family. See, here I am, and here is V, and here are the twinnies, and Mommy and Daddy. I'm big because I'm special. I am the second baby and a big sister . . . and that's important."

Maddie has a happy sense of self. As a preschooler, she is beginning to define who she is and who she is not and where she fits in the social world. Initially, that world consisted primarily of her family. Now it includes her preschool classroom too. As she interacts with people within these contexts, Maddie is expanding her understanding of self.

© Cengage Learning

Figure 4-1 Maddie and Her Family.

Children's Emerging Sense of Self naeyc

Children are not born knowing "who they are." That knowledge grows over time and comes about, not in isolation, but through interactions with others (Rose-Krasnor & Denham, 2009). The whole time children are navigating the social environment, they are gathering information about themselves, interpreting it, and incorporating that data into their understanding of self: *"How am I my own person? Can I make things happen? How do people react to me when I...? What do I know how to do? What do people like about me? What are things I like about myself?"* Gradually, these bits of information combine to help children develop a deeper answer to the question: "Who am I?" This increasingly complex self-definition is both a social and cognitive construct (Harter, 2012; Widen & Russell, 2003).

Children's interactions with people and objects, along with their intellectual interpretation of those experiences, contribute to each child's formation of a stronger more nuanced understanding of self (Lewis & Carpendale, 2004). Such understandings ultimately affect how children feel about themselves, how they interact with peers and adults, their expectations regarding the potential success or failure of social interactions, and their motivation to explore and learn new things (Thompson & Virmani, 2010; Domitrovich, Moore, & Thompson, 2012). The degree to which children believe they can influence their immediate environments and whether or not they think they can make contributions to society are also affected by the image they have of themselves and how they evaluate that self-image. Let's explore each facet of how the self operates, beginning with self-awareness.

Self-Awareness

The first and most basic social knowledge children acquire is that they are unique individuals separate from the people and environments that surround them. This understanding is termed **self-awareness** (Marsh, Ellis, & Craven, 2002). Newborns begin life closely merged with their caregiver. Gradually, through the process of individuation and separation (see Chapter 2), infants and young toddlers construct a rudimentary awareness of self that is increasingly discrete, physically and psychologically, from everyone else (Thompson & Goodman, 2009). For instance, at around 18 months, many children can look into a mirror and realize they are looking at themselves (Nielson, Suddendorf, & Slaughter, 2006). Within another six months, most children can point to themselves in a photograph. Two-year-olds' physical self-awareness is correspondingly evident in their language. They refer to themselves by name—"Me Michael!"—and use personal pronouns to claim favored possessions—"Mine" (Harter, 2012; Thompson, 2006). They also use labels such as "you," "he," and "she'" when referring to others, providing further evidence that they recognize, "I am me. I am not you. You are someone separate from me." By the end of their second year, children have a well-established sense that they are their own person, with the power to influence the people, things, and events around them (Laible & Thompson, 2008). This change from a helpless newborn, who cannot distinguish where she or he ends and the world begins, to a self-aware individual is a remarkable milestone of development (Bjorklund, 2012). It underlies all the growth in social understanding and social competence that follows, including each child's construction of a unique self-concept.

Self-Concept

Marc is creating a "ME Book" with the help of his teacher. He says,

I am five.

I have blonde hair.

I have an Angry Birds blanket.

I like to play hockey.

I didn't used to skate backwards, now I can!

These statements reflect Marc's self-concept. Whereas self-awareness is the recognition that one is an individual separate from other people, **self-concept** involves the combination of physical and psychological attributes, abilities, attitudes, and values that define a person and make him or her an individual (Shaffer, 2009). As with most developmental processes,

To describe himself, this preschooler says, "I have brown hair and a yellow shirt. I jump high."

© Cengage Learning

self-concept proceeds from concrete, simplistic definitions to more abstract, complex conceptualizations. Developing one's self understanding starts early and continues throughout childhood and adolescence.

Very early childhood. When children first acquire language, they use age and gender as obvious attributes to describe who they are (Derman-Sparks & Edwards, 2010). Toddlers proudly announce: "Me two." "I a boy." Gradually, children ages 2, 3, and 4 expand these categories and begin defining themselves in tangible, observable terms (Harter, 2012). Their self-descriptions include the following:

- Physical attributes ("I have brown eyes.")
- Abilities ("I can climb the ramp.")
- Possessions ("I have a bike.")
- Relationships ("I have a big sister.")
- Preferences ("I like ice cream and chocolate.")

It is common for children's verbal declarations to spill over into actual demonstrations such as drawing a picture of themselves and their family, climbing the ramp, or "showing off" on the bike. Although young children also identify what they like or do not like about certain objects or activities ("I like playing baby dolls," and "I don't like peas"), rarely do preschoolers provide psychological descriptions of themselves (such as, "I'm sad," or, "I'm a friendly person"). Their thinking, and therefore, their self-concept is immediate, concrete, and tied to specific experiences, not internal states (Bjorklund, 2012). For the same reason, children this age make no real connection among the multiple facets of the self they identify. Instead, just like the individual pages of his ME Book, Marc treats each self-reference as highly individualized and isolated from the rest. This is because very young children do not have a fully integrated or cohesive self-concept (Harter, 2012). That comes later.

Early to middle childhood. Age, gender, possessions, abilities, relationships, and preferences continue to be features for defining "me" and "not me" during the early elementary years. However, at ages 5, 6, and 7, children shift from their previous here-and-now focus to thinking about past, present, and future. They expand their definitions of self to include comparisons of what they can do currently versus what they could do at earlier ages (Harter, 2012). Typical statements are "I can run faster now than I used to," or "When I was little I was scared of the dark, but I'm not scared anymore." These contrasts occur as children see the growth in themselves and are not intended as boasts but rather as descriptors of changes in their development. Children also begin to project what they might do in the future, "When I grow up I'm going

to be a chef!" or, "Next year I'll be big enough to ride a horse." Simultaneously, children start to string together related actions to describe a more complete self. As a second grader, Marc might say, "I can run, jump, and climb." Or, "I know how to read, and I'm good in math." In this way, the isolated fragments that typified prior self-understandings start to come together more comprehensively and cohesively. (See the downloadable ME Book directions for a template you can share with young children as they practice describing who they are.)

ME Books

Goal: For children to define essential attributes, abilities, actions, and preferences that make them unique

Directions: Assist children in describing themselves on paper. Children may dictate words, use photographs from home or school, use pictures from magazines, or draw. Bind the individual pages together into a ME Book. Encourage children to refer to and update their ME Books throughout the year by adding to the lists on each page or adding new pages to the books as relevant. Keep the books available for children to refer to and use in talking about themselves.

Sample Pages: This is "me"—self-portrait or digital photo
I am or I have… (child's self-description in words, e.g., I am a boy, I have red hair, etc.)
This is my family—family portrait
Here is my hand/foot—hand or foot tracing
Here are things I can do….
These are things I like….
This is what I like to do at school…
These are my friends….
I used to… now I….

Digital Download   Download from CourseMate

Middle to later elementary age. A significant shift in children's self-concept occurs between the ages of 8 and 11. Now their answers to the question, "Who am I?" encompass not only visible characteristics but also internal qualities and emotional references (I am dependable, I am happy) (Harter, 2012). In the school years, besides using their former self as a benchmark for comparison, children compare themselves with their peers in terms of appearance, abilities, and accomplishments. Marc says, "I run faster than PJ. Rebecca spells better than me." Such contrasts help children bring their own attributes into sharper focus and further distinguish them from others. Continuing to refer to their abilities, children categorize them into specific areas of competence—such as academic, social, or physical—and then differentiate among them. This enables children to see variations within their performance as components of their self-definitions. "I'm good at math. I'm not so good in sports" (Harter, 2012). In addition, interpersonal relationships are more essential features of self-concept: "I am Sarah and Josie's friend"; "I'm Jerome's sister's friend." This more sophisticated view is possible because children's perceptions are influenced by what they have done in the past as well as by what they might do or be like in the future. Eventually, their self-descriptions refer to patterns of behavior that have been established over time and that they perceive will continue (I am smart; I am shy; I am a hard worker). Thinking of the self in these terms represents a more abstract internal orientation, which has become possible through increased experience and more advanced cognitive powers. Hence, children enter adolescence with much greater self-awareness and a more integrated self-concept than was evident earlier in their lives.

By the early elementary years children make differing judgments about their abilities in one area, such as music, versus another, such as athletics.

© Cengage Learning 2015

▶❚❚   TeachSource Video 4-1

5–11 Years: Self-Concept in Middle Childhood

Go online and view *5–11 Years: Self-Concept in Middle Childhood*.

In this video, you will observe children describing how they view themselves.

1. What information is in the video that you have read about in relation to how children think about who they are?

2. What do the children seem to know now that might not have been part of their self-concepts three years ago?

3. Three years from now, what characteristics might children add to their notions of self?

Watch on CourseMate

Self-Esteem

Aren't you the best baby!

How many times have I told you to stop fidgeting! Now stop it.

Wait. Let's give Manny a chance to tell us his story.

Rochelle, you're back! We've missed you.

Self-esteem is a product of social experience. As children interact with family members, other familiar adults, and their peers, each person serves as a "mirror" through which children see themselves and then judge what they see (Epstein, 2009). Accordingly, how people relate to children, talk about them, and react to their successes and mistakes send powerful messages to children about their value and capabilities. If what is reflected is perceived by the child to be good, children make positive evaluations of the self. If the image perceived by the child is negative, then children make less favorable assessments. Beginning at birth, children build a history of experience that eventually leads some to conclude the following:

- I am someone people like.
- I know lots of things.
- I can do many things.
- I can choose and make decisions.
- I like myself.

Other children may decide the following:

- I am not someone people like.
- I don't know many things.
- There's a lot I can't do.
- I can't make choices or decisions.
- I don't like myself very much.

This evaluative component of the self is **self-esteem**. Self-esteem has three dimensions: worth, competence, and control (Bagwell & Schmidt, 2011). Each contributes to whether or not children see themselves as likeable, capable people who have some power over the world in which they live (Hewitt, 2002).

Worth. The extent to which people value and like themselves, as well as perceive that they are valued by others is a measure of their **worth**. Worth prompts the questions we have all heard children ask (in words or through their actions): *"Do you like me?" "How much do you like me?" "Why do you like me?" "Would you like me even if I…?" "Do I like myself?"* Relationships are a particular sign of worth and are measured by answering, "Who cares about me?" and in turn, "Who are the people I care about?" Consequently, children calculate their value by the relationships they have or don't have: *"You're MY mommy!" "Miss Amy is my teacher." "I am a big sister." "Shelia is my friend." "Carla doesn't want to be friends with me."*

Competence. The degree to which individuals believe that they can accomplish things and achieve their goals represents **competence**. When children act on objects, try new tasks, explore their emerging capabilities, and interact with peers and adults, they are learning, *"What can I do? How well can I do it? Can I be successful? Do people approve of what I am doing?"* The answers children acquire through their day-to-day activities either support or detract from their feelings of competence.

Control. The dimension of **control** refers to how much influence individuals have on outcomes and events in their lives. Exercising control is something children practice in many realms—an infant prolongs an interaction with the caregiver by smiling and cooing; a toddler chooses the red cup, not the green one; a preschooler manages to fasten his own coat; a vhome from the library; and, a school-age child

The playground offers many opportunities for Elka to practice skills that contribute to her sense of competence and control.

constructs a small engine that works! As children act on the world and observe the impact of their actions, they form beliefs about how much, when, and what kinds of control they can exercise.

"Trio of self-esteem." Each time children encounter a new situation, they make three judgments: Am I valuable? Am I capable? What can I influence and how? These internal reflections provide a personal assessment of worth, competence, and control. Sometimes their evaluations are conscious and sometimes not. In either case, the answers children glean provide important information that they add to their store of self-knowledge and personal standards. The three dimensions of self-esteem are depicted in Figure 4-2. Note that they are portrayed within a circle and that they are described as a "trio" to reinforce the notion that they are interrelated and all three are equally important. Take a moment to consider how these three dimensions operate in combination to influence Teresa's evaluation of her "self" on her first day in a new school. Her internal judgments regarding her worth, competence, and control are presented in Highlight 4-1.

Teresa interpreted her first contact with her new teacher as an affirmation of her worth, competence, and control. However, with a different set of experiences, she might have come to different conclusions. For instance,

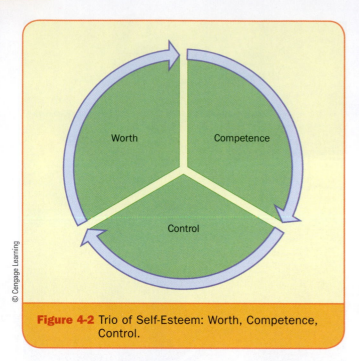

© Cengage Learning

Figure 4-2 Trio of Self-Esteem: Worth, Competence, Control.

Teresa and the Trio of Self-Esteem

Seven-year-old Teresa enters the room of her second grade class for the first time mid-year, having just moved to the community. She glances nervously as she surveys the space. A smiling adult approaches her. She squats down to Teresa's eye level and greets her with, "Well, Hello. You must be Teresa! We are so happy you will be joining our class. We have lockers back here. Here is yours. It has your name on it. Later, I'll take your picture and put it up on the board with the other children's. Let me show you and your mom some of the interesting things around the room. We are working on projects right now. You can check things out and then decide where you'd like to start."

Simultaneously, Teresa's brain is analyzing the situation and helping her interpret and assess her relative worth, competence, and control in this new place. Although she is not necessarily mindful of her thoughts, they are contributing to her self-evaluation.

Teresa's assessment of worth, "Am I valuable?"

Teresa thinks: The teacher was glad to see me, I have my own locker, and she's going to take my picture . . . I could "belong" here.

Teresa's assessment of competence, "Am I capable?"

Teresa thinks: There seem to be many things going on around the room. I've seen some of this before in my old school. I think I could try . . .

Teresa's assessment of control, "What can I influence and how?"

Teresa thinks: I get to pick where I'd like to start! This sounds great!

if the teacher was preoccupied when she greeted the newcomer, Teresa might have assumed that she was not valued. If Teresa had few prior experiences working with children in small groups, she may have concluded that getting acclimated to the new routine would require new skills she did not yet have. Or, if the free movement of the children from one area to another was unlike her old second-grade class, she might have interpreted the situation as chaotic and difficult to control. Whatever Teresa ultimately concludes will depend on her perceptions of the situation in light of her prior experiences, culture, temperament, relationships with others, language, and her current definition of self.

What Teresa experienced in her new school will contribute to, but not solidify, her self-esteem. It takes hundreds and hundreds of occurrences large and small for children to gradually construct an enduring sense of self. Self-esteem like all other aspects of child development is an evolving concept that comes about through the interplay of development and experience.

The Evolution of Self-Esteem

Making judgments about the self begins early and becomes increasingly elaborate as children mature. Very young toddlers manifest their first self-evaluations when they smile as they complete a task given to them by an adult, such as stacking the cubes or putting a shape in the right space. They register negative self-appraisals when they look away or frown if they fail (Berk, 2013). As soon as preschoolers can use words to express self-judgments, they do. We hear this when children say things like, "I'm a good boy" or, "Those kids like me."

Such comments illustrate this age group's global estimations of self-esteem and underscore the fact that they do not make distinctions among individual components of the self, such as the social self versus the physical self. Those distinctions start to emerge as 4- and 5-year-olds reflect on individual actions, such as how well they can throw a ball or how high they can count. Initially, children's judgments are mostly positive, and it is not uncommon for them to overestimate their abilities, "I can throw this ball over the house" or, "I can count to 100; want to hear me?" (Harter, 2012). Such inaccuracies reflect children's cognitive limitations and inexperience, not deliberate self-deception. Most children this age tend to be incredibly pleased with themselves and proud of their newly developing powers. They perceive little differentiation between the "real self" and the "ideal self" they envision. This is vividly illustrated in Veronica's self-portrait shown in Figure 4.3.

Figure 4-3 Veronica's View of Self at Age 5.

© Cengage Learning

During the early elementary years, children begin to compartmentalize their self-evaluations. They make different judgments about the self in at least four categories of competence—social, academic, physical/athletic, and physical appearance (Harter, 2012). By age 8, most children make essential distinctions about their abilities in each of these areas. From then on, self-esteem is a multifaceted combination of perceptions (Harter, 2012). Within this context, a child may have positive feelings in relation to academics, while feeling less adequate athletically. Recognizing perceived inadequacies in a particular realm contributes to the "reality checks" children make during this period but does not necessarily contribute to a diminished sense of self. The relative significance of a particular category to an individual child also factors into his or her self-judgment. Consequently, a child may conclude, "I'm not good at fixing things and that's okay." By middle to late childhood, most children make both positive and negative evaluations of the self, and they do so with greater accuracy than was true early in life (Harter, 2012).

This more advanced level of self-evaluation goes hand in hand with children's deepening self-awareness and self-concept. Take a moment to review the developmental progressions associated with all three facets of children's emerging sense of self as outlined in Table 4.1. Notice how the evolution of self-awareness, self-concept, and self-esteem parallel one another.

Table 4-1 The Emergence of the Self

Age	Birth to 1	2–4	5–7	8–11
	Infancy	Very early childhood	Early to middle childhood	Middle to later childhood
Description of Self	Emerging sense of self as separate from caregiver	Self is defined by concrete, observable attributes. Child focuses on one attribute at a time. Self is located in the here and now.	Self is defined by concrete, observable attributes. Child strings related concrete attributes into more comprehensive descriptions (I can run fast. I jump high. I can throw the ball.) Self involves current self, past self, and future self.	Self is defined using internal as well as external attributes. Child assigns attributes to categories: social, academic, physical, and appearance. Self includes enduring traits and longstanding patterns of behavior.
Use of Comparisons	None	None	Child makes comparisons with current self and former self.	Child makes social comparisons between self and others.
Self-Evaluations	Beginning awareness	Overall positive view. Doesn't see negatives of self. Overestimates abilities.	Overall positive view. Doesn't see negatives within self. Overestimates abilities. Child sees real self and ideal self as the same.	Aware of multiple aspects of self: positive and negative. Evaluates self in terms of categories: social, academic, physical, and appearance. Differentiates evaluations among the categories. More self-critical than previously; more accurate in personal assessments.

Source: Based on Harter (2012)

Variations in Children's Self-Esteem

Although all children go through similar developmental sequences on their way to better self-understanding, each child comes to his or her own conclusions regarding the trio of self-esteem. Some children will enter adolescence with a strong sense of worth, competence, and control, and other children will have less favorable self-perceptions. These variations have significant ramifications for each child. Consider how variations in self-esteem may be affecting how Amalia and Ronda respond to building towers in the preschool.

> Using empty grocery containers of different sizes, Amalia and Ronda place one container on top of another until the uppermost one reaches four feet in the air. Three times, when the structure gets this high, it falls down. After the third spill, Ronda howls, "I'll never get this to stay up!" She leaves the area in distress. Amalia has also tried different approaches—none is working. She looks over at Soo-Young's structure, then says, "I know…," and tries something else.

Amalia and Ronda have both experienced frustration, but each reacted in a different way. Ronda tried and then gave up. Amalia persisted despite difficulty. In this situation, Amalia's inner store of self-perceptions and skills enabled her to persist regardless of the immediate setbacks she was experiencing. Scientists observing this episode might say that Amalia, more so than Ronda, exhibited behaviors indicative of healthy self-esteem (Gartrell, 2012).

People whose self-judgments lead them to believe that they are loveable human beings, with useful knowledge and skills, and the ability to influence some of the events in their lives are said to possess healthy self-esteem. Children who feel rejected or ignored, who believe they do not possess the skills to succeed in life, and who feel helpless to influence what happens to them, are described as having poor self-esteem. Which of these perceptions dominate a child's thinking over time will profoundly affect his or her happiness and well-being (Furnham & Cheng, 2000).

Healthy self-esteem. Children whose self-evaluations are mostly positive feel good about themselves (Harter, 2012). They see themselves as likeable, capable people, whose decisions and actions make a positive difference in their own lives and in the lives of others. Their feelings of worth, competence, and control prompt them to regard most social encounters as potentially rewarding and most tasks as ultimately doable (NICHD, 2002). When confronted with obstacles, children with healthy self-esteem draw on rewarding feelings from the past to help them get through difficult times. And, because they are hopeful and confident in their abilities, they stick with difficult tasks rather than giving up when not immediately successful (Baumeister et al., 2003). By the later elementary years, children with healthy self-esteem are able to appraise their abilities and limitations realistically and are able to separate weaknesses in one area from successes in others (Harter, 2012). This gives them valuable tools for recognizing their strengths, rather than dwelling primarily on their weaknesses, and for using those strengths to solve problems and test alternatives. For all these reasons, healthy self-esteem is related to happiness, positive life satisfaction, and good mental health.

Poor self-esteem. In contrast, poor self-esteem is associated with depression, anxiety, suicidal thinking, and maladjustment (Harter, 2012; Leary & McDonald, 2003). It is also related to aggression, antisocial behavior, and delinquency (Donnellan et al., 2005). Children whose estimations of worth, competence, and control are generally negative, experience feelings of inadequacy, incompetence, fear, and rejection. They are less likely to be objective about their capabilities and to focus mostly on their weaknesses. Such children have little hope that they can influence others and anticipate that most interactions will be costly for them. They are convinced that no matter how hard they try, their efforts will usually go unrewarded. This gloomy outlook often leads them to build elaborate defenses as a way to protect their fragile egos or to ward off expected rejection. Typical means of self-protection include putting themselves down, keeping people at a distance, or building themselves up by hurting others physically or psychologically (Berk, 2013). In all these ways, poor self-esteem detracts from children's quality of life and that of the people around them.

Self-esteem is not all or nothing. At one time, people envisioned healthy self-esteem and poor self-esteem as two sides of a balance scale with individuals clustered entirely on one side or the other. In actuality, people's self-evaluations tend to fall along a continuum of perceptions between two opposite ends—positive and negative (Denham, Bassett, & Wyatt, 2008). Children with healthy self-esteem make more self-judgments within the positive range than within the negative range. Children with poor self-esteem have the opposite pattern of self-evaluations. It is important to note that no single event determines whether a child's self-esteem is more or less healthy. Accumulated experience is what counts, both plus and minus. For instance, not being invited to another child's birthday party may hurt for a while but will probably not cause permanent damage to a child's self-esteem. However, a child who is subjected to constant rejection by his or her peers could develop lasting feelings of inadequacy (Brown, Odom, & McConnell, 2008).

In the early years, self-esteem is malleable, with children making both positive and less positive self-assessments, depending on the circumstances. Gradually, as children mature, previous experiences set the tone for how they interpret new ones. If the preponderance of their interpretations have been toward the healthy end of the spectrum, children are likely to anticipate positive outcomes and to behave in ways that support that belief. On the other hand, if children's evaluations are concentrated more within the poor self-esteem range, children tend to expect more of the same, and behave in ways that fulfill those expectations (Frost, Wortham, & Reifel, 2011). As this happens again and again, children's self-esteem becomes more enduring in one direction or the other.

Seeing self-esteem in action. Children don't generally verbalize their self-evaluations. More commonly, they manifest self-esteem through observable behaviors (Harter, 2006, 2012). Typical behaviors associated with variations in self-esteem are reflected in Figure 4-4.

Reconsider the example of Amalia and Ronda building towers. Which of the outcomes cited in this chart do you see reflected in their behavior? If you were their teacher, what might you do to support the children's development? In thinking about your response, you may wonder where self-awareness and self-understanding fit in the P–K curriculum. Or you may ask, as important as it seems, how does this facet of child development and learning stack up against all the other curricular standards early childhood programs and schools must address? Recently, the Collaboration for Academic, Social, and Emotional Learning (CASEL) reviewed state standards for learning across the United States and identified self-understanding as the first and most crucial social-emotional learning standard most states have for

Children Who Exhibit Healthy Self-Esteem Tend to:	Children Who Exhibit Poor Self-Esteem Tend to:
• Demonstrate confidence in their own ideas	• Lack confidence in their own ideas
• Approach challenges with confidence	• Avoid challenges
• Initiate activities and interactions	• Fail to initiate activities or interactions
• Set goals independently	• Hang back
• Express curiosity	• Wait for someone else to take over or set the goal
• Explore and question	• Withdraw and sit apart
• Try new things eagerly	• Describe self in negative terms ("I'm so dumb." "I'll never learn how to do this!")
• Describe self in positive terms ("I can do it!" "I am learning a new way to do math.")	• Fail to show pride in own work
• Show pride in work	• Give up quickly
• Persist at difficult tasks	• React to stress with immature behavior
• Tolerate frustration	• Engage in antisocial behavior in response to accidents or others' mistakes
• Adjust to changes and transitions	

Figure 4-4 Behaviors Associated with Healthy and Poor Self-Esteem.

Source: Based on Harter (2012)

children from preschool through elementary school (Domitrovic et al., 2012). The nationwide components of this standard are presented in Figure 4-5. Notice how these national standards align with the three components of self-understanding you have just been reading about: 1) self-awareness, 2) self-concept, and 3) self-esteem.

Recognizing that self-understanding is a key curriculum standard nationwide is valuable knowledge;

Domain	Social-emotional learning standards
Self-Understanding	1. Child perceives and values self as a unique individual.
	2. Child demonstrates awareness of abilities, preferences, and characteristics.
	3. Child demonstrates belief in abilities, self-confidence.

© Cengage Learning 2015

Figure 4-5 State Standards.

Source: Based on Domitrovic et al. (2012)

however, it is not enough to ensure best practice. You must also know what skilled teachers and caregivers do to translate that knowledge into action. That is what the rest of this chapter will be about.

How Adult Practices Influence Children's Self-Esteem

Adults who demonstrate warmth, acceptance, genuineness, empathy, and respect (WAGER) are most likely to foster positive self-judgments in children. Parents and teachers exhibit these esteem-enhancing qualities when they show affection toward children, when they take an interest in what children are doing, when they give children opportunities to create and do things, and when they give children chances to plan, make decisions, and carry out projects (Eccles, 2007). In contrast, children who experience adults who are rejecting, emotionally unavailable, or nonsupportive, construct a model of the self that is unlovable, incompetent, and helpless. Adults display these negative attitudes when they ignore or are indifferent toward children and when they are impatient, discourteous, or harsh toward them (Harter, 2012).

Although adults communicate their attitudes toward children in many ways, the most obvious and powerful sign is how they talk to them. Language influences children's sense of self. What adults say to children and how they say it can deeply affect children's ideas of who they are and who they might become. Thus, adult words have a special power that should not be underestimated (Denton, 2007). Consider the following scenario:

> You are invited to visit a program for children. When you arrive, you are asked to wait until the youngsters return from a field trip. As you survey your surroundings, you notice natural wood furniture comfortably arranged, sunlight softly streaming through the windows, children's artwork pleasingly displayed, attractive materials that look well cared for, green plants placed about the room, and a large, well-stocked aquarium bubbling in a corner. You think to yourself, "What a pleasant place for children!" Just then, a child bursts into the room crying. An adult follows her, who snaps: "Rose, you're being a big baby. Now, hush." As the other children file in, you hear one say, "Look what I found outside!" An adult replies: "Can't you see I'm busy? Show it to me later." After a while, you overhear a child ask, "When do we get to take these home?" He is told, "If you'd been listening earlier, you'd know."

Your favorable impression is ruined. Despite the lovely surroundings, the ways in which adults are talking to children makes the setting seem cold and unfriendly. Adult comments have caused you to question whether it is possible for children to feel good about themselves in this program. What you have overheard has revealed an invisible but keenly felt component of every childhood setting—the verbal environment.

The Verbal Environment naeyc

The verbal environment encompasses all the verbal exchanges that take place within a given setting. Its elements include words and silence—how much is said, what is said, how it is stated, who talks, and who listens. The way in which these elements are used and combined dictates whether the environment is one in which children's sense of worth, competence, and control are strengthened or diminished. Thus, not all verbal environments are the same; some can be characterized as negative, whereas others can be described as positive. The differences between the two extremes are highlighted in Table 4-2. In each instance, how adults use language and what they expect from children's communications are the key differentials between them. As you will see, adult words can either open doors for children to learn more about themselves in positive ways, or adult talk can preclude such discoveries. Even worse, some adult talk may actually harm children's sense of self. Consider the distinctions between the two, and then we will focus on each verbal environment in turn.

Table 4-2 Contrasting Negative and Positive Verbal Environments

Negative Verbal Environments	Positive Verbal Environments
Adult language is hurtful (accusatory, demeaning, disrespectful).	Adult language promotes a sense of community and belonging (encouraging, responsive, respectful).
Adults use language to discourage child talk.	Adults use language to invite children to talk to the adults and to each other about things that interest them and what is happening in their lives.
Adults ignore child talk.	Adults listen carefully to children and respond to them in meaningful ways.
Adults use language primarily to keep children "in line," that is, to manage them.	Adults use language to build relationships with children and to help them learn new skills.
Children are passive receivers of information.	Adults use language to support children's autonomy and appropriate control (to help children make choices and decisions; use words to express wants, needs, and feelings).
Children mostly respond to adult directives.	Adults use language to help children become aware of themselves— what they are interested in, what they are feeling, what they are doing, how they are changing.
Children have few opportunities to talk with their peers.	Adults use language to promote peer conversations and to help children learn more about themselves through their interactions with each other.
Children use hurtful language in their interactions with peers; adults fail to redirect such behavior.	Adults use language to help children learn more effective interaction techniques and intervene when child talk becomes hurtful.

The Negative Verbal Environment

In negative verbal environments, children feel unworthy, incompetent, or ineffectual as a result of what adults do or do not say to them. You can readily identify the most extreme illustrations of these. Adults screaming at children, ridiculing them, cursing at them, or subjecting them to ethnic slurs are blatant examples of hurtful behaviors that could damage children's sense of self. Yet there are less obvious, more common adult behaviors that also contribute to negative verbal environments and that ultimately detract from children's self-awareness and self-esteem. Specific examples of these are presented in Table 4-3.

Negative verbal behaviors like the ones highlighted in Table 4-3 convey adult attitudes of aloofness; lack of acceptance, genuineness, and empathy; and disrespect. They cause the program to be dominated by adult talk and deprive children of natural opportunities to learn more about the self in all of its dimensions. Under such conditions, children quickly learn that their ideas, thoughts, and concerns are not valued, nor are they important enough to merit the courtesy and respect one would anticipate if held in high regard. The aversive use of language that characterizes a negative verbal environment tends to make children feel inadequate, confused, or angry (Jimerson, Swearer, & Espelage, 2010). If conditions such as these become the norm, then children's self-understanding is likely to suffer.

A different set of circumstances exists in programs characterized by a positive verbal environment.

© Cengage Learning 2015

Adults create a positive verbal environment by talking with children about the things that interest them.

Positive Verbal Environments

Classrooms characterized by a positive verbal environment are often filled with the pleasant hum of language—children talking to one another, children talking with adults about their experiences and things that matter to them, and adults using language to extend children's self-understandings and skills. Children who spend their time in such environments experience socially rewarding interactions with caregivers, teachers, and peers. Because adults use words to acknowledge and reach out to children, children feel valued (Thompson & Twibell, 2009). Adults listen carefully to children and respond to their messages thoughtfully. At all times when speaking with children, they concern themselves not only with the content of their words but also with the affective impact their messages will convey. Adult goals focus on helping children develop genuine feelings of worth, competence, and control, and adults use words to address this purpose. Some of the specific strategies teachers use to establish positive verbal environments are outlined in Table 4-4.

Positive verbal environments are beneficial to both the adults and children who participate in them. The strategies that define such settings provide obvious ways for adults to communicate warmth, acceptance, genuineness, empathy, and respect to children. This makes it more likely that children will view their caregivers and teachers as sources of comfort and encouragement and that they will experience the classroom as a secure place in which to live and learn (Epstein, 2009). In addition, adult–child interaction patterns enable children to learn more about themselves and to feel good about the self they are coming to know. For all these reasons, positive verbal environments are favorably associated with self-awareness, self-concept, and healthy self-esteem (Meece & Soderman, 2010).

Establishing a Positive Verbal Environment naeyc

Most teachers and caregivers would not knowingly act in ways to inhibit children's self-awareness or damage their self-esteem. However, at times, any one

Table 4-3   Adult Behaviors in a Negative Verbal Environment

Adult Behavior	Examples
Adult ignores children and neglects opportunities to talk with them.	• Fails to greet children or acknowledge them • Fails to talk with children or show interest in their activities • Responds grudgingly or with indifference when children approach him or her
Adult is preoccupied and pays superficial attention to children.	• Doesn't listen attentively to what children have to say • Asks irrelevant questions that show inattention • Has poor eye contact, and doesn't focus on child in front of him or her
Adult speaks discourteously to children.	• Cuts children off when children are talking to him or her, another adult, or other children • Insists children respond immediately to shifts in routine or new directions; does not allow children to finish what they are saying or doing • Uses impatient, demanding, or quarrelsome voice tone • Makes sarcastic remarks to child ("Did you leave your brain at home?") • Neglects social niceties such as "please" "thank you," and "excuse me"
Adult uses judgmental vocabulary to describe children.	• Describes children to other adults using negative terms and labels: hyper, selfish, lazy, pushy, and so on • Labels children negatively either directly or within child's hearing: ("You're so lazy." "You're such a baby." "Samantha is so selfish.") • Puts children "in their place" or makes fun of children: ("She thinks she is so smart that she doesn't have to pay attention.")
Adult ignores or demeans children's interests.	• Brushes off child's statement or question • Tells children to talk about something else ("I'm tired of hearing you tell me about Rory and your troubles. Talk about something else, or be quiet.") • Frequently tells children to stop what they are doing to follow the adult agenda ("You've seen the butterfly long enough. Now come sit down.")
Adult relies on giving orders and making demands as his or her primary means of relating to children.	• Verbalizations consist mostly of giving directions ("Sit in your chair. Open your book to the first blank page. Draw a line. Draw your picture ...")
Adult discourages children from expressing themselves.	• Asks questions that children are not really expected to answer ("What is your problem today?") • Tells children "Hush, talk to me later" (but later never comes) • Enforces long periods of silence
Adult uses children's names in a punitive way.	• Uses children's names to mean NO and DON'T and STOP (*DAVID!*) • Uses children's names mostly to correct them or in negative situations but not so often in positive ones ("David, how many times have I told you...?")
Adult use of praise is insincere or hurtful.	• Links positive behavior with negative put-down ("I'm glad you are sitting now, you've been out of your seat all day.") • Uses the same compliments with everyone for everything ("nice job," "good," "great") • Builds up one child at the expense of the others ("Jenna, you did so well; too bad no one else studied.") • Uses fake sweet voice
Adult allows children to contribute to a negative verbal environment as they talk to or about one another.	• Fails to intervene when children ignore or exclude other children • Fails to act when children speak hurtfully to one another or use sarcasm and judgmental words

Table 4-4 Adult Behaviors in a Positive Verbal Environment

Adult Behavior	Examples
Adult uses words to convey warmth to children.	• Greets children by name, invites them to interact with self or others • Responds to children cheerfully when approached or invited to interact • Uses words to show enjoyment of children's company ("That was fun" "I'm glad we had a chance to look at this book together.") • Laughs with children
Adult uses words to demonstrate interest in children.	• Remarks on children's activities ("You've been working hard on that puzzle.") • Notes children's accomplishments ("You've been waiting patiently for a turn with the iPad. Now it's time!") • Answers children's questions with relevant information or follow-up queries
Adult treats "child talk" as important.	• Makes eye contact and mirrors child's demeanor to demonstrate understanding • Listens attentively to each child—keeps focused on child • Invites children to elaborate on ideas • Allows children to finish telling "their story"
Adult speaks courteously to children.	• Allows children to complete what they are saying to others without interrupting • Uses social amenities such as please, thank you, and excuse me when talking to children • Uses objective language, not judgmental labels, when talking to or about children (Says, "Samantha wanted all the trucks for herself." Instead of, "Samantha is so selfish.")
Adult speaks with children conversationally throughout the day.	• Talks with individual children about their current needs/interests throughout the day (e.g., eating, painting, feeling anxiety about an upcoming test or the bus, etc.) • Has a minute or two of one-to-one conversation with each child each day • Creates routines that allow time for individual, small group, and whole group conversations
Adult uses language to build relationships with children.	• Nurtures children • Guides children's behavior • Expands children's verbal skills • Demonstrates interest in and respect for each child's family and culture
Adult encourages children to express themselves.	• Acknowledges children's comments, ideas, and feelings • Elicits children's observations, ideas, and opinions • Follows children's lead in conversations • Asks relevant questions for which real answers are desired • Nods, uses pauses, and says "Tell me more," to keep the conversation going
Adult uses children's names in a positive way.	• Pronounces children's names correctly (calls a Chinese child named Li Young by her full name rather than renaming her Lily) • Helps children learn each other's names • Refers to children by name in positive circumstances ("Mica, you did that all by yourself!")
Adult is genuine in his or her praise.	• Individualizes praise to fit specific situations • Acknowledges children's positive behaviors • Uses an enthusiastic voice tone that is sincere
Adult helps children develop verbal skills that contribute to a positive verbal environment.	• Encourages children to use words to show interest in one another • Provides scripts for children to use who are not sure of what to say • Intervenes when children use hurtful language and redirects their actions into more constructive directions

of us could unintentionally slip into negative verbal habits (Kostelnik & Grady, 2009). The following lists the most common reasons this happens:

- We underestimate the impact our words have on children.
- We speak without thinking.
- We get caught up in the hurried pace of the job and miss opportunities to have more personal and positive verbal interactions with children.
- We rely on our everyday ways of talking, rather than developing specific skills for talking to and with children.

Research tells us that positive verbal environments do not happen automatically or consistently without intent and forethought (Meece & Soderman, 2010). They require purposeful planning and careful implementation to become commonplace. They also oblige adults to learn new skills. Fortunately, the strategies associated with positive verbal environments are not difficult to acquire. However, to be effective, they must be used often and consistently. This takes practice and conscious effort. Some of the most useful strategies include behavior reflections, effective praise, conversations, open-ended questions, paraphrase reflections, and shared narratives. See Figure 4-6 for a graphic representation of these and then let's examine each one, beginning with behavior reflections.

Behavior Reflections

Behavior reflections are nonjudgmental statements to children regarding some aspect of their behavior

or person. The adult observes a child and then comments to the child about her or his physical attributes or activities. Such statements do not express opinion or evaluation but are exactly about what the adult sees in the child's actions (Tu & Hsiao, 2008).

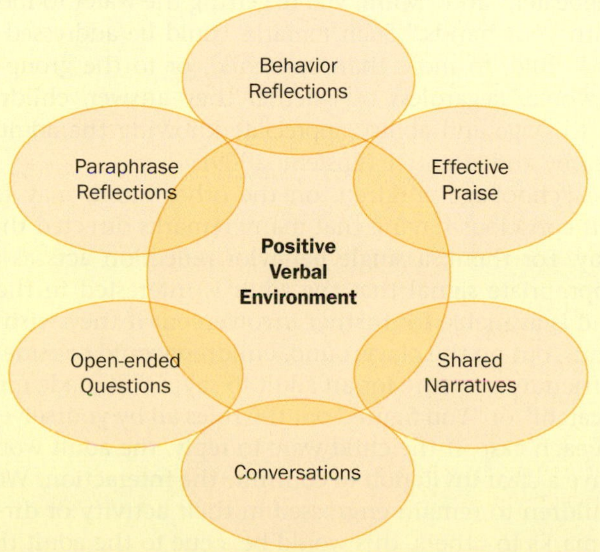

Situation: A child is coming down a slide on his stomach.

Adult: You're sliding down the slide. (Or: You found a new way to come down—you're sliding headfirst.)

Situation: Joe and Melissa are drawing a mural together.

Adult: You two are working together. (Or: Each of you has figured out a way to contribute to the mural; You're concentrating on what you are doing; You are cooperating—each of you has a part in the picture.)

Situation: A child arrives at a childcare center.

Adult: Jason, you're wearing your tennis shoes today. (Or: You look all ready to go; You look like you're carrying a heavy load!)

Notice that in each of the examples, the adult began with the child (You or name). Then, the behavior or concrete aspect (shoes) was observed. No action was taken to change the behavior. Of course there will be times to take action too, but not here, in the behavior reflection. This is simply a form of "reporting" what is evident without additional commentary.

The value to children of using behavior reflections. Behavior reflections are a powerful way to show an interest in children and to narrate their experiences. When adults reflect what children are doing, they talk about actions and experiences that have the most meaning for children—those in which they themselves are involved (Jalongo, 2008). Verbal observations such as these add to children's self-concept and help children build autobiographical memories to which they can refer over time. Behavior reflections also contribute to children's feelings of worth and competence because the adult notices them and takes the time to say aloud something they have done (Thompson, 2006; Tice & Wallace, 2003).

From these reflections, children learn that their everyday actions are important enough to be noticed and that extreme behavior is not needed to gain appropriate attention. This is an important concept for children to grasp because they sometimes assume that adults will only notice behavior that is out of the ordinary (Essa, 2008). Children's interpretations of "out of the ordinary" might include excelling in a particular area or acting out. Such conclusions are not surprising because in many group settings, you have to be the birthday child, or the one who gets all A's, or the child who pinches a lot in order to receive individual

Figure 4-6 Positive Verbal Environment Strategies.

(Figure contents: Behavior Reflections, Paraphrase Reflections, Effective Praise, Open-ended Questions, Shared Narratives, Conversations, surrounding Positive Verbal Environment)

© Cengage Learning

attention from adults. By reflecting, adults instead make note of such commonplace events as: "You're sharing the paint with Wally," or "You're trying hard to snap your coat," or "You noticed our math books are brand new." Simple comments such as these say to the child, "You are important." Because each takes only a few seconds to say, these comments are particularly useful to helping professionals who must work with more than one child at a time. Thus, while helping Nakita with her coat, the caregiver also can attend to Micah and Leon by saying: "Micah, you have almost every single button done," and "Leon, you wore your brown coat today," and to Nakita, "You figured out which arm to put in first." This spreads the attention around and helps Micah and Leon as well as Nakita perceive that the adult has taken them into account. An added benefit is that the children hear not only the messages directed at themselves but also those intended for children close by. This expands their opportunities to hear relevant language and to recognize verbal connections between their own experiences and those of their peers (Meece, Colwell, & Mize, 2007).

Because reflections do not evaluate behavior, children learn not to feel threatened by adult attention. The nonevaluative nature of the reflection enables adults to actively and concretely demonstrate acceptance of children; children interpret reflections as the adults trying to understand them better. Further, when used appropriately, behavior reflections require adults to consider the child's perspective within an interaction. Understanding what is important to a child about a particular activity by seeing it through the child's eyes sets the stage for adults to be more empathic in their responses to children (Epstein, 2009). Also, observing closely and taking cues from the children makes it more likely that children will feel good about the interactions that take place with the adult. Thus, an adult watching children dancing in a conga line might reflect: "You formed a really long conga line," or "Everybody's figured out a way to hang on," or "Everyone's smiling. You look like you're having fun." These are child-centered remarks that correspond to the children's agenda in that situation rather than the adult's.

Behavior reflections can also increase children's receptive language skills because children learn word meanings from hearing the words used to describe their immediate experiences (Epstein, 2007; Meece, 2009). This type of contextual learning occurs when children hear new words and varied ways of putting words together to describe day-to-day events. For instance, young children who hear the childcare provider observe on different occasions: "You are walking to the door," "You and Jeremy walked into the coatroom together," and "We were walking along and found a ladybug" will begin to comprehend the meanings of different verb forms based on their own direct involvement in each situation. When children experience new words or a range of new vocabulary, they become better able to

understand others and explain themselves (Byrnes & Wasik, 2009; Thompson, 2006).

Finally, the sheer act of directing language to the child using a behavior reflection increases the number of words in the child's world. The more language children experience directly, the easier it is for them to acquire new language and concepts, and the better they will do in future cognitive and social endeavors (Hart & Risley, 2003 Nemeth, 2012).

An added benefit of using behavior reflections is that they may serve as an opening for children to talk to adults if they wish. Often, children respond to the adult's reflections with comments of their own. Thus, a verbal exchange may develop that is centered on the child's interests. On the other hand, children do not feel compelled to answer every reflection they hear. For this reason, reflecting does not interrupt children's activities or make them stop what they are doing in order to respond to an adult query. Even when children remain silent, they benefit by being made aware of the adult's interest in them. Behavior reflections are ideal for talking to children as well as with them.

When to use behavior reflections. Behavior reflections can be used singly, in succession, and with other skills you will learn about. When interacting with toddlers, preschoolers, children whose primary language is not English, and children whose receptive language development has been delayed, it is appropriate to use a series of behavior reflections. For example, in a 10-minute interaction at the water table, the teacher might say: "You're pouring the water down the hose and watching it come out the other end," "You found a funnel to use," "You all remembered to put your smocks on," "Lucy, you're churning the water with an eggbeater," and "Mimi, you're getting the water to move with your hands." Such remarks could be addressed to one child, to more than one child, or to the group as a whole. Regardless of whether they answer, children of this age and ability appreciate knowing the adult is nearby and attentive (Epstein, 2009).

School-age children, on the other hand, may feel self-conscious having that many remarks directed their way. For them, a single behavior reflection acts as an appropriate signal that the adult is interested in them and is available for further involvement if they wish it. Thus, out on the playground, children would consider it a friendly overture for an adult to say: "You made quite a catch!" or "You figured out the rules all by yourselves." In each case, if the child were to reply, the adult would have a clear invitation to continue the interaction. Were children to remain engrossed in their activity or direct remarks to others, this would be a cue to the adult that a prolonged interaction was not desired at that time.

Both children and adults benefit when helping professionals use behavior reflections in their repertoire of

What behavior reflections might you use with these children?

communication techniques. Most importantly, behavior reflections afford adults an excellent means to show children they care about them (worth) and are interested in their activities (competence). Another purposeful skill to use in speaking to children is effective praise.

Effective Praise

Everyone knows children need lots of positives; therefore, it is logical to assume that praise favorably influences children's self-esteem. However, research makes it clear that this is not always so. If teachers commend children indiscriminately, children discount the praise (Alberto & Troutman, 2009). Children may also treat the adult offering insincere praise with suspicion, which has a negative impact on the adult–child relationship. When children experience excessive praise, their intrinsic motivation and interest is reduced, and their overall sense of autonomy is undermined (Hester, Hendrickson, & Gable, 2009; Lepper & Henderlong, 2000). Furthermore, certain kinds of praise actually have the potential to lower children's self-confidence, to inhibit achievement, and to make children reliant on external rather than internal controls (Leary & McDonald, 2003). All of these conditions contribute to poor self-esteem.

In contrast, meaningful feedback pertinent to the task at hand in the form of effective praise is more likely to foster healthy self-esteem (Katz, 1993; Kerns & Clemens, 2007). For this reason, educators have investigated the characteristics that distinguish effective praise from ineffective praise.

For praise to be considered effective, it must meet three criteria. It must be selective, specific, and positive.

Selective praise means the praise is reserved for situations in which it is genuinely deserved. It is not given in all situations or in blanket statements to all children. It is more likely to be directed at an individual or small group of children at a given moment in time, rather than at the entire class. Providing explicit information about what is being lauded makes the praise specific. Finally, praise must be positive. There are no negative comparisons, and no one is being put down as a result of someone else being elevated. A comparison of ineffective praise versus effective praise is summarized in Table 4-5. As you read through the examples of effective praise, you will probably notice that most are either reflections or simple informational statements to children. None make any reference to the teacher's feelings or evaluate the child in any way. When used skillfully, effective praise is a powerful contributor to children's developing self-concept and social understanding because it helps children see themselves from someone else's perspective.

Praise is most effective at fostering a positive self-identity when it is delivered in close proximity, not from across the room (Gable et al., 2009). Also, when praise is administered immediately after the "good" behavior, the child praised and other children nearby are more likely to engage in that behavior again (Hester, Hendrickson, & Gable 2009; Kerr & Nelson, 2010).

Finally, researchers have found that teachers and caregivers overestimate how often they praise children in the classroom. Many teachers, when asked, report that they use praise quite frequently. However, when these same adults are observed, this is often not the case (Hester, Hendrickson, & Gable, 2009). In other words, teachers do not use effective praise very often

Table 4-5 Comparisons of Ineffective and Effective Praise

Ineffective Praise	Effective Praise
Evaluates children "You draw beautifully."	*Acknowledges children* "You used a lot of colors in your picture."
Is general "Good job." "Nice work."	*Is specific* "You worked hard on your painting." "You spent a lot of time deciding what to draw."
Compares children with one another "You wrote the most interesting story of anyone."	*Compares children's progress with their past performance* "You wrote two words in this story that you have never used before."
Links children's actions to external rewards "You read three books. Pick a sticker from the box."	*Links children's actions to the enjoyment and satisfaction they experience* "You read three books. You seem pleased to have read so many."
Attributes children's success to luck or to ease of task "That was a lucky catch."	*Attributes children's success to effort and ability* "You tracked that ball and caught it."
Is offhand in content and tone	*Is thoughtful*
Is offered in a falsetto or deadpan tone	*Is offered in a natural-sounding tone*
Is always the same	*Is individualized to fit the child and situation*
Is intrusive—interrupts the child's work or concentration	*Is nonintrusive*

© Cengage Learning

or as often as they think. However, when they do, two very powerful things occur. First, the use of effective praise leads to overall better academic performance and classroom behavior (Sutherland, 2000). Second, teachers who use effective praise report feeling more empowered and successful in their classrooms (Hester et al., 2009). Effective praise, it appears, is good for both children and teachers' sense of worth and competence!

Conversations

One of the most valuable ways adults promote children's positive sense of self is to engage in conversations with children about things children want to discuss. We all know the best conversations require good listening. In adult–child conversations, the main responsibility for listening rests with the adult (Jalongo, 2008). Thus, adults must enter their conversations with children expecting to do more listening than talking and prepared to let the child's needs and interests drive the exchange. When adults are attentive and respond meaningfully to what children have to say, they demonstrate interest in them. Because adults represent authority figures, this clear sign of adult attention conveys a powerful message to children that they have value (Jalongo, 2008). In addition, conversations that center on topics in which children

are absorbed are more likely to produce spontaneous and lengthier discussions than those focused on adult-directed or selected topics (Jalongo, 2008).

In child-centered conversations, children feel more confident about expressing their thoughts, ideas, and feelings. As adults become actively involved with children in this manner, children come to view them as trustworthy people and as potential sources of information and guidance. Thus, the foundations for positive adult–child relationships are strengthened through child-led talk. Conversations also provide a powerful means through which children enhance their self-understanding. As children explore topics ranging from what happened on the playground, to why the gerbil died, to who wants to be their friend, they are exploring ideas, thoughts, and feelings in concert with others. These experiences add to children's store of self-knowledge and provide natural opportunities for social comparisons that give them a better idea of who they are, what qualities make them unique, and what attributes they have in common with others (Jenkins et al., 2003; LaBounty et al., 2008; Lewis & Carpendale, 2004). As you know, these are critical elements that contribute to children's self-understanding.

Conversation stoppers. Not all adult–child talk prompts conversation and self-understanding. Some ways of talking actually inhibit the give and take of "true communication." Conversations with children can be stymied in a variety of ways, as follows:

- Adults cut children off before they have finished talking.

- Adults interrupt children's stories to correct their grammar.

- Adults ask too many closed-ended questions or too many questions in a row.

- Adults finish children's sentences for them.

- Adults ask leading questions to make the conversation go in a certain direction ("Don't you think..." Wouldn't it be a good idea if we...").

- Children get the message that what they have to say is not important.

- Children get the message that the structure of their words is more important than the content they are sharing.

- Children feel like they are being interrogated, not like they are involved in a genuine conversation.

- Children get the message that speed is more important than the ideas they are trying to convey.

- Children get the message that what they really think does not matter.

Poor conversational habits like these interfere with adult–child communication and detract from children's feelings of worth, competence, and control. Children leave such interactions thinking, "I am not important. He or she is not really interested in me." Conversation stoppers such as those in the preceding list, prompt children to exit the conversation more quickly, and if habitual, make it less likely that children will develop the feelings of confidence and optimism associated with healthy self-esteem (Denton, 2007). Two verbal strategies that will help you avoid this dilemma and will enrich your conversations with children are open-ended questions and paraphrase reflections.

Questions

Questions can be a useful way to invite a child into a conversation if they are used thoughtfully and skillfully. The kinds of questions adults ask, however, dictate the quality of the answers they receive (Cassidy, 2003; Denton, 2007).

Open-ended questions. To stimulate verbal exchanges, the best questions are those that draw children out and prompt them to elaborate. These are called open-ended questions or creative questions (Weissman & Hendrick, 2014). **Open-ended questions** have many possible answers, but no single correct answer. Their purpose is to get children to talk about their ideas, thoughts, and emotions. Open-ended questions ask children to do the following:

- Predict *("What will happen next?")*
- Reconstruct a previous experience *("What happened when you visited your grandma?")*
- Make comparisons *("How are these animals the same/different?")*
- Make decisions *("What do you think we should do after lunch?")*
- Evaluate *("How do you think Sara is feeling?")*
- Imagine something *("What would it be like if the dinosaurs were alive today?")*
- Propose alternatives *("What is another way you could cross the beam?")*
- Plan next steps *("What's one thing you might do next?")*
- Solve problems *("What can we do to find out how many marbles are in this jar?")*
- Generalize *("You worked out a way to share the paints yesterday. How might you share the play dough today?")*
- Increase awareness *("What have you learned so far?")*
- Reason *("How did you decide those went together?")*

All of these questions invite a wide variety of answers and allow children to express whatever is on their mind. As a result, children are able to choose the direction the dialogue will go. This makes it more likely that they will remain interested and involved in the give and take of true conversation. Such questions promote thinking and problem-solving skills (Denton, 2007). They also communicate acceptance of the child, thereby promoting positive adult–child relationships (Marion, 2011). Most importantly, because children are encouraged to lead the conversation, open-ended questions enhance children's feelings of worth, competence, and control!

Closed-ended questions. The opposite of an open-ended question is a closed-ended one. **Closed-ended questions** call for one-word answers. Although useful in some situations ("Do you have your bus pass?"), they are not intended to promote conversation or self-discovery. When teachers ask: "Are you rooting for the Tigers?" "Do you like peaches?" "What kind of bird is this?" children may answer, but, after the answer is given, they often have nothing else to say. This makes closed-ended questions less useful

© Cengage Learning

"What will you do if your baby gets hungry while you're at the grocery store?" is an open-ended question you might ask this child.

as a relationship-building strategy or one that helps children develop greater self-understanding.

There are obviously times to use both open-ended and closed-ended questions. When selecting which is most useful for the given situation, consider the purpose of the question. See Table 4-6 for a comparison of these two types of questions.

The intent of using open-ended questions is to enhance children's understanding of themselves, to support the trio of self-esteem, and to increase their language abilities. Another powerful verbal strategy that encourages children to expand their self-knowledge is a paraphrase reflection.

Paraphrase Reflections

A **paraphrase reflection** is a restatement, by the adult, of something a child has said. The adult listens carefully to what the child is saying and then repeats the statement to the child in words slightly different from those the child originally used. As with behavior reflections, paraphrase reflections are nonjudgmental statements. Adults *do not* express personal opinions about what the child is trying to communicate. Rather, paraphrase reflections send signals to the children that the adult is listening attentively. Examples might include the following:

Abigail: Teacher, see my new dress and shoes!
Adult: You have a new outfit on today. (Or either of the following: You wanted me to see your new clothes; you sound pleased about your new things.)
Matt: (At lunch table) Oh no! Macaroni, again.
Adult: You've had more macaroni than you can stand. (Or: Macaroni's not your favorite; you thought it was time to have something else.)
Samson: Is it almost time for us to get going?
Adult: You think we should be leaving soon. (Or: You're wondering if it's time to go yet; you'd like to get started.)

In each of the preceding situations, the adult listened to the child, and then paraphrased the child's statement or inquiry. Note that there was more than one appropriate way to reflect in each situation.

Using paraphrase reflections. Paraphrase reflections can be used any time a child addresses a comment to an adult. They may consist of a single phrase or multiple statements (Meece & Soderman, 2010). Sometimes, a simple verbal acknowledgment of something a child has said is all that is required.

Barbara: I'm up to page 15.
Adult: You've gotten pretty far in a short time. (Barbara resumes reading.)

Consider the following two conversations. The first involves Chris, who is 5. The second is his 6-year-old brother, Kyle. Both discussions were spontaneous.

Conversation with 5-year-old Chris:

Chris: We got a new dog over the weekend!
Adult: You sound excited. Tell me more.
Chris: Well, he's got a flat nose...well, ah...he's been biting a lot...and, he's ah, he's cute... you know, he's ugly and homely. He's cute... and, ah...he's in a biting mood...you know, he has to chew on something a lot of times, he's just, he's going to be...ah, October... um, August 7th was his birthday! Not his real birthday. His real birthday was... what was his real birthday? His real birthday ...was February 7th, I think.
Adult: Ah, but you celebrated his birthday at a different time even though it wasn't his real one.
Chris: August, uh huh, August. He's only 6 months old. Six months....

Table 4-6   Comparisons of Closed-Ended and Open-Ended Questions

CHARACTERISTICS	
Closed-Ended Questions	**Open-Ended Questions**
Require a nonverbal response or a one-word or two-word answer from children	Promote multiword, multiphrase responses from children
Tend to have right or wrong answers	Have more than one correct answer
Are ones for which adults already know the answers	Are ones for which adults do not know what children's answers might be
Require a "quick" response	Allow children time to formulate and collect their thoughts
Focus on facts and similarity in thinking	Focus on ideas and originality in thinking
Ask for information	Ask for reasoning
Focus on labeling or naming	Focus on thinking and problem solving
Require the child to recall something from memory	Require the child to use his or her imagination
EXAMPLES	
Closed-Ended Questions	**Open-Ended Questions**
What shape is this? … Square.	What do you think will happen next?
How many cows did you see? … None.	How else could we …?
What street do you live on? … Gunson.	What's your idea?
How are you? … Fine.	How did you …?
Who brought you to school today? … Mom.	What would happen if …?
Where is your backpack? … Home.	What do you think about …?
Do you know what this is? … Yes.	What do you suppose would explain …?

Adult: Oh, he's only 6 months old. He's just a small dog.

Chris: No, he's not a small dog. He's about, you know, from here to here (child spreads arms to indicate size)…you know… he's….

Adult: Oh, he's a pretty large dog.

Chris: Yeah. He's pretty large, all right! He's got a fat stomach and tiny legs! (Laughs)

Adult: (Laughing) He sounds comical, with a flat nose too.

Chris: Yeah, and…you know, he has knots on his head … and he has a face like he's real sad, and…um….

Adult: Sad-faced.

Chris: Uh huh.

Adult: Sad-faced dogs are really cute sometimes.

Chris: Yeah.

Conversation with 6-year-old Kyle:

Kyle: Know what? Our dog's really cute, and… we keep him in one of those kinds of pens where you keep, like, babies when you want to keep them from falling down the steps or something. Well, we… we keep him in one of those. We keep him in our laundry room and, uh…we got him from North Carolina. My dad says that he was…he, his father, um, was registered as Nathan Hale. Well…he was the champion bulldog of the nation... and, uh...we got him for free because we know the people who know the owner of Nathan Hale.

Adult: Sounds like you were pretty lucky to get such a special dog.

Kyle: Yeah. We are....We got him from North Carolina.

Adult: He came from far away.

Kyle: Yeah. We, they took him...they took him on a trip for eight hours...and, he threw up about four times.

Adult: That must have been a long trip.

Kyle: Yeah, when he got out, um... he just sorta laid there, and he was...he really looked sick, and um...this is the stage when he has long legs, but you should see his stomach!

Adult: It's really something else.

Kyle: Yeah.

As demonstrated, children may pursue the same topic in very different ways. Each child talked about the same dog, but chose a different feature to discuss. By paraphrasing, the adult was able to respond to Chris and Kyle individually. She also was able to attend to what interested each child most. If she had led the conversation by asking a series of questions, such as: "What kind of dog did you get?" "How big is he?" "What's his name?" "What color is he?" and "Where did you get him?", the two interactions would have been similar, rather than unique as they were. In addition, it is unlikely that the adult would have thought to inquire about the knots on the dog's head or how many times it threw up, which were important considerations to the boys. Note, too, that Chris felt comfortable enough to correct an inaccurate response. This occurred when the adult's interpretation that a 6-month-old dog was small (meaning "young") did not match what Chris wanted to convey. Because paraphrase reflections are tentative statements of what the adult thinks she or he heard, children learn that the reflections are correctable. Directing the conversation in these ways makes children feel worthwhile and capable. It also gives children an opportunity to exercise appropriate control within the interaction.

Another benefit of paraphrasing is that it has the power to enhance children's expressive language, an important skill for the developing child. There are two ways to enrich children's language while also enhancing their self-esteem: expansion and recasting.

Expansion To fill in or extend what the child is saying is called **expansion**. This type of paraphrasing is slightly different from and more complex than the child's speech and has been shown to stimulate children to produce lengthier, more varied sentences (Kontos & Wilcox-Herzog, 1997). Between the ages of 18 months

and 36 months, simple expansions work well (Thiemann & Warren, 2010).

Child: Kitty sleep.
Adult: Yes, the kitty is sleeping.
Child: Me eat.
Adult: You are eating a sandwich.

In each of these examples, the adult has expanded the child's telegraphic message to include appropriate connecting words in the same tense as the child's.

Recasting Recasting refers to actually restructuring the child's sentence into a new grammatical form. Children aged 4 and older profit from this more elaborate variation (Tsybina et al., 2006):

Child: The cat is sleeping.
Adult: Snowball is asleep on the windowsill.
Child: This car goes fast.
Adult: Your car is going very fast around the track. Soon it will have gone the whole way around.

Recasting preserves the child's meaning but rephrases it in a way that is moderately new. Novelty can be introduced by changing the sentence structure, by adding auxiliary verbs, or by using relevant synonyms. This helps the child to notice the more complex grammatical form. Recasting works best when adults make modest changes in the child's words but do not alter them entirely. If the restatement is too complex, children will overlook the new grammatical or syntactical structure, making it unlikely that they will use it themselves.

Although paraphrase reflections are all similar in form, the content of each depends on the adult's interpretation of the child's message. Thus, no one reflection is correct for every situation, and many are possible.

Why paraphrase reflections benefit children. For true communication to take place, it is important that adults listen to what children have to say. Real listening involves more than simply remaining silent. It means responding to children's words with words of your own that imply, "I hear you, I understand you," (Jalongo, 2008). Paraphrase reflections are an ideal way to get this message across.

Sometimes called active, reflective, or emphatic listening, paraphrase reflections are widely used in the helping professions to indicate warmth, respect, and understanding. When adults use these statements, children interpret them to be sensitive, interested, and accurate listeners. The result is that children talk more freely, and interactions are more rewarding for both participants (Gazda et al., 2006.) In addition, children gain a better understanding of themselves by hearing their own thoughts mirrored back to them in words that are similar but not exactly the same as the ones they

© Cengage Learning 2015

Taking the time to sit with a child and engage in conversation tells the child he is valuable.

have used. Such talk expands children's self-awareness, affirms their sense of worth, and expands their verbal competences—all key elements in the developing self.

Shared Narratives

**Our Snowy Day
Ms. Reynold's Butterfly Group**

Ms. Reynolds begins with these familiar words:

Remember that time when we all went outside to dance in the snow?

Individual children pick up the narrative:

Yeah.

We wore our boots.

Angie had red boots on.

Sarah's were green with frogs.

We stomped a big circle in the snow.

Some of us had two socks on in our boots.

We made a circle and went all the way around.

It was cold!

(Teacher says, "What happened next?")

We said we needed hot chocolate.

Then, we got some.

Mine had marshmallows.

Me, too.

Yeah.

(Teacher says, "Then what?")

Jack spilled his.

Nancy got a towel.

You (Ms. Reynolds) fixed it.

My hair got snowy and so did Sam's.

I went around and around in the snow.

Me, too.

We had fun!

The children in Ms. Reynold's Butterfly Group (the 4-year-olds) have told the Our Snowy Day story several times this year. It always begins with, "Remember that time when we all went outside to dance in the snow?" The children add events as they remember them with a little prodding from their teacher. Some events change a little with each telling, but the details remain roughly the same and emerge in a similar order. This tale makes the children laugh and remember a good time shared by all.

Every family has stories its members tell over and over again. Some are funny, some are sad, some recount unfortunate events, and others tell of family triumphs. One way members of the family know they "belong" is that they are familiar with these stories and have opportunities to join in the telling, the embellishing, and the debates over details. The same is true for children as they participate in the "family" group of their classroom. The classroom stories they tell are called **shared narratives**. Just like other family stories, shared narratives contribute to children's

This teacher uses a tablet device to make a record of a story that will form the basis for a shared narrative in the group.

© Cengage Learning 2015

self-awareness and self-identity as members of the group. Children and teachers create shared narratives by telling a story using the children in the class as the main characters. The "plot" may revolve around a typical event that happened within the group (how several children built a "boxasaurus" or "our trip to the pumpkin patch"). Alternately, the story might highlight an important group accomplishment and the contributions of individuals to that outcome.

As children retell a real event that has happened within the class, the adult solicits and acknowledges their perspectives. These are all woven into the narrative (Shiel, Cregan, McGough, & Archer, 2012). Teachers take the role of co-narrator (along with other children), asking questions to keep the story moving and helping to connect one child's idea to the next. As the stories from these shared narrations are retold over and over again, they often take on a life of their own whereby the new versions become much different from the original event. There is no need to point out inaccuracies in these new tales. The children have reformulated the narratives to serve a special purpose, that of being in control of how the story unfolds and of solidifying their identities within the group. When children have opportunities to co-create shared narratives, they feel valued as members of the group, and they have opportunities to expand

their skills in expressing themselves as well as working with others (Bohanek et al., 2006). Some shared narratives are strictly oral and are sustained by simply being retold many times. Others are recorded aurally or visually. In each case, the focus is on the children's retelling of the event with themselves as the "featured" players.

All the verbal strategies discussed in this chapter are appropriate for all children, regardless of their primary language or their language abilities. As an early childhood professional, you will likely encounter many children whose home language is not English. Additional strategies are available to enhance such children's sense of self and healthy self-esteem. Let's consider these children more closely.

Supporting Linguistically Diverse Children: Verbal Strategies

"Have you ever experienced a setting where the people did not speak your language? How did you feel? What do you think that experience might feel like to a child?"

–Adapted from Derman-Sparks & Edwards (2010, p. 65)

The term **dual-language learners (DLLs)** is used to describe children enrolled in educational programs who are growing up with two or more languages

Learning a few words of comfort in a child's home language communicates your caring and affirms the child's worth.

(Nemeth, 2012). In the United States, many children speak a language other than English at home, and many are in the early stages of proficiency in English in speaking, listening, reading, and writing (What Works Clearinghouse, 2007; Soderman, Gregory, & McCarty, 2005). The notion of home language is also important for speakers of English who have regional or ethnic dialects or other distinct speech patterns. In every case, children's self-concept and self-esteem are strongly tied to their home language (Thompson & Virmani, 2010). The primary language that a child speaks serves as the mediator between children's development in social, emotional, and cognitive areas (Hammer, Scarpino, & Davison, 2011). Long before children ever enter formal schooling, they are busy using their home language for interactions with others (Genishi & Dyson, 2009). Children whose home language is treated with respect feel valued. Those who receive the message that their home language is unimportant, or even worse, a "problem," are less likely to feel good about themselves (Derman-Sparks & Edwards, 2010). Thus, it is potentially harmful to deny children access to their home language in the formal group setting of childcare or school. This has sometimes been done in the mistaken belief that "English

only" rules promote speedier acquisition. The research does not support this assumption. A more natural approach to second-language acquisition makes better sense.

We promote respect for linguistic diversity in children when we are sensitive to variations in how children acquire English as a second language. Some children may experience a silent period (of 6 or more months) as they acquire English; other children may practice their knowledge by mixing or combining languages (e.g., "Mi mama put on mi coat"); still other children may seem to have acquired English language skills (appropriate accent, use of vernacular, vocabulary, and grammatical rules) but are not truly proficient; yet some children will quickly acquire standard English-language proficiency. Each child's way of learning language should be viewed as acceptable (Genishi & Dyson, 2009).

One of the most concrete ways formal group settings demonstrate acceptance is to have people who speak children's home languages on staff or as volunteers in the program. When staff is bilingual or when the staff includes both English-speaking members as well as persons who speak the children's home language, children have many opportunities to speak and hear speech that is familiar to them (Genishi &

Dyson, 2009). In addition, they have the chance to hear languages other than their own. This increases children's involvement in learning and validates the importance of the children's home language as well as English (Berk, 2013). Other visible signs of acceptance include making available an assortment of multilingual story tapes, song discs, books, wall hangings, signs, and posters. Singing and reciting in a variety of languages are additional strategies that convey the value of children's home languages. Additional ideas for celebrating the cultural and ethnic heritage of linguistically diverse children are presented in Chapter 14.

Exposing children to English in the formal group setting can be carried out through a combination of formal instruction and informal conversation. All of the skills outlined in this chapter are useful in the latter approach. Behavior and paraphrase reflections extend children's language skills and also indicate interest in and acceptance of all children. Behavior reflections are particularly effective when working with children who are in the early phases of English proficiency. Simple words and phrases accompanied by gestures and demonstrations help to get the message across. Teaching children simple scripts in English, such as "my turn," "I'm next," or "show me," provide children with basic words they need to function socially. This contributes to children's feelings of worth, competence, and control.

In this chapter, we have discussed a variety of ways to enhance children's understanding of self. We've focused on promoting positive relationships and creating a positive verbal environment. The teaching and coaching techniques associated with these include fundamental strategies, such as greeting children

and calling them by name, as well as the more complex skills of positive verbal environments: behavior reflections, effective praise, open-ended questions, paraphrase reflections, conversations, and shared narratives. All of these are summarized in the Social Support Pyramid depicted in Figure 4-7.

Let us now examine how these global techniques can be translated into specific skills you can learn and use in your interactions with children and families.

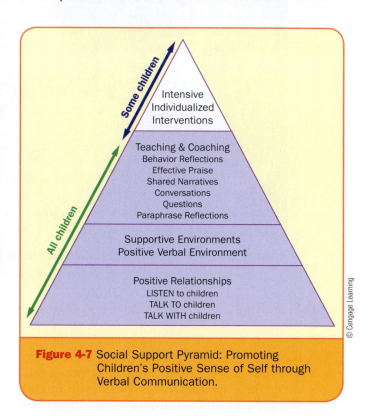

Figure 4-7 Social Support Pyramid: Promoting Children's Positive Sense of Self through Verbal Communication.

SKILLS FOR PROMOTING CHILDREN'S SELF-AWARENESS AND SELF-ESTEEM THROUGH VERBAL COMMUNICATION naeyc

Using the Skills Associated with a Positive Verbal Environment

1. **Greet children when they arrive.** Say "Hello" to children at the beginning of the day and when they enter an activity in which you are participating. Show obvious pleasure in their presence through the nonverbal communication skills you learned in Chapter 3.

2. **Use children's names.** When speaking to children, say their names as part of the conversation. This lets children know that you have remembered them from one day to the next; that you perceive them as individuals, unique from others in the

group; and that your message is aimed especially at them. Take care to pronounce each child's name correctly. Refrain from giving children nicknames or Americanized names to make their names easier for you.

3. **Invite children to interact with you.** Use phrases such as: "We're making play dough. Come and join us," "There's a place for you right next to Sylvia," "Let's take a minute to talk. I wanted to find out more about your day," or "You look pretty upset. If you want to talk, I'm available."

4. **Speak politely to children.** Allow children to finish talking before you begin your remarks. If you must interrupt a child who is speaking to you

or to another person, remember to say, "Excuse me," "Pardon me," or "I'm sorry to interrupt." Thank children when they are thoughtful or when they comply with your requests. If you are making a request, preface it with, "Please." Use a conversational, friendly voice tone rather than one that is impatient and demanding.

5. **Listen attentively.** Show your interest through eye contact, smiling, nodding, and allowing children to talk uninterrupted. Verbally indicate interest by periodically saying, "Mmm-hm," "Uh-huh," or "Yes." If the child has more to say than you can listen to at the moment, indicate a desire to hear more, explain why you cannot, and assure the child that you will resume the conversation at a specific point later in the day. Be sure to follow up with the child.

6. **Provide verbal encouragement to children as they refine and expand their skills.** Do this by giving children relevant information such as, "Just one more piece and you'll have the whole puzzle complete." Share your confidence in their ability with them. "This project will be challenging, but I'm sure you can do it."

Formulating Behavior Reflections

1. **Describe some aspect of the child's physical being or actions in a statement to the child.** After observing a child carefully, select an attribute or behavior that seems important to him or her and remark on it. Focus on the child's perspective of the situation, not your own. An appropriate behavior reflection to Manny, who is tying his shoes, would be: "You're working on your left shoe," or "You know how to make a bow."

2. **Phrase behavior reflections as statements, not questions.** Questions imply that children must respond; reflections do not.

3. **Direct reflections to the child.** Use the word "you" somewhere in your statement so that the child recognizes that your reflection is aimed at her or him.

4. **Use descriptive vocabulary as part of your reflection.** Including adverbs, adjectives, and specific object names as part of the reflection makes them more meaningful and valuable to children. Saying, "You put the paints on the widest shelf," is more language-rich than, "You put it on the shelf."

5. **Use a nonjudgmental vocabulary and tone when reflecting children's behavior.**

Reflect only what you see, not how you feel about it. "You're using many colors in your painting," is a reflection; "You used too much gray," is not.

6. **Use a conversational tone when reflecting.** Use an expressive voice tone when reflecting either children's behavior or language. Adults who reflect in a monotone or singsong voice sound condescending and disrespectful.

7. **Summarize children's actions and words.** Summarizing is more effective than reflecting each individual behavior or idea expressed. Formulate reflections that tie together a series of actions or statements. For instance, if Malcolm is playing with colored blocks say, "You're using many colors in your structure," rather than saying each color of each block being used.

Formulating Effective Praise Statements

1. **Use behavior reflections to acknowledge children's efforts and accomplishments.** "You've been working on that a long time."

2. **Make nonevaluative comments.** "You found a new way to make a tunnel," or "You did it."

3. **Note positive changes you've observed in children's abilities over time.** "You've been practicing a lot and now you can make it across the whole beam without falling off," or "You're getting very fast at matching those shapes."

4. **Point out to children the positive effects their actions have on others.** "You noticed Marcel was having a hard time getting the computer going. You gave him some help, and now it's working fine."

5. **Focus on some positive aspect of children's efforts to do something, not simply the product they achieve.** It is better to say, "Look at how you made those brush strokes sweep across the page. You've worked for 10 minutes on that," than to say, "Nice picture."

6. **Be honest in your praise, and offer children authentic feedback.** For instance, if Elliot has just struggled through reading a page aloud, say something like, "You're learning to read some new words," or "You read that whole page by yourself." This is more honest than "Great reading," or "That was terrific." Elliot is probably quite aware that his reading is not yet fluent. The latter comments lack credibility and may sound patronizing to the child. Adult praise means more when it is believable.

7. **Challenge yourself to use more effective praise daily.** Monitor yourself to see if you are praising children frequently. Consider recording yourself in action to check to be sure you're praising effectively and often. This sample self-observation record will help you get started.

Effective Praise Classroom Record

Directions: Choose three children to focus on today. Record how many times you offer effective praise to each child and when during the day you do so. At the end of the session, analyze the frequency and timing of your praise statements. What does this tell you about your use of effective praise? What if any adjustments do you think you need to make?

Portion of Day	Mandy	Dion	Liz
Free Choice	✓		
Snack Time		✓	✓
Large Group		✓	
Small Group			
Outdoors			✓
			✓

Digital Download **Download from CourseMate**

Creating Conversations

1. **Invite children to elaborate on what they are saying.** Prolong verbal exchanges with children by saying: "Tell me something about that," "Then what happened?" or "I'd like to hear more about what you did."

2. **Consider conversation openers in advance that focus on interests previously expressed by children.** Generate ideas ahead of time for one or two topics that might pick up on children's interests. ("Tell me about last night's game," "How's that new brother of yours?" or "I was really interested in your report on Martin Luther King, Jr. Tell me what you liked best about him.")

3. **Use silence to invite conversation.** Remain silent long enough for children to gather their thoughts. Ask or comment, and then pause (at least to the count of five). Children need time to think of what they are going to say next, especially if they have been listening carefully to what you were saying, because their attention was on your words, not on formulating their subsequent reply. Children

who have language delays or are dual-language learners may require even more time to formulate their responses. Don't rush into your next statement or question. This overwhelms children and gives them the impression that the adult has taken over completely rather than becoming involved with them in a more participatory way.

4. **Engage children in conversation frequently.** Spontaneously converse with children. Look for times when you can talk with children individually, both planned and unplanned. Informal times or transitions are great times for conversations. Remember, not only the quality of the talk impacts children's self-identity but also the quantity!

5. **Refrain from speaking when talk would destroy the mood of the interaction.** Talk can sometimes take away from the positive verbal environment. When you see children deeply absorbed in their activity or engrossed in their conversations with one another, allow the natural course of their interactions to continue. Keep quiet. The absence of talk in situations like these is also a sign of warmth and respect.

6. **Structure situations and times for children to engage in conversations with you and with each other.** Create opportunities within formal routines such as meal time, group time, and small-group activities to promote conversation. Take advantage of conversations that come up informally. Build on these at the time and, if appropriate, at other times in the day.

Formulating Effective Questions

1. **Monitor the questions you ask.** Use open-ended questions to promote conversation. Use closed-ended questions when a specific answer is needed.

2. **Carefully choose when to use open-ended questions.** Consider the time available and the circumstances under which the question is to be asked. Pick an unhurried time, giving children ample opportunity to respond to avoid frustration (yours or the child's).

3. **Emphasize quality over quantity in using questions with children.** Measure the effectiveness of the questions you ask by listening to children's answers in regard to both content and tone. If responses become monosyllabic or the child sounds weary of answering, stop. If answers are lively and lead to elaboration, continue.

4. **Wait for the child's answer.** Give children a minimum of at least a minute to respond to your question. The time is often well spent when you hear the thoughtful reply.

Formulating Paraphrase Reflections

1. **Listen closely to the child's words.** Consciously pay attention to the child's message. Look at the child and listen to his or her entire verbalization without interrupting. Concentrate on the child's ideas, not your response.

2. **Restate in your own words what the child has said.** Make sure that your rewording maintains the child's original intent. Don't include your opinion.

3. **Rephrase erroneous reflections.** At times, children give signs that your reflection was not in keeping with their intent. They may correct you directly by saying, "No," or "That's not what I meant." Other, subtler cues are children repeating themselves, adding new information, or sighing in exasperation. Use a corrected variation of your statement.

4. **Match your reflection to each child's ability to understand language.** Use simple, short reflections with toddlers. Construct these by adding one or two connecting words to the child's telegraphic utterances. Go beyond simple expansions, however, when working with children aged 4 and older. Recast the child's message by adding auxiliary verbs or relevant synonym phrases. Periodically, use multiple phrase reflections when working with school-age children:

   Child: There's Brownies on Tuesday, and all the kids are going. Me, too.
   Adult: Sounds like you've got a special meeting coming up. Lots of your friends are going.

   Be aware of how well children understand spoken English. Accompany your words with gestures and demonstrations to enhance your communications.

5. **Select one idea at a time to paraphrase.** Pick one main idea that stands out to you from what the child has said and reflect that. If this is not the child's major focus, he or she will tell you or restate the intent. Avoid trying to paraphrase every single word.

6. **Add interest to your reflections by periodically phrasing them in a form opposite of that used by the child.** If Sunil says, "I want the door open," it would be appropriate to say, "You don't want the door closed." If Matt announces, "I want another helping of everything," you could say, "You don't want to miss anything."

Creating Shared Narratives

1. **Engage children in telling and retelling stories about classroom events to which they contributed.**

- Encourage children to reminisce about past classroom/center events (Remember that time when…). Share stories about what happened in the past to individual children and the group.
- Use open-ended questions and paraphrase reflections to keep the language/story flowing. Invite children to take turns telling.
- Act as narrator, weaving parts of the children's stories together into a cohesive whole.
- Invite children's opinions into the interactive narration. Invite differing points of view.
- Discuss thoughts, desires, and emotions of the "actors" involved in the events. When children correct or disagree with the story, change it to suit "public" opinion.
- Refer to previously shared narratives when pertinent to help children see connections between the experience being discussed and prior ones.

2. **Take photographs of events within the classroom to use as narrative prompts.** Use these for current and future narratives. Encourage children to generate stories about "self" and "us."

3. **Create a classroom photo album, display board, or blog to further the notion that all children contribute to the social environment.** Use this to prompt stories about past events in which children can describe the part they played in each one.

Supporting Linguistically Diverse Children

1. **Become familiar with ways in which your environment is designed to support children's linguistic diversity.** Notice how the professionals in your setting provide opportunities for different languages to be used in daily activities. Look around your setting for materials that reflect children's home languages and cultures.

2. **Evaluate your sensitivity to children's use of home languages.** Ask yourself the following questions: Do I know what home languages are represented within the group of children with whom I am working? Do I respond respectfully to children when they talk to me in their home language? Do I feel confident interacting with children whose language I do not speak fluently? If you are answering "no" to any of these items, review the skills you have learned so far. Identify specific strategies you can use to interact more sensitively with linguistically diverse children.

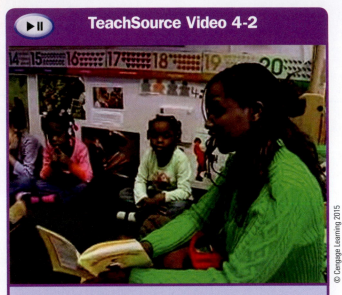

TeachSource Video 4-2

Language Development: Oral and Literacy-Related Activities – Bonus Video 3

Go online and view *Language Development: Oral and Literacy-Related Activities – Bonus Video 3.*

In this video, you will observe a teacher talking to a child in the child's native language.

1. Based on what you know about children's self-concept, how might the teacher's verbalizations influence this child's concept of self?

2. Based on what you know about children's self-esteem, how might the teacher's verbalization influence this child's self-esteem?

3. Describe three additional verbal strategies the teacher might use to promote this child's self-awareness.

Watch on CourseMate

© Cengage Learning 2015

3. **Learn relevant words in the home languages of the children in your group**. Look up phrases. Ask colleagues and parents to help you. Ask children to teach you a few key words if possible.

Communicating With Children's Families About Children's Self-Understanding

1. **Apply the principles of a positive verbal environment in your interactions with family members.** Greet family members. Learn the names of the families in your program. Use adults' last names as well as their appropriate social address such as Dr., Mr., Ms., or Mrs. If you aren't familiar with family names, greet them as the parent/guardian/grandparent of their specific child. Then, introduce yourself. For instance, "You must be with Elise. I'm Ms. Murray." If children are present, greet them too.

2. **Invite family members to enter the room, to watch their child, and to speak with you.** Use such phrases as, "You've come to see Jose. He's in the group area looking at books. You are welcome to join him there," or "Welcome to the classroom. We're almost finished with story time. Here is a comfortable place to wait," or "Thank you for coming in to speak with me. Let's watch Jose for a while and then I'd be happy to answer any questions you have about his time at school."

3. **Allow family members to finish their requests or comments before introducing your own.** Be attentive. Demonstrate interest nonverbally and by listening carefully.

4. **Use paraphrase reflections and open-ended questions while interacting with family members.** Adapt your use of paraphrase reflections to demonstrate respect for and interest in adults. Paraphrase reflections can be very effective with adults when used carefully. First, mix your reflections with other verbal strategies. Second, make sure not to "mirror" an adult's words or exact style of speech. Vary your word choice using some of the techniques outlined earlier in this chapter, such as reversing the word order, saying the opposite of what the speaker has stated, and using multiple sentences. Although reflecting is suitable for all kinds of interactions, it is particularly useful when family members are expressing concern. This strategy helps to clarify the information they are attempting to convey, so that you can respond to needs and desires more effectively. Rephrase the speaker's sentences to demonstrate your understanding of the message being delivered. Do not hesitate to correct yourself if the speaker indicates that you misinterpreted his or her intent.

5. **Use commonly understood language, not jargon.** When speaking with family members, clearly describe the issue at hand in natural, unaffected vocabulary and sentences. Use the principles of good verbal and nonverbal communication to both talk and listen. If you sense a misunderstanding, find alternate words or phrases to clarify your meaning. If you think you have misunderstood what others are saying, verify your perception with phrases, such as, "What I think you are saying is ..." or "It sounds as if you think ...."

6. **Allow sufficient time for family members to gather their thoughts.** It is not always easy for parents and other family members to come to

CHALLENGING BEHAVIOR

Meet Celia

Celia is the youngest of six children. She is delighted to be a big first grader. However, after a month in the classroom, she has yet to talk to anyone. She appears to be painfully shy. She will smile at you, her teacher, but she doesn't seem to want to speak. You phone her mother at home to casually learn about her language. Her mother is slightly surprised to hear that Celia is not speaking. She reports that every night at the dinner table, Celia fights to be the first to share about her day and that her narrations are lengthy. You decide that you are going to find a way to encourage her to talk. Considering all of the strategies outlined in this chapter, which one(s) will you try with Celia and why?

a program to speak with professionals about their children. They may therefore be hesitant in their speech, fumble for words, or stammer. Be patient and refrain from finishing their sentences or interrupting them.

7. **Use effective praise to acknowledge family participation in the program.** Respond genuinely to helpful family involvement. When parents and other family assist in a meaningful way, acknowledge their efforts honestly and specifically. *"I really appreciated your helping us work on the journal project. It meant that more of the children were able to write their ideas down. Thank You."*

8. **Collaborate with family members in supporting linguistically diverse children.** Ask family members to teach you some words and phrases that could be useful in interacting with their child. Invite family members to the program to share and discuss oral traditions, music, artifacts, or foods. When working with older children, provide ways in which family members can use their primary language to help their children with program-related assignments/ activities at home. Create a school-to-home library from which families can check out resources to share with their children.

Pitfalls to Avoid in Using Skills to Promote Children's Self-Understanding naeyc

As you try out new skills associated with a positive verbal environment, there are certain hazards to avoid.

1. **Parroting.** A common way adults initially paraphrase children is to duplicate exactly the child's words and voice tone. This type of parroting is often offensive to children because it makes the adult sound insincere or condescending. Although parroting is a natural first step for people just learning how to paraphrase, you should intentionally vary your responses as quickly as possible.

2. **Reflecting nonstop.** It is a mistake to reflect everything children do or say. The purpose of behavior and paraphrase reflecting is to give adults opportunities to observe children, to listen to them, to understand their point of view, and to provide them with more information about themselves. None of these goals can be accomplished with

nonstop talking. Using summary reflections is a good alternative.

3. **Perfunctory reflecting.** Reflecting without thinking is not appropriate; it is another form of parroting. If you find yourself simply "going through the motions" or responding absentmindedly to children, stop, and then intensify your efforts to attend more closely to what children are really saying or showing through their actions.

4. **Speaking to children in the third person.** There are times when adults make comments about the child that they intend for the child to hear, but that are not personally addressed to the child. For instance, Miss Long is playing with 2-year-old Curtis in the block area. No one else is nearby. She says things like: "Curtis is building with square blocks. Curtis is making a tall tower. Oops, Curtis' tower fell." If other children were close at hand, her remarks might be a useful bridge between Curtis and his peers. But, as the situation stands, her impersonal running commentary on his activity is not conversational and leaves no real openings for a response from Curtis should he choose to make

one. Miss Long's remarks could be turned into reflections by the insertion of "you" in each one: "Curtis, you're building with square blocks. You're making a tall tower. Oops, your tower fell."

5. **Correcting children's overestimation of their abilities.** Sometimes in an attempt to be factual, adults feel compelled to correct children's inaccurate statements about themselves. For instance, when Tyrell states, "I am a perfect speller," the adult replies, "Well, most of the time you do fine, but you do get some words wrong." In early and middle childhood, it is common for children to overestimate their abilities. Correcting children does not assist them in developing a more accurate picture of themselves. It is more helpful to reflect the emotional content of the statement instead. In this situation, the adult could respond, "You are proud of how well you spell."

6. **Turning reflections into questions.** Phrases such as "aren't you?", "didn't you?", "don't you?", "right?", or "okay?" tacked to the end of a sentence transform reflections into questions. A similar result occurs when the adult allows his or her voice to rise at the end of a sentence. Falling into this habit changes the nature of your words from signaling interest to making a response sound mandatory. This is one of the most common misuses of reflecting and occurs because adults want some sign from the child that their reflection is right. Yet, rarely does one hear:

Jack: I'm at the top.
Adult: You're excited to be so high, aren't you?
Jack: You're right, Teacher.

The real confirmation of appropriate reflecting is that children continue their activity or conversation. If children stop or correct you (Jack says, *No, I'm scared!*), that is what will tell you that your original reflection was off target. Otherwise, a nonresponse, is often a sign that your reflection was okay. If you find yourself experiencing this pitfall, interrupt yourself and repeat the reflection correctly.

7. **Answering your own questions rather than waiting for children to answer.** Adults answer many of the questions they pose themselves. For instance, Ms. Cooper asks, "Who remembered to bring their permission slips back?" Without a moment's hesitation, she says: "John, you've got one. Mary, you've got one, too." Later, she inquires, "Why do you think birds fly south for the winter?" Before children have a chance to even think about the question, she supplies an answer: "Usually, they're looking for food." In both instances, Ms. Cooper inhibited children's answers by responding too quickly herself. Unfortunately, as this

becomes a pattern, Ms. Cooper may conclude that children are incapable of answering her questions. The children translate her actions as lack of interest in what they have to say. If you catch yourself answering prematurely, say so out loud; then, repeat your question with a pause so children can answer: "Oops. I didn't give you a chance to answer. What do you think about …?"

8. **Habitually answering children's questions with questions of your own.** Sometimes, when children ask a question, adults automatically echo the question back to them:

Child: Where do bears sleep in the winter?
Adult: Where do you think they sleep?

Echoing causes children to form negative impressions of adults. The question sounds like a put-down; children translate it to mean: "You're dumb. You should know that," "I know and I'm not going to tell you," or "I'm going to let you make a fool of yourself by giving the wrong answer. Then, I'll tell you what the real answer is." Although this may not be the adult's intent, it is often the result. To avoid these unfavorable impressions, either supply the needed fact, or reflect the children's questions ("You want to know more about bears.") and then help them discover the answer by looking it up or asking an expert.

9. **Using ineffective praise.** When adults catch themselves praising children indiscriminately or falling back on overused, pat phrases, the best strategy is to stop talking, and then refocus on what the child is actually doing. Rephrase your statement so it conforms to the guidelines for effective praise presented earlier in this chapter. If an on-the-spot correction seems too difficult, simply remember the situation and during a quiet moment later in the day, reconsider what you might have said. On another day, in a similar activity, see whether any of the alternatives you thought about might fit. If so, use one or a variation of it.

10. **Interrupting children's activities.** Reflecting or asking a question when a child is obviously engrossed in an activity or is absorbed in conversation is intrusive. At times like these, adults can exhibit interest in children by observing quietly nearby and responding with nonverbal signs such as smiles, nods, or laughter at appropriate moments. When children are working very hard at something, an occasional reflection that corresponds to their point of view is appreciated; constant chatter is not.

11. **Hesitating to speak.** At times, you may fumble for the right words when trying to implement the skills presented in this chapter. By the time you think of a response, the opportunity to use the skill

The teacher watches and listens but does not interrupt the boys' conversation about their ramp.

© Cengage Learning 2015

like themselves and that they have to think about what they are saying more than they ever have in the past. They become discouraged when their responses sound repetitive and lack the warmth and spontaneity they have come to expect from themselves. When this happens, some people give up, reverting to old verbal habits. As with any new skill, proficiency develops only through practice.

Learning these verbal techniques is similar to learning to ice-skate. Beginning skaters have a hard time keeping their balance, shuffle along, and fall down periodically. They have enough trouble going forward, let alone going backward, doing turns, or making spins. If people only ice-skate a few times, chances are they will continue to struggle and feel conspicuous. If these feelings cause them to give up skating, their progress is halted, and they will never improve. However, they should keep on practicing because not only will their skill increase, but they will also be able to get beyond the mechanics and develop an individualized style.

may have slipped by or the words that come out may sound stilted. Don't give up! The best way to find the right words is to keep practicing. In fact, in the beginning, it is better to talk too much than to neglect using these skills. After you become more comfortable with the mechanics, you can fine-tune your timing and rate of response.

12. **Sounding mechanical and unnatural while trying new verbal skills.** Implementing reflections, effective praise, and open-ended questions may feel awkward and uncomfortable at first. Beginners complain that they do not sound

The process is the same for all the skills taught in this chapter. If you are willing to practice and continue working through these difficulties, noticeable improvement occurs. The artificial speech that marks the early stages of acquiring these verbal skills gradually gives way to more natural-sounding responses. With time and practice, the words will flow more easily, and you will develop your own individual style.

Summary

Children's developing knowledge of self and subsequent social understanding directly contributes to their social competence. Children's cultures, temperament, relationships, and language experiences combined with their social interactions help them formulate a sense of their worth, competence, and control in the world. There are three components of self-understanding: self-awareness, self-concept, and self-esteem. Self-awareness involves recognizing that one is an individual, separate from other people and the environment. This is what babies and toddlers are most involved in figuring out. Self-concept is the descriptive portion of the self. Beginning with toddlerhood, children describe themselves in physical and concrete ways, one attribute at a time. By the end of middle childhood, children's self-concepts are primarily defined by psychological traits and are characteristically more comprehensive.

Self-esteem represents the evaluative component of the self. It has three dimensions: worth, competence, and control. Children who judge the elements of these three dimensions positively are said to have healthy self-esteem; those who do not are described as having poor self-esteem. Individuals with healthy self-esteem lead happier lives than those whose self-judgments are negative. The development of self-esteem follows a normative sequence, evolving from assessing oneself in the here and now as a preschooler to a more compartmentalized view of the self as a young grade-schooler to a general index of one's value as a person by middle-school age. This predominantly positive or negative view remains relatively constant throughout life.

Children's self-understandings are greatly influenced by the adults with whom they interact. Adult behaviors contribute to children's either making positive or negative judgments about themselves. Favorable self-judgments of competence, worth, and control are likeliest in children who interact with adults who demonstrate warmth, acceptance, genuineness, empathy, and respect. What adults say to children conveys these messages or the opposite ones. A significant way such messages are delivered is through the verbal environment. Verbal environments can be either positive or negative. Continual exposure to a negative verbal environment diminishes children's self-concept and self-esteem, whereas exposure to a positive verbal environment enhances children's positive self-judgments.

The strategies associated with a positive verbal environment include behavior reflections, effective praise, conversations, open-ended questions, paraphrase reflections, and shared narratives. These strategies are effective not only in supporting children's understanding of self and others but also in scaffolding language development for beginning and dual-language learners. Furthermore, it is useful to tailor these strategies in your interactions with family members as a means of developing and maintaining positive relationships.

Finally, certain pitfalls are to be avoided, such as parroting, reflecting too often or perfunctorily, talking to children in the third person, using inappropriate questioning methods, and interrupting children. Hesitating to speak and sounding mechanical at first are common challenges encountered by individuals who are just beginning to learn these skills. All can be overcome with thoughtful practice.

Key Terms

behavior reflections
closed-ended questions
competence
control
dual-language learners
effective praise
expansion

healthy self-esteem
negative verbal environment
open-ended questions
paraphrase reflections
poor self-esteem
positive verbal environment
recasting

shared narrative
self-awareness
self-concept
self-esteem
verbal environment
worth

Discussion Questions

1. Describe the normative sequence of the development of self-concept in children from birth to early adolescence. Why is this important for you to know in your work with children?

2. Describe an incident from your childhood that enhanced your self-esteem. Describe another that detracted from it. How did the first incident enhance your self-esteem? What does it say to you about your behavior with children? Use the information in the chapter to assess the negative incident and how it could have been transformed into a positive experience.

3. Review the characteristics of the positive and negative verbal environments. Discuss any additional variables that should be added to both lists.

4. Describe the emotional climate of your current setting with children. Name three ways in which you could improve the verbal environment of a setting in which you currently interact with children.

5. Refer to Appendix A, the NAEYC Code of Ethical Conduct, when responding to the following: One of your colleagues talks about "those children" when referring to children who are just beginning to learn English. Consider her point of view as well as what she is communicating to children.

6. Describe at least four benefits of using behavior reflections with young children.

7. Describe how the adult's use of paraphrase reflections affects children's self-awareness and self-esteem.

8. Describe the characteristics of an open-ended question, and discuss how the use of this technique relates to self-awareness and self-esteem in children.

9. Describe how interaction strategies that are used with children can be applied to interactions with adults.

10. Talk about the differences between effective and ineffective praise. Using examples from your

past experience, describe times when you were praised effectively and/or ineffectively. What was your reaction at the time? What do you think about it now?

Case Study Analysis

Refer to the case study about Seth in Appendix B. Consider the following issues:

1. Based on your reading about Seth, which skills presented in this chapter would best help him develop a deeper concept of self? Explain your choices.

2. Read the teacher observations dated March 7 through June 21. What skills presented in this chapter do you see being used?

3. Using the teacher observations as a reference, how might adults in the classroom make better use of behavior and paraphrase reflections in interacting with Seth? What purpose would such reflections serve? How might these skills relate to the goals his parents have for him?

4. Make an assessment as to whether or not the verbal environment makes a difference to children like Seth. Provide a rationale for your response.

5. How might the skills in this chapter be used to facilitate interactions between Seth and his peers?

Field Assignments

1. Identify three strategies you used with children that are associated with the creation of a positive verbal environment. For each situation, briefly describe what the children were doing. Summarize the strategy you used. (Describe it and quote the words you said.) Discuss the children's reaction in each case.

2. Keep a record of the behavior reflections and paraphrase reflections you use with children. When you have a chance, record at least four of your responses. Begin by describing what the child(ren) did or said that prompted your response. Next, quote the words you used. Correct any inaccurate reflections as necessary. Finally, write at least two alternate reflections that fit the situations you described.

3. Focus on using open-ended questions and effective praise as you work with the children. Describe at least four situations in which you used these skills. Begin by describing what the child(ren) said or did to prompt your response. Next, record your exact words. Correct any mistaken responses by rewriting them. Finally, write at least two alternate ways of phrasing your remarks, regardless of their accuracy.

4. Describe an interaction you heard or observed involving a child's adult family member. Include positive verbal strategies that were used, including behavior and paraphrase reflections, open-ended questions, and conversation extenders. Give a summary of your assessment of the interaction.

Reflect on Your Practice

Here is a sample checklist you can use to reflect on your use of the skills as a beginning professional. A more detailed classroom observation tool is available in Appendix C.

Teachers do the following to promote children's positive sense of self through verbal communication:

✓ Greet children, and invite children to participate.

✓ Listen to children, and let children finish what they are saying.

✓ Use behavior reflections to promote self-awareness.

✓ Use open-ended questions to encourage conversation.

✓ Use effective praise to acknowledge children's accomplishments.

✓ Paraphrase children's remarks.

✓ Discuss events that occurred in the classroom to promote children's self-identify and form group memories.

✓ Engage dual-language learners in conversation and play.

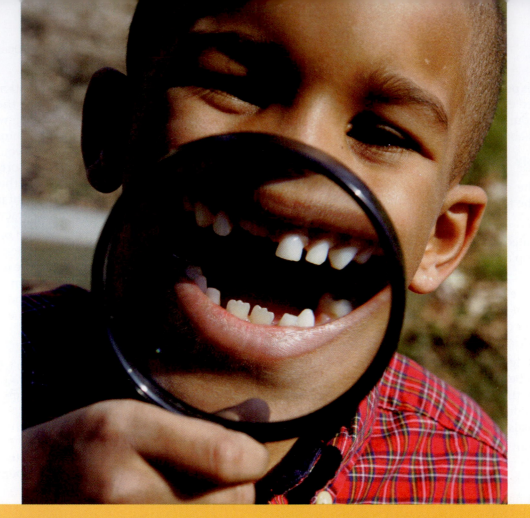

5 Supporting Children's Emotional Development and Learning

OBJECTIVES

On completion of this chapter, you should be able to:

Define emotions.

Describe how emotions influence people's lives.

Sequence key benchmarks in children's emotional development from birth through middle childhood.

Contrast how individual children experience and express emotions.

Identify emotional challenges children face.

Discuss ways adults help children deal with emotions effectively.

Demonstrate skills that support children's emotional development.

Recognize pitfalls in responding to children's emotions.

NAEYC STANDARDS

1. Promoting Child Development and Learning
2. Building Family and Community Relationships
3. Using Developmentally Effective Approaches to Connect with Children and Families
4. Using Content Knowledge to Build Meaningful Curriculum
5. Becoming a Professional

A butterfly lands on Sean's hand—his eyes widen in **amazement.**

On her first day at the center, Maureen sobs **miserably** as her mother attempts to leave.

Emily makes a diving catch and is **elated** to find the ball in her mitt.

Tony is **frightened** by the escalating sounds of angry adult voices in the other room.

When Larry calls her stupid, Jennifer yells **furiously,** "No, I'm not!"

Children experience hundreds of different emotions each day. Emotions are linked to everything children do and are prompted by many things, large and small. They are what cause children to be affected by the people and events around them. How well children express their emotions and understand the emotions of others are key elements of social competence.

What Emotions Are and Where They Come From naeyc

People in all cultures experience emotions. Joy, sadness, disgust, anger, surprise, interest, and fear seem universal (Ekman, 2007; Wellcome Trust, 2010). Although there are obvious differences among these emotional states, they have certain characteristics in common. Each is triggered by *internal or external events* that *send signals to the brain* and central nervous system. This initial reaction occurs within milliseconds, without a person even knowing it is happening.

As a result of these signals, people become aroused, and their bodies respond with physiological changes. Their hearts may beat faster, their palms may sweat, or their throats might become dry. This is the *physical* part of emotion. Such sensations usually are accompanied by observable variations in facial expression, posture, voice, and body movement.

Smiling, frowning, and laughing are visible signs of how people feel. Actions like these represent the *expressive* side of emotion. As this is going on, individuals interpret what is happening to them. Their interpretations are influenced by the context of the situation, their goals, and past experiences (Calkins & Williford, 2009). Combining these factors, people make a judgment about whether they are experiencing some degree of happiness, sadness, anger, or fear. This is the *cognitive* part of emotion.

Although scientists vary in their beliefs about the order in which physical sensations, expressive reactions, and cognitive interpretations occur, they generally agree that all three unite to create emotions

(Aamodt & Wang, 2008). To understand how these elements work together, consider what happens when Kitty, age 8, is called on to read her report aloud:

Signals to Kitty's brain: Teacher speaking Kitty's name; the other children's silence; a giggle from the back of the room.

Physical response: Kitty's mouth dries up; her pulse beats rapidly; her stomach contracts.

Expressive response: Kitty scowls; her shoulders slump.

Cognitive response: Kitty thinks about past difficulties in front of an audience as well as her desire to do well in class.

Emotion: Kitty feels nervous.

If Kitty's cognitive response had focused on past public speaking triumphs, she might interpret the emotion she is experiencing as excitement, not nervousness. In either case, Kitty makes the ultimate judgment about how she feels. Even if others expect Kitty to do well, if she perceives the situation as threatening, she will be nervous. Different cognitive responses explain why two people may have opposite emotional reactions to the same event. Although Kitty feels *nervous*, another child in the group may be *eager* to read his or her report to the class. Neither interpretation is right or wrong; each simply defines that child's current reality. Because emotions are tied to everything people do, emotional episodes like this take place many times each day.

Why Emotions Are Important naeyc

Children's emotions run the gamut from joy and affection to anger and frustration. Some emotions are pleasant, some are not, but all emotions play an essential role in children's lives.

At their most fundamental level, *emotions help children to survive.* Jumping out of the way of a speeding tricycle or forming attachments with the important people in their lives are instances in which expressive reactions overshadow a person's cognitive response. In these cases, emotions instinctively propel children toward self-preservation without their having to "think" about what is happening (Ekman, 2007).

When they do have a chance to think, *emotions provide children with information about their well-being* (Lewis, 2007). This often results in children taking some action to maintain or change their emotional state. Feelings such as happiness and trust give children a sense of safety and security. Affectionate feelings tell children they are lovable and that others value their love. Feelings of pride suggest that they are competent. All these positive emotions give children a sense of security and prompt them to continue or

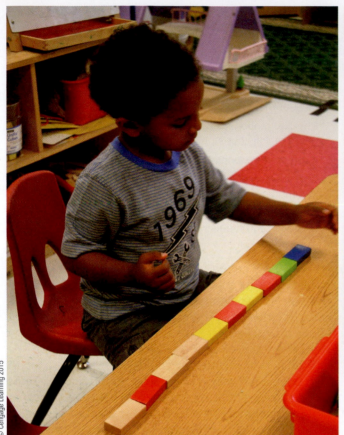

These children's expressive behaviors are signaling very different emotions.

repeat pleasurable experiences. On the other hand, some emotions signal discontent, misfortune, or danger. They alert children that something is wrong. Anger prompts children to try to overcome obstacles. Sadness brings a drop in energy, allowing children time to adjust to loss or disappointment. Fear prompts children to avoid, escape, or otherwise protect themselves from something. In every case, emotions help children interpret what is happening to them and cue them to adapt to changing circumstances. These interpretations are depicted in Table 5-1.

In addition, *emotions serve as a form of communication.* Emotional displays, such as smiling or crying, provide the first language with which infants and adults communicate before babies learn to talk. This communication function continues over the life span as people use words and nonverbal cues to express what they are feeling and to better understand the feelings of others (Jaswal & Fernald, 2007; Widen & Russell, 2008).

Emotions also influence children's cognitive functioning (Steedly, Schwartz, Levin, & Luke, 2008). Recent scientific evidence shows that the neural circuits in the brain that regulate emotion are highly interactive

Table 5-1 What Emotions Signal to Children about Their Well-Being

Emotion	Message to Child
Happiness	I am safe. All is right with the world. I need to continue or repeat this.
Affection	I am lovable and valuable.
Pride	I am competent.
Anger	Something is wrong. I need to overcome this obstacle.
Sadness	Something is wrong. I have suffered a loss. I need to adjust to this loss.
Fear	Something is wrong. I am in danger. I must escape. I need to protect myself.

© Cengage Learning

© Will Hart/PhotoEdit

What do you think this child's emotions are telling her about her current well-being?

with those associated with intellectual activities such as attending to details, setting goals, planning, problem solving, and decision making (National Scientific Council on the Developing Child, 2006). As a result, emotions can either support or interfere with these cognitive tasks. Poorly controlled emotions and negative feelings tend to detract from intellectual functioning; strong positive emotions and emotions that are well regulated support more advanced cognitive activity (Raver, Garner, & Smith-Donald, 2007).

For all of these reasons, we cannot afford to ignore children's emotional development and learning throughout the day. In fact, evidence suggests that deliberate attention to such learning needs to permeate children's experiences at home, in the center, and at school (Steedly et al., 2008).

Where Emotions Fit in the Curriculum

As an early childhood educator, you have many opportunities to help children:

- Better understand their emotions.
- Become more sensitive to the emotions of others.
- Find effective ways to manage the many different emotions they experience.

These understandings and skills are core competencies associated with emotional development and learning. As such, they inform program content for children from pre-kindergarten through grade 12 and are incorporated in the Learning Standards for most states. See Table 5.2 for typical examples.

You can teach children about emotional competence in many ways—through day-to-day interactions, intentional coaching, and planned activities. Regardless of which strategies you choose, to do the job well, you must have a thorough understanding of the developmental aspects of children's emotions.

What Early Childhood Professionals Need to Know about Children's Emotional Development naeyc

Beginning at birth and continuing through the early elementary years, emotional development is determined by the following:

- How children's emotions emerge
- How children develop emotional self-awareness
- How children come to recognize other people's emotions

Table 5-2   Examples of State Learning Standards Associated with Emotional Development and Learning

State	Ages	Expectations	Benchmarks/Learning Outcomes
Tennessee	3–4	Children verbalize feelings, needs, and wants.	The child: · Talks to others (including dolls, puppets, imaginary friends) about what she is thinking about and how she feels · Uses physical ways to express self when feelings are intense
Missouri	3–5	Children express feelings through appropriate gestures, actions, and language.	The child: · Identifies emotions (e.g., says, "I'm really mad." or "The story makes me sad.") · Shares happiness or success of another · Offers to help someone who is hurt · Uses pretend play to understand and respond to feelings
Illinois	9–10	Children identify and manage their emotions and behavior.	The child: · Identifies a range of emotions · Describes situations that trigger various emotions · Recognizes mood changes and the factors that contribute to them · Depicts a range of emotions (e.g., make a poster, draw a picture, participate in role play) · Demonstrates ways of dealing with upsetting emotions

Sources: Illinois State Board of Education (2010, June); Missouri Department of Elementary and Secondary Education (2012, January); Tennessee Department of Human Services, Adult & Family Services Division Child Care Services Section (2009, April)

● How well children learn to regulate what they are feeling

● How well children address the emotional tasks of childhood

All of these developmental processes are influenced by maturation and experience. Understanding them will help you respond to children in ways that promote their social competence.

How Children's Emotions Emerge and Mature

Nadia was born 2 days ago. She grimaces when her older brother quickly shifts from holding her upright to laying her down in his lap. Some scientists argue that Nadia is showing true emotion (Izard et al., 1995; 2000). Others believe that the newborn's grimace is just a reflex. They contend that real emotions do not appear until weeks later when children's cognitive processes are developed enough to allow them to interpret what they are experiencing (Sullivan & Lewis, 2003). Despite these differing perspectives, researchers agree

that within their first year, babies will experience multiple emotions. However, infants do not display all the emotions they will ever have. Instead, emotions increase in number and complexity as children mature. Emotional maturation emerges according to a developmental sequence as predictable as those associated with language and physical development (Copple & Bredekamp, 2009). Before she is 12 months old, baby Nadia will clearly express joy (at about 6 weeks), anger (at approximately 4 to 6 months), sadness (around 5 to 7 months), and fear (between 6 and 12 months).

Joy, anger, sadness, and fear are considered **primary emotions**, from which other related, but distinct emotions eventually develop (Widen & Russell, 2008). For example, joy is seen in the baby's first social smile. This is an unmistakable sign of infant pleasure, usually prompted by the face of a primary caregiver and welcomed by families worldwide as a significant social event (see Highlight 5-1).

Gradually, joy branches out to include wonder, affection, and pride. Likewise, the primary emotion of anger serves as a foundation for the eventual development of frustration, annoyance, envy, fury, and disgust.

The Appearance of Joy Is Celebrated in Traditional Navajo Families

A Laughing Baby

In the traditional Navajo (or Dine) culture, custom dictates that the friend or family member who witnesses a baby's first laugh has the honor of hosting a celebration called *A'wee Chi'deedloh* ("The Baby Laughed"). This festive event, honoring the appearance of joy in a baby's life, marks his or her birth as a true social being and family member.

Combinations of these feelings produce more complex reactions, as when annoyance and disgust together lead to feelings of contempt. Four primary emotions and their corresponding emotional clusters are depicted in Figure 5-1.

Even as later emotions are surfacing, earlier ones are becoming more differentiated. By the end of the first year, a child's repertoire of emotions has moved beyond the primary four to include surprise, elation, frustration, separation anxiety, and stranger distress. Further diversity and greater specificity of emotion is seen in the second year (Ekman, 2007). At that age, children are more self-conscious, and emotions such as embarrassment, affection, envy, defiance, and contempt enter the picture. By 3 years of age, children become increasingly focused on others, exhibiting initial signs of empathy and a difference between their affection for children and for adults.

Around age 3, children also start to make judgments about their actions, demonstrating signs of pride when they succeed (smiling, clapping, or shouting "I did it"), as well as shame when they are not successful (slumped posture, averted eyes, declaring "I'm no good at this") (Harter, 2012; Widen & Russell, 2008). The general order in which emotions appear during the first 3 years is depicted in Figure 5-2. By the time children are in elementary school, the number and variety of emotions they experience is even greater.

Early in life, the primary emotions are very intense. The dramatic outbursts so common among infants and toddlers underscore that intensity. However, as children's emotions become more differentiated, their reactions also become more varied.

Thus, as children mature, rather than relying on screaming to express every variation of anger, they may shout in fury, pout in disappointment, whimper in frustration, or express their upset feelings in words. This expanded repertoire of emotional expression is a result of several interacting factors—the presence of the primary emotions, the context of each situation, and children's developing cognitive and language capacities. These elements also contribute to children's understanding of emotions in themselves and in others.

How Children Develop Emotional Self-Awareness

"I'm mad at you, Teacher—go away!"

Alec—3 years old, Philadelphia

"All the kids look at me and say: Look at that ugly boy with a hump. That makes me mad, and it makes me sad. Just because I have a hunchback does not mean that my ears don't hear and my heart doesn't hurt."

John—11 years old, London

These comments illustrate the dramatic change that occurs in children's understanding of their emotions during childhood. Over time, the simplistic declarations of the toddler give way to more complex reasoning and greater breadth of understanding. It all begins with children thinking that their emotions happen one at a time. When toddlers and preschoolers are angry, they are

Figure 5-1 Primary Emotions and Corresponding Emotional Clusters.

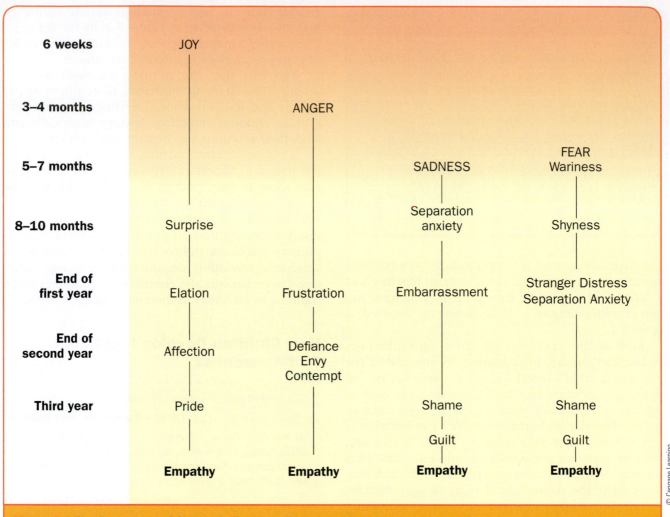

Figure 5-2 The Emergence of Children's Emotions During the First Three Years of Life.

© Cengage Learning

intensely angry; when they are pleased, they are entirely pleased (Harter, 1998). These emotional responses alternate rapidly. One minute a child may scream, "No!"; a few minutes later, he or she may laugh at something else that has happened. The quick changes children make from one emotional state to another are typical for children of this age (Gonzalez-Mena & Eyer, 2012).

By ages 5 or 6, children label their emotions and report that they can hold more than one feeling at a time as long as those feelings come from the same emotional cluster. Thus, a kindergartner might say that he is feeling happy as well as excited about going to a birthday party (Saarni et al., 2006). In contrast, he would not suggest that he could feel both happy and nervous about the party because he would expect such opposing feelings to be directed toward different things.

Sometime between the ages of 8 and 11, children come to understand that multiple and contrasting feelings toward the same event are feasible. With this new thinking, a child might suggest that staying home alone prompts both scary feelings and proud ones (Harris, 2008; Copple & Bredekamp, 2009). Initially, children perceive these feelings as occurring in succession, not simultaneously. One feeling replaces another rather than coexisting with it. So it is possible to be both happy and sad about the same event, but not at the same time.

By ages 10 to 12 years, children recognize that they can hold two or more very different feelings toward the same object or situation at the same time. This marks the first time that they become consciously aware of "mixed emotions." Initially, this mix can produce confusion. As a result, children this age often express anxiety about such feelings or distress that their emotions are "arguing with one another" (Whitesell & Harter, 1989). Learning to sort out mixed feelings accurately requires additional maturity and experience. It isn't until later adolescence that young people are able to do this reasonably well (Larsen, To, & Fireman, 2007). Another emotional characteristic of children in the later elementary grades is that they do not shift emotional states as rapidly as toddlers and preschoolers. Their emotions last longer and are rooted in the past and future, as well as in the here and now. In fact, older children often describe themselves as being in a good or bad mood, meaning they expect their general emotional state to remain relatively stable for some period of time. The developmental sequence described here is depicted in Figure 5-3.

How Children Learn to Identify Other People's Emotions

Three-year-old Maggie notices another child sobbing, with tears running down her face. Pointing to the crying child she says, "Teacher, look at Rosie. She's sad."

A mother leaves her toddler with Max, her 6-year-old, while she goes to get a soft drink from the ice chest at a school potluck. The 2-year-old begins to whimper. Max surveys the situation, grasps the younger child's hand and says, "Oh, that's all right. She isn't going far. She'll be right back. Don't be afraid. I'm here."

The ability to recognize and interpret other people's emotions is an important skill that becomes more fine-tuned over time. As illustrated by Maggie and Max, in just a few short years, children shift from focusing on obvious physical cues to more subtle contextual ones to interpret other people's emotions and respond to them. Beginning slowly in the first three years of life, emotion recognition progresses rapidly during the preschool and grade-school years.

© Cengage Learning

These first grade boys can't imagine being happy and nervous at the same time.

All one emotion	Multiple emotions from the same emotional cluster	Multiple emotions from opposite emotional clusters in succession	Multiple emotions from opposite emotional clusters simultaneously
Below 5 years	5–7 years	8–11 years	10–12 years and older

© Cengage Learning

Figure 5-3 Developmental Sequence of Children's Understanding of Emotion.

Prior to age 3. Although infants and toddlers react to other people's emotions, they are not very adept at accurately interpreting them. Their lack of experience and limited vocabulary contribute to this circumstance (Widen & Russell, 2008).

Ages 3 through 5. Preschoolers become increasingly accurate at identifying other people's positive and negative emotions (Berk, 2006). In doing so, they rely mostly on facial expressions and tone of voice to tell them how someone else is feeling. Their assessments are based more on how a person looks and sounds than on the context of the situation (Harris, 2008). Relying on expressive cues, preschoolers are likely to decide that a crying peer is sad based on the tears streaming down her face rather than on knowing what happened. Not too surprisingly, the primary emotions are consistently easier for preschoolers to identify than emotions characterized by more subtle cues (Thompson & Lagattuta, 2008). Younger children also focus on only one emotion at a time in others, just as they do in themselves (see Figure 5-4). This makes it hard for them to recognize the complex blend of emotions that other people experience.

The primary years. During the primary years, children combine physical, situational, and historic information to understand and interpret emotions. With maturity and experience, children come to recognize that a child may be sad because her toy is broken or because her dog is lost, not simply because she is crying. They also discover that the same child's feelings could change to happiness if the toy were repaired or if the lost pet found its way home. Such sources of emotion are depicted in the children's drawings presented in Figure 5-5. Gradually, children learn that the source of a person's feelings may be internal as well as physical and situational (Calkins & Williford, 2009). For instance, they become aware that memories may produce feelings even though the original event is long past. When 10-year-old Janelle says, "Tom's sad. He's lonesome for the dog he used to have," she is demonstrating an increasingly mature concept of how and why emotions occur. Furthermore, by this age, Janelle can imagine the succession of emotions or even the mixed emotions that Tom may experience, such as feeling sad about his lost dog but also pleased that his family is talking about getting a new puppy soon (Pons et al., 2003). By the end of this period, most children realize that the same events do not always lead to the same outcomes. Similar situations may prompt different responses in different people or different responses from the same person on separate occasions. For example, loud music may prompt happy feelings in Tricia but make Katrina feel overwhelmed. The same music may cause Janet to feel exuberant on Monday but on edge on Tuesday. Because of these variations, even though elementary-aged children increase in their ability to recognize another person's emotions, doing so continues to be a challenge.

How Children Learn to Regulate Their Emotions

At the same time that children are developing greater emotional understanding, they are also becoming better able to regulate what they feel. That is, children

© Cengage Learning

Figure 5-4 Children Focus on Facial Expressions to Signal Emotion. See the Variations in Expression in These Children's Drawings.

© Cengage Learning

Figure 5-5 It should read: Eventually Children Identify Emotions and Their Source

gradually learn to manage their emotions so they are not totally overwhelmed by them and so they can interact with others more effectively. Emotional regulation requires putting emotional awareness to work in real-life situations that may be upsetting, frustrating, or embarrassing (Gross, 2008; Ekman, 2007). Even positive emotions require regulation: exuberance, for example, is appropriate in some situations but not in others. At times, emotional regulation involves suppressing certain emotions (such as getting one's anger under control in order to deal with an unfair situation). At other times, it involves intensifying them (as when a child marshals his anger to stand up to a bully).

The process of emotional regulation begins in infancy. Babies learn to elicit comfort from a caregiver through the sounds they make or to turn away if an interaction is too emotionally intense. Toddlers can be seen rocking themselves when they are upset and distracting themselves in frustrating circumstances or when they have to wait. By the time children go to kindergarten, they have many more strategies at their disposal and are more proficient in using them. Words become more central to their repertoire, and children become better able to use internal strategies to moderate their feelings in various situations (Calkins & Williford, 2009). Typical emotion-regulating strategies children may acquire over time include the following:

- Suppressing the expression of certain emotions; for example, Tom doesn't show his disappointment over not coming in first as he congratulates the winner.

- Soothing one's self; for example, Gloria talks to herself as she goes into a dark part of the basement; Spencer carries around his teddy whenever he feels tired or sad.

- Seeking comfort; for example, a toddler crawls up in the lap of her caregiver after another child takes her toy.

- Avoiding or ignoring certain emotionally arousing events; for example, Connie covers her eyes with her hands during an unpleasant part of the movie.

- Changing goals that have been stymied; for example, Larry abandons his efforts to make the wrestling team and concentrates on his digital photography instead.

- Interpreting emotionally arousing events in alternate ways; for example, when his brother is abrupt with him, Calvin doesn't take it personally because he assumes his brother is still upset over a recent argument with their mom.

Emotional IQ. Children's emotional self-awareness, their understanding of other people's feelings, and their ability to manage what they feel all contribute to their social competence. This combination of knowledge and action is popularly termed **emotional IQ** (Goleman, 2011). The fundamental lessons associated with emotional IQ are learned during childhood and are summarized in Highlight 5-2.

We have become increasingly aware that children who have well-developed emotional understandings and skills (or high emotional IQ) are more successful

HIGHLIGHT 5-2

The Emotional Lessons of Early Childhood

1. **Everyone has emotions.** I feel happy this morning. So does Nicole, and so does Lisa. Ms. Bernaro, my teacher, has feelings too. Sometimes she is excited or pleased, and sometimes she is unhappy or annoyed.

2. **Emotions are prompted by different situations.** Lots of things make me happy: wearing my favorite shirt, getting an extra cookie at snack, having all the blocks I need to build a road that goes all around the rug. When someone walks through my road, or when I fall on the playground, I get angry or sad.

3. **There are different ways to express emotions.** Sometimes when I am happy I sing a little song, sometimes I laugh, and sometimes I just sit and smile to myself.

4. **Other people may not feel the same way I do about everything.** When the garbage truck came to school, I wanted to climb right up and sit on the seat behind the wheel. It felt exciting. Janice stayed back with Ms. Klein. She thought it was scary.

5. **I can do things to affect how I feel and how others feel.** When I'm sad, I can go sit on Aunt Sophie's lap or in the big chair, and after a while I feel better. Sometimes when baby Camilla is fussing, I make funny faces at her, and she starts to laugh.

Source: Based on Hyson (2004).

HIGHLIGHT 5-3

The Costs of Emotional Illiteracy Are High

Children who never learn to regulate their emotions grow up to become adults who experience one or more of the following conditions:

- High levels of anger, frustration, depression
- Abusive behavior toward self and others
- Inept parenting
- Higher rates of addiction
- Higher rates of crime and violence

Sources: National Research Council and the Institute of Medicine (2000); Goleman (2007); Garbarino (2006).

The Emotional Tasks of Childhood

Currently, many people believe that human beings work through a series of emotional tasks over the course of their lives. The person who has most influenced our understanding of what these tasks are is Erik Erikson (1950, 1963). The eight emotional stages he proposed more than half a century ago remain central to our current understanding of children's emotional development (Berk, 2013).

Each stage is characterized by positive and negative emotions as well as a central emotional task. This task is to resolve the conflict that arises between the two emotional extremes. Although all children experience a ratio between both poles of a given stage, optimal emotional development occurs when the proportion is weighted toward the positive. These stages build on one another, each serving as the foundation for the next. Table 5-3 lists all eight of Erikson's stages.

Four of the stages outlined in Table 5-3 take place during childhood. Let's look at these more closely.

Trust versus mistrust. The first stage of emotional development takes place during infancy. The emotional conflict during this stage is whether children will develop self-confidence and trust in the world or develop feelings of hopelessness, uncertainty, and suspicion. Children who develop positive feelings in this stage learn, "I am lovable, and my world is safe and secure." They are supported in this learning when adults develop positive relationships with them and attend to their needs from the earliest days.

Autonomy versus shame and doubt. Sometime during their second year, toddlers who have developed a strong sense of trust begin to move away from the total dependency of infancy toward having a mind and

in life than children who do not. For instance, when children exhibit a high degree of emotional awareness, peers and adults view them as likeable, cooperative, and friendly. Children who lack these understandings are not perceived in the same positive light (Rose-Krasnor & Denham, 2009). Similarly, children who learn how to manage their emotions well have an easier time with the disappointments, frustrations, and hurt feelings that are a natural part of growing up. Such children also tend to feel happier overall and have a better trajectory for a happy life in adulthood. On the other hand, children who lack the ability to regulate their emotions are more prone to emotional outbursts, to elicit negative responses from others, and to experience lack of emotional self-satisfaction (Orpinas & Horne, 2010). If these children continue along a path of emotional "illiteracy," their prognosis for a happy future is poor (see Highlight 5-3).

The degree to which children develop their emotional IQ is influenced to a great extent by how well they address the emotional tasks of childhood. Let's consider those next.

Table 5-3   Summary of Erikson's Stages of Development

Approximate Age	Stage	Task	Key Social Agents
Birth to 1 year	Trust vs. mistrust	To establish a trusting relationship with a primary caregiver—to develop trust in self, others, and the world as a place where needs are met	Parents/Family/Caregivers
1–3 years	Autonomy vs. shame and doubt	To strive for independence	Parents/Family/Caregivers/Teachers
3–6 years	Initiative vs. guilt	To plan and carry out activities and learn society's boundaries	Family/Teachers
6–12 years	Industry vs. inferiority	To be productive and successful	Family/Teachers/Peers
12–20 years	Identity vs. role confusion	To establish social and occupational identities	Peers
20–40 years	Intimacy vs. isolation	To form strong friendships and to achieve a sense of love and companionship	Friends/Lovers/Spouse/Partner
40–65	Generativity vs. stagnation	To be productive in terms of family and work	Spouse/Partner/Children/Culture
65+	Ego integrity vs. despair	To look back at life as meaningful and productive	Family/Friends/Society

© Cengage Learning

will of their own. The struggle throughout this period is whether the child will emerge feeling independent and self-directed or harbor fundamental misgivings about self-worth. Autonomous children do what they can for themselves, whereas nonautonomous children doubt their ability to control their world or themselves and so become overly dependent on other people. Children who develop a dominant sense of shame and doubt are those who have few opportunities to explore, to do for themselves, to experiment with objects, or to make decisions. Their attempts at exploration and independence are met with impatience, harsh criticism, ridicule, physical restraint, or resistance. In contrast, children who develop a healthy sense of autonomy are given numerous opportunities for mastery, are permitted to make choices, and are given clear, positive messages regarding limits to their behavior. Children who successfully navigate this stage learn, "I can make decisions; I can do some things on my own."

Initiative versus guilt. During their fourth or fifth year, children develop a new sense of energy. The emotional conflict during this stage is whether this energy will be directed constructively and be valued by others, or whether it will be nonproductive and rejected. Throughout the preschool and early grade-school years, children have experiences with both initiative and guilt by doing the following:

- Putting plans and ideas into action
- Attempting to master new skills and goals
- Striving to gain new information
- Exploring ideas through fantasy
- Experiencing the sensations of their bodies
- Figuring out ways to maintain their behavior within bounds considered appropriate by society

Children who have opportunities to engage in such experiences with adult support and acceptance are more likely to develop a strong sense of initiative. They take pleasure in their increasing competence and find ways to use their energy constructively. They become better able to cooperate and to accept help from others. They also learn that they can work for the things they want without jeopardizing their developing sense of correct behavior. On the other hand, children whose efforts fall short of their own expectations or adult expectations develop a sense of guilt. Adults compound this sense of guilt when they make children feel that their physical activity is bad, that their fantasy play is silly, that their exaggerations are lies, that their tendency to begin projects but not always complete them is irresponsible, and that their exploration of body and language is totally objectionable. Which kinds of experiences dominate children's interactions with others and the world strongly influences children's self-judgments. The optimal outcome of this stage is a child who thinks, "I can do, and I can make."

Industry versus inferiority. The fourth stage of emotional development takes place throughout middle childhood (approximately 6 to 12 years of age). During this phase, children become preoccupied with producing things and with adult-like tasks. They also are more interested in joining with others to get things done and in contributing to society as a whole. The central emotional issue is whether children come away feeling competent and able, or whether they believe that their best efforts are inadequate. Although all children have times when they are incapable of mastering what they set out to accomplish, some experience a pervasive sense of failure. This happens when adult, peer, or school standards are clearly beyond their abilities or when they have an unrealistic view of what is possible to achieve. Strong feelings of inferiority also arise when children believe that mastery only counts in areas in which they are not skilled.

Industriousness is fostered when adults recognize and praise children's success, when they encourage children to explore their skills in a variety of areas, when they help children set realistic goals, and when they set up tasks so children experience mastery. Providing guidance and support to children whose efforts fail eases the pain and gives children the confidence to try again. This is also an important time for adults to encourage children to work with one another in order to experience the satisfaction of working in a group as well as to learn the skills necessary to do so. When feelings of industry outweigh those of inferiority, children emerge into adolescence thinking, "I can learn; I can contribute; I can work with others."

Children explore the emotional tasks of childhood continuously through their daily activities, conversations, and interactions with others (Epstein, 2009). In addition, early childhood professionals deliberately address these tasks as part of the children's involvement in a variety of subject areas. Consider the lesson in "initiative" the 5- and 6-year-olds in Kathryn Brown's class are gaining as they also develop important literacy skills (see Highlight 5-4).

School-age children enjoy mastering new tools and skills.

HIGHLIGHT 5-4

A Lesson in "Initiative"

The children in Kathryn Brown's kindergarten are learning to be authors. They decide that one thing all authors need to know is how to tell when their book is finished. Today the children discuss this at group time. Susan says, "We need a date on our book, like books have in front." Alvin mentions that authors need to make sure their names are on the cover, "just like the books we have in school." The children also discuss the importance of filling books with writing and illustrations. With their teacher, they create a chart entitled, "I know I'm finished when . . ." listing this information. During writing conferences with the teacher, the young authors refer to the chart to check that they have done everything necessary to complete their books. They add two more things: sharing the finished book with their classmates, individually or in a small group, and then taking the book home or putting it in the classroom library. All of these steps give children a chance to put plans and ideas in action as well as master new skills and goals, leading them to feel, "I can do, and I can make."

I know I'm finished when . . .

- All my pages are FULL of writing and illustrations.
- I have a date stamp and my name.
- All my pictures go along with my words.
- I have shared it with someone.

Source: Based on Brown (2010).

In this portion of the chapter, we have considered five developmental sequences that characterize children's emotional maturation: (1) how emotions evolve from the primary emotions to their more varied forms, (2) how children come to understand what they are feeling, (3) how children recognize other people's emotions, (4) how children learn to regulate their emotions, and (5) the emotional tasks of early childhood. All of these processes underscore emotional similarities among children. Now we will look at ways in which children differ from one another emotionally.

Individual Variations in How Children Express Emotions naeyc

Although all children experience emotions, the intensity of what they experience and how they express their emotions to others is unique to each child. This is a result of natural variations in children's expressive styles, gender differences, and the unique lessons children learn within their families and cultures.

Differences in Children's Expressive Styles

If you were to use feeling words to describe some of the children you know, you might say things like: Tanya is usually "quiet and shy"; Georgio is generally "exuberant and eager to try new things"; Brandon tends to be "prickly and easily offended." Descriptions such as these are referring to children's patterns of emotional responsiveness, or their expressive style (National Scientific Council on the Developing Child, 2006; Hyson, 2004). Children's expressive style is influenced by their temperament and results from unique combinations of the following factors.

The proportion of positive and negative emotions children typically exhibit. Some children are more optimistic, some are more neutral, and some are more downhearted much of the time. Although everyone experiences many different emotions each day, all of us have a certain emotional tenor that determines how we handle most emotion-arousing events.

The frequency with which children show certain emotions. Children have certain ways they tend to react from one situation to another. For instance, Felix may react with caution each time he encounters something new. His brother may have the opposite reaction, often responding with eagerness to novel circumstances.

The intensity with which children express their emotions. Although two children may respond with a similar feeling to a particular situation, the intensity of their responses may vary. Sue and Ricardo are both pleased to have been invited to the school talent show. Sue claps her hands and giggles with joy. Ricardo gives a slow smile to show his pleasure.

How long certain emotional states last. Some children hang on to their emotional reactions longer than others do. For instance, Sarah may become upset over not getting to go first in line, and then quickly move on to enjoying a game of catch outdoors. Lisa, on the other hand, may remain unhappy for most of the afternoon, brooding over not being chosen as line-leader.

The degree to which children's emotional responses are dominated by primary or mixed emotions. Although all children become capable of more complex emotional expression as they mature, some continue to exhibit the primary emotions most frequently, whereas others generally exhibit more complicated combinations of feelings. This explains why Kyle's teacher describes the 7-year-old as an "easy read." You know he is happy or angry just by looking at his face. His twin brother Raymond, on the other hand, is harder to decipher because he often displays a complicated mix of feelings that are not so readily interpreted.

How quickly children's emotions are activated. Some children are quick to exhibit an emotional response. Others take much more time to show any emotional reaction. These distinctions are exemplified by Sandra, who has a "short fuse," reacting with anger at minor provocations; and Bethany, who is slow to anger and is seldom out of sorts.

Such variations in emotional responsiveness are not inherently good or bad, just different, and they are all perfectly normal (Ekman, 2007). Adults who are tuned in to the children in their care recognize and respect each child's unique expressive style. They understand that such differences give clues as to what each child is feeling and a basis for determining the kinds of emotional support each child needs.

Gender Differences in Children's Emotional Expression

Conventional wisdom says that females are more emotionally expressive than males and that females are the more sensitive of the two genders to other people's feelings. Research tends to support these popular beliefs (Bajgar et al., 2005). From their first year, girls smile more and cry more than boys do. Girls use more

Young children take pleasure in their increasing competence.

© Cengage Learning 2015

Family and Cultural Variations in Children's Emotional Expression

Two 8-year-olds are racing down the hall. A teacher stops them and tells them she is disappointed that they forgot the rule about walking inside. Andrew stops laughing and says, "Sorry." Wu Fang smiles, says nothing, and then walks slowly to his classroom. Both boys are expressing regret according to the customs of their family and culture.

To become successfully integrated into society, children must learn certain display rules regarding how emotions are exhibited and which emotions are acceptable in certain situations and which are not. Such learning is influenced by family expectations and by culture (Galinsky, 2010). For instance, in many European-American families, when children are being reprimanded, they are expected to maintain eye contact to show respect and to adopt a solemn expression to communicate remorse. Mexican-American and African-American children, on the other hand, often are taught to avert their gaze to indicate respect. Chinese children learn to smile as an expression of apology when being scolded by an elder, whereas Korean children develop a demeanor referred to as *myupojung*, or lack of facial expression, which they are expected to display in similar situations (Lynch & Hanson, 2011).

Children learn these expressive variations at home and in the community. They absorb them through observing and interacting with others. At first, children obey display rules to avoid negative reactions or to gain approval from the important people in their lives. Gradually, they come to accept them as the natural order of things in the family and culture in which they live. As with many other social lessons, this learning comes about through imitation, feedback, and direct instruction (Cole & Tan, 2008; Ekman, 2007).

Imitation. At the lunch following her grandmother's funeral, 3-year-old Meridith turns to see her mother grimace and begin to cry. Mom searches for her tissues, sobs, and blows her nose. Meridith runs to the buffet table. Grabbing a paper napkin, she begins to cry and blow her nose. In this case, Meridith was clearly imitating her mother's emotional expression to guide her own response.

A similar but more subtle form of **social referencing** occurs when Jorge falls down while running across the playground. He looks up to see how the nearby adult reacts to his fall. If the adult's face registers alarm, Jorge interprets this as a worrisome event and begins to cry in response. If the adult's reaction is matter-of-fact, Jorge may register the idea that the fall is no big deal and simply pick himself up to continue

emotion-related words in their conversations with peers and adults, and girls are more likely than boys to figure out what other people are feeling. These tendencies continue throughout the teenage years.

Although biology likely plays a role in such gender differences, scientists believe that most of these variations are the result of social influences, such as modeling and reinforcement (Chaplin, Cole, & Zahn-Waxler, 2005). For instance, throughout the United States, parents use more expressive facial expressions with their infant daughters than with their infant sons. Similarly, adults use feeling words more often in conversations with girls than with boys. In line with these behaviors, adults encourage females to express a wide range of emotions but are less likely to do this with males (MacGeorge, 2003; Fivush et al., 2000). Outcomes like these help us to understand that boys and girls may manifest emotions in different ways. They also remind us that how we interact with children affectively makes a difference in their emotional behavior.

his play. As children gain experience in the world, they use circumstances like these to experiment with various forms of emotional expression.

Feedback. Adults also provide feedback to children regarding the appropriateness of the ways they choose to express their emotions. Such feedback is offered through gestures, sounds, and words. For instance, when a baby's smile is greeted with the excited voice of the caregiver, the adult's tone serves as a social reward. If this happens often, the baby will smile more frequently. If the infant's smile is consistently ignored, his or her smiling behavior will decrease. Likewise, when Carmen giggles out loud at a funny cartoon, her teacher laughs along with her. However, when she laughs at another child who is struggling to recite a poem by heart, her teacher frowns slightly and shakes his head no.

In both cases, Carmen was given feedback regarding her emotional reaction. Scenarios like these are repeated many times throughout childhood. Based on the feedback they receive, children gradually come to know better as to where, when, and how to express their emotions.

Direct instruction. Sometimes, adults give children specific instructions about how they should express their emotions. They do this when they point out appropriate and inappropriate reactions of others as well as when they tell children how to react in certain circumstances:

"John did a good job of speaking up for himself at the meeting. He was angry, but he didn't lose his temper."

"You shouldn't laugh at people in wheelchairs."

"You just won first place. You should be smiling."

Children absorb hundreds of such lessons growing up. Gradually they interpret emotions and express them in ways that fit family and cultural norms. Because families and cultures are not all the same, children vary in their emotional expressiveness too.

Up to now, we have addressed common developmental benchmarks in emotional maturation and we have focused on the individualized nature of children's emotional learning. Now we will speak to typical age-related challenges children face in dealing with their emotions.

Challenges Children Encounter When Dealing with Emotions naeyc

Martin is so excited about going to the zoo that he keeps interrupting his father, who is trying to get directions for the trip.

Andrea has been waiting a long time to use the kite. Frustrated, she grabs it from Barbara and dashes to the other side of the playground.

Fred is worried about what will happen when his mother goes into the hospital. Rather than letting anybody know his fears, he pretends he doesn't care.

None of these children are handling their emotions particularly well. That is, none of them are dealing with their emotions in a way that will lead to greater personal satisfaction, resolution of a dilemma, or increased social competence.

Emotional Difficulties Experienced by Children from Infancy through Age 7

Children are not born knowing how to manage their emotions. Sometimes they rely on strategies that are not helpful to themselves or others (Kaiser & Rasminsky, 2012). For instance, because of their lack of social skills and immature language capabilities, young children often act out how they feel. They may pout when angry or jump up and down when excited. In these situations, children expect others to interpret their emotions accurately and to respond in supportive ways. Unfortunately, nonverbal expressions of emotions may be misunderstood. For instance, an adult may assume that a crying child is tired, when frustration is really the source of the child's distress. Putting the child to bed, which is a reasonable way to support tired children, is not the best strategy for helping children cope with frustration.

Another problem for children 2 to 7 years of age is that they sometimes choose inappropriate actions to show how they feel. Their poor choices may be due to poor modeling, lack of know-how, or immature understandings (Cole & Tan, 2008). Finally, even when young children are able to express how they feel in words, they still may not know what to do about it. This is demonstrated by Sam, a talented, but often fearful child (see the Challenging Behavior box).

Emotional Difficulties Experienced by Children Ages 7 to 12

Children in the later elementary years are more aware of their emotions and how to communicate them in words. However, they are less likely to be open about their emotions than younger children. Children ages 7 to 12 may try to hide or minimize their emotions (Denham, Bassett, & Wyatt, 2008). This happens because they are aware of the social rules governing emotional behavior and because they want to avoid the negative social costs associated with expressing certain feelings. Unfortunately, the discrepancy between their real emotions and what children think their emotions

CHALLENGING BEHAVIOR

Meet Sam

Four-year-old Sam was enrolled in a preschool for gifted and talented children. Sam had many fears and often said he was afraid. Anticipation played a big part in Sam's fears. He worried about what was going to happen and how to avoid anything he thought might be bad. His teacher found that the following strategies helped Sam cope with his fearful feelings:

- Explain things to Sam in advance.
- Give him a chance to participate in activities with an exit strategy in mind.
- Give him scripts to express his feelings.

Here are excerpts from notes his teacher sent to Sam's parents during the year to keep them informed about Sam's progress in relation to his fears:

Jan. 25—Sam cried during the story *Maia* (a chapter book about a dinosaur). He was afraid of the dinosaurs in the story but stayed at group, sitting close to an adult and was okay.

Jan. 26—Sam greeted me by saying he didn't want to hear Chapter 2 of *Maia*. We talked, and I persuaded him to listen to part of it, saying he could bail out at any time. He stayed for the whole chapter.

Jan. 27—We did the Dinosaur Dance in the gym. Sam thought he'd be afraid, saying dinosaurs are big and

scary. I told him he could stand near me if that happened, but it didn't. He had fun.

Jan. 28—I read another "scary" dinosaur book during large group today. Before I began reading, I talked about how funny it was going to be. Sam enjoyed it a lot.

Feb. 24—Outside, Mike P. was growling at Sam. Sam was "scared" at first. When Mike and I reminded Sam that Mike was playing dinosaurs again, he stopped being afraid and played dinosaurs with Mike most of the morning.

March 3—Sam is a little afraid of Erik, a loud child in our class who is very active. Erik also intrigues him. Outside today we practiced saying loudly, "Stop it. I don't like that." Of course, after one successful use, Sam wanted to say it often—not always when called for. The whole group talked about thumbs up and thumbs down as another signal to help each other know when something was getting to be too intense or uncomfortable. We all agreed to try this. Sam said it was a good plan.

Source: Based on Kostelnik, M., et al. (2002). *Children with special needs: Lessons for early childhood.* New York, NY: Teachers College Press. Copyright © 2002 by Teachers College Press. All rights reserved.

---

should be can cause great emotional distress. When children hide their emotions, they don't discover that they have experiences in common with other people. This leads to feelings of isolation, self-doubt, and inferiority (Goleman, 1995). Children in these circumstances think of their emotions as unnatural and different from everyone else's. The more intense this perception is, the more damaging the outcome. A dramatic example of the harm that can come from trying to hide emotions is illustrated by Cathleen Brook's description of her life in an alcoholic home:

When I was growing up in an alcoholic home, one of the things that I was acutely aware of was that when I felt sad, or angry, or panicked, or hurt, there was no place—and no one—where I was safe enough to talk about how I felt.

I really believed that noise and upsetting and making people uncomfortable was what made things so bad in my house. So I spent my life trying never to make noise and always to be good, and never making anyone uncomfortable.

And it didn't work.

And then I found alcohol, and it worked.

It's amazing how well that stuff works. I spent 11 years of my life without it, and at 11, I put it in my body, and I became who I had wanted to be. It was amazing. Alcohol was the only thing that made a great deal of sense to me. Had you been there to try to talk me out of using alcohol, I want to assure you that you would have been ignored and probably ridiculed.

But had you been there to tell me you cared what I was feeling, you might have made all the difference. Had you been there to tell me you might even know a little bit of what I was feeling, I might have believed that there was some human being in the world I could count on. (Woll, 2009, p. 1)

Not all children resort to drugs and alcohol to deal with difficult emotions. However, the fact that some do tells us that emotional development is not always an easy, healthy process.

Counterproductive Ways of Responding to Children's Emotions

The difficulties children naturally experience in handling their emotions are compounded by inappropriate adult responses. Imagine what might happen to Pedro when he declares his pride in having won honorable mention in the writing contest. If his teacher responds with a comment such as, "Awesome!" or "You're really excited," Pedro's pride is acknowledged, and he receives the message that feeling proud is okay. In contrast, if the teacher says, "You shouldn't be so boastful. No bragging!" Pedro learns that feelings of pride and accomplishment are inappropriate. Being told that his feelings are bad may cause the child to evaluate himself negatively for having experienced them. Because children naturally experience a wide range of emotions, if this trend continues, Pedro may come to view a natural part of himself as unacceptable.

When children arrive at such conclusions, they often choose maladaptive ways of coping. Pedro may become boastful to bolster his sagging confidence. He may reject compliments in an effort to adhere to an expected code of emotional conduct. Pedro may stop trying to excel as a way to avoid pride and achievement. He may develop a headache or stomachache in response to situations in which he might otherwise feel proud, or he may continually put himself down in an effort to look modest. All of these strategies detract from Pedro's future happiness.

Four ways of responding to children's emotions that are ineffective or potentially harmful include ignoring children, lying to children, denying children's feelings, and shaming children. All of these strategies cause damage and make it unlikely that children will view the adult as a source of future emotional support.

Ignoring children's emotions. Sometimes adults assume that if they ignore children's emotions, those emotions will simply go away. This does not happen. The emotions remain but, regrettably, children have no better way of coping. To make matters worse, children are left with the impression that their feelings are unimportant. Neither outcome leads to greater social competence or positive self-esteem (Ahn & Stifter, 2006).

Lying to children about emotional situations. Sometimes, in an effort to "protect" children from difficult emotional experiences, adults tell untruths. For example, 3-year-old Nina is about to have her blood drawn at the clinic. She is teary and somewhat fearful. Even though the needle is sure to prick, the adult says, "This won't hurt a bit." Such lies fail to prepare children for the actual situations they are facing and damage adult credibility. Bonds of trust, which take time to establish, are weakened (Marion, 2011).

Denying children's emotions. Adults deny children's emotions in many ways. Sometimes, they actually forbid children to have certain feelings. Phrases like "Stop worrying," "Don't be angry," or "You shouldn't be so scared" are examples of denying. At other times, adults dismiss the importance of a child's emotion, as when Lucas cried, "Look, there's blood on my finger," and the adult responded: "It's just a little cut. You won't die." On other occasions, adults tell children they do not really have the emotion they claim to be experiencing: "You know you aren't really mad at each other," "Let's see you smile." When adults deny children's emotions, the message they are sending is that these emotions are wrong and that children are bad for experiencing them. Neither message is true or helpful (Katz & Katz, 2009).

Shaming children. Making fun of children or attempting to shame them is destructive. Adults demoralize children when they say things such as "What are you

Selena hides her eyes when the firefighter puts on his hat and oxygen mask.

crying for? I can't believe you're being such a baby about this"; "All the other kids are having a good time. Why are you being so difficult?"; or "Manny isn't afraid. What makes you such a scaredy-cat?" As with lying and denying, shaming prompts feelings of doubt, guilt, or inferiority. It does not cause children to respond positively or make them feel better. For this reason, it has no place in a helping professional's collection of skills (Hyson, 2004).

Adults who resort to ignoring, lying, denying, and shaming often are trying to avoid a scene or comfort children by minimizing the intensity of the moment. Such strategies have the opposite effect. They not only make matters worse, they prevent children from learning more effective ways to handle emotional situations.

In place of such destructive practices, adults can use a variety of strategies to promote children's feelings of trust, competence, and worth, as well as help them increase their skills in dealing with emotions.

Constructive Ways of Responding to Children's Emotions naeyc

Adults can use many strategies to help children cope more effectively with their emotions. Rather than trying to eliminate or restrict children's feelings, adults should accept those feelings, even as they attempt to change the behaviors children use to express them. Adults are better able to do this when they remember the following facts:

- Children's emotions are real and legitimate to them.
- There are no right or wrong emotions. All feelings stem from the primary emotions, which occur naturally.
- Children are not adept at regulating their emotions, nor can they simply change their emotions on command.
- All emotions serve useful functions in children's lives.

Words are satisfying, more precise ways to express emotions and frequently are appropriate substitutes for physical action. That's why, in working with preprimary or school-age children, an obvious way to address the emotional challenges children face is to encourage them to talk openly about what they are feeling.

Talking to Children about Their Emotions

Strong evidence suggests that when adults talk with children about their emotions, children's emotional competence increases (Epstein, 2009; Calkins & Williford,

2009). Such conversations can take place throughout the day in a variety of contexts. A simple way to get emotion-focused conversations started is for adults to identify the emotions children are expressing (Thompson & Twibell, 2009). Because children learn best from firsthand experience, they benefit when emotions are named and described to them as they happen. For instance, if Matt is angry, and an adult identifies his emotion ("Matt, you look angry"), the child has a hands-on experience with the concept of anger. Not only does Matt find out that his emotional state can be described, but he also becomes more aware of the internal and situational cues related to that emotion. Teachable moments such as these combine all three elements of mature emotional understanding—a situation, a physical reaction, and an interpretation. A basic strategy adults use to name and describe children's emotions is called an affective reflection.

Affective Reflections

Affect refers to people's feelings or moods. **Affective reflections** involve recognizing the emotions a child may be experiencing and then using a reflective statement to name the emotions.

Situation A: Barry climbs to the top of the jungle gym. With a big smile on his face, he announces, "Hey, everybody, look at me!"

The Adult Says: "You're proud to have climbed so high." (Or, either of the following: "It feels good to be at the top; You made it! That's exciting.")

Situation B: Marlene complains that she had to clean up before her turn was over.

The Adult Says: "You wish you didn't have to clean up yet." (Or: "You didn't get to finish your turn; that's annoying; It's frustrating to be interrupted.")

Situation C: Earl is embarrassed about having to take a shower with the other boys after gym class.

The Adult Says: "It makes you uncomfortable to take a shower in public." (Or: "You wish you didn't have to take your clothes off in front of everybody; It really seems unfair to you that this is what you have to do.")

Affective reflections like these acknowledge and help to define children's emotions. In each situation, the adult's words and voice tone matches the emotion being described, enhancing the completeness of the message.

How children benefit when you use affective reflections. Labeling children's emotions using affective reflections makes abstract, internal states more tangible; that is, naming something helps it to become more concrete (Epstein, 2009; Gergen, 2001). In addition, known events are easier to comprehend than unknown ones. Labels allow sensations to become more familiar. Because emotions cannot be touched or held and have elements that are not directly observable, labeling them is a particularly important strategy.

Verbal labels also are the primary means by which people recognize and recall past events (Thompson & Twibell, 2009). An irritated child who has heard irritation described in the past is better able to identify her or his current emotional state. This recognition helps the child draw from past experience to determine a possible course of action.

Furthermore, language labels help to differentiate emotions that are perceptually similar but not entirely the same (Denham, Bassett, & Wyatt, 2008). On hearing the words "annoyed," "disgusted," and "enraged," you think of slightly different emotional states. All of these are variations on anger, yet they are distinctive in their own right. Hearing different affective reflections enables children to be more precise in understanding what they are feeling. Moreover, as children hear alternate feeling words, they adopt many of them for their own use. The broader their vocabulary, the more satisfied children are in using feeling words to express their emotions to others. They also are likely to exhibit more varied emotional reactions. Annoyance, disgust, and rage, for instance, may cause a child to envision different behavioral responses. Support for this line of reasoning comes from language research that shows that as people learn new words, their understanding of experience and ability to categorize events is strongly influenced by speech (Domitrovitch, Moore, & Thompson, 2012).

When adults acknowledge children's emotions using affective reflections, they exhibit sensitivity and caring in a way children understand. This acknowledgment makes children feel heard and accepted (Duffy, 2008). Not only do children recognize that the adult respected their emotions, but as they hear their own and other people's emotions being described, they discover that their emotions are not so different from anyone else's. This reduces the chance that they will view their own emotional experiences as out of the ordinary. Affective reflections help children comprehend that all emotions, both pleasant and unpleasant, are an inevitable part of living. The many benefits of using affective reflections with children are summarized in Highlight 5-5.

Affective reflections are fundamental to enhancing children's emotional development. They can be used with children of all ages and in a wide array of circumstances. At times, the adult's purpose in using this skill is to focus more closely on the emotional aspects of an interaction. At other times, affective reflections are used to acknowledge the child's feelings while also dealing with other kinds of issues, such as making a rule or enforcing a consequence. Using this skill contributes to a positive verbal environment and gives children more information as they form their sense of self as described

HIGHLIGHT 5-5

Benefits of Reflecting Children's Emotions

Affective reflections

- Help children better understand what they are feeling.
- Make it easier for children to draw on past emotional learning.
- Help children differentiate one emotion from another.
- Enhance children's vocabulary and the ability to express themselves.
- Demonstrate adult caring and respect.
- Show children that emotions are a normal part of living.

© Cengage Learning

"What feelings could the teacher acknowledge for this child?"

© Cengage Learning

© Cengage Learning

Take advantage of teachable moments to name children's emotions. What might these children be feeling?

in Chapter 4. Finally, as you progress through this book, you will see that affective reflections are a foundation on which many other skills are based.

Helping Children Use Words to Express Their Emotions to Others

In addition to helping children recognize emotions through affective reflections, adults can also coach children in how to talk about their emotions and how to express them in acceptable ways. Children who are able to describe their emotions in words make it easier for others to know what they are feeling. Miscommunication is less likely, and the chances of gaining necessary support are better.

This type of emotional sharing is often referred to as **self-disclosure** and is considered a basic interpersonal skill. Interaction theories that stress open and honest communication all describe skills similar to or synonymous with this concept (Gazda, Balzer, Childers, & Nealy, 2006). This is because strong evidence supports that the degree to which people are able to express their emotions to others influences their ability to maintain close personal ties (Ladd, 2005). Also, when children learn to use words, they are less likely to resort to physical means to express negative feelings. Children who learn to say, "I'm angry," gain satisfaction from being able to capture their feelings in words. They also come to realize that they do not have to shove or hit to make their emotions known.

Children become better skilled at describing emotions when adults provide appropriate information about what people are feeling and why, rather than expecting children to know these things automatically (Thompson & Twibell, 2009). Younger children benefit from information related to expressive and situational cues (e.g., "Corine sure looks excited. She is laughing and jumping," or "Rafe dropped the ball. He looks upset"). Older children profit from input related to people's internal affective states (e.g., "Esther is still upset about the score from yesterday," or "Keisha, you enjoyed describing our picnic last year"). Additionally, children increase their social competence by learning actual phrases and scripts to use in emotional situations (Hyson, 2004). For instance, phrases such as "I'm still working on this" or "You can have it when I'm finished" give children tools to express their needs when they do not want to give something up. Children who have no such tools may resort to less acceptable physical actions or give way unnecessarily, leaving them frustrated or upset. Likewise, scripts such as "I want a turn" or "I'm next" make it easier for children to negotiate in highly charged situations such as deciding who gets the next turn on the tricycle or the computer.

Children in intense emotional circumstances become more adept at coping when, in addition to helping them acknowledge their own feelings, adults instruct them in how to make such situations more manageable. This can be accomplished by teaching children specific behaviors that fit the situation or by supporting children as they work out such issues for themselves (Epstein, 2009; Denham, Bassett, & Wyatt, 2008).

With this in mind, it is time to turn your attention to acquiring the teaching skills necessary to promote children's emotional competence. They are strongly tied to the first three levels of the Social Support Pyramid (see Figure 5-6) and can be used with all children. These new skills will deepen your capacity to accomplish the following:

- Establish positive relationships with children.
- Create emotionally supportive environments.
- Implement teaching and coaching strategies that help children recognize, express, and cope with the hundreds of emotions they experience each day.

Most children will respond well to these skills and gradually increase their emotional competence over time. However, some children will display emotional behaviors that are self-destructive or harmful to others and will need more support than these skills alone can provide. When that happens, Intensive Individualized Interventions are warranted. These will be discussed later in this text.

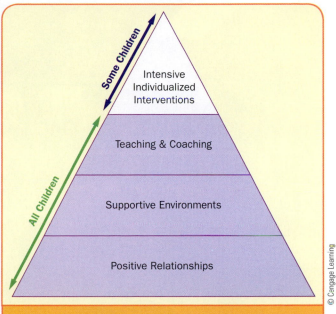

Figure 5-6 Social Support Pyramid: Supporting Children's Emotional Development and Learning.

SKILLS FOR SUPPORTING CHILDREN'S EMOTIONAL DEVELOPMENT AND LEARNING naeyc

Formulating Affective Reflections

1. **Observe children carefully before saying anything.** The context of a situation is important to its meaning. Pay close attention to children's facial expressions, voice tone, and posture as well as their actual words. Because younger children tend to be more open about what they are feeling, the behaviors they display may be easier to interpret than those exhibited by older children. With older children, pay particular attention to nonverbal cues. A child who is talking "happy" but looking "distressed" is most likely distressed.

2. **Be sensitive to the wide range of emotions children exhibit.** Children manifest numerous emotions. Some are extreme, and some are more moderate; some are positive, and some are negative. All emotions are important. If you only take time to notice intense emotions or focus solely on the negative ones, children soon learn that these are the only emotions worth expressing. They get a broader perspective when all sorts of emotions are noticed and described.

3. **Make a nonjudgmental assessment of what the child is experiencing.** Form your impres-

sion of the child's feelings using only evidence about which you are certain. Avoid jumping to conclusions about why children feel the way they do. For instance, you may observe Jack entering the room crying. It is obvious that he is either sad or angry, but why he is so distressed may not be evident.

Although you may assume that he is missing his mother, he might really be upset about having to wear his orange sweater. Because you cannot be sure what is bothering him, an appropriate affective reflection would be "You look sad," rather than "You're sad because you miss your mom." Opening the interaction with the first statement is potentially more accurate than using the second one.

4. **Make a brief statement to the child describing the emotion you observed.** Keep your reflection simple. Do not try to cram everything you have noticed about the child's emotional state into one response. Young children understand short sentences best. This also is true for children for whom English is not their home language. Older children will appreciate longer sentences or combinations of phrases but will resent being overwhelmed with too much adult talk.

Elena, a fourth grader, is invited to read to children in the preschool. How might she be feeling?

5. **Use a variety of feeling words over time.** Employ many different words to describe children's emotions. This expands children's vocabulary of feeling words and makes your responses more interesting.

Begin by naming the primary emotions (happy, mad, sad, afraid). Gradually, branch out to include related words that make finer distinctions. Next, think in advance of two or three words you have not used recently and plan to try them on a given day. Each time a situation arises for which one of your words is suited, use it. Repeat this process with different words on different days.

Finally, when you reflect using one of the more common feeling words in your vocabulary, follow it with a second reflection using a slightly different word ("You seem sad. It sounds like you're disappointed because the model didn't fly"). Below is a downloadable list of emotion words you might use.

6. **Acknowledge children's emotions even when you do not feel comfortable with them.** At times, children express emotions adults find unreasonable, hard to understand, or uncomfortable to address. For instance, Shaundra comes to the recreation center furious. Snarling through clenched teeth, she hisses, "I hate that teacher. All she knows how to do is give homework, and there's no time for anything else." At this point, it may be tempting to do any one of the following things:

COMMON FEELING WORD	Happy	Mad	Sad	Afraid
VARIATIONS	Contented	Irritated	Disappointed	Concerned
	Pleased	Frustrated	Dismayed	Uncomfortable
	Satisfied	Annoyed	Upset	Uncertain
	Hopeful	Displeased	Distressed	Worried
	Glad	Disgusted	Discouraged	Terrified
	Proud	Disgruntled	Dejected	Anxious
	Delighted	Jealous	Embarrassed	Alarmed
	Excited	Angry	Sorry	Fearful
	Thrilled	Indignant	Unhappy	Cautious
	Elated	Envious	Ashamed	Scared
	Relieved	Furious	Depressed	Doubtful
	Grateful	Irked	Sorrowful	Hesitant
	Confident	Bothered	Worried	Skeptical

Lecture: "I've told you never to say 'hate.' That's not a nice way to feel about anyone."

Rationalize: "Well, she really has to do that so you'll learn your math."

Deny: "You couldn't hate anybody, could you?"

Ignore: "Well, enough of that negative talk. Go pick out a game to play."

Unfortunately, all of these responses disregard Shaundra's perspective and make it less likely that she will share her feelings with you in the future. Additionally, such responses may cause her to react defensively or resort to more extreme measures to make her true emotions clear. Her impression probably will not be changed, and she has not learned constructive ways of handling her rage. A better response would be: "It doesn't seem fair to have to do so much homework," or "It sounds like you had a rotten day at school." Affective reflections like these prompt you to get beyond your own emotions and help you to recognize a viewpoint very different from your own. This must be accomplished if children are to trust you and give you access to their private selves.

7. **Revise inaccurate reflections.** Affective reflections are tentative statements of your perceptions of the child's emotional state. If you reflect, "You seem worried," and the child says something like, "No" or "I'm just thinking," accept the correction gracefully: "Oh, I misunderstood you," or "I'm sorry. I didn't mean to interrupt."

8. **Work up to using affective reflections gradually until the child's emotions become clearer.** Emotions that are not extreme are sometimes difficult to interpret, and some children are less expressive than others. If you do not know the child well, or there are no outward signs to guide you, use a behavior or paraphrase reflection as an opening to your interaction with a child. Wait, and then use an affective reflection after you gain more clues about what the child may be feeling.

Situation: Child is sitting on steps alone. (no overt signs of emotion)

Adult: "You're sitting by yourself." (behavior reflection)

Child: "I'm resting."

Adult: "You're taking some time to catch your breath." (paraphrase reflection)

Child: "They say I can't play 'til they're done!"

Adult: "You sound unhappy about that." (affective reflection)

▶❚❚   **TeachSource Video 5-1**

© Cengage Learning 2015

2–5 Years: Language Development for Early Childhood

Go online and view *2–5 Years: Language Development for Early Childhood.* In this video, you will observe children at play. View the video and listen to the narrative one time through. Listen again, but this time, ignore the adult narrative and concentrate on the children.

1. Go through the video and identify the variety of emotions children are exhibiting through their behavior and words. Make a list.

2. For each word, write two alternate emotion words.

3. Develop at least three affective reflections you might use in response to the children you observed.

Watch on CourseMate

Promoting Children's Understanding and Communication about Emotions

1. **Use stories, books, and songs to prompt discussions about emotions.** Read a book such as Judith Viorst's *Alexander and the Terrible, Horrible, No Good, Very Bad Day* (Macmillan, 1987) or *Diary of a Wimpy Kid* by Jeff Kinney (Amulet Books, 2004). Point out emotions experienced by characters in the story. Ask children to identify emotions they observe, explain the source of a character's emotions, or predict how a character might feel in a certain situation. Any kind of story can serve as a prompt for this type of discussion ("Goldilocks was pretty frightened," or "Laura Ingalls felt excited about going to town with her pa"). Make sure to address both positive and negative emotions. Retrieve here a downloadable sample of verbal prompts for talking about emotions with children based on a story you are reading. Refer to the website for this textbook to get titles of relevant books for children of different ages.

This list proceeds from concrete to more abstract and from simple to more complex suggestions. Choose two or three prompts per conversation rather than trying to use all of them in a single discussion.

	Prompts for talking about emotions using a narrative picture book	Examples based on *Alexander and the Terrible, Horrible, No Good, Very Bad Day* by Judith Viorst (for children ages 5 to 9)
1.	Look at the pictures in this book. What feelings do you see?	Look at Alexander in this picture. How is he feeling? Look at Anthony and Nick. How are they feeling? Are Anthony and Nick feeling the same as Alexander is feeling at breakfast? How do you know?
2.	Find a happy (sad, mad, afraid) face/character in this book.	Find an angry Alexander. Find a happy Alexander. Who looks happy at breakfast? Take a look at the people in the car. Find a happy face. Find an angry face.
3.	Find happy (sad, mad, afraid) words in this book.	Let's find some unhappy words—"terrible, horrible, no good, rotten."
4.	Look at XX – how is she/he feeling?	Look at Alexander's teacher's face and body. How is she feeling?
5.	Listen to XX – how is she/he feeling?	Alexander says, "I said I was being scrunched. I said I was being smushed. I said if I don't get a seat by the window I am going to be carsick. No one even answered." How is Alexander feeling?
6.	How do you know XX is feeling…?	How do you know Alexander is feeling sad?
7.	What is happening that is making XX feel…?	What is happening that is making Alexander feel so upset? Why is Nick happy?
8.	Why is XX feeling…?	Why is Alexander disappointed?
9.	What could happen to make XX feel…?	What could happen to make Alexander feel better?
10.	What could XX do to feel…?	What could Alexander do to make himself feel better?
11.	How do you think XX will feel if he/she…?	How do you think Alexander would feel if he found a prize in his breakfast cereal? How might Alexander feel if he had pizza for supper instead?
12.	How do you think that will make XX feel?	How might Alexander feel if he got a seat next to the window?
13.	Let's see if you are right. What do you think?	What will Alexander do next? Let's see.
14.	How might you feel if you were…?	How might you feel if you were Alexander and didn't get a prize in your cereal? Have you ever felt like Alexander is feeling? When? What did you do?

Songs can provide similar resources for expanding children's understandings and vocabulary. Consider the following adaptation of the song "If You're Happy and You Know It," as an example.

"If You're Happy and You Know It"

If you're happy and you know it, say I'm glad.
  I'm glad.
If you're happy and you know it say, say I'm glad.
  I'm glad.
If you're happy and you know it, then your words will surely show it.
If you're happy and you know it, say I'm glad.
  I'm glad.
If you're angry and you know it, say I'm mad.
  I'm mad.
If you're angry and you know it, say I'm mad.
  I'm mad.
If you're angry and you know it, then your words will surely show it.
If you're angry and you know it, say I'm mad.
  I'm mad.

2. **Set an example for talking about emotions by bringing up your own feelings.** Include emotions in your casual conversations. Talk about how everyday events affect you ("What a great day. I'm so happy to see the sun out," or "I hate it when this plumbing keeps backing up"). Discuss events in terms of how they will affect people's feelings ("It sounds like if we don't have macaroni for lunch, everyone will be disappointed," or "If we were to leave without telling Ms. Jones, she might be worried"). Ask children how they might feel about particular events as they arise ("Oh, it's raining. Who here likes rain? Who here doesn't like rain?"). Discuss emotions experienced by people children know or people they have heard about in the news ("Mr. Sanchez, our principal, feels really good today. He became a grandfather," or "It was scary for the people along Spring Creek when the flood came").

3. **Help children recognize opportunities to describe their emotions to others.** Children often mistakenly believe that what they are feeling is obvious to everyone around them. Explain this is not always true ("You're disappointed that Melinda didn't help you like she'd promised. She doesn't know that's how you are feeling. Tell her so she'll know," or "You didn't want Claudia to take the hammer just yet. She didn't know. Say that to her").

4. **Provide children with sample scripts to help them talk about their emotions.**

Sometimes, children fail to express their emotions verbally because they lack the words or they are too emotionally involved to think of them. If this happens, do one of the following:

a. **Suggest words to the child that fit the situation.** In other words, offer a verbal script (Kathy could be advised to say: "Claudia, I wasn't finished with the hammer," or "Claudia, I don't like it when you grab"). Younger or less experienced children benefit from brief phrases. Older or more experienced children are better able to consider longer sentences and more than one potential script. After children become more comfortable and adept at using the scripts you provide, help them think of some of their own ("You're upset with Claudia. Tell me words you could use to let her know that").

b. **Ask children questions that prompt them to describe how they feel.** Begin with simple yes-and-no questions ("Marco took your pliers. Did you like it when he did that?"). Over time, advance to more open-ended inquiries ("Marco took your pliers. How did that make you feel?").

5. **Help children figure out how another person is feeling based on that person's actions.** Children are not always aware of what other people are feeling, nor are they completely accurate in their interpretations. Point out specific signs of people's emotional expression to toddlers and less experienced preschoolers ("Pearl is crying. That means she is unhappy"). Prompt older, more experienced children to notice these cues for themselves ("Look at Pearl. Tell me what she is doing and what she might be feeling"). If a relevant answer does not follow, provide the appropriate information yourself.

6. **Draw children's attention to situational cues that contribute to people's emotions.** Tell toddlers and preschoolers what features of a situation triggered an emotion ("Julie and Chris both wanted the last cupcake. They decided to split it. They're pretty happy. People feel good when they can work things out," or "Garland, you had been waiting a long time to use the easel, and now it's all drippy. You look disappointed"). Ask older children to tell you what it was about a situation that they thought prompted the emotional reaction. This strategy can be applied both to situations in which the child is an observer and to those in which the child is directly involved.

In addition, point out similarities and differences in children's reactions to the same event ("You both saw the same movie, and it sounds like each of you enjoyed it," or "You both saw the same movie. Emma, it sounds like you really thought it was funny. Janice, you're not so sure").

7. **Help children sort out mixed emotions.** Begin by listening to the child describe the situation. Acknowledge each of the emotions you hear or observe when multiple emotions are evident. Tell children that it is normal to have different feelings at the same time. Also, point out discrepancies between the child's words and what he or she might be expressing in nonverbal ways ("You're *telling* me everything is fine, but you *look* miserable").

8. **Make deliberate efforts to talk with both boys and girls about their emotions.** As mentioned earlier in this chapter, this is not something adults do automatically, and there is a tendency to talk more with girls than with boys about emotions. Pay attention to your remarks during the day. If possible, keep a simple tally of the number of times you use emotion-talk with the males and the females in your group. Adjust your interaction patterns as necessary to include everyone and to cover the full range of emotions children experience.

9. **Learn more about the cultural variations in emotional expression represented by the children and families within your group.** Do this by observing how children and adults in the family/culture express emotions. Read journal articles or books that describe cultural communication. A good resource is *Developing Cross-Cultural Competence: A Guide for Working with Young Children and Their Families*, written by Eleanor Lynch and Marci Hanson (Paul H. Brookes Publishing Company, 2011). Recognize that children will use different display rules depending on their age and what they have learned at home. Respect these differences. Avoid trying to make children react in uniform ways, and do not ignore signs of affect that may differ from what you grew up learning.

Helping Children Cope with Strong Emotions

1. **Acknowledge children's strong emotions.** Stop destructive behaviors. Begin with an affective reflection followed by a statement in which you make clear that hurtful actions are not allowed. Suggest or demonstrate a more appropriate strategy children could use to express their feelings. For instance, "You're really angry. I can't let you hit. Hitting hurts. Say, 'I don't like that,'" or, "You're excited. I'm worried you are choking the gerbil, and it could stop breathing. Hold it gently like this." (More about this type of intervention will be presented in later chapters.)

2. **Comfort children who are sad or afraid.** Offer physical as well as verbal consolation.

3. **Redefine events to help children manage strong emotions.** Sometimes children react strongly because they have misinterpreted other people's actions or intents. New information, delivered on the spot, can help children reconsider or moderate intense responses. Point out facts about a situation children may have misjudged or overlooked: "You thought Andrew was making fun of you. He was laughing at a joke he just heard, not at you," or, "You thought Melba was pushing ahead in line. She's been waiting a long time, and it's really her turn now."

4. **Anticipate new situations that may cause some children to feel insecure or that could provoke intense reactions.** Talk with children about new or potentially difficult circumstances and describe what to expect. Offer explanations for events as children experience them. "When you hear the fire alarm, it will make a loud sound.

© Cengage Learning 2015

What is this child learning about sad or angry feelings?

Some of you said you didn't like it being so noisy. The bell is loud like that so no matter where we are in the building, we can hear it. That alarm tells us to leave. We will walk outside quickly and quietly all together. I'll be with you the whole time."

5. **Teach children self-regulating strategies they can use to manage their emotions more effectively.** Do this directly through conversations, on-the-spot coaching, and demonstrations. When you observe children using effective strategies independently, bring them to their attention, either at the time or later in the day. This reinforces children's developing skills and helps them to recognize successful strategies in relevant situations.

Sample strategies include the following:

a. **Restricting sensory input:** Covering their ears or eyes to blunt emotional arousal. Looking away. Distracting themselves with something else.

b. **Watching others manage in situations that prompt strong emotions in themselves:** Noting the coping strategies other children use in fearful or angry encounters.

c. **Talking to themselves:** "Mom will be back soon." "The water is fun." "I can do this." "Stop. Take a breath. Relax."

d. **Changing their goals:** Deciding to play something else after being told there's no room for them in a game or that it isn't their turn.

e. **Problem solving:** A child who is frightened about going to a new school draws a map showing the way from the main office to her room. A child who is easily angered plans to take three deep breaths before responding to peers who are teasing him.

f. **Redefining difficult situations in more optimistic terms:** "Things could be worse." "I'll get another chance tomorrow." "She isn't the only one who could be my friend."

6. **Give children many opportunities to experience joy, happiness, and humor.** All children need opportunities to have pleasant emotional experiences. Happiness is contagious and promotes children's sense of well-being. Take time to laugh with children. Play games, tell jokes, act silly, and engage in spontaneous merriment. Joyful experiences like these build up children's resilience and help them to see that the emotional world is not entirely bleak. When children see joy in your face as you interact with them, they also get a message that they are enjoyable companions and that the difficult emotions they have experienced are not the only lens through which you see them.

Communicating with Family Members about Children's Emotions

1. **Provide information to family members about the emotions children experience during their time with you.** Focus on everyday affective happenings; do not wait for a crisis or for something extraordinary to prompt messages home from you ("Jamal built a city with all the blocks today. He was excited to have found a way to use every single block," or "Today, Ted was very absorbed in writing in his journal about his time in New Jersey. Later he read his entry to the group. The other children asked him a lot of questions about his trip. He seemed pleased with their interest"). Such information can be shared in person, through short written notes, or through periodic calls home. Make it a goal to communicate with every family in your group at least once a month in this regard. Keep an informal record of your communications to make sure you are not giving a lot of information to some families and very little to others.

2. **Ask family members about children's emotional lives at home.** Stay attuned to changes in children's home lives. Day-to-day events such as a disrupted night's sleep, an anticipated trip to the store after school, or a friend coming over later in the afternoon prompt emotional reactions in children. Likewise, more dramatic happenings such as an impending divorce, mom being away on a trip, dad's girlfriend moving in, or an upcoming family event influence how children feel during their time with you. Let families know that this kind of communication enables you to respond with greater understanding to the children.

3. **Help family members better understand children's emotional development.** Mr. Ramirez mentions that his seemingly happy 3-year-old became hysterical at the sight of a clown giving out balloons at the mall. He wonders what might have prompted such a strong reaction. During a parent conference, a mother remarks that her fourth-grade daughter is in a quandary about an upcoming dance recital. The parent says, "One minute she's excited; the next minute she's terrified. She seems so moody." Use what you have learned in this chapter to help parents recognize that such behaviors have their roots in child development. For instance, explain that it is normal for young children to become wary of masks and dramatic makeup during the preschool years. Likewise, having mixed emotions is a common circumstance during the elementary years and one that children often find confusing. Hearing that

their child's behavior is developmentally based often gives family members welcome assurance. If the circumstances seem appropriate, convey to families some strategies you have learned to deal with emotional situations like these.

4. **Pay attention to the emotions family members express.** The grown-ups in children's lives experience many emotions. These may be communicated verbally and nonverbally. Watch for these cues and use affective reflections as appropriate. ("You look excited today," or "You seem upset.")

    Follow up with a question. ("Would you like to talk about it?" or "Is there something I can do to help?") Wait for the person to respond. Do not try to push parents or other family members into talking further.

    Respect their right of privacy. If a response is forthcoming, listen carefully and use the skills you have learned in Chapters 4 and 5 to convey interest, warmth, acceptance, genuineness, empathy, and respect.

5. **Accept family member emotions, even when those emotions make you uncomfortable.** There will be times when the emotions family members express are at odds with your own or with what you believe their reactions should be. For instance, when telling a mother about her son's excitement in using certain art materials, a kindergarten teacher was surprised that the mother reacted with irritation saying, "I don't want him wasting his time making pictures. I want him to concentrate on learning to read." A scout leader felt dismay when a parent announced with pride that his 10-year-old son had "thrashed a cousin good." An infant/toddler teacher became upset when a parent asked that the staff keep her 14-month-old child away from another toddler who experiences epileptic seizures. In cases such as these, your first task is to demonstrate understanding by paraphrasing or acknowledging directly the feelings expressed. ("You'd rather Hyuk Jun not paint," or "It sounds like Raymond really stood up for himself," or "You're worried about Jessie having too much contact with Ronda.") Acknowledging the parent's perspective in a matter-of-fact way requires you to put aside your own feelings for the moment and concentrate on the parent's point of view. This may be difficult, but it is crucial if family members are going to trust you and feel comfortable expressing themselves honestly in your presence. Information about how to follow up on your reflection and how to remain true to your values while demonstrating respect for family positions is presented in Chapter 15.

6. **Put a check on defensive reactions when family members express anger toward you or the program.** A parent angrily confronts you in the hall: "I told you to keep Jessie away from Ronda, but I just saw them playing together in the housekeeping area. Don't you people know how to listen?" You answer a furious telephone call from a grandmother: "This is the third time Teisha has come home with paint on her sleeves. She's ruining all her good clothes. I don't have money to keep buying new. Why aren't you paying more attention to what happens in your program?"

    When you receive family messages like these, you may feel attacked and defensive.

    This defensiveness is sometimes translated into dismissing family concerns, formulating rationales and justifications, or counteraccusations. After all, you only have the children's best interests at heart. How could parents judge your intentions so poorly? How could they be so narrow-minded in their thinking? How can they expect you to be responsible for everything?

    When you begin to experience these kinds of reactions, take a moment to gather your thoughts and gain control of your response. Try to reinterpret the situation from the family's point of view—the feelings behind such accusations are often focused on protecting the child or furthering the child's opportunities. Considered in this light, the feelings are justified—a parent made a request, which she perceived as having been ignored; it does create a hardship when children come home with soiled or damaged clothing.

    In these situations, it is best to acknowledge the family member's sense of anger or injustice, and then work to resolve the issue in ways that are mutually beneficial. Even when the source of familial anger is difficult to fathom or seems unreasonable, remember that family members are entitled to their emotions. Moreover, they cannot be expected to always express anger in ways that avoid hurting your feelings. On the other hand, as a professional, it is expected that you will respond with respect and understanding despite the circumstances. This is a hard job, but it is part of the ethical code of conduct that separates professionals from laypersons.

    The first step in any angry encounter is to move from an impulsive, quick reaction to a more measured one. If possible, take a moment to cool off before responding. Second, try to see things from the family's perspective. This is best accomplished if you treat the family member's remarks as a source of information about his or her point of view instead of as a cue to defend your behavior. Third, approach the problem by accepting the family members' rights to have their own feelings. Finally, move into a problem-solving mode, as described in Chapter 15.

Pitfalls to Avoid in Dealing with Children's Emotions naeyc

Regardless of whether you are responding to children's emotions individually or in groups, informally or in structured activities, there are certain pitfalls you should avoid. These pitfalls also apply to your communication with adults.

1. **Sounding "all-knowing."**

   "You must be feeling sad."
   "I know you're feeling sad."
   "You're feeling sad, aren't you?"

   All of these phrases make you sound all-knowing and make it difficult for children to correct mistaken reflections. Because reflections are supposed to be tentative and correctable, phrases such as these should not be used.

2. **Accusing children.** Words like vicious, stubborn, uncooperative, nasty, greedy, manipulative, and belligerent are not feeling words, even when used in the form of an affective reflection. They are accusatory terms based on adult evaluations of child behavior rather than accurate interpretations of children's emotions, and they should be avoided. For instance, a child who wants all of something may feel justified, wishful, or entitled, but certainly not greedy, which implies getting more than he or she deserves. Likewise, a youngster who remains fixed on doing something a certain way may feel determined but would not identify his or her feelings as stubborn, meaning obstinate. If you find yourself employing such a word, stop. Observe what the child is really trying to communicate, and then restate your reflection nonjudgmentally.

3. **Coercing children into talking about their emotions.** In an effort to show concern, adults may probe into children's emotional states, ignoring signs that such inquiries are frustrating for the child or unwelcome. With preschoolers, repeated questions such as "Are you disappointed?" or "Why are you so upset?" may be beyond the child's ability to answer, creating pressure that children find stressful. Similarly, older children may find these probes intrusive, preferring to keep their reactions to themselves. When children obviously are distressed but do not want to talk, it can be effective to say: "You seem pretty angry. It looks like you don't want to talk about it right now. I'll be around if you want to talk later," or "I'll check back with you to see if you change your mind."

   The best way to avoid these negative circumstances is to remain alert to actions by children indicating they are not ready to talk. Turning away, pulling back, vague answers, mumbled replies, increased agitation, and verbal statements such as "I don't know" or "Leave me alone" should be respected.

4. **Failing to introduce new feeling words to children.** Sometimes adults stick with a few tried and true feelings words for every reflection. They worry that children may be unfamiliar with a word and avoid words they think children may not already know. One way to help children understand new feeling words is to use your body, face, and voice to illustrate the affective state to which you are referring. For example, if Tyra seems to be frustrated, say, "You look very frustrated," and accompany the words with a serious tone, a frown, and a shrug of the shoulders. A second approach is to tell Tyra what it is about her behavior that leads you to believe she is frustrated: "You seem frustrated. Your body is very tense, and you are frowning." Another effective strategy is to use the unfamiliar word in a short reflection and then follow it with a second sentence defining the word you have used: "You seem frustrated. It can be discouraging to work and work and still the pieces don't fit," or "You're disappointed. You wish we didn't have to stay inside because of the rain."

Summary

Emotions are universal. They are triggered by events to which the body responds. People interpret what they are experiencing and take action based on their interpretation.

Emotions are an important part of children's lives. Positive emotions, such as joy and affection, feel good. They encourage children to reach out and to be receptive to people and experiences. Negative emotions, such as fear and anger, feel bad, inducing children to avoid, escape from, or surmount difficulties.

Emotions develop in a predictable sequence and arise from such primary emotions as joy, anger, sadness, and fear. Clusters of related emotions and combinations of them emerge over time to form more complex emotional reactions. The events that prompt particular clusters of emotion are essentially similar over the life span. Cognitive maturity and experience affect an individual's interpretation of these stimulus events.

People are thought to work through a series of emotional tasks over the course of their lives. Optimal growth occurs when the balance is toward the positive of the opposite poles in each stage. The developmental stages during which children work through emotional tasks are known as trust versus mistrust, autonomy versus shame and doubt, initiative versus guilt, and industry versus inferiority. In addition, changes in how children think about their emotions as they mature influence their emotional development. The youngest children believe that only one emotion can be experienced at a time; 5- and 6-year-olds begin to recognize that two emotions can be experienced simultaneously (but about different things); and 10- to 12-year-olds begin to identify multiple reactions to the same event. Children's recognition of emotions in others follows a similar trend. However, even older children may not be accurate interpreters of others' emotions because similar behavior cues may represent different feelings, and the same stimulus may prompt varying responses among different people or within the same individual at different times. Adults are the most significant teachers of what emotions society values and appropriate emotional expression.

Children express their emotions uniquely depending on their expressive style. Expressive style is influenced by the proportion of positive and negative emotions children exhibit, by the frequency with which they display their emotions, by the intensity of their emotions, the mix of primary emotions, and how quick they are to react. Gender and cultural differences also influence individual expression of emotions.

Children encounter difficulties dealing with their emotions. They often rely on others' recognition of their nonverbal cues, which may be overlooked or misinterpreted; they may choose inappropriate actions to show how they feel; and they may try to hide, minimize, or avoid their emotions. Inappropriate adult responses such as ignoring, lying, denying children's emotions, or shaming children compound these problems.

It is supportive and helpful to talk to children about their emotions by using affective reflections. Affective reflections involve recognizing the emotions a child may be experiencing and then using a reflection to name them. Affective reflections make abstract, internal states more concrete. Verbally labeling emotions helps children recall past events, helps them to differentiate emotions that are similar but not identical, allows adults to demonstrate caring and understanding, and contributes to a positive verbal environment. Other ways to help children cope with their emotions are to use strategies that prompt them to talk with others about emotions and deal with strong emotions, and to communicate with family members regarding the emotional aspects of children's lives.

Adults who support children's emotional development avoid the pitfalls of sounding all-knowing, of using accusatory language with children, and of coercing children into talking about their emotions before they are ready to do so.

Key Terms

affective reflections
emotional IQ

expressive style
primary emotions

self-disclosure
social referencing

Discussion Questions

1. Discuss the role of emotions in children's lives. Give examples based on your own childhood or on your observations of young children.

2. Malcom is 3 years old, and his brother, William, is 10. Discuss how each of them probably thinks about his own emotions and how aware each might be of his brother's emotional reactions.

3. Refer to Highlight 5-4, "A Lesson in Initiative." How might you support the children's development of initiative using skills presented in this chapter?

4. Describe at least three ways in which affective reflections benefit children's emotional development.

5. Discuss ways in which you could make your own affective reflections more effective.

6. In each of the following situations, describe:
   a. What emotions the children involved might be experiencing.
   b. How you would use strategies presented in this chapter to help the children become

more aware of their own feelings and the feelings of others, and how you would help them cope effectively with the situation.

Situation A: Calvin and George are playing in the sandbox. Calvin wants George's pail, so he takes it. George begins to cry, but Calvin continues to play, unperturbed. George comes running to you, saying, "He took my pail!"

Situation B: Sandy has been standing watching the others jump rope. It seems as if she'd like to join in, yet she makes no move to do so.

Situation C: Curtis has a dilemma. He was just invited to a barbecue at Steven's house, but his best friend, Travis, has not been asked to come.

7. Describe typical problems children experience in dealing with their emotions. Identify strategies adults can employ to help children cope more effectively.

8. Take five minutes to write down as many affective words and phrases as you can think of. Compare your list with classmates' lists.

9. Refer to the NAEYC Code of Ethical Conduct presented in Appendix A. Find the sections of the code that provide insight into the ethics of the teacher's behavior in the following situation.

Situation: When Mrs. Huong, a parent, tells the teacher she is worried about her son sucking his thumb, the teacher offers her an article about thumb-sucking to read. The teacher also refers her to another parent who had that same concern last year.

Case Study Analysis

Refer to the case study about Adriana in Appendix B, and respond to the following issues:

1. How would you describe Adriana developmentally in terms of her emotional self-awareness and empathy toward others?

2. If you were developing a plan to improve Adriana's emotional IQ, where would you begin?

3. What strategies did the teacher use to promote Adriana's emotional awareness?

4. If you were Adriana's teacher, how would you work with Adriana's parents to have them implement at-home strategies that are similar to the ones you will use at school to help Adriana become more aware of typical emotions? How would you discuss this with Adriana's family— exactly what would you say?

5. What signals will you look for in Adriana's behavior that will tell you she is making progress?

Field Assignments

1. Keep a record of all the affective reflections you use when working with children. When you have a chance, record at least four of your responses. Identify what the child was doing or what the child said and your response. Write at least two alternate reflections you could have said in that circumstance.

2. Describe one pitfall you have encountered using the skills presented in this chapter. Brainstorm ideas with classmates about how to avoid it in the future.

3. Describe a situation in which a child expressed his or her emotions. Discuss how you or another adult responded and the child's reaction. Critique the effectiveness of the approach. If it was ineffective, what strategies might have been better?

4. Identify one family communication strategy you heard or observed related to emotions. Describe the circumstances in which it was used and the family member's reaction. How effective do you think the interaction was?

Reflect on Your Practice

Here is a sample checklist you can use to reflect on your use of the skills as a beginning professional. A more detailed classroom observation tool is available in Appendix C.

Teachers do the following to support children's emotional development and learning:

✓ Name children's emotions.

✓ Point out things that prompt children's emotions.

✓ Interpret one child's emotions to another child.

✓ Introduce new feeling words.

✓ Talk about their own feelings.

✓ Give children scripts to express feelings.

✓ Ask children to say how they are feeling.

✓ Ask children to name another child's feelings.

Digital Download   **Download from CourseMate**

CourseMate. Visit the Education CourseMate for this textbook to access the eBook, Digital Downloads, TeachSource Videos, and Did You Get It? quizzes. Go to CengageBrain.com to log in, register, or purchase access.

6 Building Resilience in Children

OBJECTIVES

On completion of this chapter, you should be able to:

Define resilience.

Describe how resilience develops.

Tell how stress, risk factors, and adversity influence resilience.

Discuss the role of assets and protective factors in building resilience.

Partner with families in developing resilience.

Demonstrate skill in developing stress-hardy and resilient children.

Avoid pitfalls when building resilience in children.

NAEYC STANDARDS   naeyc

1. Promoting Child Development and Learning

2. Building Family and Community Relationships

3. Observing, Documenting, and Assessing to Support Young Children and Families

4. Using Developmentally Effective Approaches to Connect with Children and Families

5. Using Content Knowledge to Build Meaningful Curriculum

6. Becoming a Professional

Selena, a second-grader, has attended a small school in southwest Arizona since kindergarten. Despite coming from one of the poorest neighborhoods and a highly troubled family, she does well in school and is well liked by other children. Recently chosen as the "banker," a coveted position in a class simulation activity, her peers say that she's "really good in math and knows how to do everything." Selena's teacher adds privately, "Sometimes, it's hard to remember what she deals with everyday when she leaves school – and she's been doing it a long time."

The concept of childhood resilience is drawing accelerated interest among researchers and practitioners in education today, and these studies are taking a new and more promising direction than 20 years ago. Instead of focusing only on the risks children encounter and "fixing" resulting deficits, there is greater emphasis on variables that predict children's abilities to survive adversity and thrive.

No longer are children like Selena seen as simply "invulnerable" to stress and trauma. Instead, *every* child is thought to be capable of developing a resilient mindset (Goldstein & Brooks, 2013). Enhancing children's social competence and strengthening cumulative protections for children now constitute the most promising frameworks for resilience policy and practice (Masten & Powell, 2003). In this chapter, we will explore these latest ideas about building resilience, its relationship to stress, adversity, and protective factors—and ways we can work better with families and children to build their capacities to deal with adversity.

Defining Resilience naeyc

Resilience is defined as "the capacity to rise above difficult circumstances. This is the trait that allows us to exist in this less-than-perfect world while moving forward with optimism and confidence even in the midst of adversity" (Ginsburg, 2006, p. 4). An inherent "bounce factor" is described in almost all definitions of resiliency—a buoyancy or righting factor that allows some children and adults to deal more effectively with challenge. Some individuals do appear to have personality factors that allow quicker or greater capacity to recover from stressful events. However, the term *resilience* is now more broadly applicable to a combination of inherent traits *and* acquired strengths in individuals. Both internal and external factors influence identity and self-esteem, shaping a child's self-esteem over time.

What Do Resilient Children Look Like?

Children who demonstrate resilience are not all alike; nor are they resilient in every circumstance. However, despite their many differences, they do share a number of characteristics of **socially competent children** and can often be described as "doing okay" in spite of significant adversity (Masten & Powell, 2003). They have purpose, feel valued (not necessarily by their parents, but by some adult), enjoy being helpful to others, and demonstrate age-appropriate self-control, independence, and taking of responsibility. These characteristics transcend ethnic, social class, and geographic boundaries and have the capacity to cascade over time into related characteristics that are highly valued by others (Werner, 2013). We see them in children who are generally happy and optimistic. More often than not, they comply with parental, school, and community rules, behave appropriately, and get along with others. They are able to focus well in school and cope well with grade-level targets to effectively use the language and math symbols in their culture (Masten, 2009). In short, they are emotionally, physically, cognitively, and socially "put together."

Resilient children are emotionally, physically, cognitively, and socially "put together."

How Does Resilience Develop? naeyc

Though we will deal more with external markers and environmental influences on children's resilience in this chapter, there is strong evidence that genetic contributions should not be discounted and that conditions in the womb can affect the health not only of the fetus but well into adulthood (Cloud, 2010). For example, studies document the greater vulnerability of children who are the offspring of alcoholic and schizophrenic mothers (Werner, 2013); children whose parents and grandparents have been exposed to war, social violence, or environmental disasters; and children exposed to many biological and psychosocial risk factors, such as genetic susceptibility to substance abuse. Boys' resilience in comparison to that of girls is more fragile and because of societal expectations, **vulnerability** is more hidden by males (see Figure 6-1). As a result, it may be more difficult to detect when they are feeling troubled, depressed, and isolated (Pollack, 2006). Admittedly, we also need to know more about qualities within children that influence their dispositions. Continued research will expand our knowledge of how internal factors have the capacity to interface with external adaptation and vice versa (Masten, 2009).

The good news is that although genetic information strongly affects brain development, environmental influence has proven to have a more significant effect on neural structures and resulting behavior than previously thought (Luthar, 2008). As with other areas of development, there is now little doubt that the early

Figure 6-1 | I Am Strong.

childhood years are extraordinarily important in laying a foundation for later resilience in an individual.

An important primary task in the years before formal school entry is the development of self-regulation and executive function, both of them highly predictive of academic success and later well-being in life (Bredekamp, 2014; Calkins & Williford, 2009). **Self-regulation** assists children in being able to adapt or control their emotions, thinking, and behavior in difficult situations (Bodrova & Leong, 2012). It grows out of the development of the prefrontal cortex and resulting **executive function (EF)**, which determines how responsible children are in controlling their emotions, focusing attention, planning, exercising memory, incorporating feedback from others, working in a sustained way toward a goal, and monitoring their own cognitive processes (Obradovic, Portilla, & Boyce, 2012). Deficits in EF have been found to be strongly correlated with autism and Asperger's Syndrome, though the direction of the relationship has not been established (Pennington & Ozonoff, 1996). The outcome is that children with EF impairment suffer from mind blindness or an inability to recognize that others may have thoughts, feelings, or intentions different from theirs; they may also be less able to determine whether another child's actions are intentional or accidental (Pellicano, 2012).

Children observed at age 2 who display more **autonomy** or independence and social maturity than their peers are more likely to report fewer stressful life events and higher scholastic competence at age 10. This translates into a smoother adolescence, with greater **self-efficacy** (ability to plan and cope well) in the young adult years (Werner, 2013). When children have consistent and supportive care in their earliest years, it has a powerful and enduring influence on their adaptation at later stages in the life cycle, even if they temporarily get off track in the adolescent years (Goldstein & Brooks, 2013).

University of Minnesota researcher Ann Masten has concluded that resilience is not the result of any special trait or unique advantage that exists in certain individuals. Rather, she believes it is the "ordinary magic" that results from most children growing up amid well-operating fundamental **adaptive systems**— the many different physical and cultural systems in which they develop over time. These systems constitute all those that surround children and include family, peer groups, schools, communities, and societies that function potentially to buffer stress and adversity during a child's developmental trajectory. When the systems are strong and resilient, children are more likely to be healthy and capable. To the extent that the systems become damaged or undermined, resilience in children embedded within them becomes cumulatively more vulnerable, resulting in less capacity to stay on track developmentally (Masten, 2009).

© Cengage Learning

As you will see next, resilience results from the dynamic, shifting interplay between adversity and protective factors that are present at any particular time during a child's development. It is important to understand that children can usually cope with low to moderate stress but may be overwhelmed when multiple stressors are present, potentially creating risk factors. Similarly, although one risk factor does not necessarily create the kind of adversity that will challenge normal **homeostasis** or the ability to return to good functioning, a *pileup* of challenges to a child's competence may result in significant vulnerability and the need for intervention.

The Influence of Stress, Risk Factors, and Adversity on Resilience naeyc

David is entering fifth grade at Hambly Middle School. He's never experienced a school as large as Hambly and is worried about remembering his locker combination, finding all of his classrooms, and undressing in front of everyone for gym. Lately, he feels dizzy and shaky and wonders if everyone else knows how he's feeling inside.

Three-year-old Karen has begun following her mother closely and crying inconsolably whenever they are separated. She thinks about the violent fights her mother and father have had and knows that is why her father doesn't come home anymore. She wonders if her mother will go away, too.

Kevin, who is 6, has come to dread going to school and especially fears reading time. He has a hard time doing what his teacher wants him to do. He would if he could, but he can't. He wonders how other kids can make sense of the letters and words in the reader. His stomachaches are becoming frequent.

Although David, Karen, and Kevin differ with respect to gender, age, family situation, and many other characteristics, they do have one thing in common: childhood stress. Experts agree that for some children, growing up in today's world may be tougher. As many as 25% of all children are at risk of academic failure because of physical, emotional, or social problems and are less able to function well in the classroom because they are hungry, sick, troubled, or depressed. Children seem to have fewer sources of adult support than in the past, and many are being pressured to grow up faster (Honig, 2009; Marks, 2002).

We need to be concerned about accumulated **childhood stress** and to be watchful about the types of stress-coping responses children are developing. These are learned very early when children watch how their parents, siblings, extended family members, teachers, and peers cope when under pressure. Either positive or negative behaviors then become ingrained through habitual practice. When learned coping patterns are positive and useful, they become lifelong resources for a child, increasing what is known as "**stress hardiness**," that is, the child's ability to adapt to and cope with psychosocial **adversity** (accumulated risks), keep on track relative to developmental tasks, and maintain good health during and after the event. When coping patterns are negative, they serve only to increase the demand in a child's life, making the child more vulnerable in the future (Aldwin, 2007).

The Concept of Stress

Stress is neither good nor bad. It is simply excess energy that develops to help us meet unusual demand. This can come in the form of anything new or different in our life that forces us to draw on our energy reserves. These events are termed **stressors** and may result from significant change, feelings of overload or boredom, situations in which we feel uncertain about what might happen, or whenever we feel afraid or out of control. Children experience *all* of that from time to time in growing up. The birth of a sibling, the death of a pet,

Jeremy has a new baby brother—sometimes a joyful event and sometimes a stressful one.

© Cengage Learning 2015

birthday parties, breaking a favorite toy, getting caught stealing or lying, an overnight at a friend's, carelessly spilling milk, losing a grandparent, or bringing home a bad report card—all can be either opportunities for growth or highly negative experiences. When a child has access to caring and responsive adults and a strong repertoire of stress-coping mechanisms, or ways to contend successfully with difficulties, long-lasting or negative outcomes are highly unlikely. Some events, however, such as the recent Haiti earthquakes, ongo-

ing poverty, or family violence, are significantly more serious and may carry additional risks that even competent children and families cannot easily surmount.

When Stress-Coping Mechanisms Fail

Young children today are living in complex circumstances, as can be seen in the ecomap (diagram of her social contexts) of Kelsey, the 7-year-old depicted in Figure 6-2. When Kelsey was enrolled in first grade last year, her teacher saw some red flags that told her Kelsey

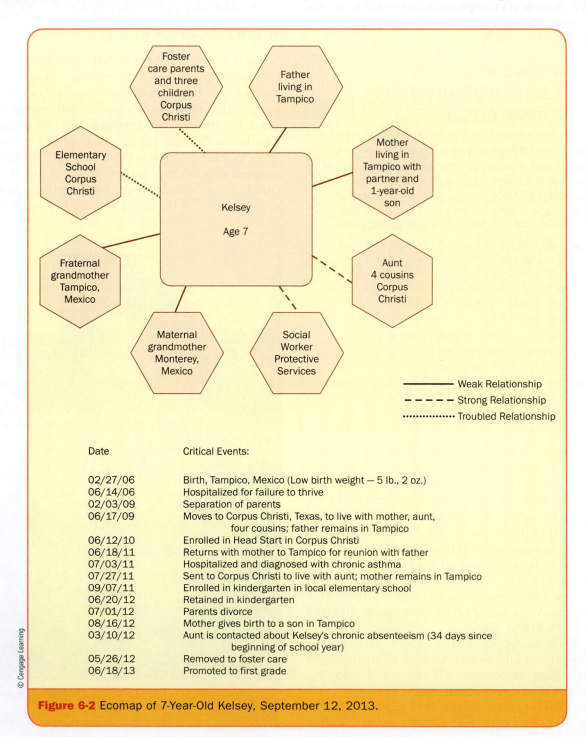

Date	Critical Events:
02/27/06	Birth, Tampico, Mexico (Low birth weight — 5 lb., 2 oz.)
06/14/06	Hospitalized for failure to thrive
02/03/09	Separation of parents
06/17/09	Moves to Corpus Christi, Texas, to live with mother, aunt, four cousins; father remains in Tampico
06/12/10	Enrolled in Head Start in Corpus Christi
06/18/11	Returns with mother to Tampico for reunion with father
07/03/11	Hospitalized and diagnosed with chronic asthma
07/27/11	Sent to Corpus Christi to live with aunt; mother remains in Tampico
09/07/11	Enrolled in kindergarten in local elementary school
06/20/12	Retained in kindergarten
07/01/12	Parents divorce
08/16/12	Mother gives birth to a son in Tampico
03/10/12	Aunt is contacted about Kelsey's chronic absenteeism (34 days since beginning of school year)
05/26/12	Removed to foster care
06/18/13	Promoted to first grade

© Cengage Learning

Figure 6-2 Ecomap of 7-Year-Old Kelsey, September 12, 2013.

might need more support that year than some of the other children in the classroom. She noted Kelsey's chronic health problems, long-standing family issues and poverty, higher mobility than usual, and academic failure. She also observed a depressed little girl who seemed disconnected from any friends. On the bright side, she noted that Kelsey spent a lot of her leisure time with books and seemed determined to learn how to read. Her foster parents—both of them—appeared at the fall conference, invited Kelsey's teacher to make a home visit, and told her, "We're going to make this work, and we need you to stay in close contact with us about how she's doing."

Resiliency must always be understood in the context of accumulated stressors or risks that are not being handled well and the protective factors in that child's life that can buffer them. In the case of Kelsey, the accumulated pileup definitely had become what is defined as risk, a condition in an individual with an "elevated probability of an undesirable outcome" unless alleviated. In turn, when a number of **risk factors** (e.g., Kelsey's academic lag, parents' marital situation) are present and interfere with or threaten the accomplishment of developmental tasks, the resulting condition is then referred to as adversity (Wright & Masten, 2013). The most common risk factors associated with the development of later adjustment problems and possible mental health problems are summarized in Table 6-1. As can be seen, Kelsey had suffered from a number of them.

Multiple Risk Factors

Multiple risk factors have the potential to disrupt children's academic or social achievement, limit a child's ability to meet the major requirements of childhood, and even lead to psychopathology. Educators who are hopeful about building resilience must be knowledgeable about and fully understand the ramifications of (1) the acute stressors or challenges faced by many children today; (2) environmental contexts in which they take place; (3) individual characteristics of children that lead to resilience or impairment; and (4) likely outcomes resulting from overwhelming risk (Goldstein & Brooks, 2013).

Socioeconomic disadvantage. One of the greatest risks for children is the lack of family income. According to the National Center for Children in Poverty (NCCP), everyday poverty significantly compromises the well-being of children. We have good evidence that children in poor families are less able to function well academically, socially, and physically. Despite this, 16 million children in the United States (22%) live in poverty, a disproportionate of them being Black and Hispanic (US Bureau of the Census, 2010). Many of these children are homeless, and it is estimated that if all homeless families were gathered in one city, they would represent the population of Atlanta or Denver. However, because they are "scattered over a thousand

Table 6-1   Generic Risk Factors That Are Predictive of Later Adjustment Problems in Children

Type of Risk Factor	Characteristics/Potential Outcomes
Exposure to low socioeconomic disadvantage	Complex systemic interactional issues: physical health issues, poor access to educational opportunity, neighborhood gang involvement, overcrowding, homelessness
Dysfunctional child-rearing environment	Impaired parenting or child-rearing: exposure to neglect and inconsistent care; sexual, emotional, and/or physical abuse; inconsistent discipline and poor supervision; admission to foster care (an additional risk factor)
Family conflict and marital dysfunction	Exposure to parental divorce or separation, high levels of family discord and domestic violence
Parental mental health or adjustment problems	Substance abuse disorders, criminality, and psychiatric disorders
Organic/genetic factors	Gender (more males are at risk than females), poor physical health, below-average intelligence, difficult temperament (irregular eating and sleeping patterns, frequent negative emotion, difficulty adapting to new situations), heritability (predisposition to mental disorder), low birth weight, fetal drug/alcohol effects, and other neurological impairment
Peer factors	Substance abuse
Traumatic life events	Death of a parent, war, terrorism, serious accidents, violent crime, natural disasters, and political, religious, or racial persecution

Source: Adapted from Resiliency Resource Center (2007). Mental Health Foundation of Australia.

cities, they are easily unseen" (Kozol, 2006, p. 3). Many children live in families that are typically plagued with high levels of substance abuse, domestic abuse, and mental health problems. Not surprisingly, poor children are more inclined to have developmental delays and behavioral and disciplinary problems than other children. They experience malnutrition, health problems, and below-average school performance. Many need psychiatric help.

Children in mother-only families are among the most impoverished demographic group in the nation, with approximately 60% of children in these families falling below the poverty line as compared with only 11% in two-parent families (Kirby, 2004). The stress a child encounters while living in a single-parent family clearly has less to do with the marital status of the parent than with the resources available to the family. Of the children who are living with single parents, some will suffer little stress. They are the children of parents who have the necessary resources to cope effectively with single parenthood—positive self-esteem, financial security, a supportive network of family and friends, parenting skills, and, in many cases, a workable relationship with their ex-spouse. They are resilient.

As would be expected, child health, emotional, and cognitive outcomes are deeply embedded in social and economic factors, such as family income and structure, parental employment and education, childcare, and housing (Fass & Cauthen, 2008). Children engulfed in poverty are exposed to a variety of adversities. Poor health and dental care, as well as high mobility rates, negatively affect their school performance. A lack of material resources in a consumer-conscious world causes them to become ashamed of how they are dressed and the way they live. Their parents are less likely to advocate for them, may suffer more frequent crises than middle-class families, and may experience poorer mental health (Shipler, 2005). There is little doubt that families in poverty are struggling to do the best they can for their children. Sometimes, however, their best will not be enough.

Family conflict and marital dysfunction. The divorce of their parents is one of the most confusing and disturbing events most children will ever experience. More than 1 million children a year continue to go through this pain. Family stress can go on for long periods before one or both adults finally make a decision to end the marriage. Accompanying these changes are all the problems associated with the breakdown, breakup, and restructuring of the relationships involved: loneliness; poor coping skills on the part of the adults; fractured ties with siblings, peers, neighbors, schools, churches, and extended family members; and greater complexity in the maintenance of significant relationships.

Two myths seem to persist about children's views of their parents' divorce. The first is that they are probably just as relieved to see the end of a bad marriage as are their parents; the second is that so many of their friends' parents are divorcing that the trauma probably has been reduced considerably. Neither of these ideas is true (Soderman, 2006). Young children are unable to intellectualize divorce. Their focus tends to be on their own families, not on the record high numbers of families "out there" whose foundations are crumbling. Although seeing their parents argue is tremendously stressful for children, being separated from a parent ranks even higher as a stressor, particularly before the age of 5.

Because attachments at early ages often are intense, fear of abandonment may cause a child to cling to the remaining parent. The child may throw an unexpected tantrum about going to school or to the childcare center and may begin tagging after the custodial parent, not wanting to allow him or her out of sight.

Much of this tension in children is caused by uncertainty about what the separation or divorce means with respect to their own security. Will they get up in the morning and find the other parent gone, too? Does the separation mean that they will have to move to another neighborhood or go to a different school? Will the parent who left come back and take the dog? Did the parent leave because she or he is mad at the child? Parents add to children's stress when they fail to sit down

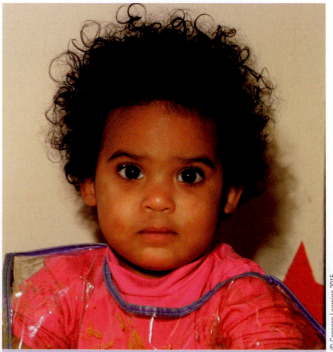

Gabby is afraid when she hears her parents fight with each other.

with their children and explain, in an age-appropriate way, the changes that are in store for the family because of the change in the spousal relationship.

Because children's thinking at early stages tends to be egocentric and "magical" in nature, children younger than 6 years of age tend to feel somewhat guilty about certain events that happen in family life. Some children believe they may have caused their parents' separation or divorce by something they did—because of naughty behavior or wishing a parent away for one reason or another.

Children's problems are intensified when alienated parents are unable to successfully restructure family life following divorce. Parents may continue to hurl insults at each other when possible, using their children as an audience. Children may be used as hostages to obtain child-support payments, as spies to find out what the ex-spouse is doing, or as messengers to carry information back and forth. Young children can become confused when they are forced to adjust to the different lifestyles or parenting approaches they encounter when moving between two households. Additional pressure is felt by the parent and child who may want visitations to go perfectly. Neither may feel comfortable about "just hanging around" with each other, as ordinarily happens in intact families. A feeling often exists that to maintain the relationship, the time spent must be "high quality" because there now is so little of it.

Tension also can be created by what "can't be talked about." Children wrestle with the dilemma of feeling disloyal to one parent if they appear loyal to the other. When a parent is openly hostile about the other parent, discusses the "sins" of that parent with the child in an attempt to vent some of his or her own feelings, or asks the child to keep certain information from the other parent, additional stress is induced as the child is forced unfairly to deal with the worry and guilt of handling adult-size problems (see Figure 6-4) (Soderman, 2003).

Even more stressful for some children, however, is the lack of opportunity to see the noncustodial parent or related grandparents because of continued hostility on the part of the custodial parent or severed affection by noncustodial family members. Adults who terminate relationships in an attempt to reduce their own pain can seriously add to a child's loss of self-esteem and loss of support networks.

Frequently, the transition time needed for most families to equilibrate following divorce is at least two years. During this period and afterward, we know that it is not the event of the divorce itself that harms a child but rather the continued conflict between parents that results in childhood problems such as anger, depression, and poor grades. When parents

learn to set aside their own conflicts, increase their awareness about how divorce can affect their children, and restructure their family relationships in a new and healthy way, the future for their children has been proven to be happier and more secure.

Almost all children, however, even those whose parents handle the transition well, manifest some signs of **psychological disequilibrium** or feelings of instability. For this reason, divorce has been targeted as the single largest cause of childhood depression.

Risk caused as a function of the dissolution of the family is confounded by the tendency of large numbers of households to drop into poverty because the income once shared by all is not available to the custodial parent.

The eventual remarriage of one or both of their parents has the potential of spawning a whole new set of stressors in some blended families: weakened sexual taboos, biological ties that predate the new spousal ties, different life histories, matters of loyalty and affection, and difficulty in deciphering roles. For example, Lynn had been the oldest child in her family until her mother remarried, but now she is in the middle with an older brother as well as a younger brother and she is having problems figuring out just how to fit in. Also, the competition between natural parents and stepparents and between stepsiblings can be problematic.

TeachSource Video 6-1

Video supplied by the BBC Motion Gallery.

Divorce and Children

Go online and view *Divorce and Children*. In this video, you will learn about one family's decision for child custody arrangements.

1. What were the particular stressors the children were experiencing in the 50/50 joint parenting arrangement?

2. What were the advantages for the children?

Watch on CourseMate

Figure 6-3 "I Don't Want My Mom and Dad to Get Divorced." Drawn by a Third Grader.

© Cengage Learning

Death as a stressor/risk factor. Generally, teachers of young children do a good job of helping children develop healthy understandings about day-to-day events. However, many of these same professionals feel uncertain about how to comfort children who have experienced the loss of a beloved grandparent, parent, or pet. There are religious constraints on professionals as well because the various beliefs of each family must be considered when answering children's spontaneous questions about death.

Before age 2, children understand very little about death. Beginning at about 3 years of age, however, children proceed through three overlapping developmental stages before achieving a realistic view of death (see Table 6-2).

Because children's experience with loss is so limited, they may feel that their overwhelming feelings of sadness and the urge to cry will never end. Other intense feelings may include guilt, anger, and resentment, and children who realize that their visible hurt may be causing discomfort in adults may tend to hide their feelings. Children in these situations need the protection of responsible adults who can help them understand that unhappy times have endings as well as beginnings. In these situations, even family members who are ordinarily supportive of their children

Four-year-old Cameron and his 19-month-old sister, Amy, probably are not articulate enough to express their feelings about the quality-versus-quantity issue. They have become somewhat accustomed to the rushed exits in the morning and the noise and confusion in the childcare setting where, from infancy, they have spent their days separated for long periods from their parents and from each other. They endure, sometimes not very graciously, the equally rushed times when they are picked up at 6:00 P.M. to make the trip home, often with stops at the supermarket, drugstore, and cleaners.

By 8:00 P.M., both children are in bed. Cameron and Amy's parents are genuinely concerned about the quality issue; in fact, it causes them a great deal of stress. Their commitment to quality time with the children, however, constantly is usurped. Realistically, "high-quality parenting" competes with the needs for day-to-day living tasks such as taking care of the laundry, responding to e-mail, preparing the report that has to be ready for a client the next day, attending a Tuesday night meeting at their church, going to a retirement dinner for someone at work, handling a flooded basement, and cleaning the bathroom.

Next door to Cameron and Amy, another family wrestles with the dilemma of fitting family life into demanding work schedules. They have decided this year that rather than contending with the hassle of finding someone to come in before and after school, they will experiment with leaving 6-year-old Sammy by himself until they arrive home at 5:30 p.m. Sammy has found that he becomes afraid only occasionally in the morning after his parents leave and before he leaves for school; however, he has come to really dread the after-school period. Rather than tell his parents about his fears, he has begun a ritual of turning on all the lights and the television set as soon as he arrives home. He fantasizes about what he would do if a "burglar got in" and how he could escape.

At least 7 million children like Sammy care for themselves before and after school in this country (Hymowitz, 2012). We now have some reliable evidence that self-care poses developmental risks for children, particularly those from low-income families. Studies of later primary children who have spent grades 1 to 3 largely unsupervised before or after school indicate that children in self-care are less socially competent and obtain lower grades and achievement test scores than their classmates who are not in early self-care. However, some of the potentially negative impacts can be ameliorated. In many communities, efforts are expanding rapidly to offer all-day kindergartens and before-school and after-school care for children. Well-designed programs are tailored to the needs of the children and youth they serve, providing children with a comfortable environment and opportunities to move about and choose from a variety of games and activities.

Highly stressed children often look stressed and benefit from supportive adults.

© Cengage Learning

may themselves be so distressed that they are unable to provide the protective factors their children need.

Working parents. Whether children live in intact families, single-parent families, or blended families, an additional stressor today is the trend toward greater involvement in the workforce by parents. Today, according to the U.S. Bureau of Labor Statistics (2012), at least 64% of mothers with young children are employed outside the home, most of them returning to work before their child is 3 months of age. Because this is a time when children's dependency needs are the highest, there is great potential for stress on both the working parent and the child.

Demands are growing for early childhood professionals, parents, and business and community leaders to work together to be responsive to the needs of children with working parents. Frantic juggling of family and work responsibilities often leaves parents feeling exhausted, anxious, and guilty.

Table 6-2 Stages in Children's Understanding of Death

Stage	Characteristic Thinking	Behavior
Stage 1: 3–6 years of age	Death is temporary and reversible, not final. People who are dead can become alive again. People who are dead still eat, sleep, and walk around. Death is like sleep or going away on a trip.	May not react immediately and may delay grief, with full understanding coming even years later. May appear to be through mourning before they actually are. There may be little crying, and the child may seem almost untouched. Children in this age group cannot yet grasp the permanence and extent of loss. They demonstrate great curiosity about the details, such as the funeral and coffin. They focus on what happens now instead of what led to the death and how it could have been prevented.
Stage 2: 4–10 years of age	Realization that death is final and irrevocable. Do not recognize own mortality. Believe life is given and taken away by external forces and agents, such as fires, guns, cars. Death can be eluded if one is clever and careful. Continued confusion about what death truly means, despite more concrete understanding of the event.	May personify death in form of bogeyman, ghost, or angel of death. Children play games in which killing plays a role (e.g., cops/robbers; soldiers/enemy; good guy/bad guy). May have nightmares in which death is confronted in some form.
Stage 3: 9 years of age and older	See death realistically as personal, universal, inevitable, and final. Understand all living things must die, including themselves. Realize that internal forces (old age, heart attacks, sickness) are also responsible for death in addition to external forces.	May become intrigued with meaning of life and develop philosophical views about life and death. Need greater support in event of death of a loved one because they understand irrevocable nature of death. Children in this age group are at greater risk for developing depression and other psychological impairment. Grief may be intense when an unexpected death occurs (Kastenbaum, 2004).

© Cengage Learning

They have a safe place to learn new skills, interact with friends, read, do their homework, or just relax.

Where such resources are unavailable, or for children who prefer to go home after school, community and school professionals are providing information to children about self-help and safety procedures in case of emergency, hoping that such dialogue will minimize some of the strain children are feeling.

Children in violent, abusive, or neglectful families. The personal transitions that many adults face today, when coupled with the strains of parenting, can have devastating effects on children. An estimated 3–10 million children are exposed regularly to domestic violence. It happens in every segment of the population, and the children involved are at risk for lessened short-term and long-term well-being, safety, and stability (Hamel & Nicholls, 2006; Miller, 2010). It is not something that children talk freely about to others because they feel ashamed, afraid, and feel uniquely alone. Living in an atmosphere of constant terror and tension, their home life is characterized by verbal abuse, insults, threats, rejection, humiliation, and disrespect. The physical aggression and beatings, which frequently result in psychological and behavioral problems, are the most frightening. Probably most damaging, however, is their developing sense that this is what home is like, and violence is the way you solve problems (Bancroft & Silverman, 2004).

Children in foster care. Although there are currently no reliable figures on the numbers of children in foster care services, it is estimated that as many as 500,000 children are currently moving in and out of foster care. Although the provisions of the Adoption and Safe Families Act of 1997 mandated shorter time frames for making permanency decisions and facilitating adoption for children in foster care, most continue to be in foster care for a significant portion of their life (Mapp & Steinberg, 2007, p. 29). Foster families are, by definition, temporary, and professionals must recognize that foster children continually experience loss: loss of family members again and again; loss of clothing, toys, and personal belongings; and loss of housing, neighborhoods, and schools. These are children who may have experienced physical abuse, sexual abuse, maltreatment, or have parents who are unable to provide even minimally adequate care. Many of these children exhibit problem behaviors that result from short- or long-term family disruption and histories of neglect or abuse: picking fights with other children, an inability to form friendships with other children, attention-getting and disruptive classroom behavior, sadness, academic failure, school phobia, and truancy. In addition to a marked lack of appropriate social skills, foster children are overrepresented among those who require special services. Unfortunately, foster children often do not stay in one place long enough to receive the help they need. Also, because many of them bounce from place to place, foster care workers may have limited ability to understand or evaluate the child's behavior problems.

Educators who hold reasonable expectations and focus heavily on teaching problem solving and building self-esteem will make the greatest strides with children in the foster care system. Tasks the children are given to complete must be developmentally appropriate rather than age appropriate; that is, expectations must be closely matched with the abilities and the capabilities children have at that particular time. You can be a powerful protective force in the lives of many of these children by making sure they receive proper assessment to diagnose needs, as well as speedy referral and follow-up when necessary.

Involvement with the child's foster family as a partner is critical. There must be acknowledgment that simply being in a foster family is a dilemma for many children. They are embarrassed to let their peers know about their situation sometimes, and they frequently think about their biological parents. You will want to keep the child's family status in mind when making arrangements involving family projects. Be sensitive in selecting classroom materials—for example, books that represent children who live with others who are not biological relatives. When we look at children who are resilient and become successful adults despite tough childhood experiences, the one thing they share in common is a significant adult. Often, that person is a teacher.

The lucky few children who find their way early to supportive and nurturing families have a fairly good chance to recover and develop positively. For those who are passed on from one foster care household to the next because of multiproblem social and academic development, however, the prognosis is far less satisfactory.

Health-related assaults. Coping with poor health and health care continues to be a major risk for growing numbers of children in the United States, particularly those in poor, urban neighborhoods. The physical environments in which many children grow up can be a significant health hazard, leading to chronic disease. Increasingly, poor air quality, toxic chemicals, and other contaminants pose special risks to young children because their organs and immune systems are still developing. Unfortunately, the parks, playgrounds, and neighborhoods where children congregate may be the places that are contaminated.

Asthma now affects 4.8 million children in the United States. The disease, which is caused by obstruction in the airways of the lungs, producing difficulty in breathing, is the leading cause of school absence. Prevalence, hospitalization rates, and mortality are all on the rise, with black children more likely than white children to be affected and four times more likely to die. Triggers can be prolonged physical activity and stressful events such as test taking. Adults must be knowledgeable about causes and signals that an asthma attack is coming or already underway by the characteristic patterns of coughing and labored breathing that an asthma attack presents. They should also be knowledgeable about the administration of antihistamines that are used to treat the condition and the policies in their setting for doing so. In the National Cooperative Inner-City Asthma Study (NCICAS), children with asthma were especially at increased risk for psychological/social maladjustment and death when their caretakers had less effective parenting styles, lack of social support, and significant life stress (Montes et al., 2012). Our growing understanding of the lifelong penalties to vulnerable children because of environmental contaminants has led to important legislation to structure protective measures and tougher regulations. To protect children, these regulations must be monitored and enforced.

Other **chronic illnesses** experienced by children include cancer, sickle cell disease, cystic fibrosis, diabetes, hemophilia, and juvenile rheumatoid arthritis. Each of these chronic conditions differs with respect to the daily challenges, stress, trauma, and demand placed on the affected child and family. Pain, hospitalization, lengthy doctor visits, treatment side effects, and limitations imposed by the medical condition are among the challenges that must be faced along with the other developmental tasks experienced by typical healthy children (Brown et al., 2008). In particular, a child's positive self-identity may be impeded if children see themselves as powerless or see the situation as hopeless.

One of the greatest health threats to children today is a lack of exercise and inadequate nutrition. Childhood obesity, which has been linked to poor cardiovascular health (hypertension and increased cholesterol) and endocrine abnormalities (particularly type II diabetes and impaired mental health) now affects over 14% of children aged 2 to 5 and 17% of children 6 to 11 years of age (CDC, 2011). Obesity also interferes with peer acceptance and inclusion in social settings where interpersonal skills are needed.

Far more serious are the results of vulnerable child syndrome (VCS) that we continue to see from maternal substance use and abuse during pregnancy, including all the problems related to low birth weight, infections, pneumonia, congenital malformations, and drug withdrawal. **Fetal alcohol syndrome** (FAS) is now the nation's leading known cause of mental retardation in children. The most severe cases leave children coping with physical malformations such as distinctive facial anomalies and short stature.

Although facial characteristics associated with FAS become less distinctive as children approach adolescence and young adulthood, effects related to intellectual, academic, and adaptive functioning do not disappear. These include IQ scores of about 68, with only 6% of the children later able to function in regular classrooms without supplemental help. Reading, spelling, and arithmetic grade levels average no higher than fourth grade, with arithmetic deficits most problematic. Socialization and communication skills and capabilities are notably deficient. Childhood adversity can arise from the child's failure to consider consequences of action, lack of appropriate initiative, unresponsiveness to subtle social cues, and lack of reciprocal friendships.

Because of a marked increase in cocaine and crack use among child-bearing adults, greater numbers of children are exposed in the prenatal period of their lives. However, initial concerns that arose in the 1990s about numbers of "crack babies" that were about to flood society and the problems that would bring to educators and care providers were somewhat overblown. Still, exposed children have been observed by professionals as being in constant motion, disorganized, impulsive and explosive, overly sensitive to stimuli, and generally less responsive to their environment. They have marked difficulty with transitions and are more inclined to test limits. Some refuse to comply and are less able to self-regulate their behavior. They have trouble making friends because smiling at others and eye contact are noticeably absent.

More seriously confounding the child's development are the interactional effects of the social environments in which these children are reared. Continued postnatal drug exposure may include passive inhalation, direct ingestion that is intentional or unintentional, or through breast feeding, resulting in a variety of neurobiological effects. Most problematic are the added problems related to parents' potential for continued addiction, leading to preoccupation with supporting their drug habits at the expense of the child's safety, home environment, nutrition, and intellectual and sensory stimulation.

Rather than lamenting the source of the child's difficulties, it has been proven to be more useful to observe the child carefully to detect what triggers negative responses and what seems to work best to get that individual child focused and back on track. Direct instruction to teach behaviors that other children seem to pick up "naturally" is often necessary and beneficial, as are specific tips and prompts for more socially rewarding behavior.

Natural disasters, war, terrorism, and violence. As was seen with the numbers of families displaced recently by Hurricane Sandy, a young child's world can suddenly

Children are thrown out of balance when instability occurs.

© Cengage Learning 2015

be turned upside down through natural disasters such as earthquakes, floods, fires, tornadoes, or hurricanes, causing loss of possessions, their home, or loved ones. This is where each of the protective systems surrounding children become especially critical. For example, in Haiti, the infrastructure relative to education, housing, roads, government, health, and other systems was not strong to begin with, leaving significantly greater chaos and adversity in the wake of the earthquake.

Children are thrown most out of balance when unpredictability and instability occur, resulting in high levels of stress and anxiety caused by fear and ambiguity. Children's sense of place and well-being are replaced by profound feelings of disorientation and a need to get back into control. Often, parents, teachers, and community leaders who normally could bring their world back into focus are similarly powerless, at least in the short run.

Human-created social traumas, however, are much more frequent and increasingly affect more of our children. Some children live in communities that have been labeled war zones, where children become victims of or witness the use of weapons, rape, robbery, or assaults. These children have night terrors, become afraid to play outside, and come to believe early that life has little purpose and meaning or that they have no future. Anxiety, lack of impulse control, poor appetite, and poor concentration are characteristics of these children. School phobias and avoidance are also common.

Intervention can take place at several levels. In classrooms, professionals can be available to children who need to talk about worries or painful memories and to feel safe with a caring adult. Children can experience, first hand, social values of caring, equity, honesty, and social justice within the immediate setting. Families can be helped to develop more appropriate coping strategies, and communities can be encouraged to upgrade services for children and families and to upgrade the quality of the neighborhood (Linares, 2004).

Even when children do not personally experience violent events, the stark reality of what such events can mean for young children is brought directly into their lives through electronic media. Children spend more of their time viewing media than in school or with parents. Up to 80% of the primetime shows they watch include beatings, shootings, and stabbings, which occur approximately every six minutes. They hear about situations such as the terrorist incidents that forever change lives and security and watch them being played again and again, not understanding they are replays. They view newscasts where adults are discussing the shooting of one child by another. Continually, they witness the gory details of the assassinations of political leaders and the "scariness" of war in terms of extreme grief of family members, children made homeless, cold, hunger, disease, and the loss of limbs and eyes (see Figure 6-4). On milk cartons, they see pictures of children who have

Figure 6-4 Child's Perception of War: "Dangerous, Not Funny, Sometimes Importan[t], Always Scary."

© Cengage Learning

been abducted and stories in the news about young children drowned by their own mothers.

Child psychologists worry about a redefinition in children's minds about self-regulation and how we should treat others—that it is okay to "'diss' one another, push, shove, hit, and kick." In fact, the influence of this "normalization" of violence can be seen increasingly in the violence that young children, especially boys, bring to their play and in the kinds of toys they request. Later, it is again enacted in the growing rate of violent crime among American youths, now the highest in the industrialized world.

Table 6-3 depicts Levin's construction of a developmental framework for understanding the overall impact of this violence on younger children and how professionals can mediate the negative effects.

There is evidence that the *number* of these risk factors (e.g., poverty, large families, absent fathers, drug-infested neighborhoods) is probably the most important factor in predicting whether there will be a "self-righting" or recovery of a child in the long term. When there are eight or nine risk factors operating, nobody does well, according to ongoing studies (Sameroff, 2005; Olsen & Sameroff, 2009).

Assets and Protective Factors naeyc

Not all children are traumatized in highly stressful situations just described, nor do effects necessarily become lifelong. Why some children have lasting scars and others are quite resilient has been the focus of longitudinal research by psychologist Emmy Werner (2013) and others who report that approximately two-thirds of the people they followed since 1955 were not able to overcome circumstances enough to be successful later in life; on the other hand, one-third were able to skirt the learning and behavior problems, delinquency, mental health problems, and early pregnancies found in the others.

Research in the field of resilience has now documented repeatedly that certain **assets** and **protective factors** can help children and their families recover and distinguish this group from those who fall prey to adversity. Access Digital Download 6.1 to see examples of assets and protective factors. This has become known as "The Short List" (Wright & Masten, 2013) that will give you a sense of what can be structured in your classroom to increase children's resilience and how you can work effectively with parents and your community:

HIGHLIGHT 6-1

Examples of Assets and Protective Factors

Child Characteristics
- Social and adaptable temperament in infancy
- Good cognitive abilities and problem-solving skills
- Effective emotional and behavioral regulation strategies
- Positive view of self (self-confidence, high self-esteem, self-efficacy)
- Positive outlook on life (hopefulness)
- Faith and a sense of meaning in life
- Characteristics valued by society and self (talents, sense of humor, attractiveness to others)

Family Characteristics
- Stable and supportive home environment
  - Low level of parental discord
  - Close relationship to responsive caregiver
  - Authoritative parenting style (high on warmth, structure/monitoring, and expectations)
  - Positive sibling relationships
  - Supportive connections with extended family members
- Parents involved in child's education
- Parents have individual qualities that have been identified as protective for child
- Socioeconomic advantages
- Postsecondary education of parent
- Faith and religious affiliations

Community Characteristics
- High neighborhood quality
  - Safe neighborhood
  - Low level of community violence
  - Affordable housing
  - Access to recreational centers
  - Clean air and water
- Effective schools
  - Well-trained and well-compensated teachers
  - After-school programs
  - School recreation resources (sports, music, art)
- Employment opportunities for parents and teens
- Good public health care
- Access to emergency services (police, fire, medical)
- Connections to caring adult mentors and prosocial peers

Cultural or Societal Characteristics
- Protective child policies (child labor, child health, and welfare)
- Value and resources directed at education
- Prevention of and protection from oppression or political violence
- Low acceptance of physical violence

Digital Download Download from CourseMate

Table 6-3   A Developmental Framework for Understanding How to Counteract the Negative Effects of Violence

How Children Are Affected by Violence	How to Counteract the Negative Effects
• Sense of trust and safety is undermined as children see the world as dangerous and adults can't keep them safe.	• Create a secure, predictable environment, which teaches children how to keep themselves and others safe.
• Sense of self as a separate person who can have a positive, meaningful effect on the world without violence is undermined.	• Help children take responsibility, feel powerful, positively affect their world, and meet individual needs without fighting.
• Sense of mutual respect and interdependence is undermined—relying on others is a sign of vulnerability; violence is modeled as central in human interactions.	• Take advantage of many opportunities to participate in a caring community where people help and rely on each other and work out their problems in mutually agreeable ways.
• Increased need to construct an understanding of violent experiences in discussions, creative play, art, and storytelling.	• Provide wide-ranging opportunities to develop meanings of violence through art, stories, and play (with adult help as needed).
• Endangered ability to work through violence as mechanisms for doing so are undermined.	• Actively facilitate play, art, and language so children can safely and competently work through violent experiences.
• Overemphasis on violent content as the organizer of thoughts, feelings, and behavior.	• Provide deeply meaningful content that offers appealing alternatives to violence as organizers of experience.

Source: Adapted with permission from *Teaching Young Children in Violent Times* by Diane E. Levin © 2003 Educators for Social Responsibility, Cambridge, MA.

Developing Stress Hardiness and Resilience in Children

Each year, you will likely have a new group of children, and they will bring with them their histories of being in a variety of adaptive systems. It doesn't take long to discover the typical ways in which they interact with others in the school setting, view themselves and their peers, and handle learning and social challenges. Hopefully, you will have a chance to meet individually with each family before or slightly after the year begins to learn more about each child's world outside of the classroom. For example, completing a home visit or an ecomap (refer to Figure 6-2) during a parent conference may furnish you with vital information you need to effectively assess children's strengths and limitations. You will discover what interests the children, any trauma they've experienced, and clues about what additional support they will need (see Table 6-4). This may allow you to be more influential in your school or community if, by chance, protective factors are weak or missing.

Even when you are unable to significantly change any negative contexts in which children spend time outside of your classroom, you will have countless spontaneous and planned opportunities each day to increase every child's stress hardiness. Included will be practices relative to monitoring children's health; teaching decision making and the value of optimism;

Grandparents can be a source of comfort to children coming from abusive or neglectful families.

Building friendships creates stress hardiness in children.

what he calls "soft skills"—completing work on time, resilience, perseverance, punctuality—and the active engagement of parents and families (Friedman, 2013).

You can structure targeted interactions with individual children, small groups, and the entire class to build these strengths. Important aspects of stress hardiness and resiliency can be taught with every age group, beginning with nursery children, into middle childhood, and beyond. To be successful, you will need to approach and respond to children in the many warm, nonthreatening, friendly, and helpful ways that have been described in the various chapters in this text.

Monitoring Children's Health

Cierra attends a local elementary school in an industrial city that has deteriorated because of severe unemployment. Her parents have been caught in a downward spiral of depression that is reflected in the faces of their four children who have had inadequate nutrition and health care. Because of concern registered by the children's teachers, the school system has begun providing breakfast and lunch for the children, as well as sponsored after-school activities where they can complete homework and participate in large-motor activities before returning home. The parents have been given information about a clinic that provides free health care for children and the number of a volunteer who will provide transportation when needed.

fostering self-efficacy, friendship building, and making connections with others; and helping children work toward mastery in many different domains.

Distinguished columnist Thomas Friedman has said that the best schools in this country have cultures that believe anything is possible with any student. In addition to hiring strong teachers who have good content knowledge and a dedication to continuous academic improvement, these schools also center around

Children's health in early childhood has been significantly correlated with coping problems in adolescence and adulthood. A child's health history (serious or chronic illnesses, accidents, referrals to health care providers, pediatrician's low-rating of physical status at age 2, presence of pregnancy and birth complications) should be part of the information gathered for ongoing

Table 6-4 The Relationship between Stress, Risk, and Adversity and Children's Need for Support

Degree of Stress, Risk, and Adversity	Likely Response from Child	Needed Support
Normal Stressors (e.g., losing a hockey game)	Developmental competence and on-track development; resilience	Normal protective factors
Risk Factor (e.g., divorce of parents)	On-track development and resilience over time	Adequate protective factors
Multiple Risk Factors (e.g., mother with mental health problem; parental abuse; poverty)	Threatened resilience; increased vulnerability; indications of off-track development	Increased protective factors and surveillance
Adversity (e.g., Haiti earthquake—Loss of a parent, home; inadequate health care and nutrition; disease)	Predictable vulnerability and loss of resilience; negative outcome	Intervention needed to regain on-track development and avoid negative outcomes

surveillance of development in the early learning context (Werner, 2013).

High levels of stress can affect children physically as well as psychologically, and highly stressed children often look stressed. When compared with more relaxed children, they frequently exhibit slumped posture or a noticeably rigid body carriage. The child may appear to be "charged up" (one or more body parts in constant motion) or peculiarly passive. The voice may have an explosive or shrill quality, and speech may be accelerated. In children who have experienced prolonged or intense risk factors, the hair often is dull, and there may be dark circles under the eyes (not usually seen in healthy children). Frequency and/or urgency of urination may increase significantly, as do numbers of somatic complaints such as headaches, stomachaches, and earaches. Appetite may increase or decrease dramatically, with accompanying gain or loss in weight. There may be vomiting, diarrhea, difficulty in swallowing, unexplained rashes on the face or other parts of the body, and frequent wheezing and/or coughing. The child may develop problems sleeping and be particularly susceptible to colds, flu, and other viral infections, causing them to miss school frequently (Aldwin, 2007).

If you have children in your classroom who are exhibiting numbers of these symptoms, investigate by talking with the family about whether they share your concerns and how other adults may become involved to help relieve whatever is bothering the child and family. Our responsibility in ensuring that every child is learning sometimes takes us outside of our own classroom so that we can serve as an advocate for a child whose family system is unable to provide the protection that child needs and deserves.

Also, in the early years, children are developing attitudes and habits related to nutrition, personal hygiene, rest and sleep, relaxation, and fitness and exercise. As you work with children throughout the day, try to build in certain practices (e.g., hand washing) or knowledge and activities about nutrition and the value of daily exercise and rest so that all children grow in their understanding about how to take care of their bodies.

Kay Clevenger, a kindergarten teacher at 3e International School in Beijing, China, appreciates the benefits of teaching children how to calm themselves, enjoy quiet, and how to relax when they are feeling tense. Every day, right after lunch, she brings out a little brass gong and mallet. Children sit with legs crossed and hands on knees. They wait for the gong and then close their eyes in complete silence, paying attention only to their breathing and the quietness in the room. After one or two minutes, Kay strikes the gong, and the afternoon begins.

Early in the year, Kay invites children to investigate their bodies to find out where all their "hinges" are (neck, elbow, wrist, fingers, pelvis, knees, ankles). She has them practice "bending" these hinges, then "locking them up" one at a time to develop an awareness of how their bodies feel when tense and when loose. She invites them to turn themselves into "floppy dolls" who become increasingly limp as they unlock one hinge after another, folding themselves into the carpet. She then transforms them magically and instantly into soldiers as they lock the hinges back up and march around the room with straight backs and stiff legs and arms.

Coaching Children in Decision Making, Planning, Implementing, and Evaluating

Sophie and Maggie are excited because they are both turning 6 years of age on the same day—until they are confronted with the problem of who gets to sit in the special birthday chair the teacher provides for recognition during large group. When they ask the teacher what to do and who "gets to sit in the chair," Mr. Kent asks, "Hmmm.... what do you both think we should do to solve this problem? Do you have some ideas?"

"We could have two special chairs," the girls agree, "and we could decorate a new one." After an additional birthday chair has been created, the problem takes a different turn: both girls want to sit in the new chair, not the old one. "What do you think we should do to solve the problem?" Mr. Kent asks again. The girls generate some solutions and listen to solutions generated by some of the other children. Finally, and very seriously, they come to the resolution that they will put two slips of paper in a box. One will be marked with an X, and that will tell who will sit in the new chair. When they draw, Sophie gets the slip without an X and immediately registers her disappointment by folding her arms across her chest, looking at the floor, and pouting, saying, "It's not fair!"

"Remember that it's important to be a good winner and a good loser and to accept the results of our agreements," offers Mr. Kent, with a smile. "Let's get over our disappointment so that we can move on with the fun that is coming. Girls, please take your special chairs."

In this classroom, the teacher allows children to figure out solutions to problems whenever appropriate but also teaches them that they must deal gracefully with the consequences of their decisions. Children feel good about themselves when they can practice **decision making**. It allows them to expand the skills they will need again and again to cope effectively with learning and life challenges: generating alternatives, seeking information, considering consequences, acting on their plan, and eventually accepting responsibility for the outcome (Hendrick & Weissman, 2014).

Between ages 2 and 3, children are able to begin this process, and adults can offer simple either/or choices between two acceptable alternatives. For example, children can select playthings from an array of toys and play contentedly. By the time children are 4, they might be able to generate some of the alternatives themselves when confronted with a problem. For example, four girls in the sandbox are frustrated and arguing over not having enough shovels in the sandbox. Karouko asks an adult for spoons, scoops, or little cans so everyone could play, "Cause then I don't have to give them the red shovel." Wise teachers know that the adult's role is to demonstrate, explain, and guide the process whenever possible, not to dictate the solution. In this case, her teacher reinforced Karouko's resilient thinking, "Good for you, Karouko, you thought of a way your friends can also carry sand. Let's all go look in the equipment shed and see what we can find." Children learn to make choices by thinking about what is possible and are more likely to "own" the decisions they themselves make. Involved children are less likely to resent the consequences of decisions that turn out to be less desirable than anticipated when they have made them themselves.

All children need close guidance in learning to make decisions. The younger children are, the more difficulty they have with understanding that their goals are not always the same as other peoples' goals. Perspective taking is most difficult with scarce resources, especially when the goal of another child is in conflict with the child's own purposes. As children mature, they are increasingly able to understand the purposes of another person and, by virtue of greater experience in making decisions, they often are able to generate more alternatives to problems. This process develops gradually over time and depends on opportunities to first make small decisions and, gradually, larger ones. Follow through to see how children in your classroom are taking responsibility for decisions they make and whether they need support in carrying them out. Comfort children who are unhappy about the results of their decision but allow them to experience the disappointment that comes with decisions they have made, assuring them that it's the way we learn better ways of doing things in the future.

Group decision making takes more time than individual decision making, and supporting the process with a group of children takes even longer. When you decide to let the children choose as a group, you also commit a substantial time resource to the process. Extensive communication is usually required to arrive at a decision. However, the time is well spent because children are more committed to a course of action if they have participated in determining it. Some decisions that groups of children might make are which song to sing, which game to play, whether to participate in a fund-raising activity, or how a holiday should be celebrated. Some groups of children are allowed to participate in choosing displays to make, rearranging furniture, and organizing storage.

Two- and three-year-olds are capable of making short-term, simple plans when asked what they might like to play. The time between choice and action is a few moments. Four- and five-year-olds, on the other hand, might verbalize about the blocks they want to use in building a structure, about the colors to select for a painting, or about the choice of play partners for climbing on the outdoor structure. These are the beginnings of plans. As children mature, if given some experience with the process, they will increase their planning for longer time periods and further into the future. The plans will be for increasingly complex tasks as well. Whereas a 4-year-old can participate in making and implementing a plan to share riding vehicles outdoors, 12-year-olds who have had many previous planning experiences are capable of creating a plan for a full camp evening activity using a variety of materials and equipment.

Both younger and older age groups require supportive and informative adults to assist them in thinking about the consequences of each decision and anticipating how the action will be implemented. To do this, adults must help children clearly do the following:

- Define the problem (or what the goal will be).
- Obtain information about the resources available.
- Generate possible alternatives.
- Make choices among the alternatives and stick to them.
- Gather materials and equipment as necessary and arrange the physical environment.
- Carry out the plan.
- Discuss and evaluate the activity.

Older children may be led through this planning process formally. For example, a group of third-grade children made board games that included developing the playing boards, the rules for play, and the social rules to guide behavior. After playing several of the board games, children made modifications in their games. They also discussed what made a game fun (evaluation criteria). Children learn these skills gradually through the guidance of adults who provide them opportunities to go through the full process of planning, choosing, and evaluating.

Sharing the Value of Optimism

To be hopeful in bad times is not just foolishly romantic. It is based on the fact that human history is a history not only of cruelty, but also sacrifice, courage, kindness. What we choose to emphasize in this complex history will determine our lives. If we see only the worst, it destroys our capacity to do something. If we remember those times and places—and there are so many—where people have behaved magnificently, this gives us the energy to act, and at least the possibility of sending this spinning top of a world in a different direction. And if we do act, in however small a way, we don't have to wait for some grand utopian future. The future is an infinite succession of presents, and to live now as we think human beings should live, in defiance of all that is bad around us, is itself a marvelous victory.

—**Howard Zinn, Filmmaker**

Think about the people you most enjoy spending time with. They are likely to be upbeat most of the time, have a sense of humor, and be involved in pursuits they enjoy. They definitely have a positive outlook on life (see Figure 6-5) and while they are likely to experience as many challenges as anyone else, they consistently anticipate an "okay" outcome.

Others who anticipate the worst in similar situations, spend a great deal of time focused on the stressful event itself rather than the possibilities for relief, redirection, reframing the event, or leaving it behind

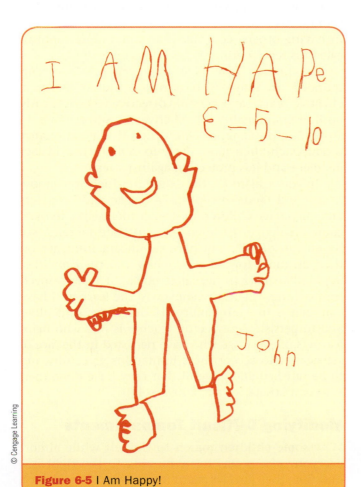

Children who learn to be optimistic are more resilient.

© Cengage Learning 2015

and getting on with life. Marvin Seligman (2007) sees this quality in people as partly the result of heritable temperament (about 50%), circumstances (as little as 10%), and taking active control of our thoughts and actions (as much as 40%). He and other researchers who have studied resilience believe that people have more control than they think over activating their own happiness.

We can teach children, and particularly those whose disposition is more negative in quality, that optimism versus pessimism is something that we have a fair amount of control over. Drawing from children's literature is an excellent way to introduce real-world situations in which characters experience problems, don't give up, and find satisfying outcomes (Forgan, 2003). Also, this is an area that is strengthened by teachers who encourage **positive self-talk** in children ("I'm scared, but I can handle this," "I can do this. I can stay calm," "I made a lot of new friends this year!") and discourage any negative references to themselves or others ("I just know this is going to turn out awful," "Nothing I do ever makes any difference," "No one really likes me around here.").

Optimism has been an observed characteristic in resilient children from a variety of backgrounds (Mandleco & Peery, 2000). As part of that optimism, they demonstrate behaviors that say, "I am a motivated, creative, flexible, adaptable, open-to-change person. I take an active approach toward solving problems, am a self-starter, and like people!" Teachers like Sherry Davis believe that a resilient mindset can be fostered; she makes sure that activities promoting the development of optimism are included in her classroom. For instance, Sherry makes a habit of ending each school day by having children write just one thing that day that made it a pretty good day for them and sign their name. They do this on "happy slips,"

Figure 6-5 I Am Happy!

© Cengage Learning

small yellow pieces of paper that they drop in a box by the door as they prepare to go home. Sherry takes them out before leaving for home and pins each of them on a board for children to read when they come in the next morning. Children write about having fun with a particular friend, about something they learned, about a book they enjoyed, that they got to play a game they liked, and that snack was good. She says, "It's the first thing they run to when they come in the next morning, just to see what everyone had to say, and it gets our day off to a great start!"

Fostering Self-Efficacy and Self-Determination

Closely related to optimism is self-efficacy, or the extent to which we believe our goals can be accomplished even when frustrations get in the way. This is another important component in creating the resilient mindset that we want children to develop and maintain (Wang & Deater-Deckard, 2013).

Even infants express their needs. Babies cry when they are in pain, hungry, bored, or tired. If their needs are responded to in healthy ways, optimism is developed over time, leading to later strengths such as self-determination or self-efficacy. If their needs are ignored, **learned helplessness** (Seligman, 2007) develops, leading to poor psychological health and predictably poor outcomes relative to building resilience. Very early on, such children feel powerless to change their situation or anything about themselves. They feel ineffectual in trying to control aspects of their environment or interactions with others.

Conversely, healthy children make their needs known to others. Toddlers point to the refrigerator when hungry or the faucet when thirsty. Preschoolers express their wants and needs for affiliation (relating to others) rather directly. These are usually expressed very simply, such as when Diana approached Mrs. Sturgeon and said shyly, "I want to play with Jake." "Well," said Mrs. Sturgeon, "Let's see what *you* can do about that. I see that Jake is busy building with blocks. What if you ask him if you can gather some of the red ones he needs and roll them over in that dump truck right there? Do you think that could work? Try it and see." What was happening here is that Mrs. Sturgeon was recognizing that Diana had an objective but didn't have the necessary interpersonal skills to approach another child to get what she wanted. Luckily, Jake responded positively, and Diana saw that other people (in this case, her teacher) could be a resource to help her if she just asked. By involving Diana in the problem-solving process instead of simply asking Jake if he would let Diana play with him, Mrs. Sturgeon was building additional resilience in Diana for the future—thinking about how she could be helpful to others.

Important in self-efficacy and self-determination is the healthy development of self-esteem and self-worth (see Chapter 4), which comes from our feeling that we are valued by and valuable to other people in the contexts in which we spend most of our time. Out of this comes the confidence to relax with others, to make suggestions, take suggestions, and to become increasingly adept at controlling our circumstances (Wang & Deater-Deckard, 2013). One teacher uses this concept in February when creating a predictable chart, which she calls "What We Can Do Now That We Couldn't Do in September." Thom says, "I couldn't ride a two-wheeler, but I can now—after falling off a million times!" and everyone laughs in a good-natured way, including Thom, as his teacher documents his accomplishment on the chart.

Having children as young as 3 years of age keep samples of their work from September to spring in a portfolio and then going over it with them also raises their self-awareness that attempting something hard at a particular time and practicing it can pay off in personal growth. Looking at self-portraits he had drawn in preschool, kindergarten, and another one he had completed at the end of first grade as part of a brief autobiography prompted Andrew to say, "I was such a baby then! I couldn't even write my name." The grin on his face reflected the great satisfaction he felt in having others recognize how much more sophisticated his representing skills had become.

As children grow older and continue to be surrounded by adults who provide genuine feedback, effective praise, and helpful corrective feedback, early positive emotionality is predictive of resilience in 8- to 10-year olds (Lengua, 2009); negative emotionality produces children more likely to demonstrate maladjustment and less protection against stressors.

In your classroom, the extent to which you choose to use and model accepting language and behaviors and encourage children to stretch themselves to overcome challenges ("C'mon—try just one more.... see if you can do it!") will have significant influence on their attitudes toward themselves and their abilities. Says Lillian Katz in her latest book: "It takes respectful teaching, where you convey to the learner: 'I have confidence in your ability to overcome difficulties and to persist.' A respectful teacher is one who helps learners of every age who have persisted in the face of setbacks... to accept these limitations gracefully and to be satisfied and grateful that they have done their very best" (Katz & Katz, 2009, p. 49).

Modifying Difficult Temperaments

Why some children march to the left while almost everyone else seems to be moving to the right is a question that puzzles many of us who interact on a regular basis with young children. There are always children who do not appear to be comfortable in any program, no matter how wide the range of offerings. They have noticeable trouble getting along with family members, peers, and people in general, and they demonstrate far more unpredictability, intensity, and negative emotion. As they grow older, without intervention to modify those behaviors, they often continue to struggle with poorly developed social skills, difficult personal interactions, and low self-esteem—all of which tempers resilience in a negative direction. We need to make the effort to provide children with better skills to ward off these outcomes.

Children who have been observed to demonstrate early difficult temperament appear to be hypersensitive to the external environment and have more difficulty regulating both their emotions and their behavior. The quality of a child's parenting, which has been shown to be an important protective factor in developing resilience, will be crucial in determining an additional protective factor—the child's positive adjustment to school (Stright, Gallagher, & Kelley, 2008). Early on, both in the home and school setting, the child needs

TeachSource 6-2

0–2: Temperament in Infants and Toddlers

Go online and view *0–2: Temperament in Infants and Toddlers.*

In this video, you will observe examples of differing temperaments in young children.

1. What characteristics did you see in children defined with difficult temperament? With easy temperament?

2. What were some of the strategies used by the caregivers to support the children?

3. What was the most predictive factor in determining long-term outcomes for children who might have difficult or slow-to-warm-up temperament?

Watch on CourseMate

© Cengage Learning 2015

CHALLENGING BEHAVIOR

Meet Julie

Life in 4-year-old Julie's family revolves around her. Repeated power struggles usually end in tantrums. She refuses to wear any clothes she calls "itchy," which includes anything new, and often wants to sleep in what she's wearing. She is described by her parents as unable to sit still to play with a game or puzzle but wants to watch MTV with its flashy, loud rock videos and will scream until she gets her way. The constant battles are taking their toll on Julie as well as on her family. On an ordinary day in the life of the Johnson family, Julie is always at center stage, and her parents, brother, grandparents, friends, schoolmates, and teachers all seem to be "supporting" players. It sometimes seems to her mother that the world revolves around her difficult child and, in a sense, it does—with everyone reacting to Julie's actions, which are often negative and which leave a string of negative reactions in their wake. (Adapted from Turecki, 2000, pp. 86–90).

to interact with adults who have an extra store of patience and are able to provide the kind of predictable structure, clear limits, reinforcement of positive and/or adaptable behavior, and play outlets needed. Also, the skills that were outlined in the preceding chapters on communication and emotional development are highly applicable here in helping children learn to better regulate their behavior and deal with intense emotions. Consider how you might use what you have learned so far to work with a child such as Julie, whose difficult temperament translates into a variety of challenging behaviors.

Strengthening Skills of Friendship Building and Social Connections

A noted psychologist often spoke about the powerful effect friendships (or lack of them) have on resilience. As troubled individuals would come to him for counseling and advice, the first question he would ask is, "Who are you able to go to for support when you have a problem?" Those who had little resilience were often silent for a moment and would then admit that they had "no one" they could think of. Those who eventually recovered from the adversity they were experiencing could readily offer a number of names (Broderick, 2008). In regaining wellness and our developmental footing, it is often our ability to connect to others that can help with necessary social system modification, reorganization, and reclaiming of a resilient mindset. Ultimately, the key component in resilient processes is our connection to people (Goldstein & Brooks, 2013).

Free play and the encouragement of playfulness in the school context that characterized American early childhood has increasingly disappeared in the wake of growing competitiveness. Researchers have documented that the result has been that children are more aggressive, more selfish, less cooperative, less egalitarian, less peaceful, and less willing to share. There is less concern among children for the feelings and well-being of others and greater selfishness—all part of "a society that has forgotten how to play." The most important skill for social competence is to be able to please other people while still gratifying your own needs. When children are able to play freely with others and keep others interested in playing with them, they have learned the skill of seeing the world from another person's perspective. That, along with a sense of humor, fosters a child's ability to exist harmoniously with others, to counteract tendencies toward arrogance, and to build autonomy (Science Daily, 2009).

Children who are in playful settings are less aggressive, more cooperative, and more willing to share.

As children move outward from the family, some will need more support than others in forming friendships with other children and adults. Teachers who care about helping children with this task are central to empowering children with the skills to make solid connections with others—a critical protective factor in the building of resilience. When you take time in your teaching to provide children with the tools they need to navigate the peer environment, including issues surrounding fairness, diversity, prejudice, and power, they are better equipped to overcome daily challenges (Derman-Sparks & Edwards, 2010). In Chapters 7 and 8, you will learn more about strategies for enhancing and expanding children's play, as well as ways in which you can create a climate in your classroom to promote friendship skills in children that will last into adulthood.

Scaffolding Children's Intellectual and Scholastic Competence

The literacy study was winding down, with only three more children to assess. The researcher called for Marcus to read and, as he sat down and opened the book, it was clear this was a child who was neglected. He was extremely dirty, thin, and looked fatigued. These were usually signs of children who were predictably poor readers.

Marcus brightened up as he opened Leo Leonni's *Fish is Fish* and sped through the first hundred words without a single error. "Whoa," the surprised researcher said to him as she recorded his score "You're a reader! Who reads to you?"

"No one reads to me. I read to me," said Marcus, slowly pushing the book back to her.

A child's intellect and school achievement is a major buffer against adversity, and a lack of ability to keep on track in school is often one of the first indicators that some sort of adversity has become a barrier to a child's ongoing development. Resilient children often score well on educational achievement and scholastic aptitude tests, have better reading scores, and demonstrate greater abilities to reason and regulate their own behavior (Mandleco & Peery, 2000; Bernard, 2004). It could also be said that having someone who was willing to keep them on track at the first sign of failure, to teach them to be reflective, and to be good at self-regulation allowed them to develop the characteristics that later resulted in their being labeled "resilient."

Children such as Marcus, who come from poverty and highly dysfunctional situations, may be *expected* to fail by teachers who have low opinions or stereotyped views about his ability to learn or to exercise an internal locus of control. Fortunately, many more teachers believe that *all* children have the capacity for healthy development and successful learning (Espinosa, 2010). They understand that high expectations and opportunities for participation in meaningful, engaging activities draw all children into the learning process. They also don't give up on the family's capacity to rebound to change the life trajectory of their children. They work closely with one or both parents (or grandparents) to make sure that children get to school every day, have the books and supplies they need to keep up with learning, have a healthy diet and enough sleep so their brains are functioning well, and a peaceful place to go after school.

Good intellectual functioning in children encompasses abilities such as planning, flexible thinking, resourcefulness, critical thinking, and insight. Holding all of these together as a category is a "figuring-things-out" quality that develops in the resilient child's thinking (Bernard, 2004). *Planning* was discussed earlier as part of the reflective process that children must go through to make more formalized decisions. It enables children to have a sense of being in control and leads to "planful competence" that they need before entering adolescence. *Resourcefulness* happens when children seek help and also develop the "street smarts" that are essential for children growing up without family protection. This also emerges out of children's autonomy when they are provided opportunities for independent self-care and taking of responsibility. *Critical thinking*, higher-order thinking skills, and analytic habits of thinking develop when teachers draw children's attention to *how* they are thinking and solving problems, as well as the efficiency and effectiveness of the outcomes associated with their thinking. Such intellectual skills cannot be taught by themselves but evolve out of the purposeful activities that teachers plant in high-quality learning contexts. Finally, *insight* is most helpful to children who live in troubled situations fraught with adversity. It is the filter that children need to figure out that the problems experienced in their families (not enough food to eat, abusive or bizarre behavior) are not common to all families and that their lives can be different eventually (Bernard, 2004). They learn this through books that teachers can introduce them to, discussions with caring peers and adults, and the kindness that is demonstrated daily in the educational setting.

Admittedly, no matter how adept children become at coping with stress and warding off adversity, it is never possible for them to be completely successful, to avoid all negative consequences, and to be able to take everything that comes their way. Children, and especially very young children, cannot cope with stress on a daily basis without help and support from at least one caring adult. For some children, your classroom and the school may be the only place where they can find such help.

Working with Families as Partners in Developing Resilience naeyc

Ellie is a second grader who has tremendous difficulty recovering from any kind of disappointment. Recently, the children began a project in the classroom where they had to prepare a written "application" for a class job in a simulation to understand earning and spending dollars. She wanted the job as banker, but it went to her best friend Selena. Ellie was given her second choice, the job of gathering books in the library. That evening, she complains to her mother that "everyone has to do something really stupid in class…," that she hates school, and that she's not going anymore. Ellie's mother is distressed and has contacted the school about why teachers are spending their time on something that is not only upsetting the "children" but is also a "useless" exercise.

Mrs. Vetter and her assistant are discussing 4-year-old William's lingering sadness about his father moving out of the home and whether or not to meet with his parents to talk about some ways they can be more supportive. "He's usually able to handle things as they come," says Mrs. Vetter. "But this time, it's different."

After children move into a situation in which they receive a significant portion of their care from adults other than their parents, *all* of the adults then become linked in the delicate responsibility of guiding a child's socialization—and, in this case, fostering resilience.

For this link to be strong and effective, you must be willing to share information that you believe the family needs to know about a child to best support the child's needs—and vice versa. This calls for frank, open communication that is conducted in a nonthreatening, nonjudgmental manner, even when parents' behavior in a difficult situation is less than optimal. When one adult seeks to place blame or to unfairly criticize another adult's genuine attempts to be supportive, the thread that links them together is weakened significantly. You can be most helpful to parents when you do the following:

- Let them know if their child is manifesting signs of undue stress.
- Remain alert for signs of parental stress.
- Treat parents respectfully.
- Share information with parents about the effects of childhood/adult risk and adversity through seminars or newsletters.

- Listen empathically to parents when they speak of their own stress and acknowledge their efforts to reduce their child's level of distress.

- Let parents know you want to work cooperatively with them to support them and their child during thorny times.

- Talk to separating or divorcing parents about the importance of explaining to their children how divorce will affect their daily living and that the children played no part in the adults' problems. Explain the necessity of keeping children's routines as regular as possible and providing children with reassurance and extra emotional support (though this may be difficult when parents, themselves, are experiencing high levels of stress).

Now that you have learned how adversities lead to less desirable outcomes and about resilience in children, ask yourself the following questions:

- What can I do to further develop resilience in the children in my classroom?

- How can I make a difference in the lives of children even when I can't change their home environments?

- Do I need to link with other professionals to build some additional protective factors for a child (see Figure 6-6)?

To find out how to translate these questions into action, study the following skill section carefully.

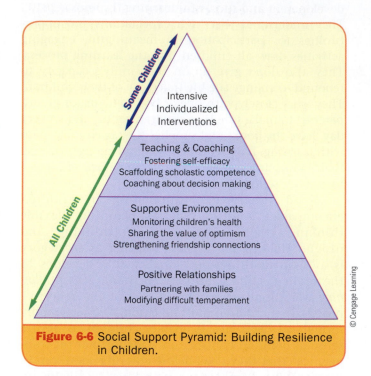

Figure 6-6 Social Support Pyramid: Building Resilience in Children.

© Cengage Learning

SKILLS FOR DEVELOPING STRESS HARDY AND RESILIENT CHILDREN naeyc

1. **Set realistic goals for children that take into consideration variations in temperament and abilities.** Rather than focusing solely on the end result, consider where the child's current functioning is and determine the steps a child will need to take to move toward the ultimate outcome. See the child as an individual, at one point in time in his or her development, and with potential to achieve greater capability if given adequate support.

2. **Help children learn how to reframe upsetting experiences.** For example, for children experiencing their parents' divorce or separation, explain that these are the result of "grown-up problems." Tell children that adults get divorced because they no longer find happiness in being together. Reassure youngsters that they are not responsible for the divorce, nor is it possible for them to bring their parents back together. Explain that although family members will be living in different households, they are

still family, and the mother and father are still the child's parents and will continue to be.

3. **Link to other supportive contexts in the community that provide protective oversight for children and families experiencing cumulative stress, adversity, and trauma.** Know where your expertise is limited and where it would be helpful to the child and family to expand and link protective factors.

4. **Observe for early signs of excessive and cumulative stress in children.** Watch for the withdrawn child as well as for the child who more openly displays negative feelings or behaviors. Both may require tremendous patience on your part because children may resist your initial attempts to make them more comfortable. The withdrawn child may become more intensely avoidant; the angry, aggressive child may refuse, at first, to work at controlling hostile behavior. Giving in to or ignoring such behaviors, rather than building

these children toward more productive coping, only reinforces their feelings of insecurity.

5. **Teach strategies to help children handle undue stress before they find themselves in highly stressful situations.** Coach children about what to do in potentially frightening situations or emergencies. Discuss potentially stressful or risky situations. Use Persona Dolls, puppets, and role plays to expand awareness of positive coping mechanisms and prepare children for chance encounters. For example, ask, "What would you do if you got separated from your parents in a department store?" or "What would you do if someone older and bigger than you tried to take your lunch money away?"

6. **Respect children's viewpoints about situations as well as their coping modalities.** This does not mean that you will always agree with how they are handling their problems, but it is where empathy on your part will be important. It will enable you to see the stressor through the child's eyes. Moreover, a holistic look at the stressor in terms of what other demands the child and family are facing is necessary to avoid simplistic "solutions."

7. **Convey to children that they do have self-control and can practice positive self-talk in tense situations.** Children cannot control their feelings, but they can learn to control their behavior. Help them to develop and practice positive self-talk described earlier in this chapter that is appropriate to the particular problems they may experience.

8. **Encourage children to view themselves in a more positive light.** When children have developed the habit of focusing verbally or mentally on the negative aspects of an experience ("No one likes me," "I'm so dumb," "I knew everyone would laugh at me," "I can never remember anything!"), positive behavior changes can happen when you verbalize positive aspects. Avoid denying children's feelings ("You shouldn't *feel* that way," "It's not that bad"). Rather, point out the genuinely potential benefits or good in a situation. Discourage children from ever saying how stupid, incompetent, or helpless they are when in the middle of a difficult situation. For instance, after missing the word *chaotic* in a spelling bee, Alvin sits down saying, "I'm not any good at spelling, anyway!" At this point, you could say: "You're disappointed that you missed a word. You lasted for five rounds. That's pretty good."

9. **Instruct children in specific relaxation techniques and imagery.** Provide a brief period in the school day to have children practice exercises such as deep muscle relaxation and relaxed breathing daily so they become habitual. Also, children who have very limited skills in a particular area or poor self-esteem often foresee themselves as performing poorly in a particular situation before they even begin. This tends to decrease their potential for performing at least adequately, if not well. Suggest that children imagine that they are going to perform very well in the particular task that worries them. Teach them to begin the task in their minds and go through it step by step until it is successfully "completed." Have the children pretend with all their senses; for example, they might imagine themselves preparing for an oral presentation, reading, writing note cards, walking to the front of the group, and seeing classmates listening attentively. Encourage them to envision success and competence for any potentially threatening experience. Tell children to use this technique whenever they have to do something that worries or frightens them.

10. **Teach children the power of being an effective decision maker, thereby supporting the development of executive functioning.** Start with giving children small choices, and involve them in solving real, genuine problems:

- Offer many different choices to children each day. Anticipate situations in which choices could be offered, and plan what those choices will be. For instance, if you know you will be reading a story to the group, consider giving children a choice about where to sit, whether they would like to follow up the story by writing a poem or drawing a picture, or what character they would like to portray in a reenactment of the tale.

- Take advantage of naturally occurring situations in which to offer choices. Ask if the child would prefer to pass out plates or napkins. Even if materials all look the same, give children a choice of which one to use, or ask children whether they'd like to work with someone this time on a particular task or get the job done by themselves. Let a child decide whether he or she will put away the large blocks or the small blocks first.

- Offer choices using positive statements. Give children acceptable alternatives rather than telling them what they cannot choose. It would be better to say "You can use the blocks to make something like a road, a house, or a rocket" than to say, "You can make anything except a gun." The former statement helps children to recognize what alternatives are available; the latter directs children's attention to the very thing you do not want them to consider.

- Offer choices for which you are willing to accept either alternative the child selects. Pick alternatives with which you are equally comfortable. If you say, "You can either water the plants or feed the fish," you should be satisfied with either choice the child makes. If what you want is for the child to water the plants, do not make plant watering optional. Instead, offer a choice *within* the task, such as watering the plants in the morning or just after lunch. These choices are offered as either-or statements or "you choose" statements. For example, "You can water either the big plants or the little plants first" or "You choose: big plants or little plants first?" Avoid the tag question, "OK?" to a statement for which a child has no choice. It implies a choice, and the child may say "No!"

- Allow children ample time to make their decisions. When making choices, children often vacillate between options. Without rushing them, give them a time frame within which to think, saying: "I'll check back with you in a few minutes to see what you've decided," "While you're finishing your painting, you can decide which area to clean up," or "You ask Suzanne what she wants to do, and then get back with me to let me know what you've decided."

- Allow children to change their minds if the follow-through on the decision has not yet begun. If Camille is trying to decide between the blue cup and the red cup and initially chooses the blue one, she should be allowed to switch to the red cup as long as her milk has not already been poured or the red cup has not been given to someone else.

- Encourage children to carry out and complete the implementation of their plan by themselves. Permit children to act on their choices. Provide the necessary demonstration but still ask the child to complete the follow-through of the plan. For example, a child chooses a book by picking it up, chooses a play partner by offering to share materials, and so on. Avoid doing tasks for children that they can do for themselves because it implies that the child is not competent and undermines self-esteem.

- Allow children to accept responsibility for the choices they make and to experience the positive and negative consequences of their decisions unless doing so would endanger their safety or physical or emotional health. When children have made a decision and it is in process, help them stay with it and follow through on their choice.

- Help children learn to evaluate their own accomplishments. Focus on what has been accomplished compared to what was intended. "Did this picture turn out the way you planned?" "What can you do differently next time?" Point out that the child was ultimately successful because of the effort, "You tried twice to get those boots on, but you did it in the end." Sometimes children need to have feedback on how to assess if they have accomplished the task. Ask them in advance questions such as, "How will you know if the dishes are really clean?" or "How will you know that the story you've written is ready for publication?" Ultimately, children will learn to provide feedback to themselves, but this takes much practice and experience. Avoid any comparisons between children.

11. **Provide children with many opportunities to do things for themselves.** Do not do things for children in your classroom that they are capable of doing independently or you undermine their ability to build needed resilience capability. Take the time needed in the classroom to have children think through and implement plans to carry out goals they want to achieve.

12. **Provide additional support for children who have chronic or potentially life-threatening disease (e.g., cystic fibrosis, cancer), but do not overprotect them.** Children who are in remission or well enough to attend school may need some privileges not accorded to other children related to the need for additional rest, medication, and nutritional limitations. Like other children, however, they need consistent limits on their behavior, appropriate and reasonable academic expectations, and occasional help in forming classroom friendships.

13. **Explain to children about the concept of "bouncing back" from setbacks.** Help them understand that we cannot make ourselves completely invulnerable, but we can come back from disappointments and adversity. Coach them in asking for help from others when getting back on track looks overwhelming. Provide scripts for younger children to use. Help older children figure out what they might say or do.

14. **Provide support for children coping with death and loss:**
    - Use appropriate vocabulary when discussing death and dying (e.g., use "dead," "dying,"

and "died" rather than analogies such as "Dying is like going to sleep" or euphemisms like "passed on," "lost," or "gone away").

- Explain why death has occurred, giving children accurate information (e.g., living things get sick sometimes, mostly they get better, but sometimes their bodies can't function anymore; the body wears out sometimes; sometimes there are accidents).

- Describe death in terms of familiar bodily functions (e.g., the guinea pig's heart stopped beating, his lungs stopped breathing, and he doesn't feel anything).

- Answer children's questions about death matter-of-factly. Respond calmly and honestly to questions about cemeteries, coffins, tombstones, funerals, ghosts, and skeletons.

Pitfalls to Avoid When Building Resilience naeyc

All children and all families experience upsets and problems. Others endure highly adverse situations. As has been pointed out, their reactions depend heavily on individual and familial assessment of resources to meet these demands. Following are some pitfalls you may experience in working with children and families under stress:

1. **Blaming the victim.** Always remember that you carry with you your own perceptions (and possibly very different resources) and must be careful not to stereotype families based on intellectual abilities, achievement, composition, ethnicity, financial resources, or protective factors. Much of a family's response in a stressful or adversarial situation will depend on how they perceive a particular demand or crisis together with what they feel they can do to counter it and still maintain their balance. Although some individuals and families make what seem to be terribly poor decisions, they are doing the best they can given their current perceptions of their options and resources. In other words, people do not purposely or consciously "mess up" their lives.

   Avoid lumping stressed children all together (e.g., "all those foster kids," "children from that part of town"). Stereotypes can be made of classes of children without any true understanding of the group in question. Professionals deal with children experiencing adversity individually to help them become more resilient.

2. **Allowing children complete freedom to choose.** No one can do whatever he or she wants

- Avoid religious explanations and respect family differences in perspectives about death.

15. **Confer with family members to coordinate strategies and diminish the effects of adversity.** Family members who are themselves under stress are still concerned about the well-being of their children. Engage them in a dialogue, and, if possible, develop joint strategies that will support the children. Recognize verbally the efforts that families are engaged in.

16. **Seek information about community resources and the resources available at your school or agency that can be brought to bear in specific situations.** Refer families to other professionals according to the policy in your setting.

to do. There are limits to all things. Children need to collaborate and be involved in decisions, but giving them complete freedom places a burden on them that they are likely not yet prepared to carry. Children who are given the opportunity to "do anything" may not even be able to generate choices. Complete freedom of choice is stressful for children, and they may become confused and distressed.

3. **Assuming that family members understand the principles of decision making and know how to structure decisions for their children.** Though professionals learn specifics about decision making and can teach this to children, parents may not even think of providing their smallest children with simple choices such as which sock to put on first. Sharing and modeling such strategies with parents supports the continuity between home and school.

4. **Not acting on suspected abuse.** You do not determine whether or not abuse has occurred. Other professionals do so after an investigation. Your role is to report your concerns according to your school or agency policy and to adhere to state laws governing for reporting of abuse.

5. **Making skewed and inappropriate responses.** Adults tend to respond first to children who irritate them or cause them stress and to ignore the more compliant ones. Because withdrawn children cause us fewer problems in the classroom, there often is a tendency for helping professionals to see the aggressive or overly dependent child as the one who most needs help. In these cases, we probably are responding as much to our own needs as to the needs we see in the children. Their

behavior increases our own stress levels, prompting us to do something about it.

The children who suffer quietly may be particularly vulnerable, and we need to be alert for the subtle cues they present. They may need your help in dealing with overwhelming thoughts and feelings or additional support in learning to communicate what is bothering them. If they are to become resilient, they must learn to cope with these stressors rather than run away from them.

Problems in the educational setting occur when we see only the irritating behavior in a child, not the child's distress. When we find ourselves getting angry about a child's negativism, we need to remember that this is the child's strategy for coping with a particular situation. Effective behavior changes do not occur overnight. They require patience, consistency, and firmness on our part and the development of trust on the child's part. A sensitive approach to troubled children need not be seen as a "soft" approach. Children do feel safer with a strong adult; what they do not need, however, is a punitive adult who strips them of their faulty defense mechanisms without providing anything more effective. This only makes an already vulnerable child feel more bankrupt and out of control.

6. **Dictating "appropriate" responses.** Although everyone experiences the same range of feelings, reactions to particular situations vary among individuals. Situations arise in which you expect a certain reaction, such as remorse, sadness, or tension. When the person does not respond in the expected manner, the reaction may be perceived as "inappropriate." Remember, there are no right or wrong feelings. Your role is not to tell children or members of their family how to feel but rather to help them learn constructive ways of making their feelings known to others.

If a child or family rejects your offer for help, you may feel annoyed and unappreciated. Keep in the back of your mind that, in most cases, an individual's response is based on his or her reaction at the moment and has nothing to do with you. Children often show their distress through their behavior rather than through words. Although talking can help a troubled child, it must take place when the child is ready. Children vary in the time it takes them to reach this point.

Let children know you are available, but do not pressure them into talking or make them feel obligated to talk to obtain your approval. You can say things like "If you want to talk, I'll be around," or "Sometimes people feel better when they talk about their feelings." If a child seems hesitant or expresses a desire to be left alone, respect his or her need for privacy by following up with a statement like "I'll still be here if you want to talk later; and, if you don't, that's all right, too." Use affective reflections to help children cope with emotions of all kinds.

7. **Making a perfunctory diagnosis of a child's behavior.** When helping professionals know that a child and his or her family are going through a stressful time, they may erroneously assume that all of the child's inappropriate behavior is a direct result of a particular stressor. For example, adults often are quick to say: "He's biting because his mother went back to work," "She has trouble making friends because her parents are divorced," or "She's complaining about an upset stomach—it must be because of jealousy over the new baby." Although the stressful situation at home may be contributing to these behaviors, there is a chance that other factors are involved. It is necessary to carefully consider the range of possibilities. For instance, the child who is biting may not know an alternative way of getting what he wants; the friendless child may not recognize other children's attempts to make contact or may lack basic conversational skills; and the child with the stomachache may, in fact, be simply reacting to something she ate.

8. **Looking for a "quick fix" or a superficial solution.** When we feel we do not have the time, the energy, or a ready solution to a particular problem, we sometimes fall into the trap of trying to get the situation over with as quickly as possible. This can be difficult for children because the adult's notion of a solution may not match the child's real need. For example, all of us, at one time or another, have seen adults trying to cajole or shame a crying child into being quiet. When this strategy fails, it is not unusual to hear the adult say coercively, "Either you stop crying, or I'll give you something to cry about!" At other times, adults may force children to prematurely confront a situation in the mistaken belief that this will make the child "get over" feelings of fear, revulsion, or unhappiness. Statements like "There's nothing to be afraid of," "Just get in there and do it," and "You'll get over it" are typical of this approach. In any case, the child's real feelings are neglected, and the adult is focusing on his or her own convenience. Helping others is not always convenient and providing emotional assistance takes time and energy. In addition, solutions do not necessarily come about within one encounter and may require repeated effort.

9. **Failing to recognize your own limitations.** It is not always within your power to eliminate the

source of a child's distress. Although you perform an important function when you provide emotional support, it may not be possible to alter the child's environment or to change the behaviors of others in the child's environment who are negatively affecting the child. It's also important for you to know where your sphere of influence ends and when it is time to link families with other helping professionals. When behaviors are "extreme," involve credentialed professionals beyond the classroom.

10. **Forgetting that parents have other roles that require their time and energy.** The reaction of young children who run into their teachers at the supermarket or elsewhere in the community is often amusing to adults. The children seem absolutely amazed that the teacher can be anywhere but in the classroom and in the role of teacher. Ironically, professionals and parents hold like perspectives, unless they happen to travel in similar social circles that allow them to meet one another frequently outside the educational setting. Parents and professionals tend to think of one another narrowly and only in terms of the role each plays in their interactions. Thus, when parents think of you, they may forget that you may also be a parent, spouse, adult child, voter, and homeowner. Similarly, you could forget that although parents may play the parenting role 24 hours a day, other roles can and do become more dominant in their lives during that 24-hour period. They, too, experience the pressure of meeting job demands, maintaining a home, nurturing intimate relationships with persons other than their children, furthering their education or training, responding to their own parents' needs, and performing a wide variety of community obligations.

11. **Being inflexible and/or insensitive to the needs of financially troubled parents, working parents, single parents, teenage parents, divorced parents, stepparents, parents of handicapped children, and bilingual or migrant families.** Professionals sometimes are seen as distant and unfeeling about the pressures many parents face in their everyday lives. Notices arrive home regularly reminding parents to put their children to bed early, to provide a quiet place to study, and to be sure that children eat a balanced diet. Parents whose homes are small and crowded, those who are unemployed, and those who are going through painful marital transitions or other unexpected crises experience additional distress when receiving these reminders. To be sensitive to the total ecosystem or context in which children are developing, learn about each family. Understanding, flexibility, and insightfulness can ease their burdens.

12. **Overreacting to negative parents.** The less confident we are in our own position regarding a controversial issue, the more we tend to become defensive when our views are challenged. As experience and continuing education allow us to integrate what we know about children and families with what others know, we will become more relaxed and open when others present a different, even hostile viewpoint. When we overreact to a critical and negative parent, we exhibit our fear of being proven wrong, our uncertainty, and our confusion.

A parent can make an important point, one that is based on very good intentions and might truly be helpful; however, she or he may deliver it in such a negative manner (blaming, sarcastic, derisive) that we fail to really listen. A message delivered in such a way that it puts the receiver in a highly charged emotional state often fails to be heard. Work hard to stay calm in such a situation; actively listen and perhaps reflect to the parent: "You're really angry. I think we need to talk about that, but I am hearing what you're saying about the need for a better information-delivery system, and I believe you're right." Occasionally, hostile remarks and behavior by a parent may have little to do with you or with what is really going on in the program. The parent may be feeling overwhelmed or out of control in other important areas and may see no other outlet for expressing his or her frustrations. Some careful probing, combined with understanding on your part sometimes can help such a person understand what is happening and reevaluate his or her behavior.

Summary

Resilience, or the capacity to rise above adverse circumstances, can be seen in children who are socially competent, have purpose, and who demonstrate a number of characteristics of social maturity.

Resilience emerges from both inherent and external factors. The accumulation of stress and risk factors may lead to adversity, which creates elevated possibilities of undesirable outcomes for children when coping mechanisms fail.

Protective factors, on the other hand, which include characteristics internal to the child, family, community, and society, can buffer adversity. Within the school setting, educators can increase these protective factors through the following:

- Monitoring children's health
- Coaching children in decision making
- Sharing the value of optimism
- Fostering self-efficacy
- Modifying difficult temperaments
- Strengthening friendship connections
- Scaffolding scholastic competence

Families may be effective partners in developing important resiliency strengths and attitudes in young children when information is shared openly between home and school, where there is respect, and where parents and teachers work together cooperatively to build resilience in children.

Building stress-hardy children calls for setting realistic goals, employing useful stress-management strategies and effective decision making, and encouraging independence wherever possible.

Pitfalls include blaming, failing to set limits, not acting on suspected abuse, looking for quick fixes, and other unhelpful responses.

Key Terms

adaptive systems
adversity
assets
autonomy
childhood stress
chronic illnesses
coping
decision making
executive function

fetal alcohol syndrome
homeostasis
learned helplessness
optimism
positive self-talk
protective factors
psychological disequilibrium
resilience
risk factors

self-efficacy
self-regulation
socially competent children
stress
stress-coping mechanisms
stress hardiness
stressors
vulnerability

Discussion Questions

1. With three or four others in a small group, compare one another's most common physical, emotional, and behavioral reactions when under pressure. How are your reactions similar? How are they dissimilar?

2. A parents' group requests that you bring a speaker in to discuss helping children to build resiliency. What aspects of the topic do you believe ought to be covered if the speaker has only an hour?

3. In your own childhood years, were there any significant problems that you can remember that you were able to overcome? Were there any protective factors that helped you do that?

4. A parent approaches you about the fact that she is going through a divorce and is worrying about the possible effects on her 5-year-old son. What can you tell her about ways to support him while going through this family transition?

5. With two to three others, consider a continuum of optimism from 1 to 10 (1 = pessimism or low optimism; 10 = high optimism). Where would you place yourself on the continuum? Where do the others place themselves? Has the presence of optimism or pessimism had any effect on life choices?

6. Consider this statement: "No matter what, they just land on their feet." Give evidence from the chapter about why that is or is not true.

7. Discuss (a) as many aspects of poverty as possible that you believe can contribute, either directly or indirectly, to increased adversity in children's life, and (b) aspects of middle-class children's lives that differ from the experience of poverty but that also may create stress.

8. Return to Chapter 2 to review the elements of difficult, slow-to-warm-up, and easy

temperaments. In what category would you place the oldest child in your classroom? What evidence do you have for that?

9. Often, professionals focus on children of divorced families as children who may be distressed. Discuss the kinds of significant stressors that may exist in families that are intact but troubled—stressors that may be somewhat hidden.

10. Consider the concept of "adaptive distancing" described in the chapter. Do you know any adult who has done this or would have benefited by doing so?

Case Study Analysis

Read the case study in Appendix B about Marco, age 22 months, and consider the following:

1. How did the teacher encourage Marco's progress toward developmental milestones?

2. What were Marco's parents doing that hampered independence and self-control?

3. If you were Marco's teacher, how would you work with his parents to have them implement practices at home that were similar to those at school to encourage autonomy and social development? What, exactly, would you say?

4. Extended family members care for Marco when parents are working. What effect might this have on his development if all of the adults treat him differently and have different expectations for him?

5. Given what you learned in this chapter about protective factors when there is stress in a child's life, how would you assess the stress Marco might be experiencing and the presence or absence of protective factors?

Field Assignments

1. Go to a local bookstore or library. Find at least three current books that address one of the family stressors discussed in the chapter (e.g., working parents). What new information can you gain so you can better support children in your classroom?

2. Examine the ecomap in Figure 6-1. Carry out this exercise with a parent in your classroom to discover as much as you can about her child from birth to the present.

3. Observe a professional working with children. Describe incidents in which children were offered

a choice. Record how the choice was worded and how it was implemented. Describe in what way the children were allowed, encouraged, and supported in order to manage their own activity. Conclude with any errors you think the adult made and what corrections might be possible.

4. Visit a homeless shelter in your community. Find out from the director how the shelter facilitates children's school participation and enrollment when necessary. How much support is given to a family and for how long?

Reflect on Your Practice

Here is a sample checklist you can use to reflect on your use of the skills as a beginning professional. A more detailed classroom observation tool is available in Appendix C.

I influence children's social development by building resilience in the following ways:

✓ I set realistic goals for children in my classroom.

✓ I help children learn how to reframe upsetting experiences.

✓ I link to supportive organizations in my community that provide protective oversight for stressed children and families.

✓ I observe for early signs of excessive and cumulative stress in children I am teaching.

✓ I teach children strategies they can use to handle undue stress.

✓ I teach children to be effective decision makers.

✓ I provide children with many opportunities to do things for themselves.

✓ I provide support for children who are coping with loss.

✓ I partner with family members to coordinate strategies to help their child cope with adversity.

Digital Download   **Download from CourseMate**

CourseMate. Visit the Education CourseMate for this textbook to access the eBook, Digital Downloads, Teach-Source Videos, and quizzes. Go to CengageBrain.com to log in, register, or purchase access.

7 Play as a Context for Social Development and Learning

OBJECTIVES

On completion of this chapter, you should be able to:

Describe the nature of play and how it relates to social competence.

Explain how various types of play develop over time.

Articulate how adults guide and facilitate children's play.

Identify pitfalls to avoid in facilitating children's play.

NAEYC STANDARDS naeyc

1. Promoting Child Development and Learning
2. Observing, Documenting, and Assessing to Support Young Children and Families
3. Using Developmentally Effective Approaches to Connect with Children and Families
4. Using Content Knowledge to Build Meaningful Curriculum

Situation:	Two children are playing family roles of husband and wife.
Anne:	(looking at rocking horse) Gotta go.
Phillip:	Go?
Anne:	Gotta go to work.
Phillip:	No, you cook.
Anne:	Can't cook, gotta go to work. (climbs on the horse and begins to rock)
Phillip:	No, you cook and stuff. I'll go to work. (holds the reigns of the rocking horse)
Anne:	Gonna be late for work. You stay and cook.
Phillip:	Don't you know? You cook, and I go to work.
Anne:	(trying unsuccessfully to rock) Drop you off on my way to work.
Phillip:	(mounts the horse behind her)

The play of these children nearly floundered for lack of a shared meaning about the roles that they were playing. Fortunately, they were able to agree on both riding the horse to work even though they did not fully realize the difficulty of their differing perceptions of the roles of wives. Anne's mother had been employed throughout Anne's 4 years of life, and Phillip's mother was a full-time homemaker. Yet, through play, these two children discovered a means for coping with their differing points of view.

Play is both common and complex. It is the predominant social activity of early childhood and continues to provide a vehicle for social interaction as children mature. Within the context of play, children decide the details of what to play, determine how to play, negotiate the rules of play, and develop roles to carry out within their play. Because play is such an important aspect of children's lives, adults need to understand the nature of play and their part in supporting play throughout childhood. Unfortunately, play is frequently misunderstood, neglected, ignored, or replaced with adult-driven agendas. Parents who are concerned for children's safety restrict play, and schools concerned with short-term achievement goals mistakenly restrict play in many programs. Play is brain food, however, with children achieving physical fitness, performing executive functions, engaging in complex communications, and practicing social skills. As you read the rest of this chapter, ask yourself what would happen to the children and to society if children did not play.

The Nature of Play and Social Competence naeyc

Any definition of play must take into account the gleeful chase of toddlers, the intense dramatization of an irate customer played out in the pretend grocery,

the boisterous, roughhousing of young boys, the concentrated practice of a 10-year-old shooting basket after basket, the chanting cadence of the jump-rope rhyme, and the patience and strategy of the school-age child accumulating wealth in a Monopoly game. Play events are separated from everyday experiences by a play frame that lets all players know it is "not for real" (Johnson, Christie, & Wardle, 2005). Play has certain definitive characteristics (Hughes, 2010).

Players may begin, end, or alter the activity in progress consulting only the other players. Adult-directed activity is not play, though it may be enjoyable. The opposite of play is reality, or seriousness, rather than work. People play at their work, enjoying it thoroughly, and work hard at developing play skills necessary for a sport. Six- and seven-year-old children readily distinguish between work and play, yet they describe "in between" characteristics of play that are more "work-like" and work that is fun (Wing, 1995). See Highlight 7-1.

Genetic Foundations

Play is a species behavior (Power, 2000). All mammals, including humans, play. Adaptability, behavioral flexibility, and physical fitness have had great survival value and are practiced and enhanced throughout play. Overall, the individual animals that play a lot appear to be in better physical condition, have stronger social networks, and are more socially adjusted to their group (Bekoff & Pierce, 2009). Play has its own distinct communication signals and social conventions. Similarly, object play, play-fighting, and play-chasing behaviors are common among children as well as other primates (Power, 2000; Hughes, 2010). Children and other animals learn to interpret signals and actions of others; mental and emotional mastery; cooperation and leadership skills, and other social skills such as negotiating and problem solving (Frost, Wortham, & Reifel, 2012). Most importantly, play is essential to the growth and development of the social brain (Panksepp, 2008).

HIGHLIGHT 7-1

Characteristics of Play

Play is:
- Fun
- Active and involved
- Intrinsically motivated
- Voluntary
- Not serious
- Process oriented
- Determined by the players

Where Play Fits in the Curriculum

As an early childhood educator, you have many opportunities to help children:

- Enhance their social competence through play.
- Practice communication skills.
- Improve their level of social participation.
- Become master players enacting a full story.

Play is a way to meet the social development education standards of Wisconsin and one of the language and literacy standards of Minnesota (see Table 7-1). These skills and knowledge inform educational program content for children and are incorporated in the learning standards of these states.

Social Development and Play

Gary saw Charles enter the 3- to 4-year-olds' classroom with anticipation and excitement. Gary ran toward him, eager to play, and tackled him around the knees, sending him to the floor with a crash. Charles cried and sought to get away from Gary. In dismay, Gary noted, "He don't want to play with me."

Linda entered the playground holding a rope long enough for two others to swing for jumping rope. She told the other girls that she had learned how to jump doubles from her older cousins. As Olivia and Angeline twirled rope, Linda started to jump, inviting Kathleen to join her. With many stops and starts and Linda's coaching, the girls finally began rhythmic jumping together. Franny stood by, waiting and watching. After a long jumping sequence, Kathleen made a misstep, and Franny got her turn. Angeline and Olivia turned the rope more smoothly at an even, slow pace. Franny started jumping right away without the missteps that Kathleen made at the beginning.

Fergus and Paul were at the water table in the kindergarten room. Pouring water into containers holding 8 ounces of fluid, Fergus noticed that Paul kept pouring water into an overflowing salad dressing bottle and said, "When it's full, it's full. You can't fuller it no more. Dump it or use another one." Paul noticed his full bottle, dumped it, and began filling it again.

Gary learned from the consequences of his own behavior that a tackle is not a suitable approach to initiate play. Linda learned to coach others as they attempt new skills and also how to keep the other players interested. Olivia and Angeline cooperated in twirling the rope, delaying gratification in anticipation of their own turns. Franny learned how to jump doubles from the errors of Kathleen. Fergus learned that he can give information that can help another, and Paul learned to accept help.

Each child in these examples has either learned a new social skill or practiced one. Play and social learning have a complex relation, with new learning being both generated in the context of play and practiced on other play occasions. Play leads development and calls forth opportunities for new competencies to be explored, modified, practiced, or even discarded for more effective strategies. For instance, as children mature, they recognize fair and unfair treatment, and they gradually develop ethical identities (Edmiston, 2008). They plan ahead for their play, as Linda did when she brought the long jump rope to school. Ultimately, they learn self-control and to influence their playmates so that the play continues smoothly. In fact, there is no element of social competence to which play does not contribute (See Figure 7-1).

As you read this chapter, you will gain further insights into the particulars of how play supports each category of social competence. Let us begin by exploring how the spontaneous play of children is impacted by children's gender, their degree of social participation, and their status in the playgroup.

Gender. There are no gender differences in play in the first 18–24 months (Power, 2000; Hughes, 2010). After children establish their gender identity and can reliably identify others as boys and girls, the nature of their play changes forever (Fagot & Leve, 1998). The choices of play themes, preferred roles, and mode of expression differ, although the amount of play is the same. Most boys tend to play more vigorously and more aggressively than girls. They also range further away from adults than do girls. Social culture for boys tends to be organized into competing groups

Table 7-1   Play in the Curriculum

State	Age	Standard
Wisconsin	3–5	· Engages in social interaction with others aged 3–5 · Participates in parallel play with others for longer periods of time · Participates in cooperative play with others
Minnesota	2nd grade	Identifies the actions and feelings of the characters in a familiar story

Sources: Wisconsin Child Care Information Center (2011); Minnesota Department of Education (2005).

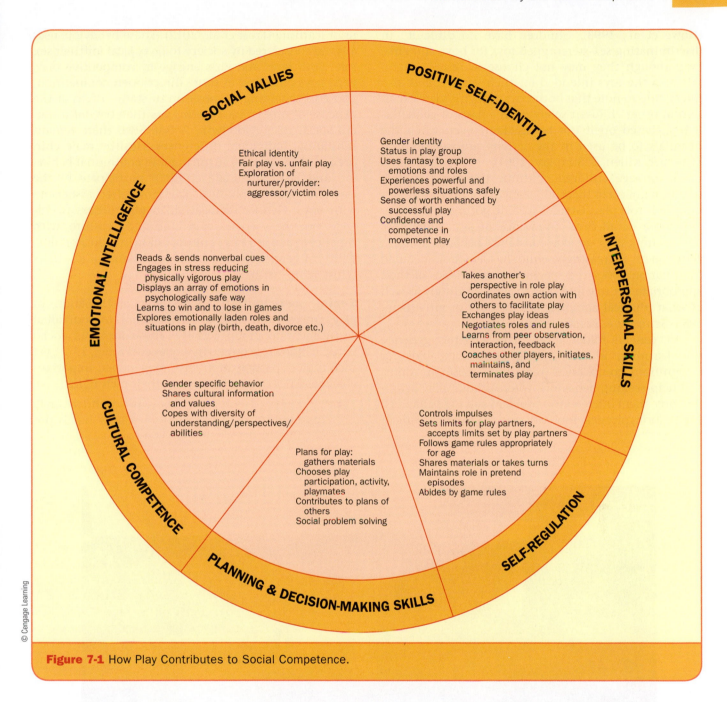

Figure 7-1 How Play Contributes to Social Competence.

or coalitions, whereas the social culture for girls is consistently more communal. Girls tend to focus on relationships and social support, demonstrating more nurturing and empathy in their play (Geary, 2004). These naturally occurring gender differences are reinforced through social learning. While children are growing up, family members, the media, and other social institutions provide clear cues as to appropriate gender behavior. Thus, boys and girls receive strong messages about appropriate play for a child of their sex. Through words and actions, adults let children know what is expected. Moreover, parents (and fathers in particular) discourage the play of both daughters and sons that falls outside of gender stereotyped roles (although greater latitude is offered for girls to play with trucks than for boys to play with dolls) (Honig, 1998; Freeman, 2007). Media and toy manufacturers reinforce stereotypical gender-related behavior in the play materials created for this age group (Willis, 1999; Hughes, 2010).

Regardless, children as young as 2 seem to prefer to play with gender-specific materials and with same-sex peers. Girls participate more frequently in housekeeping settings enacting social roles, and boys engage in pretend play in garage, spaceship, or work-related settings focusing on power relationships

(Howe et al., 1993). Children have no difficulty in discriminating sex-stereotyped toys for boys and girls, even though they may not choose to restrict themselves to the toys intended for their gender. It is also interesting to note that both boys and girls view exclusion of other children solely on the basis of gender as wrong, based on it not being "fair," even when the materials to be used in the activity are stereotypical (Theimer, Killen, & Strangor, 2001).

School-age children continue the trend in role selection but often incorporate media or literary figures into their role play. Gender-specific portrayal is clearer and more detailed as knowledge of sex stereotypes and awareness of gender constancy become uniform above age 7. Increasingly, children have more detailed information about the specific characteristics of their appropriate sex role and how to act accordingly as well as what physical activities are for boys or girls (Bem, 1985; Schmalz & Kerstetter, 2006).

In general, older girls' play activities generate rule learning, imitation, task persistence, bids for recognition, compliance, remaining close to adults, and help-seeking behaviors, whereas boys' play activities force them into creative problem-solving behaviors, exploration, physical mobility, and the restructuring of

prior learning (Frost et al., 2012). These behaviors usually are considered by society to be typical for their sex role. Both boys and girls engage in competitive play, with boys engaging in more direct open competition, and girls scheming for position or status, often at the expense of others' hurt feelings as they try out different social roles (Goodwin, 2006). Still, there remain substantial individual differences. Healthy male children often engage in nurturing and communal behavior, and healthy female children participate in the assertive vigorous physical play most often associated with boys. Gender segregation in play occurs worldwide, but the specifics vary culture by culture, with American mainstream culture allowing greater flexibility in gender-specific behaviors than many others (Frost et al., 2012).

Social participation.   Children's participation in play ranges from lack of involvement to individual engagement to group activity. These forms of social participation are acquired in sequence (Parten, 1932), yet each type of participation has independent, important characteristics that have value in their own right:

1. **Unoccupied behavior:** The child wanders, may casually finger materials momentarily but is not

Solitary play may enable the child to explore, to imagine, and to act on her own, even when other children are available.

© Cengage Learning 2015

engaged in play. Most of the time, the child does not appear to attend to others beyond a glance.

2. **Onlooker:** The child is a spectator observing other children but is not engaged in any task or social participation. Most of the time is spent looking at what others are doing rather than doing something himself or herself.

3. **Solitary play:** The child plays with toys or materials alone and independently, without interacting with others. Children use their intelligence and problem-solving abilities to engage with objects or to pretend alone (Bornstein, 2007).

4. **Parallel activity:** The child plays independently, but other children engaged in the same activity are nearby. Nonverbal contact is common, and the presence of peers appears important to them. Two children putting puzzles together on the same table is typical of this type of play. Occasional glances and smiles are common.

5. **Associative play:** The child interacts with other children around a similar but not necessarily identical activity. There may be a considerable amount of sharing of materials, lending (e.g., a shovel in the sandbox), taking turns, and watching others' activities and conversation (e.g., from each side of an art easel) (Hughes, 2010). No shared goals, themes, or roles are involved. For example, Niki rides his truck back and forth near a block construction where Dennis and Mark are working together. Occasionally, he stops to comment and then continues his "deliveries."

6. **Cooperative or organized supplementary play:** The child plays in a group to make some material product or to strive for some common goal such as engaging in competition, playing a game, or engaging in pretend that is only possible if each one enacts the agreed-upon roles. Ring-around-a-rosy is cooperative play, as is the play of Dennis and Mark, who are engaged in building.

Solitary play and the various forms of group play are not hierarchical categories. In fact, solitary play fosters the formation of novel behavior patterns and exercises creativity, whereas social play serves to enhance the bonds between individuals (Dolgin, 1981). Solitary play is the most common form of play for toddlers, partly because they lack experience and opportunity to interact with peers and partly because there is a point at which toddlers switch from treating peers as objects. Midway through the second year, toddlers are capable of mutual involvement, turn-taking, and repetition in playful activities between two children (Hay, Ross, & Goldman, 2004).

You may see all forms of social participation in play in any setting. For example, the onlooker, although not socially involved, may be acquiring knowledge that later will enable him or her to participate more directly. Some children need time to wander through the play setting to see what their choices are before making a decision. Parallel play frequently occurs prior to an episode of cooperative play. Therefore, each kind of social participation has something to contribute to the child's social development.

Social status. When children play together, they invariably learn about status in the group, dominance roles, and other power relationships. Their play provides a safe way to explore their own position among the players and also to indirectly comment on the existence of power relationships (Pellegrini, 2004). Children also may resort to applying specific classroom rules in situations where another player might thwart their wishes. For example, a child might call forth the rule of "no guns" when another child has constructed a weapon and playmates are intrigued. Such assertions as "Only four can play," "Take care of what you get out," and

▶❚❚ **TeachSource Video 7-1**

© Cengage Learning 2015

2–5 Years: Play in Early Childhood

Go online and view *2–5 Years: Play in Early Childhood*.

In this video, you will see a variety of types of play and differing levels of social participation. As you view the film, ask yourself the following questions:

1. What resources in the environment were needed to elicit the play?

2. How did the children coordinate their social interactions during the play in each small segment?

3. Did you notice any metacommunication strategies or nonverbal signals that enabled the play to continue?

Watch on CourseMate

"First come, first served" may be recalled and applied by young children only when they serve the purposes of the child calling on the rule (Jordan, Cowan, & Roberts, 1995; Winther-Lindqvist, 2009). Other less overt strategies are equally effective. For example, Toby, who faces Jeanette and announces, "Let's play house," is communicating her desire to play but also is excluding Marie, on whom she has turned her back. This message is equally clear to all concerned. Toby has established her role of leader by initiating the play activity and may continue by defining the ongoing play.

Children who have high status in the group tend to direct their messages to specific players. Often they do this with more than one playmate, each in turn. Preferred players, though, must be contingently responsive to other children to maintain the play. Even when rejecting a play idea, the high-status child may offer an explanation or an alternative rather than an outright rejection, thus continuing the interaction (Hazen & Black, 1989). High-status players also decide which rules apply to a particular game. For example, the rule of equal numbers of players per team may be ignored if a friend of the dominate child wants to play, making one team larger (Winther-Lindqvist, 2009).

Competent school-age children behave in ways that are relevant to the ongoing activity, are sensitive to the nonverbal cues of playmates, and responsive and appropriate to the social initiations by their peers. Less-effective children have poor emotional regulation and situation knowledge, are less attentive to social cues, and are much more likely to engage their peers in aggressive or coercive cycles. They are frequently rejected or isolated by their playmates. These lower-status children appear to be less connected to the group and unable to "read" the social situations or the emotional tenor of the group in order to coordinate their activities with others (Pettit & Harrist, 1993). Children use all social participation strategies and incorporate their social identities, such as status in the group, special skills, and friendship networks, into all types of play.

Types of Play naeyc
Exploratory Behavior

> Renzell, age 4, picked up a stethoscope, blew into the bell, looked at the earpieces, put the earpieces in his ears, tapped the bell, and then walked over to a doll and announced that he was a doctor. He played out this role with several dolls, listening to their bodies all over. When Michael entered the area, Renzell said, "I think you are sick," and began to listen to Michael's arm. Michael told him, "Listen right here," pointing to his

Exploratory play occurs during planned and unplanned activities as children expand their understandings.

> chest. Renzell listened to Michael's chest and said the thing didn't work. He then listened to Michael's chest in different places, asking, "Can you hear that?" every now and then. He also listened to the radiator, to the hamster, and to other children, momentarily forgetting his doctor role.

Children engaging in exploratory behavior are scanning the environment, scrutinizing, feeling, smelling, mouthing, shaking, hefting, moving, operating, probing, or otherwise investigating the nature of the objects at hand. Exploratory play precedes true play and generally consists of three general patterns: procuring objects, investigating manually, and asking questions (Power, 2000). The questions being addressed are the following: What can this do? How does it work? What is the nature of this object or situation? Exploratory behavior of novel objects precedes true play behavior (Hutt, 1971; Hughes, 2010). The **complexity** and **novelty** of materials affect how long children need to explore before they can use the objects in social play. The strategies that they use become more systematic over time (Power, 2000).

The complexity of objects increases with the number of parts (consider the variety of puzzles or model cars), responsiveness or pliability (sand or water is more pliable than a toy truck), and the number of possible uses (a ball is more versatile than a hockey stick). Children show wariness of objects that are too novel. Children still explore familiar objects but take less time with repeated exposures. Electronic games incorporate both novelty and complexity with the many options built within some of the software, stimulating both exploration of the software program and game play. Therefore, adults should provide ample materials and time for exploration before they expect children to engage in social play.

Babies explore with mouths, hands, and feet using all their senses. Prekindergarten children explore paste by tasting, smelling, and smearing before using it to adhere pieces of paper. Water and sand are poured, patted, tasted, and smelled. Six- to seven-year-olds are more precise in manipulating things and engage in careful visual or auditory exploration as well. For example, when they encounter a manual potter's wheel, children will swirl it around with their fingers, examine it closely to see how it works, and try it out with a bit of clay before trying to make something with the wheel. Older children explore very deliberately but are quicker. All children explore alone and in small groups, frequently shifting between examination and calling on friends to share discoveries.

Children shift from the question, "What does this object do?" to a slightly different question, "What can I do with this object?" Children incorporate objects into their play, where they determine the meanings and uses of the artifact. Like Renzell and his stethoscope, children shift from exploration to imaginative play repeatedly during a single episode. Adults play multiple roles in enabling the play of children, including intensive intervention for those children whose play skills interfere with their social development. These are summarized in the Social Support Pyramid shown in Figure 7-2.

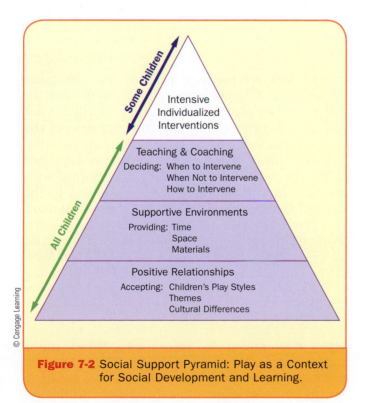

Figure 7-2 Social Support Pyramid: Play as a Context for Social Development and Learning.

Play with Objects

Children of all ages will play with anything: real things (utensils, furnishings, leaves and sticks, animals); reconstruction materials or instructional materials (memory games, puzzles, stacking toys); construction materials (blocks, paints, clay, cardboard); fluid materials (water, sand, snow); toys (cars, dolls, and other miniature replicas); sports equipment (balls, mallets); board games (Monopoly, Chutes and Ladders); and media games (handheld electronic games, computer games). Play behavior occurs everywhere: the bus, yard, playground, prekindergarten, lunchroom, classroom, or hallway. The play context includes space, materials, time, and other people. The experiences of all the children as well as the terrain, plants, or other objects in the physical space suggest content and type of play outdoors (Reifel & Yeatman, 1993). In addition, the quality of the play context is highly associated with children's social problem solving (Goleman, 2011).

Playthings are reduced in size and simplified (such as a toy stove), replicated (such as a toy truck), or structured to make basic concepts clear (such as a set of various-size colored rings on a cone-shaped holder). They vary from very realistic (miniature furniture for toddlers) to more abstract forms (sculpted animals for older children). Toys are also symbolic: They represent family relationships, provide cues for appropriate sex-role behavior, represent the child's own self-identity, and transmit cultural values. For example, children learn social values when they recognize that other children from around the world play with toys that they enjoy as well.

Objects are the currency of social play—solitary, parallel, associative, and cooperative modes—and by their very nature, objects form an overall context for the play to occur. Children's motor competence, cognitive functioning, and social skills affect how they actually use objects in the play with others.

Developmental changes in the use of objects. Objects are first explored, then combined with other things functionally related, and then used in pretend. Toddlers use objects in bids for interaction with agemates. Having possession of desired objects or play space keeps even a low-status player in the game or pretend play. Following is the sequence of object use that you will see if you work with young children. Older children continue to use objects in play similarly, with ease.

1. Motor behavior is repetitive, and mouthing is used.
2. Objects are systematically explored.
3. Actions begin to be appropriate for objects.

Objects are systematically explored and actions are appropriate for the object from an early age. This behavior continues whenever children encounter novel objects.

© Cengage Learning 2015

4. Objects that have functional relationships are combined.

5. Action patterns are combined to form larger sequences (stirring in, pouring from, and washing a bowl).

6. Action patterns are applied to self (may be simple pretending—e.g., eating or sleeping).

7. Action patterns are applied to others or to replicas (doll "eats").

8. The ability to act is attributed to replicas (doll "feeds" teddy bear).

9. Objects that are not present but are needed to complete a logical sequence are "invented" (pretends a spoon to stir with).

10. Objects are transformed for use in sequences (uses pencil for spoon).

Transform means to substitute one object for another. For example, a 3-year-old might use a pencil, a stick, a tongue depressor, or a screwdriver in the absence of a spoon to stir a drink or to feed a doll.

The first six behavior patterns are sometimes combined and practiced to gain mastery over an object. Mastery play or practice play is repetitious but may have slight variations until the properties of the object are understood and thoroughly mastered. One 2-year-old manipulated a set of seven nesting cubes in 30 different ways. Each cube was combined with one, two, and three other cubes, in addition to the full set. She also tried stacking the cubes. Mastery play, as well as exploratory behavior, is common when people of any age encounter objects that are novel and complex. Older children engage in similar play with newly introduced technologies. Children, as young as 30 months, cooperate in attaining mastery over playthings.

Style differences in object use. When adults understand the preferred play style, they grasp the child's point of view on how the materials are to be used as well as interpret it to other players. Children's play **style** appears to develop between ages 2 and 3 and to carry on as a preferred mode of play throughout childhood (Shotwell, Wolf, & Gardner, 1979). Some children respond to the symbolic potential of objects more readily than others and use objects to further the pretend narrative. Their play style has been called the **dramatist style**. The dramatist builds simply, just enough to construct the house or store where the people live and shop, and approaches materials with the question, "What story can I tell with these things?" Children of the same age using the **patterner style** are interested in the color, texture, shape, and form, and they communicate meaning by the spatial location of objects. The patterner approaches the materials with the question, "How can I arrange these things so that they are beautiful?" and is concerned with design elements. A child who is a patterner may use all the trucks and arrange them by size, color, function, or other criteria. Adults who do not recognize this style of play sometimes expect the child to give up some of the trucks to other players, who could be satisfied with using one if they use the dramatic style. However, the removal of several units of the design would totally disrupt the purpose of the other child's play. Observant adults who supervise children should note which style the child appears to be using before insisting that children divide up the materials and share them. A better approach to a patterner is to suggest the sequential use of materials. A dramatist is unlikely to be disturbed by sharing the material as long as there is enough to enact the story he or she has in mind. These children also find it easier to put materials away because their imagination is the true source of the play, not the materials themselves.

Dramatic Play

Dramatic play, or pretend play, probably is one of the most apparent forms of play seen in children. Pretend play may begin at about 1 year of age, and the amount of time spent at it peaks between the ages of 5 and 6, and then drops off as children are in school for longer periods of time. Pretend continues throughout childhood as older children engage in literary fantasy play or fantasy media play. If time and opportunity permits, school-age children can maintain the story line over several days or weeks.

Pretend play with others, or **sociodramatic play**, in which children share goals, themes, and materials, is possible by age 3 (if children have acquired the skills

Young children need concrete materials with which to enact pretend scenarios.

to do so) and will continue throughout childhood. Onset of this challenging form of play is delayed for those children whose opportunities are more limited. Adults are able to successfully coach children in developing the play skills that they have not already acquired.

Style differences in dramatic play. There are differences in style in pretend play as well as object play, as detailed in Table 7-2 (Rosenberg, 2001). Style refers to features of the behavior that occur independently of the content of the play and tends to be consistent over time with a player. Some children use both styles or do not appear to have a preferred mode. By noting the typical dramatic play style of children, adults are able to be more successful in making transitions and in supporting another child's entry into the play.

When interrupted for a transition in a group setting, the **pragmatist** simply stops and complies with adult requests. The **fantasizer**, however, has difficulty leaving the imaginative mode and may resist change by ignoring the adult and may appear distracted or distressed at the interruption when forced to comply. Such children need sufficient warning to complete their imaginative episode prior to transition. The fantasizer incorporates other children if they are able to fit into the story narrative early in the play episode. The pragmatist can include others with adult support after play has begun more easily as they are generally less intense.

Regardless of the child's characteristic style of dramatic play, all children use the same basic skills to pretend. Children learn skills from parents, siblings, peers, and teachers, which are then used in social encounters.

Object substitution. First, children must learn to substitute one object for another or transform one object into another. In **object substitution**, the closer the substituted object resembles the object needed for the dramatization, the more likely the child will be to use it. A shell can be substituted for a cup, but not for a bat. Between 2 and 3 years of age, children substitute one object in their play, but not two. For example, an abstract wooden object might be used for a horse and a cup for a drinking trough, but the play breaks down if the child is given the abstract wooden object and a shell. In the third year, children will substitute a cup for any container: potty-chair, bowl, hat, or dish. Adults know the child is substituting because the object is renamed

Table 7-2   Dramatic Styles of Children in Imaginative Play

	Characteristic Traits
Fantasizer	1. Child is thoroughly into the imaginative play. She cannot be distracted, has no concern about failure, and lacks self-consciousness. She is focused and riveted.
	2. There is an internal locus of control with a lack of concern for the adult leader or supervisor, who seems to be ignored.
	3. There is self-talk during the play where the child appears to have conversations with his "other self." He may take multiple roles.
	4. She usually has vivid images with details drawn from her own experience but frequently imagines what has never happened. She oscillates between memory and fantasy with the memories providing a stimulus for elaboration.
	5. Fantasizers jump right into the activity and begin to play, or they choose not to participate.
	6. They seem to be very sensitive to sensory cues and won't engage when there is a bad smell or they do not feel well.
Pragmatist	1. This child is concerned with the real world around her and can be distracted by nearby activity.
	2. There is a concern for the audience. He may seek approval and may need to be encouraged by the caregiver.
	3. She may ask for clarification or permission from the adult in the midst of play and then start up again. The play is less intense.
	4. He engages in self-talk, but it is generally self-evaluative or a comment on what he has done, "I really don't like this hat."
	5. The pragmatists enact what has happened in their lives. Their imagery is general, such as any cat, rather than a specific cat.
	6. She will play under more adverse conditions and does not appear to be concerned with the temperature or sensory characteristics of the space.
	7. She tries hard to find a useful procedure to carry out the activity, is predictable, and seeks adult approval.

Children use what is at hand as a substitute for what they need when they play.

© Cengage Learning 2015

Between 3 and 4 years of age, they pretend with nothing to hold onto. School-age children do it readily.

Children who have not learned how to pretend may approach toys in an exploratory mode and then respond to them as if they were real. In one preschool room, Emily entered the housekeeping area and examined the model stove, turning the knobs, gingerly touching the burners, and opening the oven to peer inside. Then, she pulled the stove from the wall and examined the back. Putting her hands on her hips in great disgust, she addressed the teacher, "This damned stove won't work!" She was upset when the adult responded that the toy stove was not supposed to work like a real stove.

Changes of time and place. Children also learn to transform time and settings. They might substitute a climber for a spaceship in flight or pretend that the sandbox is a beach during the period when prehistoric animals lived. Players are very aware of this convention and tend to play consistently with it. For example, Debbie, the "baby," climbed out of her bed to iron on the ironing board. Her "mother" admonished her that babies can't iron because they'll get burned. Debbie climbed back into her bed, said: "Grow, grow, grow. I'm the big sister now," and returned to the ironing board, condensing many years into a few seconds. Time and place have no restrictions except in the information of the players.

Role-playing. The young player must learn to take on a role. The simplest kind of role is the **functional role** (Watson & Fisher, 1980). The child becomes a person who is driving a truck. This role does not contain a permanent identity or personality but is defined by the person in the present situation. A child taking on a **character role**, however, engages in many behavioral sequences appropriate for the part. Character roles include family roles (mother, father, sister), occupational roles (firefighter, doctor), and fictional roles (superhero, witch). Family roles are played with much more detail than the others. Younger children tend to limit themselves to roles with which they have had direct experience (baby, parent), but older children are more likely to act out roles that they have observed (husband, wife) and try more occupational roles. Lastly, preschool children are able to portray multiple roles. One 30-month-old girl was observed playing "mother" to "baby" and "wife" to "husband" while coaching "husband" in how to perform the role of "father" (Miller & Garvey, 1984). Upper-elementary children are capable of assuming a broad variety of character roles. Role and action representations initially are affected by the availability of realistic props. The following observation checklists should assist you in keeping track of children's developing skills.

or because the action with the object is clearly an action appropriate for the object being substituted for. However, 4-year-olds tend to use objects more realistically (Trawick-Smith, 1990). They are more likely to engage in sociodramatic play, in which all the players must agree on the meaning of each pretend object. There are obvious complications in having many substituted objects during group play.

Object invention. Next, children need to be able to invent an object—to imitate its use through actions even when no object is at hand. **Object invention** is simple pantomime, and in its simplest form, only one pretend object at a time is used. A child may use a stirring action above a bowl to invent a spoon or twirl an arm above the head to symbolize a rope. Younger children find it very difficult to mime without a placeholder object (a real object that takes the place of another real object, such as a stone used as a car).

Observation of Dramatic Play Skills for Younger or Less Experienced Children

Name	Object Substitution	Object Invention	Transforms Setting/Time	Takes on Role	Level of Social Participation
1.					
2.					
3.					
4.					
5.					
6.					
7.					
8.					
9.					
10.					
11.					
12.					
13.					
14.					
15.					

© Cengage Learning

Observation of Dramatic Play Skills for Older or More Experienced Children

Name	Constructs Materials for Pretend Play	Transforms Time, Setting	Strong Story-like Narrative	Duration 10 Minutes or More	Number of Children in Sociodramatic Play
1.					
2.					
3.					
4.					
5.					
6.					
7.					
8.					
9.					
10.					
11.					
12.					
13.					
14.					
15.					

© Cengage Learning

Cultural and experiential differences in children.

There appears to be variations in the timing of skill development and in the preferences for particular themes in cross-cultural studies, as well as those of subpopulations inside the United States (Power, 2000; Gaskins, Haight, & Lancy, 2007). The child's culture (economic conditions, characteristics of the community, the value placed on play by adults, and child-rearing practices) influence both the skills of the players and the content of the play (Göncü, Jain, & Tuermer, 2007). Apparently pretend play is more sensitive to encouragement than are other forms of play (Smith, 2005). However, there appears to be little difference in the types of play children choose when all types of play are available (Ramsey, 1998).

Children bring to the play experience their cultural background and lifestyle as sources of information. They may play out life experiences that are unfamiliar to their teachers, such as cocktail parties, cruises, foreign travel, being evicted, gang fighting, family violence, and burglaries, as well as explicitly sexual activities. Adults may not feel comfortable with some of this play in the group, but children may need to play out their experiences. Children may be redirected into other aspects of family role behavior such as going to work or cleaning house. However, for play to flourish, they should not be scolded or shamed about theme or role depiction.

In addition, the ways boys and girls establish common ground necessary for sociodramatic play are quite different. Boys tend to use statements about themselves or about what they are going to do to define a common play situation: "I am the bus driver," acclaimed Milton as he manipulated chairs and blocks to form a bus. Other boys joined the play theme by either assisting in the construction of the bus or sitting in it. On the other hand, girls usually focus on the group or the relationship and frequently establish the relationships between players as a means to begin play. "Let's pretend we are lost and scared," quivered Jean to her companion. The girls took hands and hid under the table.

Accepting the cultural diversity in a group of children is basic to accepting the children. Race, ethnicity, religion, age, gender, family composition, lifestyle, economic circumstances, presence of disabling conditions, sexual preferences of familiar adults, as well as specifics related to the local community may appear in children's play content. One 11-year-old sought information about what to call the grandchildren of her father's second wife by her first husband and whether or not they should be invited to the wedding that she was enacting with adult figures. Adult responses of surprise, shock, or confusion can usually be reduced when such adults seek to understand the cultural milieu of all the children. Play behavior is built on variations of serious behavior, then repeated, combined in a number of ways, reduced to unimportance through humor, or magnified through play ritual. Children must use what they know, regardless of content. Less-experienced children usually play like younger children until they acquire the skills that others of the age group demonstrate. Experienced, knowledgeable adults take gender and cultural expectations into account when setting up and guiding play.

Rules children construct for themselves in social pretend play.

Between 2 and 6 years of age, children gradually generate rules to allow them to engage in pretend play in groups. Two- and three-year-olds do not see the need for the rules until they begin to engage in more sophisticated themes and stories or with more players. Some who have difficulty in entering and maintaining complex social play have not yet perceived the need for some rules, do not know the rules, or have not quite understood how to put the rules into operation. There may also be variations among groups of children as they develop the social rules. Needless to say, children need time and opportunity to interact with each other in supportive play settings to construct or modify the internal rules of social play (see Table 7-3).

Table 7-3 Explicit and Implicit Rules

Explicit Rules	Implicit Rules
1. A child who is first to arrive in the dress-up area or who first proposes an idea for a game becomes the director of the play. 2. All children must ask to play. 3. All children must take on some role within the story. 4. All children must play fairly (although what is fair is not clearly defined; it is usually used in the context of taking turns, sharing, and not being bossy).	1. Children maintain the distinction between fantasy and reality while operating within the fantasy context. 2. Unless playing alone, children engage others in the pretend game in progress. 3. Children maintain the pretend sequence by creating and continuing an adequate story line and by accepting the fantasy proposals of others. (Curran, 1999, p. 49)

Two sets of play frames are visible here. The foreground has three boys, blocks, cars, and space to build. The background has two boys, blocks, and miniatures. In addition, there is a boy in the background who is in neither play frame.

Peer communication about pretend play. Metacommunication—that is, communication about communications—refers to either statements or actions that explain messages about how a behavior should be interpreted (Farver, 1992; Whitebread & O'Sullivan, 2012). They indicate if the behavior should be taken seriously or playfully. Verbal metacommunications often set the scene or conditions for play: "Let's pretend this fire is real." Nonverbal metacommunications are less explicit, such as a child "shoveling snow" in the middle of summer. Metacommunications explicitly separate the real from the pretend and work frequently to maintain the play (Göncü, Patt, & Kouba, 2004). Even when players step out of the play frame or outside the adopted roles to provide information or a rebuke, other players do not seem to experience confusion (Dockett, 1998). Examine Table 7-4 carefully. You will see how the child's purpose for using metacommunication to further the play works with samples of verbal and nonverbal communications. Messages about the narrative or the setting frame play so that it is socially defined as play and is not, therefore, "for real." To maintain play, some messages must be said "out of frame" to share information so that the play can continue.

Older children try to integrate the ideas of the players within the shared text by using implicit signals to regulate the play drama (Dunn, 2009). Explicit metacommunications are used when the narrative and roles are negotiated during a preparation phase, when players are not familiar, with fantasy themes, and where there is disagreement among players (Whitebread & O'Sullivan, 2012). During the enactment phase, children try to maintain the illusion of a different reality using mime, nonverbal cues, role enactment, and storytelling strategies. More explicit strategies are sometimes used if they encounter a breakdown in the story line, and also in the concluding phase where a problem is resolved (Dunn, 2009). Each player has to adjust what he or she does to all of the other players' roles as well as to the narrative. This requires considerable complex thinking and self-regulation.

The **play frame** encompasses the scope of the play event. Included in the play frame are all the objects and people relevant to the play scenario. Players within the frame are linked by communication and by their shared goals. For example, if a child is involved in an episode where he or she must leave the "restaurant" to get some more "food" from across the room, the

Table 7-4 Purpose of Metacommunications about Play with Verbal and Nonverbal Examples

Child's Purpose	Verbal Communication	Nonverbal Communication
Initiating the play	"Wanna play?" "Let's run."	Enters a play setting and engages in behaviors that start the play such as "cooking" or "offering" blocks to another child
Establishing a theme	"Let's pretend we are in space and we get lost." "I am the doctor. Is your baby sick?"	Uses props that suggest a theme such as a menu for a restaurant or a cash register for a store
Transforming settings or inventing them	"It's night, and dark here." "This can be my house and over there is your house." "Mission control is at the table."	Engages in actions that suggest a setting, such as making water-flow noises while aiming a hose
Establishing a role	"I'm the mom." "I'll get this ship working." "This will be the biggest building I ever did!"	"Comforts" a doll Carries the "tool box" over to the ship Builds with blocks
Establishing another's role	"You better watch where you are going." "You be the daddy."	Hands another child the objects to be used, such as the flowers in a "flower shop"
Establishing joint roles	"We are just kids, and we are running away." "You get to be the monster, then I do."	(Used only with children who play together frequently) Acts as though experiencing great pain and falls to the ground in front of another player
Transforming objects or inventing them	"Take this ship to Mars" (while sitting in a nest of large blocks). "Here is the money" (while the child gestures only).	Uses a teacup to feed or water model animals in the "farm" constructed of blocks
Making plans about the feelings or the behavior of another	"Let's say you are really mean."	Uses facial expressions and gestures to convey feelings
Making plans about his or her own feelings or behavior	"This place is really scary so I better hide."	Uses voice and gesture to convey feelings
Establishing their joint feelings or behavior	"We can put this fire out really fast. Get another hose."	Uses voice and body movement to convey feelings and ideas
Terminating play with communication about theme, role, props, or settings	"I don't want you to chase me anymore." "Let's play . . ." "Put the stuff in the box and let's have a snack."	Walks away Looks away, attends to something else Shakes head or uses other gestures to indicate disengagement

© Cengage Learning

child is still in the frame. If a photograph were taken of the pretend play episode described at the beginning of the chapter, the photographer would automatically move back to include the children and the rocking horse. This would be so, even though other persons might be in either the foreground or background of the photo. Persons and objects nearby—but not linked by communication and common goals that further the play—are out of the play frame. Children in the play frame send and receive messages that allow them to function harmoniously. Children's play frames also allow for humor and the interpretation that what is in the play frame is not serious.

Influencing the direction of play. Children tend not to expose their pretend illusion unnecessarily. If possible, they keep their communications "within frame," but metacommunications lie on a continuum from deeply within frame to completely out of frame (Griffin, 1984).

Children use **ulterior conversations**, which might appear to be role enactment, but do alter the course of the play. The query "Is it nighttime?" from the "baby" effectively initiates a caregiving sequence from the "mother."

Underscoring provides information to other players ("I'll get the dinner now," spoken in character voice). One example is "Wash, wash, wash" for dishes or laundry. This making of "magic" is done in a rhythmic, singsong voice.

Storytelling frequently is couched in the past tense and often is spoken in cadence. It allows for the development of more elaborate plots: "Let's say this spaceship went up, way up . . . and the computer went out . . . and the moon wasn't there."

Prompting is a technique in which one player instructs another on how to act or what to say, often in a stage whisper or a softer voice: "I'm ready for breakfast now; . . . (whispering) no, you have to cook the eggs before I eat."

Formal pretend proposals sometimes are embedded into ongoing play, as in "Let's pretend the family goes to the beach." The suggestion for play variation usually is used when the play scenario is becoming repetitive or falling apart. Usually, the more indirect methods are preferred after a play sequence is begun. These are summarized in Table 7-5.

When children pretend using small figures and blocks or a dollhouse, nearly all of the story line is provided by narrative rather than by the action of the dolls. When children themselves are the actors, however, they are more able to use nonverbal communicators as well to supply the content of the play.

Role selection. The social relationships in a group of children are reflected in their play. High-status children join ongoing play by imperiously adopting a role or defining an activity ("I'll be the aunt, coming to visit"). Lower-status children must ask permission to join the play ("Can I be the sister?") and may be restricted to particular roles. Often, higher-status children will assign lower-status children to the roles they may play ("You can be Grandma, who's sick"). The roles assigned may reflect actual status in the group. Play leaders also use rejection statements ("You can't play here") and counter defining statements ("We aren't in a forest—we're in a jungle").

The role play of children is very complex. They must participate as writer-directors of their imaginative play from outside the play frame and enact make-believe roles and events within the play frame.

Children tend to resist certain kinds of make-believe. They are much more willing to change generations than to change gender. Boys prefer male roles, whether they are baby or grandparent roles. High-status children tend to resist taking a lower-status role in the make-believe play, preferring to be the parent rather than the baby, the captain rather than the seaman. When one player refuses to play an unsatisfactory role, she or he usually is incorporated into the more desirable role. For example, a child unwilling to be the victim becomes one of two monsters, and the victim is invented.

Table 7-5 Summary of Strategies Children Use to Redirect Play within the Play Frame

Strategies	Description	Example
Ulterior conversations	Statements are a part of pretend play and also suggest what the other players should do next.	"These children are really very hungry."
Underscoring	Statements made by one player to inform the others about what they are doing are usually used when nonverbal enactments may not work.	"I will go to work, then I will come home again."
Storytelling	Statements elaborate the theme or set up a problem that must be solved within the theme.	"Smoke! Smoke! The house is on fire, and we gotta get out of here fast!"
Prompting	One player informs another on what to do or say. This is often in a stage whisper but may be mimed or communicated through gestures.	(Whispered) "That's the bride hat. If you want a hat, put on this one for the groom."
Formal pretend proposals	One player suggests a major shift in the play to the other players. The intent is to remain in the play sequence with all the players but change the theme.	(During house play) "What do you say that this family goes on a vacation to the beach?"

Children resist interrupting pretend play with reality. For example, if a child trips and falls down, he or she is likely to pretend a hospital-doctor sequence rather than interrupt the flow of the play to seek adult help. The child simply incorporates the event into the play if at all possible.

Combining the pretend play skills. After children have become skillful players, they modify and extend their pretend play. Children first use the pretend skills in short sequences and then combine them into more complex sequences. These **play schemes** are named by topic such as "cooking," "playing babies," or "driving the car." Generally, these schemes combine pretend play with action or object and role play into action-based portrayals of real-life situations (Roskos, 1990). As children gain in maturity and skill, they join a group of related play schemes and transform the play into a more elaborate **play episode** that is socially organized and has a specific problem to solve inherent to the plot such as a family going on vacation with no suitcases. Episodes are tied together through the topic and rely on language to integrate and hold the play sequence together.

An episode is played out in stages. First, the children ready the play area by handling the materials and moving the props. Second, children share directing the course of play when the roles are determined, the ground rules are established, the problem is stated or implied, and the story is narrated (Roskos, 1990).

Both schemes and episodes are commonly called dramatic play or thematic play and may portray a variety of topics. However, in the episode, there will be a problem to resolve. Problems such as relatives coming to visit (but there are not enough beds), playing store (where no one comes to buy), or playing post office (where there is an insufficient number of stamps) are typical. Favorite schemes such as "comforting the baby" could appear in all of these, and often do, as children signal each other to repeat a preferred sequence. Episodes tend to have a story-like structure with a clear beginning, development of the problem, resolution of the problem, and an end. When children know each other well, have many shared play schemes, and have had the opportunity to develop all of the skills mentioned in this section, the pretend play can extend for substantial periods of time.

School-age children play more elaborately, with more characters, and with more detail when they are in an environment that allows them to pretend (Curry & Bergen, 1987). They also select more dramatic problems, such as capture and rescue, and select themes that are more fantastic. Seven- to twelve-year-olds increase the

Boys are more likely to display metacommunication skills outdoors and in other settings than the housekeeping area.

layers of pretend play, such as when writers and actors are performing in the theater. The pretend play of rehearsal and script writing may take much longer than "the play" they are producing. They may also engage in improvisational contests or act out storybook or television themes. The pretend play of children requires cooperation, coordination of effort, organization of resources, and complex social interactions.

Master players. Children learn to play from family members, neighborhood children, peers, and teachers. As you work with children, you will encounter children with minimal skills such as those who wander and finger materials, or those who "hit and flit" without really engaging in play, and those that have some but not all of the basic skills. The intellectual and social advantages of play come to those who play with several others; use active imagination; are creative rather than repetitive; maintain (10 minutes or more) or reignite play over time (days or months); challenge others to use optimal skills; and act out a story line constructed with others during play (Bredikyte & Hakkarainen, 2011). Skillful boys often display their mastery outdoors or with blocks and vehicles; girls are more likely to display it with housekeeping or other nurturing themes.

A master player is fluent in all the basic skills of pretend:

- Exploring and playing with objects
- Substituting and inventing objects
- Imagining time and place appropriate for the theme
- Taking on and maintaining a role while engaging with others
- Complying with the rules that peers agree to
- Using metacommunications to influence the play and maintain the play frame
- Engaging and maintaining play with other participants at least 10 minutes
- Constructing whatever is needed to use to play with others

Construction Play

Objects stimulate pretend play and also construction. Some aspects of this have previously been described as children's handling of objects as dramatists or as patterners. **Construction play** occurs when children make or build something. All forms of social participation are common depending on the setting, materials, and available players.

Young children. Real construction begins during the second year when the child learns to connect objects together (such as threading beads or attaching

the pieces of a train) and develops the corresponding ability to disjoin objects (such as snap beads). Children also learn to stack and knock down blocks and to build both vertically and horizontally.

Between 2 and 3 years of age, children make constructions and name them "houses" and may combine various construction materials, such as mixing blocks with cars or toys. This often is done for the purpose of initiating pretend play. Given the guidance of supporting adults, they also will learn tool use, such as knives and rollers for clay, cookie cutters, scissors, and hammers and nails to make things. At this age, children's constructions are very simple; they are more interested in the process than the product.

By the time children are 4, their constructions become more detailed and elaborate. They might construct a house of blankets, boxes, and blocks, or a toy world with miniature trucks and soldiers. They

Children often construct something to enact their pretend scenarios. This may be with any kind of materials.

© Cengage Learning 2015

also make music, particularly with percussion instruments. They begin to show interest in their paintings as products and to cut paper designs. Their strategies are more organized. Parallel play and associative play is common as children build, and some building in blocks is also sociodramatic play at the same time.

Between 5 and 7 years of age, children have sufficient small-muscle control to plan and make a variety of things. Constructions are increasingly elaborate and often require social collaboration. At this time, they also begin to make costumes or other supplementary props for their pretend play.

Older children. Children in elementary school may be interested in model construction, handicrafts, weaving, woodworking, metalworking, bookbinding, basketry, carving, and a variety of other projects. They also construct some of their own games and do creative writing. Skillful pretend players also build sets, make costumes, and put on their own plays; the planning of scripts, actors, action, props, and sets may take hours, days, or weeks, whereas the production itself may be less than 10 minutes long. This also is the period of collecting and hobbies. School-age children extend their interests in constructions using a wide variety of materials, becoming increasingly scientific and experimental (Johnson, 1998).

Children who are inexperienced in social settings or who seem to have difficulty getting along with others often find parallel play with construction materials satisfying. It provides for conversation now and then and does not demand the integrated social skills of pretend play in a group.

Check Your Understanding

What are the sources for individual differences in the play of children?

- Age and experience with other players

- Gender

- Culture of the family

- Preferred styles with materials

- Preferred styles with pretend

- Level of basic play skills

- Availability of familiar playmates versus new playmates

- Information of the players

Play with Movement

You are familiar with the joyous running, jumping, and laughing of children coming outside for recess. Most physical play improves strength, endurance, balance, and coordination while children are showing off skills and attaining social status. For example, maintaining balance and just hanging on is the first stage of swinging. Less skilled children imitate peers in repeated attempts, but their movements are not synchronized, and they have limited success, usually "stomaching" the swing but are eager for their turn. Eventually, they adapt their strategies to suit their own abilities and limitations, frequently kicking the ground to increase their swinging speed. Then the timing improves so the swing may be pumped, with unskillful jumping from the moving swing attempted. With practice, they delight in demonstrating their prowess to their peers, sometimes competing, even though optimum amplitude is not achieved. Refinement and efficiency of movement occurs as children eventually attain security in their own skills and become capable of experimenting with "bumping" or other possibilities with the motion or the swing itself (Fox & Tipps, 1995). In a safe setting, with opportunities to observe more skilled players, and with practice and time, children attain movement skills that tend to be admired by peers and make positive social interaction more likely.

The feeling of sheer splendor experienced by a child racing down a hill, feet thudding on turf, wind blowing through the hair and on the skin; the careful placement of each step as a timid child threads the way up to the top of the climber; the amazingly empty feeling in the stomach of a child on a zooming sled, all involve play with motion itself. The children are exquisitely satisfied and pleased with their performance, which contributes to their self-esteem. Less-able children are often most successful in movement play with age-mates where demands for emotional regulation, language, and social skills are lessened, and they can engage successfully with others.

Play with movement, which begins in infancy and continues throughout adulthood, provides for the context of social interaction, as is evidenced in the popularity of swimming pools, ski facilities, and bowling alleys. Four aspects of movement play will help you better understand how to safely supervise children's play: practice play, challenge, risk taking, and rough-and-tumble play.

Respecting repetitious activity. Practice play is play with movement or an object repeated over and over, usually in the presence of peers. For example, Esther, age 5, wanted to try the high slide in the park. An adult went with her and offered to catch her the first time. Hesitant and timid at first, Esther went up the slide and down with growing satisfaction

© Cengage Learning 2015

Movement play in swinging requires physical skills and often involves cooperation and the pleasure of social interaction.

and pleasure. She took 21 turns on the slide without ever repeating exactly her previous performance. She varied the placement of hands and feet; went down on her belly, bottom, and back; climbed up the slide forward and backward; and went down feet first and head first. The adult observed her, commented on her performance, and stood close to the slide when concerned for Esther's safety. This child, who began hesitantly, left the experience with satisfaction and greater confidence in her ability.

From infancy to adolescence, what the child practices varies, but the process remains much the same. Toddlers march, throw, climb, and dance. Between 2 and 3 years, children jump from low heights, balance on a beam, and hang by their arms. Between the ages of 3 and 4, they begin to catch balls, climb jungle gyms, and ride tricycles. Between 4 and 5 years of age, they roller skate, swim, ride vehicles, dance to music, bounce balls, and play catch. Between 5 and 7 years, they use stilts, swing and pump the swing, and jump rope. Older children are likely to practice for specific sports. Skilled performance is often a means of engaging in social interactions that might otherwise be unavailable. It requires technique,

memory, practice, and, as children are older, competition, which by its nature requires cooperation. It contributes to a child's identity and sense of competence among their friends.

Maintaining interest in movement play. The selection of a play activity usually is based on its potential challenge for the child. Self-selected challenges require slightly greater skill than the child already possesses. Usually, the child observes the action, tests his or her ability to do it, seeks help if necessary, and then practices the skill until it has been mastered. Children who are obese, clumsy, or disabled find the natural movements of much younger children challenging and need additional support and encouragement to attempt even those simpler skills (Javernik, 1988).

Because play is not "for real," children are free to drop a task that is too difficult for them without loss of self-respect. Sometimes, this is verbalized as "just playing around." Interest remains high until mastery is complete. If a mastered skill, such as dribbling a ball, can be varied and incorporated into other skills, such as evading and running, interest may remain with the activity for years. In this sense, challenge comes from within the players and is a test of their own skills. When small groups of fifth graders created their own games with various bats and balls, they strove to build in enough challenge in the way the rules were made to keep peers interested (Hastie & André, 2012). At its best, challenging play helps children to understand themselves and to recognize their own accomplishments against the background of previous behavior.

Understanding risk. There frequently is some risk in play with motion. Skiing is definitely more risky than running. Some children seem like monkeys, climbing high into trees; others of the same age are frightened of simple climbing frames with padded mats beneath. Temperament and previous experience influence the willingness of children to take risks in play. Toddlers have little sense of potentially dangerous situations

Children test what they can do, challenging themselves and taking risks. Adults provide safe equipment, supervision, and guidance to ensure safety.

and must be protected. Preschool children, however, should be provided many opportunities to try skills in supervised play to learn just how competent they are.

By the age of 7, most children can judge the risk involved in any activity and are unlikely to go beyond their ability unless urged to do so. For example, Gwendolyn was well coordinated for a 7-year-old, was an excellent swimmer, and could ride a two-wheel bike. Jeff, only 2 weeks younger, moved easily enough but couldn't swim or do gymnastics. He spent more of his time at indoor activities. When the children were playing together outside, Gwendolyn climbed a tree and invited Jeff up. After being urged and called a scaredy-cat, Jeff attempted the climb. He fell three times because he couldn't catch the branch with his hands and pull himself up by his arms as Gwendolyn could. Bruised and shaken, he clung to the trunk once Gwendolyn had pulled him up. Apparently realizing that the tree was too risky for Jeff, Gwendolyn swung down and procured a ladder to help his descent. Children frequently assume that an activity that is easy for them will be easy for an age-mate and may need guidance in recognizing the difference between being supportive to peers and challenging them to perform potentially dangerous activities. Children rarely attempt feats that are beyond their abilities unless pressured to do so.

Supporting social and physical testing. Many children participate in rough motor play, which increases both the challenge and the risk. At a high pitch of activity, children run, hop, jump, fall over, chase, flee, wrestle, hit, laugh, and make faces, which is sometimes embedded in superhero play (Pellegrini, 2007). Played in a group, **rough-and-tumble play (R&T)** differs from aggression, which includes such behaviors as pushing, taking things, grabbing, genuine intimidation, and staring down another in a real confrontation (Pellegrini, 2004). Adults can identify distinctive behaviors in children's play to distinguish between rough and tumble play and aggression (Carlson, 2011; Pellegrini, 2009):

- Facial expressions are relaxed, smiling, or excited during R&T, but they are scowling, rigid, controlled, or stressed during aggression.
- Children invite others to do R&T and intend to have fun. There are no angry words or threats.
- Players usually want to return to the play if interrupted and engage in it regularly. In real fighting, children flee from the aggressor.
- High-energy behaviors, exaggerated movements, open-handed hits or kicks that do not connect combined with a playful expression and a role announcement, "I'm the Viper!" occur only in R&T.

Participants in R&T play know it's not real. For example, a child will say "Bam!" while striking at another, but without following through with physical contact. Children learn to read nonverbal signals of other players, but in some cases, the invitation to play is unambiguous. For example, one third-grade child passed a note to another girl, making her intentions quite clear (see Figure 7-3).

All preschool children engage in rough-and-tumble play, although boys do so more often than girls. Boys tend to play in larger groups with other boys at the perimeter of the play yard with very vigorous movements, and girls are more likely to carry out rough-and-tumble play near equipment with more restrained actions. Shrieks, shouting, howling, and laughter accompany this play. Rough-and-tumble play at this age frequently is combined with character roles of superheroes. Usually, young children spend more time watching this kind of play than participating in it.

School-age children usually play with children of the same sex, unless the play specifically requires a member of the opposite sex. One game, called "kiss or kill," requires one player to chase another of the opposite sex, get him or her down, say, "Kiss or kill?" and proceed with the kiss or the "strike" as the downed player prefers. Rough-and-tumble play is most likely

to occur after the children have been engaged in set tasks or after prolonged sedentary activity. When older children participate in rough-and-tumble play, it most frequently flows into games with rules, not aggression (Pellegrini, 2004). Children play with friends peaking in frequency during middle childhood (Smith, 2005) and dropping off in early adolescence. Tag or other running games often follow rough-and-tumble chasing. Interestingly, rough-and-tumble play is closely associated with social competence and high status in older boys.

Unpopular boys, on the other hand, don't seem to be able to discriminate between aggression and rough-and-tumble play. Apparently, they have not learned to distinguish the appropriate cues, and they respond to playful acts with aggressive ones (Pellegrini, 2004). Adults should point out the play cues and closely supervise it so that they can learn from their peers. The differences often are apparent only in facial expression, such as a smile, a silly face, or a frown. Laughter and noisemaking (such as "monster sounds") often signify that an activity is playful. Other play signals also are used to indicate the intent to play rough-and-tumble, such as "Let's play chase!" The adult's task is to help children indicate to peers whether or not they want to play ("Don't chase me—I'm not the dragon anymore," or "I'm not playing"). Often, safety zones must be established to avoid inadvertent involvement of unwilling players.

Rough-and-tumble play contributes to the development of a number of social and emotional skills such as reading and sending nonverbal cues, emotional regulation, social affiliation and cohesion, abilities for initiating and maintaining interactions with peers, and attaining and maintaining social status in male groups (Pellegrini, 2009). Rough-and-tumble play contributes to making and keeping friends. In addition, children establish and maintain dominance within their groups during rough-and-tumble play, which in the long run contributes to reducing conflict by clearly defining the social structure. There is more R&T play when new groups are formed, such as in the fall of the year and when children start middle school (Pellegrini, 2009). Rough-and-tumble play also contributes to motor training, particularly in physical fitness and strength, which in turn enables the children to be successful in game play during adolescence (Pellegrini, 2007).

Adults usually want to squelch rough-and-tumble play, perceiving it as aggression. Experienced professionals note that children not allowed rough-and-tumble play in one setting (school yards, recreational settings) do so in others (bus, neighborhood, backyards). It is better to supervise this play to minimize the risks to children's safety.

© Cengage Learning

Figure 7-3 A Written Play Signal for Rough-and-Tumble Play That Was Passed Between Two 9-Year-Olds in School.

Vigorous play, such as chasing, requires close supervision. Young boys often chase each other at the edges of the playground and well away from supervising adults.

Games

Games involve other players, have rules, and are eminently social. Generally, there are social sanctions for those not following the rules although older children may not implement them for players who are younger and don't know any better (Pellegrini, 2009). Games develop gradually as children's social skills mature, from the simple turn-taking of toddlers to the complex games of older children. What makes a game fun? Movement play in the game, a sense of inclusion with other players, and often the element of surprise or chance enhances the enjoyment of children between ages 3 and 8. Seven- to twelve-year-olds are pleased to show off their skills and physical or mental competence, and actually winning becomes increasingly important as children mature. They achieve acclaim and status through performance (Winther-Lindqvist, 2009).

Children between the ages of 3 and 5 play hide and seek or any number of games with a central person, such as tag or simple games with spinners or lotto (Frost et al., 2012). They take turns if the wait isn't too long. With more experience, they change roles, playing various versions of hide and seek such as "kick-the-can." Between 5 and 7 years of age, children play games of acceptance and rejection, such as "farmer in the dell," and of attack

and defense, such as snowball fighting. Seven-to nine-year-olds add games of dominance and submission such as "Mother may I," complex card and board games, and sandlot sports such as modified forms of softball and kickball. Young school-age children make mistakes based on their excitement and impulsiveness such as all the basemen running after the ball rather than staying on base to catch it after someone else has retrieved it (Davies, 2010). Older children, more concerned with outcomes, enjoy intellectual games such as charades or trivia and are more likely to participate in organized teams. The roles older children take in games are likely to depend on special skills, such as playing guard in a basketball game. Children who frequently ignore the rules, blow up in the middle of a game, or otherwise disrupt everyone's play risk peer rejection (Davies, 2010).

Games are based on chance (most dice games), skill (baseball), or strategy (checkers). Primary-age children invent games and discuss rules with other players using their experiences with pretend and movement play (Frost et al., 2012). Small groups of fifth graders are capable of creating new ball games given the time, support, and materials to do so (Hastie & André, 2012). Many games of motor skill (e.g., softball) have become sports in which the play is administered and directed

Games of strategy require following the rules, cooperation and self regulation generally achieved by children 7 years old and older.

by adults rather than by the children. Both the content of the rules and the process of playing are external to the children. In this book, we will focus on the informal games in which children can follow, make, modify, or change the rules themselves.

Young children do not approach a game in the same way that adults and older children might. Children aged 3 to 5 play games in much the same fashion that they participate in movement play. They observe a particular way to move and imitate it. They are, in fact, frequently confused. In the game of tag, for example, a young child will run to avoid getting caught but is likely to have difficulties if tagged and declared to be "It." At this point, a very young child may refuse to play or may just stand there. If older players are willing, they may allow the little one to tag them so the game can go on.

Three- and four-year-olds frequently perceive rules as an interesting example of how to play rather than a required behavior. When playing together, they have difficulties regulating sequential turn-taking. Nor are they concerned with what other players do; they simply are interested in their own actions. Each player is on his or her own. This is not the same as cheating, although you might interpret it as such. Kindergarten-age children understand clearly that a cheater cheats to achieve a favorable outcome. Some children believed that cheating in a board game was appropriate in some circumstances, particularly playing with someone else who cheated (Holmes, Valentino-McCarthy, & Schmidt, 2007). They tended to view fair play as malleable rather than static, and they could identify players and actions that violated the rules of games, as well as realize that pressures can be applied on others to play fairly, most typically calling "no fair" (Holmes, Valentino-McCarthy, & Schmidt, 2007).

Seven- and eight-year-olds begin to be concerned with problems of mutual control, winning, and losing. They are likely to discuss the rules before play but may have conflicting notions on what the "real" rules are. Conflicts may break out; these can be handled as discussed in Chapter 8. Children of this age often regard rules as sacred and untouchable, emanating from adults and lasting forever (Piaget, 1976; Sutton-Smith & Sutton-Smith, 1974). Rules may vary for some games, especially those that are passed on verbally by children themselves. The game rules may be followed, changed, ignored, enforced, and invented according to the context of the game or what children think is fun, fair, or acceptable. Usually no single person is in control of the rules, and group consent to alter the play is necessary. For example, if all the skilled players are on one side in a softball game, some may switch in the middle because there is no real competition. How play rules are altered also contributes to the social hierarchy of children's groups and establishes ideas of what is and is not acceptable (Winther-Lindqvist, 2009). Children develop skill in negotiation as they decide among themselves what the rules are to be.

Games are varied and are combined with many other forms of play. There are singing and dancing games, games using a variety of objects, movement games, games associated with dramatics (charades), language games (Scrabble), and games that involve construction (Bug). Similar games are available electronically with applications for TV, iPads, or smartphones. Even motor play is available on the Wii. Fortunately, most public libraries have good collections of books on traditional games suitable for children to play in groups or individually, and many electronic games are easily found in the Internet.

Adults provide materials, space, and time for play for children of all ages. They explain how the game is

Older children use the skills learned from earlier play with movement and rough and tumble play to engage in more formalized games or sports such as soccer.

played and what the rules are as well as demonstrating as necessary to show children how to play. Playing as one of the players is also very helpful in the earlier phases of learning the game. When the children seem to have the idea, take on an observer's role, preferably at some distance, but within sight of the action. Help children identify the problem when there are different interpretations of the rules, and ensure the safety of children (such as when a ball rolls into a street or parking lot). Otherwise, children should play independently.

Humor

Adults usually do not find the humor of the very young amusing, even if they recognize that the child is trying to joke. Children's humor is limited by their experience and their cognitive development, so their performance changes over time. Humor strengthens group bonds, provides relief from stress and strain, allows for self-effacement or celebration of life, rechannels feelings of aggression into socially acceptable humor, and provides a way for children to control people and situations (Scarlett et al., 2005; Klein, 2003). A sense of humor is a life-long social asset. Understanding that humor is always dependent upon the context and the development of children's use of incongruity will help you appreciate attempts at humor by the very young (McGhee, 1979).

Incongruity in children's humor. When an arrangement of ideas, social expectations, or objects is incompatible with the normal or expected pattern of events, it is incongruous. Although incongruity is not the only ingredient in humor, it may be the most common element in children's humor. Incongruity does not always elicit amusement, however. Children may react with interest, curiosity, anxiety, fear, or amusement.

Humor, like other play forms, is framed by clear play signals. The younger the child, the clearer the play signals need to be—laughter or a traditional joke opening such as "Knock, knock"—if the incongruous statement is to be treated as humor. Otherwise, the child will ignore it or treat it with curiosity.

Exaggeration. The enlarging of the story or motion so that it is beyond belief is **exaggeration**. Children often engage in slapstick actions or draw gigantic ears on a dog and laugh at their own joke or at others' antics. Older children use exaggeration in their verbal jokes, such as when a 10-year-old imitated the "announcement voice" from a public speaker at school: "Will the person with the license plate BL 72958109936210 please remove it from the parking lot? It is blocking the drive."

Humor is social. Children laugh longer in a group than when alone. Humor is dependent on the ability of the child to pretend and to have a playful orientation toward the situation in which humor occurs. If children do not have a playful orientation, they may enjoy exaggeration or incongruity, but not find it funny. Children also try to share their jokes with people with whom they already have a close bond. Playful attitudes or moods are more easily maintained in a social group than when alone, as well. Parents often are the ones selected to hear a joke, as Chukovsky (1976, p. 601) reports:

One day in the twenty-third month of her existence, my daughter came to me, looking mischievous and embarrassed at the same time—as if she were up to some intrigue. . . . She cried to me even when she was still at some distance from where I sat: "Daddy, oggiemiaow." . . . And she burst out into somewhat encouraging, somewhat artificial laughter, inviting me to laugh at this invention.

Developmental trends in children's humor. Humor, like other aspects of development, proceeds sequentially. In Table 7-6, the ages at which types of humor are likely to begin are provided, though children continue to enjoy the humor of previous stages. Children must be in a playful state of mind and be at a stage of cognitive development to engage in humor or to appreciate it. For example, preschoolers are perceptually oriented and are likely to laugh at people with disproportionate facial features, disfigurements, or noticeable handicapping conditions. They also laugh when someone falls in a funny way. Because of their cognitive limitations (very young children are less able to empathize in unfamiliar situations), it is not intended to be cruel. Older school-age children, having well-developed cognitive abilities, are able to enjoy humor based on illogical behavior. They prefer an element of intellectual challenge. Younger children imitate older ones in attempts to generate humor. However, they frequently forget the punch line or substitute a logical answer to the question, thereby "destroying" the joke.

Valuing children's humor. Accepting adults who understand the child's attempts at humor listen attentively and smile or laugh at their jokes. Admonishing children to stop being silly or quit fooling around inhibits the development of humor. Because children frequently imitate humor, adults who also use simple exaggeration or incongruity humor during the day provide a model to emulate. Humor helps define the child as a member of a group, enhance the member's position in the group, or increase morale. In the early phases, children's humor isn't recognizable to many adults, who may then ignore, suppress, or even reprimand children for attempts at humor. Although the content of humor changes as the individual matures, the skill and confidence that children develop in this area enables them to participate successfully in a variety of social situations.

Table 7-6 The Development of Children's Humor

Stage	Age	Description	Example
0	Young infants	No humor; smiles and laughs	Returns smile of adult
1	Older infants	Laughs in response to the caregiver trying to be funny	Playing peek a boo Playing "Where is the baby? (blanket over baby's head is suddenly removed)
2	During second year	Using an object in a way known to be inappropriate	Child uses a shoe for a phone: a bowl for a hat—followed by laughter
3	Older toddlers to age 4	Incongruity with objects or actions Nonverbal humor Exaggeration Visual distortions Calling a person or object a wrong name	Calls the cat "dog" and laughs Pratfalls and slapstick Laughs at drawings of person with very long legs Laughs at drawing of cat with no ears Laughs at odd movements/disfigurements Laughs at calling Henry, "Winnie"
4	4 and up	Silly words, Nonsense words Jokes around inappropriate desires/topics Gender role confusion	Asks for a wortzel at lunch time. Peers laugh when child says, "Doo Doo" or "Pee Pee" or "Poopie poo" Man walking in high heels
5	About 7	Multiple meaning of words Traditional joke lines Puns Illogical behavior Literary humor Begins to take audience into account	Man is working in the garden and asks child to bring him the hose. Child brings a ladies stocking. Knock, knock jokes Question jokes Buying a cat to use up the cat food that was on sale.
	10–12 years		Silverstein poetry or other children's literature

Sources: Chukovsky,1976; McGhee(1979); Scarlett, et al., 2005; Fuhler, Farris, & Walther, 1999, wrote about children's humor and some of their ideas influenced the table.

Even though each type of play has its own sequence of development in childhood, all require the support and guidance of caring adults if the quality of the play is to become optimal for each child. Adults coach children in the strategies that they have not yet developed as well as providing the time and materials to develop complex play. Are you ready to assist a child who wants to play and does not know how to do so? Think about how you might carry out these roles using the skills that are described next.

SKILLS FOR SUPPORTING, ENHANCING, AND EXPANDING CHILDREN'S PLAY naeyc

Setting the Stage for Children's Play

1. **Demonstrate warmth, acceptance, genuineness, empathy, and respect in children's attempts at humor, pretend, or game play.** Relax and enjoy the children.

Children play best when they are relaxed and without external pressures.

2. **Provide a variety of quality playthings to encourage exploration and imagination** (Klein, Wirth, & Linas, 2004). Children will play with anything, and some of the most interesting are from nature, such as sand, water,

and mud. Provide materials for construction, such as bristle blocks, unit blocks, paints of various types, paper, musical instruments, clay, and dough. Give young children realistic props; offer older children less realistic materials. Offer jump ropes, balls of various sizes, and other appropriate materials such as tricycles, ice skates, or basketball hoops for movement play. Provide different types of games: those that require cooperation (lifting one child in a parachute); those that encourage competition; some that are played in small groups indoors, such as checkers; and others that are played in larger groups outdoors, such as volleyball. Use real things such as dishes, hammers, and baby blankets in the pretend play area.

3. **Provide the props, the materials, and the necessary information for children to create a variety of sociodramatic play scenarios.** Offer props that support play themes revolving around family activities (camping, gardening, traveling), community activities (postal services, hospital, veterinarian clinics), and literary characters (Three Pigs, Goldilocks, or Madeline). Read and reread good children's literature and information books that provide the background for play. Record favorite stories so that children can listen independently. Provide specific props critical to the stories.

4. **Encourage exploration of materials.** Use nonverbal strategies such as smiling, watching, and offering or accepting materials. Assume children may use the materials in any way not expressly prohibited by the setting, unless the well-being of others is at stake or property could be damaged. Delay any demonstration of material use until children ask for assistance. Refrain from setting limits until children actually misuse the materials. Point out new or interesting uses of materials by other children when appropriate.

5. **Ensure the physical and psychological safety of all children.** Involve children in determining rules for keeping safe to prevent physical and psychological injury for themselves and for others. Encourage children to paint, tell stories, or deal with issues of violence that emerge in their play.

6. **Stand or sit near children at play.** Keep children in view from a little distance. Remain adjacent to the play space for children of all ages. Avoid hovering over children because it stifles their play. However, avoid standing at one end of the play yard while children are dispersed far away from you.

Maximizing the Play Potential of the Materials Available

1. **Mix unrelated toys together.** Fasten butcher paper onto the wall of the building outdoors where children usually ride tricycles, and provide paints. Put Lego® blocks and other small construction toys into a pretend play area set up as an office or hospital. Think of all the possible and then the not-so-possible combinations of materials. Materials need not have any obvious relationship. Stimulate the creative potential of the children.

2. **Introduce novel toys and materials gradually.** Avoid putting out all the new things at the same time. The stimulus value of each one competes with the others, becoming stale too soon.

3. **Rotate playthings.** Remove some play materials. When brought out again, they will generate increased interest. Similar to simple rotation is the practice of having a special set of toys in the child-care center that are used only in the late afternoon. The "new" materials, although similar to those used in the morning, generate much better play than would the same materials played with earlier.

4. **Provide culturally relevant materials.** Select play materials related to the occupations in the community, the family traditions of children, the geographic location of the community, or the group membership of children in the program. For example, preschool children in fishing villages will find more play potential in fishing-related objects than children from the southwestern plains. Make sure that the culturally relevant materials from all groups are represented over time (Jones, 2004).

5. **Encourage social interaction among children.** Set out two sets of Lego blocks instead of one. Have enough dress-up clothes for several children to play. When too many children want to play in the housekeeping area, suggest that some of them construct a home next door so that they can play neighbors. Other children are by far the most novel, interesting, and complex resources for play. Older children enjoy many games that emphasize cooperation and working together. As children mature, they are able to play in larger groups, and materials such as cards and board games can be played with as many as six players.

6. **Help children identify problems with their play and to seek information or help from peers.** For instance, "It seems your car does not roll very far on the carpet. Ask Soo-Jin what she thinks might be used to make it go farther." Soo-Jin might suggest a cardboard runway, boards, or movement of the car to a harder surface, or the

adult might do this. Let the children try things out, even if they try something like a scarf, which you already know will not work. Make a general request for new play ideas: "Angelo needs some money. Does anyone have an idea of what to use?"

7. **Encourage children to communicate in writing as well as orally.** Add writing and literacy materials to all play centers. Use blueprints of buildings in the block area and provide the appropriate paper, pencils, straight edge, and other related tools. Use grocery list note pads in the kitchen area as well as real cookbooks. Many kinds of writing implements and papers can be incorporated into children's play.

Helping Children Acquire Skills through Your Direct Involvement as a Player

1. **Play with materials**. Children love to see adults smear the finger paint or build in the sandbox. Comment on your play, saying things like: "I'm smearing my paint all over," or "I'm glad the sand is wet so my house stays up." Then, wait for children to comment on what they are doing. When modeling, respect your own play. Bring your play to some closure: Flatten the sand castle or announce that you are through. Children should not expect you to give way to them automatically when they want to play or when they just grab your materials. Simply tell them, "I'm nearly finished, and then you can have this place," as you complete whatever you are doing.

2. **Use verbal or nonverbal prompts from outside the play frame**. Mime the action that might be appropriate to the child after you have

caught his or her eye. This is especially useful for children who are about to move to another level of play on their own or to those who really do not want adults to interfere. Such actions are "throwing" in movement play, big smiles in humorous situations, or a physical enactment in pretend play. Using a stage whisper for giving direction or prompting also is helpful for some children.

3. **Take a role to encourage pretend play**. Select either a behavioral role, such as saying "Varoom, varoom" as you "drive" a truck down a block highway, or a character role, such as becoming the parent or the spaceship captain. Use a variety of techniques to influence the direction of the play, such as engaging in ulterior conversations or storytelling. Respond to the role cues of other children, and remain in character while in the play frame. Gradually take a less active part until you can exit the play frame altogether. Give a clear metacommunication to indicate that you are leaving the play, "This lunch was good. I have to be a teacher again."

4. **Enter into play imaginatively when play between children appears to disintegrate** (Trawick-Smith, 2013). Take action and use scripts to enter the play. For instance, knock on the door and say, "I am a traveler and am lost and hungry."

5. **Demonstrate movements as necessary**. If you should see a 2-year-old attempting to jump down a step but walking it instead, the most playful thing to do is to jump yourself, with feet together, landing with knees slightly bent and using your arms for balance. Demonstrations provide information, and if briefly and playfully done, it can be a part of the ongoing play. Give prompts, such as "Bend your knees when you land," and then resume the game or movement play.

6. **Participate fully in the game.** Play by the rules as you understand them and participate fully, taking turns, or running. Children learn some games, especially games of strategy such as chess, only by observing better players. Discuss the play as other players do, pointing out what you did and why, if appropriate. Be careful not to become so engrossed in your play that you forget that your goal is to support the play of the children.

Helping Individual Children Change the Level of Social Participation in Play

1. **Note patterns of play alone and with others.** Consider age, experience, and culture in deciding whether to intervene. For example, if a child

between 24 and 30 months spent most of the time watching older children play, this level of play is very appropriate. Except for exhibition games or waiting for turns, prolonged observation by a 10- or 11-year-old is not. Children who demonstrate skills in all levels of social participation should be left alone to choose how to play.

2. **Focus on the process of play so that the play may be extended or elaborated** (Klein, Wirth, & Linas, 2004). To provide the child clues for imaginative play with others, use statements such as "Do you need help with this crying baby?" or "What will happen to these animals when it rains? You could ask Brian to help build a barn."

3. **Note cues that a child is unsatisfied with his or her level of social engagement**. Cues indicating that children need help might be prolonged observation of a group at play (more than 10 minutes); following more skillful players from one activity to another; forceful crossing of the play boundaries or disruption of others' group play; crying, complaining, or stating that they want to play, too. Allow children who appear to be satisfied with their level of participation to continue if they appear to be relaxed, happy, and fully involved in what they are doing.

4. **Encourage children to observe other more-skilled children at play when they are learning a skill, "See how Laurie moves the pieces of the puzzle around."** Traditional games are handed down locally from one child to another, so this pattern of the observer continues throughout childhood.

5. **Match the play participation goal to the child's level of skill**. Allow children to practice playing alone or in parallel play until they are comfortable. If a child cannot catch a ball that he or she is bouncing, it is unlikely the child will be able to play catch. Notice when individuals shift from parallel play to short episodes of greater social interaction. Usually, parallel play is unstable and will shift into more direct interaction or solitary play.

6. **Play with the child yourself**. Less-skilled players perform more easily with a predictable, responsive adult than with other children. Give clear play signals, and use a variety of metacommunications. Pay attention to subtle cues and modify your involvement. Remember that a substantial number of children enter school without knowing how to so this.

7. **Invite the child and a second, similarly skilled player to play with you, and then ease yourself out of the situation.** Avoid

trying to match the best player or the most popular child with the least-skilled player. The disparities in skill may be too great for the play to continue. Remember that children are sensitive to social status in developing their play roles.

Escalating the Quality of Play Gradually by Varying Your Play Performance or by Giving Cues through Play Signals or Metacommunications

1. **Extend object play by imitating what the child is doing, and then vary the activity a little**. Incorporate the child's ideas into your modeling. Use the same object in a slightly different way, such as tapping a maraca with your hand instead of shaking it, or talking to a doll in an emotionally expressive tone of voice instead of a normal tone or monotone.

2. **Suggest that children use specific play signals to initiate or sustain play.** Tell the least-skillful player what to say, "Tell James, 'I'll be a policeman.'" This active approach is more likely to lead to success than the more general question, "Do you want to play?" Select the type of play signal that is commonly used by other players in the group. Consider *ulterior conversations, underscoring, storytelling, prompting, or formal pretend proposals.* For example, when one player seems exasperated with the inability of another to play a role correctly, lean over the props and stage whisper directions: "Whisper to the mail carrier that she is supposed to give the letters to other people, not read them herself." Or perhaps if the play theme seems to be floundering, suggest the storytelling approach to one of the players: "Think what would happen if there were an earthquake, and the city had to be rebuilt. Tell the story."

Demonstrate how to use nonverbal play signals when they would facilitate the play. For instance, show a child how to "fall ill" just outside the pretend hospital by making moans and holding a part of the body as if in pain. Show a child how to portray being a sad "baby" outside the housekeeping area as a way to get a response from other players. Some children may need much more support and direction than others, but play skills can be learned and enhanced.

3. **Encourage 9- to 12-year-olds to "go with the flow" when their ideas for the text or narrative of the play are denied or rejected by other players.** Suggest that they use mime

or actions to contribute to the story agreed upon, adjusting it by increments. Once started, older children prefer less explicit statements to maintain the illusion that the play is for real.

4. **Withdraw from the play and resume the role of observer after the play is well underway.** Think of a way to exit the game gracefully ("Let's pretend that I am a teacher, and I have to go to work now"), or step out of the play and state clearly that you aren't playing anymore. If you have a central role, such as pitcher in a softball game, you might just say that your turn is up, and ask who would like to pitch.

Becoming Directly Involved in Children's Playfulness

1. **Demonstrate a nonliteral approach to resources.** Playfully respond to the environment and to commonplace situations. For example, Mr. Phipps used to sing little songs or make up verses about ordinary things as they occurred during the day: the rain on the windowsill, blocks falling down, parents going to work, or children not wanting naps. He did this quite unconsciously to amuse the children. No one noticed until parents commented that their children could make up songs and poetry by themselves and wondered what the school was doing to promote such creativity.

   Another way to do this is to propose impossible conditions: "I wonder what if . . . ?" What would happen if so much snow fell that the houses were covered? What would happen if all of us grew wings and could fly? Encourage children to be expansive and to try to imagine all the possibilities. This often generates a lot of laughter. Show your interest in each child's contribution regardless of how silly it is.

2. **Be accepting of young children's humor.** Smile and show interest even if you do not have the least idea of what the joke is. When group glee strikes, with every child laughing uproariously, laugh along with it. They will quiet themselves down eventually. It is not at all unusual for the children not to know what they are laughing at either.

3. **Explain that a child was only joking when someone misinterprets the meaning of what was said or did not recognize a play signal.** Help less-mature children recognize play signals. For example, to call a boy a girl is a serious insult, except in a joke, which is typical of children age 4 or 5. Nonsense names or other names used to

address people may be very distressing to children not in on the joke or too young to understand it. Tell them that it is a joke, and point out the play signal if necessary.

4. **Use affective reflections when preschool children laugh at disfigurement, falls, or handicapping conditions, and then provide brief, but accurate information.** Say, for example, "You thought Mr. North walked very funny. He cannot help that because one leg is shorter than the other. People who cannot help the way they walk feel sad when other people laugh at them."

5. **Point out other children's play signals to children with special needs.** Children with autism, learning disabilities, or developmental delays often have difficulty understanding nonverbal cues and words not taken literally. Point them out quietly, "Jacob does not really think that John is a rotten turnip. See how they are both laughing."

Coaching Children Occasionally from Outside the Play Frame

1. **Suggest a related theme.** Extend the theme by suggesting that children go on a picnic, go to a movie, go on vacation, or engage in some other family-related activity if the housekeeping play is disintegrating.

2. **Add a necessary prop.** Children "going on a vacation" need a suitcase, and the play may break down without it. Get the suitcase from storage, and place it near the play area. Do not leave children unsupervised for long periods of time while you search for materials, but when possible, make such impromptu additions.

3. **Introduce new players from outside the play frame.** Say something simple and direct, like "Mary has been watching you play and would like to play, too." The children participating in the play may or may not accept Mary. It's their choice. Should they not want Mary to play at this time, help Mary find another place to play, providing several alternatives. Small-group games and pretend play are much more difficult to enter than are activities such as artwork or block construction because the children have already established roles and relationships. Do not force acceptance of another player; the play may completely disintegrate if established roles, themes, and relationships are disrupted. Play, by definition, is child directed and voluntary.

Offer a new character role for a player joining the group ("Here is the grandmother, coming to visit"). Additions of mail carriers, meter readers, relatives, guests to a party, and so on, can be incorporated into the ongoing play. Do not give the entering child a role that overshadows the other players, such as a spaceperson landing in the yard. The new player is likely to be "killed off" or rejected.

4. **Teach players to use a clear signal when leaving the play frame**. Say: "Tell Sarah you don't want to be the monster anymore," or "John doesn't know you don't want to chase him. Tell him that." Such suggestions will allow children to exit the play and will reduce the likelihood of the nonplaying child responding to rough-and-tumble play with aggression.

5. **Offer specific help when it is needed to maintain play**. For example, if a child's block construction is wobbling, point out the area where the problem is occurring. If children are confused about how a game should proceed, restate the relevant rules. When children are involved in superhero play, suggest that they think about the problem and talk about the characteristics of the true hero. Identify ways other than physical might to solve problems, or remind them to identify children who are and are not playing.

6. **Talk about play events that disintegrate for older children who are rejected playmates or isolated by their peers**. Assist them in identifying the social cues that they misinterpreted, and suggest alternative behaviors. Ask them to tell you what they think happened. Probe for details. Correct misinterpretations, and point out the behaviors that would lead to more acceptable responses and the maintenance of play. Initiating the social interactions, entering an ongoing play frame, and participating during rough-and-tumble play are particularly difficult for many children.

7. **Teach children games when necessary.** Have all materials set up, and know the rules. Invite the children to participate. Then, give brief directions, one at a time. For example, in the game of "Duck, duck, goose," say, "Take hands" (to form a circle). You may have to help by giving more specific directions, such as, "Jacob, hold Susan's hand." When the children are in a shoulder-to-shoulder circle, ask them to sit down. After they are all seated, stand up and announce that you will be "It" the first time. Walk around the circle, tapping heads and saying "Duck, duck, duck, goose!" When the word "goose" is said, direct the child to chase you, and then run

around the circle, sitting in the child's empty space. Then, direct the standing child to be "It." With very young children, go with the child who is "It" for the first time as he or she taps heads and says, "Duck, duck . . . goose," and then run with the child to the empty space of the new person who is "It." Give directions and demonstrate in alternating patterns. With young children, don't give all the directions at once.

Allow the children to play until all have had a turn or their interest diminishes. Repeat the directions as necessary each time you play the game until the children can play it by themselves.

8. **Encourage children to solve their own problems and create their own rules during pretend play or with informal games.** Use behavioral and affective reflections to help children clarify social conflicts or problems. Frequently, the problems stem from different perspectives: "Barbara, you think that everyone

▶❙❙ **TeachSource Video 7-2**

© Cengage Learning 2015

Young Children's Stages of Play: An Illustrated Guide

Go online and view *Young Children's Stages of Play: An Illustrated Guide.*

1. Identify examples of exploratory, solitary, parallel, associative, and cooperative play.

2. What instances of construction did you see?

3. How did the teachers enter into the play of the children in or out of the frame?

4. Describe what the teachers did and how children responded. Do you think that the play would continue if the adult left?

5. How do the children coordinate their play during cooperative play? Give examples.

Watch on CourseMate

should play the game the same way; Jason thinks that the rules should be changed a little for the younger children because they cannot run as fast. Tell me how you think you can work this out." Respect children's decisions as they interpret, comply with, alter, or create rules for pretend play and games that may be different from the ones that are familiar to you.

Guiding Children's Rough-and-Tumble Play

1. **Decide whether rough-and-tumble play is to be allowed, and if so, when, where, and under what conditions such play will be permitted**. Make your expectations clear and consistent. Consider limiting such play to a specific area or space as well as allowing it only during specified periods of the day. After clear limits as to time and place for rough-and-tumble play are made, use the following guides to help children toward more pleasant experiences.

2. **Decrease the violence in all play instead of trying to eliminate rough-and-tumble play.** Avoid toys that suggest violence or themes that lead to violence. When children "make" weapons of blocks, sticks, wads of paper, or anything else, remind them that they may not "kill" anyone or use a weapon. Avoid cartoons and television programs that are violent. Treat threats and verbal aggression as suggested in Chapter 12.

3. **Ask children to use specific, verbal play cues to initiate rough-and-tumble play.** All children must agree to be players to minimize being frightened or feeling that they are being attacked. Individuals have a right to say no to this type of play.

4. **Coach children in how to say no.** Give scripts to children who do not care to engage in rough-and-tumble play. "No," "I don't want you to chase me," or "I want to play something else," are all statements that children can be taught to use to decline play.

5. **Provide a "safety zone" so that when a child enters the zone, rough-and-tumble play stops.** This is similar to tag games where some object becomes a "safe" place. Children who are playing rough-and-tumble games sometimes frighten themselves and need an easy way to stop playing.

6. **Provide information about heroes.** Frequently, superhero play focuses on the most violent aspects of fantasy character dramas. Point out the protection of the victim, the plot, and the array of nonviolent characters in the media portrayal. Helping, protecting, and honorable motives are central to superheroes, but young children often omit these aspects. If children portray real superheroes, their play resembles pretend play with bouts of chasing.

7. **Suggest that the villain or victim be imaginary.** This way all of the children can be runners, and no one needs to be chased.

8. **Remain in close physical proximity to children engaging in rough-and-tumble play.** Move toward the action if you see three or four children running in a pack, distant from the other children and the play equipment, because this is probably the beginning of a rough-and-tumble play sequence. The episode is more likely to remain playful than degenerate into overt aggression when an adult is close by.

9. **If the rough-and-tumble play ceases to be fun, and someone is hurt or frightened, stop the behavior.** It is no longer play. Playing must be fun and voluntary for everyone. Protect the children from hurting others or being hurt themselves. Strategies for doing this are discussed in Chapters 4, 5, 10, and 11.

Demonstrating Awareness of Individual Differences

1. **Accept the young child's approach to games with rules**. Little children are not cheating or committing a moral error if they don't play precisely by the rules. Simply restate the rule in question, and go on with the game. Children learn to play games with rules by playing with better players who know the rules.

2. **Provide the time, materials, and coaching that each child needs to improve his or her performance.** All children should begin with simple games, roles, and constructions and then move on toward more challenging activities as their skills develop.

3. **Allow some of the less-skilled players to move into the play setting or attain play equipment for outdoor play from time to time.** This will enable them to initiate the social play experience and make them less likely to be excluded from the play.

4. **Accept the child's play-style preferences.** Both patterners and dramatists engage in high-quality play. Both children with strong fantasy and those with a more pragmatic approach benefit from their pretend play. Observe the play style of

children from cultural groups that are different from your own before intervening. If the children are joyful and socially engaged in a nonviolent way, refrain from trying to change it.

5. **Provide support for younger boys when girls outperform them in movement play.** Girls' motor skills often develop faster than boys' motor skills do until the later elementary grades, when the trend is reversed. Boys may be vulnerable to feelings of failure when the girls run faster, jump farther, and ride bikes earlier. Reassure them that they too will be able to do all of these things soon. Use similar strategies for developmentally delayed children.

6. **Support children in their choice of play activities; do not limit play to gender stereotyped choices.** Encourage children to explore a wide array of materials and roles. Respect playmate choices whenever possible as both boys and girls develop gender role-related skills in their play. Count out the teams so that they are evenly balanced for gender and skill.

7. **Respect cultural and experiential differences in children.** Allow children to explore play themes that might be unfamiliar to you. Encourage children to freely express their ideas and emotions in their play. Refrain from responses that automatically reject or diminish others' cultural experience.

Adapting Play Experiences for Children with Special Needs

In addition to using all of the skills previously mentioned, the following skills will assist you in supporting children who have special needs (Sandall, 2004):

1. **Use information from family members, specialists, and your observations to identify the child's competencies.** Avoid focusing on what the child cannot do. Use previously suggested strategies to find a co-player, select materials, and guide play.

2. **Simplify activities.** Break down activities into component parts, reduce the number or complexity of the materials used, simplify directions and vocabulary, or adjust the way the activity is carried out. For example, reduce the number of cards in a memory game that has a total of 40 pairs to 5 or 10 pairs of cards. Use a series of photographs of a sequence of steps to paint; this is easier for some children to understand than a series of oral directions.

3. **Provide a psychologically safe environment in which to play.** Use explanations such as, "Dakin has not learned to do that, yet," to explain why a child cannot do everything others can do. Note carefully that the child with special needs is not systematically excluded from play. Intervene as appropriate, providing assistance and support. Maintain similar expectations for the use of materials. For example, a child who has difficulty hearing should be expected to pick up toys and wait for the use of materials until others are finished (Sluss, 2005).

4. **Encourage the children to play with preferred materials.** If a child has an interest in trains, alter the nature of the activity over time by adding materials (train tracks or tickets) or encouraging other players to also play with trains. Incorporate trains one way or another in a variety of play opportunities.

5. **Use special equipment to enable the child to gain access to peers and materials.** Obtain a beanbag, which will allow a child typically in a wheelchair to be at the same level of other players. Help typically developing children to understand specialized equipment used by one child such as a hearing aide. Incorporate samples of special tools into exploratory play when possible.

6. **Encourage peer support.** Assign a job as helper for the day. Eric could not grasp the die or markers or move his marker when it was his turn. Ned was his partner for the day and would place the die in Eric's hand, then move the marker as indicated looking back at Eric for approval. Eric played, and Ned helped.

Sharing Information with Family Members about Children's Play

1. **Respond with information about the value of play to children's overall development when family members ask, "Why do they spend time playing?"** Provide information and then follow it up with specific details relevant to the child's development in your program. Remain calm and present your response with logical statements. Respect the right of the parent to have a different perspective from your own.

2. **Write notes about children's success in a play episode informally throughout the time the child is in the program.** Share photos of children's constructions with a few comments about the developmental significance of the event. Write glad notes when a child finally

participates successfully in a game with others. Let adult family members know where budding friendships might be encouraged through discussion at home. Describe a play event that illuminates the child's comprehension of ideas.

3. **Provide information about suitable play materials for the age group with whom you are working.** Written resources are available from your state cooperative extension service, as well as from the Association for Childhood Education International and the National Association for the Education of Young Children. In addition, many good articles are published in family magazines in November of each year.

4. **Encourage families to participate in community-wide events that support children's play informally for all age groups.** Send information about events in the community home during breaks or holidays. When other agencies or groups participate in park cleanup days, attend yourself and ask families to join you.

5. **Ask about the child's play at home and in other settings, as well as what the child mentions about play in your setting.** Parents' observations are likely to be very useful to you and may help in the planning and supervision of each child at play.

Pitfalls to Avoid

When you try to use the skills described here, sometimes certain attitudes and behaviors may interfere with your ability to carry them out in a truly playful spirit.

1. **Believing that children learn only what they are taught**. Learning is something that children do for themselves. Adults may structure the learning, but the information learned by direct instruction is limited compared with what children acquire from the environment, from their families and friends, and at play. Adults can facilitate children's learning to play, but they should not require children to perform to specification.

2. **Organizing play primarily to meet academic ends.** Children learn from all of their play experiences. Play is only play when it belongs to the children, is voluntary, and is fun. If children happen to count hats as a part of store play, fine, but they should not be required to do so. If children choose to put together an alphabet puzzle, fine; however, a clown puzzle is just as good from a playful perspective.

3. **Watching for mistakes.** Play is not serious, so mistakes in play simply do not count. By all means, assist a child when asked to do so, but never point out mistakes to a playing child. Let the child discover the error independently. Many interesting products were invented out of mistakes that someone played with.

4. **Making demands for specific responses.** Lessons about materials, for example, should not be substituted for play with materials. For example, you may present a lesson on the effects of mixing paint colors and ask the child to predict the color to be produced. The scientific approach to pigments should be separated from the creative activity of painting a picture, in which some paints might become mixed. Answer questions if asked; otherwise, leave the child alone. The distinction between curious investigation from a scientific perspective and playful exploration often is not clear. If the child has control, and you only respond to inquiries, then you are behaving appropriately. However, if the child is passive, and you are talking quite a bit, requiring answers from the child, or giving a series of directions, then this is a lesson, not play.

5. **Expecting the play performance to be the same within a group.** Cultural differences become apparent in play. So do differences in style. Though there are general differences between boys and girls, the range of individual differences are very great. Having uniform expectations of children is not appropriate.

6. **Setting too many restrictions.** Children cannot play if they are expected to maintain silence, not move, never touch one another, remain clean and tidy, and never create a mess. Play requires action. Action inevitably leads to disorder, messes, noise, joy, conversation, and, usually, jostling about. When adults set unreasonable restrictions on play, they simply are trying to prohibit play altogether. Of course, even the youngest player can be expected to clean up after the play, but that is a task in social responsibility, not play.

7. **Squelching the creative use of materials.** Consider whether there actually are reasons of safety or economics that restrict the

use of a particular material. For example, poker chips make better money to carry in purses than do puzzle pieces, most children would rather use them, and puzzles are ruined if pieces are missing. However, the same thing does not apply to macaroni, strings, Lego blocks, or other small items. The challenge is in planning to manage the proper return of the items after play is finished for the day. One teacher maintained a pail for small items, and children deposited them there whenever they were found. Later, they were returned to the appropriate storage area.

8. **Having no constraints at all.** Play is planned disorder, or organized, rule-governed interactions that do not fit adult predetermined conceptions. Play simply does not flourish when there are no rules or means of controlling its scope or parameters. Rules regarding safety, rights and feelings of others, and other necessities of group living are essential prerequisites of quality play. Children who do not have limits spend most of their time in social testing to see just where the boundaries of acceptable behavior are rather than in productive play. You will learn about setting limits in Chapters 10, 11, and 12.

9. **Ignoring play.** Given the right conditions, play probably will develop without adult prodding. However, quality play—that which stretches the imagination and the social and cognitive abilities of the player—does not develop in a vacuum. Writing lesson plans, cleaning cupboards, or chatting with other adults unrelated to the ongoing activity while the children are engaged in play is inappropriate.

10. **Interrupting play.** Stopping play to meet an adult agenda is an interruption. For example, stopping play with blocks to ask children to look for scissors is disrespectful. Make suggestions or requests, give directions, and provide information before or after play has begun. Stop play when it is clear that safety is an issue, "Put the rock on the ground. What else could you use for a rocket?" or "The hamster does not know how to swim. You can play with him on the floor (not in the water table)" (Jones & Reynolds, 2011). Occasionally sensitive, out-of-the-frame coaching is helpful, but it should never stop the ongoing flow of play. It is usually used when the play is disintegrating or not going well.

11. **Directing play or games too soon.** Children learn from the process of deciding on rules or setting up a fantasy play situation. It may take longer to do these tasks than you think is necessary. Unfortunately, adults often move in too soon and usurp the planning and organizational functions. Unless children ask for help, or unless conflict erupts that the children are unable to resolve themselves, you should show interest, but remain uninvolved.

12. **Asking children to explain their humor.** This quickly kills all the fun of a joke. If you do not "get" the joke, a social smile, social laughter, or a simple pleasurable expression are all appropriate responses.

13. **Admonishing children to be quiet or to quit being silly when engaged in humor.** Sometimes, adults are annoyed by children's laughter, especially if it occurs in the wrong time and place. In such cases, let children know you understand their merriment ("You kids are having a great time telling jokes"), and then explain why their humor is inappropriate ("I'm concerned that the bus driver won't be able to drive safely in this traffic with all the distraction"). Do not just set limits on children's humor in a general, disapproving way.

14. **Becoming too involved in the play yourself.** You may find yourself having so much fun playing that you forget that the purpose of participation is to stimulate children's high-quality play. Play should go on nicely after you have ceased to be so active. If it does not, you might have been dominating the play, the activity might have been above the children's level, or the role you had chosen might have been so central to the theme that the play cannot continue without it.

15. **Restricting the activity of children with special needs to "lessons" or ignoring these children as they play.** All children benefit from play, and children learn from engaging in play with more skilled peers. Avoid scheduling specialists during free play all the time. Some children may need assistance or coaching during play, and some activities may need to be adapted. Plan for individual needs for play. Play is one area in which most children can experience some success.

16. **Omitting mention of play performance when conferencing with families.** Parents are interested in the social relationships of their children, which are typically displayed during play. They can best support their child's development if they understand what skills their children do or do not have.

Summary

Play is the context of social engagement during childhood and has a foundation in genetics. Age of children as well as gender play contribute to choice of activities and playmates. Play is voluntary, fun, and involves children in using all of their physical, mental, and emotional resources. Play contributes to all aspects of social competence and there is variation in the levels of social participation

There are several types of play: exploratory behavior and object play, play with movement, construction play, and imaginative play. Within each play form, sequences of development were suggested through which children pass before they become skillful players. Most of these sequences occur in early childhood, with older children using early skills in new combinations for more complex forms of play.

The rules children create to further their play and the strategies that they use to initiate, develop, or change their play were discussed as well as some suggestions as to how adults might use their understanding of play to assist less-skilled children.

Individual differences in the ways in which children play were highlighted. The strategies that children use to frame the play, move the story forward, and terminate play were described. Humor is an additional aspect of playfulness that contributes to the child's social position in the group.

The role of the adult is to facilitate play for all the children in the group. This means that the adult must establish an atmosphere conducive to play, provide appropriate materials and facilities, and guide the skill development of the children toward increasing levels of performance. Responsiveness to children's observed behaviors is essential to this role, as is communication with the children's parents.

Several pitfalls were identified so that you can avoid them as you begin to support children's play.

Key Terms

associative play	metacommunication	prompting
character role	novelty	rough-and-tumble play
complexity	object invention	sociodramatic play
construction play	object substitution	solitary play
cooperative play	onlooker	storytelling
dramatic play	parallel activity	style
dramatist style	patterner style	transform
exaggeration	play episode	ulterior conversations
fantasizer	play frame	underscoring
formal pretend proposals	play schemes	unoccupied behavior
functional role	practice play	
games	pragmatist	

Discussion Questions

1. Why is it unlikely that play can ever be eliminated as a human behavior?

2. Look at Figure 7-1, How Play Contributes to Social Competence. What do you think would be the consequences if children do not have sufficient time to play? Project what these consequences might be for the child, the schools, and the community.

3. Describe the characteristics of play, and give examples of playful and nonplayful behavior.

4. Why aren't the concepts of work and play opposites? Why is it more accurate to contrast play with seriousness than with work? Use your own life experience to elaborate on this topic.

5. List the skills needed for children to participate in dramatic play. Give examples of each skill.

6. Describe style differences in object and pretend play.

7. What does metacommunication mean? Describe play signals that are nonverbal and verbal.

8. When a young child starts to tell a joke but forgets the punch line and then laughs, how should you respond?

9. When a group of school-age children of mixed ages are playing softball and are not following the Little League rules on their own, how should you respond?

10. When older children are fully involved in play, and everything is running smoothly, what should you do?

11. Explain the contribution of play to the seven elements of social competence (social values, positive self-identity, interpersonal skills, self-regulation, planning and decision making, emotional intelligence, and cultural competence). Use your own life experience for examples or observations from children's play.

12. Referring to Appendix A, NAEYC Code of Ethical Conduct, determine if the following situations pose an ethical dilemma. Identify the section that influences your answer.

   a. A teacher leaves the children unattended on the playground with the intent of watching them from a window and assumes that, if there is an emergency, one of the children will come to get her.

   b. Three children are having a noisy confrontation while engaged in dramatic play. The teacher does nothing.

   c. One teacher complains to a colleague that Ms. Gace (another colleague) runs a room that is just too structured, and the children don't get any real play time.

   d. A little girl is playing house, and another child comes in and wants to be the mother. The children agree to have two mothers playing in one house. The adult intervenes and insists that families have one father and one mother in each house.

Case Study Analysis

Read the case study on Eisa in Appendix B, and answer the following questions.

1. Examine the case study of Eisa and list any instance in which play is described.

2. What is the level of social participation in play in each instance?

3. Given what you know about her circumstances, would you expect Eisa to play at that level in a group of Spanish-speaking children? Why would you infer that?

4. Write a brief plan that would facilitate play for Eisa. Indicate the centers, settings, and children, or types of children, you would include in the plan to enhance her social play.

5. List eight skills from the skills section of the text that you think would be helpful in implementing the plan.

Field Assignments

1. Using simple, direct statements that you would use with the children, write out the directions to a game. Indicate where you would demonstrate what to do or play along with the players for them to get the idea of the game. Then try out the game with a group of children. How well were they able to follow your directions? What would you do differently?

2. Observe a group of young children over several days. Record whether or not you have observed the following behaviors for each child:

   a. Substitutes an object for another during pretend play

   b. Invents objects and uses gestures or movements to indicate existence

   c. Transforms time or age of player(s) or self

   d. Transforms place

   e. Takes on a behavioral or functional role

   f. Takes on a family or fantasy character role

   Now arrange to play with these children, and devise strategies to encourage the development of these skills. What materials will you need? How will you coach them? If they can perform the basic skills, what should your role be?

3. Collect materials that would be useful to parents in making toy selections for specific age groups.

4. Become directly involved in play with children. Use the techniques suggested in the text to influence the direction of play. Note the effect that your participation has on the children.

Reflect on Your Practice

Here is a sample checklist you can use to reflect on your use of the skills as a beginning professional. A more detailed classroom observation tool is available in Appendix C.

Teachers do the following to promote children's play:

✓ Takes cues from children; interprets cues to other children.

✓ Responds to children's humor playfully, smiles and laughs.

✓ Willingly plays with children and materials, and invites children to play.

✓ Facilitates changes in the level of play, and encourages children playing together.

✓ Coaches children from outside the play frame, making suggestions, providing props, or introducing new players.

✓ Uses silence to facilitate children's play.

✓ Instructs, stimulates, and extends children's play as appropriate.

CourseMate. Visit the Education CourseMate for this textbook to access the eBook, Digital Downloads, TeachSource Videos, and Did You Get It? quizzes. Go to CengageBrain.com to log in, register, or purchase access.

8 Supporting Children's Peer Relationships and Friendships

© Cengage Learning

OBJECTIVES

On completion of this chapter, you should be able to:

Describe the importance of children's relationships with peers and friends.

Explain how children think about friends and friendship.

Discuss the criteria children use in choosing friends.

Identify essential friendship skills.

Talk about where friendship development fits into the early childhood curriculum.

Demonstrate effective teaching strategies for enhancing children's peer relationships and friendships.

Recognize pitfalls to avoid in supporting children's friendships.

NAEYC STANDARDS naeyc

1. Promoting Child Development and Learning
2. Building Family and Community Relationships
3. Using Developmentally Effective Approaches to Connect with Children and Families
4. Using Content Knowledge to Build Meaningful Curriculum
5. Becoming a Professional

Rose and Mitzie ran toward their teacher. They were smiling. Mitzie shouted: "We're twins! We're twins!" The teacher looked at them and wondered how they arrived at that conclusion. Mitzie was tall, slim, and fair, with blue eyes and blonde hair. Rose was small, Asian with dark hair, and big brown eyes. The teacher asked, "What makes you twins?" Giggling, they opened their mouths, and lo and behold, each had a missing front tooth! It was as simple as that. No concern about racial, cultural, or developmental differences—just friends enjoying something they had in common—sharing an experience that had meaning for them, that delighted them, that strengthened their relationship.

(Zavitkovsky, 2010)

Rose and Mitzie are enjoying one of the happiest of all childhood moments—making a first friend, a new friend, a best friend! For children, gaining peer acceptance and establishing friendships are critical milestones in their social development and learning (Caspi & Shiner, 2006). Working out peer relations, finding friends, and maintaining friendships are complex social processes that involve knowledge and skills children only gain through interactions with others. In fact, these activities require children to develop abilities associated with every element of social competence described in Chapter 1, including the following:

- Positive self-identity
- Interpersonal skills
- Self-regulation
- Planning and decision making
- Cultural competence
- Emotional intelligence
- Social values

At one time, it was believed that becoming "friends" just happened. We now know that being a friend and making friends are not automatic and that not all children are equally successful in achieving the status of "friend." Fortunately, there are things children can learn to think about and do to increase their friendship potential. Adults can influence the development of these important capabilities in children through day-to-day interactions with children as well as specialized interventions (Gallagher & Sylvester, 2009; Hemmeter & Conroy, 2012). That is where you come in. As an aspiring early childhood professional, you have a significant role to play in helping children develop positive peer relations and friendships.

The Importance of Children's Relations with Peers and Friends naeyc

Children are involved in many relationships as they grow up. Some are with adults, some are with peers, and some may be with friends. All relationships engage children in human society and help them define who they are, what they can become, and how and why they are important to other people (National Scientific Council on the Developing Child, 2009). However, each of these relationships differs in closeness, the status of children in the relationship, and the extent to which children believe they can shape the outcome of their interactions (Rose-Krasnor & Denham, 2009). Consequently, children's relationships with adults differ from their relationships with peers. In turn, not all peer relations are defined as friendships.

Adult–Child Relationships

Secure, stable relationships with caring adults are essential to children's optimal development. Yet, society has certain expectations for these relationships, and the interactions between adults and children are characterized by clear differences in status and influence (Siegler, DeLoache, & Eisenberg, 2011). Adults' greater knowledge, skills, and experience make them authority figures to children. Whether the relationship involves parent and child, coach and player, or teacher and student, it is expected that the adult will be the expert and leader and that the child will be the learner and follower. Although adult–child relationships serve critical functions in children's lives and may be marked by love and respect, adults and children do not have equal power. Adults have the "upper hand," and children have few chances to change this. For instance, Jillian loves Ms. Cheryl, the lunchroom aide. She likes to talk with her and sing the songs she has learned in her classroom. Though Jillian may call Ms. Cheryl her friend, it is not a true friendship. They do not play equivalent roles in their interactions. It is Ms. Cheryl who determines the rules and who has the final say in most of what she and Jillian do together.

Peer Relationships

As children mature, they spend more and more time in the company of peers (Rubin, 2003). **Peers** are typically age-mates. Frequently, they share a common interest and meet to engage in particular activities like going to school, going to temple, singing in the church choir, or playing T-ball. However, beyond the pursuit that draws them together, little or no contact occurs otherwise, and they are not especially affectionate in their feelings for one another (Bukowski, Motzoi, & Meyer, 2009). In this case, Jillian and Dakota are classmates, but outside of school they do not interact and are not close companions. This makes them peers.

How peers function in children's lives. As peers, Jillian and Dakota have much to learn from one another and their classmates. Throughout the school day, the girls will have opportunities to share and take turns, consider the needs and desires of other children, and work on managing their impulses (NSCDC, 2009). In response to peer reactions, they will practice regulating their emotions (learning when to show their feelings and what feelings to reveal) and regulating their behaviors (learning what actions to display and which ones to inhibit) (Rubin, Bukowski, & Parker, 2006). These are all important social skills.

Peers expose each other to the finer points of current child culture (what games to play, what snacks to crave, what superstitions to hold, what jokes to tell, what movies to see, what heroes to admire, and so on). These are important cues that children use to initiate and maintain friendly interactions within their cohort group. Likewise, peers often serve as an appreciative audience for childhood accomplishments, such as Jillian's talent for making silly faces or Dakota's ability to build ramps and jump bikes. In these circumstances, children recognize what is relevant to other children and are able to offer support and admiration for skills, not necessarily appreciated by adults. Through interactions like these, peers add to children's self-identity and help one another develop a sense of where they fit in the social world of the classroom, the choir, or the T-ball team (Howes, 2009).

As children relate to their peers, they also learn how "being social" works among equals. This means paying greater attention to skills such as bargaining, debating, compromising, and developing shared

Peer relationships provide an opportunity for children to achieve a sense of belonging.

> **Things children can learn from each other!**
>
> - Starting conversations
> - Inviting others to play
> - Responding to play invitations
> - Using a not too loud nor too quiet speaking voice
> - Matching facial expressions, body movements, and words
> - Keeping a conversation going
> - Answering another child's questions
> - Expressing appreciation
> - Expressing affection
> - Recognizing other people's feelings and needs
> - Waiting and taking turns
> - Following game rules
> - Sharing materials
> - Offering to help or comfort
> - Listening to other people's ideas
> - Suggesting ideas
> - Making plans
> - Resolving conflicts without hitting, hurting, or retreating
> - Controlling angry outbursts
> - Acknowledging mistakes
> - Excusing others' mistakes

© Cengage Learning 2015

Figure 8-1 What Peers Can Learn from One Another.

agendas—things less practiced in adult–child relationships. They also get a chance to try out different social roles without great risk (NICHD, 2008). For instance, children can experiment with being a leader one day and a follower the next. They can take on the persona of jokester or see what it feels like to be "all business." They can also switch between being bold and being cautious. Gradually, these lessons help children learn what is effective social behavior and what is not; which behaviors fit them well, and which ones are not for them (Gest, Graham-Bermann, & Hartup, 2001).

Refer to Figure 8-1 for the things researchers tell us children learn through their interactions with peers (Kostelnik, Rupiper, Soderman, & Whiren, 2013). It is an impressive list!

Through peer interactions children connect to others their age and achieve a deeper sense of belonging. In time, children begin to select friends from this important social network.

Friendships

The bonds of friendship are more special and more personal than those among people who are simply peers. **Friends** choose to be with one another as specially chosen companions. They have warm feelings for one another and share responsibility for the relationship. In true **friendships**, both parties describe the other as a friend and are committed to resolving conflicts in an effort to continue their association with one another (Rubin et al., 2006). Although Jillian has friendly interactions with her teacher, her dentist, her soccer coach, her babysitter, and her classmates Maria and Dakota, she only experiences Juanita as a true friend.

Why children need friends. Friends have fun together and enjoy one another's company. Most importantly, friends supply affection and comfort. They reinforce children's notion that someone their "equal" cares about them, not because they "have to" but because they "want to." This factor of "choice" is at the heart of every friendship and can serve as an emotional buffer against other sources of stress in children's lives (Bukowski et al., 2009). All of these factors make friends an important source of security and social support.

Friends also provide cognitive stimulation and relevant measures of social comparison. In the course of their interactions, friends compare possessions and abilities, and discuss their outlooks on life. They express their opinions, openly criticize one another's ideas, clarify and elaborate on their own ideas, and seek feedback. This give and take among friends provides children with valuable information about their own attitudes, ideas, and skills, and increases their self-awareness (Harter, 2012).

Within the context of friendship, children refine existing social skills, try out new ones, and practice the difficult task of balancing personal wants and desires with those of others (Rubin et al., 2006). It is with friends that children are most apt to develop and refine prosocial skills such as cooperation and altruism. In addition, friends practice social problem-solving skills such as communicating, managing conflict, and creating and maintaining trust in spite of periodic differences of opinion. Although friends are more likely than nonfriends to argue, they are also more likely to resolve their arguments in proactive ways such as negotiating, striving for equitable outcomes, or trading off a victory today for a more positive outcome tomorrow (Siegler et al., 2011). Being able to share one's most personal feelings, manage disputes, and resolve interpersonal dilemmas provides excellent preparation for future intimate relationships in adulthood.

Children who have friends have a lot going for them. Because they have many chances to practice social skills, they enlarge their repertoire of problem-solving strategies and expand their capabilities in every dimension of social competence listed on the first page of this chapter. As a result, they are more accepted by peers and they experience fewer instances of rejection. This pleasant state of affairs translates into greater

When peers play together, they practice friendship behaviors.

happiness and confidence at home and at school. Under these conditions, children with friends perform better academically too (Rubin Bukowski, & Laursen, 2009; Sebanc, 2003). It is easier for them to learn to read, explore science, or carry out math activities when they are not preoccupied with fear of rejection or unsure about how to get along with others. This is why children who come to school looking forward to being with friends have more positive attitudes toward school, fewer absences, more classroom participation, and higher grades than children whose peer relations are rocky and friendships are few (Hyson, 2008; Epstein, 2009). All of these advantages contribute to children's healthy self-esteem. The benefits of having friends are summarized in Figure 8-2. Every way you look at it—from a personal, interpersonal, or academic perspective—having friends makes a positive difference in children's lives. This is why children want and need friends. It is no surprise that much of their time and energy is devoted to answering the question, "Who will be my friend?"

Children with friends are more likely to...

Be **happy** and have:
- Greater **social competence**
- Better **problem-solving skills**
- Greater **self-confidence**
- Better **academic** performance
- **Healthy** self-esteem

Figure 8-2 Benefits of Having Friends.

What Happens When Children Cannot Find a Friend

> Jessie wails, "Teacher, he won't be my friend!"
>
> Frustration is evident on Jessie's face and in his voice.

Because all relationships have their ups and downs, most children eventually experience the sorrow of being rejected by someone they wish would be their friend. This is a normal part of growing up and for many children represents a time to cope with disappointment but eventually bounce back socially. Some children, however, are consistently left out of friendship pairings and for whom friends are hard to come by (Hemmeter & Conroy, 2012). Such children do not have the opportunity to enjoy the benefits that befriended children experience. Friendless children are unhappy children and have more than their share of difficulties as they grow older. These children are more likely to suffer lifelong problems such as depression, mental illnesses, heart disease, and hypertension in adulthood (Bukowski et al., 2009; Ladd & Troop-Gordon, 2003). Later in life, they are also more likely to become juvenile delinquents, drop out of school, and commit suicide (Ladd, 2005). No one knows for sure whether friendlessness causes these serious problems or whether the behavior traits that contribute to antisocial behavior and emotional instability also lead to peer rejection. Whatever the case, there is a strong relationship between children's inability to form close friendships and later feelings of self-dissatisfaction and sometimes despair. A summary of these ill effects is offered in Figure 8-3.

Although completely friendless children are rare, many children grow up feeling lonely and wishing they had more friends. Clearly, having friends is important, and children think about friends a lot. How and what they think about friends is influenced by age and experience.

Children without friends are more likely to...

Be **unhappy** and:
- Be **lonely**
- Experience **depression and anxiety**
- Display **poor** social skills
- **Lack** self-confidence
- Perform **poorly** in school
- Have **poor** self-esteem
- **Drop out** of school
- Have **mental health problems** in adulthood

Figure 8-3 Problems with Being Friendless.

Children's Ideas About Friends and Friendship

> The teacher asks, "Who is your friend?"
>
> Four-year-old Terry says, "Gillie is my friend. He plays blocks with me."
>
> Ten-year-old Sandie says, "Audrey is my friend. We have fun playing soccer together. Sometimes we stay at each other's houses overnight—that's fun. We keep each other's secrets, and if one of us is lonely, we ride bikes 'til we feel better. We're really good to each other!"

Terry and Sandie have very different ideas about friends. Children's concepts about friendship—their notion of how it works, their expectations, and the rules that govern their actions toward friends—are influenced by their age and experience.

Friendship Framework

Young children are drawn to their peers. Babies like to be with other babies, and toddlers enjoy one another's company. By 18 months of age, children imitate other children and play simple social games such as peek-a-boo or look-for-the-toy (Wittmer, 2008). Children as young as 2 proudly proclaim of another child, "Her my friend." These are all early signs of affiliation.

Researchers have studied children's friendships for the past 20 years and describe a hierarchy of phases that characterize children's thinking about friends. They refer to these as the **Friendship Framework** (Selman, Levitt, & Schultz 1997; Kennedy-Moore, 2012). This framework begins with 3-year-olds—when children begin to seek out peers in earnest. It coincides with children's emerging understanding of other people's perspectives and a corresponding increase in self-awareness (Gallagher & Sylvester, 2009). From this time onward, children's ideas about friends proceed through a series of five overlapping levels, each characterized by its own logic. In each level, children's understanding of what a friend is, the value placed on friendship, and the friendship skills required to make and keep friends look different.

Let's consider these levels in turn, beginning with Level 0, the time of Momentary Playmates.

Level 0—Momentary Playmates: Ages 3 to 6. Young children call "friend" those peers with whom they play most often or who engage in similar activities at a given time. This was evident in 3-year-old Maddie's answer to the question about her friendship drawing: Why are they your friends? "Because we play Polly Pockets together and all wear pink dresses" (see Figure 8-4 for her drawing of playing together with friends). At this level, children view friends as children who are conveniently

Figure 8-4 Maddie and Her Friends—Level 0.

nearby ("He's my friend; he lives next door"). Friends are also valued for their possessions ("She's my friend; she has a Barbie") or because they demonstrate visible physical skills ("He's my friend because he runs fast").

Children at this age like the idea of having friends, and they definitely have preferences for some playmates over others, but they are not necessarily reliable friends themselves. They are egocentric, thinking only about their own side of the relationship and what other children can do for them. They do not consider their responsibility to the friendship or how to match their behaviors to another child's needs. ("She lets me play with her Barbie" but not necessarily, "I let her play with my Barbie.") Likewise, it is common for children in this level to assume friends think just the way they do. If this proves false, they may feel surprised or upset.

Children in Level 0 are better at initiating an interaction than they are at responding to others' overtures. They may inadvertently ignore or actively reject other children's attempts to join their play, especially if it has been going on for a while and "everyone" has an established role already (mom, baby, big sister, or players and scorekeeper). Once a child or group of children has centered on carrying out the play episode in a particular way, it becomes difficult for the players to expand their thinking to envision how a newcomer could be

included. The refusal to allow another child access to their play is a cognitive dilemma, not a deliberate act of cruelty. Tomorrow, the child who is rebuffed may be deeply involved in the play, and another latecomer may be the child for whom "there is no room." All of these things underscore the momentary nature of children's earliest thinking about friends.

Level 1—One-Way Assistance: Ages 5 to 9. At Level 1, children understand that friendship goes beyond their current activity, but they still think in very practical terms. Friends are people whose behavior pleases them. As 6-year-old Veronica drew the friends walking dogs together, she smugly explained that her friend Kelly in the picture was going to get her a Pinkalicious doll for her birthday party (see Veronica and Kelly in Figure 8-5). For some children, good feelings are prompted by a playmate who will give them a turn, share gum, offer them rides on the new two-wheeler, pick them for the team, save them a seat on the bus, or give special birthday presents. For others, pleasure comes from having another child accept the turn, the gum, the ride, the invitation to join the team, the seat, or the present. Because each friend is concerned about whether his or her wants are being satisfied, neither necessarily considers what to do to bring pleasure to the other. If, by chance, their individual

© Cengage Learning

Figure 8-5 Veronica and Kelly on Their Play Date—Level 1.

wants and behaviors are compatible, the friendship lasts. If not, the friendship will likely dissolve.

Another characteristic of this level is that children try out different social roles: leader, follower, negotiator, instigator, comic, collaborator, appeaser, or comforter. They experiment with a variety of behaviors that may or may not match their usual manner. That is, a child who wants to be more assertive may become bossy and overbearing; a child who discovers the benefits of comedy may become silly or outrageous.

By the time children reach Level 1, their desire to have a friend is so strong that many prefer to play with a "not so nice" companion rather than play alone. They will try almost anything to initiate a relationship and may attempt to bribe or coerce another child to like them by saying: "If you'll be my friend, I'll invite you to my party," or "If you don't let me have a turn, I won't be your friend." Children who resort to such tactics are not trying to be mean but are merely experimenting with what works and what does not.

Level 1 is also notable for the fact that boys play with boys and girls play with girls. This occurs because children continue to focus on outward similarities, and gender is an obvious way of determining likeness. School-age friends are observably similar to each other in many additional outward ways as well—clothes, hair styles, ways of talking, and so on (Rubin et al., 2006).

Although children concentrate much of their energy on the friendship process, they have difficulty maintaining more than one close relationship at a time. During this phase, children often discuss who is their friend and who is not. Children can be overheard to

▶❚❚   **TeachSource Video 8-1**

© Cengage Learning 2015

5–11 Years: Peer Acceptance in Middle Childhood

Go online and view *5–11 Years: Peer Acceptance in Middle Childhood*.

In this video, you will see factors that influence children's relationships with their peers.

1. The video states that peer relationships become more important during this stage. Why do you think this is true?

2. Based on what you observed in the video, what factors do children consider when choosing friends?

3. Based on the factors described by the children in the video and what you have read so far, how would you help a child develop friendships?

Watch on CourseMate

Figure 8-6 The Cool Cat Club. Who's in! Who's Not!—Level 2.

© Cengage Learning

say, "You can't be my friend; Mary's my friend." Pairs change from day to day and frequently are determined by what people are wearing, by a newfound common interest, or by convenience (who shows up first). Thus, friends change frequently, although some friendship pairs remain relatively stable over time, as long as the two children see each other often (Rubin et al., 2011).

Level 2—Two-Way, Fair-Weather Cooperation: Ages 7 to 12.

Children at Level 2 are able to consider both points of view in the friendship, but alternately, rather than simultaneously. Children expect friends to be "nice" to each other and often trade favors as a way of helping each other satisfy their separate interests: "You helped me yesterday—I'll help you today"; "We're playing my game first and then your game." They recognize that each person should benefit from the relationship and that the friendship will end if this does not occur: "If you call me names again, I won't be your friend"; "That's not fair! I waited for you yesterday." Friends are very concerned about what each thinks of the other, and they evaluate their own actions as they feel the other might evaluate them: "Steve will like me if I learn to catch better"; "Nobody will like me with this ugly haircut." Conformity in dress, language, and behavior reaches a peak as

children try to find ways to fit in with the group. As a result, it becomes very important for children to carry a backpack that looks like everyone else's, wear their hair in certain ways, and take the same lessons or join the same out-of-school activities as their friends.

The emphasis throughout this period is sameness, and forming clubs is a natural outgrowth of this. Clubs tend to be formed by a small number of "friends," and although short lived, have elaborate rules. The major activity in such clubs involves planning who will be included and who will be excluded (see Figure 8-6 for Cauleen's Cool Cat Club). To further confirm their unity, friends share secrets, plans, and agreements.

When children reach level 2, they become very possessive of each other, and jealousy over who is "friends" with whom is common. Having a friend, and a best friend at that, provides self-affirmation and helps children move more confidently within the larger peer group (Siegler et al., 2011).

Level 3—Intimate, Mutually Shared Relationships: Ages 8 to 15.

Level 3 marks the first time that children view friendship as an ongoing relationship with shared goals, values, and social understanding (Rubin et al., 2006). Now, children are more willing to compromise rather than simply cooperate. This

Figure 8-7 JJ and His Best Friend—Level 3.

means they are not concerned with the emphasis on reciprocity that marked the previous phase; rather, they become involved in each other's personal lives and have a stake in each other's happiness. They gain satisfaction from the emotional support they enjoy within the relationship. On this basis, friends share feelings and help each other solve personal conflicts and problems. They reveal thoughts and emotions to each other that they keep from everyone else.

Friendship has now become intimate, and the best-friend relationship is a crucial one. Because this is such an intense learning experience, children often only focus on one best friend at a time, as is evident in JJ's picture of he and his best friend Steve (see Figure 8-7). It is natural for them to become totally absorbed in each other. Such friendships are both exclusive and possessive. In other words, friends are not supposed to have another close friend, and they are expected to include each other in everything. Friends do share approved acquaintances but are not allowed to pursue a relationship with someone one of them does not like. The greatest betrayal comes when a friend breaks these rules. Only after children have developed friendship to this point are they able to branch out and have close ties with more than one peer at a time.

Level 4—Mature Friendships: Ages 12 and Older.
For individuals at the mature-friendship level, emotional and psychological benefits are the most valued qualities of friendship. Friends are not as possessive of each other as they were in previous levels; they can have some dissimilar interests and can pursue activities separately. Children at this level are able to allow their friends to develop other close relationships as well. Thus, they can have more than one friend at a

time and can have friends who are not friends with each other. At this level, friendship becomes a bond that involves trust and support. As a result, friends are now able to remain close over long distances, over long periods of time, and in spite of long separations (represented by Rachel's picture of friends talking on the phone; see Figure 8-8).

Why the framework matters. The friendship framework shows us that children think about friends and friendship in qualitatively different ways at different ages (Kennedy-Moore, 2012). Although there is no guarantee that all children will reach the highest levels of friendship development, the framework makes clear the path to getting there and gives us clues as to how we might support children along the way. We cannot necessarily accelerate children's progress through the sequence, but we can better understand children's behavior by knowing more about their philosophy of friendship at each level. This knowledge also helps us to recognize that some of the poor social behaviors children display in their quest for friends is the result of immaturity and limited understandings, not poor character. Such mistaken behaviors can be addressed through the developmentally appropriate teaching strategies you will learn about later in this chapter. In the meantime, see Figure 8-9 for a brief summary of all five levels of the framework.

How Children Choose Their Friends naeyc

> Eric and Steven are like two peas in a pod; they dress alike; they talk alike; they act alike; they are the best of friends.
>
> Sasha and Tabitha are as different as day and night. One is short, one is tall; one is boisterous, one is quiet; one likes cats, one likes dogs. Still, they are inseparable.

Adults often wonder why children choose the friends they do. Physical appearance, ethnicity, gender, age, behaviors, and attitudes or preferences are cues children consider in selecting a potential friend (Howes, 2009; Bukowski et al., 2009).

Physical Appearance

One factor that contributes to children's friendship selection is personal appearance. Children are naturally attracted to those who look like them—same hair, same skin color, and same physical traits (Rubin et al., 2006). Children also attach the positive qualities of friendliness, intelligence, and social competence to those they consider attractive. Likewise, they associate negative attributes with peers they think of as unattractive.

Figure 8-8 Long Distance—Level 4.

© Cengage Learning

FRIENDSHIP LEVEL	NAME	APPROXIMATE AGES	CHILDREN'S MAIN WAY OF THINKING
Level 0	Momentary Playmates	3 to 6 years	"Today, my friend is you!"
Level 1	One-Way Assistance	5 to 9 years	"It's all about me!"
Level 2	Two-Way, Fair-Weather Cooperation	7 to 12 years	"I scratch your back, you scratch mine."
Level 3	Intimate, Mutually Shared Relationships	8 to 15 years	"Friends do EVERYTHING together."
Level 4	Mature Friendships	12 years and older	"BFF—through thick and thin, near and far."

Figure 8-9 Summary of the Friendship Framework.

© Cengage Learning 2015

Ethnicity

Children tend to pick their friends based on ethnicity and are most likely to choose friends from their own racial group (Graham, Taylor, & Ho, 2009). However, family attitudes do influence how children feel about making friends with someone of another race or culture. If children perceive their family members as accepting of racial differences, they are more likely to include children of different racial or ethnic backgrounds among their friends. Also, if classrooms and play settings are more ethnically diverse, friendships tend to be more mixed (Howes & Lee, 2007).

Gender

Gender is another dominant consideration in who becomes "friends" with whom. There is an expectation in children for how one should act based on gender. Girls viewed as "tomboys" seem to fare well and are liked regardless, but boys who violate gender stereotypes are

Girls like to play in pairs.

likely to be disliked and shunned (Rubin et al., 2006). Children prefer same-sex playmates throughout childhood and even at a very early age tend to exclude the opposite sex. At age 2, girls prefer to play with girls. By age 3, boys begin to prefer to play with boys, although this preference is not set until around age 5 (Fabes et al., 2003a). Girls tend to play in pairs and small groups; boys tend to form packs and engage in larger group activities (Rose & Smith, 2009). Females often reveal personal information whereas males usually engage in physical activities that do not require personal sharing (Rubin et al., 2006). Although friendships between males and females do occur, same-sex friendships tend to be more lasting and stable over time.

Age

Children are most likely to select friends who are close to their own age (Siegler et al., 2011). When friendships develop between children of different ages, it usually is because the participants are developmentally similar in some way. For instance, shy children who have less confidence in their interaction skills may seek out younger friends with whom they feel more comfortable socially.

Behavior Characteristics

The likelihood that two children will become friends is closely linked to the number of behavioral attributes they share (Bukowski et al., 2009). In both Western and Eastern cultures, similarities between friends can be found with regard to their level of prosocial behavior, antisocial behavior, shyness, depression, popularity, and achievement (French et al., 2000; Barbu, 2005). Friends also tend to resemble one another in terms of physical or cognitive skill, and degree of sociability (Coplan & Arbeau, 2009). Consequently, it is not unusual to see children choose friends who share their

▶❚❚ TeachSource Video 8-2

2–5 Years: Gender in Early Childhood

Go online and view *2-5 Years: Gender in Early Childhood*.

In this video, you will see children discussing ideas of gender roles.

1. Based on what you observed in the video, how do you think children's ideas about gender roles might influence their choice in friends?

2. Describe two implications of children's concept of gender roles on peer relationships.

3. Describe what strategies you might use to help children develop a broader understanding of gender roles.

Watch on CourseMate

love of sports, reading, chess, or stamp collecting. It is also common for bright, agile, impulsive, or outgoing children to seek friends much like themselves.

Children sometimes choose friends whose characteristics complement their own personality and capacities (Rubin et al., 2006). This often involves attributes that they themselves lack and for which the other child can serve as a model. Thus, loud children and quiet children, active children and passive children, serious children and "class clowns" may choose one another as friends. Yet, even when this occurs, one must remember that these children have found enough common ground that they see more similarities than differences in each other. Children are seldom attracted to those whom they view as total opposites (Hartup & Abecassis, 2004; Kennedy-Moore, 2012).

Attitudes/Preferences

When children who are dissimilar in some way discover that they share like attitudes or preferences, they feel more positive about one another. This awareness facilitates friendly relations between children who initially perceive themselves as totally different. Such knowledge has been found to promote increased friendships among children of differing ethnicities and between children with disabilities and their more typically developing peers (Hemmeter & Croyer, 2012). When two children discover that they both like math, or that they are equally excited about dogs, or that they each have a desire to be firefighters, physical differences become less important, and shared interests may open the door to a new relationship (see Figure 8-10). This is why adults who want children to experience the rewards of friendships with children of the opposite sex, of another ethnicity, or children of differing abilities provide opportunities for these children to

recognize similarities as they interact with one another in day-to-day interactions and in planned activities.

Social Competence

For each of the dimensions we have discussed so far, sameness and commonalities have been the key attributes that children look for in a possible friend. However, one quality attracts children to their peers more than any other—social competence (Bagwell & Schmidt, 2011). Children are attracted to their socially competent peers. It is more rewarding to spend time with children who are kind, keep their angry emotions under control, and know how to compromise than to interact with someone who displays the opposite characteristics. Thus, peers view socially competent children as desirable companions for many reasons.

First and foremost, children value fun. "He's fun," or "We have fun together" are among the earliest reasons children give for choosing a playmate. Because socially competent children are spontaneous and playful in their interactions, they are enjoyable to be with. They have the social skills and language abilities to greet others, invite others to play, and to respond positively to a newcomer's request to join a game. They are adept at cooperating and negotiating (Hebert-Meyers et al., 2009). These attributes prompt peers to see them as approachable and engaging.

Socially competent children are also perceptive. They recognize social cues that indicate another person's reactions to their social approaches and they adjust their emotions and behaviors to match the needs of the situation (Biddle, Garcia-Nevarez, Henderson, & Valero-Kerrick, 2014). Such children also infer what might be pleasant to others and act on this understanding in mutually beneficial ways. The ability to manage their emotions, to recover from setbacks, and to behave in ways that minimize conflict are further plusses that enhance children's value as potential friends and play partners.

Finally, socially competent children demonstrate acceptance of a wider range of variation in people than is true for other children, and they are able to tolerate more differences in preferences and opinions among potential friends (Rubin et al., 2006). They stand up for their friends and recognize social injustice aimed at peers and others in their immediate circle. Their loyalty and affection for peers make them dependable comrades, a key requirement for friendships at higher levels of the friendship framework. You will see all of these qualities reflected in Table 8-1, in which we summarize how development influences social competence and how those abilities affect their friend potential.

All of the qualities outlined in Table 8-1 make children who are socially competent desirable candidates for friendship (Rose-Krasnor & Denham, 2009). Consequently, developing qualities and skills associated with social competence are central to children establishing

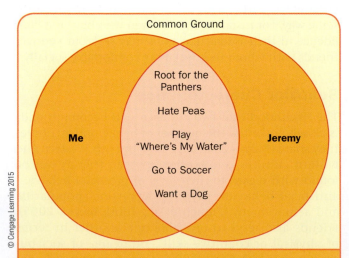

© Cengage Learning 2015

Figure 8-10 Children Who Can Find "Common Ground" Are More Likely to Become Friends.

Common Ground

Me · Jeremy

Root for the Panthers

Hate Peas

Play "Where's My Water"

Go to Soccer

Want a Dog

Table 8-1   Developmental Profile of Socially Competent Peers

Developmental Focus	Ability in Relation to Social Competence	Peer Relation and Friendship Benefits
Social	• Recognizes and accommodates other children's needs and interests • Regulates own behavior (knows what actions fit certain situations and uses them) • Demonstrates caring and helpfulness • Recognizes and responds to unfair treatment of others	Viewed as approachable and caring, not disinterested or unkind
Emotional	• Recognizes emotions in self and others • Regulates own emotions (knows what emotions to express, when to express them, and how) • Demonstrates empathy	Viewed as friendly and self-controlled, not remote, hostile, or impulsive
Language	• Initiates interactions • Knows words to use in different situations • Understands other people's messages and intents • Uses words to keep the interaction flowing • Uses words to negotiate and compromise	Viewed as socially connected and cooperative, not isolated or oppositional
Cognitive	• Imagines the thinking and needs of others and adjusts behavior accordingly • Contemplates alternate interpretations, strategies, and potential outcomes • Sees connections and similarities less obvious to others	Viewed as a good player, not awkward or unskilled

© Cengage Learning 2015

positive peer relations and friendships. This is an easier task for some children than for others.

Unsuccessful Peer Interactions

Four-year-old Alisha is reserved and very quiet around her peers. She often can be seen standing on the fringe of an activity simply watching. Even when invited to join the play, she usually shakes her head "no." Following several such refusals, children have stopped asking and now generally ignore her.

Randy, 8-years-old, is the terror of the school playground. He regularly pushes, hits, and trips his classmates. During group games, he runs to the center of the circle, grabs the ball, and challenges other children to catch him. His loud aggressive behavior has earned him a reputation as a bully, and most children avoid him whenever they can.

To the casual observer, Alisha and Randy seem worlds apart. Yet, both are examples of children who have difficulty interacting with their peers. Children who habitually experience unsuccessful peer interactions fall into two categories: peer neglected and peer rejected. Such children are at risk for the many negative outcomes associated with friendless children that were identified in Figure 8-3.

Peer-neglected children. Peers often neglect children who are typically shy and passive (Coplan, Schneider, Matheson, & Graham, 2012.) Such **peer-neglected children** are not talkative. They make very few attempts to enter play and dislike being the focus of attention. They are less outgoing and prosocial with others and are ignored and overlooked by peers. Frequently, children are neglected simply because they do not know or do not use socially accepted ways of attracting other children's attention (Ladd, 2005). As a result of being neglected by peers, these children often expect to be overlooked and back away further from interactions. This cycle results in neglected children missing opportunities to interact successfully with peers and the chance to learn new patterns of interaction.

This leaves peer-neglected children feeling increasingly isolated. For example, Rudy watches Steven and Jamie play space rangers under the climber outside. His caregiver, Mr. Rogers, suggests that Rudy go play too. Rudy replies, "Nah, I'm no good at that game," and backs away. Rudy doesn't believe that he can enter the play and would rather not even try.

Peer-rejected children. These children are actively shunned by peers and have difficulty finding playmates (Ladd, 2005). When children experience rejection from peers, they are more likely to become aggressive, especially if they already have a tendency toward aggression. This combination of early aggression and rejection is likely to lead to antisocial behavior (Jimerson, Swearer, & Espelage, 2010). Such children may exhibit behavior based on the desire to get even or defeat their peers. Clearly, neither retaliation nor aggression is useful for promoting social relationships. **Peer-rejected children** seem to follow two patterns of behavior: rejected-withdrawn or rejected-aggressive. Each comes with its own set of problems.

Rejected-withdrawn children are socially awkward. They display immature or unusual behavior and are insensitive to the expectations of their peer group. They know that they are not liked by others and expect to be ignored or ejected from social situations (Damon, Lerner, & Eisenberg, 2006). For instance, Janelle, age 6, observes her peers playing house. She wants to play too, but she does not think the others will let her. Instead of asking to play, she gets on all fours and barks her way into the scene, irritating the others and disrupting the play. The children give her dirty looks and proceed to ignore her. She goes off and plays alone. Rejected-withdrawn children are lonely. They tend to exhibit low self-esteem, depression, negative social-emotional functioning, and other emotional disorders. These children are targets for bullies, frequently falling victim to the hurtful behaviors of others (Rubin et al., 2006).

Rejected-aggressive children are just the opposite. Often, they are the bullies. Rejected-aggressive children alienate themselves from their peer group through the use of force. They try to dominate interactions, are critical of others, and typically are uncooperative (Alsaker & Gutzwiller-Helfenfinger, 2010). They interpret the behavior of others as hostile toward them. For example, Josh wants to play soccer with the neighborhood boys. He approaches the game on his bike. When no one invites him to join, he rides his bike through the middle of the game. He gets off on the other side, letting his bike fall onto the edge of the field, knocks another player down, and kicks the ball away, making a goal. Part of the difficulty lies in these children's inability to grasp the consequences of their own behavior on others and the corresponding peer reactions. Because they don't make the connection, they fail to take responsibility for their actions, believing that the fault lies with everyone else (Jimerson et al., 2010).

Although rejected-withdrawn children expect others to dislike them, rejected-aggressive children believe themselves to be socially popular when in fact they are not (Ladd, 2005). These children are more likely than all others to become chronically hostile, develop conduct disorders, and engage in criminal violence. Whether withdrawn or aggressive, rejected children, without intervention, are likely to continue their counterproductive patterns throughout life (Rubin, Bowker, & Kennedy, 2009).

Both neglected and rejected children possess an inaccurate perception of others, misreading or misunderstanding the social cues of other children (Hay, Ross, & Goldman, 2004). This leads to very lonely children. Of all the children who experience peer interaction difficulties, rejected-withdrawn children report having the greatest amount of loneliness and stress (Asher & Paquette, 2003). Results like these help us to better understand the importance of helping children improve their chances to demonstrate friendly behavior and learn better ways to make friends.

The Friendship Skills Every Child Needs to Know naeyc

When Jonathan, age 7, was asked to author a "how-to" book, he decided to write the directions for "how to make a friend." Here is his step-by-step description:

1. *First you talk to them.*
2. *Then, you ask them if they want to play something.*
3. *Then you just get to know them.*
4. *Then, if you get upset, mostly you try to work things out.*

Jonathan's directions show he knows what he is talking about! He identified all three essential **friendship skills** children must master if they are to figure out how to make friends well (Rubin et al., 2011). These include the following:

1. Making contact with a potential friend
2. Maintaining positive relationships
3. Negotiating conflict among friends

Making Contact

Before a friendship can begin, one person must make an approach and another must accept. How this contact is carried out influences each child's perception of the other. Children make good impressions when they act and talk as follows:

- **Smile and offer greetings:** "Hi," "Hey!" or "What's up?"
- **Ask for information:** "What's your name?" or "Where's the cafeteria?"
- **Respond to others' greetings:** "I'm new, too," or "Come with me. I'll show you."
- **Offer information** "My name's Rosalie. This is my first day at Central."

- **Invite participation:** "Wanna play catch?" or "You can be on our team."

- **Take on a role or carry out a simple job:** "I'll help keep score," or "I'll help you put these away." (Shapiro, 1997; Evans, 2002)

At other times, friendly children rely on nonverbal cues to signal interest and make contact. They approach ongoing social interactions by watching, listening, moving closer, and easing into the situation rather than simply rushing in (Rubin, 2003). They may imitate what other children are doing to show they are following another's lead (such as joining a game of chase or pretending to shop at the make believe grocery store). They may also simply play side by side with active players and gradually become absorbed in the play through friendly offers to share or work together if the opportunity arises. Through signals like these, children let others know they want to be friends. Children universally interpret pleasantness and kindness as friendly behaviors. Thus, children who are cordial elicit positive reactions and are better accepted by their age-mates (Kennedy-Moore, 2012). This is true whether the genial child is the initiator or the respondent.

These research findings underscore the old adage, "You catch more bees with honey than with vinegar," meaning you attract more friends by being nice than by being rude or unkind. Yet, many children fail to make the connection. These are children whose timing is off or who have the right idea but an inappropriate way of showing it. They may be truly unaware of the importance of positive strategies or may fail to recognize how or why their mismatched or ill-mannered behavior affects others as it does. Whatever the explanation, such children often attempt to make contact by grabbing, pushing, barging in, whining, threatening, ignoring, begging, criticizing, or being bossy (Ladd, 2005). Children who rely on these approaches are frequently rejected. As their lack of success becomes more habitual, they tend to withdraw or become hostile. Over time, they develop a reputation of being unfriendly or undesirable as a playmate, continuing the problem. In such cases, adults will need to intervene to help children learn to make more positive contacts and improve their chances of finding a friend.

Maintaining Positive Relationships

The positive behaviors that characterize successful beginnings continue to be important as the relationship grows. Peers at every level of the friendship framework describe likeable children as fun to be with, sensitive, positive in their outlook, and kind (Rubin et

▶⏸ **TeachSource Video 8-3**

© Cengage Learning 2015

Including Students with Physical Disabilities: Best Practice

Go online and view *Including Students with Physical Disabilities: Best Practice.*

In this video, you will observe a child with spina bifida and her teachers.

1. In the video, you see Marianne's teachers emphasizing the importance of social development. Why is it important to consider social development and the opportunity to interact with others for children with special needs?

2. What strategies did the teachers in the video use to help support Marianne's interactions with peers?

3. Describe two additional strategies you might use to help Marianne make friends.

Watch on CourseMate

al., 2006). In particular, how well children communicate both verbally and nonverbally influences their attractiveness as a potential friend (Hebert-Meyers, 2009). Children who speak directly, are attentive to everyone involved in an interaction, respond with interest, acknowledge the play signals of others, and offer fun ideas are sought after as friends. The following techniques characterize such children's interactions with others:

- **Expressing interest:** Smiling, nodding, establishing eye contact, asking related questions.

- **Cooperating:** Taking turns, sharing, working together.

- **Expressing acceptance:** Listening to another child's ideas, adopting another child's approach to a play situation.

- **Expressing affection:** Hugging, holding hands, or saying: "I like you" or "Let's be friends."

Max and Justin have an ongoing friendship in first grade. They often spend time together at free-choice time.

© Cengage Learning 2015

- **Expressing empathy:** "That's a neat picture you made," "You look sad; want me to sit with you while you wait?"
- **Offering assistance and helpful suggestions:** "If you like, I can hold the box while you tie it. It may need some string on top of the tape."
- **Praising playmates:** "That was a great hit," "Neat idea! I think it'll work."

Children who use these tactics actively demonstrate respect and affection for others, qualities that contribute to long-term relationships (Rubin et al., 2006). Also, positive behaviors like these elicit positive responses from others, which reinforce children's efforts and prompt them to continue their successful actions.

In the same way that positive cycles are established, so are negative ones. Children who are aggressive, uncooperative, act silly, show off, or display immature behavior may irritate, frustrate, and offend their peers. Similar problems arise when children misjudge how to act appropriately. They may rely on insincere flattery, express their affection too roughly (giving bear hugs), or communicate their appreciation too effusively. Others miss the mark by constantly correcting rather than suggesting, or taking over instead of merely helping. In any case, these behavior patterns sabotage children's efforts to maintain the friendships they had begun.

Negotiating Conflict

Perhaps the most severe test of a relationship occurs when friends disagree. How both parties manage the conflict determines, to a large extent, whether or not the friendship will continue. Children who use constructive ways of resolving differences, while still meeting their own needs, are most successful in maintaining lasting relationships (Rubin, Bukowski, & Laursen, 2009). This is because they are able to preserve their dignity and at the same time take into account another person's perspectives. Children who are so passive that they never stand up for themselves lose self-respect and, eventually, the respect of peers. Those who respond aggressively also are rejected. Neither extreme is conducive to eliciting positive reactions from others (Rubin et al., 2006).

There is a strong correlation between children's effective use of language skills and their ability to negotiate well (Hebert-Meyers, 2009). In order for conflict to be successfully negotiated, all parties need to understand the source of the problem and be able to express their ideas for a solution. Children who use threats, shame, or coercion to force a solution violate these fundamental requirements. Consequently, other children begin to avoid them or retaliate in kind. Those who are most successful are children who implement the following negotiation skills (Stocking, Arezzo, & Leavitt, 1980; Evans, 2002):

• Express personal rights, needs, or feelings:	"I want a chance to pick the movie this time."
• Listen to and acknowledge others' rights and feelings:	"Yeah, you have been waiting a long time to see that movie."
• Suggest nonviolent solutions to conflicts:	"Let's flip for it."
• Explain the reasoning behind a proposed solution:	"This way, we each get a chance."
• Stand up against unrealistic demands:	"No, you got to pick the last time. Now it's my turn."
• Accept reasonable disagreement:	"Okay, I hadn't thought of that."
• Compromise on solutions:	"Let's see both, or go swimming instead."

These are all skills children can learn with support from early childhood professionals like you.

Where Friendship Development Fits in the Curriculum naeyc

With our society's obvious interest in literacy and numeracy for even the youngest children, you may wonder if friendship has any place in the formal school curriculum. In reality, interacting effectively with peers and developing friendships are considered crucial benchmarks in children's social development and

as such, are incorporated in the Learning Standards for most states. See Table 8-2 for examples.

Typical Challenges Children Face in Meeting Friendship-Related Learning Standards

Children are not born knowing the best ways to make and keep friends. Such lessons are learned by observing others, by practicing, by experimenting with a variety of social behaviors, and by experiencing the consequences of their actions. Children who are better observers and more accurate evaluators of what is effective

Table 8-2   Examples of State Learning Standards Associated with Friendship

State	Ages	Expectation	Benchmarks/Learning Outcomes
Nebraska	3–5	Receives social support and shows loyalty to a friend	The child: Notices who is absent from circle time and asks about it, showing concern for others. Develops close friendships with one or two children as well as plays with many children.
Illinois	Grades 6, 7, and 8	Uses communication and social skills to interact effectively with others	The child: Practices strategies for maintaining positive relationships (e.g., pursuing shared interests and activities, spending time together, giving and receiving help, practicing forgiveness).
Alaska	60 months to kindergarten entry	Develops friendships with peers	The child: Gives social support to others (e.g., offers to help a peer who cannot find his or her toy). Follows suggestions given by a peer about how to proceed in their play. Have friends in different settings (e.g., neighborhood, school, extended family).

Sources: Nebraska Department of Education (2005); Illinois State Board of Education (June 2010); Alaska Department of Education and Early Development Division of Teaching and Learning Support (December, 2007).

and what is not acquire friends more easily than those who make poor observations and assessments or those who have poor role models among the adults and peers with whom they spend time. This does not mean that children who experience challenges in the friendship arena have no chance for improvement.

On the contrary, there is encouraging evidence that all children can learn essential friendship skills with the help of socially adept peers and caring adults (Frankel & Myatt, 2003). This is true even for children who are neglected or rejected. Favorable results have been reported for such children when they have undergone intensive interventions designed to increase their awareness, teach them targeted social behaviors, and decrease their aggressive and otherwise nonproductive responses (Ladd, 2005).

Regardless of their degree of need, the most typical stumbling blocks for children of all ages are that they do not always know:

- What is appropriate friend behavior
- What friendship-related skills to use or how to use them
- How to monitor or modify their behavior while interacting with peers (Bagwell & Schmidt, 2011).

These are things all children can learn to do better. However, they make the most progress when caring adults guide the way.

The Adult Role in Supporting Children's Friendships naeyc

As an early childhood professional, your support of children's friendships begins by observing children carefully and paying close attention to their play patterns, social status, and overall behaviors that support or detract from friendship opportunities (Thompson & Twibell, 2009). The knowledge you gain will help you better understand what children already know and what they might need from you to develop stronger friendship skills. The teaching strategies you have learned in previous chapters are useful in promoting social competence as well as positive peer relations. Those skills will also address learning standards focused on friendship such as those presented in Table 8-2. For instance, creating a positive verbal environment, helping children learn how to express their emotions constructively, developing stress hardiness and resilience in children, and supporting and expanding children's play skills all contribute to enhanced opportunities for interaction and the development of friendly relations in the classroom. Five additional strategies are strongly associated with improving children's friendship skills (Mize & Ladd, 1990b; Epstein, 2009). These

include creating friendship-supportive classroom environments, demonstrating friendship skills with puppets and props, having children role-play friendship skills, engaging children in buddy skills training, and providing intensive one-on-one coaching for children who need more targeted interventions (Hemmeter & Conroy, 2012). As a classroom teacher or caregiver, you could use any one or combination of these strategies to meet the needs of the children with whom you work. Let's consider what each one entails.

Creating Friendship-Supportive Classroom Environments

Children vary in what level of adult support is necessary and beneficial for friendship development. However, all children profit when adults create environments in which children's friendships are respected and encouraged. Such environments prompt children to engage in productive peer interactions and to develop the skills that children find most attractive in a potential friend (Hamre, 2008).

One way in which adults create the kinds of social environments children need is to provide them with many opportunities to interact with peers informally. It is hard to make friends with children you don't know. It is harder still to practice friendship skills within the confines of teacher-directed activities. Children need chances to get to know one another, talk together, and explore how social relationships work. They need time, space, and materials that are open-ended and self-directed in order to explore various social roles and to practice essential social skills within the equality of the peer group. When adults set up play and loosely structured experiences between children and assist them in learning to interact with one another, positive peer relationships are likely. One of the most fruitful mediums for this kind of activity is pretend play (Epstein, 2009; Bodrova & Leong, 2007). In fact, researchers tell us that children's early pretend play behaviors with peers strongly influence friendship behaviors later in life (NICHD, 2008). Play is so vital to friendship formation that when pretend play is not supported, it can interfere with harmonious peer relations throughout childhood (Hay et al., 2004). These findings have important implications for the kinds of activities and routines children need to experience from preschool through the elementary grades. Free-choice time, recess, project work, and creative dramatics provide many chances for children to exercise their "friendship muscles" and to further develop the skills they need to grow into socially competent adults.

A second way adults create supportive environments is when they treat children's day-to-day experiences as opportunities for children to learn how to get along and

To foster children's friendship, pair children with similar abilities. Point out their common strengths and interests, and invite them to work together to accomplish a task.

become more friendship savvy. These adults do more than simply bring children together. They observe and take advantage of teachable moments to facilitate new skill development. Adults do this by helping children interpret the social cues and feelings of their peers and adjusting their behavior accordingly. They translate children's experiences and guide them toward social proficiency. They also supplement these on-the-spot lessons with planned activities that emphasize the learning standards presented earlier in this chapter. One such activity is to carry out friendship skits.

Demonstrating Friendship Skills with Puppets and Props

Even the youngest of children enjoy watching a story being acted out with puppets or toy figures as the "actors." These items can be used in friendship skits designed to promote children's recognition and understanding of essential friendship skills and the emotions associated with peer interactions. Demonstrations initially carried out by an adult and later enacted by children are effective ways to demonstrate friendly behavior and prompt discussion (Joseph & Strain, 2003). One approach is for teachers to create scripted skits that illustrate a particular skill. Go to Figure 8-11 for an example of a friendship lesson focused on making effective

Teachers can use persona dolls to demonstrate problem-solving strategies to children.

SAMPLE SKITS FOR TEACHING A FRIENDSHIP SKILL: SIGNALING YOU WANT TO PLAY

Materials
Two people puppets (or human figurines or dolls); several small, colored blocks; markers and poster paper or a smart board

Procedure
Adult: Today, we are going to talk about friends. Here are two puppets. We are going to pretend that these puppets are real children just like you. Their names are Max and Gus. They are 4 years old and go to a school just like ours. Who is this? (Adult holds up one puppet, and children answer with name.) Who is this? (Adult holds up second puppet, and children answer with name.) Watch carefully and see what happens when Gus and Max try to be friends.

Skit #1
(Set up one puppet [Gus] as if "playing" with several blocks. Place the second puppet [Max] facing Gus, but at least a foot away.)

Adult: Here is Gus. He is playing alone with the blocks and is having a good time. Max sees Gus and would really like to play with him, so he watches Gus very carefully. Gus keeps playing; he doesn't look up. Max feels sad. He thinks Gus doesn't want to be friends.

Question for Discussion:
1. Who was playing?
2. Who wanted to play?
3. Did Gus know Max wanted to play? How do you know?
4. What else could Max do to let Gus know he wanted to play?

   As children answer these questions, provide information to help in their deliberations: "Gus was so busy playing, he didn't look up. That means he never even saw Max standing there. He didn't know Max wanted to play. Watch again and see what Max does differently this time."

Skit #2
Adult: Here is Gus. He is playing alone with the blocks and is having a good time. Max sees Gus and really would like to play with him. So, he watches Gus very carefully. Gus keeps playing. He doesn't look up. Max walks over to Gus and says: "Hi. I like your building. I'll help you get some more blocks."

Questions for Discussion:
1. Who was playing?
2. Who wanted to play?
3. Did Gus know Max wanted to play?
4. How could he tell?
5. What will Gus do next?
6. Let's think of some other ways Max could let Gus know he wants to play.

Suggestions for Leading the Discussion
As children suggest ideas, paraphrase them and write them down where all the children can see them. Accept all ideas regardless of originality, correctness, or feasibility. If children have difficulty thinking of ideas, prompt them by providing information: "Sometimes, when people want to play, they can say: 'Hi. I want to play,' or they can ask a question like, 'What are you building?' This lets the other person know they want to be friends. What do you think Max could do?" Once children have suggested their ideas, replay the scene using each suggestion, one at a time. Ask the children to predict how Gus will react in each case. Play out the scene as they suggest. Provide further information as appropriate: "John, you said Max could help Gus build. Let's try that." (Maneuver the puppets and provide appropriate dialogue). "Tell me what you think Gus will do now."

Figure 8-11 Sample Friendship Skits.

Digital Download   **Download from CourseMate**

contacts with potential playmates. It is built around two skits, one that demonstrates a lack of social skills in approaching a potential friend and a second skit that shows effective skill use. With a few modifications in language, this skit is suitable for children ages 3 to 8 years. In this case, the teacher uses friendship skits at least once a week at circle time, sometimes addressing the same skill under different circumstances, and sometimes presenting another skill such as negotiating a disagreement about what game to play.

   Another use of friendship skits is more open ended and takes its plot from teacher observations of real child challenges in the classroom (Luckenbill, 2011). When using this approach, teachers craft social stories to help children think about actual classroom events and potential solutions. Each skit is structured around a six-step problem-solving sequence:

- Identify the problem.
- Talk about emotions.
- Generate solutions.
- Talk about the potential solutions.
- Agree on a solution.
- Follow through in the classroom.

See Figure 8-12 for an example of how teachers at the Center for Child and Family Studies at the Univer-sity of California, Davis, use **Persona Dolls** to carry out a friendship skit in this way.

Skits like the ones presented in Figures 8-11 and 8-12 help to make abstract concepts such as empathy and kindness more concrete. Using puppets or figures, instead of focusing on the real children involved, allows the children to adopt the issue as a group prob-lem, which means the group also takes responsibility for its resolution (Luckenbill & Nuccitelli, 2013). This brings more skilled children and lesser skilled chil-dren together, enriching the conversation and adding more "helpers" to remind one another of potential solutions when disagreements arise in the classroom. Friendship skits have been found to be effective with children from preschool though the upper-elementary

Problem	The teacher observed the block area and saw …	That a child who had difficulty controlling his body was often told, "You can't play—you always knock down my blocks. I hate you—you aren't my friend."
Desired Outcome	The teachers in the class-room agreed on these goals for the children.	Children will be able to identify feelings in relation to exclusion and will problem-solve strategies. Children will include others in their play regardless of disability and consider individual strengths.
Preparing for the Skit	The teachers write this social story about two puppets, Emily and Zeke (these are not the real names of any children in the class). The teacher's role is played by an adult in the classroom.	Emily is stacking blocks and Zeke knocks them down. Emily becomes angry because Zeke has done this before. Zeke apologizes. Emily is still upset, and tells him that he always does this and that she hates him. Zeke says that makes him sad. Emily calls for teacher help, "I have a problem; he can't be my friend." The teacher restates the problem, and then talks about their upset feelings. She begins to generate alternative solutions, focusing on Zeke's strengths and times when the two children had played. Another teacher adds some observations. The children sitting in the circle are asked to suggest some as well.
Carry Out Skit	Circle Time—children in semi-circle, adults with dolls at front.	Teachers introduce the dolls and act out the script.
Problem-Solving Conversation	Work through problem-solving steps.	Teachers call on the children and reflect children's comments back to them. Teachers use open-ended questions and paraphrase reflections to move the discussion forward.
Closure	Based on the children's discussion, the dolls close the session.	Emily evaluates what she hears to Zeke. She proposes that they play a game that is not blocks. They can still be friends. Zeke agrees that this is a good idea and says that they have solved the problem. They begin to play another game.

Figure 8-12 Developing a Social Problem-Solving Skit.

Source: Based on Luckenbill & Nuccitelli (2013).

© Cengage Learning

grades. They are especially useful in promoting the speech development and social skills of children with autism as well as children with speech and language challenges (Frandsen, 2011). Thus, skits represent an inclusive way to address children's friendship needs. They are usually introduced at circle time. However, small group instruction is also possible. Another way adults support children's development of friendship knowledge and skills is through teaching children to role-play.

Teaching Friendship Skills Through Role-Playing

Children are naturally drawn to role-playing—it is fun, entertaining, and educational. It is also a variation on the pretend play scenarios children enjoy creating for themselves. As children engage in pretend play, they make up stories and they create a setting, characters, and dialogue, as well as beginnings and endings of scenes (Dombro, Jablon, & Stetson, 2011). These same features are incorporated into role-playing designed to help children learn friendship skills.

Teaching social problem-solving skills through role-playing is a powerful method for improving children's abilities in the friendship process (Thompson & Goodman, 2009). Children take turns acting out social situations while their peers observe. In friend-related scenarios, the role-players get to practice the language of problem solving and the behaviors of friendship. Observers have a chance to see friendship skills in action. After the role-play, the actors discuss emotions felt while playing the characters or their reactions to other players' behaviors and words. The audience offers observations too. By acting out social dilemmas and their potential solutions, children obtain concrete examples of friendship-related behaviors that are easier to recognize than those offered through discussion alone. Although most children ages 4 through 12 enjoy role-playing, it cannot be assumed they necessarily know how to do it purposely or in front of an audience. Many children benefit from instruction on how to role-play for instructional purposes. Further guidelines for how to do this are presented in the skills section of this chapter.

Buddy Skills Training

A fourth method of assisting children in developing friendship skills is **buddy skills training or peer-pairing**. At its simplest, buddy skills training involves putting a more friendship-savvy child with a less-skilled child. In these circumstances, the adult serves as a "coach" before, during, or after the children have had an opportunity to work or play together. Simply putting children together is not enough to make much of a difference in friendship skill development. The "target" child often requires help knowing what to expect or translating what is happening, so the adult serves this function. Such pairings have been found to be particularly useful in improving the social skills and status of neglected children (Zimbardo, 1999; Bagwell & Schmidt, 2011). Often, socially neglected children do not know how to keep up with their age-mates. For this reason, it is sometimes useful to pair them with younger children to help them gain practice using appropriate contact and relationship-building behaviors (Rubin, 2003). Adults can pair children by developing small-group assignments or activities in which children work together. This might involve having Tim (a more socially competent child) pair with Gregory (a less socially skilled child) in carrying out a 10- to 15-minute block building project each day, or by asking a third grader to read to a second grader, or by designing special jobs that pairs conduct together, such as collecting the scouting dues and reporting the results to the pack. Whatever the circumstance, the goal of the intervention is to enhance children's friendship skills, not to require them to become best friends.

For example, children with autism often show delays in their friendship skills and can benefit greatly from social skills training. Simply pairing children with autism with children who are more socially skilled, however, is not sufficient to change a child's behavior. Children with autism may not recognize the relevant aspects of social interchanges or imitate the positive social behavior of others without prompting. Adults may supply such prompting but so may the more socially skilled child of the pair. Typically developing children can receive explicit training in how to interact with a child with autism to draw that child's attention to the details of the play. For example,

Pair a less popular child with a more popular child.

© Cengage Learning 2015

a child with more developed social skills may verbally describe the play ("Now we're building the house. See? Look here. See our house?"). They may also observe and comment on the play of their peers ("Rosa is making dinner for us. Try some. Pretend like this."). Thoughtfully pairing children for certain activities with the expectation that children "stay with their buddies, play with their buddies, and talk with their buddies" improves children's level of social interaction and play (Laushey & Heflin, 2000; Hughett, Kohler, & Raschke, 2011). The best pairings are between children who are different in social skills but not so far apart that the socially skilled child will find no satisfaction in the relationship. Improving these skills helps all children see commonalities with one another and increases the chances for developing friendships. See the Challenging Behavior box and consider how you might help Jacob gain friendship skills by using buddy skills training.

One-on-One Intensive Coaching

When children exhibit a destructive pattern of interactions, or are unhappy with their inability to make friends and are unsure about what to do, they may benefit from intensive one-on-one coaching (Bagwell & Schmidt, 2011). This level of coaching is an example of intensive intervention. It consists of short, regularly scheduled sessions in which an adult and a single child work on one friendship skill at a time to help the child improve his or her performance with peers (Bierman & Powers, 2009). The session involves a planned lesson that takes place outside of the context of naturally occurring peer interactions, either off to the side or in

---

HIGHLIGHT 8-1

Coaching to Enhance Peer Communication

Two kindergartners are building with blocks. One of the two, Matthew, often yells and uses harsh language in interacting with peers, causing the other children to avoid or reject him as a potential friend. His teacher has begun simple and short coaching sessions with Matthew to help him learn more friendly language. She also uses some on-the-spot coaching in the block area to reinforce this skill.

Matthew: (pointing to his block structure, in a loud tone) Jason! Look!

Jason: (does not look up from block building, says nothing)

Matthew: (in a loud, angry voice) Jason!

Teacher: (quietly to Matthew) You want Jason to look. Try talking to Jason in a quiet voice. Say, "Jason, look at what I built."

Matthew: (in a quieter voice) Jason, look.

Jason: (looks up briefly) Yeah. (returns to his building)

Teacher: Maybe you could tell him what you made. Say it in a quiet voice. Say, "I made this highway. See?" Maybe he'll listen if you say it like that.

Matthew: Jason, this is the highway. See?

Jason: (looks at Matthew). Oh, yeah. Where are some cars though?

The two children begin to work on the highway; the teacher steps back to let them work things out.

CHALLENGING BEHAVIOR

Meet Jacob—a Child with No Friends

Jacob is a student in your kindergarten classroom who has Asperger's syndrome, a developmental disorder that affects a person's ability to socialize and communicate effectively with others. Jacob is quite intelligent and has good language skills, but he rarely interacts with other children. You tried pairing him with Jonathan, a very gregarious boy, thinking Jacob and Jonathon might become friendly. Although Jonathan seems willing to play with Jacob, they have little in common and have difficulty finding things to do together.

Consider all that you have read in the chapter so far. What will you think about as you consider your next steps? What strategies could you use to assist Jacob with making friends?

---

a separate area. A typical coaching "session" includes the adult identifying the skill to be addressed and why it is important, demonstration of a skill, practice by the child, and evaluation. The content of these sessions may also be reinforced as teachable moments arise in the classroom. See Highlight 8-1 for an example of this kind of reinforcement.

The five strategies described previously vary in their intensity and fall within different parts of the Social Support Pyramid. See Figure 8-13 for a visual depiction of this.

As you can see, the most basic strategy is to create friendship-supportive environments in which adults provide opportunities for children to interact freely with peers and also take advantage of children's day-to-day interactions to promote friendship development.

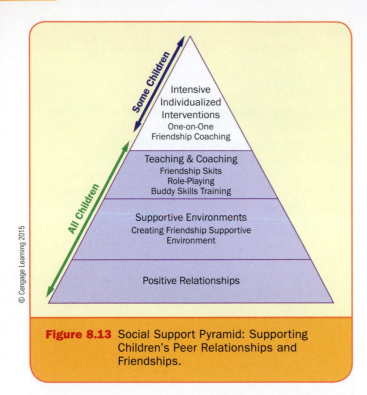

Figure 8.13 Social Support Pyramid: Supporting Children's Peer Relationships and Friendships.

© Cengage Learning 2015

Here are examples of chants and songs incorporating children's names to help children become acquainted with one another.

Chant #1

Friends, friends, one, two, three.

All my friends are here with me.

Mary is my friend, Sasha is my friend, Deshawn is my friend. (Point to each child as you say his or her name.)

Friends, friends, one, two, three.

All my friends are here with me.

(Repeat verse substituting names of other friends present.)

Chant #2

Hicklety, ticklety bumble bee

Can you say your name for me?

(Child responds by saying name.)

Hello, _____!

Song #3

Greeting song (sung to tune of Goodnight Ladies)

Hello _____. Hello _____.

Hello _____. We're glad that you are here!

Digital Download   **Download from CourseMate**

Friendship skits, role-playing, and buddy skills training provide multiple options for teaching and coaching the essential skills children need to know. For children who need more intensive intervention, one-on-one coaching offers a way to address the most serious friendship-related challenges some children face. Now that you know about these effective teaching strategies, we will give you step-by-step guidelines for how to enact the specific skills associated with each one.

SKILLS FOR SUPPORTING CHILDREN'S PEER RELATIONSHIPS AND FRIENDSHIPS naeyc

Creating Friendship-Supportive Environments

1. **Provide many opportunities for children to be with their peers informally** to talk, to play, and to enjoy one another's company. Develop a daily routine that includes planned times when children can interact with and respond to one another freely. These opportunities should include both structured activities, such as large group time or meals, and less structured parts of the day, such as free-choice and outdoor time. Be careful not to take over and have adult talk dominate these times. Observe and listen.

Allow children to talk without redirecting the conversation toward something you want to talk about.

2. **Encourage all children to participate in pretend play.** Provide props and space for make-believe play indoors and outside. Invite children to participate or direct them to the area, "It looks like Sam and Celia are playing in the grocery store. You could do some shopping too." If children are hesitant to get involved, move into the play with them. "I need some eggs. Come with me and help me fill my grocery bag." Use reflections and other play-enhancing strategies you learned about in Chapter 7 to keep the play going. Bow out if the

players are able to sustain the play themselves. Use this strategy with all children but especially with peer-neglected or peer-rejected children.

3. **Help children learn each other's names.** Use each child's name frequently so that names become familiar. With younger children, play name games or sing songs that incorporate each child's name. For both younger and older children, create displays that include named portraits of children in the class (digital photos or self-portraits).

4. **Carry out small- and large-group discussions to help children discover similarities between themselves and their peers.** Set the scene by having children discuss their reaction to topics such as, "Things I like best." Then invite each child to identify another child who expressed an interest that matches one of their own such as, "Paul and I both like . . . " or "I like the Mets and so does . . . ."

5. **Point out friendly interactions between peers as they occur.** Use behavior reflections or give children information to reinforce friendly interactions. "You are helping Jamie put the blocks away." "Michael passed you the crackers. That was a friendly thing to do."

6. **Help children get involved as play groups and work groups are forming each day.** Observe children's typical approaches. If you notice that certain children are hesitant to become involved and subsequently are shut out of peer group activities, try one of the following strategies:

   - **Plan ahead** with the child to identify an activity to choose as soon as playgroups begin to form. If this is too difficult for the child, an alternative is to help her or him move into the group with you. To do this, you might choose a potential role and approach the activity within the role. For instance, if several children are pretending to fly to the orbiting space station, you could walk toward them, saying: "Carol and I will be Mission Control. We'll talk to you up in the space station." Back out of the play gradually as Carol becomes more comfortable and the group becomes more accepting of her. Do not be surprised if at first Carol walks out when you do. With your continued support, she eventually will feel more relaxed and be able to maintain her membership in the group on her own.

   - **Help players see what the newcomer can contribute** to the existing play. For example, if Jonathon and Dante are building a barn in the block area, suggest Cohen bring plastic animals to the area saying something like, "Here come some animals to live in the barn." Be prepared to offer support to the children involved.

   - **Advise a hesitant child to play near the desired group** and at the same type of activity. Gradually, the group may allow that child to join them and become their friend. An alternative to this approach is to help the child build a new group by inviting other children to draw, build, compute, or cook with her or him.

7. **Help children recognize the friendly overtures of others in the course of their day-to-day interactions**. Be alert for situations when children misunderstand each other's intentions in the contact phase. Step in if you see a child rebuff another's efforts to make contact without giving a reason. Paraphrase the newcomer's positive purpose. Respect the child's decision for whether the contact is welcome. Children will often be more receptive to another's overtures after the friendly intentions are made clear.

For example, Matt was an active 4-year-old who longed for a friend. He frequently talked with teachers about who his friends might be. Yet, his actions often contradicted his words. One day, he had the entire block area to himself. He worked for a long time building a bus. As he was busily "driving to Chicago," Courtney arrived on the scene and asked if she could go, too. Matt scowled and said, "No." Courtney repeated her request and was again rebuffed. This time she said: "Well, I'll just stand here on the corner until someone gets off. Then, I'll get on." Matt looked confused. At this point, an adult approached and said: "Matt, you're having fun driving to Chicago. Courtney is telling you she would like to play. She wants to be a passenger on your bus. That way, she can be your friend." Matt looked pleased and relieved. He had not recognized the cues Courtney was using to signify her interest in his game. He had thought she was going to take over his play. Information provided by the adult put a whole new light on the situation, and the two children played "bus" for most of the morning.

8. **Help children recognize how their behavior affects their ability to make and keep friends.**

   - **Offer information** to help children better understand how their peers are interpreting their behavior. For instance, Steven pushed Daisy to get her attention. She stalked off. He became angry when she rejected him. The adult noted Steven's surprise, took him aside, and said: "It seems as if you want to be friends with Daisy. Pushing hurts. When you push her, it makes her so angry that she doesn't want to play with you. Friends don't hurt each other. Next time, say her name and tell her what you want." The adult gave Steven important information that he had not acquired on his own. This information would have to be repeated several times and in several different circumstances before Steven could really follow the advice. If the negative pattern persisted, Steven would be a likely candidate for the coaching strategies described earlier.

- **Tell children about the positive skills they exhibit** so they can repeat them at another time. For example, if you notice children sharing, taking turns, smiling at each other, or coming to a compromise, point out the positive effects these actions have on their relations with one another: "You two figured out a way that you could both wash the blackboards. That was a friendly way to settle your disagreement."

9. **Connect children with peers by referring children's questions and comments to one another.** For example, if Jeremy approaches the block area where other children are working and says to you, "Can I build?" refer his question to one of the builders. "Jeremy, you want to build. Tell Russell." Provide a script if necessary: "Say, 'I'm ready to help you.'" If Russell fails to respond, offer information to one child or the other to help the interaction along. "Jeremy, Russell didn't hear you. Get closer to him and tell him again." Or "Russell, Jeremy is trying to tell you something. Stop, look at him, and listen to his words."

10. **Assist children in keeping their verbal interactions going.** Listen without interrupting as children talk to one another. Intervene if the interaction falters, using reflections of any kind or open-ended questions. If, for instance, children lose track of the topic and no longer seem to be connecting, help them refocus. "Jeremy and Russell, you were talking about how to get the arch to balance. Russell, tell Jeremy what you discovered." Sometimes, children who are not yet conversant benefit from having their rudimentary language interpreted by the teacher to the other children. Thus, when Melissa asks Jane, "Do you want orange juice?" and Jane responds, "Ju," Melissa may not understand. Pause to see if she responds. If Melissa seems confused, paraphrase Jane's words, "She said, 'Juice.'" On the other hand, if Melissa addresses a

question to Jane, "How about some juice?" and Jane does not answer, again, act as an interpreter. "Jane, did you hear Melissa's words? Look at her and she'll ask you again." When children begin talking to one another, bow out of the conversation so you do not become the focus of their attention.

11. **Teach children the language of negotiation and compromise.** Use naturally occurring situations to model relevant words or offer scripts to help children resolve the typical conflicts that arise among peers. For example:

- Words to express rights: "I had it first. You can have it next."

- Words for suggesting solutions: "Maybe we could…," "Sometimes when this happens people…," "Here's an idea," "What's your idea?"

- Words for standing up against unreasonable demands: "No, I haven't had my turn yet."

- Words for compromising: "A little for me, a little for you. Now we both have some."

Interject this language as soon as children begin experiencing difficulties. Do not wait for a full-blown argument to ensue. In Chapter 12, you will learn more about how to mediate more serious and aggressive conflicts. However, that model is most effective when children have experience with words associated with problem solving and getting along.

12. **Help children endure the sorrows of friendship.**

- Listen without judgment as children air grievances or sorrows related to an offending peer or lost friend.

- Use affective reflections and open-ended questions to identify and talk about children's friendship-related emotions.

- Offer your condolences: "I'm sorry you and Tricia weren't able to patch up your differences. It's really sad to lose a friend."

- Allow children some time to grieve over a lost friendship, don't push too quickly for children to forget or find a new friend right away.

- Brainstorm activities and/or people the child could explore as possibilities for establishing new relationships.

Introducing Buddy Skills Training

1. **Pair children for various activities.** Assign children to do jobs together or have them carry out a joint project as a way to create common

experiences. Set the expectation that during these activities children should "stay with their buddy, play with their buddy, and talk to their buddy."

2. **Pair a shy child with a younger playmate who is less sophisticated socially.** Begin by pairing the child with a younger child of the same gender. Gradually, include age-mates of the same and opposite sex. This enables the shy child to practice social skills with a nonthreatening, often openly approving, younger admirer.

3. **When you first team children, point out the similarities** you have observed or give them a chance to discover some mutual interests.

4. **Assist both parties in learning and implementing social skills.** For example, less skilled children may not know how to appropriately gain others' attention while more skilled children can learn to better observe the actions of others and comment on what they see.

Designing Skits that Demonstrate Friendship Skills

1. **Choose a friendship skill to teach.** Focus on one skill per demonstration (making contact, maintaining a friendship, or negotiating). Identify the skill being demonstrated so children know what to look for. "Today I'm going to show you a story about a child who wants to play."

2. **Choose characters and props for the demonstration.** Puppets, miniature figures, and pictures all are good choices for portraying the characters. Remember to use concrete props children can point to, handle, and discuss.

3. **Outline a script that includes each of the following:**

   - Demonstrate poor skill use or no skill use (e.g., character not making contact, but hoping other child will notice that he wants to play).
   - Explain why the action did not work.
   - Demonstrate the skill (e.g., character making contact effectively).
   - Explain why the skill worked.
   - Discuss the skit with the children, relating it to experiences in their world.
   - Encourage the children to use the props to recreate the skit or to develop their own versions.

   Keep skits short to hold children's attention. The best skits are only a few lines long.

4. **Write out the statements and questions you will use to stimulate discussion.** Focus on identifying which character was demonstrating the skill and which was not, how viewers arrived at their conclusions, and what skill they would suggest the characters use the next time.

5. **Rehearse the skit.** Gather your props and practice the skit. Revise the skit until you can do it from memory and feel comfortable about carrying it out.

6. **Present your skit either in a small-group situation or in a one-to-one interaction.**

   - Seat the children in a semicircle, making sure everyone can see your face and hands and the space directly in front of you. If you are sitting on the floor, it is useful to kneel so you are more easily visible to the children. If you are sitting in a chair, use a low bench or table on which to display the props. As the script unfolds, manipulate the puppets in corresponding actions. Be expressive with your face and your voice. Use dialogue for the characters that seems appropriate for the situation; use different voices for each character.
   - Introduce the characters. Have the children repeat the character names so you are sure they know which character is which.
   - Introduce the story line. Use words like this: "Today, we are going to talk about friends. Here are two puppets. We are going to pretend that these puppets are real children just like you. Their names are X and Y (choose names that *do not* sound alike). They are X years old and go to a school just like ours. Watch carefully and see what happens when X and Y try to be friends."
   - Speak clearly and with expression. Elicit group discussion. Listen carefully and accept children's answers nonjudgmentally. If children are way off track, give them information that will clarify the situation, and make a mental note to revise your skit to make the point more clear next time. Praise children as they watch and again as they discuss what they have seen.

7. **Evaluate the effectiveness of your skit.** Do this later in the day. If children appeared interested and were able to generate relevant conversation about the selected topic, plan to repeat the same skit next time using different props and dialogues. Over time, gradually introduce new information for children to consider. If children were uninterested, determine whether things in the environment distracted them or whether your activity was unappealing. Observe children carefully or ask their opinions as a way to find out.

8. **Encourage older children to make up skits of their own that dramatize a problem**

with friends. Sometimes, children between 10 and 12 years of age will be willing to enact their skits for peers or for younger children. The same procedures just discussed apply, regardless of the age of the skit planner.

9. **Develop open-ended social problem solving skits in response to classroom problems involving peer relations.** Watch for potential problems that arise among peers in the classroom. Develop a social story in response. Make sure to address all six problem-solving steps: identifying the problem, talking about emotions, generating solutions, discussing the solutions, agreeing on a solution, and following through.

Teaching Children to Role-Play

1. **Explain role-playing.** Define role-playing as a particular way of pretending to learn or practice something. Describe roles as parts children play in a scene. Tell children they will act out how they would feel in a given situation or how they think another person might feel under those circumstances. Point out to the children that for each role-play episode, some children will be taking on roles while others watch, and everyone will have a chance to discuss the results. Show them the boundaries of the physical area in which the enactment will take place as well as any props available to the actors.

2. **Set the scene.** Present a theme, script, or problem. You may also suggest certain emotions for them to portray. Give each child a specific role to play and a few hints about related actions or words that might characterize their role.

3. **Help the role-players get into character.** Allow children to select a prop or costume item as a way to further establish their roles. This step is critical for children younger than 7 years of age who otherwise might have difficulty enacting and sustaining a role. Young children may need to hang a picture or symbol around their neck if the role is abstract or a good prop is not available.

4. **Observe attentively.** Applaud the efforts.

5. **Discuss events in the role-play.** Elicit comments both from the participants and the observers.

6. **Ask children to develop alternate scenarios.** Have children act these out, and then discuss the varying outcomes.

7. **Summarize the key points of the discussion.** Identify similarities in their thinking as well as differences. Highlight the one or two major points that seemed most important to the group.

Carrying Out Intensive One-on-One Friendship Coaching

1. **Select a friendship "skill for improvement" that addresses the child's particular difficulty.** It can be challenging to narrow your choice to one skill if you see a child who seems to be doing "everything" wrong: ignoring peers, rejecting them, grabbing, pushing, interrupting, taking over, teasing. It is tempting to plan a complete makeover. However, trying to do too much all at once usually ends in frustration and failure. A better approach is to work on one problem area at a time. In this way, both the child and you experience success each step of the way, encouraging continued efforts.

2. **Initiate coaching.** Select a neutral time to begin coaching rather than immediately following a disagreeable encounter. Take the child aside at some dispassionate time and explain what will happen: "Robert, today you and I are going to have a special time together. Come with me and I'll tell you all about it."

3. **Introduce the skill** by describing it in specific terms rather than generalizations.

    For example: "When you want someone to be your friend, it is important to listen to his (her) ideas. That means looking at him (her) and not talking while he (she) is trying to tell you something." (Notice the specific behaviors described).

    NOT: "When you want someone to be your friend, you should act more interested." (This is not specific enough for the child to know behavior expectations.)

4. **Demonstrate the skill.** Model the behavior or point it out in other children who are playing so the child can see skill in action: "Here, I'll show you. Tell me one way we could play with these puppets, and I will listen to your idea," or "Look at Jeremy—he's listening very carefully to what Sondra is saying."

5. **Provide a reason the new behavior is important.** "When you listen to people's ideas, it makes them feel good. That helps them to like you better."

6. **Practice the skill with the child.** Show/give examples of good and poor skill usage using puppets: "Here are two puppets, Ray and Gina. Ray is telling Gina an idea. Watch and listen.

Tell me how well Gina shows Ray she wants to be friends." After several demonstrations, offer the child the opportunity to rehearse the new behavior by role-playing with you or another child, or by using the puppets. Time to practice helps children feel more comfortable with their new skills. This gives them experience at what it is like to be both the recipient and the initiator of varying social behaviors. Invite children to suggest their own ideas about other ways to demonstrate the skill, ask questions, or discuss their emotions and reactions.

7. **Evaluate the child's use of the skill.** Praise children's efforts and improved performance throughout the practice session. Point out instances of the child's appropriate use of the skill. Commend the child for trying. Provide physical support through smiles and hugs. Offer corrective feedback aimed at improving the child's use of the skill. Focus on behaviors: "You focused on his eyes this time. That was a great improvement. Tomorrow we'll add in a new piece."

8. **Repeat the coaching procedure several times.** Change the props and the hypothetical circumstances more than once. As you see each child increase the use of the targeted skill in day-to-day interactions, praise efforts and offer on-the-spot information to help refine performance. With improvement, plan to introduce a new skill for the child to work on or gradually fade out the coaching sessions.

9. **Continue feedback and reinforcement to maintain the child's use of each skill.** Be careful not to introduce a new skill until the current skill is well established.

Communicating with Children's Families

Help family members understand and support children's friendships using the following strategies:

1. **Talk with family members about the normal course of children's friendships.** Listen carefully to what they have to say and reflect their thoughts and emotions. Explain the characteristics of the particular friendship stage their child is experiencing. Suggest strategies described in this chapter to help family members better understand children's actions and deal with unacceptable behaviors in positive and supportive ways. Explore other issues with family members as they arise, such as having "best friends" or the disappointment of failed friendships. Offer suggestions in terms of the ideas presented in this book. For instance, instead of offering children advice, suggest families engage in active listening; give parents a brief "script" in which you outline this technique.

2. **Offer parent workshops about children's friendships. Highlight specific friendship skills.** Brainstorm with family members ways they could enhance children's friendship-making opportunities and abilities.

3. **Help families facilitate children's friendships beyond school time.**

   a. When adult family members are looking for a new friend for their youngster, suggest other children in the group who you believe might be potential friends. Consider the children's age, gender, proximity, relationship in the program, interests, and stage of friendship to determine which children might be suitable friends for a particular individual.

   b. **Encourage parents to make play dates for children.** Work with families to establish "helpful hints" or guidelines, so visits will be fun for children and livable for adults.

4. **Establish a policy for out-of-school party invitations.** For example, unless all children in the group were to be included, invitations to parties are offered by mail or phone, so as not to hurt other children's feelings and to avoid the confusion of a message getting into the wrong child's hands.

5. **Initiate classroom events that enable families to get to know one another.** Parents and guardians may be understandably hesitant to invite a child to their home or to allow their child to visit a family with whom they are unfamiliar. Invite family members to a sing-along or potluck dessert function to offer families the opportunity to get acquainted. Encourage children to introduce their families to each other. These casual events help people feel more comfortable and may result in "play dates" for the children.

6. **Talk to adult family members about their peer-neglected or peer-rejected children.** Speak openly and compassionately with the adults in a private setting, listening carefully to what they say. Respond to their anguish or uncertainty using affective reflections. Inquire about the child's friendships beyond the school setting and within the family (siblings, cousins, etc.). Be aware that some children have strong friendships out of school and may not feel the desire to have a special school friend. Keep this in mind in your

conversations with parents. Document examples of the child's unsuccessful attempts at making friends or rebuffs of the overtures of others. Try all the strategies suggested in the text. If, over a sufficient period of time (weeks or months), the child fails to move forward, take the issue seriously and recommend further intervention. Help families seek community resources, such as counselors, social workers, or psychologists, who might be available to give assistance.

Pitfalls to Avoid in Promoting Peer Relations and Friendships naeyc

Regardless of whether you are supporting children's friendships individually or in groups, informally or in structured activities, there are certain pitfalls you should avoid.

1. **Intervening too quickly.** When adults see children struggling over friendship issues, it is tempting to step in immediately. No one likes to see children in distress. Unless there is some physical danger that should be dealt with quickly, it is important to take a moment to observe the situation and to thoughtfully determine what form of intervention is best. At times, simply moving physically closer to the situation defuses it. In other instances, direct use of the strategies described in this chapter is more appropriate. Regardless of which course you follow, remember that the more children practice friendship skills with the least help from you, the more quickly they will learn how to be successful in their interactions with peers. Children benefit when they have an opportunity to try out strategies and solutions on their own.

2. **Missing opportunities to promote friendly interactions among children.** Adults sometimes become so centered on interacting with the children themselves that they fail to recognize opportunities to help children increase their friendship skills with peers. For example, an adult who is carrying on a conversation with one child may view the arrival of a second child as an interruption or may carry on two separate conversations simultaneously. A better approach would be to use reflections, ask open-ended questions, or provide information to encourage the children to talk to each other as well as to the adult.

3. **Insisting that everyone be "friends."** Although it is natural for adults to want children to like each other, it does not always turn out that way. Instead, children tend to form close relationships with only a few children at a time. Insisting that everyone like each other is unrealistic and denies children's real emotions. In every group, there are people who rub each other the wrong way. Help children learn to interact constructively with the people they like best and the people they like least. Show children acceptable ways of acting on their preferences.

4. **Requiring everyone to be together all the time.** It is a mistake to think that friendship is built on constant companionship. Although familiarity does breed common interests, forcing children to play together when they do not want to detracts from, rather than enhances, their relationships. With this in mind, allow children opportunities to engage in solitary activity and constructively explain their desire for privacy to curious or well-meaning peers. In addition, aid the child who is rebuffed by a peer who would rather be alone. This can be accomplished by explaining the other's desire for privacy and by helping the child who is turned away to find an alternate activity or companion.

5. **Breaking up children's friendships.** Children who have developed a best-friend relationship may become inseparable. Adults often worry that this closeness is interfering with the children's ability to develop other friendships. As a result, adults may decide to intervene by limiting the children's time together. This is a mistake. As children begin to develop "special relationships," it is natural for them to center on the object of their admiration. It must be remembered that when children first become interested in making friends, their main goal is simply to be included in peer activities with multiple players.

   However, after this has been accomplished, children begin to want to have an influence on their relationships. In other words, they want others to listen to their ideas, accept their suggestions, and involve them in decision making. From the children's viewpoint, this is a relatively risky process. So, they seek the security of a one-to-one relationship within which to test their skills. In friendship pairs, risks are reduced because the two children involved come to know each other well and therefore are more accurate in predicting another's reaction. In addition, they share a history of good times, helping them weather the bad times that are sure to occur. It takes a long time for children to work through these needs. When adults interrupt the process, they deprive children of important opportunities to learn the true meaning of friendship. Adults should allow children to experience this important phase of relationship building.

6. **Failing to recognize children's mistaken behavior as an effort to make friends.** Children may use inappropriate behaviors in their efforts to make friends. For instance, children may taunt to initiate an interaction, physically force other children out of an area to have exclusive access to a favored peer, or try to coerce a friend into rejecting another as a way of confirming their own friendship bond. On the surface, these may appear to be straightforward situations of poor behavior requiring negative consequences. Observant adults recognize the issue relates to a lack of skill or understanding. They use such situations as opportunities to help the child learn more constructive friendship skills, rather than simply stopping the negative behavior or punishing the child.

7. **Ignoring the signs of lonely children and those who are rejected.** At one time, we thought children could work out such dilemmas on their own. Today we know such children need comfort and assistance to change their skills and prospects. This requires adults to observe carefully and step in as necessary using skills described in this chapter, starting at the base of the Social Support Pyramid and working upward. If none of these strategies makes a difference, adults can solicit help from other professionals as described in the last chapter in this text. It is imperative not to let such problems fester.

Summary

Peer relationships and friendships are important events in the lives of children. They offer children unique opportunities to develop socially, emotionally, and intellectually. Both peer relationships and friendships serve as places to practice social competence skills. Some children make friends easily; others do not. The repercussions of not having a friend or of being dissatisfied with the relationships one does have represent severe difficulties in childhood that can last through adulthood. Completely friendless children are rare; however, evidence does indicate that many children wish they had more or better friends.

Adults may wonder whether children really understand what friendship means. Although children's ideas about what constitutes friendship are different from adults' and change as children mature, it is clear that even very young children are interested in having friends. Researchers theorize that children progress through a sequence of five overlapping levels of friendship understanding, which becomes increasingly complex as children mature. In the early levels, children rely on proximity and convenience in choosing friends. They focus on their own point of view, the outward characteristics of their companions, and with what is happening right now! In the later levels, children are more sensitive to the desires and concerns of others, they appreciate psychological traits such as humor and trustworthiness, and they think about the future of their relationships as well as the present.

When first choosing a friend, children focus on obvious attributes such as physical appearance, race, gender, age, ability, and attitudes. In general, it can be said that children seek out friends whom they perceive as being similar to themselves. At times, these likenesses are apparent only to the children involved.

The social skills children display also have a major impact on their ability to make and keep friends. Making friends is not an automatic or magical process. Children who "win friends and influence people" know how to make contact, maintain positive relationships, and negotiate the inevitable conflicts that arise. Although some children learn these skills on their own, many children need help. Consequently, friendship development is a key component of preschool and elementary school curricula in most states.

Adults can play a vital role in increasing children's friendly behavior. This can be accomplished through informal, day-to-day techniques, planned activities, and structured coaching sessions. Family members may also be involved in promoting children's friendships both in and out of the formal group setting. Professionals can be of great help in supporting children and families in their efforts.

As adults take on the role of friendship facilitator and coach, there are certain pitfalls they need to avoid. These include not giving children opportunities to develop friendship skills and missing chances to support friendship development among children. Likewise, insisting that every child be friends with every other child, requiring children to spend all their time with others, keeping friends apart, and failing to recognize that children sometimes engage in inappropriate actions as they explore the world of their peers, stymy rather than enhance children's ability to find and keep a friend.

Key Terms

buddy skills training

friends

friendships

Friendship Framework

friendship skills

one-on-one coaching

peers

peer-neglected children

peer-pairing

peer-rejected children

Persona Doll

rejected-aggressive children

rejected-withdrawn children

Discussion Questions

1. Abraham Lincoln said, "The better part of one's life consists of his friendships." React to this statement, discussing the reasons why people need friends.

2. Think about a childhood friend. Describe what attributes made that person important to you.

3. Describe how children's ideas of friendship change over time. Identify children you know who fit into each stage, and explain your conclusions.

4. Describe two children you know—one who seems to have many friends and one who seems to have no friends. Discuss what variables might be influencing each child's situation.

5. As a group, develop a friendship skit aimed at teaching children how to make contact with a potential friend. In addition, generate at least five discussion questions.

6. Pretend you have been invited to a parent meeting to describe friendship coaching. Outline what you might say to parents regarding the rationale for this technique as well as its component parts.

7. Referring to Appendix A, NAEYC Code of Ethical Conduct, judge the ethics of the following situation: You and your best friend work in the same program. One evening your friend tells you that sometimes when the children are happy, she goes outside for a cigarette, leaving the children unattended.

8. Identify a child you know who might benefit from friendship coaching. Describe the area in which coaching would be most useful, and explain how you would implement the coaching procedure.

9. Pretend that a child's parent has spoken with you about concerns regarding his or her child's peer relationships. What information would you require to give an appropriate response? What suggestions could you make to the parent to help foster this child's friendships outside of school?

10. Identify the pitfall in this chapter to which you are most susceptible, and describe ways to avoid it.

Case Study Analysis

After reading the case study of Seth in Appendix B, consider the following:

1. Describe the behaviors Seth exhibits that may influence how he is viewed by his peers. Consider the variables discussed in this chapter: social cognition, emotional regulation, play experiences, and language.

2. Describe how you might use each of the following methods to assist Seth in improving his social interactions: shaping, modeling, coaching, and peer teaching.

3. Think of some cooperative play activities you could design to encourage Seth to interact with his peers. How would you choose activities? Are there certain materials that might reinforce Seth's participation? How would you decide which peers to include in the activities?

4. Think about the Social Support Pyramid in relation to the case study. Point out potential opportunities to increase Seth's interaction with his peers. What skills would you want to teach Seth to take advantage of these opportunities? What skills would you want to teach Seth's peers so that they would be more successful in interacting with Seth?

5. What pitfalls might you encounter when working with Seth? How might you avoid experiencing these pitfalls?

Field Assignments

1. Discuss three situations in which you supported children's friendships. Describe what the children were doing. Next, talk about what you did, making specific reference to the skills you have learned in this chapter. Explain how the children reacted to your approach. Conclude by evaluating your skill usage and describing any changes you might make in future situations that are similar.

2. Choose a friendship skill. Design an activity through which you will teach the skill to children. Write down your plan in detail. Also, include a description of how you expect children to react to the activity. Carry out the activity with a small group of children.

   Evaluate in writing your presentation, state any unexpected outcomes, and describe any changes you would make if you were to repeat this activity in the future.

3. Select three children. Describe their interactions with peers. Using Figure 8-9, choose the level of friendship in which each child is functioning, giving your rationale for each choice using descriptions from the chapter. Suggest one thing that could be done with each child to improve his or her peer relationships.

Reflect on Your Practice

Here is a sample checklist you can use to reflect on your use of the skills as a beginning professional. A more detailed classroom observation tool is available in Appendix C.

Teachers do the following to support children's development of friendships:

✓ Facilitate interaction among and between children.

✓ Allow children to engage in peer interaction without intrusion.

✓ Help children recognize their emotions and the emotions of others.

✓ Help children who are on the fringe of an activity to become involved.

✓ Help children initiate contact with others, providing scripts as needed.

✓ Help children recognize friendship signals.

✓ Help children problem-solve or negotiate conflicts.

✓ Support children who experience rejection or the end of a friendship through listening, reflecting, discussing, and redirecting to other peers as potential friends.

Digital Download **Download from CourseMate**

CourseMate. Visit the Education CourseMate for this textbook to access the eBook, Digital Downloads, TeachSource Videos, and quizzes. Go to CengageBrain.com to log in, register, or purchase access.

9 Influencing Children's Social Development by Structuring the Physical Environment

OBJECTIVES

On completion of this chapter, you should be able to:

Describe what structuring is and how structuring can enhance children's social competence, independence, self-direction, and self-control.

Plan how to use time, space, and furnishings to enhance children's social development.

Structure the physical environment to foster social competence and prevent or diminish undesirable behaviors.

Avoid pitfalls in structuring the physical environment.

NAEYC STANDARDS   naeyc

1. Promoting Child Development and Learning
2. Building Family and Community Relationships
3. Observing, Documenting, and Assessing to Support Young Children and Families
4. Using Developmentally Effective Approaches to Connect with Children and Families
5. Using Content Knowledge to Build Meaningful Curriculum
6. Becoming a Professional

Grace, age 2 years and 7 months, enters the classroom after playing outside. Hungry and excited that snack is next, she moves to the sink and looks at the pictograph above it showing the steps for washing hands. She turns on the water, pumps liquid soap from the container, and washes her hands while singing her own version of the ABC song. She turns off the water, glances again at the pictograph, and pulls a paper towel from the holder. She reaches for another and then remembers that her teacher has asked them to use just one towel and looks at the number 1 above the picture for selecting a paper towel. She finds a dry spot on the towel she has and wipes the remaining moisture from her hands.

Jerry, 3-and-a-half years old, sits quietly on the rug placing blocks carefully on a tower. His friend walks past carrying a sign saying "CLEAN UP 5 minutes" and ringing a small hand bell. Jerry surveys his structure and then carefully removes the blocks, replacing them on open shelves that are marked with the silhouette of each shape.

Mitsy, age 5, hurries to her cubby and removes her one-piece snowsuit. Spreading it out on the floor, she promptly sits in the middle. With quick efficiency she puts on her clothing and prepares to go outside, announcing, "I'm done. I zipped!"

Edward, age 7, scans his personal weekly plan folder to be sure that he has completed all of the starred activities for the week. Now that it is Thursday, he smiles because all of the required activities have been completed, and he can do whatever he chooses. He watches other children for several minutes, then moves into the science area where one of his friends is observing the guinea pig and taking notes in his science journal. Edward records his participation on the science pictograph with a marker and comments to his friend, "He's a lettuce pig, not a guinea pig!"

Each of these children is functioning independently in an environment designed to foster autonomy and a sense of competence and control. The pictograph featuring steps in washing hands that has been placed above the sink reminded Grace not to waste paper towels. The open storage for blocks with the shelves clearly marked enabled Jerry to put away his materials. Convenient coat storage and instruction in putting on winter clothing helped Mitsy to move efficiently from the indoors to outside. The use of an individualized weekly planning folder for Edward assisted him in checking on "must-do" tasks before moving on to another activity. In every case, the physical environment positively influenced these children's social competence. This did not happen by chance. The deliberate organization of the environment provides the visual cues and resources so that children function with as much independence as possible. This aspect of guiding children's social development and learning is called structuring.

Structuring is the management of time, space, and materials to promote children's social competence. Other aspects of child development and skills are also influenced by environmental factors. However, in this chapter, we will focus on the social domain.

Early childhood professionals structure the physical environment for three reasons. First, adults try to anticipate children's behavior and then prepare the setting before children arrive to promote desirable actions and minimize undesirable ones. This is the most common form of structuring. It requires adults to consider in advance what social goals to emphasize with the children and how time, space, and materials might best be arranged to help children pursue those goals. Secondly, adults structure on the spot to resolve problems as they arise. This strategy minimizes frustration and conflict among children as well as between adults and children. A quick environmental adjustment may alter the context sufficiently to minimize children's difficulties and improve social outcomes. Finally, adults structure to enhance communication and social interaction among children as well as to promote appropriate on-task behavior. Used in these ways, structuring can enhance all seven elements of social competence shown in Table 9-1.

Structuring Space and Materials naeyc

One of the ways that adults prepare the surroundings to promote desirable social behavior is by structuring space and materials. Buildings, furnishings, materials, and elements of the natural environment are concrete, visible resources that can be manipulated to facilitate the social competence of children. The physical environment in which children play and

Adults structure to enhance communication and social interaction among children.

Table 9-1 The Relationship among Social Competence Goals, Forms of Structuring, Teaching Goals, and Adult–Structuring

Element of Social Competence	Form of Structuring	Goals for Children	Structuring Example
Social Values	In advance	Put away materials that they use.	Provide easy access to well-organized storage.
Positive Self-Identity	In advance	Contribute to the group and receive recognition.	Display artwork, projects, or other work.
Interpersonal Skills	On the spot	Work together toward a common goal.	Add supplies to accommodate the numbers of children who want to work on a group project.
Self-Regulation	On the spot	Attend during whole-group efforts.	Cover a shelf of toys during group time or turn the shelf around.
Planning and Decision Making	In advance or on the spot	Choose between competing materials or activities.	Provide (or add) appropriate materials or activities from which to choose.
Cultural Competence	In advance	Recognize that people have various cultural backgrounds.	Add photos and other materials to learning centers depicting various backgrounds and abilities.
Emotional Intelligence	In advance or on the spot	Use a variety of feeling words to describe their reactions to new materials.	Add novel tools and materials a few at a time; post signs in the area on which a list of emotion words are written.

© Cengage Learning

learn has much to do with the presence or absence of disruptive behavior. Many "discipline problems" in classrooms can be traced directly to the arrangement and selection of furnishings and materials (Weinstein & Mignano, 2010). On the other hand, self-control develops in a well-designed and well-arranged physical space. Friendships flourish in cozy, comfortable rooms where informal exchange is planned for. Overall, professionals want the spaces in which children work and play to provide a sense of belonging and connection to others in the group. A flexible space with many open-ended materials that can be used to meet a multitude of goals is desirable. In addition, natural materials engage the senses and generate a sense of wonder and curiosity in the most effective spaces (Curtis & Carter, 2003).

Building and Grounds

Architects, landscape designers, interior designers, and program administrators have the responsibility to create safe environments for children. Guidelines for these have been developed by most state legislatures or state departments of education. For example, Michigan passed Public Act 16 in 1997, which outlines playground equipment safety (www.legislature.mi.gov).

The Florida Department of Education has established an Office of Safe Schools to promote and support safe learning environments for all of its students (www.fdoc.org/safeschools/). Safety, convenience, durability, maintenance, beauty, accessibility, and specific adaptations for use are all considerations in this process. Playgrounds usually need fencing. All states have standards for safety and health for those facilities that serve children. Although the fixed features (doors, ceiling heights, room dimensions, etc.) of facilities have impact on children's social behavior, practitioners who are working within programs cannot alter or change facilities easily by themselves. On the other hand, professionals may alter less permanent features such as furniture arrangements, lighting, or the amount of color in a room.

Maintaining health and safety. Children and adults alike have responsibility to maintain the physical environment to promote health and safety. Children learn social values of cleanliness, order, safety, and consideration of others through exposure to adults who practice safe and healthy maintenance. Having been coached to do this earlier, Laurel wiped her place at the snack table so that Jason had a clean spot for his snack. Having observed the teacher doing this on other occasions, David and Mickhail set orange cones across part of the open field to clarify a boundary and to avoid running into others during a chasing game that they were starting. Safety and health come first in programs for children, with children learning these strategies themselves gradually. When the environment is organized for health and safety, adults are free to relax and interact with children. The need for safety must also be balanced with the children's desire to attempt reasonable challenges (Kostelnik & Grady, 2009).

Adjusting interior spaces to promote social development. Supportive learning environments come in all shapes and sizes. Some classrooms were originally designed for children, but many (especially those for very young children) are located in space initially created for other purposes. Fortunately, modifications can be made to make spaces more hospitable (Knapp & Hall, 2010). Most of these alterations are done as a part of the preparation of the environment, although opportunities and needs do occasionally arise for on-the-spot changes.

Walls. Color influences mood and the climate of the space. Warm colors such as orange or red are more stimulating; cooler colors such as blue or green are more calming; and white, black, and brown may be depressing or unattractive (Knapp & Hall, 2010). Adults can modify the walls by adding bulletin boards or corkboard strips to display children's work, placing furniture against the walls, or by hanging appropriate prints of quality art or other displays in the spaces. The most engaging classrooms are those that children "own"; that is, they display children's productions instead of commercial products (Sansing, 2012). This personalizing of space indicates that the territory belongs to them, which prompts children to be more comfortable and forthcoming socially (Trenholm & Jensen, 2011). A loft or an indoor climber with an elevated platform provides interest and possibilities for enclosures for personal spaces.

Light. Lower lighting and lighting dispersed around the room are most conducive to social interaction (Bogle & Wick, 2005). Adding lamps and turning some overhead lighting off tends to have this effect in institutional spaces. More intense lighting is needed for close work such as reading. Either too bright or too meager light is associated with disruptive behavior (Tanner, 2009). Turning the lights off to reduce heat during hot weather

© Cengage Learning

Carpets are easier to sit on.

This teacher is providing clear directions to expand the child's ability to be independent.

the block corner, a firm-surfaced carpet reduces noise without reducing the stability of blocks. One enterprising teacher hung three tumbling mats on a cement wall. This solved the problem of storing the mats when they were not in use, decreased the reverberation of noise in the basement room, and added color and texture to the wall. Most administrators will allow staff to bring additional rugs into such settings. Some examples of adjusting the interior are given in Table 9-2.

Adjusting Exterior Spaces to Promote Social Development

- Making it to the top of the climber
- Running and chasing friends
- Working together to build an "oversized" structure with plastic PVC pipe
- Making "rivers" and dams in the sandbox
- Reading books in pairs under the shade of the trees

These are some of the delightful experiences children can have outdoors, all of which contribute to their emerging social competence. Because outdoor time has been found to be so essential to children's development and learning, national accreditation and most state licensing guidelines require that a fenced outdoor play area be made available to young children at the center or school. This area must provide at least 75 square feet of space per child and must include equipment and materials suitable for children from birth to age 8. It is expected that children will have access to outdoor activity regularly (NAEYC, 2009).

All children from infancy to adolescence need opportunities to play outdoors. A wider array of motor and social play opportunities and greater independence are often more available outdoors. Natural areas particularly seem to reduce fatigue and enhance affect and emotional self-regulation, especially for those with attention deficit-hyperactivity disorder (Evans, 2006). Human beings need contact with the natural environment to maintain their mental health. Quite often, a child's judgment of self-competence in movement is acquired outside and constitutes part of the sense of self-efficacy and body image. Freedom of movement in a safe environment allows children of all ages to explore what they can do as they investigate nature and practice their motor skills. Outdoor play spaces, like other areas, should be developmentally appropriate, scaled to the size of the children, and designed to promote success and independence.

Children have opportunities to help and encourage their peers in outdoor play (Hearron & Hildebrand,

and adjusting blinds to control the amount of natural light coming into the room increases comfort. Evidence suggests that excessive heat reduces social interaction and makes aggression more likely, particularly in crowded spaces (Burgoon, Guerrero, & Floyd, 2010).

Sound control. Rugs and carpets can be added to decrease noise, which in turn reduces stress and supports conversation. Area rugs can be removed so that cleanup of messy activities is easier. A certain level of noise is to be expected as children talk and move about. Noisy learning environments lead children to tune out speech and contribute to children's annoyance and fatigue (Evans, 2006). One way to determine if the environment needs changing is to listen carefully as children and adults are behaving appropriately. If the room still seems too noisy, additional sound-absorbing, soft materials should be added.

Carpets are easier to sit on and are softer to land on if a child falls from an indoor climber. In

Table 9-2 Adjusting Aspects of the Facility to Influence Children's Social Behavior

Condition Observed	Adjustment	Impact on Children
The room is hot and stuffy.	Open windows, turn down heat.	Reduces stress and potential aggression; promotes greater comfort and more positive social interaction.
Block area is only large enough for two children at a time.	Increase amount of floor space devoted to blocks.	Encourages more opportunities for social interaction among children.
Playground gate latch is broken.	Tie a rope or bungee cord on the gate to keep it closed during session; report for repair.	Prevents children from leaving supervised area; enables adults to interact more comfortably with children rather than standing guard at the gate.
Children avoid the manipulative toy area.	Cover the room divider with cherry or orange construction paper using two-sided tape for temporary change.	Children are attracted to bright colors and are more likely to move to the area.
Noise of hammering on the "Pound a Peg" toy resting on a table is excessive.	Place a folded section of newspaper under the toy.	Child enjoying the pounding toy can continue without distracting others.
Children's boots are on top of books in lockers or scattered across the floor near the lockers.	Add long narrow trays to the hallway to hold boots.	Classroom is more attractive, and children's books are preserved. Adult admonitions eliminated.

© Cengage Learning

2012). Often the social constellation of children changes as the activities move outdoors. For example, boys tend to engage in more pretend play when outdoors than when inside. Leadership and playgroups may change in the outdoor spaces.

To enable all children to participate fully, adults should plan multiple opportunities for small and large motor play, construction play, and pretend play, as well as other program activities (Hohmann, Weikart, & Epstein, 2008). Indoor activities can be moved outdoors, and natural materials moved inside (Oliver & Klugman, 2005). Active adult planning and supervision is as important outdoors as indoors, as failure to do so may result in having youngsters afraid to go outside, behavior outdoors becoming more aggressive, children becoming bored, or children clinging to adults (Bilton, 2010). Children outdoors need the support of adults in successfully negotiating social challenges that emerge as a result of greater space and mobility.

Plants are an important feature in the outdoor environment. Sod absorbs some of the stress when children are running or falling and is ideal for group games or rough-and-tumble play. Hedges around the perimeter reduce traffic noise and dust, and provide increased privacy at the same time. Sometimes practitioners add grass or clover seed to areas getting a lot of hard use. Children can contribute to the beauty of the environment while cooperating in developing a garden. Adult guidance is needed so that only nonpoisonous plants are put in

the garden, and plants such as poison ivy are removed. Shade trees provide excellent group meeting spaces, and some groups of children have planted seedlings as part of their learning experiences. A thoughtful arrangement of bushes can provide enclosed places for small groups of children to play. Yard fencing is excellent to support pole beans, squash, or trumpet vines. With variations of climate and soil type, the modifications to the outdoor play space using plants is very large in scope, and other professionals or master gardeners may need to be consulted.

A permanent climbing apparatus is a feature of many playgrounds in schools, parks, and childcare environments where children learn to take turns, move safely on the structure, and engage one another successfully. Movable outdoor equipment such as ladders, crates, and boards encourages cooperative play and allows children to alter their environment themselves (Felstiner, 2004).

Toys and equipment that are readily added or deleted according to the plans of the day promote the developmental competence of children. Sleds replace tricycles during the winter. During pleasant weather, any toy or material that is typically indoors may be used outdoors.

Generally speaking, the strategies for supporting social interaction outdoors are the same as those indoors. A few adaptations of nonverbal communications might be needed as children move more quickly and farther away when outside. Additionally, it is sometimes difficult to hear directions and guidance given the distances involved.

Structuring the indoor and outdoor facilities minimizes the numbers of rules that adults must set to keep children safe. In a well-structured place, interactions between adults and children are supportive, positive, and focused on achieving social competence.

Arranging Furnishings and Equipment

A supportive environment allows children to control their surroundings when appropriate and permits and encourages movement so that children can interact freely with objects and people (Marion, 2011). Because safety always is of highest priority, adults should plan environments to minimize risk for children.

A supportive environment is arranged into **learning centers**, or areas that provide for individual, small-group, or large-group activities (Stuber, 2007). When these are organized, physical limits are clear and regulate the use of materials and the behavior of children. Conflict between children is reduced, and conditions for high-quality learning or play are established. The needs of children with disabilities must be kept in

mind so that they are able to function as independently as possible (Sutterby & Frost, 2006).

The number and kinds of areas needed are determined by the age of the children and the size of the group. If an **activity space** is defined as that occupied by a child using a material, then the number of activity spaces for a block area may be 4 or 6 because that number of children could reasonably use the blocks at one time. To prevent waiting, it is recommended that there be roughly one-third more activity spaces than there are children (Marion, 2011). A minimum of 27 activity spaces for a group of 20 children would be needed. Realistic estimation based on the physical space and the children's age is necessary to attain the desired outcome. Generally speaking, preschool children play more successfully in groups of 2 to 4, and school-age children may organize some of their play in slightly larger groupings. When individual materials are involved, such as a puzzle or watercolor materials, then the number estimated should match exactly the number of materials. Do not count on children sharing except when the supply of materials is large, such as with blocks. Most manipulative sets of construction materials are suitable for 1 or possibly 2 children, so multiple sets are needed if you intend for

Some activity areas work better when the number of children is limited.

© Cengage Learning 2015

more children to play. Activity spaces can be estimated as follows:

Sensory tables	2–4
Pretend play	4
Blocks	4–6
Six puzzles	6
Board game	2–4
Listening center with six headphones	6
Writing center	1–4
Reading area	2–4
Easel painting	1–2

Similar planning for outdoor play is necessary. The numbers for each zone, enclosure, or play area should be estimated carefully because they vary greatly. Some simple structures are suitable for one or two children; other complex combinations of equipment provide play space for many children.

Private space. A **private space** is an area designed for one child, or maybe two, where a child can retreat for a reasonable period of time from social interaction. In one second-grade classroom, the teacher had painted an old bathtub red and filled it with pillows. A child in that area, usually reading or simply watching others, was always to be left undisturbed. A private area of this type is never to be used for punishment or time-out; instead, it should be used to provide a sense of relaxation, comfort, and privacy in the midst of a public environment. The use of private space may reduce stress and eventually help a child attain higher levels of self-control. Children can briefly escape the noise and activity to a space that provides comfort and security (Frost et al., 2008).

Small-group space. A **small-group space** is designed for fewer than eight children. In most programs for young children, four to six children may be playing together (housekeeping, blocks, water play) or engaged in studying (insect collections, number lotto, weighing cubes). A small-group work area should have spaces for sitting and a surface for working. Primary-school teachers generally conduct reading groups in a small-group area with the children sitting in a circle or around a table. Older children may have four desks clustered together for most of the day. Some areas of this type, such as an art area, are specialized so that materials may be stored on adjacent shelves. Other small-group spaces need easy access to water or electricity and should be placed in the room where these are easily accessible. Areas are more flexible when their use is not predetermined and where materials may be brought into or removed from the area. Opportunities for social interaction abound in small-group settings.

Large-group space. Most settings have a **large group space** that can accommodate all of the children at one time. Usually this space has bulletin boards, large book easels, and audio-visual equipment. This type of indoor space is normally used for a variety of activities: language arts, creative dance, group discussion, games, and music. Participation in whole-group activities helps children to see themselves as a part of the larger social network.

Density. The number of children per unit of space refers to the density of the environment. The total room could be very dense with furniture and children being crowded together. High classroom density impacts negatively on behavior as youngsters tend to defend their territory or withdraw. Less desirable behavior is diminished if children get access to materials that they want. Dense classrooms also lead to shorter interactions, more aggressive incidents, and less social cooperation (Evans, 2006). Crowding can occur in private spaces if two or three children enter a space suitable for one, in

© Cengage Learning 2015

High classroom density impacts negatively on behavior.

small-group spaces if either the numbers of children are great or the space taken up by furniture is too great, and in large-group spaces if children are bumping into each other. Adjusting the amount of space in the activity area is one way to keep crowding limited. For example, moving a divider back 12 inches or removing some furniture can decrease the density of a small-group space sufficiently for comfort and for improved interactions (Maxwell, 2003; Knapp & Hall, 2010).

Boundaries and activity areas. Clear, physical boundaries tend to inhibit running, provide cues to where the child is supposed to participate, curb intrusions and interruptions, and designate appropriate pathways for children to move throughout the room. Usually, furnishings and low room dividers are used to mark separations in areas. Most youngsters under age 8 forget or ignore unclear boundaries, such as those formed by floor tape, or those described verbally such as telling the children not to play with the trucks when the area is used for large-group activity. Placing fabric over the shelf housing the trucks is a clearer restriction. Each learning center may be further defined by distinctive materials, such as books and cushions in one area, and child-size tables and chairs with board games in another.

Areas also should be arranged within the room so that activities do not conflict with one another or offer distractions. Quiet activities should be separated from more vigorous ones. For example, it is better to locate a study carrel near a work area or the independent reading area than near the block or game area to avoid setting limits for children who unintentionally intrude. In addition, two learning centers may be side by side and deliberately left permeable to encourage small groups of children to interact (Hohmann et al., 2008). The number, type, and arrangement of activity areas are within the control of the helping professional. Activity areas can be added, removed, or relocated to facilitate the achievement of program goals.

Activity areas are as useful outdoors as indoors. Boundaries can be established outdoors by varying the surface or dividing areas using plantings. Asphalt may be used on a ball court or a tricycle path, grass on the playing or running field, and sand or other resilient materials under climbing equipment. Resilient surfaces promote safety, decreasing the frequency of adult cautions and limit setting. Constructed boundaries, such as fences and pathways, are clear to children and provide them with clues to appropriate behaviors, as well as providing greater safety. Within well-defined areas, adults can influence social interaction by the use of mobile equipment and materials, such as the addition of water or shovels and pails to a digging area. Temporary boundaries may be added as needed to diminish reprimands and reminders, such as when orange traffic cones mark off a big puddle of rainwater on the playground.

Pathways. Activity areas also must be arranged so that movement between areas is easily accomplished without interfering with the activities in progress. Such pathways need to be sufficiently wide to allow children to pass one another without physical contact. Wider pathways outdoors are necessary to avoid collisions where children run. Pathway width may need adjustment if a child needs a walker or a wheelchair. In some rooms, the area designated as the large-group area also serves as a means of access to other activity areas.

Sometimes, the pathway is like a hallway without walls, with the large-group area at one end and small-group and private spaces arranged on either side of a central pathway. This arrangement may encourage running by toddlers, but a central pathway may be more effective for older children.

Storage. Accessible storage promotes responsibility for the materials and encourages children to care for their environment independently. Stored items should be sorted, placed at the point of first use, and arranged so that they are easy to see, reach, grasp, and replace by those who use them most often (Berns, 2012). Like items should be together. Materials that are used regularly should be readily accessible from pathways or activity areas. Storage of equipment and materials used outdoors should be suitable in size and accessible from the playground areas.

Adult storage space that is inaccessible to children also is desirable for safety. Cleaning compounds, medicines, power tools, and potentially harmful substances and equipment should be stored in locked cupboards where children cannot get to them. Sharp-pointed scissors, electric fry pans, and other potentially hazardous materials should be stored out of the reach of children. Such items are sometimes stored centrally for a number of classrooms, outside of areas used by children.

Controllable Dimensions

The physical setting is composed of a number of dimensions involving the facility, the furnishings, and the materials used by children: soft–hard, open–closed, simple–complex, intrusion–seclusion, and high mobility–low mobility (Prescott, 2008). The particular combination of these dimensions varies according to the type of program (classroom, hospital, playroom, YMCA recreation area) as well as the goals of the program and the philosophy of the adults. These dimensions determine the overall comfort and atmosphere communicated by the physical environment. The dimensions are briefly defined with typical examples seen in many programs in Table 9-3.

Table 9-3   Controllable Dimensions in the Physical Environment

Dimension and Definition	One Extreme	Middle	Other Extreme
Softness: Responsiveness of the texture to touch	**Soft:** Pillow Upholstered chair	**Malleable materials:** Sand, water, and dough Grass or lawn	**Hard:** Cement Tricycle Walls
Openness: Degree to which the material itself restricts its use	**Open:** Blocks, toy stove Clay, ball	**Semiopen/semiclosed:** Accessible cabinet with doors, playing cards	**Closed:** Puzzle, tracing patterns, form boards
Complexity: The number of components and their variety	**Simple:** Ladder, wind-up car Doll dress	**Moderately complex:** Jump rope Simple toy car Unit blocks Erector set	**Complex:** Large climber with multiple possible activities Computer
Seclusion: Permeability between boundaries	**Seclusion:** Study carrel; private space learning center Single stall toilet with door Large block building with roof A box or tent where children can close themselves in	**Semisecluded:** Bushes where children play, but adults can see easily Climber where toddler can crawl under and peek out Sunglasses or mask	**Intrusion:** Open windows in a classroom; sounds of children moving outside the room Lab schools with visitors
Mobility: Degree of opportunity for children to physically move their bodies in a learning center	**High mobility:** Gym; playground; tricycle; indoor climber; indoors during transitions	**Moderate:** Garden with pathways and boundaries Most early childhood classrooms; pretend play area; block area; often science areas	**Low mobility:** Nailed-down seats in a room; writing center; reading center; sometimes math center

© Cengage Learning

Qualities of the physical environment have a continuing impact on the quality of interpersonal interaction within it. In the soft–hard dimension, hardness usually is associated with efficiency and formality, and softness is associated with relaxation and comfort. Younger children are more at ease in a softer setting and gradually learn how to behave in the more formal hard settings. Regarding the open–closed dimension, when a material is closed, there is only one way to use it, but when it is open, neither the alternatives nor the outcomes are limited. More open settings encourage curiosity, exploration, and social interaction, and completely closed settings prohibit such behavior altogether. The simple–complex dimension describes the material in terms of the number of alternatives that can be generated. Children tend to play cooperatively with complex and super units more frequently than with simple units, which often elicit solitary or parallel play activity. Complexity encourages deep exploration, and variety encourages broad exploration. School

settings need some of each so that children will focus on an activity for an extended period of time, which is more likely with complex activities but also allows for movement to other alternatives for a change of pace.

The intrusion–seclusion dimension describes the permeability between the program and the things and people outside it and the boundaries between people and things inside the program. Many classrooms have no seclusion within them and may be very fatiguing to young children. Children who are overcome by the stress of continuous interaction act up, cry, or daydream to escape for short periods. Private areas, as described earlier, are spaces in which children can have a degree of seclusion. Small-group spaces are partially secluded and enable children to moderate their level of seclusion. The high-mobility/low-mobility dimension comes into play when children who have the opportunity to choose some sedentary activities and some active pursuits usually choose both in the course of the day. Prolonged sedentary activity

Planning for outdoor play and the number of children using equipment is necessary when structuring the physical environment.

© Cengage Learning

causes children to wiggle to ease their muscles and to become bored and restless regardless of the interest or importance of the activity. They frequently engage in inappropriate behavior, irritating peers and adults and necessitating limit setting. To prevent this, daily **schedules** should provide for a balance between vigorous movement, moderate activity, and more quiet pursuits. When children's need for mobility is taken into account, the selection of equipment and the use of space usually are changed.

Each of the dimensions varies by degrees and may change over the course of a year or within a single day. Each dimension affects the social relationships of children in the setting. An open, moderately secluded, soft environment with low-to-moderate mobility is a conversation area, much like a living room, in which children can relax and interact informally.

Continuous evaluation of the effectiveness of the space to support children's social development requires flexible thought. Sometimes adults continue to function in ineffective settings simply because the classroom or playground has "always been this way." Sit at the child's eye level and appraise the environment from various perspectives when children are using it and when it is empty. Highlight 9-1 provides guidelines for evaluating the childcare setting as a place that supports social competence.

Choosing Appropriate Materials

Adults can promote competent and independent behavior in children by providing a moderately rich assortment of exploratory materials (Dodge, Colker, & Heroman, 2008). The goal in careful selection, maintenance, display, and storage of materials is to have resources that children can use in cooperative or independent activity. Carefully selected materials that meet the interests of children and support program objectives contribute to overall functioning, emotional adjustment, and the development of self-concept and self-control (Frost et al., 2008). The equipment and materials that children use also affect the quality of social interactions during play (Sutterby & Frost, 2006).

Developmentally appropriate materials. Materials should reflect the levels of competence of children in the program. A range of activities that are challenging and can be completed eventually support children's self-esteem. Adults would think it strange if someone gave a chemistry set to a 5-year-old. Not only would the child be at risk of swallowing some of the chemicals, but also, in all probability, the set would quickly be destroyed, and the child frustrated with failure. However, the same set given to a 12-year-old could provide hours of pleasure and instruction. Frequently, materials intended

HIGHLIGHT 9-1

Evaluating the Effectiveness of the Space

Does the environment offer cues for appropriate social behavior?
- Clear boundaries between learning centers or project areas
- Pathways designed so that children do not interrupt other's activities
- Quiet and vigorous activity areas separated spatially
- Adequate number of activity spaces for the numbers of children
- Minimal wait times for materials and equipment
- Storage that is labeled and accessible

Does the environment provide opportunities for conversations among children?

- Places that are soft, comfortable, and informal
- Small group spaces in which only a few children participate at a time
- Private spaces for one or two children
- Spaces that are attractive, inviting, pleasant
- Materials and activities that promote cooperation; working together

Does the environment minimize the need for adult direction or correction of behavior?

- Hard surface flooring in messy areas (easy to clean)
- Softer surface flooring to minimize normal noise (block area)
- Learning centers well maintained and orderly
- Childproofing for safety (wall plugs, electric cords, appliances, and medications put away; doors closed; etc.)
- Self-care possible (toileting, hand washing, putting on and taking off wraps)

Does the environment promote the self-identity of the children?

- Regularly changed displays of children's art, projects, work
- Photos depicting all racial groups, abilities, and occupations for men and women
- Artifacts and pictures that represent the cultures of children in the group
- Learning centers accessible to all children regardless of ability or disability
- Opportunities for children to explore, experience challenge, and be successful

Does the environment promote individual responsibility for the environment and for others?

- Supplies available for cleaning up indoors
- Trash cans and gloves for playground cleanup
- Pictographs available for routine maintenance and cleanliness
- Movables stored in marked containers
- Adequate storage indoors and out

for older children create potential risks and failure for younger ones. In addition, when older children use equipment and materials designed for young children, they lose interest because there is no challenge, and they find new, often destructive ways to use them.

Structurally safe materials. Materials should be examined for potential safety hazards. Sturdiness, durability, craftsmanship, and appropriate construction materials all contribute to safe products. For example, tricycles available in local stores are not as sturdily constructed as those designed specifically for use by groups of children. Care also should be taken to see

that materials are not likely to cause choking. If an object is small enough to get into a toddler's mouth and has a diameter between that of a dime and a quarter, it might get stuck in the throat. Safe materials enable independent use without multiple cautions from adults.

Materials that work. Children become frustrated when equipment and materials do not operate, which sometimes leads to disruptive behavior. The wheels of trucks should turn; scissors should cut; finger paint should be thick, books should have all the pages to the stories, and the paper should be heavy enough or glossy so that it doesn't fall apart. It is nearly impossible to trace accurately through standard typing paper; tracing paper and paper clips make the job much easier. Children cannot use basketballs, kickballs, or volleyballs that are underinflated. Children's sense of competence is enhanced when they are successful, rather than experiencing failure due to inoperable tools and materials.

Materials that are complete and ready to use. Puzzles should have all their pieces. If one gets lost, it can be replaced by molding in some plastic wood (available in most hardware stores) to fit the hole. Incomplete materials lead to unnecessary feelings of failure and frustration and loss of self-esteem.

In addition, some materials should be assembled in advance so that children do not have to wait while the adult rummages around in a cupboard or drawer for a pair of scissors or make children wait while they get a necessary item for a science experiment. Waiting children usually lose interest or become disruptive.

Complete advance preparation includes some plan for cleaning up, so having a damp sponge in a pan would be appropriate preparation for a messy activity. In this way, the adult never needs to leave the group of children and can offer continuous guidance while

children are able to complete projects with a sense of competence.

Organizing materials storage. Storage should be where the material is most frequently used. If children know where something is located, they can go and get it independently, especially common items such as paper, crayons, and scissors. Materials also should be stored so that children can take care of them. For example, taping shapes of unit blocks on the back of a cupboard so that children know where to put each size and shape encourages independence, as does labeling or color coding the difficulty of books on plastic bins. Materials that have many pieces, such as beads, small math cubes, or Cuisenaire® rods, should be placed in sturdy containers such as clear plastic shoeboxes or tiny laundry baskets because the cardboard boxes soon wear out. In this way, children can keep all materials that go together in one place and demonstrate their responsibility for their own classroom.

Attractively displayed materials. Neatness and orderliness are aspects of attractiveness. Attractiveness affects the mood of children and also leads to treating their work spaces with responsibility. Both adults

Sand provides protection from falls, as well as opportunities for children of all ages to play. Because it is loose and malleable, it is excellent as a learning material as well.

© Cengage Learning

and children are more at ease with one another in warm, comfortable, and attractive spaces. Materials that are displayed in a moderately empty space on an accessible shelf are most likely to be used and are more appealing. Young children simply have difficulty in selecting materials on crowded shelves. Puzzles in a puzzle rack or laid out on a table ready for use are more appealing than a large, heavy stack of them. As many books as possible should be displayed with their covers showing, rather than spines. This is especially important for very young children.

Appropriate size of equipment and materials.
Tables, chairs, desks, or other equipment add to the comfort and decrease the fatigue of children if they are sized correctly. Adults also should have at least one chair that fits them to sit on occasionally (Knapp & Hall, 2010).

Fewer problems are encountered at mealtime if preschool children are offered 6-inch plates, salad forks, and 4- or 5-ounce glasses to use. Serving dishes (soup bowls) with teaspoon servers would enable young children to serve themselves amounts of food that they can reasonably consume. Using small, unbreakable pitchers for milk and juice encourages independence as well. When children determine portion size for themselves, there is less wasted, and children feel they have control. Equipment and all materials should be appropriate for the size and age of the children in the program to promote independence of action and children's comfort.

Quantities appropriate to the number of children.
If there are enough materials for a particular activity, children can work cooperatively successfully. If there is an insufficient supply, either the number of materials should be increased or the number of children using them decreased. For example, if a third-grade teacher has 12 books and 14 children, she can either hold two consecutive sessions of 7 children and use the books on hand or get 2 more books. Either solution is better than having children rush to the reading area to get a book for themselves. Toddlers as well as some inexperienced preschool-aged children do not comprehend sharing. In addition, a toy being played with by another child is more appealing than one on a shelf. Duplicate toys allow the desires of the youngest children to be met without conflict.

Adequate supplies of materials are necessary for any program regardless of the children's age if children are to be reasonably successful. This will determine how well children get along with each other as well as influence the quality of interactions. Materials should be accessible to all children, including those with special needs. This fosters independent action and allows children to work together peacefully.

Adding or Removing Materials, and Childproofing the Environment

Purchasing materials and equipment and the initial furniture arrangement or materials storage is usually the responsibility of administrators in the organization. Selecting specific materials appropriately and organizing and displaying them carefully are strategies teachers use to prevent frustration, interpersonal conflict, property damage, and physical risk. These strategies are the result of advanced planning with ultimate goals of supporting positive social interactions and appropriate behavior. Helping professionals, who are working directly with the children, structure the specific materials to meet their immediate needs and ensure that the physical environment is conducive to the development of social competence (Kostelnik, Soderman, & Whiren, 2011). In addition, supervising adults must make adjustments based on individual or group needs as children interact within the space, use equipment, and engage in the activities with materials in meaningful ways. The most common adjustments that adults make to the environment in support of children's interpersonal engagement are to add materials, take them away, or childproof the environment.

Adding to the environment.
Adults add to the environment in many ways. A photograph of each child's family or of the local community might be hung and discussed with the children. An artifact or an article of clothing representative of the cultural heritage of one of the children might be brought in to share. Fresh flowers or living plants and animals might be added temporarily in the setting to soften the environment and to add interest.

These additions are typical of the general strategy of preparing the environment. However, on-the-spot adjustments of adding to the environment occur daily. For example, if two children want to look at one picture book about trains, offer a second book with pictures of trains. If children are waiting a long time to use glue sticks, provide either school paste or glue. If Alyce is arguing with Theresa about leaving the store without "paying," ask them what they think could be used for money and then help them to obtain the material if necessary. Such on-the-spot actions usually rectify the situation sufficiently for the children to move forward in their social interactions as well as support their problem-solving skills.

Taking away from the environment.
Often, after initially arranging their classrooms for the year, teachers do not think about removing materials, equipment, or furniture from a particular area. However, by doing so, we can provoke children's interest in newly

Animals can be added temporarily in the setting to add interest.

© Cengage Learning 2015

introduced activities or learning opportunities. For example, Mrs. Sisco removed everything normally in the housekeeping area over the weekend, storing the equipment temporarily to set up the rudiments of a grocery store. Children noticed the change immediately on Monday morning, became excited about participating in the newly equipped center, and added other "furnishings" as their play developed.

Removing materials and equipment when young children are misusing them or not understanding their purpose is sometimes necessary. For example, if children are handling books in a disrespectful manner, pushing and shoving one another at the sensory table, teasing the guinea pig, or throwing cars in the block center, the learning resources should be temporarily removed. You can then return them after informing children about your expectations and demonstrating how to use them appropriately. Always follow up to see that children are responsive to these guidelines.

Generally, the adding or deleting of materials is done to enhance play, minimize potentials for frustration or conflict, and promote cooperation and self-control. The environments in which we live and work affect our mood and our behaviors with each other and are relatively easy to change either before the program is in session or during it.

Childproofing the environment. Adding materials, taking them away, and altering them are necessary for childproofing the environment. Childproofing means providing the necessary adjustments to ensure the safety of the children. It is usually done before children enter the environment but may occur on the spot when safety risks are detected. Several examples of this are illustrated in Table 9-4.

The amount of space necessary may have been incorrectly estimated for an activity. For example, Mr. Bongard placed an indoor climber about 18 inches from an open, screened window one hot summer day because he thought that the vigorous activity would benefit from the potential air circulation. However, as he was watching Brad and Doug climb to the top between the window and the climber, they attempted to stand on the nearby windowsill. He hastily lifted Brad down and asked Doug to climb down before he moved the climber at least 3 feet away from the window. The quick adjustment to increase safety was essential.

Other adjustments. Sometimes space should be limited instead of increased. Miss Adkins took her kindergarten children to the gym to run simple relay races. At first, she set the activity up so that children would run the length of the gym. She noticed that

Table 9-4 Examples of Adjusting Materials to Increase Safety

Observation	Action Taken
A toddler pokes the electrical outlet in the hallway.	Add an outlet cover, and remove the child from the hallway.
A 3-year-old puts the hot water on at full force to wash her hands.	Adjust the water temperature and flow.
A group of third graders leave boxes and papers in the hallway blocking a door.	Remind children to collect the trash and assist with removal as needed.
A cord to the coffee pot is hanging over the edge of a counter in the teachers' area, but it is in sight of children.	Fold the cord loosely, and fasten it with a wire twist or rubber band.
A mother gives her kindergarten child a plastic bag with medications and directions for administering them and sends her into the primary classroom.	Take the medicine from the child immediately, and place it in a safe spot.

they were quickly tired and restless, as they had to wait too long for a turn. She made a mental note to shift the races across the width of the gym next time instead of the length, which would still gave ample room to run but cut down the waiting time. Adjustments by moving equipment or by increasing or decreasing space most appropriate for an activity are fairly typical of most child-centered programs.

Sometimes adjustments are made in the ways in which directions are given. At the beginning of this chapter, Grace used a pictograph to guide her hand-washing and use of paper towels. Using sequenced photographs or drawings for routine activities such as returning materials, tying shoes, or taking off outdoor clothing are easy structuring strategies that support directions already given to children on how to do the task.

In addition, individual children may not understand the directions on the use of equipment or materials, so additional explanations and demonstrations may be necessary for each person to be successful. For example, today, a variety of new technologies is being added to all early childhood classrooms, including prekindergarten contexts. Teachers are finding developmentally appropriate ways to extend children's repertoire of cultural, literacy, and communications knowledge and practices through the use of tablets, electronic art galleries, global online communities, smart boards, and iPods. While many of us today may have grown up with only *Sesame Street* and other television programs as our major childhood link to technology, the children in our classrooms have been labeled "netizens" (Luke, 1999; Vasquez & Felderman, 2013). Teachers are being challenged to capitalize on opportunities to understand and make technology more accessible to all children. Mr. Rock has found just one demonstration to the group in using a new technology comfortably and independently is generally

inadequate, particularly with children who have little or no access at home. He therefore adjusted his strategy of encouraging usage to one of training a few of the children in the kindergarten with new equipment and software and then asking those children to give demonstrations to their peers. This "each one teach one" adjustment also supported social interaction and contributed to the prosocial goal of helpfulness.

Occasionally, a center is adjusted by simply closing it. Mrs. Perry temporarily closed the thematic play center "Seed Store" when children were just throwing the seeds around instead of engaging in productive play. Upon close appraisal, she decided that the children didn't have the necessary understandings about seeds, their use, or how they were bought and sold to engage in the play. After children learned more about shopping for seeds, the center was reopened successfully several days later. Most frequently, adjustments are very simple interventions that help the children be more successful in learning and in their interactions with each other.

Mr. Turkus responded to the frustrated cry of 3-year-old George, who slapped his painting with the paintbrush and exclaimed, "Is not red." The red drippings on the outside of the jar did not match the muddy, purplish red color of the paint inside. Mr. Turkus showed George how to rinse the brushes and jars, and provided a small amount of the three primary colors. He then demonstrated how to keep the red paint red by using a separate brush for each color. George resumed painting happily.

Ms. Polzin noticed Nicholas riding his truck through the block area and ramming into block structures that Claire and Raphael were building. When they moved to hit him, he seemed oblivious to the cause of their anger. After a settlement between the children was complete, Ms. Polzin provided masking tape to mark off a road for the truck where block structures could not be built.

In each of these instances, the adults altered the environment to enhance the success of the children in their care. Structuring the furnishings, equipment, and materials of the physical environment prepares the setting for effective interactions by providing visual cues for behavior and materials needed for success. The impact of the learning environment is significant in that in a large study of 3- and 4-year-olds, the researcher concluded that children's perceptions of the physical environment were related to measures of the children's cognitive and social competency, particularly in the 3-year-olds (Maxwell, 2007).

CHALLENGING BEHAVIOR

Children "Running Wild"

Sometimes adults blame children for problems that are really the fault of poorly designed physical environments. Consider this situation at the Happy Days Childcare Center.

The Center is located in a church fellowship hall. The doors from the parking lot open into a very large tiled floor room (used on weekends as a mini-gymnasium) with six small classrooms coming off the huge open space. Wooden cubbies are located at the far end of the hall in the smallest classroom. Children have to cross through the entire big space to put away their coats. All 50 children arrive at about the same time.

Four activity areas (whole group, blocks, pretend play, and art) are widely separated in the four corners of the room with an eating area near the end where the kitchen is located. There is a large empty space in the middle of the hall. Three quieter learning centers (books, manipulatives, and a listening center) are located in the smaller classrooms. Two classrooms are reserved for naptime.

One teacher told the new director, "The children are completely out of control when they arrive every morning. They burst from the vans yelling and running. They don't seem to be able to settle down all day long and we are constantly reprimanding them to stop running and shouting. I've never worked with such 'wild' children. We need to get a grip on things here."

Following a few days of observation, the director recommended that the program not jump immediately to the topmost tier of the Social Support Pyramid to address children's out of control behaviors. She suggested they begin by creating a more supportive physical environment. Together the staff decided to try these initial changes:

- Move the cubbies to create an initial entry to the hall. This will encourage children to stop as they enter to remove coats.

- Place large area rugs under the learning centers in the hall. This will reduce noise and make the spaces seem cozier.

- Cluster the centers in the hall closer together and eliminate the space in the middle to diminish the visual invitation to run from place to place.

- Revise the transportation schedule so that the vans arrive a few at a time, allowing children to enter the space a few at a time and to be greeted individually by the adults.

- Divide the children into three distinct groups so that one-third begin the day outdoors, one-third begin in the smaller classrooms, and one-third begin in the hall.

- Provide the extra supervision necessary so that children walk from the cubbies area to the place where they are scheduled to be until they have learned the new routine.

Look at each of the tiers in the Social Support Pyramid displayed in Figure 9.1. What additional adjustments do you think the staff could make to remedy the situation?

Figure 9-1 Social Support Pyramid: Influencing Children's Social Development by Structuring the Physical Environment.

© Cengage Learning

Apply what you have learned so far to the challenging circumstances teachers in the Happy Days Childcare Center faced in working with children running "wild" in the classroom.

In addition to planning for the physical environment, adults plan in advance for the use of time in programs and an orderly, predictable sequence of events for children. This sets the stage for the quality of interpersonal experiences adults and children experience.

Structuring Time naeyc

Adults value time as a resource and are concerned with helping children to function within the cultural definitions of time that adults use. One way adults help children to use time efficiently is by teaching them a habit for routine activities that are repetitious and used regularly. Health habits regarding hand washing, toileting, and tooth brushing are routines in many early childhood programs that are formed with clear directions, consistent practice, and an understanding of their purpose (Oshikanlu, 2006). Sometimes, adults become annoyed with children when they are slow to develop a desired habit. At such times, a child either may not know an appropriate sequence of behaviors, or the sequence is so new that he or she must concentrate closely on each action. A typical example of not knowing an appropriate sequence is when a kindergarten child puts on mittens or boots before the snow pants. Adults sometimes become irritated when such incidents make the group wait, mostly because they do not realize that the situation requires teaching rather than demanding and limit setting. Another way adults help children learn the cultural meaning of time is by organizing events into a predictable sequence.

The Daily Schedule

Schedules are organized time segments that pertain to the particular program and reflect its philosophy and goals. These blocks of time are arranged in an orderly way, with children moving from one activity to another in an unsurprising pattern. When teachers establish reasonable routines that make sense to children, the daily schedule or routine supports children's ability to act autonomously and to proceed at their own pace (Gestwicki, 2011). Events can be predicted; expectations for behavior are clear. All routines contribute to the children's sense of safety and security. The need for constant guidance in what to do and how to do it is minimized, so children's dependence on adult direction is decreased. The following are guidelines teachers use in developing a daily schedule that promotes social competence (Bullard, 2010; Kostelnik et al., 2011):

- Design the schedule for the age of the children in the program and their interests and needs, making sure that it encourages the development of each child's sense of competence (maximum independence) and worth (opportunities to display work, chart progress, see own culture represented in the physical environment, etc.).
- Provide a balance of child-initiated (free choice) and adult-initiated (small-group and large-group times) activities with ample opportunities for children to have some control (choice) over what they do.
- Provide a variety and balance of small-group and whole-group experiences that support social interaction.
- Alternate quiet and vigorous activities so children can experience privacy and rest as well as opportunities to be actively engaged with others.
- Provide for in-depth experiences and cooperative activities that engage children for longer periods of time, build concentration, and encourage children to work together to accomplish a task.
- Make specific provisions for transitions that are predictable and that involve minimal wait times.
- Make the daily schedule visible to the children and others through posted photographs, pictographs, or writing; add oral directions when needed to help children recognize the routine of the day and to have a resource for figuring out "what comes next."
- Regularly evaluate and adjust the schedule to be responsive to children's changing needs.

When a child first enters a new group setting, the familiar patterns developed within previous settings (including the home) may need to be altered to fit the new situation and expectations. Initially, the needed changes can result in distress and confusion for a child. The problems of adjustment are reduced as children become used to and accept the new pattern.

Routines must be learned. Adults first must adapt to the toddler's schedule and then gradually teach children to function within a group schedule. Children under 6 years of age may take as long as a month to adapt to a new daily schedule. Children in the elementary grades often adjust in two weeks or less; at this age, pictorial charts or posted schedules may help them to adjust more quickly. Routines may be flexible, allowing a little more time to finish an activity if the change is compatible with the requirements of other program segments. Sometimes, however, as when large groups of children must use the same resources, schedules must be quite rigid. The use of the swimming area in a summer camp requires that all children must arrive, enter, and leave the water in an orderly fashion if standards of safety are to be maintained; every group must operate on clock time if all groups are to be able to swim each day. In contrast, in an after-school program, children may move indoors and outdoors whenever adult supervision is available; a rigid clock-time schedule is unnecessary.

The predictability of a routine offers emotional security to young children. After a distressing encounter with another child, Cara, age 4, chanted the daily schedule several times: "First we play, then we wash, then we have a snack, then we hear a story, then we go outside, and then my mama comes to take me home." After each repetition, she appeared more cheerful and ultimately was able to participate comfortably for the rest of the day. Young children also will comprehend the sequence of the daily routine before understanding the concept of time. Ross, 3-and-a-half years old, was distressed when his mother left him at the childcare center. He played for about 45 minutes, and then asked if the children could go outside. This was a drastic change of schedule—usually, outside play was the last activity of the day—but the teacher allowed Ross and two other boys to go outside with an assistant. Ross played happily for a few minutes, and then informed the adult that his mother would be there soon to pick him up! He had erroneously inferred that playing outside caused his mother to arrive because of the contiguity of the events. Older children rely on regular routines as well. Jen knew her "hard" work was done by noon; with her reading tasks finished, she could then pursue math and science the rest of the small-group time!

Transitions. A good schedule is continuous, fluid, and goal directed. Blocks of time allow children to finish tasks and provide for individual differences in speed. Waiting is minimal, and the transitions in which the whole group must participate are as few as possible. A group **transition** occurs when one time block is finished and another begins. These transitions usually occur when children move from one room to another or when there is a complete change of activity. In Cara's verbalization of her routine ("First we play, then we wash . . .," she located all the group transitions by saying "then." In elementary schools, transitions occur before and after recess and lunch and also may occur between activities, such as between math and social studies. An individual transition is when a child is finished with one activity and moves on to another within a scheduled time block.

Generally, there is a marked increase in the number of interaction problems between children and between adults and children during group transitions. Children may be confused about how to behave after one activity is over and before another begins. Sometimes, youngsters deliberately run, call out to friends, or wander during a transition. Older school-age children use this time for conversation and play, with a resulting increase in noise. Therefore, decreasing the number of transitions results in the lower probability of interaction difficulties.

Short attention spans and differences in working speed can be managed by grouping a variety of activities together in a larger time block and allowing children to change activities individually. For example, in a second-grade room, a teacher combined reading groups, workbook activities, and selected games involving one or two children into one block of time. In programs for very young children, a large variety of materials usually is available at any one time. Individual transitions are generally smoother, with children most successful if they have decided what to do next. In general, the schedule should be adapted to the length of time children need to complete tasks rather than to rigid periods, with particular attention to the age of children and time of year. Children tend to focus on their tasks longer as they mature, and from fall to spring have a longer attention span.

In any case, the goal is to meet the individual needs of children; strategies and standards for doing so differ according to program demands. However, there are general guides that will help support transitions for all age groups:

- **Plan carefully** so that you consider just what each child is supposed to do and how the child is supposed to do it. Teach repeating transitions carefully so that each child develops relevant habits related to that transition. Entering the building is one of these regular transitions that can be taught so well that it becomes a habit. For example, children should know which door to enter and which staircase (if you use one) to use, which side of the staircase to walk on, how to walk safely using the handrail, how to remove outdoor wear and where to put it, to wash and dry their hands on entering the classroom (reduces transmitting colds), and where in the room to congregate or begin the first activity. This kind of instruction with appropriate ongoing supervision tends to reduce problems such as running in hallways, fooling around in stairwells, and congregating in bathrooms or locker areas. Treat transition as a skill to be taught.

- **Provide enough time** so that the transition can be accomplished without rushing, yet eliminate waiting as much as possible (Lamm et al., 2006). Children can use sign-up sheets when more youngsters want a material than can be accommodated. Specific materials such as picture books might be used while children gather for a group experience. Making children wait for the adult is disrespectful and wastes children's time (Bullard, 2010).

- **Give clear, precise directions**. Be specific and direct. Offer three or fewer directions stated at one time. For example, when it was time for a group transition from learning centers to another group setting or activity, Ms. Swanson approached a small group who had been using a lot of blocks and said, "Put each block on the shelf where it matches the shape" (pointing to the silhouette). She stayed nearby to make sure these young children understood. Then she said, "Place all of the blocks on the shelves." Seeing the children engaged, she moved on to another area to give directions to those children using paints. If necessary, this adult would return to the block area to give the same directions or a demonstration if needed.

- **Alert children that a transition is coming** soon so that they can either complete an activity or organize the materials so that completion is possible later. Use the same signal every day such as having a child ring a hanging wind chime used only to announce clean up or having a helper carry around a sign that reads "5 minutes to play."

- **Plan for the movement of children** through pathways when the whole group is in transition. Dismiss children in small groups or individually to avoid congestion in bottleneck areas such as doorways. Consider the size of the pathway and whether one child will be walking past other children. In spacious outdoor areas, small groups of older children should be able to pass each other without physical contact.

- **Engage in active supervision during transitions**. Children need support and assistance to engage in socially appropriate behavior when the whole group is moving within the space. Scan the whole room, move toward children who are disruptive, and give directions to those who are wandering, disengaged, withdrawn, or unable to identify opportunities for helping so they can contribute to the group effort. For example, "Frank, put away 20 blocks. Count them as you go." This supports prosocial behaviors such as helping and cooperating with others.

- **Tell children what is coming next** if it is a group transition, or ask children what they plan to do next if it is an individual transition. This helps children to develop planning skills and increases their ability to predict what will happen sequentially.

- When children are engaged in a free-choice activity, **start the transition to cleaning up the room by the whole group gradually**. Ask small groups of children with the greatest number of materials to take care of to begin cleanup before

the other children. Then move to other small groups so that the whole group finishes about the same time.

- **Always send children to something or someone** that is prepared for them. Aimless wandering or dabbling with numerous materials is not desirable during individual or group transitions. Assure that each child knows where to be and what he or she should be doing at the end of the transition. Ambiguity often leads to uncertainty and contributes to overstimulation or the perception that things are out of control.

- **Adapt transition strategies for children with special needs**. Children who have ADHD, those who are autistic, or those who use hearing aids may be particularly vulnerable to the noise that comes when children are on the "move" during a transition.

All whole group transitions are noisy. Books are closed. People move from place to place. Children interact with one another. Transitions take longer initially

---

Warning Signs That the Physical Environment Is Problematic

The following behaviors signal that the physical environment is not working well for children and teachers.

Children:

- Wander aimlessly around or have difficulty finding something to do that interests them
- Frequently run in the classroom
- Repeat the same activities over and over again
- Become frustrated because materials are lost or broken or because activities are too difficult for them to handle on their own
- Continually fight over materials and space
- Use materials destructively
- Yell to the teacher or to one another from across the room
- Crawl under tables and shelves
- Consistently depend on adults to reach for things or do things for them

Teachers:

- Continually complain about children's behavior
- Have to shout to get children's attention
- Lose track of what children are doing and where children are
- Feel uncomfortable working with individual children or children in small groups even for a little while

Digital Download **Download from CourseMate**

and are much shorter after the specific transition habit is acquired. However, if children are milling around, pushing and shoving, engaged in boisterous play and generally disorganized, then the adult should take immediate action. When this happened in Ms. Haden's group, she flicked the light, asked all of the children to lie on the floor where they remained until the room was quiet. Then said, "Lie still until I ask you to stand up. You will be quiet as mice and not touch anyone. When I touch you, stand up and put away the materials you have been using and come sit in the group area." She paused, then asked them to stand up and move quietly like mice. Her voice was soft and firm. Later she provided an opportunity for children to discuss what happened during that transition. She discouraged blaming others and helped children to think about what they did to contribute to the bedlam. She neither shamed nor scolded them. Later, she evaluated her instructional strategies, directions, and transition planning.

A number of red flags or warning signs signal inadequate structuring of the physical environment (Dodge, Colker, & Heroman, 2008; Kostelnik & Grady, 2009). These can be seen in Highlight 9-1 and can be downloaded for your use in evaluating whether the climate in your classroom is a positive one or one that needs additional attention.

Rate and Intensity of Programs

The number of transitions that take place during the day determines the rate or pace of a program. For example, some children may experience three or more transitions in a single hour. This is a fast pace with a rapid rate of change, providing only 15 to 20 minutes for each segment. A moderate pace would have at least one activity period of 45 to 60 minutes and others of varying length of time. A low-pace program would have few group transitions and two long periods in a half-day program.

The intensity of the program generally refers to the amount of change within a time segment and the degree to which children must attend to an adult. High-intensity programs have three to five novel experiences per week with fewer opportunities to repeat or practice skills. The adult–child interaction is high and the number of adult-initiated activities greater. In low-intensity programs, children have one or two novel activities per week and many opportunities to repeat and vary familiar activities; the role of the adult is that of observer and facilitator. Children may be overstimulated, rushing from one thing to another, or they may be bored with a very low-intensity program. In either extreme, children find it difficult to have congenial, easygoing interactions with their peers. Both

Transitions take longer initially until habits are established and acquired by the children.

overstimulation and boredom generate fatigue, which limits children's ability to cope with social interactions. A child who is able to solve interpersonal problems when rested may simply cry or become distraught if required to face the same situation when tired.

Some elementary programs require a 2-hour block devoted to reading. Direct instruction in reading groups are high intensity with lower intensity options designed for practice available for the other children. Regardless of the age of children and the nature of the program, teachers must balance components to minimize fatigue.

It is quite possible to have some children in a program frustrated, others bored, and still others exhausted from the stress of working under pressure to keep up. Factors that influence the rate at which

children can function are motivation, health, knowledge, skill, practice, age, stamina, habit, and the number of people involved in an activity (Berns, 2012). Crowded conditions are more tiring than those in which the density is lower. Interacting continuously with someone is more tiring than sporadic contact during the day. In a daylong program, if the pace and intensity of the schedule are low to moderate, children are more likely to experience only the normal fatigue that is the result of normal activity. This can be reduced for very young children by napping, and they will be able to engage in more pleasant social experiences during the rest of the day.

The skills section that follows should help you to move from simply knowing about these things to actually being able to carry out the tasks.

SKILLS FOR STRUCTURING THE PHYSICAL ENVIRONMENT TO FOSTER SOCIAL DEVELOPMENT AND PREVENT OR DIMINISH UNDESIRABLE BEHAVIOR naeyc

Arranging the Room to Support Social Development and Learning

Classrooms, playrooms, gymnasiums, and other spaces are used for children's activities. Following are some general guidelines for initially setting up a room. Remember that the nature of the program and the nature of the space will greatly influence these specifics.

1. **Survey the space**. Note the placement of potential hazards such as electrical outlets and probable pathways such as doorways, water sources, and windows. Sit on the floor and look around. Is the space inviting or attractive? Does it stimulate curiosity and promote order?

2. **Imagine how children might move within this space, and try to predict the problems they might encounter that are likely to require setting limits**. Can children change from one play space to another easily? Is it likely that children will walk? Is the space organized to prevent hazards? Spilling or dripping paint is not unusual. Extension cords are a trip hazard for children and adults. Even older youngsters have poked things into uncovered electrical outlets. Surfaces on stairwells and next to other areas where children form lines are usually touched, leaving dirty fingerprints. Young people frequently run and mill about during arrival and dismissal as well as other scheduled transitions.

3. **Evaluate the placement of furnishings in terms of social development goals**. If peer conflict regularly occurs in the same place, consider reorganizing the space. Are children able to move through the space with confidence and ease without interrupting someone else? Where do most of the limit-setting instances occur? Use the answers to these questions to help you restructure the area.

4. **Adapt the room arrangement as needed to meet the needs of children experiencing physical or mental challenges**. Children in wheelchairs must have more space in pathways than children who are independently mobile. Children with broken limbs who are temporarily experiencing limitations in mobility may also require space adjustments so they may do what they can for themselves. Children with sensory or mental impairments may require greater attention to maintaining clear walkways or opportunities for seclusion from time to time. Parents and specialists usually can provide suggestions for meeting the special needs of individuals. In principle, adults structure the environment to enable the successful participation of all the children within it.

5. **Adjust furnishings and equipment as necessary to support children's social behavior on the spot**. Move tables or other large equipment a few inches so that youngsters

can move freely without interfering with another person. Observe for pushing, shoving, loud voices of protest, or other disruptions, and consider alternatives in the physical environment to change the conditions before setting limits. Change the location of the activity if it is too close to other activities that interfere with the children's success and enjoyment.

6. **Add or subtract objects** in the physical environment to achieve specific goals related to children's social development.

7. **Share your observations of children's use of space and room arrangement with program leaders** if children's interactions indicate a consistent or ongoing problem. Cooperate with fellow team members by discussing structuring issues. As a group, view the room at the level of the children and evaluate whether or not it supports the social competence of the children or if it generates potential problems for them.

Maximizing Safety

The safety of children is every adult's responsibility, regardless of role. Usually, the adults in charge of a program will check the environment and childproof it so it is safe. Occasionally, however, people overlook less obvious risks or forget to follow through in making the adjustments. Thus, all adults must make it a habitual part of daily practice to apply the principles of childproofing the environment. Taking simple precautions is much better than telling children to be careful or scolding them for playing near something hazardous. You always have the option of inquiring about a situation you think is unsafe.

1. **Scan the environment inside and out for potential safety hazards when supervising children**. Remove hazards promptly. Sometimes, when other people use space during other time periods, materials and equipment are left out that may pose a danger to the children. People passing or using a playground during nonoperation times may leave inappropriate or dangerous materials on the ground.

2. **Keep safety in mind when supervising activities**. Some materials are potentially hazardous if used improperly but otherwise are safe. A stapler used properly is safe, but little fingers can get under the staple. Large blocks usually are safe, but a tall construction may require an adjustment of a lower block to ensure balance of the whole structure. Remain alert and observant throughout the day.

3. **Act promptly when a safety hazard is noticed**. Act conservatively and, if your judgment is at fault, it is better to be more protective than less protective in an ongoing program for children. For example, if three preschool children are at the top of a slide all trying to come down at once, climb the slide, help one child to go down at a time, and monitor how many children are able to get to the top to take a turn. Do not hesitate to act.

4. **Review any actions during the program day with other adults**. For example, plants not known to be safe can be removed or fencing can protect the area. Adults who are not with the children for the full time they are in session also need information so that the same hazardous situation does not reoccur.

5. **Know the local and state legal guidelines** and periodically check that they are being maintained.

Managing Materials to Promote Independence

Organizing according to the following guidelines can minimize problems with cleanup done by children.

1. **Store materials to be used by children in durable containers near the point of heaviest use** so that they are easy to reach, grasp, and use. Help children place materials in the correct storage container, if necessary.

2. **Establish a specific location for materials so that children will know where to put them**. Mark storage areas with words, colors, symbols, or pictures as needed to identify materials that should be located there.

3. **Check equipment and materials** to be sure they are complete, safe, and usable.

4. **Demonstrate the proper care of materials**. If necessary, tell the children exactly what to do while demonstrating step by step, and then take the materials out again so that the children can imitate the behavior.

5. **Give reasons for the standards that you set**. For example, say: "Put the pieces in the puzzle box before putting it in the rack. That way, the pieces won't get lost."

6. **Supervise the process of putting materials away**, giving reminders as necessary; praise children who are achieving the standard and those who are helping others to do so. Allow children to choose between two or three tasks. If they are unwilling to choose which task to do, assign a task and support the child through the process. Check periodically to see that there has been follow-through. (These skills are discussed in Chapters 10 and 11.)

Arranging Space and Materials So Children Have Clues for How to Behave

1. **Provide only enough chairs or activity spaces for the maximum number of children that can participate in an activity**. Children become confused if there are five chairs at a table, but only three children may participate in the activity. To avoid this problem, remove extra chairs.

2. **Use signs, labels, or pictographs placed so that children understand what is expected from these visual cues**. For example, put one colored cube in a plastic bag and tape it to the exterior of the opaque bin that holds the cubes. Place a label on the container as well. Then draw a cube, color it, and label the shelf where the bin is stored. Children will know how and where to place the cubes when pickup time occurs.

3. **Use more floor area for larger groups and less space for smaller groups**. For example, the computer, table, and two chairs can be placed in a small area near the library comfortably. However, the thematic play space should be three to four times larger as more children are likely to play there. Usually children move through large open space or bring materials into the space to use them there.

4. **Make all activities appealing and attractive**. Add color to attract children such as placing a piece of construction paper under a puzzle, much like a placemat. Opening a few books with lovely illustrations and arranging them so that children can see them from afar might draw children into the library area. When initially arranging your classroom and periodically thereafter, sit on the floor or in a small chair and really look to see if all of the activity areas are equally appealing.

5. **Encourage children to personalize their space by making room decorations, using the bulletin boards, or having a display area**. Keep written messages, pictures, and photographs at children's eye level. Put child photographs on the locker or cubby or place family photos on bulletin boards where children may talk about their families with each other.

6. **Provide activities for private spaces**. Plan activities that children may do alone. Permit the child who needs some seclusion an opportunity to withdraw occasionally from the main flow of action.

7. **Provide materials and activities that are developmentally appropriate**. Avoid offering activities that are too simple or too difficult. Modify the planned activity if you observe children struggling or 'breezing through it" with little real engagement.

8. **Have all the materials ready and all the equipment and furnishings in place when the program begins**. Supervise the children continuously rather than being distracted by having to constantly replenish supplies. Check the materials for usability, quantity, and safety ahead of children using them to ensure the smooth functioning of activities. Then you are free to interact with the children.

9. **Organize materials so that physical work is minimized both for children and for you**. Observe children and other adults for ways to eliminate or simplify unnecessary work. For instance, use a tray to carry several items instead of making many trips. Offer suggestions to help children make their own work much more efficient.

10. **Send children to an activity or an area rather than away from one**. Give children a clear notion of what alternatives they may pursue. Give a direction, such as "Put away your books and come to the large-group area," or ask the child what he or she plans to do next. Avoid statements such as, "You should finish up," or "You're all done." Neither statement helps the child decide what activities are open for him next.

Minimizing Potential Conflict over Materials

1. **Provide materials in an appropriate number for the task and situation**. In a classroom, use the ratio of 1.5 to 2.5 play spaces per child. Check the number of spaces and the amount of materials available when mobility is excessive or when child-to-child conflict occurs. Either too many or too few activities can produce this effect. Add or remove activity areas and play units, based on your assessment.

2. **For young children, especially toddlers, provide duplicate or near duplicate play materials**. Substitute a duplicate or similar object for the one under contention.

3. **Arrange the space so children can get materials and take care of them without interfering with other children**. Place furnishings so children can move to and from storage without bumping into other people or asking them to move their activity.

Supporting and Working within the Daily Schedule

1. **Know the time schedule for your work or participation hours and be on time.** Check the environment when you arrive to be sure it is acceptable for children and the necessary materials that you need are there. Notify the program if you are going to be late or absent due to illness.

2. **Know the children's daily schedule and the schedules for any other groups of children when common spaces or equipment are shared**. Make sure that you understand where you are supposed to be at any given time. Find out about any anticipated changes in the schedule for special events. Refer to the daily schedule in talking with children. For example, if there are less than 10 minutes until cleanup, the child who has decided to carry a tub of digging equipment to the sandbox may need guidance: "I notice that you want to use some digging tools. It is nearly time for cleanup. Take out one shovel and one pail. Then there will be less to put away."

3. **Know how all normal routines are implemented in the program in which you are working**. Learn the typical ways of handling arrival or departure, diapering or toileting, meals, naps or rests, movement in hallways, all group assemblies, and other regular program events. Adhere to established routines as much as possible. After children learn the routines and understand the behavioral expectations, they will most likely behave in socially appropriate ways.

4. **Make on-the-spot adjustments as needed to support children's appropriate behavior.** Refrain from rushing or hurrying children during transitions. Instead, start the cleanup or the beginning of the transition sequence earlier than the scheduled time if the activity is obviously going to take longer than normal. Make small adjustments on your own, or check with other staff for anything greater than 5 to 10 minutes.

Supporting Children's Attempts to Plan, Implement Plans, and Assess Them Using Environmental Resources

Children have their own social goals and their own ideas of how, when, where, and with whom resources should be used. This means that there are many opportunities for adults to help children in making plans throughout the day and from day to day in their programs. Planning for the use of resources is one of the most useful skills that children can develop.

1. **Identify opportunities for children's participation in planning**. Help children identify problems in the course of daily activity (Who gets the next turn? How many people can be at the snack table at once? What will we build with the blocks?). Let them solve these dilemmas for themselves when they cannot endanger themselves or others. Assist them in reflecting on their choices and the consequences of what they have chosen to do.

2. **Use behavior and affective reflections to help children clarify the problem**. Use reflections to assist children in sorting out the feelings of the moment, which get in the way of children's clear thinking. Observe, listen, and consider what the children's purposes are, and construct your reflections accordingly.

3. **Assist children in identifying possible alternatives**. Use open-ended questions as necessary. "What ideas do you have?" "What do you think we can do about this?" "How long do you think that will take?" "What other people might like to do this or play?" "Is there another alternative?" and "How much more room do you need to do that?" are examples of open-ended questions. Avoid contributing your ideas to the solution of their problem. Do not take the initiative and the ownership of the problem away. Help children identify possible alternatives. Listen respectfully to their ideas, even the unlikely ones. For instance, Kendal and Erica were putting train tracks down that ran into the pathway where other children were passing. After the problem was pointed out to them, they suggested several alternative ideas to the congestion in the pathway:

- Continue building as they had, but let others step over their train.
- Move a table to deflect the people traffic around them.
- Make signs about a railroad crossing and put them on chairs on either side of the intersection.
- Change the direction of the railroad to avoid getting in the pathway.

4. **Encourage children to make specific plans to implement their decisions**. Ask leading questions such as: "How will you do this?" or "What materials will you need?" or "Are there other ways to accomplish the same thing?" or "What steps will you need to take to be able to do this?"

What choices might you offer this child?

5. **Provide sufficient time for children to cooperate in planning group efforts or making complex plans**. Listen attentively to ideas; avoid rushing to completion. Schedule planning time into the day to avoid the sense of being hurried. Make decisions yourself if there is not time for the group to carry out the process. Avoid imposing your choices on children when you have told them that they can choose.

6. **After children have generated alternatives and determined the plan of action, review the plan with them**. If there are several hours between planning and implementation, review it again. Write down what they are planning to do. Draw a plan if space and furnishings are involved. Such drawings are very rough but can convey the idea. For example, some 4-year-olds want two "houses" to play neighbors. When they ask the teacher, she asks them to share their ideas with her and eventually with the larger group of children. To do this, they sketch a map of where things might be put.

   Ask older children to discuss with you or write out a plan to correct their own behavior when they have difficulty with their social interactions with others. Assist them to organize and think through a course of action in regard to their behavior and to develop a concrete map to follow.

7. **Use reflections and open-ended questions to support children's evaluations of their plans**. For example, was the child satisfied with the process? ("You figured out a way to . . .") Did the outcome meet his or her expectations? ("You have rearranged the playhouse into two playhouses. Tell me how you think that is working.") Consider the process successful if the plan is satisfying to the children and the implementation of it meets the needs that generated it "well enough." Accept their plans, even though they are not likely to be what you imagine. Assist the child in the group who is less satisfied than another. This, too, is typical of any planning group. Allow older children more time to assess their plans to foster transfer in future challenges they will meet.

Supporting Children's Social Competence through Careful Supervision

1. **Maintain a global perspective of all people in the environment as well as those closest to you**. Observe all children carefully by rapid scanning, being alert to noise and smell. Note all children and adults present before focusing in on the children nearest you. Watch for

children having difficulties with materials or other children. Note the needs of other adults as they are engaged in interactions so that you may supply materials or give assistance as needed. Try to avoid daydreaming or other intruding ideas when supervising children as needs arise quickly that require your attention. Turn your cell phone off, and do not text while with the children!

2. **Situate your body so that you can view the whole area and all of the children**. Usually have your back to a wall, a corner, or a boundary. If seated in an area where visibility is limited, stand up occasionally. Reorient when you hear unusual noise or notice unexpected movement.

3. **Take action if necessary to protect children**. Adjust the blocks if they appear to be unstable. Retrieve a toddler if the child has managed to open a gate and go through. Ask unfamiliar adults if you can help them if they remain in the vicinity of the playground awhile. (The person may or may not be a threat to the children.) If safety is the issue, always act without delay. If another adult is closer and is moving into the situation, return to your place, scan the whole area, and continue your activity. If an accident should occur, reassure the other children, and continue with the program.

4. **Check carefully that all adults and children are present and accounted for during "inclement weather" drills and fire drills**. Count them before you leave the classroom to move to a safer area and when you get there. (When children are frightened, they may hide in a place that makes them feel secure rather than moving with the group.) Regular drills enable children to predict the sequence of events.

5. **Modify the use of materials, space, or equipment as needed to support social goals for children**. There are only three things you can do: You may add materials, equipment, or space, you may remove or limit materials, and you may alter the space in some way. Review the guidelines that were set forth earlier in this chapter for making modifications to the environment.

Sharing Useful Structuring Ideas with Families

1. **Suggest structuring strategies to behavioral problems that parents bring to your attention.** Structuring the environment to promote appropriate behaviors is applicable to many situations that parents encounter. Strategies that are used for children in groups may be modified and applied to family situations. Following are some fairly typical experiences with some structuring possibilities that might make family life more pleasant.

2. **Share ideas about dealing with behavioral issues.**

   - **Toileting accidents:** Can the child easily walk to the toilet, remove clothing, and get on and off the toilet easily and independently? Do these accidents generally occur at the same time of day or in the same conditions, such as when they are outside? Modify clothing, add a small stool, or monitor the reminders given children.

   - **Rough-house play or noisy interaction in the car:** This behavior is very distracting and potentially dangerous. Family members may add something for the children to do. There are numerous small games that children can play while riding.

   - **Sibling fighting or older children hitting younger ones:** This usually occurs when the younger child intrudes on the older child's space or possessions. Parents can clarify which things are personal possessions, which belong to both, and where each is stored. They also can provide opportunities in which either child is free from intrusion.

   - **Cleaning up play space:** Principles related to storage and schedules apply here. Children need a warning that play is finished at home as well as school and are able to learn a standard that is acceptable at home. Young children should help, and eventually they will learn how to do this if they can see where things are to be placed. Open shelves and plastic containers at home work well.

3. **Communicate with family members about any major changes in the child's group membership, room arrangements, daily schedule, or equipment and furnishings**. When parents know about changes in advance, they are able to reassure the child. They are also less likely to experience distress than if they discover the changes all on their own. In childcare or school settings, when older toddlers move from the comfortable room they know into a new group of preschool children, both the children and the parents should be part of this transition. Adding a loft to a kindergarten in the middle of a semester is stressful, although usually it is seen very positively. Usually changes that involve the group are communicated in a newsletter, and changes that involve an individual are communicated in person or on the phone.

4. **Tell family members how structuring is used to support the children's appropriate behavior in the group setting**. After listening to your ideas, parents can adapt them at home. For example, seating in a classroom often supports friendship. Noting this effect of physical closeness, parents might consider inviting children who live nearby to come to their homes for play. Separating materials for older and younger children is another easily transferable idea.

5. **Structure family members' arrival, observation or participation, and dismissal so that they and their children have a successful experience**. Some mothers breastfeed their infants in workplace childcare programs; therefore, a secluded area and a chair with armrests are most comfortable. New parents may want to observe their children, whereas others may want to visit the program for short periods and leave again. Parents who volunteer in grade school may want to observe their child during a session. Regardless of parental needs, professionals should structure these events so that parents, children, and staff are all comfortable with the plan.

6. **Invite parents to participate in events that contribute to the maintenance and beauty of the facility**. Periodic yard cleanup days or paint-and-fix days (held for 3 or 4 hours, two to four times a year) contribute to the quality of the program at a lower cost than if carried out by contractors or hiring additional employees. These events are usually done by nonprofit organizations but may also be implemented by public schools or public parks. If carefully structured, adults enjoy themselves and feel very positive about contributing to their child's program.

7. **Ask family members to contribute materials or equipment to the program**. Paper rolls, fabric scraps, wood scraps, plastic food trays, baby food jars, film canisters, wrapping paper, holiday cards, and many other materials that are often discarded can be used for activities with the children. Dress-up clothing, computers, toys in good repair, or surplus household items that might be sold may also be willingly contributed. If you are soliciting contributions, write a very specific request to parents.

   - State clearly the acceptable conditions such as "a doll carriage in good working order," "clean baby food jars with the labels removed."
   - Accept all contributions with thanks, gracefully and individually.
   - Avoid making an issue if parents are unable or unwilling to provide materials requested by the program that may be costly, such as snacks, crayons, paper, glue sticks, pencils, cleaning supplies, and so on. Make sure that all children have access to resources equally.

Pitfalls to Avoid naeyc

In structuring the physical environment to enhance children's social development, there are certain pitfalls you should avoid.

1. **Making too many changes at once**. Children need security and predictability. Even though you may think of several major alterations to make, such as making adaptations to the daily schedule or rearranging the room, it is best to implement one change at a time.

2. **Expecting children to adapt to change instantly.** Younger children are more upset than older children by major changes in routine and environment. Sometimes, when new materials are added, rooms are changed, or schedules are altered, children experience feelings of confusion or disruption. With patience and structuring support from you, children will eventually adapt to the change, and activities will proceed more smoothly. This takes time, so it is important not to "give up" too soon.

3. **Failing to supervise**. Never leave children unattended by an adult. Children may misuse materials usually considered safe. Even if you are gone just for a minute, a situation that could endanger a child may occur at that time. In addition, children may lose interest and behave inappropriately.

4. **Directing rather than guiding when supervising children**. Occasionally, adults are more focused on the product than on the children doing the activity. Therefore, they tend to make all the decisions, establish the standards of what is good enough, and tell children what to do and how to do it at all points. Directing is only the best choice when an issue of health or safety is involved. If adults direct too much, they diminish children's autonomy, confidence, and feelings of competence.

5. **Inserting your own alternatives for decisions or contributing too much to children's planning too early**. Adults tend to take over the process of the planning from children by offering too much help too soon. Wait for the children to ask, then review some of their ideas, and

ask for other ideas. Let them develop and discard unworkable solutions. Approach this knowing that lots of ideas can be considered, even those that are unlikely to work. Taking over undermines children's self-confidence and their trust in you.

6. **Giving unnecessary or overly detailed directions**. Adults sometimes give too many directions when children are already competent to do the task. This may lead to children tuning out the adult. Keep directions simple and direct. When in doubt, ask children if they know how to do the task.

7. **Confusing situations that require setting limits with those that require giving directions**. If a child knows how to do a task or knows the expectations of behavior and chooses not to follow through, then limit-setting is appropriate. Do not give directions repeatedly as a means of trying to achieve compliance; however, if the child does not appear to know how to do the task, give directions repeating them if necessary. The key here is to judge the child's previous experience and knowledge.

8. **Assuming that a child knows how to do a routine**. Learn to distinguish whether a child does not know how to do something or is refusing to do it. Children do not automatically know how to dress, undress, wash, put away materials, get food in a school cafeteria, or clean cupboards. If you are supervising a child, teach the child how to do a task correctly rather than criticizing the child's best effort. Comments such as "Didn't your mother teach you anything?" "If you can't do it right, don't do it at all" or "Can't you even wipe a table? I'll do it myself" are all inappropriate. Instead, use comments like, "You are having a hard time with that. I'll show you how, and you can finish it."

9. **Assuming that the observations of support staff are not important**. Support staff members are usually working near the children and can see how they are functioning in an area and with the materials. It is their responsibility to share this information with the group leader who then can work toward more effective planning. If you are the head teacher, encourage support staff to share what they observe and find ways to make this a regular part of the program. If you are in a support role, be observant and share your observations with your head teacher or others in charge.

Summary

The processes of structuring to achieve the goals of social competence were discussed in this chapter. Preparing a physical environment that is efficient and pleasant reduces fatigue, promotes independent behavior, and facilitates interaction. Organizing the materials, furnishings, and equipment can minimize interpersonal conflict in the group as well as support safe learning opportunities. Planning and implementing change that is goal-directed may be time consuming, but it leads to satisfaction for both children and adults.

General structuring processes were applied specifically to time management in programs for children. Special consideration was given to the importance of predictability and routine for children's sense of security and emotional adjustment to the environment.

Transitions are generally unsettling for children, but there are strategies to promote appropriate behavior.

Principles of structuring also were applied to the selection, storage, and use of materials and to the arrangement of space. The quality of the environment influences social interaction among children and adults. Skills were described for establishing and changing room arrangements, supervising children, and promoting efficient use of materials. Techniques were presented for adding to or subtracting from the environment as a means to facilitate social interaction.

Finally, pitfalls were introduced to highlight potential problems in altering the environment, possibly making it more challenging for the children and adults interacting within the setting. With practice and patience such pitfalls can be avoided.

Key Terms

activity space	large-group space	simple–complex dimension
boundaries	learning centers	small-group space
directing	open–closed dimension	soft–hard dimension
high mobility–low mobility	private space	structuring
intrusion–seclusion dimension	schedules	transition

Discussion Questions

1. Explain why professionals structure the environment and how they do it as simply as they can so that someone who is a novice in working with young children can understand.

2. Describe how you would apply the structuring process to the problem of disruptive, noisy, or difficult transitions from free play to a story-listening experience.

3. Why might the standards of order and efficiency differ among similar kinds of programs in different settings?

4. Explain the role of communication between adults who rearrange a room or make major changes in the schedule of the day. Identify various strategies by which ideas can be shared and situations in which the adult-to-adult communication about structuring might be problematic.

5. Discuss the importance of knowing and following a predictable schedule. Why would it be important not to ignore it or to deviate from it frequently?

6. Explain how the management of time is related to children's social and emotional development. Is it important throughout childhood? Why?

7. Explain the importance of having a private space in programs for groups of children.

8. Think back over your own childhood and recall instances in which you were denied opportunities to make choices. How did you feel? How did you behave? Did the adults make explanations to you? How did they behave?

9. Write a letter that could be sent to family members asking for materials for the program or asking them to participate in a volunteer workday. Make the letter friendly and inviting, as well as very specific. Exchange your letter with a classmate and discuss the differences and reasons for those differences.

10. Referring to Appendix A, NAEYC Code of Ethical Conduct, determine which of the situations listed here would constitute an ethical problem, and identify the principles and ideals that influence your thinking.

    a. Showing up 20 minutes after you were expected without calling in advance in a program with young children

    b. Failing to mention that the gate to the fenced playground is broken

    c. Letting a preschool child carry a pot of very hot water

    d. Scooping the pieces of many sets of materials together and dumping them in one container to make cleanup faster

    e. Failing to have images of adults and children of all racial groups and some disabling conditions available to children

    f. Moving a toddler from the infant/toddler room to a preschool room without informing the parent or preparing the child

Case Study Analysis

Read the case study in Appendix B about Eisa, a dual-language learner, and consider the following:

1. How did the teacher structure the situation prior to Fan joining the classroom in order to make Eisa more comfortable?

2. How might the teacher structure Eisa's time in the classroom differently from the other children's at the beginning to make her more comfortable and to make learning more developmentally appropriate?

3. How/when can the teacher possibly structure dyads of children to work together so that Eisa is able to get acquainted with her classmates?

4. In what ways did the teacher create pathways for communication with Eisa's parents? What suggestions did she give to Fan's parents that could have a positive influence on Eisa's success in the classroom?

5. What could the teacher add to the classroom to reflect Eisa's culture?

Field Assignments

1. Supervise a group of children doing a simple activity. Later, write out a description of how you checked, adjusted the environment, and guided the children. Evaluate your own performance.

2. Observe any program for children, and note the daily schedule as posted. Compare it to what actually happened. What adjustments were made and why? How did the children know when to make a transition? Describe in detail the transitions you observed, identifying what adults said and did and how children responded.

3. Make a visit to an early childhood program. Draw a detailed floor plan of one of the rooms. List the strengths and weaknesses of the room arrangement in relation to children's social development. Suggest improvements in the physical layout.

Reflect on Your Practice

Here is a sample checklist you can use to reflect on your use of the skills as a beginning professional. A more detailed classroom observation tool is available in Appendix C.

Teachers who structure the physical environment to support children's social development and learning:

✓ Develop a prepared, safe environment.

✓ Participate in all aspects of daily classroom activity.

✓ Demonstrate the ability to coordinate own actions with those of other teachers in the classroom.

✓ Foresee potential problems and act to prevent them.

✓ Maintain a global view of the environment.

✓ Prepare children for major changes in the day.

✓ Childproof the environment.

✓ Present alternatives to children.

✓ Break tasks into manageable steps for children to accomplish.

✓ Offer children appropriate choices.

✓ Give children appropriate responsibilities.

CourseMate. Visit the Education CourseMate for this textbook to access the eBook, Digital Downloads, TeachSource Videos, and quizzes. Go to CengageBrain.com to log in, register, or purchase access.

© Jacky Chapman/Janine Wiedel Photolibrary/Alamy

10 Fostering Self-Regulation in Children: Communicating Expectations and Rules

OBJECTIVES

On completion of this chapter, you should be able to:

Define self-regulation and describe how it comes about.

Discuss how development influences children's capacity for self-regulation.

Explain how experience impacts children's self-regulating capabilities.

Analyze how different approaches to child guidance affect children's behavior and outlooks on life.

Describe what personal messages are and when and how to use them.

Demonstrate effective personal messages in interactions with children.

Identify pitfalls to avoid in communicating expectations and rules.

NAEYC STANDARDS naeyc

1. Promoting Child Development and Learning

2. Building Family and Community Relationships

3. Using Developmentally Effective Approaches to Connect with Children and Families

4. Using Content Knowledge to Build Meaningful Curriculum

5. Becoming a Professional

Help put the blocks away.

Catch your sneeze in your sleeve.

Pet the puppy gently.

Wait your turn.

These are typical expectations children encounter growing up. Although no single standard of behavior is universal, every society has rules like these to keep people safe and to help them get along (Berns, 2013). Adults have primary responsibility for passing this information on to the next generation. We often refer to this as teaching children to behave. Socialization is another term we use to describe this process. Adults socialize children to carry out desirable actions such as sharing, answering politely, and telling the truth. We also socialize children to avoid inappropriate behaviors such as shoving, tattling, spitting on the sidewalk, or taking all the chocolate-covered cherries for themselves. Lessons like these play a key role in children's development of social competence.

How well children learn to adapt their behavior to societal expectations influences how well they function at home, at the center, in school, and in the community at large. Initially, adults play a major role in teaching children right from wrong. In time, we hope children will become more independent, thinking for themselves and monitoring their actions without constant supervision. When that happens, children will have achieved a significant benchmark in human development—self-regulation.

What Is Self-Regulation? naeyc

Casey and William, both third-graders, rush to get to a ball game at the Y. On the way, they come to a huge patch of ground that has been freshly seeded and covered with straw. A large sign announces, "PLEASE STAY OFF THE GRASS." Casey looks around. He's anxious to get to the game but doesn't want to get in trouble for disobeying a rule. Seeing no adults in sight, he quickly cuts across the newly seeded area.

William is in a hurry too. He also notices that no one is around but concludes that stepping on the newly planted grass could damage it. Although he is tempted to take the shortcut across the seeds, he suppresses the impulse and quickly walks around, even though it takes a little more time.

In this situation, both boys were tempted to disregard the sign. Casey gave in to that temptation because no one was there to enforce the rule or to help him choose a better response. His reasoning and actions demonstrated his lack of maturity and self-regulation. William, on the other hand, controlled his desire to dash across the new grass. He made a decision to go around, based on his personal sense of what was right, not because his actions were being monitored by anyone else. This kind of thinking and behaving illustrates self-regulation.

People demonstrate **self-regulation** when they decide that certain actions are right or wrong and then voluntarily behave in ways that match their beliefs (Calkins & Williford, 2009). As you can see, children who regulate their own behavior make judgments based on reasoning, concern for others, and an understanding of acceptable and unacceptable conduct. They do not rely on someone else to make them do the right thing or forbid them from behaving inappropriately. This degree of self-monitoring involves initiating some behaviors and inhibiting others. Consequently, children carry out positive social interactions and implement constructive social plans without having to be told they must. They also resist temptation, curb negative impulses, and delay gratification independent of supervision (Rose-Krasnor & Denham, 2009; Wagner & Heatherton, 2011). Refer to Table 10-1 for examples.

How Self-Regulation Evolves

Self-regulation emerges gradually throughout childhood in an "outside" to "inside" developmental process. Initially, children depend on others to regulate their behavior for them. With time and practice, they eventually demonstrate greater degrees of self-direction (Eisenberg, Smith, & Spinrad, 2011). In this text, we describe this progression as advancing from an amoral orientation to internalization.

Amoral Orientation (No Regulation)

Babies have no inborn concept of right or wrong; they are **amoral**. That is, they are not able to make ethical judgments about their actions or consciously control their behavior in response to moral demands. For instance, baby Leroy reaches for his mother's glasses as they sparkle close by. He does not think about the potential pain he might cause her if he is successful in pulling them off. Nor can he end his investigation merely because his mother frowns or warns him to stop. Leroy has not yet learned how to interpret these parental behaviors or how to adjust his actions in response.

Gradually, through maturation and experience, this complete lack of self-monitoring begins to change. Most toddlers and young preschoolers learn to respond to external cues supplied by parents, caregivers, and teachers to guide their actions. This type of regulation is called adherence.

Table 10-1   Signs of Self-Regulation

Behavior	Examples
Children carry out positive social interactions.	Walter comforts Latosha who is sad over missing her mom. Michael shares his headphones with a newcomer to the listening center.
Children implement constructive social plans.	Marcus wants a turn with the watercolors. He figures out a strategy for getting some, such as trading chalk for paint, and then tries bargaining with another child to achieve his goal. Courtney recognizes that Graham is struggling to carry a dozen hula hoops down to the gym. She helps Graham by taking several hoops from his arms and walking with him downstairs.
Children resist temptation.	Woo-Jin walks all the way over to the trash can to dispose of her sandwich wrapper, although she is tempted simply to drop the crumpled paper on the ground. Juan turns in a change purse he found in the hallway, even though he is tempted to keep it for himself.
Children curb negative impulses.	Ruben suppresses the urge to strike out in anger when Heather runs into him during a soccer game. LaRonda refrains from teasing Richard about the "awful" haircut he got over the weekend.
Children delay gratification.	Carla waits for Tricia to finish talking to the 4-H leader before announcing that she is going to Disney World. Lionel postpones taking another brownie until everyone gets one.

© Cengage Learning 2015

Adherence (External Regulation)

Adherence is the most superficial degree of self-regulation and occurs when people rely on others to monitor their actions for them. Early in life, children need physical assistance in learning how to behave appropriately. Here are some examples:

Baby Leroy's mother puts her glasses beyond the child's reach. Leroy can no longer pull at them.

Three-year-old Nary is running in the classroom. The teacher takes her hand and walks with her to the block area, helping her to slow down.

The playground supervisor separates two kindergartners who are pushing to get on the swing next. The children stop pushing.

Gradually, children also learn to respond to verbal cues about what to do and what not to do. For example:

When Gary, age 4, takes three cookies at snack, the provider says, "Remember you may have two cookies to start." Gary puts one cookie back.

When Nary runs in the classroom, the teacher reminds her to walk. Nary slows down.

The teacher's aide provides Morris with a script he can use to tell another child he wants a turn on the swing instead of pushing. Morris says, "Can I go next?"

In each of these situations, adults provided controls children were unable to supply completely on their own.

Another form of adherence occurs when children act in certain ways either to gain rewards or to avoid negative consequences (Laible & Thompson, 2008; Bear, 2010). For instance, 3-year-old Hannah has had numerous "sharing lessons" in her short lifetime. She has been rewarded with smiles and praise when she voluntarily hands a toy to a peer or sibling. She also has experienced negative consequences, frowns and warnings, for failing to share with playmates or for wrenching toys from others. Based on episodes like these, Hannah is slowly beginning to differentiate desirable and undesirable behaviors. However, rewards and consequences alone do not provide enough information for Hannah to acquire all the reasoning she will need to act appropriately on her own. At adherence, she has no real understanding of why sharing is good; she simply knows it is expected. Although she may share her crayons with a peer, her behavior is influenced by her desire for a reward, not by concern for the other child's rights. Under these circumstances, Hannah will likely share when an adult is present. However, if mom or the teacher is unavailable to monitor the situation, Hannah may find it difficult to share and resort to hitting or grabbing to protect her crayons.

This is the drawback to adherence. Children who rely on external controls need constant support and

These children identify with their teacher and try to clean the brushes just like she showed them.

supervision to behave appropriately. When such controls are missing, they do not know what to do. Thus, adherence is an important step in the maturation process but does not represent a desirable end unto itself.

Identification (Shared Regulation)

A more advanced degree of self-regulation occurs when children adopt certain codes of behavior so they can be like someone they admire. Through the process of identification, children imitate the conduct, attitudes, and values of important people in their lives (Kalish & Cornelius, 2006). Children's compliance with certain expectations may also be a strategy for establishing or preserving satisfying relationships with these special people. In either case, children adopt certain mannerisms, words, and ways of behaving to feel closer to people they revere.

Typically, children identify with parents or other family members. Teachers and caregivers are also sources of identification. In every case, the persons with whom children identify are nurturing, powerful people—usually adults or older children (Maccoby, 2007; Bjorklund, 2012).

Identification advances children's development. It moves them beyond the simple formula of rewards and punishments and provides them with many of the ideals and standards they will carry with them into adulthood. However, children who share things as a result of identification use sharing as a way to further personal aims—confirming their similarity to an admired person who advocates sharing or pleasing that person through their actions. They still do not recognize the inherent fairness in sharing or the real needs of the person to whom they lend something briefly. Also, children governed by identification rely

on second-guessing how someone else might behave in a given situation. If they have never seen the model in a similar circumstance, children may not know what to do and lack the means to figure it out on their own.

Internalization (Internal Regulation)

Internalization is the most advanced degree of self-regulation. When people treat certain expectations as logical extensions of their own beliefs and personal values, we say they have internalized those expectations (Epstein, 2009). It is this internal code that guides their actions from one circumstance to another. The course of action they choose is aimed at avoiding self-condemnation rather than acquiring external rewards or gaining approval from others. People whose behaviors fall within the internalization category understand the reasons behind certain behavior standards and feel a moral commitment to act in accordance with those standards. They also recognize how specific actions fit into larger concepts such as justice, honesty, and equity. Individuals who reason according to internalized beliefs take into account the impact

Ian waits patiently for Xavier to finish. This is an example of self-regulation.

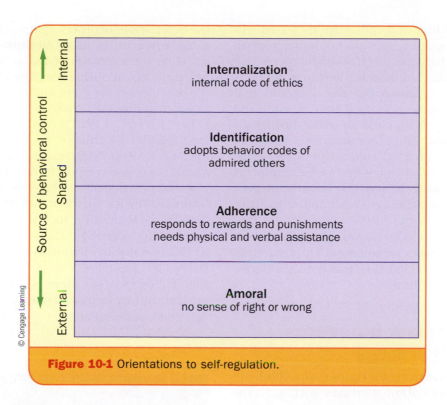

Figure 10-1 in box:

- **Internalization** internal code of ethics
- **Identification** adopts behavior codes of admired others
- **Adherence** responds to rewards and punishments needs physical and verbal assistance
- **Amoral** no sense of right or wrong

Left axis: Source of behavioral control; Internal ↑ / Shared / External ↓

© Cengage Learning

Figure 10-1 Orientations to self-regulation.

their behavior will have on others. For instance, Mariah, who has internalized the value of sharing, will offer to give another child some of her crayons, not because the teacher said so or because anyone else is watching, but because sharing seems the appropriate thing to do. Engaging in this positive action makes Mariah feel good. She enjoys knowing another child will have a chance to draw too. Similarly, Ian wants a turn with the drum synthesizer, but Xavier is using it. He watches and waits as Xavier explores the different sounds. Eventually, it is his turn. His waiting without prompting from anyone else is a sign of self-regulation and social maturity.

After children have internalized an expectation, they have a guide for how to behave appropriately in all kinds of circumstances, even unfamiliar ones. Understanding the reasons for certain rules enables children to weigh the pros and cons of alternate actions and to choose behaviors that match their ideals. This eliminates the need for constant supervision. Children can be depended on to regulate their own behavior. Most importantly, internalized behaviors are long lasting. Children who adopt beliefs in justice, honesty, or fairness as their own abide by those ideals long after their contacts with certain adults are over and in spite of temptation or the opportunity to break the rule without being discovered (Rose-Krasnor & Denham, 2009). Thus, Mariah may eventually adopt additional prosocial behaviors beyond sharing (such as cooperating or comforting) because helping others

feels like the "right" thing to do. Ian may exercise patience and delay gratification in other circumstances because he thinks it's important for people to get a "fair" turn.

Figure 10-1 provides a summary of the amoral, adherence, identification, and internalization orientations to self-regulation just described.

Self-regulation evolves gradually. It takes many years for children to develop an internalized code of conduct. Preschoolers show lesser degrees of self-regulation than do children in the upper-elementary grades (Epstein, 2009). Although toddlers are able to comply with simple requests and commands, they mostly rely on external controls to guide their actions. As children form relationships with nurturing adults, identification gradually becomes a more significant factor in what motivates children to behave in certain ways. With time (there is no way to predict exactly how much), increasing numbers of children demonstrate internalization of commonly held rules, such as taking turns at the snack table or walking in the hallway. By the later elementary years, children's capacities for self-regulation have expanded greatly, and they are better able to monitor their own actions in both typical and novel situations (DeVries & Zan, 2003; Siegler, DeLoache, & Eisenberg, 2011).

Children progress toward self-regulation at varying rates and in varying degrees. Even though we can expect children to demonstrate increased self-regulation as they mature, they do not move from an amoral orientation to higher levels of conduct according to a strict age-related timetable. Research supports a developmental progression but also indicates that children achieve greater self-regulation at rates and in degrees that vary from child to child (Kochanska & Aksan, 2006; Bear, 2010). For instance, 4-year-old Lucille may require physical support to share, while Sandra, also 4 years of age, may find verbal reminders enough to do the same. It may take months or even years before Carl learns to curb his impulse to strike out at someone who teases him, whereas Joseph may grasp this notion much sooner. Throughout childhood, such behavior differences are common. This means the children you encounter will vary widely in the degree of self-regulation they display.

How Development Influences Self-Regulation naeyc

There are many developmental reasons why children's capacity for self-regulation increases with age. The most notable of these are changes in children's emotional development, cognitive development, language development, and memory skills.

Emotional Development

Emotions provide children with strong internal signals about what is appropriate or inappropriate behavior. As children learn to pay attention to these signals, their ability to monitor their actions increases. Two emotions that strongly contribute to self-regulation are guilt and empathy (Kochanska & Aksan, 2006; Eisenberg, Fabes, & Spinrad, 2006). **Guilt** feelings warn children that current, past, or planned actions are undesirable. These feelings serve as a brake, telling children to slow down or reconsider what they are doing. **Empathy**, which involves understanding other people's emotions by experiencing those same feelings oneself, conveys the opposite message. It prompts children to initiate positive actions in response to someone's feelings. We can see empathy at work when a child comforts an unhappy peer or offers to share or take turns so another child will not be disappointed. Children as young as 3 years are capable of both guilt and empathy (Pinker, 2008). However, these emotions are aroused by different events for younger and older children.

Guilt. The situations that arouse guilt evolve from simple, concrete incidents in toddlerhood to abstract, complex situations in later adolescence (Thompson, 2006). Initially, children feel guilty over their transgressions—actions that violate known rules and

the expectations of others. Spilling their milk, damaging a toy while using it, or stealing something from a classmate are examples of the actions children might feel guilty about during the early childhood period. In the later elementary years, children report feeling guilty when their inaction leads to distress for others. This is why Thomas, a fifth grader, might feel guilty when classmates tease a child on the playground, and he does nothing to stop it. By middle school, an increasing number of children report feeling guilty over neglecting responsibilities, such as forgetting to let the dog out before leaving for school or failing to attain ideals they have set for themselves such as making the track team or achieving a certain grade point average (Mills, 2005). As children mature, the main things that make people feel guilty are related to personal standards, rather than failing to satisfy other people's expectations. This gradual shift in focus contributes to the inner controls needed for self-regulation.

Ramone mirrors Jemma's delight in choosing a shape. This is an example of empathy.

© Cengage Learning

Empathy. The beginnings of empathy are also present early in life (Thompson & Goodman, 2009). For instance, many babies cry upon hearing or seeing the cries of other babies. They also laugh when other babies laugh. In other words, infants mimic other children's emotional states. Between 1 and 2 years of age, infants' imitative reactions grow into more genuine feelings of concern for a particular person. At this age, children also recognize that some action is required as part of their response. This is demonstrated when one toddler pats another who is crying as a result of falling down. In the later preschool and early elementary years, children make more objective assessments of other people's distress and needs (Eisenberg et al., 2006). They begin to recognize emotional reactions different from their own, and they become more adept at responding in a variety of ways to provide comfort and support. By the time children reach the age of 10 to 12 years, they demonstrate empathy for people with whom they do not interact directly—the homeless, the disabled, or the victims of a disaster. This increased sensitivity to the plight of others contributes to children's expanding capacity for self-regulation.

Cognitive Development

Children's ability to distinguish between appropriate and inappropriate behavior evolves in line with their cognitive powers. As children's cognitive capacities expand, so does their ability to regulate their behavior internally. These evolving capabilities are influenced by children's changing notions of right and wrong, by how well they comprehend other people's perspective, and by the cognitive characteristics of centration and irreversibility.

Children's notions of right and wrong. In toddlerhood, children use rewards and punishments to figure out if their actions or those of another child are right or wrong. They determine that sharing is "good" when sharing is praised, and they find out that writing in picture books is "wrong" when they are corrected for such behavior. As these lessons unfold, children also discover that not all transgressions are treated equally.

By 3 and 4 years of age, children realize that punching your sister elicits a much stronger negative reaction from adults than does something like coming to the table with dirty hands. Through many such experiences, preschoolers begin to make distinctions between moral violations (lying, stealing, hurting others) and social-conventional infractions (poor table manners, greeting someone improperly, or speaking rudely) (Smetana, 2006; Yau & Smetana, 2003). By the time they reach kindergarten, children classify actions as "very wrong" if they result in physical harm to people or property (hitting people or breaking things) or if they violate people's rights such as someone missing a turn or not

getting an equal share of something (Turiel, 2006). On the other hand, children categorize actions that disrupt the social order of the group, such as forgetting to say "please" or not putting toys away as "not very wrong." In both cases, children's focus is on the here and now, and they do not routinely think about how their current actions might impact people or property in the future.

Older children (ages 8 and up) use more sophisticated reasoning in thinking about rules and expectations. They expand their definitions of hurtful behavior beyond physical actions to include psychological impacts such as hurting people's feelings, betraying secrets, or violating another person's trust. They recognize the need for maintaining some form of social order to protect the rights of individuals and the group. Children at this stage also take into account long-term as well as immediate outcomes in judging if an action is right or wrong. Thus, fourth graders recognize that cheating at a game may yield a short-term positive result such as winning but ultimately lead to dishonor for yourself and for your team, making cheating a "wrong" choice.

Refer to Highlight 10-1 to see how children's thinking about right and wrong relates to their day-to-day behavior.

© Cengage Learning

HIGHLIGHT 10-1

The Link between Moral Thinking and Moral Behavior
Thinking and doing are not the same!

At circle time, Ms. Wilson asks a group of 3-year-olds, "Is it okay to hit people to get what you want?" The children answer in chorus, "NO!" Ms. Wilson makes another query. "Is it a good idea to share?" In unison, the whole group shouts, "YES!" The children clap their hands in approval.

Conversations like this show that even very young children recognize the desirability of moral standards such as human welfare, justice, and preserving people's rights. In fact, these are moral orientations children share worldwide (Neff & Helwig, 2002). Yet, early in life, knowing what is right and doing what is right are not synonymous. Young children are impulsive; their actions are not always guided by rational thought. What is easy for them to say in the relaxed atmosphere of circle time is quickly forgotten in the heat of an action-filled encounter. This makes the link between moral thinking and moral action weak for preschoolers and children in the early elementary years. As children mature and gain the developmental understandings and skills described in this chapter, the connection between thinking right and doing right becomes stronger and stronger.

Table 10-2 The Emergence of Perspective Taking

3 to 6 years	6 to 8 years	8 to 10 years	10 to 12 years
All ways of seeing the world are like mine.	You would see things my way if we both had the same information.	I can see multiple perspectives but only one at a time.	I can see multiple perspectives simultaneously.

© Cengage Learning

Perspective-taking. To interact effectively and to make accurate judgments about how to behave in particular situations, children must understand what other people think, feel, or know. This requires children to form a mental image of what the world looks like to someone else (Epstein, 2009). Called **perspective-taking**, the capacity to consider others' points of view is not fully developed in young children. As is true for other dimensions of development, children gradually progress from simplistic, egocentric notions to more sophisticated, other-oriented understandings (Johansson, 2006).

Children 3 to 6 years of age and younger are relatively unaware of perspectives other than their own. As a result, they often have difficulty putting themselves in another person's shoes. This is especially true when that person's views conflict with the child's own. Children erroneously assume that their interpretation of events is universal. ("I think building a road with these blocks is a good idea. You must think so too.")

Between 6 and 8 years of age, children are more likely to realize that someone else's interpretation of a situation may be different from their own. However, they commonly assume that such variations exist only because each person has access to different information. ("If you just knew how many cars we could fit on this road, or how big a road we could build, or the awesome tunnel we could add to this road, you would want to build a road too.") It is hard for them to realize that people can genuinely come to different conclusions.

Eight- to ten-year-olds recognize that their own perspectives and the perspectives of another person may be contradictory, even if they both possess the same information. However, they tend to think about their own view and other people's views alternately, making it hard for them to address multiple perspectives within the same situation ("I think we should divide the tickets. Jerome says that's unfair. This is confusing.")

Ten- through twelve-year-olds are able to differentiate their own perspective from that of other people and are able to consider the two points of view simultaneously. They can also speculate about what other people currently are thinking or what they might think in the future. These abilities help children bet-ter determine how to behave in an increasingly varied number of situations. ("Jerome and I have different ideas about how to solve this problem. If I insist on my idea, that might hurt Jerome's feelings. We could combine our ideas, or we could try one and then the other to see which one works best.")

The developmental sequence of children's perspective-taking abilities is summarized in Table 10-2.

Centration. Early in life, children tend to direct their attention to one primary attribute of a situation, ignoring most others (Shaffer, 2009). This phenomenon, known as **centration**, restricts children's ability to see the big picture and to generate alternate solutions to problems. Thus, young children have a limited rather than comprehensive perception of events. This explains why children may try the same unsuccessful strategy repeatedly (e.g., saying "please" over and over even though the other children keep saying "no"). It is also why they have difficulty shifting their attention from one facet of an interaction ("She knocked over my blocks" or "He has all the gold glitter paint") to another ("She was trying to help me stack the blocks higher" or "There are several other colors of glitter paint from which to pick").

Even when children recognize that actions such as whining are inappropriate, they may be unable to generate suitable alternate behaviors at the moment such thinking is needed. The younger the child, the more this is so. Likewise, the more emotional the situation is for the child, the more difficult it is for him or her to think about other approaches. Decentering occurs only gradually, as children are confronted with multiple perceptions and methods of resolution. Adults enhance the process when they point out options to children and when they help children brainstorm suitable alternatives as relevant circumstances arise (Goleman, 2006). Such supports continue to be helpful well into adolescence.

Irreversibility. Toddlers and preschoolers do not routinely mentally reverse actions they initiate physically (Shaffer, 2009). In other words, their thinking is **irreversible**. This means they are not proficient at readily thinking of an opposite action for something they are actually doing. If they are pushing, it is hard for them to pull instead; if they are reaching for something, it's a challenge to draw back. Young children also have difficulty spontaneously interrupting an ongoing behavior. For example, if a child is in the act of hitting, she might complete the hitting action before reversing it either by taking her hand away or dropping it to her side. Irreversibility is evident in Jennifer's reaction to her caregiver's directions at the art table.

Jennifer, a 3-year-old, was busy gluing dry leaves to her collage. In her effort to get to the bottom of the glue bottle, she tipped it upside down, and the glue ran all over. The caregiver said, "Don't tip the bottle." Jennifer continued gluing, and the glue kept dripping.

When the adult called out her warning, she assumed Jennifer knew how to reverse tipping the bottle. To the adult, it was obvious that returning the jar to an upright position was the reverse of holding it upside down. However, young children have not had enough experience to picture in their minds how to transpose a physical action. For this reason, adults must help preschoolers reverse inappropriate acts by showing them or telling them how to do it. The same holds true for older children in unfamiliar situations. For instance, elementary-aged children are better able to halt or slow down if an adult says, "Don't run in the hall"; they are less likely to respond successfully in a situation that is new to them or that takes place in unfamiliar surroundings.

Language and Memory Development

Not only is the capacity for self-regulation affected by children's emotional development and cognitive capabilities, but language, private speech, and memory play roles in the process too.

Language. The phenomenal rate of language acquisition during the early childhood years plays a major role in the development of internal behavior controls. This is because language contributes to children's understanding of why rules are made and gives them more tools for attaining their goals in socially acceptable ways. By the time they are 3 years old, most children have command of a well-developed receptive vocabulary and the ability to express their basic needs. However, they are not always successful at responding to verbal directions or at telling others what they want (Jalongo, 2008). As a result, it is not unusual for younger children to resort to physical actions to communicate. They may grab, jerk away, fail to respond, push, or hit rather than use words to express themselves. At such times, they benefit from adult assistance in determining what to say.

As the elementary years progress, children learn to use language more effectively. They become increasingly successful at telling others what they want and better equipped to understand and respond to verbal instructions, requests, explanations, and reasoning as guides for behavior (Marion, 2011). Consequently, children find words a more satisfactory and precise way to communicate. When this occurs, their physical demonstrations become less frequent and intense. However, there are still times when children in the elementary grades need guidance in determining the best words to use in emotionally charged encounters or in unfamiliar situations.

Private speech. Children also use **private speech** to regulate their behavior (Bodrova & Leong, 2007; Winsler, Naglieri, & Manfra, 2006). That is, they talk out loud to themselves to reduce frustration, postpone

Marcella uses private speech to remind herself of how to put on her socks and shoes.

Table 10-3   Links between Child Development and Teacher Behaviors that Foster Self-Regulation

Because of These Immature Self-Regulation Capacities in Children...	Teachers...
Guilt	Discuss how children's behavior affects themselves and others.
Empathy	Talk about emotions—the child's and others'—and coach children in responding to emotions.
Notions of right and wrong	Provide reasons for expectations and rules.
Perspective taking	Help children recognize how their view of the world may be the same or different from someone else's.
Centration	Help children see the "big picture" and generate alternative solutions in problem situations.
Irreversibility	Show children what to do and phrase their rules in positive terms.
Language	Reason with children, talk children through problem situations, provide physical assistance as necessary, and provide children with relevant scripts.
Private speech	Allow children to talk things through aloud; coach children in self-talk.
Memory	Remind children of expectations and rules.

© Cengage Learning

rewards, or remind themselves of rules. Olga sits down in the writing center and says to no one in particular, "Hmmm, what do I need? I know: paper, pens, and tape." When Abbas begins losing patience putting a model together, he quietly repeats to himself, "Slow down, take your time. You'll get it." This kind of talk is common in early and middle childhood. The normal developmental progression is for toddlers and 3-year-olds to repeat audible rhythmic sounds. Children ages 4 to 7 or 8 years "think out loud" in conjunction with their actions. They generate whole phrases to plan strategies and monitor their actions. Children in the later elementary years mutter single words in barely discernible tones (Winsler & Naglieri, 2003). Studies of children's behavior in problem-solving situations indicate that they rely on private speech most when a task is difficult. Moreover, children's performance typically improves following the self-instruction they provide themselves (Bailey & Brookes, 2003; Winsler, Nagieri, & Manfra, 2006). In adolescence, private speech becomes the silent, inner speech that people use throughout their lives to organize and regulate day-to-day activities. Although private speech is a naturally occurring phenomenon, it appears that children also can be taught to use "self-talk" as a way to help them gain control of their actions.

Memory skills. Memory is another variable that influences self-regulation. Although scientists have not yet determined whether memory actually increases from one year to the next, it does seem that as children grow older, they become better able to use the information they have stored in their memory as a resource for determining future behavior. Consequently, they become less dependent on others to show or tell them how to respond to each new situation. Instead, they use remembered information to guide their actions (Bjorklund, 2012; Golbeck, 2006). This means adults working with children in formal group settings should expect that children will periodically "forget" the rules. Also, children may be unsure of how to respond in unfamiliar circumstances. From toddlerhood through 8 to 9 years of age, children often need frequent reminders about rules and procedures and clear explanations about what to expect when routines change or new activities are introduced.

Older children benefit from periodic reviews of the rules but are better able to remember them without continual adult support. See Table 10-3 for a summary of all the developmental influences just discussed.

How Experience Influences Self-Regulation naeyc

Because most young people experience the developmental changes described previously and thus acquire some of the basics for internalization, the reasons why they vary in compliance can best be attributed to differences in experiences. Children learn the rules of society from others through direct instruction, observation, reinforcement, and negative consequences (Thompson & Twibell, 2009). Infants and preschoolers are chiefly responsive to parents and other adults with whom they have a positive relationship; grade-school children are also influenced by peers.

Direct Instruction

As mentioned earlier in this chapter, adults regulate children's behavior using physical and verbal controls. These are forms of **direct instruction**. At first, adults rely mainly on bodily intervention to keep children safe and help them get along. They separate squabbling siblings, remove dangerous objects from reach, extract forbidden items from children's grasp, and restrain them from dashing across busy streets. These actions usually are accompanied by brief verbal commands such as "Stop," "No," "Give me that," or "Wait for me." Gradually, physical interventions give way to greater reliance on verbal directions and warnings, to which children become increasingly responsive. Typical adult instructions usually fall into the categories outlined in Table 10-4. Verbal instructions are the quickest way to let children know what the appropriate, inappropriate, and alternate behaviors are. They are particularly effective when combined with modeling.

Modeling

Adults **model** a code of conduct through their own actions (Fox & Lentini, 2006). Returning library books on time, helping an injured animal, or resisting the urge to eat a candy bar before supper all convey messages to children about desirable behaviors. Setting a good example is critical in teaching right from wrong. In fact, modeling positive attitudes and constructive ways of interacting with others is the single most effective

© Cengage Learning 2015

Showing children what to do and talking them through your actions is effective modeling.

Table 10-4   Examples of Adult Instruction

Telling Children What Is Right and What Is Wrong

"It hurts the cat when you pull her tail."

"Share your toys."

"Stealing is bad."

Informing Children of Expected Standards

"Pet the cat gently."

"Put your toys away."

"Give Grandma a kiss."

Restricting Certain Behaviors

"Five more minutes on the swing."

"Put on a smock before you start painting."

"Use this tissue, not your sleeve."

Offering Children Strategies for How to Meet Certain Standards

"You could stack all the big plates on one side and the little plates on the other, like this."

"You could use the ball together, or you could take turns."

"If you think about something else, that will make the waiting go faster."

Redirecting Children's Behavior

"Go outdoors. Don't bounce that ball inside."

"That spoon is too big. Try this one."

"Tell him you're angry. Don't bite."

Providing Children with Information about How Their Actions Affect Themselves and Others

"He hit you because you hit him."

"Every time you tease her, she cries."

"Mr. Martin really appreciated you helping him rake the leaves."

Giving Children Information about How Their Behavior Looks to Others

"Comb your hair. People will think I don't take good care of you."

"When you don't say 'Hi' back, he thinks you don't like him."

"When you forget to say 'Thank you,' people don't know you appreciated what they did."

© Cengage Learning

means for transmitting these facets of social competence to young children (Thompson & Twibell, 2009).

Children naturally imitate much of what they see; however, modeling has the most impact when the model's behavior is obvious to children. This means children are better able to imitate a model with whom they can interact or whose behavior is pointed out to them (Kostelnik, 2005). Such coaching helps children to recognize important details that they might otherwise not notice. For instance, if the object is to demonstrate gentle handling of animals, it is best to work directly with the child and demonstrate the task while describing it aloud. "See, I'm touching the guinea pig very gently so I don't hurt him. Look at how softly I'm stroking his back." Simply showing children the proper procedure without a direct explanation may not prompt them to imitate the appropriate behavior themselves later.

Verbal descriptions of modeled behaviors are especially valuable when adults hope children will recognize that someone is resisting temptation or delaying gratification. Those are subtle behaviors that children may not recognize unless they are pointed out. This teacher is verbalizing what she sees to help others recognize Raymond's efforts to delay gratification: "Raymond really wants to use the picture dictionary, even though the college dictionary is available now. He is waiting until Karen has finished with it so he can use it next." This kind of narration goes a long way toward helping children incorporate the model's behavior into their own social strategies.

Reinforcement and Negative Consequences

In addition to instructing children about how to act and modeling appropriate behavior, adults reinforce desirable deeds and penalize those they consider unacceptable. **Reinforcement** involves providing some consequence to a behavior that increases the likelihood the child will repeat that behavior in similar situations. **Negative consequences** are ones that reduce the probability of a particular behavior being repeated. Although the principles of reinforcement and negative consequences are relatively straightforward, appropriate use is complex. For this reason, Chapter 11 is devoted entirely to this subject. For now, it is important merely to recognize that children experience both reinforcement and negative consequences as a result of their behavior and that these play a major role in their becoming self-regulating.

Integrating Development and Experience

The individual interactions children experience each day help them create a unique mental map of the social environment (Coie & Dodge, 1998; Goleman, 2006).

That is, children mentally chart their experiences and make note of which behaviors make them feel guilty, which make them feel good, which are rewarded and which are not, and under what circumstances those conditions apply. Gradually, this map grows in breadth and complexity. Over time, children catalogue a growing number of experiences and make finer discriminations among events. They draw on information gleaned from these episodes to fit their behavior to situational demands rather than depending on other people to direct them. In addition, their increased developmental competence enables them to interpret more accurately the cues they receive and to envision more varied responses to those cues. As a result, they become progressively more successful in monitoring their own behavior.

Gradually, peers also contribute to children's understanding of what constitutes desirable and undesirable behavior. The combined experiences with adults and age-mates lead to greater self-regulation. Interactions

▶❙❙   **TeachSource Video 10-1**

© Cengage Learning 2015

5–11 Years: Moral Development in Middle Childhood

Go online and view *5–11 Years: Moral Development in Middle Childhood*.

In this video, you will see and hear children reason about what makes someone's behavior right or wrong.

1. Which of the four levels of self-regulation (amoral, adherence, identification, or internalization) are represented in the children's rationales?

2. Describe two implications these levels of moral reasoning have in terms of how children might behave?

3. Describe two implications these levels of moral reasoning have for how adults would need to interact with children who reason at these levels.

Watch on CourseMate

with adults teach children about obligations, responsibility, and respect; peer relations give children first-hand experience with cooperation and justice. This difference in perspective is a result of children's general interpretation that positive behavior with adults means obedience, and positive behavior with peers involves reciprocal actions such as sharing or taking turns. This chapter and the next concentrate on the adult's role in helping children achieve self-regulation.

Adult Approaches to Child Guidance naeyc

> Two preschoolers are ramming their trikes into each other on the trike track. What had started as a playful interaction is becoming more forceful and out of control.
>
> Adult 1: Says sternly, "No more ramming. Stop that now!"
>
> Adult 2: Thinks, "They'll work it out. Kids always do."
>
> Adult 3: Barely notices the children's activity.
>
> Adult 4: Carefully pulls the children apart and says in a calm voice, "This started out as fun. Now it looks unsafe. I'm worried someone might get hurt. Let's think of another way to use the trikes."

These adults are exhibiting four different approaches to child guidance. Even though all adults use instruction, modeling, rewards, and negative consequences to teach children how to behave, the combination of techniques they use and the way in which they apply them differ. These variations have been the subject of research since the 1960s. It has been found that the blend of socializa-

tion strategies adults adopt has a major influence on children's personality development and whether children follow rules due to adherence, identification, or internalization. Both short-term and long-range effects have been recorded (Eisenberg et al., 2011; Kochanska et al., 2008). Although most research has focused on parent–child relationships, other adult–child interactions, including ones between children and teachers, have been examined. Much of this work has yielded similar results.

In a series of landmark studies, researchers identified four common adult discipline styles: authoritarian, permissive, uninvolved, and authoritative (Baumrind, 1967, 1991; Maccoby & Martin, 1983). These four styles continue to be the standard for comparison today (Eisenberg et al., 2011). Each is characterized by particular adult attitudes and practices related to the dimensions of control, maturity demands, communication, and nurturance.

- **Control** refers to the manner and degree to which adults enforce compliance with their expectations.
- **Maturity demands** involve the level at which expectations are set.
- **Communication** describes the amount of information offered to children regarding behavior practices.
- **Nurturance** refers to the extent to which adults express caring and concern for children.

Differences among the four styles of child guidance are reflected in the combinations of these dimensions depicted in Figure 10-2. Authoritarian adults are high in control, high in maturity demands, low in communication, and low in nurturance. Permissive

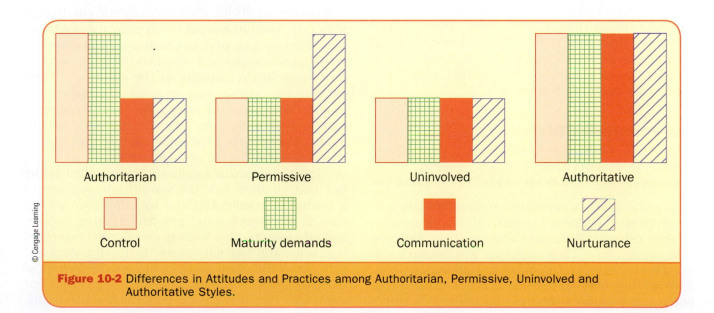

© Cengage Learning

Figure 10-2 Differences in Attitudes and Practices among Authoritarian, Permissive, Uninvolved and Authoritative Styles.

adults are low in control, low in maturity demands, low in communication, and high in nurturance. Uninvolved adults are low in every category. Adults high in all four dimensions are described as "authoritative." Although few people exhibit a "pure" style, adult behaviors tend to cluster according to one pattern or another. Understanding the characteristics of each style and their impact on children will help you begin to develop a style of your own.

The Authoritarian Style

"Do what I tell you," and "Do it because I said so!"

Demands such as these typify the **authoritarian style**. Adults who display this style value children's unquestioning obedience above all else. To achieve the high standards they have for children's conduct, adults become vigilant rule enforcers and spare little time for relationship building. Explanations and reasoning do not fit into their view of themselves as the ultimate authority. Broken rules are dealt with swiftly and forcefully, frequently through ridicule, shame, or physical punishment. Not too surprising, authoritarian adults tend to have cold, distant relationships with children. Children view them as harsh taskmasters who focus more on finding mistakes than on recognizing their attempts to comply. This approach, sometimes referred to as power-assertive discipline, keeps children at the adherence level of moral reasoning (Eisenberg et al., 2011; Dodge, Coe, & Lynam, 2006). Children follow rules out of fear or blind obedience, not out of empathy or concern for others. This hampers their ability to develop the reasoning skills and emotional sensitivity necessary for internalization. In addition, children who interact mostly with authoritarian adults generally become unfriendly, suspicious, resentful, and unhappy. They tend to be underachievers, to avoid their peers, and to exhibit increased incidents of misconduct, as well as more extreme acting-out behaviors (Kochanska et al., 2002, 2008).

The Permissive Style

"Love you! Do what you want."

Adults who display a **permissive style** have warm relationships with children but establish few boundaries on their behavior. Permissive adults are the opposite of authoritarian ones. They emphasize relationship building at the expense of taking action to guide socialization. They see themselves as loving resources to children but not as active agents responsible for shaping children's

present or future behavior. They accept a wide range of children's actions based either on the conviction that external controls thwart children's development or out of uncertainty about how to achieve compliance (Oyserman et al., 2005). Consequently, permissive adults offer little instruction about how to behave. They ignore children's transgressions, make few demands, and seldom give children opportunities to assume responsibility. At those infrequent times when they feel compelled to administer a penalty for gross misconduct, the favored technique is temporary love withdrawal ("I don't like children who hurt people").

Unfortunately, children subjected to this approach show few signs of internalization. Because they receive almost no cues about which behaviors are socially appropriate and which are not, they fail to develop mental guidelines or strategies to draw on in their day-to-day social encounters. Moreover, they have little chance to develop feelings of empathy for others because cause-effect relationships are not explained. Peers and adults often view their unrestrained behavior as immature, inconsiderate, and unacceptable. Such negative perceptions contribute to children's feelings of anxiety and low self-esteem.

As a rule, a child whose world is dominated by permissive adults tends to be withdrawn, unproductive, and unhappy. In adolescence, this style is frequently associated with delinquency and poor academic performance (Hart, Newell, & Olsen, 2003; Steinberg, Blatt-Eisengart, & Cauffman, 2006).

The Uninvolved Style

"Whatever."

Uninvolved adults are indifferent to the children in their care. They do not put much energy into relating to children or into guiding children's social behavior. These grown-ups are self-absorbed, focusing on their own needs at the expense of the children's. Their extreme egocentrism may be a result of depression or stress. Whatever the cause, the **uninvolved style** leads to many of the same outcomes described for children subjected to a permissive approach (Collins & Steinberg, 2006; Kochanska et al., 2008).

Those problematic results are compounded by the fact that children lack the warmth enjoyed within a permissive relationship and so suffer even greater feelings of alienation and problems relating to peers and other adults. This leads to moodiness, feelings of insecurity, and low self-esteem. Disruptive, detached behavior is the norm early in life. As children grow older, they tend to be noncompliant, irresponsible, and immature. They also are low performers academically.

Truancy, delinquency, drug use, and precocious sexuality are common difficulties during the teenage years (Aunola & Nurmi, 2005; Clark & Gross, 2004; Kochanska et al., 2002, 2008). As you might guess, such children lack important experiences that could help them move toward internalization. They tend to remain at the amoral or adherence stages of self-regulation instead.

The Authoritative Style

"I care about you, and I will teach you how to behave."

Adults who adopt an **authoritative style** combine the positive attributes of the authoritarian and permissive styles, while avoiding the negative ones. They also employ some strategies that none of the other styles use, such as clear communication and other-oriented reasoning. Teachers and caregivers who use an authoritative approach encourage children to assume appropriate responsibility and get what they need in socially acceptable ways. When children attempt a new skill, adults acknowledge their efforts; when children face challenges, adults help them develop alternate approaches. Such strategies contribute to children's feelings of competence and worth. At the same time, authoritative adults establish high standards for children's behavior and become actively involved in teaching them how to pursue those standards successfully. Explanations, demonstrations, suggestions, reasoning, and redirection are examples of the strategies they use. When children misbehave, authoritative adults treat such episodes as teachable moments in which to discuss guilt, empathy, and the perspectives of others (Russel, Mize, & Bissaker, 2004; Bear, 2010). They also provide on-the-spot coaching to help children recognize acceptable and unacceptable behaviors as well as potential alternatives. This non-punitive form of child guidance is sometimes called *inductive discipline* because adults induce children to regulate their behavior on the basis of the impact their actions will have on themselves and others.

The authoritative approach to child guidance is the style most strongly related to the development of self-regulation (Domitrovich et al., 2011; Fox & Lentini, 2006; Milevsky et al., 2007). Children feel secure in the knowledge that there are people in the world who care for and about them. They know what is expected of them and have many chances to learn how to behave accordingly. Most importantly, children have access to the information and models they need to progress from adherence, to identification, to internalization. Under these circumstances, children tend to be sensitive to others' needs, happy, and coopera-

Authoritative adults combine the positive attributes of the authoritarian and permissive discipline styles while avoiding the negative ones.

© Cengage Learning 2015

tive. They are well equipped to resist temptation, delay gratification, and control their negative impulses. They are also better able to maintain positive social interactions and initiate constructive social plans on their own. Unsurprisingly, their behavior is the most internalized of the four patterns of self-regulation described in this text. For all these reasons, children benefit when early childhood professionals adopt an authoritative style.

Refer to Table 10-5 for a summary of all four guidance styles and the corresponding profiles of child behavior with which they are associated. Research evidence indicates that these outcomes tend to endure from early childhood into later maturity (Eisenberg et al., 2011; Kochanska et al., 2008; Pratt, Skoe, & Arnold, 2004).

The Dynamic Interaction between Children's Temperament and Adult Approaches to Guidance

Jessie is a quiet 9-year-old, somewhat fearful of new situations and timid with people. In terms of temperament, she could be described as slow to warm up.

Raelynn, on the other hand, is impulsive and fearless in her social interactions. She is a contentious child, who many would call temperamentally difficult.

Evidence based on differences in temperament show that children like Jessie find it easier to exercise self-regulation than do children like Raelynn (Rothbart, Ellis, & Posner, 2011; Kochanska et al., 2002). This does not mean that Jessie will achieve self-regulation automatically nor that Raelynn will never develop self-control. It does mean that the road toward

Table 10-5	Adult Discipline Styles and Associated Patterns of Child Behavior
Discipline Style	**Children's Behavior Profile**
Authoritarian	Aimless
	Fearful, apprehensive
	Hostile
	Low self-reliance and self-control
	Moody, unhappy
	Suspicious
	Unfriendly
	Withdrawn
	Aggressive
Permissive	Aggressive
	Aimless
	Domineering
	Immature
	Impulsive
	Low achiever
	Low self-reliance and self-control
	Rebellious
	Unhappy
	Withdrawn
Uninvolved	Aggressive
	Immature
	Impulsive
	Insecure
	Irresponsible
	Low achiever
	Low self-esteem
	Low self-reliance and self-control
	Moody
	Noncompliant
Authoritative	Cooperative
	Curious
	Empathic
	Friendly
	Goal oriented
	Happy
	High achiever
	High self-reliance and self-control

© Cengage Learning

ences in how adults interact with each child to promote self-regulation. For instance, Jessie is likely to respond most favorably to gentle, psychological strategies that emphasize nurturance and communication with a modest focus on maturity demands and control. Fearful children like her are highly anxious and often burst into tears at the slightest hint of a reprimand. When this happens, it is difficult for them to absorb desired moral lessons. Thus, adults must tread lightly in helping Jessie learn the "rules." Addressing Raelynn's needs also requires a warm, secure relationship between adult and child. However, the mild directives that work best with fearful children may be insufficient to capture a fearless child's attention. Raelynn will also need clear and firm (not harsh) messages of what is expected and how to best maintain the warm, mutually cooperative relationship she has with the significant adults in her life. As you can see, these two approaches are variations on the authoritative discipline style.

Authoritarian techniques, on the other hand, are not likely to work well with either girl. Clearly, such strategies would overpower Jessie, causing her to withdraw even more. Children with difficult temperaments like Raelynn tend to act out when power assertion is used. That reaction typically prompts adults to increase their demands for control with increasingly poor results (Kochanska, Padavic, & Koenig, 1996; Kochanska et al., 2002). In both instances, adults and children have contributed to a counterproductive cycle that is hard to break and could contribute to increased behavior problems later.

The most favorable outcomes occur when adults strive to maintain a corresponding fit between their discipline styles and children's dispositions (Rothbart et al., 2011). Adults who are able to accommodate the fearful child's need for loving support and modest demands promote the emergence of self-regulation and their own feelings of competence in working with the child. Those who strive to maintain positive relationships with children in spite of children's irritable contentious demeanors find that the going gets better over time. Difficult children, treated with patience, warmth, and firm guidance, become better able to moderate their reactions and develop self-regulating strategies associated with social competence. When a corresponding fit between temperament and adult style is absent, both children and adults suffer.

A cross-cultural perspective. Some people wonder whether authoritative child guidance represents the needs of people of varying ethnic/cultural and socioeconomic backgrounds. In the United States and Canada, research with Euro-American children, African-American children, middle-class children, and children from lower socioeconomic backgrounds all

internalization is usually easier for the quiet, more reflective child than for the child whose approach to life is naturally impulsive, rebellious, and headstrong.

How adults approach the two girls will be a factor in the children's emerging self-regulatory capabilities as well. There should be similarities as well as some differ-

yield similar results. When adults combine warm, affectionate relationships; high standards; clear expectations; and reasonable boundaries on child behavior, children demonstrate high rates of positive self-esteem, autonomy, prosocial conduct, and behavioral self-discipline (Domitrovich et al., 2011; Ladd, 2005). These results hold true for other Western cultures as well. Consequently, the authoritative style is the most commonly practiced approach to child guidance in these communities (Rothbaum & Trommsdorff, 2008). On the other hand, some East Asian and other non-Western cultures do not prize personal autonomy and independence as much as they do group responsibility and social obligation. In these culture groups, adult socialization styles tend to emphasize the control and maturity demands dimension very highly. However, within these cultures, adult control is likely to be seen by children as an expression of concern, caring, and involvement (Rothbaum & Trommsdorff, 2008; Eisenberg et al., 2009). In other words, caring is in the "eyes of the beholder." One's culture influences which behaviors children interpret as fitting the dimensions associated with the styles we have just discussed. Thus, readers are reminded that each child lives in a contextual niche unique to that child. The details of how relationships are established and how compliance is achieved vary. Behaviors that appear one way to an outsider may not have the same interpretation within a particular culture group or family.

In addition, alternative life conditions may call for techniques that differ in form but correspond in concept to those associated with an authoritative perspective. For instance, the Green family lives in a housing project riddled with drugs and violence. Mrs. Green is faced with having to keep her son safe in a hostile environment. She may demand quicker compliance and more absolute obedience in that environment than she would if she lived elsewhere. Moreover, what children and the significant adults in their lives interpret as warm and supportive depends on past experiences and current interpretations (Rothbaum & Trommsdorff, 2008). This means one child may interpret teasing from adults as a positive relationship-building strategy, whereas another views teasing as a strategy of rejection. Likewise, sarcasm may be understandable to some children as a gentle admonition to be taken seriously ("Go ahead, make me tell you a second time"), whereas other children would miss the message entirely. Children's comprehension is tied to the customs of speech and interaction with which they are familiar.

For this reason, helping professionals are cautioned not to judge other adults' socialization styles too narrowly and to seek ways to adapt their skills to meet the needs of children and families whose backgrounds vary widely.

> **HIGHLIGHT 10-2**
>
> ## Becoming an Authoritative Adult
>
> When children don't know how to wash their hands, we teach them.
>
> When children don't know how to say the alphabet, we teach them.
>
> When children don't know how to multiply, we teach them.
>
> When children don't know how to dance, we teach them.
>
> When children don't know how to behave, we teach them.
>
> **Source:** Adapted from Herner (1998, p. 2).

Becoming Authoritative

At one time, it was thought adults were instinctively authoritarian, permissive, or authoritative. We now know that although some people's personality or temperament seem more aligned with one style or another, anyone can learn to be more authoritative through training and practice (Fox & Lentini, 2006; Epstein, 2009). Authoritative adults think of themselves as teachers. They assume that "teaching" children to behave is as natural as teaching them anything else (see Highlight 10-2).

To develop an authoritative teaching style, you must pay attention to how you establish relationships with children, the kind of climate you create in the classroom, and how you communicate your expectations to children. Skills presented in previous chapters have focused on relationship enhancement as well as creating supportive environments in which children can safely explore behavioral boundaries. This means you have already learned some elements of the authoritative style. The skills presented in this chapter will help you address expectations and rules.

Stating Your Expectations naeyc

A developmentally appropriate way to express expectations and rules for children's behavior is through a **personal message**. A personal message consists of three parts. In the first step, you will use a reflection to acknowledge the child's point of view. In the second portion, you will identify your emotional reaction to the child's behavior, name the specific action that prompted those feelings, and explain why. The third segment, used only in situations in which behavior change is desired, involves describing an alternate behavior for the child to pursue. This last step is, in fact, a statement of a rule that the child is expected to follow for that situation. Here is an example:

> Five-year-old Kayla is using a plastic butter knife to cut a banana for fruit salad. Playfully, she begins swiping the air with the knife as though it were a pretend sword. The teacher worries that Kayla might hurt herself or another child and so he says, "Kayla, you're having fun. I'm worried someone could get hurt when you wave the knife around. Keep the knife low like this." (The teacher demonstrates what to do).

Personal messages give children the information they need for both current and future reference. They also help children better understand how their actions affect others and provide them with cues about desirable and undesirable behaviors (Kaiser & Rasminsky, 2012).

In favorable circumstances, personal messages tell children what they are doing right so they can repeat the behavior in subsequent interactions. For instance, an adult who values cooperation may acknowledge two children's efforts to share by saying: "You're working together. It makes me feel happy to see you sharing. Sharing is one way to cooperate."

In problem situations, personal messages set the stage either for children to comply on their own or for the adult to impose consequences when children fail to obey. For example, adults who want to redirect a child's anger away from hitting and toward talking could say: "You're angry. It upsets me when you hit. Hitting hurts. Tell Stuart what he did that made you so mad." For now, we will turn our attention to personal messages aimed at changing problem behaviors; later, we will consider how to use them in positive situations.

Knowing When Behavior Change is Necessary

Every day, teachers and caregivers are faced with situations in which they must decide whether or not a child's behavior is appropriate. If a behavior is not acceptable, they must also determine what conduct would be more suitable. To make these decisions, adults ask themselves the following questions:

1. Is the child's behavior unsafe either for self or others?
2. Is the child's behavior destructive?
3. Does the child's behavior infringe on the rights of someone else?

The rule is that children must sit on the swings, not lay on them to swing. Does this rule meet the criteria for deciding behavior change is necessary?

© Cengage Learning 2015

If the answer to any of these questions is yes, it is time to intervene (Levin, 2003; Malott & Trojan, 2008). If the response is no, then intervention is unnecessary.

For example, concern about safety is the reason why children are stopped from running with scissors, prevented from dashing across a busy street, or kept from playing with matches. Similarly, the sanctions adults impose on graffiti or writing in library books are aimed at protecting property. When children are rebuked for copying from someone else's paper or for bullying a timid classmate, adults are making an effort to teach children respect for others' rights. In all of these situations, there are legitimate grounds for trying to alter children's behavior.

Finally, adults must decide whether a problem behavior is important enough to warrant persistent attention (Denno, Carr, & Bell, 2011; Edwards, 2007). This can be described as *the criteria of importance*. In other words, is the behavior serious enough to deal with each and every time it happens? When a behavior meets these criteria, a personal message is in order.

For example, when Mr. Smith sees children throwing rocks on the playground, he takes action to stop it regardless of when he sees it or how tired or preoccupied he is. Because rock throwing is so dangerous, preventing it is a top priority for Mr. Smith. In this case, a personal message that forbids rock throwing is appropriate.

On the other hand, it annoys Mr. Smith when children pile their backpacks on the floor rather than hanging them up on the hooks provided. Some days, he makes and enforces a rule that all backpacks have to be up off the floor and on the hooks so people won't trip over them. However, if he has a headache or has put in a long day, Mr. Smith pretends not to see the backpacks on the floor rather than dealing with the problem. The intermittent nature of Mr. Smith's attention to the backpack standard is a sign that it is not important enough, at least for now, to warrant a personal message.

Because adults differ, their interpretations vary as to what constitutes a dangerous situation or a potential threat to another's self-esteem. For instance, one adult may limit children climbing up the front of the slide based on safety considerations. Another adult may decide that such climbing is a good gross-motor activity and simply restructure the activity so there is only one child on the slide at a time. People's personal standards are uniquely influenced by past experience, family, community, and culture. This means that no two adults' standards match exactly. However, when adults relate the rules they set to the standards of safety, protecting property, and protecting people's rights, they are operating from a common set of values, making it easier for children to understand why certain behaviors are acceptable and others are not. These standards are simple and all encompassing. They provide basic guidelines by which to judge children's behavior and are applicable to children of varying ages and abilities, including children with special needs (see Highlight 10-3—Setting Limits with Rosie: A Child with Special Needs).

Part One of the Personal Message

To successfully teach children how to achieve social goals appropriately, adults must first understand what children are trying to accomplish (Kaiser & Rasminsky, 2012; Dowling, 2005). After this has been established, it is easier to determine an acceptable alternate behavior that will satisfy both the adult and the child. Based on this rationale, the first step of the personal message is to recognize and acknowledge the child's perspective using a behavior, paraphrase, or affective reflection.

A personal message begins with a reflection for several reasons. First, in problem situations, adults and children often have very different points of view. For example, when 4-year-old Allison lifts her dress up over her head in the supermarket to show off her new panties, she feels proud, but her mother is mortified. At times like these, adults wish children would act differently, so it is common for them to center on this desire and forget that children's emotions are legitimate, although contrary to their own. Reflecting helps adults avoid this pitfall. It compels them to remember that each child has a unique perception that must be considered prior to subsequent action.

Another advantage of reflecting first is that the reflection is a clear signal to the child that the adult is actively attempting to understand his or her position (Calkins & Williford, 2009). Children are more willing to listen to adult messages when they think their own messages have been heard. Even when children have chosen a physical means to express their desires, knowledge of adult awareness reduces their need to escalate the behavior to make their feelings known. For instance, if Sam is angry, he may be ready to fling a book across the room to make his point. When the adult reflects, "Something happened that really upset you," Sam may not feel so compelled to throw the book to show his anger because someone has already acknowledged it.

A third value of reflecting first is that it is a way to mentally count to 10 before committing yourself to a particular line of action. It offers a moment in which adults can sort out their emotions, organize their thoughts, or readjust their approach. It reduces the risk of overreacting or responding thoughtlessly. For instance, from across the room, Ms. Romano notices Danny painting a picture with tempera dripping all over the floor. Her first reaction is one of annoyance.

She hurries to the easel, a reprimand on her lips. However, as she approaches, she becomes aware

HIGHLIGHT 10-3

Setting Limits with Rosie: A Child with Special Needs

Meet Rosie

Four-year-old Rosie Carmassi attends preschool with other typically developing children her age in the morning and attends a special education program in the afternoon. Rosie was born with cerebral palsy. She is an intelligent little girl who enjoys music, storybooks, and dress-up play with scarves and hats. Currently, Rosie can't walk, can't talk, and can't voluntarily control any part of her body other than her eyes and her lips.

Over the year, Rosie became an integral member of the preschool group, participating fully in classroom life and making friends. However, it took some time for her teachers to figure out that Rosie needed limits as much as she needed other learning opportunities each day.

Rosie's morning teacher tells about early efforts to help Rosie learn to behave in the classroom.

Rosie could make some limited sounds but didn't have enough control so that she could use them to communicate. She really depended on her eyes. She could roll her eyes upward for yes and downward for no. She could also move them left and right to signal direction and look at something to make her needs known.

Initially, Rosie had a picture board that we used. It was a circular board with pictures displayed in wedges, kind of like a pie. She had a few pictures of typical things she might need or want in the classroom, such as water or the toilet, and some pictures for areas in the room, such as blocks or pretend play. The board was always available, and she would look at a part of it to indicate what she wanted.

We had some frustrating times early in the year. Rosie would want something and neither the teachers nor the children would know what it was. Then she'd get frustrated and cry or shriek. She also did this whenever she didn't want to do something. At first, when Rosie got upset about things, all the adults in the classroom would try to give her anything she wanted. Everyone just felt so sorry for this little girl in the wheelchair, who couldn't talk or move about freely. As a result, Rosie was getting rewarded for some very inappropriate behavior, and it was getting worse. One day at our before-school meeting I said, "We are not helping Rosie when we give in to her every whim." I asked them if they would say "yes" to some of the things she wanted if other children asked for them (such as not washing her hands before snack or not waiting her turn with a hat). Everyone agreed they wouldn't. Then I said, "We are here to help Rosie. The way we are going to help her is to not let her behave like that." We decided to use the *principles of safety and protecting property and rights* (just as we did with the other children) to guide our decisions when it came to determining expectations for Rosie. We worked hard at making those expectations clear and consistent. It was challenging for all of us, but after several weeks, we saw a change in Rosie. She was more relaxed and more successful in the classroom. She learned what the boundaries were and that we cared enough to keep her safe and treat her like the other kids. This was an important lesson for all of us.

Source: Rosie's story was adapted from a case study included in *Children with Special Needs: Lessons for Early Childhood Professionals* written by Kostelnik, Onaga, Rohde, and Whiren (Teachers College Press, 2002, pp. 32–48).

of Danny's obvious pride in his work and his total absorption in his painting. By reflecting, "You're really excited about your painting," she is able to put a check on her initial response. Instead of blurting out, "How many times have we talked about keeping the paint on the paper," she is able calmly to provide him with important information. "Some paint dripped on the floor. I'm worried someone might slip and get hurt. Get a sponge, and we'll clean it up." In this way, the reflection served as a reasoned entry into what could have been an emotionally charged situation.

Finally, reflecting is a way for adults to show respect and caring for children (Denham, Bassett, & Wyatt, 2007). This demonstration of positive regard must continue, particularly when disciplinary action is in order. When used in conjunction with the other portions of the personal message, reflecting unites the two components of the authoritative style: affection and clear behavioral expectations.

All of the reasons for reflecting before acting are summarized in Highlight 10-4.

To summarize, in problem situations, the child has one perspective, and the adult has another. For a resolution to take place, each must accurately and correctly take into account the other's attitudes. This mutual understanding forms the basis for a shared response that will join the two separate lines of thought. The reflection represents the adult's effort to assess the child's attitude; the second portion of the personal message will help the child recognize the adult's perspective.

Why adults should talk about their emotions.

Helping professionals often have an emotional reaction to children's behavior. They feel pleased when children cooperate, distressed when they fight, and annoyed when they procrastinate. Emotions are just as natural for adults as they are for children. Experienced practitioners learn to use their own emotions as a guide to interacting more effectively with children. They do this by talking about their emotions as they happen (Miller, 2013).

When adults disclose their emotions to children, they illustrate the universality of feelings. They demonstrate that at different times, everyone feels unhappy, pleased, frustrated, worried, proud, satisfied, or angry. This helps children realize that all human beings experience emotions and, as a result, makes them more willing to accept feelings in themselves and to recognize them in others (Hendrick & Weissman, 2011). Talking about emotions also aids children in learning that people have different reactions to the same situation. They find out that what makes them happy may prompt sadness in others or that something which causes them anxiety is welcomed by someone else. Due to their immature social perspective-taking abilities, children do not automatically know this. As they hear more about other people's emotions, they gradually become aware that more than one interpretation is possible. Another advantage is that adults serve as a model for using words to express emotional states. Children discover that people can have a variety of reactions and still be capable of verbalizing how they feel (Thompson & Twibell, 2009). Eventually, children find that emotions can be put into words and that words offer a satisfying way to communicate with other people.

Adults who want to maintain positive relationships with children also should keep in mind that sharing their feelings with children promotes closer ties. People who talk honestly about their emotions are considered more trustworthy and helpful by the persons with whom they interact, than people who avoid such conversations (Gazda et al., 2006). When adults reveal something personal about themselves, children see it as a positive sign of engagement. In addition, when such revelations are the norm, children find it less threatening to reveal their own emotions. This leads to greater mutual understanding and respect.

Finally, children are interested in how the significant adults in their lives react to what they say and do. They care about how adults feel and are responsive to their emotions. In fact, adults who describe their own disappointment or disapproval regarding a particular child's behavior place that child in an optimal state of arousal for receiving the rest of the information contained in their message (Kochanska et al., 2008). Without this type of information, children will not

The teacher begins her personal message by saying, "You're having fun with the orange paint."

HIGHLIGHT 10-4

Why Reflections Come First in the Personal Message

Benefits of Reflecting First
- Helps you see child's point of view
- Signals child you are trying to understand
- Helps you mentally count to 10
- Shows respect for child

Part Two of the Personal Message

The second portion of the personal message describes the adult's emotions, identifies the child's behavior that led to those feelings, and gives a reason for why this is so:

"I feel annoyed when you hit. Hitting hurts."

"It upsets me when you interrupt. I keep losing my place."

be induced to seriously consider the adult's reasoning. On the other hand, adults who depend on power assertion or love withdrawal as a way to communicate concern provoke such strong reactions in children that they are unable to attend to the specific content of the message. Thus, when children refrain from hitting because it would upset their teacher, or when they share materials because the caregiver has advocated cooperation, they are demonstrating identification. It is from this base that they eventually begin to internalize some of the behavior expectations adults think are important.

Focusing on children's behavior. After adults have described their emotions, it is important that they tell the child which behavior has caused them to react. Children often do not know which of their behaviors is prompting the adult's reaction. This means identifying by name the undesirable behavior that the child is displaying. This helps children pinpoint actions to avoid (Essa, 2008; Malott & Trojan, 2008). For example, a personal message that includes the statement "It bothers me when you keep jumping out of your seat" tells the child what behavior prompted the adult's irritation and describes an issue that can be resolved. On the other hand, remarks such as "It annoys me that you're showing off" or "I get upset when you're such a slob" are accusations that attack a child's personality and do not further mutual respect and understanding.

Behaviors are actions you can see. Taking turns, hitting, kicking, and coming on time are all visible, objective ways to describe children's conduct. On the other hand, descriptors such as lazy, uncooperative, hyperactive, stubborn, greedy, hostile, and nasty are all subjective and accusatory labels. They make children feel defensive without giving them clear cues as to which specific actions are the focus of your message. If such labels are used, children may become hostile or think that satisfying the adult is beyond their capability. In either case, effective behavior change is more difficult to achieve. To avoid such adverse reactions, use objective words to describe children's actions rather than subjective labels when talking to children about problem behaviors.

The importance of giving children reasons. Children are better able to understand and respond to adult expectations when these expectations are accompanied by reasons (Helwig & Turiel, 2002; Denno et al., 2011). This is why the second portion of the personal message also includes giving children an explanation for the adult's reaction.

Why are adults upset when children hit?

Because hitting hurts.

Why are they frustrated when children dawdle?

Because they may be late for something important.

Why do they become annoyed when children interrupt a story over and over again?

Because interrupting interferes with their train of thought or makes it difficult for others to concentrate.

Although such conclusions may be perfectly clear to adults, they are not so obvious to many children.

When adults give children reasons for their expectations, they help them recognize that behavior standards have a rational rather than arbitrary base. Reasons help children see the logic of expectations that they might not discover on their own. In addition, reasons offer children information about the effect their behavior has on others. This increases their understanding of interpersonal cause and effect, that is, the relationship between their own acts and the physical and psychological well-being of another person (Wells, 2009). Reasons make the connections among actions clearer (see Highlight 10-5).

HIGHLIGHT 10-5

Reasons Strengthen Cognitive Connections!

Toddler Mia stuck her finger into the electrical outlet. Her dad told her that her fingers would get hurt and to keep them away from the outlet. Then she touched the outlet with her elbow; Dad moved closer, repeating the reason and the limit. Then she turned around and put her bottom on it! He scooped her up and talked firmly to her about keeping every part of her body away from the electricity.

Mia treated each body part and each action as a separate event. Although her dad understood that fingers, elbows, and bottoms all fell under the category "Keep away from outlets," Mia did not see the connection among them. Her dad offered a reason, getting hurt, to make that connection for her. Adults who use reasons to point out the similarities among different actions (e.g., finger poking and elbow touching are both unsafe) help children make such associations more easily.

When children hear reasons over and over again, they gradually make connections that help them determine for themselves whether certain actions are acceptable or not. This is illustrated when a child reasons to herself: "Hitting is wrong because it hurts people. Biting must be wrong because it hurts people too." In this way, children eventually use reasons to guide their judgments about what is right and what is wrong (Thompson & Twibell, 2009). Likewise, a child who says to himself, "I shouldn't eat a candy bar before supper because it will spoil my appetite" is relying on reasons he has heard previously to self-regulate his current behavior.

Reasoning is the hallmark of the authoritative adult. Children who see adults model reasoning as a way to resolve problem situations demonstrate more self-regulation and less aggression than do children for whom such models are not available (Epstein, 2009). In addition, children can only internalize standards that make sense to them and that help them to predict the possible aftermath of the things they do or say. Reasoning fulfills these criteria and leads to the establishment of long-term behavior controls. Stating a reason for why a rule is necessary also helps adults determine if that rule is important enough to implement and enforce.

Matching reasons to children's understanding. A child's current developmental level has an impact on what types of reasons will make the most sense to him or her. For instance, preschoolers are most responsive to demonstrable object-oriented rationales, such as "Be careful with the magnifying glass. It's fragile, and it might break." They also understand reasons that emphasize the direct physical effects of their actions: "If you keep pushing him, he'll fall down and cry" (Hoffman, 1983). Young children are less able to comprehend explanations that focus on ownership or the rights of others, such as "That's Timmy's magnifying glass from home. Ask him first before you touch it." On the other hand, children 6 years of age and older are more receptive to reasoning that focuses on the rights, privileges, and emotions of other people. The most effective reasons at this age emphasize the psychological effects of children's actions ("He feels sad because he was proud of his tower and you knocked it down") as well as explanations that focus on the fairness of the child's actions in terms of someone else's motives ("Wait before you holler—he was only trying to help." A depiction of the developmental differences in what reasons make sense to young children is shown in Figure 10-3.

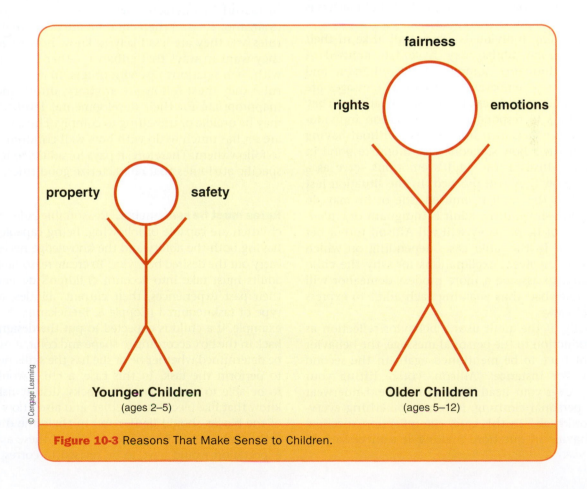

Figure 10-3 Reasons That Make Sense to Children.

Variations in part two of the personal message. As we have discussed, the second portion of the personal message consists of a statement of the adult's emotion, a reference to the child's behavior, and a reason for this reaction. These three components can be arranged in any sequence after the reflection. Adults should always reflect first and then proceed with the second part in a way that seems most comfortable for them. There is no one correct order. For example, in the case of Allison, who was lifting her dress over her head in a proud display of her underwear, more than one response is appropriate:

> Option 1. "Allison, you're proud of your new underwear. Underwear is very personal clothing. It's not meant for everyone to see. It upsets me when you lift your dress so high."
>
> Option 2. "Allison, you're proud of your new underwear. It upsets me when you lift your dress over your head. Underwear is very personal clothing and is not meant for everyone to see."

How adults decide to articulate the second part of the personal message will depend on what they think of first and their own individual style. What matters is that all the components are included.

In addition, individuals are not all alike in their reactions. Some adults may have felt amused at Allison's performance, some would be indignant, and others might be embarrassed. Personal messages are ideally suited to account for these variations. They enable adults to respond to each situation individually based on their own impressions, without having to second-guess how someone else might respond in their place. Instead, the adult's emotions serve as a guide for how they will proceed. In the situation just discussed, if the adult is amused, she or he may do nothing but smile; if the adult is indignant or embarrassed, she or he probably will tell Allison to put her dress down. In the latter case, depending on which emotion is involved, explanations for why the child is required to assume a more modest demeanor will differ somewhat, thus enabling each adult to express personal views.

Finally, if the adult uses a behavior reflection as an introduction to the personal message, the behavior does not have to be mentioned again in the second portion. For instance: "Allison, you're lifting your dress up over your head. That upsets me. Underwear is very personal clothing; it is not something everyone should see." In this case, the reflection specified the behavior in question, making it unnecessary to repeat.

Part Three of the Personal Message

Telling children an appropriate course of action for a particular circumstance is the function of the third portion of the personal message. Due to children's relative lack of experience and the influence of centration and irreversible thinking, it is not enough to tell them which behaviors are unacceptable. They must also be told what to try instead (Curwin, Mendler, & Mendler, 2008; Bear, 2010). This appropriate substitute behavior serves as a rule for children to follow. Thus, the "rule or redirection" portion of the personal message is a guide for behavior—it tells children what to do.

Some examples are

> "Walk."
>
> "Keep your dress down."
>
> "Turn your homework in as soon as you get to school."
>
> "Share the jump ropes."
>
> "Talk quietly in the lunchroom."

Rules make the world more predictable because they help children recognize what they can and cannot do. This knowledge enables them to be more successful in interacting with both peers and adults (Marzano, 2003). When children are not sure what the rules are, they are less likely to know how to get what they want in ways that enhance rather than interfere with their relationships with others. In addition, if the rules they must follow are arbitrary, unreasonable, or inappropriate for their developmental level, children may be unable or unwilling to comply. Thus, how rules are set has much to do with how well children are able to follow them. Therefore, it pays for adults to learn the specific attributes that characterize good rules.

Rules must be reasonable. Reasonable rules are rules children are capable of following. Being capable means having both the ability and the knowledge necessary to carry out the desired behavior. To create reasonable rules, adults must take into account children's development, their past experiences, their current abilities, and the type of task required (Copple & Bredekamp, 2009). For example, if a child is expected to put the design blocks back in the box according to shape and color, it must first be determined whether he or she has the skills necessary to perform the task. In this case, a child would have to be able to manipulate the blocks, distinguish color, know that like pieces go together, and also know that all of the blocks should lie flat and in the same direction. If the child lacked know-how in any of these areas, the expectation would have to be revised to correspond to what the child could do. This might mean telling the child to simply gather the blocks, or to pile them in the box randomly, or to work with another person to collect the materials.

Rules must benefit the child. Rules must have long-term positive effects that benefit the child, not just the adult (Katz, Chard, & Kogan, 2013). Hence, adults must decide whether a rule enhances a child's development or hinders it. Development is enhanced when expectations promote significant increases in children's interpersonal, academic, or life skills. Development is hindered when adults fail to take into account children's individual needs and abilities or when they prohibit children from engaging in constructive activities. Such instances occur when adults set standards indiscriminately or solely for their own convenience. Thus, forbidding all the children in a mixed-age group from climbing on the high jungle gym because the youngest ones are afraid, preventing a crying child from clutching a blanket for comfort because the adult thinks it is high time she grew up, forbidding a boy from using a loom because the leader sees weaving as too feminine, or demanding that children be silent during lunchtime because the principal wants to make sure they do not yell across the table, are all growth-inhibiting measures. These are all examples of depriving children of potentially beneficial experiences.

Adults avoid such problems when they recognize that each child is an individual and that although some standards are appropriate for a group (such as walking rather than running inside), others are best applied on a child-by-child basis. For instance, because physical mastery is important for everyone, younger children could be encouraged to tackle a low climber, while older children could attempt a more challenging apparatus. Moreover, adults should examine their own attitudes for biases that curtail children's exposure to a wide range of opportunities. Intolerance and sexism, as illustrated in the preceding blanket and loom incidents, are examples of these. Additionally, in an effort to deal with definite problem behaviors, such as shouting during lunch, adults must be careful not to exact a standard that is unnecessarily extreme. Because children benefit from peer interaction, they should be encouraged to talk informally with classmates. Teaching children to monitor the volume of their voices is a better approach to the problem of too much noise than eliminating conversation altogether. Finally, adults must continually reexamine their rules in an effort to keep them up to date. A rule that is appropriate for a child of 4 may be inhibiting at age 6.

Rules must be definable. Rules are definable when both the adult and the child have the same understanding of what the rule means (Malott &

Trojan, 2008). Good rules specify the exact behavior that adults value and find acceptable. It is confusing to children when adults use language that is open to many interpretations. This is exemplified when adults tell children to "behave," "act nice," "be good," or "act like a lady." Such phrases mean different things to different people. The child may construe these generalizations in one way, and the adult may think of them in another. Children who make genuine attempts to carry out the instructions become frustrated when their efforts fall short of the expected standard. For example, the teacher's notion of "nice" might mean sitting quietly with hands in lap, while the fidgeting child thought that he was complying by not spitting at a teasing classmate.

The difficulty is compounded when adults assume that because they use the same phrases over and over, children must know what they mean. For instance, a teacher tried to stop two children from fighting. She said: "You're angry. I get upset when you fight. Someone could get hurt. Use your words." Following her directions, one child said to the other, "Okay, you $#%@#!" The adult did a quick double take! She certainly didn't mean those words! Adults who want children to use words to express their emotions, who want children to cooperate, or who want children to stop acting up must tell them a specific way to accomplish these things.

Rules must be positive. Children are most successful at following positive rules that tell them what to do rather than what not to do or what to stop doing (Marion, 2011). In other words, it is easier for children to respond appropriately when they are told "Put your hands in your pockets" rather than "Stop pushing"; "Walk" rather than "Don't run"; and "Eat your food" rather than "Don't play with your food." This is because the irreversible aspects of children's thinking make negative commands difficult for them to comprehend. Children are much more successful in following rules that help them redirect an action, rather than reversing or interrupting ongoing behaviors.

A shorthand method for remembering all the necessary components is to think of each personal message as containing three parts and four R's: part one—Reflect; part two—React and give a Reason; and part three—state the Rule or redirect the child's behavior. The steps that make up a complete personal message are summarized in Highlight 10-6.

Articulating the Entire Personal Message—The Four R's

The following situations illustrate the integration of all three parts of the personal message, including all four R's.

HIGHLIGHT 10-6

Creating a Complete Personal Message

Part 1 —**R**eflect

Use a behavior, paraphrase, or affective reflection.

Part 2 —**R**eact

Describe your emotion and the child's behavior.

Reason

Give a reason for your message.

Part 3—**R**ule or redirection

Tell children what to do versus what not to do.

Situation 1: A child is poking Mr. King to get him to listen to her story.

Adult: You're anxious to tell me something. I don't like it when you poke me to get my attention. It hurts. Call my name or tap my shoulder lightly.

Situation 2: Several children have left their gym towels scattered about the locker room.

Adult: You're in a hurry to get back to class. It bothers me when you leave your dirty towels all over the locker room because then I have to pick them up. Put them in the laundry basket before you leave.

Situation 3: It is a hot, humid day. The class is restless and children are beginning to fidget and whisper while a classmate is reporting on the life of Sojourner Truth.

Adult: You're hot and uncomfortable. It's distracting to Karl when you whisper while he's giving his report. I'm concerned his feelings will be hurt. He worked hard to find this information. Sit quietly until he is finished.

Messages such as these can be given to individual children or to groups. In addition to being used to correct children's behavior, personal messages should also be implemented as a way to reinforce appropriate actions.

Positive Personal Messages

A positive personal message contains only parts one and two of the format just described. Our previous emphasis on problems should not be taken to mean that you should expect children to engage only in negative behavior. In reality, the evidence is to the contrary.

Children often strive to comply with adult expectations and, in fact, frequently initiate constructive actions on their own. As a result, not all of the emotions prompted by children's behavior are ones of anger or concern. For this reason, personal messages should be used to identify adults' positive reactions as well. Adults must "catch" children being "good"—displaying behaviors that are socially desirable—and tell children what those behaviors are: "You made a rule to take turns in the space shuttle. I'm pleased you all talked it over and figured out a way to give everyone a chance" or "You cleaned up all the art scraps without anybody reminding you. I'm delighted. Now, this table is ready for making popcorn."

A message used in this way is a special kind of praise. Adults go beyond telling children that they have done a "good job" or "great work." Instead, they are saying that the child's specific behavior had special meaning for them. Research has shown that this type of response is very effective because it describes the impact a particular behavior has had on the person offering the praise. General terms such as "good," "nice," or "pretty" soon lose their meaning for both children and adults if they are used over and over again or applied indiscriminately. Moreover, children interpret effusive remarks that glorify them, rather than their behavior, as insincere or "too gushy." Thus, it is more effective to say: "You worked hard on your essay. I really liked it. It made me want to know more about Harriet Tubman" than to say, "You are a born writer." In the same vein, children learn more about their behavior from a statement such as, "You're trying to comfort Andrew. It makes me feel good that you noticed he was so sad. He needs a friend right now," than from a comment like "You're a terrific kid." When adults identify behavior they are pleased to see children display and tell them why, they encourage children to repeat those actions another time. All too often, adults take children's proactive behaviors or compliance for granted; they simply expect children to do as they are told or to automatically behave in an appropriate fashion. When this happens, adults have failed to recognize that it takes effort for children to achieve these productive outcomes.

Positive personal messages share many of the characteristics cited earlier regarding effective praise. Both are useful tools for helping children recognize the positive behaviors they demonstrate. The difference between the two is in who evaluates the child's behavior, the child or the adult. Effective praise prompts self-evaluation by the child because the adult acknowledges the effort or accomplishment solely from the child's viewpoint, without offering any opinions about it. Positive personal messages, on the other hand, offer a more direct way for adults to tell children what they think about children's appropriate behavior. These are most useful when children are first learning how to behave in a particular circumstance and are looking to

Emily has been working on a craft project for most of the morning. When the clean-up bell rings, she does not want to clean up. The teacher says:

R1 You're not quite finished.
R2 I'm concerned that if you keep working
R3 you'll miss time outside.
R4 Find a spot on the shelf to keep your project until tomorrow.

adults for specific cues in this regard (Miller, 2013). As children become more adept at complying with rules on their own, most positive personal messages should give way to effective praise statements. This allows children to judge for themselves the extent to which their conduct is in keeping with the internalized codes they are beginning to develop. However, it is always appropriate for grown-ups to let children know when their behavior has affected the adult personally and positively. Children appreciate hearing statements such as, "You helped me shelve a lot of books. I appreciate it. That saved me hours of work," or "You remembered I had a hoarse voice and were very quiet while I read the story. I'm glad. That made it easier for me to talk."

Stating positive personal messages. Positive personal messages begin with a reflection. This step clarifies the situation from the child's point of view and alerts children that the adult has noticed what they are doing. Next, the adult identifies a personal emotion regarding the child's action and gives a reason for it. In addition, the specific behavior that prompted the adult's emotional reaction is described.

This may seem like a lot of words when a simple "Thank you" or "Good" would do. However, the purpose of a positive personal message is to teach children which behaviors they should retain for future use. Thus, positive personal messages help children internalize the constructive behaviors they display. Again, the emphasis is on helping children move from adherence to higher levels of social conduct.

Children need reasons why they should behave in certain ways as much as they need to know why they should not engage in particular actions. They also need to know that the adults with whom they identify are sources of approval as well as correction.

The Connection between the Authoritative Style and Developmentally Appropriate Practice

Take a moment to compare the authoritative strategies we have been discussing with the DAP guidelines for creating caring communities depicted in Figure 10-4. What parallels do you see?

At this point, you have learned about parts one, two, and three of the personal message. Now you need to translate that understanding into skilled behavior. Following are specific guidelines for how to make personal messages an effective part of your approach to guiding children's social behavior and learning. As you read about these skills, hopefully you will notice a clear relationship to the DAP guidelines offered in Figure 10-4.

Teachers in classrooms using developmentally appropriate practices do the following:

· Help children develop responsibility and self-regulation.
· Supervise, monitor, anticipate, prevent, and redirect behaviors that interfere with learning.
· Teach positive behaviors.
· Set clear and reasonable limits on children's behavior and consistently apply them.
· Listen to and acknowledge children's emotions and frustrations.
· Help children resolve conflicts.
· Model skills that help children solve problems on their own.

Figure 10-4 DAP Guidelines for Creating Caring Communities.

Source: Based on NAEYC, 2009, p. 16.

SKILLS FOR EXPRESSING EXPECTATIONS AND RULES TO CHILDREN naeyc

Reflecting in Problem Situations

1. **Observe children carefully before talking.** Consider what the child may be trying to achieve and why.

2. **Use reflections to accurately describe the child's perspective.** Remain nonjudgmental as you strive to capture the child's point of view. Try reflections such as, "You wanted another turn at bat" or "You don't think you had a fair turn." Avoid thinly veiled accusations such as, "You just don't want to cooperate today" or "You thought you could pull a fast one."

3. **Remind yourself to describe the child's point of view before your own.** In problem situations, it is natural to want to express your reaction immediately. As we've discussed, this is not effective. To avoid this reaction, take a deep breath prior to speaking. That breath will serve as a cue that the reflection comes first. If you catch yourself skipping the reflection, stop and begin again. Later, think of alternate reflections you might use should the situation arise another time. This type of mental practice will help you in future encounters.

4. **Pay attention to children's age when deciding which type of reflection to use.** Affective reflections generally are most effective with children under 8. For instance, if two first graders have come to blows over who will get the next turn at bat, it would be accurate to say, "You're hitting," and then proceed with the rest of the personal message. However, it is closer to the mark to reflect: "You're really angry. You each thought it was your turn next." This acknowledges what the children consider to be the real problem (the dispute over turns) and provides a more helpful introduction to the subsequent message. On the other hand, older children sometimes resent having an adult interpret their feelings in front of others. It seems too personal. In such cases, the more neutral behavior reflection or paraphrase reflection is more appropriate.

5. **Avoid using "but" as a way to connect the reflection to the rest of the personal message.** The word "but" means "on the contrary." When it is used to connect two phrases, the second phrase contradicts the first. For example, if a friend were to meet you on the street and say, "You look wonderful, but . . ." you would know that the initial praise was a perfunctory introduction to what the person thought was really important. The same is true when it comes to the personal message. Adults who say, "You wish the story would end, but I want to finish it" are telling children that their feelings do not count. This betrays the true spirit of the reflection.

Expressing Your Emotions to Children

1. **Identify the emotions you experience.** State your emotions clearly to the child. Do not rely on nonverbal cues alone. Adults sometimes tap their fingers to show irritation, wrinkle their nose to convey disgust, or sigh to indicate exasperation. Children often misinterpret these signs or miss them altogether. They do not automatically know how you feel and, in fact, are often surprised to find that your feelings may be quite different from their own. Subtle hints will not get your message across. Children benefit from the explicit communication that words provide. Words are specific and to the point. They help children know how you feel and why you feel that way:

"I feel pleased . . ."

"It makes me angry . . ."

"I'm annoyed . . ."

"It's important to me . . ."

"I wish . . ."

2. **Become sensitive to your own internal cues that signal a particular emotion.** Perhaps your cheeks get hot when you start to feel angry, your stomach gets jumpy when you are anxious, or your head seems heavy when you are overwhelmed. At first, it will be the more extreme emotions, such as anger, fear, or excitement, that will be the easiest to discern and express. Eventually, you will become better able to recognize and talk about more moderate emotions such as contentment, irritation, discomfort, or confusion.

3. **Use a wide range of feeling words of differing intensities.** Purposely select an assortment of feeling words. The greater the vocabulary at your disposal, the more likely you are to be attuned to the array of emotions these words represent. If you find yourself using the same few words over and over, select variations to use in the future and then do it.

Identifying Behaviors

1. **Name the behavior that is affecting you.** Be specific. Describe actions you can see or hear. Avoid generalities that clump several behaviors together or that are open to misinterpretation. Rather than saying, "I get upset when you do mean things," say "I get upset when you (hit me; throw things; tease Jacquie; punch Frank)." Both you and the child must know exactly what you find acceptable or unacceptable.

2. **Describe the behavior, not the child.** It is inappropriate to tell children that they are "not nice," bad, nasty, a hard case, hyper, or that they should know better. All of these descriptions attack children as persons and should not be used.

Formulating Reasons

1. **Give children specific reasons for why you approve or disapprove of their behavior.** Link those reasons to safety, protecting property, or protecting people's rights. Rationales such as "Because I said so," "Because I want you to," "Because it's important," "Because it's not nice," "Because that's the rule," or "Because that's how we do things around here" are not effective. They do not clearly relate to any of the criteria for deciding when behavior change is appropriate. Adults often use phrases like these when they cannot think of anything else to say. If you cannot think of a legitimate reason for your reaction, reexamine the situation to determine whether your expectations really are appropriate.

2. **Phrase reasons in terms children understand.** Use familiar language and short, simple sentences. Focus on one main idea rather than offering an explanation that incorporates several ideas.

3. **Give reasons every time you attempt to change a child's behavior.** Do not assume that because you gave an explanation yesterday for why running is prohibited, the children will remember today. Children often forget the rationale or may not realize that the reason still exists after a lengthy time lapse. They must hear the same reasons repeatedly before they are able to generalize from one situation to another.

Enacting Rules

1. **Use safety, protection of property, respect for others, and the principle of importance to determine what rules to make.** If the child's behavior cannot be linked to any of these, reconsider making a rule.

2. **Tell children what the rules are.** Rules should be explicit rather than implicit. Do not assume that children know a rule just because you know it or that they remember it from past experience. Remind children of what the rules are at times when the rules are not an issue. Calm, rational discussions of why certain rules are enforced help children understand the value of and reasons for specific expectations. Also, remind children of the

rules in situations in which those rules apply. For instance, it is more effective to say in part three of the personal message, "Remember to walk in the classroom," when a child is caught running than to say, "How many times have I told you about running indoors?" The latter remark assumes that the child knows that the rule is "walk." Although the child may recognize that running is not allowed, there is no guarantee that he or she remembers the rule that specifies what to do instead.

3. **Be specific when making rules.** Name the behavior you expect children to see: walk, put the ball down, turn in your homework first-thing in the morning, wait until the speaker is finished talking. Avoid generalities such as "be nice," "don't be mean," "don't act up," "act your age," "make me proud of you," "behave yourself," "be good at school," "don't make me ashamed of you," or "mind your manners." Not only are these expressions vague, but also children's interpretation of what they mean may differ from yours, leading to misunderstandings and mistaken behavior.

4. **Revise unreasonable rules.** If you become aware that a child is not able to follow a rule as

you have stated it, do not press on in the mistaken notion that rules must be absolute. It is better to revamp the rule at a level at which the child is able to comply. For example, this would mean changing a rule from "Everyone must raise his or her hand and wait quietly to be called on before speaking" to "Everyone must raise his or her hand to be called on." The "wait quietly" portion of the rule should be added only after most children have demonstrated an ability to raise their hand.

5. **Reward children's approximations of the rule.** Do not expect children to comply perfectly with all rules every time. Recognize behaviors that show that children are attempting to follow the rule, although they may not be totally successful. For instance, if the rule is that children must raise their hands and wait to be called on to talk in a group, you should not expect perfect silence as you survey the waving hands before you. That would be too much for children to accomplish all at once. At first, it is likely that raised hands will be accompanied by excited vocalization as children attempt to gain your attention. Rather than focusing on the infraction of talking, it would be better to praise them for remembering to raise their hands. Gradually, with time and many reminders, fewer children will call out when they raise their hands to speak.

6. **Use positive personal messages often.** When children follow a rule or act in other appropriate ways, draw their attention to their desirable acts with a personal message. Point out to them the favorable effect their behavior had in terms of safety or preserving people's rights or property. These on-the-spot observations are memorable to children and make it more likely that they will remember the rule in the future. As children demonstrate increasing skill at following rules independently, shift to more frequent use of effective praise.

7. **Point out when children demonstrate delay of gratification, impulse control, or resistance to temptation, or when they carry out prosocial plans.**

- "You're waiting patiently."
- "You wanted that extra cupcake, but you let Carol have it instead. That was hard to do, and you did it."
- "You put a check on yourself when you were going to hit Anthony. That took a lot of control."
- "You remembered the guinea pigs had no water. It was very responsible of you to come back over lunchtime to fill their water bottle."

8. **Determine whether children have the same understanding of the rule that you do.** Ask

---

Analyzing Potential Rules and Expectations

Think of an activity that you have planned or in which you will participate with children. Name one rule that relates to that activity. Write it down and then analyze your rule using the following criteria.

Rule: _____

1. Is this rule reasonable developmentally for the children involved? Yes No
   If no, revise.

2. Is this rule definable/specific? Yes No
   If no, revise so that both you and the child will know what the rule means.

3. Is this rule stated positively? Yes No
   If you answered no, revise your rule.

4. What is the reason for this rule (health and safety, property, rights?)
   If no reason fits, revise your rule.

5. Here is what I will say. (How will you state your rule to children?)

children to repeat the rule in their own words, or get them to demonstrate their comprehension in some manner. Watch to see how well they follow through. If children have not understood the rule, make the rule clearer. Some things to try include the following:

- Repeat your words more slowly and articulate more clearly.
- Rephrase your message in simpler, more familiar language and emphasize key words.
- Restate your message using a combination of gestures and words.
- Take the child to an area where there is less interference from noise and other distractions.
- Emphasize your message using physical prompts such as pictures or objects in combination with gestures.
- Demonstrate what you want by doing it yourself.

9. **Catch yourself saying "No" or "Stop."** Rephrase your negative instruction as a positive statement. This may mean interrupting yourself in the middle of a sentence. Another variation is to couple negative instructions with positive ones, such as saying: "Walk. Don't run." Ask a colleague to help you monitor your "Do's and Don'ts" using this simple downloadable observation tool or record yourself for a short time as you are

teaching. Analyze your use of positive and negative statements.

10. **Tell younger and less experienced children what to do instead. Let older or more experienced children generate alternatives for themselves.** If a young child is pushing to get out the door, you could say:

> *"You're anxious to get outside. I'm worried that when you push, someone will get hurt. Take a giant step back away from the door and try again."*

> The message to an older child might be:

> *"You're anxious to get outside. I'm worried that when you push, someone will get hurt. Let's think of a way everyone can get outside safely."*

> Select one response or the other by considering children's previous experience and their potential readiness to negotiate. Two-year-olds, a fifth-grade class that has come together for the first time, or a group of children frenzied with excitement probably will have neither the skill, the patience, nor the trust necessary to work out a compromise.

> However, children who have had lots of practice generating ideas and alternatives and who are calm are likely to rise to the challenge.

11. **Talk and act simultaneously.** Immediately stop children's actions that may be harmful to themselves or others. Use physical intervention if necessary. For example, if two children are fighting, stop the hitting by grasping their hands or separating them. If a child is about to jump off a too-high step, move quickly to restrain him or her. If children are using the saw inappropriately, gain control of it. After the dangerous situation has been neutralized, children are better able to hear what you have to say. It is at this point that personal messages have their greatest impact.

12. **Ask children to help make the rules.** Gather the children in a group, and ask them to help create rules for the group or a particular activity. Record their ideas on paper, and post them for all to see. Refer back to the children's rules as the year goes by. Periodically discuss whether or not revisions are necessary. Participating in the self-governance of the group increases children's understanding of rules and promotes their feelings of internal control. They receive clear evidence that their ideas are worthwhile and that they can influence events in the classroom.

Do's & Don'ts Analysis

Directions: Choose a 20-minute portion of the day on which to focus. Ask a colleague to record how many times you say a do or a don't to children and to write down your actual words in each instance. At the end of the time, analyze the frequency of each kind of statement. Change the don'ts to do's as examples for the future.

Portion of Day (Circle One)	Do's	Don'ts	Correction
Free Choice			
Meal Time			
Circle Time			
Small Group			
Outdoors			
Your Words	Put on a smock		
		Don't get paint on the floor.	Keep the paint on the paper.

▶‖ **TeachSource Video 10-2**

Guidance for Young Children: Teacher Techniques for Encouraging Positive Social Behaviors

Go online and view *Guidance for Young Children: Teacher Techniques for Encouraging Positive Social Behaviors.*

In this video, you will hear a teacher describe the strategies she uses to help children better understand rules and expectations in the classroom.

1. Identify two rules or expectations the teacher has for the children's behavior in her classroom.

2. Identify two strategies the teacher uses to help children meet classroom rules and expectations.

3. Name two additional strategies the teacher might use, based on your understanding of Chapter 10.

Watch on CourseMate

plan to carry out discipline in the formal group setting. This includes the kinds of rules you will enforce with children and how that enforcement will take place.

Such information may be shared with families at an introductory orientation, in a parent handbook, in newsletters sent home, at conference time, or in informal conversations with family members. See the following example.

Dear Families of Children in the 6-Year-Old Class

Something many families want to know is how children are supposed to behave at our school. Here are some basic expectations I have for children in our first grade. All of them are designed to keep children safe, protect the rights of everyone in the class, and safeguard belongings. The children and I will talk about these expectations in more detail over the next few days. In the meantime, I would be happy to answer any questions you have and to hear your comments about our classroom rules.

- Children will walk, not run, indoors.
- Children will use materials in a safe manner.
- Children will keep from hurting other children and will express their feelings in words.
- Children will participate in clean-up every day.

Throughout the year, the children and I will discuss these rules and others that they think are important. We will work on varying ways to make our classroom a safe, caring, happy place to live and learn.

Digital Download   **Download from CourseMate**

Communicating with Families

1. **Find out what expectations families have for their children's behavior.** Every family has certain ways in which they expect their children to act at home and away from home. Knowing what these expectations are helps early childhood professionals to better understand individual families and to support families in their child-rearing role. Obtain such information through individual and group discussions held during the year, ask families to complete a brief written form on which they identify some of the "home rules" they have for their children, and talk with families informally as related circumstances arise. Remain open and accepting. Avoid making judgments regarding the merit of certain family rules.

2. **Communicate your discipline approach to families.** Families have a right to know how you

3. **When talking to family members whose discipline style differs from the authoritative one you are learning, emphasize similarities rather than concentrating on differences in philosophy.** Professionals sometimes believe they have little in common with family members who hold nonauthoritative attitudes toward discipline. Likewise, family members who espouse more authoritarian or permissive philosophies may question the authoritative techniques you use. Under these circumstances, the most effective approach is to emphasize the common ground between these approaches, not the discrepancies (Derman-Sparks & Edwards, 2010). With this in mind, remember that authoritarian and authoritative styles both advocate firm control and high standards; permissive and authoritative styles promote warm, accepting relationships between children and

What rules might you and the children create for playing with the parachute?

adults. Discussing authoritative strategies in terms of how they support these overarching principles provides some common ground between them. For instance, family members with more authoritarian attitudes may believe that reasoning is unnecessary or undesirable because children should simply do as they are told. To help such persons feel more comfortable with your giving reasons to children, point out that you will establish boundaries on the child's behavior by stating a rule and that you are prepared to enforce that rule as necessary. Further explain that the reasons you offer children will help them make sense of the rule at the time and be better able to follow the rule in the future. This explanation combines an authoritative value (helping children think through a problem) with an authoritarian one (achieving compliance) and builds a bridge between the two.

Pitfalls to Avoid naeyc

Regardless of whether you are fostering children's development of self-regulation individually or in groups, informally or in structured activities, there are certain pitfalls you may fall into at first but which you should eventually avoid.

1. **Talking in paragraphs.** Effective personal messages are brief and to the point. However, beginners who are struggling to include all four R's often add extra words or sentences. An awkward example would be: "You seem really unhappy about not getting a turn. I'm sorry you didn't get a turn, but you are hitting Tanya with a stick. When you hit her with a stick, I'm afraid she could get hurt. I'd like you to hand the stick to me." Children are not likely to pay attention to all this talk. They cannot distinguish the main point and may forget what was stated in the beginning. Laborious personal messages are ones children ignore. They get tired of listening and tune out.

When first learning this skill, talking too much is better than forgetting an important element. If adults find themselves delivering a particularly long personal message, they should think afterward of a more concise way of expressing it. For instance, the preceding example could have been condensed to: "You're upset. It worries me that if you hit Tanya with a stick, you could hurt her. Hand the stick to me."

2. **Failing to use the personal message for fear of making a mistake.** Adults may become tongue-tied at moments when a personal message would be appropriate. They dread stumbling over the words, getting the order wrong, or forgetting parts. Unfortunately, the more adults remain quiet, the less practice they get, and so

improvement and comfort with the skill does not develop. The only remedy is to make fledgling attempts whenever the opportunity arises. It often is easier to begin with positive personal messages because there is less risk involved. After these flow smoothly, corrective messages seem less difficult.

3. **Talking about personal feelings only in problem situations.** Some adults focus primarily on children's mistakes. They are quick to express their dissatisfaction, and focus on admonishing children who fall short of their expectations. This outlook fails to recognize that behavior change is not solely a product of telling children what they are doing wrong but is also a function of strengthening positive behaviors children already display. For children to keep certain behaviors in their repertoire, they must hear that adults feel pleased, excited, amused, appreciative, comforted, or supported by their actions.

4. **Giving up midway.** Children do not always wait patiently to hear an entire personal message. They may turn their heads or simply walk away. Sometimes when this happens, adults become flustered and give up. A better approach is to use the nonverbal strategies presented in Chapter 3. Adults should lightly hold onto an uninterested child or pursue children who dash off in an attempt to avoid confrontation. This does not mean jerking children around or forcing them to establish eye contact.

   It does mean trying to gain the child's attention for the entire duration of the message. It also is important for children to be told that adults become annoyed when children do not listen. "You don't want to hear what I'm telling you. It upsets me when you walk away while I'm talking. Stand still and listen."

5. **Focusing on short-term goals rather than long-term goals.** In problem situations, adults sometimes find it easier to simply say "No" or "We don't do that here." Occasionally, these shortcuts have the desired effect: Children stop what they are doing. Unfortunately, such success usually is temporary because it does not prompt children's internalization of the rule. Instead, adults have to repeat their admonitions over and over again. Moreover, children may not comply without direct supervision. Personal messages are worth the time they take because they contribute to increased self-regulation.

6. **Making expectations known from a distance.** When adults see children in threatening situations, their first impulse is to shout a warning: "Look out! You'll drop the fish tank" or "Watch it! The floor is slippery." In cases such as these, children frequently ignore the message because they do not

realize it is directed at them. The adult's loud voice may cause alarm or stimulate children to become louder or more active themselves. In either case, the adult's message is not received adequately. A better approach is to move quickly over to the child and state expectations in a face-to-face interaction. The benefits of such a direct approach outweigh the seconds lost to achieve it.

7. **Waiting too long to express your emotions.** In an effort to avoid committing themselves to a line of action, some adults refrain from expressing less intense emotions and allow their emotions to build up over time. When they do react, it is often when they have reached the limit of their endurance. Then, their irritation explodes into fury, concern blossoms into real anxiety, or confusion escalates into panic. None of these are constructive responses because they are so intense that rational action becomes difficult. In addition, children usually are shocked at such extreme reactions and are genuinely uncertain as to what led to the eruption. Adults who rely on this approach also model that only extreme emotions are worth expressing. They should not be surprised when children copy their example. This pitfall can be forestalled by discussing your emotions when first aware of them.

8. **Disguising expectations.** When adults feel nervous about telling children what to do, they often disguise their rules. The most common tactic is to phrase the rule as a question. Instead of saying, "It's time to clean up," they cajole: "Don't you want to clean up, now?"; "Clean up, okay?"; "You wouldn't want us to have a messy room would you?"; or "We want a clean room, right?"

   In every case, adults are hoping children will see things their way. Yet, children usually interpret these messages not as rules that they are obligated to follow, but as questions, which are optional and that can be answered with either "Yes" or "No." Adults who are unwilling to hear "No" eliminate ambiguity when they phrase their rules as statements: "Start cleaning up"; "It's time to clean up."

   A final error that obscures rules is for adults to include themselves in the rule when they have no real intention of following it. For instance, adults say, "Let's wipe our bottom until it is clean," when what they mean is, "Wipe your bottom," or they say, "Let's brush our teeth," rather than "Brush your teeth." Adults who do this imply that children should look to them as a model of the behavior in question. When this does not mirror reality, the statement is confusing.

   Adults who use disguising tactics limit children's chances to be successful. Rules should be phrased as statements rather than questions, using words with precise rather than ambiguous meanings, and in a way that leaves no doubt as to who is expected to follow them.

Combining Personal Messages with Other Skills You Have Learned

Personal messages are effective for establishing expectations and for reminding children about important rules. They are especially useful when combined with other skills associated with the Social Support Pyramid described in Chapter 1 and depicted in Figure 10-5. Note that these strategies encompass a variety of skills you have learned in previous chapters.

If, in spite of all these strategies, Ethan continues to leave the classroom unattended, his teachers will apply consequences and, if necessary, develop an Intensive Individualized Intervention to address the problem behavior. These latter techniques are addressed in Chapter 11, Fostering Self-Discipline in Children: The Role of Consequences.

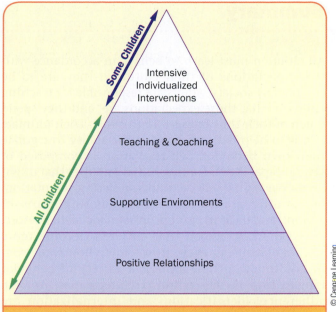

Figure 10-5 Social Support Pyramid: Fostering Self-Regulation in Children: Communicating Expectations and Rules

© Cengage Learning

CHALLENGING BEHAVIOR

Meet Ethan

Combining personal messages with other skills is illustrated in how teachers at Ocean View Center approached a challenging behavior demonstrated by Ethan, a 4-year-old who sometimes left the classroom unattended.

Staff observations indicated that Ethan had moments in the day when he began to miss his mom and would "take off to find her." Ethan's teacher understood his distress. Even so, leaving the room was unsafe. She used the following personal message to remind Ethan about why it was important to stay in the room.

> "Ethan, you miss your mom. I worry when you leave our room. It is not safe for me not to know where you are. Stay in the room unless a teacher is with you."

In addition to a personal message like this, staff members implemented a variety of strategies within the first three levels of the Social Support Pyramid to help Ethan stay in the classroom. Here are a few examples:

Teaching and Coaching

- Adults used affective reflections to acknowledge that Ethan missed his mom. They comforted him and then redirected his attention to activities he enjoyed.
- Adults offered Ethan choices of things he might like to do to give him a greater sense of control over his surroundings.

- Adults used peer coaching to help Ethan "connect" with other children and to begin to find a special friend in the classroom.

Creating Supportive Environments

- Teachers included activities each day that Ethan especially enjoyed.
- Ethan's family had him bring his "RoboBear" from home to ease the transition from home to school. He kept it in his cubby but could go and get it whenever he felt sad.
- Teachers kept the classroom door closed. One adult was stationed in an activity area near the door. The school installed a "safety cap" on the interior doorknob to make it harder for Ethan to open the door on his own.
- Teachers periodically reminded Ethan about the schedule of the day so he had an idea of when the time was getting closer for his mom to pick him up.

Establishing Positive Relationships

- The same teacher greeted Ethan each day and checked in with him frequently throughout the session.
- Adults in activities used invitations, behavior reflections, and effective praise to help Ethan become involved with the materials.
- The teacher sent a short note home each day so mom knew what Ethan was doing at school and could talk about what he had done as well as what he might be doing the following day.

Summary

All children must learn to behave in accordance with the expectations of their culture if they are to be accepted by society. Adults are responsible for teaching children what those expectations are, and they spend much of their time engaged in this role. Their ultimate aim is to help children develop the ability to regulate their own behavior. Self-regulation is composed of several capabilities: curbing initial impulses that might be damaging to self or others, resisting temptation, postponing gratification, implementing plans of action, and initiating appropriate social behaviors. It is generally agreed that children become more self-regulating as they grow older; however, even in adulthood, people exhibit a variety of behavior ranging from no self-control to self-regulation. Amoral, adherence, identification, and internalization are terms used to describe these variations. Individuals' behaviors generally fall into one or another of these categories, although it should be noted that everyone at different times and in different circumstances may display any of them.

Guilt and empathy are emotional factors that influence self-regulation. Cognitively, children's developing notions of right and wrong, their social perspective-taking abilities, centration, and irreversibility also figure into the process. Language and memory skills play a role too.

Children learn the values and expectations of society through direct instruction, observation, rewards, and negative consequences. Adults tell and show children what is expected of them—explicitly in words and implicitly by their own behavior.

Different approaches to child guidance—authoritarian, permissive, uninvolved, and authoritative—have been linked to emotional and behavioral outcomes in children. The authoritative mode produces children who feel good about themselves and are most likely to internalize standards of behavior. Therefore, it is the style of interaction we recommend in this text.

Authoritative adults often express their expectations through a personal message. This consists of a reflection acknowledging the child's point of view, a statement to the child that describes the adult's reaction to a specific behavior of the child and the reason for the reaction, and, finally, an alternative, desirable behavior in which the child is to engage. This last step is used only in situations focusing on behavior change and serves as a rule that governs the child's behavior for that situation. Circumstances under which rules are appropriate deal with safety, protection of property, and the rights of others. The rule portion of the personal message must be reasonable, beneficial to a particular child, definable, and positive. Personal messages are also used to reinforce children's constructive behavior.

Personal messages are most effective when used in combination with other skills you have learned related to establishing positive relationships with children, creating supportive environments, and teaching and coaching to help children gain social competence. In this way, personal messages become a key skill in helping children achieve greater self-regulation. In addition, it is important to communicate with families regarding one's approach to child guidance as well as to elicit information from families about their philosophies and strategies.

Difficulties students encounter when first learning how to express their expectations to children (such as too much talk, forgetting parts of the message, or using ambiguous language) can be overcome through practice and self-reflection.

Key Terms

adherence
amoral
authoritarian style
authoritative style
centration
communication
control
definable rules
direct instruction
empathy

guilt
identification
internalization
irreversible
maturity demands
model
moral violations
negative consequences
nurturance
permissive style

perspective-taking
personal message
positive rules
private speech
reasonable rules
reinforcement
self-regulation
social-conventional infractions
uninvolved style

Discussion Questions

1. Define self-regulation, and describe its component parts.

2. Jamal is a preschooler. His brother Ahmed is 10 years old. Discuss how guilt and empathy would figure into each child's thinking.

3. It has been shown that children become more capable of self-regulation as they mature. Explain the developmental changes that contribute to this increased capacity.

4. Define amoral, adherence, identification, and internalization. Then, discuss which behavior cues tell you when a person is operating at any one of these levels.

5. Name three rules you had to follow as a child. Talk about whether your compliance with each rule was at the adherence, identification, or internalization level.

6. Describe all of the things you could do in relation to instruction and modeling to teach a child how to handle guinea pigs safely. Make sure you take into account children's varying levels of maturity.

7. Think about a teacher you had while growing up. Describe that person's behavior to someone else, keeping in mind the four discipline styles discussed in this chapter. See if the listener can categorize the teacher's behavior based on your description. Then, discuss the effect that style had on your learning.

8. Describe what changes you might have to make in your own interaction style to make it more authoritative.

9. With classmates, identify the three parts of the personal message, and provide no less than three reasons per part for why each is included.

10. Refer to the NAEYC Code of Ethical Conduct presented in Appendix A. Find sections that address the following situations related to rules.

    a. The Brown family and the Smith family both have children in your class. Mrs. Brown approaches you, saying that she doesn't want her child to interact with the Smith child. She expects you to enforce this rule.

    b. One of the families in your group is from another country. The father approaches you, saying he wants his 4-year-old daughter to learn to act in the ways of her culture. This means she must be very deferential in her interactions with adults. He is disturbed that she calls out at group time, seems bossy in her play, and makes decisions such as where to play. In all of these cases, he believes that she should be more submissive. He wants you to support his family's expectations.

Case Study Analysis

Read the case study in Appendix B about Adriana and consider the following:

1. At what level of self-regulation do you think Adriana is currently operating? Select three pieces of evidence that contributed to your conclusions.

2. What are three strategies you could use to help Adriana move to the next level of self-regulation?

3. Identify strategies the teachers have used to help Adriana exhibit greater self-regulation. How effective do these strategies seem to be?

4. Are there any rules you might develop to help Adriana become more involved with the other children?

5. Look through the case study for evidence of adults communicating with one another about their expectations for Adriana. What would you add or change to make the communication more effective?

Field Assignments

1. Keep a record of the personal messages you use in your field placement. When you have a chance, record at least three of your responses. Begin by describing what the child(ren) said or did to prompt your remarks.

   Next, write the exact words you used. Critique your effectiveness and correct any inaccurate personal messages.

   Finally, record two alternate personal messages you could have tried in each situation. Make sure to identify both personal messages used to change children's behavior and ones used to reinforce positive actions.

2. Describe a situation in which your use of a personal message was effective, both from your point of view and the child's. Next, describe a situation in which your use of a personal message was ineffective. Analyze what went wrong and how your response could be improved in the future.

3. Identify a situation involving the children with whom you work, in which it may be necessary for you to establish a rule. Write out your rule. Record how well it fits the criteria for an effective rule described in this chapter. If necessary, change your rule to make it more appropriate. Next, talk about what you will do and say to remind children of the rule and to enforce it as necessary.

   Later, discuss whether or not you had to use the rule you made. Describe any changes you enacted in carrying out the rule and why. Conclude by describing the children's reactions to your rule.

4. Read program materials designed to acquaint families with program policies regarding their participation and that of the child (e.g., enrollment materials, program handbook, introductory newsletter). List at least five rules, policies, or expectations for families and describe the reasoning behind these. If the reasoning is not obvious to you, talk to someone in the program to find out more about why the policies have been made.

Reflect on Your Practice

Here is a sample checklist you can use to reflect on your use of the skills as a beginning professional. A more detailed classroom observation tool is available in Appendix C.

Teachers who support children's development of self-regulation through effective rule setting, do the following:

✓ Ask children to help make classroom rules.

✓ Intervene when safety, property, or rights are in jeopardy.

✓ Implement rules that are definable and reasonable (children know what is expected and are capable of doing it).

✓ Reflect (acknowledge) children's perspectives in rule-setting situations.

✓ Describe their reactions to children's behavior.

✓ Give reasons for rules (focused on safety, property, or rights).

✓ Redirect children's mistaken behavior by telling children what to do as well as what not to do.

✓ Revise or discard unreasonable rules.

CourseMate. Visit the Education CourseMate for this textbook to access the eBook, Digital Downloads, TeachSource Videos, and quizzes. Go to CengageBrain.com to log in, register, or purchase access.

11 Fostering Self-Regulation in Children: The Role of Consequences

OBJECTIVES

On completion of this chapter, you should be able to:

Explain why children sometimes act inappropriately and what adults can do to help children be more successful.

Identify four kinds of consequences—positive, natural, logical, and unrelated—and the difference between these and punishments.

Explain how to combine personal messages and consequences effectively.

Describe the need for intensive individualized intervention, how to plan for it, and how to use it to enhance children's social competence.

Discuss how to adapt rules and consequences for children with special needs.

Demonstrate skills for implementing consequences.

Recognize pitfalls to avoid in implementing consequences.

NAEYC STANDARDS naeyc

1. Promoting Child Development and Learning
2. Building Family and Community Relationships
3. Using Developmentally Effective Approaches to Connect with Children and Families
4. Becoming a Professional

The following episode takes place in a Pre-K class

Teacher: You're enjoying painting. It's time to clean up now and get ready for lunch. Please cap the paints or tag the projects that are already dry.

Ralph: I'm not done yet.

Julie: I don't want to.

Jacob: (Says nothing; continues to paint at the easel.)

Learning to voluntarily comply with reasonable rules and requests is an important component of social competence. Yet, as everyone knows, there are times when children refuse to do what they are asked to do, when they behave inappropriately, or when they fail to follow a given rule. What to do in such situations is a common concern of teachers, caregivers, and parents (Charles, Seuter, & Barr, 2014). On the one hand, adults want children to comply; on the other hand, they are often unsure of how to achieve this goal in developmentally appropriate ways. This chapter will address both concerns.

Everything you read will be based on three assumptions. First, very young children are novices when it comes to social behavior, and while most children generally want to act in ways that adults and peers find acceptable, they are not always successful. Second, learning the rules of society is a complex process that takes time and practice to master. It is not automatic; nor is it easy. Third, children make mistakes.

Children's mistaken behavior can come about for several reasons:

- Children are not sure of what the rules are.
- Children are not sure how to follow the rule.
- Children don't know appropriate actions to substitute for unacceptable ones.
- Children do not have the ability or instrumental know-how to follow a particular rule.
- Children think the rule is meaningless.
- Children have no investment in the rule.
- Children are gaining positive payoffs from negative actions.
- Children are getting mixed messages about the importance of certain rules.
- Children are testing adults to see how far they will bend regarding rule enforcement.

In most instances, any one or a combination of these reasons may be why children act inappropriately. Children's misbehaviors often improve when adults adjust their approach to setting and enforcing rules. Let's consider each of these problems further.

Problem Behaviors and Their Potential Solutions naeyc

Problem 1: Uncertainty about What the Rules Are

Problem 2: Uncertainty about How to Follow a Certain Rule

Problem 3: Confusion Over What to Do Instead

Problem 4: Lack of Ability or Instrumental Know-How

These four problems result from poor rule making (MacKenzie & Stanzione, 2010). In each case, children make mistakes because they are incapable of following a particular rule, not because they are unwilling. Poorly constructed rules actually increase children's chances of misbehavior because children lack the knowledge and skills necessary to succeed.

Solution. As described in Chapter 10, effective rules are ones children are capable of following. This means children are developmentally able to meet the expectation and are clear on what they must do to comply. Effective rules also tell children appropriate behaviors to substitute for inappropriate ones (this is the fourth R of the personal message). If children lack appropriate knowledge or skills, adults help them learn these things. Rules that are reasonable, definable, and positive meet these criteria and make it less likely that children will continue mistaken behavior.

Problem 5: Meaningless Rules

Problem 6: No Ownership of the Rules

Children often reject rules that seem irrelevant or unnecessary (Kohn, 2006). Rules that make no sense from the child's point of view are ones they may ignore. Similarly, rules in which children have had no say elicit less support than expectations and solutions that involve child input.

Solution. Adults minimize children's rejection of rules when they give reasons for their rules and requests. As noted in Chapter 10, the reasons that make sense to very young children are ones that focus on keeping people safe and those that protect property. Eventually, protecting people's rights and fairness also become understandable rationales for certain expectations.

In addition, children are most willing to adopt a code of behavior in which they have some say. Children benefit from participating in discussions about problem situations in the classroom and their potential solutions. Such discussions often highlight why rules are important to groups of people living and working together and what rules children think

Our Rules
1. Don't step on people's fingers if they are sitting on the floor.
2. Write in your own journal.
3. Take turns with iPads.
4. Give Chip fresh water every day.
5. Everyone help with clean-up.
6. Say 'hi' to new kids.

© Star City Photography

First-grade rules developed by the children.

should be observed (Epstein, 2009). When children have opportunities to define problems they would like to see resolved as well as identify rules to abide by, they perceive those rules as legitimate social agreements and themselves as partners in those agreements. This prompts children to become invested in helping create an environment in which rules are honored.

Problem 7: Positive Payoffs for Negative Actions

Sometimes inappropriate behaviors get children what they want (Allen & Cowdery, 2012). Kendra's hitting prompts Juan to give up a toy; Sarah's taunting makes Ellie give up a chance to go first; Jim's badgering gets him 15 more minutes on the computer. In each case, the child's poor behavior helped him or her achieve a desired outcome. Alternately, poor behavior can help children avoid things they do not want to do. Crying may circumvent having to follow a rule; wandering may get a child out of clean-up; shouting out at group time may grant the child a "get out of jail free" card from an activity she does not enjoy when she is told to leave the group for a while. A child who is bored may add some excitement to his day by teasing, chasing, or pinching someone secretly.

Solution. To counter the hidden benefits inappropriate behavior can bring, adults must observe children carefully to determine what those benefits are. Based on these observations, teachers introduce alternate strategies that yield similar payoffs in more constructive ways (Dunlap & Fox, 2009). To do this well involves collecting data about the mistaken behavior, analyzing what prompts it, and determining what happens after it occurs. Only then will appropriate substitute actions become clear. You will learn more about how to do this later in this chapter.

Problem 8: Mixed Messages

Even when a rule is appropriately stated to children, adult actions may undermine it. This happens when adults fail to acknowledge compliance, ignore broken rules, or give in to noncompliance (MacKenzie & Stanzione, 2010; Miller, 2013). Such acts create an unpredictable environment in which children cannot be sure what the real expectations are. For example, a rule in the preschool room is that children should wear a paint shirt to paint at the easel. Some days, adults enforce the rule regularly; on other days, adults pay little attention, and many children paint without paint shirts. It is not surprising that children are unsure of the rule and seldom remember to use a paint shirt on their own. Similarly, at Roosevelt Elementary School, it is expected that children will clean their places at the lunch table before leaving the cafeteria. Students are understandably confused when, on the days they bus their trays, no one notices. Additionally, on some days, they are scolded for leaving food wrappings on the table; on other days, they are urged to "just leave their trays there" (adults are running late); and on still other days, they are ignored when they fail to throw away their food wrappings (adults are too tired to cope). Adult actions have made rule enforcement arbitrary. Over time, youngsters conclude that the rule has no real meaning and do not feel obliged to uphold it.

Problem 9: Testing the Limits

Children constantly try to determine what constitutes in-bounds and out-of-bounds behavior. The only way they can discover these differences is to test them out by repeated trial and error (Denno, Carr, & Bell, 2011). Because adults vary in their willingness to obtain compliance, children test each adult with whom they come in contact to discover that person's limits. Both forms of testing frequently result in inappropriate behavior.

Solution. The way to resolve behavior problems related to mixed messages and limit testing is to enforce rules consistently through the use of consequences. The following portion of this chapter focuses on this important skill.

Consequences naeyc

Consequences are events that make a particular behavior more or less likely to happen in the future. Positive consequences increase the chances that behaviors will be repeated; natural, logical, and some unrelated consequences reduce the chances.

Consequences that Increase Desirable Behaviors

Positive consequences are ones that reinforce children for maintaining a rule or encourage them to repeat a positive behavior in the future (Marzano, 2003). One of the most common and most effective is to reinforce children's behavior with a positive personal message. For instance, when Mr. Moore says, "LaTisha, you remembered to raise your hand before talking. I'm pleased. That gave me a chance to finish what I was saying," his message is highlighting the child's appropriate behavior in

When the children put the blocks away, their behavior could be reinforced with a positive personal message.

© Cengage Learning

a way that will make an impression on LaTisha. In addition, it acknowledges that following the rule took effort.

When adults affirm children's compliance using personal messages, children are likely to comply again in the future. This is because positive personal messages remind children of rules and their rationales at times when children have demonstrable proof that they are able to follow them. This type of confirmation is beneficial to children of all ages.

Another positive consequence, covered in Chapter 4, is effective praise. An example is when the adult points out, "You've been reminding yourself to bring your homework every day this week. You've made it to Thursday already with homework every day." This nonevaluative acknowledgment of children's rule-related behavior underscores their growing ability to act in socially acceptable ways.

Similarly, when adults acknowledge the accumulated benefits of following a rule over time, they promote children's feelings of self-satisfaction and pride in their own performance. For instance, if the rule were "Practice the piano every day," the adult might say, "You were a big hit at the recital. All of your practicing really paid off."

Positive consequences can take the form of earned privileges too. For instance, the rule is "Handle library books carefully." When children can demonstrate this skill, they are permitted to use the books without adult assistance. This type of reward actually formalizes the natural aftermath of their positive behavior. It also emphasizes the positive outcomes that result from their actions. When this information is articulated, the link between behavior and outcome becomes more evident.

Finally, there are times when positive consequences take the form of tangible rewards such as stickers or stars on a progress chart (Essa, 2008). For example, a child may receive a sticker for each day she is able to get through the morning without hitting another child. Such tangible rewards serve as concrete evidence of positive behavior and help some children recognize their accomplishments. Although tangible rewards are not used very often or in every setting, they are used in some situations with beneficial outcomes.

See Highlight 11-1 for several possibilities of verbal and nonverbal reinforcers.

Consequences that Reduce Mistaken Behaviors

Social scientists commonly refer to all actions that reduce problem behaviors as punishments. However, research shows that some uses of punishment are effective in promoting self-regulation, and others are not. To clearly distinguish between the two, we will label strategies that enhance self-control as **corrective consequences**, and we will label strategies that detract from

Potential Reinforcers

Early childhood teachers can offer children positive reinforcement in many ways.

Using nonverbal signals:

- Give a child a high-five.
- Give the thumbs-up sign.
- Smile.
- Pat the child on the back.
- Listen intently.
- Fulfill a child's request.
- Join a child's activity.
- Ask to keep a copy of the child's work.
- Display a child's work.

Using words:

- Invite children to interact and talk with you.
- Talk with children about what they are doing.
- Ask the child to explain how he or she did something.
- Inquire about the child's family, pets, interests, or activities at home and school.
- Share jokes.
- Ask the child for help for yourself or another child.
- Paraphrase children, allowing them to lead the conversation.
- Ask children what they would like to do.
- Use effective praise and positive personal messages.
- Point out how much you or others appreciate the child and see him or her as a good friend.

Source: Based on *Challenging Behavior in Young Children: Understanding, Preventing and Responding Effectively*, by B. Kaiser and J. S. Rasminsky, 2012, Boston, MA: Pearson.

children desirable alternatives to their misbehavior (Sigsgaard, 2005; Bear 2010). Consequently, children who are punished on a regular basis tend to adopt the coercive manner to which they have been subjected, becoming increasingly defiant and hostile (Beaudoin & Taylor, 2004). Much of their time also is spent figuring out how to do what they want without getting caught (McCord, 2005). For all these reasons, punishments lead to short-term compliance only. Children remain at adherence because they do not acquire the tools necessary for internalization (empathy, reasoning, new behaviors).

Corrective Consequences. The rule in Ms. Weichart's classroom is that children must wash their hands before lunch. As Marit approaches the lunch table, she is reminded to wash her hands with soap. When she fails to do so, Ms. Weichart intervenes. She calmly talks to the child about why washing hands is important.

When Marit forgets to use soap on her hands, the teacher physically helps her "rehearse" the appropriate actions.

self-control as **punishments**. There are significant differences between the two, as summarized in Table 11-1.

Punishments. Punishments such as hitting children, yelling at them, or shaming them make children suffer in order to teach them a lesson (Kohn, 2006). These are harsh, unreasonable actions that rely on power and force to change children's behavior or get them to do something. They may be carried out with no warning or in a threatening manner that frightens or humiliates children. As described in Table 11-1, punishments focus on making children "pay" for their misdeeds, rather than teaching them how to behave more appropriately. Punishments do not emphasize reasoning or the development of empathy for others. Nor do they teach

Table 11-1 Differences between Corrective Consequences and Punishments

Corrective Consequences	Punishments
Indicate to children that they are valued, even when their behavior is not	Reject children
Are instructive—they teach children how to correct problem behaviors	Are not instructive—they inform children that a problem has occurred, but do not teach them how to correct it
Focus on mistaken behavior	Focus on "bad" child
Have a clear link to the mistaken behavior	Have no relationship to the mistaken behavior
Are thoughtfully implemented	Are arbitrary and demeaning
Communicate that children have the power to correct the mistaken behavior	Communicate the personal power of the adult
Enable children to change their own behavior	Require adults to assume the entire responsibility for behavior change
Focus on prevention of future mistakes	Focus on retaliation for mistakes
Are applied matter-of-factly	Are applied with obvious resentment, anger, indifference, or contempt
Are applied in proportion to the severity of the mistaken behavior	Are severe and exceed the severity of the mistaken behavior
Rely on reasoning	Rely on coercion

Sources: Curwin, R. L., Mendler, A. N., & Mendler, B. D. (2008). Discipline with Dignity: New Challenges, New Solutions. Alexandria, VA: ASCD; Malott, R., & Trojan, E. A. (2008). Principles of Behavior 6E. Upper Saddle River, NJ: Pearson; Gartrell, D. (2011). A Guidance Approach to the Encouraging Classroom. Clifton Park, NY: Delmar Learning.

Then she helps Marit go back into the bathroom to wash. The act of washing her hands with the teacher's help enables Marit to rehearse the desired behavior and may remind her to wash her hands in the future. As such, it acts as a consequence that teaches the child "how" to behave.

Corrective consequences for mistaken behavior are constructive actions that help children recognize the impact their actions have on themselves and others. They are implemented with the long-term goal of teaching children self-regulation (Thompson & Twibell, 2009; Bear, 2010). Consequences help children learn acceptable conduct from the experience of being corrected. They enable children to approximate desired acts. They also serve as practice for the future and make it more likely that children will succeed in repeating appropriate behaviors independently. When used properly, consequences encourage children to think about dimensions of problem situations, which may be useful to them in future encounters. For example, what prompted the episode, how and why did people react to the child's behavior, and what acceptable alternatives were suggested? This self-analysis is possible because corrective consequences do not elicit intense feelings of fear or shame, both of which interfere with children's ability to reason.

Another attribute of consequences is that they make the children's world more predictable; children know exactly what will happen when a rule is broken. Infractions are dealt with matter-of-factly and consistently, no matter who the perpetrators are or how often they have broken the rule before. This makes it easier for children to recognize the link between actions and reactions and to gradually internalize acceptable codes of conduct (Denno, Carr, & Bell, 2011).

Types of Corrective Consequences

Consequences that address mistaken behavior effectively come in three varieties: natural, logical, and unrelated.

Natural consequences. Natural consequences happen without intervention by an adult (Nelsen, 2006). They are a direct result of the child's behavior alone. As such, natural consequences signal children that their actions matter and that they have the power to influence outcomes. For instance, if children fail to hang their jackets in their cubbies, the natural consequence may be a misplaced jacket. Children who come late for lunch may experience the natural consequence of eating cold food or eating alone because everyone else is finished. Natural consequences are most effective when they are obvious to children and when children care about the outcome. Eventually children will learn to put their jackets away if they want to find them easily or come on time for lunch if they prefer warm food or eating with friends.

Logical consequences. Logical consequences are "logically" related to the rule, meaning there is an obvious connection between the child's behavior and the corrective action (Fields, Merritt, & Fields, 2014). When Jamie draws on a tabletop in her classroom, an adult talks with her about her actions and their impact on classroom materials. Then she helps Jamie gather what she needs to scrub the table clean. Scrubbing helps Jamie restore damaged property and makes an obvious connection between the inappropriate behavior of drawing on the table and the consequence of cleaning it (Gartrell, 2014). This makes scrubbing the table a logical consequence. **Logical consequences** generally take one of three forms:

- Rehearsal: Children approximate or practice a desired behavior.

- Restitution: Children make genuine amends for their misbehavior.

- Temporary loss of privilege: For a brief time, children forfeit a privilege they have abused.

Rehearsal If Rudy is running down the hall, a logical consequence would be to have him go back and walk. The act of walking serves as a more relevant reminder of the rule than scolding him or making him sit out for several minutes. Walking actually enables Rudy to "rehearse" the appropriate behavior he is expected to use in the future. Having children practice rules you want them to remember increases their likelihood of following the rule another time on their own.

Restitution At times, rehearsals are not feasible, so restitution is more appropriate. Jamie, who drew on the table, then scrubbed away the marks, returning the table to its original condition, demonstrated this. Similarly, the logical consequence when children throw food

A logical consequence for not putting the books away earlier is to return them to their proper place now.

The logical consequence for forgetting to flush the toilet is to go back and flush the toilet.

© Cengage Learning 2015

© Cengage Learning

on the floor is to have them clean it up. This act restores the situation to a more acceptable state and shows children that the unacceptable behavior of throwing food will not be allowed. In this way, restitution improves a problem situation or repairs damage done.

Rehearsal and restitution are the most common forms of logical consequences (Charles et al., 2014). They support the development of self-control among children of all ages and are well suited for most situations in which consequences are needed. Because they are so tangible, rehearsal and restitution dominate our work with toddlers and children whose thinking is characteristically described as preoperational. As children begin to think more abstractly, temporary loss of privilege is another form of logical consequence that can help children develop greater powers of self-regulation.

Temporary loss of privilege In Mr. Li's class, the children are allowed to go into the hall unaccompanied to retrieve things from their lockers. When second-grader Corinne begins wandering the corridors while asking to get something from her backpack, the teacher temporarily revokes her privilege to be in the hall on her own. She is given another chance the next day to see if she can assume the privilege responsibly. Going into the hall unsupervised involves both privilege and responsibility. When children demonstrate that they are not capable of handling the two successfully, a logical consequence interrupts the problem behavior and helps children recognize that if they want to have certain privileges, they will have to assume the responsibilities that go with them. Withholding small privileges like this is especially effective when adults are also warm and clear about the rules and when they give children opportunities to try again another time (Bee & Boyd, 2009).

An important benefit of using logical consequences is that they teach children behaviors that are incompatible with the problem behaviors children are displaying (Stormont et al., 2008; Bear, 2010). For instance, cleaning a table is incompatible with drawing on it; cleaning food off the floor is incompatible with throwing it there. As incompatible responses like these are strengthened through practice and positive consequences, the less desirable behaviors that they replace are weakened. If such instances are noted and praised, eventually youngsters learn to replace the taboo behavior with the more desired action. Further examples of logical consequences are described in Table 11-2. As you will see, there may be more than one option for a particular situation. In these instances, adults choose just one, not multiple consequences per situation.

Unrelated consequences. The third type of corrective consequence is an **unrelated consequence**. Unrelated consequences involve the introduction of a penalty unrelated to the mistaken behavior. As the name implies, these consequences are not the natural outgrowth of a child's behavior, nor do they enable children to approximate desired behaviors or rectify less desirable ones. Instead, they are outcomes manufactured by the adult in response to children's misbehavior (Malott & Trojan, 2008). Examples might include forbidding Lisa to watch television until she brushes her teeth or to choose a learning center until she hangs up her coat. Brushing teeth has nothing to do with watching television, so denial of television neither teaches Lisa how to brush her teeth nor improves her unclean mouth. However, if Lisa really values her TV time, she will learn that watching television is contingent on tooth brushing. The same is true regarding the coat. Forbidding Lisa to choose a learning center does not give her practice in hanging up her coat, but it does create an aversive situation that the child can make more positive by doing what is required.

It is the unrelated nature of the penalty that distinguishes these consequences from the loss of privilege variation of logical consequences. Because they have no relation to the broken rule, adults must take particular care to enforce these in the true spirit of consequences, not punishments. Furthermore, the most beneficial unrelated consequences are those that, although dissimilar in content, are linked in time to the infraction. For instance, it is more effective to withhold the next event in a sequence than one far in the future. Therefore, it is better to deprive Lisa of participating in some portion of the free-choice period for forgetting to hang up her coat than to keep her in from recess several hours later. Of the three types of corrective consequences described here, unrelated consequences are used least often. However, there are times when they are appropriate and fulfill the goal of helping children learn more acceptable behavior through the guidance process.

Deciding which Corrective Consequences to Use

Adults must carefully determine which corrective consequence is most suitable for a given situation. To do this, they think about all three consequences, beginning with natural consequences, then logical ones, and then unrelated actions. The ultimate aim is to choose the consequence that addresses the mistaken behavior appropriately while at the same time giving the child the most opportunity to exercise self-direction.

Step one. Natural consequences are always considered first. Adults ask themselves the following questions:

- *Is the outcome acceptable to me?*
- *Will the child recognize that a consequence has occurred?*
- *Will the consequence make a difference to the child?*

> **Table 11-2** Examples of Logical Consequences

Problem Behavior	Logical Consequence	Form of Logical Consequence
Lacey knocks over another child's blocks.	Lacey helps rebuild the block structure.	Restitution
Lindsey makes a mess.	Lindsey cleans it up.	Restitution
Chris hits another child in anger.	Chris gets a tissue to soothe the victim's tears.	Restitution
	Chris is separated from the victim and must remain near an adult to be reminded not to hit.	Rehearsal
	Chris must develop a plan for what to do when angry rather than hitting.	Rehearsal
	Adult provides Chris with a script to use in lieu of hitting and has Chris practice using it.	Rehearsal
Taylor rips pages out of a book.	Taylor repairs the book.	Restitution
	Taylor replaces the book.	Restitution
	Taylor helps pay for the book.	Restitution
Lonnie misuses instructional time.	Lonnie makes up the time immediately.	Rehearsal
Gena says she finished her work so she can go to another activity, but she really didn't.	Instead of moving from one activity to another independently, Gena must show her finished work to the adult before moving on.	Temporary loss of privilege
Leah keeps talking to her friends during an assembly.	Leah must sit apart for a while.	Temporary loss of privilege
	Leah sits next to an adult who can help her focus on the speaker.	Rehearsal
Nine-year-old Mavis repeatedly cheats while playing a game with her peers.	Mavis is asked to leave the group and play on her own for a while. She may return to the group when she can assure them she will play fairly.	Temporary loss of privilege
Instead of remaining with her partner, Bethany repeatedly runs ahead of the group on a field trip.	Bethany must walk with an adult for the rest of the field trip.	Rehearsal Temporary loss of privilege.

© Cengage Learning

Obviously, a consequence that would result in physical harm to a child is unacceptable. The natural aftermath of a child drinking poison or playing in traffic are clear examples. Yet, things other than safety also influence acceptability. What might be acceptable to one adult might be unthinkable to another. As mentioned earlier, the natural consequence for children who arrive late for a meal is to eat cold food or eat alone. Some caregivers might view these outcomes as reasonable; others would find themselves reheating the meal or keeping the child company. If adults know they will be unable to sustain a hands-off policy, the natural consequence is not the consequence of choice. The same is true if the consequence is so subtle the child will never notice it happened (e.g., family members always eat independently,

so this time is no different) or if the consequence is one the child doesn't care about (child prefers eating alone.) All of these conditions diminish the power of the natural consequence to inhibit children's behavior in the future. Under these circumstances, a logical or unrelated consequence is better.

Step two. If a natural consequence is unsuitable, logical consequences are considered next. The questions to ask now are these:

● *Would the child benefit from rehearsal?*
● *Does this situation call for restitution?*
● *Is the child developmentally able to see a connection between the infraction and a loss of privilege?*

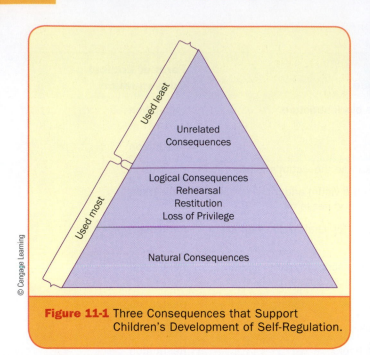

Figure 11-1 Three Consequences that Support Children's Development of Self-Regulation.

© Cengage Learning

If the answer to any of these queries is yes, then a logical consequence is an appropriate teaching tool.

Although logical consequences take more imagination than do unrelated penalties such as sitting in isolation or staying in for recess, they are much more effective in helping children learn appropriate alternate behaviors (Gartrell, 2014).

Step three. Unrelated consequences are the consequences of last resort. These must be used sparingly because their primary value is in curtailing behavior for the moment. For long-term change to occur, children must learn acceptable substitutes for which logical consequences are preferable. Unrelated consequences should be implemented only when no logical consequence is available. See Figure 11-1 for a depiction of how the three corrective consequences described here relate to one another.

Implementing Corrective Consequences

Several children are crowded around the water fountain. They begin to push and shove. Seeing that someone could get hurt, Mr. Wilson decides to intervene.

When children are engaged in potential problem situations like this, adults begin by reminding them of the rule in a matter-of-fact tone using a personal message (Charles et al., 2014). The rule portion of the personal message serves as the reminder. In this case, Mr. Wilson says, "It looks like everyone wants a drink at the same time. I'm worried someone will get hurt when you are pushing like this. Take turns. One person at a time at the front." Often, such prompting is all that is needed for children to comply. If children obey at this point, they should be reinforced with effective praise. However, if they continue to disregard the rule, the adult must implement an appropriate corrective consequence.

The consequence is first stated to the child in the form of a warning (Curwin, Mendler, & Mendler, 2008). The **warning** is phrased as an either-or statement that repeats the rule and then tells the child what will happen if he or she does not follow it. Mr. Wilson's rule is "Take turns. One person at a time at the front." He might state a warning such as, "Either wait your turn, or you will have to go to the end of the line." This warning gives children an opportunity and an incentive to change their behavior in accordance with adult expectations. It also notifies children that this is the last chance for them to comply prior to further adult intervention.

The warning is not intended to be frightening, abusive, or threatening. Rather, it is a plain statement of fact. This means adults warn children calmly. They do not yell at children or use threatening gestures to make their point.

Sample Warning:

"Either" (adult describes the expected behavior)

OR

(Adult states what the consequence will be)

Example: Either take turns or go to the end of the line.

After the warning is given, the adult pauses to give children an opportunity to comply. Children's reaction times are somewhat slower than adults sometimes want them to be. Adults have to take care not to jump in before the child has had time to respond (Denton, 2007). For instance, Alexia continues to push in the line at the water fountain. Mr. Wilson tells her to wait her turn or go to the end of the line. It may take Alexia several seconds to decide what to do. Alexia's delay poses no real threat to those around her, so it can be tolerated for a few moments to give her a chance to abide by the rule on her own.

Sometimes, when safety is jeopardized, immediate physical intervention is necessary. In such cases, the warning is said at the same time the adult is implementing the consequence. For example, if Marla is about to throw a stone, the adult should quickly catch her hand while saying, "You can either put the stone down yourself, or I will take it from you." As the adult grasps Marla's hand, he or she allows a moment's verbal pause to give Marla a chance to drop the rock herself. During this moment, the adult tries to sense Marla's intention, based on whether she remains tense or begins to relax, as well as by what she might be saying. If Marla were capable of releasing the stone, she would be displaying a little self-control. If she were not, the adult would exert the maximum external control by taking the stone away from her. This last step is a follow-through on the stated consequence.

Following Through with Consequences

It is not enough simply to tell children what the consequences of their actions will be. Adults must enforce consequences if children do not comply (Deno, Carr, & Bell, 2011). This is called the **follow-through**. Based on this step, if Alexia continues to push in line at the water fountain, Mr. Wilson will follow through by escorting her to the back of the line, as noted in the warning. The follow-through is a critical part of the guidance process because it involves the enactment of the corrective consequence.

Because appropriate consequences are instructive, the follow-through provides children with valuable information about how to redirect inappropriate behavior. It also demonstrates that adults are predictable,

that they mean what they say, and that there is a limit to the amount of out-of-bounds behavior they will tolerate. From social encounters such as these, children begin to build an accurate picture of their effect on the world and its reaction to them.

When adults find themselves in situations that demand a follow-through, there are certain things they must say so that the reasoning behind their actions is clear to the child. It is important for children to recognize that corrective consequences are a result of their own behavior; they are not arbitrary or vengeful actions on the part of the adult.

The follow-through begins with a brief reflection that summarizes the situation from the child's point of view. Next is a sentence that restates the warning. This often is prefaced by the words, "Remember, I told you . . .." Then the adult repeats the consequence as a statement of what will happen next as a result of the child's behavior, often beginning with the word, "now."

Sample Follow-Through:

Reflect,

Remind (state the warning: either enact behavior or consequence will happen),

Now (implement consequence)

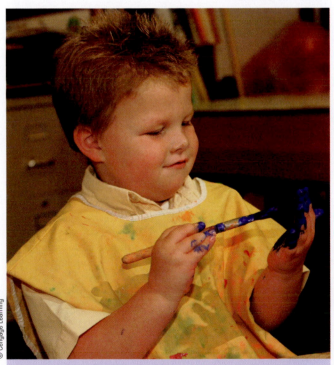

Mark enjoys making handprints. He wants to keep the paint on all day. The teacher uses a personal message to remind him that the rule is, "Wash your hands before lunch."

The teacher warns Mark that he can "either wash his hands on his own, or she will help him." When he does not comply, she gently leads him to the sink.

Thus, a typical follow-through might sound like this: "Alexia, you're still anxious to get ahead in line. Remember, I told you, either wait your turn or go to the back. Now, go to the back." While this is being said, Mr. Wilson escorts Alexia to the back of the line.

When to Implement Consequences

Two key factors influence how well children learn from the consequences they experience: consistency and timing. Consistency involves how often the rule is enforced. Timing refers to the period between when the rule is broken and when enforcement is initiated. Rule enforcement must be consistent (Conroy, Brown, & Olive, 2008; Bear, 2010). Every time the rule is broken, the adult must be prepared to enact appropriate consequences to ensure compliance.

Rules that are administered one day and neglected the next are ineffective. Because children cannot be sure whether or not the rule is in operation, they are not likely to follow it. As a result, youngsters who experience erratic rule enforcement tend to demonstrate more incidents of mistaken behavior than do children whose experience has been more regular. Because consistency is so important, adults are cautioned to insist on only a few rules at a time. It is better to unwaveringly enforce one or two important rules than to halfheartedly attempt many rules.

In addition to being consistent, rule enforcement must be immediate. Long delays between the moment when the child breaks the rule and the moment when the follow-through takes place weaken the impact of the consequence (MacKenzie & Stanzione, 2010). In other words, it would be ineffective for Mr. Wilson to tell Alexia that if she continued to push at the water fountain, she wouldn't get a treat later in the day. Helping Alexia to back away from the fountain soon after the pushing occurred would help Alexia focus more clearly on the problem behavior and its logical solution. Children must have an opportunity to associate their inappropriate behavior with an immediate consequence. The further removed the consequence is in time from the act itself, the more difficult it is for children to make a connection. For these same reasons, consistency and immediacy are important to the implementation of positive consequences as well.

Combining the Warning and Follow-Through with the Personal Message naeyc

Up to this point, we have focused on the appropriate use of both positive consequences and natural, logical, and unrelated ones. The latter take place in a sequence of skills that enhance children's development of self-

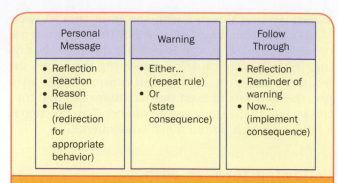

Figure 11-2 The Entire Sequence for Supporting Children's Development of Self-Regulation.

© Cengage Learning

control. This sequence consists of a personal message succeeded by a warning and then, if necessary, a follow-through. You learned about personal messages in Chapter 10. The warning and follow-through were just outlined. Here is what they look like all together (see Figure 11-2).

The sequence is illustrated in the following situation.

Mr. Howard, a student teacher, enters the bathroom to find Alan stuffing several paper towels down the toilet, laughing at the loud sound the toilet is making. Water and towels are all over the floor. The child does not see the adult come in.

Personal message: Mr. Howard quickly approaches Alan and stands close to him. He catches Alan's hand just as the child reaches for another towel. Mr. Howard says, "Alan, you're having fun. I'm worried that with this water all over the floor, someone will slip and get hurt. Start cleaning up this mess." Mr. Howard pauses a moment and waits for Alan to comply. Instead, Alan tries to move toward the door. Mr. Howard stops him.

Warning: "You'd rather not clean up. Either you figure out where to start cleaning, or I'll tell you where to start." Again, Mr. Howard waits a few seconds in the hope that Alan will begin. The child just stands there. Mr. Howard calmly hands Alan a bucket and a sponge.

Follow-through: "It's hard for you to make a choice. Remember, I said either you choose, or I'd choose. You can start in this corner." Mr. Howard places the sponge in Alan's hand and edges him toward the puddle.

Rationale for This Verbal Sequence

By combining a personal message with a warning and follow-through, Mr. Howard was using a step-by-step sequence designed, in the short run, to change Alan's unacceptable behavior. Its long-range objective is to provide a structure through which Alan eventually achieves greater self-discipline.

Table 11-3 Short-Term Benefits of Using a Personal Message, Warning, and Follow-Through

	Short-Term Benefits for Mr. Howard	Short-Term Benefits for Alan
Step 1a: Personal message	Has a way to enter the situation calmly and rationally	Is treated with respect and acceptance
	Has a means of communicating respect and acceptance of the child, but disapproval of the behavior	Is alerted that his behavior is inappropriate and is told why
	Has a blueprint for what kinds of information to provide the child initially	Is informed via the rule of what to do instead (clean up the mess)
Step 1b: Pause	Has a chance to see if Alan can comply before he exerts further external control	Is given a chance to change the inappropriate behavior on his own, thereby exercising internal control
	Has a moment to think of an appropriate consequence to use if necessary	
Step 2a: Warning	Has a constructive way to exert increased external control over Alan's behavior	Is reminded of the rule
	Establishes a legitimate foundation for carrying out the follow-through if necessary	Gains a clear understanding of what will happen if he does not comply
Step 2b: Pause	Has a chance to see if Alan can comply before he exerts further external control	Is given a chance to change the inappropriate behavior on his own, thereby exercising internal control
Step 3: Follow-through	Has an authoritative way to resolve the situation without becoming abusive or giving in	Is able to rehearse an acceptable behavior he was not able to carry out on his own
	Has been able to stop the negative behavior as well as remedy the problem situation	Has evidence that the adult means what he says and is predictable in his actions
	Has had an opportunity to demonstrate that he means what he says, increasing his predictability in the eyes of the child	

© Cengage Learning

Short-term benefits. The immediate advantages to both Mr. Howard and Alan of the sequential use of a personal message, warning, and follow-through are outlined in Table 11-3.

Long-term benefits. The skills just described offer short-term advantages to adults and children, but they provide long-term benefits as well. Combining a personal message, a warning, and a follow-through helps adults deal with children's inappropriate behaviors consistently, both for the same child over time and among different children. This consistency enables helping professionals to establish an authoritative pattern of interaction with children in formal group settings. In addition, the time adults initially invest in using the sequence with children pays off later in fewer future mistaken behaviors (Denno, Carr, & Bell, 2011).

Children also profit when their confrontations with adults are eventually reduced. They feel more successful and better able to satisfy their needs in ways that result in social rewards rather than social costs.

The resulting positive self-appraisal enhances their feelings of self-esteem. Moreover, as children experience this self-discipline sequence on a variety of occasions, they gradually shift from complete dependence on external, adult control to greater internal control.

When the sequence is first introduced, most children will test the adult's predictability and resolve. They will often test through the entire sequence: personal message (with no change in behavior), warning (with no change in behavior), and follow-through in which the consequence is implemented. As children become more familiar with both the adult and the sequence of steps described here, children often respond to the warning without having to experience the follow-through directly. This happens because they have learned that the adult means what he or she says and that a warning indicates that a follow-through is forthcoming unless the behavior is changed. Behavior change at this point shows that children are beginning to exercise some self-regulation. They are at the adherence level, focused on avoiding a consequence or gaining the benefits of compliance.

Eventually, children reach a point at which a personal message is all that is needed to guide their actions. In this way, they begin to exert greater control over their behavior, while the adult exerts less. Initially, this change occurs because children respond to the emotions of the adult with whom they identify. Gradually, however, they take into account the reasoning behind the expectation and, as a result, consider the effects their actions have on those around them. Such reasoning ultimately leads to internalization.

As this occurs, it is the child who assumes the greatest responsibility for his or her conduct, not the adult. Thus, the adult's use of the skill sequence in any given situation will match the child's ability to exercise inner control. If the child is able to comply based on the reasoning of the personal message, further intervention is unnecessary. However, should a youngster need more support, it is provided. The relationship between children's degree of self-regulation, as discussed in Chapter 10, and the skill sequence is depicted in Table 11-4.

Successive Use of the Skill Sequence

It is not unusual for children to resist complying by attempting to divert the adult's attention from the issue at hand. Shouting, protesting, escalating the problem behavior, or running away are strategies children might use to try and avoid corrective consequences (Divinyi, 2011; Calkins & Williford, 2009). Unfortunately, if adults give up, they are teaching children that these tactics work. As a result, children begin to rely on inappropriate strategies more and more frequently.

This dilemma must be avoided because the more ingrained an inappropriate behavior becomes, the more difficult it is to change. The best way to deal with such situations is to defuse them right at the start. This means always following through after a warning has been stated and the child has failed to demonstrate compliance. For example, if the warning is "Either walk, or I will help you," that is exactly what must happen. If Ginger runs away, she must be retrieved; if Saul become stiff or goes limp, his feet should be shuffled along. Even a few steps are enough to make the point.

Sometimes one problem behavior will lead to another. When this happens, adults should repeat the sequence and follow through each time it is needed. For instance, 4-year-old Kayla is in a small group activity peeling vegetables for vegetable soup. Giggling, she pokes Charlie with her plastic peeler. Charlie protests. Kayla laughingly pokes him again and again. The teacher intervenes, using a personal message and then this warning: "Either keep the peeler to yourself, or you will lose the privilege of using it." Kayla tries to poke Charlie one more time. As the teacher follows through, Kayla angrily pushes all the vegetable peels onto the floor. This represents a new problem behavior. The adult responds with a new personal message, "You are upset about having to give up the peeler. Those scraps on the floor worry me. Someone could slip on them and get hurt. Put them in the trash instead." If the child refuses, the teacher goes on to a relevant warning and follow-through, remaining calm and matter-of-fact. For instance, the warning is "Either put some peels in the trash, or I will help you." The follow-through is "You are pretty upset. Remember I said put some peels in the trash or I would help you. Now, I will help you." The adult puts some peels in Kayla's hand to put in the trash.

When adults enforce rules each time they are broken, they create a predictable, stable environment for children and leave no doubt in children's minds about what happens when rules are followed or not. This consistency is absolutely necessary if children are to learn that adults always respond fairly and rationally. Maintaining a calm rationale approach is always important. However, this is especially true when children lose their own rationality in the heat of a temper tantrum.

What to Do about Young Children's Temper Tantrums

Most people know a **temper tantrum** when they see one. There is no mistaking the physical signs: red face, flailing arms and legs, screaming, and crying. Any child, at any time, may become involved in a tantrum, and although such behavior is most common in children ages 1 through 4, kindergartners as well as school-age children may resort to these volcanic outbursts when "life" becomes overwhelming.

Children have tantrums for several reasons. They initially appear when urgent wants are not immediately

Table 11-4 The Link between Children's Degree of Self-Regulation and this Verbal Skill Sequence

Child's Degree of Self-Regulation	Stage of the Sequence that Applies
Amoral–None	Child requires a follow-through
Adherence	Child responds to warning
Identification	Child responds to personal message
Internalization	Child monitors self

© Cengage Learning

gratified. Later, tantrums may occur because children are fatigued or not feeling well, because they are stressed from multiple demands in their day, because they receive little attention for positive behavior, because they are continually subjected to unrealistic adult demands, because rule enforcement is unpredictable, because they need more structure in their lives, or because adults have given in to tantrums in the past (Brooks, 2011).

Many of the factors that spark temper tantrums are preventable. The best preventative measures are to make sure children's physical needs are met, acknowledge children's feelings before they become intense, establish predictable routines, teach children alternate ways to get what they want, respond positively to children's appropriate behavior, and make reasonable rules and enforce them consistently using positive and appropriate corrective consequences (Harrington, 2004). Yet, children occasionally will resort to temper tantrums in spite of all these precautions.

Whenever a child throws a tantrum, it is such an intense emotional and physical event that children's normal thought processes are no longer available to them. Impassioned children cannot hear or respond to adult directions or efforts to comfort; they cannot think out a logical, more socially appropriate sequence of actions; and they can no longer gauge the effect of their behavior. Under these circumstances, the adult's goal is to help the child regain self-control.

In the case of toddlers, whose outbursts are extreme but short lived, the best way to restore calm is to ignore their outrageous behavior and let them quiet down in their own way and time. Older children, whose emotional states are longer lasting, benefit from having a chance to recover in private, away from the stimulation of group activity. Some teachers refer to this as "cool down time," "time away," or even "time-out" (Kaiser & Rasminsky, 2012). Whatever term is used, the goal is the same: to help children regain their composure without any shameful or punitive repercussions. Instead, the cool down time is treated as a logical consequence in which children rehearse the skills necessary to calm down.

Cool down time.
Cool down time is implemented in a place that is safe, easily supervised, and affords the child some privacy as well as minimal distractions. Children are never put in complete isolation, and there are no designated "cool down chairs" in a corner somewhere to which children are banished to get them out of the way (Warner & Lynch, 2004). At the same time, the adult is careful not to give the child undue attention. That only prolongs the tantrum by further stimulating the child or reinforcing his or her behavior. If another child approaches, the teacher

quietly moves that child away, assures him or her that the upset child is unharmed and that he or she will be returning to the group when ready. The usual length of cool down time ranges from only a minute or two for preschoolers to five minutes or so for older children. When the child feels ready, he or she can reengage in classroom activities (Essa, 2008). The adult does not lecture. Instead, teachers reinforce the child as soon as possible for demonstrating appropriate behavior of any kind. They also make sure to have a positive interaction with the child to signal that things have returned to normal. If the child reenters the classroom routine prematurely and falls back into inappropriate behavior, the adult says, "I guess you're not quite ready to join us," and takes him or her back to the cool down area to try again before rejoining the group activities.

Sometimes children initiate a cool down time themselves because they are on the verge of losing control. Younger children might retreat to their cubby for a while. Older children may go to a quiet part of the room or ask to take a break away from the hubbub of the classroom in order to regain their bearings. When this happens, use positive personal messages and effective praise to underscore children's efforts to control their own behavior.

Sitting apart.
A variation on cool down time is **sitting apart** (Reynolds, 2008). Sitting apart involves temporarily removing a child from an activity or group time because he or she is causing harm or disruption but is not having a temper tantrum. The following scenario illustrates sitting apart.

> During circle time, Elka is enjoying tapping Brandon's back with her feet. She has been told to scoot back and keep her feet still. She refuses. Her kicking is becoming more vigorous, and Brandon is becoming unhappier. In this case, Mrs. Ortega says, "Either keep your feet still, or you'll have to sit away from the group so you can't kick Brandon anymore." Elka continues her kicking. Mrs. Ortega follows through. Elka is moved a little away from the circle to a spot where she can still see the story but where she has no physical contact with the others in the group. She is told she may return when she can sit without kicking.

Elka will remain there until she signals that she is ready to return or the story is over, whichever comes first. Thus, she is able to practice the desired behavior in a setting in which she will have success. Sitting apart used in this manner is a way to rehearse sitting without kicking people, making it one more logical consequence to add to your tool kit of effective guidance strategies.

Where Consequences Fit in Your Daily Repertoire of Guidance Strategies

Consequences help children to maintain or change their actions in response to rules and expectations. This makes them valuable tools for guiding children's social behavior and learning on a daily basis. To use consequences effectively, it is best to consider the context in which they are applied. Sometimes, children's behavior is so clearly unsafe, or damaging to people or property, that immediate adult intervention is necessary. In situations like these, you will use the skill sequence (personal message, warning, follow-through) described in this chapter. At other times, problem behaviors are less pressing, and it is possible to rely on more subtle means of adult intervention to guide children toward more positive actions. Several of these have been described in previous chapters in this text. Thus, there is a continuum of guidance strategies focused on solving behavior problems in the classroom. These range from ones in which children behave constructively with minimal adult support to ones in which adults exert greater control through the enforcement of consequences. This guidance continuum is illustrated in Figure 11-3 with the kinds of supports adults provide all children in their quest to achieve greater social competence.

The strategies outlined in Figure 11-3 are ones teachers use every day with all children. They do not merely restrict children's undesirable actions; they teach children how to be more successful. There is a strong body of evidence that these practices are effective for *most children most of the time* (Dunlap & Fox, 2009). Some children, however, need even more specialized support to achieve greater self-discipline. For these children, Intensive Individualized Interventions provide that support.

The Need for Intensive Individualized Intervention naeyc

All children have their ups and downs—times when they behave well and times when they engage in mistaken behavior. However, some children's mistaken behavior becomes so pervasive and so resistant to change that it interferes with their learning, development, and success in getting along. This puts children at risk for future social problems and possible school failure (Kaiser & Rasminsky, 2012). For instance, any child might hit another in the heat of a conflict, but some children use hitting as their typical mode of interaction. Likewise, a child might disrupt group time on a day when she is upset over not getting a turn to speak,

but this behavior is episodic, not routine. However, some children disrupt group activities so predictably (e.g., rolling around on the floor, talking loudly during the story, or getting up and walking away), that every group time becomes an ordeal for that child and everyone present. When children adopt challenging behaviors like these as their normal way of interacting, other children avoid them. Adults dread interacting with them or feel at a loss for what to do to help them behave more productively. None of these reactions improve the child's chances for success. A better approach is to initiate an Intensive Individualized Intervention, the top tier of the Social Support Pyramid shown in Figure 11-4.

Intensive Individualized Interventions

As the name suggests, **Intensive Individualized Interventions** are specifically designed to suit a particular child. They are intensive because they require the child's everyday caregivers to apply similar strategies across multiple microsystems. This level of intervention requires adults to come together to create a plan and then purposefully coordinate their efforts to support the child in developing new abilities to replace inappropriate behaviors (Hemmeter & Conroy, 2012).

The process for creating Intensive Individualized Interventions involves five steps:

1. Create a Positive Behavior Support team for the child.
2. Make a functional assessment of the situation to better understand factors that contribute to the child's challenging behavior.
3. Develop a behavior hypothesis that identifies the meaning of the child's behavior and provides a basis for planning.
4. Design a Positive Behavior Support plan.
5. Implement and monitor the planned intervention.

Let's consider each step more fully with a real child in mind. Her name is Katie, and her story begins below.

Convening a team. It takes a group effort to make Intensive Individualized Interventions work (Stormont et al., 2008). Everyone who interacts with the child regularly has potentially valuable information to share in developing a **Positive Behavior Support plan**, carrying it out and judging its success. This includes family members, teachers and other classroom staff, administrators, specialists, cooks, bus drivers, playground supervisors, and anyone else who has regular contact with the child. You might find yourself a member of such a team.

THE GUIDANCE CONTINUUM

Greatest Self-Regulation

1. **Watch and listen**. Observe children from nearby. Make yourself available if children want to come to you, but let them work things out for themselves if they can.

2. **Add or take something away** to make it easier for children to manage on their own. For instance, too few objects for children at the art table could lead to arguments. Adding a few more might be all that is needed for children to share more successfully. On the other hand, too many objects on the table might make it difficult for children to work without getting in one another's way. Removing a few items could make it easier for them to use the materials cooperatively.

3. **Describe what you see:** "It looks like two people want to use the scissors at the same time." Or, "You decided to share the glitter. I'm pleased you found a way to work together."

4. **Provide information.** "You thought she spilled the glue on your picture on purpose. She was trying to get the glue back into the bottle and some spilled out. It was an accident." Or, "Sometimes when two people want the same thing at the same time, they decide to share or take turns."

5. **Pose questions.** "What could you do to solve this problem?" Or, "What could you do instead of hitting her to show you're angry?"

6. **Give choices.** "John is using the skinny paintbrush now. You may use the thick brush or the charcoal" Or, "It's clean-up time. You may put away the smocks or stack the trays."

7. **Physically intervene.** Stop hurtful actions such as hitting by catching the child's hands. Hold onto a wiggling child to help him or her hear what you are saying. Separate two children who are pushing.

8. **Help children negotiate problems.** Serve as a translator in the situation. "Did you like it when he pushed you? What could you say to him about that?" Or, "Kali, you think it would be okay to take turns. What do you think, Melanie?" (You will read more about this strategy in Chapter 12.)

9. **Remind children of rules using a personal message.** "You really wanted the glitter. It bothers me when you grab to get what you want. Someone could get hurt. Ask Lisa for a turn next."

10. **Connect actions to consequences via a warning or effective praise.** "Either take turns with the glitter or you'll have to choose something else to work with." Or, "You decided to trade the glitter shaker for the glue. That solved the problem."

11. **Enforce logical consequences.** "You're having a hard time remembering to share the glitter cans. Let's find another material for you to use." Or, "You accidentally dripped glue on Morgan's picture. Let's get some towels and blot it off."

12. **Use "cool down" time for children who are having a temper tantrum or who are on the verge of losing control of their emotions.**

Greatest External Regulation

© Cengage Learning

Figure 11-3 Guidance Continuum for All Children.

Meet Katie

Katie is a second grader, whose frequent whining annoys her classmates and also interrupts their activities. She seldom makes it through a day without three or four whining episodes. Peers have begun steering clear of Katie and adults are finding that much of their time is being spent dealing with Katie's high-pitched outbursts.

Her teacher believes Katie's behavior is interfering with people's rights and with Katie's ability to get along with classmates. She has established a rule that Katie must express herself without whining but has been unsuccessful in implementing consistent consequences herself. She suspects the same is true for other adults who interact with Katie.

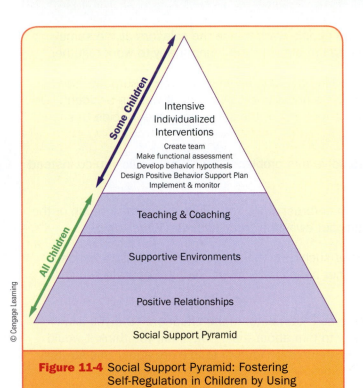

Figure 11-4 Social Support Pyramid: Fostering Self-Regulation in Children by Using Consequences.

© Cengage Learning

The team that meets to discuss how to support Katie includes her classroom teacher, the paraprofessional that helps in the room, the teacher and the aide in the after-school program she attends, and her mom.

Making a functional assessment. Before team members can create a Positive Behavior Support plan, they need to answer four important questions:

- What conditions typically trigger the challenging behavior?
- What are the precise behaviors the child exhibits that are problematic?
- What happens in response to the child's inappropriate actions that reinforces and keeps the challenging behaviors going?

- What does the child gain from engaging in the challenging behavior (e.g., power, attention, task avoidance, stimulation, etc.)? In other words, what function does the challenging behavior serve in the child's life?

These questions can be addressed through an A-B-C analysis (O'Neill et al., 1997).

A stands for antecedents Antecedents are what happen immediately before the challenging behavior occurs that contribute to the child's inappropriate actions. Almost anything can "trigger" a challenging behavior. Some possibilities are adult directives, peer actions, variations in routine, transitions, features of the physical environment, time of day, and lack of stimulation or too much stimulation. Figuring out what "sets off" a particular problem behavior is essential information that must be determined before a proper plan can be developed.

B stands for behavior Behaviors are the actions a child employs to pursue his or her goals. This part of the analysis identifies the challenging behavior in observable measurable terms. For instance, hitting is an observable, countable action. You can see a child hit, and you can count how many times it happens. Moreover, one child might hit and then look around hoping that an adult was watching. Another child might hit and then flee the area to avoid adult scrutiny. Although the two situations are similar, they are not the same and call for different responses. Being specific about the behavior assures that there is common understanding among team members about the true nature of the problem and makes it more likely that the team will create a meaningful individualized plan for each child who needs one.

C stands for consequences In the context of an A-B-C analysis, consequences comprise what happens immediately after the child engages in challenging behavior. How do people react? Does the child get what he or she wanted? Does the child get out of doing something he or she did not want to do? This information gives the team clues about what might be contributing to the persistent nature of the challenging behavior and what payoff the child may be gaining from his or her inappropriate actions.

Data to answer these questions is gathered by observing the child on several occasions and by recording factual information through notes, running records, anecdotal records, checklists, and rating scales. Enrollment forms, medical forms, and incident reports are other useful sources of data. Interviews with relevant individuals (the child himself or herself, peers, and adults) can be helpful too.

> Team members agree to observe Katie for at least one hour per day for three days to make their A-B-C analysis. These observations take place at school, in the after-school program, and at home.

Developing behavior hypotheses. After the data has been gathered, group members reconvene to sift through the evidence and come to some conclusions about what it shows (Duffy, 2010). Sample observations can be depicted in an A-B-C chart like the abbreviated example offered in Table 11-5. Studying these observations gives the team a factual basis for understanding the challenging behavior more fully and for recognizing what function it plays in the child's life (Hanline et al., 2009). The most common functions of challenging behavior (such as gaining attention, avoiding undesirable activities, or responding to too much or too little stimulation) were described in the opening pages of this chapter. Teachers must take function into account when creating intervention strategies so their plans do not inadvertently address the "wrong" problem or make matters worse. For instance, if Katie whines to get attention, a plan that includes long discussions with an adult whenever she whines would provide social rewards that could prompt Katie to whine more often. On the other hand, if Katie whines because she lacks the skills to comply, verbal coaching could increase her ability to work through an activity with less frustration and less whining. Look over the evidence in Table 11-5, what do you see? Do you agree with the behavior hypothesis Katie's team has made?

Based on the evidence in Table 11-5, Katie's Positive Behavior Support team believes that the "pay off" for Katie's whining is that it gets her out of things she does not want to do. Katie also is learning that adults do not consistently enforce expectations and that they will "bend" the rules a lot if she whines. All of this will have to change if Katie's behavior is to improve.

Designing a Positive Behavior Support plan. Based on the understandings they gain through the functional analysis, team members create a Positive Behavior

---

Table 11-5 Functional Analysis of Katie's Whining

Katie		
A **Antecedents/Triggers**	**B** **Behavior**	**C** **Consequences of Katie's Behavior**
Silent reading time: Teacher asks Katie to find a book to read.	Katie whines that she can't find any book she likes.	Adult walks away. Katie does not read a book.
Transition time: Teacher tells Katie to put on her coat to go home.	Katie whines that her coat is too heavy and itchy to put on.	Adult says, "You'll be cold." Katie leaves her coat in her locker.
Class meeting time: Katie wants to sit next to Candy, but all the seats at Candy's table are taken.	Katie whines that she really wants to sit next to Candy.	Madison gets up and lets Katie sit next to Candy. The teacher conducts the class meeting.
After-school program: Assistant teacher asks Katie to wipe down two snack tables before choosing a free-choice activity.	Katie whines that she is too tired to wipe tables.	Adult decreases demand to only one table.
At home: Mom announces, "Time to eat. Come to the table."	Katie whines that she isn't finished using the computer.	Katie eats in front of the computer.

Behavior hypothesis: A primary function of Katie's challenging behavior is avoidance—whining helps Katie avoid situations and tasks that are unappealing to her.

Support plan for the child. Such plans include six elements (Fox et al., 2009):

- An objective for the intervention that focuses on a desirable child behavior
- Prevention strategies that address the conditions that trigger the challenging behavior
- Replacement behaviors that are alternatives to the challenging behavior and that help the child achieve his or her goals more appropriately
- Strategies to reinforce appropriate behavior
- Strategies to ensure that the challenging behavior is not being reinforced
- Ways to track the child's progress

Typical plans involve a combination of guidance strategies, including rules and consequences. The characteristics that make a Positive Behavior Support plan specialized are its highly coordinated nature and the systematic data gathering that contributes to its development and implementation.

A Positive Behavior Support plan for Katie is offered in Table 11-6.

Implementing and monitoring the Positive Behavior Support plan. A Positive Behavior Support plan, no matter how well crafted, is only effective if it is carried out accurately and systematically by all members of the team. Thus, adults have to monitor their own behavior and carry out the replacement, reinforcement, and nonreinforcement strategies every time they are applicable. While the plan is in action, adults collect data about the child's behavior, including times when she is successful and times when she is not. They also meet periodically to discuss the strategies they are using and how the child is progressing across settings. During these debriefings, team members make adjustments in the plan or in their own behavior as necessary to increase the child's chances of success. Gradually, as the child's behavior improves, he or she will need less intensive individualized support and will be able to maintain desired behaviors in response to

Table 11-6 Katie's Positive Behavior Support Plan

OBJECTIVE	Katie will comply with reasonable requests without whining.
PREVENTION	Give Katie her own special warning five minutes before the general warning to the class/family about upcoming transitions. Coach her in bringing her activity to an end. Give Katie choices when compliance is not an issue. Structure situations to avoid direct confrontations related to compliance.
REPLACEMENT BEHAVIOR	Give Katie choices within situations requiring compliance: · Coat: Put on your coat. You can zip it or leave it unzipped. · Sitting next to Candy: The red table is full. You can sit at the blue table or the green table. You decide. · Book: You can read this one or this one. You pick. Make a rule that you will only listen to Katie's communications when she uses a normal tone. The first time Katie whines each day say, "I cannot understand you when you whine. Please tell me again without whining." Model how to speak without whining. Ask her to rehearse the message in a normal tone.
REINFORCEMENT	Use effective praise when Katie complies without whining. Use a positive personal message when Katie expresses her "wants" using a normal tone of voice. Ask Katie to repeat her statement in a normal tone. If she restates her comment without whining, say, "Good, now I can understand you."
AVOID REINFORCEMENT FOR INAPPROPRIATE BEHAVIOR	Follow through on reasonable expectations matter-of-factly (use a brief personal message, warning, and follow-through).
TRACK PROGRESS	Observe Katie one hour per day for three weeks. Use a checklist and anecdotal records to record her behavior. Use the following indicators to determine to what extent Katie's behavior is improving: · Katie requires the follow-through stage of the limit-setting sequence less frequently. · Katie's use of whining to avoid an expectation decreases.

the more universally applied strategies found within the Guidance Continuum for All Children outlined in Figure 11-3.

> Potential Outcome for Katie: If the adults remain true to their plan, Katie will eventually respond at the warning or personal message stage to reasonable requests for compliance ('Come to group" or "Sit down for supper"), and she will use whining less frequently to escape such requests. As this is happening, Katie also will be acquiring new skills that will help her behave more productively and experience greater social success with peers.

Intensive Individualized Interventions are effective with children in early childhood and elementary settings as well as with children who are older (Stormont et al., 2008). They are particularly suitable for use with that smaller number of children whose challenging behaviors need specialized attention. These are children whose behavior initially prompts adults to wonder, "What should I do?" Another group of children you may wonder about when it comes to applying rules and consequences are children with special needs.

Adapting Rules and Consequences for Children with Special Needs naeyc

> At greeting time, the teacher reviews the steps for painting at the easel, including putting on a paint smock. As soon as free-choice starts, 3-year-old Kenyon begins painting without covering up first. He continues painting even after the teacher reminds him of the rule.
>
> What should the teacher do?
>
> In the kindergarten, Devonne has difficulty sitting through group time. She frequently interrupts the story, stands up in front of the other children, and laughingly pokes at children nearby.
>
> What should the teacher do?
>
> Gerald, a third grader, is reading a book and saying "hooey boy" over and over, sometimes loudly and sometimes under his breath. His actions could distract the other children.
>
> What should the teacher do?

Based on everything you have read in this chapter, you might consider intervening in these situations, reminding each child of the appropriate rules and applying consequences as necessary. Would any of that change if you were to learn that one or more of these children

had some type of disability—a hearing impairment, Down syndrome, or Tourette's syndrome?

All young children need to learn limits, sharing, and turn-taking, as well as appropriate behavior for different settings. This includes children with disabilities, although in some instances, it will take them longer to learn and consistently apply these skills (Odom, McConnell, & Brown, 2008). Most of the guidance strategies you are acquiring are universally applicable. However, adaptations may be necessary to accommodate children's special needs. Some accommodations will be tailored to meet the unique characteristics of each child's condition. For instance, certain strategies you would use to support a child with a hearing impairment are different from others you might use to guide the behavior of a child with a visual impairment or traumatic brain injury.

Specific ideas about how to work with a child who has a particular special need can be developed by consulting with family members and specialists in the field, by reading, and by contacting professional organizations dedicated to supporting people with particular conditions. In addition, there are a number of generic strategies that special educators suggest in adapting rules and consequences for any child who has special needs. Some of these are listed in Highlight 11-2.

Now that you have reviewed general strategies to guide the social behavior of children with special needs, let us revisit Kenyon, Devonne, and Gerald in their classrooms.

Kenyon has a hearing impairment. This makes it difficult for him to respond to verbal communication. He is better able to get the message through visible communication such as pictographs, demonstrations, sign language, or Cued Speech (using hand signals in combination with mouth movements to make the sounds of spoken language look different from each other) (National Dissemination Center for Children with Disabilities, 2004). Initially, Kenyon's teacher uses visible communication to make sure Kenyon is aware of the rule (drawing his attention to the steps for painting shown in a pictograph and physically offering him a paint shirt to put on). If Kenyon continues to paint without a paint shirt, the teacher warns Kenyon that if he doesn't put on a paint shirt, he will have to leave the easel until he does. If Kenyon ignores the warning, the teacher leads him away from the easel and helps him put on a paint shirt (rehearsal) before he is allowed to continue.

Devonne has Down syndrome. This disorder, caused by a chromosomal anomaly, involves a combination of birth defects, including some degree of mental retardation and often visual as well as hearing impairments (March of Dimes Birth Defects

HIGHLIGHT 11-2

Strategies for Adapting Rules and Consequences for Children with Special Needs

- Observe children carefully.
  - Determine if there are sights, sounds, smells, sensations, people, routines, or times in the day that seem to trigger a child's misbehavior or make it more difficult for him or her to behave successfully.
  - Determine what delights each child and what he or she might view as a positive consequence.
- Head off problem behaviors in advance.
  - Reduce sensory overload.
  - Make adjustments in environments, routines, and schedules to avoid triggers that prompt mistaken behavior.
  - Increase supervision and social support as necessary.
- Get children's attention before stating rules and consequences. This may require specific strategies uniquely suited to each child.
- Use repetition to enhance children's understanding of rules and consequences.
  - Create predictable routines that enable children to follow rules more successfully. Provide numerous cues (visual and verbal) about the order of the day.
  - Repeat the same few rules often.
  - Use the personal message, warning, and follow-through consistently.

- Break rules/expectations into manageable steps. These may be smaller chunks than would be true for typically developing children.
  - Teach one step at a time.
  - Reward small steps.
  - Do not expect 100% compliance 100% of the time.
- Give children additional time to respond to rules and warnings.
  - Become familiar with each child's response pattern.
  - Avoid demanding instant compliance.
- Apply demands for compliance wisely.
  - Ignore some behaviors that are annoying but that do not threaten safety, property, or rights.
  - Choose logical consequences that help a child and those around him or her be more successful in doing what needs to be done. Be prepared to take extra time to enforce such consequences.
  - Avoid shame as a consequence to get children to behave.

Source: Adapted from Klein, Cook, & Richardson-Gibbs (2001); Stephens (2006); Brown, Odom, & McConnell (2008).

Foundation, 2007). Devonne's interruptions at group time are good-natured but disruptive to the other children. Her teacher establishes a few important rules for everyone—sit on your bottom and keep your hands to yourself. She repeats these before and during each group time. An aide sits near Devonne. When Devonne gets up, the aide quietly reminds her of the rule in an abbreviated form (Devonne, remember the rule is "sit" so everyone can see). If Devonne continues to stand, she is warned that she will have to sit at the back of the group with an adult where she can practice listening without disturbing the others (rehearsal). The aide follows through as necessary. In addition, Devonne's kindergarten teacher and the after-school childcare teacher have collaborated on this strategy, so Devonne experiences the same rule and consequences in her kindergarten classroom as in her after-school childcare setting.

Gerald has Tourette's syndrome, a neurological disorder characterized by tics—involuntary, sudden motions or vocalizations—which are completely meaningless but which the child experiences as irresistible urges that must be expressed (National Institute of Neurological Disorders and Stroke, 2005). Although

children can control such tics (from seconds to hours at a time) with great effort, suppressing them may merely postpone more severe outbursts. Tension increases the rapidity and severity of children's tics; tics are less pronounced when children are relaxed. Knowing this, Gerald's teacher does not make a rule forbidding Gerald from expressing his verbal tic "hooey boy" and provides him a more private study area in a quiet part of the room during reading so as to be less distracting to others. At the same time, she helps Gerald work on more controllable social behaviors such as taking turns and collaborating on projects by coaching him and by making rules and enforcing them as she would with any child.

These examples have illustrated some ways in which rules and consequences can be used to help children with disabilities become more socially competent. Chapters 14 and 15 offer more information about working with children with special needs.

We have covered a lot of territory in this chapter regarding how to use consequences effectively with children at all levels of social development and learning. Now it is time to address the actual skills involved in creating appropriate consequences.

SKILLS FOR IMPLEMENTING CONSEQUENCES naeyc

Creating Appropriate Consequences

1. **Anticipate consequences that fit the rules you make.** Think ahead about possible consequences for common expectations in your program. For example, if you are working with preschoolers, think about the consequences you could use to enforce rules about sharing, sitting through group time, and keeping quiet at nap time. If the children in your group are older, consider consequences for resolving playground conflicts with peers and to enforce rules for paying attention, turning assignments in on time, and doing one's own work. These are all typical situations in which rule enforcement may be necessary. Think first of the natural consequences you might use. Then, consider possible logical consequences. Figure out an unrelated consequence last. Generate ideas for positive consequences as well; consider forms of praise as well as earned privileges. Use both verbal and nonverbal reinforcers to get across that positive behaviors matter too.

Anticipating Consequences that Fit the Rules You Make

Rule	Positive	Rehearsal	Restitution	Loss of Privilege

2. **Give children opportunities to generate their own ideas for solutions to problems or potential consequences.** Just as children benefit from formulating some of the rules that govern their lives, they can also learn from helping to generate potential solutions and consequences. Introduce potential problem situations at a time when mistaken behavior is not an issue, and help children consider open-ended questions, such as "What should we do when people knock down other people's blocks?" or "What should we do when people keep wandering around the room and interrupting those who are working?" When youngsters weigh out the value of the rule and what action might lead to better compliance, they are directly experiencing the causal relationship between behavior and outcome. They also have an opportunity to explore why the rule is important and to discuss the role of consequences. It is not unusual for such talks to begin with children suggesting unkind or totally unfeasible penalties. Do not reject these outright but include them for analysis along with the other suggestions. Experience has shown that once the novelty of such outrageous notions has worn off, children settle down to serious discussion.

In addition, encourage the children to identify their own ideas about problems they would like to see resolved by the group. As children generate ideas, post them on a list specified for this purpose (John wants to talk about problems at lunchtime. Jamal wants to talk about people calling names). Create a forum, such as a daily class meeting, in which to discuss such issues. Avoid naming any individual wrongdoers or developing consequences for a particular child. Instead talk about ways any child in the group might respond to such problems in the future. Record potential solutions on chart paper or in a notebook to which children have continual access. Encourage children to make a sustained effort to try the solution for a week, and then evaluate how the solution is working. Make revisions as necessary.

3. **State corrective consequences in the form of a warning.** Link the rule and the consequence in an either-or statement to the child: "Either choose your own place in the circle, or I will help you choose one," "Either put that puzzle together, or you won't be allowed to get another off the shelf," or "Either stop whispering, or I'll have to separate you."

4. **Give warnings privately.** Children who are preoccupied with saving face as a result of public humiliation are not inclined to comply with rules. When giving warnings, move close to the child and stoop down to his or her level. Use a firm, quiet voice to explain what will happen should the misbehavior continue.

5. **Point out the natural consequences of children's actions.** Provide information to

children about the natural consequences of their behavior in a matter-of-fact, nonjudgmental tone. Children benefit from factual information, such as "When you shared the paste with Tim, he was willing to share the glitter with you" or "When you forgot to feed the fish, it meant they went hungry all day." Children tune out when they catch a hint of "I told you so" in your words or demeanor. Resist the temptation to tell children how smart you were all along. They will learn more from supportive explanations of the facts. Thus, instead of saying, "See. Those were never intended to go every which way in the box," say, "You've discovered that when the pieces go every which way, they don't fit in the box."

6. **Use the personal message, warning, and follow-through in order.** Stick with the sequence and keep all the steps. Skipping parts invalidates both the short-term and long-term benefits described earlier in this chapter.

7. **Allow children enough time to respond to each step of the sequence.** Approach discipline encounters with the idea of spending at least a few minutes. At each phase of the sequence, wait at least several seconds so children have time to comply if they are able. In situations you consider dangerous, stop the action physically and watch for signs that the youngster will obey. In less pressured circumstances, a time lapse of a few minutes between

personal message and warning, then warning and follow-through may not be too long. For instance, Mr. Gomez has decided it is time for Lou Ellen to choose a workstation rather than flitting in and out, disrupting everyone. He says: "Lou Ellen, you haven't found an activity that really interests you yet. It bothers me when you wander around because it is distracting. Pick one spot where you would like to work. I'll check on you in a minute or two to see which you decide on." Three minutes later, Mr. Gomez checks and finds that Lou Ellen still is unoccupied. Approaching her, he says: "Lou Ellen, you're still looking for something to do. You can either select a station now, or I'll pick one for you." He stands by her for 30 seconds or so, and she does not move. At this point, Mr. Gomez enforces the rule by stating: "You still can't decide. Remember, I said you choose, or I'd choose. Now, we'll try birdcalls." Mr. Gomez takes Lou Ellen by the hand and heads in the direction of the birdcall station.

Notice that in the prolonged interaction, a reflection prefaced each portion of the sequence. Reflecting helped to reclarify the situation each time and provided continuity from one step to the next.

Helping professionals who work in a team should be alert to fellow team members who are caught up in a limit-setting situation. When this occurs, other adults should provide supervision

Don't rush children through the skill sequence. Give them time to respond to your words.

© Cengage Learning

to the group until the follow-through has been completed. Professionals who work alone may have to follow through while simultaneously maintaining a global view of the room throughout the procedure. In addition, they should be prepared to tell other children in the group what to do until the situation is resolved. ("Dolores and I have to work this out. Keep working on your math journals until we are through.")

8. **Finish the follow-through once you begin it.** Although it is important to give children enough time to respond, it also is critical to enforce rules once you progress to the follow-through phase of the sequence. If you have begun to say, "Remember, I told you . . .," and the child vows never to do it again or says, "Okay, okay, I'll do it," continue to implement the consequence calmly and firmly. Do not get sidetracked at this phase by other issues. Reflect the child's concern or promise, thereby acknowledging it, and then point out that the consequence is for current behavior, not future actions.

9. **Communicate with other adults regarding rule enforcement.** Sometimes, children push the limits with one adult and then move on to someone else when a follow-through is forthcoming. In this way, the same child may engage in problem behavior all over the room with no real enforcement. Prevent this from happening by alerting other adults about the warning you have given a certain child. Do this within the child's hearing so that she or he is aware that the warning remains in effect even though the location has changed. Be receptive when other adults advise you of their warnings. Follow through on their warning if necessary. For example, if Kathleen has been warned that if she pushes another child on the playground one more time, she will have to sit on the side for five minutes, tell other adults that this is the case. Thus, anyone seeing Kathleen push again can enforce the consequence. This creates a predictable environment for Kathleen in which she will learn that pushing is unacceptable and that all the adults are united in their efforts to keep children safe.

10. **Avoid power struggles.**

Adult: Yes, you will.

Child: No, I won't.

Adult: Yes, you will.

Child: No, I won't.

This is the common language of a power struggle. It typically occurs when adults try to implement consequences, and children refuse to comply (Essa, 2008; Miller, 2013). The situation escalates when both become more adamant about their positions. Power struggles usually involve a verbal battle and often happen in front of an audience. Unfortunately, there are no winners—both parties stand to lose something. The adult may gain temporary adherence but may well have lost the respect of the child. On the other hand, if the child gains superiority for the moment by having the adult back down, he or she may suffer future repercussions from an adult who feels thwarted or ridiculed. There are a number of strategies you can use to avoid this problem:

a. Avoid making unnecessary rules.

b. Do not embarrass children—keep all communication between you and the child as private as possible.

c. Remain calm.

d. Avoid contradicting children's assertions.

For instance, if the warning is "Either take a drink without snorting, or I will take your straw," and the child snorts, reach for the straw. If the child says, "But I didn't mean it," do not debate the purposefulness of the act. Instead, acknowledge the child's contention with the words, "That may be . . ." and continue to implement the consequences: "You didn't snort on purpose. That may be. Remember, I told you, any more animal sounds, and I would take the straw away. Now, I'm taking the straw."

e. Stick to the main issue. Do not allow yourself to become involved in an argument over extraneous details.

f. Discuss the power struggle privately with the child. This strategy is particularly effective with older children who have learned some methods of compromise.

Tell the child directly that a power struggle seems to be developing and that you would like to work out the issue in another way.

g. Avoid entrapment. When children begin to argue, refuse to become involved. You can do this either by quietly repeating the rule and the consequences and then resuming your normal activity, or by telling the children that you would be willing to discuss it later when you all are calmer.

11. **Acknowledge children's compliance with rules and expectations.** Use positive personal messages, effective praise, and earned privileges to help children recognize and repeat socially acceptable conduct. Do this for all children in the group, especially those who frequently misbehave.

12. **Use cool down time with children who are having a temper tantrum.** Remember that cool down time is a logical consequence only in this circumstance. Avoid implementing

it indiscriminately. Do not use it when another, logical consequence could better teach the child how to follow the rule. For instance, if Benny forgets to raise his hand before blurting out an answer, it would be better to tell him that he won't be called on until he does raise his hand than to send him into another area of the room for cool down time.

Participating in Intensive Individualized Interventions

1. **Observe children who exhibit challenging behaviors carefully to get a bigger picture of their overall experience in the classroom.** Ask yourself the following questions (Kaplan, 2000; Hanline et al., 2009):

   a. Which of the child's behaviors are challenging, and what does that behavior look like?

   b. When and where does the child behave appropriately?

   c. Who is present when the child is behaving appropriately?

   d. When and where does the child exhibit the challenging behavior?

   e. Which activities/routines/parts of the day does the child seem to enjoy and find easier to manage?

   f. Which activities/routines/parts of the day does the child seem to find less enjoyable and more difficult to manage?

   g. Which approaches seem to work well with the child, and which are less successful?

   h. Who are people with whom the child gets along best?

2. **Observe children's challenging behaviors in targeted situations to get a better understanding of the context in which they occur.** Make a written record to answer these queries (Stormont et al., 2008):

   a. When and where does the challenging behavior happen?

   b. Who is there when the challenging behavior happens?

   c. What activities, events, and interactions happen just before the challenging behavior occurs?

   d. What happens after the challenging behavior happens? How do people react? What do people do? What does the child do?

   e. What does the child seem to be trying to achieve?

   f. What alternate skills might the child need to replace the inappropriate behavior?

Use an A-B-C analysis to help you organize this information. A downloadable A-B-C analysis template is provided here to help you with this process.

A-B-C Analysis Template		
A Antecedents/ Triggers	B Behavior	C Consequences of Child's Behavior

Behavior Hypothesis:

Digital Download   Download from CourseMate

3. **Use the written evidence to conduct a "reality check" on your perceptions.** Sometimes children's challenging behavior is so perplexing that adults get the feeling that the child is "misbehaving all the time." Count how often the behavior occurs. You may be surprised to see that it happens less often than you thought or only in certain situations—not all the time.

4. **Use nonjudgmental language to talk about children's challenging behaviors.** Just as we do not refer to children with disabilities as, "my autistic child" or "that hearing impaired child," it is inappropriate to label children who exhibit challenging behaviors as, "my challenging child" or "that oppositional child." Avoid labeling the child as "out of control," "high needs," or "antisocial." This implies that this facet of the child's being is all there is. Discuss explicit behaviors, "Katie whined when she had to wait to pet the rabbit."

5. **Participate fully in the team effort to create, implement, and monitor Positive Behavior Support plans for children.** Use agreed-upon strategies, including appropriate personal messages, warnings, and the follow-through, as necessary. Make sure to reinforce the child's appropriate actions whenever

you can. If you find yourself inadvertently reinforcing the challenging behavior, talk with other team members about ways to avoid this. Here is a Positive Behavior Support plan template you may download to help you with this planning.

Positive Behavior Support Plan Template	
Objective (focused on desirable behavior)	
Prevention Strategies	
Replacement Behavior	
Reinforcement	
How to Avoid Reinforcing Inappropriate Behavior	
How to Track Progress	

Digital Download   **Download from CourseMate**

6. **Be sure to have a positive interaction each day with children whose behavior is challenging.** Find something to say or do that is friendly and affirmative. Show the child through your behavior and words that there are some things about him or her that are likable and worthy. It often takes imagination and effort to identify such qualities, but if you cannot see these possibilities, it is much harder for children to see them in themselves.

Communicating with Families

1. **Listen empathically to family members who express frustration about their children's misbehavior.** There are times when parents and guardians need a chance to talk about their children's negative behavior without feeling guilty or embarrassed. At other times, they benefit from the opportunity to explore their concerns and to determine the relative seriousness of certain behavior problems they are encountering. In all of these circumstances, your role is to listen. Refrain from giving advice. Sometimes, family members just need to talk things through. Refer really troubled family members to program personnel whose job responsibilities include counseling.

2. **Help family members recognize signs that their children are achieving greater self-control.** Provide information to parents and guardians illustrating children's increasing abilities to delay gratification, resist temptation, curb their impulses, and carry out positive plans. Short notes home or brief verbal comments are ideal ways to convey such messages. "Today, Leanne offered her turn at the easel to a child who was anxious to paint before time ran out. She decided this all on her own. I thought you'd enjoy hearing about her growing awareness of the needs of others," or "Perry was very angry that our field trip was canceled. He wrote about this in his journal and suggested that our class develop a backup plan for next time. I was impressed that he used such constructive strategies to deal with his frustration and just wanted you to be aware that he is making great progress in this regard."

3. **Clarify who will enforce rules when both family members and staff members are present.** Family members and professionals often feel uncertain about who should step in when both witness an incident in which the family member's child engages in disruptive behavior, such as refusing to cooperate during a "family night" program, resisting coming out of the bedroom during a home visit, or hitting another child in frustration. To avoid such confusion it helps to have preestablished guidelines for what to do when these things happen. Many families and professionals have found the following guidelines both fair and useful:

   a. Parents are in charge of the "home front." When a professional is making a home visit or meets a parent and child in a public setting such as a store or at a concert, parents are in charge of their own children.

   b. Program staff are in charge during program hours in program-related environments, including field trip sites.

   c. Parents who are acting as volunteers or aides in the program take responsibility for children other than their own and leave the handling of their own children to another volunteer or the professional.

   d. When confronted with a situation in which you must intervene with a family member's child in that person's presence, act matter-of-factly and use the skills you have learned in this chapter. Say something to alert the person to your intentions if the conditions seem appropriate for such a remark. For instance, if Jeremiah is trying to follow his mom out the door, you might say to his mom, "I'll help Jeremiah find something fun to do. We'll stay together here in the classroom." Give Jeremiah a personal message and a warning. If you must proceed to the follow-through, calmly help him remain in the classroom, even if he is crying hard. Thank the parent and assure her that you will let her know how Jeremiah is doing later in the day.

4. **Discuss with family members mutual ways to help children achieve self-discipline.** This may take place informally or as part of an Intensive Individualized Intervention plan. Interact with family members to identify strategies for use both at home and in the formal group setting to promote children's positive behaviors and to address problematic ones. Ask if such behaviors occur at home and what family members do about them. Make note of these strategies and whenever possible use them in creating a plan for working on the behavior in the formal group setting. If the behavior is not evident at home, talk with family members about what is happening in the program, describe current strategies, and ask for feedback and/or additional recommendations. Similarly, listen attentively when family members describe behaviors they observe in their children. Talk about the extent to which such actions appear away from home and what people in the program may be doing about them. Agree on one or two common strategies that family members and program professionals will use. Discuss a timetable for checking in with one another to determine progress and alterations. If you are the professional in charge, carry out your plan. Confirm the results with family members and make adjustments as necessary. If you are a student participant and a family member mentions such an instance to you, acknowledge the person's concern and say that you will bring the matter to the attention of the head teacher or some other appropriate person in the program. Follow through on your conversation. Later, get back to the family member, letting him or her know that you informed the appropriate person as promised.

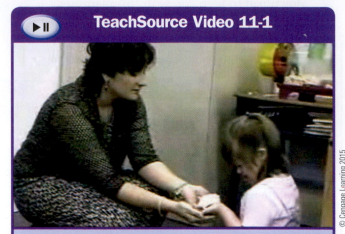

TeachSource Video 11-1

Lauren and Beth: Serving Students with Special Needs in Inclusive Environments

Go online and view *Lauren and Beth: Serving Students with Special Needs in Inclusive Environments.*

In this video, you will hear a teacher and a parent describe their expectations for a child with special needs and how they work together to help her learn to follow rules and meet social expectations.

1. Name two expectations the parent and teacher have for the child's behavior.

2. Describe two ways the parent and teacher are working together to help the child learn to "behave."

3. Based on what you have read about rules and consequences, identify two additional strategies the adults might use to support this child's social learning.

Watch on CourseMate

© Cengage Learning 2015

Pitfalls to Avoid naeyc

Regardless of whether you are helping children develop self-regulation as one-to-one individuals or in a group, informally or in structured activities, there are certain pitfalls you should avoid.

1. Reluctance to follow through.

Jonathan, you're having a good time up there. I'm worried you might fall. Climb down, please.

Jonathan, I mean it: climb down.

Jonathan, I really mean it this time.

Jonathan, how many times do I have to tell you to climb down?

Jonathan, am I going to have to get angry?

Jonathan, I'm getting mad.

OK, Jonathan, I'm really mad now—climb down.

Jonathan, that's it! I'm going to carry you down.

This scenario illustrates a common problem for many adults: their reluctance to follow through on the limits they set. In an effort to avoid a confrontation, they may find themselves repeating a warning or some variation of it numerous times. This confuses children. They have no way of telling when adults finally mean what they say. In Jonathan's case, will that point be reached after the third warning, the fifth, or the sixth? Perhaps yesterday, the adult waited until the fifth warning; tomorrow, he or she may stop at the second. Children are not mind readers and cannot predict when the adult's patience may run out. The one way to avoid this situation is always to follow through after you give the first warning. In this way, children learn that the description of the consequence is a cue for them either to change their behavior or to expect the consequence to happen.

2. **Relying on convenient or familiar consequences rather than finding one best suited to the situation.** Some adults utilize the same consequence over and over. When corrective action is necessary, frequently they choose an unrelated consequence, like removing children from a situation or having them lose a particular privilege. Although such consequences may stop the behavior for the moment, they do not teach appropriate alternatives for children to use in future situations. Over time, children may learn to anticipate the consequence and may decide that certain misbehaviors are worth experiencing it. This problem can be avoided by varying consequences to fit the situation at hand.

Use a wide range of positive consequences too. Children are less responsive when the same few reinforcers are used for everything. Refer to Figure 11-2 for examples of a wide range of verbal and nonverbal reinforcers adults can use to support children's efforts to achieve self-discipline.

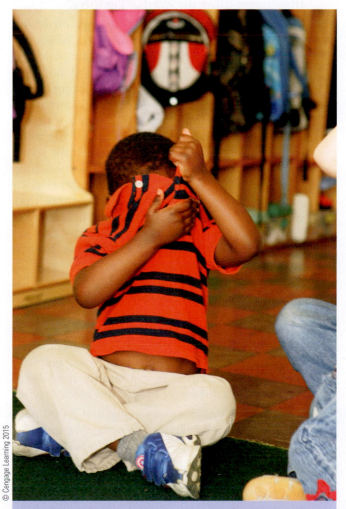

What consequence will you use when Dani sings into his shirt while you are telling a story at group time?

What consequence will you use when Rochelle keeps wiping her nose on her sleeve?

3. **Ignoring natural consequences.** Sometimes adults fail to recognize that a natural consequence has taken place and so institute additional, unnecessary consequences. For instance, Peggy accidentally stepped on her guinea pig. She was upset over the possible injury and attempted to soothe the animal. Her distress was the natural consequence of her error. The 4-H leader completely missed the natural consequence and proceeded to scold Peggy for being so careless. Then she told her she was not to hold the guinea pig for the next hour, even though Peggy already had recognized the negative results of her actions. Because a consequence is imposed to help children become aware of the impact of their behavior, no further penalty was called for. Instead, the adult could have talked with Peggy about ways to avoid future injuries.

Unfortunately, many adults cannot resist the desire to drive the point home by lecturing, moralizing, or instituting more drastic consequences. However, children who feel victimized are less able to change their behavior. The best way to avoid this pitfall is to survey the situation carefully and note any natural consequences that may have occurred. If these are evident, point them out to the child rather than imposing more consequences.

4. **Demanding cheerful compliance.** When adults follow through with a consequence, they should not expect children to comply cheerfully. This means that a child may pout, complain, mutter, or stomp as he or she adheres to the rule. Adults must keep in mind that the aim of the follow-through is to enforce the consequence. It is too much to insist that a child also put a smile on his or her face when doing something he or she really does not want to do. Adults create unnecessary confrontations when they insist that youngsters obey with pleasure. Although it may be annoying when children show their obvious distaste for the rule, attitude is not something over which adults have control, and it should not become a major issue in adult–child interactions.

5. **Harboring grudges.** After imposing a consequence, the adult's motto should be "forgive and forget." It is counterproductive to allow feelings of anger, resentment, or hostility for past actions to color present interactions. After a consequence has been imposed, that is the end of it. Treat each new day as a fresh start. Furthermore, if on a particular day, one adult has had continual confrontations with the same child or is feeling frustrated or overwhelmed, she or he should take a break, or, in a team-teaching situation, ask someone else to deal with the child for a while.

6. **Insisting that children apologize.** Frequently, adults think that if they can just get children to say they are sorry, the problem is solved. With this in mind, they may force children to say "sorry" even when they do not really mean it. Unfortunately, this causes children to conclude that apologizing takes care of everything. They figure they can engage in any behavior they like as long as they are prepared to express their regret at the end. They also learn that insincerity is okay. Sorrow and remorse are emotions. We cannot make children experience these emotions on demand.

Children can, however, be taught to make restitution for a wrong they have committed. This may involve having the child soothe the victim, get a wet cloth to wash the victim's bruised knee, or repair a broken object. Research has shown that children definitely grasp the concept of restitution prior to understanding the true significance of an apology (Weissman & Hendrick, 2014). As a result, concrete restitution has the most meaning for children. Only when children feel genuine remorse should they be encouraged to express their regret using the words, "I'm sorry."

7. **Overlooking the positive things children with challenging behaviors do.** When the same child misbehaves again and again, it is easy to fall into the trap of thinking that is all he or she is capable of doing. Adults must be aware of this pitfall because a child who gets the idea that she can never "make good" will stop trying (Curwin, Mendler, & Mendler, 2008). Likewise, the adult who sees a child as "hopeless" often stops trying too. The best way to avoid over-generalizing one's negative perceptions is to intentionally look for children's strengths. Having more than one adult watch the same child at the same time and record what they see increases the chances that constructive behaviors and abilities may be "captured." Collecting even just a few positive examples gives adults a sense of hope about the child, making it easier to deal with the stress that surrounds challenging interactions. It also helps adults to see the child more holistically, providing clues about behaviors and conditions that may be key to turning the child's challenging behavior around. Consider how seeing Sammy as a "whole child" made a difference to his third-grade teacher.

"Ms. Crowe, Ms. Crowe, what's purple and 5,000 miles long?" Sammy, the child who was often impulsive or defiant in class bounced up and down on his toes while he waited for me to answer. "I don't know," I said. "What?" "The grape wall of China," he crowed with excitement. Although Sammy was often a challenge for me to work with, he had a zeal for history and a wacky sense of humor. Our shared laughter helped us begin to bond. I began to see him as more than just my "challenging" child.

—Caltha Crowe, third-grade teacher, 2010

Summary

There are times when children do not follow the rules set by adults. They may engage in mistaken behavior because they lack the capability or the understanding to follow the rules, because adults have given mixed or unclear messages, or because they believe the rule is unnecessary. Adults can avoid or counteract these problems by making rules that take into account children's development, by clarifying or rephrasing their expectations, and by helping children develop positive and appropriate alternative behaviors. In addition, adults can monitor their own behavior so that their words are congruent with their actions, offer explanations for rules, and provide opportunities for children to become part of the rule-making process.

Adults enforce rules through the use of positive or corrective consequences. These help children recognize the impact of their behavior on self and others. Positive consequences reinforce appropriate behavior. Corrective consequences reduce children's mistaken behavior. They are instructive, rely on reasoning, and are humanely and matter-of-factly administered. They are categorized as natural, logical, or unrelated. Natural consequences happen without direct adult intervention, logical consequences are directly related to a particular rule, and unrelated consequences are manufactured by adults. The latter should be used sparingly and be linked, at least in time, to the rule infraction. Adults must carefully weigh many factors in deciding which consequences to use in particular situations.

Adults implement corrective consequences by reminding children of the rule. If children do not comply, the adult repeats the rule and states a warning as an either-or statement. Adults pause long enough to give children an opportunity to correct their behavior on their own. If children do not, adults follow through with the consequence. All consequences should be implemented consistently and immediately.

Personal messages combined with the warning and follow-through help children learn to regulate their own behavior. As children become more accustomed to this process, they learn to respond to earlier phases in the sequence, decreasing the necessity for adults to go through all three steps.

At times, when one problem behavior leads to another, adults must exercise patience and implement appropriate consequences for each problem behavior. The logical consequence of cool down time is used infrequently and only when children are out of control. The response to other challenging behaviors is Intensive Individualized Interventions. These consist of five steps: creating a Positive Behavior Support team; making a functional assessment; developing behavior hypotheses; designing a Positive Behavior Support plan; and, implementing and monitoring the planned intervention.

All young children need to learn limits, sharing, turn-taking, and appropriate behavior in various settings. This includes children with special needs. Most of the guidance strategies presented in this chapter can be adapted for children whose abilities vary, although it may take children with special needs longer to adapt to certain rules and gain greater social competence.

In this chapter, you learned how to create appropriate consequences and how to participate in Intensive Individualized Intensive planning for individual children. You also learned that it is important to join with parents as partners in helping children develop self-control.

Some pitfalls to avoid in using consequences include being reluctant to follow through, using the same few consequences over and over again, ignoring natural consequences, and demanding that children obey every rule cheerfully. Harboring grudges, insisting that children say, "sorry," or focusing only on negative behaviors and overlooking the positive actions of children whose behavior is sometimes challenging are additional pitfalls to watch out for.

Key Terms

corrective consequences	natural consequences	temper tantrum
follow-through	Positive Behavior Support plan	unrelated consequences
Intensive Individualized	positive consequences	warning
Intervention	punishments	
logical consequences	sitting apart	

Discussion Questions

1. Describe five reasons why children behave inappropriately and their corresponding solutions.

2. Discuss the hidden payoffs that may prompt children's misbehavior. Describe (without naming) a child you have observed whose behavior might indicate that such a payoff was in operation. Explore strategies that might be employed to alter the child's behavior.

3. Discuss the similarities and differences between positive consequences, corrective consequences, and punishments.

4. Generate ideas for positive consequences and for natural, logical, and unrelated consequences for the following rules:

   a. Walk, don't run, down the hall.

   b. Throw the ball, don't kick it.

   c. Use your own gym towel.

   d. Handle the computer keyboard gently.

   e. Walk on the sidewalk, not in the flowerbed.

   f. Tell someone when you need help.

   g. Call people by their real names don't mock people's names.

5. Discuss the importance of following through on consequences as well as the results of not doing so.

6. Referring to the NAEYC Code of Ethical Conduct in Appendix A, identify the principles or ideals that will help you determine an ethical course of action in the following situations:

   a. A parent is walking with her child to the car. Suddenly the child dashes away from her into the busy parking lot. The parent, obviously frightened, grabs the child and smacks her three times saying, "You scared the life out of me. Never do that again." You are getting out of your car nearby when this happens and witness the interaction.

   b. You notice a colleague in the hallway arguing with her own child (4 years old) who is enrolled in the program. The child is screaming and trying to pull away as the adult escorts him toward the door. Suddenly the adult turns the child around and gives him two swats on the bottom. You and several children from your class see the incident.

   c. A large group of third graders are playing T-ball on the playground. Another adult comes to you and says, "I have to go in now. I told Jeff he couldn't play T-ball any more today because of his fighting. Please make sure he doesn't play T-ball." The adult goes inside. There are 20 minutes left to play. A few minutes later, Jeff, who has been watching from the sidelines, is called into the game by his friends. He looks to you and says, "I've learned my lesson. Can't I play?"

7. How would you respond to another helping professional who said: "The personal message, warning, and follow-through takes too long. Besides, children can't respond to so much talking. Just tell them what's not allowed and be done with it"?

8. Compare the Guidance Continuum (Figure 11-3) with the strategies for adapting rules and consequences to suit children with special needs presented in Highlight 11-2. In what ways are the figures congruent? Discuss how some of the strategies on the Continuum could be further adapted for children with special needs.

9. Describe a child's challenging behavior you have observed. Discuss how adults addressed the behavior. Was their approach effective or not, and why?

10. Pretend you have been assigned to describe your center's use of Intensive Individualized Intervention to a group of parents. Give a five-minute presentation to a group of your classmates. Then, generate a list of questions parents might ask and discuss how you would respond.

Case Study Analysis

After reading the case study about Adriana in Appendix B answer the following questions:

1. The teachers have decided to use logical consequences to help Adriana develop less aggressive behaviors. Go through the behavior records provided and identify a logical consequence for each example of mistaken behavior you find.

2. Do you think Adriana is a candidate for an Intensive Individualized Intervention? What is the basis for your conclusion?

3. If you were doing an A-B-C analysis, would the teacher records provided here give you enough information to develop a behavior hypothesis? If yes, what would your behavior hypothesis be? If no, what further information would you need?

4. Describe how you might organize a formal A-B-C analysis for Adriana. Where and when might you observe her behaviors to get a better picture of what is happening.

5. Consider the "team" that is working on Adriana's behavior plan. Are all the "right" people included? If not, whom might you add? What will each team member need to do to maximize Adriana's social competence?

Field Assignments

1. Briefly describe a situation in which you will be working with children in the coming week. Identify any potential behavior problems that could arise within that circumstance. Using the entire skill sequence discussed in this chapter, write out the step-by-step process you would go through should such a problem actually occur. Later, record whether or not the issue came up. If it did, discuss how you handled it. Talk about any changes that were made in your original script and why they were made. Identify ways you will improve your performance the next time.

2. Write down three situations in which, as you worked with children, you did or could have used the entire sequence of skills from personal message to warning to follow-through. Begin by describing what the child(ren) said or did to prompt your response. Then, record your exact remarks (regardless of their correctness). Briefly discuss the child's reaction. Next, discuss the strengths and weaknesses of your approach. Conclude by describing an alternate strategy that might fit the situation or another way you could have phrased your message.

3. Observe another adult in your field placement handle a child's inappropriate behavior. Describe the situation and how it was addressed. Describe the adult's approach and discuss how it compared with the strategies you have been learning about in this book.

4. Discuss your use (or a supervisor/colleague) of one of the family communication strategies listed in this chapter. Describe what you (or he or she) did, the role of the family member, and the outcome. Critique how the skill was used. Suggest how you would handle the situation if it were to happen again.

Reflect on Your Practice

Here is a sample checklist you can use to reflect on your use of the skills as a beginning professional. A more detailed classroom observation tool is available in Appendix C.

> **Teachers who support children's development of self-regulation through the effective use of consequences, do the following:**
>
> ✓ Use positive consequences to reinforce children's appropriate actions.
>
> ✓ Remind children of rules (usually through a personal message) before administering a corrective consequence.
>
> ✓ Tell children in advance of what the consequence will be (through an appropriate warning).
>
> ✓ Use logical consequences to help children practice more appropriate behaviors.
>
> ✓ Remain calm in limit-setting situations.
>
> ✓ Apply consequences consistently and in a timely manner.
>
> ✓ Follow through on limits set.
>
> ✓ Coordinate actions with other adults to best support children's development of self-regulatory skills.

CourseMate. Visit the Education CourseMate for this textbook to access the eBook, Digital Downloads, TeachSource Videos, and quizzes. Go to CengageBrain.com to log in, register, or purchase access.

12 Handling Children's Aggressive Behavior

OBJECTIVES

On completion of this chapter, you should be able to:

Define aggression and distinguish it from assertiveness.

Discuss the factors that contribute to aggression.

Describe how aggression emerges during childhood.

Identify adult actions that increase aggression.

Analyze strategies that reduce aggression.

Explain what bullying is and what to do when bullying occurs.

Demonstrate skills for preventing and handling aggressive behavior.

Recognize pitfalls to avoid in addressing aggression.

NAEYC STANDARDS naeyc

1. Promoting Child Development and Learning
2. Building Family and Community Relationships
3. Observing, Documenting, and Assessing to Support Young Children and Families
4. Using Developmentally Effective Approaches to Connect with Children and Families
5. Using Content Knowledge to Build Meaningful Curriculum
6. Becoming a Professional

HEY! You wrecked it!

No, I didn't!

Yes, you did!

Teacher, he hit me!

He started it!

Scenes like this are not uncommon. After all, children are just learning the skills they need to get along. Due to their relative lack of experience, there are times when they resort to aggression to express themselves or to get what they want. Left unchecked, aggression hurts people, damages property, disrupts daily activities, and creates negative group environments. Furthermore, children who display high rates of aggression when they are young are very likely to experience future problems interacting with others and feeling competent at home, at school, and in the community (Alsaker & Gutzwiller-Helfenfinger, 2010). All of this makes aggression a significant issue for aspiring professionals like you to think about and learn to handle effectively.

Defining Aggression naeyc

Aggression is antisocial behavior that damages or destroys property or that results in physical or emotional injury. It can be verbal or physical (Dodge, Coie, & Lynam, 2006). Slapping, grabbing, pinching, kicking, spitting, biting, threatening, degrading, shaming, snubbing, gossiping, attacking, teasing, and demolishing are all examples of aggressive acts.

Types of Aggression

In this chapter, we will discuss two types of aggression: instrumental and hostile. Knowing their similarities and differences will enhance your ability to respond effectively when children are aggressive.

Instrumental aggression. There are times when children are so intent on getting what they want or defending something that their physical or verbal actions inadvertently result in someone getting hurt. This is **instrumental aggression** (Ladd, 2005). For instance, when Marsha and Celeste struggle over a rolling pin, the physical push-pull of their argument leads to Marsha being scratched and Celeste having her fingers smashed. The outcome is two unhappy children, both of whom have been injured. Neither child started out trying to hurt the other; each simply wanted the rolling pin first.

Unfortunately, Marsha and Celeste relied on force to stake their claims. In this case, the resulting aggression was a byproduct of the girls' interaction, not its main purpose. Lack of premeditation and lack of deliberate intent to harm are the two factors that distinguish instrumental aggression from purposeful attempts to hurt people or reduce their self-esteem. Most instrumental aggression is prompted by quarrels over objects, territory, or rights (Doll & Brehm, 2010).

Instrumental aggression over objects Jessica and LaTesha both run to the swing at the same time. Each wants it for herself. Soon they are tussling over who will get it. The goal of the children's actions is to gain possession of the swing. In the process of their struggle, aggression results.

Instrumental aggression over territory Raymond has taken over a large part of the block area to build his airport. He becomes upset when other children's structures edge into his space. In the subsequent dispute over who can build where, children start hitting. Although the goal of the children's actions is to simply establish control over territory in the block area, the unfortunate result is that children get hurt.

Instrumental aggression over rights An argument breaks out as several children rush to the door to go outside. Each wants to be "line leader." In this situation, the children's main goal is to establish who will have the right to be first in line. The aggression that comes about is a by-product of their efforts to achieve that goal.

Hostile aggression. Children who display **hostile aggression** deliberately inflict pain on others (Doll & Brehm, 2010). Their hurtful actions or words are intentional attacks aimed at retaliating for perceived insults or at getting a victim to do what the aggressor wants. Hostile aggression is expressed in two different ways:

- **Physical aggression**—harm to others through physical injury or the threat of such injury
- **Relational aggression**—damage to another person's status or self-esteem through gossip, lies, or other forms of social manipulation

In both cases, the purposeful nature of hostile aggression differentiates it from instrumental aggression.

Several fourth-graders are rushing to get to their lockers before the bell rings. In her effort to get in and out on time, Jean accidentally knocks Claudia into the wall. Before anyone can respond, Claudia, red-faced, jumps up and runs into the classroom. Later, as the children line up at the water fountain, Claudia shoves Jean and says, "There, see how you like it."

Initially, Jean's behavior was inadvertent. However, Claudia interpreted it as a deliberate blow to her ego, which required her to retaliate later in the day. By pushing Jean, Claudia felt they were "even," and her honor was restored. In this case, the act of pushing Jean was a purposeful attempt to hurt her, an example of hostile aggression. The same would be true if Jean retaliated against Claudia's shove by telling everyone on the playground, "Don't let Claudia play. She's no good."

Assertiveness

A socially appropriate alternative to aggression is **assertiveness**. Children are assertive when they express themselves or protect their rights while respecting the rights and feelings of others (Ostrov, Pilat, & Crick, 2006). Assertive children do the following:

- Resist unreasonable demands: "No, I won't give you the brush yet. I still need it."

- Refuse to tolerate aggressive acts: "Stop calling me names." or "No pushing."

- Stand up against unfair treatment: "You forgot my turn." or "Hey, no fair cutting in line."

- Accept logical disagreements: "Okay, I see what you mean."

- Suggest solutions to conflict: "You can have it in a minute." or "I'll use it again when you're through."

Children demonstrate greater social competence and develop more positive feelings about their abilities when they can express themselves effectively and when they can exert some control and influence over others. As children mature, they try out many strategies to express that influence. However, because they are social novices, children's efforts to be assertive are sometimes mistaken or unsuccessful. They may even take the form of aggression. Ultimately, through observation, instruction, feedback, and practice, children can gradually learn the more constructive behaviors associated with assertiveness.

In this chapter, you will learn how to help children become more assertive and less aggressive. To begin, it helps to understand why and how aggression develops in the first place.

Why Children Are Aggressive naeyc

In explaining the roots of aggression, scientists do not know exactly how much can be attributed to biology and how much is a result of learning. However, there is general agreement that, from infancy onward, both factors shape children's aggressive behavior (Moffitt & Caspi, 2008).

These children are learning assertiveness as they practice making suggestions and listening to each other's ideas.

© Bill Aron/PhotoEdit

Biology

People sometimes wonder, "Is there some biological trigger that prompts people to be aggressive?" This question has yet to be fully answered. So far, scientists have not found a "super" gene that is responsible for human aggression. However, studies conducted around the world do indicate that a person's tendency to be more or less aggressive is genetically influenced (Dodge et al., 2006; Xu, Farver, & Zang, 2009). This is especially true when it comes to physical (versus relational) aggression (Brendgen et al., 2005). Some studies have shown that up to 50% of the variability in a person's aggressive impulses can be attributed to his or her genetic make-up (Rhee & Waldman, 2002). Researchers also have found that high levels of androgen and testosterone (male sex hormones) are associated with higher levels of aggressive behavior (Hermans, Ramsey, & van Honk, 2008). This is not to say that male hormones cause aggression, only that they appear to be linked to aggression in some way. Temperament also seems to play a role in people's aggressive tendencies (Denham, Bassett, & Wyatt, 2008; Rothbart, Ellis, & Posner, 2011). Some children come into the world more emotionally intense than others. Their reactions to events are more extreme, and they have greater difficulty letting go of strong emotions. This may contribute to aggressive responses in highly charged situations. Some children who are temperamentally boisterous or distractible or who have difficulty adjusting to changes in routine resort to aggression more so than children whose temperaments are mellower. Raucous children also are prone to physical interaction that includes touching, hitting, and grabbing to satisfy their needs. In contrast, their quieter peers stay more physically distant, avoiding interactions that may lead to aggressive outcomes. Findings like these help us to see that biology contributes to childhood aggression; however, it is not the only factor involved.

The Frustration-Aggression Hypothesis

Four-year-old Jackie can't get her block tower to stay up! According to the frustration-aggression hypothesis, she could become aggressive if her frustration with the tower's instability gets the better of her. When this hypothesis was first posed, people thought that aggression was an inevitable response to frustration and that frustration was at the heart of most aggressive acts (Dollard, Doob, Miller, Mowere, & Sears, 1939). Gradually that notion has been revised. Today, scientists believe that a frustrated child is more likely to be aggressive than one who is contented (Rothbart, Ellis, & Posner, 2011). However, we also know that frustrated people do not always act aggressively. For instance, Jackie may react to her frustration by trying harder, requesting help, simplifying the task, giving up, or taking a break. Thus, frustration may contribute to aggression, but it is not its only source, nor does frustration automatically result in hurtful behavior.

The Distorted-Perception Hypothesis

Some children see hostile intent where none exists (Hubbard et al., 2002; Nelson, Mitchell, & Yang, 2008). For instance, a ball hits Trevor from behind as he walks across the play yard. He assumes that someone hit him on purpose even though the action was really the result of a wild throw. He responds with a yell and an aggressive gesture. Any child could react to an unexpected violation of personal space in this way. However, some children are more prone than others to respond as though others' actions are deliberate and hostile. Such children are generally poor social observers. They find it difficult to accurately interpret other children's expressive cues, such as facial expressions or words that would help them to understand no harm was meant (Zins, Weissberg, Wang, & Walberg, 2004).

Even if the other children apologize for the wild throw, Trevor may feel obligated to retaliate. That aggressive response could trigger counter-aggression from the other children, reinforcing Trevor's impression that peers are hostile toward him. This is how vicious cycles get started, increasing the antagonism that exists between Trevor and the children with whom he must interact each day. Additionally, as Trevor's reputation for aggression becomes more firmly established, classmates may become less patient in dealing with him and be quicker to resort to physical force than they would with a less aggressive peer. The end result is increased aggression among all the children involved.

Reinforcement and Direct Experience

There is convincing evidence that reinforcement and direct experience play a key role in shaping and maintaining aggressive behavior in children (Frick et al., 2003). For instance, children may hit, bite, scratch, taunt, or threaten in order to get their way. When other children or adults give in by withdrawing from the conflict or yielding to the aggressor's wishes, the child's aggression is rewarded. Situations like these teach both aggressors and victims that hurtful actions are effective. If such behavior continues to be rewarded, children who demonstrate aggression develop feelings of power that further reinforce their negative actions. Aggressors may even achieve a certain notoriety that underscores the value of behaving aggressively. All of these factors reinforce rather than inhibit aggressive actions.

Modeling and Observational Experience

Another explanation for why children behave aggressively is that they learn how to be aggressive by watching others (Goleman, 2006; Dogan, Conger, Kim, & Masyn, 2007). The models they observe may be adults or peers in their family, at the center, at school, or in the community. Such models may be live or in the media. For instance, children see television programs in which disputes are settled by violence; they observe a mother shake Tony in order to make her point; they watch peers and siblings use physical power as a successful means of getting what they want. Children experience aggression directly when they are smacked, shaken, or shoved as punishments for misbehavior.

All of these examples illustrate to children that aggression is an effective way to assert one's will. They also break down inhibitions children may have regarding the use of force (Garbarino, 2006). It makes little difference that adults frequently admonish youngsters not to resort to violence or advise them to "act nice." For children, "seeing is believing." Unfortunately, children exposed to aggressive models retain the effects of that modeling long after a particular incident is over. They remember what they see and hear and are able to imitate it months later (Bell & Quinn, 2004). All of these factors contribute to the enormous influence aggressive models have on children's lives.

Lack of Knowledge and Skills

Children sometimes succumb to aggression because they don't know what else to do when their goals are blocked or when they come under attack by another child. Children may resort to physical violence after they run through their entire repertoire of social skills and still fail to get what they want or protect something important to them (Crothers & Kolbert, 2010). Immaturity contributes to this problem but so does lack of experience. Children who have few opportunities to practice nonviolent strategies or learn the skills associated with assertiveness are most likely to be aggressive (Levin, 2003).

The Emergence of Aggression naeyc

As you can see, the sources of aggression are varied and complex. Any combination of the factors just described may result in antisocial behaviors. How children express aggression and the amount of aggression they exhibit is further influenced by age, experience, and gender.

Changes in Aggression over Time

Three trends characterize childhood aggression from the time children are toddlers through middle childhood:

- Younger children often resort to physical force to get their way. Older children rely more on verbal tactics.
- Younger children most often engage in instrumental aggression. Hostile aggression becomes more common in later childhood.
- For most children, aggression peaks around age 3 and then gradually declines after that.

These developmental shifts occur for several reasons.

Sahid protests loudly when Lenny wants to use more green paint. He shouts, "There's not enough."

© Cengage Learning 2015

The teacher shows the boys how to mix another batch. Sahid and Lenny learn a new skill (mixing paint) and see a different way to resolve an angry confrontation.

© Cengage Learning 2015

A Toddler's View of "WHAT'S MINE!"

If I like it, it's mine.

If it's in my hands, it's mine.

If I can take it from you, it's mine.

If it's mine, it must never be yours in any way.

If I'm doing or building something, all the pieces are mine.

If it looks like mine, it's mine.

If I saw it first, it's mine.

If you are playing with something and you put it down, it automatically becomes mine.

If it's broken, it's yours.

Author Unknown

The earliest forms of aggression. Toddlers and young preschoolers are impulsive. When they want something, they go after it immediately. Children this age have immature language skills and know only a few strategies for getting what they want. If their limited tactics fail, they often resort to physical force to get what they need or to defend whatever they believe is theirs. When asked to share, their egocentric view of the world makes it hard for them to give up objects. See Highlight 12-1 for a humorous but reasonably true description of how toddlers think about their toys. All of these developmental characteristics increase the likelihood that young children will hit, grab, or bite to resolve disputes over sharing and ownership (Baillageon, et al., 2007). As a result, there is a high rate of instrumental aggression, most of it physical, among children this age. In fact, instrumental aggression is so prevalent in early childhood that most children will experience more aggressive encounters during the preschool years than at any other time in their lives (Bell & Quinn, 2004).

Aggression among 4-, 5-, and 6-year-old children. Older preschoolers and young grade-school children have greater impulse control and are better able to communicate their needs in words. They have heard "the rules" about sharing and taking turns many times, and have had some experience settling disputes peacefully and successfully. Given these conditions, physical aggression begins to

decline and the total number of altercations goes down as well (Alink et al., 2006). Conflict, however, does not disappear. Arguments still erupt over objects, rights, and privileges with children substituting verbal insistence, taunting, tattling, and name-calling for hitting or shoving (Dodge et al., 2006). The friendship threat also appears during this time, "I won't be your friend," as does social exclusion, "You can't play if you …" (Wheeler, 2004). In this way, children's repertoire of social strategies keeps expanding, including both positive and less constructive options.

Aggression during the elementary years. The good news in grade school is that as children's cognitive and verbal skills grow, their ability to peacefully resolve instrumental disputes improves. They become more adept at negotiating conflict and find problem solving an effective way to achieve goals they previously addressed through more forceful means (Levin, 2003; Alink et al., 2006).

Unfortunately, advances in cognition and language also contribute to a rise in hostile aggression within this age group (Laursen & Pursell, 2009). Cognitively,

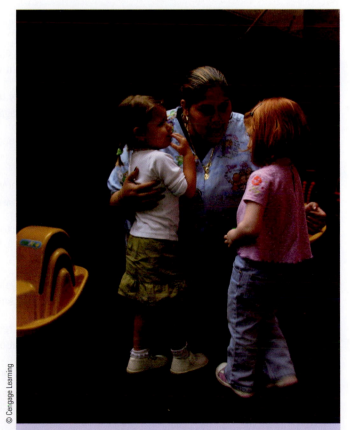

© Cengage Learning

Young children need adult support to resolve instrumental aggression.

children recognize negative intentions of others ("He tripped me on purpose." "She wanted everyone to laugh at me."). Children's developing **perspective-taking abilities** play a part in their ability to be aggressive, too, which helps them to successfully predict what will "get" another person. Their well-developed memory skills also help them recall hurtful encounters long after they are over. These capacities, along with a developing belief that social relationships demand reciprocity, provoke some children to retaliate if they perceive they have been wronged. Children see such retaliation as justified if it is done to maintain "face" with one's peers (Olweus, 2010). Such slights may be real or happen when children erroneously assign hostile motives to their peers (Hubbard et al, 2002). Under such circumstances, minor disagreements or misunderstandings can quickly escalate into expressions of hostile aggression through insults, baiting, or rejection (Garbarino, 2006). Antagonistic interactions can last days or months as children "get even" over and over again (Nelson, Robinson, & Hart, 2005). The

result is that physical fighting lessens during elementary school, but verbal disputes and relational aggression become more pronounced.

Gender Differences in Aggression

Who tends to be more aggressive—boys or girls? At one time, the common answer was that boys were more aggressive from the earliest days onward. Today, researchers are revisiting that assumption. A summary of current thinking in the field is presented in Figure 12-1.

As Figure 12-1 illustrates, all children are aggressive at one time or another, and males and females are equally capable of aggression. Consequently, both boys and girls need support in learning effective ways to meet their needs more constructively.

How well children learn alternatives to aggression depends a great deal on adult intervention. Most adults agree that this is an important responsibility for them to assume, but they often are at a loss about what to do. Unwittingly, they may choose strategies

---

MALE/FEMALE DIFFERENCES IN AGGRESSION

Year one, little girls and little boys are equally aggressive.

Between 15 months and 2 years, sex-linked differences in aggression become apparent. Both boys and girls are aggressive, but they express their aggression in different ways. These differences continue throughout childhood.

- **Males are more physically aggressive than females.** They use physical force and verbal threat more often than females do and are more likely to strike back when aggression is aimed at them.

  Similar differences in physical aggression are found between the sexes across social classes and cultures worldwide.

- **Females are more relationally aggressive than males.** They are more likely to gossip, snub, or ostracize a peer, or say mean things to assert their power or respond to insult/injury.

  Relational aggression by females appears at levels equal to the physical aggression more typical of males.

Sex-related differences in aggression are related to:

Biology: Males' greater concentrations of testosterone, physical strength, and more vigorous motor impulses may contribute to higher levels of physical aggression.

Social learning: Physical aggression is more approved and reinforced for boys than girls. Alternately, it is more socially acceptable for girls to manipulate and sabotage an adversary's self-esteem or status.

Both males and females who display high levels of aggression tend to be rejected by their peers.

Figure 12-1 Sex-Related Differences in Childhood Aggression.

Sources: Based on Garbarino, J. (2006). See Jane Hit: Why girls are growing more violent and what we can do about it. NY: Penguin Group; Olweus, D. (2010). Understanding and researching bullying. In S. R. Jimerson, S. W. Swearer & D. L. Espelage (Eds.) Handbook of Bullying in Schools: An international perspective. New York, NY:Routledge, 9–33.

that stimulate or prompt aggression rather than diminish it. Thus, early childhood professionals must learn not only which strategies are useful but also which ones are not.

Ineffective Strategies Adults Use to Handle Children's Aggressive Behavior naeyc

Fortunately, substantial research data are available that clearly differentiate effective techniques from those that are detrimental. We will explore each of these, beginning with those that should be avoided. In that category are ignoring aggression, displacement, inconsistency, and physical punishment.

Ignoring Aggression

> Ethan and Anthony are arguing over who will be captain of the "ship." Gradually, their angry words escalate into shouting and name-calling. The adult sees the incident but deliberately looks away. She thinks, "If I just ignore them, maybe they'll stop fighting on their own."

Sometimes, adults ignore children's aggressive behavior hoping that eventually it will go away. This is a mistake. Research shows that when adults disregard children's antisocial acts, aggression increases (Espelage & Swearer, 2004). Ignoring aggression creates a permissive atmosphere in which both aggressor and victim learn that aggression has its rewards. Aggressive children continue unabated, and those being hurt eventually give up or counterattack. When children give up, the aggressor "wins," and everyone, including those not directly involved, knows it. Alternately, when children's counterattacks are successful, they have first-hand evidence that aggression works. These former victims sometimes become aggressors themselves as a way to stay safe and gain status with peers (Rigby & Bauman, 2010). In both cases, unrestricted aggression is self-perpetuating and leads to more, not fewer, incidents of hurtful behavior among children.

Displacement

> Orville and Dan are arguing over who will be captain of the "ship." Gradually, their angry words escalate into shouting and name-calling. The adult separates the children and has each child go to "an angry corner" in the room to pound on a pillow to get his "anger out." After complying, the children are allowed to resume their play.

The boys' teacher is using **displacement**. This involves having children who are angry and aggressive "displace" their anger from its original source (each other), to some "safe" target (a pillow). The adult assumes that pounding the pillow helps each child rechannel and discharge his anger, thereby blunting future aggression. The evidence is to the contrary.

Children who displace angry feelings are not learning how to deal with the real problem at hand, in this example, a peer with conflicting needs (Berkowitz, 1993). Children also fail to develop problem-solving strategies or the means to prevent future conflicts. That can lead to frustration. One other negative possibility is that children may shift the "safe target" chosen by an adult to one of their own choosing, such as a child down the street, a family pet, or a younger sibling (Slaby, Roedell, Arezzo, & Hendrix, 1995). Each of these outcomes makes further aggression likely.

Inconsistency

A third ineffective means of dealing with childhood aggression is to be inconsistent. Adults who are haphazard in their approach promote increased aggression (Snyder, Reid, & Patterson, 2003). Consider this situation between Ms. Cannon and Jacob:

> Day 1 – Ms. Cannon thinks, "I've got to be firm about stopping Jacob's taunting today."
>
> Day 2 – Ms. Cannon thinks, "I'm too tired to deal with Jacob's taunting today."
>
> Day 3 – Ms. Cannon thinks, "I've had too many run-ins with Jacob today. This time I'll just look the other way."
>
> Day 4 – Ms. Cannon thinks, "I've got to be firm about stopping Jacob's taunting today."
>
> Days 1 through 4 – Jacob thinks, "I don't know what will happen until I "diss" somebody!"

Sticking with the rules today and ignoring them tomorrow or coming down hard on one child while avoiding confrontation with another, leads to confusion and frustration for children. Because adult reactions follow no stable pattern, the only way children can tell if their aggressive actions will be ignored or condemned is to be aggressive and see what happens each time. Under these circumstances, aggression goes up, not down.

Physical Punishment

Some adults believe in the old adage "Spare the rod and spoil the child." To discourage childhood aggression, they rely on practices that cause children physical discomfort, such as swatting children or shaking them roughly (Gershoff, 2008). The assumption is that children will become less aggressive in order to avoid a spanking or other such consequence (Lessin, 2002). The evidence shows that physical punishment often has the opposite effect.

For instance, in a meta-analysis of 27 empirical studies conducted on children's aggressive behavior in the United States, every single one found that physical punishment was associated with *more* not less childhood aggression (Gershoff, 2008). Similarly, international research points to a strong relationship between physical punishment and high rates of aggression in children (Nelson, Hart, Yang, Olsen, & Jin, 2006; Lansford et al., 2005; Paganini et al., 2004). A substantial body of evidence also shows that the more often children experience physical punishment when they are young, the more defiant and aggressive they become as they grow older. In contrast, although physical punishment may get short-term compliance, there is little research evidence that it improves children's behavior in the long run (Afifi, Dasiewicz, MacMillan, & Sareen, 2012). Several factors contribute to these outcomes. Let us consider the following interaction between Ms. Johnson, Olivia's teacher, and Olivia's mother to better understand what they are.

> Olivia's mother approaches Ms. Johnson. She has tried many ways to get 6-year-old Olivia to stop pinching other children when she is frustrated. She has talked to Olivia, denied her treats, scolded her, and warned her that her peers will not want to play with her, but Olivia continues to pinch. Olivia's mother says, "When I was little, my parents would have pinched me back. Is that what we should do?"

Olivia's mother wonders if by pinching Olivia, the child could learn two important lessons ("Pinching hurts," and, "Pinching is not a good way to express yourself"). Unfortunately, Olivia probably might learn some lessons but not necessarily the ones her mom intends. Consider what else Olivia could be learning.

Lesson 1: Aggression Looks Like This

Pinching Olivia will give Olivia an "up close and personal" lesson in how to be aggressive. From what we know about aggressive modeling, Olivia is more likely to mimic the adult's hurtful actions than to abandon her own (Gershoff, 2008; Bear, 2010).

Lesson 2: Might Makes Right

The adult who pinches is demonstrating that physical pain is an effective tactic for getting your message across and that powerful people use pain against weaker people to gain compliance (Alsaker & Gutzwiller-Helfenfinger, 2010). The take-away message to Olivia is that it is okay to hurt people who are younger, weaker, or less powerful than yourself to get them to do what you want.

Lesson 3: Aggression Is the Only Option

Olivia pinches to express frustration. She does not know how to satisfy her needs in more constructive ways. Unfortunately, the adult would be pinching for the same reason. She is at her wits end and does not know what else to do. Pinching Olivia back reinforces the notion that frustration justifies hurting others. It also fails to demonstrate suitable alternatives (Malott & Trojan, 2008; Gershoff, 2008).

Lesson 4: This Adult Can't Be Trusted

When subjected to physical punishment, some children attribute hostile motivation to the adult ("The adult has it in for me."). Other children become afraid. Neither of these reactions prompts feelings of trust or respect between children and adults. Such mistrust prompts children to reject the corrective message the adult is trying to convey (Gershoff, 2008)

Lesson 5: Watch Out for Number #1

Developmental research tells us that if an adult pinches her, Olivia is likely to center on her own reactions (e.g., pain, anger, or a desire for revenge). In this state, she is less apt to take into account other people's needs or to develop empathy for her victims. Without those emotions to guide her actions, it is harder for Olivia to achieve the more advanced levels of thinking and feeling that could lead to reduced aggression (Society for Adolescent Medicine, 2003; Bear, 2010).

Lesson 6: Don't Get Caught!

A powerful lesson some children learn from physical punishment is that the best way to avoid it, is not to get caught. These children become covert or deceitful in their aggression, paying more attention to avoiding detection than to finding constructive ways to interact with others (McCord, 2005; Rigby & Bauman, 2010). Thus, Olivia may comply when authority figures are nearby but pinch when no adults are looking. Such thinking drives aggression underground but does not eliminate it.

As you can see, if the adults in Olivia's life carry out a pinching campaign, Olivia's aggressive behavior could escalate rather than end. In addition, Olivia's relationship with her parent and teacher could be damaged inhibiting her learning overall. Most importantly, Olivia is not learning what to do instead, nor is she developing the inner controls she needs to become more socially competent (Gershoff, 2008; McCord, 2005). Negative outcomes like these make physical punishment a poor choice for countering childhood aggression.

At this point, you might be wondering, "If physical punishment has such detrimental potential, what happens when entire programs institutionalize physical punishment through the use of corporal punishment?" Let us consider that question next.

Corporal punishment in U.S. schools and childcare programs.

> Olivia's teacher marches her down the hall to the principal's office. The principal talks to her about how her pinching hurts others. He then explains, "Pinching is not allowed in our school. To help you remember the rule, you will get a swat with the paddle."

Legally, **corporal punishment** involves the use of "reasonable force and physical pain" to address students' misbehavior and maintain discipline in a school or childcare center (Fatham, 2006). Most commonly, this involves some form of paddling. Most programs that permit paddling spell out its procedures and require written permission from children's parents before it can be used.

Schools report that paddlings are typically administered for offenses such as disrespect to teachers, disturbing the class, foul language, or tardiness (Dobbs, 2004). According to statistics from the U.S. Department of Health and Human Services (2010), the following children are most likely to be paddled at school:

- Kindergartners
- Children in the early elementary grades
- Children with disabilities
- Children of color
- Children from single-parent and low-income families

Many people (including parents, teachers, and administrators) hold strong opinions about corporal punishment, both pro and con. Advocates believe that school spankings get children's attention and keep them from "acting up" so they are better able to learn. Opponents contend the practice gets in the way of learning and undermines children's development of internal behavior controls (McCord, 2005; Bear, 2010). Based on opinion alone, the issue is a divisive one. The research however, is not so divided and provides a factual basis from which to consider this matter.

Studies conducted by medical, psychology, and education scientists consistently report that school-based corporal punishment yields negative outcomes. These findings are in line with the results of physical punishment reported earlier in this chapter. The evi-

dence shows that many children subjected to corporal punishment become increasingly aggressive, coercive, and destructive (American Academy of Pediatrics, 2006; Gershoff, 2008). This includes children who experience physical punishment directly and others who simply attend the programs in which it is implemented. Furthermore, schools practicing corporal punishment generally report higher incidents of vandalism, attacks against teachers, and more disruptive student behavior than is true for schools in which it is not practiced (Society for Adolescent Medicine, (2003).

As outcomes like these have become better known, there has been a steady decline in the number of programs advocating corporal punishment in the United States. As recently as the early 1970s, corporal punishment was available in every state as a disciplinary tool for workers in schools, childcare centers, and family childcare homes (Center for Effective Discipline, 2013). Today, the picture has changed. Thirty-one states have laws or regulations banning corporal punishment in public schools (see Figure 12-2). Paddlings are barred in Catholic school systems nationwide. Even in states where corporal punishment is still allowed, many schools are voluntarily discarding its use. All but three states, Idaho, Louisiana, and South Carolina, forbid physical punishment in childcare centers, and forty-six states prohibit physical punishment to be used in Family Child Care Homes (Center for Effective Discipline, 2013).

Alternatives to corporal punishment.
The move away from corporal punishment has been accompanied by a move toward more effective program-wide strategies for addressing aggression and managing children's behavior (Center for Effective Discipline, 2013; Bear, 2010; Zins et al., 2004). Some of these include the following:

- All students receive social skills instruction and coaching.
- Character education is included in the curriculum.
- Students help create the rules.
- Rules and their reasons are clear to all.
- Rules are enforced consistently, fairly, and calmly.
- Aggression is always addressed immediately.
- Positive social behaviors are reinforced.
- Educators, families, and other community professionals work together to address problem behaviors, including aggression.
- Educators and families participate in continuing education about positive behavior management.
- Peer and cross-age counseling, conflict mediation, in-school suspension, Saturday School, parent pick-up programs, and therapeutic interventions are additional strategies that might be employed.

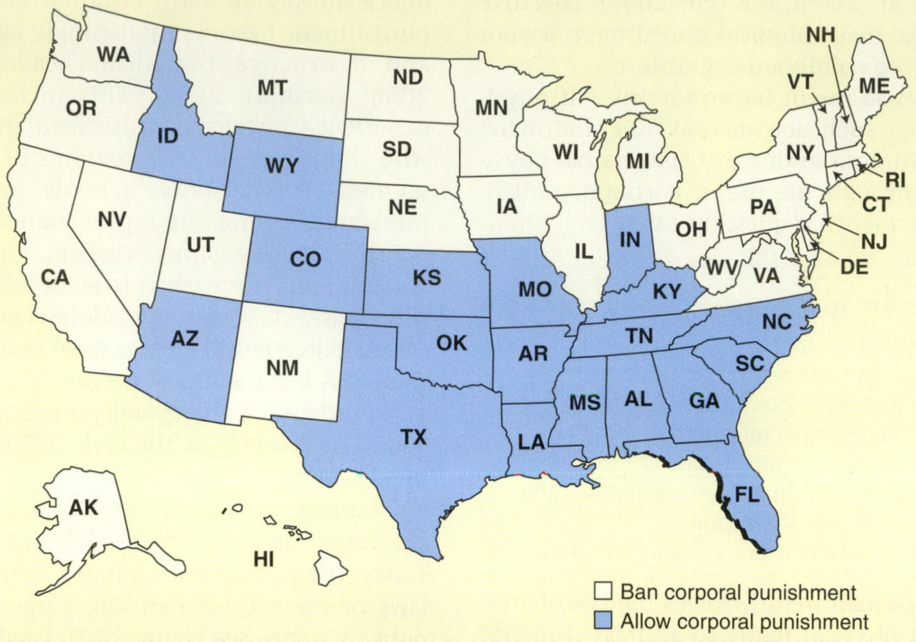

Figure 12-2 Status of Corporal Punishment in U.S. Public Schools.

Source: U.S. Department of Health and Human Services (2010).

Even if you are in a state that condones corporal punishment in schools or childcare settings, as an early childhood professional, you have an obligation to explore alternatives to physical punishment. This obligation is referred to in the NAEYC Code of Ethical Conduct (see Figure 12-3).

From an early childhood perspective, physical punishment violates this ethical code. More than 40 professional organizations have written official statements that echo the NAEYC stand on this issue.

The four strategies we have just discussed—ignoring aggression, displacement, inconsistency, and physical punishment—all increase, rather than reduce, aggressive behavior in children. Those methods fail because they allow aggression to continue and because

they do not help children learn acceptable alternatives to hurtful behavior. Now we will turn our attention to more productive ways of dealing with the challenge of childhood aggression.

How to Effectively Address Childhood Aggression

A group of 4-year-old girls is trying to keep another classmate from joining them. As she approaches, one of the group announces, "Here comes trouble!" The girls move away from their classmate, purposely excluding her.

If you were a teacher observing this episode what might you do? Let the children work things out for themselves? Talk to the group about the hurtful impact of their name-calling? Demand that everyone play "nicely"? Or, does something else come to mind?

Here is how the children's teacher responded.

Seeing the children's behavior, the teacher moves closer to the group and announces, "My name is Trouble. Who wants to play Follow the Leader with me?" All the girls happily fall in line behind her. The excluded girl joins the game too. (*Wheeler, 2004, p. 230*)

The NAEYC Code of Ethical Conduct states

". . . we shall not harm children. We shall not participate in practices that are disrespectful, degrading, dangerous, exploitative, intimidating, psychologically damaging, or physically harmful to children."

Figure 12-3 Excerpt from the NAEYC Code of Ethical Conduct.

© Cengage Learning 2015

In just a few seconds, the teacher redirected the children's relational aggression into a more constructive interaction. Exclusions and alliances were redefined, and the name-calling was defused. This was not just a "lucky" happenstance, nor was it random communication on the adult's part. The teacher intervened intentionally. She purposely de-escalated the children's aggressive play and modeled how to include a less popular child in the game. She gave the aggressors a chance to interact more inclusively and provided an opportunity for their potential victim to practice play skills that might improve her attractiveness to peers in the future. All of these strategies are among those known to reduce aggression in young children and to enhance children's ability to interact more productively (Jimerson, Swearer, & Espelage, 2010; Epstein, 2009).

Through numerous social exchanges, children learn alternatives to aggressive behavior. Of course, there is more than one approach to a situation like this. However, no matter the circumstance, teachers have to consciously decide about whether, when, and how to intervene (Epstein, 2007). That decision depends on your goals, your knowledge of the children involved, and your awareness of potentially beneficial strategies for reducing childhood aggression. Luckily, there are many useful strategies from which to choose.

In this portion of the chapter, we will examine three types of countermeasures to aggression. First, you will learn more about strategies that are either preventative or remedial and that are useful regardless of what form aggression takes. These are all-purpose tactics based on what we know about why children are sometimes aggressive as well as how children develop and learn in the social domain. Next, we will discuss the number one strategy for reducing instrumental aggression, conflict mediation. Mastery of this skill will give you a powerful tool for turning squabbles into meaningful learning opportunities for children. Third, we will examine what to do when aggression turns hostile and becomes bullying. This form of aggression is the most challenging you will face and specific skills tailored to address the needs of bullies, their victims, and others who witness hostile behavior are necessary to deal with it effectively. Let's get started!

All-Purpose Strategies to Counter Aggression

The key to reducing children's aggressive behavior is to help children internalize values and methods of interacting that are incompatible with violence (Levin, 2003). The most successful strategies are ones that do the following:

- Make clear that aggression is unacceptable.
- Teach children how to meet their needs constructively.
- Teach children how to respond to the aggression of others.

A wide array of strategies that meet these criteria and that have research evidence to back their effectiveness is presented in Table 12-1. These strategies are linked to the sources of aggression you just read about.

Chances are, as you examined the interventions outlined in Table 12-1, you recognized some as ones with which you are already familiar. Many aggression-reducing strategies are rooted in concepts and skills you have learned through previous chapters. In fact, you already have a formidable repertoire of approaches you can use to deal with aggressive child behavior. These foundational skills correspond to the four phases of the Social Support Pyramid introduced in Chapter 1 and are depicted in Figure 12-4.

As you can see, addressing aggression begins with establishing positive relationships in the classroom. This includes adult–child relationships and relationships among peers. We know this is important for all children, but it is especially so for children who display aggressive tendencies and for children who respond violently or who appear helpless in the face of aggression (Miller, 2013). Such children often find themselves isolated or receiving attention mostly for inappropriate behavior. When children are treated as outsiders in the classroom, they feel no responsibility to the group and are disinclined to pay attention to nonaggressive messages. Changing these patterns and reaching out to children begins with the adults. It requires intentional effort to befriend children whose behavior is often unappealing or damaging. It takes great patience and skill to "catch" children in nonaggressive situations and to support them during those times so they can experience the rewards of pleasant human interaction (Crothers & Kolbert, 2010). The skills presented in Chapters 2, 3, and 4 provide a base for addressing children's needs for positive affiliations.

Well-planned, orderly, developmentally appropriate programs set the stage for nonviolent, caring behavior (Kaiser & Rasminsky, 2012). Such classrooms encompass both the positive verbal environment, described in Chapter 4, and the safe, well-organized physical spaces and routines covered in Chapter 9.

Teaching and coaching strategies aimed at skill development are essential in helping children move to less aggressive patterns of behavior. Children who rely on aggression tend to lack communication skills, emotional skills, play skills, and the skills necessary to make friends (Frey et al., 2010). The same is true for

Table 12-1 Effective Strategies for Handling Children's Aggressive Behavior

Development and Learning Principle	Teaching Practice
Because biology contributes to aggression...	• Adults adapt activities and routines to meet the needs of children who are active, impulsive, and emotionally intense.
Because frustration contributes to aggression...	• Adults create environments that minimize children's frustration. • Adults help children find constructive ways of dealing with frustration. • Adults provide children with opportunities to become more competent.
Because distorted perceptions contribute to aggression...	• Adults help children interpret social situations more accurately.
Because reinforcement and direct experience influence aggression...	• Adults set limits on aggressive behavior and follow through using appropriate consequences. • Adults assist children in de-escalating aggressive play. • Adults reinforce children's nonaggressive actions and problem-solving efforts.
Because modeling and observational experience influence aggression...	• Adults model caring, respectful behavior and respond to aggression calmly and rationally.
Because lack of knowledge and skills contributes to aggression...	• Adults teach children emotional skills (e.g., how to understand their own and others' emotions). • Adults teach children appropriate play and friendship skills (e.g., how to enter a group and how to take turns). • Adults teach children assertive communication skills. • Adults teach children alternatives to aggression. • Adults teach children effective responses to aggression.
Because ignoring aggression increases aggressive behavior...	• Adults stop children from hurting each other or damaging property. • Adults elicit children's help in stopping aggression.
Because displacement strategies increase aggression...	• Adults help children confront problems directly. • Adults teach children how to work through conflicts peaceably.
Because inconsistency increases aggression...	• Adults consistently follow through on rules forbidding aggression. • Professionals and family members work together to address children's aggressive behaviors.
Because physical punishment increases aggression...	• Adults use logical and appropriate unrelated consequences to correct aggressive behavior. • Adults seek alternatives to corporal punishment.

Sources: Based on Brown, Odom, & McConnell (2008); Crothers & Kolbert (2010); Frey, Edstrom, & Hirschstein (2010); Kaiser & Rasminsky (2012); Orpinas & Horne (2010).

the children who often find themselves on the receiving end of children's aggressive attacks. Children who are aggressive also lack the internal controls they need to curb impulsive behavior or delay gratification. They lash out quickly and often without thought. Most importantly, they have no grasp of how to solve problems amicably or how to follow rules that keep children safe, protect property, or preserve the rights of others. Although no child automatically knows how to do these things, aggressors need significant assistance in learning such behaviors (Orpinas & Horne,

2010). The strategies outlined in Chapters 5, 6, 7, 8, 10, and 11 provide a strong foundation for addressing this task.

Finally, some children need the extra support that comes through the development of Intensive Individualized Interventions. Readers were introduced to the mechanics of these plans in Chapter 11. An example of how one teacher used such a plan to reduce a child's aggressive behavior in concert with that child's family and other helping professionals is presented in Brian's story in Challenging Behavior.

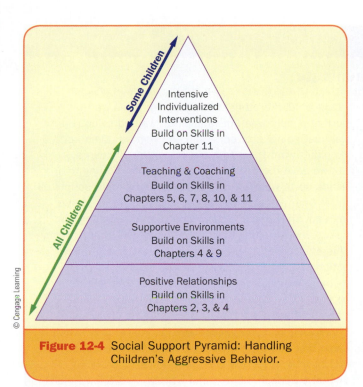

Figure 12-4 Social Support Pyramid: Handling Children's Aggressive Behavior.

Brian's teacher made use of several of the intervention strategies covered in Table 12-1. As Brian makes progress, his teacher might also consider whether he

and his classmates are ready to engage in conflict mediation as an additional approach to enhancing social competence.

The Special Case of Instrumental Aggression

The most prevalent form of aggression early childhood professionals encounter is the instrumental form. Even children who are able to talk about sharing and taking turns in conversations sometimes forget and resort to instrumental aggression in the heat of real-life confrontations. At times like these, adults may be tempted to simply separate the children or remove the disputed object. Although such tactics halt the aggression, they do not teach children better ways to handle conflict. A more effective strategy is to use such occasions to help children practice nonviolent approaches to conflict resolution (Epstein, 2009). In this process, your role is to support children as they attempt to resolve their differences.

To do this effectively, it helps to remember that conflict is not necessarily negative and is not always violent. Differences of opinion and ways of doing things are normal aspects of community living. In fact, conflict offers children a natural means for improving their social competence (Laursen & Pursell, 2009). Sometimes children are able to work

Tina is a victim of accidental aggression at the sand table. The teacher checks her eye and says, "That surprised you. It's no fun to have sand in your face. Joe didn't mean to hurt you. It was an accident."

Joe gets Tina a tissue to make amends.

Meet Brian: A Child Struggling to Communicate

Brian's Teacher Narrates

Brian entered my classroom as a 3-year-old, having been identified as needing special education for speech and language. His official diagnosis was *apraxia.* This meant it was difficult for him to produce language. Because of brain damage or lack of brain development, he had to consciously work (both mentally and physically) at making sounds that come naturally to most children.

In the classroom, if someone had a toy Brian wanted, he took it. He would pinch. Or, he would step on somebody's foot. This kind of aggression was frequent. By closely observing him, I realized that these hurtful acts were related to Brian's inability to communicate. His actions were saying, "I have no way to communicate with you. I have no way of getting your attention or getting you to do what I want."

Goals and Strategies for Brian

One goal I had in working with Brian was to help him become less aggressive. A second was to enhance his communication skills. These two goals were complementary.

Whenever Brian would hurt someone, I interceded. I would take his hand, draw him close to the other child and say, "Look, look what you did! See her face. She is crying. You hurt her. Did you want to tell her something?" Next, I suggested words that I thought he wanted to say, for example, "I want it." At first, Brian would try to pull away. However, as time went on, he'd squeeze up against me during these little conversations. He'd make sounds and point to things he wanted. I made sure to repeat the same few words over and over again. At first, it felt like this was all my aide and I were doing all day long.

Over time, the other children came to realize that hurting people was not what Brian wanted to do. He was just going after something he wanted. Even so, we didn't want them to feel like perpetual victims. So, we gave them gestures, for example, putting their hands up to ward off his grabbing, and simple scripts to let Brian know how they felt and what he could do instead. They became more adept at anticipating his needs and at telling him "no" if he began to hurt them. This empowered them and interrupted his aggressive actions.

Other strategies we used included establishing consistent expectations for Brian's behavior (coming to group time, sharing toys, staying in the classroom), introducing sign language (signs for "more" and "want" came first and were especially useful), combining signs and sounds, rewarding tiny improvements, providing intensive speech therapy, and working with Brian's mom and dad to ensure consistency between home and school.

Epilogue

Brian's aggression did not stop immediately. His behavior change was gradual. It took a year for the aggression to pretty much disappear. Today, Brian is in a class for 4-year-olds with special needs. His aggression appears only sporadically.

Childhood apraxia is not something children grow out of. However, with proper intervention early in life, children like Brian can learn to speak more clearly and to communicate more effectively.

Source: Brian's story was adapted from a case study included in Kostelnik, Onaga, Rohde, & Whiren (2002, p. 120–135).

out solutions without direct adult intervention. Keeping this in mind, watchful teachers allow children to argue as long as their actions do not turn to violence and their language does not become abusive. If a resolution comes about, they use positive personal messages to identify children's appropriate behaviors and bring them to their attention. However, if aggression occurs or children seem at a loss for what to do next, you can become directly involved as a conflict mediator.

Conflict mediation involves walking children through a series of steps beginning with problem identification and ending with a mutually satisfactory solution. The adult provides more or less direction as necessary until some conclusion is reached. The goal is not for adults to dictate how children should solve their problem but to help them figure out a solution of their own. Children experience several benefits from working through their differences in this way (Epstein 2009; Wheeler, 2004).

Conflict mediation has the following characteristics:

- Contributes to more peaceful program environments
- Builds trust among children and between children and adults
- Teaches constructive ways of dealing with highly emotional situations
- Teaches children problem-solving strategies and gives children a chance to practice those strategies in the heat of real disagreements
- Promotes friendliness among children
- Promotes feelings of competence and worth among children

During conflict mediation, children learn the skills necessary to reach peaceful resolutions. These skills involve compromise and the ability to consider their own perspective as well as that of another person (Levin, 2003). At first, children need a lot of support to proceed all the way to a negotiated settlement. The mediator provides this support, serving as a model and as an instructor. As children learn problem-solving procedures and words, they become increasingly capable of solving problems for themselves. There is also evidence that these childhood lessons are maintained into adulthood (Rimm-Kaufman & Wanless, 2011).

As with any other social skill, children require numerous opportunities to practice conflict resolution under the guidance of a more experienced person (Beane, 2005). In most cases, this is an adult. However, over the past decade 10-, 11- and 12-year-olds have been taught to mediate peer conflicts on the playground and in the lunchroom. Regardless of whether the mediator is an adult or older child, most conflict-resolution models involve similar steps (Epstein, 2009; Kaiser & Rasminsky, 2012). Here is a practical, systematic model that can be used to mediate children's disputes while teaching them appropriate problem-solving skills.

A Model for Conflict Mediation naeyc

Several girls are working out a dance routine. Suddenly, Mrs. Woznawski, the after-school supervisor, hears Sarah shout, "Give me that hoop—I need it!" Bianca screams back: "Use something else! I'm not done." Alerted to the difficulty, the adult watches from a distance as the children continue their argument. However, as the dispute heats up, the children begin to grab and pull on the hoop. This is an opportune time for Mrs. Woznawski to begin conflict mediation.

Step 1: Initiate the Mediation Process

The first step in approaching a conflict situation is to assume the role of mediator. Stopping the aggressive behavior, separating the combatants, and defining the problem accomplish this: "You both want the hoop. It looks like you each have different ideas about what to do." You may have to position yourself between the children as you help them focus on the mutual problem rather than on the object or territory they are defending. It is helpful to neutralize the object of contention by temporarily gaining control of it and assuring the children that it will be safe until the conflict is resolved: "I'll take care of the hoop until we can decide together what to do." This stops Bianca and Sarah from continuing to grab, helps them to hear you and each other, and sets the stage for them to approach a highly emotional situation more objectively.

Step 2: Clarify Each Child's Perspective

Clarifying the conflict based on the children's perspective is step 2. Ask each child in turn to state what he or she wants from the situation. It is important to allow each child ample opportunity, without interruption, to state his or her ultimate desire. This might involve possession of a toy or getting a turn. Some sample statements might include, "You both seem very angry. Sarah, tell me what you want. Bianca, you can tell me what you want when Sarah is finished." This step is critical because the children must trust you not to make an arbitrary decision in favor of one child or the other. You establish neutrality by withholding any evaluation of the merits of either child's position. Paraphrasing each child's view to the other child is also essential. This ensures that you correctly understand each child's perspective and helps the children to clarify both positions. Children who are very upset or quiet may require several opportunities to describe their position. It must be emphasized that, depending on the level of the children's distress, this step may take several minutes. Children may need help articulating their desires. Try to be as accurate as possible in paraphrasing, checking back with each child in turn.

Step 3: Sum Up

The third step occurs when you have enough information to understand each child's perception of the conflict. When this happens, define the problem in mutual terms, implying that each child is responsible for both the problem and its solution: "Sarah and Bianca, you each want to use the hoop all by yourself for your dance number. That is a problem. We need a solution that will satisfy each of you." In other words, state that a problem exists and that a solution must be found.

Step 4: Generate Alternatives

Generating several possible alternatives takes place in stage four. Suggestions may come from the children themselves or from bystanders. Each time a child suggests a solution, you paraphrase it to the children directly involved: "Jonathan (a bystander) says you could figure out a way for both of you to use the hoop together in your routine." At this point, each child is asked to evaluate the merits of the recommendation: "What do you think, Sarah? What do you think, Bianca?" Elicit as many divergent ideas as possible and have no stake in which solution is eventually selected. Each child should be a willing participant in the outcome, and no alternative should be forced on any child. It is typical during this phase for children to reject certain possibilities that they may later find acceptable.

Therefore, when a suggestion is repeated, present it again rather than assuming it will be rejected a second time. If the children are not able to originate alternatives, help them out by saying something like: "Sometimes when people have this problem, they decide to use it together somehow, take turns, or trade things back and forth. What do you think?" Sometimes during this step, children tire of the process, and one or the other says something like, "I don't want it anymore" or "It's okay, she can have it." Other times, one of the children will simply walk away. If this happens, reflect and provide information, "This is hard work."

or "You're getting tired of trying to solve this problem. Working things out can take a long time." If the child insists that he or she would like to solve the problem by giving up, respect his or her wishes. With practice, children increase their skills and are better able to tolerate the time involved in reaching a negotiated settlement. In the meantime, both children have witnessed the mediation process up to a certain point, and each will have a better idea of what to expect the next time.

Step 5: Agree on a Solution

Children will reject certain suggestions outright and will indicate that others seem more acceptable. The ultimate goal of step 5 is for the children to agree on a plan that is mutually satisfying. Your job as mediator is to help the children explore the possibilities that seem most acceptable to them. The plan should not include any alternatives that either child vehemently opposes. The final agreement usually involves some concessions from each child and may not represent the action a child would take if she or he did not have to consider another person's needs. Eventually, the children will exhibit behaviors that indicate that each can find a way to accept one or a combination of ideas.

Continue the mediation process until the possibilities have been narrowed down to a workable solution. When this finally occurs, it is important to acknowledge that a resolution has been achieved. For example: "You think you can take turns with the hoop and add the jump rope too. It sounds like you've solved the problem! Try out your idea."

Mediation gave these girls practice in problem solving.

Step 6: Reinforce the Problem-Solving Process

The purpose of mediation step 6 is to praise the children for developing a mutually beneficial solution. The message to be conveyed is that the process of reaching the solution is as important as the solution itself. The way to achieve this is to acknowledge the emotional investment each child had in the original conflict and the hard work involved in reaching an agreement: "It was important to each of you to have the hoop. You worked hard at figuring out how to do that without hurting each other."

Step 7: Follow Through

The conclusion of the mediation process involves helping the children carry out the terms of the agreement. This is accomplished by reminding the children what the terms were and, if necessary, physically assisting or demonstrating how to comply. At this point, an adult should remain in the vicinity to determine the degree to which children carry out the agreement. If the plan begins to falter, the children should be brought together again to discuss possible revisions.

The seven steps involved in conflict mediation are summarized in this downloadable reminder (Highlight 12-2).

Conflict Mediation in Action

The following is a transcript of an actual conflict between two children, both 5 years old, in which the helping professional used the model just described.

HIGHLIGHT 12-2

Summary of Conflict Mediation Model

Step 1: Initiate mediation

Step 2: Clarify each child's perspective

Step 3: Sum up

Step 4: Generate alternatives

Step 5: Agree on a solution

Step 6: Reinforce problem-solving

Step 7: Follow through

© Cengage Learning 2015

Step 1: Initiate Mediation

Angela: Mr. Lewin, Evan and Aaron are fighting.

Adult: Aaron and Evan, you're both trying to put on that stethoscope. (Restrains the two children, who are pulling on the stethoscope, crouches to the children's level, and turns each child to face him.) I'll hold it while we're deciding what to do about it. I'll hold it. I'll make sure it's safe. I'll hold on to it. (Removes the stethoscope from the children's grasp and holds it in front of him.)

Step 2: Clarify

Aaron: I wanted that!

Adult: You wanted the stethoscope. How about you, Evan?

Evan: I want it.

Adult: You wanted the stethoscope, too. (Another child offers a stethoscope.)

Evan: I don't like that kind.

Aaron: I want it.

Adult: Aaron says he really wants that stethoscope. What about you, Evan?

Evan: I want it!

Step 3: Sum Up

Adult: You want it, too. Evan and Aaron, you both want to play with one stethoscope. We have a problem. What can we do about it? Anybody have any ideas?

Step 4: Generate Alternatives

Aaron: He can have Angela's.

Adult: You think he can have Angela's. It looks like Angela still wants hers. (Angela backs away.)

Evan: I still want mine, too.

Adult: Evan, you want yours, too. Sometimes when we have a problem like this, we can figure out a solution. Sometimes we share it; sometimes we take turns. Anybody have any ideas?

Another child: Share it.

Adult: Shanna thinks you can share it. What do you think Aaron?

Aaron: Take turns.

Adult: Aaron thinks we should take turns. What do you think, Evan?

Evan: Unh uh (shaking his head from side to side).

Adult: You don't think we should take turns.

Evan: Then I just want it.

Adult:　Then you just really want it, hmm. That's still a problem.

Aaron:　I want it.

Adult:　You really want a turn with it. How about you, Evan? What do you think?

Step 5: Agree

Evan:　No. Aaron can have one turn.

Adult:　You think Aaron can have one turn.

Evan:　Yes, guess so.

Step 6: Reinforce

Adult:　Thank you, Evan.

Evan:　Not a long turn.

Adult:　Not a long turn. You want to make sure that you get it back. Aaron, Evan said you could have one turn, and then you'll give it back to him.

Evan:　A short turn.

Adult:　A short turn. Aaron, you may have a short turn. Thank you very much, Evan. That was really hard to do.

Step 7: Follow Through

Adult:　It's about five minutes 'till it's cleanup time. So Aaron can have a two-minute turn, and you can have a two-minute turn.

Adult:　(two minutes later) Aaron, two minutes are up. Now, it is time for Evan's turn. Thank you, Aaron. You kept your part of the bargain, and Evan kept his.

How Children Think about Conflict Resolution

Three-year-old	Give me that. I want it!
Six-year-old	We could take turns! First me, then you!
Twelve-year-old	We could combine our ideas. If that doesn't work, we could vote for the best one.

Children's ideas about conflict resolution evolve as their understanding of relationships becomes more sophisticated and as their language and cognitive skills grow. Understanding age-related perceptions will help you recognize what may constitute "reasonable" solutions from the children's perspective. It will also help you appreciate the progress children are making as they practice conflict resolution.

Toddlers: It's all about me! Initially, very young children see their own needs as paramount. Physical force, verbal insistence, and withdrawal are typical ways in which they handle disagreements over toys. This simplistic view can be summed up as "fight or flight." When two toddlers argue over a toy, they might grab or protest to address the situation. Most often, however, children simply give up if a peer refuses to yield a favored item, shifting their attention to something else nearby (Wheeler, 2004). In either case, conflicts tend to be settled through parallel but separate outcomes rather than joint agreements.

Preschool – early elementary: It's all about what's fair! The strategies children use to resolve conflicts at this age may be physical or verbal, aggressive or nonaggressive. The outcomes may be unresolved or culminated as a result of adult-imposed solutions, submission of one child to another, or compromises reached through mutual strategizing by children within the dispute or with help from peers (Charlesworth, 2011). Children judge how to proceed within a conflict based on the idea that peer interactions are reciprocal. If the first move a child makes in a disagreement is conciliatory, the follow-up response by the other child is likely to be the same. Conversely, if the first step toward resolution is aggressive, children believe it is perfectly "fair" for other participants to retaliate in kind. Although random aggression is frowned upon by children starting around age 5, aggression for the purpose of defending one's rights or reacting to another's aggression is treated as acceptable under the circumstances (Wheeler, 2004). This thinking leads children to say things like, "He hit me first," or "I had it" as reasonable rationales for reacting aggressively within a contested situation. In the same vein, children expect to get some restitution from the offending party if the disagreement is to end satisfactorily. This can take the form of acknowledging the victim's rights or some action to reverse the hurtful words or deeds. You hear this belief reflected when children demand, "Say you're sorry" or "You give that back!" The most satisfactory resolutions at this age are ones in which both children participate in the outcome.

Older elementary: Reasoning and persuasion are key! Around third grade, nearly all children reject physical aggression as a way of settling differences over objects, territory, or rights. They expect peers to resolve arguments more constructively and tend to dislike children who engage in physical aggression to get what they want (Ladd, 2005). During these years, children gradually conclude that both participants in a conflict bear some responsibility for the dispute and that both could benefit from a mutually satisfying settlement (Orpinas & Horne, 2010). They also understand that more than one solution may be possible. See Table 12-2 for how one group of 12-year-old children described the different ways they could resolve conflicts.

Table 12-2 12-Year-Olds' Ideas for Solving Disputes

Solution	Sample Comments
Discuss	We should debate and see the problems with both our ideas.
	Have a group discussion and share our thoughts and ideas. Then we could agree on one.
	We could vote.
Defer to someone else	We could let "C" decide.
	Go with "B's" idea so he doesn't get mad or feel bad.
	Tell the teacher if we can't work it out.
Combine ideas	Combine both of our ideas.
Persuade	I would try to persuade people that my idea is best.
	Find other people to help you out or support your opinion.
Search for an alternative	Find an idea we both like and use that one.
	Brainstorm and come up with something better.
Compare and evaluate	Test his idea first, then test mine.
	Try to do both ideas and see which one does better.

Source: Adapted from Kuhn (2005).

Does Conflict Mediation Work?

At this point, you may be wondering whether conflict mediation actually reduces children's aggression or expands their ability to resolve conflicts on their own. Studies do indeed show that children who participate in mediated disputes get better at resolving disagreements amicably (Crothers & Kolbert, 2010). In addition, children increase the number and variety of solutions they suggest and decrease the amount of time they need to negotiate a settlement (Evans, 2002; Kuhn, 2005). Over time, as the negotiation process becomes more familiar, onlookers along with the children in conflict become more actively involved in suggesting ideas and reasons for particular courses of action. Gradually, children also become better able to resolve conflicts independently, without the help of a formal mediator (Epstein, 2009). Finally, there is promising evidence that in groups of children in which mediation is used, not only does instrumental aggression diminish, but positive prosocial behaviors also increase (Lopes & Salovey, 2004; Orpinas & Horne, 2010). Thus, conflict mediation, combined with the other strategies suggested in this chapter, goes a long way toward decreasing children's aggressive interactions.

The mediation model outlined here can be adapted for children as young as 3 or as old as 12 years of age. The steps of the model are similar to many mediation programs currently available commercially as well as others described in the literature. It can be adapted for use by an adult in a single classroom, by an entire program staff, and by children serving as peer mediators in formal group settings.

The teacher mediates an argument between Turell and Ernesto about the two-person bike. The boys decide Turell will drive first, with Ernesto in the back. After two times around the playground, the boys are to switch places. When it's time to switch, Turell becomes upset. The teacher comforts him, and then helps him follow through with the mediation agreement.

Conflict mediation is well suited for dealing with incidents of instrumental aggression. Hostile aggression requires additional skills.

When Aggression Turns into Bullying naeyc

Four-year-old Selena has developed a pattern of picking on Cammy, a younger, physically smaller child in her childcare home. The provider notes that Selena seems angry much of the time and that she hits anyone who disagrees with her; she is especially aggressive toward Cammy. Selena calls Cammy names and physically torments her.

Cammy has begun to exhibit signs of anxious behavior, such as crying when her mother leaves in the morning and clinging to the caregiver throughout the day.

Tristan's parents are thinking about pulling him out of Elmwood School. The fourth-grader complains that a certain group of boys continually threaten him in the hallways and on the playground. They play cruel pranks such as trashing his locker or spilling food on him in the cafeteria. The boys tell him that he smells bad and warn other children not to associate with him. They make fun of his family, his culture, and his abilities. Their tactics have made life miserable for Tristan, yet his teacher does not feel comfortable intervening. She believes adult intervention will only make things worse and has told Tristan he will have to "work things out for himself."

All children have times when they exhibit aggressive behavior. However, some children routinely and deliberately use hurtful actions such as rejection, name-calling, or physical intimidation to exert power over others. Such incidents go beyond the simple clashes common among children; they represent prolonged misuse of influence by one person or group of persons over another. This form of hostile aggression is traditionally called bullying.

Bullying is most prevalent in the later elementary years, yet even preschoolers can exhibit early signs of hostile behavior (Gartrell, 2014). Children as young as 3 years of age talk about bullying and recognize its characteristics:

Deliberate: "He did it on purpose."

Imbalanced: "Unfair—the bully is bigger or more powerful than the victim."

Continuous: "It happens a lot."

These concepts are illustrated in Figures 12-5 and 12-6, children's drawings of bullies.

Victims of Bullying

Being bullied happens to just about everyone. It is estimated that as many as 80% of all children experience bullying sometime during early and middle childhood (Hanish, Kochenderfer-Ladd, Fabes, Martin, & Denning, 2004). Children harassed by bullies report physical injuries and/or feelings of frustration, fear, humiliation, and vulnerability. None of these conditions promote constructive peer relations or positive program environments. For some children, bullying happens only once in a while, but for approximately 10 to 15% of children, bullying is pervasive, and they become chronic victims (Craig et al., 2009). The misery of such children is profound. They live with the immediate effects of being bullied regularly—physical hurt, shame, helplessness, rejection, and unhappiness. Even worse, they go through each day knowing that these indignities will be repeated many times.

Chronic victims tend to be the children least able to respond effectively to taunts and physical assaults. Their communication skills are limited, and they have few social skills. Temperamentally, most are socially withdrawn, anxious, submissive, and insecure. Physically, they are generally weak (Olweus, 1993; Stassen Berger, 2007). They are the last to be chosen in any game and the first to be eliminated from the play. They have few friends and often spend their time alone or apart from the group. Most are passive victims. They seldom initiate the hostile attack and rarely assert their rights when it happens. However, a few children are better described as provocative victims. They incite aggressive reactions from others by their volatile but ineffective responses to social situations. These are the children who argue incessantly about every little thing, who lose their tempers, whine, or cry easily in frustration. They are also the ones who overreact to joking or teasing, treating it as verbal aggression even when that is not its intent (Toblin, Schwartz, Hopmeyer Gorman, & Abou-ezzeddine, 2005). Regardless of the cause, each time passive or provocative victims become involved in aggressive incidents, their ineffectual responses reinforce the bully's behavior, prompting the cycle of aggression to continue.

Generally, chronic victims of bullying are disliked and elicit little sympathy from peers who observe their predicament (Veenstra et al., 2007). For instance, victims who provoke attack through ineffective or irritating behaviors are often viewed as "getting what they deserve" (Society for Adolescent Medicine, 2003). In addition, both aggressive and nonaggressive children anticipate potential rewards from interacting with chronic victims in terms of getting what they want. In other words, classmates see victims as patsies who can be easily taken advantage of and made to give up coveted items. It is no surprise, then, that victims of bullying experience a severely diminished sense of competence and worth.

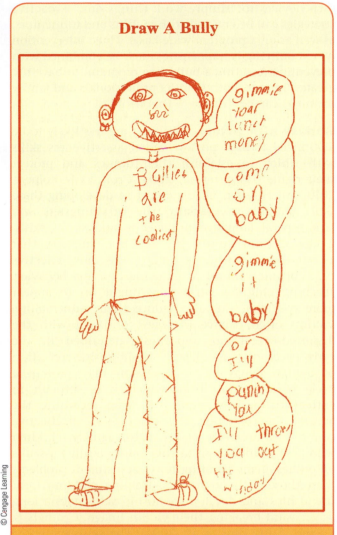

Figure 12-5 Child's Depictions of Bullies. University of Nebraska, Lincoln (Swearer, 2012).

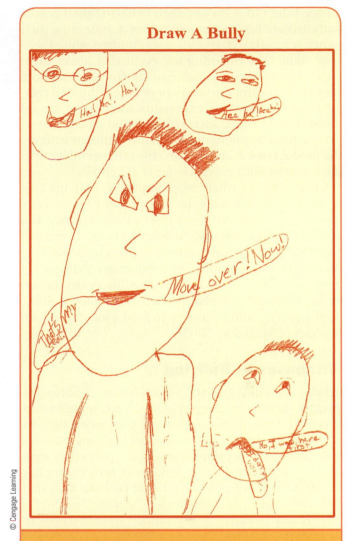

Figure 12-6 Child's Depictions of Bullies. University of Nebraska, Lincoln (Swearer, 2012).

They may express their discomfort through lack of appetite, disturbed sleep, real or imagined illnesses, inability to concentrate, increased fear of facing others, unexplained bouts of crying or extremely anxious behavior, reluctance to go to the center or school, or unusually aggressive behavior toward others less powerful than themselves (often younger peers, siblings, or pets) (Troop-Gordan & Ladd, 2005). This often adds up to low self-esteem and a poor prognosis for the future. Unfortunately, patterns of behavior related to victimization start as early as year three. If they persist, children may become "locked into" the persona of chronic victim by 8 or 9 years of age (Pepler, Smith, & Rigby, 2004). Thus, early childhood is a time when children either begin to develop ineffectual responses to the aggression of others or more productive strategies.

Bullies

The most common type of bully is fearless, coercive, and impulsive. They use aggression to achieve a goal and revel in their success. Such children often have high self-esteem based on their powerful status. Other bullies feel inferior and insecure. They use aggression to mask these feelings and dominate others. All bullies value aggression and the power it gives them over other people. They expect aggression to get them what they want and feel justified using hostile acts to assert their will (Horne et al., 2004). A look into their background sometimes reveals that they have been victims of bullying themselves in another time and place, making them bully/victim. Some bullies are children who have experienced few boundaries, gaining an impression that they can do anything they like. Other children become bullies as a result of attributing hostile intent to peers and then believing their hostile outbursts are justified as a means of maintaining their rights. A fourth scenario involves children who experience some overwhelming life event that leaves them angry and confused. Unable to control the situation, they try to control the behavior of others through coercion. Rather than risk expressing their anger toward those close to them, such children find a "safe" target among their acquaintances. Finally, children who are the product of a coercive home life often exhibit bullying behavior with peers (Dodge et al., 2006).

Regardless of what has prompted it, bullying that is allowed to continue in the preschool and early elementary years manifests itself as delinquency and academic failure by middle school (Troop-Gordan & Ladd, 2005). Moreover, children for whom bullying becomes a standard mode of conduct are significantly more likely as adults to be involved in violent crime, be imprisoned, be involved in domestic violence, abuse their children, and be unable to hold a job (Society for Adolescent Medicine, 2003).

Witnesses to Bullying

Besides the bully and the victim, other children frequently observe bullying episodes. Such witnesses are affected by this hostile aggression, even when they are not directly involved. Witnesses see bullying modeled and reinforced. They learn that bullying pays off for some people. They may develop feelings of fear, frustration, hopelessness, or anger based on what they see. They may feel guilty about not doing more to help another child or tangentially powerful if they support the bully's behavior from the sidelines. They may fear for their own safety or worry that they will become targets of the harassment (Beaudoin & Taylor, 2004). Conversely, witnesses can influence what happens when bullying takes place. They may function as supporters of the bully or supporters of the victim. If they ignore what is happening, they send a message to bully and victim that bullying is okay with them or that there is nothing that can be done to change the situation. On the other hand, when children stand up for the victim, the bullying often ends (Hawkins, Pepler, & Craig, 2001; Kaiser & Rasminsky, 2012). Consequently, witnesses play an important role in determining to what extent bullying is accepted or rejected as a way of life in formal group settings.

The Role of Adults in Bully Prevention

Both victims and bullies are vulnerable people whose long-term prognosis for social and academic success is negative. Witnesses are also impacted negatively. The adults in children's lives must take such destructive behavior seriously. Children cannot be left to their own devices to "simply work things out." Proactive strategies can be enacted with victims and tormentors, as well as on a program-wide basis. Thus, intervention (when bullying is happening) must be combined with prevention (creating a bully-free program) to have the greatest impact. Both helping professionals and family members can contribute to this effort.

Working with victims. Children are less likely to be victimized if they possess verbal assertiveness skills with which to establish their desires and protect their rights (Horne et al., 2004; Crothers & Kolbert, 2010). All children need support in developing these skills, but this is especially true for youngsters who lack general language proficiency and social skills. Evidence from continuing research suggests that assertiveness training is among the most effective types of intervention in reducing bullying behavior. Teaching children what they might do to appear more confident can also reduce their vulnerability. Victims often behave in ways consistent with the distorted-perception hypothesis described in the early pages of this chapter. Their misinterpretation of benign behavior as aggression may prompt a cycle of aggression from which it is difficult to extract themselves. Adult coaching regarding the accurate interpretation of social cues is an effective countermeasure (Frey et al., 2010). Finally, children who have friends seem to cope better against assaults by bullies, demonstrating fewer adjustment problems than those with no friends. Helping children form friendships and develop friendship skills goes a long way toward breaking their victim image (Crothers & Kolbert, 2010; Zins et al., 2004). The skills presented in Chapter 8, Supporting Children's Peer Relationships and Friendships, are useful in this regard.

Dealing with bullies. Bullies cannot simply be ignored by adults at the center or school. Such tactics push them beyond the bounds of normal social circles, reinforcing their defiant style. Thus, clear boundaries and consistent expectations are prime ingredients for working with perpetrators of hostile aggression. Children must be told that such behavior will not be tolerated. Hostile youngsters must also be helped to control their angry impulses (Essa, 2008). Strategies such as self-talk, identification of emotions, figuring out behavioral cues that tell how others are feeling, and logical consequences have been described in previous chapters and are effective tools related to impulse control. In addition, many aggressors also benefit from the same strategies that support victims—assertiveness training, social skills training, cooperative learning activities, and coaching to help them develop more accurate interpretations of social encounters (Frey et al., 2010).

Children with friends are better able to cope with bullies.

fifth grade decided that rejecting another child's bid to play was a form of hostile aggression (Paley, 1992). They agreed to create a rule, "You can't say, you can't play," meaning that no one could be left out of group activities and group games based on how they looked, how they talked, or because they were not a favorite or appealing peer. This rule came about after much discussion among the children and adults about how to create a safe, nurturing environment in which all children would feel valued. Simply formulating the rule was not enough. Together the children and their teacher explored its meaning, practiced following it, and continually discussed the impact the rule was having on their lives as individuals and on the climate in their classroom and the school overall. In time, the climate improved, and instances of rejection were reduced.

This example illustrates that hostile aggression can be effectively addressed when many children are involved in creating a new environment and when bully-prevention techniques move beyond the bullies and victims alone. In addition, though the individual strategies described so far are effective, they are most powerful when combined in a comprehensive approach to bully prevention that includes children and adults in the program as well as children's families. Thus, our best means for reducing the hostile aggression of bullying is to work out program-wide solutions.

Program-wide solutions to bullying. Willow Creek School and Walnut Hills School look very much the same from the outside, but inside there is a significant difference between them.

At Willow Creek School, there is little talk about bullying. Students seldom tell adults if they are bullied. They believe it won't make a difference; they fear it will make things worse. Adults don't act on what they learn, or they tell children to "work things out for themselves." Bullying takes place in the hallways, the bathrooms, and on the playground. When asked if there is a problem with bullying at their school, everyone is quick to say, "no." But the truth is, several children are bullies; more are victims; and even more children witness bullying every day.

The picture is different at Walnut Hills School. The focus here is on prevention. Children, staff, and family members talk about bullying and what they might do to reduce bullying in the program. In every classroom, there is a Bully Buster poster that summarizes the philosophy at Walnut Hills.

Bullying is not cool at our school.

We don't tease, call names, or put people down.

We don't hit, shove, kick, or punch.

Working with other children in the program. Any child may witness bullying at any time, so every child needs to know there are protections in place so they will not be victimized themselves or left feeling helpless in the face of hostile aggression. Most important, witnesses need to know what to do when they see or learn about someone bullying someone else. The first and most important step is to "break the code of silence" that surrounds bullying (Beane, 2005). That is, practitioners must talk about bullying openly and find ways to involve all the children in helping to create a bully-free environment. Children who are witnesses can be empowered to support victims in a variety of ways, to find new approaches to interacting with bullies, and to help create an inclusive program in which no one feels threatened or left out.

The notion of inclusion was the basic tenet of Vivian Paley's celebrated book, *You Can't Say, You Can't Play*, in which children from kindergarten through

If we see someone being bullied, we speak up and stop it (if we can) or go for help right away.

When we do things as a group, we include everybody and make sure no one is left out.

We have the power to stop bullying! We are working together!

There is very little bullying at Walnut Hills and when it does happen, children and adults know what to do to make things safer for everyone.

Willow Creek School and Walnut Hills School have chosen different approaches to dealing with bullying in their programs. The outcomes are quite different as well. Such results could be predicted by the research (Espelage & Swearer, 2004; Olweus & Limber, 2010).

Bullying is most likely when the following occur:

- Children are frequently left unsupervised.
- Behavior expectations are unclear and inconsistent.
- Adults rely on autocratic or permissive discipline strategies.
- Adults ignore bullying behavior.
- No preventative measures are taken to address bullying.
- Children and adults lack the knowledge and skills to be bully-free.
- There is poor communication between home and the formal group setting.

Programs characterized in this way tend to be "bully laboratories," in which everyone suffers (Beane, 2005). On the other hand, bully-free programs incorporate the same elements that characterize schools implementing alternatives to corporal punishment. The emphasis in such programs is on authoritative discipline strategies that demonstrate respect for children and require them to take responsibility for their actions. Staff members model the behaviors they want children to adopt, are consistent in their approach to discipline, and provide

adequate supervision for children at all times. Strong home–program partnerships are valued and nurtured.

Most importantly, bullying is taken seriously. Adults and children join forces to confront bullying in constructive ways and to create a bully-free environment. Many of the strategies you have learned about in this text support that goal. How to implement some of the key skills you have just read about is described next.

TeachSource Video 12-1

© Cengage Learning 2015

School Age: Emotional Development (Bullying)

Go online and review *School Age: Emotional Development (Bullying)*.

In this video, you will observe a teacher talking to children about bullying and playing a game to reinforce the lesson.

1. Identify at least two lessons the teacher is trying to get across.
2. How effective do you think the teacher's game is in teaching about bullying?
3. Name three additional ways the teacher might work with children to address issues of bullying in the classroom or at school.

Watch on CourseMate

SKILLS FOR HANDLING AGGRESSIVE BEHAVIOR naeyc

Dealing with Aggression in Formal Group Settings—All-Purpose Strategies

1. **Coach children in how to control their angry impulses.** Talk with them about their strong feelings—what those feelings are and what prompts them. Work with children to recognize signs that their emotions are escalating beyond their control. Teach children self-talk to help them maintain their composure. Point out the feelings of victims to assist angry children in empathizing with people who are hurt, unhappy, or angry too. Teach children to slow down. Provide verbal cues, "Slow down." "Take a breath." "Wait a moment before you get back in the game." Use

physical intervention as necessary—catching a child by the hand, turning a child toward you, or taking the child to the side. Show children how to break tasks into individual steps to slow the pace of their activity. Acknowledge children's attempts at impulse control through reflections and effective praise: "You waited very patiently," "You're picking up the books, one at a time. That keeps them from getting ripped." Consider short-term use of tangible rewards to assist children in recognizing and practicing nonaggressive responses in provocative circumstances.

2. **Structure the environment to minimize potential frustration for children.** Check equipment to make sure that it works. Determine whether materials are appropriate for the children's developmental stage. If they are not, revise them. If a piece of equipment does not function, repair it or replace it with something else. Have enough materials that youngsters do not have to wait for long periods of time to gain access to them. Allow children to have things long enough so that they feel satisfied.

Arrange the classroom to give children easy access to functional activity spaces. Make these areas large enough for more than one child to occupy comfortably. Survey the space to make sure children can move about freely without accidentally bumping into peers or objects or otherwise interfering with one another's activities.

Alert children to upcoming changes in routine so that they are not surprised when such changes occur. Warn them prior to transitions between activities so they can finish what they are doing before going on to the next thing.

3. **Remain alert to children for whom frustration is building.** Watch children for signs of frustration. When it is evident that a child is becoming distressed, intervene. Offer comfort, support, information, or assistance as befits the situation. Help children reevaluate their goals or break the task into more manageable steps. Encourage children to cope directly with the source of frustration. "You're upset! That model keeps falling apart. The glue you are using works better on paper than it does on plastic. Let's look for a different kind of glue." If circumstances allow, ask the child in question what he or she can think to do—take a break, get help from another child, go to another resource for information, watch someone else for a while, and so on. Support children when they attempt one of these solutions. If the child is stumped, ask other children to suggest a way to resolve the dilemma: "Raul is feeling frustrated. The paint is soaking all the way through his paper and spoiling his picture. Sam and Carlos, what do you think Raul could do about this problem?" In this way, teachers have a chance to turn frustrating situations into useful learning opportunities.

4. **Provide children with opportunities to develop competence.** Assign them age-appropriate responsibility: watering the plants, feeding the fish, checking that the computer is turned off at the end of the day, and so forth. Give children chances to make choices and to try a variety of tasks and experiences independently. Structure these so children feel challenged but not so overwhelmed that success is unlikely. Teach children the skills they need to achieve their goals: how to use tools, how to play games, and how to work with others. Do not deny these privileges to children who are aggressive. They are among the ones who most need alternate ways of exercising power and achieving appropriate social status in the group.

5. **Help children learn to more accurately interpret social cues.** Provide them with practice recognizing social cues such as voice tone, facial expressions, and words that differentiate aggressive actions from nonaggressive ones. Pose hypothetical situations, enact short skits with puppets, or use role-play to demonstrate these variations. Next, ask children to interpret what they have observed. Point out that there may be more than one interpretation for each event: "You think he bumped her because he didn't like her. Another reason might be that there were too many people crowded around the table. There wasn't room for everybody to stand without touching each other." Encourage children to practice taking the perspective of the victim, to get a sense of how aggressors are perceived when they resort to coercion: "How do you think Marvin felt when Geraldine shoved him and yelled at him?" After they become somewhat accurate in their conclusions, invite children to generate nonaggressive reactions to the scenarios you pose: "When Marvin stepped on Geraldine's backpack, what could she do instead of shoving him so hard?" or "What would happen if she did that?" or "What will happen next?" Make sure to have the children critically evaluate each proposed response: "Why do you think that is a good idea?" or "Why don't you think that will work?" or "Which of our ideas seems best?" This final step helps children move beyond generating random suggestions to consciously weighing the merits or disadvantages of each—a skill they must possess to successfully control aggression in real-life circumstances.

In addition, use on-the-spot coaching in actual social situations to help typically aggressive children go through the steps just described (recognizing cues, interpreting them accurately, generating nonaggressive responses, choosing a response, enacting it). Refer to Chapter 8 for more information about such coaching. Notice when children put a check on initial aggressive impulses or react in nonaggressive ways at times when formerly they may have responded with aggression. Use effective praise to help children recognize the progress they are making.

6. **Set consistent limits on aggression.** Stop aggressive behavior, relying on physical intervention if necessary (e.g., catching a child's hand or separating children in a heated argument). Acknowledge the aggressor's emotions, express your concern, and explain why the behavior is unacceptable. Suggest specific alternative behaviors for younger children to pursue; help older children generate their own ideas for a solution to the problem. Clearly state the consequences for continued aggression, and follow through immediately should children persist. Implement this strategy in response to cases of instrumental aggression in which children are developmentally unable to negotiate or there is no time to do so. Use the same tactic when you observe children using hostile aggression as a way to "save face." For example, children who shove in reaction to being jostled themselves, or those who get into a teasing interchange, are exhibiting signs of being provoked and benefit from having their point of view acknowledged while at the same time hearing that aggressive behavior is forbidden.

7. **Help children de-escalate potentially aggressive play.** Keep an eye on children as they play and watch for early signs of difficulty. When a child stops laughing; when voices become upset or complaining; when facial expressions show fear, anger, or distress; and when words are becoming hurtful, step in. Redirect the play or become involved in the play yourself to help defuse potential aggression.

    Be more direct if you observe young children pretending to use blocks, sticks, or their fingers as weapons. Step in immediately and redirect the action. Say something like: "You're having fun. You're using the stick as a gun. It upsets me when you pretend to shoot someone else. Guns are dangerous. They are not toys. Use the stick to dig with. You may not use it as a weapon." Do not be sidetracked by children's protestations that they were "just pretending." Reflect their assertion: "You weren't shooting each other for real. That may be. It bothers me when children pretend to hurt others. There are better ways to play. Let's figure one out."

8. **Reinforce children's behaviors that are incompatible with aggression** (Epstein, 2009). Acknowledge their helpful, cooperative, empathic responses. Make a special effort to note such behaviors in children who are typically aggressive. Although all children benefit from positive reinforcement, more aggressive children particularly need to hear that they are capable of appropriate behavior. It is all too easy to get into the rut of expecting aggression from certain children and failing to recognize the more positive things they do. Avoid this by assigning yourself the task of purposely looking for nonaggressive behaviors and telling children your favorable observations.

9. **Model the core elements of nonaggressive behavior—respect, empathy, and reasoning—in your day-to-day interactions with children** (Wheeler, 2004). Remain calm and rational when confronting children or adults whose behavior angers or frustrates you. Keep your voice level and your movements controlled. Take the time to acknowledge the perspectives of others when they conflict with your own. Work out compromises and talk things through, especially in difficult situations. Follow up on promises you make so children know that you can be trusted to do what you say.

10. **Encourage children to predict the consequences of their aggressive actions** (Miller, 2013). Ask questions such as, "What do you think will happen if you knock her tower down?" "How will your friend feel if you call him Georgie Porgie?" How would you feel if someone called you a hurtful name?"

11. **Intervene when a child accidently hurts another.** Use this as an opportunity to promote empathy and to forestall potential retaliation. Comfort the victim and explain the accidental nature of the aggression. If the aggressor does not realize the results of his or her actions, point them out in concrete, nonjudgmental ways: "Look at Susan. She is crying. When you knocked over the chair it hit her in the back. That hurt." Teach the aggressor to use such phrases as "It was an accident," "I didn't mean it," or "It wasn't on purpose." When appropriate, assist the aggressor in finding ways to make restitution. This is a good time to teach the words, "I'm sorry" if the aggressor truly regrets his or her actions. Sometimes victims can contribute ideas for restitution as well: "Susan, what could Kathleen do to help you feel better?"

12. **Attend to the victims of aggression.** Comfort the victim in front of the aggressor, and help the child generate ideas of how to respond to similar aggressive acts in the future. "You're upset.

© Cengage Learning

Comfort victims of aggression.

assertively. Take advantage of teachable moments throughout the day to teach these same lessons. Chapter 8 provides examples of how skits might be used to teach such scripts. Refer to Chapter 13 for guidelines about how to plan activities and use on-the-spot coaching with similar goals in mind. Sample scripts include:

- "I'm still using this."
- "You can have it next."
- "I want a turn."
- "When will I know that your turn is over?"
- "Stop calling me names."
- "Please stop grabbing."
- "This is mine. It's not for sharing. Sorry."
- "I'm not ready yet."

15. **Explore alternatives to corporal punishment if it is practiced in your setting.** Most schools and centers do not require that all helping professionals use corporal punishment, even though some on the staff may. Prior to accepting a position, ascertain whether you will be expected to paddle children. If this is a requirement of the job, consider seeking another. If it is not, discuss with your supervisor ways in which you can use your disciplinary approach within the confines of the system.

Jemma hit you. The next time she tries that, put up your hand and say, 'Stop.'" In addition, whenever possible, involve the aggressor in helping the victim as well. Avoid humiliating the aggressor or coercing her or him to apologize in your attempt to assuage the victim's distress.

13. **Praise children when they attempt non-aggressive solutions to difficult situations.** Use positive personal messages and effective praise when you observe children settling a potential dispute, refraining from hitting to resolve a conflict, or coming to the aid of a victim of hostile aggression. Compliment children's efforts to be nonviolent even if their approach has been rebuffed by others. Offer comfort and suggestions for how their performance could improve in the future.

14. **Teach children assertive language.** Plan discussions and formulate activities to highlight sample words children might use when they want to express themselves or maintain their rights

Dealing with Instrumental Aggression

1. **Provide children with practice sharing, taking turns, trading, bargaining, and negotiating to get what they want.** Accomplish this through games, role-playing, and skits. Use a variety of strategies, including on-the-spot coaching as well as planned activities. Address these skills every day.

2. **Mediate children's conflicts.** When incidents of instrumental aggression occur, use the conflict mediation model described in this chapter. Carry out each step in order:

Step 1: Initiate mediation	Establish the mediator role and neutralize the object, territory, or right.
Step 2: Clarify	Clarify the conflict based on each child's perspective.
Step 3: Sum up	Define the dispute in mutual terms; make clear each child has responsibility for both the problem and its solution.

Step 4: Generate alternatives	Ask for suggestions from the children involved and from bystanders.
Step 5: Agree on a solution	Help children create a plan of action that is mutually satisfying.
Step 6: Reinforce problem-solving	Praise children for developing a mutually agreed-on solution and for working hard to achieve it.
Step 7: Follow through	Help children carry out the terms of the agreement

Make sure you allow yourself enough time to work through the entire process. If you have less than five minutes available, do not begin negotiation. Implement the strategies of the personal message and corrective consequences presented in Chapters 10 and 11 instead. For example, "You both want another turn with the balance scale. That's a problem. I wish we had time to work this out between you. I'm concerned you have to be outside for the bus right now. Put the scale away. You can both use it again tomorrow."

Responding to Hostile Aggression

1. **Talk about bullying with everyone.** Define bullying with the children. Share stories about bullying. Give children opportunities to draw pictures, write in their journals, or read stories about bullies to provide an opening to discuss these matters. Invite children to describe what bullying looks like and how it feels to be a victim, a bully, or a witness.

2. **Make specific rules about bullying and follow through on them.** Rules communicate that bullying is unacceptable and that it is everyone's responsibility to create a bully-free setting. Ask the children to help you create rules similar to the ones written by the children at Walnut Hills School (described earlier in this chapter). Establish a few simple rules that children describe in their own words. Talk about what will happen if people break the rules. If you see bullying, follow through on the rules you set. If you hear about bullying in your program, intervene. Work with bullies, victims, and witnesses to increase their skills and to follow the rules. Conduct a variety of conversations with children one-on-one, in small groups, and with the group as a whole to gauge to what extent you are maintaining a bully-free environment.

3. **Help children distinguish between tattling and telling about bullying.** Crucial to establishing a bully-free environment is for everyone to join forces to stop bullying. Because much bullying occurs when and where adults can't see it and intervene, children who see bullying need to tell a trusted grown-up that bullying is happening. Allan Beane (2005) has created some simple rules to help children understand the importance of telling adults about bullying (p. 43). Here they are in a downloadable Bully Buster checklist.

BULLY BUSTER Checklist

- If you see someone being bullied, tell the teacher.
- If you know that someone is being bullied, tell the teacher.
- If you think someone is being bullied, tell the teacher.
- If you do nothing about bullying, you're saying bullying is okay with you.
- We have the power to stop and prevent bullying in our classroom, but we have to work together.

Digital Download Download from CourseMate

Though younger children often feel comfortable telling a teacher when problems arise, older children will need to be reminded of the distinction between tattling and telling. Define tattling as about behaviors that are not dangerous. Describe telling as letting adults know about dangerous situations such as bullying. Tattling simply gets people in trouble. Telling keeps people safe.

4. **Talk with the child who bullies.** Stop aggression where and when it happens using personal messages and a relevant follow-through. Later, take the aggressor to a private spot to discuss the incident or the pattern of behavior you are seeing. Remind the child of the rules (anti-bullying and keeping people and property safe). Talk about how his or her behavior is affecting others and how it might affect him or her in the future (e.g., loss of potential friends, continued consequences in the classroom, etc.). Make sure the child has a chance to express his or her wishes and goals. Work on these with the child. If possible, find

ways for the bully to make amends. This provides a replacement behavior for the aggression and gives the child a more socially acceptable way to gain status with his or her peers.

Focus on conveying the message that bullying is unacceptable and must stop. Avoid hostile reactions such as yelling, using sarcasm, threatening, or trying to humiliate the perpetrator (Kaiser & Rasminsky, 2012). Remember, your effectiveness will depend on your ability to establish a relationship with the child as well as how well you can help the child achieve his or her goals in more constructive ways.

5. **Conduct follow-up conversations with children who have been victimized.** Carry out this conversation privately. Reaffirm that every child has the right to feel safe and that no one deserves to be bullied (Olweus & Limber, 2010). Use open-ended questions to discuss the child's reactions to what happened. Explore ideas for improving the situation, and choose one or two things the child will try to do (Kaiser & Rasminsky, 2012). Provide coaching (e.g., assertiveness scripts, play strategies, as needed). Describe how you and/or others will help with the follow-through on this plan.

6. **Help children explore ways to avoid becoming victims of bullying and what to do if they are victimized.** Conduct group discussions as well as individual coaching sessions as appropriate. Explore such strategies as staying away from bullies, looking confident, taking a big breath before responding to verbal aggression, walking away, saying "Stop," telling a grown-up, asking for help, and bunching together with friends.

7. **Help children develop a repertoire of strategies for what to do if they witness bullying.** Some strategies bully-prevention experts recommend include refusing to join in with the bullying, speaking out and saying that bullying is not okay, reporting bullying that witnesses know about or see, inviting the person who is being bullied to join the witness and his or her friends, offering support to the victim in the presence of the bully, supporting a victim in private, and gathering several witnesses together to protect a victim (Beane, 2005; Jackson, 2003).

Communicating with Families

1. **Communicate to family members how you intend to deal with aggression in your setting.** Explain what you will do as well as what you will not do. Provide a rationale for your

choices. Do not try to coerce parents into adopting your methods for themselves, but do make it clear that in your setting, certain adult practices are acceptable and others are inappropriate. If parents tell you to spank their children if they misbehave, say something like: "You're really anxious for your child to behave at school. That's important to me, too. I will be making it clear to children what the rules are, and I will be using consequences to enforce them. However, paddling is not one of my consequences." Briefly describe a sample disciplinary encounter, using the skills you have learned, to demonstrate what you mean.

2. **Listen thoughtfully if family members report that other children are bullying their child.** Respond with appropriate action. It has been reported that commonly when parents mention that their child is being bullied, program personnel minimize the importance of this problem, maintain that such predicaments are beyond their jurisdiction, or shift the conversation to other difficulties the child might be having (Roffey, Tarrant, & Majors, 1994). The denial that surrounds bullying is detrimental to child development. That is, adults who pretend bullying is not happening or who think of it as mere child's play are not doing all they can to help bullies and victims develop more appropriate interaction strategies. If you become aware that a child is being bullied, talk with parents about possible ways to address the issue, both at home and in the program. If a child or parent complains of bullying about which you have been unaware, promise to observe the situation more closely. Develop a plan for how you will respond using strategies outlined in this chapter. Address concerns related both to the victim and the bully. Ask family members for input and ways the plan might be generalized for home use. Carry out the plan, offering and getting periodic feedback from home. Support parents as they express their frustration or concern throughout the process. Keep family members apprised of children's progress.

3. **Talk with families of children who demonstrate bullying behavior.** If a child is beginning to establish a pattern of bullying in the program, bring this to his or her parents' attention (Crothers & Kolbert, 2010). Do this in a no-nonsense factual way. Avoid using a tone that implies blame. Provide anecdotal records and narrative examples to illustrate your concerns. Make clear that such aggression is unacceptable, both for the child's sake and for the sake of others

in the program. Share with family members what you regard as the child's strengths and invite them to do so as well. Ask them what they believe their child needs to learn at this point in his or her development. Use this information as you work with family members (and other professionals as appropriate) to create an Intensive Individualized Plan to address the child's aggression. Check in with parents regularly to discuss the child's progress.

Pitfalls to Avoid ♦♦♦♦♦

The major pitfalls in handling children's aggressive behavior have already been covered in the section on ineffective strategies (e.g., physical punishment, ignoring aggression, displacement, and inconsistency). However, conflict mediation is a new skill for many people, and there are several pitfalls you can fall into when first learning to mediate. The following list describes common mistakes adults make when mediating children's conflicts.

1. **Failing to lay the groundwork.** Prior to initiating conflict mediation, the adult must have established himself or herself in the children's eyes as someone who cares about them, who will keep them safe, and who is predictable in reacting to children's actions. As you learned in previous chapters, warmth, acceptance, genuineness, empathy, and respect (WAGER) are the foundations on which effective mediation builds. Failure to establish these conditions undermines the spirit of the process. Therefore, the mediation model is most effectively implemented only after children are comfortable and familiar with their caregivers, the surroundings, and the daily routines.

2. **Ignoring developmental considerations.** In order to successfully participate in conflict mediation, children must be able to indicate acceptance or rejection of proposed alternatives. Children whose age or development has not reached the point at which they can state their desires, or children who do not speak the same language as the mediator, are not yet ready to engage in this model. Children can communicate verbally or by using an effective substitute such as signing.

   In addition, adults who try conflict mediation are cautioned to remain sensitive to children's tolerance for frustration. Not all children are ready to go through all of the steps at once. Most children calm down as mediation proceeds. Those whose behavior becomes increasingly agitated are demonstrating a lack of readiness. At that point, the procedure should be terminated, with the adult enforcing a limit to resolve the original conflict: "You both want the stethoscope. I can't let you hurt each other as a way to decide who gets

it, so I will have to decide. Evan, you can have the stethoscope for two minutes, and then Aaron, you can have a two-minute turn." At the same time, children should be praised for their hard work up to that point: "Evan and Aaron, you worked hard at telling me what you wanted. That helped a lot." Gradually, children will be able to proceed further in the process.

3. **Skipping mediation altogether.** Adults sometimes avoid conflict mediation because they feel uncomfortable taking their attention away from an entire group to focus on only one or two children. They worry that the mediation process requires more time than they can spare. Instead, they may separate children, remove the disputed toy, and dictate an expedient solution. This approach undoubtedly works in the short run. However, it does not provide an opportunity for children to practice problem-solving strategies. As a result, over time, the adult continues to bear the primary responsibility for conflict resolution rather than gradually transferring this responsibility to the children.

   It is important to consider the fact that mediation takes place where the conflict occurs; disputing children are not removed from the group. As a result, children who are not directly involved in the conflict frequently participate as observers or advisors. In this way, the teaching that is taking place affects several children at once. Also, because children become so engrossed in the process, another conflict rarely erupts elsewhere in the room during this time.

4. **Denying children's legitimate claims.** In his or her zeal to reach a compromise, a helping professional may inadvertently deny a child's legitimate right to maintain possession of a desired object. The mediator may hear such statements as "I had it first," or "She took it from me." When this occurs, the focus shifts to helping the perpetrator generate appropriate strategies, such as asking, trading, or bargaining, to achieve his or her goal. There also will be times when a child has used an acceptable strategy for obtaining the object, and the child in possession refuses. In these cases, the mediator can help the children develop a suitable

time frame for the exchange to take place. If the mediator does not know who has the legitimate claim, this can be stated in a personal message that also stresses the inappropriateness of any violent solution to a difference of opinion.

5. **Laying blame.** Sometimes when adults hear a commotion, their first impulse is to say: "Okay, who started it?" or "Haven't I told you not to fight?" Children's responses to these queries frequently take the form of denial or accusation, neither of which leads to clarification or constructive problem solving. It is better to approach the conflict saying "You both seem very upset" or "It looks like you both want the stethoscope at the same time." These statements focus on the problem that exists between the children rather than attributing sole responsibility to either child.

6. **Taking sides.** In order to establish credibility and be accepted as a mediator, the adult must be perceived as impartial. For this reason, she or he should avoid indicating initial agreement or disagreement with any position that is stated. This means strictly avoiding giving nonverbal cues such as nodding, frowning, and finger tapping as well as refraining from verbal indications of support, sympathy, disdain, or revulsion.

7. **Denying a child's perspective.** There will be times during conflict mediation when a child expresses a point of view that seems ludicrous or untrue. In those circumstances, it is tempting for the adult to try to correct the child's perception: "You know you really don't hate John," or "You shouldn't be so upset about having to wait your turn," or "You should feel pleased that John wants to play with you at all after the way you've been acting." Although any one of these statements may seem accurate to the adult, they do not correspond to the child's perception of the situation.

As a result, what began as mutual problem solving will end in fruitless argument. As hard as it may be, it is the adult's responsibility to exercise patience and allow children to work through their own feelings about the problem under discussion.

8. **Masterminding.** It is natural for adults to want to resolve conflicts quickly. Sometimes, to accelerate the mediation process, they step in with their own solution rather than permitting children to work out the problem themselves. A related tactic is to force children toward a preconceived conclusion by asking such questions as "Don't you think . . . ?" or "Doesn't it seem that you should . . . ?"

When Toby and Myra argue over whose book to read, their teacher remains neutral as she assumes the mediator role.

or "Wouldn't it be nice if we . . . ?" If the teacher has chosen to initiate the mediation process, he or she should allow it to proceed to a mutual resolution. Otherwise, children become frustrated at being led to believe that they are responsible for reaching a decision when, in reality, they must acquiesce to the teacher's conclusion.

When this occurs, the chances for continued conflict are high because children do not feel a real commitment to an approach that is dictated to them. In addition, coercive strategies do not help children practice the problem-solving skills they will need to reconcile future disagreements. Finally, the use of such autocratic techniques seriously jeopardizes the adult's credibility in subsequent attempts to mediate children's conflicts.

Summary

Aggression is any verbal or physical behavior that injures, damages, or destroys. Two primary types of aggression have been identified: instrumental and hostile. In instrumental aggression, hurtful outcomes are unintentional by-products of an interaction; hostile aggression is a purposeful act. Assertiveness and aggressiveness are two different things. Although both involve exerting influence over others, assertion does not include any intent to injure or demean. There is no single factor that causes violent behavior in children.

Current research shows that aggression is influenced by biology and is learned through modeling and reinforcement as well. The way children express aggression changes over time due to cognitive maturation and experience. Instrumental aggression (arguments over objects, territory, or rights) dominates the early years; hostile aggression (deliberate intent to be hurtful) becomes more evident as children mature.

Both boys and girls demonstrate aggressive behavior, although the tactics they use are somewhat different. Males tend to be more overt and physically abusive, and females rely on relational and verbal strategies.

Adults have tried different ways to reduce children's aggression. Ignoring aggression, displacement, inconsistency, and physical punishment actually increase children's antisocial behavior. These behaviors are best avoided.

Effective preventive techniques take into account the reasons why aggression occurs and put into place conditions that make aggression less likely to happen. When aggression does erupt, adults draw on a wide range of all-purpose strategies that make clear that aggression is unacceptable, that help children find alternative means of dealing with their aggressive impulses, and that support children in learning productive ways of responding to the aggression of others. To do this effectively, adults must first build positive relationships with children, create supportive environments, and employ teaching and coaching strategies that help children develop the skills they need to make their desires known and get what they want in amicable ways. Sometimes, it is necessary to create Intensive Individualized Plans so professionals and families can work together to address children's most challenging behaviors.

Bullying is a form of hostile aggression in which one or more people deliberately use hurtful actions to exert power over others. Attention must be paid to bullies, their victims, and any witnesses to aggression. Program-wide strategies for dealing with hostile aggression are also important to develop. Quite importantly, working with family members is essential for reducing childhood aggression of all kinds.

When it comes to instrumental aggression in particular, adults help children negotiate their differences through on-the-spot conflict mediation. This turns children's day-to-day arguments into valuable teachable moments. Eventually, children become better able to resolve such disputes constructively on their own. When hostile aggression occurs, adults must be quick to respond with firm limits and strategies aimed at teaching children how to curb angry impulses, interpret social cues more accurately, and replace their aggressive reactions with less violent ones.

The ineffective strategies for dealing with aggression are the key pitfalls to avoid. In addition, when mediating children's conflicts, it is best to avoid failing to develop relationships with children prior to trying conflict mediation, ignoring developmental considerations, failing to take the time to try mediation, denying children's legitimate claims, blaming one child or another, taking sides, denying the child's point of view, and trying to coerce children into agreeing with your personal solution—sometimes called masterminding.

Key Terms

aggression
assertiveness
bullying
conflict mediation
corporal punishment

displacement
hostile aggression
instrumental aggression
passive victims
physical aggression

provocative victims
relational aggression
perspective-taking abilities

Discussion Questions

1. Describe the two types of aggression. Discuss behaviors that differentiate them from one another. Present examples of behavior you have witnessed that fit into each category.

2. Describe an interaction in which you have observed either a child or an adult being aggressive. Discuss what changes in that person's behavior would have made the actions assertive instead.

3. Choose a fictional character or a public figure you consider aggressive. In a small group, identify some of that person's characteristics. Apply your knowledge of learned aggression to offer some explanation for the person's behavior.

4. Describe the emergence of aggression in children. Discuss how maturity and experience influence the types of aggression children display at different ages.

5. In this book, we have taken a stand against corporal punishment in professional settings. Discuss your reactions to that position.

6. What are two ways in which adults might model nonaggressive behavior in a classroom? What will children learn from this? How could you make these lessons more powerful?

7. Describe an aggressive behavior exhibited by a child without revealing the child's identity to the group. Refer to the strategies and skills outlined in this chapter to assist you in formulating a plan for reducing the unwanted behavior.

8. Two children come to the program with toy swords they got over the weekend. They want to play with them in the classroom. Using the content of this chapter as background, discuss what you would do in this situation.

9. Read Meet Brian (Challenging Behavior). Identify which of the effective strategies for reducing aggression described in this chapter that the teacher used. Are there any you would add if you were Brian's teacher?

10. Share with the group your experience in attempting the conflict mediation model presented in this chapter. Describe children's reactions, your own reactions, and the eventual outcome. Brainstorm with classmates ways to improve your technique.

Case Study Analysis

Read the case study in Appendix B about Adriana, and consider the following:

1. Review the teacher observation records. What evidence do you see of aggressive behavior between Adrianna and her classmates? What kinds of aggression does she appear to engage in? Provide a rationale for your response.

2. On September 10th and 27th, Adrianna has conflicts involving other children's possessions. Would conflict mediation be an appropriate strategy in these situations? Why or why not?

3. Adrianna's parents wonder whether they should let her cousins "hit her back" when she hurts them or damages their things. They are thinking that perhaps she does not realize how painful her actions have become and that she may deserve a "taste of her own medicine." What would you advise and why?

4. Does Adrianna fit the definition of a "bully"? Why or why not?

5. Based on what you have learned about victims and onlookers, what strategies might you suggest that other children use in interacting with Adrianna? How would you determine the effectiveness of your plan?

Field Assignments

1. Describe an incident of childhood aggression that occurred in your field placement. Discuss how another adult handled it. Evaluate the effectiveness of the approach that was used. Next, describe how you handled an aggressive

incident involving a child in your setting. Evaluate the effectiveness of your approach.

2. Interview two community professionals who work with young children. Obtain information from them regarding the strategies they use to help children who exhibit aggressive behavior. Report your findings.

3. Describe a situation in which you were involved in conflict mediation. Begin by discussing what prompted the conflict. Next, talk about the children's reactions to the mediation process and what final outcome occurred. Identify two things you did well during the process and one thing you would like to improve the next time such a situation arises. Conclude by discussing your reaction to your role as a mediator.

4. Watch a child's television show (cartoon) or movie and record the frequency of aggressive or violent acts. Discuss possible effects on children.

5. Review the parent handbook for the program in which you are participating. Identify policies and procedures aimed at reducing childhood aggression.

Reflect on Your Practice

Here is a sample checklist you can use to reflect on your use of the skills as a beginning professional. A more detailed classroom observation tool is available in Appendix C.

Teachers who handle childhood aggression constructively do the following:

✓ Design opportunities for children to practice sharing, taking turns, trading, bargaining, and negotiating.

✓ Use proximity control (move closer to children) to be available to provide nonverbal and verbal cues to children as needed to reduce aggressive actions.

✓ Intervene when children are hurting someone or damaging something.

✓ Reinforce children's behavior that is incompatible with aggression.

✓ Model nonaggressive ways of resolving conflict.

✓ Support children's problem-solving skills through conflict mediation.

✓ Address bullying directly in classroom conversations and activities.

✓ Intervene directly with bullies, victims, and onlookers to bullying.

CourseMate. Visit the Education CourseMate for this textbook to access the eBook, Digital Downloads, TeachSource Videos, and Did You Get It? quizzes. Go to CengageBrain.com to log in, register, or purchase access.

13 Promoting Prosocial Behavior

OBJECTIVES

On completion of this chapter, you should be able to:

Describe examples of prosocial behavior.

Identify factors that influence prosocial behavior.

Demonstrate skills that support children's prosocial behavior.

Recognize pitfalls to avoid while promoting children's prosocial behavior.

NAEYC STANDARDS naeyc

1. Promoting Child Development and Learning

2. Building Family and Community Relationships

3. Using Developmentally Effective Approaches to Connect with Children and Families

4. Using Content Knowledge to Build Meaningful Curriculum

Defining Prosocial Behavior naeyc

Helping	Sharing
Sacrificing	Aiding
Sympathizing	Encouraging
Volunteering	Giving
Reassuring	Inviting
Rescuing	Defending
Cooperating	Comforting
Donating	Restoring

All of these terms describe prosocial behaviors and represent positive values of society. They are the opposite of antisocial conduct, such as selfishness and aggression. **Prosocial behaviors** are voluntary actions aimed at helping or benefiting others (Hearron & Hildebrand, 2013). They often are performed without the doer's anticipation of any personal benefit (Penner & Orom, 2010). At times, they also involve some physical or social risk to the individual performing them, such as when a person defends someone who is being bullied or falsely accused. Prosocial behaviors emerging in childhood are likely to carry over into adulthood (Eisenberg, 2010). Evidence suggests that the roots of caring, sharing, helping, and cooperating are in every child. Although older children demonstrate a wider range of prosocial behaviors, even very young children have the capacity to demonstrate prosocial responses in various circumstances (Eisenberg, Fabes, & Spinrad, 2006).

Prosocial behavior is a significant component of social competence. Regardless of age, children's interactions tend to be more positive than negative. For instance, studies dating back 30 years suggest that the ratio of children's prosocial behaviors to antisocial acts is no less than 3:1 and may be as high as 8:1 (Moore, 1982). This means that for every negative behavior, children average three to eight positive actions. More recent research confirms this pattern (Dovidio, Pillavin, Schroeder, & Penner, 2010). For instance, preschoolers routinely attempt to help, show sympathy, or engage in other prosocial behaviors much more often than they are aggressive. These tendencies to be helpful and kind remain relatively stable throughout the preschool and elementary years (Rose-Krasnor & Denham, 2009). Thus, childhood is an optimal period for the development of prosocial attitudes and conduct.

Benefits of Prosocial Behavior

Being kind has social, emotional, and academic advantages. Children who engage in prosocial acts develop feelings of satisfaction and competence from assisting others. When children help with the family dishes, share information with a friend, comfort an unhappy playmate, or work with others to achieve a final product, they come away thinking: "I am useful. I can do something. I am important." The resulting perception of being capable and valuable contributes to a healthy self-image (Trawick-Smith, 2014). Kindness also communicates affection and friendship. It contributes to positive feelings in both doers and receivers, providing entry into social situations and strengthening ongoing relationships (Hartup & Moore, 1990).

Children whose interactions are characterized by kindness maximize the successful social encounters they experience. This increases the likelihood that their kind acts will continue in the future. In fact, children's natural sharing behavior at age 4 has been linked with prosocial behavior into adulthood (Eisenberg et al., 1999). Prosocial behavior also increases children's chances for receiving help or cooperation when they need it. Children who are more prosocial are more likely to be on the receiving end of prosocial acts (Persson, 2005).

Children who are the beneficiaries of any type of prosocial action get a closer look at how such behaviors are carried out. Each episode serves as a model from which they derive useful information to apply to future encounters. Recipients also have chances to learn how to respond positively to the kindness that others extend to them. Individuals who never learn this skill eventually receive fewer offers of comfort and support.

Children who are prosocial are more likely to be in supportive peer relationships (Hughes & Ensor, 2010). They tend to have at least one or two friends, engage in less aggression and conflict with others, and are more popular with peers (Eisenberg et al., 2006). Adults often describe prosocial children as socially skilled.

Finally, there is clear evidence that early prosocial behavior strongly predicts current and future academic achievement (Wentzel, 2009). This may be because children who are prosocial are more able to ask for assistance from peers and adults, further developing their cognitive abilities and thus creating a more positive school climate for themselves. Highlight 13-1 summarizes the benefits of prosocial behavior.

Besides benefiting the individual, prosocial behavior has advantages for groups as well. Group settings in which children are encouraged to be cooperative and helpful result in more friendly interactions and productive group efforts than settings in which little attention is paid to these values (Dovidio et al., 2010). Moreover, routine or tedious chores, such as cleanup, are more easily managed. When everyone pitches in, tasks are quickly accomplished, and no one person feels overly burdened. An added benefit is that children begin to develop a positive group image in which they view both themselves and other group participants as genial and competent (Marion, 2011).

HIGHLIGHT 13-1

Benefits of Engaging in Prosocial Behavior

1. Creates feelings of satisfaction
2. Builds perceptions of competence
3. Provides entry into social situations
4. Promotes ongoing relationships
5. Increases popularity among peers
6. Increases chances of receiving help or cooperation
7. Increases academic performance
8. Leads to positive group atmosphere

Children's Motivation to Act in a Prosocial Way

Children are kind, helpful, or cooperative for multiple reasons. Some may be acting to prevent harm (inviting a child to play so her feelings aren't hurt). Others react spontaneously to an event (Jerome falls off of the swings. Fred runs over yelling, "Are you okay?"). Still others want to make up for the distress their own behavior caused (Kurt knocked Jeremy aside to get the robot he wanted first. He then notices that Jeremy is near tears and hands over a second robot smiling, "You can have this one."). A prosocial behavior may occur because someone has directed the child ("Give her some of your blocks, please."). A plea for help may be yet another reason for prosocial behavior ("Could you please get the teacher for me?"). Finally, a child may act simply for the benefit of someone else, no strings attached (Hastings, Utendale, & Sullivan, 2008).

Children's inspiration to be prosocial is influenced by developmental factors such as age, ability to think of others, level of sympathy toward the victim, and moral motivation (Malti et al., 2009; Vaish, Carpenter, & Tomasello, 2009). It is also influenced by experience—observing prosocial acts, experiencing kindness, and experiencing reactions to their own efforts to be prosocial. In the early years, children practice kind acts with their parents and then peers. Preschoolers and early elementary students use self-centered or needs-oriented reasons for action, selecting behaviors to make themselves feel better (to stop the crying, or to get praise from adults). This reasoning decreases in the later elementary years. Over time, the reasons for prosocial behavior become more abstract, relying on principles and moral standards as a guide for taking action (Eisenberg et al., 2006).

Steps to Becoming Prosocial

At one time, it was thought that if children were taught to think in prosocial ways, the appropriate actions would automatically follow. Unfortunately, kind thoughts have not been significantly linked to prosocial acts. Although even older toddlers and preschoolers can explain that sharing, taking turns, and working together are good things to do, they do not necessarily act in these ways when doing so would be appropriate. For example:

> While pretending to be a police officer, Brian would look his teacher in the eyes and clearly state: "The rule is: Keep your hands to yourself. Hitting other children hurts." He would then walk away from this recitation, see someone doing something he interpreted as wrong, grab the block from his belt (his billy club), and conk the offender over the head.

Brian had the right idea, but the wrong follow-up actions. To be truly prosocial, children must get beyond simply thinking about what is right to doing what is right. That involves the following three steps, progressing from thought to appropriate action:

1. **Becoming aware** that sharing, help, or cooperation is needed.
2. **Deciding** to act.
3. **Taking appropriate action** to be prosocial.

Figure 13-1 provides examples of these three steps in action. Review the figure carefully to see how a child's abilities, the situation at hand and potential challenges influence each step.

Step 1: Becoming aware. First and foremost, children must become aware that someone would benefit from a prosocial response (Schwartz, 2010). This requires accurately interpreting what they see and hear, which means recognizing typical distress signals such as crying, sighing, grimacing, or struggling—as well as correctly identifying verbal cues—"This is too much for me to do all by myself," or "If we work together, we'll finish faster." Unclear or subtle signals are more difficult for children to interpret than direct ones. For instance, if Patty observes Duwana fall and moan, it may not be clear to her that Duwana needs assistance. However, if Duwana cries and calls for help, Patty will comprehend her distress more easily. Likewise, Patty might enter the awareness phase of prosocial behavior if an adult pointed out to her the signs of distress exhibited by Duwana. In most cases, people who come upon a problem situation look both to the victim and the reactions of others nearby to determine if a real problem exists.

Prosocial Step	Necessary Developmental Abilities	Potential Challenges	Situation	Translation	Possible Strategy
AWARENESS	Child must tune-in to the other person. Child must accurately interpret the body language, actions, and words he sees and hears.	Child may be too focused on own needs to recognize the needs of others. Child may not notice cues or may not interpret them accurately.	Jorge is struggling to carry an overflowing bucket of water to the sand area. He keeps readjusting the bucket so he doesn't drop it. He becomes frustrated when water splashes out and sets the bucket down. Reba is standing nearby simply watching.	Reba does not recognize Jorge's nonverbal behaviors as signals that he needs help. She is unaware that Jorge needs assistance.	Teacher points out Jorge's need for help. "Reba, look at Jorge. He is having a hard time carrying that bucket. He needs our help." Or, Teacher says to Jorge, "You look like you need help. If you say, 'I need help,' other people will come quick."
DECISION MAKING	Child must figure out what the other person needs.	Child may not know what is needed. Child may misinterpret what is needed.	Ladonna is an active 3-year-old whose left leg is much shorter than her right leg. She is capable of moving around the classroom on her own, but Darlene often picks Ladonna up and bodily moves her from one spot to another. When the teacher asks Darlene what she is doing, she proudly says, "I'm helping!"	Darlene has decided to help but does not understand what Ladonna needs.	Teacher says, "You want to help. Let's ask Ladonna if she needs you to pick her up." Or, Teacher says, "You want to help Ladonna. Ladonna likes to walk on her own. Let her do that. She does want a friend though. You could help by asking her to play a game with you instead."
DOING	Child must have the ability to do what is needed.	Child may not have the necessary skills.	The children are working together to build a marble maze out of cardboard tubes. Tenshi becomes upset when she tries to glue two tubes together and they keep coming apart. Carter comes over and tries to tape the boxes together, but the tape is too flimsy, and his fingers keep getting "stuck" in it.		The teacher points out that Carter has a good idea, but the tape is too thin. She shows Carter and Tenshi how to use duct tape instead to hold the tubes together.

Figure 13-1 Steps to Prosocial Behavior.

Source: Based on Kostelnik, Rupiper, Soderman, & Whiren (2014).

This is especially true when the situation is ambiguous or vague. If onlookers appear unfazed, a potential helper may remain unaware that intervention is needed. This is illustrated when Abdul's construction crashes to the floor. Abdul appears unhappy but makes no sound. Several children nearby look up, but seeing no tears or other overt signs of distress, return to their play. Roger, observing the entire scene, may also assume that assistance is unnecessary because no one else made a move to help. However, he might think differently if an adult or other child said something like, "Are you okay?" or "That's too bad your tower fell." These comments prompt awareness that the situation could indeed be distressing to Abdul.

All children benefit from direction to notice those who could use some help. For young children who are hearing impaired and do not hear cues of distress, adult intervention is particularly useful. Each year, Ms. Barkley teaches her entire kindergarten class the American Sign Language signs for "stop" and "look" and uses these daily to point out helping opportunities with peers. Whenever a potential situation occurs, she says the word while simultaneously signing, "Stop. Look." This benefits all of the students in her room.

As children become aware of cues that someone is in distress, they may feel sympathy or empathy for that person, or they may feel personal distress over the situation. Feeling distress for the other person is more likely to lead to prosocial action, whereas feeling distress for one's self is less likely to lead to such action. Initially, a very young child's emotional reaction is to mimic the distress signals by crying or sighing. As children mature, they become more able to feel empathy and are more adept at coupling their emotional response with some gesture of assistance. In fact, the more empathy and sympathy a child feels for the person, the more likely they are to take action (Eisenberg et al., 2006).

Step 2: Deciding to act. After children identify a person in need, they are faced with the decision of whether or not to act. Three factors that influence this decision include children's relationship to the person in need, their mood, and whether they perceive themselves as basically prosocial beings (Dovidio et al., 2010).

Relationship Children of all ages are most likely to respond with kindness to people they like and with whom they have established relationships (Eisenberg et al., 2006). Although children may react compassionately to unfamiliar people, friends are more often kinder to one another than they are to strangers. Prosocial acts such as sharing are also more likely to occur if the recipient is someone who has shared with the giver previously or if sharing will require the receiver

to do likewise in the future (Dovidio et al., 2010). Under these circumstances, children feel obligated to one another based on their notions of fairness and reciprocity. Common group membership also increases an individual's likelihood of helping. For example, children may be more likely to assist a peer whom they identify as a member of "our class" than a child from a class other than their own (Dovidio et al., 2010).

Feelings Our behavior is greatly influenced by our feelings. One might feel distressed when witnessing an emergency situation or discomfort at a perceived injustice. When you choose to help another person, you eliminate the negative feelings experienced by viewing that person's distress. People who are more empathic are more likely to respond prosocially in the future (Dovidio et al., 2010). Mood also affects whether or not children decide to pursue a prosocial course of action. Children of all ages who are in a positive frame of mind are more likely to be prosocial than those in a negative or neutral mood (Ladd, 2005). When children are happy, they become optimistic about the outcome of their efforts. They may even undertake difficult or socially costly prosocial actions with the expectation of ultimate success. On the other hand, children who are angry or sad often cannot see beyond their own unhappy circumstances to aid others, or they may believe that their actions will fail anyway. Exceptions to this rule occur when older children who are in a bad mood perceive that kind behavior will actually improve their state of mind. Their subsequent acts of kindness may be carried out in the hope of making themselves feel better. However, if they see no self-serving benefits to their actions, such children will decide not to engage in prosocial activities.

Self-perception Decisions to behave in prosocial ways may be influenced by how kind children consider themselves. Children who frequently hear themselves described as cooperative or helpful believe they are and often choose to act in ways that support this self-image (Paley, 1992). Children who have no such self-perceptions may shy away from deciding to carry out a prosocial act because such behaviors do not fit the way they see themselves in relation to others.

Social and personal norms As children observe the prosocial acts of others, they begin to learn that helpful behavior is valued. Through experience and learning, children begin to make judgments about what is right and what is wrong. Over time, children acquire social norms regarding what behavior is appropriate and expected in different situations. As they mature and develop moral reasoning skills, they will adopt a personal code regarding helping others. A child's decision to act will be influenced by these social and personal norms (Dovidio et al., 2010).

Step 3: Taking action. If children assume responsibility for sharing, helping, or cooperating, they must then select and perform a behavior they think is appropriate to the situation. Their conduct in such circumstances is influenced by two abilities: perspective-taking and instrumental know-how (Berk, 2013).

In **perspective-taking**, children recognize what would be useful to someone else whose needs may not mirror their own at the moment. Very young children have limited perspective-taking skills. For instance, when 2-year-old Juanita offered her caregiver the bunny blanket when the door shut on the adult's hand, she meant well, but did not understand what was truly needed to rectify the situation. Her ineffectiveness is not surprising. However, as these abilities emerge, children in the lower elementary grades become better equipped to help and to cooperate. This is especially true in situations in which the setting is familiar or the circumstances of distress resemble something they themselves have experienced. By the age of 6, perspective-taking skills begin to improve along with children's social cognition. They become increasingly able to project appropriate responses in unfamiliar situations (Carlo et al., 2010).

Instrumental know-how involves having the knowledge and skills necessary to act competently (Brown, Odom, & McConnell, 2008). Children who have many skills at their disposal are the most effective in carrying out their ideas. Those who have few skills may have good intentions, but their efforts often are counterproductive or inept. Moreover, younger children who are the most prosocial also are the most likely to engage in some antisocial behaviors. Due to their inexperience, they cannot always discriminate appropriate actions from inappropriate ones. Gradually, children become more aware of what differentiates these two types of behavior and become better able to initiate actions that are useful and appropriate.

Children may experience difficulty in proceeding through any one of the three steps just described. For instance, children may overlook or misinterpret cues that convey another person's need for a prosocial response. They also may choose an inappropriate action when trying to help. A child who is trying to comfort may shove a favorite storybook in another child's face, hug so hard that it hurts, or say something lacking tact, like "Well, you don't smell THAT bad." Young helpers may miss the mark by adding water to the acrylic paint to make it go further or by using toothpaste to scrub the whiteboard because they believe it cleans well. At times, children may assume that cooperation means giving up all of one's own ideas or settling for mediocrity in an effort to please everyone. These are all natural mistakes children make in learning how to be kind to one another. As children mature and gain experience, these become less frequent.

► ‖   **TeachSource Video 13-1**

© Cengage Learning 2015

Maddie: Positive Collaboration between School Professionals and Parents to Serve a Student with Physical Disabilities

Go online and view *Maddie: Positive Collaboration between School Professionals and Parents to Serve a Student with Physical Disabilities*.

In this video, you will see Maddie, a first grader with cerebral palsy who is educated in an inclusion environment. Her parents describe Maddie's experiences in the classroom and how they have partnered with educational professionals to make decisions about her education.

1. In the video, Maddie's parents state that the children in her classroom have been very kind to and accepting of Maddie. Based on what you have read in this chapter, how might having Maddie as a classmate influence children's prosocial behavior?

2. What obstacles might Maddie encounter in developing and practicing prosocial behaviors? If you were Maddie's teacher, what opportunities could you provide for Maddie to be helpful to others in her class?

3. Maddie's parents stressed the importance of ongoing communication with the teacher and school. What information would you provide her parents regarding Maddie's developing prosocial behaviors?

Watch on CourseMate

Influences on Children's Prosocial Behavior naeyc

Two fourth graders are sitting at the lunch table waiting for their friends to arrive. They witness a second-grade boy spill the contents of his lunch box all over the floor right next to their table. One child giggles. The other smiles, but gets up to help him.

What makes one person act with kindness and another not? As with many other areas of development, scientists have tried to determine the factors that contribute to prosocial behavior beyond daily interactions with peers. Such factors include elements of biology, social-cognitive understanding, language, social experiences, cultural expectations, and adult behaviors.

Biology and Prosocial Behavior

Prosocial behavior may be due in part to biology (Simpson & Beckes, 2010). Studies provide evidence for biological links to the development of empathy, sympathy, and prosocial behavior (Eisenberg, 2013; Hastings, Zahn-Waxler, & McShane, 2005).

Temperament. It appears that the combination of temperament, sensitivity to the emotions of self and others, and the regulation of emotions is connected with an individual's ability to react to situations in a prosocial manner (Eisenberg et al., 2006). For instance, children who are prone to pleasant dispositions, recognize the distress of others, but are not overly upset by this distress, are likely to react in a prosocial manner. In contrast, children who see the world in a bleak manner or become overly upset by another's distress are not as likely to take appropriate, helpful actions. In addition, children who are able to regulate their emotions and take action tend to be more prosocial (Eisenberg et al., 2006).

Gender. The majority of studies have shown no gender differences in children's willingness to engage in prosocial behavior. It would seem that both boys and girls have an equal capacity to be prosocial. Some research has found there is a difference in gender in the occurrence of prosocial behavior. Girls have been found to engage in prosocial behaviors more often than boys (Keane & Calkins, 2004; Russell et al., 2003). Others have found no difference (Hastings, Rubin, & DeRose, 2005).

Age. In general, children's capacity for prosocial behavior expands with age. Infants and toddlers may recognize and react to a companion who is crying or in obvious distress by crying themselves or attempting to comfort the upset child (Thompson, 2006; Wittmer, 2008). During the preschool years, children become more aware of and intentional about prosocial behaviors (Eisenberg et al., 2006). Behaviors such as sharing, helping, cooperating, donating, comforting, and defending become much more common as children mature (Pratt, Skoe, & Arnold, 2004).

Social Cognition and Prosocial Behavior

As children grow older, their ability to understand the thoughts and feelings of others and regulate their own behavior contributes to their increasing prosocial behavior. Social cognition requires some degree of sympathy, empathy, perspective-taking, and theory of mind, all of which are linked to prosocial behavior (Carlo et al., 2010; Hastings, et al., 2008). Thus, children who can understand the emotions of others are most likely to carry out prosocial acts and to demonstrate greater overall social competence (Hughes & Ensor, 2010).

Language and Prosocial Behavior

Language is powerful. Children's ability to understand and use language is very important in communicating needs and getting those needs met. In particular, as children expand their use of emotion words, they learn more about themselves, come to better understand the behavior of others, and respond empathically and sympathetically to others (Saarni et al., 2006; Epstein, 2009). As children acquire early language abilities to discuss, think about, and reflect on behaviors of self and others, they demonstrate greater prosocial behavior and fewer problem behaviors (Hughes & Ensor, 2010).

Sharing

Sharing is a voluntary distribution of resources. By definition, children are not really sharing if they are forced or required to share by others. Sharing provides a good example of the combination of the influence of biology, social-cognitive understanding, and language in children's growing prosocial development. After a child understands the need of the other as well as understanding the request to share, a course of action becomes apparent to even very young children. In a typical early childhood program that serves toddlers and preschoolers, you are bound to see examples of children sharing. Children as young as 2 years old will offer playthings to one another (Rose-Krasnor & Denham, 2009). They find sharing with adults easier, and their frequency of sharing is relatively low compared with older children. This is because younger children are by nature territorial and egocentric (Reynolds, 2008). They highly prize the possession of the moment, making it difficult for them to relinquish objects, even when they are no longer using them. This explains why 4-year-old Michael, who rides the tricycle and then runs off to dig in the sand, protests loudly when another child gets on the tricycle. To Michael, the tricycle is his, and he dislikes giving it up even though he had lost interest in it.

© Cengage Learning

Dramatic play is a great place to practice sharing. These boys are sharing the task of cooking.

Additionally, young children lack the verbal negotiation skills necessary to resolve disputes over possessions or reach mutually satisfying compromises with others. Consequently, their initial reasons for sharing focus on self-serving interests, such as sharing now so the recipient will be obliged to share with them in the future or to appease a peer who threatens, "I won't be your friend if you don't gimme some."

Throughout the later preschool and early elementary years, children come to realize that sharing leads to shared activity and playing with another person is often more fun than playing alone (Reynolds, 2008). During this time, children's peer interactions increase, and their sharing abilities become greater. The most dramatic changes occur between 6 and 12 years of age, which is also when perspective-taking skills greatly expand (Carlo et al., 2010).

Older children share more easily for several reasons. First, their more advanced intellectual abilities enable them to recognize that it is possible for two people to legitimately want the same thing at the same time, that possessions shared can be retrieved, and that sharing often is reciprocated (Berk, 2013). They also understand that there is a difference between sharing (which means temporary loss of ownership) and donating (which is permanent), and they can understand, as well as make clear to others, which of the two

is intended. In addition, they have more skills at their disposal that allow them to share in a variety of ways. If one approach, such as taking turns, is not satisfactory, they may try options such as bargaining, trading, or using an object together. Finally, older children find it easier to part with some items because they differentiate among the values of their possessions.

Children in the early elementary years are also motivated to share by a desire for acceptance from others. Prosocial acts such as sharing are seen as good, making it more likely that children who engage in such behavior will enjoy the approval of their peers. The self-sacrifice that comes with sharing is compensated by that approval.

Gradually, as children mature, their reasoning also becomes influenced by the principle of justice. Sharing becomes a way to satisfy that principle. At first, children define justice as strict equity, meaning that everyone deserves equal treatment regardless of circumstance. When sharing is called for, children figure that each person must have the same number of turns, that each turn must last the same amount of time, and that everyone must receive the same number of pieces.

Eventually, children come to believe that equity includes special treatment for those who deserve it—based on extra effort, outstanding performance, or disadvantaged conditions. Under these circumstances, children decide that sharing does not have to be exactly the same to be fair. They recognize that a person who has fewer chances to play may require a longer turn, or they may reason that someone who worked especially hard on a project deserves to go first. This reasoning is sometimes evident in children as young as 8 years of age, but for others, it appears much later. In either case, such thinking deepens children's understanding of prosocial behavior, leading to more frequent instances of kindness than is possible earlier in life.

The differences between older and younger children in their ability to share underscore changes in their general development and reasoning abilities. Thus, children gradually move from self-oriented rationales ("He'll like me better if I share.") to other-oriented reasoning ("She'll be unhappy if she doesn't get a turn.") and from concrete rationales ("I had it first.") to more abstract ideals ("She needs it."). Ultimately, children become better able to "put themselves in another person's shoes" and do so to support their self-respect. The latter achievement tends to occur in later adolescence and is seldom seen in children younger than 12 years of age. Finally, there is evidence that the levels of reasoning described here relate to the actual behaviors children display (Eisenberg et al., 2006). Children who use more mature levels of moral reasoning display a greater repertoire of prosocial skills and are more likely to engage in prosocial behavior than children at lower stages (see Table 13-1). Children's behavior is determined by their maturity and by their social and cultural experiences.

Table 13-1 Comparison of Age and Sharing

Younger (Ages 2 to 6)	Older (Ages 6 to 12)
Self-oriented motives	Other-oriented motives
Recognize own claim	Recognize legitimacy of other's claims
Prize the possession of the moment	Differentiate value among objects
"Here and now" thinking	Thinking of future benefits; past experience may be used to guide behavior
Few verbal skills with which to bargain or negotiate	Well-developed verbal skills
Some difficulty seeing more than one option	Many alternative solutions

© Cengage Learning

Social Experiences and Prosocial Behavior

The experiences children have in the social environment of family, peers, and school play a role in their prosocial development. In the family, as early as birth, the environment begins to impact prosocial behavior. The emotional attachment that occurs between baby and parent is believed to be the basis for prosocial development (Diener et al., 2007). Also, the conversations that parents have with young children are linked with the development of empathy (Garner, Dunsmore, & Southam-Gerrow, 2008; Thompson, 2006). When parents engage in prosocial acts themselves, encourage similar behavior in their children, and explain the rationale for such acts, children are more likely to be prosocial (Hastings et al., 2008). In the later years, in homes where children are given chores to do and in which everyone works to help for the good of the family, children demonstrate increased prosocial behavior (Eisenberg et al., 2006). As one mother said to her toddler and preschooler, "Everyone works and then everyone plays" as she assigned simple household tasks.

Children learn from each other. Thus, peers provide great opportunities for both giving and receiving prosocial behavior. Most importantly, interacting with age-mates offers chances to practice positive acts of all kinds. Peers tend to "rub off" on each other, acquiring the behavior characteristics of the other (Bukowski, Velasquez, & Brendgen, 2008). Simply being exposed to prosocial peers has been shown to produce children who are more prosocial over time (Fabes et al., 2005). Further, having at least one reciprocal friendship is related to higher levels of prosocial behavior (Wentzel, Barry, & Caldwell, 2004).

The overall quality of the school environment, particularly the interactions between teacher and child and between child and child, are linked to children behaving in more or less prosocial ways. For instance, the higher the quality of care children receive in childcare, the greater the amount of prosocial behavior they exhibit (NICHD, 2002). Further, there is an association between the quality of the school and children's self-regulation, empathy, and social competence (Eisenberg et al., 2006; Wilson, Pianata, & Stuhlman, 2007). Finally, teacher attitudes and behaviors contribute significantly to children's prosocial actions in the classroom. When teachers reportedly like their students, they generally attribute prosocial behavior intentions to their actions and respond in a positive manner toward their students. However, when they feel the opposite and respond more negatively, aggression is more common in student behavior (McAuliffe, Hubbbard, & Romano, 2009). It takes thoughtful, purposeful action to create quality interactions that promote prosocial behavior.

TeachSource Video 13-2

Benefits of Preschool

Go online and view *Benefits of Preschool.*

In this video, you see a report indicating that children attending British nursery schools have higher academic achievement at age 7 than children who did not attend such schools.

1. In the video, you learn that quality early childhood programs benefit children's academic performance. Would you expect children who attended nursery school to exhibit more prosocial behavior? Why or why not?

2. Based on what you have read, how might children's prosocial behavior be impacted by attending nursery school?

Watch on CourseMate

Creating opportunities for children to help or cooperate in real-life situations enhances their prosocial skills.

Adult Behavior and Prosocial Behavior

Adults have a major impact on the degree to which children learn to be helpful and cooperative, and they use many means to exert their influence. The most effective strategies fall within the first three tiers of the Social Support Pyramid you have been reading about in this text (see Figure 13-2).

As you might assume, the most fundamental way adults promote prosocial behavior is through the relationships they develop with children. When adults are

Cultural Expectations and Experiences and Prosocial Behavior

Cultures differ in the emphasis they place on prosocial behaviors such as sharing, helping, or cooperating. Some emphasize competition and individual achievement, whereas others stress cooperation and group harmony. Some have a high tolerance for violence; others do not. In any case, cultural influences play a role in the extent to which kindness is a factor in human interactions.

Children growing up in societies that value kindness, helpfulness, and cooperation are apt to internalize those values and display corresponding behaviors in their daily living. Additionally, cultures that promote warm, loving relationships between adults and children, as well as the early assignment of tasks and responsibilities that contribute to the common good are likely to produce prosocial children (Hastings et al., 2008).

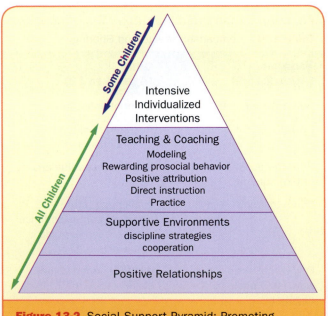

Figure 13-2 Social Support Pyramid: Promoting Prosocial Behavior

warm and supportive, children become more securely attached to them and are more likely to behave in prosocial ways (Hastings et al., 2008).

Creating environments that either facilitate or inhibit the development of children's prosocial behavior is another way adults influence the degree to which children are helpful and kind (Laible & Thompson, 2008). In group settings, the atmosphere most likely to promote nurturing, sharing, cooperating, and rescuing has the following characteristics (Bronson, 2006):

- Participants anticipate that everyone will do his or her best to support one another.
- Both adults and children contribute to decisions made, practices, and procedures.
- Communication is direct, clear, and mutual.
- Individual differences are respected.
- Expectations are reasonable.
- People like one another and feel a sense of belonging to the group.
- There is an emphasis on group as well as individual accomplishments.

Adults shape such an environment by using an authoritative discipline style, modeling prosocial behavior, rewarding children's attempts at prosocial actions, instructing children in prosocial values or skills, and providing children with practice of prosocial behaviors.

Discipline strategies. The authoritative approach to discipline espoused in this text can be a positive and powerful component to learning to behave in a prosocial manner (Hastings et al., 2008; Laible & Thompson, 2008). Talking through situations and giving reasons for reactions and compliance leads to internalized values in children (Eisenberg et al., 2006; Hastings, McShane, Parker, & Ladha, 2007). When adults maintain high expectations for children to engage in prosocial behavior and enforce rules that support this philosophy, kind and fair behavior toward peers occurs in the present and in the years that follow (Pratt et al., 2003). However, when adults use withdrawal of love or assertion of power techniques, the results may be the opposite (Knafo & Plomin, 2006). Refer to Chapters 10 and 11 for more on these approaches and their results.

Modeling. Children who frequently observe people cooperating, helping, sharing, and giving are most likely to act in those ways themselves (Hastings et al., 2008). When adults model such actions with other adults or children, they help to increase children's prosocial conduct now and into the future (Ladd, 2005). This modeling is even more effective when it

is explained how the act will benefit the other person (Hastings et al., 2008). Saying, "This will really make Janet feel better to know that we took the time to make her a get-well card," instead of "It is kind to send a card," puts the focus on the other person, not on the self.

Children emulate those models in their lives that are skilled in their behavior, are considered to be of high status by the observer, are helpful and friendly, and are in a position to administer both rewards and consequences (Thompson & Twibell, 2009). Models who are aloof, critical, directive, punitive, or powerless commonly are ignored. In addition, prosocial modeling has its greatest impact when what adults say is congruent with what they do (Shaffer & Kipp, 2013). Researchers have found that when there is inconsistency between words and deeds, the model is less credible and may even prompt children to engage in fewer prosocial acts. Hence, adults who urge children to lend one another a hand but seldom offer assistance themselves or do so grudgingly, show children that helping is not really a high priority. On the other hand, when children observe adults acting with kindness and deriving obvious pleasure from their actions, imitation becomes more likely (Fox & Lentini, 2006).

Reinforcing prosocial behavior. A prosocial environment is one in which such conduct is likely to be reinforced. When children's prosocial behaviors are highlighted, they are likely to increase their use of such actions within the same environment (Eisenberg et al., 2006). Technically, all adults have to do is watch for instances of children being kind and then enact positive consequences. Yet, adults commonly fail to make the most of this strategy. This happens when they take children's prosocial behaviors for granted and do not acknowledge them adequately or often enough. It also happens when adults inadvertently reward actions that actually counteract helpful or cooperative behavior. Tangible rewards such as candy or stickers may actually lower the occurrence of prosocial behavior (Ramaswamy & Bergin, 2009).

Keep in mind that prosocial behaviors are learned and are subject to the same conditions that characterize other learning episodes. That is, children must be motivated to learn and to feel successful. Neither of these criteria is met when adults ignore children who are trying to figure out what the positive expectations are or spend the majority of their time correcting them. Instead, adults must take as much care to enact positive consequences as they do with corrective ones.

Prosocial attribution. As mentioned earlier, people's self-definition of how helpful they are is another factor that influences how much prosocial behavior they demonstrate. When children consider themselves kind, generous, or compassionate, it is more likely they will behave in these ways toward others (Bronson, 2006). Therefore, one way to promote prosocial acts is to encourage children to think of themselves in positive ways using **prosocial attributions** (also called **character attributions** or **dispositional attributions**). A prosocial attribution is a statement to a child in which the adult attributes a prosocial behavior to a child, such as "You shared because you like to help others," (Wittmer & Honig, 1994). When children view themselves as helpful or kind, they are more likely to behave in ways that support this self perception. Therefore, prosocial attributions make future prosocial behavior more likely. To be effective, attributions must be specific and closely related to what the child has done or said. In addition, they should refer to the child's dispositional kindness or internal motives, rather than simply labeling the actions as a positive thing. For instance, stating, "You are a good helper" or "You helped put away the toys" is not as effective as saying, "You put away the toys because you are a helpful person." Using simple praise without the internal attribution makes it less likely that the behavior will transfer to new situations in the future (Eisenberg et al., 2006). However, when the praise and prosocial attribution are combined, the probability of the kind act occurring in another situation is increased.

Cooperation. When children cooperate, they may share ideas or materials in order to work together toward a common job or task. Teachers set the stage for cooperation and can model and guide this behavior. Cooperation among children is undermined if adults rely on competition as their primary means for motivating children. Children are encouraged to compete rather than cooperate when they are told: "Let's see who can put the most blocks away," or "The nicest picture will go in the showcase." In each instance, children are quick to determine that there will be only one winner and helping or cooperating with someone else will sabotage their own chances for coming out on top. On the other hand, such situations could be modified to encourage the children to cooperate by focusing on group accomplishments rather than on individual achievement: "Let's see how well we can all work together to put these blocks away," or "When you're finished painting your pictures, we'll go out and hang them in the hall." These conditions inspire children to come to one another's assistance or to work together as appropriate.

In addition, group-administered rewards encourage children to work as a team to achieve a common aim. Recording each book read by the group or tallying each act of kindness helps keep track of the children's progress as a whole and directs their attention to what the entire

These children are working as a team to create a block structure.

group can achieve. Thus, it is effective to monitor the group's progress and then enact positive consequences when certain benchmarks are obtained rather than always rewarding children individually. This approach has been found to lead to friendlier, more cooperative behavior among the participants (Crothers & Kolbert, 2010). When adults try to administer tangible rewards to encourage prosocial behavior among children, the results are usually counterproductive. Children who are bribed in these ways attribute their actions to the tangible rewards rather than to the needs of others or their own inclinations to treat others kindly. In addition, children may actually behave less prosocially when the expected rewards are no longer available.

Direct instruction. Children's prosocial behavior increases when they are taught to think and act in kind, helpful, and cooperative ways (Dovidio et al., 2010; Brown, Odom, & McConnel, 2008). Such teaching focuses on the individual skills that lead to helping and cooperating. Recognizing prosocial behavior when it is displayed, identifying the needs of another, anticipating the consequences of acts, and generating multiple solutions to interpersonal problems are all prosocial skills. A variety of strategies have been used to teach these skills to children of varying ages, including the following:

- Discussing the value of prosocial behavior and giving examples of how children can act accordingly
- Telling stories that illustrate prosocial principles
- Demonstrating prosocial behavior using small figures, dolls, puppets, video vignettes, or live models
- Reenacting previously observed prosocial actions
- Role-playing situations in which children take on the behaviors of helper and person in need of assistance

- Playing games that promote cooperation and awareness of others
- Creating opportunities for children to help or cooperate in real-life situations

Children who actively participate in tasks or situations that enable them to rehearse prosocial skills demonstrate the greatest instances of such behaviors in similar circumstances (Ladd, 2005). These findings hold true from preschool through preadolescence, particularly for children younger than 6 years of age. The opportunity to physically reenact appropriate behaviors in relevant situations helps children better remember both the behavior and the cues that signal what conditions apply in a given circumstance (Alsaker & Gutzwiller-Helfenfinger, 2010). For example, when Heidi watches a skit in which she must use a variety of cues to decide which puppet needs help, she is better equipped to recognize when help is needed in a real-life situation. Thus, the most productive approach for direct instruction is to combine verbal descriptions and explanations with practice of corresponding actions.

Practice with prosocial behavior. Actual participation in prosocial activities seems to foster prosocial behavior in the future (Eisenberg et al., 2006). Many researchers believe that for children to see the value of prosocial acts, they must actually engage in the behavior and experience firsthand the empathic rewards it can offer. When children practice behaving with kindness and caring, they also experience the satisfaction of social approval from adults. Finally, when children act in a prosocial manner, they come to believe that they are capable and competent beings. They begin to identify themselves as prosocial people.

All of the adult practices previously described can be translated into more specific intervention skills that may be used individually or in combination to positively influence children's prosocial behavior. Read the following skill section carefully and think about how you might use each skill with children you know. In addition, review the Challenging Behavior, which describes Courtney, whose "helpful" behavior is challenging to the other children and to the teachers with whom she interacts each day.

CHALLENGING BEHAVIOR

Meet Courtney

Courtney, age 8, loved everything about helping! She was the first one with a sponge whenever anything spilled. She was quick to offer a suggestion if peers seemed stumped about what to do next. She could be depended on to comfort others in distress. Lately, however, her teachers noticed that on the playground (shared with a younger class), she had taken to picking up the youngest children and bodily moving them from place to place to "help" them get around. She was also seen forcing younger children to sit on her lap so she could "help" them read a story. She "helped" children in the sandbox and on the swings, even when they said they wanted to

do things themselves. If children protested, Courtney became upset. Her behavior became more coercive and her actions more rough. Her teachers wondered what to do. They didn't want to squelch Courtney's desire to be helpful, but her overpowering behavior was becoming a challenge for herself, the other children, and the supervising adults.

If you were Courtney's teacher, how might you approach this situation? As you read through the skills portion of the chapter, think about Courtney and her classmates. Which of these skills might you employ to help Courtney get her "helping behavior" on the right track?

SKILLS FOR PROMOTING PROSOCIAL BEHAVIOR IN CHILDREN 🅝🅐🅔🅨🅒

Creating a Prosocial Environment

You will want to use the skills learned from pervious chapters to help you create an atmosphere that is conducive to the development of prosocial behavior. Some additional strategies include the following:

1. **Label prosocial acts as they occur naturally.** When children clean the guinea pig's cage, tell them they are showing concern for the animal's well-being. When Theresa announces

that she received a get-well card during her recent absence, point out that sending the card was the way someone chose to comfort her. Explain that children who remain quiet while a peer gives a report are helping him or her to concentrate. When children take turns, mention that this is a way of cooperating with one another. All of these instances enable you to highlight prosocial behavior rather than lecturing or moralizing about it.

2. **Point out instances in which an unintentional lack of kindness was shown, and describe an alternate, prosocial approach.** Through inexperience or thoughtlessness, people sometimes are inconsiderate, selfish, uncooperative, or uncharitable. When this happens, point out to children the effects that behavior had on the person to whom it was directed, and describe a more appropriate action. Rather than labeling the child as "selfish," say, "When you didn't give her any, it hurt her feelings." Thus, if children laugh when one of them trips and drops his or her lunch tray, say, "It embarrassed Sam when you laughed. He feels really uncomfortable. Help him to pick up the tray."

3. **Create opportunities for children to co-operate.** Each day, include projects and routines that require the efforts of more than one person. Feeding classroom pets or setting up experiments can provide children the opportunity to work together to accomplish a task. Encourage children to help one another as occasions arise. Ask children with special needs to assist their peers whenever appropriate. When children ask you to help, try instead to find another child who could fulfill that role. Use the list of examples in the downloadable tool to get started planning cooperative activities in your classroom.

Activities that Encourage Cooperation and Sharing

- Use toys and materials that promote cooperation such as parachutes, rocking boats, and teeter-totters.

- Provide giant floor puzzles or marble mazes that children can work on together.

- Encourage murals made by groups of children instead of individual artwork made by each child.

- Play games that encourage taking turns.

- Put a mound of play dough in the middle of the table for children to share.

- Encourage children to set up a chore list and have daily helpers for different tasks.

- Discuss how space or materials should be used so that all get access, for example, sharing blocks or space in the art area.

- Point out when children are considerate of others such as when they replace the pieces of puzzles or keep the brushes in the appropriate paint jars.

- Set up routine jobs that children complete together (e.g., setting the table for lunch).

- Read books on the topic of sharing (e.g., *The Boy Who Wouldn't Share* by Mike Reiss).

Digital Download Download from CourseMate

4. **Use prosocial reasoning when talking with children.** Offer explanations for classroom expectations that are prosocial in nature. For instance, explain that turn-taking gives everyone a chance to try a new object or experience. Point out that comforting a friend in distress makes the unhappy child feel better and often makes the comforter feel better, too. Focus on other-oriented rationales as well as benefits to the doer. Discuss the unique needs of each child and how fairness requires taking into account individual circumstances. Ask children to identify the prosocial reasons behind certain activities in the classroom, such as why people wait to tell their idea until after another person has finished. Set aside time to talk with children about specific incidents in which they and their peers were kind to one another. Help children reflect on these circumstances, and discuss how prosocial acts make people feel.

5. **Reward prosocial behavior.** Remain alert to children's attempts to be helpful, cooperative, or kind. Avoid taking these actions for granted or waiting for dramatic episodes before reinforcing the behavior. Instead, acknowledge small kindnesses, such as when children move out of the way, help to carry something, play together without bickering, share an idea, or offer encouragement to someone else. Show approval and appreciation by smiling and using positive personal messages and prosocial attributions.

6. **Administer group recognition.** Identify situations where children can work together. These may be newly introduced conditions (such as a special project) or circumstances usually focused more on individual achievement. For instance, if you have emphasized each child taking care of his or her own area or materials, change this routine and encourage children to work together to clean up a larger area. Afterward, use effective praise with children to reinforce their cooperation and helpfulness.

7. **Demonstrate a variety of prosocial behaviors.** Carefully examine your own behavior with children and with other adults and set an example for children to follow. Although it may seem easiest to comfort, rescue, or help children, do not forget to share and cooperate as well. Highlight this modeling by commenting on what you are doing. "I see Ramón needs help. I'm going to help him carry that box." Be sure to model prosocial behaviors in your interactions with colleagues and family members as well.

8. **Demonstrate constructive ways of responding to other people's prosocial behavior.** A positive response to offers of help from others

contributes to the prosocial environment. If you desire the help that is offered, say, "Thank you" with a pleased expression on your face. If you would rather do something on your own, or if the proposed assistance would not be helpful, do not simply brush the child or adult aside. Instead, acknowledge the kindness and explain that this is something you would like to do yourself or describe an action that would be more useful. In both cases, you are modeling appropriate ways of either accepting or declining help.

9. **Be positive when engaging in prosocial behavior.** Because children tend to imitate adults who seem to enjoy giving help and cooperation, exhibit obvious pleasure in prosocial situations. Smile and say things like, "It makes me feel good to help you."

10. **Point out the prosocial behaviors modeled by yourself and others.** Children will better understand the prosocial behaviors they see when their model's behavior is explained. Provide children with such information by saying things like, "Arthur was having a hard time coming up with words for his song, so Lamont is helping him by making a list of some words that rhyme," or "Randi and Mike have decided to use the workbench together. Randi will use the hammer while Mike uses the saw. Then, they'll trade."

11. **Use positive attribution to increase children's prosocial self-images.** Say specific things, such as, "Elke, you were really helpful to Danielle when you reached up high for the dictionary she needed," or "Lonny and Javon, you were cooperative when you worked together on the diorama. That made the work easier for both of you," or "Jackson, you showed a lot of kindness when you wiped your sister's tears. It made her feel better knowing you were concerned about her."

Using Teaching and Coaching to Promote Prosocial Behavior

Direct training in helping and cooperating can be provided through on-the-spot teaching and coaching in naturally occurring situations or through preplanned activities. In both cases, the role of the adult is to teach children basic facts about kindness, to demonstrate applications to real-life situations, and to give children a chance to rehearse related skills. Each approach has certain elements in common but also unique characteristics that must be understood to implement them successfully.

Providing On-the-Spot Instruction

As you will recall, three steps are involved in developing prosocial behaviors: awareness, decision making, and action. The focus of on-the-spot instruction is to assist children at any point beyond which they seem unable to proceed.

1. **Observe children for signs of prosocial behavior.** Carefully watch and take note when children show consideration for another person, attempt to assist someone, or join forces, even briefly.

2. **Ask children directly to help you.** This is particularly important when working with preschoolers who have not yet developed the observational skills to accurately recognize when help is needed. Pointing out your need for assistance gives them practice in recognizing situational cues and performing corresponding behaviors related to kindness.

3. **Make children aware when someone else needs help or cooperation.** There are times when children fail to recognize distress signals or other signs that indicate that help or cooperation is desired. Rectify this by giving children relevant information to assist them in becoming more attuned to the present circumstances. If Marianne seems oblivious to Barney's struggle to carry a heavy board, say, "Look at Barney. He's working awfully hard. He looks like he could use some help." Likewise, if DaShawn was absentmindedly singing aloud while listening to his iPod, but others were trying to concentrate on their reading, others might respond with statements such as "pipe down," or "shut up." Such comments could easily be misinterpreted by DaShawn or even seen as a challenge to continue. Information from you at this point would be useful: "You are enjoying your music. It's hard for other people to concentrate. They're just asking you to cooperate by being a little quieter."

4. **Teach children signals they might use to elicit help or cooperation from others.** In the preceding example, children were trying to get DaShawn to cooperate using an antagonistic strategy, which could have backfired. They, too, could benefit from some basic information, such as "DaShawn didn't know he was bothering you. Instead of yelling at him, you can walk over and explain why you want him to be quiet." Toddlers and preschoolers, as well as children in highly charged situations, respond best to direct suggestions. Offer these in the form of a script or sample words that they might use: "Tell Marianne, 'This board's too big for me to carry alone.'" With your support and

encouragement, most school-age children who are not passionately involved in a situation will be able to generate their own ideas for what to say.

5. **Point out situations in which people could decide to help or cooperate.** At times, children are aware that someone needs their help or cooperation, but they don't know what to do next. Point out that a prosocial decision can be made by saying something, such as "Janice looks like she needs your help. We can decide to help her," or "Mr. Crouch wants us all to work together on this project. We'll have to decide whether or not to do that."

6. **Discuss situations in which cooperation would not be prosocial.** These would involve circumstances in which people or property are endangered or moral codes are violated. For example, joining together for the purpose of stealing, cheating on an exam, or damaging property would be inappropriate cooperative efforts. With school-age children, discuss peer pressure and generate strategies and scripts children might use to cope in uncomfortable peer-related circumstances.

7. **Assist children in determining what type of help or cooperation is most suitable for a particular situation.** After children show some signs of wanting to help or cooperate, assist them in deciding how to take action. Provide information such as "Sometimes, when people are unhappy, it helps when someone hugs them or says nice things to them," or "Sometimes, people feel satisfaction from attempting to do something that is difficult, and their pleasure is spoiled if another person takes over."

8. **Demonstrate helpful behaviors.** Showing a child how to unlock the wheelchair of a classmate in need, illustrating to children how one person can steady a doll while another puts on the clothes, or demonstrating how it takes two people to make the computer game work are all ways to make these types of discussions more concrete. In addition, discuss ways children can support another person's effort without offering direct, physical assistance.

Point out the importance of a reassuring smile, the "thumbs-up" sign, or cheering from the sidelines. These are all ways children can provide comfort and encouragement. Finally, teach children to ask questions such as: "Do you want help?" "How can I help you?" "What do you need?" and "What would you like me to do?" This enables children to acquire information about what kind of behavior another person might perceive as helpful or cooperative in a given situation.

9. **Teach children how to share.** Teaching children how to share is not accomplished by simply telling them to do it. Children may need guided experience with sharing before they will readily share objects and territory. Use planned activities and on-the-spot instruction to acquaint children with many different ways to share such as taking turns, using an object/place simultaneously, dividing materials/territory, finding a substitute object/place, or compromising. See Highlight 13-2 (which can also be downloaded for on-the-spot reference) for strategies that can be used to teach children to share.

Teach children who are waiting for a turn to ask, "How will I know when your turn is over?" This requires the child in possession of an item to designate a signal for completion and gives the waiting child something specific to look for. Older children appreciate being able to say, "Okay, but I get it next." Establishing their turn in the order of possession satisfies their need for some control in the situation.

Finally, help children recognize legitimate instances in which sharing can be expected (e.g., using class materials) and other times when sharing cannot be expected (e.g., using someone else's private property). All of these techniques touch on nuances of sharing that cannot be conveyed by simply demanding that children "share."

10. **Work at increasing children's perspective-taking skills.** For children to understand when help or cooperation is needed or when an act of kindness is called for, they must learn to

put themselves in the place of another person. Although this skill will often emerge around age 6, it can be taught to children who are as young as 3, 4, and 5 years of age. Promote children's conscious understanding of prosocial behavior by using open-ended questions, such as "How did you know that would happen?" or "What made you think of trying that?" Promote children's consequential thinking by asking such questions as, "What will happen if . . .?" or "What will happen next . . .?" Finally, promote children's alternative thinking with such statements as, "William wants to finish the project himself. What could you do to help him do that?" or "What's another way you could help?"

11. **Provide opportunities for children to increase their instrumental know-how.** Teach children these strategies:

- Help children put feelings into words so they are able to express their own emotions and understand the expression of other people's emotions.

- Provide numerous formal and informal opportunities for children to make decisions in the classroom. This gives children practice in generating alternatives to problems and in developing confidence in their abilities to find positive solutions.

- Finally, give children chances to learn useful skills. Sorting and organizing materials in the classroom, holding doors while others carry things, and using actual tools to fix broken toys are only some of the possibilities.

12. **Work with children to evaluate the results of their actions.** Children learn a lot from taking a retrospective look at what they have done as close to the event as possible: "Did jumping on the box solve the problem?" "Were there enough of you, or did you need more people to work on that project?" "Were you able to give Raymond all the information he needed?" or "How do you think it worked out for everybody to have a five-minute turn with the microscope?"

If children are unable to assess their own performances, offer some information yourself or help them gather information from others. This evaluation could be conducted during a private conversation with a child or as a group assessment of group effort. Regardless of how well their prosocial venture worked out, praise children for attempting it.

13. **Encourage children to accept kindness from others.** Sometimes, children are unaware of or misinterpret other children's attempts at prosocial behavior. Thus, Tricia may not realize that when Audrey takes over, she is actually trying to help, nor may she understand that Sam's apparent lack of decisiveness is his way of trying to cooperate. In situations like these, point out what is really taking place.

In addition, there are children who, wanting to be independent or self-sufficient, actively reject assistance, reassurance, or sympathy. Frequently, they neither cooperate nor expect cooperation from others. Their rationale is that they expect nothing and give nothing. In reality, such children often fear rejection or "taking a chance" on someone. These children need to experience kindness before they can extend it to those around them. Because their actions put other children off, you are the one who must reach out.

Do not fail to provide unreceptive children with the same courtesies or offers of help and encouragement that you might grant to a more appreciative child. This is the first step in helping them become more accepting of prosocial behavior from someone else.

14. **Support children when their attempts at kindness are rebuffed.** At times, children's enthusiasm is dashed if their offer of help is refused or an action they thought was helpful turns out otherwise. If this happens, acknowledge the child's disappointment or frustration and discuss the situation. Offer information that might assist the child in understanding the outcome. If you do not know why the child's attempt failed, be supportive and sympathetic.

All of the preceding strategies can be used individually, on separate occasions, or in combination. Which specific technique is called for depends on the particular circumstance in which you are involved. This is illustrated in the following real-life example.

Situation: Kenton and Josh, two 6-year-olds, are playing with a construction toy that has many interconnecting pieces. Josh builds an elaborate vehicle, which Kenton admires.

Kenton: Make me one like yours.

Josh: Well, if I make it, it'll be mine.

Kenton: But I want one. Make me one.

Josh: Then it'll be mine!

Kenton: You make it. I can't get the pieces to fit.

At this point, it is obvious that Kenton is unsuccessfully trying to elicit Josh's help. Adult intervention is appropriate.

Adult: Josh, Kenton is asking you for help. Sometimes, when people help, they do the job for someone. However, it sounds like you think if you make the car for Kenton, it will have to be yours. Another way people help is by showing someone how to do it. That way, Kenton can make his own with your help. How does that sound to you?

Josh: Okay.

Kenton: Yeah.

Josh demonstrated how his car went together. After this was well underway, the adult commented briefly on the boys' cooperative behavior as well as on Josh's willingness to help a friend.

In this situation, the adult enabled one child to become aware of another child's signals and provided information about a possible course of action. She also rewarded the children for demonstrating prosocial behavior. Later in the day, she could take a moment to informally talk with Kenton and Josh about their reactions to the helping episode.

Coordinating Planned Activities to Teach Prosocial Behavior

Planned activities are lessons adults develop in advance and carry out with children individually or in groups. The best activities are not necessarily the most elaborate; rather, they are those that have been well prepared and then implemented in ways that are sensitive to children's interests and needs. The following list illustrates how best to accomplish this.

1. **Decide what prosocial skill you want to teach.** Choose one of the skills described in this chapter, such as becoming aware that someone needs help, deciding to help, or taking action to help.

2. **Consider multiple optional lessons for the skill.** Lessons that include both discussion and active participation are the most effective. Active participation means physically involving children in the activity by handling props, moving about, and talking rather than simply listening. Some examples of successful activities include the following:

   a. Reading and telling stories that have a prosocial theme.

   b. Dramatizing prosocial situations through skits or through use of puppets, dolls, or stand-up figures.

   c. Discussing with the children prosocial events that have occurred in the formal group setting.

   d. Role-playing prosocial episodes. Sample topics might include how to ask for help or cooperation, how to decide whether help

or cooperation is needed, determining what type of action would be most helpful or cooperative, and how to decline unwanted help.

   e. Discussing scenes from magazines, books, or posters. The discussion might involve identifying who was helped, who provided help, how the help was carried out, or pointing out cooperative and uncooperative behaviors.

   f. Playing cooperative games such as ring-around-a-rosy with preschoolers or carrying out a scavenger hunt with older children in which groups of children search for things as a team rather than competing as individuals.

   g. Turning traditionally competitive games such as bingo into cooperative group efforts.

      To adapt this game, have one card for every two or three children. The object is to help one another find the matching numbers or pictures rather than competing to be the first to complete a card. When one group's card is complete, those children may move to another group to help them. Several game books are available that emphasize cooperative efforts.

   h. Creating group projects, such as a class book or mural, to which everyone contributes.

3. **Select one of your activity ideas to fully develop.** Make a realistic assessment of what props are available, how much time you will have, the physical setting, and the number of children you will be working with at one time. For instance, do not choose a story that takes 20 minutes to read if you only have 10 minutes in which to work.

4. **Develop a plan of action that outlines the prosocial activity from start to finish.** Write this plan down as a way to remember it and further think it through. Include what you will say to introduce the activity, any instructions you may have to give, how you will handle materials, how you will have children use them, the sequence of steps you will follow, and how you will close. Anticipate what you will say or do if children seem uninterested or unable to carry out your directions. See Highlight 13-3 for a sample activity plan.

5. **Gather the materials you will need.** Make any additional props that are necessary.

6. **Implement your plan.** Use skills you have learned in previous chapters related to nonverbal and verbal communication, reflecting, asking questions, and playing to enhance your presentation.

7. **Evaluate your activity in terms of immediate and long-term prosocial outcomes.** Typical evaluation questions include the following: Who were the children who participated? What did children actually say or do in this activity?

HIGHLIGHT 13-3

Sample Activity to Promote Prosocial Behavior

Activity	Sharing a Lump of Play Dough
Goal:	To help children practice sharing
Materials:	A 2-pound lump of play dough, a table with five chairs (one for an adult, four for children), one plastic knife, one pair of scissors, one 12-inch length of wire
Procedure:	

1. Place a lump of play dough in the center of the table.
2. Neutralize the dough by keeping one hand on it. Say, "I have one big ball of play dough, and there are four children who want to use it. Tell me how everyone can have a chance."
3. Listen to children's ideas; elicit suggestions from everyone.
4. Clarify each child's perspective by paraphrasing his or her ideas to the group. Follow up with, "And what do you think of that?"
5. Remain impartial throughout this process. Do not show disapproval of any child's idea, regardless of its content.
6. Remind children as necessary that the first step in playing with the dough is deciding how that will take place.
7. If children become bogged down, repeat pertinent helping facts and principles.
8. Summarize the solution when it has been achieved.
9. Praise children.
10. Carry out the agreed-upon solution.

How did children demonstrate interest or lack of interest? Later in the day, did children refer either to the activity or the prosocial skill covered in the activity in their conversation or play? Over time, do children spontaneously demonstrate prosocial behaviors highlighted by the activity?

8. **Repeat the same prosocial activity, or a variation of it, at another time.** Children learn prosocial concepts through repeated exposure over time. Therefore, do not expect to see immediate behavior change or the adoption of prosocial skills in their everyday interactions after just one or two presentations of a particular skill.

Communicating with Children's Families

Children's prosocial behaviors within the family setting can and should be encouraged by family members. Following are some strategies that will enable you to join forces with parents and other significant people in children's lives to promote children's prosocial behavior.

1. **Communicate your classroom philosophy of cooperation to families**. Cooperative activities, group projects, and individual work give children a message that each person in the classroom has an important role in the smooth functioning of that setting. Communicate your philosophy to parents in the form of a newsletter in which you describe what prosocial behavior is and how it is encouraged in the classroom.

2. **Invite family members to help in the formal group setting.** At the beginning of the program year, send out a "family interest survey" eliciting information about things adult family members are interested in doing, such as repairing toys, sewing, accompanying field trips, designing bulletin boards, or telling stories. Among the most valuable contributions families can make to the classroom are activities that represent their cultural heritage that may be unfamiliar to many students. Families may be reluctant to respond in writing, so carry out conversations with parents at informal times as a way of both finding out information and encouraging them to participate.

Provide opportunities that require varying expertise to encourage a range of participation. Certain family members may welcome ongoing opportunities to contribute whereas others prefer short-term projects. Some adults may be more comfortable helping "behind the scenes," whereas others may be able to take advantage of working directly with the children. Remember to point out to the children the helpful actions carried out by their family members, and be sure to acknowledge all help in writing and verbally. Children will benefit from sending a thank-you note to the family.

3. **Answer families' questions about the role of competition and cooperation in their children's lives.** At the same time that cooperation is being fostered in the classroom, some parents may express concern that to be "successful in life" their children need to feel competitive.

   Hold discussions with family members on this topic or introduce it as part of a newsletter to families. Encourage parents to express their views and acknowledge their perceptions. Point out some of the differences between "doing one's best" and "beating the opposition." For example, give families some specifics as to how children's achievement may be measured in many ways such as reviewing how much better they did this time than last. Suggest keeping journal entries regarding the emotions of the individual when working toward an identified goal. Help parents understand how to support their children through the disappointments and hard times that inevitably come with competition and comparisons. Rather than denying their children's perceptions of "failure," aid parents in understanding how to use affective reflections and continuing responses to encourage children to reveal and, therefore, better understand their emotions at such times. Point out developmental norms with regard to how children at various ages assess their success or failure. In addition, mention, if appropriate, that while some children become more motivated to do as the adult wishes when prompted by a competitive statement or challenge, friction among children also increases.

4. **Assist adults in figuring out how their children can be helpful at home.** In many families, certain routine chores are assigned to the youngest members. Jobs such as making

one's own bed in the morning, clearing dishes from the table, meal planning, and even simple meal preparation are well within the abilities of most children. Responsibility for these tasks gives children a sense of contributing to the life of their family, as well as increasing their self-perceptions of competence and worth.

Encourage adult family members to have discussions with their offspring as to the ways in which the children can be helpful at home. Suggest the family draw up a list of chores to be done and let young family members choose from among the list. Sometimes children prefer doing the same task over and over; at other times, they would rather change jobs frequently. Suggest that the family make a decision about this, and explore the possibility that the same strategy need not necessarily apply to every child. In other words, some children in a family may hold the same responsibility while others may switch. Offer a visible means of letting everyone know that a job is done, such as crossing off a completed chore and a weekly jobs list.

Caution parents against fostering competition among their children. Negative comparisons have the effect of discouraging rather than encouraging participation. Suggest instead that some chores may be more efficiently handled when several people cooperate. Also include standards for completion to avoid misunderstandings. For example, in one family, 8-year-old Aaron was to sweep the kitchen after dinner. His father was cross with him for not returning the broom and dustpan to the closet. After some discussion, both parties realized that although the adult assumed that putting things away was part of the job, the child did not see that as part of his responsibility. As a consequence, the chore was changed to sweeping the floor and putting away the tools.

Finally, explain to adults the importance of not taking children's work for granted. Children are more likely to continue their efforts when their assistance has been acknowledged, and the positive influence of their contributions on the operations of the family has been appreciated.

Pitfalls to Avoid naeyc

Whether you are teaching children prosocial behavior by creating an atmosphere that is conducive to acts of kindness, providing on-the-spot instruction, or using planned activities, there are certain mistakes to avoid:

1. **Failing to recognize children's efforts to be prosocial.** Children who are just learning to help and cooperate may be awkward in their

attempts or may initially pursue a course of action that at first bears little resemblance to kindness. When this happens, adults may misinterpret these behaviors as purposefully uncooperative or unhelpful. Harmful behavior should be limited, but children should receive support for their positive goals as well as information on how to improve their performance. This means it will be necessary to ascertain children's intentions before taking corrective action. Thus, if children are adding water to the acrylic paint or scrubbing the window with toothpaste, don't assume their motives are to ruin the materials or annoy you. Instead, ask questions such as: "What were you trying to do?" "What did you think would happen?" or "Why are you . . .?" If they give an indication that their intent was to be helpful, acknowledge their efforts and explain why the action wasn't helpful, suggesting alternative actions that would be useful. Make sure that your voice tone is sincerely questioning and not accusatory.

These same strategies can be employed in any situation in which a child is attempting to help, cooperate, comfort, or rescue via some inappropriate means. If you set a limit or enforce a consequence only to discover later that the child truly was trying to help, go back to the child, explain that you now understand what he or she was trying to do, and discuss why corrective action was necessary. Give the child specific ideas about what to do instead.

2. **Bringing a prosocial model's behavior to a child's attention through negative comparison or through competition.** As has been stated previously, children are more likely to imitate models whose behavior is pointed out to them. However, adults should not use these situations to make unfavorable comparisons between the model's behavior and that of the child. Statements like, "Look at Roger. He's so polite. Why can't you be more like that?" make the child feel defensive rather than receptive and do not make imitation likely. A better approach would be to say: "Roger accidentally bumped into Maureen, so he said, 'Excuse me.' That was a very polite thing to do." This latter statement provides factual information in a nonjudgmental way.

3. **Coercing children to engage in insincere prosocial behavior.** Sometimes adults who are trying to teach children consideration manipulate them into expressions of kindness that the children do not really feel. This is illustrated by the parent who insists that 12-year-old Raymond "be nice and give Aunt Martha a kiss," even though the child has protested that he doesn't like to do it. He complies, not to be kind to Aunt Martha, but to avoid trouble. Similar difficulties arise when children are prodded into saying they are sorry when they are not. They learn that apologizing is the quickest way out of a dilemma rather than a sincere expression of remorse. Likewise, children who are urged to bestow false compliments on others as a way to charm them are learning that hypocrisy is acceptable.

To avoid these undesirable outcomes, adults must refrain from being preoccupied with the illusion of kindness at the expense of helping children develop the empathy necessary for true kindness to occur. Hence, it would be better to give the child information about the other person that might prompt empathic feelings: "Aunt Martha is glad to see you. She loves you very much. It would make her feel good to know that you care about her, too," "When you were trying to practice with your crutches, you banged Jerry in the leg. That hurt a lot," or "You told me you thought Carrie's spider was neat. She'd probably like to hear that from you."

4. **Making children share everything all the time.** There is no doubt that sharing is an important interpersonal skill that children should learn. Unfortunately, there are times when adults promote this virtue too enthusiastically. For instance, Elizabeth was using three grocery bags to sort the food in her "store." One bag was for boxes, one was for cans, and one was for plastic fruit. She needed all three bags. Helen approached and asked if she could have one of the bags. Elizabeth protested, but the adult insisted that Helen be given a bag. The adult dumped out the fruit and gave a sack to Helen.

In this case, Elizabeth had a legitimate right to finish using the bag. It would have been easier for her to share it willingly after her game was over. A better approach would have been to say: "Elizabeth, when you are finished playing, Helen would like a chance to use a bag. Tell her when you are ready." A variation of this problem occurs when adults arbitrarily regulate turn-taking as a way to get children to share. For example, as soon as a child gets on a tricycle, the adult admonishes, "Once around the yard, and then you'll have to get off so someone else can have a turn." This approach is used in a well-meaning effort to avoid conflict or to be fair. However, it often ends up with no child feeling truly satisfied. Furthermore, it requires constant adult monitoring.

Instead, allow children to fully use the materials to which they have access. It would be better, if at all possible, to expand the amount of equipment available so that children are not pressured into having to give up something with which they are deeply involved. If this is not possible, prompt empathic feelings by pointing out that others are waiting and would like a turn, too. Help children develop a strategy to share materials that is agreeable to all parties. Finally, remember to praise children when they finally relinquish what they have been using to someone else. Point out how their actions pleased the child who wanted to be next.

Summary

Prosocial behaviors are voluntary actions to aid or benefit others. Prosocial behavior is a significant component of social competence and has many benefits for children. Children who are kind develop feelings of satisfaction and competence, have many successful encounters, and get help and cooperation from others in return. Groups in which prosocial behavior is fostered are friendlier and more productive than those in which it is ignored.

To behave in ways perceived as prosocial, children first must become aware of situations in which such acts would be beneficial. Then, they have to decide if and how they will act and finally, take the action (or lack of action) they have decided on. Desiring to act with prosocial intent and knowing how best to do it are not necessarily learned at the same time.

As children mature and gain experience, they become more proficient at matching their prosocial actions to the needs of others. Children's abilities to take on another's perspective also affect their prosocial behavior; that is, children with good role-taking abilities are generally more inclined to engage in prosocial behavior. This link becomes stronger with age. Age, family, peers, school, and culture influence children's prosocial behavior. Particular societal characteristics either promote or inhibit prosocial conduct. For example, the emphasis placed on prosocial or antisocial behaviors may vary among cultures.

The most profound influences on children's helpful and cooperative behavior are adults: the warmth of their relationship with children, the discipline strategies, the behaviors they model, the behaviors in children they reward, and the prosocial values and skills they teach. Teaching children kindness can be accomplished through creating an atmosphere conducive to prosocial actions, through on-the-spot instruction, and through planned activities. Partnerships between the family and the professionals who work with the children enhance children's intentions and skills toward prosocial behavior.

There are certain mistakes professionals may make in regard to children's prosocial behavior. Failing to recognize children's positive intentions to be helpful or insisting that children share everything all of the time are common pitfalls. These difficulties can be avoided with practice and self-reflection.

Key Terms

character attributions
dispositional attributions
instrumental know-how
perspective-taking
prosocial attributions
prosocial behavior

Discussion Questions

1. Identify several aspects of prosocial behavior. Discuss their similarities and differences using examples from real life.

2. In small groups, talk about the benefits and risks of behaving in prosocial ways. When appropriate, tell about some personal instances in which you did or did not behave this way and the consequences of those behaviors.

3. Geraldo is working hard at constructing a bridge out of tongue depressors. He seems to be having difficulty getting it to stay up. Patrick is watching.
   a. Describe the steps Patrick will go through in acting with kindness toward Geraldo.
   b. Discuss all the possible choices Patrick will have to make and the potential outcomes of each decision.

4. Describe the influence of age on children's prosocial behavior. Discuss the emergence and the increase or decline of particular types of prosocial behaviors as children get older. Give reasons based on your understanding of children's development.

5. Discuss cultural influences on children's prosocial behavior. Describe experiences in your own upbringing to illustrate. Describe particular family or social values that had an impact.

6. Describe the attributes of the atmosphere of a formal group setting that facilitate the development of children's prosocial behavior. Discuss specifically how the discipline strategies you have learned thus far contribute to this atmosphere.

7. Describe six ways in which adults can model cooperation in the formal group setting and in the home. Discuss how children can translate these techniques into their own behavior.

8. Using examples from the formal group setting in which you work, describe instances in which adults did the following:

    a. Rewarded children's prosocial behavior

    b. Overlooked children's prosocial behavior

    c. Inadvertently punished children's prosocial behavior

    Discuss any aftermath you observed, either immediately or within a short time.

9. Discuss the role of direct instruction on children's prosocial behavior. Relate specific skills that foster helping and cooperating to particular strategies for teaching these skills.

10. Referring to Appendix A, NAEYC Code of Ethical Conduct, find the principles and ideals to use in judging the ethics of the following situation: Two teachers in your program are excited about an activity they heard about at a recent workshop. Each time children do a kind act, they earn a point. The child with the most points at the end of the week is named "kindness kid" for a day.

Case Study Analysis

After reading the case study for Adriana in Appendix B, consider the following:

1. What opportunities would you create for Adriana to play and work with others? What difficulties might she have in engaging in cooperative activities?

2. Identify strategies described in this chapter you would use to assist Adriana in becoming more prosocial.

3. Describe prosocial actions you might engage in as a way to model appropriate behaviors for Adriana. What steps would you take to ensure that Adriana is aware of your actions?

4. Think about the Social Support Pyramid in relation to the case study. Describe what actions you would take in each level of the pyramid to assist Adriana in becoming more prosocial.

5. What pitfalls might you encounter when working with Adriana? How might you prevent experiencing these pitfalls?

Field Assignments

1. Choose a prosocial skill. In a few sentences, describe an activity you will use to teach children about the behavior you have selected. Carry out your plan with children. Describe how you carried out your plan and how the children responded. Briefly talk about how you might change or improve your plan for repetition in the future.

2. Identify a job you ordinarily carry out yourself in your field placement. Describe at least three ways you could get children involved in helping you. Implement one of your strategies, and then describe what actually happened. Discuss what it is about your plan that you might repeat in the future and what you might change.

3. Focus on modeling prosocial behavior. Describe a prosocial behavior that you modeled and how you did it. Next, discuss a situation in which you pointed out prosocial modeling by yourself or by another person. Write the words you used.

4. Select a prosocial skill to teach children. Use the on-the-spot strategies identified in this chapter. Document children's progress over time.

5. Describe a conversation between you (or another professional) and an adult family member in which a child's prosocial behavior was discussed. Outline the nature of the behavior as well as any strategies that were suggested to encourage the prosocial actions. Write a brief evaluation based on the material covered in this and earlier chapters.

Reflect on Your Practice

Here is a sample checklist you can use to reflect on your use of the skills as a beginning professional. A more detailed classroom observation tool is available in Appendix C.

Teachers who support children's prosocial development do the following:

✓ Facilitate interaction among and between children.

✓ Help children recognize their emotions and the emotions of others.

✓ Help children develop problem-solving strategies.

✓ Acknowledge children's prosocial behavior using attributions and effective praise.

✓ Encourage acts of kindness and cooperation.

✓ Eliminate unnecessary competition and promote cooperative play.

✓ Model prosocial behavior themselves.

CourseMate. Visit the Education CourseMate for this textbook to access the eBook, Digital Downloads, TeachSource Videos, and quizzes. Go to CengageBrain.com to log in, register, or purchase access.

14 Fostering Healthy Attitudes about Sexuality and Diversity

OBJECTIVES

On completion of this chapter, you should be able to:

Discuss aspects of children's psychosexual development.

Identify outcomes related to the development of ethnic identity, preferences, and attitudes in young children.

Explain issues surrounding inclusion of children with exceptional needs.

Talk about the impact of precocious behavior, shyness, and difficult temperament on children's social development.

Demonstrate skills for effective handling of developmental issues related to children's sexuality, ethnicity, exceptional needs, and other differences.

Describe strategies for communicating with families about children's individual differences.

Avoid pitfalls in the handling of issues related to variations in children's development.

NAEYC STANDARDS   naeyc

1. Promoting Child Development and Learning
2. Building Family and Community Relationships
3. Observing, Documenting, and Assessing to Support Young Children and Families
4. Using Developmentally Effective Approaches to Connect with Children and Families
5. Using Content Knowledge to Build Meaningful Curriculum
6. Becoming a Professional

A 4-year-old boy in the housekeeping area of a large childcare center suddenly announces that the dolls are "going to make a baby." Putting one doll on top of the other, he tells two other children who are playing nearby, "Watch this!" and proceeds with a fairly demonstrative performance. The other two children watch with obvious fascination. As the teacher approaches, the child quickly picks up one of the dolls, purposefully ending the play episode.

Several young children begin arguing over selection of a variety of dolls representative of different ethnic groups. The hands-down favorites are the White and Asian dolls. An adult cheerfully suggests that no one has chosen any of the Black dolls lying on the bottom of the box. "We can't! They're dirty and bad," responds one of the children. The adult is particularly surprised because the statement is made by an African-American child.

Kathy, a student who is visually impaired, is being mainstreamed into a fifth-grade classroom. She watches tensely as two teams are chosen for kickball during recess. When she is not chosen by either team, the teacher announces, "Kathy will want to play, too." There is an embarrassing silence, but no offer is made by either team to have Kathy join them.

Episodes like these commonly arise as children navigate the social environment. How we respond to them influences the lessons children learn and how children feel about themselves and others in the process.

When adults are able to maintain a sensitive, nonreactive, and matter-of-fact approach in handling sensitive issues, social competence is promoted in children, including values of social justice, healthy attitudes toward sexuality, and the ability to interact effectively with people of varying cultural, ethnic, and racial backgrounds. Over time, children who develop strength in social competence become adults who are better able to read social situations accurately, give and receive emotional support, and develop a positive self-identity.

However, because none of us escapes developing stereotypes or misconceptions about various aspects of human diversity, there may well be times when we feel genuine embarrassment, irritation, discomfort, and uncertainty in handling sensitive situations such as these (Derman-Sparks & Edwards, 2010). Because of personal emotions that automatically arise in response to our own moral sensibilities and past experiences, we may find ourselves reacting too intensely, avoiding or ignoring negative behaviors, or feeling momentarily confused about what might be the most effective response.

A serious byproduct of excessive adult anxiety or avoidance in such situations is the potentially negative effect on children's development—primarily the production of guilt, loss of self-esteem, or the reinforcement of negative attitudes, misinformation, and maladaptive behavior.

In this chapter, we will suggest ways in which you can grow and empower both yourself and the children you teach to handle intricate issues surrounding sexuality and diversity in healthy and socially productive ways.

Children's Psychosexual Development naeyc

As children develop a sense of themselves, it's important for them to feel comfortable about their sexuality. The following discussion includes the manner in which children come to understand their own psychosexual development, that is, the gender role they will play as a male or female, stereotypes and behaviors they may attach to these roles, and adult responses to these behaviors.

Gender-Role Development

We want to distinguish at the outset the difference between **gender identity** (biological, male–female

© Cengage Learning

Randy refuses to share the camera with Rosalie. He says, "Only boys can be cameramen." What will you do?

Table 14-1 Overview of Gender Typing

Age in Years	Gender Identity	Gender Stereotyping	Gender-Typed Behavior
0–2½	Ability to discriminate males from females emerges and improves. Child accurately labels self as a boy or a girl.	Some gender stereotypes emerge.	Gender-typed toy/activity preferences emerge. Preferences for same-sex playmates emerge (gender segregation).
3–6	Conservation of gender (recognition that one's gender is unchanging) emerges.	Gender stereotyping of interests, activities, and occupations emerges and becomes quite rigid.	Gender-typed play/toy preferences become stronger, particularly for boys. Gender segregation intensifies.
7–11		Gender stereotyping of personality traits and achievement domains emerges. Gender stereotyping becomes less rigid.	Gender segregation continues to strengthen. Gender-typed toy/activity preferences continue to strengthen for boys; girls develop (or retain) interest in some masculine activities.
12 and beyond	Gender identity becomes more salient, reflecting gender-intensification pressures.	Intolerance of cross-sex mannerisms increases early in adolescence. Gender stereotyping becomes more flexible in most respects later in adolescence.	Conformity to gender-typed behaviors increases early in adolescence, reflecting gender intensification. Gender segregation becomes less pronounced.

Source: Shaffer, 2008.

identification) and **gender-role identification**, which refers to the behaviors, abilities, and characteristics associated with a particular gender. This begins a great deal earlier than previously thought and continues even into adulthood (Berk, 2013). Parents play a particularly important role but so do teachers, peers, and siblings.

Children progress through a series of stages in acquiring gender-typed behavior (see Table 14-1), and we see it reflected in their choice of playmates, selection of playthings, and later in gender segregation. The sequence remains the same for all children but is dependent also on the experiences they have and their intellectual maturity.

Observations of children's play shows that they are aware of socially defined behaviors and attitudes associated with being male or female, and this knowledge is reflected in their "gender-doing," that is, the gender-related behaviors reflected in their play. We hear them make comments such as "Daddies are strong," "Mommy cooks the dinner," and "I get to be the nurse because I'm a girl." Also seen in preschoolers is an ability to use "gender-bending" in their play dynamics when necessary. This happens when, for example, a young preschool boy is willing to play the role of "mommy" if no one else is willing or available to take the role. However, as children grow older, they exhibit more discomfort in taking on roles of the opposite gender

(see Figure 14-1). This signals that they are no longer in process of exploring gender roles because this part of their social learning has become more inflexible. This is true for boys earlier than for girls (Hyun & Choi, 2004).

Gender-role development has a major effect on children's understanding of their place in society as a male or female and also in the roles they take on to express their maleness or femininity. However, social identity and role-taking are shaped as well by children's environments and their experiences within those environments. For example:

Amid nudges Carrie out of the way, saying, "Boys always get to go first." (Amid comes from a family culture in which his statement is true.)

Jaxon and Kirk are in the pretend center, cooking. Jaxon says, "We are chefs, not just cooking, right?" "Yeah," responds Kirk, "We get a lot of money for cooking up this stuff!" (Jaxon and Kirk understand the difference between cooking at home, which may be female dominated, and cooking for a job, which is male dominated.)

Belinda shares her aspiration to be a firefighter at group time when community helpers are being discussed. Richard calls out, "You can't be a fireman. You're a girl." (Richard has not yet learned that both men and women can be firefighters.)

Figure 14-1 An Example of Developing Gender Segregation.

Source: From "Psychosexual development in infants and young children," by A. S. Honig, September 2000, *Young Children*, 55(5), p. 71. Reprinted with permission from the author, A. S. Honig.

Adult Responses to Young Children's Psychosexual Behavior and Development

From infancy, all human beings have sexual feelings. A positive attitude toward sexuality means accepting these sensual feelings and urges as natural rather than shameful. Children's subsequent ability to handle such feelings depends on their earliest experiences. Early encounters involving psychological intimacy with significant others teach a child that interpersonal involvement is safe or dangerous, pleasurable or not pleasurable. Similarly, children develop positive or negative attitudes toward their own bodies and bodily functions depending on adults' verbal and nonverbal reactions as they help children with everyday functions such as bathing, dressing, and elimination.

If adults use words such as *nasty*, *yucky*, or *dirty* to describe genital areas or elimination, children are apt to develop feelings that there is something unacceptable about them. Conversely, when adults respond in a matter-of-fact tone of voice, use appropriate labels for body parts, and use behavioral and affective reflections, then children develop a healthier approach to their sexuality. In essence, children learn about sexuality just as they learn about everything else: through words, actions, interactions, and relationships. Some children will express more interest in sexual words, touching genitalia, or in masturbation than do others (Couchenour & Crisman, 2013).

Masturbation. Although childhood masturbation is a fairly universal human experience, it elicits major concern in some adults. Most children discover their genital areas quite by accident during infancy as they become acquainted with their own bodies through poking into openings and exploring their own extremities. Young children can be seen occasionally rubbing or patting their genitals prior to napping, while adults are reading to them, or when watching television. This is usually little more than normal, self-soothing activity. At other times, children seek to derive comfort or enjoy similar sensations by stroking other less provocative body parts such as their noses and ears, twisting locks of their hair, or rubbing pieces of soft material between thumb and finger.

Children between the ages of 3 and 5 years of age often experience growing emotional attachment to the opposite-sexed parent and express residues of these feelings by leaning their bodies against a favored adult, sitting very close, touching, combing or brushing his or her hair, or playing tickling games. At any age, children may engage in masturbation consciously or unconsciously, as a source of comfort when feeling tired, tense, anxious, stressed, bored, or isolated from others; when needing to go to the bathroom; to get attention; or because it simply feels pleasurable. Young boys often unknowingly clutch at their genitals when worried, tired, or excited.

The time to be concerned about masturbatory play or self-manipulation is when it goes on for a large part of the day, when there is infection in the genital area, or when children are being exposed to adult sexual activity, pornography, or sexual abuse. Adults who view masturbatory behavior as abnormal or precocious sexual behavior, and therefore wrong, may actively attempt to discourage such exploration through shaming, threatening, or punishing the child. Instead, good observation skills are called for to document the frequency and normalcy of the behavior (Honig, 2000).

Sex play among young children. By 3 to 5 years of age, children have learned that there is an opposite sex. Most also have discovered that this opposite sex is equipped with different genitalia, which are interesting not only because of their markedly different appearance, but also because they are used in a different way for elimination.

Because children are curious beings as well as sexual beings, it should come as no surprise that they may want to explore these differences and that they commonly do so during the course of playing "house," "doctor," and other childhood games. At this stage of development, children show interest in adult heterosexual behavior. Those who are exposed to media depictions of sexuality or real-life encounters occasionally use dolls and other toys to reconstruct remembered acts. If they have witnessed the actual birth of a younger sibling or watched representations of a birth on television, they sometimes extend sex play to act out the birth process.

A potentially serious problem can occur when children sometimes choose to insert objects into each other's genital openings as part of their sex play. Although adults should acknowledge children's curiosity in such situations, they also should explain the harm that can be caused by putting objects into body openings, including other openings such as the eyes, mouth, nose, and ears. Adults should calmly set limits about sex play and redirect inappropriate behavior to another activity.

Children's curiosity about the human body should not be dismissed, and you can help satisfy children's natural desires to learn more about their bodies and the bodies of others by answering questions in a simple and forthright manner. Some excellent picture books that provide satisfactory answers to many of the questions children pose about sexual differences and where babies come from include Patricia Pearse's *See How You Grow*, Angela Rayston's very simple *Where Do Babies Come From?*, or the more explicit book by Peter Mayle & Arthur Robins, *Where Did I Come From?* These and others can be suggested for use by parents. Using correct terminology (e.g., penis rather than wee-wee) is also an important part of teaching physiological facts and takes away the aura of secrecy about sexual differences.

Peeping or voyeurism by children. Often considered in the category of "sexual disturbances," voyeurism usually occurs when children's natural curiosity about sexual differences has been seriously stifled. Some children who do not have opposite sexed siblings (a natural laboratory for learning about sex differences) may use the childcare center or school bathroom to satisfy some of their curiosity. For this reason, directors of preprimary centers often purposely choose to leave the doors off toilet stalls.

This can be upsetting for some parents who feel that such practices promote precocious interest in sexuality, although there is evidence to the contrary. Also, young children who have been taught that toileting should take place in absolute privacy may be somewhat stressed. For this reason, at least one stall should have a door.

Peeping or sexually aggressive behaviors such as intimate touching also can occur in older children who have been sexually abused or chronically overstimulated sexually by witnessing adult sexual activity. These children may go beyond covert behavior and become more openly aggressive sexually. When such behavior occurs in very young children, it can be shocking, particularly if you view such children as entirely "innocent" and incapable of such thoughts and actions. A childcare aide described the experience of having a 4-year-old boy begin unbuttoning her blouse as he sat on her lap listening to a story she was reading. When she asked him to stop what he was

---

HIGHLIGHT 14-1

Responding to Unexpected Behaviors

1. Maintain a calm demeanor when responding to children's sex play.
2. Redirect children's behavior that may be perfectly normal but makes others feel uncomfortable.
3. Always intervene in cases where behavior is clearly intended to shock or entertain in inappropriate ways or where behavior seems to be "oddly unchild-like" (Miller, 2012).
4. Express clear expectations for future behavior and reasons why a particular behavior is not appropriate.
5. Investigate when you suspect negative influences on the child that may be taking place in other environments in which the child plays and lives.
6. Use correct vocabulary when referring to body parts.
7. Provide natural opportunities for children to learn more about their sexual development.

doing, he grinned and told her, "I want to see your boobies." She notes: "I was amazed and shaken that this little 4-year-old knew exactly what he was saying and doing. I'm still having a hard time dealing with it, and I find myself avoiding him."

Although we can be thrown temporarily off balance when children unexpectedly display behaviors such as exhibitionism, peeping, public masturbation, homosexual acts, and sexually explicit language, several "rules of response" should be kept in mind. These are summarized in Highlight 14-1 and elaborated on later in the skills section of this chapter.

Stereotypical behaviors. While effeminate boys or excessively tomboyish girls worry some adults, so do children at the other end of the continuum. These are children who seem to play extremely stereotypical and rigid sex roles at the expense of developing a wider range of androgynous behaviors— that is, behaviors that are viewed as not sex-specific. For example, an androgynous male would not see childcare as solely a woman's responsibility; similarly, an androgynous female would view learning how to change a tire as beneficial and appropriate rather than as "masculine." Adults who hold more androgynous views and see these as appropriate may be uncomfortable seeing children developing what they feel are narrow psychosexual viewpoints. There is evidence that no matter how carefully parents guard against their children developing traditional male/female stereotypes, 4- and 5-year-old children move in that direction anyway. Their determination seems fueled by gender stereotypes that continue to be promoted on television, in books, and in all of the many contexts in which children develop.

The difference in male/female aggressive behavior seems to be the most troublesome for some adults to deal with. While overt aggression in girls has been increasing, researchers continue to document that boys' behavior is significantly more aggressive (Card et al., 2008). Adults who are particularly threatened by a lot of vigorous activity may tend to suppress boys' natural vigor rather than providing effective outlets for their energy. The fact that boys are more energetic and often harder to control than their sisters "does not mean that masculinity itself is pathological. What boys need is clear moral guidance and healthy outlets for their natural energy and competitiveness" (Charen, 2000). Also, rough and tumble play is a natural outlet for such energy. See Chapter 7 for more information about how to supervise this.

One third-grade teacher made wrestling and chasing games off-limit activities on the playground for the boys in her class. No other suggestions were made about what might replace such play, and when two of the boys in the class continued wrestling, she would order them to stand quietly against the building until they could think of something else to do other than "bully one another." Other children in the class who had been more compliant soon began to tease the two boys, who became labeled as the "bullies," with no intervention on the teacher's part. When one of the boys' parents expressed concern over the reputation her son was earning, the teacher countered with the explanation, "If other children can control themselves and find more acceptable outlets for their energy in using the playground equipment provided, so can these boys." This unwillingness or inability of classroom teachers to deal with boisterous behavior has contributed to the overrepresentation of boys in special-education classes for the emotionally impaired and learning disabled. Males consistently outnumber girls in such programs by a ratio of 3:1 and, in some school districts, the ratio is as high as 20:0 (Soderman, Gregory, & McCarty, 2005).

For children whose sexual behavior or gender role identification seems to be on a divergent track, you must sort out those behaviors that seem to be consistent with normal development and those that are not. Although we are living in an era of significant change regarding sexual values and roles (Levin & Kilbourne, 2009; Deveny & Kelly, 2007), the restructuring of what constitutes healthy sexuality does not call for the abandonment of all current social definitions. You must, however, be aware of how your own personal convictions may affect your responses to children and your instructional planning for them. When behavior is inappropriate, the child will need understanding as well as supportive intervention. If you are unsure about how to evaluate a child's behavior objectively or how to provide necessary guidance, always consult professionals who have additional expertise.

Ethnic Identity, Preferences, and Attitudes in Children naeyc

Just as gender-role development appears to be age specific and stage specific, so is the development of ethnicity and cultural awareness. Sometimes, we are caught off guard by disparaging remarks children make about a person of differing racial or ethnic origin. Such remarks can be quite innocent in nature, simply reflecting the child's lack of experience and information. Other times, children may be more intentionally hostile, such as when they demonstrate a style of "humor" that debases different races, nationalities, or religions. This type of humor depends on a negative conceptualization of the disparaged group and

© Cengage Learning 2015

Children who enjoy playing together are less likely to develop ethnocentrism or an exaggerated preference for their own ethnic group.

cannot succeed unless the child has learned to think in terms of "good guys" and "bad guys." There also are conscious slurs that result from a child's developing **ethnocentrism**, the exaggerated preference for one's own group and a concomitant dislike of other groups (Wolpert, 2005).

Because of their own ethnocentrism, professionals may occasionally find themselves fighting feelings of mild dislike or even strong hostility toward children, parents, or colleagues who belong to other racial or ethnic groups. These feelings can also stem from socioeconomic differences. Whatever the source, such feelings affect our interactions, causing patronizing behavior, avoidance, or even aggressiveness.

Valerie Polakow describes a scenario in which three African-American preschoolers were constantly and exclusively singled out as "Mrs. Naly's Black (and deviant) troublemakers":

Jomo goes over to the piano and sounds a note. Mrs. Naly rushes over. "Can you tell me what that says?" she says, roughly pulling Jomo so that he turns and faces a hand-lettered sign that has a frowning face. "No playing," he says, squirming under her grasp. "Right," she responds and walks back to the art table. Danny and Ryan, who are playing on the floor, tickle

Jomo, and he falls on top of them laughing. The three boys roll on the floor giggling and tickling each other, and Ryan's foot catches a shelf with stacking blocks. The blocks fall on top of the boys, and more giggling ensues as Ryan says, "Quit it man—I'm building," and starts to build a structure on the floor. As the other two follow, Mrs. Naly approaches from the other side of the room. "You three are misbehaving again—you're just going to have to learn to settle down, and until you do, you'll be in trouble with me—no outside time today!" For the third day that week, the three "troublemakers" are kept inside while the other children go out. Mrs. Naly tells me that none of those three is ready for kindergarten: "They're real problem kids, and their families are a mess." (Polakow, 1994, p. 25)

Conversely, teachers who have become skilled in the principles and "doing" of **antibias education** create more optimistic futures for children. This calls for being willing to confront the harmful effects of misinformation, stereotypes, **biases**, prejudice, and fear when we see or experience it in either ourselves or in others. In doing so, we have to be aware of the dynamics of **internalized privilege** or internalized superiority (economic, social, or cultural advantages that come from belonging to a particular social identity). We must be equally aware of **internalized oppression** or inferiority that has

HIGHLIGHT 14-2

Identifying Your Social Identity

Instructions: Circle those identities in columns 2 and 3 that apply to your life. Look at the pattern of circles in the two columns. Either with a talking partner or in writing, describe the following for each of the circled identities: In what ways have you experienced either privilege and visibility or prejudice and discrimination? Which identities opened doors for you, and which ones made life harder?

Social Identity	Groups Defined as the Norm; Recipients of Societal Advantages	Groups that Are Targets of Institutional Prejudice and Discrimination
Race	White	People of color; biracial or multiracial people and families
Ethnicity/Heritage	European American "Melting pot"	All other defined or recognizable ethnicities
Language	English	Home language other than English
Gender	Male	Female, intersex, transgender
Economic class (in childhood, now)	Middle to wealthy	Poverty or working class
Religious beliefs	Christian or Christian tradition	Muslim, Jewish, Buddhist, Hindu, pagan, atheist, and so on
Age	Productive adults (ages 20–45 for women, 20–60 for men)	Children, adolescents, women over 45, men over 60
Sexual orientation	Heterosexual	Asexual, bisexual, gay, lesbian, transgender
Education	College degree Highly literate	High school or less Literacy struggles
Body type, size	Slim, fit Medium height for women; tall for men	Large, overweight Very short or very tall
Able self (physical, mental, emotional)	Healthy Functional, no apparent disability	Any form of disability, physical, mental, emotional stability; learning; behavior controls
Family structure (in childhood, now)	Married Parent with one to three biological children	Unmarried Single parent divorced, relative's children; adoptive, foster, or blended family

Source: Derman-Sparks & Edwards, 2010, p. 31.

Digital Download   **Download from CourseMate**

developed because of limited access to opportunities and constant negative messages about one's own group or **social identity** (see Highlight 14-2). We must develop the courage to speak up, get beyond worrying about offending someone, revisit events that don't go the way we had hoped, and get beyond believing that intervention might

"make things worse" suggest Derman-Sparks & Edwards (2010) who provide another real-life example:

The student teacher had been videotaped during circle time. The circle had fallen apart, with children getting up, running away, and refusing to participate. That evening, the class discusses what happened. The student teacher complains about the disruptive behavior of two African-American boys who had "ruined" the circle. Then the teacher plays the tape. Everyone is shocked to see that the real disruption had come from two White boys, that one of the African-American boys had joined in later, and the second had been almost entirely a bystander. "But I remembered it as Alec and William!" the student teacher says in tears, "How could I have been so wrong?" (p. 21)

Because children's developing self-concept is heavily influenced by the interactions they have with others, including peers and nonfamilial adults, the attitudes others hold about the child's racial group, social class, or religious sect will be critical. As soon as children achieve a basic sense of self as distinct from others (15 to 18 months), they are capable of being shamed and feeling ashamed (York, 2003). As a result, when children perceive they have negative social status, basic feelings of self-worth will suffer.

Factors that lead to the development of racist attitudes clearly have their origin in early childhood and

Table 14-2 Acquisition of Racial Awareness

Age	Characteristics/Behaviors of Racial Awareness
2–3	More aware of others' physical characteristics and cultural behaviors, as different from themselves May be afraid of others who are different in skin color or who exhibit physical disabilities
4	Growing curiosity about how they are like or different from other children Think about and develop reasons for the cultural/physical differences they see Can be confused about what "goes together" ("Why are children called Black when their skin isn't black?" "Girls are supposed to have girl names, so how can 'Sam' be a girl?") Beginning to classify people by physical characteristics (gender, color, appearance) Growing interest in cultural difference related to lives of children and adults they know (where they live and work, who is in the family, what language is spoken) Thinking and behavior becoming more reflective of societal norms, interaction with others, and learned negativity/fears related to differences ("If I play with the child who has a disability, I might catch it too." "Hispanics talk funny.")
5	Deepening awareness of general, racial, ethnic, and ability differences and similarities Growing awareness of socioeconomic class, age, aging Heightened awareness of themselves and others as members of a family ("How come Sara doesn't have a daddy?") Continued reflection about reasons why people differ from one another Greater absorption and use of stereotypes "to define others and to tease or reject other children"
6	Likely to share family's classification for people but may still be uncertain about why "specific people are put into one category or another" Exercise discrimination against others, based on identities Beginning to understand own emerging group identity and that others have an ethnic and lifestyle identity as well
7–8	Increased interest in others' religions, lifestyles, and traditions Beginning "to appreciate deeper structural aspects of culture" (i.e., human connection to land, influence of the past on current ways of life) "if presented concretely through stories about real people" Growing cognition allows understanding that there are different ways to meet common human needs Increased in-group solidarity May experience tension or conflict with others based on gender, race, ethnic identity, socioeconomic class, as well as biases against certain groups because of disabilities or ethnic, religious, or socioeconomic differences

Source: Adapted from Derman-Sparks, 2010.

include elements of direct learning, personality, cognition, perception, communication from the media, and the important people in children's lives who reinforce their behavior—for good or for bad. As early as 2 or 3 years of age, children begin to notice differences in the way people look and the way they behave. Early positive or negative attitudes tend to increase with age, clearly showing more consensus and reliability at 4 years of age than at 3 and becoming fairly well ingrained in all children by the age of 6 (see Table 14-2).

As children respond to their observations, they receive verbal feedback from others that is both informational and evaluative. For example, Martin became very friendly with Eugene, a light-skinned African-American classmate. When he asked his mother if Eugene could come home to play after school, she responded negatively, saying she preferred that Martin not invite Black children home. Martin, later appealing again to his mother, challenged her statement that Eugene was Black, noting that he didn't have black skin. "Yes," replied his mother. "But that isn't the only way you can tell someone is Black. He has very broad lips and a Black person's hair. He's Black, all right. You just play with your own kind." Thereafter, Martin began looking at Eugene and children like Eugene in a different way. A very different scenario is found in the home of Chi Yun, whose parents actively encourage her friend-

ships with children from several ethnic groups. Their goal is that she grows to value people based on shared interests and respect, rather than on family class or birth place.

When you observe confusion, misconceptions, or negativity related to children's perspectives of racial and ethnicity in your classroom, a helpful strategy is to confront this through children's books that depict various aspects of diversity through engaging storytelling (see NAEYC's website at www.naeyc.org for a listing of these).

Persona dolls can be used to selectively address children's questions or events that happen in the classroom or on the playground, as well as issues you want children to explore to promote healthier attitudes and social behavior (Brown, 2001; Derman-Sparks & Edwards, 2010). Persona dolls are special dolls that you keep separate from the other dolls in your classroom. You introduce them individually to the children, building a personal identity and social identity about each doll—their name, age, gender, family members, and what they like to do—making them more real to the children. Then, when you want to introduce an issue, you can bring out one of the dolls, tell a brief story about what happened to the doll and how the doll feels about the situation, and invite the children to discuss the situation and how it could be handled more fairly.

Usually at about 5 years of age, the child begins to develop an established concept of "us" and "them"

Mica's and Rosa's parents encourage their developing in-school friendship by scheduling play dates outside of school.

© Cengage Learning 2015

related to racial cues. This is a time when children begin to expand their perception of the differences that characterize particular groups. At the same time, intra-group differences become less important. For example, children may focus on the general differences among African Americans, European Americans, and different Asian groups in terms of skin color, eye color and shape, hair texture, shape of lips, and other facial characteristics and become less discerning about the wide variations among individuals within these out-groups. Unfortunately, this tends to build later faulty perceptions that "they all look alike." It is also at this age that a "rejection" stage begins, when children begin to rationalize their feelings and preferences aloud. Children of this age can be very rule bound and rigid in their behavior (York, 2003). As a result, they are likely to choose friends that are alike in gender and race. Verbal aggression increases but can be effectively moderated by engaging 5- and 6-year-olds in discussions about fairness.

It is difficult to gauge the ratio of prejudicial (i.e., preconceived hostile attitudes, opinions, feelings, or actions against another person or race) and nonprejudicial experiences a child may have when developing particular racial and ethnic concepts. Unless more opportunities for positive examples are actively provided, children can become victims of a pileup of negative experiences. An African-American educator noted: "Many Black children spend all day long in environments where they feel they are not valued. But when they get home and back in their own neighborhoods, they know they're accepted, that they're all right." There is evidence that what goes on in the classroom in the relationships between teachers and certain students may either reinforce negative attitudes about minority-group membership or modify them in a positive direction.

There is little research that looks at the effects of "transplanting" single children from one culture to another, as has been the case with many Korean and Chinese children adopted by American Caucasian families. Questions must be asked about the timing and effect of interrupting the sequence of development of ethnic identity and racial attitudes in such children, many who find themselves members of what ordinarily would constitute an out-group. Increases in the numbers of adoption cases involving African-American children and their Caucasian adoptive parents raise similar questions. In addition, children with mixed-race parents may have difficulty in identifying with *either* racial group, or finding acceptance in either group.

Prejudice can be the outcome as the child's attitudes and preferences grow more rigid. However, children can emerge into adolescence and young

Children form racial concepts through their ongoing interactions with peers and adults.

© Cengage Learning

adulthood free of the limiting and distorted perspectives that ultimately lay the foundation for hurtful social behavior. To do so, they must be challenged appropriately to examine their feelings and attitudes, remain open to new information, and have opportunities to become familiar with and enjoy interacting with a variety of people.

Inclusion of Children with Exceptional Needs naeyc

Another potentially vulnerable group of children in educational settings includes those who are disabled in one way or another. Although it has been estimated that approximately 10% of all children have exceptional needs, disabilities, and/or developmental delays, it is difficult to determine an exact number. Some disabling conditions, such as Down syndrome, cerebral palsy, missing body parts, and severe visual or speech impairments, are easy to spot. Others, such as mild or moderate emotional impairment or learning disabilities, are more difficult to determine. When including children with exceptional needs in the everyday classroom, it is often the latter disabilities—those that are more "invisible"—that are not as readily embraced by other children and adults in the setting.

Because of the remarkable advances in medical technology, greater numbers of children born with disabling conditions are surviving and eventually entering our childcare and educational systems, many requiring special services. Although all children have unique needs, children with exceptional needs are those whose well-being, development, and learning would be hampered if needed support in terms of adjusting the environment is not provided in the early years.

A study of teacher candidates' perceptions about inclusion (Horne & Timmons, 2009) indicated that although they held positive self-perceptions about their beliefs, attitudes, and knowledge related to inclusion of children with disabilities, they worried about planning time and about meeting the needs of all children, and felt they needed ongoing professional training to "make it work" in the regular classroom.

One of the first steps in professional preparation to provide for effective inclusion is to be aware of our own stereotypes. Are we inclined to look negatively on those who are overweight, too short, more ragged and dirty than other children, who speak "funny," are timid, physically weak, pimply, or "too" smart? What about our reaction to children who are not yet toilet-trained, those who take longer to catch on to simple information or routines, or who come from "problem" families (Honig, 2004)?

Given the comprehensive services provided today to children with disabling conditions, it is difficult to believe that prior to 1975, many American children with impairments were denied enrollment in public schools. Between 1960 and 1975, various states in the United States had begun to recognize the benefits of providing early intervention and were pushing for federal support. This came in the form of Public Law 94-142, the Education for All Handicapped Children Act (later renamed in 1990 as the Individuals with Disabilities Education Act or IDEA). It provides services for children between the ages of 3 and 21, but focuses largely on children 6 years of age or older. In 1986, Public Law 99-457 was enacted, enlarging the scope of PL 99-142 with a downward extension that now ensures services for all children with disabilities, including at-risk infants and toddlers with handicapping conditions and special needs (Part H) and preschoolers in need of services (Part B). Also, in 1990,

PL 101-476 added the categories of autism and traumatic brain injuries for the purposes of part B.

Assistance for Education of Children with Disabilities mandates the following:

1. The state will guarantee a free, appropriate public education to all eligible children with disabilities, "including children with disabilities who have been suspended or expelled from school."

2. The state will ensure that each child with a disability receives an **Individualized Education Program (IEP)**.

3. The state and local education agencies will place children with disabilities in settings that also serve children without disabilities to the extent that such placements do not compromise the right of children with disabilities to receive an appropriate education that meets their unique needs.

4. The state will act to protect the due-process rights of children with disabilities and their parents.

5. The state will take whatever steps are necessary to ensure an adequate supply of special educators and related services personnel.

6. The state will set "performance goals and indicators" for improving special education, particularly in the areas of district-wide assessments of academic performance. (Bowe, 2007, p. 117)

Council for Exceptional Children (CEC) Standards of Professional and Ethical Practice for Teachers of Children with Disabilities

While there are comprehensive federal and state guidelines for services provided to children with disabilities, in October 2011, the Council for Exceptional Children (CEC) developed standards of professional and ethical practice for teachers. Teachers of children with exceptional needs are expected to do the following:

- Systematically individualize instructional variables to maximize the learning outcomes of individuals with exceptionalities.

- Identify and use evidence-based practices that are appropriate to their professional preparation and are most effective in meeting the individual needs of individuals with exceptionalities.

- Use periodic assessments to accurately measure the learning progress of individuals with exceptionalities, and individualize instruction variables in response to assessment results.

- Create safe, effective, and culturally responsive learning environments that contribute to fulfillment of needs, stimulation of learning, and realization of positive self-concepts.

- Participate in the selection and use of effective and culturally responsive instructional materials, equipment, supplies, and other resources appropriate to their professional roles.

- Use culturally and linguistically appropriate assessment procedures that accurately measure what is intended to be measured, and do not discriminate against individuals with exceptional or culturally diverse learning needs.

- Only use behavior change practices that are evidence-based, appropriate to their preparation, and that respect the culture, dignity, and basic human rights of individuals with exceptionalities.

- Support the use of positive behavior supports and conform to local policies relating to the application of disciplinary methods and behavior change procedures, except when the policies require their participation in corporal punishment.

- Refrain from using aversive techniques unless the target of the behavior change is vital, repeated trials of more positive and less restrictive methods have failed, and only after appropriate consultation with parents and appropriate agency officials.

- Do not engage in the corporal punishment of individuals with exceptionalities.

- Report instances of unprofessional or unethical practice to the appropriate supervisor.

- Recommend special education services necessary for a child with an exceptional learning need to receive an appropriate education.

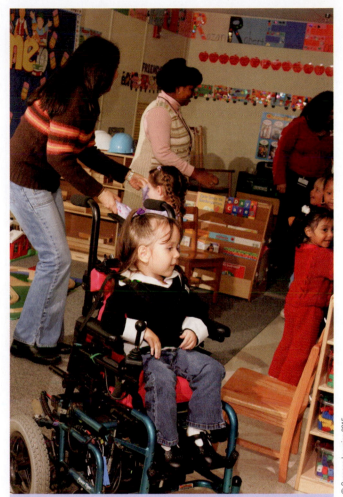

A special focus must be directed toward specifically organized and adjusted environments for children with special needs.

© Cengage Learning 2015

Developing Individualized Family Service Programs (IFSPs) and Individualized Education Programs (IEPs)

Like other families, those who have children with exceptional needs have hopes and aspirations for their children that need to be encouraged and enabled. An **individualized family service program (IFSP)** developed for children from birth to 3 years is meant to do just that. It requires a highly collaborative process between the family and a service coordinator to identify and organize the most effective resources available to support a child's optimal development. This is an example of where the more intensive, individualized support depicted in the Social Support Pyramid

in Chapter 1 must be applied (see Figure 14-2). If the plan is to fulfill its promise, it must include a family-directed assessment of the family's resources, priorities, and concerns. At every step in the ongoing process, it must also be respectful of the family's beliefs and values (Cook, Klein, & Tessier, 2008).

Forms for the IFSP differ from state to state and area to area, but they usually include outcome statements for each of the following:

- The family's strengths and preferred resources (e.g., a preference for home-based services versus center-based services)

- The family's concerns and priorities

- The child's strengths and present levels of development

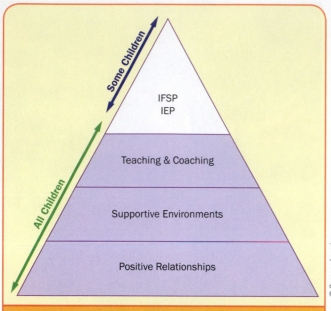

Figure 14-2 Social Support Pyramid: Fostering Healthy Attitudes about Sexuality and Diversity.

- IFSP outcomes (e.g., goals the family would like to work on in the next 6 months that are directly related to their stated priorities and concerns)
- A transition plan to the next set of services
- Statement of eligibility
- Family permission for implementation of the plan (signatures)
- A list of the IFSP participants

The Individualized Education Programs (IEP)

An IEP is a written plan for children older than 3 years of age, and it broadens the collaboration beyond family members, the service coordinator, and those persons directly providing services to the child. It usually includes a multidisciplinary assessment team to determine the appropriate educational goals and objectives for a child. Usually included are at least one general education teacher (if the process is based on inclusion), at least one special education teacher or provider, any other member of the school staff required to meet the child's unique needs, an individual who can match evaluation outcomes to specific instructional strategies, the school administrator, and other individuals whose expertise is valued by the parent or school, such as a childcare provider.

Required contents of an IEP are as follows:

- A statement of the child's present levels of educational performance (based on results of norm-referenced and criterion-referenced tests)
- A statement of annual goals and related benchmarks or short-term behavioral objectives
- A statement of the specific education and related services and supplementary aids to be provided for the child, and a statement of the program modifications or supports for school personnel that will be provided
- An explanation of the extent, if any, that the child will not participate with typically developing peers in the regular classroom

---

CHALLENGING BEHAVIOR

Social Goal for Gavin, a Kindergarten Child with Down Syndrome: Eating Snack at the Table

Current situation: Gavin has been unwilling to join the other children at the table at snack time and insists on eating while sitting on the floor. When encouraged to join the other children, he dissolves into a tantrum. When asked about eating behaviors at home, his parents admit that they allow him to eat while sitting on the floor in order to avoid his tantrums. Gavin has no hearing problems, understands language at an age-related developmental level, follows two-step directions, and does other tasks at the table without difficulty.

Teacher Strategy to Implement on 1/11/10: Gavin will be encouraged to make a choice between sitting at a table at snack time or waiting for lunchtime to eat. He may sit at a table by himself or with the other children but having snack will require him to sit at a table and not on the floor.

If he has a tantrum, it will be ignored other than keeping him and other children safe. When he is calm, the opportunity to have a snack while sitting at a table will again be offered.

Parent Strategy to Implement on 1/11/10: Parents will also give Gavin a choice between eating at the table or not having a snack. A tantrum will be ignored, and when he is calm, a snack at the table will be offered again. No snack will be provided if he is unwilling to sit at the table.

Reevaluate on 1/18/10 with parents: If he is eating snack at the table, wait for two more weeks to have him internalize the behavior and then require that he sit at the table for all meals.

- The projected dates for initiation of services and the anticipated frequency, location, and duration of services
- The appropriate objective criteria and evaluation procedures
- The schedule for determining whether the short-term instructional objectives are being achieved (each child's program must be reevaluated at least once each year) (Cook et al., 2008)

Categories of Disabling Conditions

A disability is not necessarily a handicap and becomes one only when the child experiences a problem functioning or interacting in the environment because of the impairment. We want to emphasize that children with exceptional needs are individuals with as much variety in ability and personality as typically developing children. Also, because they may have more than one disability, impairment, or compromised health condition, precise diagnosis is often difficult. Disabling conditions are categorized in various ways depending on whether the categorizing group is medically, educationally, or legislatively oriented. The highest incident of disabilities

in school-age children is that of learning disabilities, constituting almost half of all disabilities. The major categories that seem most useful to teachers, parents, and childcare personnel are those that have been outlined by the National Dissemination Center for Children with Disabilities (NICHCY) and IDEA. These can be seen in Digital Download 14-2, and include the following:

- **Autism Spectrum Disorders**
- **Deaf-Blindness**
- **Deafness**
- **Developmental Delay**
- **Emotional Disturbance**
- **Hearing Impairment**
- **Intellectual Disability**
- **Multiple Disabilities**
- **Orthopedic Impairment**
- **Other Health Impairment**
- **Specific Learning Disability**
- **Speech or Language Impairment**
- **Traumatic Brain Injury**
- **Visual Impairment, Including Blindness**

Categories of Disabilities

1. **Autism Spectrum Disorders** include developmental disabilities significantly affecting verbal and nonverbal communication and social interaction, generally evident before age 3, that adversely affect a child's educational performance. Characteristics often associated with autism are engaging in repetitive activities and stereotyped movements, resistance to environmental change or change in daily routines, and unusual responses to sensory experiences. The term autism does not apply if the child's educational performance is adversely affected primarily because the child has an emotional disturbance, as defined in #5 below. A child who shows the characteristics of autism after age 3 could be diagnosed as having autism if the criteria above are satisfied. Children within the spectrum differ greatly in the severity of their condition. For example, in Asperger's syndrome, a fairly mild form of autism, children have normal language skills and average or above-average intelligence; however, social interaction and social cognition (e.g., perspective taking) are problematic (Ormrod, 2011).

2. **Deaf-Blindness** means concomitant (simultaneous) hearing and visual impairments, the combination of which causes such severe communication and other

developmental and educational needs that cannot be accommodated in special education programs solely for children with deafness or children with blindness.

3. **Deafness** is a hearing impairment so severe that a child is impaired in processing linguistic information through hearing, with or without amplification, which adversely affects a child's educational performance.

4. **Developmental Delay** for children from birth to age 3 (under IDEA Part C) and children from ages 3 through 9 (under IDEA Part B), as defined by each state, means a delay in one or more of the following areas: physical development, cognitive development, communication, social or emotional development, or adaptive (behavioral) development.

5. **Emotional Disturbance** means a condition exhibiting one or more of the following characteristics over a long period of time and to a marked degree that adversely affects a child's educational performance:

   (a) An inability to learn that cannot be explained by intellectual, sensory, or health factors

   (b) An inability to build or maintain satisfactory interpersonal relationships with peers and teachers

(c) Inappropriate types of behavior or feelings under normal circumstances

(d) A general pervasive mood of unhappiness or depression

(e) A tendency to develop physical symptoms or fears associated with personal or school problems

The term includes schizophrenia. The term does not apply to children who are socially maladjusted, unless it is determined that they have an emotional disturbance.

6. **Hearing Impairment** is an impairment in hearing, whether permanent or fluctuating, that adversely affects a child's educational performance but is not included under the definition of "deafness."

7. **Intellectual Disability** is characterized as significantly subaverage general intellectual functioning, existing concurrently (at the same time) with deficits in adaptive behavior and manifested during the developmental period, which adversely affects a child's educational performance. Note that "Intellectual Disability" is a new term in IDEA. Until October 2010, the law used the term "mental retardation." In October 2010, Rosa's Law was signed into law by President Obama. Rosa's Law changed the term to be used in the future to "intellectual disability." The definition of the term itself did not change and is what has just been shown above.

8. **Multiple Disabilities** are concomitant (simultaneous) impairments (such as intellectual disability-blindness, intellectual disability-orthopedic impairment, etc.), the combination of which causes such severe educational needs that they cannot be accommodated in a special education program solely for one of the impairments. The term does not include deaf-blindness.

9. **Orthopedic Impairment** means a severe orthopedic impairment that adversely affects a child's educational performance. The term includes impairments caused by a congenital anomaly, impairments caused by disease (e.g., poliomyelitis, bone tuberculosis), and impairments from other causes (e.g., cerebral palsy, amputations, and fractures or burns that cause contractures).

10. **Other Health Impairment** means having limited strength, vitality, or alertness, including a heightened alertness to environmental stimuli, that results in limited alertness with respect to the educational environment, that:

(a) is due to chronic or acute health problems such as asthma, attention deficit disorder or attention deficit hyperactivity disorder, diabetes, epilepsy, a heart condition, hemophilia, lead poisoning, leukemia, nephritis, rheumatic fever, sickle cell anemia, and Tourette's syndrome; and

(b) adversely affects a child's educational performance.

11. **Specific learning disability** is a disorder in one or more of the basic psychological processes involved in understanding or in using language, spoken or written, that may manifest itself in the imperfect ability to listen, think, speak, read, write, spell, or to do mathematical calculations. The term includes such conditions as perceptual disabilities, brain injury, minimal brain dysfunction, dyslexia, and developmental aphasia. The term does not include learning problems that are primarily the result of visual, hearing, or motor disabilities; of intellectual disability; of emotional disturbance; or of environmental, cultural, or economic disadvantage.

12. **Speech or Language Impairment** is a communication disorder such as stuttering, impaired articulation, a language impairment, or a voice impairment that adversely affects a child's educational performance.

13. **Traumatic Brain Injury** is an acquired injury to the brain caused by an external physical force, resulting in total or partial functional disability or psychosocial impairment, or both, that adversely affects a child's educational performance. The term applies to open or closed head injuries resulting in impairments in one or more areas, such as cognition; language; memory; attention; reasoning; abstract thinking; judgment; problem-solving; sensory, perceptual, and motor abilities; psychosocial behavior; physical functions; information processing; and speech. The term does not apply to brain injuries that are congenital or degenerative, or to brain injuries induced by birth trauma.

14. **Visual Impairment, Including Blindness** means an impairment in vision that, even with correction, adversely affects a child's educational performance. The term includes both partial sight and blindness.

Digital Download Download from CourseMate

Source: National Dissemination Center for Children with Disabilities (NICHCY) (2012).

Children with attention-deficit/hyperactivity disorder (ADHD). ADHD, a neurobehavioral syndrome, is the most common reason for referral of children to pediatricians, educational specialists, and child mental health professionals (Glanzman & Blum, 2007). With- out a doubt, there has been a dramatic and troubling increase in the numbers of young children diagnosed in this category, with more than 4 million children being seen in pediatric clinics and almost 2 million taking stimulant medication to control their behavior.

Although a specific cause has not been firmly established, it is thought that the inattention that characterizes ADHD is caused by a malfunction in the brain's executive system. This, in turn, interferes with the child's willpower and ability to regulate his or her behavior and deal with challenging tasks (Bramer, 2006). A biochemical theory suggests that there may be a problem in the reticular activating system of the brain so that neurotransmitters fail to fire unless medication is given to stimulate them. Because it is often seen in parent and child, there is some evidence of a genetic link. Little evidence supports theories that diet is an important factor or that psychogenic or family dynamics cause the disorder.

While ADHD itself is not listed as a disability under IDEA, children with ADHD are twice as likely to be diagnosed as learning disabled (LD), making them eligible for special education. Others are made eligible for services under Section 504 of the Rehabilitation Act. According to the American Psychiatric Association's Diagnostic and Statistical Manual of Mental Disorders (DSM-IV), the essential feature of ADHD is a "persistent pattern of inattention and/or hyperactivity-impulsivity that is more frequent and severe than is typically observed in individuals at a comparable level of development." The four criteria for diagnosis are listed here:

1. Some symptoms must have been present before age 7.
2. Some impairment must be present in at least two settings (e.g., home/school).
3. There must be clear evidence of interference with developmentally appropriate social, academic, or occupational functioning.
4. The disturbance does not occur exclusively during the course of other specific disorders.

Symptoms of inattention include difficulty in organizing task and activities, being easily distracted, or inability to sustain attention.

According to the Center for Disease Control, in 2010, 8.4% of children or 5.2 million between the ages of 3 and 17 were diagnosed with ADHD, most of them receiving some form of medication. Concern about misdiagnosis of the condition is warranted, as there are a number of medication contraindications, including loss of appetite and weight, sleep difficulties, stomachaches, headaches, tics, Tourette's syndrome association, emotional liability and cloudy cognitive ability, height and growth impairments, generalized anxiety, and abuse of the drug.

Overall, in addition to the need for sensitive practitioners, a child's future is more positive if hyperactivity and aggression are a minimal part of the condition, if IQ is higher, and if family strengths are well developed.

Social skills will be an important and powerful predictor of the child's ability to cope and be successful.

It is important to remember that children continue behaviors that work for them. In the case of some of the maladaptive behaviors often seen in children diagnosed with ADHD, such behaviors have a purposeful communication function: "You're asking me to do something that is too difficult. . . . I don't understand what you want. . . . I want a certain thing, and I want it now. . . . I'm bored; pay some attention to me" (Cook et al., 2008).

To help children with ADHD reach maximum potential, strategies include the following:

- Provide more frequent feedback for their behavior than for more typically developing children.
- Consistently provide natural and logical consequences.
- Draw children's attention to the consequences of their actions, and help them identify and state potential consequences of actions.
- Anticipate potential problem situations and communicate with children ahead of time about what may happen and what will be needed from them (e.g., "Jason, when we go into the large gym for assembly, it will be noisier than usual, and there will be many, many children. I will need to have you hold my hand until you are seated to watch the performers, and you will need to stay seated until our class stands to leave the gym").
- Review rules that the child may have trouble following: "Jason, what are the rules for entering the gym? That's right, holding my hand until you are seated and no moving to another spot until we are all ready to go."
- Remember that the child is not purposefully trying to annoy you; because of brain functioning that is different from typically developing children that age, additional support is needed.
- Maintain a predictable daily schedule.
- Give children simple, step-by-step directions when guiding them through activities and routines, and allow ample time for completion of tasks.
- Limit the number of choices and activities offered at one time.
- Document problematic behaviors in a daily log to identify what triggers antisocial behaviors, and modify the classroom to reduce triggers.
- Provide quiet, less distracting areas of the classroom where the child can complete tasks requiring close attending skills.
- Coach children toward self-control by mastering language for expression of feelings and desires,

© Cengage Learning 2015

Children diagnosed with ADHD may exhibit constant "on the go" behavior, fidgeting, and excessive talking.

and provide numerous instances of positive reinforcement.

- Remember that establishing good rapport with children is critical. Forms of positive attention, such as genuine praise, a smile, nod, or pat on the back are some of the most basic but powerful management tools.

- Involve parents; encourage them to be partners in their child's experience. Hold frequent conferences to coordinate classroom practices with home practices. Keep family members fully informed.

- Make and maintain connections to special education personnel when a child's behaviors impact negatively on classroom performance (Miller, 2012; Kostelnik & Grady, 2009).

Children with autism spectrum and Asperger's syndrome disorders. The rise in incidence and prevalence of autism has been called startling, with the Centers for Disease Control and Prevention reporting that autism spectrum disorders in 2006 occurred in 1 out of 110 U.S. children (1 in 70 boys and 1 out of 315 girls). In 2002, the number was reported to be 1 in every 150 children, and the increase cannot be fully accounted for by broader diagnosis or earlier diagnosis (Falco, 2009).

Earlier, there was suspicion that growing rates of **autism** were linked to vaccines given to children, specifically because the vaccines contained thimerosal, which is 50% ethyl mercury. However, mercury has now been removed from the vaccines, and there has been no corresponding decline in the rates of autism (Gurian, 2009). Tragically, we do not currently have an answer, either, to the cause of autism or to the apparent increase.

Though the major causative factor is yet to be determined, research points strongly toward a genetic predisposition and neurological disorder. What is known is that it is a complex, severe pervasive developmental disorder that usually becomes apparent between 18 months and 3 years of age. It is manifested in difficulty in social interaction, communication skills, ritualistic/compulsive behavior, and almost always in impaired intellectual functioning. Symptoms vary widely from child to child, making it difficult to design a standard educational approach. In the social realm, red flags include an inability of a child to read nonverbal clues, not responding when called by name, lack of eye contact, inappropriate responses, a lack of play skills, unreasonable fears in new situations, a resistance to change, a preference for isolated play, little recognition of cause/effect, and lack of facial expression. The child may wander off, unaware of being separated from the group, may not develop empathy for others, may be aggressive and/or destructive toward self and others, and throw unexplained tantrums.

If you are working with children who exhibit the disorder, you will be more successful when you ease the child into new situations. Strategize to capture the child's attention without forcing it. Teach and model social and play skills purposefully, and redirect swiftly by giving clear verbal signals. Distract the child away from negative behaviors, fixations, and withdrawal from others by encouraging involvement in more acceptable activity. It's also very important to coach other children as well. For example, if the child with autism doesn't respond when you call his name, tap him on the shoulder and repeat his name. If other children give up easily, it makes it even more difficult for the child with autism to be included.

Children with **Asperger's syndrome disorder**, a milder form of autism that is often not diagnosed until about age 6, often share many of the same communication, physical/motor, and social/emotional adaptive behaviors as children with autism. However, with Asperger's syndrome, there do not appear to be significant intellectual or language delays (Paasche, Gorrill, & Strom, 2003). Children with Asperger's syndrome often have average or above-average intelligence; yet, because of brain abnormalities (that often go undiagnosed), they frequently have a difficult time making friends and "fitting in." There may also be a tendency to blurt out inappropriately, act in ways their peers find silly or offensive, or completely misinterpret oth-

ers' behaviors and body language. As a result, they can be seen as simply disruptive, disorganized, and poorly socialized when, in fact, they are in need of planned intervention to help them behave in more productive and socially acceptable ways (Ormrod, 2011).

Inclusion

The severity of any of these disabling conditions and the availability of community, school, and family resources will determine whether a child will attend a special school or be included in the social, recreational, and educational activities that other children experience. The purpose of inclusion is twofold: (1) to enhance their social competence so they can later live more comfortably and successfully in the mainstream of society, and (2) to promote the acceptance of children with disabilities through reducing and removing social stigma. Making this a reality requires a collaborative approach with constructive attention to ensuring access to services, developing and enforcing quality assurance standards, and training personnel and administrators in appropriate strategies for meeting the needs of extremely diverse populations of children (Deiner, 2012).

Personnel in public schools, childcare centers, and other programs for children have made great strides in making these mandated "least restrictive environments" as available as possible to children with a

© Cengage Learning 2015

With support, many children with disabilities successfully meld into the mainstream.

variety of disabling conditions. Architectural barriers and problems with transportation and toilet facilities have dramatically improved despite the expense involved. Formal preparation and in-service education for professionals who work primarily with typically developing children now regularly include information and skill training regarding disabling conditions, strategies for supporting the social integration of children, and techniques for modifying curricula for children with exceptional needs. In-service programs to upgrade professional knowledge and skills are increasingly directed toward enhancing professional competencies in classroom management of children with exceptional needs, screening and evaluation, interpretation of clinical reports, agency referral, and the structuring of IEPs and IFSPs.

The challenges you may encounter in the inclusion of children with disabilities will likely be similar to those in racial integration: successfully melding those who are different from the majority into the mainstream. Some children accomplish this with few problems; others experience increased conflict, isolation, and accompanying loss of self-esteem. Placing a student with exceptional needs into the regular classroom can result in both opportunities and risks for the child who is being integrated. If the process is well monitored and structured, it can result in the growth of true understanding and friendships between nondisabled children and the child with exceptional needs. If the process is not well structured and monitored, the child could very well become the victim of inattention, be stereotyped, or be treated in a paternalistic manner—all of which are worse than not including the child in the first place. When skilled professionals truly value inclusion, there is good evidence that all children in the setting—both with exceptional needs and without—have positive experiences in planning and learning with those who one day will be their coworkers and neighbors.

Children's Perceptions of Disabling Conditions

Social acceptance by other children depends not so much on a child's limitations as on individual characteristics such as independence, friendliness, and other social skills. Successful integration also will depend on your ability to structure the environment, paying as much attention to the social dynamics of the integration as to the physical facilitation and curricular aspects. As pointed out earlier, young children are keenly aware of differences in other children and react in a variety of ways when they encounter a child who acts, moves, looks, speaks, or thinks differently. Because young children are still learning the "rules" of life and generalize about the rest of the world from their own experience, they often are strict conformists about what is acceptable and what is not. They tend to explain disabilities in terms of what they already know. Sometimes, their attempts to resolve their own curiosity result in their identifying with the child who has a disabling condition ("When I was a baby, I didn't have any fingers on my hands, either"); creating explanations for a disability (in reference to a 4-year-old classmate who could not walk, "When Cierra grows up, then she'll be able to walk!"); and handling fears about their own intactness by avoiding other children with a disability or making statements such as, "My legs might get broked, too."

Children's Attitudes toward Peers Who Have Special Needs

Young children who have not learned negative social attitudes toward disabling conditions will not automatically reject a child simply on the basis of a disability. They are open to social models portrayed by adults and more apt to learn positive attitudes toward disability when you provide a positive model through your actions, words, nonverbal behaviors, and explanations.

Negative attitudes toward atypical peers exhibited by children aged 5 and older often exist before these children have experiences with mainstreaming. These are natural responses to first impressions and to the labeling process that fosters stigmatization. Acceptance results from mutual interaction and experiences where (1) children have to depend on one another for assistance; (2) feelings of psychological safety are present, and rejection and threat are absent; (3) differences are seen realistically and accepted as natural and okay; and (4) perceptions about working and playing with one another in the setting—no matter what the existing differences—are upbeat and generally rewarding rather than distasteful and unpleasant.

An actual observation of the process of peer acceptance over a period of time was made by a researcher when Chris, a preschooler with a moderate-to-severe hearing loss, was being mainstreamed into a university preschool setting. To date, he had not been well accepted by the other children. Because he chanced to begin a spontaneous play episode that caught the interest of some of the children, he eventually "earned" his way into the group:

March 2. Chris spots a purple cape hanging in the dramatic play area. He puts it on and begins pretending he is a vampire, moving about the room flapping his wings and "scaring" other children. He draws the attention of several other children who decide they, too, want capes so they can be vampires.

"Vampire play" grew in popularity for several days afterward. The head teacher allowed the children to wear the capes about the room instead of confining their play to the dramatic-play corner, which usually was encouraged.

March 7. Cameron takes Chris up to a student teacher, telling her, "I have a whole team of vampires. He's (pointing to Chris) on my team." Cameron then "attacks" a helping adult standing nearby. Chris copies him. Cameron spreads his "wings" over Chris, catching him and saying, "Gotcha, little vampire." He takes him to a locker and puts him inside roughly. Chris tries to "break out." Cameron indicates the other children to Chris and says, "Let's suck their blood." They are joined by David. Cameron catches Chris again, saying to David, "I caught the little bat; I caught the little vampire!" He then lets Chris go, saying to Chris and David, "C'mon, team. We're a whole team."

Chris is definitely a member of the team now and, thus, is on his way to becoming an integrated, mainstreamed member of the class. Should the head teacher have insisted that the play be maintained in the dramatic-play area or asked the boys to play something else "nicer" than vampire play, the moment may have been lost. The fragile nature of the process, chance happenings, and sensitivity on the part of the supervising adults can be seen in a subsequent observation and example of expectations for reworking future interaction with classmates:

March 8. Chris has his "bat cape" on again. It is precious to him, and he searches for it as soon as he enters the room. It has been his key to getting into the group. When he attempts to climb on some larger equipment with it, a student teacher asks him to remove the cape because of safety. He declines to play on the equipment, rather than give up the cape. The student teacher is aware of the cape's importance and does not push the issue. If Chris takes the cape back to the dramatic-play corner while he climbs, someone else may take it, and he will have lost his key.

In classrooms where teachers are open to and encourage child-initiated activity, children's naturally evolving play can sometimes be more powerful than

Teachers may need to consult with other professionals about particular disabilities or special needs.

our carefully planned activities to foster peer acceptance and appreciation of children with disabilities:

Because Chris's classmates were curious about the hearing aids he wore, the teacher set up a display of vibrating objects on one of the tables, including a tuning fork and xylophone, which she invited the children to examine. While she was working with some of the children and the tuning fork, Chris began looking at the xylophone, which also was a wheeled toy that could be pulled with a string. Instead of using the striking mallet on the toy, he put the xylophone on the floor and began pulling it across the room, marching as he went. Several atypical children fell in line after him, marching and singing, "Down by the station, early in the morning . . ." The children who had been observing the tuning fork activity also fell in line, leaving the teacher and her carefully constructed display of vibrating objects in favor of the march.

Guidelines for Integrating Children with Disabling Conditions into Formal Group Settings

The quality of the integrative process will differ significantly depending on the extent to which you make the additional effort needed to go beyond the mere maintenance of students with exceptional needs in the nonspecialized setting.

The skills you must master as a teacher in dealing with common variations among typically developing children are needed even more when dealing with those who have exceptional needs. Admittedly, each situation may be so different that it will call for you to educate yourself on the particular disability and to seek advice from a consultant teacher. However, there are some very general considerations for supporting commonly experienced disabilities, as can be seen in Table 14-3. There is no set formula for successful inclusion. What is clear is that it must be made a priority by the administrators, parents, and professionals who are involved.

The Impact of Precocious Behavior, Shyness, and Difficult Temperament on Children's Social Development naeyc

Disabling conditions are not the only differences that present challenges for developing children in educational settings. Less attention is paid frequently to providing the support needed by advanced and precocious children, children who are truly gifted, those who are excessively shy, and those who exhibit difficult temperament.

Advanced and Precocious Children

Over the years, Harvard psychologist Howard Gardner has made us more sensitive to children's multi-learning capabilities and the fact that some children will be more highly developed than others in any one of the eight multiple intelligences described in Chapter 1. Such individuals may be termed **precocious children**. These individual differences may result in noticeable limitations, average abilities, or advanced development because of a rich variety of educational and family experiences, precocious development, or "gifted and talented" characteristics.

Giftedness has been defined as the brain's ability to integrate functions in an accelerated manner, and is present when a person is especially precocious in one area, has a drive to master that area, and thinks in unusual ways about that area (Conklin & Frei, 2007). Adults can use the following guidelines when trying to assess whether a child is truly gifted, talented, or has some kind of outstanding potential (Ormrod, 2011, p. 172):

- Advanced vocabulary, language, and reading skills
- Extensive general knowledge about the world
- Ability to learn more quickly, easily, and independently than peers
- Advanced and efficient cognitive processes and learning strategies
- Considerable flexibility in ideas and approaches to tasks
- High standards for performance (sometimes to the point of unhealthy perfectionism)
- High motivation to accomplish challenging tasks; boredom during easy tasks
- Positive self-concept, especially with regard to academic endeavors
- Above-average social development and emotional adjustment (although a few extremely gifted students may have difficulties because they are so *very* different from their peers)

Gifted learners are quite different from children who are obviously bright. For example, the bright child knows the answers, but the gifted learner asks the questions. The bright child has good ideas and works hard, but the gifted learner may have wild and silly ideas, play around, and yet test well. Bright children still enjoy playing with peers, but the gifted child frequently prefers adults. We also need to remember that bright children are often pleased with their own learning, but gifted children can be highly self-critical, have strong feelings and opinions, and be quite intense (Allen & Cowdery, 2012).

Obviously, not all children who seem advanced are truly gifted or talented, but practitioners must be

Table 14-3   Supporting Commonly Experienced Disabilities

Orthopedic Impairments and Developmental Disabilities

1. The pace of classroom activity may need to be adjusted.
2. Position children so they can feel as secure, comfortable, and involved as possible in activities and routines.
3. Make space adjustments as necessary to address safety issues and facilitate freedom of movement.
4. Support, encourage, and facilitate interactions with materials and equipment while accepting levels of interaction that are appropriate for each individual.
5. Protect children who are not mobile or cannot speak from loud noises and other sensory discomforts.
6. Adapt materials, toys, and utensils for easier use (e.g., nonskid materials, larger handles, Velcro, or magnetic blocks).

Emotional/Behavioral Challenges

1. Teach clear, consistent, predictable limits.
2. Make explanations brief and direct.
3. Model behaviors you want to establish.
4. Provide "retreat" spaces.
5. Provide very concrete cues for transitions.
6. Build children's vocabularies to express feelings.
7. Observe interactions and behaviors closely to prevent provocations.
8. Reduce noise and movement as necessary and be aware of individual stimulation thresholds.

Visual Impairments

1. Minimize clutter.
2. Familiarize the child with the environment.
3. Help the child use auditory or tactile clues to increase independence.
4. Support, encourage, and facilitate interactions with peers.
5. Place materials within reach and increase cues such as texture, smell, and high contrast to make toys and objects more identifiable.

Children's Strengths

1. Support successes by giving approval without distracting the child from a task.
2. Break tasks into smaller steps and scaffold learning.
3. Provide for open-ended play and exploration but be ready to model, stimulate, and encourage.
4. Support child–child interaction and facilitate child–object involvement.
5. Allow for extra time to complete tasks and for practice.
6. Encourage children to stay engaged while working toward mastery of a task.

Hearing Impairments

1. Use multisensory cues (tactile, visual, good lighting, picture cues) and optimal positioning of materials for sight.
2. Check hearing aids and batteries daily.
3. Capitalize on residual auditory abilities (e.g., use a bell).
4. Use simple sign language with all children in the room.

Source: Based on Gonzalez-Mena, 2007.

alert for children who demonstrate these characteristics. Because young children are in the process of developing their abilities and capabilities in many areas, there is a real danger that children may be tagged as either "slow" or "advanced" when time and further observation of their development may prove the diagnosis is untrue (McAfee & Leong, 2010). In addition, cognitive "gifts" in one area may occasionally come at the cost of proficiency in other developmental areas. Some of the world's brightest and most talented individuals, including Albert Einstein, Thomas Edison, Lewis Carroll, Winston Churchill, Jay Leno, Whoopi Goldberg, and Tom Cruise, were,

in fact, thought to be seriously "learning disabled" in their early years. None of these individuals' strong interests and needs as children were recognized; instead, they were overlooked by adults who equated intellectual prowess, giftedness, and talent with conformity, neatness, good behavior, rapid learning, and early maturation.

When children appear truly advanced in one area, there is always the temptation to believe they are generally advanced in all areas, and this may not be so. Children who are large for their age, have well-developed vocabularies, or who are more cognitively sophisticated than their peers are sometimes expected by adults to excel in *all* areas and are reprimanded when they fall short.

Rather than placing advanced and precocious children in specialized settings, heterogeneous grouping that allows for diverse abilities and variety in developmental growth patterns, cultures, languages, temperaments, and individual needs is the strongest model for nurturing human development (Wallace et al., 2005). The best approach for supporting the potential of any child with special needs, whether delayed or advanced, is to pair that child with a professional who is highly knowledgeable about child development and skill emergence in young children and well trained in developing effective programming for a range of abilities in a group of young children. Best practice—whether for children with special needs, average abilities, or advanced capabilities—involves providing engaging, interdisciplinary experiences in all areas of developing intelligences and respecting the experiential and developmental differences children bring with them into any context.

Excessively Shy Children

Almost all children will exhibit shyness at some point in their lives. About 20% of children are inherently shy, however, and another 20% develop shyness because of situational happenings in family life such as a divorce or a move. Thus, it is a personality style shared by a sizeable number, ranging on a spectrum from only moderately shy to severely shy (Adelman, 2007). Children who have this personality style are fairly easy to spot. They may avoid eye contact in order to reduce the tension they feel in being around others who are unfamiliar. They may hide or cry when encountering a new situation or act as if the situation does not even exist—or occasionally explode into an unpredictable temper tantrum to release their anxiety. Though normally talkative around family and friends with whom they are comfortable, they can "shut down" almost completely in less familiar contexts, refusing to speak or answering only in monosyllables to questions from others. Shy children may go without what they need or want, rather than summon up the courage to make a simple request. They experience a variety of uncomfortable responses when they feel they are "on stage"—flushing of their skin, dry mouth, stomachaches, and stage fright that may be so severe that it interferes with their ability to demonstrate their true abilities.

Shy children may also be hypersensitive to even the smallest slights from others, whether imagined or real. While they would like to escape from others in social situations, they also long to be as well liked and socially competent as other children. Unfortunately, their tendency to misinterpret social signals from others often leads to feelings of being left out, incorrect perspectives about how others view them, and eventually true shunning by other children.

Although it may be impossible to eliminate shyness altogether in such children, it is useful to help them become more aware of the connections between self-talk and their emotional responses. Self-talk is the constant "background talk" that goes on in the brain in any particular situation, and it can range from highly negative to highly positive. Shy children and adults tend to bombard themselves with negative self-talk in negotiating stressful events. When we experience any kind of perceived threat or demand, within milliseconds, we automatically connect it to our perceived resources to handle it. Thus, the child who has to give a report in front of his classmates and realizes he is anxious and inhibited about it can be taught to recognize when negative self-talk is taking over ("I can't do this because I'll forget what I'm saying, and everyone will laugh at me!"), which increases anxiety and diminishes his self-confidence in the situation.

Learning to imagine or pretend and practice thinking about successful outcomes rather than dwelling on the worst possible scenario are also helpful. Shy children can be given helpful scripts that can get them through the initial stages of situations that are particularly stressful for them—entering an ongoing playgroup, meeting new people, and asking for what they need. It is also important to debrief about situations that were particularly difficult for them, to focus on any successes they had, and to plan for ways they can restructure similar experiences in the future in order to be more comfortable, thereby increasing their self-confidence and social competence (Adelman, 2007).

Temperament and Individuality

As children become increasingly aware of ways in which they differ from others, they begin to evaluate the meanings of these differences through a value-plus and value-deficit lens. Evolving self-identity depends a great deal on self-esteem. This, in turn, results from clues received from others in response to their behavior and developing abilities.

Children who are perceived by others to be extremely challenging often have temperamental characteristics that place them at extreme ends of a normal continuum of behavior responses. They appear predisposed to be more negative in mood, more

Labeling a child as "difficult" can be damaging.

impulsive or unpredictable, and given to more intense reactions when under stress. They may also have a tendency to withdraw or explode when confronted with unfamiliar people, activities, or stimuli. These unique characteristics, which begin as inherited traits, may be somewhat modified over time in a more positive direction or become established behavioral patterns that place such children in a special-needs category. The outcome will depend on the particular combination of difficult traits and how long an established pattern has existed. When behavior is extreme, an intensive individualized intervention may be called for (refer to Table 14-3).

Children who have difficult temperaments have greater potential to be classified as having ADHD or autism, due to their extreme behavior. In the case of Adam, his parents had been to a series of professionals who disagreed about the causes of his behavior. The parents had rejected advice from those who suggested that Adam had become increasingly defiant and oppositional because he was allowed and "encouraged" to be and that changing his behavior would require them to change their way of "handling him." Though there had been no definitive assessment that would document any brain disorganization that was causative (e.g., fMRI or a PET scan), Adam's parents had excused his explosiveness as something he just couldn't control and had continued with their pattern of avoiding any confrontations with him. Keys that had gone unnoticed were that he really wanted to make friends with other children in the classroom and clearly wanted to be in school. He also had age-appropriate language skills. The professionals in his new school saw those

CHALLENGING BEHAVIOR

Meet Adam

Adam, a 5-year-old, had been diagnosed as autistic and had already been dismissed from two preschool programs because he was unpredictable and violent toward other children and adults. He seemed to enjoy shoving other children down on the playground without any apparent provocation, and he frequently hit without warning in the classroom when he wanted something another child had and was challenged by that child. When adults tried to redirect his behavior, a full-blown temper tantrum resulted, requiring restraint by an adult in order to protect others from his fury. Adam's parents admitted that they "walked on eggshells" around him, doing anything to avoid these tantrums and often gave in to what he asked for or

ignored his unresponsiveness to their requests because they didn't want to confront him. They had been doing so since he first began throwing the tantrums at age 2. His mother shared that she was "at the end of her rope" and was worn out trying to effect any change in his behavior. Fortunately, because teachers in his new school were skilled in working with parents as partners to increase a child's ability to regulate his behavior, Adam began to make progress both at home and in the classroom. It was not an overnight change and required ongoing patience and persistence on the part of all the adults in his life; Adam's responses, however, provided evidence that the situation was not "hopeless" as his parents had thought earlier.

characteristics as contrary to the autism diagnosis, and that's when Adam's hopeful future began.

Some scientists question the desirability of labeling children "difficult." They maintain that such identification may not be valid; it can, in fact, be damaging, given a caregiver's resulting expectations for such children. Reality reminds us, however, that although serious issues continue to surround valid assessment of difficult temperament, there is no question that certain children are far more challenging than others. Whether their difficulties are a reflection of their own constitutional characteristics, disturbed caregiver–child interactions, or other environmental stressors, the fact remains that difficult traits do appear early in some young children. Equally important is our knowledge that difficult behavior may be modified or intensified by life experiences. The child, as an active agent in his or her own socialization, plays an important part in flavoring those experiences.

Important "others" in a child's life also play ongoing roles in the dynamic unfolding of his or her individual personality. This concept of mutual influence is important. When children are difficult to handle, less confident caregivers often develop self-doubts, feelings of guilt, and anxiety over what the future holds for the child and their relationship with the child. Unless difficult behaviors, or caregivers' perceptions of those behaviors, can be satisfactorily modified, a sense of

helplessness often begins to pervade all interactions with the child. Dreams of being a competent parent or teacher may yield to the hard reality that the child is unhappy, out of control, and moving in a negative direction developmentally. Attitudes toward the difficult behavior may move swiftly from early amusement or pride over a child's "assertiveness" to disapproval and even rejection by the adult.

Adult responses, in turn, have a marked effect on whether additional stress will be imposed on the child or whether the child will be guided successfully toward developing greater self-regulation and more positive coping behaviors. Positive, respectful interaction, which builds resiliency and inner strength in all children, is absolutely essential for children who have difficulty with adaptive interaction. Caregivers who acknowledge that diverse temperament patterns do exist but who persist in encouraging healthier behaviors in a sensitive and supportive way bolster children's protective factors that enhance their development. They help children understand cause and effect, become better problem solvers, and view themselves and others in a more positive light (Gonzalez-Mena & Eyer, 2012).

Now consider all you have learned as you read the following skills designed to translate theory into practical strategies. These skills will help you progress from knowing to doing.

SKILLS FOR FOSTERING HEALTHY ATTITUDES ABOUT SEXUALITY AND DIVERSITY naeyc

Communicating with Children about Sexuality and Diversity

1. **Become acquainted with persons of varying cultural, religious, racial, and developmental backgrounds, and use some of the following experiences to broaden your understanding:**

   - Participate in community, social, or cultural events that represent different groups.

   - Find ways to become personally acquainted with at least one family of each racial and cultural group in your community.

   - Go beyond seeking information only related to foods and holidays.

   - Find out as much as possible about subtle social conventions that sometimes cause

   irritation when not understood: concepts of family, time, nature, gender roles, aesthetics, ecology, dress, and safety (Trawick-Smith, 2013).

   - Take advantage of opportunities to broaden your familiarity with other groups through ethnic festivals, community-awareness programs involving those with disabilities, or open events sponsored by religious groups other than your own.

   - Seek out establishments in your area, such as stores and restaurants that offer artifacts and food representative of particular cultures.

   - Look for organizations and institutions in your community that focus on international programs.

- Visit a medical supply store that caters to the disabled, and examine the different equipment that some individuals use to function more effectively.

- Volunteer in programs in which you are likely to interact with people who are different from yourself.

- Explore your own background and culture.

- Relate your differences to those of other groups in order to better understand and value similarities and differences.

- Pay careful attention to your nonverbal behaviors as well. If you find yourself drawing away, making a face, or avoiding eye contact with a child who falls into any of the categories discussed or to one who brings up sensitive subjects, stop.

- Watch out for any tendency on your part to blame whole groups of people for what individuals do, and demand proof when you hear children repeat rumors that reflect on any group.

- Do not tell stories, however funny, that reflect on any group, and do not laugh when others tell them. Show disapproval when others use hateful terms that slur any group.

- Monitor your verbal responses, making sure you do not dismiss or deny children's feelings and verbal expressions of these feelings.

- Discuss situations that are difficult for you with a colleague or classmate as a way to clarify your own attitudes as well as to elicit further suggestions.

2. **Build a positive social climate in which both similarities and differences are valued.**

- Emphasize that each person has something valuable and unique to contribute to the group.

- Take advantage of the many children's books about individual differences as well as puppet play, films, videotapes, and filmstrips to promote growth in the understanding of others.

- Use resource people from the community, including those with varying racial and ethnic origins and disabling conditions.

- Take advantage of video technology to allow children to visit other countries and explore differing lifestyles without leaving the classroom.

- Foster positive attitudes and attitude changes in school-age children through role-playing and disability simulations. For example, wheelchairs can be borrowed from equipment companies to allow students to understand the difficulty involved in maneuvering a wheelchair. Glasses can be made with layers of yellow cellophane to simulate visual impairment. One creative teacher had a student who was visually impaired demonstrate her ability to get around the room and explain the kinds of cues in the room on which she relied for help. Students then were blindfolded and, with the help of another student to keep them safe, tried their luck at negotiating the same path, relying not on their sight but on the cues their classmates had identified.

3. **Build a cooperative rather than competitive spirit within the group by purposely planning activities that will highlight, at one time or another, the skills of all children in the program.**

- Discuss similarities between people. We all need friends, we all have similar emotions, and we all have both positive and negative qualities.

- Encourage children to rely on one another and to seek each other's help in solving problems rather than depending on the adults in the setting.

- Use small, heterogeneous groups to foster the development of acceptance, rapport, and mutual understanding among children of different racial, ethnic, and developmental backgrounds.

- Structure activities in which children have opportunities to establish eye contact, talk with one another, and develop common goals. Provide needed support to guide these groups toward success.

4. **Address children's stereotypical remarks directly and in a nonjudgmental manner.** When children make stereotypical remarks such as, "Only boys can be doctors," help them develop more accurate understandings by using the following strategies:

- Challenge children by using open-ended questions. ("Why do you think only boys can be doctors?")

- Provide accurate information in matter-of-fact ways. ("Some doctors are men; some doctors are women.")

- Point out examples to counter children's mistaken ideas. ("Daniel said his doctor is a woman." or "Here is a picture of a woman doctor.")

- Talk over children's ideas in class meetings. ("Jimmy thinks only boys can be doctors. What do you think?")

- Use props that counter stereotypes (e.g., puzzles, pictures, books, and dress-up clothes for both genders). Follow up with field trips or visitors. (Visit a female doctor's office, or have a female doctor visit the classroom.)

5. **Respond thoughtfully to children's questions about sexuality, ethnicity, disabling conditions, and other differences.**

- Listen carefully to determine what it is they really want to know.

- Clarify the question by reflecting before answering. For example, if a child asks the question "Is Timmy still a baby?" about a 7-year-old who cannot walk, you would want to clarify with, "You mean, 'How come Timmy can't walk yet?'"

- After determining the child's purpose, answer the question at a level he or she can understand. Often, in an effort to be comprehensive, adults give children more information than they need or can manage. Give short, precise, clear answers in language that the child understands. Use simple phrases and familiar analogies.

- Check to see what the child thinks you have said by asking him or her to paraphrase your answer. "Tell me in your own words why Sandy talks the way she does." Work from there to expand the child's understanding, if necessary. Do not give more information than children ask for; allow them time to assimilate what already has been said.

- Reassure children when they seem to be overly concerned. Watch for evidence that the child is more comfortable after he or she has been given an explanation. You may have to answer the same question several times for very young or overly fearful children. When questions about another child's physical, ethnic, or developmental differences are repeatedly asked in that child's presence, redirect the curious child to discuss the issue with you privately.

6. **Use correct vocabulary when referring to body parts, cultural groups, or disabling conditions.**

- Words like vagina, penis, and breast describe specific parts of the body, which should be as accurately labeled as other body parts. To do otherwise demeans the body and teaches children that genital organs are not natural but are things to be ashamed of.

- Certain groups prefer to be called by a particular name. For instance, some people prefer to be known as Black Americans, others as African Americans or people of color; some as Indians, some as Native Americans; and some prefer the term Latino whereas others favor Hispanic or Mexican American. Dwarfs prefer to be called little people or dwarfs, not midgets. If you are not sure about the preferences of the families in your group, find out. Similarly, describe a child as having a hearing impairment rather than saying that her ears are broken. In each of these situations, it is better to be truthful and precise when speaking with children than to try to sidestep the sensitive arenas through euphemisms or inaccurate terminology. Rephrase statements made by children using offensive terms.

7. **React calmly to children's sex play.**

- Reflect children's interest in their own bodies and the bodies of others.

- Give them information that will satisfy their curiosity, such as the names of their body parts and how they function.

- Set limits on behavior that is inappropriate or dangerous, such as fondling another child's genitalia, masturbating in public, or putting something in a child's vagina or anus.

8. **Provide natural opportunities for children to learn more about their sexual development.**

- For very young children, the bathroom at the preschool or childcare center is an ideal place to ask questions, observe similarities and differences, and learn that body parts and body functions do not have to be hidden behind closed doors. Allow preschoolers to use the bathroom in one another's presence if they wish.

- Provide dolls with anatomically correct genitalia for them to play with.

- With parents' permission, use books to communicate information to older children.

- Answer questions honestly, and clear up any misunderstandings.

9. **Be as gender fair as possible in your day-to-day interaction with children.**

   - Actively nurture "opposite gender" characteristics to encourage full human development—gentleness, nurturance, cooperation, and communication in males, and courage, competence, and independence in females.

   - Be aware of and avoid adult tendencies that have been documented—that is, tendencies to interrupt girls more frequently when they are speaking and/or providing boys with more help, attention, information, and encouragement to solve problems.

   - Present important concepts in many diverse ways and repeatedly. Encourage visual-spatial activity and logico-mathematical experiences in early childhood for girls (mazes, maps, blocks, geo-boards, and more practice in noting likenesses and differences). These may be helpful in shoring up abilities that are often needed later in fields where few women excel. Similarly, boys may benefit from more active involvement in language activities and experiences, as well as help in stress and conflict management, and intrapersonal and interpersonal skill building.

10. **Remain alert for valuable learning experiences that may be created spontaneously by the children.** At times, children's interactions with materials and with one another capture their interest to such an extent that our own best-laid curricular plans should be laid aside. Assess whether allowing children to deviate from intended activities will allow other learning or needed social adaptations to occur. Sometimes, a spontaneous event can be a far more valuable learning experience than the planned one.

11. **Help children develop pride in their own cultural heritage, language, and traditions.**

    - Pronounce a child's name as his or her family pronounces it rather than anglicizing it.

    - Serve foods that are familiar to the children's particular backgrounds, asking for suggestions and recipes.

    - Allow children to bring in articles that are used in family celebrations and to explain to the group how they are used. Include dress-up clothes from a variety of cultures.

    - As a part of the daily routine, sing songs, tell stories, play games, and engage in other activities that relate to the cultures represented by the children and staff in your group. It is better to integrate such activities into the ongoing curriculum rather than to occasionally have a "Mexico Day" or "Black American Week." The latter approach sensationalizes and makes artificial what, to the culture itself, is just a natural part of living.

12. **If your group is homogeneous, introduce other customs anyway.** It may be best to begin with groups that can be found in the wider community rather than cultures with whom children are unlikely to interact.

13. **If children reject other children because of their gender, ethnicity, or special needs, deal with the situation calmly, using one or more of the following strategies:**

    - Reflect the victim's feelings: "You look really upset, Jerome. It hurt your feelings when Samuel called you a name."

    - Express empathy: "Jerome, I know it hurts when people call us names."

    - Protest: "Samuel, I don't like it when you call Jerome 'four-eyes.' That hurts his feelings."

14. **Give accurate information.** "Jerome is wearing glasses to help him see better."

15. **Describe alternate strategies for expressing feelings.** "You were upset because Jerome bumped into what you were building. It's hard to remember what to say when you're angry. Say, 'I'm angry' instead of calling Jerome the name 'four-eyes.'"

16. **Describe the behavior you expect.** "In our room, we are respectful toward one another. You may tell other people how you feel about something they've done, but you may not call one another hurtful names."

17. **Use rules and consequences to let children know that purposeful slurs and unkind references to particular children or groups will not be tolerated.** If youngsters seem to be using terms such as "homo," "wop," or "honky" without knowing what they mean, provide pertinent rationales for why such behavior is unacceptable to you. When children deliberately use such tactics to wound the self-esteem of another, they are engaging in hostile aggression. This should be stopped with a personal message, warning, and follow-through as necessary, carried out in a calm, matter-of-fact, and firm tone.

18. **Monitor all teaching materials and activities for racial, cultural, gender-role, religious, and developmental stereotypes.**

Continuously watch for ways in which the curriculum may influence children's perceptions of their own or others' roles and abilities. Encourage them to participate in a wide range of enriching activities on the basis of their interests and skills rather than on outmoded ideas.

19. **Assess your classroom environment for antibias and culturally relevant materials. Ask yourself:**

   - What groups are represented by pictures and photographs displayed (e.g., race, culture, gender, family structures, lifestyles, age, physical disabilities)? Is any one group dominant? Do they represent real or stereotyped individuals? Are they contemporary or historical?

   - What genders and cultures are included in music activities, displayed artwork (prints, sculpture, textiles, artifacts), dress-up area, and reading corner?

   - What changes do I need to make to provide more balance and broader representation?

20. **Honor and highlight individual families in your program.**

   - Interview family members to explore their culture, asking about special days and family celebrations. Ask how they guide behavior and recognize special achievement or rites of passage.

   - Take pictures and display them where children and their parents can look at them together.

   - Feature each family individually in your newsletter, providing them with an opportunity to share a favorite family story with others in the program.

Communicating with Families about Children's Individual Differences

1. **Actively listen to family members to discover their agenda and wishes concerning their child's experience in the program.** For example, an African-American mother is concerned that there were no other minority children in the program. A father expresses worry about his young son's gender orientation because of the amount of time the child spends dressing up in feminine clothing in the pretend play area. Parents of a bright 4-year-old ask what you were doing to teach her how to read. Be clear about the parent's thoughts and feelings. Explore what they believe your responsibility is in relation to their concerns.

2. **Respond with empathy and honesty to family members' concerns.** Realize that parents or grandparents often are seeing a problem in terms of what it means for the future of a child, whereas you may be more concerned about the child's present functioning and behavior. Often, the two most common concerns of family members of children with disabilities are the social acceptance and future of the child.

   Professionals can gain a great deal of insight into how a child functions by learning more about the parents' feelings, thoughts, behaviors, and values. How do they feel about this child? Are they proud or disappointed? What are their hopes for him or her? Let parents know that their concerns are important to you before outlining intervention strategies you believe best match their child's needs. Follow through responsibly in giving parents the information they need on an ongoing basis.

3. **When integrating children with exceptional needs, use the family as a primary resource.** With respect to at least one child in the program, each parent is an unqualified expert. You can make this concept work for you and the child by forming partnerships with parents and other family members. As well as providing advice to them when they ask, you can ask their advice when having a difficult time figuring out what to do with their child (e.g., "How do you get Jenny to hang up her coat? I'm having a tough time helping her remember to do that!"). With especially shy children, most of the year could go by before you get a handle on the child's likes, dislikes, and interests. A parent often can provide a valuable shortcut to a workable strategy.

4. **Be supportive and responsive to family members of typically developing children who have questions and concerns about the presence of children with exceptional needs in the group.** Such concerns are to be expected. Parents or grandparents may worry that their own child may not get enough attention or will regress in his or her own development. If you become defensive or intimidating or make parents feel guilty for having "negative" feelings, you probably will construct unwanted barriers. Respond as honestly as possible to both open and hidden concerns.

HIGHLIGHT 14-3

Letter to Parent from International School Principal

Dear Mrs. _____:

We were disappointed to learn that you are withdrawing your son's application for our nursery classroom because the teacher is Indian. She is a native English speaker who has a great deal of early childhood education experience and excellent references from past employers. That is the reason she was hired, and we feel grateful that we were able to hire her.

Ours is a multicultural, bilingual school. One of our guiding principles is respect for people from all cultures, and we welcome both families and faculty from many parts of the world. Currently, we have families from 22 different nations enriching our school. We would hope that all adults here will model genuine respect for others so that children may learn to move easily from one culture to another and work easily with others as they grow older.

You have asked to have your application fees transferred to our preschool class for next fall. Since we cannot promise that you would not experience similar issues like this in the future in our school, we would like to refund all of your fees at this time. It would be unethical of us to accept your application under the circumstances. Please stop by our reception desk, and we will have a full refund ready for you. Should you change your mind about this, we would welcome you and your son Harrison into the nursery program where we believe he could have a wonderful school experience this year.

With kind regard,

_____, Principal

For example, a parent might ask, "Are things going pretty smoothly this year with all the changes?" If you were to respond, "Not bad," leaving it there, you may cut off an opportunity to have the parent share his or her concerns. If, however, you respond: "Not bad. How are parents looking at the changes?" you leave an opening for the parent to bring up a concern with a general response.

Make yourself available to answer questions, and invite parents into the classroom to observe for themselves. Let family members know you are interested in their questions and feedback and that you value openness.

5. **Stick to the issue when challenging parents who are advocating nonacceptance of others to their children, based on bias.** If you have direct evidence that a family member is actively teaching nonacceptance based on ethnic/racial or disability differences or is blaming every negative occurrence on race or disability, ask to have a private discussion about the situation. Stick to the issue and, without being argumentative, firmly provide reasons why bias is harmful and cannot be tolerated in a developmentally appropriate learning context where respect is essential (see Highlight 14-3).

Pitfalls to Avoid naeyc

When using the skills described, there are common pitfalls to avoid.

1. **Overprotecting the child who is atypical or from a minority group.** If you give special privileges to one child and not to others, you always run the risk of alienating other children and hampering the potential development of the favored child. Rules should be changed to accommodate individual children only when safety issues are involved, when the child's learning modes are inadequate for the task at hand, or when children are not emotionally able to meet the challenge set before them. When rule changes are necessary, give simple, matter-of-fact explanations to the other children. In addition, you can draw children into a discussion about how to make the rule change palatable, given the circumstances. Children's sense of fairness, particularly when they are asked their opinion about a problem, almost always inclines them toward helpfulness.

When rules are changed arbitrarily, however, and without apparent fairness, children can become resentful, rejecting, and hostile toward the other child and/or the supervising adult.

2. **Failing to see negative interactions because they are not part of the success picture you have in mind.** It can be tempting to overlook negative incidents that happen or to make light of them because we want to build a positive picture that everything in the classroom is going well. However, honest, ongoing evaluations of inclusiveness are essential. Incidents in which a child is being exploited, manipulated, isolated, or harmed (physically or psychologically) by children or adults in the setting must be addressed immediately by (a) interrupting the incident; (b) acknowledging the emotions of all individuals involved; (c) stating that exploitive and harmful behavior is not allowed under any circumstances; and (d) structuring alternatives that will lead not only toward promoting interaction and feelings of psychological safety but also toward positive acceptance of one another.

3. **Inadvertently using stereotypical language.** All people have phrases in their vocabulary that they use unthinkingly. Some of these may be unintentionally offensive. Referring to someone as an "Indian giver," describing the haggling process as "Jewing someone down," saying you'll go out "Dutch" with someone, or asking children to sit "Indian style" are examples. In addition, referring to workers as "firemen," "postmen," and "salesgirls" reinforces sex-role stereotypes. More egalitarian terminology would include "firefighters," "postal workers," and "salesclerks." Similarly, beware of segregating males and females unnecessarily. It is not constructive to pit boys against girls in games or have children retrieve their art projects by having one gender go before the other. Use other attributes to designate subgroups, such as "Everyone with green socks may get their coats." or "All the people at this table may be dismissed."

4. **Failing to plan for and evaluate student progress effectively.** Children's programs almost always have an evaluation component attached to them. Usually, these are summative in nature and based on predetermined, normative criteria, measuring how much a child is able to accomplish against a given standard in a given period of time. However, children who have ability deficits for one reason or another are certain to measure up poorly unless they are given reasonable mastery objectives based on their own ability. Similarly, children who consistently need more challenging activities than most of the children must have their progress evaluated more frequently to make sure they are progressing.

5. **Failing to seek the support of administrators, family members, other professionals, and community members.** Just as children work within a team situation in the classroom, professionals are part of a larger team of adults who affect what goes on in the program. If you are working with children who require additional resources, such as more time, understanding, patience, staff, and materials, you may have to justify those needs to other adults who are in positions to help. Often, without additional support, there will be a tendency toward burnout and a feeling of being overwhelmed and inadequate in meeting the children's needs. When there is effective communication between helping professionals and the other adults with expertise, these feelings can be minimized.

6. **Responding only to the needs of family members with whom you feel comfortable and avoiding those with different values or differing racial, ethnic, or cultural backgrounds.** Family members who are different from the majority of the other families or who do not speak fluent English may shy away from becoming involved because they feel they have little to offer or that what they have to offer will not be valued. Some may sense, fairly or unfairly, a condescending or standoffish attitude on the part of the professional. For example, one young woman who applied for a Head Start position was excited about working with "those" children.

What she failed to consider was that her job also required her to work with "those" parents. Armed with some of her best ideas from a parent–teacher interaction class she had taken in college, she came in the first evening, excited to share some of her expertise. The parents had not come prepared to receive it and had other things on their minds. She said the next day to one of her colleagues, "All they wanted to do was sit and talk and drink coffee!" She and the parents never were able to get beyond that, and the young woman lasted only the rest of the year in that position. Instead of working to meet parents where they needed her to meet them, she indignantly waited for them to "show some interest in their kids." However, their need to talk to one another about their concerns had to come first. Professionals who have had few personal experiences with certain ethnic groups and cultures can gain new understandings by making a genuine effort to study ethnic groups and cultures different from their own.

Summary

Sensitive issues surrounding children's sexuality, ethnicity, exceptional needs, and personality differences may sometimes cause you discomfort, irritation, embarrassment, or confusion in choosing the most effective ways to support children and their families. When these feelings lead to avoidance, rejection, aggressiveness, or overprotectiveness, your ability to support children's development and competency building is significantly diminished.

Sexual behavior in children such as public masturbation, sex play, peeping, sex-oriented language, and sexually assertive moves toward another child or adult should be handled as matter-of-factly as possible as you calmly guide the child toward more appropriate behavior. Apparent deviations in **psychosexual development**, although sometimes troublesome to adults, may not be subject to alteration and call instead for understanding and a more thorough knowledge of the child's perspective. Severe sexual deviations should be handled by seeking the expertise of other professionals.

Children's attitudes toward other racial and ethnic groups are age-specific and stage-specific. When working with children and parents of other racial and ethnic origins or socioeconomic status, you may occasionally find yourself dealing with negative feelings based on your own ethnocentrism and experiences. An inability to rise above these feelings would undermine your professional effectiveness or negatively affect children's self-esteem and developing ethnic attitudes. Conversely, positive behaviors on your part will serve as an important prerequisite to prejudice prevention and reduction.

Inclusion of children with exceptional needs also is an area requiring additional sensitivity on your part. Remember that the objective of integrating children with disabling conditions is twofold: to promote acceptance of atypical children through stigma reduction and removal, and to enhance their social competence so they can later live more comfortably and successfully in the mainstream of society. The challenge for inclusion of children with disabling conditions is similar to that of racial integration—that is, melding those who are different from the majority successfully into the mainstream.

When working with children who are precocious, shy, or difficult in temperament, you may encounter stigmatization, stereotyping, and rejection on the part of some children and families. This will require you to be able to facilitate supportive interaction in the group between typically developing children and children with exceptional needs.

Success in handling developmental issues related to children's sexuality, ethnicity, exceptional needs, and other differences will depend on your commitment to successful integration, an ability to structure the environment, and attention to the developing social dynamics in the learning context. Respecting the uniqueness of all persons is a positive statement confirming our ability to be truly human toward one another. When you create an accepting, nurturing, growth-enhancing environment, it allows children to see themselves and others as fully functioning, competently developing human beings.

It will be important to hone your skills in communicating with families about children's individual differences and to respond to their concerns with empathy and honesty. Those parents of children with exceptional needs should be viewed as a primary resource.

Finally, when fostering healthy attitudes about sexuality and diversity, you will want to avoid such pitfalls as being overprotective, overlooking negative interactions, inadvertently using stereotypical language, failing to evaluate children's progress effectively, and not working with family members and others in an ineffective manner.

Key Terms

antibias education
Asperger's syndrome disorder
autism
biases
deaf-blindness
deafness
developmental delay
disabling conditions
emotional disturbance
ethnicity
ethnocentrism
gender identity
gender-role identification
giftedness
hearing impairment
Individualized Education Program (IEP)
Individualized Family Service Program (IFSP)
intellectual disability
internalized oppression

internalized privilege
multiple disabilities
orthopedic impairment
other health impairment
Persona dolls

precocious children
psychosexual development
shyness
social competence
social identity

specific learning disability
speech or language impairment
traumatic brain injury
visual impairment

Discussion Questions

1. The parent board of an all-White cooperative nursery school is considering offering a scholarship to an African-American preschooler for the coming year. What advantages and disadvantages do you see in such an arrangement? What kinds of preparation do you feel should be made prior to implementing such a procedure?

2. You have a Korean-American child in your third-grade classroom and find that he is being harassed on the way home by three of the more popular boys in the classroom. You arrange to meet with the three boys. How do you begin your discussion with them? Role-play this situation with three classmates who can take the part of the students.

3. You are teaching in a large, urban middle school. An 11-year-old girl approaches you during lunch hour, saying that a young male security guard in the school tried fondling her and has been asking her if he can take her home after school. How do you respond to her? What action, if any, do you take?

4. You are holding an open house for parents. The father of a 5-year-old boy approaches you and asks what you think about letting boys play with dolls. He also asks, "How early can you tell whether or not a male is going to be gay?" State your initial response to him exactly as you would make it. Review the normative sequence in the development of gender identity as you might relate it to the father.

5. You have observed that one of the parents who has volunteered to tutor children with reading problems appears to be highly impatient with Kevin, a second-grader. This morning, you overhear her saying to him: "Your problem is laziness. That's why a lot of you Black children aren't able to ever finish school. Is that what you want to happen to you?" How do you handle this situation?

6. As you round the corner into the "quiet" area reserved for reading, you discover two 5-year-old boys examining each other's genitals. What are your initial thoughts? What do you say to the boys? Do you take any further action? If so, what?

7. One of the boys in your Cub Scout group appears to be extremely nervous. On picking him up after a meeting, his mother notices him touching his genitals. In front of the other boys, she crudely quips: "For crying out loud, Terry, quit playing with yourself. You're going to make it fall off!" You ask her if you can talk privately with her for a moment. What do you say to her?

8. You see one of the White preschoolers vigorously rubbing the arm of a Black aide. When you ask about it, the aide laughs and says, "He's trying to rub off the dark color of my skin." How do you respond?

9. In the middle of the morning's activity, one of the children unexpectedly has a grand mal seizure. Following the episode, the rest of the children are visibly shaken, and some are crying. What do you say to them?

    Afterward, with the potential of it happening again, how do you prepare the classroom and the children for the possibility?

10. Children in the childcare center are having a snack of raisin toast and peanut butter. The student teacher has been instructed to serve only one piece to each child until all children have been served. You notice that Kendra, a child with Down syndrome, has been sitting at the table for quite a long time and is on her second piece of toast. When you ask the student teacher about the situation, she says, "I know the rule, but I feel sorry for her." Verbalize your response exactly as you would make it to the student teacher.

11. Read the following ethical scenario. Refer to the NAEYC Code of Ethical Conduct presented in Appendix A. Find the section(s) that provides insight into the professional responsibilities related to the following situation:

    Jessica, a child with cerebral palsy, uses a wheelchair. She attends Maple Avenue Child Development Center. During outdoor time, she is wheeled into the teachers' lounge and left there to watch television while the other children play outside. Her caregiver explains, "TV is a good activity for her because there's nothing for her to do on the playground. This way, she doesn't get hurt."

12. If you were to assess your own personality type based on the brief discussion of temperament in this chapter, would you say you were an easy child to raise, a slow-to-warm-up child, or a difficult one? If someone were to interview your family, what kinds of specific examples might they provide to support or dispute your conclusions?

Case Study Analysis

Read the case study in Appendix B about Seth, a child diagnosed with autism, and consider the following:

1. What were some of Seth's characteristics that fit the description of autistic behavior described in this chapter?

2. What worried Seth's parents the most?

3. How did Seth's teachers respond in a supportive way to help Seth with these issues?

4. What specific strategy did Seth's special education teacher use to encourage social interaction between Seth and Nicholas in the grocery store in dramatic play? How was this different from what a teacher might do with a typically developing child?

5. Because changes are difficult with Seth and most other children with autism, what strategies did his teacher use to provide support prior to the field trip to the zoo?

Field Assignments

1. To become more skillful in handling others' responses, it is important to examine your own feelings about the sensitive areas that are the focus of this chapter. Respond as honestly as possible to the following.

    With respect to your own sexuality, differing ethnic, religious, racial persons or groups, and disabled persons or populations:

a. Cite any negative childhood experiences you had.

b. Identify any faulty or stereotypic information you remember receiving.

c. On a scale of 1 to 10, 10 being most comfortable, describe how comfortable you are related to your own sexuality and interaction with people different from you.

d. Describe any negative adult experiences you have had related to these areas.

e. Have your beliefs and thinking about individual differences changed during your adult years? If so, how?

f. What social changes do you think need to take place in order to have less biased behavior related to these issues?

2. Become familiar with some of the screening tools used to assess growth and development. These are tools that can be simply administered without specialized knowledge or clinical experience. They are available through universities, colleges, intermediate school districts, hospitals, and clinics. The ESI (Early Screening Inventory) and DDST II (Denver Developmental Screening Test II) are two examples. Arrange to obtain one of these tools and use it to test three different children in the age range indicated. Obtain permission from the child's parents prior to testing the child. Because you are probably not experienced in assessment at this point, do not share the results of the test with the child, the child's parents, or other professionals. Remember to keep the results confidential.

3. Constantly monitor and evaluate your teaching materials and classroom activities for racial, cultural, gender-role, sexual, religious, and developmental stereotypes. Examine the following:

- Textbooks or children's books
- Assessment tools
- Religious holidays observed in programming
- Foods served
- Responsibilities delegated to children for care and management of the environment
- Activities planned onsite and off
- Rules and regulations
- Resource people invited to participate in the program
- Makeup of professional and paraprofessional staff

4. Adapt a previously developed lesson plan for a particular child with exceptional needs, and carry out the modified plan. What modifications were necessary? What additional modifications would you make if using the adapted plan for a child with a different set of exceptional needs?

Reflect on Your Practice

Here is a sample checklist you can use to reflect on your use of the skills as a beginning professional. A more detailed classroom observation tool is available in Appendix C.

Teachers who foster healthy attitudes about sexuality and diversity do the following:

✓ Build a positive social climate in which similarities and differences are valued.

✓ Communicate with families about children's individual differences.

✓ Address children's stereotypical remarks directly and in a nonjudgmental manner.

✓ Provide natural opportunities for children to learn more about their sexual development and react calmly to children's sex play.

✓ Help children develop pride in their own cultural heritage, language, and traditions.

✓ Be as gender fair as possible in their day-to-day interaction with children.

✓ Describe alternate strategies for expressing emotions.

✓ Describe the behavior they expect to children.

Digital Download   **Download from CourseMate**

CourseMate. Visit the Education CourseMate for this textbook to access the eBook, Digital Downloads, TeachSource Videos, and quizzes. Go to CengageBrain.com to log in, register, or purchase access.

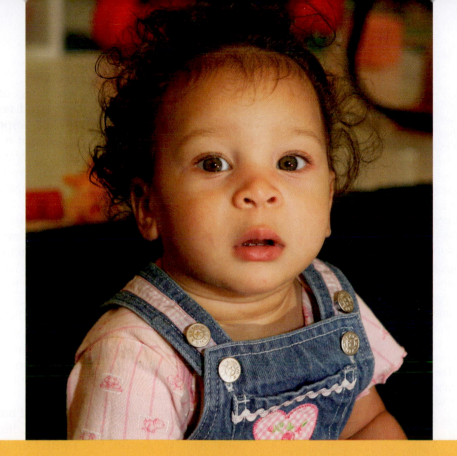

15 Making Ethical Judgments and Decisions

OBJECTIVES

On completion of this chapter, you should be able to:

Describe ethical judgments and the variables that influence making such judgments.

Discuss the principles involved in making ethical judgments.

Make ethical judgments related to children's extreme behavior.

Adhere to ethical codes of conduct focused on child abuse and neglect.

Describe ethical dimensions of working with families.

Demonstrate skills for making ethical judgments.

Avoid pitfalls in making ethical judgments.

NAEYC STANDARDS naeyc

1. Promoting Child Development and Learning
2. Building Family and Community Relationships
3. Observing, Documenting, and Assessing to Support Young Children and Families
4. Using Developmentally Effective Approaches to Connect with Children and Families
5. Using Content Knowledge to Build Meaningful Curriculum
6. Becoming a Professional

The children in the hospital playroom are reminded that at the end of the session, everything must be put back where they found it. When cleanup time is announced, all the children pitch in to help. When they proclaim the job finished, Mr. Walters, the child-life specialist, surveys the room. He notices that although tables are clean and everything has been put away, the cupboards are disheveled, and not all of the markers have been capped. Looking at the children's beaming faces, he ponders, "Should I make them do more, or should I accept the job they've done?"

Two children in an English-immersion preschool are playing with blocks together. They are speaking French to one another, their primary language. Andy, a Korean 5-year-old, approaches and stoops down, intending to get involved. "Only French or English to play here!" says Julian. Andy speaks neither French nor English very well but understands from Julian's body language and tone that he's not welcome. The teacher, overhearing, knows that an intervention is called for but wonders what the most effective approach would be.

On the playground, Myron drops a hard line-drive. "Oh, damn," he says, looking embarrassed that he has dropped the ball. He is seemingly unaware of the epithet. Miss Delmar, who overhears this, considers many options: lecturing Myron, sending him off the field, or ignoring the incident.

For the second time this month, Stuart comes to the center badly bruised. When asked what happened, he claims that he fell down the stairs. The director muses, "Is this really the result of an accident, or could it be a sign of abuse?"

none at all. When these choices affect others, we draw on what we believe about right and wrong, honesty, justice, kindness, reciprocity, and respect for others. This is the essence of ethical decision making.

Essentially, the best ethical judgments are those that we make consciously and involve the same series of steps found in any decision-making model. In Table 15-1, we see how Mr. Walters, the teacher who opened our chapter, reached his decision to praise the children for their less-than-perfect cleanup job.

Formulating an ethical judgment carries with it certain risks and no guarantees. Yet, as uncertain as the process is, we're more likely to make a better choice when we do so consciously, rather than in an arbitrary fashion. Going through these steps makes it more likely that our actions will match our aims. Furthermore, evaluating the outcomes that actually occur after an option is carried out provides additional information that can be used as input for future judgments we make.

Ethical judgments are influenced both by the situation and by the person who is deciding how to proceed. Any two persons faced with formulating a choice about the same circumstance might make entirely different, yet equally good or equally poor, decisions. Because ethical judgments are so personal and so situation specific, it would be unwise here to suggest prescribed answers to a variety of scenarios. Rather, our goal in this chapter is to point out what variables to consider when making a sound judgment as well as how to think through the process involved in making ethical judgments.

Ethical Judgments and the Variables that Influence Making Such Judgments naeyc

Every day, professionals working with children and families are faced with making sound, sensitive ethical judgments such as these. Ethics, the basic principles that guide our day-to-day conduct and assist us in resolving the dilemmas we encounter, will be the result of shared ideals coming from our own profession, community, colleagues, family, and peers, as well as our own evolving values, morals, and virtues (Miller, 2013).

While our decision making usually involves simply making a choice between alternatives, making ethical judgments requires us to sort out conflicting values we may have relative to the situation and to prioritize them. Some of the situations we encounter demand on-the-spot decision making; others allow time for longer deliberation. Some call for maximum intervention; others for only minimal interference or

How Program Goals, Strategies, and Standards Relate to Ethical Judgments

Situations that call for sensitive judgments usually involve the enacting of goals, strategies, or standards.

Goals. One of the goals we have in almost all programs involving children is that of enhancing children's social competence. Typical goals include fostering their self-regulation, interpersonal skills, positive self-identity, social values, cultural competence, and planning and decision-making skills. Each of these represents a desired outcome: the achievement of increased social competence. None of these goals is wholly attained within the setting or time period during which we work with a particular child. However, when adults establish goals, their interactions with children gain purpose, and there is usually progress. There is an end result to work toward, rather than operating haphazardly with no purpose in mind. Goals can be general or specific, long range or short range, more or

Table 15-1   Steps in Making an Ethical Decision

Procedure
WHAT MR. WALTERS DOES TO REACH HIS DECISION

1. Assess the situation.

Mr. Walters formulates a picture of what is happening, taking into account the children's lack of familiarity with the hospital playroom, the anxiety many of them are feeling at being in a hospital setting, his supervisor's desire for neatness, the importance of what's been left undone, the children's display of pride, his knowledge that no one will be using the playroom again until tomorrow, and his own feelings of pleasure that the children have worked together.

2. Analyze possible strategies in response to it.

Mr. Walters thinks about the possible responses. Some of these include accepting the children's work without comment, having them redo the work, singling out particular children on the basis of their contributions, scolding them all for not doing enough, and praising the children for working together willingly. He takes into consideration whether making the children redo the work would seem reasonable to them or make them feel defeated. He considers the fact that he is unfamiliar with the youngsters and doesn't know how they will react to a scolding. He wonders if he praises the children for their efforts, some will recognize the discrepancy between their performance and a really clean room and view his words as false.

3. Select and implement a strategy or combination of strategies.

On the spot, Mr. Walters chooses to praise the children for their cooperation in working together.

4. Evaluate the outcome.

Mr. Walters is satisfied that his response best supports his overall aim that children feel comfortable in the hospital environment and that they have made an earnest effort to replace materials.

© Cengage Learning

This teacher develops goals for individual children as well as goals for the entire group in her classroom.

© Cengage Learning

less important, and independent of or interdependent of other aims (Goldsmith, 2013). Furthermore, we develop goals for individual children as well as goals for the entire group. Sometimes these multiple aims are compatible, and sometimes they are in direct opposition to one another. Some of the questions related to goal setting include the following:

- What are the appropriate goals for each child?
- Is a goal that is appropriate for one child also suited for another?
- What should be done when pursuit of a goal for an individual runs counter to one established for the group?
- Is a particular goal still valid?
- What should be done when one goal for a child seems incongruent with another?
- What factors necessitate changing a goal?
- What makes one goal more important than another?

Mrs. Torez must consider questions such as these when, during a class discussion, Jesse blurts out an answer without raising his hand. Her goal for the group has been for children to exercise greater impulse control and demonstrate it by waiting to be called on. Yet, Jesse is a shy child whom Mrs. Torez has been encouraging to become more assertive. Should her response be geared toward supporting the group goal or the one established for Jesse? Is there a way to address both goals without compromising either? What Mrs. Torez does will be based on her judgment of the situation.

Strategies. To pursue their goals for children, adults implement particular **strategies**. Some of these involve determining the following:

- Which strategy is best suited to achieving a particular goal?
- Is the strategy that is most potentially effective actually feasible?
- How compatible are the strategies implemented for one goal with those for another goal?
- How long should a strategy be continued before judging its effectiveness?
- Can a planned strategy be carried out as originally intended?
- Can a strategy stand alone, or should it be carried out in conjunction with other strategies?

A situation in which an ethical judgment about strategies must be made arises when Mr. Sears considers T. J.'s persistent antisocial behavior in the group. For the past several months, he has been trying to get T. J. to handle his frustration in a more constructive manner. Though Mr. Sears has tried several options, none has had the desired effect.

Recently, he has begun to wonder whether he has used too many different approaches and too rapidly. He also wonders whether his efforts to contend with T. J. have led him to neglect other children, prompting them to act out. The conclusions Mr. Sears reaches and what he will do about them depend on the soundness of the judgments he makes.

Standards. Success in accomplishing goals is assessed using **standards**. People establish standards when they decide that a certain amount of a behavior or a certain quality of behavior represents goal attainment. For example, as long ago as 1857, groups of educators came together to form the National Education Association (NEA). They subsequently published a set of standards that was prefaced with the following statement:

> The educator, believing in the worth and dignity of each human being, recognizes the supreme importance of the pursuit of truth, devotion to excellence, and the nurture of the democratic principles. Essential to these goals is the protection of freedom to learn and to teach and the guarantee of equal educational opportunity for all. The educator accepts the responsibility to adhere to the highest ethical standards.

In addition to the various national professional groups publishing standards for educators, each state has produced its own code of ethics. For example, Georgia has produced a code of ethics that contains principles that include a commitment to the student and to the profession. Principles related to commitment to the student include the following expectations for all educators:

1. Shall not unreasonably restrain the student from independent action in the pursuit of learning.
2. Shall not unreasonably deny the student's access to varying points of view.
3. Shall not deliberately suppress or distort subject matter relevant to the student's progress.
4. Shall make reasonable effort to protect the student from conditions harmful to learning or to health and safety.
5. Shall not intentionally expose the student to embarrassment or disparagement.

The measurement of standards may be formal or informal, known by children or unknown by them, and purposeful or intuitive on the part of the adult. Questions that focus on ethical judgments about standards are as follows:

- What standards should be established?
- Should the same standard apply to all children?

- When or why should a standard be changed?
- When competing standards exist, which standards should prevail?
- How well does a child's behavior meet a given standard?

Think back to Mr. Walters, the child-life specialist. He was making an ethical judgment about standards when deciding whether the children's definition of a clean room was good enough to accept. Ms. Heller, a first-grade teacher, is also thinking about standards when she tries to determine whether to accept Gavin's second attempt at editing the story he is writing. Her dilemma is whether to hold Gavin to the standards she usually has for her first graders at this time in the school year or to consider the improvement he has made and the considerable effort it took for Gavin to produce the work. In each case, final determinations regarding an acceptable level of performance will come about as the result of adult judgments.

Variables that Affect Ethical Judgments

Goals, strategies, and standards must continually be evaluated. Goals that are accomplished are replaced by other goals, and those that obviously are unattainable or need to be adapted are revised; strategies that are outmoded or ineffective are updated. Because none of these remains constant forever, helping professionals continually make ethical judgments about them. Their judgments are influenced by three variables: their values, their knowledge of how children learn and grow, and their assessment of the situation at hand. Let's examine each of these influences more closely.

Values. Underlying each ethical judgment are personal values. Values are the qualities and beliefs you consider desirable or worthwhile (Berns, 2012). As such, values are deeply internalized feelings that direct your actions.

To achieve these goals, these adults implement related strategies such as rewarding children who tell the truth, separating children who are taking tests, and teaching children appropriate sources for getting help as a substitute for copying. In addition, they apply related standards to determine how well their goals have been met. Not only do adults' values influence their goals for children, but they also affect how adults interpret and appraise children's behavior. As a result, an adult may view children who tell tall tales with less favor than children who don't.

Because values cannot be seen, their presence can only be inferred from what people do (Goldsmith, 2013). For instance, Linda Hong frequently reminds children about the value of telling the truth and doing

Eventually, the children and adults will have to decide, "Is our room clean enough?" This is a question of standards.

© Cengage Learning 2015

their own work. She often carries out activities in which children must discriminate between fact and fantasy. She reveals her emotions rather than hiding them, and she encourages children to describe their true reactions even when they are in opposition to her own. If a child copies another's work, he or she is told to do it over. Based on her actions, you might conclude that the value of honesty is important to her. On the other hand, were she to ignore minor incidents of cheating, tell fibs herself, or attempt to deny children's emotions, her behavior would indicate that honesty was not critical to her. Even if she were to say that it was, her actions would belie her words.

How values develop. Values are a product of early and continued socialization. Families, society, culture, teachers, religion, friends, professional colleagues and organizations, and mass media all contribute to one's belief system. In this way, every facet of a person's environment has a direct or indirect impact on his or her thinking. Because value acquisition starts in infancy, it is the family that has the first and most profound influence on the fundamental dispositions of young children. However, our core values are not static and as we mature, our beliefs are supplemented by inputs from all of the contexts in which we live, work, and play with others. These combine eventually to form a particular orientation that we internalize, that provides meaning to our lives, and serves as a guide throughout our life.

Because the overall environment in which each of us grows up is unique, no two people have exactly the same value system. Values differ across cultures, between families in the same culture, and among individual family members. This means there is no one correct set of values to which all persons subscribe.

Prioritizing values. People develop a system of values that often is ranked, ranging from most critical to least important. The order of importance is determined by whether a person treats a particular value as basic (a value that is fixed or unconditional, regardless of context) or relative (one that depends on the context for interpretation). **Basic values** usually take priority over **relative values**, and relative values take on more or less importance, depending on the situation (Deacon, 2002). In Linda Hong's case, for example, the basic value of honesty pervades everything she does. Therefore, when she must choose between being up front, circumspect, or deceitful, she usually selects the first option.

A value's hierarchy is not always so linear, with each value being placed above or below another. Rather, several values may occupy the same level of importance at the same time. These values may be compatible or contradictory. The similar weight shared

by a cluster of competing values explains why people sometimes experience value conflicts in particular circumstances. For instance, you may equally value honesty and kindness. However, have you ever been caught in the dilemma of whether to tell the truth or to be less than honest to keep from hurting someone's feelings?

Recognizing our own values. The more we are consciously aware of our own personal values, the better we are able to examine them. Only then can we determine when conflicting values exist within ourselves or between others and ourselves and then take systematic steps to resolve the dilemmas that result.

Additionally, we need to determine whether our actions are the same as the values we espouse. This makes it more likely that we will be consistent in our interactions with children and their families. For all of these reasons, clarifying our values is an important facet of professional life (see Highlight 15-1).

Knowing the values supported by our profession. In addition to personal values, values adopted by the profession at large provide useful guides for making judgments. Such values are usually identified in the ethical codes of conduct adopted by professional organizations or societies.

A code of ethical conduct to which members are committed represents the collective wisdom of the field regarding common ideals, aspirations, values, required practices that support those values, and prohibited practices that undermine them. In other words, a code of ethics provides a tangible framework for thinking about professional values and how those values might influence our behavior in the formal group setting. When we keep that code in mind at all times, we then have a credible foundation for the judgments we will have to make (Miller, 2013).

HIGHLIGHT 15-1

The Public Rates Teachers Highly on Ethics and Trustworthiness

Research indicates that the public considers teachers to be highly ethical and trustworthy. The public believes teachers take seriously their responsibility to adhere to the highest ethical standards and rate them second only to doctors in terms of telling the truth, placing the needs of children at the center of their work, and giving the needs of children priority over their own needs (Koch, 2009).

Source: Koch, 2009.

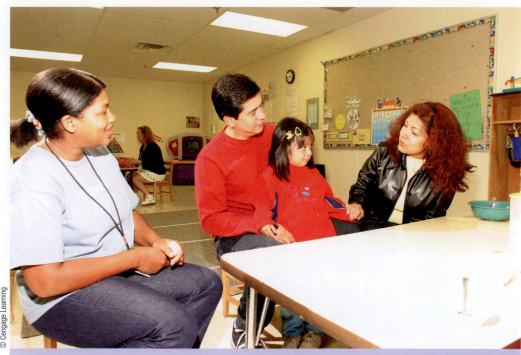

Helping professionals must be sensitive to the differing values held by the children and families with whom they work.

© Cengage Learning

Respecting clients' values. It's important to be sensitive to the differing values held by the children and families with whom we work. We cannot expect clients' values to exactly mirror or always be compatible with our own, and we may be confronted with dissimilarities between our values and those of our clients. If so, our task becomes one of finding ways to work with others that demonstrate respect for their belief systems, regardless of what action is eventually taken.

Separating values from goals, strategies, and standards. Occasionally, professionals mistake differences in goals, strategies, and standards for value conflicts. In reality, it is possible for dissimilar goals, strategies, and standards to be applied in response to the same value. For example, Mrs. Williams values competence and has a goal for her son, DeRon, to be able to handle social situations with greater skill. She teaches him to establish his rights through physical force and considers his winning a fight as a positive indication of his abilities. Mrs. Pritchard, his teacher, shares the same value and goal for DeRon with his mother, but her tactics and standards differ significantly. She teaches DeRon to use words to establish his rights and views his avoidance of physical confrontation as a measure of achievement rather than weakness.

In this case, the dissimilar approach between parent and teacher is based not on conflicting values but on differing means. Although values are almost impossible to debate, strategies can be negotiated. The two adults do have common ground. If Mrs. Pritchard recognizes this, she will have a positive base from which to approach the parent. If she does not see this shared perspective, her efforts to influence the parent could result in failure. In addition to an understanding of values, there are two other variables that affect the ethical judgments professionals make. The first involves how well they take into account children's current level of functioning; the second is whether they look at each situation in context.

Knowledge of child development and learning affects judgments. When adults make ethical judgments about goals, strategies, and standards related to children's behavior, they must weigh such variables as the child's age, what the child's current level of comprehension might be, and what experiences the child has had.

Although age is not an absolute measure of a child's capabilities and understanding, it does serve as a guide for establishing appropriate expectations. For instance, adults who know that preschoolers do not yet have a mature grasp of games with rules would not view a 4-year-old who spins twice or peeks at the cards

Preschoolers may not have a mature grasp of games with rules.

© Cengage Learning 2015

in a memory game as a cheater. Subsequently, they would not require very young children to adhere to the rules of a game in the same way they might expect grade-schoolers to. Likewise, awareness that 7- and 8-year-olds normally spend lots of time talking about who is and is not in their friendship circle keeps adults from moralizing to children when they hear such discussions going on. Rather, their strategy for improving peer relations might consist of group discussions aimed at encouraging children to discover similarities with others in the group.

The types of previous knowledge and skills a child brings to a situation should also be taken into account. Obviously, children with little or no exposure to a particular situation or skill should not be expected to pursue exactly the same goals or perform at the same level of competence as youngsters whose backlog of experience is greater. For instance, goals for a field trip to a farm for children from the inner city would be different from those a teacher has for youngsters from a rural area. Standards related to dressing independently would be different for a 2-year-old from those for a 6-year-old, not only because of differences in age, but because the older child has had more practice.

The situational context. The judgments we make never take place in a vacuum. Rather, they are influenced by several factors. Some of these include time, human resources, material resources,

the physical environment, and the specific details of the behavioral episode itself. The goals, strategies, and standards finally decided on are all affected by these constraints. For instance, under normal circumstances, Ms. Krikke's goal is to foster independence among the children in her class. Ordinarily, children are given the time to make their own decisions, to repeat a task to gain competence, and to do as much as possible for themselves. However, these goals and strategies have to be modified during a tornado drill, when the goal of safety supersedes that of independence. Under such circumstances, children have no choice about taking shelter; nor can they take their time dressing themselves. As a result, slow dressers get more direct assistance than is customarily provided.

Similarly, Mr. Ogden might think that the best strategy for helping an impulsive child is constant, one-to-one monitoring by an adult. Yet, he concludes that he would be unable to implement this approach because of demands on his own time and the lack of other adults who might serve in this role.

Physical resources and available time also affect ethical judgments. This explains why the presence of a huge mud puddle on the playground could be viewed as either a place to avoid or an area of exploration. Which judgment is made depends in part on what kind of clothing the children are wearing, whether soap and water are available for cleanup, and whether there is enough time for children to both play in the mud and get cleaned up before the next activity period.

As you can see, your values, knowledge of child development and learning, and the situational context all influence the kinds of ethical judgments you will make as a professional. They also affect sensitive judgments about ethical behavior, judgments involving one's priorities, judgments about extreme behavior, and judgments related to child abuse and neglect.

Principles Involved in Making Ethical Judgments naeyc

Helping professionals continually confront ethical dilemmas in their daily work:

Ms. Skegel, a Head Start teacher, runs into a parent in the local grocery store who asks her how well the "situation is going" with the inclusion in the classroom of a child with autism.

Craig DeLong, who teaches first grade at Challenger Elementary School, has been asked to give the children in his classroom a group-administered standardized test, which he knows will produce inordinate stress in the children.

Ms. Satton, an aide in a kindergarten classroom, watches as the teacher passes out worksheets to the children; she knows these take up a lot of the children's time and produce little real learning.

The new administrator of a childcare program learns that the building is in violation of the state fire code but is told by the board president that it would be too expensive to remedy the situation and that his cooperation would be appreciated.

Three-year-old Tomeko Kenyon's mother asks Ms. Levinger not to allow Mr. Kenyon to pick Tomeko up after school because the parents are separated, and he is abusive. When Ms. Levinger asks if she has a court order to support this, Mrs. Kenyon says, "No, but I know you'll help me out for Tomeko's sake."

Concerns arise from incidents professionals witness or experience directly, as well as ones they hear about. These predicaments can affect children, families, colleagues, supervisors, or other community members. Ultimately, the basic judgments to be made center on which actions are right and which are wrong.

These are moral judgments, with no middle ground, requiring the application of one's professional code of ethics. In this text, we have used the *NAEYC Code of Ethical Conduct* (2005) as a guide for professional behavior. Lillian Katz has been a pioneer in developing ethics in early childhood education, saying that codes of ethics give us courage to act in terms of

what we believe to be in the best interests of the client rather than in terms of what will make our clients like us. These codes are about what is right, rather than expedient; good rather than simply practical; and spell out acts in which early childhood educators must never be accomplices, bystanders, or contributors (Katz, 1991; Feeney & Freeman, 2012). Up until this point, however, our primary focus has been on recognizing circumstances addressed by the code. Although familiarity with the code is essential, it is not sufficient to ensure that practitioners will always act ethically. For this to occur, ethical principles and codes must be embedded into all professional thinking (Newman, 2002). Effectively using the code is a skill that can be learned just as other skills are learned through direct instruction, modeling, and positive reinforcement.

Personal reflection on ethical dilemmas (both hypothetical and real) and conversations with colleagues about such dilemmas are essential strategies for building a strong foundation on which to make future professional judgments. Time must be set aside during preservice classes, staff meetings, or other training sessions to talk about the components involved in building a strong conceptual framework of the knowledge, skills, and dispositions involved in making ethical judgments (see Figure 15-1).

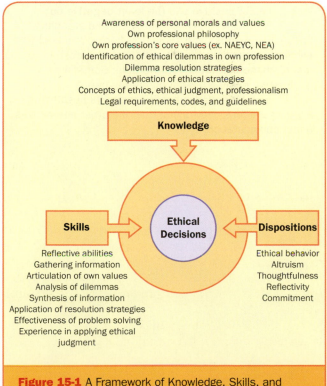

Figure 15-1 A Framework of Knowledge, Skills, and Dispositions for Making Ethical Judgments.

Source: Adapted from Newman (2002).

The ability to make a sound professional judgment also involves establishing priorities from among competing interests. Some of these include self-interest versus children's interests, individual interests versus group interests, and the interests of one person versus those of another. People also may experience conflicts within their own value system that cloud their ability to make a definitive judgment. Although there are no absolute rules for distinguishing among these, there are some general principles helping professionals can use when faced with difficult decisions.

Priority Principles

Six principles are arranged in a hierarchy in Table 15-2, from most to least important. Each one has higher priority than those that follow it. All of them serve as guideposts for which priorities take precedence in

Table 15-2   Priority Principles

Prioritized Principles	Example of Application of Principle
Principle 1. Children's safety takes precedence. The overriding concern of every helping professional is children's physical and mental welfare. If you must choose between an option in which a child's health and well-being can be maintained and other, more efficient, easier, or less involved options in which safety is a question, there is no choice. You are ethically and morally obligated to pursue the safest alternative.	The fifth-grade science class is doing an experiment with heat that involves the use of Bunsen burners. The children, working in small groups, are running behind schedule in their task. Another class is to arrive in five minutes. While surveying the room, the teacher notices that a few children, still working, have taken off their protective goggles. The adult feels caught between wanting them to get the experiment over with in time and feeling that she should enforce the safety standards. Even though there are only a few minutes remaining, and making the children don the goggles will cause a delay, the appropriate course is clear, as mandated by principle 1: safety first.
Principle 2. Give priority to the approach that promises the most positive and the least negative outcomes. Although all goals, strategies, and standards have some benefits and some drawbacks, it is best to eliminate the most negative options and choose from among those that are most favorable. Sometimes, the best option has the largest number of benefits. Sometimes, an option is best because its negative aspects are less detrimental than the other alternatives under consideration.	During a conference with the director of the childcare center, Mrs. Leeper (a parent) reveals that her father is terminally ill and is not expected to live much beyond the new year. She has not yet shared the news with her children and has approached the center director for advice. Together, they identify the benefits of telling the children about the situation right away, such as giving the children lead time to deal with the tragedy, a chance to say goodbye to their grandfather, and an opportunity to share in a family experience; a chance for Mrs. Leeper to gain family support; and the relief of not having to keep it a secret. Drawbacks to telling the children include causing everyone to feel sad during the holiday, as well as the difficulty of introducing a topic about which Mrs. Leeper feels uncomfortable and with which her children have had little experience. The two adults also explore the pros and cons of not telling. Favorable aspects of postponing the disclosure are the children probably will have an uninterrupted holiday and that the mother will not have to deal with the issue right away. The negative aspects of this approach include the mother's growing anxiety, her inability to share a very traumatic period of her life with her loved ones, the potential shock to the children, and their probable distress over sensing that something is wrong but not knowing what it is. Taking all of these factors into account, Mrs. Leeper makes the judgment that it is better to tell them than to remain silent. In her opinion, the benefits of telling right away outweigh both the benefits of not telling and the negative aspects of making the announcement.

© Cengage Learning

(Continued)

Table 15-2   (Continued)

Prioritized Principles	Example of Application of Principle
Principle 3. When a child's needs and an adult's needs differ, give priority to the child's needs whenever possible. Children's interests always take higher priority, unless the adult would find pursuit of those needs unlivable or contrary to his or her basic values.	Children at the Jefferson School are rehearsing for a spring concert. The music teacher is especially eager for the youngsters to put on a good show because music teachers from several other districts are in the audience. While listening to the opening number, she realizes that Sandra is singing loudly and enthusiastically but is off key. She debates whether to allow the child to sing. She knows that other teachers have told such youngsters to mouth the words without making a sound. At the same time, she is aware of how much Sandra is anticipating singing at the concert. Based on her understanding of principle 3, she rejects restricting Sandra's participation in favor of allowing her to sing, putting Sandra's needs before her own.
Principle 4. When goals of equal weight conflict, give priority to the goal that is least often addressed in day-to-day encounters. Often, situations arise in which it is possible to concentrate on reinforcing only one of several competing goals. When this happens, it is best to pursue the goal that is less often addressed.	Jorge received $10 from his grandmother for his birthday. He took the entire amount and bought his mother a change purse painted with a half-naked woman in a suggestive pose. He is proud of his purchase and pleased to be giving his mother a gift. His mother is touched that he so selflessly used his money for someone other than himself but also is concerned with his poor choice and lack of fiscal awareness. She realizes that she must focus on one aspect of the situation or the other. If she tries to deal with both by thanking him and then having him return the inappropriate purchase, she would, in fact, diminish the genuineness of her praise. She must choose between the value she places on prosocial behavior and her value related to money management. After much thought and following the premise of principle 4, she thanks Jorge for the change purse and says nothing about the inappropriate image or the way he spent the money. She decides that she will have many future opportunities to teach fiscal responsibility, but fewer chances to reward Jorge's generosity.
Principle 5. When a strategy supports a short-term objective but interferes with long-term goals, give priority to pursuing the long-term goal.	Children from the center have been on a walking field trip. They are tired, and the adults want to get back. It's been a long afternoon. The group reaches the middle of the block. The center is right across the street, and no traffic is in sight. The leader considers jaywalking but realizes that such an action would detract from her long-range goal of teaching children the safe way to cross the street. Her decision to have the children walk several extra yards to the corner is based on her understanding of principle 5.
Principle 6. When group and individual needs compete, give priority to the approach that best satisfies each. This may involve a compromise that addresses both sets of needs simultaneously. If this is not possible, competing needs may have to be addressed sequentially, knowing that the final result may not be completely satisfactory to all. In either case, strive to achieve win-win solutions, as opposed to outcomes in which either the individual or the group is perceived as a "winner" or a "loser."	Vito has little self-confidence. The one area in which he excels is building with blocks. Day after day, he builds elaborate structures and then begs that they remain standing, undisturbed. At first, the adult honors Vito's wishes, even though it limits other children's access to the blocks. She reasons that it is more important for Vito to feel good about an accomplishment than for the group to use the materials. However, over time, the adult notices that the youngsters are becoming increasingly upset and feeling short-changed about their limited opportunities to build. Using principle 6, the adult decides to limit how long a structure can remain standing, as well as Vito's monopolization of the blocks. She offers him a choice of using the blocks exclusively for a few minutes or using them for a longer time in conjunction with other children.

a given circumstance. These principles came about as a result of our experiences with families and children and through discussions with numerous professionals who were faced with making ethical judgments in a wide variety of situations. The principles are equally useful in making on-the-spot decisions as in longer-term deliberations. Moreover, they are valid in dealing with issues of varying magnitude. For this reason, we feel they can be generalized to most of the day-to-day sensitive judgments you will have to make.

Ethical Judgments Related to Children's Extreme Behavior naeyc

Sometimes, early childhood educators find themselves in a dilemma, trying to decide whether a child's behavior merits the attention of additional behavioral or medical experts. On one hand, a child's actions may be so baffling or so dysfunctional that the adult fears that ignoring them could have serious consequences. On the other hand, he or she worries about alarming the family, offending them, or asking them to commit to what may be a significant outlay of time or money. Torn between both sides of the issue, the helping professional may find it impossible to make a conscious decision. Fortunately, guidelines are available to enable professionals to make such ethical judgments with more assurance.

What Constitutes Extreme Behavior?

Criteria have been developed for determining what behaviors should be considered extreme (Guerney, 2004). Some behaviors are extreme by virtue of their mere presence. Others are designated as extreme because they exceed the normal boundaries you would expect in relation to a child's age. How intense a behavior is and how generalized it becomes are additional factors that must be taken into account when determining whether behavior is extreme. Other variables that influence decision making include the effect the behavior has on the child's present or future functioning and how resistant the behavior is to modification.

Presence of self-destructive behaviors and cruelty to others/animals. Self-destructive acts are danger signs. Their very appearance should prompt immediate intervention. Self-destructive acts are those that children inflict on themselves and that result in physical injury or mental damage. This is exemplified by the youngster who disfigures herself by scratching or pulling out her hair; by the child who bangs his head, causing contusions; and by the child who deliberately courts danger as a thrill-seeking device. In

each case, the behavior is too serious to be allowed to continue.

Similarly, children who repeatedly engage in unprovoked acts of cruelty toward others and/or the animals in their lives are displaying antisocial behaviors that are more often than not linked to serious future problems. As many as half of all sex offenders self-report a history of animal cruelty, and in most incidents of recent school shootings, the juveniles involved had documented histories of animal cruelty. Though childhood animal cruelty does not inevitably lead to later violence toward people, early displays of such behavior require speedy consultation with a behavior expert. This is especially true when children claim that such acts are accidental or put the blame on others, all the while seeming to enjoy the havoc that results. If such actions become customary, either at home or in the program, the child is exhibiting signs of extreme behavior.

Sudden drastic changes in behavior patterns. Another cause for concern is when a child's normal behavior pattern changes suddenly or radically. A generally happy, responsive child who becomes withdrawn and fearful, a habitually mild-mannered child who overnight becomes volatile, and a child who begins complaining of unrelenting stomachaches are all showing evidence of extreme behaviors. Because these actions are so out of character, they signal a need for closer scrutiny.

Age-atypical behavior. Frequently, a behavior is considered extreme if it reappears or continues to exist long after one would expect a child to have outgrown it. Although it is typical for 2-year-olds to have temper tantrums, even frequent ones, 9-year-olds do not usually behave this way. Thus, if a 9-year-old repeatedly resorted to explosive outbursts, it would be obvious that the behavior should be categorized as extreme. Likewise, if an 8-year-old suddenly begins bed-wetting after having been dry at night since toddlerhood, this would deserve serious attention.

Intense behavior. Problem behaviors are generally considered normal if they appear only occasionally or briefly. However, they are labeled extreme if they occur frequently or if they last for prolonged periods of time. For instance, it is not unusual for preschoolers to periodically seek the comfort of blanket and thumb when frightened or tired. On the other hand, were 3-year-old Michael to spend the majority of his waking hours pacifying himself in this manner, the behavior would be considered extreme. Likewise, everyone has times when they want to "sneak" an extra cookie or snack item. However, the child who regularly steals or hoards food is exhibiting signs of extreme behavior. Whether parents or the professional with whom the

It's cleanup time. These boys have newly discovered one another and are engrossed in their conversation. What judgment principles apply here?

© Cengage Learning

CHALLENGING BEHAVIOR

Meet Adrian

Adrian, a first grader, was observed by his teacher jabbing a pencil at the classroom guinea pig, which was huddled in the corner of the cage, squealing loudly. His teacher moved quickly to correct the situation but was concerned when Adrian offered the explanation that he was "just having fun" with the distressed animal. This incident, along with one noted just a month earlier where Adrian had hurt a kindergartner on the playground and had seemed relatively unconcerned, were signals to his teacher that she had to contact his parents for an immediate conference.

child comes in regular contact should seek outside help would depend on how long the problem lasts. There are times when extreme behaviors are short lived. That is, they appear for a few days, and then children gradually return to their original behavior patterns. Such instances are viewed as temporary crises that require adult support but not necessarily outside intervention. However, should the behavior endure, some serious exploration of the child's situation, with the help of an expert in such matters, would be in order.

Indiscriminate and pervasive behavior. Certain actions that might be considered normal if their appearance were limited become abnormal when they pervade all aspects of a child's life. For instance, it is common for youngsters aged 4 through 9 to tell untruths to protect themselves in incriminating situations or to make themselves seem more interesting. Although hardly exemplary, their resorting to lies under duress or in moments of self-expansiveness should not be categorized as extreme.

On the other hand, there are a few children who rely on falsehoods in virtually all situations, regardless of whether they are in obvious trouble or in a circumstance in which absolute adherence to the facts is unimportant. These youngsters tend to lie about many things even when the truth would serve them better. In these cases, a behavioral expert should be consulted to determine how it could be modified.

Behaviors that hamper children's functioning. Behaviors that have the potential to hamper children's growth or development should be treated as extreme. This is exemplified by children who repeatedly force themselves to throw up after eating, those who are so hostile or lacking in affect they do not let anyone get close to them, and youngsters who become so centered on getting good grades that they resort to cheating, lying, and sabotage of others' work to better their own standing. Likewise, diabetic children who deliberately avoid their medication or habitually eat forbidden foods fall into this category. Young people who are so shy or standoffish that they literally have no friends or acquaintances also are enmeshed in extreme, counterproductive patterns of behavior. In each case, consultation with parents and behavioral experts is recommended.

Resistance of the behavior to change. Resistance for more than a short time (usually several weeks) to reasonable efforts to correct a common, everyday problem is a sign that the behavior has become extreme. "Reasonable efforts" refer to adult use of relevant, constructive strategies aimed at eliminating negative actions while simultaneously promoting desirable alternate behaviors. It also implies consistency. That is, the problem behavior must receive attention on a predictable basis, and the strategies employed must be used often enough and long enough that a behavior change is likely.

Within this definition, a child who periodically experiences negative consequences for being out of his seat, but who at other times is inadvertently rewarded for wandering, is not demonstrating resistant behavior, but rather the effects of the adult's unpredictable responses. Conversely, if the child experiences appropriate consequences over a two-month span but still habitually wanders the room, this is evidence that the behavior has become extreme.

Similarly, a developmental task for all young children is to become toilet trained. Although the optimal period for this to occur varies among individuals, it is accepted that by about 3 years of age, most children will have begun or completed this training. Yet, some children resist learning to use the toilet. Initial resistance is common and should not be a signal for alarm. However, there are youngsters whose resistance continues to mount such that bladder or bowel control is still not achieved into the grade-school years. Under these conditions, the behavior can appropriately be described as extreme.

Frequently Reported Sources of Extreme Behavior

When adults are confronted with children's extreme behavior, they often wonder where it comes from and why it occurs. Although the variables influencing any single child may differ widely, three of the most commonly reported sources include physiological factors, childhood fears, and childhood depression (Goleman, 2011).

Physiology. It has been suggested that some children who exhibit extreme behavior do so as a result of protein, vitamin, or mineral deficiencies in their diet (Santrock, 2008). For instance, children who are deprived of essential B vitamins have impaired concentration, resulting in a shorter attention span and a lack of task commitment. Over the past several years, scientists also have hypothesized that some genuinely extreme, noncompliant behavior is related to neurological dysfunction. Hyperactive behavior, sometimes diagnosed as attention-deficit disorder (ADD) or attention-deficit/hyperactivity disorder (ADHD), is the most common of these. Brain damage, which may result from birth complications or a later head injury, can also make it difficult for a child to sit still, and chemical imbalances in the brain may

interfere with the transfer of signals from one cell to another. Either way, brain dysfunction may contribute to a child's need for constant motion and an inability to relax (Berger, 2008).

Another extreme behavioral problem that results from neurological difficulties is Tourette's syndrome. Children with this condition display tics (repeated involuntary movements, such as eye blinking), which may be accompanied by the shouting of obscenities and the production of loud and/or strange noises. All of these behaviors are actually beyond the child's ability to control. When related to neurological dysfunction, assistance from specially trained professionals is necessary.

Childhood fears. Another source of extreme behavior in children is fear. All children at one time or another become afraid of certain places, people, things, or events. Even if extreme in intensity for days or sometimes weeks, these fearful episodes usually are of a relatively short duration. Time, along with adult empathy and support, will dissipate most of these. Yet, there are times when fears persist for such long periods and permeate so many areas of a child's life that they interfere with the child's ability to function. Such extreme fears are called **anxiety disorders**. They are persistent, unfounded, out of proportion to the actual danger or threat, and lead to maladaptive behavior (Berns, 2013).

Most often, this maladaptation takes the form of extreme withdrawal. For example, 7-year-old Veronica reached a point where she was terrified at the mere prospect of coming in contact with anything fuzzy. Initially, Veronica had expressed a fear of mice. Gradually, her fear extended to encompass most fuzzy objects, such as stuffed animals, blankets, and the fur collar on her coat. As time went on, she became hysterical at the touch of a cotton swab and when asked to use yarn in a weaving project. Ultimately, her anxiety prompted her to resist leaving the sanctuary of her home, from which most of the offending items had been eliminated.

School Phobia. A common anxiety disorder during the grade-school years is known as school refusal, or **school phobia** (Papalia, Olds, & Feldman, 2008). Although many youngsters experience some anxiety about school, about 16 of every 1,000 develop such severe anxieties that they become physically ill at the prospect of going to school each day (Gelfand & Drew, 2003). Their resistance to school becomes extreme. Screaming, crying, and tantrums are common, as are severe stomachaches, headaches, and sore throats. The child's distress may be directly related to incidents at school (inability to perform the work expected or being made fun of by other children). It also may be caused

© Cengage Learning

It is important to communicate concerns to the child's family about potentially extreme behaviors.

by other factors not so easily discernible, such as fears that develop from a misunderstood conversation or the chance remark of another child. In either case, the child's reaction is to attempt to withdraw from all school contacts.

Occasionally, rather than trying to resolve fear through withdrawal, some youngsters try to master it directly. In the process, they often overreact, engaging in potentially harmful activities. For example, following a period of extreme fear of fire, some children set fires. They reason that their ability to produce a flame at will and to extinguish it themselves demonstrates their power over it.

Another worrisome way that some children cope with fear is to develop an obsession or a compulsion. Undesired recurring thoughts are called **obsessions**. These are persistent preoccupations or ideas children cannot get out of their heads. Impulses to repeatedly perform certain acts are called **compulsions** (Berns, 2012). Everyone exhibits some obsessive or compulsive behavior at some time, and in their mildest forms, neither of these is a problem.

However, if a compulsion or obsession begins to interfere with a person's functioning and is one from which he or she derives no pleasure or social benefits, it is judged extreme. For instance, 10-year-old Jessica was obsessed with the thought of having to urinate even though there was no physical basis for her

concern. Her obsession caused her to make as many as 50 trips to the bathroom each day. Often, after she got there, she was unable to produce even a drop. When Jessica was denied access to the bathroom as often as she wanted, her anxiety over a possible accident drove her to tears. She became so preoccupied with this one biological function that she was able to think of little else. As with other fear-related circumstances that exceed the bounds of normalcy, behaviors such as Jessica's require the attention of a behavioral expert.

Childhood depression. A source of extreme behavior that has become increasingly prevalent in children ages 2 to 12 is childhood depression (Papalia et al., 2008). Behaviors associated with this phenomenon range from affective ones, such as sadness, continual crying, withdrawal, inability to concentrate, lack of interest in life, and feelings of defeat, to physical manifestations, such as severe and frequent stomachaches or headaches for which there seems to be no physiological basis. Sometimes, extreme misbehavior can be a symptom of depression as well. It shows itself in such acting-out behaviors as stealing, fighting, or defiance.

These and other destructive acts are characterized by excessive disobedience and unrelenting resistance to change. It must be remembered that all children occasionally disobey for a variety of reasons and that

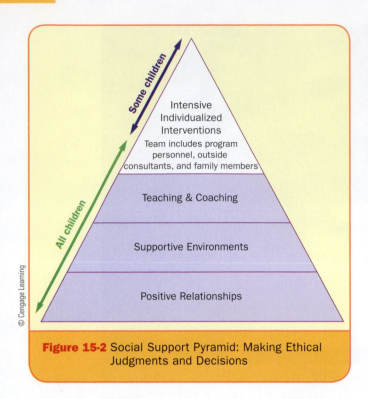

Figure 15-2 Social Support Pyramid: Making Ethical Judgments and Decisions

noncompliance does not, in and of itself, mean that a child is suffering from depression. Rather, outside help is warranted when unremitting, intense, hostile disobedience occurs over a long period of time. Such extreme behavior signals the need for Intensive Individualized Intervention (see Figure 15-2). Such interventions require the participation of adults within the program, consultants from beyond the program, and members of the child's family. Children experiencing extreme behaviors benefit greatly from the consistent, cohesive approach this kind of intervention affords them. Working with a wide array of childhood professionals whose expertise complements—but does not duplicate—your own, provides new perspectives to consider and greater possibilities for success than would be true if you simply tried to tackle such problems on your own.

Ethical Codes of Conduct Focused on Child Abuse and Neglect naeyc

When you suspect that a child in your care has suffered the trauma of child abuse or neglect, your emotions may run high. Your initial responses may include disbelief, horror, anger, or panic and may detract from your ability to deal with the situation coherently. At times like these, it is critical that you control your emotions and make a calm, rational judgment about whether there is a possibility of child abuse. To make such a judgment, you first must understand the nature of child abuse and the signs to look for.

Defining Abuse and Neglect

The mistreatment of children includes both abuse—actions that are deliberately harmful to a child's well-being—and neglect—failure to appropriately meet children's basic needs (Berger, 2008). Legally, every state has its own definition of these acts. However, there is general agreement that abuse and neglect most often take the following forms.

Physical abuse. These are assaults on children that produce pain, cuts, welts, bruises, broken bones, and other injuries. Whipping children, tying them up, putting tape on their mouth, locking them in closets, throwing them against walls, scalding them, and shaking them violently are common examples.

Sexual abuse. This includes molestation, exploitation, and intimidation by an adult (95% of reported cases are by men) to dominate or control a child. Sexual abuse is accomplished through force, coercion, cajoling, enticement, and threats, and because children generally trust, respect, and love the adults in their lives, they are easy to manipulate (Crosson-Tower, 2009). Children who are sexually abused may also be subjected to obscene phone calls or sexually explicit language; they may be made to exhibit themselves or to watch the exhibition of an adult.

Physical neglect. Neglect includes failure of adults to provide adequate food, clothing, shelter, medical care, and supervision for children. Neglected children starve because they are not fed, freeze when they are left without clothing in frigid temperatures, and may perish in fires when left unsupervised (Papalia et al., 2008).

Emotional abuse. This kind of abuse includes actions that deliberately destroy children's self-esteem. Such abuse is usually verbal and may take the form of scapegoating, ridiculing, humiliating, or terrorizing children.

Emotional neglect. This means failure of adults to meet children's needs for affection and emotional support. Emotionally neglected children are ignored or subjected to cold, distant relationships with adults.

Medical neglect. Adults might fail to meet children's need for medical attention in cases of acute or chronic disease.

Other maltreatment. Abuse and neglect includes cases where there is abandonment, threats of harm, and congenital drug addiction.

In each of these cases, children's current levels of functioning are damaged, and there is a potential

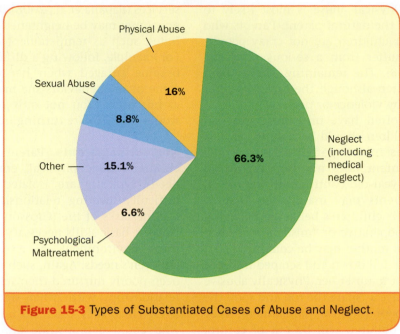

Physical Abuse

Sexual Abuse

16%

8.8%

Other — **15.1%**

66.3%

Neglect (including medical neglect)

6.6%

Psychological Maltreatment

Figure 15-3 Types of Substantiated Cases of Abuse and Neglect.

Source: U.S. Department of Health and Human Services; Karageorge & Kendall, 2009.

threat to their future well-being. At one time, it was thought that such negative acts occurred rarely and were perpetrated by a few "sick" people in our society. We now know better.

Scope of the Problem

Child abuse is a very serious problem that is more widely recognized today than ever before. Figure 15-3 shows types of substantiated cases of abuse and neglect documented by the U.S. Department of Health and Human Services (Karageorge & Kendall, 2009). Latest data available indicate that 10.6 of every 1,000 children in the United States are abused (48.2% boys; 51.5% girls) and that each year, more than 1,000 children die as a result of abuse and neglect. Younger children are the most likely victims, with 31.9% of maltreatment under 4 years of age. Under 1 year, 22.2 per 1,000 male children are mistreated, and 21.5% of female children are estimated to be abused or neglected. These figures are based on reported cases, with 25.4% of the cases reported by teachers; the real numbers undoubtedly are higher because much abuse is never brought to the attention of the authorities (NCANDS, 2007).

Such documentation suggests that at least 1 of every 10 young people will experience violation of their person during the childhood years. According to the law of averages, this means that you may come in contact with about 2 or 3 such children during a 12-month period. This is not to say that an abused child will be found in every formal group setting. It does underscore the fact that sometime during your career, you will have to make a judgment about whether a child is a victim of abuse. In fact, the problem has become so widespread that all 50 states now have laws requiring that suspected cases of child abuse be reported by doctors, teachers, and other helping professionals who work with children. Furthermore, in most states, helping professionals are legally responsible for any injury to a child that comes about because the professional failed to make such a report (NCANDS, 2007).

The Abusers

Who would beat, bash, burn, choke, neglect, starve, rape, sodomize, or otherwise assault a child? Are the perpetrators of such hideous deeds psychopathic monsters? Overwhelmingly, the evidence says no. Rather, they are ordinary people who, for any number of reasons, subject children to humiliating or physically injurious acts. Child abuse cuts across all ages, both genders, all races, all social classes, all family structures, and all socioeconomic groups.

There are no characteristics that infallibly separate abusers from nonabusers, victims from nonvictims. Although certain conditions may be more or less highly related to abuse, their existence alone is not an absolute indicator of whether or not abuse will occur. Rather, it is a combination of variables that determines actual outcomes.

Physical abusers. Physical abuse is most likely to occur at the hands of the natural parent. Parents who physically abuse their children are not crazy people. Only 10% actually suffer from a serious psychotic disorder (Berger, 2008). The remaining adults claim to care for their children although the care they offer frequently is marred by violence or neglect.

Abusive parents often have unrealistic expectations about what children should be able to do at a particular age. For instance, a parent might become incensed when an infant does not stop crying on demand or when a 2-year-old continues to wet or soil her pants. These parents may inaccurately assume intentionality in their children's behavior, believing that the child is uncooperative or "misbehaving" just to be difficult. Thus, a mother may be convinced that a school-age child who fell down and scraped his knee did so deliberately, just to upset her. Physically abusive parents also tend to have a "spare the rod and spoil the child" philosophy about physical punishment; they are afraid that their children will be out of control unless they spank them, even for small infractions. Unfortunately, because these parents often have a low tolerance for stress, usually possess a poor repertoire of life skills, and are frequently unhappy about being a parent, their intentions to be an effective parent result in physical abuse of their children. In an overwhelming number of these cases, the adults have experienced poor relationships with their own parents, often having been abused as children themselves (Goleman, 2007).

Finally, situational factors within and outside the family play a significant role in the likelihood of abuse occurring. For example, abuse is most common in families in which finances are severely strained (regardless of socioeconomic status). Other stressful life events such as divorce, unemployment, family conflict, overcrowding, lack of a support system, or drastic changes in status and role create the conditions in which abuse may eventually take place (Berk, 2013). The results of the latest nationwide survey by the National Committee to Prevent Child Abuse also linked child abuse with homelessness and substance abuse by parents (Children's Defense Fund, 2013). Abusive families frequently are isolated families; that is, they have little access to parenting information that might be of use to them or to potential resource people and have no real means of social comparison, either for their children or for themselves. This isolation heightens, and sometimes causes, many of the problems they experience.

Increasingly, scientists believe that abuse occurs as a result of an interactive effect among all of the variables just described: the adult's personality, lack of parenting skills, unrealistic expectations, situational characteristics, and lack of community support

services (Papalia et al., 2008). The volatile nature of the encounter may be heightened by the child's own attributes, such as temperament or physical appearance. For example, following a difficult divorce, Sonia often became enraged when her youngest son displayed some of the behaviors she had come to dislike in her ex-husband. "You not only *look* like your dad," she would yell. "You're turning out to be just like him!"

Neglectful parents. Parents who fail to meet their children's basic physical, emotional, or educational needs typically are isolated individuals who have difficulty forming relationships or carrying on the routine tasks of life (Crosson-Tower, 2009). They also lack the basic skills necessary to organize a safe, warm home environment. As a result, they ignore their children's needs. Again, such parents are likely to have been poorly nurtured themselves and to have stressful relationships with other significant adults in their lives. Thus, they often do not have access to models who could demonstrate more appropriate forms of engagement with children.

Sexual abusers. For many years, parents and helping professionals have warned children to stay away from strangers. Most often, the child molester has been portrayed as a classic "scary person": an unfamiliar, middle-aged male in a raincoat who hangs around parks or schools waiting to tempt a lone child with candy. Unfortunately, this scenario does not cover the most common situations in which children are at risk. In reality, in 80% of child sexual abuse cases, the child knows the offender, and more frequently than not, the offender is a member of the child's own household. When sexual abuse by strangers does occur, it is most likely to happen in a single episode, during warm-weather months, outside, in an automobile, or in a public building. On the other hand, abuse perpetrated by family members or acquaintances is apt to occur repeatedly, at any time, and at home (Shaffer & Kipp, 2013). In these cases, force or bribery seldom is used. Instead, the child may submit to the adult's requests in deference to the adult's perceived status in the family, from a desire to please, or fear about what will happen if they don't agree.

Families in which the father or father figure abuses a daughter represent the most common incidents of abuse. These families often are plagued by dysfunctional relationships, especially between spouses. The adult male frequently has low self-esteem and is weak and resentful rather than virile or oversexed as is the common stereotype. Most mothers are aware of the situation but are unable to face their predicament and so deny what is happening. In fact, after the abuse becomes known, it is not uncommon for family members to turn against the victim, blaming her for the disruption. Circumstances such as these can go on for years if no intervention is forthcoming.

The Victims

The majority of physical-abuse cases are initiated during the preschool years. Though the phenomenon has been tied to abuse in future generations, it is important to point out that individuals who were abused or neglected do not necessarily grow up to abuse or neglect their own children. Though it is true that many of those who abuse children were abused themselves as children, it does not hold true that because a child is abused, he or she will automatically become an abuser in the future. Other myths often attached to children who are abused and neglected are that they become deviant adults who are involved in crime, drugs, or prostitution, or that the effects of abuse or neglect are irreparable and render victims incapable of leading a fulfilling and happy life (Croson-Tower, 2009).

Individuals can and do break the cycle of earlier maltreatment, and that is most likely to occur if there is early detection, support from a nonabusive adult during childhood (and therapy when indicated), and when they later have a satisfying, nonabusive relationship with a spouse (Shaffer & Kipp, 2013).

Although 10% of all victims of sexual abuse are younger than 5 years of age, the majority are children between the ages of 9 and 12 (Santrock, 2008).

Although females are primary targets, it should not be forgotten that boys also are victims of abuse and that adult females can be abusers. Unlike physical abuse, child sexual abuse often extends to more than one victim within the same family.

These sexual encounters frequently begin with innocent touching and progress to fondling and then to overt sexual stimulation. Forcible rape rarely occurs. Instead, there often are pleasurable overtones to the interactions, which contribute to children's confusion over what is happening to them. The most likely victims are those who lack information about sexual abuse and what to do if it occurs. Children who have low self-esteem and those who are physically weak and socially isolated are the most likely candidates for victimization.

Effects on victims. An obvious outcome of either physical or sexual abuse is injury. For example, it has been reported that abusive acts are the fourth most common cause of death in children 5 years of age and younger (Children's Defense Fund, 2013). Other problems include fractures, lacerations, internal injuries, pregnancy, and venereal disease. In addition, we can only begin to calculate the cost to society of caring for victims, incarcerating perpetrators, and the loss of productive family functioning. Because of the close contact helping professionals enjoy with the children in their care, they play an important role in identifying victims of abuse.

© Cengage Learning 2015

Signs of physical trauma in a child do not automatically signal abuse but warrant ongoing attention.

Signs of abuse. Several signs may indicate possible child abuse. Some relate to the child's appearance, others to the child's behavior, and still others to what the child says. Certain family indicators also should be considered. For example, does the child receive a lot of spankings at home or complain that the parents are always angry? Does the child come to school early and find reasons to stay after school as long as possible? Abused children may role-play behaviors displayed by abusive parents when they are involved in dramatic play, or they may represent the abuse in drawings they make. They may abuse younger children, exhibit aggressive behavior, be self-abusive, or express suicidal ideas. There may be frequent absences from school with no explanation (Driscoll & Nagel, 2007).

The presence of one sign alone does not automatically signal abuse. However, if one or more are present, they should be interpreted as a warning that additional attention is warranted (Berk, 2013). More specific signs are summarized in Highlight 15-2, Highlight 15-3, Table 15-3, and Figure 15-4.

HIGHLIGHT 15-2

Signs of Physical Abuse and Neglect

Physical Indicators

- Bruises
  - Bruises on the face, lips, or mouth; on large areas of the back, torso, buttocks, or thighs; on more than one side of the body
  - Bruises of different coloration, indicating that they occurred at different times
  - Bruises that are clustered
  - Bruises that show the imprint of a belt buckle, coat hanger, strap, or wooden spoon
- Welts
- Wounds, cuts, or punctures
- Burns
  - Rope burns on arms, legs, neck, face, or torso
  - Burns that show a pattern (cigarette, iron, radiator)
  - Burns on the buttocks or genitalia
  - Caustic burns
  - Scalding-liquid burns
- Fractures
  - Multiple fractures in various stages of healing
  - Any fracture in a child younger than 2 years of age
- Bone dislocations
- Human-bite marks
- Neglect
  - Child is consistently dirty, hungry, or inappropriately dressed for the weather.
  - Child has been abandoned.
  - Child has persistent medical problems that go unattended.

Behavioral Indicators

The child:

- Is wary of physical contact with adults
- Flinches when adults approach or move
- Exhibits a dramatic change in behavior
- Shows extreme withdrawal or aggression
- Indicates fear of parents or caregivers
- Consistently arrives early and stays late
- Is consistently tired or falls asleep during the day
- Is frequently late for school or absent
- Is under the influence of alcohol or drugs
- Begs or steals food
- Shows a limited capacity for experiencing pleasure or enjoying life

Verbal Indicators

The child:

- Reports injury by parents or caregiver
- Offers inconsistent explanations for injuries or condition
- Offers incredible explanations for injuries or condition
- Makes comments such as: "Can I come and live with you?," "Do I have to go home?," "My mom/dad doesn't like me"
- Reports not having a place to sleep and/or enough to eat

Family Indicators

The family:

- Maintains a filthy home environment
- Is socially isolated from the rest of the community
- Is extremely closed to contacts with school or child's friends
- Refuses to allow child to participate in normal school activities (physical education, social events)
- Offers inconsistent, illogical, or no explanation for child's injury or condition
- Shows lack of concern about child's injury or condition
- Attempts to conceal child's injury or condition
- Describes the child as evil, monstrous, or incorrigible
- Reports or uses in your presence inappropriate punishments (denial of food, prolonged isolation, beating)
- Consistently speaks in a demeaning way to the child
- Abuses alcohol or drugs
- Reacts defensively to inquiries regarding the child's health

Signs of Sexual Abuse

Physical Indicators

The child:

- Is pregnant
- Shows signs of venereal disease
- Has blood in urine
- Has genitals that are swollen or bruised
- Shows presence of pus or blood on genitals
- Has physical complaints with no apparent physical cause
- Has torn or stained underclothing
- Shows rectal bleeding

Behavioral Indicators

The child:

- Persistently scratches genital area
- Has difficulty sitting on chairs or play equipment (squirming, frequently readjusting position, frequently leaving seat)
- "Straddle walks" as if pants were wet or chafing
- Suddenly loses appetite
- Suddenly reports nightmares
- Shows extreme withdrawal or aggression
- Shows wariness of contact with adults
- Shows inappropriate seductiveness with adults or other children
- Shows a sudden lack of interest in life
- Withdraws into fantasy behavior
- Regresses to infantile behavior such as bed-wetting, thumb-sucking, or excessive crying
- Shows limited capacity for enjoying life or experiencing pleasure

- Is promiscuous
- Runs away
- Is frequently truant
- Exhibits knowledge of sexual functions far beyond other children in his or her peer group
- Suddenly withdraws from friends

Verbal Indicators

The child:

- Complains of pain in the genital area
- Reports incidents of sexual contact with an adult or older child
- Reports having to keep secret a game with an adult or an older child
- Expresses fear of being left alone with a particular adult or older child
- Reports: "She/he fooled around with me," "She/he touched me," or "My mother's boyfriend/my father/my brother/my aunt does things to me when no one else is there"

Family Indicators

The family:

- Exhibits an obvious role reversal between mother and daughter
- Is socially isolated from the rest of the community
- Is extremely closed to contacts with school or child's friends
- Demonstrates extreme discord
- Refuses to allow child to engage in normal social interactions

Table 15-3 Signs of Emotional Abuse and Neglect

Physical Indicators
- None

Behavioral Indicators

The child:

- Does not play
- Is passive and compliant or aggressive and defiant
- Rarely smiles
- Has poor social skills
- Is socially unresponsive
- Avoids eye contact
- Seeks attention constantly and always seems to want and need more
- Relates indiscriminately to adults in precocious ways
- Shows reluctance to eat or fascination with food
- Is prone to rocking, thumb-sucking

Verbal Indicators

The child:

- Reports problems sleeping
- Continually describes self in negative terms
- Is reluctant to include family in program-related events

Family Indicators

The family:

- Conveys unrealistic expectations for the child
- Seems to rely on the child to meet own social and emotional needs
- Shows indifference or lack of interest in child
- Lacks basic knowledge and skills related to child-rearing
- Describes child in primarily negative terms
- Seems focused more on meeting own needs than those of the children
- Blames child

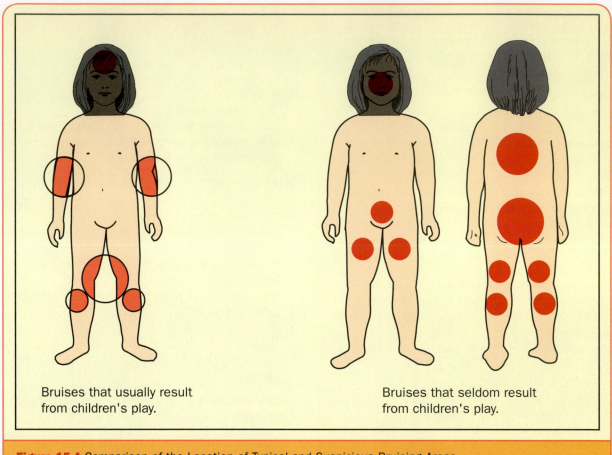

Bruises that usually result from children's play.

Bruises that seldom result from children's play.

Figure 15-4 Comparison of the Location of Typical and Suspicious Bruising Areas.

Source: Head Start Bureau, 1977.

Reporting Child Abuse

Individuals usually designated as mandated reporters of child abuse include the following:

- Childcare providers
- Pediatricians and other health care workers
- Law enforcement officers
- Mental health professionals
- Clergy
- School personnel
- Social workers

Such reports signal only the suspicion that abuse has occurred, and the latest data we have is that 6 million referrals were made in 2006 but there were only 905,000 convicted cases (Karageorge & Kendall, 2008). However, when you see clear signs of abuse and document and relay them to the proper authorities, you will be acting as an advocate for the child. Often, there may be no one else in the child's life willing to do so.

The reporting process is straightforward. Although particular institutions and government jurisdictions have their own individual procedures, most include the following:

1. A disclosure of the suspicion to a designated person within the program: social worker, principal, or director.

2. A verbal report to the social agency responsible for children's protective services in a particular community. This report is conveyed either directly by the individual who has the suspicion or indirectly through a designated spokesperson. In either case, the identity of the person who originally suspected abuse is kept confidential and is revealed only with his or her consent.

3. A written report to the social agency with which verbal contact was initiated. This usually occurs within two to three days. The written statement contains essential information, usually is brief, and is written in the person's own words rather than in legalistic terms.

4. An interview with the child. This is most common when sexual abuse is suspected. Youngsters usually are interviewed in the presence of someone they trust; in many cases, this is the helping professional in whom they confided.

5. Continued investigation. From this point on, the case falls within the jurisdiction of a protective service worker. Although contact with the helping professional is desirable, the burden of responsibility has now shifted to the protective service worker.

Despite the fact that professionals must report suspected child abuse, doing so is always stressful, often confusing, and even traumatic. Some of the unfortunate realities that accompany the tough judgments that must be made in these situations, and sometimes cause professionals to second-guess themselves, are described by Nunnelley & Fields (1999, p. 75):

Chindwin, a new employee in a childcare facility, discovered what appeared to be cigarette burns on a toddler assigned to her room. She showed them to the director who informed her that she didn't want to hear about such incidences (because it would mean loss of the child's weekly tuition). . ... Chindwin felt bewildered and confused. She knew she should report the problem, but she wanted to keep her job.

Tarrissa was concerned about one of the girls in her first-grade class. The child was somewhat obsessed with keeping her hands clean and was reluctant to ever go to the bathroom with other children. Following the established procedure in her school, Tarrissa discussed her concerns with the school counselor. Unfortunately, the information became buried on the counselor's desk, and Tarrissa's suspicions of sexual abuse were never reported.

Margaret, the owner of a family childcare home, had worked for months with a family experiencing domestic violence. After a particularly bad incident, the mother sought refuge in a shelter and, fearing for her children's lives, sent the police to retrieve her daughters from Margaret's care. The girls were terribly frightened to go with the officers and cried and clung to Margaret. The experience was traumatic for everyone.

Child Abuse Prevention in the Formal Group Setting

Less than 3% of all substantiated cases of child abuse occur in formal group settings. Although this is a relatively small portion of the total cases, we must do all we can to reduce the possibility that abuse will happen when children are in our care. Hiring procedures for new staff and policies focused on day-to-day operations and family communication can all be designed with child abuse prevention in mind. A summary of strategies that make abuse less likely to occur on the job is presented in Figure 15-5.

So far, this chapter has focused on factors that influence ethical judgments that helping professionals

Ethical dilemmas may arise when parents expect special treatment for their child.

© Cengage Learning 2015

HIRING PRACTICES

- Applicants are carefully screened. This includes all staff members, substitutes, and volunteers—people who work with the children directly and those who provide support services to the programs such as cooks, bus drivers, and custodians.

- Screening strategies include signed written applications, personal interviews, on-site observations with children, verification of personal and professional references and education qualifications, criminal record checks (see Chapter 1), and signed declarations related to previous convictions of any crime against children or other violent crime. A person's failure to fully disclose previous convictions is cause for automatic dismissal.

- New employees are oriented to the job and are informed of the child abuse prevention procedures to follow.

- Mandatory probation periods for new employees are instituted, during which time they are paired with seasoned employees who provide modeling and consultations. New employees are observed frequently to assess their interactions with children.

DAY-TO-DAY OPERATIONS

- The program's discipline policies are clearly defined.

- Programs create conditions that alleviate staff fatigue and burnout, such as limiting the number of children for which each adult is responsible, keeping group sizes within established bounds, providing adequate breaks, and offering refresher training related to discipline, classroom management, parent relations, staff conflict, and child abuse prevention.

- Programs are structured to avoid the possibility of private, hidden opportunities for child abuse to occur. All early childhood spaces are regarded as public. Daily routines and the physical environment (both indoors and outdoors) are reviewed to eliminate the possibility that staff members have solitary access to children with no possibility of being observed by others. Program policies encourage parental drop-in visits and provide ongoing supervision by qualified personnel throughout the day.

Figure 15-5 Preventive Strategies That Reduce the Probability of Child Abuse in Formal Group Settings.

Source: Data adapted from *Position Statement on the Prevention of Child Abuse in Early Childhood Programs and Responsibilities of Early Childhood Programs to Prevent Child Abuse,* NAEYC, 1998; Click, 2011; Prevent Child Abuse America (formerly National Committee for the Prevention of Child Abuse), 1996.

make. We have concentrated on ethical judgments in day-to-day encounters, considerations about children's extreme behavior, and those regarding child abuse and neglect. Following are suggestions for working ethically with family members, specific skills for making ethical decisions, and pitfalls that should be avoided.

Ethical Dimensions of Working with Families naeyc

Family members should be welcome at all times. Success of a program depends on communicating with families regularly and establishing warm, caring relationships with family members. Families need information on all components of a program, including philosophy, goals, discipline strategies used, child abuse prevention measures taken by the program, and methods for reporting suspected child abuse. They

should also understand that in the interest of keeping their children safe, they will only be released to parents, legal guardians, and the people parents have identified in writing.

Despite every effort to communicate well with families, teachers do encounter ethical issues with families. Occasionally, parents may not be aware of a problem. When they are alerted, they may disagree about the seriousness of an issue, may not believe their child could be at fault in any way, or may be confused about what they can possibly do to support the school. This is why anything important enough to contact parents should be well documented. Also, it should only be an issue where the child's present or future functioning will be at stake without parental assistance (Allen & Chowdry, 2012). For example, Ms. Reif grew exasperated when 4-year-old Kelly continued talking out loud to other children during story time, despite her efforts to redirect the behavior. She contacted Kelly's parents for a conference to "deal with it." Though Kelly's parents were unhappy to learn about this, they were also confused about how they might effectively control the situation.

When surveyed about the most frequent ethical dilemmas with children's families, educators have reported the following:

- How to handle cases of possible child abuse and neglect
- Challenges created by the custody disputes of parents who are divorcing
- Parents' demands to treat children in ways that teachers, in their professional judgment, believe are harmful
- Requests to share information that they fear parents may use as justification to harshly punish their children
- Encounters with parents who expect special treatment for their children
- Demands that make the teacher vulnerable to burnout or even disciplinary action (Freeman & Swick, 2007, p. 164)

Undoubtedly, one of the thorniest situations in dealing with families is that of filing a child abuse report. Still, if you find it necessary to do so, ethical behavior mandates that you contact the family immediately after it has been made. The purpose of this contact is not to humiliate them or to try to get them to repent, but to indicate that you respect them enough that you would not do something behind their backs.

Inform them that you suspect that their child has been subjected to physical or sexual abuse. Explain that you are legally bound to report such suspicions and that you wanted them to know you

had done so. Indicate that you would like to be supportive of the family in any way they might find acceptable. Expect a hostile or incredulous reaction, particularly if the parents themselves have been involved in the abuse.

Avoid berating the family or spending a great deal of time trying to justify your actions to them. Should parents choose to respond to you, either in defense of their actions, to explain extenuating circumstances, or to accuse you of misrepresenting them, listen in a nonjudgmental way. Use the reflective listening skills you have learned to accomplish this.

Keep confidential all matters related to the case. Do not gossip or disclose tantalizing tidbits to other parents or to staff members who are not directly involved. Refuse to answer questions from curious people who have no legitimate right to the information.

If you are in a situation that requires continued contact with the family, treat them casually and civilly. Acknowledge their presence, speak to them, and be genuine in your interactions. This means not being effusive or friendlier than you have been in the past. Talk about day-to-day affairs rather than "the case."

In all situations that call for considering ethical decision making with families, you must move beyond your own moral and idiosyncratic reactions to a particular situation and rely explicitly on the professional code of conduct, "using the 3Rs of parental relationship: respecting, responding, and reflecting on the strengths, hopes, and dreams of each family" (Freeman & Swick, 2007, p. 169).

In the following section, a summary of the skills you will need to formulate ethical judgments is outlined. Included are skills for making ethical and day-to-day judgments, managing children's extreme behavior, and contending with abuse and neglect. All will be extremely important in your work with young children.

SKILLS FOR MAKING ETHICAL JUDGMENTS naeyc

How to Make Ethical Judgments

1. **Identify situations that have ethical implications.** This may encompass both hypothetical and real circumstances. Refer to the journal *Young Children* for sample cases illustrating ethical dilemmas. Think about ways to approach these. Refer to the sample answers in each issue, comparing your response to those of others in the field. In addition, keep a journal of your experiences with children and families. Catalog

examples from real life to discuss with colleagues in an appropriate setting.

2. **Become familiar with the NAEYC Code of Ethical Conduct. Review the code.** Know what it contains. Refer to it often when faced with perplexing situations that challenge your personal and professional values.

3. **Practice using the NAEYC Code of Ethical Conduct in response to ethical dilemmas.** You may find that some circumstances are easily

categorized as ethical or unethical because they clearly support or run counter to the code. Others are not so obvious. This may be due to their complexity or the subtle nature of the incident. In either case, practice will improve your skills and confidence using the code. Both students in training and practitioners in the field report that such practice is most beneficial when carried out regularly and in small groups of colleagues.

- First, decide what makes a troubling situation an ethical dilemma. Remember, not all worrisome situations are ethical in nature. Ethics implies right and wrong.

- Identify signals that alert you to potential ethical issues. Listen carefully to the signals other people say they use. Compare these with your own, and add or subtract ones that would be helpful for future use.

- Next, sort out matters that must be addressed by different people. The response to an ethical dilemma may require varying actions by more than one person. Explore what these responses might be.

- Finally, refer to the code for help in thinking about priorities and responsibilities in determining a plan to address the situation.

The point is not to achieve unanimous agreement on a single course of action but to generate one or more strategies that support ethical approaches to the problem. Identify those strategies that seem most congruent with your own thinking. Consider what you would say and do to carry out your plan.

Keep a record of typical responses to hypothetical circumstances. In real-life situations in which you are involved, carry out your plan. Then make note of the outcomes for future reference.

4. **Refer to the code when talking about why you carry out certain practices in your work and why you refrain from using others.** Such conversations may be with parents, colleagues, or laypersons. Explaining to others that we have a code of ethics is a valuable sign of professionalism. It also provides justification for judgments and decision making that goes beyond intuition. For instance, the reason early childhood professionals do not deprive children of food or use of the toilet as a means of punishment is that such behavior is unethical according to principles set forth in the code. As a profession, we have agreed that ethical behavior requires us to inform parents of accidents involving their child and to maintain family confidentiality. Referencing the code periodically is a good way to keep its standards in the forefront of your thinking.

How to Make Day-to-Day Judgments

1. **Become aware of values that are important to you.** Think about decisions you have made in your own life in terms of the values they represent. Try to determine what basic beliefs govern your interactions with children and their families. Figure out if there are discernible patterns to the kinds of choices you make. Discuss your ideas with friends and colleagues. Compare your reactions with theirs, and try to articulate why you have chosen a particular path. Take advantage of formalized opportunities to engage in values clarification.

2. **Comprehensively assess situations in which a judgment must be made.** Make an initial survey that includes the following factors: recognition of the child's perspective, awareness of your own affective state, consideration of the child's age and past experiences, and an analysis of the situational context.

   If you are in a situation in which you are an observer and in which safety is not in question, take a few moments to sort out the issues prior to acting. Should you be in a circumstance in which an immediate response is expected, use an affective reflection and the middle portion of the personal message (i.e., your emotions and the reasons for them) to identify aloud the child's perspective and your own. If, at that point, you need a few more moments to think, tell the children, "Let me think about it for a minute, and then I'll decide what to do."

3. **Consider alternative strategies in terms of their potential outcomes.** Imagine various responses to a particular situation. Predict the possible impact of each on the child, on yourself, and on others. Think about how each outcome would either support or impede your current goals for all parties.

4. **Select and implement a strategy or combination of strategies that supports your overall goals for children and that is based on your priorities for the situation.** Keep in mind the goals you are working toward for each child and for the group as a whole. In addition, use the priority principles outlined in this chapter to help you sort out what is most important in a given instance. Use the goals and priorities you identify as the basis for action.

5. **Include nonintervention as a strategy option.** Taking no action in a situation can be the result of a considered judgment on your part. Some incidents, particularly when they have no effect on others, do not require a response.

6. **Adopt standards that take into account children's age and experience.** Apply your understanding of child development and learning to your expectations for children's performance. Do not expect children to perform perfectly the first few times. Allow them to make mistakes. Observe youngsters carefully to determine what they can and cannot do, and then set your standards accordingly. As they become more adept, increase your expectations gradually.

7. **Reassess situations in light of new information.** Remember that you can make different judgments regarding your goals, strategies, and standards as you acquire new knowledge. This may mean selecting an option you had previously discarded or developing an entirely new one.

8. **Evaluate the ethical judgments you make.** Take time to assess the effectiveness of your thinking and of corresponding actions. Consider whether the potential outcome became reality. If so, ask yourself whether it contributed to progress toward a desired goal. If the anticipated effect did not occur, reflect on what contributed to the incongruous result and what might be done instead. Discuss your deliberations with a colleague or supervisor.

9. **Learn from judgment errors.** Sooner or later, you will make a judgment that you will come to regret. When this happens, mentally review the circumstances under which you made it. Consider what prompted your response and what other options were available to you at the time. Try to determine what went awry, and figure out what you might do if you had the decision to make again. Sometimes, you will conclude that you made a bad judgment and that another option would have been better. On other occasions, you will deduce that the judgment was right at the time, even though the outcome was negative or stressful. Mentally catalogue relevant information for future use. Then, move on. It is counterproductive to unceasingly agonize over a past judgment.

10. **Support colleagues who have made poor judgments.** When fellow staff members have made a judgment that has turned out poorly, offer comfort and encouragement. Be available as a sounding board and listen to their evaluation of what went into their decision. Help them sort out what went wrong, and brainstorm remedial strategies or alternate approaches for the future.

11. **Identify values you and colleagues or parents hold in common when differences in goals, strategies, and/or standards**

exist. Talk over conflicts in approach that arise. Explore thoroughly other people's perceptions by asking them to describe their understanding of the situation and overall purpose within it. Listen carefully and quietly, avoiding jumping to conclusions, interrupting, or giving your opinion prematurely.

Use the reflective listening skills you have learned to convey interest and acceptance. Look beyond the details of what people are saying to the essence of their message.

Find common aims at this level. Then, proceed to negotiate the goals, strategies, and standards that might be acceptable to both of you. In most cases, this type of clarification should contribute to mutual understanding and a more unified approach. If you recognize that you have a true conflict in values, acknowledge this state of affairs. Then, determine what you will have to do to make the situation livable.

How to Deal with Children's Extreme Behavior

1. **Get to know the children in your group prior to making a judgment that any one of them is exhibiting extreme behavior.** Although the mere presence of some behaviors is enough to signal a problem, it is important that you give yourself enough time to determine what is typical or atypical for each child.

2. **Make a concerted effort to change a behavior by using appropriate guidance techniques before judging it extreme.** Use the skills you have learned in previous chapters as your initial means of addressing problematic behavior. Be consistent in your approach, and allow enough time (usually several weeks) for your strategies to have a fair chance of success. Ask a colleague to review your plan and/or to observe its implementation to judge whether it is appropriate and whether you are carrying it out effectively. If you discover that a child's continued exhibition of a problem behavior is the result of a faulty plan or ineffective implementation, make the necessary revisions.

3. **Confirm your judgment that a child's behavior is extreme.** Make an objective record of the child's behavior over time. Use the A-B-C approach to Functional Assessment described in Chapter 11. Then, refer to resources that describe age or behavioral norms. If the behavior appears to be inappropriate, carefully observe how often it can be seen in other children of comparable age while they are both active and quiet. If no

other children manifest the behavior in question, talk to an experienced and trusted colleague who has worked with many children effectively. Also, consult your supervisor, a reputable professional, or other coworkers whose job responsibilities encompass this type of consultation. If others agree that the behavior seems extreme, set up an appointment with the child's parents.

4. **Communicate to the family your concern that their child's behavior is extreme.** When making the initial contact, whether in person, by telephone, or by written message, express your concern matter-of-factly and request a meeting with the parent(s). Avoid going into elaborate detail or sounding secretive and mysterious in the initial contact with parents so that you do not alarm them or make them feel defensive. You might say something like: "I've been observing Charles for the last several days and have become concerned about his sudden lack of interest in interacting with the other children. Normally, he's quite outgoing, and his withdrawal has persisted for some time. I'd like to set up a time to discuss this with you in more detail."

When the meeting takes place, be prepared to provide documented and concrete examples of the behavior in question. Find out if the same behavior occurs at home and whether or not the parent considers it atypical. If, as the conference proceeds, you reach the conclusion that indeed, the behavior is extreme, share this concern with the parent(s) and provide a rationale for your judgment. Be prepared to suggest specific courses of action the parent(s) could take, including consultation with a reputable professional.

5. **Recommend the type of professional who could deal most appropriately with a particular problem.** Determine with the family who will contact the consulting professional. If the behavior may be physically based, as in problems with eating, elimination, sleeping, too much or too little energy, or obvious depression, the family should first contact a physician. If an extreme behavior is determined to be unconnected to physical sources, begin with a behavioral expert trained in dealing with the behavior of concern. Such an expert is more likely to be familiar with behavioral problems than would many physicians. Further, reputable, competent behavioral specialists would be aware of conditions to which physical difficulties could contribute and would suggest medical consultation in such instances.

Check on potential community resources such as child guidance clinics, college psychological clinics, school guidance counselors, community mental health agencies, social service agencies in your area, intermediate school districts (umbrella agencies that offer special services across school districts), and programs specializing in youngsters whose problems are similar to the one you have tentatively identified for a particular child. Even when an individual program may not exactly suit your needs, personnel there may be able to direct you to a more appropriate source.

6. **Provide emotional support to families who are seeking outside help for their child's extreme behavior.** The referral process often takes a long time, resulting in anxiety or frustration for families. Offer words of encouragement or sympathy, and be willing to listen to familial complaints and lamentations. Use reflective listening skills to communicate your understanding. Take additional action, if possible, to speed up the process.

7. **Follow up on your recommendation that a child or family should receive outside services.** If you have agreed to provide a contact for a medical or behavioral expert, do so promptly. Make the contact directly or through the channels dictated by your agency or program. Periodically check on the progress of your referral, and make sure that contact actually is made. Should the family assume primary responsibility for seeking help, communicate with them regularly to ascertain what has happened.

8. **Provide accurate, relevant information to the consulting professional.** Share your observations of the child's behavior, either verbally or in writing. Make available records you have kept regarding his or her behavior pattern, or summarize them in a report.

Invite the outside expert to observe the child within the formal group setting. Offer to meet with him or her and the family.

9. **Coordinate the way you deal with the child's extreme behavior in the formal group setting with the way it is being handled by the family and by the consultant to whom the child has been referred.** Find out what action has been recommended. Discuss with the consultant and the family the feasibility of adapting your program to the consultant's recommendations as well as ways in which your actions can complement theirs. For instance, if it has been decided that certain behaviors will be rewarded and others ignored at home and in the therapy session, follow the same guidelines, if possible.

Provide feedback to all adults involved in the plan regarding the child's progress in your setting. Make relevant suggestions for changes and revisions in the plan. Also, ask for feedback regarding your own performance. Maintain periodic contact with both the consultant and the family throughout this time.

How to Deal with Child Abuse and Neglect

1. **Find out the appropriate procedures for reporting child abuse and neglect in the state in which you are currently working.** Read the laws regarding child abuse and neglect, including what constitutes abuse, the persons or agencies to whom such cases should be referred, who is legally obligated to report abuse, and what safeguards exist for those reporting. Although all 50 states mandate reporting suspected cases and protect helping professionals from legal prosecution when making reports in good faith, the specifics of who is bound to report, who is notified, and how it is done vary. It is likely that your state requires all school administrators, teachers, counselors, social workers, nurses, physicians, dentists, audiologists, law enforcement officers, and duly-regulated childcare providers to make an oral report of suspected child abuse or neglect to the local department of social services.

    In addition to obtaining this legal knowledge, find out the reporting protocol of the formal group setting in which you are employed. If you are required to make a report through a designated person, determine how you will know that your report has been filed. Also, ask what role you are expected to play in subsequent action. Should the policy require that you report your suspicions directly to the authorities, find out who they are. (Often, these are described as "Children's Protective Services.")

2. **Watch for signs of child abuse and neglect.** Use the physical, behavioral, verbal, and family indicators outlined in Highlights 15-2 and 15-3.

    Pay attention to children. Look at them. Listen to what they say. Disclosure may be accidental or embedded in statements they make about other events (Austin, 2000). Be alert for changes in a child's physical condition or demeanor. Believe children when they persistently complain that they are hungry, that they "hurt down there," or that Uncle Billy beat them with a strap (Hendrick & Weissman, 2011). Most children do not make up stories about abuse or molestation.

3. **Document your suspicions.** Keep written notes about the sign that caused you to suspect child abuse or neglect and the date on which it occurred. If more than one sign is present, record each of them.

4. **Respond appropriately when children disclose abuse**, as follows:

    a. Remain calm and reassuring, maintaining an open, relaxed posture.

    b. Take the child to a private space to talk out of the earshot of others.

    c. Use language appropriate to the child's developmental level, and do not use words that the child has not already used. Begin with general, open-ended questions or statements. Refrain from asking "why" questions. "What" and "how" questions are preferable.

    d. Use reflective listening and minimal prompts ("um hmm," "I see.").

    e. Take the child seriously.

    f. Allow the child to talk about feelings (e.g., guilt, shame, fear, ambivalence), and let the child know that such feelings are normal.

    g. Assure the child that he or she is not alone and that you are willing to help. However, do not make false promises (e.g., "It will be all right." "Nothing bad is going to happen.").

    h. Obtain only the information necessary to make a report.

    i. Reassure the child that the abuse is not his or her fault. Thank the child for confiding in you about the problem.

    j. Do not condemn the alleged abuser.

    k. Help the child devise a safety plan if the abuse happens again by telling a trusted adult. (Austin, 2000, pp. 3–5)

5. **Promptly report suspected cases of child abuse or neglect.** Should a child or family display a combination of signs that you have been trained to recognize as indicative of child abuse, report it. Do not delay in the hope that conditions will change or that you were wrong. Do not vacillate about what to do. Once the suspicion is there, the subsequent action you will need to take is clear.

6. **Reassure children who have revealed that they are victims of abuse or neglect.** Say something like: "It was hard for you to tell me your mother knocked your tooth out. I'm really glad you told me." Let them know that you believe what they have said and that no harm will come to them from you for reporting the incident. Reflect their feelings of confusion, worry, anger,

or guilt. Allow them to talk out their feelings and to describe individual incidents with as much or as little detail as they want. Remain receptive and supportive of abused children no matter how uncomfortable or distressed you may feel.

On the other hand, avoid pumping children for details that are beyond their capacity or willingness to reveal at a given time. Express your sympathy about what has happened, but at the same time, do not berate the child's family. Even youngsters who have been ill-treated often feel a loyalty to family members. They may withdraw if they perceive that they must defend their family to you.

Many children feel guilty regarding their role in the abusive situation. They may conclude that because they are "no good" or "ugly" or "so bad," the adult had no choice but to abuse them. Attempt to rectify these misperceptions by stating that what happened was not the child's fault. Instead, it was the adult's behavior that was inappropriate.

Explain that sometimes adults become angry, confused, or lonely, but that beating children, tricking them, or subjecting them to unwanted fondling is wrong.

7. **Talk to children about physical touching.** Begin with infants, and continue throughout the childhood years, to use feeling words to describe physical interactions. Provide children with information about how touching affects them and others. Say things like: "A hug feels good," "Pinching (or biting) hurts," "You were happy when Jeremy scratched your back," or "You didn't like it when Marion hit you." Such statements form the foundation for a "touch vocabulary" that can be expanded as children develop.

Familiarizing children with these specialized words is the first step in teaching personal safety.

8. **Teach children personal safety.** It is widely believed that children benefit when they are taught ways to avoid exploitive touching. Prepare relevant activities and skits as a way to share accurate facts and information about personal safety with children. Adapt your presentation to match children's understanding and experience. For example:

a. Initiate a discussion in which children talk about touches that make them feel good and touches that make them feel bad. Introduce the idea of confusing touches: those that start out feeling good, but that eventually become uncomfortable (tickling, bear hugs, petting). Point out that no one has the right to use bad touch or confusing touch with another

person. Tell children that if someone tries to touch them in ways they do not like, they can say "No, get away!" and then tell someone they trust.

b. Set up a skit in which one character tries to trick another character into doing something. With very young children or older youngsters who have had little prior training, begin with obvious tricks unrelated to sexual abuse. As the children begin to understand the notion of a trick, introduce skits that address inappropriate touching (e.g., bribery, keeping a "secret," or flattery). Emphasize the point that it is not okay for people to force children to touch them or to trick children into touching them. Teach children that if a person tries to trick them into touching him or her or into doing things the child does not understand, the child can say, "No, get away!" and tell someone he or she trusts.

c. Play the "What if . . . ?" game as a way to check children's understanding of how to respond in dangerous situations. Make up pretend episodes, such as "What if the man down the street asks you to come in and see the new puppies?" "What if your babysitter asks you to keep a secret, especially from your mom and dad?" or "What if you have a fight with your friends in the park, and a nice lady you don't know offers you a ride home?" Reflect children's answers and provide accurate information as appropriate. Ask open-ended questions to further extend the discussions.

9. **Treat families with sensitivity even when child abuse is suspected or has occurred.** Be aware of help available in your community for parents who indicate they are on the brink of abuse. Promising studies show that many abusing parents can be helped so that they no longer resort to physical violence (Shaffer, 2009). This is an indication of how important it is to refer parents to people and programs designed to assist them. Find out as much as you can about such support programs in your area. Identify short-term alternatives such as hotlines, sources of respite care, parent groups, educational opportunities, and workshops. In addition, keep a file of long-term options, including local individual and family therapists, mental health agencies, and religious and social service programs, as well as such nationally recognized groups such as Parents Anonymous and the National Committee to Prevent Child Abuse.

Pitfalls to Avoid naeyc

There are many guidelines to remember in deciding how to make an ethical judgment. The skills just covered describe the behaviors you should exhibit. The pitfalls that follow describe behaviors you should avoid.

1. **Failing to make a conscious judgment because of time pressures.** Sometimes, early childhood educators are so rushed that they think they cannot take the time to figure out what to do. Instead, they react instinctively. Occasionally, their intuitive responses are correct and fit well into a comprehensive approach to the child and the group. More often, they satisfy short-term ends, but do not comprehensively address long-term goals. Although it is not always feasible to ponder over what to do, it is possible to incorporate the ethical judgment process somewhere in the situation. Even if this can be done only in retrospect, assessing your judgment is a valuable professional skill.

2. **Staying with a poor judgment too long.** At times, people become wedded to a selected option because they have invested so much time and energy in making that judgment. They fail to recognize signs that a goal or standard does not fit, that a strategy useful under other circumstances is not effective in this instance, or that a plan simply is not working. If they continue to ignore these cues, the situation will deteriorate. The best way to avoid this pitfall is to keep alert to changes in the situational context and to remain receptive to new information.

3. **Failing to recognize your limitations.** This mindset can be the result of any of the following potential errors of judgment:

   - Thinking you are the only one who cares enough to handle the child appropriately or who understands the child well enough to know what to do

   - Jealously guarding your role in the child's life and perceiving other helping professionals as interlopers

   - Not recognizing the seriousness of the child's situation

   - Interpreting the need to consult with an outside expert as an indication of your own inadequacy

   - Thinking you possess skills that, in fact, you do not

   In any case, this type of thinking is not conducive to creating the most favorable climate for the child's development. If you find yourself resisting making a referral, even when all signs indicate that doing so is in the best interest of the child, examine your attitude. If you find that your lack of enthusiasm relates to any of the reasons just described, reconsideration is in order.

4. **Neglecting to clarify your own role in relation to the consulting professional.** Working with an outside consultant requires coordination of efforts. Children benefit most when they are handled consistently. This means that professionals in the formal group setting must have a clear understanding of what expectations, if any, the consultant has for their performance. It is not enough to have a vague picture of what is required. Instead, you must clarify mutual goals as well as the strategies and standards that will support them.

5. **Not following the recommendation of a consultant long enough to allow it to work.** One of the most common pitfalls in working with an outside consultant is to prematurely abandon a mutually agreed-on plan. Having finally taken the step of calling in an outsider, the helping professional may expect instant results. When these are not forthcoming, he or she gives up in disappointment. To avoid succumbing to this form of disillusionment, it is best to formulate, in conjunction with the consultant, a timeline along which progress will be measured. Knowing that a particular approach might have to be employed for several weeks or even months before a change can be expected increases your patience and makes setbacks easier to tolerate.

6. **Ignoring signs of abuse.** Sometimes, in an effort to avoid dealing with a difficult situation or because they wish it were not so, helping professionals overlook obvious cues that abuse has occurred. If a child exhibits bruises and reports that his mother beat him, the professional may think, "Oh, all children get paddled sometimes." When a youngster's vagina is raw and bleeding, the adult attributes it to masturbation. Should a child continually be dirty and smell bad, the adult passes it off as typical of that cultural group or social class.

   Children are not served well when adults reach these conclusions, which are based not on the facts, but on their own psychological and emotional defenses. Every sign that could indicate abuse must be taken seriously. Children should not be made to suffer because adults are afraid to face reality.

7. **Threatening families you suspect of child abuse.** Occasionally, rather than reporting a case of probable child abuse, helping professionals

try to intervene directly with the family. They confront family members, saying things like: "If I see this again, I'll have to report you" or "Promise me you'll stop, and I won't report you." Their motives may be self-serving (wishing to avoid legal entanglements) or well meaning (hoping to save the family embarrassment). In either case, these tactics are ill advised and should not be used. Instead, you should follow the procedures outlined in the child abuse section of this chapter.

8. **Purposely frightening children as a way to teach personal safety.** Adults who are trying to teach children to be careful about strangers and exploitive touching may deliberately overgeneralize their warnings so that youngsters become fearful of everyone and all forms of physical contact. Describing in lurid detail horrible incidents of abuse, treating all situations as unsafe, and failing to distinguish "good touch" from "bad touch" contributes to this negative perception. It is not healthy for children to feel in constant jeopardy. Instead, they must be exposed to a balanced view in which caution is promoted while avoiding terror and distrust.

9. **Assuming personal safety training will automatically protect children from sexual abuse.** Even with personal safety training, many children will have trouble saying "No" to adults, especially people with whom they have a close relationship. Young children should not be expected to handle the full burden of protecting themselves. Treat personal safety training as one potential tool children have at their disposal, not as a one-time inoculation against all potential abuse. Throughout childhood, children continue to need the watchful eye and support of caring adults. Remain alert to signs of sexual abuse regardless of whether or not children have had any training in this regard.

Summary

Helping professionals continually make ethical judgments for and about the children with whom they work. These encompass long- or short-range judgments—those that adults have time to evaluate carefully and others that must be made immediately. Some judgments will have profound effect; others will be relatively minor. However, all ethical judgments must be made consciously. Program goals, strategies, and standards relate to ethical judgments, and variables that influence those will include professionals' values, values of the profession, knowledge of child development and learning, and the situational context.

Six prioritized principles are involved in making ethical judgments, requiring professionals to be acquainted with NAEYC's Code of Ethical Conduct as a guide.

The discussion in Chapter 15 has dealt with everyday and special kinds of ethical judgments. Two arenas requiring specialized judgments are that of children's extreme behavior and child abuse or neglect. Extreme behavior may be attributed to physiological causes, children's fears, and childhood depression.

Ethical judgments about suspected child abuse or neglect are critical for children's health and well-being. This calls for understanding the scope of the problem, the abusers, the victims, the signs of abuse, and how to report it.

The success of your program will depend on how well you are able to work with family members, sharing information on all components of your program, including your philosophy, goals, discipline, communication, and ways of keeping children physiologically and psychologically safe.

There are specific skills you can learn to enable you to make ethical day-to-day judgments, some involving children's extreme behavior and others concerning child abuse and neglect.

In addition, there are behaviors that you will want to avoid when making judgments.

Key Terms

anxiety disorders
basic values
compulsions
ethical judgments
ethics

goals
intentionality
neglect
obsessions
relative values

school phobia
sexual abuse
standards
strategies
values

Discussion Questions

1. Discuss the relationship between helping professionals' values and their goals, strategies, and standards for children. Give some examples from your own life.

2. In a small group, discuss a value that you hold. As best you can, trace its origin and how it has affected a judgment you have made.

3. Consider the following cases. Use the NAEYC 2005 Code of Ethical Conduct (Appendix A) to help you make a judgment about the ethics or lack of ethics displayed. First, identify parts of the code that pertain to each case. Next, determine whether the person(s) acted in an ethical or unethical way. Finally, discuss possible responses.

   a. Cecile Matthews was recently hired as assistant teacher in the 3-year-old room at the McMillan Childcare Center. Her room is next to the toddler room. She notices that although the legal ratio is 1 adult for every 4 toddlers, the 12 children are frequently left with 1 adult in attendance. When she mentions this concern to the director, she says, "You pay attention to what goes on in your room. I'll worry about the rest." Cecile observes no change in the supervision pattern for toddlers over the next several weeks.

   b. The parent council for a cooperative nursery school decides not to interview James Beck for the job of head teacher in the toddler group because they believe women are the best caregivers for children that age.

4. Discuss the priority principles outlined in this chapter. Make comments either in support of or in opposition to the following:

   a. The order in which they are presented

   b. A specific principle or principles

   c. How they should or should not be applied

5. Define what is meant by extreme behavior. Describe four factors that must be taken into account when making an ethical judgment about whether a behavior is extreme. Discuss three pitfalls to avoid in making this kind of judgment.

6. Discuss how a child's fear may result in extreme behavior. Describe the ethical judgments a helping professional must make in such a case.

7. Define what is meant by physical abuse and neglect. Discuss who are the most likely victims

and the most likely perpetrators. Discuss what you would do if you suspected physical abuse.

8. Define what is meant by sexual abuse. Discuss who are the most likely victims and the most likely perpetrators. Discuss what to do if you suspect sexual abuse.

9. You help a 3-year-old with toileting and notice what appear to be welt marks on her buttocks and legs. Find the place in the NAEYC Code of Ethical Conduct (Appendix A) that offers professional guidelines in such a situation. What should you do, based on the code?

10. Discuss the similarities and differences in ethical judgments you would make on a day-to-day basis and those you would make when dealing with extreme behavior or child abuse.

Case Study Analysis

Read the case study in Appendix B about Seth, a child diagnosed with autism, and consider the following: Seth arrives at school one morning with a bruise on his face that looks like he has been slapped extremely hard. You ask him about it, having him look in the mirror and saying, "Seth, what happened here with your face?"

Because of his difficulty in communicating, he only responds, "Mama says 'Bad Seth. Seth bad.'" You suspect the likelihood of abuse.

1. Who would you contact first about this possibility?

2. If it turns out that you are asked to make a verbal report to children's protective services, what would you include?

3. Given your past relationship with Seth's parents, why would this be stressful, and how might it affect your relationship?

4. What factors would cause you to second-guess yourself in this particular situation?

5. If protective services investigates and Seth remains in your program after this incident, what behavioral indicators would you look for in the future while being observant about the situation?

Field Assignments

1. Interview an early childhood professional about ethical decisions he or she has made. Without betraying the rule of confidentiality, ask the person to describe a situation requiring

an ethical judgment in which he or she was involved. Ask: What made it an ethical dilemma? How was the situation handled? Looking back on the outcome, would he or she do anything differently if the same circumstance arose again?

2. Describe at least two situations that occurred during your field placement in which you made a conscious judgment using the priority principles identified earlier in this chapter. Describe each situation and what you did. Identify the priority principle(s) you used. Discuss your response with classmates. Would you handle the situation the same way again? Why or why not?

3. Name the person in your field placement to whom you would report a suspected case of child abuse. Outline the child abuse reporting procedures required in your agency or state. Name the governmental agency responsible for dealing with child abuse in your community. Identify at least three agencies, services, or programs available to parents who are on the brink of child abuse or who have committed child abuse.

4. Look up the law of your state regarding the reporting of child abuse and neglect.

Reflect on Your Practice

Here is a sample checklist you can use to reflect on your use of the skills as a beginning professional. A more detailed classroom observation tool is available in Appendix C.

I influence children's social development by making ethical judgments in the following ways:

✓ I make decisions by assessing the situation, analyzing possible response strategies, selecting and implementing the best one, and evaluating the outcome.

✓ My actions are congruent with the values I espouse to others.

✓ When I make judgments about goals, strategies, and standards related to children's behavior, I take a child's age, level of comprehension, and experiences into consideration.

✓ I have a professional code of ethics that I use for making moral judgments.

✓ Children's safety and well-being always takes precedence when I am choosing between options.

✓ I know the signs of child abuse or neglect and am knowledgeable about the rules and procedures for reporting it.

✓ I make a concerted effort to change a child's behavior by using appropriate guidance techniques before judging it extreme.

✓ When a child's behavior is extreme, I communicate my concerns to the child's parents.

Digital Download   **Download from CourseMate**

CourseMate. Visit the Education CourseMate for this textbook to access the eBook, Digital Downloads, Teach-Source Videos, and quizzes. Go to CengageBrain.com to log in, register, or purchase access.

Appendix A

Code of Ethical Conduct and Statement of Commitment

A position statement of the National Association for the Education
of Young Children *Revised April 2005*

Preamble

NAEYC recognizes that those who work with young children face many daily decisions that have moral and ethical implications. The NAEYC Code of Ethical Conduct offers guidelines for responsible behavior and sets forth a common basis for resolving the principal ethical dilemmas encountered in early childhood care and education. The Statement of Commitment is not part of the Code but is a personal acknowledgement of an individual's willingness to embrace the distinctive values and moral obligations of the field of early childhood care and education. The primary focus of the Code is on daily practice with children and their families in programs for children from birth through 8 years of age, such as infant/toddler programs, preschool and prekindergarten programs, child care centers, hospital and child life settings, family child care homes, kindergartens, and primary classrooms. When the issues involve young children, then these provisions also apply to specialists who do not work directly with children, including program administrators, parent educators, early childhood adult educators, and officials with responsibility for program monitoring and licensing. (Note: See also the "Code of Ethical Conduct: Supplement for Early Childhood Adult Educators.")

Core Values

Standards of ethical behavior in early childhood care and education are based on commitment to the following core values that are deeply rooted in the history of the field of early childhood care and education. We have made a commitment to:

- Appreciate childhood as a unique and valuable stage of the human life cycle
- Base our work on knowledge of how children develop and learn
- Appreciate and support the bond between the child and family
- Recognize that children are best understood and supported in the context of family, culture,* community, and society

* Culture includes ethnicity, racial identity, economic level, family structure, language, and religious and political beliefs, which profoundly influence each child's development and relationship to the world.

- Respect the dignity, worth, and uniqueness of each individual (child, family member, and colleague)
- Respect diversity in children, families, and colleagues
- Recognize that children and adults achieve their full potential in the context of relationships that are based on trust and respect

Conceptual Framework

The Code sets forth a framework of professional responsibilities in four sections. Each section addresses an area of professional relationships: (1) with children, (2) with families, (3) among colleagues, and (4) with the community and society. Each section includes an introduction to the primary responsibilities of the early childhood practitioner in that context. The introduction is followed by (1) a set of ideals that reflect exemplary professional practice and (2) a set of principles describing practices that are required, prohibited, or permitted.

The ideals reflect the aspirations of practitioners. The principles guide conduct and assist practitioners in resolving ethical dilemmas.** Both ideals and principles are intended to direct practitioners to those questions which, when responsibly answered, can provide the basis for conscientious decision making. While the Code provides specific direction for addressing some ethical dilemmas, many others will require the practitioner to combine the guidance of the Code with professional judgment. The ideals and principles in this Code present a shared framework of professional responsibility that affirms our commitment to the core values of our field. The Code publicly acknowledges the responsibilities that we in the field have assumed and in so doing supports ethical behavior in our work. Practitioners who face situations with ethical dimensions are urged to seek guidance in the applicable parts of this Code and in the spirit that informs the whole. Often, "the right answer"—the best ethical course of action to take—is not obvious. There may be no readily apparent, positive way to

** There is not necessarily a corresponding principle for each ideal.

handle a situation. When one important value contradicts another, we face an ethical dilemma. When we face a dilemma, it is our professional responsibility to consult the Code and all relevant parties to find the most ethical resolution.

Section I: Ethical Responsibilities to Children

Childhood is a unique and valuable stage in the human life cycle. Our paramount responsibility is to provide care and education in settings that are safe, healthy, nurturing, and responsive for each child. We are committed to supporting children's development and learning; respecting individual differences; and helping children learn to live, play, and work cooperatively. We are also committed to promoting children's self-awareness, competence, self-worth, resiliency, and physical well-being.

Ideals

I-1.1—To be familiar with the knowledge base of early childhood care and education and to stay informed through continuing education and training.

I-1.2—To base program practices upon current knowledge and research in the field of early childhood education, child development, and related disciplines, as well as on particular knowledge of each child.

I-1.3—To recognize and respect the unique qualities, abilities, and potential of each child.

I-1.4—To appreciate the vulnerability of children and their dependence on adults.

I-1.5—To create and maintain safe and healthy settings that foster children's social, emotional, cognitive, and physical development and that respect their dignity and their contributions.

I-1.6—To use assessment instruments and strategies that are appropriate for the children to be assessed, that are used only for the purposes for which they were designed, and that have the potential to benefit children.

I-1.7—To use assessment information to understand and support children's development and learning, to support instruction, and to identify children who may need additional services.

I-1.8—To support the right of each child to play and learn in an inclusive environment that meets the needs of children with and without disabilities.

I-1.9—To advocate for and ensure that all children, including those with special needs, have access to the support services needed to be successful.

I-1.10—To ensure that each child's culture, language, ethnicity, and family structure are recognized and valued in the program.

I-1.11—To provide all children with experiences in a language that they know, as well as support children in maintaining the use of their home language and in learning English.

I-1.12—To work with families to provide a safe and smooth transition as children and families move from one program to the next.

Principles

P-1.1—Above all, we shall not harm children. We shall not participate in practices that are emotionally damaging, physically harmful, disrespectful, degrading, dangerous, exploitative, or intimidating to children. This principle has precedence over all others in this Code.

P-1.2—We shall care for and educate children in positive emotional and social environments that are cognitively stimulating and that support each child's culture, language, ethnicity, and family structure.

P-1.3—We shall not participate in practices that discriminate against children by denying benefits, giving special advantages, or excluding them from programs or activities on the basis of their sex, race, national origin, religious beliefs, medical condition, disability, or the marital status/family structure, sexual orientation, or religious beliefs or other affiliations of their families. (Aspects of this principle do not apply in programs that have a lawful mandate to provide services to a particular population of children.)

P-1.4—We shall involve all those with relevant knowledge (including families and staff) in decisions concerning a child, as appropriate, ensuring confidentiality of sensitive information.

P-1.5—We shall use appropriate assessment systems, which include multiple sources of information, to provide information on children's learning and development.

P-1.6—We shall strive to ensure that decisions such as those related to enrollment, retention, or assignment to special education services, will be based on multiple sources of information and will never be based on a single assessment, such as a test score or a single observation.

P-1.7—We shall strive to build individual relationships with each child; make individualized adaptations in teaching strategies, learning environments, and curricula; and consult with the family so that each child benefits from the program. If after such efforts have been exhausted, the current placement does not meet a child's needs, or the child is seriously jeopardizing the ability of other children to benefit from the program, we shall collaborate with the child's family and appropriate specialists to determine the additional services needed and/or the placement option(s) most likely to ensure the child's success. (Aspects of this principle may not apply in programs that have a lawful mandate to provide services to a particular population of children.)

P-1.8—We shall be familiar with the risk factors for and symptoms of child abuse and neglect, including physical, sexual, verbal, and emotional abuse and physical, emotional, educational, and medical neglect. We shall know and follow state laws and community procedures that protect children against abuse and neglect.

P-1.9—When we have reasonable cause to suspect child abuse or neglect, we shall report it to the appropriate community agency and follow up to ensure that appropriate action has been taken. When appropriate, parents or guardians will be informed that the referral will be or has been made.

P-1.10—When another person tells us of his or her suspicion that a child is being abused or neglected, we shall assist that person in taking appropriate action in order to protect the child.

P-1.11—When we become aware of a practice or situation that endangers the health, safety, or well-being of children, we have an ethical responsibility to protect children or inform parents and/or others who can.

Section II: Ethical Responsibilities to Families

Families* are of primary importance in children's development. Because the family and the early childhood practitioner have a common interest in the child's well-being, we acknowledge a primary responsibility to bring about communication, cooperation, and collaboration between the home and early childhood program in ways that enhance the child's development.

* The term family may include those adults, besides parents, with the responsibility of being involved in educating, nurturing, and advocating for the child.

Ideals

I-2.1—To be familiar with the knowledge base related to working effectively with families and to stay informed through continuing education and training.

I-2.2—To develop relationships of mutual trust and create partnerships with the families we serve.

I-2.3—To welcome all family members and encourage them to participate in the program.

I-2.4—To listen to families, acknowledge and build upon their strengths and competencies, and learn from families as we support them in their task of nurturing children.

I-2.5—To respect the dignity and preferences of each family and to make an effort to learn about its structure, culture, language, customs, and beliefs.

I-2.6—To acknowledge families' childrearing values and their right to make decisions for their children.

I-2.7—To share information about each child's education and development with families and to help them understand and appreciate the current knowledge base of the early childhood profession.

I-2.8—To help family members enhance their understanding of their children and support the continuing development of their skills as parents.

I-2.9—To participate in building support networks for families by providing them with opportunities to interact with program staff, other families, community resources, and professional services.

Principles

P-2.1—We shall not deny family members access to their child's classroom or program setting unless access is denied by court order or other legal restriction.

P-2.2—We shall inform families of program philosophy, policies, curriculum, assessment system, and personnel qualifications, and explain why we teach as we do—which should be in accordance with our ethical responsibilities to children (see Section I).

P-2.3—We shall inform families of and, when appropriate, involve them in policy decisions.

P-2.4—We shall involve the family in significant decisions affecting their child.

P-2.5—We shall make every effort to communicate effectively with all families in a language that they understand. We shall use community resources for translation and interpretation when we do not have sufficient resources in our own programs.

P-2.6—As families share information with us about their children and families, we shall consider this information to plan and implement the program.

P-2.7—We shall inform families about the nature and purpose of the program's child assessments and how data about their child will be used.

P-2.8—We shall treat child assessment information confidentially and share this information only when there is a legitimate need for it.

P-2.9—We shall inform the family of injuries and incidents involving their child, of risks such as exposures to communicable diseases that might result in infection, and of occurrences that might result in emotional stress.

P-2.10—Families shall be fully informed of any proposed research projects involving their children and shall have the opportunity to give or withhold consent without penalty. We shall not permit or participate in research that could in any way hinder the education, development, or well-being of children.

P-2.11—We shall not engage in or support exploitation of families. We shall not use our relationship with a family for private advantage or personal gain, or enter into relationships with family members that might impair our effectiveness working with their children.

P-2.12—We shall develop written policies for the protection of confidentiality and the disclosure of children's records. These policy documents shall be made available to all program personnel and families. Disclosure of children's records beyond family members, program personnel, and consultants having an obligation of confidentiality shall require familial consent (except in cases of abuse or neglect).

P-2.13—We shall maintain confidentiality and shall respect the family's right to privacy, refraining from disclosure of confidential information and intrusion into family life. However, when we have reason to believe that a child's welfare is at risk, it is permissible to share confidential information with agencies, as well as with individuals who have legal responsibility for intervening in the child's interest.

P-2.14—In cases where family members are in conflict with one another, we shall work openly, sharing our observations of the child, to help all parties involved make informed decisions. We shall refrain from becoming an advocate for one party.

P-2.15—We shall be familiar with and appropriately refer families to community resources and professional support services. After a referral has been made, we shall follow up to ensure that services have been appropriately provided.

Section III: Ethical Responsibilities to Colleagues

In a caring, cooperative workplace, human dignity is respected, professional satisfaction is promoted, and positive relationships are developed and sustained. Based upon our core values, our primary responsibility to colleagues is to establish and maintain settings and relationships that support productive work and meet professional needs. The same ideals that apply to children also apply as we interact with adults in the workplace.

A—Responsibilities to co-workers

Ideals

I-3A.1—To establish and maintain relationships of respect, trust, confidentiality, collaboration, and cooperation with co-workers.

I-3A.2—To share resources with co-workers, collaborating to ensure that the best possible early childhood care and education program is provided.

I-3A.3—To support co-workers in meeting their professional needs and in their professional development.

I-3A.4—To accord co-workers due recognition of professional achievement.

Principles

P-3A.1—We shall recognize the contributions of colleagues to our program and not participate in practices that diminish their reputations or impair their effectiveness in working with children and families.

P-3A.2—When we have concerns about the professional behavior of a co-worker, we shall first let that person know of our concern in a way that shows respect for personal dignity and for the diversity to be found among staff members, and then attempt to resolve the matter collegially and in a confidential manner.

P-3A.3—We shall exercise care in expressing views regarding the personal attributes or professional conduct of co-workers. Statements should be based on firsthand knowledge, not hearsay, and relevant to the interests of children and programs.

P-3A.4—We shall not participate in practices that discriminate against a co-worker because of sex, race, national origin, religious beliefs or other affiliations, age, marital status/family structure, disability, or sexual orientation.

B—Responsibilities to employers

Ideals

I-3B.1—To assist the program in providing the highest quality of service.

I-3B.2—To do nothing that diminishes the reputation of the program in which we work unless it is violating laws and regulations designed to protect children or is violating the provisions of this Code.

Principles

P-3B.1—We shall follow all program policies. When we do not agree with program policies, we shall attempt to effect change through constructive action within the organization.

P-3B.2—We shall speak or act on behalf of an organization only when authorized. We shall take care to acknowledge when we are speaking for the organization and when we are expressing a personal judgment.

P-3B.3—We shall not violate laws or regulations designed to protect children and shall take appropriate action consistent with this Code when aware of such violations.

P-3B.4—If we have concerns about a colleague's behavior, and children's well-being is not at risk, we may address the concern with that individual. If children are at risk or the situation does not improve after it has been brought to the colleague's attention, we shall report the colleague's unethical or incompetent behavior to an appropriate authority.

P-3B.5—When we have a concern about circumstances or conditions that impact the quality of care and education within the program, we shall inform the program's administration or, when necessary, other appropriate authorities.

C—Responsibilities to employees

Ideals

I-3C.1—To promote safe and healthy working conditions and policies that foster mutual respect, cooperation, collaboration, competence, well-being, confidentiality, and self esteem in staff members.

I-3C.2—To create and maintain a climate of trust and candor that will enable staff to speak and act in the best interests of children, families, and the field of early childhood care and education.

I-3C.3—To strive to secure adequate and equitable compensation (salary and benefits) for those who work with or on behalf of young children.

I-3C.4—To encourage and support continual development of employees in becoming more skilled and knowledgeable practitioners.

Principles

P-3C.1—In decisions concerning children and programs, we shall draw upon the education, training, experience, and expertise of staff members.

P-3C.2—We shall provide staff members with safe and supportive working conditions that honor confidences and permit them to carry out their responsibilities through fair performance evaluation, written grievance procedures, constructive feedback, and opportunities for continuing professional development and advancement.

P-3C.3—We shall develop and maintain comprehensive written personnel policies that define program standards. These policies shall be given to new staff members and shall be available and easily accessible for review by all staff members.

P-3C.4—We shall inform employees whose performance does not meet program expectations of areas of concern and, when possible, assist in improving their performance.

P-3C.5—We shall conduct employee dismissals for just cause, in accordance with all applicable laws and regulations. We shall inform employees who are dismissed of the reasons for their termination. When a dismissal is for cause, justification must be based on evidence of inadequate or inappropriate behavior that is accurately documented, current, and available for the employee to review.

P-3C.6—In making evaluations and recommendations, we shall make judgments based on fact and relevant to the interests of children and programs.

P-3C.7—We shall make hiring, retention, termination, and promotion decisions based solely on a person's competence, record of accomplishment, ability to carry out the responsibilities of the position, and professional preparation specific to the developmental levels of children in his/her care.

P-3C.8—We shall not make hiring, retention, termination, and promotion decisions based on an individual's sex, race, national origin, religious beliefs or other affiliations, age, marital status/family structure, disability, or sexual orientation. We shall be familiar with and observe laws and regulations that pertain to employment discrimination. (Aspects of this principle do not apply to programs that have a lawful mandate to determine eligibility based on one or more of the criteria identified above.)

P-3C.9—We shall maintain confidentiality in dealing with issues related to an employee's job performance and shall respect an employee's right to privacy regarding personal issues.

Section IV: Ethical Responsibilities to Community and Society

Early childhood programs operate within the context of their immediate community made up of families and other institutions concerned with children's welfare. Our responsibilities to the community are to provide programs that meet the diverse needs of families, to cooperate with agencies and professions that share the responsibility for children, to assist families in gaining access to those agencies and allied professionals, and to assist in the development of community programs that are needed but not currently available. As individuals, we acknowledge our responsibility to provide the best possible programs of care and education for children and to conduct ourselves with honesty and integrity. Because of our specialized expertise in early childhood development and education and because the larger society shares responsibility for the welfare and protection of young children, we acknowledge a collective obligation to advocate for the best interests of children within early childhood programs and in the larger community and to serve as a voice for young children everywhere. The ideals and principles in this section are presented to distinguish between those that pertain to the work of the individual early childhood educator and those that more typically are engaged in collectively on behalf of the best interests of children—with the understanding that individual early childhood educators have a shared responsibility for addressing the ideals and principles that are identified as "collective."

Ideal (Individual)

I-4.1—To provide the community with high-quality early childhood care and education programs and services.

Ideals (Collective)

I-4.2—To promote cooperation among professionals and agencies and interdisciplinary collaboration among professions concerned with addressing issues in the health, education, and well-being of young children, their families, and their early childhood educators.

I-4.3—To work through education, research, and advocacy toward an environmentally safe world in which all children receive health care, food, and shelter; are nurtured; and live free from violence in their home and their communities.

I-4.4—To work through education, research, and advocacy toward a society in which all young children have access to high-quality early care and education programs.

I-4.5—To work to ensure that appropriate assessment systems, which include multiple sources of information, are used for purposes that benefit children.

I-4.6—To promote knowledge and understanding of young children and their needs. To work toward greater societal acknowledgment of children's rights and greater social acceptance of responsibility for the well-being of all children.

I-4.7—To support policies and laws that promote the well-being of children and families, and to work to change those that impair their well-being. To participate in developing policies and laws that are needed, and to cooperate with other individuals and groups in these efforts.

I-4.8—To further the professional development of the field of early childhood care and education and to strengthen its commitment to realizing its core values as reflected in this Code.

Principles (Individual)

P-4.1—We shall communicate openly and truthfully about the nature and extent of services that we provide.

P-4.2—We shall apply for, accept, and work in positions for which we are personally well-suited and professionally qualified. We shall not offer services that we do not have the competence, qualifications, or resources to provide.

P-4.3—We shall carefully check references and shall not hire or recommend for employment any person whose competence, qualifications, or character makes him or her unsuited for the position.

P-4.4—We shall be objective and accurate in reporting the knowledge upon which we base our program practices.

P-4.5—We shall be knowledgeable about the appropriate use of assessment strategies and instruments and interpret results accurately to families.

P-4.6—We shall be familiar with laws and regulations that serve to protect the children in our programs and be vigilant in ensuring that these laws and regulations are followed.

P-4.7—When we become aware of a practice or situation that endangers the health, safety, or well-being of children, we have an ethical responsibility to protect children or inform parents and/or others who can.

P-4.8—We shall not participate in practices that are in violation of laws and regulations that protect the children in our programs.

P-4.9—When we have evidence that an early childhood program is violating laws or regulations protecting children, we shall report the violation to appropriate authorities who can be expected to remedy the situation.

P-4.10—When a program violates or requires its employees to violate this Code, it is permissible, after fair assessment of the evidence, to disclose the identity of that program.

Principles (Collective)

P-4.11—When policies are enacted for purposes that do not benefit children, we have a collective responsibility to work to change these practices.

P-4.12—When we have evidence that an agency that provides services intended to ensure children's well-being is failing to meet its obligations, we acknowledge a collective ethical responsibility to report the problem to appropriate authorities or to the public. We shall be vigilant in our follow-up until the situation is resolved.

P-4.13—When a child protection agency fails to provide adequate protection for abused or neglected children, we acknowledge a collective ethical responsibility to work toward the improvement of these services.

NAEYC has taken reasonable measures to develop the Code in a fair, reasonable, open, unbiased, and objective manner, based on currently available data. However, further research or developments may change the current state of knowledge. Neither NAEYC nor its officers, directors, members, employees, or agents will be liable for any loss, damage, or claim with respect to any liabilities, including direct, special, indirect, or consequential damages incurred in connection with the Code or reliance on the information presented.

Statement of Commitment*

As an individual who works with young children, I commit myself to furthering the values of early childhood education as they are reflected in the ideals and principles of the NAEYC Code of Ethical Conduct. To the best of my ability I will

- Never harm children.
- Ensure that programs for young children are based on current knowledge and research of child development and early childhood education.
- Respect and support families in their task of nurturing children.
- Respect colleagues in early childhood care and education and support them in maintaining the NAEYC Code of Ethical Conduct.
- Serve as an advocate for children, their families, and their teachers in community and society.
- Stay informed of and maintain high standards of professional conduct.
- Engage in an ongoing process of self-reflection, realizing that personal characteristics, biases, and beliefs have an impact on children and families.
- Be open to new ideas and be willing to learn from the suggestions of others.
- Continue to learn, grow, and contribute as a professional.
- Honor the ideals and principles of the NAEYC Code of Ethical Conduct.

Glossary of Terms Related to Ethics

Code of Ethics. Defines the core values of the field and provides guidance for what professionals should do when they encounter conflicting obligations or responsibilities in their work.

Values. Qualities or principles that individuals believe to be desirable or worthwhile and that they prize for themselves, for others, and for the world in which they live.

Core Values. Commitments held by a profession that are consciously and knowingly embraced by its

* This Statement of Commitment is not part of the Code but is a personal acknowledgement of the individual's willingness to embrace the distinctive values and moral obligations of the field of early childhood care and education. It is recognition of the moral obligations that lead to an individual becoming part of the profession.

practitioners because they make a contribution to society. There is a difference between personal values and the core values of a profession.

Morality. Peoples' views of what is good, right, and proper; their beliefs about their obligations; and their ideas about how they should behave.

Ethics. The study of right and wrong, or duty and obligation, that involves critical reflection on morality and the ability to make choices between values and the examination of the moral dimensions of relationships.

Professional Ethics. The moral commitments of a profession that involve moral reflection that extends and enhances the personal morality practitioners bring to their work, that concern actions of right and wrong in the workplace, and that help individuals resolve moral dilemmas they encounter in their work.

Ethical Responsibilities. Behaviors that one must or must not engage in. Ethical responsibilities are clear-cut and are spelled out in the Code of Ethical Conduct (for example, early childhood educators should never share confidential information about a child or family with a person who has no legitimate need for knowing).

Ethical Dilemma. A moral conflict that involves determining appropriate conduct when an individual faces conflicting professional values and responsibilities.

Sources for Glossary Terms and Definitions

Feeney, S., & N. Freeman. 1999. *Ethics and the early childhood educator: Using the NAEYC code.* Washington, DC: NAEYC.

Kidder, R.M. 1995. *How good people make tough choices: Resolving the dilemmas of ethical living.* New York: Fireside.

Kipnis, K. 1987. How to discuss professional ethics. *Young Children* 42(4), 26–30.

Appendix B

Case Studies

Seth J.   Age: 4 years 5 months   Autism

History: Seth is the only child of Maria, a high school science teacher, and Walt, a banking administrator. Maria and Walt first began to worry about Seth's development when he didn't do many of the things they had seen other infants do such as playing peek-a-boo or mimicking facial expressions or gestures. When they would try to engage Seth with toys, songs, or games, he would show little to no interest. He rarely made eye contact. Seth didn't babble or make other baby noises, or respond when his parents called his name. Seth acquired early motor milestones within the typical range but was delayed in communication skills, having no words by the time he was 2. Shortly before his third birthday, he was referred to a university-based speech and hearing clinic for evaluation. His hearing was checked and appeared normal. Seth was diagnosed with autism and began receiving services through his public school when he was 3.

Currently: Despite Seth's difficulties, he has been successfully integrated into a full-day community-based preschool program in his neighborhood. Seth enjoys being read to and exploring books on his own, especially books related to his favorite topics, animals and vehicles. He enjoys playing outdoors and activities that include physical movement, such as dancing.

In addition to attending preschool, Seth receives speech and language intervention each week at the university-based clinic, and his individualized special education teacher visits his classroom twice each month. During these visits, the special education teacher observes Seth during classroom routines and activities and works with Seth's preschool teachers to find ways to engage Seth in what is taking place. Seth currently responds well to familiar verbal requests and is able to follow predictable routines with little support or guidance, although he becomes upset if unexpected changes occur.

Seth has difficulty communicating with others, especially his peers. Seth rarely makes eye contact with others. He uses some gestures, such as reaching for desired objects or shaking his head "no." He responds well to prompts to use verbal language; for example, if he points to a desired food, and his mother tells him "Seth, say 'I want peaches,'" he will repeat "want peaches," but he seldom makes verbal requests without being prompted. He will comment with one- or two-word utterances on things in his environment in which he is interested, such as vehicles he notices on the road outside the classroom window. These comments often seem directed at himself instead of another person. During much of the day, Seth plays alone in areas of the classroom with relatively few peers present. If peers come to the area where Seth is playing he will often leave and go to an unoccupied area of the classroom.

Maria and Walt, Seth's parents, are primarily concerned with Seth's social skills and want him to develop friendships with some of his peers. They would like to see him respond positively when a peer approaches him and to initiate interactions with his peers at school. Maria and Walt would also like to see Seth increase his verbal vocabulary and make requests without being prompted.

Over time, Seth's teachers have learned to predict situations in which he becomes upset and better read his behavioral cues. Seth's teachers share Maria and Walt's goal of increasing Seth's peer interactions and relationships. They have developed a binder containing social stories for Seth. The social stories describe a situation or skill such as greeting a peer or responding to a peer's request in a story-like format that is interesting to Seth and easy for him to understand. The stories model appropriate social interaction by describing the situation, others' perspectives, and suitable responses. Seth's teachers use the social stories to remind him of appropriate strategies he can use to meet his needs.

Examples of Teacher Observations

March 7

Seth played in the block area for the entire choice time today. He pulled a basket of small cars from the shelf and placed the cars in a long line. He then picked up one car at a time and spun each wheel of the car, placed it back in line and picked up another car. He continued to do this for about

10 minutes. Darrin came into the area and said, "Let's build a garage for the cars!" and began to build with wooden blocks next to Seth. Seth did not look at Darrin or respond to his statement. Seth moved over to the Lego table and began snapping the Legos together. He continued to build with the Legos for the next 30 minutes.

April 23

I set up an obstacle course in the hallway today because we weren't able to go outside due to the rain. Seth began to whine loudly when we went into the hallway. He began screaming "No, no, no!" and ran away from the group, back toward the classroom. He ran to the door to the playground and stood by the door screaming. I knelt next to him and pointed out the window saying, "We can't go outside, it's raining." Seth screamed again, and I reached over and rubbed his back and said, "Look, Seth, it's raining," and pointed out the window. He repeated "raining" in a whiny voice, and I responded, "You want to go outside. Look, it's raining." He quietly repeated "raining." We sat together and looked at books until he was calm.

May 12

We set up a grocery store in the dramatic play area this week. Seth seemed to enjoy pushing the small grocery cart around but hadn't done much else in the store area. Today, Carmen (Seth's special education teacher) joined Seth in the store. When he began to push the cart, she handed him a plastic banana and said, "Put the banana in the cart." Seth took the banana from her and put it in the cart. She did this for several more items, and Seth took each one and placed it in the cart. She then announced, "It's time to buy the food." Seth repeated "buy the food," and Carmen responded, "That's right, time to buy the food." She told Seth, "Push the cart to Nicholas" (who was standing at the check-out counter) and pointed to Nicholas. Seth pushed the cart toward the counter. Carmen prompted Seth to hand the banana to Nicholas, and Seth complied. Carmen did this with two other items, and Seth complied each time. She then paused, and Seth took an item from the cart on his own and handed it to Nicholas. He continued until the cart was empty. Then Carmen handed him some play money and said, "Give the money to Nicholas." Seth took the money from Carmen and handed it to Nicholas saying, "To Nicholas" as he did so. This afternoon Seth filled his cart with items without any prompting. I told him "buy the food," and he pushed the cart to the counter and handed each item to Deidre.

June 21

When Seth arrived this morning I reminded him that we were taking a field trip to the zoo. I showed him the picture schedule and pointed out the picture of the zoo after the picture of morning circle time. Each time we transitioned between activities, I reminded Seth of the trip to the zoo and pointed to the picture. I noticed at circle time, he began to rock back and forth and whine. I know this is a sign he is becoming agitated, so I whispered, "You are nervous about going to the zoo. Let's go look at a book about the zoo so we know what we'll see." We went over to the book area and looked at the social story I made about Seth at the zoo. Seth seemed to calm down as we read about riding the bus and seeing the animals. Seth named each animal in the book when I pointed to the pictures.

Eisa R.   Age: 6 years 7 months   Dual Language Learner

History: Eisa joined our first-grade classroom in January. She and her family have come from Chihuahua, Mexico, so that her father can study engineering. They expect to be in the United States for only two to three years and then plan to return to Chihuahua. Previously, Eisa had attended a nursery school in Mexico and then a local elementary school in Chihuahua for kindergarten and the first semester of first grade where children were exposed to English for two hours per week. Her mother described this as "just learning numbers, color words, body parts, some songs, and shape words.... nothing where they had to learn how to make conversation." Still, Eisa had very little understanding of English or ability to express it. Her mother and father speak English but, to date, had spoken only Spanish to Eisa and to one another at home. In Mexico, Eisa had little experience with English speakers and played only with other Mexican children.

On her first day, Eisa clung to her mother, cried on entering our classroom, and initially balked for several weeks at coming to school at all. She would refuse to get dressed in time to catch the school bus, pretend that she didn't feel good and had a stomachache, and cry that she was afraid of the other children. By early February, her mother reported that Eisa had begun to accept the situation but remained unhappy, saying often that she wanted to go back to her "old school" where she had two friends that she continued to miss. Her mother had considered returning to Chihuahua with Eisa but has begun hoping that the situation will improve so that the family can stay together.

Currently: Eisa has now been in the classroom for about 3 months. She has moved beyond using common phrases such as "good morning" and is venturing to express what she needs or wants, though she cannot always be understood. When this happens, she sometimes becomes frustrated, turning away from the person she's trying to communicate with and saying it loudly and angrily in Spanish. She is now fully familiar with and follows routines without prompts from the teacher or classmates and is clearly enjoying music and physical education periods where she participates fully. Her drawings in her journal are quite detailed, and she has begun to write some English words, although she is still inserting Spanish words.

Eisa's parents have hired a tutor for her who comes after school two afternoons a week. In their sessions, the tutor always includes the reading of some of the more familiar books from the classroom that Eisa has come to enjoy. She has also adopted some of the literacy activities we use here at the school to teach phonemic awareness and vocabulary development. They go on walks in the neighborhood, where the tutor plays "I spy" games with Eisa. The tutor reports that Eisa has become more motivated recently to learn English and is asking questions about pronunciation and syntax or how to say or write something she's struggling with. In response to Eisa's parents' question of whether or not they should begin speaking only English in the home, I said that it is important that they continue to use Spanish with Eisa and to have her respond in Spanish in order to maintain her native language along with the second language she is learning. I suggested that some of the stories Eisa is hearing in English are now also available in Spanish and that it would be good if they would check some of them out at the local library. Marcus Pfister's *Rainbow Fish* and *Rainbow Fish to the Rescue* (*El Pez arco iris; El Pez arco iris al Rescate*) are Eisa's favorites. I have also suggested that it might be good to have Eisa communicate in Spanish by email with the friends in Chihuahua that she misses and to send some pictures to them about what she is doing in Colorado.

Eisa's parents meet frequently with me, and I have sent them brief notes to share her progress and growing comfort with her classmates and the language she is learning. They have indicated that Eisa is forming a friendship with another little girl in their apartment building who is also a first-grader at our school but in a different classroom. The girls ride their bikes together and play with the paper dolls Eisa brought with her from Chihuahua. Language between them, which had been missing, is growing markedly. Both are attending a gymnastics class together on Wednesday afternoons after school, and the parents of both girls have begun to develop a friendship so that the families are now seeing each other socially where everyone speaks English.

Examples of Teacher Observations

January 7

I'm glad I took the time to learn a few words in Spanish over the holidays so that the children and I could greet Eisa in Spanish when she entered the classroom. I think she was too upset to notice, but we made another attempt in large group and got a little smile out of her. I asked Carly to sit next to Eisa at their table and to help her with transitions. Carly showed her where to find materials and took Eisa's hand on the way to music class. Eisa didn't join in with anyone on the playground but had stopped crying by the middle of the morning and was watching what the children were doing. Before class got started again, I gave her mother a call to let her know that Eisa was no longer as upset as when she left her. During writing workshop this afternoon, everyone created a page for a class book to give to Eisa before she went home. They had drawn a self portrait of themselves, pasted on a real photograph as well, and had written "Hi, Eisa. My name is _____. I'm glad you're here." We all worked together to make a cover for the book, and Eisa took it home with her so that she could become more acquainted with her classmates.

January 9

Eisa did not say a word to anyone all day. She did watch what others were doing and would move to be near them, sometimes participating in parallel play—especially with Carly and Jenna.

January 10

Eisa ate little during snack and lunch again today, and I made a note to ask her parents if they would like to send snack and lunch until she becomes more familiar with foods the school serves. Several children already do this, so she wouldn't be the only one bringing her own lunch. She has enjoyed listening to books read on tape, and this requires her to sit next to other children who also like this activity. She can be with other children but not have the pressure of having to speak in English, which gives her a little rest while still having her spend time on the new language. The pictures help a lot, and I've begun using more visual aids and modeling in the morning meeting where I introduce the different center activities I've planned for them. This actually helps the other children better understand how to use the materials and equipment. Sometimes I forget that Eisa might not be the only one who needs additional support in understanding what I am asking of them.

February 12

Eisa had a difficult time today, staying by herself. While she didn't cry, she was a bit teary. I asked her if she was okay, but she didn't respond, so I just left her with a hug. When I called her mother at noon, she shared with me that Eisa's father had left that morning for Chihuahua because of a business matter and would be gone for at least a week. During writing workshop in the afternoon, I said, "Write father a message. Make a picture for him. Mother will send it." Eisa got busy with the task. She's been in the United States for less than two months, so any change at home or at school is likely to be stressful for her.

March 21

Eisa brought back her permission slip for our first-grade camping trip today, and her mother has agreed to go, too. She and Carly have become fairly good friends, and they were excited when I asked the children to work with a partner to prepare a list in their journals of what they planned to take for the overnight. Eisa still inserts Spanish words occasionally in her expressive speaking and writing, but the amount of English she has learned in less than three months is quite amazing. She went through a period when she first joined the class in January of not speaking at all to anyone, but evidently her motivation to be part of the group and play with Carly and Jenna was greater than her fear of making a mistake.

Adriana L.   **Age: 5 years 0 months**   **Lack of affect, lack of empathy for others, hurtful behaviors toward peers**

History: Adriana lives at home with her mother, her father, and her 9-year-old brother. She was adopted at 3 years of age from an orphanage in Bulgaria. According to her parents, the orphanage was a very sterile environment, and children did not get personal attention or stimulation beyond the most basic physical care. Adriana's parents were glad to get her out of the orphanage—they are sure a loving home will make up for the neglect they believe Adriana experienced early in life. Adriana was enrolled in a different preschool last year. Her parents report that she began the program there as a quiet child. However, by the end of the year, she had become very aggressive toward other children. Her former teachers told them that Adriana's aggressive actions often happened without warning. They did not seem to be related to anything obvious other children did, such as taking a toy or violating Adriana's personal space. Most troubling to the teachers was that Adriana seldom registered any emotion in the course of the day, including when she hurt someone or spoiled their play. The teacher and assistant teacher in that class used time-outs (removing Adriana from the group for 5 to 10 minutes) each time she was aggressive. Adriana's parents say that the time-outs did not change her antisocial behavior as the year went on. They also report that Adriana has exhibited aggression with neighborhood children and that they have decided to keep her from playing with peers at home because they are not sure how to handle these destructive incidents. They are hoping a new school will give her a fresh start.

Currently: Adriana enrolled in our preschool program in August. Although she is kindergarten eligible, her parents want her to have one more year of preschool before going to the elementary school. Initial observations during a home visit and in the classroom over the past three months have helped us (the assistant teacher, an aide, and me) see that Adriana has the following **strengths:**

- She has a good command of English and is very verbal in her solitary play; especially when she is involved in make-believe play with small figures and props.

- She spends about 90% of her free choice time in the art area. She likes to draw and make things. She takes something home from this learning center many days.

- She can carry out an art project that lasts more than one day, such as developing a collage that has multiple steps (gluing, then painting, then drying, then framing with craft sticks). Such projects are self-initiated.

- She does not "give up" when she wants to learn something new. For example, she spent almost three weeks learning how to cut out a paper snowflake. She returned to this task daily until she could produce snowflakes that satisfied her.

The teachers have also noted two key **areas of concern.** First, in the early days after she arrived in our program, several children approached her and asked her to play. She ignored them—never saying anything, just looking past them or turning away. Since then, her unpredictable aggressive outbursts have prompted children to avoid her, and most children no longer seek her out. Some children say they are afraid of her. Second, Adriana seems detached from people emotionally. The adults in our classroom as well as her parents have noticed a consistent lack of affect with children and adults too. We do not know whether Adriana doesn't feel things the way most people do or if she just doesn't know how to respond. Regardless, her failure to read social cues and her own lack of emotional responses is getting in the way of her ability to get along with others and to function successfully in the classroom. Her parents and our teaching team have agreed on the following strategies to address these concerns:

1. We will help Adriana begin to match feeling words with specific situations as a way to build her affective awareness. We will talk about what she might be feeling in a given situation (even if we can't be sure what her actual feelings are), and we will point out other children's feelings using words and verbal cues.

2. We will set consistent boundaries on Adriana's aggressive behavior through means other than time-outs (our main strategy will be to use logical consequences that focus on restitution—tending

to a victim and/or repairing damage). We will intervene when she is aggressive (stop the behavior), and we will ask children to tell her how they feel when she hits them or breaks their things. We will then administer a logical consequence.

3. We will "catch" Adriana being good and reinforce her neutral or positive actions when she plays without harming other children.

4. We will all meet (mom, dad, assistant teacher, paraprofessional, and me) every two weeks to discuss Adriana's experiences and our observations. We will refine our goals and strategies as the year progresses.

Examples of Teacher Observations

September 10
Adriana is outdoors in the sandbox sifting sand and making tunnels with her hands. Caleb, a 3-year-old, walks along the edge of the sandbox. Without warning, Adriana leaps up and shoves Caleb forcefully to the ground. (I intervene, stop the pushing, and comfort Caleb.) Afterwards, I ask Adriana why she pushed him. She responded: "I don't know." I said, "Caleb was surprised and hurt when you pushed him. It is not okay to hurt children at school."

September 27
Adriana is at the art table drawing with chalk on black paper. Lindsey sits beside her. Suddenly, Adriana reaches over and makes a zigzag line of heavy chalk across the top of Lindsey's picture. Lindsey makes a loud sound in protest, gets up, and moves to the other side of the table. Adriana continues her drawing without speaking or looking up. Livvy (our paraprofessional) notices and moves over to talk to the children about the incident.

October 5
Adriana is playing pirates on the playground, using sticks and leaves and stones as characters and props. She does not interact with any other children. Five-year-old Silvia asks if she can play. Adriana turns her back to her and continues her pretend game. Silvia leaves. Adriana plays multiple characters with different voices to act out the parts. She uses long sentences (7 to 12 words) and varied vocabulary to supply scripts for the pirates. Inside, Adriana goes straight to the art center and begins building a boat out of things in the scrap box.

October 12
Jocelyn is building a bridge out of blocks. Adriana walks across the block area. Without a word, she brings her fist up high above her head and smashes it down on Jocelyn's structure. The blocks fall. Jocelyn looks shocked. Adriana walks away to the science center.

October 24
Today at the art table, Tonia became excited because her watercolor paints soaked through her coffee filter paper creating a fuzzy effect she liked. She showed the paper to several children, including Adriana. Adriana had no reaction. Her face looked blank. (I could not tell if she didn't notice, didn't care, or didn't know how to respond.)

November 6
Emory is running across the play yard. He trips over the edge of the trike path and falls forward on the cement. As he gets up, there is a large scrape on his knee oozing blood, and he is crying loudly. Adriana is nearest to him, standing about four feet away. She glances over but remains where she is. Her face is expressionless. Ms. Jackson goes to Emory and comforts him. As she takes him inside to wash the scrape, she catches Adriana's hand and says, "Emory is hurt. See, he is crying. I need a helper to hold the bandages while I clean his knee. You will be my helper." Adriana goes inside with her. Sara (Jackson) reports that Adriana held the bandages as requested and watched silently as she (Sara) cleaned the scrape, wiped Emory's tears, and talked to him about feeling upset or hurt.

November 18
Adriana is intently focused on building pirate boats in the art center. It is time to clean up and go to group. I say, "You are disappointed. You didn't get to finish your boat." Adriana says nothing, and her face registers no expression. On the playground that day, I overhear her in her pirate play have one character say to another, "You're disappointed—don't cry!"

November 22

At clean-up time today, Adriana said she didn't want to clean up, she wanted another piece of tape for her project. I answered, "Okay, one more, but that's all." She put the piece on her paper and then demanded another. I said, "You really want another piece. I told you just one more. Please put your project on the shelf until tomorrow." She said several times, "Let me have it." I had said no, and I wanted her to realize I meant what I said, so, I did not give her another piece. Jerome, who was finishing his own project, had a piece of tape and gave it to Adriana. She put it on her project in real triumph—a clear and genuine emotion!

February 7

Jerome was building a tower in the block area. It fell down more than once. He began to cry. Adriana came over, looked at him and said, "I'm so sorry you don't have enough blocks." He wasn't crying over not having enough blocks, but she thought that was why he was upset. (What was important, however was that she noticed another child's feelings!)

March 18

We are getting our coats to go outside. James says to Adriana, "You're that girl who hurts people." Adriana puts her hands on her hips and says in a loud voice, "I don't do that anymore!"

April 4

Adriana's mom comes in to the room to pick her up. She asks Adriana if she wants to walk out with her or with the other children. Adriana says, "I want to go with my friends." Although Adriana still does not play with the other children, I am pleased to hear her use the word "friends."

Marco B.   Age: 22 months   Socialization

History: Marco is the only child of professional parents and the first grandchild for both sides of the extended family. His mother took family leave following his birth and returned to teaching when he was 7 months old. His father took family leave to take care of him until he was 10 months old. For the next 12 months, parents, grandparents, and other family members cared for him by fitting him into their very busy schedules sometimes with three or more caregivers on any given day. When Marco entered the center, his parents reported that he wore all of them out, and it had become too difficult to continue. They spoke of him as "the prince"; indicating that he had not begun toilet learning, did not pick up toys, and tended to ignore adult requests. This family is seeking more regularity for Marco in the hopes that it would help him to "mind" better and achieve other toddler milestones of greater independence. Explicitly, they want him to come when called, stop when asked to, use the toilet, and be mannerly when eating. I gave them the handout on toilet training and a flyer about our parent program on guidance.

Currently: Marco is a healthy, vigorous toddler who entered the program with confidence. He is curious, moving at speed from one thing to another at the beginning of the session until he has very briefly checked out every center before he begins to play. Marco has a very expressive face and generally cheerful demeanor. He talks, laughs, and cries loudly.

Examples of Teacher Observations

August 23
Marco left his seat during lunch only four times today. Each time was when I focused on another child.

August 24
Ms. Ott patted Marco, and he stayed on his mat but squirmed around for about 10 minutes. He fell asleep holding his lamb as soon as he stopped moving and slept more than 2 hrs.

August 27
I spoke quietly to Marco when he was playing in the sensory table, "Your turn for a diaper change is in 2 minutes." He screwed up his face and howled as if crying. When I stood up to get his supplies, the howling stopped suddenly and he grinned. The cry face and howling resumed as I took him by the hand and told him it was a time for a change. He rolled, wiggled, and waved his arms and legs when he lay on the changing table. I fastened the strap and put my hand on his belly, "Marco you are making a lot of noise. I can't tell what you want when you make so much noise and wiggle."

Suddenly silent, he shouted, "Down."

I replied, "You want to get down and play. You will be down faster if you pull the diaper tabs then lift your legs." He did.

August 29
Marco ate only from his own plate. When he started to get up during lunch, I put my hand on his shoulder, and he sat down again, repeatedly. He ate everything offered and did not ask for different food.

August 30
I spoke to Marco's mom about his pattern of eating. They regularly fix something else for him to eat if he decides he does not want what was served. They either tie him into his high chair or let him roam around and "eat on the run." I suggested that they try seated meals with small servings and a regular snack with nothing else but water between meals and planned snacks. They expressed concern that he would be hungry. I assured them that he would eat more at meals if he was not nibbling during play, and they could supervise what he ate more easily.

September 1
Conrad came up behind Marco who was sitting on the large bus. Conrad bent down and pulled the bus from under Marco who plopped down on the sand. Marco's eyebrows went up and his mouth opened, looking surprised, then he scowled. Miss Snyder said, "Conrad, you want the bus. Marco is using it. You can use the blue truck."

Marco leaned into Miss Snyder as she put her arm around him. Pulling the bus further away from Conrad, he grumbled, "Mine."

September 2

Conrad, Izzie, Marco, and James run rapidly toward the fence of the playground before swerving to avoid a tree. James, in the lead, stumbles falling down, and the others fall down nearby laughing. They run and fall, over and over with much laughter.

September 6

Marco enters the room and moves through it rapidly, looking at all the centers. Within two minutes he stops, touches Ruth's red curls. She ignores him. Miss Snyder invited, "You can glue these pieces on a paper, Marco," as she moved supplies toward him. He dropped several colored scraps of paper on a larger piece, poured a puddle of glue (about 2 inches across) on top, and smeared it over the paper pieces. Smiling, he smeared the glue back and forth with both hands, even up into the corners. He smeared some on the back of his hand and also on the back of Ruth's hand. She said, "No!" He squeezed more glue on his paper and moved his arms with large arcs back and forth, chuckling to himself. Ruth turned slightly, and Marco lifted two glue-coated hands toward her hair. Miss Snyder, who had been helping the other three children, darted toward him and grasped his hands, "You want to touch Ruth's hair. Glue goes on the paper not on hair. It is very hard to get glue out of hair." Marco smiled. Lifting his paper up, some pieces fell to the floor. He stomped on them, laughing. Miss Snyder asked him to put the paper on the rack and wash his hands. He shook his paper. Miss Snyder said, "Marco, you are enjoying playing with a paper dripping with glue. I am concerned that it will get on other people. Put your paper on the drying rack." He continued to shake the paper distributing lots of glue on the floor. Miss Snyder said, "Marco, you can put your paper on the rack, or I will help you do it." He looked at her and grinned. Miss Snyder responded, "You didn't put the paper on the rack so I will help you," as she firmly but gently led him to the drying rack and then on to the sink to wash up. Ms. Ott noticed and moved into the area to supervise the other children and to begin wiping up the glue with a damp sponge.

November 2

Miss Snyder sits on the floor with Ruth and plays with the train and tracks. Izzie joins them and tries to put a track together himself. Marco runs up, observes Ruth a few minutes, and just takes one of Izzie's train cars. Izzie screams. Miss S. said, "You want to play with the train. That one is Izzie's, and he is angry that you took his. Get one from in the bucket." Marco looked up at Izzie as if he just noticed him, turned, and took a car and some tracks from the bucket. Marco, Ruth, and Izzie play several minutes side by side. Marco looks up at the others occasionally. Says nothing.

November 28

Ruth's mother brings her inside. Marco goes to his locker and approaches her saying, "I have this for Ruth." The mother thanks Marco and fastens Ruth's hairclip into her hair saying, "You found it."

Summary of notes related to social play: Marco plays near Ruth, Izzie, James, or Conrad most frequently. He runs fast with James, tries art projects when Ruth is there, and approaches Izzie or Conrad when they have trucks or cars. He watches and imitates. Rarely, he will engage in one activity for more than 10 minutes and that is when Ruth is there.

Samples of language:

"Don't."

"That's mine."

"I like peas."

"I have big boy underwear now."

"Read me the bears one....please."

"I ran fast, faster than James."

"Ruth is crying. She fell down! Come!"

Summaries from toileting chart:

September 10

Marco typically has a BM between 8 and 8:30. He is dry at 10 but usually wet by 10:30. Dry after lunch and always wet after nap. Protests changes.

October 12

Marco was successful with BM in toilet three times this week and urinated in the toilet at least once a day for the past week. Wet after nap.

December 20

Marco uses the toilet for BM most of the time. He urinates in toilet midmorning and after lunch regularly. Some difficulty managing snaps on pants, still. Needs reminding to wash hands. Wet after nap.

January 30

Pull-ups. Demonstrates ability to do all toileting steps but is inconsistent. Needs the pictograph and reminding. Parents are cooperating in avoiding jeans with snaps. Wet after nap.

March 15

Pull-ups. Uses toilet consistently for BM and urination. Needs reminding to go. Needs reminding to wipe and wash hands. Talked to father about shift to underwear, except for naptime.

April 12

Underwear. Marco grinned ear to ear when he showed his cloth underwear. He went to the toilet several times on his own. Washes hands without reminding occasionally. Used a pull-up for nap.

Appendix C

....

Professional Skills Inventory Rating Form

Term/Semester
Student's Name
Field Placement
Supervising Teacher's Name
Attendance: Sessions (Circle sessions attended) 1, 2, 3, 4, 5, 6, 7, 8, 9, 10, 11, 12, 13, 14, 15

Midterm Evaluation	Score Description	Final Evaluation
Strength = S	Excellent skill usage: student performs the skill correctly and uses the skill in an appropriate situation about 90% of the time; very little need for improvement of this skill.	4
Good = G	Good skill usage: student usually performs the skill correctly and uses the skill in appropriate situations about 80% of the time; student should continue to practice this skill to polish his or her performance.	3
Common Practice = CP	Basic or average skill usage: student demonstrates a basic understanding of the skill 70% of the time but does not perform the skill correctly or as often as would be appropriate; student should continue to work on and practice this skill.	2
Minimal = M	Less than average skill usage: student seldom performs the skill or skill usage is incorrect (uses the skill about 50–60% of the time); student needs lots of extra attention to this skill to improve.	1
Unsatisfactory = U	Unsatisfactory skill usage: student performs the skill poorly in many situations or demonstrates no performance of the skill in appropriate situations (uses the skill less than 50% of the time).	0
Not Applicable = NA	Need for student use of the skill was not present in this field placement.	

(continued)

Professional Skills Inventory Rating Form—continued

Total Points for Each Category	Midterm Evaluation	Final Evaluation
(16) 1. Participates in planning and evaluation sessions.	_____	_____
A. Takes the initiative in finding out his/her responsibilities for the day.	_____	_____
B. Helps prepare and maintain the environment as needed.	_____	_____
C. Assesses own performance.	_____	_____
D. Assists in evaluation.	_____	_____
(16) 2. Is dependable in the position assigned.	_____	_____
A. Carries out assigned duties.	_____	_____
B. Arrives promptly, calls early if not coming, makes up absences, stays during entire session.	_____	_____
C. Participates in all aspects of daily classroom activity.	_____	_____
D. Remains available for interaction with children.	_____	_____
(12) 3. Cooperates as a team member.	_____	_____
A. Replaces another adult when needed.	_____	_____
B. Supports other adults in group activities, during transitions, and within activity areas or outside.	_____	_____
C. Demonstrates ability to coordinate own actions with those of other teachers in the classroom.	_____	_____
(20) 4. Uses skills related to principles of positive communication.	_____	_____
A. Demonstrates positive nonverbal behaviors.	_____	_____
B. Demonstrates positive verbal communication.	_____	_____
C. Takes cues from children.	_____	_____
D. Adapts methods of communicating to the age, experience, and temperament of the children.	_____	_____
E. Observes and responds to nonverbal communication of all children.	_____	_____
(28) 5. Uses language effectively with individual children and in small groups of children for the purpose of:	_____	_____
A. Demonstrating interest in and respect for children.	_____	_____
B. Helping children recognize their emotions and the emotions of others.	_____	_____
C. Facilitating interaction among children and between children and adults.	_____	_____
D. Expanding children's understanding of themselves.	_____	_____
E. Instructing, stimulating, and extending children's play.	_____	_____
F. Asking appropriate questions or clarifying concepts and information.	_____	_____
G. Talking to children of all ages, temperaments, and skills.	_____	_____
(12) 6. Uses silence effectively to facilitate children's play.	_____	_____
A. Allows children to engage in solitary play without intrusion.	_____	_____
B. Allows children to engage in peer interaction without intrusion.	_____	_____
C. Allows children to rest undisturbed.	_____	_____

(continued)

Total Points for Each Category	Midterm Evaluation	Final Evaluation
(16) 7. Intervenes to avoid problems *before* they happen.	_____	_____
A. Develops a prepared, safe environment.	_____	_____
B. Foresees potential problems and acts to prevent them.	_____	_____
C. Maintains a global view of the environment.	_____	_____
D. Presents alternatives to children.	_____	_____
(16) 8. Helps children learn how to develop problem-solving strategies and self-regulation.	_____	_____
A. Breaks tasks into manageable steps for children to follow and accomplish.	_____	_____
B. Offers children appropriate choices.	_____	_____
C. Gives children appropriate responsibilities.	_____	_____
D. Utilizes positive strategies for coping with stress and promoting resilience	_____	_____
(36) 9. Recognizes, interprets, and effectively uses a variety of positive guidance techniques.	_____	_____
A. Develops rules to protect children's safety, to protect property, or to help children learn to respect the rights and feelings of others as well as rules that are reasonable, definable, and positive.	_____	_____
B. Communicates expectations to children in ways that lead to the development of internal controls.	_____	_____
C. Develops consequences that are immediate, consistent, and logical.	_____	_____
D. Uses a calm, rational approach to limit-setting situations.	_____	_____
E. Uses appropriate warnings prior to enacting a consequence.	_____	_____
F. Follows through appropriately on limits set.	_____	_____
G. Ignores negative child behavior as appropriate.	_____	_____
H. Sets firm limits when children display aggression or uses sitting away or gentle restraint as appropriate.	_____	_____
I. Demonstrates flexibility in meeting the needs of individual children.	_____	_____
(8) 10. Collaborates with parents.	_____	_____
A. Gives accurate information to parents about the program.	_____	_____
B. Interacts with parents in a respectful professional manner.	_____	_____
Total Possible (180) TOTAL POINTS	_____	_____ (180)

Glossary

abusive or neglectful families   Families who maltreat children by way of psychological, physical, or sexual abuse or who do not provide for children's basic needs.

acceptance   To value children unconditionally.

activity space   Area occupied by one child using a material.

adherence   Following a rule merely to gain a reward or avoid a punishment; relying on others to monitor one's personal actions.

adversity   When risk factors interfere with the accomplishment of developmental tasks.

affect   Emotions, mood.

affective reflections   Nonjudgmental statements that describe the emotion of the child or adult.

aggression   Any behavior that results in physical or emotional injury to persons, or any behavior that leads to property damage or destruction.

amoral   Having no concept of right and wrong.

antibias education   Knowledge that helps children avoid developing or maintaining stereotyped viewpoints, biases, prejudices, and fear.

antisocial behavior   Inappropriate problem behavior.

anxiety disorders   Persistent unfounded fears that are out of proportion to the actual threat or danger and lead to maladaptive behavior.

appreciation of children's stress   Respecting children's viewpoints as well as their coping strategies.

Asperger's syndrome disorder   A developmental disorder on the autism spectrum that affects the ability to socialize and communicate effectively with others.

assertiveness   Purposeful action used to express self or protect rights while respecting the rights and feelings of others.

associative play   A situation in which a child plays with other children and interacts with them sporadically in similar but not identical activities or in activities that are loosely associated. There is no shared goal.

attachment   Reciprocal, enduring relationship between infant and caregiver, each of whom contributes to the quality of the relationship.

authoritarian discipline style   Adults vigilantly enforcing the rules typically without explanation or reasons. Punishments occur swiftly and forcefully, often using ridicule, shame, or physical means.

authoritative discipline style   Adults respond to children's needs with warmth and nurturance with high standards and expectations for behavior. Emphasis is on teaching the children to take responsibility and make good decisions. Consequences with explanations, demonstrations, suggestions, and discussions are used instead of punishments.

authority   Power that comes from specialized knowledge, role in society, and ability to distribute resources and give rewards.

autonomy   Ability to act independently.

axial space   Physical space that extends to the outer reach of the arms and legs.

baby talk   Stylized speech usually having an atypical voice pitch, in which adults use diminutive word forms, sound substitutions, and improper pronouns. Children do not talk like this.

basic values   Values that are absolute, regardless of the situation or context.

behavior reflections   Nonjudgmental statements made to children that describe their attributes or their roles in activities in which they are engaged; they begin with the child, not "I," and are descriptive.

behavioral state   Degree of arousal. Muscle tone, activity, respiration, position of the eyelids, and alertness vary in each state (i.e., sleeping or crying).

biases   Inclinations toward prejudging persons or situations not based on fact or the current situation.

blended families   Families that are reconstituted as a result of divorce and/or death; binuclear families.

boundaries   Physical or psychological barriers.

buddy skills training   Involves pairing more friendship-skilled children with children who are less skilled. The more-skilled child may also "coach" the less-skilled child in friendly behavior as they play together.

bullying   Routinely using hostile aggression to exert power over others.

centration   Directing attention to only one attribute of a situation while ignoring all others.

channel of communication   A mode of non-verbal communication (i.e., voice tone, facial expression, gesture, body position and orientation, and use of clothing or furnishings).

character attribution   Verbally assigning particular characteristics to children such as "you are kind" or "you are giving"; a verbal strategy used to affect how children think about themselves.

character role   Child takes on the behaviors and responsibilities of another role within the play scenario; may be family roles, work roles, or fantasy-based roles.

childhood stress   Things of any type that place unusual demands on a child's ability to cope with life events.

chronic illness   Long-term illnesses, such as cancer, cystic fibrosis, and diabetes.

closed-ended questions   Questions that call for a one- or two-word answer, and effectively close the door on future conversations.

coaching   An intervention tool that involves an adult working directly with a child to instruct him or her on specific skills that can be used to make and keep friends.

communication   (as related to discipline style) Degree to which adults communicate their expectations and reasoning to children in both verbal and nonverbal ways.

communicative gestures   Child points to or physically signals the caregiver to look at something. Infant checks to see if the adult is responding.

competence   The belief that one is able to accomplish tasks and achieve goals.

complexity   State of having two or more parts or multiple uses; having interrelated parts; complicated.

compulsions   Impulses to repeatedly perform certain acts.

conflict mediation   A strategy used to diffuse conflict between people in order to come to a mutually agreed upon solution to the conflict.

construction play   Occurs when children build or make something deliberately to embody an idea.

contingent behavior   Actions that respond to another person's action.

control (as related to discipline style)   The manner and degree to which adults enforce compliance with their expectations.

control (as related to self-esteem)   The feeling on the part of individuals that they can influence the outcomes and events in their world.

cooperative activity   Activity in which participants work together to complete a group goal. It is the opposite of competitive activity.

cooperative play   Two or more children maintain play that is focused on some common goal or play theme. Actions and communication are coordinated.

coping   Contending with stress.

co-regulation   Adult shares a difficult task with a child, breaking it into easily manageable parts that the child can accomplish so the child can learn the behavior to manage the task. The adult structures the situation for the child to assist him or her in becoming able to eventually self-regulate. An example of co-regulation is an adult assisting a child in asking for a toy from a peer (rather than grabbing it) by giving the child the question to use: "May I use the train when you are done?"

corrective consequences   Implemented in response to children's mistaken behavior. These constructive actions help children recognize the impact of their actions on themselves and others and are implemented with the long-term goal of teaching children self-discipline.

corporal punishment   Formalized approach to physical punishment used by some institutions such as schools and prisons and regulated by laws and institutional rules.

corrective consequences   Strategies used to help children change their behavior in ways that enhance children's self-control. Constructive actions aimed at helping children learn acceptable conduct from the experience of being corrected.

decision making   Making choices between two or more alternatives.

defense mechanisms   Strategies used to temporarily regain a sense of balance.

definable rules   Rules in which both children and adults have the same understanding of what behavior is expected.

denial   Acting as if stress does not exist.

developmentally appropriate practices   The early childhood teaching behaviors that result when adults take into account children's ages, individual needs, and the context of their lives.

dimension of high–low mobility   The degree of opportunity for the physical movement of children's bodies within a space.

direct instruction   Specific directions used by adults to regulate children's behavior through physical and verbal controls.

directing   Supervising by efficient, effective means to attain a goal; speaking or acting clearly, explicitly; telling someone what to do and how to do it. Directing uses the action dimension heavily.

disabling conditions   A blanket categorization that refers to a child's special need, which may fall under any one or more of the following categories: learning disability, developmental disability, mental retardation, serious emotional disturbance, speech and language disorders, or physical or sensory disability.

displacement   A technique in which children who are behaving aggressively are given another source at which to aim their aggression to rid themselves of the aggression.

display rules   Unspoken expectation of nonverbal behavior in response to a situation.

distal space   Physical space from the outer edges that the arms and legs can reach to the farthest that the eye and ear can perceive.

dramatic play   Pretend play; a story-like performance of a player taking on an imaginary role.

dramatist style   A mode of play during which constructions or materials are used mostly to support pretend play, and intrinsic design is less important.

dual-language learners   Children who are learning 2 languages at the same time.

duration   A period of time.

easy child   Generally happy, friendly, predictable, and adaptable.

effective praise   Praise that is selective, specific, and positive.

emblems   Specific cultural gestures that have a direct verbal referent.

emotional IQ   Measure of a person's adeptness at understanding his or her own emotions and the emotions of others.

emotions   Display of affect.

empathy   Recognizing and understanding another person's perspective.

English language learners   Those whose first language is not English.

ethical judgments   Decisions focused on ethical codes of conduct.

ethics   Basic principles that guide day-to-day conduct.

ethnicity   Ethnic classification or affiliation.

ethnocentrism   Focus on only ethnicity of self.

exaggeration   An overstatement; something that has been embellished or amplified.

expansion   A type of paraphrasing in which the respondent fills in or enhances what the child has just said.

expressive language   Verbal or written language used to communicate with others.

expressive speech   Words about emotional content.

expressive state   The typical manner in which an individual expresses his or her emotions.

expressive style   Children's patterns of emotional responsiveness.

fantasizer   A person who uses a narrative, story, or situation as a point of reference.

feedback   Information provided about performance. It includes what was done correctly, what was incorrect, and what to do next time.

follow-through   Enforcing the negative consequence set up in the warning. It is used when the child does not comply with the warning, and it includes a reflection of the child's current action, emotion, or statement, followed by a reminder of the warning and implementation of the corrective consequence.

formal pretend proposals   A straightforward request to play or to change the direction of the play within the play scenario.

friends   Two or more people in a relationship in which there is a positive connection, and each party has expectations of benefiting from the relationship.

friendship   The special positive mutually beneficial relationship between friends.

Friendship Framework   The ways in which children think about friends and friendship from the earliest years through their maturity.

friendship skills   Specific skills that are used to make and keep friends.

functional role   Simple role-play in which the child becomes the actor in the present situation; may be the role of truck driver while moving a truck around or the "motor" of the truck with appropriate sounds.

games   Group rule-governed play; usually includes a winner and loser.

gaze following   Infant looks at the caregiver's face and then orients to the same location.

gender identity   Biological, male–female identification.

gender-role identification   The behavior and characteristics associated with a particular gender.

genuineness   Honesty and sincerity communicated orally and nonverbally.

gestures   The movements of hands, arms, or body that accompany speech used to illustrate words, give emphasis, or replace words.

giftedness   The ability to solve complex problems in an effective, efficient, elegant, and/or economical way.

goals   A desired end toward which effort is directed; an end that can be attained.

goodness of fit   The degree to which the adult temperament fits the temperament of the infant.

grieving process   Behaviors used in coping with loss, including denial, bargaining, depression, and acceptance of the event.

guilt   A feeling that warns that a current or planned action is undesirable and provokes regret for past misdeeds.

Healthy self-esteem   self-judgments that lead people to believe that they are loveable human beings, with useful knowledge and skills, and that they can influence some of the events in their lives.

hesitation   A pause that is often vocalized.

high or low mobility   A person's physical activity level.

homeostasis   Ability to return to good functioning.

hostile aggression   Intended harm to things or people in which the aggressor experiences satisfaction with the harmful outcome.

identification   Following a rule to imitate or gain the approval of an individual one admires.

illustrator gestures   Movements of the hands or body that depict an object or event.

imagery   Purposefully imagined pictures in the mind.

imitative learning   Repetition of the acts of others.

impulsive acting out   Acting impulsively and often flamboyantly to avoid thinking of either the past or the consequence of current actions to conceal true feelings of misery and pain.

individualized education program (IEP)   A written plan developed for children older than 3 years to provide the most effective resources to support the child's development.

individualized family service plan (IFSP)   A plan developed for children, birth to age 3, under P.L. 99–457, to identify and organize the most effective resources to support the child's development.

individuation   Process by which the self or identity is developed.

inhibiting consequences   Consequences that reduce the probability of problem behaviors being repeated.

inhibition   Tendency to repress or show restraint.

instrumental aggression   Unintentional harm to things or people that happens as a result of the aggressor trying to get or protect something using force. Often occurs over objects, territory, or rights.

instrumental know-how   Having the knowledge and skills to act competently.

intensity   Frequency per unit of time; strength.

Intensive Individualized Intervention   Represents the top of the Social Support Pyramid.

Such intervention requires adults to come together to create a plan and then purposefully coordinate their efforts to support the child in developing new abilities to replace inappropriate behaviors.

intentionality   Uncooperativeness or misbehavior thought to be designed by a child in order to be difficult.

interaction   A two-way exchange that is reciprocal in nature.

internal space   Physical space from the center of the body to the surface of the skin.

internalization   Following rules based on an internal code of ethics; the same as self-regulation.

internalized oppression   Feelings of inferiority that develop because of limited opportunity or negative messages.

internalized privilege   Feelings of superiority that develop because of economic, social, or cultural advantages.

intrusion–seclusion dimension   Permeability of the boundaries between spaces; particularly permeable between the group and the things and people outside the group.

irreversible   Unable to mentally reverse actions that are initiated physically—not able to think of an opposite action for something one is doing; common among toddlers and preschoolers.

joint attention   Two people engage in communicating fully with each other, with each attending to the nonverbal cues of the other and focused on the same thing.

large-group space   A learning center for more than eight children, usually all of the children in the group.

learned helplessness   Feelings of powerlessness or perception of inability to change a situation for the better.

learning centers   A physical arrangement of furnishings and materials that is designed to promote learning.

logical consequences   Consequences directly related to a rule which are used to help a child learn what to do instead or repair what has been done, and include rehearsal of the appropriate action, restitution for the action, or temporary loss of privilege.

mask smile   The simple smile with an otherwise neutral expression.

masked play   Aggressive or violent behavior in which the aggressor claims to have been playing.

maturity demands   The level at which expectations are set.

metacommunication   A communication about how to communicate or talking about how to speak; requires thinking about the way one communicates; in play, it sets the frame for the fact that play is going on or a statement is meant as a joke.

mixed message   A communication in which the spoken words and one or more nonverbal channels communicate conflicting meanings.

modeling   An intervention tool involving the process of demonstration of a skill "in action."

moral violations   Lying, stealing, and hurting others.

narrative talk   The language that is used in communication between adults that serves to create a story for the child of his or her life.

natural consequences   Consequences that happen without any intervention.

negative affect   Grumpiness in babies; global mood that is unhappy.

negative verbal environment   The verbal atmosphere in which children feel unworthy, unlovable, insignificant, or incompetent as a result of what adults do or do not say to them.

neglect   Failure to appropriately meet children's basic needs.

neglected children   Children who are rarely or never selected as a friend/play partner. These children believe themselves to be less skilled than others.

negotiation skills   A specific set of behaviors that aid in resolving a conflict peacefully.

nonlexical sounds   Vocalizations without words such as throat clearing or yawning.

nonverbal communication   The transfer and exchange of messages in all modalities except words.

novelty   New; not resembling something known or previously used.

nurturance   The extent to which adults express caring and concern for children.

object invention   Imaginative creation of objects.

object substitution   The act of substituting one object for another or transforming one object into another.

obsessions   Undesired recurring thoughts.

on-the-spot coaching   Situational assistance in which the coach translates for the child (or children) the intentions and actions of his or her peers and offers suggestions for appropriate action to improve the interactions.

one-on-one coaching   Personalized assistance to improve the child's interpersonal relationships and behavior that occurs out of the situation. Child is told how to perform a skill and what not to do, and then practices doing the skill correctly with feedback provided by the coach.

onlooker   The child who watches other children, actively observes, and may briefly comment to them but does not engage with others.

open–closed dimension   The degree by which the use of materials or equipment is restricted by their design.

open-ended questions   Questions for which there are many possible answers; used to invite conversation and allow the speaker to direct the course of the conversation.

paralinguistics   Vocalizations that are not words.

parallel activity   The child plays in the presence of other children, often with the same or similar materials; nonverbal contact with other players is common.

paraphrase reflections   Nonjudgmental restatements of something the child said, but not word for word.

passive victims   Victims of bullying who do nothing to instigate the bullying. Passive victims seldom initiate the hostile attack and rarely assert their rights when it happens.

patterner style   A play style that is dependent on color, texture, shape or other physical characteristics.

patterners   Children whose preferred style of construction or materials use is to build an aesthetically pleasing design or pattern as a desired end goal.

peer teaching   An intervention tool that involves putting a more abled child with a less abled child.

peer-neglected children   Children ignored or overlooked by peers, not necessarily because of poor social skills but more due to their self-image and expectation of always being left out.

peer-rejected children   Children who are left out of activities and shunned by other children purposely.

peers   Others who are around the same age level or maturity level as the person.

perception of a stressor   A child's understanding of a perceived stressor, whether the stressor is real or not.

permissive discipline style   Emphasizes warmth and affection with little instruction on how to behave or expectations for behavior. Punishments often include love withdrawal.

Persona Dolls   Life-like dolls that are roughly the same size and age as the children involved; the dolls are given an "identity" by the teacher for the purpose of introducing social issues to the class.

personal message   A statement that expresses behavior expectations for children. It includes a reflection of what the child is doing, saying, or feeling; the adult emotional reaction and the reason for the reaction; and if it is used to change behavior, then also a direction for what to do instead (redirection).

personal space   Space within one's arm reach.

perspective-taking   The ability to think about how another person feels in a given situation.

pitch and tone   Characteristics of the voice that depict high or low and range and quality of sound.

play episode   All of the materials and equipment, the theme, and all of the players involved in a prolonged, socially organized play event.

play frames   Defines the context (people, materials, space) of a particular play scenario.

play schemes   Short sequences of pretend play such as eating, waking up, or cooking that are used in combination in dramatic play.

poor-quality program   Program that fails to meet standards outlined by the APHA and AAP. Care where the providers are untrained, where child–adult ratios and group sizes are inappropriate, or care is based on low-quality programs.

Poor self-esteem   self-judgments that lead people to feel rejected or ignored, to believe they do not possess the skills to succeed in life, and helpless to influence what happens to them.

Positive Behavior Support plan   Typical plans involve an objective for the intervention, prevention strategies, replacement behaviors, reinforcers, attention to what should not be reinforced, and ways to monitor children's progress.

positive consequences   Rewards for engaging in desired behavior.

positive rules   Statements that identify desired behaviors.

positive self-talk   Giving one's self messages to help self-manage a situation, such as "I can sit quietly" or "I can handle this calmly."

positive verbal environment   The verbal atmosphere in which children feel competence, worth, and control as a result of what the adults say and do not say to them.

practice play   Repetitive actions with materials in play; examples include repeatedly dropping balls in a container and dumping them out and repeatedly shooting hoops.

pragmatist   Focuses on the here and now, the direct and the concrete.

precocious children   Children who are more highly developed than usual.

primary emotions   The intense and relatively pure emotions that are the first to develop in infancy and from which other related emotions emerge; such emotions include joy, anger, sadness, and fear.

private space   A physical space designed for one or two children to occupy alone or together.

private speech   Talking out loud to one's self as a way to think through a problem, reduce frustration, postpone rewards, or remind self of rules. Commonly used by children for self-regulation.

professionals   People who use their skills and abilities to assist other people in improving the quality of their lives and who have access to specialized knowledge, demonstrated competence, standards of practice, continuing education, and a code of access.

prompting   A technique that people use to instruct another person on what to say or how to act.

prosocial attribution   Telling children that they have prosocial characteristics, such as "You shared because you noticed that she didn't have any dough and you like to help others."

prosocial behavior   Acts that support, assist, or benefit others without external rewards.

protective factors   Assets that help children and families recover from risks and ward off adversity.

provocative victims   Victims of bullying who prompt aggressive reactions from others by crying easily; by becoming defensive or angry when it is not appropriate; or by misinterpreting joking or teasing as verbal aggression when that is not the intent.

proximal space   Physical space from the surface of the skin to the outer edges of clothing, hair, or ornament.

psychological disequilibrium   Feelings of instability.

psychosexual development   The development of children's cognitive beliefs about sexual matters and processes.

punishments   Penalties for misbehavior and actions taken against children whose behavior is disapproved of. Punishments detract from children's development of self-regulation.

reasonable rules   Rules that a child is capable of following.

recasting   A higher form of paraphrasing in which the adult restructures the child's sentence into a new, more complex form.

receptive language   Known vocabulary.

referential speech   Words about objects, actions, and locations.

regression   Acting younger than one's age and engaging in earlier age behaviors.

reinforcement   Providing some consequence to a behavior that increases the likelihood the behavior will reoccur in a similar situation.

rejected-aggressive children Children whose attempts to enter play and make friends are rejected due to their aggressive actions. These children tend to become even more aggressive over time.

rejected children Children actively shunned by their peers.

rejected-withdrawn children Children whose attempts to enter play and make friends are often ignored because of their socially awkward and immature actions. These children tend to withdraw from social interaction over time and are often lonely.

relational aggression Damage to another person's ego or relationships as happens when children gossip or tell lies about someone.

relationships Interactions established over time that infer a sense of belonging.

relative values Values that vary, taking on more or less importance depending on the situation.

resilience Capacity to rise above difficult circumstances.

resistance to control A temperamental approach that is negative in mood, independent, and irritable.

respect Believing that children are capable of learning and making self-judgments.

responsive Reacting to nonverbal and verbal cues.

rhythm Predictable and regular timing.

risk Condition with an elevated probability of a bad outcome.

risk factors Accumulated risks.

role-playing Fictional reenactments or creations in which participants each take on a role and act out a situation.

rough-and-tumble play Movement play in which the children run, hop, fall, chase, wrestle, or kick at other children while laughing or showing pleasant expressions; may include play fighting.

scaffolding The process of linking what a person knows or can do with new information or skills he or she is ready to acquire.

schedule Planned sequence of events that are regular over a day and/or a week.

school phobia Anxiety about going to school.

self-awareness An understanding that the self is separate from others in the environment.

self-concept The combination of attributes of the abilities, behaviors, attitudes, and values that one believes defines the self and sets the self apart from others.

self-disclosure A type of emotional sharing; considered a basic interpersonal skill.

self-efficacy Ability to plan and cope well; self-determination.

self-esteem The evaluation placed on one's definition of self; composed of three dimensions: worth, competence, and control.

self-regulation The ability to behave in acceptable ways of one's own choice rather than depend on others to guide and control one's behavior.

sensitive caregiving Adult takes care of the child while observing and responding to the cues of the child. Uses both verbal and nonverbal cues to provide care and emotional support.

sexual abuse Molestation, exploitation, and intimidation of children in order to engage them in sexual activity.

shaping Involves the gradual incremental use of rewards to maintain or encourage desired behaviors.

shared attention Focus of infant and caregiver is on the same thing or event; the infant may check on the caregiver's face to make sure he or she is looking at the object of interest to the infant.

Shared narratives a group story that uses the children in a class as the main characters, which is told over and over again, and which leads to feelings of cohesion among group members.

shared regulation The ability to monitor and manage one's thinking, attention, feelings, and behavior with the help of another.

shyness A personality style ranging from moderate to severe, resulting in social discomfort and avoidance.

shyness and inhibition Fearfulness, tendency to withdraw.

silence The absence of sound

simple–complex dimension The number of alternative uses that can be generated from equipment or materials.

simultaneous bilingualism Acquisition of more than one language before age 2.

sitting apart Involves temporarily removing a child who is disruptive or causing harm from an activity or group time so that the child may regain self-control, and then allowing the child to reenter the group when calm or when the activity is done. During the sitting apart time, the child remains in the room close to the focus activity.

skills Observable actions that can be learned and evaluated.

small-group space A learning center for eight or fewer children (usually four to six children).

social cognition Knowledge and understanding of social acts.

social competence The ability to recognize, interpret, and respond appropriately in social situations.

social competencies Values of social justice, healthy attitudes toward sexuality, and the ability to interact effectively with people of varying cultural, ethnic, and racial backgrounds.

social-conventional infractions Poor table manners, speaking rudely, greeting someone improperly.

social referencing When a baby appraises a new situation by looking at the caregiver's facial expression and attending to his or her tone of voice and other nonverbal cues before responding; process becomes increasingly refined with age and experience.

social responsibility Behavior that contributes to the common good.

social understanding Comprehension of the manner in which the social world works.

socialization Capacity to cooperate in a group, to regulate one's behavior according to society, and to get along with others.

sociodramatic play Cooperative play that depicts a story line with extended communications among the players that move the story forward; a common theme and shared pretend sequences and objects.

soft–hard dimension Responsiveness of the texture to touch.

solitary play The child plays alone; no social interaction.

specific praise Praise that provides explicit information about what is being praised.

standards Method of assessing attainment of goals.

storytelling A play strategy that provides a narrative about the situation, characters, past events, or unseen objects or events; usually it is used to set the stage for play and to state the problem to be resolved during the play.

strategies Methods used to pursue goals.

stress Excess energy that helps us meet unusual demand.

stress-coping mechanisms Ways to contend successfully with difficulties.

stress hardiness Able to cope with adversity.

stressors Anything new or different in our life that forces us to draw on energy reserves.

structuring Management of time, space, and materials aimed at promoting children's social competence.

style Features of the behavior that occur independent of the content of play.

subjective time Not related to clock or calendar time; instead, it is a concept that things will occur when they are ready; readiness is determined by the people using this frame of reference.

successive bilingualism Acquisition of a second language after age 3.

temper tantrum An intense physical and emotional response in which a child has no access to rational thought processes.

temperament Describes the degree or intensity of emotional behavior and the timing and duration of response.

tempo The regular speed of something.

transform To change into something else; in play roles, the objects, situations, time, and circumstances are transformed into something else as part of pretend play.

transition A period of time between the ending of one segment in the schedule and the beginning of another.

ulterior conversations Usually whispered directions or comments about the play to another player.

underscoring Statements made by children whose pretend actions may not clearly communicate what the child is doing and how the role is being performed.

uninvolved adults Those adults who ignore children and are indifferent to them.

uninvolved discipline style Adults are indifferent to children and fail to relate well to children or to guide their behavior effectively.

unoccupied behavior The child is not engaged in any talk, object manipulation, or social activity.

unrelated consequences Consequences not related to the action but set up by an adult in response to child's misbehavior. Often involves loss of privilege unrelated to the problem behavior or the introduction of an unrelated penalty.

values The qualities and beliefs a person considers valuable or worthwhile.

verbal environment All of the verbal and nonverbal exchanges that take place within a given setting.

vulnerability Defenselessness; weakness.

vulnerable child syndrome (VCS) Problems that result from maternal substance use and abuse during pregnancy, including all the problems related to low birth weight, infections, pneumonia, congenital malformations, and drug withdrawal.

warmth Showing interest, being friendly, and being responsive.

warning An either-or statement that repeats the rule and tells the child what will happen if he or she does not follow it.

worth The extent to which people value and like themselves as well as perceive that they are valued by others.

References

Aamodt, S., & Wang, S. (2008). *Welcome to your brain*. New York, NY: Bloomsbury.

Adelman, L. (2007). *Don't call me shy: Preparing shy children for a lifetime of social success*. Austin, TX: LangMarc Publishers.

Afifi, T. O., Mota, N. P., Dasiewicz, P., MacMillan, H. L., & Sareen, J. (2012, July 2). Physical punishment and mental disorders: Results from a nationally representative sample. *Pediatrics, 130*(184); DOI:10.1542/peds.2011-2947.

Ahn, H. J., & Stifter, C. (2006). Child care teacher's response to children's emotional expression. *Early Education & Development 17*(2), 253–270.

Alaska Department of Education and Early Development Division of Teaching and Learning Support. (2007, December). State of Alaska Early Learning Guidelines. Retrieved from http://www.eed.state.ak.us/publications/EarlyLearningGuidelines.pdf.

Alberto, P., & Troutman, A. (2009). *Applied behavior analysis for teachers* (8th ed.). Upper Saddle River, NJ: Merrill.

Aldrich, J. E. (2002). Early childhood teacher candidates' perceptions about inclusion. *Journal of Early Childhood Teacher Education, 23*(2), 167–173.

Aldwin, C. M. (2007). *Stress, coping, and development: An integrative approach* (2nd ed.). New York, NY: The Guilford Press.

Alink, L. R. A., Mesman, J., van Zeijl, J., Stolk, N., Juffer, F., Koot, H. M., Bakermans-Kranenburg, M. J., & Ijzendoorn, M. H. (2006). The early childhood aggression curve: Development of physical aggression in 10- to 50-month-old children. *Child Development, 77*, 954–966.

Allen, K. E., & Cowdery, G. E. (2012). *The exceptional child: Inclusion in early childhood education* (6th ed.). New York, NY: Thomson Delmar Learning.

Alsaker, F. D., & Gutzwiller-Helfenfinger, E. (2010). Social behavior and peer relationships of victims, bully-victims, and bullies in kindergarten. In S. R. Jimerson, S. W. Swearer, & D. L. Espelage (Eds.), *Handbook of bullying in schools: An international perspective* (87–99). New York, NY: Routledge.

American Academy of Pediatrics. (2006). Policy statement on corporal punishment in schools. *Pediatrics, 106*(2), 343.

American Civil Liberties Union and Human Rights Watch. (2010). Statement before the House Education and Labor Subcommittee on Healthy Families and Communities. *Hearing on Corporal Punishment in the Schools and Its Effect on Academic Success*. April, 2010. Available at http://www.hrw.org/sites/default/files/related_material/CorpPunishStatement_041510.pdf.

Andersen, P. A., Guerrero, L. K., & Jones, S. M. (2006). Nonverbal behavior in intimate interactions and intimate relationships. In V. Manusov & M. Patterson (Eds.), *The handbook of nonverbal communication* (pp. 259–278). Thousand Oaks, CA: Sage Publications.

Arnett, J. J. (2008). Socialization in emerging adulthood: From family to the wider world, from socialization to self-socialization. In J. Grusec & P. Hastings (Eds.), *Handbook of socialization: Theory and research* (pp. 208–255). New York, NY: The Guilford Press.

Asher, S. R., & Paquette, J. A. (2003). Loneliness and peer relations in childhood. *Current Directions in Psychological Science, 12*(3), 75–78.

Aunola, K., & Nurmi, J. E. (2005). The role of parenting styles in children's problem behavior. *Child Development, 76*(6), 1144–1159.

Bagwell, C. L., & Schmidt, C. L. (2011). *Friendships in childhood and adolescence*. New York, NY: The Guilford Press.

Bailey, B. A., & Brookes, C. (2003). Thinking out loud: Development of private speech and the implications for school success and self-control. *Young Children, 58*(5), 46–52.

Baillargeon, R. H., Zoccolillo, M., Keenan, K., Cote, S., Perusse, D., Wu, H., Boivin, M., & Tremblay, R. E. (2007). Gender differences in physical aggression: A prospective population-based survey of children before and after 2 years of age. *Developmental Psychology, 43*, 13–26.

Bajgar, J., Ciarrochi, J., Lane, R., & Deane, F. P. (2005). Development of the levels of emotional awareness scale for children (LEAS-C). *British Journal of Developmental Psychology, 23*(4), 569–586.

Ball, J. (1989, February). The National PTA's stand on corporal punishment. *PTA Today, XIV*, 15–17.

Bancroft., L., & Silverman, J. G. (2004). Assessing abusers risks to children. In P. Jaffee, L. Boher,

& A. Cunningham (Eds.), *Protecting children from domestic violence: Strategies for community intervention*. New York, NY: The Guilford Press.

Barbu, S. (2005). Similarity of behavioral profiles among friends in early childhood. *Child Health and Education, 1*(1), 27–40.

Barr, R. G., & Gunnar, M. (2000). Colic: The transient responsivity hypothesis. In R. Barr, B. Hopkins, & J. Green (Eds.), *Crying as a sign, a symptom, and a signal* (pp. 41–66). London, England: Mac Keith Press.

Bates, J. E., & Pettit, G. S. (2008). Temperament, parenting, and socialization. In J. E. Grusec, & P. D. Hastings (Eds.), *Handbook of socialization: Theory and research* (pp. 153–177). New York, NY: The Guilford Press.

Bath, H. I. (2008, Winter). Calming together: The pathway to self-control. *Reclaiming Children and Youth, 16, 4,* 44–46.

Bauer, P. J. (2009). Neurodevelopmental changes in infancy and beyond: Implications for learning and memory. In O. A. Barbarin & B. H. Wasik (Eds.), *Handbook of child development & early education: Research to practice* (pp. 57–77). New York, NY: The Guilford Press.

Baumeister, R. F., Campbell, J. D., Krueger, J. I., & Vohs, K. D. (2003). Does high self-esteem cause better performance, interpersonal success, happiness or healthier lifestyles? *Psychological Science in the Public Interest, 4*(1), 1–44.

Baumrind, D. (1967). Child care practices anteceding three patterns of preschool behavior. *Genetic Psychology Monographs, 75,* 43–88.

Baumrind, D. (1991). The influence of parenting style on adolescent competence and substance use. *Journal of Early Adolescence, II,* 56–95.

Bavelas, J. B., & Chovil, N. (2006). Nonverbal and verbal communication: Hand gestures and facial displays as part of language use in face to face dialogues. In V. Manusov & M. Patterson (Eds.), *The Sage handbook of nonverbal communication* (pp. 97–118). Thousand Oaks, CA: Sage Publications.

Bavelas, J. B., Chovil, N., Coates, L., & Roe, L. (1995). Gestures specialized for dialogue. *Personality and Social Psychology Bulletin, 21*(4), 394–405.

Beane, A. L. (2005). *The bully free classroom*. Minneapolis, MN: Free Spirit Publishing.

Bear, G. G. (2010). *School discipline and self-discipline: A practical guide for promoting prosocial student behavior*. New York, NY: The Guilford Press.

Beaudoin, M., & Taylor, M. (2004). *Breaking the culture of bullying and disrespect, grades K–8*. Thousand Oaks, CA: Corwin Press.

Bee, H., & Boyd, D. (2009). *The developing child*. Boston, MA: Allyn & Bacon.

Beebe, B., & Stern, D. (1977). Engagement—disengagement and early object experiences. In N. Friedman & S. Grand (Eds.), *Communicative structures and psychic structures*. New York, NY: Plenum.

Bekoff, M., & Pierce, J. (2009). Wild justice: Honor and fairness among beasts at play. *American Journal of Play, 2*(2), 451–475.

Bell, S. H., & Quinn, S. (2004). Clarifying the elements of challenging behavior. In S. H. Bell, V. Carr, D. Denno, L. J. Johnson, & L. R. Phillips (Eds.), *Challenging behaviors in early childhood settings* (pp. 1–19). Baltimore, MD: Paul H. Brookes Publishing.

Bell, S. M., & Ainsworth, M. D. (1972). Infant crying and maternal responsiveness. *Child Development, 43,* 1171–1190.

Bem, S. L. (1985). Androgyny and gender scheme theory: A conceptual and empirical integration. In T. B. Sondergregger (Ed.), *Nebraska Symposium on Motivation* (Vol. 32, pp. 1–71). Lincoln: University of Nebraska Press.

Berk, L. E. (2006). Looking at kindergarten children. In D. F. Gullo (Ed.), *K today: Teaching and learning in the kindergarten year* (pp. 11–25). Washington, DC: NAEYC.

Berk, L. (2013). *Child development*. Boston, MA: Pearson.

Berkowitz, L. (1993). *Aggression: Its causes, consequences and control*. New York, NY: McGraw-Hill.

Bernard, B. (2004). *Resilience: What we have learned*. San Francisco, CA: WestEd.

Berns, R. M. (2013). *Child, family, school, community: Socialization and support* (7th ed.). Belmont, CA: Wadsworth.

Biddle, K. A., Garcia-Nevarez, A., Henderson, W. J., & Valero-Kerrick, A. (2014). *Early childhood education: Becoming a professional*. Los Angeles, CA: Sage Publications.

Bierman, K. L., Domitovich, C. E., Nix, R. L., Gest, S. D., Welsh, J. A., Greenberg, M. T., ... Gill, S. (2008). Promoting academic and social-emotional school readiness: The Head Start REDI program. *Child Development, 79*(6), 1802–1817.

Bierman, K. L., & Powers, C. J. (2009). Social skills training to improve peer relations. In K. H. Rubin, W. M. Bukowski, & B. Laursen (Eds.), *Handbook of peer interactions, relationships, and groups* (pp. 603–621). New York, NY: The Guilford Press.

Bilton, H. (2010). *Outdoor learning in the early years: Management and innovation*. New York, NY: Routledge.

Bjorklund, D. F. (2012). *Children's thinking: Cognitive development and individual differences*. Belmont, CA: Wadsworth Publishing Co.

Blanck, P., & Rosenthal, R. (1982). Developing strategies for decoding "leaky" messages: On learning how and when to decode discrepant and consistent social communications. In B. S. Feldman (Ed.), *Development of nonverbal behavior in children*. New York, NY: Springer-Verlag.

Bodrova, E., & Leong, D. (2007). *Tools of the mind: The Vgotskian approach to early childhood education*. Englewood Cliffs, NJ: Prentice Hall.

Bodrova, E., & Leong, D. J. (2012). Scaffolding self-regulated learning in young children: Lessons from tools of the mind. In R. C. Pianta, W. S. Barnett, I. M. Justice, & S. M. Sheridan (Eds.), *Handbook of early childhood education* (pp. 352–369). New York, NY: The Guilford Press.

Bogle, R. E., & Wick, C. P. (2005). *Report from the National Summit on School Design*. Washington, DC: The American Architectural Foundation and the Knowledge Works Foundation.

Bohanek, J. G., Marin, K. A., Fivush, R., & Duke, M. P. (2006). Family narrative interaction and children's sense of self. *Family Process, 45*(1), Research Library Core, 39–52.

Bornstein, M. C. (2007). On the significance of social relationships in the development of children's earliest symbolic play: An ecological perspective, In A. Göncü & S. Gaskins (Eds.), *Play and development: Evolutionary, sociocultural, and functional perspectives* (pp. 101–129).

Bowe, F. G. (2007). *Children with special education needs* (4th ed.). Belmont, CA: Wadsworth.

Bramer, J. S. (2006). *Attention deficit disorder: The unfocused mind in children and adults*. New Haven, CT, and London, England: Yale University Press.

Bredekamp, S. (2014). *Effective practices in early childhood education: Building a foundation*. Boston, MA: Pearson.

Bredikyte, M., & Hakkarainen, P. (2011). Play intervention and play development. *Play and Performance: Play 7 culture studies, Vol. 11*, 59–83.

Brendgen, M., Dionne, G., Girard, A., Boivin, M., Vitaro, F., & Perusse, D. (2005). Examining genetic and environmental effects on social aggression in 6-year-old twins. *Child Development, 76*, 930–946.

Broderick, C. (2008). *The uses of adversity*. Salt Lake City, UT: Deseret Book.

Bronson, M. B. (2006). Developing social and emotional competence. In D. F. Gullo (Ed.), *K today: Teaching and learning in the kindergarten year* (pp. 47–55). Washington, DC: NAEYC.

Brooks, J. B. (2011). *The process of parenting*. New York, NY: McGraw-Hill.

Brophy-Herb, H., Schiffman, R., & Fitzgerald, H. (2007). The Early Head Start Research and Evaluation (EHSRE) Project: Pathways to family health, childhood social skills linked to learning abilities. *Science Daily*. Paper presented at the annual meeting of the Society for Research in Child Development, June 21.

Brown, B. (2001). *Combating discrimination: Persona dolls in action*. London, England: Trentham.

Brown, K. (2010). Young authors: Writing workshop in the kindergarten. *Young Children, 65*(1), 24–28.

Brown, R.T., Wiener, L., Kupst, M., Brennan, T., Behrman, R., Compas, B. E., … Zeltzer, L. (2008, May). Single parenting and children with chronic illness: An understudied phenomenon. *Journal of Pediatric Psychology, 33*(4), 408–421.

Brown, W. H., Odom, S. L., & McConnell, S. R. (Eds.). (2008). *Social competence of young children: Risk, disability & intervention* (pp. 3–30). Baltimore, MD: Paul H. Brookes Publishing.

Bukowski, W. M., Motzoi, C., & Meyer, F. (2009). Friendship as process, function, and outcome. In K. H. Rubin, W. M. Bukowski, & B. Laursen (Eds.), *Handbook of peer interactions, relationships, and groups* (pp. 217–231). New York, NY: The Guilford Press.

Bukowski, W. M., Velasquez, A. M., & Brendgen, M. (2008). Variation in patterns of peer influence: Considerations of self and other. In M. J. Prinstein & K. A. Dodge (Eds.), *Understanding peer influence in children and adolescents* (pp. 125–140). New York, NY: The Guilford Press.

Bullard, J. (2010). *Creating environments for learning*. Upper Saddle River, NJ: Merrill.

Bureau of Labor Statistics. (2012, April). Employment characteristics of family summary. Retrieved from http://www.bls.gov/news.release/famee.nr0.htm.

Burgoon, J. K., & Dunbar N. E. (2006). Nonverbal expressions of dominance and power in human relationships. In V. Manusov & M. Patterson (Eds.), *The Sage handbook of nonverbal communication* (pp. 279–298). Thousand Oaks, CA: Sage Publications.

Burgoon, J. K., Guerrero, L. K., & Floyd, K. (2010). *Nonverbal communication*. Boston, MA: Allyn & Bacon.

Business Roundtable (2004). *Early Childhood Education: A call to action from the business community* (pp. 1–9). Washington, DC: Corporate Voices for Working Families.

Butterfield, P. M., Martin, C., & Prairie, A. P. (2004). *Emotional connections: How relationships guide early learning*. Washington, DC: Zero to Three Press.

Byrnes, J. P., & Wasik, B. A. (2009). *Language and literacy development: What educators need to know*. New York, NY: Guildford Press.

Calkins, S. D., & Williford, A. P. (2009). Taming the terrible twos: Self-regulation and school readiness. In O. A. Barbarin & B. H. Wasik (Eds), *Handbook of child development and early education: Research* to practice (pp. 172–198). New York, NY: The Guilford Press.

Card, P. A., Stucky, B. D., Sawalani, G. H., & Little, T. D. (2008, September/October). Direct and indirect aggression during childhood and adolescence: A meta-analytic review of gender differences, intercorrelations, and relations to maladjustment. *Child Development, 79*(5), 1185–1229.

Carkhuff, R. R. (2012). *The art of helping* (9th ed.). Amherst, MA: Human Resources Development Press.

Carlo, G., Knight, G. P., McGinley, M., Goodvin, R., & Roesch, S. (2010). The developmental relations between perspective taking and prosocial behaviors: A metaanalytic examination of the task-specificity hypothesis. In B. W. Sokol, U. Muller, J. I. M. Carpendale, A. R. Young, & G. Iarocci (Eds.), *Self and social regulation: Social interaction and the development of social understanding and executive functions* (pp. 234–269). New York, NY: Oxford University Press.

Carlson, F. M. (2011). *Big body play.* Washington, DC: National Association for the Education of Young Children.

Carpenter, M., Nagell, K., & Tomasello, M. (1998). Social cognition, joint attention, and communicative competence from 9 to 15 months of age. *Monographs of the Society for Research in Child Development, 63*(255), 4.

Caspi, A., & Shiner, R. L. (2006). Personality development. In N. Eisenberg, W. Damon, & R. M. Lerner (Eds.), *Handbook of child psychology* (pp. 300–365). New York, NY: Wiley.

Cassidy, D. J. (2003). Questioning the young child: Process and function. *Childhood Education, 65,* 146–149.

Center for Disease Control and Prevention. (2006). Child development. *Attention-Deficit/Hyperactivity Disorder (ADHD).* Atlanta, GA. http://www.cdc.gov/ncbddd/adhd/what.htm.

Center for Disease Control and Prevention. (2011). Obesity among low-income children. Retrieved June 2, 2013, from http://www.cdc.gov/obesity/downloads/PedNSSFactSheet.pdf.

Center for Effective Discipline. (2013). *U.S. corporal punishment and paddling statistics by states and race: States banning corporal punishment.* Columbus, OH: Author. Retrieved March 30, 2013, from http://www.stophitting.com/index.php?page=statelegislation.

Chaplin, T. M., Cole, P. M., & Zahn-Waxler, C. (2005). Parental socialization of emotion expression: Gender differences and relations to child adjustment. *Emotion, 5*(1), 80–88.

Charen, M. (2000, April 24). Our boys could use some help. *Lansing State Journal,* 6A.

Charles, C. M., Seuter, G. W., & Barr, K. B. (2014). *Building classroom discipline* (10th ed.) White Plains, NY: Pearson.

Charlesworth, R. (2011). *Understanding child development* (7th ed.). Clifton Park, NY: Thomson Delmar Learning.

Chiang, C., Soong, W., Lin, T., & Rogers, S. (2008). Nonverbal communication skills in young children with autism. *Journal of Autism and Developmental Disorders, 38,* 1898–1906.

Chukovsky, K. (1976). The sense of nonsense verse. In J. S. Bruner, A. Jolly, & K. Sylva (Eds.), *Play: Its role in development and evolution* (pp. 596–602). New York, NY: Basic Books.

Clark, C., & Gross, K. H. (2004). Adolescent health-risk behaviors: The effect of perceived parenting style and race. *Undergraduate Research Journal for the Human Sciences, 3,* 1–11.

Click, P. M. & Karkos, K. (2011) Administration of Programs for Young Children, 8e, Belmont, CA: Wadsworth.

Cloud, J. (2010, January). Why genes aren't destiny. *Time, 175*(2), 31–35.

Coie, J. D., & Dodge, K. A. (1998). Aggression and antisocial behavior. In N. Eisenberg (Ed.), *Handbook of child psychology Vol. 3: Social, Emotional, and Personality Development,* (6th ed., pp. 779–862). New York, NY: Wiley.

Cole, P. M., & Tan, P. Z. (2008). Emotion socialization from a cultural perspective. In J. Grusec & P. Hastings (Eds.), *Handbook of socialization: Theory and research* (pp. 516–542). New York, NY: The Guilford Press.

Collins, W. A., & Steinberg, I. (2006). Adolescent development in interpersonal context. In W. Damon & R. M. Lerner (Ser. Eds.) & N. Eisenberg (Vol. Ed). *Handbook of child psychology. Vol. 3: Social, emotional, and personality development* (6th ed.) (pp. 1003–1067). New York, NY: Wiley.

Conklin, S., & Frei, S. (2007). *Differentiating the curriculum for gifted learners.* Hunting Beach, CA: Shell Education.

Connecticut State Department of Education, Bureau of Teaching and Learning. (2013). English language arts crosswalk: Common core state standards to Connecticut state standards to district curriculum. Retrieved Feb. 9, 2013, from http://www.sde.ct.gov/sde/cwp/view.asp?a=2678&Q=320780.

Conroy, M. A., Brown, W. H., & Olive, M. L. (2008). Social competence interventions for young children with challenging behaviors. In W. H. Brown, S. L. Odom, & S. R. McConnel (Eds.), *Social competence of young children: Risk, disability & intervention* (pp. 205–231). Baltimore, MD: Paul H. Brookes Publishing.

Cook, R. E., Klein, M. D., & Chen, D. (2012). Adapting early childhood curricula for children with special needs (7th ed.). Upper Saddle River, NJ: Merrill.

Coplan, R. J., & Arbeau, K. A. (2009). Peer interactions and play in early childhood. In K. H. Rubin, W. M. Bukowski, & B. Laursen (Eds.), *Handbook of peer interactions, relationships, and groups* (pp. 143–161). New York, NY: The Guilford Press.

Coplan, R. J., Bowker, A., & Cooper, S. M. (2003). Parenting daily hassles, child temperament and social adjustment in preschool. *Early Childhood Research Quarterly, 18,* 376–393.

Coplan, R. J., Schneider, B. H., Matheson, A., & Graham, A. (2012). Play skills for children: Development of a social skills facilitated play early intervention program for extremely inhibited preschoolers. *Infant and Child Development, 19*(3).

Copple, C., & Bredekamp, S. (2009). *Developmentally appropriate practice in early childhood programs: Serving children from birth through age 8.* Washington, DC: NAEYC.

Couchenour, D., & Chrisman, K. (2013). *Families, schools and communities: Together for young children.* Belmont, CA: Wadsworth Publishing.

Craig, W., Harel-Fisch, Y., Fogel-Grinvald, H., Dostaler, S., Hetland, J., Simons-Morton, B., ... Pickett, W. (2009). A cross-national profile of bullying and victimization among adolescents in 40 countries. *International Journal of Public Health, 54,* 216–224.

Crothers, L. M., & Kolbert, J. B. (2010). Teacher's management of student bullying in the classroom. In S. R. Jimerson, S. W. Swearer, & D. L. Espelage (Eds.), *Handbook of bullying in schools: An international perspective* (pp. 535–546). New York, NY: Routledge.

Curran, J. (1999). Constraints of pretend play: Explicit and implicit rules. *Journal of Research in Childhood Education, 14*(1), 47–55.

Curry, N., & Bergen, D. (1987). The relationship of play to emotional, social, and gender/sex role development. In D. Bergen (Ed.), *Play as a medium for learning and development: A handbook for theory and practice.* Portsmouth, NH: Heinemann.

Curtis, D., & Carter, M. (2003). *Designs for living and learning: Transforming early childhood environments.* St. Paul, MN: Redleaf.

Curwin, R. L., Mendler, A. N., & Mendler, B. D. (2008). *Discipline with dignity: New challenges, new solutions.* Alexandria, VA: ASCD.

Damon, W., Lerner, R. M., & Eisenberg, N. (2006). *Handbook of child psychology, social, emotional and personality development, Volume 3.* Hoboken, NJ: John Wiley and Sons.

Davidson, T., Welsh, J., & Bierman, J. (2006). Social competence. *Gale encyclopedia of children's health: Infancy through adolescence.* Thomson Gale.

Retrieved September 23, 2009, from Encyclopedia.com: http:// www.encyclopedia.com/doc/1G2-3447200525.html.

Davies, D. (2010). *Child development.* New York, NY: The Guilford Press.

Day, M., & Parlakian, R. (2004). *How culture shapes social-emotional development.* Washington, DC: Zero to Three.

DeCapua, A., & Wintergerst, A. (2007). *Crossing cultures in the language classroom.* Ann Arbor: University of Michigan Press.

Deiner, P. L. (2009). *Infants & toddlers: Development & curriculum planning.* Clifton Park, NY: Cengage/ Delmar.

Deiner, P. L. (2012). *Inclusive early childhood education* (5th ed.). Belmont, CA: Wadsworth.

Denham, S.A., Bassett, H. H., & Wyatt, T. (2008). The socialization of emotional competence. In J. Grusec & P. Hastings (Eds.), *Handbook of socialization: Theory and research* (pp. 614–637). New York, NY: The Guilford Press.

Denno, D., Carr, V., & Bell, S. H. (2011). *A teacher's guide for addressing challenging behavior in early childhood settings.* Baltimore, MD: Paul H. Brookes Publishing.

Denton, P. (2007). *The power of our words: Teacher language that helps children learn.* Turners Falls, MA: Northeast Foundation for Children.

Derman-Sparks, L., & Edwards, J. O. (2010). *Anti-bias education for young children and ourselves.* Washington, DC: National Association for the Education of Young Children.

Deveny, K., & Kelley, R. (2007, February 12). Girls gone bad. *Newsweek,* 41–47.

DeVries, R., & Zan, B. (2003). When children make rules. *Educational Leadership, 61*(1), 64–67.

Diener, M. L., Isabella, R. A., Behunin, M. G., & Wong, M. S. (2007). Attachment to mothers and fathers during middle childhood: Associations with child gender, grade, and competence. *Social Development, 17*(1), 84–101.

Divinyi, J. (2011). *Good kids, difficult behavior.* Pahargani, New Delhi, India: B. Jain.

Dobbs, M. (2004, February 21). U.S. students still getting the paddle: Corporal punishment laws often reflect regional chasms. *Washington Post,* retrieved January 20, 2010, http://www.nospank.net/n-l51r.htm.

Dockett, S. (1998). Constructing understanding through play in the early years. *International Journal of Early Years Education, 6*(1), 105–116.

Dodge, D. T., Colker, L. J., & Heroman, C. (2008). *The creative curriculum for preschool* (3rd ed.). Washington, DC: Teaching Strategies.

Dodge, K. A., Coie, J. D., & Lynam, D. (2006). Aggression and antisocial conduct in youth. In W. Damon & R. M. Lerner (Series Eds.), &

N. Eisenberg (Vol. Ed.), *Handbook of child psychology: Vol. 3. Social, emotional, and personality development* (6th ed., pp. 719–788).

Dogan, S. J., Conger, R. D., Kim, K. J., & Masyn, K. E. (2007). Cognitive and parenting pathways in the transmission of antisocial behavior from parents to adolescents. *Child Development, 78,* 335–349.

Doherty-Sneddon, G. (2004). *Children's unspoken language.* New York, NY: Jessica Kingsley Publishers.

Dolgin, K. (1981). The importance of playing alone: Differences in manipulative play under social and solitary conditions. In A. Cheska (Ed.), *Play as context* (pp. 238–247). West Point, NY: Leisure Press.

Doll, B., & Brehm, K. (2010). *Resilient playgrounds.* New York, NY: Routledge.

Doll, B., Zucker, S., & Brehm, K. (2004). *Resilient Classrooms: Creating Healthy Environments for Learning.* New York, NY: The Guilford Press.

Dollard, J., Doob, L. W., Miller, N. E. Mowrer, O. H., & Sears, R. R. (1939). *Frustration and aggression.* New Haven, CT: Yale University Press.

Dombro, A. L., Jablon, J., & Stetson, C. (2011). *Powerful interactions: How to connect with children to extend their learning.* Washington, DC: NAEYC.

Domitrovich, C. E., Moore, J. E., Thompson, R. A., & the CASEL Preschool to Elementary School Social and Emotional Learning Assessment Workgroup. (2012). Interventions that promote social-emotional learning in young children. In R. C. Pianta, W. S. Barnett, L. M. Justice, & S. M. Sheridan (Eds.), *Handbook of early childhood education* (pp. 393–415). New York, NY: The Guilford Press.

Dovidio, J. F., Piliavin, J. A., Schroeder, D. A., & Penner, L. A. (2010). *The social psychology of prosocial behavior.* New York, NY: Psychology Press.

Dowling, M. (2005). *Young children's personal, social and emotional development.* London, England: Paul Chapman Educational Publishing.

Duffy, R. (2008). Are feelings fixable? *Exchange, 30*(6), 87–90.

Duffy, R. (2010). Challenging behavior: Step-by-step sifting, part 2. *Exchange, 32*(1), 88–91.

Dunlap, G., & Fox, L. (2009). Positive behavior support and early intervention. In W. Sailor, G. Dunlap, G. Sugai, & R. Harner (Eds.), *Handbook of positive behavior support* (pp. 49–72). New York, NY: Springer.

Dunn, J. (2009). Keeping it real: An examination of the metacommunication processes used within the play of one group of preadolescent girls. In C. D. Clark (Ed.), *Transactions at play: Play & culture studies* (Vol. 9, pp. 67–85). Lanham, MD: University Press of America.

Eccles, J. S. (2007). Families, schools, and developing achievement-related motivations and engagement. In J. E. Grusec & P. D. Hastings (Eds.), *Handbook of socialization: Theory and research* (pp. 665–691). New York, NY: The Guilford Press.

Edmiston, B. (2008). *Forming ethical identities in early childhood play.* New York, NY: Rouledge.

Edwards, C. H. (2007). *Classroom discipline and management.* New York, NY: John Wiley and Sons.

Egan, G. (2010). *The skilled helper* (8th ed.). Pacific Grove, CA: Brooks/Cole Publishing Company.

Eisenberg, N. (2013). Prosocial behavior, empathy, and sympathy. In M. H. Bornstein, L. Davidson, C. L. M. Keyes, & K. A. Moore (Eds.), *Well-being: Positive development across the life course* (pp. 253–267). Mahwah, NJ: Lawrence Erlbaum Associates.

Eisenberg, N., Chang, L., Ma, Y., & Haung, X. (2009). Relations of parenting style to Chinese children's effortful control, ego resilience, and maladjustment. *Development and Psychopathology, 21,* 455–477.

Eisenberg, N., Fabes, R. A., Shepard, S. A., Cumberland, A., & Carlo, F. (1999). Consistency and development of prosocial dispositions: A longitudinal study. *Child Development, 70,* 1360–1372.

Eisenberg, N., Fabes, R. A., & Spinrad, T. L. (2006). Prosocial development. In W. Damon & R. Lerner (Eds.), *Handbook of child psychology* (Vol. 3, pp. 646–718). New York, NY: Wiley.

Eisenberg, N., Smith, C. L., & Spinrad, T. L. (2011). Effortful control: Relations with emotion regulation, adjustment, and socialization in childhood. In K. V. Vohs & R. F. Baumeister, *Handbook of self-regulation: Research, theory and applications* (pp. 263–283). New York, NY: The Guilford Press.

Ekman, P. (2007). *Emotions revealed* (2nd ed.). New York, NY: Times Books.

Elliot, E., & Gonzalez-Mena, J. (2011). Babies' self-regulation: Taking a broad perspective. *Young Children, 66*(1), 28–32.

Epstein, A. S. (2007). *The intentional teacher: Choosing the best strategies for young children's learning.* Washington, DC: NAEYC.

Epstein, A. S. (2009). *Me, you, us: Social-emotional learning in preschool.* Ypsilanti, MI: HighScope Press.

Erikson, E. H. (1950, 1963). *Childhood and society* (Rev. ed.). New York, NY: W. W. Norton & Company.

Espelage, D. L., & Swearer, S. M. (2004). *Bullying in American schools: A social-ecological perspective on prevention and intervention.* Mahwah, NJ: Lawrence Erlbaum Associates.

Espinosa, L. (2010). *Getting it right for young children in diverse backgrounds.* Upper Saddle River, NJ: Pearson Education.

Essa, E. (2008). *What to do when: Practical guidance strategies for challenging behaviors in the preschool* (6th edition). Belmont, CA: Wadsworth, Cengage Learning.

Essa, E. (2014). *Introduction to early childhood education* (6th ed.). Clifton Park, NY: Wadsworth.

Evans, B. (2002). *You can't come to my birthday party: Conflict resolution with young children*. Ypsilanti, MI: High/Scope Press.

Evans, G. W. (2006). Child development and the physical environment. *Annual Reviews in Psychology, 57*, 423–451.

Fabes, R. A., Martin, C. L., & Havish, L. D. (2003a). Young children's play qualities in same-, other-, and mixed age peer groups. *Child Development, 74*, 921–932.

Fabes, R. A., Martin, C. L., & Havish, L. D. (2003b). Children at play: The role of peers in understanding the effects of child care. *Child Development, 74*(4), 1039–1043.

Fabes, R. A., Moss, A., Reesing, A., Martin C. L., & Hanish, L. D. (2005). *The effects of peer prosocial exposure on the quality of young children's social interactions*. Data presented at the annual conference of the National Council on Family Relations, Phoenix, AZ.

Fagot, B., & Leve, L. (1998). Gender identity and play. In D. Fromberg & D. Bergen (Eds.), *Play from birth to twelve and beyond: Contexts, perspectives and meanings* (pp. 187–192). New York, NY: Garland Publishing.

Falco, M. (2009). Study: 1 in 110 U.S. children had autism in 2006. CNN Medical News Report, available at http:// www.cnn.com/2009 /HEALTH/12/17/autism.

Farver, J. (1992). Communicating shared meanings in social pretend play. *Early Childhood Research Quarterly*, 501–516.

Fass, S., & Cauthen, N. K. (2008). *Who are America's poor children: National Center for Children in Poverty (NCCP)*. New York, NY: Columbia University.

Fathman, R. E. (2006). *2006 School corporal punishment report card*. Columbus, OH: National Coalition to Abolish Corporal Punishment in Schools, 1–3.

Feeney, S. (2010). Ethics today in early care and education: Review, reflection and the future. *Young Children, 65*(2), 72–77.

Feeney, S., & Freeman, N. K. (2012). *Ethics and the early childhood educator*. Washington, DC: NAEYC.

Fehr, B. J., & Exline, R.V. (1987). Social visual interaction: A conceptual and literature review. In A. W. Siegman & S. Feldstein (Eds.), *Nonverbal behavior and communication* (2nd ed.). Hillsdale, NJ: Lawrence Erlbaum Associates.

Feldman, R. S., Coats, E. J., & Philippot, P. (1999). Television exposure and children's decoding of nonverbal behavior in children. In P. Philippot, R. S. Feldman, & E. J. Coats. (Eds.), *The social context of nonverbal behavior*. Cambridge, England: Cambridge University Press.

Felstiner, S. (2004). Emergent environments: Involving children in classroom design. *Childcare Information Exchange, 157*, 41–43.

Feyereisen, P., & deLannoy, J. (1991). *Gestures and speech: Psychological investigations*. Cambridge, England: Cambridge University Press.

Field, T. (2007). *The amazing infant*. Malden, MA: Blackwell Publishing.

Fields, M. V., Merritt, P. P., & Fields, D. (2014). *Constructive guidance and discipline: Birth to age 8* (6th ed.). Upper Saddle River, NJ: Pearson.

Fivush, R., Brotman, M. A., Buckner, J. P., & Goodman, S. H. (2000). Gender differences in parent-child emotion narratives. *Sex Roles, 42*, 233–253.

Forgan, J. (2003). *Teaching problem solving through literature*. Westport, CT: Teachers Ideas Press.

Fox, J., & Tipps, R. (1995). Young children's development of swinging behaviors. *Early Childhood Research Quarterly, 10*, 491–504.

Fox, L., Carta, J., Strain, P., Dunlap, G., & Hemmeter, M. L. (2009). *Response to intervention and the Pyramid Model*. Tampa, FL: University of South Florida, Technical Assistance Center on Social Emotional Intervention for Young Children, http://www.challenegingbehavior.org.

Fox, L., Dunlap, G., Hemmeter, M. L., Joseph, G. E., & Strain, P. S. (2003). The teaching pyramid: A model for supporting social competence and preventing challenging behavior in young children. *Young Children, 58*(4), 48–52.

Fox, L., & Lentini, H. (2006). You got it!: Teaching social and emotional skills. *Young Children, 61*(6), 36–42.

Frandsen, M. (2011). Puppets, play therapy can improve social skills, speech for children with autism. *Examiner.com*, February 16, 2011, pp. 1–4. Retrieved February 10, 2013, from http://www.examiner.com /article/puppets-play-therapy-can-improve-social-skills-speech-for-children-with-autism.

Frank, M. G., Maroulis, A., & Griffin, D. J. (2013). The voice. In D. Matsumoto, M. G. Frank, & H. S. Hwang (Eds.), *Nonverbal communication: Science and applications* (pp. 53–74). Los Angeles, CA: Sage.

Frankel, K. A., & Myatt, R. (2003). *Children's friendship training*. New York, NY: Brunner-Routledge.

Freeman, N. (2007). Preschoolers' perceptions of gender appropriate toys and their parents' beliefs about genderized behaviors: Miscommunication, mixed messages, or hidden truths? *Early Childhood Education Journal, 34*(5), 357–366.

Freeman, N. K., & Swick, K. J. (2007, Spring). The ethical dimensions of working with parents. *Childhood Education, 83*(3), 163–169.

French, D. C., Jansen, E. A. Riansari, M., & Setiono, K. (2000). Friendships of Indonesian children: Adjustment of children who differ in friendship presence and similarity between mutual friends. *Social Development, 12*(4), 605–618.

Frey, K. S., Edstrom, L. V., & Hirschstein, M. K. (2010). School bullying: A crisis or opportunity. In S. R. Jimerson, S. W. Swearer, & D. L. Espelage (Eds.), *Handbook of bullying in schools: An international perspective* (pp. 403–415). New York, NY: Routledge.

Frick, P. J., Cornell, A. H., Bodin, S. D., Dane, H. E., Barry, C. T., & Loney, B. R. (2003). Callous-unemotional traits and developmental pathways to severe conduct disorders. *Developmental Psychology, 39,* 246–260.

Fridlund, A. L., & Russell, J. A. (2006). The functions of facial expressions: What's in a face. In V. Manusov & M. Patterson (Eds.), *The Sage handbook of nonverbal communication* (pp. 299–319). Thousand Oaks, CA: Sage Publications.

Friedman, T. (April 4, 2013). Our little school against the world. *Tampa Bay Times,* 13A.

Frost, J. L., Wortham, S. C., & Reifel, S. (2012). *Play and child development* (4th ed.). Boston, MA: Pearson.

Fuhler, C. J., Farris, P. J., Walther, M. P. (1999). Promoting reading and writing through humor and hope. *Childhood Education, 26*(1), 13–18.

Furnham, A., & Cheng, H. (2000). Lay theories of happiness. *Journal of Happiness Studies, 1,* 227–246.

Gable, R. A., Hester, P. P., Rock, M., & Hughes, K. (2009). Back to basics: Rules, praising, ignoring and reprisals revisited. *Intervention in School and Clinic, 44*(4), 195–205.

Gallagher, K. C., & Sylvester, P. R. (2009). Supporting peer relationships in early education. In O. A. Barbarin & B. H. Wasik, *Handbook of child development and early education: Research to practice* (pp. 223–246). New York, NY: The Guilford Press.

Garbarino, J. (2006). *See Jane hit: Why girls are growing more violent and what we can do about it.* New York, NY: Penguin Group.

Garner, P. W., Dunsmore, J. C., & Southam-Gerrow, M. (2008). Mother-child conversations about emotions: Linkages to child aggression and prosocial behavior. *Social Development, 17*(2), 259–277.

Gartrell, D. J. (2012). *Education for a civil society: How guidance teaches young children democratic life skills.* Washington DC: National Association for the Education of Young Children.

Gartrell, D. J. (2014). *A guidance approach to the encouraging classroom* (4th ed.). Clifton Park, New York, NY: Thomson Delmar Learning.

Gaskins, S., Haight, W., & Lancy, L. F. (2007). The cultural construction of play. In A. Göncü & S. Gaskins (Eds.), *Play and development: Evolutionary, sociocultural, and functional perspectives* (pp. 179–202). Mahwah, NJ: Lawrence Erlbaum Associates.

Gazda, G. M., Balzer, F., Childers, W., Nealy, A., Phelps, R., & Walters, W. (2006). *Human relations development—a manual for educators* (7th ed.). Boston, MA: Allyn and Bacon.

Geary, D. (2004). Evolution and developmental sex differences. In E. N. Junn & C. J. Booyatzis (Eds.), *Annual editions: Child growth and development* (pp. 32–36). McGraw-Hill Contemporary Learning Series. Dubuque, IA: McGraw-Hill.

Genishi, C., & Dyson, A. H. (2009). *Children, language, and literacy: Diverse learners in diverse times.* New York, NY: Teacher's College Press.

Gergen, K. (2001). *Social construction in context.* London, England: Sage.

Gershoff, E. (2008). *Report on physical punishment in the United States: What research tells us about its effects on children.* Columbus, OH: Center for Effective Discipline.

Gest, S. D., Graham-Bermann, & Hartup, W. W. (2001). Peer experience: Common and unique features of number of friendships, social network centrality, and sociometric status. *Social Development, 10,* 23–40.

Gestwicki, C. (2011). *Developmentally appropriate practice: Curriculum and development in early education* (4th ed.). Belmont, CA: Wadsworth /Cengage Learning.

Ginsburg, K. R. (2006). *A parent's guide to building resilience in children and teens.* New York, NY: American Academy of Pediatrics.

Glanzman, M. M., & Blum, N. J. (2007). In M. L. Batshaw, L. Pellegrino, & N. J. Roizen (Eds.), *Children with disabilities* (6th ed.). Paul H. Brookes Publishing.

Gleason, J. B., & Ratner, N. B. (2012). *The development of language* (7th ed.). Needham Heights, MA: Allyn & Bacon.

Golbeck, S. (2006). Developing key cognitive skills. In D. F. Gullo (Ed.), *K today: Teaching and learning in the kindergarten year* (pp. 37–46). Washington, DC: NAEYC.

Goldstein, S., & Brooks, R. B. (Eds.) (2013). *Handbook of resilience in children.* New York, NY: Springer.

Goleman, D. (1995). *Emotional intelligence: Why it can matter more than IQ.* New York, NY: Bantam Books.

Goleman, D. (2011). *Social intelligence: The new science of human relationships.* New York, NY: Bantam Books.

Göncü, A., Jain, J., & Tuerner, U. (2007). Children's play as cultural interpretation. In A. Göncü &

S. Gaskins (Eds.), *Play and development: Evolutionary, sociocultural, and functional perspectives* (pp. 155–178). Mahwah, NJ: Lawrence Erlbaum Associates.

Göncü, A., Patt, M., & Kouba, E. (2004). Understanding young children's pretend play in context. In P. K. Smith & C. Hart (Eds.), *Blackwell handbook of childhood social development* (pp. 418–437). Malden, MA: Blackwell Publishers.

Gonzalez–Mena, J. (2012). *Child, family, and community: Family-centered early care and education* (6th ed.). Boston, MA: Pearson.

Gonzalez-Mena, J., & Eyer, D. W. (2012). *Infants, toddlers and caregivers* (8th ed.). Boston, MA: McGraw-Hill.

Goodwin, M. H. (2006). *The hidden life of girls: Games of stance, status, and exclusion.* Malden, MA: Blackwell Publishing.

Griffin, H. (1984). The coordination of meaning in the creation of a shared make believe. In I. Bretherton (Ed.), *Symbolic play.* Orlando, FL: Harcourt Brace Jovanovich.

Guerrero, L. K., & Floyd, K. (2006). *Nonverbal communication in close relationships.* Mahwah, NJ: Lawrence Erlbaum Associates.

Gurian, M. (2009). *Nurture the nature.* San Francisco, CA: Jossey-Bass.

Gustafson, G. E., Wood, R. M., & Green, J. A. (2000). Can we hear the causes of infants' crying? In R. Barr, B. Hopkins, & J. Green (Eds.), *Crying as a sign, a symptom, and a signal* (pp. 8–22). London, England: Mac Keith Press.

Halberstadt, A. G. (1991). Toward an ecology of expressiveness: Family socialization and a model in general. In R. S. Feldman & B. Rime (Eds.), *Fundamentals of nonverbal behavior* (pp. 106–160). New York, NY: Cambridge University Press.

Hall, E. T. (2002). *The hidden dimension.* Garden City, NY: Doubleday & Company.

Hall, J. (1996, Spring). Touch, status, and gender at professional meetings. *Journal of Nonverbal Behavior, 20*(1), 23–44.

Halliday, M. A. K. (2006). *The language of early childhood, volume 4,* J. J. Webster (Ed.). London, England: Continuum International Publishing Group.

Hamel, J., & Nicholls, T. (2006). *Family intervention in domestic violence.* New York, NY: Springer Publishing.

Hammer, C. S., Scarpino, S., & Dawson, M. D. (2011). Beginning with language: Spanish-English bilingual preschooler's early literacy development. In S. B. Neuman & D. K. Dickinson (Eds.), *Handbook of early literacy research, volume 3.* New York, NY: The Guilford Press.

Hamre, B. (2008). Learning opportunities in preschool and elementary classrooms. In R. C. Pianta, M. J. Cox, & K. Snow (Eds.), *School readiness, early learning, and the transition to kindergarten* (pp. 219–239). Baltimore, MD: Paul H. Brookes Publishing.

Hanish, L. D., Kochenderfer-Ladd., B., Fabes, R. A., Martin, C. L., & Denning, D. (2004). Bullying among young children: The influence of peers and teachers. In D. L. Espelage & S. M. Swearer (Eds.), *Bullying in American schools: A social-ecological perspective on prevention and intervention* (pp. 141–159). Mahwah, NJ: Lawrence Erlbaum Associates.

Hanline, M. F., Wetherby, A., Woods, J., Fox, L., & Lentini, R. (2009). *Positive beginnings: Supporting young children with challenging behavior.* Florida State University and University of South Florida, retrieved March 1, 2010, http://pbs.fsu.edu /PBS.html.

Hansen, J. (2007). The truth about teaching and touching, *Childhood Education, 83*(3) 158–162.

Harrington, R. G. (2004). Temper tantrums: Guidelines for parents. *Helping children at home and school II: Handouts for families and educators.* Bethesda, MD: National Association of School Psychologists.

Hart, B., & Risley, T. R. (2003). The early catastrophe: The 30 million word gap by age 3. *American Educator,* available at http://www.aft.org /newspubs/periodicals/ae/spring2003/hart.cfm.

Hart, C. H., Newell, L. D., & Olsen, S. F. (2003). Parenting skills and social/communicative competence in childhood. In J. O. Greene & B. R. Burleson (Eds.), *Handbook of communication and social interaction skills* (pp. 753–798). Mahwah, NJ: Lawrence Erlbaum Associates.

Harter, S. (1998). The development of self-preservations. In W. Damon & N. Eisenberg (Eds.), *Handbook of child psychology, Vol. 3: Social, emotional, and personality development* (5th ed., pp. 553–618). New York, NY: John Wiley and Sons.

Harter, S. (2006). The self. In N. Eisenberg, W. Damon, & R.M. Lerner (Eds.), *Handbook of child psychology* (pp. 505–570). Hoboken, NJ: John Wiley & Sons.

Harter, S. (2012). *The construction of the self: Developmental and sociocultural foundations.* New York, NY: The Guilford Press.

Hartup, W. W., & Abeccassis, M. (2004). Friends and enemies. In P. K. Smith & C. H. Hort (Eds.), *Blackwell handbook of childhood social development* (pp. 285–305). Malden, MA: Blackwell.

Hartup, W. W., & Moore, S. G. (1990). Early peer relations: Developmental significance and prognostic implications. *Early Childhood Research Quarterly 5*(1), 1–17.

Haslett, B. B., & Samter, W. (1997). *Children communicating: The first five years*. Mahwah, NJ: Lawrence Erlbaum Associates.

Hastie, P. A., & André, M. H. (2012). Game appreciation through student designed games and game equipment. *International Journal of Play, 1*(2), 165–183.

Hastings, P. D., Rubin, K. H., & DeRose, L. (2005). Links among gender, inhibition, and parental socialization in the development of prosocial behavior. *Merrill-Palmer Quarterly, 51,* 501–527.

Hastings, P. D., Utendale, W. T., & Sullivan, C. (2008). The socialization of prosocial development. In J. E. Grusec & P. D Hastings (Eds.), *Handbook of socialization: Theory and research* (pp. 638–664). New York, NY: The Guilford Press.

Hastings, P. D., Vyncke, J., Sullivan, C., McShane, K. E., Benibui, M., & Utendale, W. (2006). *Children's development of social competence across family types.* Ottawa, Ontario: Department of Justice Canada.

Hastings, P. D., Zahn-Waxler, C., & McShane, K. (2005). We are, by nature, moral creatures: Biological bases for concern for others. In M. Killen & J. Smetana (Eds.), *Handbook of moral development* (pp. 483–516). Hillsdale, NJ: Lawrence Erlbaum Associates.

Hawkins, D. L., Pepler, D. J., & Craig, W. M. (2001). Naturalistic observations of peer interventions in bullying. *Social Development, 10*(4), 512–527.

Hay, D., Ross, H., & Goldman, B. D. (2004). Social games in infancy. In B. Sutton-Smith (Ed.), *Play and learning* (pp. 83–108). New York, NY: Gardner Press.

Hazen, N. L., & Black, B. (1989). Preschool peer communication skills: The role of social status and interaction content. *Child Development, 60*(4), 867–876.

Head Start Bureau. (1977). *Child abuse and neglect: A self-instructional text for Head Start personnel.* Washington, DC: U.S. Government Printing Office.

Hearron, P., & Hildebrand, V. (2013). *Guiding young children* (8th ed.). Upper Saddle River, NJ: Merrill.

Hebert-Meyers, H., Guttentag, C. L., Swank, P. R., Smith, K. E., & Landry, S. H. (2009). The importance of language, social, and behavioral skills across early and later childhood as predictors of social competence with peers. *Applied Developmental Science, 10*(4), 174–187.

Helwig, C. C., & Turiel, E. (2002). Children's social and moral reasoning. In C. Hart & P. Smith (Eds.), *Handbook of childhood social development* (pp. 475–490). Oxford: Blackwell Publishers.

Hemmeter, M. L., & Conroy, M. A. (2012). Supporting the social competence of young children with challenging behavior in the context of the teaching pyramid model: Research-based practices and implementation in early childhood settings. In R. C. Pianta, W. S. Barnett, L. M. Justice, & S. M. Sheridan (Eds.), *Handbook of early childhood education* (pp. 416–434). New York, NY: The Guilford Press.

Hemmeter, M. L., Ostrosky, M., & Fox, L. (2006). Social and emotional foundations for early learning: A conceptual model for intervention. *School Psychology Review, 35,* 583–601.

Hendrick, J., & Weissman, P. (2011). *Total learning: Developmental curriculum for the young child.* Upper Saddle River, NJ: Prentice Hall.

Hermans, E. J., Ramsey, N. F., & van Honk, J. (2008). Exogenous testosterone enhances responsiveness to social threat in the neural circuitry of social aggression in humans. *Biological Psychiatry, 63,* 263–270.

Herner, T. (1998). Understanding and intervening in young children's challenging behavior. *Counterpoint* (Vol. 1, p. 2) Alexandria, VA: National Association of Directors of Special Education.

Hester, P. P., Hendrickson, J. M., & Gable, R. A. (2009). Forty years later: The value of praise, ignoring, and rules for preschoolers at risk for behavioral disorders. *Education and Treatment of Children, 32*(4), 513–535.

Hewitt, J. (2002). The social construction of self-esteem. In C. R. Snyder & S. J. Lopez (Eds.), *The handbook of positive psychology.* New York, NY: Oxford University Press, pp. 135–147

Hinde, R. A. (2006). Ethological and attachment theory. In K. Grossman, E. Grossman, & E. Waters (Eds.), *Attachment from infancy to adulthood* (pp. 1–12). Florence, KY: Taylor & Francis Group.

Hohmann, M., Weikart, D. P., & Epstein, A. S. (2008). *Educating young children* Ypsilanti, MI: High Scope Press.

Holmes, R. M., Valentino-McCarthy, J. M., & Schmidt, S. L. (2007). "Hey, no fair": Young children's perceptions of cheating during play. *Investigating play in the 21st century: Play & culture studies, Volume 7* (pp. 259–276). Lanham, MD: University Press of America.

Honig, A. (1992, November). *Mental health for babies: What do theory and research teach us?* Paper presented at the Annual Meeting of National Association for the Education of Young Children, New Orleans, LA.

Honig, A. (1993, December). *Toddler strategies for social engagement with peers.* Paper presented at the Biennial National Training Institute of the National Center for Clinical Infant Programs, Washington, DC.

Honig, A. (1998). Sociological influences on gender role behaviors in children's play. In D. Fromberg & D. Bergen (Eds.), *Play from birth to twelve and beyond: Contexts, perspectives and meanings* (pp. 338–348). New York, NY: Garland.

Honig, A. S. (2000, September). Psychosexual development in infants and young children. *Young Children, 55*(5), 70–77.

Honig, A. S. (2004, March/April). How to create an environment that counteracts stereotyping. *Child Care Information Exchange*, 37–41.

Honig, A. S. (2009). *Little kids, big worries: Stress-busting tips for early childhood classrooms.* New York, NY: Paul H. Brookes Publishing.

Horne, A. M., Orpinas, P., Newman-Carlson, D., & Bartolomucci, C. L. (2004). Elementary school bully busters program: Understanding why children bully and what to do about it. In D. L. Espelage & S. M. Swearer (Eds.), *Bullying in American schools: A social-ecological perspective on prevention and intervention* (pp. 297–325). Mahwah, NJ: Lawrence Erlbaum Associates.

Horne, P E., & Timmons, L. (May 2009). Making it work: Teacher's perspectives on inclusion. *International Journal of Inclusive Education, 13*(3), 273–286.

Horowtiz, F. D., Darling-Hammond, L., & Bransford, J. (2005). Educating teachers for developmentally appropriate practice. In L. Darling-Hammond & J. Bransford (Eds.), *Preparing teachers for a changing world* (pp. 88–125). San Francisco, CA: Jossey-Bass.

Howe, N. Moller, L., Chambers, B., & Petrakos, H. (1993). The ecology of dramatic play centers and children's social and cognitive play. *Early Childhood Research Quarterly, 8*, 235–251.

Howes, C. (2000). Social development, family, and attachment relationships. In D. Cryer & T. Harms (Eds.), *Infants and toddlers in out-of-home care* (pp. 87–113). Baltimore, MD: Paul H. Brookes Publishing.

Howes, C. (2009). Friendship in early childhood. In K. H. Rubin, W. M. Bukowski, & B. Laursen (Eds.), *Handbook of peer interactions, relationships, and groups* (pp. 180–194). New York, NY: The Guilford Press.

Howes, C., & Lee, L. (2007). If you are not like me, can we play? Peer groups in preschool. In O. Saracho & B. Spodek (Eds.), *Contemporary perspectives on research in social learning in early childhood education* (pp. 259–278). Durham, NC: Information Age.

Hubbard, J. A., Smithmyer, C. M., Ramsden, S. R., Parker, E. H., Flanagan, K. D., Dearing, K. F., Relyea, N., & Simons, R. F. (2002). Observational, psychological, and self-report measures of children's anger: Relations to reactive versus proactive aggression. *Child Development, 73*, 1101–1118.

Hughes, F. P. (2010). *Children, play, and development* (4th ed.) Los Angeles, CA: Sage.

Hughes, C., & Ensor, R. (2010). Do early social cognition and executive function predict individual differences in preschoolers' prosocial and antisocial behavior? In B. W. Sokol, U. Muller, J. I. M. Carpendale, A. R. Young, & G. Iarocci (Eds.), *Self and social regulation: Social interaction and the development of social understanding and executive functions* (pp. 418–441). New York, NY: Oxford University Press.

Hughett, K., Kohler, F. W., & Raschke, D. (2011). The effects of a buddy skills package on preschool children's social interactions and play. *Topics in early childhood special education, 32*, 246–254.

Hutt, C. (1971). Exploration and play in children. In R. Herron & B. Sutton-Smith (Eds.), *Child's play*. New York, NY: John Wiley & Sons.

Hymowitz, K. S. (Spring 2012). American cast. *City Journal, 22*(2).

Hyson, M. (2004). *The emotional development of young children*. New York, NY: Teachers College Press.

Hyson, M. (2008). Enthusiastic and engaged learners: Approaches to learning in the early childhood classroom. New York, NY: Teachers College Press; Washington, DC: NAEYC.

Hyun, E., & Choi, D. H. (2004). Examination of young children's gender-doing and gender-bending in their play dynamics. *International Journal of Early Childhood, 36*(1), 49–64.

Illinois State Board of Education. (2010, June). Illinois Learning Standards, Stage G: Social Emotional Learning (SEL) goals, standards and descriptors. Retrieved from http://www.isbe.net/ils/social_emotional/stage_G/descriptor.htm.

Indiana Department of Education. (2013). Three to five years: Early childhood foundations. Retrieved February 8, 2013, from http://www.doe.in.gov/achievement/curriculum/archived-early-childhood-standards.

Isenberg, J. P., & Jalongo, M. R. (2012). *Creative expression and play in early childhood*. Upper Saddle River, NJ: Merrill/Prentice Hall.

Izard, C. E., Ackerman, B. P., Schoff, K. M., & Fines, S. E. (2000). Self-organization of discrete emotions, emotion patterns, and emotion-cognition relations. In M. Lewis & I. Granie (Eds.), *Emotion, development and self-organization: Dynamic system approaches to emotional development* (pp. 15–36). New York, NY: Cambridge University Press.

Izard, C. E., Fantauzzo, C. A., Castle, J. M., Haynes, O. M., Rayias, M. F., & Putnam, P. H. (1995). The ontogeny and significance of infants' facial expressions in the first 9 months of life. *Developmental Psychology, 31*, 997–1013.

Jackson, J. S. (2003). *Bye-bye, bully!: A kid's guide for dealing with bullies*. St. Meinrad, IN: Abbey Press.

Jalongo, M. R. (2008). *Learning to listen, listening to learn: Building essential skills in young children*. Washington, DC: National Association for the Education of Young Children.

Janssen, D., Schöllhörn, W. I., Lubienetzki, J., Folling, K., Kokenge, H., & Davids, K. (2008). Recognition of emotions in gait patterns by means of artificial neural nets. *Journal of Nonverbal Behavior, 32*, 72–92.

Jaswal, V. K., & Fernald, A. (2007). Learning to communicate. In A. Slater & M. Lewis (Eds.), *Introduction to infant development* (pp. 270–287). New York, NY: Oxford University Press.

Javernik, E. (1988). Johnny's not jumping: Can we help obese children? *Young Children*, 18–23.

Jaworski, A. (2008). The poser of silence in communication, In L. K. Guerrero & M. L. Hecht (Eds.), *The nonverbal communication reader* (3rd ed., pp. 175–181). Long Grove, IL: Waveland Press.

Jenkins, J. M., Turrell, S. L., Kogushi, Y., Lollis, S., & Ross. H. S. (2003). A longitudinal investigation of the dynamics of mental state talk in families. *Child Development, 74*(3), 905–920.

Jimerson, S. R., Swearer, S. M., & Espelage, D. L. (Eds.). (2010). *Handbook of bullying in schools: An international perspective*. New York, NY: Routledge.

Johansson, E. (2006). Children's morality: Perspectives and research. In B. Spodek & N. Saracho (Eds.), *Handbook of research on the education of young children* (pp. 55–84). Mahwah, NJ: Lawrence Erlbaum Associates.

Johnson, J. E., Christie, J. F., & Wardle, F. (2005). *Play, development, and early education*. Boston, MA: Allyn & Bacon.

Johnson, K. R. (1998). Black kinesics: Some nonverbal communication patterns in black culture. *Florida FL Reporter, 57*, 17–20.

Jones, E., & Reynolds, G. (2011). *The play's the thing: Teachers' roles in children's play*. New York, NY: Teachers College Press.

Jordan, E., Cowan, A., & Roberts, J. (1995). Knowing the rules: Discursive strategies in young children's power struggles. *Early Childhood Research Quarterly, 10*, 339–358.

Joseph, G. J., & Strain, P. S. (2003). Comprehensive evidence-based social-emotional curricula for young children: An analysis of efficacious adoption potential. *Topics in Early Childhood Special Education, 23*, 65–76.

Justice, L. M., & Vukelich, C. (2008). *Achieving excellence in preschool literacy instruction*. New York, NY: The Guilford Press.

Kaiser, B., & Rasminsky, J. S. (2011). *Challenging behavior in young children: Understanding, preventing and responding effectively*. Boston, MA: Pearson.

Kalish, C. W., & Cornelius, R. (2006). What is to be done? Children's ascriptions of conventional obligations. *Child Development, 78*, 859–878.

Kaplan, J. S. (2000). *Beyond functional assessment: A social-cognitive approach to the evaluation of behavior problems in children and youth*. Austin, TX: Pro-Ed.

Karageorge, K., & Kendall, R. (2009). The role of professional child care providers in preventing and responding to child abuse and neglect. *Child Welfare Information Gateway*. U.S. Department of Health and Human Services. Available at http://www.hhs.gov.

Karp, H. (2003). *The happiest baby on the block: The new way to calm crying and help your newborn baby sleep longer*. New York, NY: Bantam Books.

Karp, H. (2012). *The happiest baby guide to great sleep*. New York, NY: Harper Collins.

Kastenbaum, R. (2004). *Death, society, and human experience*. Boston, MA: Allyn and Bacon.

Katz, L. G. (1991). Ethical issues in working with young children. In *Ethical behavior in early childhood education: Expanded edition*. Washington, DC: NAEYC.

Katz, L. G. (1993). Distinctions between self-esteem and narcissism: Implications for practice. *Perspectives from ERIC/EECE. Monograph Series, 5*, Urbana, IL: Eric Clearinghouse on Elementary and Early Childhood Education. (ERIC Document Reproduction Service No. 363–452).

Katz, L. G., Chard, S. C., & Kogan, Y. (2013). *Engaging children's minds: The project approach* (3rd ed.). Norwood, NJ: Ablex.

Katz, L. G., & Katz, S. J. (2009). *Intellectual emergencies*. Lewisville, NC: Kaplan Press.

Keane, S. P., & Calkins, S. D. (2004). Predicting kindergarten peer social status from toddler and preschool problem behavior. *Journal of Abnormal Child Psychology, 32*, 409–423.

Kennedy-Moore, E. (2012). Children's growing friendships. *Psychology Today*, pp. 1–6. Retrieved February 5, 2012, from http://www.psychologytoday.com.

Kerns, L., & Clemens, N. H. (2007). Antecedent strategies to promote appropriate classroom behavior. *Psychology in the Schools, 44*(1), 65–75.

Key, M. R. (1975). *Paralanguage and kinesics*. Metuchen, NJ: Scarecrow Press.

Klein, A. M. (2003). Introduction: A global perspective on humor. In A. J. Klein (Ed.), *Humor in children's lives: A guidebook for practitioners* (pp. 1–13). Westport, CT: Praeger.

Klein, M. D., Cook, R. E., & Richardson-Gibbs, A. M. (2001). *Strategies for including children with special needs in early childhood settings*. Albany, NY: Delmar/Thomson Learning.

Knafo, A., & Plomin, R. (2006). Parental discipline and affection and children's prosocial behavior: Genetic and environmental links. *Journal of Personality and Social Psychology, 90*(1), 147–164.

Kochanska, G., & Aksan, N. (2006). Children's conscience and self-regulation. *Journal of Personality, 74,* 1587–1617.

Kochanska, G., Aksan, N., Prisco, T. R., & Adams, E. E. (2008). Mother-child and father-child mutually responsive orientation in the first two years and children's outcomes at preschool age: Mechanisms of influence. *Child Development, 79,* 30–44.

Kochanska, G., Gross, J. N., Lin, M., & Nichols, K. E. (2002). Guilt in young children: Development, determinants and relations with a broader system of standards. *Child Development, 73,* 461–482.

Kochanska, G., Padavic, D. L., & Koenig, A. L. (1996). Children's narratives about hypothetical moral dilemmas and objective measures of their conscience: Mutual relations and social antecedents. *Child Development, 67,* 1420–1436.

Kohn, A. (2006). *Beyond discipline: From compliance to community*. Alexandria, VA: Association for Supervision and Curriculum Development.

Kontos, S., & Wilcox-Herzog, A. (1997). Teacher's interactions with children: Why are they so important? *Young Children, 52*(2), 4–12.

Kostelnik, M. J. (2005, November/December). Modeling ethical behavior in the classroom. *Child Care Information Exchange*, 17–21.

Kostelnik, M. J., & Grady, M. L. (2009). *Getting it right from the start*. Thousand Oaks, CA: Corwin.

Kostelnik, M. J., Onaga, E., Rohde, B., & Whiren, A. K. (2002). Brian: Just bursting to communicate. In *Children with special needs: Lessons for early childhood professionals* (pp. 120–135). New York, NY: Teachers College Press.

Kostelnik, M. J., Rupiper, M., Soderman, A. K., & Whiren, A. P. (2014). *Developmentally appropriate curriculum in action*. Upper Saddle River, NJ: Pearson.

Kostelnik, M. J., Soderman, A. K., & Whiren, A. P. (2011). *Developmentally Appropriate Curriculum: Best practices in early childhood education* (5th ed.). Upper Saddle River, NJ: Prentice Hall.

Kovach, B., & Da Ros-Voseles, D. (2008). *Being with babies: Understanding and responding to the infants in your care*. Beltsville, MD: Gryphon House.

Kozol, J. (2006). *Rachel and her children—Homeless families in America*. New York, NY: Three Rivers Press.

Krannich, C., & Krannich, R. (2001). *Savvy interviewing: The nonverbal advantage*. Manassas Park, VA: Impact Publications.

Kraut, R. E., & Johnston, R. E. (2008). Social and emotional messages of smiling. In L. K. Guerrero & M. L. Hecht (Eds.), *The nonverbal communication reader* (3rd ed., pp. 139–143). Long Grove, IL: Waveland Press.

Kuhn, D. (2005). *Education for thinking*. Cambridge, MA: Harvard University Press.

Labile, D., & Thompson, R. A. (2008). Early socialization: A relationship perspective. In J. E. Grusec & P. D. Hastings (Eds.), *Handbook of socialization: Theory and research* (pp. 181–207). New York, NY: The Guilford Press.

LaBounty, J., Wellman, H. M., Olson, S., Lagattuta, K., & Liu, D. (2008). Mother's and father's use of internal state talk with their young children. *Social Development 17*(4), 754–774.

Ladd, G. W. (2000). The fourth R: Relationships as risks and resources following children's transition to school. *American Educational Research Division Newsletter, 19*(1), 7, 9–11.

Ladd, G. W. (2005). *Children's peer relations and social competence: A century of progress*. New Haven, CT: Yale University Press.

Ladd, G. W. (2008). Social competence and peer relations: Significance for young children and their service providers. *Early Childhood Services, 2*(3), 129–148.

Ladd, G. W., & Troop-Gordon, W. (2003). The role of chronic peer difficulties in the development of children's psychological adjustment problems. *Child Development, 74*(2), 1344–1367.

Lafrance, M., & Hecht, M. A. (1999). Option or obligation to smile: The effects of power and gender on facial expression. In P. Philippot, R. Feldman, & E. Coats (Eds.), *Social context of nonverbal behavior*. Cambridge, U.K: Cambridge University Press.

Laible, D. J., & Thompson, R. A. (2008). Early socialization: A relationship perspective. In J. E. Grusec & P. D. Hastings References (Eds.), *Handbook of socialization: Theory and research* (pp. 181–206). New York, NY: The Guilford Press.

Lamm, S., Grouix, J. G., Hansen, C. Patton, M. M., & Slaton, A. J. (2006). Creating environments for peaceful problem solving. *Young Children, 61*(1), 22–28.

Langford, S. (2013). Interpersonal skills and nonverbal communication. In D. Matsumoto, M. G. Frank, & H. S. Hwang (Eds.), *Nonverbal communication: Science and applications* (pp. 213–224). Los Angeles, CA: Sage.

Lansford, J. E., Chang, L., Dodge, K. A., Malone, P. S., Oburu, P., Palmerus, K., ... Quinn, D. (2005).

Physical discipline and children's adjustment: Cultural normativeness as a moderator. *Child Development, 76*, 1234–1246.

Larsen, J. T., To, Y. M., & Fireman, G. (2007). Children's understanding and experience of mixed emotions. *Psychology Science, 18*(2), 186–191.

Laursen, B., & Pursell, G. (2009). Conflict in peer relationships. In K. H. Rubin, W. M. Bukowski, & B. Laursen (Eds.), *Handbook of peer interactions, relationships and groups* (pp. 267–286). New York, NY: The Guilford Press.

Laushey, K. M., & Heflin, L. J. (2000). Enhancing social skills of kindergarten children with autism through training of multiple peers as tutors. *Journal of Autism and Developmental Disorders, 30*(3), 183–193.

Leary, M. R., & McDonald, G. (2003). Individual differences in self-esteem: A review and theoretical integration. In M. Leary & J. P. Tangney (Eds.), *Handbook of self and identity* (pp. 401–418). New York, NY: The Guilford Press.

Lengua, L. J. (2009, January). Effortful control in the context of socioeconomic and psychosocial risk. *American Psychological Association*, Science Briefs 1-3. Retrieved from http://www.apa.org/science/about/psa/2009/01/lengua.aspx.

Lepper, M. R., & Henderlong, J. (2000). Turning "play" into "work" and "work" into "play": 25 years of research on intrinsic versus extrinsic motivation. In C. Sanson & J. M. Harackiewicz (Eds.), *Intrinsic and extrinsic motivation: The search for optimal motivation and performance* (pp. 257–307). New York, NY: Academic Press.

Lessin, R. (2002). *Spanking, a loving discipline: Helpful and practical answers for today's parents*. Grand Rapids, MI: Bethany House Publishers.

Levin, D. (2003). *Teaching young children in violent times* (2nd ed.). Washington, DC: National Association for the Education of Young Children.

Levin, D. E., & Kilbourne, J. (2009). *So sexy so soon: The new sexualized childhood and what parents can do to protect their kids*. New York, NY: Ballantine.

Lewis, D., & Carpendale, J. (2004). Social cognition. In P. K. Smith & C. H. Hart (Eds.), *Childhood social development* (pp. 375–393). Malden, MA: Blackwell.

Lewis, M. (2007). Early emotional development. In A. Slater & M. Lewis (Eds.), *Introduction to infant development* (pp. 233–252). New York, NY: Oxford University Press.

Linares, L. O. (2004). *Community violence: The effects on children*. New York, NY: NYU Child Study Center.

Lock, A., & Zukow-Goldring, P. (2012). Preverbal communication. In J. G. Bremner & T. D. Wachs (Eds.) *The Wiley-Blackwell handbook of infant development* (pp. 394–425). Malden, MA: Blackwell Publishing.

Lopes, P. N., & Salovey, P. (2004). Toward a broader education: Social, emotional and practical skills. In J. E. Zins, R. P., Weissberg, M. C. Wang, & H. J. Walberg (Eds.), *Building academic success on social and emotional learning* (pp. 76–93). New York, NY: Teachers College Press.

Luckenbill, J. (2011). Circle time puppets teaching social skills. *Teaching Young Children, 4*(4), 9–11.

Luckenbill, J., & Nuccitelli, S. (2013). Puppets and problem solving: Circle time techniques (pp. 1–39). Retrieved February 14, 2013, from http://caeyc.org/main/caeyc/proposals/pdfs/Luckenbillpuppet.pdf.

Luke, C. (1999). What next? Toddler netizens, playstation thumb, techno-literacies? *Contemporary Issues in Early Childhood, 1*(1), 95–100.

Luthar, S. S. (2003). *Resilience and vulnerability: Adaptation in the context of childhood adversities*. New York, NY: Cambridge University Press.

Luthar, S. S. (2008, June). Conceptualizing and reevaluating resilience across levels of risk, time, and domains of competence. *Clinical Child Family Psychological Review, 11*(1–2), 30–58.

Lynch, E. W., & Hanson, M. J. (2011). *Developing cross-cultural competence: A guide for working with children and their families*. Baltimore, MD: Paul H. Brookes Publishing.

Maccoby, E. E. (2007). Historical overview of research and theory. In J. E. Grusec & P. D. Hastings (Eds.), *Handbook of socialization theory and practice* (pp. 13–41). New York, NY: The Guilford Press.

Maccoby, E., & Martin, J. A. (1983). Socialization in the context of the family: Parent–child interaction. In P. H. Mussen (Ed.), *Handbook of child psychology* (4th ed, Vol. 4). New York, NY: Wiley.

MacGeorge, E. L. (2003). Gender differences in attributions and emotions in helping contexts. *Sex Roles, 48*(3), 175.

Machotka, P., & Spiegel, J. (1982). *The articulate body*. New York, NY: Irvington Publishers.

Mackenzie, R. J., & Stanzione, L. (2010). *Setting limits in the classroom: A complete guide to classroom management* (3rd ed.). Rocklin, CA: Three Rivers Press.

Malott, R., & Trojan, E. A. (2008). *Principles of behavior* (6th ed.). Upper Saddle River, NJ: Pearson.

Malti, T., Keller, M., Gummerum, M., & Buchmann, M. (2009). Children's moral motivation, sympathy, and prosocial behavior. *Child Development, 80*(2), 442–460.

Mandleco, B. L., & Peery, J. C. (2000). An organizational framework for conceptualizing resilience in children. *Journal of Child and Adolescent Psychiatric Nursing, 13*(1), 99–111.

Mapp, S., & Steinberg, C. (2007, January/February). Birth families as permanency resources for children in long-term foster care. *Child Welfare, 86*(1), 29.

March of Dimes. (2003). Understanding the behavior of term infants, retrieved March 15, 2010, from http:// www.marchofdimes.com/nursing /modnemedia/othermedia/background.pdf.

March of Dimes Birth Defects Foundation. (2007). Down syndrome. *Quick reference & fact sheets for professionals and researchers, 681*, 1–4.

Marion, M. (2011). *Guidance of young children.* New York, NY: Macmillan.

Marks, D. R. (2002). *Raising stable kids in an unstable world: A physician's guide to dealing with childhood stress.* Deerfield, FL: Health Communications.

Marsh, H. W., Ellis, L. A., & Craven, R. G. (2002). How do preschool children feel about themselves? Unraveling measurement and multidimensional self-concept structure. *Developmental Psychology, 38*(3), 376–393.

Martin, S., & Berke, J. (2007). *See how they grow: Infants and toddlers.* Clifton Park, NY: Thomson Delmar Learning.

Marzano, R. J. (2003). *Classroom management that works: Research-based strategies for every teacher.* Alexandria, VA: Association for Supervision and Curriculum Development.

Masten, A. S. (2009). Ordinary magic: Lessons from research on resilience in human development. *Education Canada, 49*(3), 28–32.

Masten, A. S., & Marayan, A. J. (2013). Resilience processes in development: Four waves of research on positive adaptation in the context of adversity. In S. Goldstein & R. B. Brooks (Eds.), *Handbook of resilience in children.* New York, NY: Springer.

Masten, A. S., & Powell, J. L. (2003). A resilience framework. In S. S. Luthar, *Resilience and vulnerability: Adaptation in the context of childhood adversities* (pp. 1–25). New York, NY: Cambridge University Press.

Matsumoto, D. (2006). Culture and nonverbal behavior. In V. Manusov & M. Patterson (Eds.), *The Sage handbook of nonverbal communication* (pp. 219–336). Thousand Oaks, CA: Sage Publications.

Matsumoto, D., & Hwang, H. S. (2013a). Body and gestures. In D. Matsumoto, M. G. Frank, & H. S. Hwang (Eds.), *Nonverbal communication: Science and applications* (pp. 75–96). Los Angeles, CA: Sage.

Matsumoto, D., & Hwang, H. S. (2013b). Facial expression. In D. Matsumoto, M. G. Frank, & H. S. Hwang (Eds.), *Nonverbal communication: Science and applications* (pp. 15–52). Los Angeles, CA: Sage.

Maxwell, L. E. (2003). Home and school density effects on elementary school children: The role of spatial density. *Environment and Behavior, 35*, 566–578.

Maxwell, L. E. (2007). Competency in child care settings: The role of the physical environment. *Environment and Behavior, 39*, 229–245.

McAfee, O., & Leong, D. (2010). *Assessing and guiding young children's development and learning* (3rd ed.). Boston, MA: Allyn and Bacon.

McAuliffe, M. D., Hubbard, J. A., & Romano, L. J. (2009). The role of teacher cognition and behavior in children's peer relations. *Journal of Abnormal Child Psychology, 37*, 665–677.

McCay, L. O., & Keyes, D. W. (2002). Developing social competence in the inclusive primary classroom. *Childhood Education, 78*(2), 70–78.

McClellan, D., & Katz. L. (2001). *Assessing young children's social competence.* Champaign, IL: ERIC Clearinghouse on Elementary and Early Childhood Education. (ERIC Document Reproduction Service No. ED450953).

McClure, E. B., & Nowicki, S. (2001). Associations between social anxiety and nonverbal processing skill in preadolescent boys and girls. *Journal of Nonverbal Behavior, 25*(1) 3–19.

McCord, J. M. (2005). Unintended consequences of punishment. In M. Donnelly & M. A. Straus (Eds.), *Corporal punishment of children in theoretical perspective* (pp. 156–170). New Haven, CT: Yale University Press.

McCornak, S. (2012). *Reflect & Relate: An introduction to interpersonal communication.* Boston, MA: Bedford/St.Martin's.

McGhee, P. (1979). *Humor: Its origin and development.* San Francisco, CA: W. H. Freeman.

Meece, D. M. (2009). Good guidance: Show your interest in children through reflections. *Next: The Teaching Young Children Staff Development Guide, 2*(3), 3–5.

Meece, D. M., Colwell, M. J., & Mize, J. (2007). Maternal emotion framing and children's social behavior: The role of children's feelings and beliefs about peers. *Early Child Development and Care, 117*, 295–299.

Meece, D. M., & Soderman, A. K. (2010). Positive verbal environments: Setting the stage for young children's social development. *Young Children, 65*(5), 81–86.

Michigan State Board of Education. (2006). *Early childhood standards of quality for infant and toddler programs.* Lansing, MI: Michigan State Board of Education. Available at http://www.michigan.gov/ documents/mde/ECSQ-IT_Final_New _format_09_417914_7.pdf.

Miles, S. B., & Stipek, D. (Jan–Feb, 2006). Contemporaneous and longitudinal associations between social behavior and literacy achievement in a sample of low-income elementary school children. *Child Development, 77*(1), 103–117.

Milevsky, A., Schlechter, M., Netter, S., & Keehn, D. (2007). Maternal and paternal parenting styles in adolescence: Associations with self-esteem, depression, and life satisfaction. *Journal of Child and Family Studies, 16,* 39–47.

Miller, D. F. (2013). *Positive child guidance* (6th ed.). Belmont, CA: Wadsworth/Cengage.

Miller, P., & Garvey, C. (1984). Mother–baby role play: Its origins in social support. In I. Bretherton (Ed.), *Symbolic play: The development of social understanding* (pp. 101–130). New York, NY: Academic Press.

Mills, R. S. L. (2005). Taking stock of the developmental literature on shame. *Developmental Review, 25,* 26–63.

Minnesota Department of Education. (2005). Early childhood indicators of progress: Minnesota's Early Learning Standards. Retrieved from http://sped.dpi.wi.gov/sped_assmt-ccee.

Moffitt, T. E., & Caspi, A. (2008). Evidence from behavioral genetics for environmental contributions to antisocial conduct. In J. E. Grusec & P. D. Hastings (Eds.), *Handbook of socialization theory and research* (pp. 96–123). New York, NY: The Guilford Press.

Montes, G., Lotyczewski, B. S., Halterman, S., & Hightower, A. D. (March 2012). School readiness among children with behavior problems at entrance into kindergarten: Results from a US national study. *European Journal of Pediatrics, 171*(3), 541–548.

Moore, S. G. (1982). Prosocial behavior in the early years: Parent and peer influences. In B. Spodek (Ed.), *Handbook of research in early childhood education* (pp. 65–81). New York, NY: Free Press.

Morrison, G. (2012). *Early childhood education today* (11th ed.). Upper Saddle River, NJ: Prentice Hall.

Nabobo-Baba, U., & Tiko, L. (2009). Indigenous Fijian cultural conceptions of mentoring and related capacity building implications for teacher education. In A. Gibbons & C. Gibbons (Eds.), *Conversations on early childhood teacher education: Voices from the working forum for teacher education.* Auckland, New Zealand: New Zealand Tertiary College.

Nabuzoka, D., & Smith, P. (1995). Identification of expressions of emotions by children with and without learning disabilities. *Learning Disabilities Research & Practice, 10*(2) 91–101.

National Association for the Education of Young Children, (2009). *Where we stand on standards for programs to prepare early childhood professionals.* Washington, DC: Author. Retrieved October, 2009, from http://www.naeyc.org/positionstatements/ppp

National Dissemination Center for Children with Disabilities. (2004). *Deafness and hearing loss, fact sheet 3 (FS #3),* January, 1–5.

National Institute of Neurological Disorders and Stroke. (2005). *Tourette syndrome fact sheet*, NIH Publication No. 05–2163, April 1–6.

National Research Council and the Institute of Medicine. (2000). In J. P. Shonkoff & D. A. Philips (Eds.), *From neurons to neighborhoods: The science of early childhood development.* Washington DC: National Academy Press.

National Scientific Council on the Developing Child. (2006). Children's emotional development is built into the architecture of their brains. Working Paper No. 2. Waltham, MA: Brandeis University Press.

National Scientific Council on the Developing Child. (2007). The timing and quality of early experiences combine to shape brain architecture. Working Paper No .5. Available from http://www.developingchild.net.

National Scientific Council on the Developing Child. (2009). Young children develop in an environment of relationships. Working Paper No. 1. Retrieved from http://www.developingchild.net.

Nebraska Department of Education. (2005). Nebraska early learning guidelines. Retrieved from http://www.education.ne.gov/oec/pubs/ELG/B_3_English.pdf.

Neff, K. D., & Helwig, C. C. (2002). A constructivist approach to understanding the development of reasoning about rights and authority within cultural contexts. *Cognitive Development, 17,* 1429–1450.

Nelsen, J. (2006). *Positive time-out.* New York, NY: Crown Publishing Co.

Nelson, D. A., Hart, C. H., Yang, C., Olsen, J. A., & Jin, S. (2006). Aversive parenting in China: Associations with child physical and relational aggression. *Child Development, 77,* 554–572.

Nelson, D. A., Mitchell, C., & Yang, C. (2008). Intent attributions and aggression: A study of children and their parents. *Journal of Abnormal Child Psychology, 36,* 793–806.

Nelson, D. A., Robinson, C. C., & Hart, C. H. (2005). Relational and physical aggression of preschool-age children: Peer status linkages across informants. *Early Education and Development, 16,* 115–139.

Nemeth, K. N. (2012). *Basics of supporting dual language learners.* Washington, DC: NAEYC.

New Hampshire Department of Education. (2006). K-12 written and oral communication: New Hampshire curriculum framework. Retrieved February 9, 2013, from http://www.education .nh.gov/career/guidance/documents/framework_ k12.doc.

NICHCY. (March 2012). *Categories of disability under IDEA*. Available at http://nichcy.org/disability/ categories.

NICHD Early Child Care Research Network. (2002). Child-care structure—process—outcome: Direct and indirect effects of child-care quality on young children's development. *Psychological Science, 13*, 199–206.

NICHD Early Child Care Research Network. (2008). Social competence with peers in third grade: Associations with earlier peer experiences in childcare. *Social Development, 17*(3), 419–453.

Nielsen, M., Suddendorf, T., & Slaughter, V. (2006). Mirror self-recognition beyond the face. *Child Development, 77*(1), 176–185.

Obradovic, J., Portilla, X. A., & Boyce, W. T. (2012). Executive functioning and developmental neuroscience. Current progress and implications for early childhood education. In R. C. Pianta, W. S. Barnett, I. M. Justice, & S. M. Sheridan (Eds.), *Handbook of early childhood education* (pp. 324–351). New York, NY: The Guilford Press.

Odom, S. L., McConnell, S. R., & Brown, W. H. (2008). Social competence of young children: Conceptualization, assessment and influences. In W. H. Brown, S. L. Odom, & S. R. McConnell (Eds.), *Social competence of young children: Risk, disability & intervention* (pp. 3–30). Baltimore, MD: Paul H. Brookes Publishing.

O'Hair, D., & Friedrich, G. (2001). *Strategic communication*. Boston, MA: Houghton-Mifflin.

O'Hair, M. J., & Ropo, E. (1994, Summer). Unspoken messages: Understanding diversity in education requires emphasis on nonverbal communication. *Teacher Education Quarterly, 21*(3), 91–112.

Oliver, S., & Klugman E. (2005). Play and the outdoors: What's new under the sun? *Exchange, 164*, 6–12.

Olsen, S. L, & Sameroff, A. J. (2009). *Biopsychosocial regulatory processes in the development of childhood behavioral problems*. New York, NY: Cambridge University Press.

Olweus, D. (1993). *Bullying and school: What we know and what we can do*. Oxford: Blackwell Scientific Publications.

Olweus, D. (2010). Understanding and researching bullying: Some critical issues. In S. R. Jimerson, S. W. Swearer, & D. L. Espelage (Eds.), *Handbook of bullying in schools: An international perspective* (pp. 9–31). New York, NY: Routledge.

Olweus, D., & Limber, S. P. (2010). The Olweus bullying prevention program: Implementation and evaluation over two decades. In S. R. Jimerson, S. W. Swearer, & D. L. Espelage (Eds.), *Handbook of bullying in schools: An international perspective* (pp. 377–401). New York, NY: Routledge.

O'Neil, R. E., Horner, R. H., Albin, R. W., Sprague, J. R., Storey, K., & Newton, J. S. (1997). *Functional assessment and program development for problem behavior: A practical handbook* (2nd ed.). Pacific Grove, CA: Brooks/Cole.

Ormrod, J. E. (2011). *Educational psychology: Developing learners*. Boston, MA: Pearson.

Orpinas, P., & Horne, A. M. (2010). Creating a positive school climate and developing social competence. In S. R. Jimerson, S. W. Swearer, & D. L. Espelage (Eds.), *Handbook of bullying in schools: An international perspective* (pp. 49–59). New York, NY: Routledge.

Oshikanlu, S. (2006). Teaching healthy habits to young children, *Exchange, 169*, 28–30.

Ostrov., J. M., Pilat, M. M., & Crick, N. R. (2006). Assertion strategies and aggression during childhood: A short-term longitudinal study. *Early Childhood Research Quarterly, 21*(4), 403–416.

Otto, B. (2009). *Language development in early childhood*. Upper Saddle River, NJ: Pearson.

Oyserman, D., Bybee, D., Mobray, C., & Hart-Johnson, T. (2005). When mothers have serious mental health problems: Parenting as a proximal mediator. *Journal of Adolescence, 28*, 443–463.

Paasche, C. L., Gorrill, L., & Strom, B. (2003). *Children with special needs in early childhood settings*. Belmont, CA: Wadsworth.

Paganini, D. A., Tremblay, R. E., Nagin, D., Zoccolillo, M., Vitaro, F., & McDuff, P. (2004). Risk factor models for adolescent verbal and physical aggression toward mothers. *International Journal of Behavioral Development, 28*, 528–537.

Paley, V. G. (1992). *You can't say, . . . you can't play*. Cambridge, MA: Harvard University Press.

Panksepp, J. (2008). Play, ADHD, and the construction of the social brain: Should the first class each day be recess? *American Journal of Play, 1*(1) 55–79.

Papilia, D., Olds, S., & Feldman, R. (2008). *Human development* (11th ed.). New York, NY: McGraw-Hill.

Parten, M. B. (1932). Social participation among preschool children. *Journal of Abnormal and Social Psychology, 27*, 243–269.

Pellegrini, A. D. (2004). Rough-and tumble play from childhood through adolescence: Development and possible functions. In P. K. Smith &

C. Hart (Eds.), *Blackwell handbook of childhood social development* (pp. 438–454). Malden, MA: Blackwell.

Pellegrini, A. D. (2007). The development and function of rough and tumble play in childhood and adolescence: A sexual selection theory perspective. In A. Göncü and S. Gaskins (Eds.), *Play and development*. Mahwah, NJ: Lawrence Erlbaum Associates.

Pellegrini, A. D. (2009). *The role of play in human development*. New York, NY: Oxford University Press.

Pellicano, E. (2012). The development of executive function in autism. *Autism Research and Treatment*, Vol. 2012. Retrieved from http://www.hindawi.com/journals/aurt/2012/146132.

Penner, L. A., & Orom, H. (2010). Enduring goodness: A person-by-situation perspective on prosocial behavior. In M. Mikulincer & P. R. Shaver (Eds.), *Prosocial motives, emotions and behaviors: The better angels of our nature* (pp. 55–72). Washington, DC: American Psychological Association.

Pennington, B. F., & Ozonoff, S. (January 7, 1996). Executive functions and developmental psychopathology. *Journal of Child Psychological Psychiatry*, *37*, 51–87.

Pennsylvania Department of Education and Department of Public Welfare. (2009). *Infants-toddlers: Pennsylvania learning standards for early childhood*. Available at http://static.pdesas.org/content/documents/pennsylvania_early_childhood_education_standards_for_infant-toddler.pdf.

Pepler, D., Smith, P. K., & Rigby, K. (2004). Looking back and looking forward: Implications for making interventions work effectively. In P. K. Smith, D. Pepler, & K. Rigby (Eds.), *Bullying in schools: How successful can interventions be?* (pp. 307–324) Cambridge, England: Cambridge University Press.

Persson, G. E. B. (2005). Young children's prosocial and aggressive behaviors and their experiences of being targeted for similar behaviors by peers. *Social Development*, *14*, 206–228.

Petersen, S. (2012). School readiness for infants and toddlers? Really? Yes, really! *Young Children*, *67*(4), 10–13.

Pettit, G., & Harrist, A. (1993). Children's aggressive and socially unskilled behavior with peers: Origins in early family relations. In C. Hart (Ed.), *Children on playgrounds: Research perspectives and applications* (pp. 14–42). Albany, NY: State University of New York.

Piaget, J. (1962). *The origins of intelligence in children*. New York, NY: W. W. Norton.

Piaget, J. (1976). The rules of the game of marbles. In J. Bruner, A. Jolly, & K. Sylva (Eds.), *Play: Its role in development and evolution* (pp. 411–441). New York, NY: Academic Press.

Pinker, S. (2008, January 13). The moral instinct. *The New York Times Magazine*, 32–59.

Polakow, V. (1994). *Lives on the edge: Single mothers and their children in the other America*. Chicago, IL: University of Chicago Press.

Pollack, W. S. (2006). Sustaining and reframing vulnerability and connection. In S. Goldstein & R. B. Brooks, *Handbook of resilience in children* (pp. 65–77). New York, NY: Springer.

Pons, F., Lawson, J., Harris, P. I., & de Rosnay, M. (2003). Individual differences in children's emotion understanding: Effects of age and language. *Scandinavian Journal of Psychology: Applied*, *7*, 27–50.

Power, T. (2000). *Play and exploration in children and animals*. Mahwah, NJ: Lawrence Erlbaum Associates.

Pratt, M. W., Skoe, E. E., & Arnold, M. I. (2004). Care reasoning development and family socialization patterns in later adolescence. A longitudinal analysis. *International Journal of Behavioral Development*, *28*, 139–147.

Prescott, E. (2008, March/April). The physical environment: A powerful regulator of experience. *Exchange*, *2*, 34–37.

Puckett, M., & Black, J. (2013). *The young child: Development prebirth through age eight* (6th ed.). Upper Saddle River, NJ: Pearson.

Raikes, H. H., & Edwards C. P. (2009). *Extending the dance in infant and toddler caregiving*. Washington, DC: Paul H. Brookes Publishing.

Ramaswamy, V., & Bergin, C. (2009). Do reinforcement and induction increase prosocial behavior? Results of a teacher-based intervention in preschools. *Journal of Research in Childhood Education*, *23*(4), 527–538.

Ramsey, P. (1998). Diversity and play: Influences of race, culture, class and gender. In D. Fromberg & D. Bergen (Eds.), *Play from birth to twelve and beyond: Contexts, perspectives and meanings* (pp. 23–33). New York, NY: Garland Publishing.

Raver, C. C., Garner, P. W., & Smith-Donald, R. (2007). The roles of emotion regulation and emotion knowledge for children's academic readiness. In R. C. Pianta, M. J. Cox, & K. L. Snow (Eds.), *School readiness and the transition to kindergarten in the area of accountability* (pp. 121–147). Baltimore, MD: Paul H. Brookes Publishing.

Ray, G. B., & Floyd, K. (2006). Nonverbal expressions of liking and disliking in initial interactions: Encoding and decoding perspectives. *Southern Communication Journal*, *71*, 45–65.

Reifel S., & Yeatman, J. (1993). From category to context: Reconsidering classroom play. *Early Childhood Research Quarterly, 8*, 347–367.

Remland, M. S. (2009). *Nonverbal communication in everyday life*. Boston, MA: Pearson.

Reynolds, E. (2008). *Guiding young children: A problem-solving approach* (4th ed.). Mountain View, CA: Mayfield.

Rhee, S. H., & Waldman, I. D. (2002). Genetic and environmental influences on antisocial behavior: A meta-analysis of twin and adoption studies. *Psychological Bulletin, 128*, 490–529.

Richmond, V., McCroskey, J., & Hickson M. L. (2011). *Nonverbal behavior in interpersonal relations* (7th ed.). New York, NY: Prentice-Hall.

Rigby, K., & Bauman, S. (2010). How school personnel tackle cases of bullying: A critical examination. In S. R. Jimerson, S. W. Swearer, & D. L. Espelage (Eds.), *Handbook of bullying in schools: An international perspective* (pp. 455–467). New York, NY: Routledge.

Riggio, R. (2006). Nonverbal skills and abilities, In V. Manusov & M. Patterson (Eds.), *The Sage handbook of nonverbal communication* (pp. 79–96). Thousand Oaks, CA: Sage Publications.

Riley, D., San Juan, R. R., Klinkner, J., & Ramminger, A. (2008). *Social & emotional development: Connecting science and practice in early childhood settings*. St. Paul, MN: Redleaf Press.

Rimm-Kauffman, S. E., & Wanless, S. B. (2011). An ecological perspective for understanding the early development of self-regulatory skills, social skills and achievement. In R. C. Pianta, W. S. Barnett, L. M. Justice, & S. M. Sheridan (Eds.), *Handbook of early childhood education* (pp. 299–323). New York, NY: The Guilford Press.

Rochat, P. (2012). Emerging self-concept. In J. G. Bremner & T. D. Wachs (Eds). *The Wiley-Blackwell handbook of infant development* (pp. 321–344). Malden, MA: Blackwell Publishing.

Roffey, S., Tarrant, T., & Majors, K. (1994). *Young friends: Schools and friendships*. New York, NY: Cassell Publishing.

Rogoff, B., Moore, L., Najafi, B., Dexter, A., Correa-Chavez, M., & Solis, J. (2008). Children's development of cultural repertoires through participation in everyday routines and practices. In J. Grusec & P. Hastings (Eds.), *Handbook of socialization: Theory and research* (pp. 490–515). New York, NY: The Guilford Press.

Rose, A. J., & Smith, R. L. (2009). Sex differences in peer relationships. In K. H. Rubin, W. M. Bukowski, & B. Laursen (Eds.), *Handbook of peer interactions, relationships, and groups* (pp. 379–393). New York, NY: The Guilford Press.

Rose-Krasnor, L., & Denham, S. (2009). Social-emotional competence in early childhood. In K. H. Rubin, W. M. Bukowski, & B. Laursen (Eds.), *Handbook of peer interactions, relationships and groups* (pp. 162–179). New York, NY: The Guilford Press.

Rosenberg, H. (2001). Imagination styles of four and five year olds. In S. Golbeck (Ed.), *Psychological perspectives on early childhood education* (pp. 280–296). Mahwah, NJ: Lawrence Erlbaum Associates.

Roskos, K. (1990). Ataxonomic view of pretend play activity among 4- and 5-year-old children. *Early Childhood Research Quarterly, 5*(4), 495–512.

Ross, H., Vickar, M., & Perlman, M. (2012). Early social cognitive skills at play in toddler's peer interactions. In J. G. Bremner & T. D. Wachs, (Eds) *The Wiley-Blackwell handbook of infant development* (pp. 511–531). Malden, MA: Blackwell Publishing.

Rothbart, M. K., & Bates, J. E. (2006). Temperament. In Eisenberg (Ed.), *Handbook of child psychology, Volume 3* (99–166). Hoboken, NJ: John Wiley & Sons.

Rothbart, M. K., Ellis, L. K., & Posner, M. I. (2011). Temperament and self-regulation. In K. V. Vohs & R. F. Baumeister, *Handbook of self-regulation: Research, theory, and applications* (pp. 441–460). New York, NY: The Guilford Press.

Rothbaum, F., & Trommsdorff, G. (2008). Do roots and wings complement or oppose one another? In J. Grusec & P. Hastings (Eds.), *Handbook of socialization: Theory and research* (461–489). New York, NY: The Guilford Press.

Rubin, K. H. (2003). *The friendship factor: Helping our children navigate their social world and why it matters for their success and happiness*. New York, NY: Penguin Group.

Rubin, K. H., Bukowski, W. M., & Laursen, B. (Eds.). (2009). *Handbook of peer interactions, relationships, and groups*. New York, NY: The Guilford Press.

Rubin, K. H., Bukowski, W. M., & Parker, J. G. (2006). Peer interactions, relationships and groups. In N. Eisenberg, W. Damon, & R. M. Lerner (Eds.), *Handbook of child psychology, vol. 3: Social, emotional and personality development* (6th ed., pp. 571–645). Hoboken, NJ: John Wiley and Sons.

Rubin, K. H., Coplan, R., Chen, X., Bowker, J. C., McDonald, K., & Menzer, M. (2011). Peer relationships in childhood. In M. H. Bornstein & M. E. Lamb (Eds.), *Social and emotional development: An advanced textbook*. New York, NY: Psychology Press.

Russell, A., Hart, C. H., Robinson, C. C., & Olsen, F. F. (2003). Children's sociable and aggressive behaviour with peers: A comparison of the

United States and Australia, and contributions of temperament and parenting style. *International Journal of Behavioral Development*, 27, 74–86.

Russell, A., Mize, J., & Bissaker, K. (2004). Parent-child relationships. In P. K. Smith & C. H. Hart (Eds.), *Blackwell handbook of childhood social development* (pp. 204–222). Malden, MA: Blackwell.

Ryan, K., & Cooper, J. M. (2013). *Those who can, teach.* Belmont, CA: Wadsworth Publishing

Saarni, C., Campos, J. J., Camras, L. A., & Witherington, D. (2006). Emotional development: Action, communication and understanding. In N. Eisenberg, W. Damon, & R. M. Lerner (Eds.), *Handbook of child psychology* (pp. 226–299). New York, NY: Wiley.

Saarni, C., & Weber, H. (1999). Emotional displays and dissemblance in childhood: Implications for self-presentation. In P. Philippot, R. Feldman, & E. Coats (Eds.), *Social context of nonverbal behavior.* Cambridge, England: Cambridge University Press.

Sandall, S. R. (2004). Play modifications for children with disabilities. In Koralek, D., (Ed.), *Young children and play* (pp. 44–45). Washington, DC: National Association for the Education of Young Children.

Sansing, C. (2012, December). Fulfilling the needs of students and teachers in the classroom. Retrieved from http://smartblogs.com /education/2012/12/31/needs-fulfilling-chad-sansing/.

Sansone, A. (2004). *Mothers, babies and their body language.* London, England: Karnac.

Santrock, J. W. (2006). *Child development* (10th ed.). Dubuque, IA: Brown and Benchmark.

Santrock, J. W. (2012). *Children* (11th ed.). Boston, MA: McGraw-Hill.

Scarlett, W. G., Naudeau, S., Salonius-Pasternak, D., & Ponte, I. (2005). *Children's play.* Thousand Oaks, CA: Sage.

Schmalz, D. L., & Kerstetter, D. L. (2006). Girlie girls and manly men: Children's stigma consciousness of gender in sports and physical activities. *Journal of Leisure Research, 38*(4), 536–557.

Schwartz, S. H. (2010). Basic values: How they motivate and inhibit prosocial behavior. In M. Mikulincer & P. R. Shaver (Eds.), *Prosocial motives, emotions and behaviors: The better angels of our nature* (pp. 221–241). Washington, DC: American Psychological Association.

Science Daily. (2009). "Free play" for children, teens is vital to social development, reports psychologist. *Science Daily*, April 15, 2009, available at www .sciencedaily.com.

Sebanc, A. M. (2003). The friendship features of preschool children: Links with prosocial behavior and aggression. *Social Development, 12*(2), 249–265.

Segrin, C. (2008). The influence of nonverbal behaviors in compliance-gaining processes. In L. K. Guerrero & M. L. Hecht (Eds.), *The nonverbal communication reader* (3rd ed., pp. 468–477). Long Grove, IL: Waveland Press.

Seligman, M. E. P. (2007). *The optimistic child*. Boston, MA: Houghton Mifflin.

Selman, R. L., Levitt, M. Z., & Schultz, L. H. (1997). The friendship framework: Tools for the assessment of psychosocial development. In R. Selman, C. L. Watts, & L. H. Schultz (Eds.), *Fostering friendship* (pp. 31–52). New York, NY: Aldine De Gruyter.

Semic, B. (2008). Vocal attractiveness: What sounds beautiful is good. In L. K. Guerrero & M. L. Hecht (Eds.), *The nonverbal communication reader* (3rd ed., pp. 153–168). Long Grove, IL: Waveland Press.

Shaffer, D. R. (2008). (6th ed.). *Social and personality development*. Belmont, CA: Wadsworth.

Shaffer, D. R., & Kipp, K. (2013). *Developmental psychology: Childhood and adolescence* (7th ed.). Pacific Grove, CA: Brooks/Cole.

Shapiro, L. (1997). *How to raise a child with a high EQ*. New York, NY: HarperCollins.

Shaw, D. S., Gilliom, M., Ingoldsby, E. M., & Nagin, D. S. (2003). Trajectories leading to school-age conduct problems. *Developmental Psychology, 39*, 189–200.

Shiel, G., Cregan, A., McGough, A., & Archer, P. (2012). *Oral language in early childhood and primary Education (3–8 years)*. Research Report No. 14. Dublin: National Council for Curriculum and Assessment.

Shipler, D. K. (2005). *The working poor*. New York, NY: Vintage Books.

Shotwell, J., Wolf, D., & Gardner, H. (1979). Exploring early symbolization: Styles of achievement. In B. Sutton-Smith (Ed.), *Play and learning* (pp. 127–156). New York, NY: Gardner Press.

Siegler, R., DeLoache, J., & Eisenberg, N. (2011). *How children develop*. New York, NY: Worth Publishers.

Sifianou, M. (1995). Do we need to be silent to be extremely polite? Silence and FTAs. *International Journal of Applied Linguistics, 5*(1), 95–110.

Sigsgaard, E. (2005). *Scolding: Why it hurts more than it helps*. New York, NY: Teachers College Press.

Simpson, J. A., & Beckes, L. (2010). Attachment theory. In J. M. Levine & M. A. Hogg (Eds.), *Encyclopedia of group processes and intergroup relations*. New York, NY: Sage.

Slaby, R. G., Roedell, W., Arezzo, D., & Hendrix, K. (1995). *Early violence prevention*. Washington, DC: NAEYC.

Sluss, D. (2005). *Supporting play birth through age eight.* Clifton Park, NY: Thompson.

Smetana, J. G. (2006). Social domain theory: Consistencies and variations in children's moral and social judgments. In M. Killen & J. G. Smetana (Eds.), *Handbook of moral development* (pp. 119–153). Mahwah, NJ: Lawrence Erlbaum Associates.

Smith, P. (2005). Play: Types and functions in human development. In B. J. Ellis & D. F. Bjorklund (Eds.), *Origins of the social mind: Evolutionary psychology and child development* (pp. 271–291). New York, NY: The Guilford Press.

Snyder, J., Reid, J., & Patterson, G. (2003). A social learning model of child and adolescent antisocial behavior. In B. B. Lahey, T. E. Moffitt, & A. Caspi (Eds.), *Causes of conduct disorder and juvenile delinquency* (pp. 27–48). New York, NY: The Guilford Press.

Society for Adolescent Medicine. (2003). Corporal punishment in schools: Position paper of the Society for Adolescent Medicine. *Journal of Adolescent Health, 32,* 385–393.

Soderman, A. K. (2003, August). *Divorce.* Paper delivered at the 13th annual meeting of the European Early Childhood Education Research Association (EECERA). University of Glasgow, Scotland.

Soderman, A. K., Eveland, T. S., & Ellard, M. J. (Eds.). (2006). *In your child's best interest: A guide for divorcing parents.* East Lansing, MI: Michigan State University Extension.

Soderman, A. K., Gregory, K. S., & McCarty, L. (2005). *Scaffolding emergent literacy: A child-centered approach, preschool through grade 5* (2nd ed.). Boston, MA: Allyn & Bacon.

Stassen Berger, K. (2007). Update on bullying at school: Science or forgotten? *Developmental Review, 27,* 90–126.

Steinberg, L., Blatt-Eisenberg, I., & Cauffman, E. (2006). Patterns of competence and adjustment among adolescents from authoritative, authoritarian, indulgent, and neglectful homes: A replication in a sample of serious juvenile offenders. *Journal of Research on Adolescence, 16,* 47–58.

Steiner, J., & Whelan, M. S. (1995). *For the love of children: Daily affirmations for people who care for children.* St. Paul, MN: Redleaf Press.

Stephens, T. J. (2006). *Discipline strategies for children with disabilities.* Sioux Falls, SD: Center for Disabilities, School of Medicine & Health Sciences, University of South Dakota.

Stocking, S. H., Arezzo, D., & Leavitt, S. (1980). *Helping kids make friends.* Allen, TX: Argus Communications.

Stormont, M., Lewis, T. J., Beckner, R. S., & Johnson, N. W. (Eds.). (2008). *Implementing positive behavior support systems in early childhood and elementary settings.* Thousand Oaks, CA: Corwin.

Stright, A. D., Gallagher, K. C., & Kelley, K. (2008). Infant temperament moderates relations between maternal parenting in early childhood and child's adjustment in first grade. *Child Development, 79,* 186–200.

Stuber, G. M. (2007). Centering your classroom: Setting the stage for engaged learners. *Young Children, 62*(4), 58–60.

Sullivan, M. W., & Lewis, M. (2003). Contextual determinants of anger and other negative expressions in young infants. *Developmental Psychology, 39,* 693–705.

Sutterby, J., & Frost, J. (2006). Creating play environments for early childhood: Indoors and out. In B. Spodek & O. N. Saracho (Eds.), *Handbook of research on the education of young children* (pp. 305–322). Mahwah, NJ: Lawrence Erlbaum Associates.

Sutton-Smith, B., & Sutton-Smith, S. (1974). *How to play with your child and when not to.* New York, NY: Hawthorn Books.

Talwar V., & Lee, K. (2002). Emergence of white-lie telling in children between 3 and 7 years of age. *Merrill Palmer Quarterly, 48*(2), 160–181.

Tanner, C. K. (March 2009). Effects of school design on student outcomes. *Journal of Educational Administration, 47*(3), 381–399.

Theimer, C., Killen, M., & Strangor, C. (2001). Young children's evaluations of exclusion in gender stereotypic peer contexts. *Developmental Psychology, 37*(1), 18–27.

Thiemann, K., & Warren, S. F. (2010). Programs supporting young children's language development. Updated paper. In Tremblay, R. E., Barr, R. G., & Peters, R. (Eds), Encyclopedia on early childhood development [online]. Montreal, Quebec: Centre of Excellence for Early Childhood Development, 1–11. Available at http://child-encyclopedia.com/pages/PDF/Thiemann-WarrenANGxp_rev.pdf.

Thomas, A., & Chess, S. (1986). The New York longitudinal study: From infancy to early adult life. In R. Plomin & J. Dunn (Eds.), *Changes, continuities and challenges.* Hillsdale, NJ: Lawrence Erlbaum Associates.

Thompson, J. E., & Twibell, K. K. (2009). Teaching hearts and minds in early childhood classrooms: Currriculum for social and emotional development. In O. A. Barbarin & B. H. Wasik (Eds.), *Handbook of child development and early education: Research to practice* (pp. 199–222). New York, NY: The Guilford Press.

Thompson, R. A. (2006). The development of the person: Social understanding, relationships, conscience, self. In N. Eisenberg, W. Damon, & R. M. Lerner (Eds.), *Handbook of child psychology* (pp. 24–98). Hoboken, NJ: Wiley.

Thompson, R. A., & Goodman, M. (2009). Development of self, relationships and socioemotional competence. In O. A. Barbarin & B. H. Wasik (Eds.), *Handbook of child development and early education: Research to practice* (pp. 147–171). New York, NY: The Guilford Press.

Thompson, R. A., & Lagattuta, K. H. (2008). Feeling and understanding: Early emotional development. In K. McCartney & D. Phillips (Eds.), *Blackwell handbook of early childhood development* (pp. 317–337). Malden, MA: Blackwell Publishing.

Thompson, R. A., & Virmani, E. A. (2010). Self and personality. In M. H. Bornstein (Ed.), *Handbook of cultural developmental science* (pp. 195–207). New York, NY: Psychology Press.

Tice, D. M., & Wallace, H. M. (2003). The reflected self: Creating yourself as (you think) others see you. In M. R. Leary & J. P. Tangney (Eds.), *Handbook of self and identity* (pp. 91–105). New York, NY: The Guilford Press.

Ting-Toomey, S. (1999). *Communicating across cultures*. New York, NY: The Guilford Press.

Toblin, R. L., Schwartz, D., Hopmeyer Gorman, A., & Abou-ezzeddine, T. (2005). Social-cognitive behavioral attributes of aggressive victims of bullying. *Journal of Applied Developmental Psychology, 26*, 329–346.

Trawick-Smith, J. (1990). The effects of realistic versus nonrealistic play materials on young children's symbolic transformation of objects. *Journal of Research in Childhood Education, 5*(1), 27–36.

Trawick-Smith, J. (2013). Teacher-child play interactions to achieve learning outcomes. In R. C. Pianta, W. S. Barnett, L. M. Justice, & S. M. Sheridan (Eds), *Handbook of early childhood education* (pp. 259–277). New York, NY: The Guilford Press.

Troop-Gordon, W., & Ladd, G. W. (2005). Trajectories of peer victimization and perceptions of self and school mates: Precursors to internalizing and externalizing problems. *Child Development, 76*, 1072–1091.

Tsybina, I., Girolametto, L., Weitzman, E., & Greenberg, J. (2006). Recasts used with preschoolers learning English as their second language. *Early Childhood Education Journal, 34*(2), 177–185.

Tu, T. H., & Hsiao, W. Y. (2008). Preschool teacher-child verbal interactions in science teaching. *Electronic Journal of Science Education, 12*(2), 199–223.

Turecki, S. (2000). *The difficult child*. New York, NY: Bantam Books.

Turiel, E. (2006). The development of morality. In W. Damon & R. M. Lerner (Series Eds.) & N. Eisenberg (Vol Ed.), *Handbook of child psychology. Vol. 3: Social, emotional, and personality development* (6th ed., pp. 789–857). New York, NY: Wiley.

Turnbull, A. P., Turnbull, H. R., Erwin, E. J., & Soodak, L. C. (2006). *Families, professionals and exceptionality: A special partnership* (5th ed.). Columbus, OH: Merrill/ Prentice-Hall.

U.S. Bureau of Labor Statistics. (2012). Employment characteristics of families summary. Available at http://www.bls.gov.

U.S. Bureau of the Census. (2010). *Income, poverty, and health insurance coverage in the United States: 2010*. Report P60, n. 238, Table B-2, pp. 68–73.

U.S. Department of Health and Human Services, Administration on Children, Youth and Families. (2010). *Child maltreatment*. Washington DC: U.S. Government Printing Office.

Vaish, A., Carpenter, M., & Tomasello, M. (2009). Sympathy through affective perspective and its relation to prosocial behaviors in toddlers. *Developmental Psychology, 45*(2), 534–543.

van Hamond, B., & Haccou (Eds.). (2006). *Gaining and proving yourself in social competence: The Atlas Way*. Antwerpen-Apeldoorn: Fontys OSO & Garant-Uitgevers n.v.

Vasquez, V. M., & Felderman, C. B. (2013). *Technology and critical literacy in early childhood*. New York, NY: Routledge.

Veenstra, R., Lindenberg, S., Zijlstra, B. J. H., De Winter, A. F., Verhulst, F. C., & Ormel, J. (2007). The dyadic nature of bullying and victimization: Testing a dual-perspective theory. *Child Development, 78*, 1843–1854.

Vermande, M. ,Aleva, L., Olthof, T., Goosens, F., van der Meulen-van Dijk, M., & Orobio de Castro, B. (2008, July). *Victims of bullying in school: Theoretical and empirical indications for the existence of three types*. Paper presented at the 20th Biennial Meeting of the International Study for the Study of Behavioral Development (ISSBD), Wurzburg, Germany.

Vygotsky, L. (1978). *Mind in society: The development of higher psychological processes*. Cambridge, MA: Harvard University Press.

Wagner, D. D., & Heatherton, T. F. (2011). Giving in to temptation: The emerging cognitive neuroscience of self-regulatory failure. In K. V. Vohs & R. F. Baumeister, *Handbook of self-regulation: Research, theory and applications* (pp. 41–63). New York, NY: The Guilford Press.

Wallace, B., Maker, J., Cave, D., & Chandler, S. (2005). *Thinking skills & problem solving: An inclusive approach.* London, England: David Fulton Publishers.

Wang, Z., & Deater-Deckard, L. (2013). Resilience in gene-environment transactions. In S. Goldstein & R. B. Brooks (Eds.), *Handbook of resilience in children.* New York, NY: Springer.

Warner, L., & Lynch, S. A. (2004). *Preschool classroom management: 150 teacher-tested techniques.* Beltsville, MD: Griphon House.

Watson, M. W., & Fisher, K. W. (1980). Development of social roles in elicited and spontaneous behavior during the preschool years. *Child Development, 18,* 483–494.

Weinstein, C. S., Romano, M., & Mignano, A. J. (2010). *Elementary classroom management: Lessons from research and practice.* New York, NY: McGraw-Hill.

Weissman, R., & Hendrick, J. (2010). *The whole child* (10th ed.). New York, NY: Macmillan.

Wentzel, K. R. (2009). Peers and academic functioning at school. In K. H. Rubin, W. M. Bukowski, & B. Laursen (Eds.), *Handbook of peer interactions, relationships and groups* (pp. 531–547). New York, NY: The Guilford Press.

Wentzel, K. R., Barry, C. M., & Caldwell, K. A. (2004). Friendship in middle school: Influences on motivation and school adjustment. *Journal of Educational Psychology, 96,* 195–203.

Wentzel, K. R., & Looney, L. (2008). Socialization in school settings. In J. Grusec & P. Hastings (Eds.), *Handbook of socialization: Theory and research* (pp. 382–403). New York, NY: The Guilford Press.

Werner, E. E. (2005). Resilience research: Past, present and future. In R. D. Peters, B. Leadbeater, & R. J. McMahon (Eds.), *Resilience in children, families, and communities: linking context to practice and policy* (pp. 3–12). New York, NY: Kluwer Academic/Plenum Publishers.

Werner, E. E. (2013). What can we learn about resilience from large-scale longitudinal studies? In S. Goldstein & R. B. Brooks (Eds.), *Handbook of resilience in children.* New York, NY: Springer.

Whaley, K., & Rubenstein, T. (1994). How toddlers "do" friendship: A descriptive analysis of naturally occurring friendships in a group childcare setting. *Journal of Social and Personal Relationships, 11,* 383–400.

What Works Clearinghouse. (2007). English Language Learners. Retrieved February 7, 2010, from http://www.whatworks.ed.gov.

Wheeler, E. J. (2004). *Conflict resolution in early childhood.* Upper Saddle River, NJ: Pearson.

Whitebread, D., & O'Sullivan, L. (2012). Preschool children's social pretend play: Supporting the development of metacommunication, metacognition, and self-regulation. *International Journal of Play, 1*(2), 197–213.

Whitesell, N. R., & Harter, S. (1989). Children's reports of conflict between simultaneous opposite–valence emotions. *Child Development, 60,* 673–682.

Widen, S. C., & Russell, J. A. (2003). A closer look at preschoolers' freely pronounced labels for facial expressions. *Developmental Psychology, 35,* 232–245.

Willis, S. (1999). Imagining dinosaurs. In B. L. Clarke & M. Higonnet (Eds.). *Girls, boys, books, toys* (pp. 183–195). Baltimore, MD: Johns Hopkins University Press.

Wilson, H. K., Pianta, R. C., & Stuhlman, M. (2007). Typical classroom experiences in first grade: The role of classroom climate and functional risk in the development of social competencies. *The Elementary School Journal, 108*(2), 81–96.

Wing, L. (1995). Play is not the work of the child: Young children's perceptions of work and play. *Early Childhood Research Quarterly, 10,* 223–247.

Winsler, A., & Naglieri, J. (2003). Overt and covert verbal problem-solving strategies: Developmental trends in use, awareness, and relations with task performance in children aged 5 to 17. *Child Development, 74*(3), 659–678.

Winsler, A., Naglieri, J., & Manfra, I. (2006). Children's search strategies and accompanying verbal and motor strategic behavior: Developmental trends and relations with task performance among children age 5 to 17. *Cognitive Development, 21,* 232–248.

Winther-Lindqvist, D. (2009), Game playing: Negotiating rules and identities. *American Journal of Play, 2*(1), 60–84.

Wisconsin Child Care Information Center. (2011). Wisconsin Model Early Learning Standards. Retrieved from http://ec.dpi.wi.gov/.

Wittmer, D. (2012). The wonder and complexity of infant and toddler peer relationships. *Young Children, 67*(4), 16–20.

Wittmer, D. S. (2008). *Focusing on peers: The importance of relationships in the early years.* Washington, DC: Zero to Three.

Woll, P. (2009). Children of chemical dependency: Respecting complexities and building on strengths. *Prevention Forum, 11*(1), 1.

Wolpert, E. (2005). *Start seeing diversity.* St. Paul, MN: Redleaf Press.

Wright, M. O., & Masten, A. S. (2013). Resilience processes in development. In S. Goldstein & R. B. Brooks, *Handbook of resilience in children* (pp. 17–37). New York, NY: Springer.

Xu, F., Farver, J. A. M., & Zang, Z. (2009). Temperament, harsh and indulgent parenting, and Chinese children's proactive and reactive aggression. *Child Development, 90,* 244–258.

Yau, J., & Smetana, J. G. (2003). Conceptualizations of moral, social-conventional, and personal events among Chinese preschoolers in Hong Kong. *Child Development, 74,* 647–658.

York, S. (2003). *Roots and wings.* St. Paul, MN: Redleaf Press.

Zavitkovsky, D. (2010). Docia shares a story about perceptions of similarities and differences, *Exchange* archive. Retrieved January 4, 2010, from https://secure.ccie.com/catalog/search.php?search=zavitkovsky&category=50.

Zero to Three. (2008). *Caring for infants & toddlers in groups: Developmentally appropriate practice* (2nd ed.). Washington, DC.

Zimbardo, P. (1999). *The shy child.* Los Altos, CA: Malor Books.

Zins, J. E., Weissberg, R. P., Wang, M. C., & Walberg, H. J. (Eds.). (2004). *Building academic success on social and emotional learning.* New York, NY: Teachers College Press.

Ziv, Y., Oppenheim, D., & Sagi-Schwartz, A. (2004). Children's social information processing in middle childhood related to the quality of attachment with mother at 12 months. *Attachment & Human Development, 6*(3), 327–349.

Index

Tables are indicated by a t following the page number.

A

AACTE (American Association of Colleges of Teacher Education), 17
Abandonment, fear of, 164
A-B-C analysis, 348
Able self, 430
Abuse. *See* Child abuse and neglect
Acceptance, 28–29, 75–76
ACEI (Association of Childhood Education International), 17
Active listening, 112–113
Activity space, 268
Adaptive systems, 160
ADHD (Attention-deficit hyperactivity disorder), 12, 266, 438–440, 472
Adherence, 295–296, 297, 344t
Adoption and Safe Families Act of 1997, 168
Adult approaches to child guidance, 305
  authoritarian style, 306
  authoritative style, 307, 309
  interaction between child's temperament and, 307–309
  permissive style, 306
  uninvolved style, 306–307
Adult behavior, and prosocial behavior, 408
  cooperation, 410
  direct instruction, 410–411
  discipline strategies, 409
  modeling, 409
  practice with, 411
  prosocial attribution, 409–410
  reinforcement, 409
Adult–child relationships, importance of, 230
Adult–child separation, 38–39
Adult family members, support for, 54–55
Adult instruction, 303t
Adults, role of in child friendships, 246–252
Adults requests, complying with, 51
Advanced and precocious children, 444–446
Adversity, 161, 174
Affective reflections, 144–146, 147–149, 220
Age
  and friendships, 239
  as part of social identity, 430
  prosocial behavior, 405
  sharing, 406–407, 407t
Age-appropriate practices, 19–20
Age-atypical behavior, 470

Aggression, 364
  bullying, 384–388
  changes in over time, 368–370
  conflict mediation, 379–384
  definition of, 365
  earliest forms of, 369
  effective communication, 388–391
  effective strategies, 374–379, 376t
  emergence of, 368–371
  families, communicating with, 393–394
  gender differences in, 370–371, 370t
  hostile, 365–366, 392–393
  ineffective strategies, 371–374
  instrumental, 365, 377–379, 391–392
  pitfalls to avoid, 394–396
  reasons for, 366–368
  vs. rough-and-tumble play, 212
  social support pyramid for, 377
  types of, 365–366
Alexander and the Terrible, Horrible, No Good, Very Bad Day (Viorst), 149, 150
American Association of Colleges of Teacher Education (AACTE), 17
American Psychiatric Association, 439
American Speech-Language-Hearing Association (ASHA), 48
Amoral orientation, 294, 297, 344t
Anger, 131
Antecedents, in A-B-C analysis, 348
Antibias education, 429
Anxiety disorders, 472
Area rugs, 266
ASHA (American Speech-Language-Hearing Association), 48
Asperger's Syndrome, 160, 440–441
Assertiveness, 77, 366
Assets and protective factors
  children's health, monitoring, 174–175
  coaching children in decision making, planning, implementing, and evaluating, 175–176
  definition of, 172–173
  difficult temperaments, modification of, 178–179
  examples of, 172
  friendship building and social connections, 179–180
  intellectual and scholastic competence, 180–181
  optimism, value of, 176–178
  resilience, development of, 172–181
  self-efficacy and self-determination, 178
  stress hardiness and resilience, development of, 173–174

Assistance for Education of Children with Disabilities, 434
Association of Childhood Education International (ACEI), 17
Associative play, 195
Asthma, 169
Attachment, 29–31
Attention-deficit hyperactivity disorder (ADHD), 12, 266, 438–440, 472
Attention spans, 280
Attitudes, and friendships, 240
Authoritarian style, 305, 306, 308t
Authoritative style
  associated children's behavior, 308t
  attitudes and practices, 305
  becoming, 309
  and developmentally appropriate practice, 319–320
  overview of, 307
  prosocial behavior, 409
  reasoning as hallmark of, 315
Authority
  communication of nonverbally, 77–78
  conveying nonverbally, 83–85
Autism spectrum disorders
  case study, 501–502
  category of disability, 437
  executive function, 160
  friendship skills, 250–251
  overview of, 440–441
Autobiographical memories, 105
Autonomy, 160
Autonomy vs. shame and doubt, 136–137
Awareness, and prosocial behavior, 401–403
Axial space, 63–64, 66

B

Babbling sounds, 40
"Baby talk," 86
Back-to-back position, 65
Basic care, provision of, 48–49
Basic values, 464
Behavior. *See also* Aggression; Extreme behavior; Problem behaviors
  in A-B-C analysis, 348
  of adults in a negative verbal environment, 103t
  of adults in a positive verbal environment, 104t
  associated with healthy and poor self-esteem, 100
  identifying problems, 321

link between moral thinking and moral behavior, 299
resistance to change, 471–472
Behavioral indicators
of abuse and neglect, 478
of emotional abuse and neglect, 479t
of sexual abuse, 479
Behavioral states, 33–35, 34t
Behavior change, knowing when necessary, 310–311
Behavior characteristics, and friendships, 239–240
Behavior hypotheses, 349
Behavior reflections, 105–107, 117
Biases, 429
Biology, and aggression, 367
Biology, and prosocial behavior, 405
Blindness, 437, 438
Body motion, 64–65
Body orientation, 65
Body type, as part of social identity, 430
Books, to prompt discussion of emotions, 149–151
"Bounce factor," 159
Boundaries and activity areas, 270
Bronfenbrenner, Urie, 9
Bruising areas, 480
Buddy skills training, 250–251, 254–255
Bullying
adults' role in prevention, 386–388
bullies, 385–386
program-wide solutions, 387–388
victims of, 384–385, 386
video, 388
witnesses to, 386
"Bully laboratories," 388

C

Caregivers and teachers
influences of, 12–13
professionalism, 16–19
Carpets, 266
Case studies
autism, 501–502
dual language, 503–504
lack of affect and empathy, 505–507
socialization, 508–510
CEC (Council for Exceptional Children), 434–435
Center for Child and Family Studies, 249
Centers for Disease Control and Prevention, 439, 440
Centration, 300, 302t
Channels of communication, for nonverbal communication, 61–62
Character attributions, 410
Character roles, 201
Child abuse and neglect
abusers, 475–477
definition of, 474–475
prevention of in the formal group setting, 481–482
reporting, 480–481, 487–488
scope of, 475
signs of, 478–479

types of cases, 475t
victims of, 477–479
Child development, 6–9, 465–466
Child guidance, adult approaches to, 305–309
Childhood depression, 473–474
Childhood fears, 472
Childhood stress, 161. *See also* Stress
Child Life Specialist Association (CLSA), 17
Childproofing, 275–279, 277t
Child rearing belief and practices of family, 55
Chronic illnesses, 169, 184
Classroom expectations, nonverbal communication, 81t
Classroom record, of effective praise, 118
Classrooms, friendship supportive, 246–247, 252–254
Climbing apparatus, 267
Closed-ended questions, 109–110, 111t, 118
CLSA (Child Life Specialist Association), 17
Cocaine, 170
Code of Ethical Conduct, 374, 467, 483–484, 493–500
Code of ethics, 18, 19t
Cognitive connections, and reasons, 314–315
Cognitive development, 7, 241t, 299–301
Cognitive function, emotions and, 128–129
Cognitive part of emotion, 127
Colic, 35
Collaboration for Academic, Social, and Emotional Learning (CASEL), 99–100
Common feeling words, 148
Common ground, in friendships, 240
Communication. *See also* Language development; Nonverbal communication
in adult discipline styles, 305–306
effective, 388–391
emotions as a form of, 128
with infants and toddlers, 49–50
Communication competence
advanced communication, 41–42
children's communications, tuning in to, 42
in infants, 39–41
Communicative gestures, 41
Comparisons, use of in emergence of self, 98t
Competence, self-esteem and, 95–96. *See also* Social competence
Complex child temperament, 32
Complexity, and exploratory play, 196–197
Compulsions, 473
Conflict, minimizing potential conflict over materials, 285
Conflict, negotiation of, 244–245
Conflict mediation

children's thoughts on, 382
clarify children's perspectives, 379
effectiveness of, 383–384
example of, 381–382
follow through, 381
generate alternative and agree on solution, 380
model for, 379–381
overview of, 378–379
reinforce problem-solving process, 381
summarize, 379–380
Consequences
in A-B-C analysis, 348–349
adapting for children with special needs, 351–353
appropriateness of, 353–356
corrective consequences, 334–340
in daily repertoire of guidance strategies, 346
families, communicating with, 357–358
following through with, 341–342
intensive individualized interventions, 346–351, 356–357
logical consequences, 337–338, 339–340
natural consequences, 336–337, 339, 340, 360
pitfalls to avoid, 358–360
positive consequences, 334
problem behaviors and potential solutions, 332–333
punishment, 335
unrelated consequences, 338, 340
warning and follow-through, combined with personal message, 342–346
when to implement, 342
Construction play, 208–209
Contact, making and friendship, 242–243
Contingent behavior, 36–37
Continuing education, 18, 19t
Control, 95–96, 305–306
Controllable dimensions, 270–272, 271t
Conversations, 105, 108–109, 118
Conversation stoppers, 108–109
Cool down time, 345
Cooperation, and prosocial behavior, 410, 412
Cooperative or organized supplementary play, 195
Coping mechanisms. *See* Stress-coping mechanisms
Coping skills, 164
Co-regulation, 46–47
Corporal punishment, 373–374
Corrective consequences
deciding which to use, 338–340
following through with, 341–342
implementing, 340–341
overview of, 334–336
vs. punishments, 336t
types of, 336–338
when to implement, 342

Council for Exceptional Children (CEC), 434–435
Crack cocaine, 170
Criteria of importance, 311
Critical thinking, 181
Cruelty to others or animals, 470
Crying behavioral state, 34–35, 34t, 55
Cues, 31–36
Cultural competence, 4, 193, 264t
Cultural contexts, 13
Cultural expectations and experiences, 408
Culture
  dramatic play, differences in, 203
  emotional expression, 140–141, 152
  eye contact, 71
  gestures, 66
  Navajo culture, 131
  nonverbal communication, 82
  personal space, 64
  respect for families', 54–55
  smiles, 70
Curriculum
  emotional development, 129
  friendships, 245–246
  nonverbal communication, 80
  peer relationships and friendships, 245–246
  play, 192, 192t

D

Daily schedule, 272, 279–282, 286
DAP (Developmentally appropriate practices), and social competence, 18–21
DAP guidelines for creating caring communities, 319–320
Davis, Sherry, 177–178
Deaf-blindness, 437
Deafness, 437
Death
  resilience, development of, 166–167, 184–185
  stages in children's understanding of, 168t
Decentering, 300
Decision making, 175–176, 402, 403
Definable rules, 317
Demonstrated competence, 17–18, 19t
Density, 269–270
Despair vs. ego integrity, 137t
Developing Cross-Cultural Competence (Lynch and Hanson), 152
Development
  interrelated nature of, 7
  self-regulation, influence on, 298–302
  self-regulation and teacher behavior, 302t
  stages of, 137t
Developmental changes in use of objects, 197–198
Developmental delay, 437, 445t
Developmentally appropriate practices (DAP), and social competence, 18–21

Developmental trends in children's humor, 215, 216t
Diagnostic and Statistical Manual of Mental Disorders (DSM-IV), 439
Diary of a Wimpy Kid (Kinney), 149
Difficult temperament, 178–179, 446–448
Direct experience, 367
Directing, 289
Direct instruction
  emotional expression, 141
  prosocial behavior, 410–411
  self-regulation, 303
Direction of play, influencing, 205–206
Disabling conditions, categories of, 437–441
"Discipline problems," 264
Discipline styles
  associated children's behavior, 308t
  authoritarian style, 305, 306, 308t
  authoritative style, 305, 307, 308t, 309, 315, 319–320, 409
  cross-cultural perspective, 308–309
  overview of, 305–306
  permissive style, 305, 306, 308t
  uninvolved style, 305, 306–307, 308t
Displacement, in handling aggression, 371
Display rules, 81
Dispositional attributions, 410
Disrespectful nonverbal behavior, 77t
Distal space, 63
Distorted-perception hypothesis, 367
Diversity and sexuality, 423
  communicating with children about, 448–452
  ethnic identity, preferences, and attitudes in children, 428–433
  families, communicating with, 452–453
  inclusion of children with exceptional needs, 433–444
  pitfalls to avoid, 453–454
  psychosocial development, 424–428
  Social Support Pyramid for, 436
Divorce, 164–165
DLLs (Dual-language learners), 42, 114–116, 119–120, 503–504
Do's and don'ts analysis, 323
Down syndrome, 48, 351–352, 436
Dramatic play
  changes of time and place, 201
  combining pretend play skills, 207–208
  cultural and experiential differences, 203
  direction of play, influencing, 205–206
  introduction to, 199–200
  master players, 208
  object invention, 201
  object substitution, 200–201
  observation forms, 202
  peer communication, 204–205

  role-playing, 201, 250, 256
  role selection, 206–207
  rule children construct for themselves, 203
  style differences in, 200
Dramatist style, 199
Drowsiness behavioral state, 34t
DSM-IV (Diagnostic and Statistical Manual of Mental Disorders), 439
Dual-language learners (DLLs), 42, 114–116, 119–120, 503–504
Duration sounds, 71–72
Dysfunctional child-rearing environment, 163

E

Early childhood
  aggression, 369
  conflict mediation, 382
  emotional lessons of, 136
  emotions, identification of in others, 134
  gender, 239
  language development for, 149
  play in, 195
  self-concept, 93
Early learning standards, related to social competence, 14t
Early to middle childhood, self-concept and, 93
Earned privileges, 334
Easy child temperament, 32
Ecomap, 162
Economic class, 430
Education, as part of social identity, 430
Education for All Handicapped Children Act, 434
EF (Executive function), 160, 183–184
Effective praise, 105, 107–108, 108t, 117–118, 334
Ego integrity vs. despair, 137t
Elementary years
  aggression, 369–370
  conflict mediation, 382, 383t
  construction play, 209
  emotions, identification of in others, 134
  rough-and-tumble play, 212
  self-evaluations, 97
  sharing, 406
Eliason, Claudia, 22
Emblems, 60
Emotional abuse and neglect, 474, 479t
Emotional awareness, 135
Emotional clusters, 131–132
Emotional development
  abilities in social competence, 241t
  affective reflections, 144–146, 147–149, 220
  children's understanding and communication, promotion of, 149–152
  coping with strong emotions, 152–153
  in curriculum, 129

emergence and maturation of children's emotions, 130–131
emotional difficulties infancy to age 7, 141
emotional self-awareness, 131–133
emotional tasks of childhood, 136–139
identification of other people's emotions, 133–134
importance of, 127–129
influence on self-regulation, 298–299
interrelated nature of, 7
pitfalls to avoid, 155
regulation of emotions, 134–136
structuring, teaching goals, and adult-structuring, 264t
using stories, books, and songs, 149–151
what early childhood professionals need to know, 129–139
Emotional difficulties, 141–142
Emotional disturbance, 437–438, 445t
Emotional expression
counterproductive ways of responding to, 143–144
expressive styles, 139
family and cultural variations in, 140–141
gender differences in, 139–140
helping children to use words, 146–147
individual variations in, 139–141
Emotional illiteracy, 136
Emotional intelligence, 4, 193
Emotional IQ, 135–136
Emotional situations, lying to children about, 143
Emotions. *See also* Emotional development; Emotional expression
benefits of adults talking about, 313–314
constructive ways of responding to, 144–147
counterproductive ways of responding to, 143–144
denial of, 143
developmental sequence of children's understanding of, 133
emergence and maturation of, 130–131
emergence of in first three years of life, 132
expressing to children, 321–323
helping children to use words, 146–147
hiding, 141–142
ignoring, 143
nonverbal communication, 61
shaming children, 143–144
as signals to children about their well-being, 128
talking to children about, 144, 313–314
Empathy, 76, 298, 299, 302t, 505–507
Empathy, in relationships with children, 29
Emphatic listening, 112–113

English, formal instruction and informal conversation, 116
Erikson's stages of development, 137t
Ethical dilemmas, 18
Ethical judgments and decisions
child abuse and neglect, 474–482
children's extreme behavior and, 470–474, 485–487
day-to-day judgments, 484–485
goals related to, 460, 462
pitfalls to avoid, 489–490
principles involved in, 467–470
situational context, 466–467
Social Support Pyramid for, 474
standards related to, 462–463
steps in, 461t, 483–484
strategies related to, 462
values, 463–465
variables in, 463–467
working with families, 482–483
Ethics, 460
Ethnic identity, preferences, and attitudes in children, 428–433
Ethnicity, 239, 428, 430
Ethnocentrism, 429
Exaggeration, 215
Exceptional needs. *See also* Special needs
children's attitudes toward peers with special needs, 442–444
children's perceptions of disabling conditions, 442
disabling conditions, categories of, 437–441
inclusion, 441–442
individualized programs, 435–436
integration into formal group settings, 444
introduction to, 433–434
standards of ethical practice, 434–435
Executive function (EF), 160, 183–184
Expansion, 112
Expectations, stating
authoritative style and developmentally appropriate practice, 319–320
four R's, 317–318
introduction to, 309–310
knowing when behavior change is needed, 310–311
personal message, part one, 311–312
personal message, part three, 316–317
personal message, part two, 313–316
Expected standards, 303t
Experience
development, integration with, 304–305
self-regulation, influences on, 302–305
Explicit rules, 203t
Exploration and learning, with infants and toddlers, 50–51
Exploratory behavior, 196–197
Expressive language, 41
Expressive part of emotion, 127
Expressive styles, 139
Exterior spaces, promoting social development, 266–268

External regulations, 295–296
Extreme behavior
definition of, 470–472
ethical judgments related to, 470–474, 485–487
reported sources of, 472–474
resistance to change, 471–472
Eye aversion, 71
Eye contact, 70–71, 84, 85

F
Face-to-face position, 65, 82, 85
Facial expression, 68–71, 134
Families
aggression, communication about, 393–394
children's emotions, communication about, 153–154
children's self-understanding, 120–121
divorce, 164–165
ethical dimensions of working with, 482–483
family conflict and marital dysfunction, 164–165
foster care, 168–169
friendship, communication about, 257–258
individual differences, communication about, 452–453
influences of, 11–12
as partners in development of resilience, 181–182
prosocial behavior, communication about, 417–418
self-regulation, communication about, 324–325
self-regulation and consequences, 357–358
sharing structuring ideas with, 288–289
support for, 54–55
variations in emotional expression, 140–141
violent, abusive, or neglectful families, 168
Family conflict, 163, 164–165
Family indicators
of abuse and neglect, 478
of emotional abuse and neglect, 479t
of sexual abuse, 479
Family interactions, school, and community, 71
Family roles, 201
Family structure, 430
Fantasizer, 200, 200t
FAS (Fetal alcohol syndrome), 169–170
Fear, 131
Feedback, emotional expression, 141
Feelings, prosocial behavior, 403
Feeling words, 148
Fetal alcohol syndrome (FAS), 169–170
5–11 Years: Lev Vygotsky, the Zone of Proximal Development, and Scaffolding, 21
Follow-through, 341–346, 344t

Formal pretend proposals, 206, 206t, 219
Foster care, resilience, 168–169
Four R's, 317–318
Free play, 180
Friedman, Thomas, 174
Friendliness, in infants and toddlers, 43–45
Friendship Framework, 233–237
  intimate, mutually shared relationships, 236–237
  mature friendships, 237
  momentary playmates, 233–234
  one-way assistance, 234–236
  summary of, 238
  two-way, fair-weather cooperation, 236
Friendships
  adult role in, 246–252
  among infants and toddlers, 44–45
  behavior characteristics, 239–240
  buddy skills training, 250–251, 254–255
  children's ideas about, 233–237
  communication with families about, 257–258
  in the curriculum, 245–246
  definition of, 231–232
  friendship-supportive classrooms, 246–247, 252–254
  how children choose friends, 237–242
  importance of, 231–232
  introduction to, 29–30
  need for and benefits of, 232
  one-on-one intensive coaching, 251–252, 256–257
  pitfalls to avoid, 258–259
  problems with being friendless, 233
  puppets and props, using to demonstrate friendship, 247–250
  rejection, 233
  role-playing, 250, 256
  skills needed for, 242–245
  skits that demonstrate friendship skills, 255–256
  and social connections, 179–180
  state learning standards, 245, 245t
  strengthening skills in, 179–180
Frustrated-aggression hypothesis, 367
Functional analysis, 348–349, 349t
Functional roles, 201
Furnishings and equipment, 268–270

G

Games, 213–215
Gandhi, Mahatma, 11
Gaze, 70–71
Gaze following, 41
Gender
  aggression, 370–371, 370t
  differences in emotional expression, 139–140
  dramatic play, differences in, 203
  in early childhood, 239
  in Friendship Framework, 235
  and friendships, 239
  as part of social identity, 430

prosocial behavior, 405
  social development and play, 192–194
  stereotypical behaviors, 428
Gender identity, 424–425, 425t
Gender-role development, 424–425
Gender-role identification, 425
Gender segregation, 426
Gender stereotyping, 425t
Gender-typed behavior, 425t
Gender typing, 425t
Generativity vs. stagnation, 137t
Genetic foundations of play, 191
Genuineness, 76
Genuineness, in relationships with children, 29
Gestures, 65–66
Giftedness, 444–446
Goals, and ethical judgments, 460, 462
Goodbye routine, 38–39, 39t
Goodness of fit, 33
Grandparents, 173
Greene, Graham, 8
Group decision making, 176
Guidance continuum for all children, 347
Guilt, 298, 302t
Guilt vs. initiative, 137–138

H

Haiti, 170
Hanson, Marci, 152
Hartup, Willard, 5
Head Start Child Outcomes Framework, 12–13
Health, monitoring, 174–175
Health and safety, 264–265, 284
Health impairment, 438
Health-related assaults, resilience, 169–170
Healthy self-esteem, 99, 100
Hearing impairment, 351, 438, 445t
Hesitations, 72t, 73
High-intensity programs, 282–283
High-mobility–low-mobility dimension, 271–272, 271t
High risk infants and toddlers, 48
Hiring practices, 482
Home language, 115
Homeostasis, 161
Hostile aggression, 365–366, 392–393
Humor, 215–216, 220
Hurricane Sandy, 15, 170

I

IDEA (Individuals with Disabilities Education Act), 434
Identification, 296, 297, 344t
Identity and status, nonverbal communication, 61
Identity vs. role confusion, 137t
IEP (Individualized education programs), 434, 435–437, 442
IFSP (Individualized family service plan), 53, 435–436, 442
Illustrator gestures, 60–61
Imitation, 80, 140–141

Imitative learning, 41
Implicit rules, 203t
Inclusive environments, 358
Incongruity in children's humor, 215
Inconsistency, in handling aggression, 371
Indiscriminate behavior, 471
Individualized education programs (IEP), 434, 435–437, 442
Individualized family service plan (IFSP), 53, 435–436, 442
Individually appropriate practices, 20
Individual needs, detection of, 49
Individuals with Disabilities Education Act (IDEA), 434
Individuation and socialization, support of
  adult–child separation, 38–39
  differences in outcomes, 37–38
  infants, 36–37
  toddlers, 37
Inductive discipline, 307
Industry vs. inferiority, 137t, 138–139
Ineffective praise, 108t
Infant gaze and social meaning to caregivers, 36t
Infants and toddlers
  adult family members, supporting, 54–55
  adult requests, complying with, 51
  effective communication, 49–50
  emotional regulation, 135
  exploration and learning, 50–51
  guidance for, 52
  individual needs, 49
  individuation and socialization, 36–37
  interaction, being available for, 52–53
  peer relationships and friendships, 43t, 52
  pitfalls to avoid, 55–56
  prompt basic care, 48–49
  special needs, supporting children with, 53–54
  toy play, 51
Inferiority vs. industry, 137t, 138–139
Initiative vs. guilt, 137–138
Insight, 181
Instrumental aggression, 365, 377–379, 391–392
Instrumental know-how, 404
Intellectual competence, 180–181
Intellectual disability, 438
Intense behavior, 470–471
Intensity, 72t, 73
Intensity of programs, 282–283
Intensive individualized interventions
  aggression, 376
  behavior hypotheses, 349
  convening a team, 346
  emotional development and learning, 147
  ethical judgments and decisions, 474
  functional assessment, 348–349
  guiding social development and behavior, 22, 23
  handling aggression, 377

implementing and monitoring positive behavior support plan, 350–351
need for, 346–351
nonverbal communication, 60
participation in, 356–357
peer relationships and friendships, 252
physical environment, 278
play, 197
positive behavior support plan, 349–351, 350t
positive relationships, 29
prosocial behavior, 408
resilience, development of, 182
self-regulation, 327
self-regulation through consequences, 348
verbal communication, 116
Intentionality, 476
Interaction, being available for with infants and children, 52–53
Interior spaces, 265
Internalization, 296–298, 344t
Internalized oppression, 429–430
Internalized privilege, 429
Internal regulation, 296–298
Internal space, 62, 64
Interpersonal skills, 4, 193, 264t
Intimacy vs. isolation, 137t
Intimate, mutually share relationships, 236–237, 238
Intrusion-seclusion dimension, 271, 271t
Irregular sleep behavioral state, 34t
Irreversibility, 300–301, 302t
Isolation vs. intimacy, 137t

J

Jenkins, Loa, 22
Joint attention, 41
Joy, 131

K

Katz, Lillian, 178, 467
Kinney, Jeff, 149

L

Labels, 144–145
Language, 54–55, 302t, 405, 430
Language development, 7. See also Communication; Dual-language learners (DLLs)
abilities in social competence, 241t
behavior reflections, 106
children's communications, tuning in to, 42
for early childhood, 149
influence on self-regulation, 301–302
oral and literacy-related activities, 120
overgeneralization, 42
and self-concept, 93
signs, 42
typical, 48
words, 41–42
Language skills, and ability to negotiate well, 244
Large-group space, 269

Later elementary years, emotional difficulties, 141–142
Learned helplessness, 178
Learning. See also Social development and learning
multiple ways of, 9–10
and social competence, 9–11
as a social process, 6, 9
Learning centers, 268
Learning disabilities, interpreting emotions, 79
Learning through Play, 13
Light, 265–266
Limits, setting, for children with special needs, 312
Linguistic diversity, 114–116, 119–120
Logical consequences, 337–338, 339–340, 339t
Lullabies and songs, 42
Lynch, Eleanor, 152

M

Making contact, and friendship, 242–243
Mandated reporters, 480
Marital dysfunction, 163, 164–165
Mask smile, 69–70
Masten, Ann, 160
Master players, 208
Mastery play, 198
Masturbation, 426–427
Materials. See Space and materials
Maternal substance use and abuse, 169–170
Mature friendships, 237, 238
Maturity demands, 305–306
Mayle, Peter, 427
ME books, 93
Medical neglect, 474
Memory development, influence on self-regulation, 301–302
Memory skills, 302, 302t
Mental development in middle childhood, 304
Mental maps, 304
Metacommunications, 61, 204, 205t, 219–220
Michigan Board of Education, 47
Middle childhood
mental development, 304
peer acceptance, 235
self-concept, 93–94
Mind blindness, 160
Mistrust vs. trust, 136, 137t
Mixed emotions, 132–133, 152
Mixed message, 78
Modeling
and aggression, 368
and prosocial behavior, 409
self-regulation, 303–304
Momentary playmates, 233–234, 238
Moral behavior, 299
Moral thinking, 299
Moral violations, 299
Mother-only families, 164
Movement and social interaction, 36

Movement play, 209–212
maintaining interest in, 210–211
repetitious activity, 209–210
risk, understanding, 211
social and physical testing, 211–212
Multiple disabilities, 438
Multiple risk factors, 174

N

National Association for the Education of Young Children (NAEYC), 17. See also Code of Ethical Conduct
National Center for Children in Poverty (NCCP), 163
National Committee to Prevent Child Abuse, 476
National Cooperative Inner-City Asthma Study (NCICAS), 169
National Dissemination Center for Children with Disabilities (NICHCY), 437
Natural consequences, 336–337, 339, 340, 360
Natural disasters, resilience, 170–172
Navajo culture, 131
NCCP (National Center for Children in Poverty), 163
NCICAS (National Cooperative Inner-City Asthma Study), 169
Negative consequences, 295, 304
Negative verbal environment, 101t, 102, 103t
Neglect. See Child abuse and neglect
Neglectful parents, 476
"Netizens," 277
NICHCY (National Dissemination Center for Children with Disabilities), 437
Nonassertiveness, 78
Nonlexical sounds, 71, 72t
Nonverbal communication, 59
acquisition of, 80–81
body motion, 64–65
body orientation, 65
channels of, 61–74
children's acquisition of, 79–81
classroom expectations, 81t
communication of authority and security, 77–78
conveying authority and security, 83–85
in curriculum, 80
definition of, 60
enhancing through teaching and coaching, 85
facial expression, 68–71
functions of, 60–61
gestures, 65–66
interactions with family members, 85–86
metacommunications, 205t
nurturing relationships, 74–77
paralinguistics, 71–74
pitfalls to avoid, 86–87
position in space, 62–64
potential challenges of, 78–79

Nonverbal communication (*Continued*)
  Social Support Pyramid for, 60
  touch, 66–68
  tuning in to children, 82–83
Normal stressors, 174
Notions of right and wrong, 302t, 303t
Novelty, and exploratory play, 196–197
Nurturance, 305–306

O

Obama, Barack, 438
Obesity, 169
Object invention, 201
Objects
  instrumental aggression over, 365
  play with, 197–199, 216–217
Object substitution, 200–201
Observable behaviors, in socially
    competent children, 5
Observational experience, 368
Observation forms, for dramatic play, 202
Obsessions, 473
Older children, games, 213–214
"One-upmanship," 65
One-way assistance, 234–236, 238
Onlooker, 195
Open-closed dimension, 271, 271t
Open-ended questions, 105, 109, 111t,
    118, 120
Optimism, sharing the value of, 176–178
Organic/genetic risk factors, 163
Orthopedic impairment, 438, 445t
Outdoor play, 266–267

P

Paley, Vivian, 387
Paralinguistics, 71–74
Parallel activity, 195
Paraphrase reflections, 105, 110–113,
    116, 119, 120
Parental mental health, 163
Parroting, 121
Passive victims, 384
Pathways, 270
Patterner style, 199
Pearse, Patricia, 427
Peeping or voyeurism by children,
    427–428
Peer acceptance in middle
    childhood, 235
Peer communication in dramatic play,
    204–205
Peer group, influences of, 12
Peer-neglected children, 241
Peer-pairing, 250–251
Peer-rejected children, 242
Peer relationships, 29
  adult role in, 246–252
  buddy skills training, 250–251,
    254–255
  children's ideas about, 233–237
  communication with families about,
    257–258
  in the curriculum, 245–246
  friendship in infants and toddlers,
    44–45

friendship-supportive classrooms,
    246–247, 252–254
  how children choose friends, 237–242
  importance of, 230–231
  infants and toddlers, 43t
  one-on-one intensive coaching,
    251–252, 256–257
  pitfalls to avoid, 258–259
  puppets and props, using to
    demonstrate friendship, 247–250
  role-playing, 250, 256
  skills needed for, 242–245
  skits that demonstrate friendship
    skills, 255–256
  state learning standards, 245, 245t
  unsuccessful interactions, 241–242
Peer risk factors, 163
Peers, 230–231
Pennsylvania Department of
    Education, 47
Periodic sleep behavioral state, 34t
Permissive style, 305, 306, 308t
Persona Dolls, 183, 249, 432
Personal message
  adult's emotions, description,
    313–314, 321
  child's behavior, identification of,
    313, 314, 321
  definition of, 309–310
  degree of self-regulation and, 344t
  fear of making a mistake, 325–326
  importance of giving children
    reasons, 314–315, 321
  matching reasons to children's
    understanding, 315
  part one, 311–312
  part three, 316–317
  part two, 313–316
  positive, 318–319
  positive messages, 318–319, 322
  rationale for verbal sequence,
    342–344, 343t
  reflection, 311–313, 316, 320
  rule or redirection, 316–317,
    321–323
  variations in part two, 316
  warning and follow-through,
    combining with, 342–346
Personal norms, 403
Personal space, 62, 63–64
Perspective-taking, 300, 300t, 302t,
    370, 404
Pervasive behavior, 471
Physical abuse, 474
Physical abusers, 476
Physical aggression, 365–366
Physical appearance, and
    friendships, 237
Physical development, 7
Physical environment, 262–290
  adaptations for children with special
    needs, 283
  adding or removing materials,
    275–279
  adjustments to influence children's
    social behavior, 267t

appropriate materials, 272–273
  building and grounds, 264–266
  childproofing the environment,
    275–279, 277t
  children "running wild," 278
  controllable dimensions,
    270–272, 271t
  effectiveness, evaluation of, 273
  exterior spaces promote social
    development, 266–268
  families, sharing structuring ideas
    with, 288–289
  furnishings and equipment, 268–270
  independence, promoting with
    management of materials, 284
  maximizing safety, 284
  pitfalls to avoid, 289–290
  planning, implementation, and
    assessment, support children's
    attempts, 286–287
  rate and intensity of programs,
    282–283
  relationship with social competence
    goals, 264t
  room arrangement, 283–284
  Social Support Pyramid for, 278
  space and materials, structure of,
    263–279, 285
  structuring time, 279–283
  supervision, supporting social
    competence through, 287–288
  warning signs in, 281–282
Physical indicators
  of abuse and neglect, 478
  of emotional abuse and neglect, 479t
  of sexual abuse, 479
Physical neglect, 474
Physical part of emotion, 127
Physical punishment, in handling
    aggression, 371–374
Physical testing, 211–212
Physiology, and extreme behavior, 472
Pitch and tone, 72t, 73
Planning and decision-making, 4, 181,
    193, 264t
Plants, 267
Play, 190
  adaptations for children with special
    needs, 223
  adult direct involvement as a
    player, 218
  awareness of individual differences,
    222–223
  becoming directly involved in, 220
  changing the level of social
    participation in, 218–219
  characteristics of, 191
  coaching from outside the play frame,
    220–222
  construction play, 208–209
  in the curriculum, 192, 192t
  dramatic play, 198–208
  in early childhood, 195
  exploratory behavior, 196–197
  games, 213–215
  genetic foundations, 191

giving cues through play signals or metacommunications, 219–220
guiding rough-and-tumble play, 222
humor, 215–216
importance of in friendship formation, 246
maximizing potential of available materials, 217–218
metacommunications, 204, 205t
with movement, 209–212
movement play, maintaining interest in, 210–211
nature of and social competence, 191–196
with objects, 197–199
pitfalls to avoid, 224–225
repetitive activity, 209–210
rough-and-tumble play, 211–212, 222
setting the stage for, 216–217
sharing information with family, 223–224
social competence, contributions to, 193
social development and, 192–196
strategies to redirect play within the play frame, 206t
types of, 196–216
varying adult play performance, 219–220
young children's stages of, 221
Play episode, 207
Play frame, 204–205, 206t
Play schemes, 207
Play signals, 219–220
Polakow, Valerie, 429
Poor self-esteem, 99, 100
Position in space, 62–64, 81t
Positive behavior support plan, 346, 349–351, 350t
Positive consequences, 334
Positive praise, 107
Positive reinforcement, 335
Positive relationships
emotional development and learning, 147
ethical judgments and decisions, 474
guiding social development and behavior, 22
handling aggression, 377
maintaining, 243–244
nonverbal communication, 60
peer relationships and friendships, 252
physical environment, 278
play, 197
prosocial behavior, 408
resilience, development of, 182
self-regulation, 327
self-regulation through consequences, 348
sexuality and diversity, 436
verbal communication, 116
Positive relationships, establishment of, 22
Positive rules, 317
Positive self-identity, 4, 193, 264t
Positive self-talk, 177, 183

Positive verbal environment
adult behaviors in, 104t
behavior reflections, 105–107
conversations, 108–109
effective praise, 107–108
establishment of, 102–116
overview of, 101t
paraphrase reflections, 110–113, 119
praise statements, 117–118
questions, 109–110
shared narratives, 113–114, 119
strategies for, 105
using the skills associated with, 116–117
verbal strategies to support linguistically diverse children, 114–116, 119–120
Potential reinforcers, 335
Poverty, 163–164
Practice, and prosocial behavior, 411
Practice play, 198, 209–210
Pragmatists, 200, 200t
Praise statements, 117–118, 122
Precocious behavior, 444–446
Preferences, and friendships, 240
Prejudices, 429, 433
Preschool, benefits of, 408
Preschoolers
conflict mediation, 382
emotions, identification of in others, 134
rough-and-tumble play, 212
Pretending, nonverbal communication, 61
Pretend play. See Dramatic play
Pretend play skills, combining, 207–208
Primary caregivers, definition of, 30
Primary emotions, 1
Principles, 467–470
Priority principles, 468–469t, 468–470
Private space, 269, 285
Private speech, 301–302, 302t
Privilege, temporary loss of, 338, 339t
Problem behaviors, potential solutions, 332–333
Problem-solving skits, 249
Professionalism, 16–19, 19t
Professional Skills Inventory Rating form, 511–513
Prompting, 206, 206t, 219
Prosocial attribution, 409–410
Prosocial behavior
adult behavior, 408–411
attribution, 409–410
awareness, 401–403
benefits of, 400–401
and biology, 405
children's motivation, 401
cooperation, 410
coordinating planned activities, 416–417
creating a prosocial environment, 411–413
cultural expectations and experiences, 408
decision making, 402, 403

definition of, 400–404
direct instruction, 410–411
discipline strategies, 409
families, communicating with, 417–418
influences on, 404–411
language, 405
modeling, 409
on-the-spot instruction, 413–416
pitfalls to avoid, 418–419
practice with, 411
reinforcement, 409
sample activity to promote, 417
sharing, 405–407
social cognition, 405
social experiences, 407
Social Support Pyramid for, 408
steps to becoming, 401–404
taking action, 404
teaching and coaching, 413
Protective factors. See Assets and protective factors
Provocative victims, 384
Proximal space, 62–63, 64, 65, 82
Psychological disequilibrium, 165
Psychosocial development
adult responses to, 426–428
gender-role development, 424–425
Punishment, 335, 336t, 371–374
Puppets and props, 247–250

Q

Questions, 122
formulation of, 118
open-ended, 105
in positive verbal environment, 109–110
Quiet alert behavioral state, 34t

R

Race, 430
Racial awareness, acquisition of, 431t
Racist attitudes, 431–432
Rate and intensity of programs, 282–283
Rayston, Angela, 427
React, as part of personal message, 318
Reading infant/toddler cues
behavioral states, 33–35
movement and social interaction, 36
temperament, influence on social relationships, 31–33
Reason, as part of personal message, 314–315, 318
Reasonable rules, 316–317, 322
Recasting, 112
Receptive language, 41
Redirection, 303t
Referrals, 48
Reflection, 121, 122, 311–313, 318, 319, 320
Reflective listening, 112–113
Regular sleep behavioral state, 34t
Rehabilitation Act, 439
Rehearsal, 337, 338, 339t
Reinforcement, 304, 367, 409
Rejected-aggressive children, 242

Rejected-withdrawn children, 242
Relational aggression, 365–366
Relationships
   essentials of positive adult-child, 28–29
   importance of, 230–233
   influence of time on, 76–77
   nurturing nonverbally, 74–77
   prosocial behavior, 403
Relationships, establishment of with infants and toddlers
   adult family members, supporting, 54–55
   attachment as foundation of, 29–31
   communication competence, 39–42
   complying with adult requests, 51
   effective communication, 49–50
   essentials of positive adult-child relationships, 28–29
   exploration and learning, 50–51
   friendliness, 43–45
   individual needs, 49
   individuation and socialization, 36–39
   interaction, being available for, 52–53
   peer relationships and friendships, 52
   pitfalls to avoid, 55–56
   prompt basic care, 48–49
   reading infant/toddler cues, 31–36
   self-regulation, 45–47
   special needs, relating to infants and toddlers with, 47–48
   special needs, supporting children with, 53–54
   WAGER, 28
Relationships, skills for development nonverbally
   conveying authority and security, 83–85
   enhancing children's nonverbal behavior through teaching and coaching, 85
   interactions with family members, 85–86
   tuning in to children, 82–83
Relative values, 464
Relaxation techniques and imagery, 183
Religious beliefs, 430
Repetitious activity, 209–210
Resilience, 158
   assets and protective factors, 172–181
   definition of, 159
   development of, 160–161
   families as partners in development of, 181–182
   influence of risk factors on, 163–172
   influences of stress on, 161–163
   pitfalls to avoid, 185–187
   skills for development of, 182–185
Resourcefulness, 181
Respect, 29, 76, 83
Respectful nonverbal behavior, 77t
Restitution, 337–338, 339t
Rewards, 295, 334
Rhythm of speech, 71–72
Rhythm provided by listener, 72t

Right and wrong, children's notions of, 299
Rights, instrumental aggression over, 365
Rise-and-fall phrasing, 40
Risk, understanding in movement play, 211
Risk factors
   characteristics and potential outcomes, 163t
   death as, 166–167
   family conflict and marital dysfunction, 164–165
   foster care, 168–169
   health-related assaults, 169–170
   natural disasters, war, terrorism, and violence, 170–172
   needed support, 174t
   resilience, development of, 163–172
   socioeconomic disadvantage, 163–164
   violent, abusive, or neglectful families, 168
   working parents, 167–168
Robins, Arthur, 427
Role confusion vs. identity, 137t
Role-playing, 201, 250, 256
Role selection, 206–207
Room arrangement, 283–284
Rosa's Law, 438
Rough-and-tumble play (R&T), 211–212, 222
Routines, importance of, 279–280
Rules
   adapting for children with special needs, 351–353
   children construct for themselves in dramatic play, 203
   enacting, 321–323
   implicit vs. explicit, 203t
Rules and redirection, 316–317, 318, 321–323

S

Sadness, 131
Safety. *See* Health and safety
Sample scripts, 151
Sarcasm, 79
Scholastic competence, 180–181
School phobia, 472–473
Security, 77–78, 83–85
See How You Grow (Pearse), 427
Selective praise, 107
Self, 98t, 327
Self, sense of
   emergence of, 92–101, 98t
   pitfalls to avoid, 121–123
   verbal environment, 101–102
Self-awareness, 37, 92, 97, 131–133
Self-care, and working parents, 167
Self-concept, 92–94, 97, 105, 431
Self-control, physical environment, 264
Self-destructive behaviors, 470
Self-determination, 178
Self-disclosure, 146
Self-efficacy, 160, 178

Self-esteem, 94. *See also* Healthy self-esteem; Poor self-esteem
   adult practices influence on, 100–101
   evolution of, 96–98
   foster care, 169
   trio of, 95–96
   variations in, 98–100
Self-evaluations, 96–99, 98t
Self-perception, 403
Self-regulation. *See also* Consequences
   adherence (external regulations), 295–296
   adult approaches to child guidance, 305–309
   amoral orientation (no regulation), 294
   behaviors, identifying, 321
   child development and teacher's behaviors, 302t
   cognitive development, 299–301
   definition of, 294
   degree of and verbal skill sequence, 344t
   development and experience, integration of, 304–305
   development's influence on, 298–302
   direct instruction, 303
   as an element of social competence, 4, 193
   emotional development, 298–299
   evolution of, 294, 297
   expectations, stating, 309–320
   experience, influences on, 302–305
   expressing your emotions to children, 321
   families, communicating with, 324–325
   fostering, 45–47
   identification (shared regulation), 296
   internalization (internal regulation), 296–298
   language development, 301–302
   memory development, 301–302
   modeling, 303–304
   normalization of violence, 172
   orientations to, 294–297
   pitfalls to avoid, 325–327
   progress toward, 297–298
   reasons, formulating, 321
   reflection on problem situations, 320
   reinforcement and negative consequences, 304
   and resilience, 160
   rules, enacting, 321–323
   signs of, 295t
   structuring, teaching goals, and adult-structuring, 264t
   varying progress toward, 297–298
   warning and follow-through, combined with personal message, 342–346
Self-regulation strategies, 153
"Self-talk," 302
Seligman, Marvin, 177
Sensitive caregiving, 34
Separation anxiety, 38–39
Sesame Street, 277

Sex play among young children, 427
Sexual abuse, 474, 479
Sexual abusers, 476–477
Sexuality and diversity, 423
  communicating with children about, 448–452
  ethnic identity, preferences, and attitudes in children, 428–433
  families, communicating with, 452–453
  inclusion of children with exceptional needs, 433–444
  pitfalls to avoid, 453–454
  psychosocial development, 424–428
  Social Support Pyramid for, 436
Sexual orientation, as part of social identity, 430
Shame and doubt vs. autonomy, 136–137
Shared narratives, 105, 113–114, 119
Shared-regulation, 46–47, 296
Sharing, and prosocial behavior, 405–407, 412, 414
"The Short List," 172
Shush, 35
Shyness, 446
Side-by-side position, 65
Side/stomach position for holding, 35
Signs, in infant communication, 42
Silence, 72t, 73
Simple-complex dimension, 271, 271t
Single-parent families, 164
Sitting apart, 345
Situational context, 466–467
Situational cues, 151–152
Skills, 17
Skill sequence, 344
Skits that demonstrate friendship skills, 248–250, 255–256
Slow-to-warm-up child temperament, 32
Small-group space, 269
Smile, 69–70
Social cognition, 405
Social competence. See also Prosocial behavior
  benefits of, 5–6
  definition of, 2–6
  developmentally appropriate practices, 18–21
  early learning standards, 14t
  elements of, 4
  and friendships, 240–241
  individual variations in, 3–5
  and learning, 9–11
  observable behaviors, 5
  overview of, 6–9
  role of caregivers in fostering, 15–18
  sexuality and diversity, 424
  structuring and, 264t
Social connections, strengthening skills in, 179–180
Social-conventional infractions, 299
Social development, and play, 192–196
Social development and learning, 7
  abilities in social competence, 241t
  cumulative and delayed effects of, 8–9
  framework for, 21–23

optimal periods of, 8
rates of, 8
sequence of, 7–8
Social environment, 2
  caregiver and teacher influences, 12–13
  cultural contexts, 13
  family influences, 11–12
  peer group influences, 12
Social experiences, and prosocial behavior, 407
Social identity, 430
Social interaction, nonverbal communication, 61, 80
Socialization, case study, 508–510
Socialization, support of. See Individuation and socialization, support of
Socially and culturally appropriate practices, 20–21
Socially competent children, 159, 240–241, 241t
Social maturity, 160
Social norms, 403
Social participation, social development and play, 194–195
Social referencing, 41, 140–141
Social relationships, temperament, 31–33
Social status, social development and play, 195–196
Social Support Pyramid
  children's positive sense of self, promotion of through verbal communication, 116
  emotional development and learning, 147
  ethical judgments and decisions, 474
  guiding social development and behavior, 22
  handling aggression, 377
  for nonverbal behavior, 60
  nonverbal communication, 60
  peer relationships and friendships, 252
  physical environment, 278
  play, 197
  positive relationships, 29
  prosocial behavior, 408
  resilience, development of, 182
  self-regulation, 327
  self-regulation through consequences, 348
  sexuality and diversity, 436
  verbal communication, 116
Social testing, 211–212
Social values, 4, 193, 264t
Sociodramatic play, 199–200
Socioeconomic disadvantage, 163–164
Soft-hard dimension, 271, 271t
"Soft skills," 174
Solitary play, 195
Songs, to prompt discussion of emotions, 149, 151
Soothing, 35
Sound control, 266

Space and materials
  adding or removing materials, 275–279, 284
  adjusting to increase safety, 277t
  appropriate materials, 272–273
  appropriate size of equipment and materials, 275
  arrangement of, 285
  attractively displayed materials, 274–275
  building and grounds, 264–266
  independence, promoting with management of materials, 284
  interior spaces, 265
  light, 265–266
  materials, minimize potential conflict over, 285
  materials that are ready to use, 274
  materials that work, 273–274
  organization of materials storage, 274
  quantities appropriate to number of children, 275
  sound control, 266
  structurally safe materials, 273
  walls, 265
Specialized knowledge, 17, 19t
Special needs. See also Exceptional needs
  adapting room arrangement for, 283
  adapting rules and consequences for children with, 351–353
  collaboration with parents to serve student with physical disabilities, 404
  including students with physical disabilities, 243
  inclusive environments, 358
  play adaptations, 223
  play signals, 220
  relating to infants and toddlers with, 47–48
  setting limits, 312
  supporting children with and relationships, 53–54
Specific learning disability, 438
Specific praise, 107
Specific rules, 322
Speech or language impairment, 438
Stages of development, 137t
Stagnation vs. generativity, 137t
Standards, and ethical judgments, 462–463
Standards of practice, 18, 19t
Standards of Professional and Ethical Practice for Teachers of Children with Disabilities, 434–435
State Learning Standards
  emotional development and learning, 130t
  friendship-related, 245–246, 245t
  nonverbal communication, 80t
  play, 192, 192t
  self-understanding, 99–100, 100t
  social competence, 14t
State Learning Standards Associated with Infants and Toddlers, 47
Storage, 270

Storytelling, 206, 206t, 219
Strategies, and ethical judgments, 462
Stress
    coping mechanisms, failure of,
        162–163
    definition of, 161
    influence on resilience, 161–163
    strategies for handling, 183
Stress-coping mechanisms, 162–163
Stress hardiness, 161, 182–185
Stressors, 161
Strong emotions, helping children cope
    with, 152–153
Structurally safe materials, 273
Structuring. *See also* Physical
        environment
    adjustments to influence children's
        social behavior, 267t
    definition of, 263
    relationship with social competence
        goals, 264t
Style differences in dramatic play, 200
Style differences in object use, 198–199
Styles of play, 198–199, 200, 200t
Subjective time, 77
Sucking, 35
Supervision, supporting social
        competence through, 287–288
Supportive environments, 22
    creation of, 22
    emotional development and
        learning, 147
    ethical judgments and decisions, 474
    guiding social development and
        behavior, 22
    handling aggression, 377
    nonverbal communication, 60
    peer relationships and friendships, 252
    physical environment, 278
    play, 197
    positive relationships, 29
    prosocial behavior, 408
    resilience, development of, 182
    self-regulation, 327
    self-regulation through
        consequences, 348
    sexuality and diversity, 436
    verbal communication, 116
Swaddle, 35
Swing or swaying, 35
System pressures, program
        conditions that offset, 16t

T

Taking action, and prosocial
        behavior, 404
Teacher techniques, for encouraging
        positive social behaviors, 324
Teaching and coaching
    aggression, 375–376
    in decision making, planning,
        implementing, and evaluating,
        175–176
    emotional development and
        learning, 147
    ethical judgments and decisions, 474

friendships, one-on-one intensive
        coaching, 251–252, 256–257
    guiding social development and
        behavior, 22
    handling aggression, 377
    nonverbal communication, 60,
        80–81, 85
    peer relationships and friendships, 252
    physical environment, 278
    during play, 220–222
    play, 197
    positive relationships, 29
    prosocial behavior, 408, 413
    resilience, development of, 182
    self-regulation, 304, 327
    self-regulation through consequences,
        348
    sexuality and diversity, 436
    social development and behavior,
        22, 23
    verbal communication, 116
Teaching Pyramid Model, 22
TeachSource video
    *5–11 Years: Lev Vygotsky, the Zone
        of Proximal Development, and
        Scaffolding*, 21
    attachment in infants and toddlers, 31
    bullying, 388
    collaboration with parents to
        serve student's with physical
        disabilities, 404
    divorce, 165
    family interactions, school, and
        community, 71
    gender in early childhood, 239
    guidance for infants and toddlers, 52
    including students with physical
        disabilities, 243
    inclusive environments, 358
    inclusive environments for children
        with special needs, 358
    language development for early
        childhood, 149
    Learning through Play, 13
    moral development in middle
        childhood, 304
    oral and literacy-related activities, 120
    peer acceptance in middle
        childhood, 235
    play in early childhood, 195
    preschool, benefits of, 408
    self-concept in middle childhood, 94
    teacher techniques for encouraging
        positive social behavior, 324
    temperament in infants and
        toddlers, 179
    young children's stages of play, 221
Technology, 277
Temperament. *See also* Difficult
        temperament
    and aggression, 367
    definition of, 31
    influence of on social relationships,
        31–33
    interaction with adult's approach to
        guidance, 307–309

modification of difficult, 178–179
    prosocial behavior, 405
    strengths and challenges of, 32t
Temper tantrums, 46–47, 344–345
Tempo of speech, 72t
Temporary loss of privilege, 338, 339t
Territory, instrumental aggression
        over, 365
Terrorism, resilience, 170–172
Third person, speaking in, 121–122
Time, influences on relationships, 76–77
Time, structuring
    daily schedule, 279–282, 286
    transitions, 280–282
Time and place, changes in during
        play, 201
Toddlers
    aggression, 369
    conflict mediation, 382
    individuation and socialization, 37
Toilet learning, 45–46, 47
Touch
    classroom expectations, 81t
    as nonverbal communication, 66–68
Tourette's syndrome, 352, 472
Toy play, 51
Transform, 198
Transitions, 280–282
"Transplanting" a child into another
        culture, 433
Traumatic brain injury, 438
Traumatic life events, 163
Trio of self-esteem, 95–96
Trust vs. mistrust, 136, 137t
Turn-taking conversations, 42
Two-way, fair-weather cooperation,
        236, 238

U

Ulterior conversations, 206, 206t, 219
Underscoring, 206, 206t, 219
Uninvolved style, 305, 306–307, 308t
Unoccupied behavior, 194–195
Unrelated consequences, 338, 340
Unsuccessful peer interactions,
        241–242
U.S. Bureau of Labor Statistics, 167
U.S. Department of Health and Human
        Services, 373, 475

V

Values, 463–465
VCS (Vulnerable child syndrome), 169
Verbal communication,
        metacommunications, 205t
Verbal environment, 101–102. *See also*
        Negative verbal environment;
        Positive verbal environment
Verbal indicators
    of abuse and neglect, 478
    of emotional abuse and neglect, 479t
    of sexual abuse, 479
Violence, 170–172, 173t
Violence in electronic media, 171–172
Violent, abusive, or neglectful
        families, 168

Viorst, Judith, 149, 150
Visual impairment, 438, 445t
Voice, classroom expectations, 81t
Voyeurism or peeping by children, 427–428
Vulnerability, 160
Vulnerable child syndrome (VCS), 169

W

WAGER (warmth, acceptance, genuineness, empathy, respect), 28–29, 47, 60, 100–101
Waking activity behavioral state, 34t

Walls, 265
War, resilience, 170–172
Warmth, in relationships with children, 28, 75, 83
Warning, 340–341, 344t
Where Did I Come From? (Mayle and Robins), 427
Where Do Babies Come From? (Rayston), 427
Words, in early communication, 41–42
Working parents, resilience, 167–168
Worth, 95–96

Y

You Can't Say, You Can't Play (Paley), 387
Young children
  construction play, 208–209
  games, 213–214
  stages of play, 221

Z

Zinn, Howard, 177

Chapter	Developmentally Appropriate Practice (DAP) Guidelines	NAEYC Professional Prep Standards	NAEYC Preschool/Program Accreditation Standards	DEC Recommended Practices
	2F5. To strengthen children's sense of competence and confidence as learners, motivation to persist, and willingness to take risks, teachers provide experiences for children to be genuinely successful and to be challenged, pp. 196–216	**5c.** Using own knowledge, appropriate early learning standards, and other resources to design, implement, and evaluate developmentally meaningful and challenging curriculum for each child, pp. 196–216		
Chapter 8: Supporting Children's Peer Relationships and Friendships	**1B.** Relationships are an important context through which children develop and learn, pp. 230–233, 246–252 **2E.** Teachers plan the environment, schedule, and daily activities to promote each child's learning and development, pp. 245–246	**1a.** Know and understand children's characteristics and needs (0–8), pp. 230–233, 246–252 **4a.** Understanding positive relationships and supportive interactions as the foundation of their work with young children, pp. 233–244 **5c.** Using own knowledge, appropriate early learning standards, and other resources to design, implement, and evaluate developmentally meaningful and challenging curriculum for each child, pp. 245–246	**1.C.02.** Teaching staff support children's development of friendships and provide opportunities for children to play with and learn from each other, pp. 237–245 **1.C.03.** Teaching staff support children as they practice social skills and build friendships by helping them: enter into [play], sustain [play], and enhance play, pp. 237–245 **2.B.05.** Children have varied opportunities to develop skills for entering into social groups, developing friendships, learning to help, and other pro-social behavior, pp. 230–233, 237–245 **2.L.06.** Children have varied opportunities to engage in discussions about fairness, friendship, responsibility, authority, and differences, pp. 233–237, 245–252	**INS8.** Practitioners use peer-mediated intervention to teach skills and to promote child engagement and learning, pp. 233–237, 245–252
Chapter 9: Influencing Children's Social Development by Structuring the Physical Environment	**1E3.** Teachers ensure that the environment is organized and the schedule follows an orderly routine that provides a stable structure within which development and learning can take place, pp. 279–283 **2E.** Teachers plan the environment, schedule, and daily activities to promote each child's learning and development, pp. 263–279 **2E2.** Teachers present children with opportunities to make meaningful choices, especially in child-choice activity periods, pp. 272–279	**5c.** Using own knowledge, appropriate early learning standards, and other resources to design, implement, and evaluate developmentally meaningful and challenging curriculum for each child, pp. 263–283	**3.A.04.** Teachers organize space and select materials in all content and developmental areas to stimulate exploration, experimentation, discovery, and conceptual learning, pp. 263–279 **3.D.10.** Teachers organize time and space on a daily basis to allow children to work or play individually and in pairs, to come together in small groups, and to engage as a whole group, pp. 279–283 **9.A.12.** Indoor space is designed and arranged to accommodate children individually, in small groups and in a large group; divide space into areas that are supplied with materials organized in a manner to support children's play and learning; provide semiprivate areas where children can play or work alone or with a friend; and provide children with disabilities full access (making adaptations as necessary) to the curriculum and activities in the indoor space, pp. 268–279 **9.A.16.** Outdoor play areas, designed with equipment that is age and developmentally appropriate and that is located in clearly defined spaces with semiprivate areas where children can play alone or with a friend, accommodate motor experiences such as running, climbing, balancing, riding, jumping, crawling, scooting or swinging; activities such as dramatic play, block building, manipulative play, or art activities; and exploration of the natural environment, including a variety of natural and manufactured surfaces, and areas with natural materials such as nonpoisonous plants, shrubs and trees. The program makes adaptations so children with disabilities can fully participate in the outdoor curriculum and activities, pp. 266–268	**INS4.** Practitioners plan for and provide the level of support, accommodations, and adaptations needed for the child to access, participate, and learn within and across activities and routines, pp. 263–283 **INS5.** Practitioners embed instruction within and across routines, activities, and environments to provide contextually relevant learning opportunities, pp. 263–283
Chapter 10: Fostering Self-Regulation in Children: Communicating Expectations and Rules	**1C4.** Teachers listen to and acknowledge children's feelings and frustrations, respond with respect in ways that children can understand, guide children to resolve conflicts, and model skills that help children to solve their own problems, pp. 294–298	**1c.** Create healthy respectful, supportive, and challenging learning environments, pp. 294–298 **4c.** Using a broad repertoire of developmentally appropriate teaching/ learning approaches, pp. 298–302	**1.F.01.** Teaching staff actively teach children social, communication, and emotional regulation skills, pp. 298–305	**INT5.** Practitioners promote the child's problem-solving behavior by observing, interpreting, and scaffolding in response to the child's growing level of autonomy and self-regulation, pp. 305–320

Chapter	Developmentally Appropriate Practice (DAP) Guidelines	NAEYC Professional Prep Standards	NAEYC Preschool/Program Accreditation Standards	DEC Recommended Practices
	1C5. Teachers themselves demonstrate high levels of responsibility and self-regulation in their interactions with other adults (colleagues, family members) and with children, pp. 302–320 **2E4.** Teachers provide experiences, materials, and interactions to enable children to engage in play that allows them to stretch their boundaries to the fullest in their imagination, language, interaction, and self-regulation as well as to practice their newly acquired skills, pp. 302–320	**5c.** Using own knowledge, appropriate early learning standards, and other resources to design, implement, and evaluate developmentally meaningful and challenging curriculum for each child, pp. 302–320	**1.F.02.** Teaching staff help children manage their behavior by guiding and supporting children to persist when frustrated, play cooperatively with other children, use language to communicate needs, learn turn taking, gain control of physical impulses, express negative emotions in ways that do not harm others or themselves, use problem-solving techniques, and learn about self and others, pp. 305–320	
Chapter 11: Fostering Self-Regulation in Children: The Role of Consequences	**1C4.** Teachers listen to and acknowledge children's feelings and frustrations, respond with respect in ways that children can understand, guide children to resolve conflicts, and model skills that help children to solve their own problems, pp. 332–352	**1c.** Create healthy respectful, supportive, and challenging learning environments, pp. 332–352 **5c.** Using own knowledge, appropriate early learning standards, and other resources to design, implement, and evaluate developmentally meaningful and challenging curriculum for each child, pp. 332–352	**1.F.01.** Teaching staff actively teach children social, communication, and emotional regulation skills, pp. 332–333, 346–352 **1.F.02.** Teaching staff help children manage their behavior by guiding and supporting children to persist when frustrated, play cooperatively with other children, use language to communicate needs, learn turn taking, gain control of physical impulses, express negative emotions in ways that do not harm others or themselves, use problem-solving techniques, and learn about self and others, pp. 334–346	**INS7.** Practitioners use explicit feedback and consequences to increase child engagement, play, and skills, pp. 334–346
Chapter 12: Handling Children's Aggressive Behavior	**1C2.** Teachers are responsible at all times for all children under their supervision, monitoring, anticipating, preventing, and redirecting behaviors not conducive to learning or disrespectful of the community, as well as teaching prosocial behaviors, pp. 379–388 **1C4.** Teachers listen to and acknowledge children's feelings and frustrations, respond with respect in ways that children can understand, guide children to resolve conflicts, and model skills that help children to solve their own problems, pp. 371–379	**1a.** Know and understand children's characteristics and needs (0–8), pp. 365–370 **4a.** Understanding positive relationships and supportive interactions as the foundation of their work with young children, pp. 371–379 **5c.** Using own knowledge, appropriate early learning standards, and other resources to design, implement, and evaluate developmentally meaningful and challenging curriculum for each child, pp. 379–388	**1.C.05.** Teaching staff guide children who bully, isolate, or hurt other children to learn and follow the rules of the classroom, pp. 384–388 **1.E.04.** Teaching staff respond to a child's challenging behavior, including physical aggression, in a manner that provides for the safety of the child, provides for the safety of others in the classroom, is calm, is respectful to the child, and provides the child with information on acceptable behavior, pp. 371–384	**INT5.** Practitioners promote the child's problem-solving behavior by observing, interpreting, and scaffolding in response to the child's growing level of autonomy and self-regulation, pp. 371–384
Chapter 13: Promoting Prosocial Behavior	**1C2.** Teachers are responsible at all times for all children under their supervision, monitoring, anticipating, preventing, and redirecting behaviors not conducive to learning or disrespectful of the community, as well as teaching prosocial behaviors, pp. 404–411 **1C4.** Teachers listen to and acknowledge children's feelings and frustrations, respond with respect in ways that children can understand, guide children to resolve conflicts, and model skills that help children to solve their own problems, pp. 404–411	**1a.** Know and understand children's characteristics and needs (0–8), pp. 400–404 **1b.** Use developmental knowledge to create healthy environments for young children, pp. 404–411 **4a.** Understanding positive relationships and supportive interactions as the foundation of their work with young children, pp. 404–411 **5c.** Using own knowledge, appropriate early learning standards, and other resources to design, implement, and evaluate developmentally meaningful and challenging curriculum for each child, pp. 404–411	**1.F.01.** Teaching staff actively teach children social, communication, and emotional regulation skills, pp. 400–411 **1.F.02.** Teaching staff help children manage their behavior by guiding and supporting children to persist when frustrated, play cooperatively with other children, use language to communicate needs, learn turn taking, gain control of physical impulses, express negative emotions in ways that do not harm others or themselves, use problem-solving techniques, and learn about self and others, pp. 400–411	**INT5.** Practitioners promote the child's problem-solving behavior by observing, interpreting, and scaffolding in response to the child's growing level of autonomy and self-regulation, pp. 400–411